PHILIP'S

STR...S

Norfolk

www.philips-maps.co.uk

First published in 2003 by

Philip's, a division of
Octopus Publishing Group Ltd
www.octopusbooks.co.uk
2-4 Heron Quays, London E14 4JP
An Hachette Livre UK Company
www.hachettelivre.co.uk

Second edition 2006
Third impression with revisions 2008
NORBC

ISBN 978-0-540-09485-1 (pocket)

© Philip's 2008

Ordnance Survey®

This product includes mapping data licensed from
Ordnance Survey® with the permission of the
Controller of Her Majesty's Stationery Office.

© Crown copyright 2008. All rights reserved.
Licence number 100011710.

Contents

III	**Key to map symbols**
IV	**Key to map pages**
VI	**Route planning**
X	**Administrative and Postcode boundaries**
1	**Street maps** at 1⅓ inches to 1 mile
132	**Street maps** at 2⅔ inches to 1 mile
178	**Street map of Norwich city centre** at 5⅓ inches to 1 mile
179	**Index** of towns and villages
182	**Index** of streets, hospitals, industrial estates, railway stations, schools, shopping centres, universities and places of interest

Digital Data

The exceptionally high-quality mapping found in this atlas is available as digital data in TIFF format, which is easily convertible to other bitmapped (raster) image formats.

The index is also available in digital form as a standard database table. It contains all the details found in the printed index together with the National Grid reference for the map square in which each entry is named.

For further information and to discuss your requirements, please contact
victoria.dawbarn@philips-maps.co.uk

PHILIP'S MAPS
the Gold Standard for drivers

◆ **Philip's street atlases cover every county in England, Wales, Northern Ireland and much of Scotland**

◆ Every named street is shown, including alleys, lanes and walkways

◆ Thousands of additional features marked: stations, public buildings, car parks, places of interest

◆ Route-planning maps to get you close to your destination

◆ Postcodes on the maps and in the index

◆ Widely used by the emergency services, transport companies and local authorities

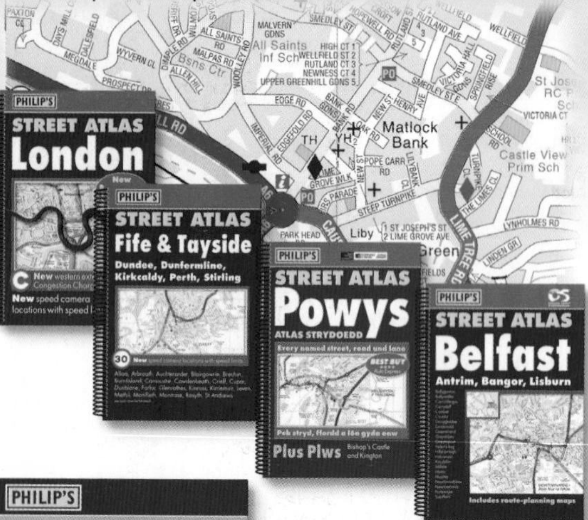

For national mapping, choose **Philip's Navigator Britain** the most detailed road atlas available of England, Wales and Scotland. Hailed by Auto Express as 'the ultimate road atlas', the atlas shows every road and lane in Britain.

'The ultimate in UK mapping'
The Sunday Times

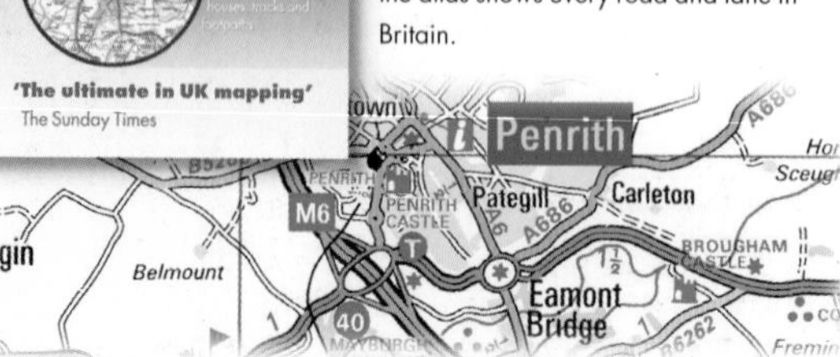

Street atlases currently available

England

Bedfordshire and Luton	Surrey
Berkshire	East Sussex
Birmingham and West Midlands	West Sussex
Bristol and Bath	Tyne and Wear
Buckinghamshire and Milton Keynes	Warwickshire and Coventry
Cambridgeshire and Peterborough	Wiltshire and Swindon
Cheshire	Worcestershire
Cornwall	East Yorkshire Northern Lincolnshire
Cumbria	North Yorkshire
Derbyshire	South Yorkshire
Devon	West Yorkshire
Dorset	**Wales**
County Durham and Teesside	Anglesey, Conwy and Gwynedd
Essex	Cardiff, Swansea and The Valleys
North Essex	Carmarthenshire, Pembrokeshire and Swansea
South Essex	Ceredigion and South Gwynedd
Gloucestershire and Bristol	Denbighshire, Flintshire, Wrexham
Hampshire	Herefordshire Monmouthshire
North Hampshire	Powys
South Hampshire	
Herefordshire Monmouthshire	**Scotland**
Hertfordshire	Aberdeenshire
Isle of Wight	Ayrshire
Kent	Dumfries and Galloway
East Kent	Edinburgh and East Central Scotland
West Kent	Fife and Tayside
Lancashire	Glasgow and West Central Scotland
Leicestershire and Rutland	Inverness and Moray
Lincolnshire	Lanarkshire
Liverpool and Merseyside	Scottish Borders
London	
Greater Manchester	**Northern Ireland**
Norfolk	County Antrim and County Londonderry
Northamptonshire	County Armagh and County Down
Northumberland	Belfast
Nottinghamshire	County Tyrone and County Fermanagh
Oxfordshire	
Shropshire	
Somerset	
Staffordshire	
Suffolk	

How to order

Philip's maps and atlases are available from bookshops, motorway services and petrol stations. You can order direct from the publisher by phoning **0207 531 8473** or online at **www.philips-maps.co.uk**
For bulk orders only, e-mail philips@philips-maps.co.uk

Symbol	Description	Symbol	Description
	Motorway with junction number	◆	**Ambulance station**
	Primary route – dual/single carriageway	◆	**Coastguard station**
	A road – dual/single carriageway	◆	**Fire station**
	B road – dual/single carriageway	◆	**Police station**
	Minor road – dual/single carriageway	✚	**Accident and Emergency entrance to hospital**
	Other minor road – dual/single carriageway	H	**Hospital**
	Road under construction	✛	**Place of worship**
	Tunnel, covered road	i	**Information Centre** (open all year)
	Rural track, private road or narrow road in urban area	🛒	**Shopping Centre**
	Gate or obstruction to traffic (restrictions may not apply at all times or to all vehicles)	P P&R	**Parking, Park and Ride**
	Path, bridleway, byway open to all traffic, road used as a public path	PO	**Post Office**
	Pedestrianised area	⚑	**Golf course**
DY7	**Postcode boundaries**	⚞	**Picnic site**
	County and unitary authority boundaries	Prim Sch	**Important buildings, schools, colleges, universities and hospitals**
	Railway, tunnel, railway under construction		**Built up area**
	Tramway, tramway under construction		**Woods**
	Miniature railway	River Ouse	**Tidal water, water name**
≷ Walsall	**Railway station**		**Non-tidal water** – lake, river, canal or stream
🚇	**Private railway station**		**Lock, weir, tunnel**
● South Shields	**Metro station**	Church	**Non-Roman antiquity**
🚊 🚊	**Tram stop, tram stop under construction**	ROMAN FORT	**Roman antiquity**
◗	**Bus, coach station**	87 246	**Adjoining page indicators and overlap bands** The colour of the arrow and the band indicates the scale of the adjoining or overlapping page (see scales below)

Camping site, caravan site

Acad	**Academy**	Inst	**Institute**	Recn Gd	**Recreation Ground**
Allot Gdns	**Allotments**	Ct	**Law Court**		
Cemy	**Cemetery**	L Ctr	**Leisure Centre**	Resr	**Reservoir**
C Ctr	**Civic Centre**	LC	**Level Crossing**	Ret Pk	**Retail Park**
CH	**Club House**	Liby	**Library**	Sch	**School**
Coll	**College**	Mkt	**Market**	Sh Ctr	**Shopping Centre**
Crem	**Crematorium**	Meml	**Memorial**	TH	**Town Hall/House**
Ent	**Enterprise**	Mon	**Monument**	Trad Est	**Trading Estate**
Ex H	**Exhibition Hall**	Mus	**Museum**	Univ	**University**
Ind Est	**Industrial Estate**	Obsy	**Observatory**	W Twr	**Water Tower**
IRB Sta	**Inshore Rescue Boat Station**	Pal	**Royal Palace**	Wks	**Works**
		PH	**Public House**	YH	**Youth Hostel**

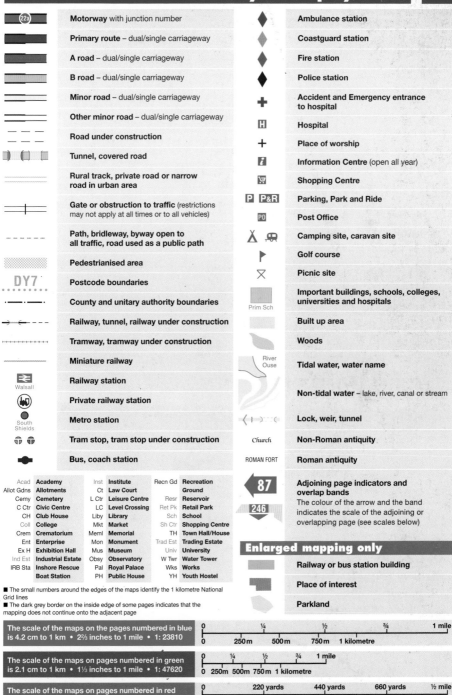

Enlarged mapping only

	Railway or bus station building
	Place of interest
	Parkland

■ The small numbers around the edges of the maps identify the 1 kilometre National Grid lines
■ The dark grey border on the inside edge of some pages indicates that the mapping does not continue onto the adjacent page

The scale of the maps on the pages numbered in blue is 4.2 cm to 1 km • 2⅔ inches to 1 mile • 1 : 23810	0 ¼ ½ ¾ 1 mile 0 250 m 500 m 750 m 1 kilometre
The scale of the maps on pages numbered in green is 2.1 cm to 1 km • 1⅓ inches to 1 mile • 1 : 47620	0 ¼ ½ ¾ 1 mile 0 250 m 500 m 750 m 1 kilometre
The scale of the maps on pages numbered in red is 8.4 cm to 1 km • 5⅓ inches to 1 mile • 1 : 11900	0 220 yards 440 yards 660 yards ½ mile 0 125 m 250 m 375 m ½ kilometre

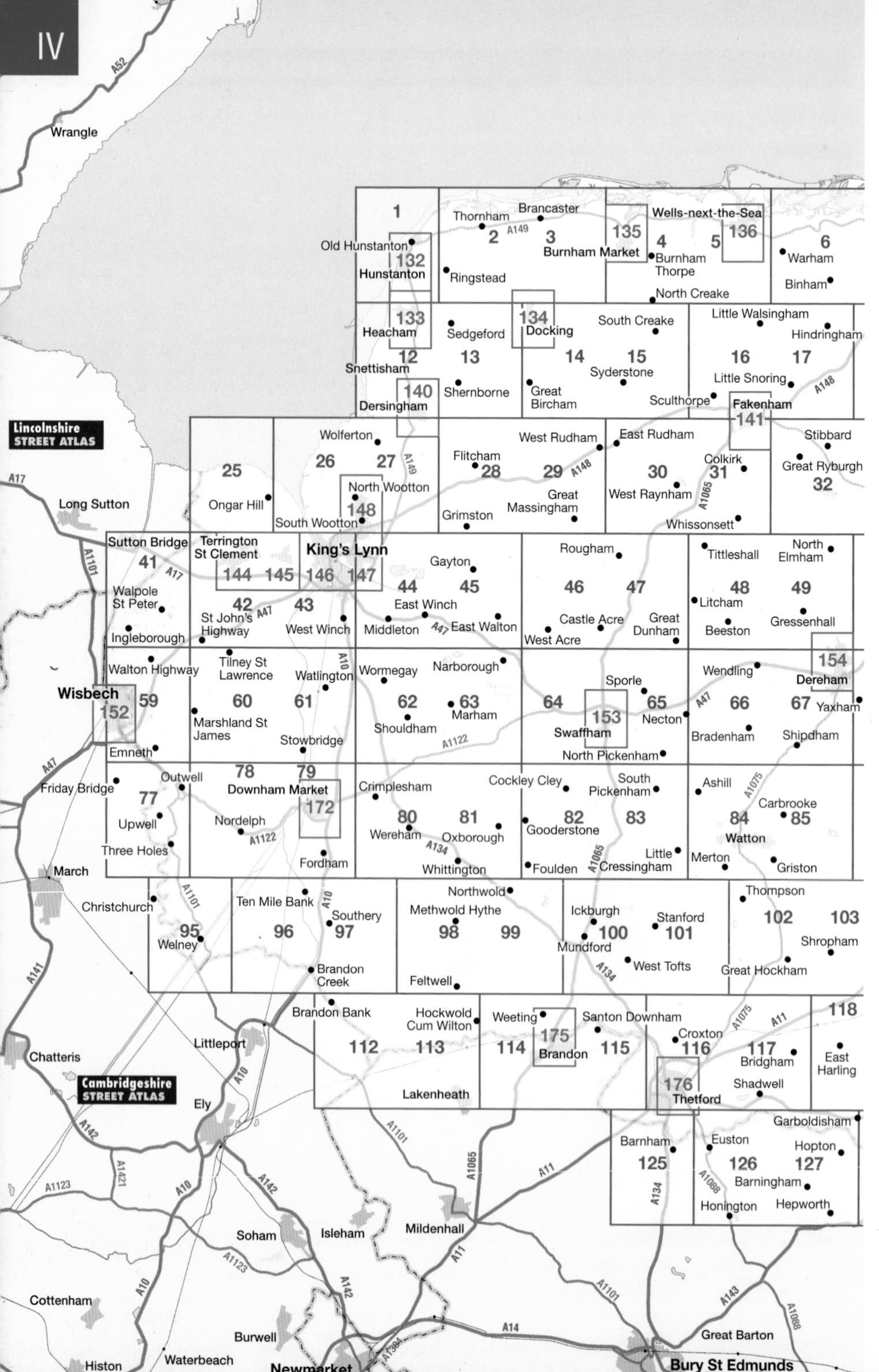

Wrangle
Lincolnshire STREET ATLAS
Long Sutton
Wisbech
March
Christchurch
Chatteris
Cambridgeshire STREET ATLAS
Ely
Littleport
Soham
Isleham
Mildenhall
Cottenham
Burwell
Histon
Waterbeach
Newmarket
Bury St Edmunds
Great Barton
Old Hunstanton
Hunstanton
Heacham
Snettisham
Dersingham
Thornham
Brancaster
Ringstead
Burnham Market
Burnham Thorpe
North Creake
Wells-next-the-Sea
Warham
Binham
Sedgeford
Docking
South Creake
Little Walsingham
Hindringham
Shernborne
Great Bircham
Syderstone
Sculthorpe
Little Snoring
Fakenham
Wolferton
Flitcham
West Rudham
East Rudham
Colkirk
Stibbard
Great Ryburgh
Ongar Hill
North Wootton
South Wootton
Grimston
Great Massingham
West Raynham
Whissonsett
Sutton Bridge
Terrington St Clement
King's Lynn
Gayton
Rougham
Tittleshall
North Elmham
Walpole St Peter
St John's Highway
West Winch
East Winch
Middleton
East Walton
Castle Acre
West Acre
Great Dunham
Litcham
Beeston
Gressenhall
Ingleborough
Walton Highway
Tilney St Lawrence
Watlington
Wormegay
Narborough
Sporle
Wendling
Dereham
Marshland St James
Stowbridge
Shouldham
Marham
Swaffham
Necton
Bradenham
Shipdham
Yaxham
Emneth
North Pickenham
Friday Bridge
Outwell
Downham Market
Crimplesham
Cockley Cley
South Pickenham
Ashill
Carbrooke
Upwell
Nordelph
Wereham
Oxborough
Gooderstone
Watton
Three Holes
Fordham
Whittington
Foulden
Little Cressingham
Merton
Griston
Ten Mile Bank
Southery
Northwold
Methwold Hythe
Ickburgh
Stanford
Thompson
Welney
Mundford
Shropham
Brandon Creek
Feltwell
West Tofts
Great Hockham
Brandon Bank
Hockwold Cum Wilton
Weeting
Santon Downham
Croxton
Brandon
Bridgham
East Harling
Lakenheath
Thetford
Shadwell
Garboldisham
Barnham
Euston
Hopton
Barningham
Honington
Hepworth
1 2 3 4 5 6 12 13 14 15 16 17 25 26 27 28 29 30 31 32 41 42 43 44 45 46 47 48 49 59 60 61 62 63 64 65 66 67 77 78 79 80 81 82 83 84 85 95 96 97 98 99 100 101 102 103 112 113 114 115 116 117 118 125 126 127
132 133 134 135 136 140 141 144 145 146 147 148 152 153 154 172 175 176
A52 A17 A1101 A47 A149 A148 A1065 A10 A1122 A134 A1075 A141 A142 A1421 A1123 A11 A1088 A1101 A143 A14 A1304

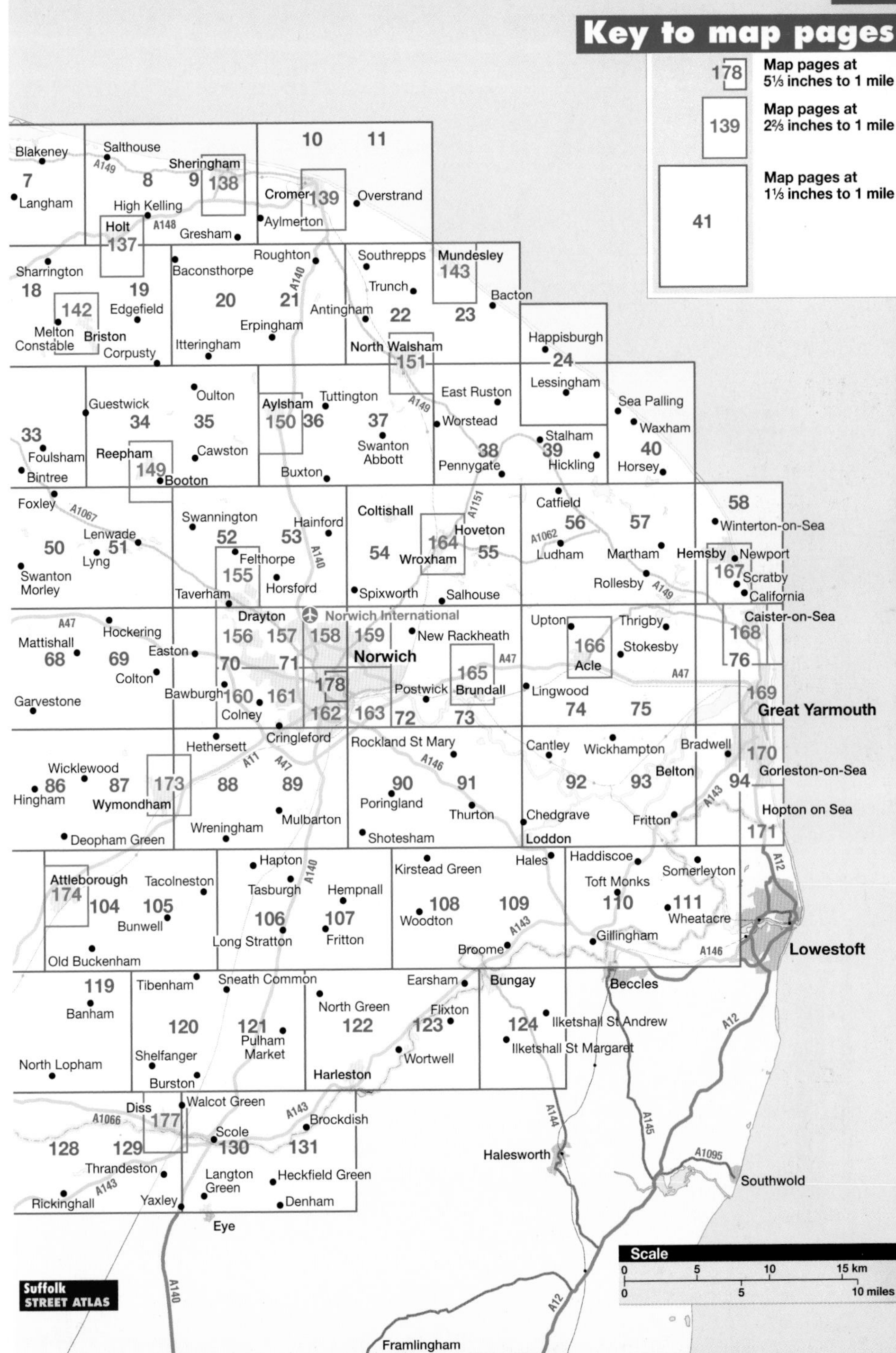

V

Key to map pages

178	Map pages at 5⅓ inches to 1 mile
139	Map pages at 2⅔ inches to 1 mile
41	Map pages at 1⅓ inches to 1 mile

Blakeney
Salthouse
A149
Sheringham
10   **11**
Langham
7
8   **9** **138**
High Kelling
Cromer **139**
Overstrand
Holt
A148
Gresham
Aylmerton
137
Roughton
Southrepps
Mundesley
Sharrington
Baconsthorpe
Trunch
143
18
19
20 **21**
Antingham
Bacton
Edgefield
22 **23**
Erpingham
Melton
Constable
142
Briston
Itteringham
North Walsham
Happisburgh
Corpusty
151
24
Guestwick
Oulton
Tuttington
Lessingham
33 **34** **35**
Aylsham
150 36
37
East Ruston
Sea Palling
Waxham
Foulsham
Reepham
Cawston
Worstead
Bintree
149
Booton
Swanton
Abbott
Stalham
Hickling
40
Horsey
Foxley
A1067
Buxton
38
Pennygate
39
Swannington
Hainford
Coltishall
Catfield
58
Lenwade
52 **53**
Hoveton
56 **57**
Winterton-on-Sea
50 **51**
Felthorpe
54
Wroxham
55
A1062
Ludham
Martham
Hemsby
Newport
Lyng
155
Horsford
Spixworth
Salhouse
Rollesby
A149
167
Scratby
Swanton
Morley
Taverham
California
Drayton
Norwich International
Upton
Thrigby
Caister-on-Sea
Mattishall
Hockering
156 157 158 159
New Rackheath
166
Stokesby
168
68 **69**
Easton
Norwich
Acle
76
Colton
70 **71**
A47
Garvestone
Bawburgh
160 161
178
Postwick
165
Brundall
Lingwood
169
Colney
162 163
72 73
74 **75**
Great Yarmouth
Hethersett
Cringleford
Rockland St Mary
Cantley
Wickhampton
Bradwell
170
Wicklewood
173
A146
Belton
Gorleston-on-Sea
86 87
88 89
90 91
92 93 94
Hingham
Wymondham
Poringland
Thurton
Chedgrave
Fritton
Hopton on Sea
Wreningham
Mulbarton
Loddon
171
Deopham Green
Shotesham
Hapton
Kirstead Green
Hales
Haddiscoe
Somerleyton
Attleborough
Tacolneston
Tasburgh
Hempnall
108 109
Toft Monks
110 111
174 104 105
106 107
Woodton
Wheatacre
Bunwell
Fritton
Gillingham
A146
Lowestoft
Old Buckenham
Long Stratton
Broome
A143
119
Tibenham
Sneath Common
Earsham
Bungay
Beccles
Banham
120 121 122
North Green
Flixton
124
Ilketshall St Andrew
A12
North Lopham
Shelfanger
Pulham
Market
123
Ilketshall St Margaret
Burston
Harleston
Wortwell
Diss
Walcot Green
A143
Brockdish
A1066
177
Scole
128 129
130 131
Halesworth
A1095
Southwold
Thrandeston
Langton
Green
Heckfield Green
A143
Rickinghall
Yaxley
Denham
Eye

Scale
| 0 | 5 | 10 | 15 km |
| 0 | | 5 | 10 miles |

Framlingham
Saxmundham
Leiston

Suffolk
STREET ATLAS

Route planning

Scale

0	1	2	3	4	5	10 km
0	1	2	3	4	5	6 miles

BRANCASTER ROADS

Holkham Bay

T H E   W A S H

Lynn Channel

Wells-next-the-Sea

Burnham Market

Docking

Hunstanton

Heacham

Dersingham

King's Lynn

Fakenham

Swaffham

Dereham

Terrington St Clement

Clenchwarton

Sutton Bridge

Long Sutton

Wisbech

Briston

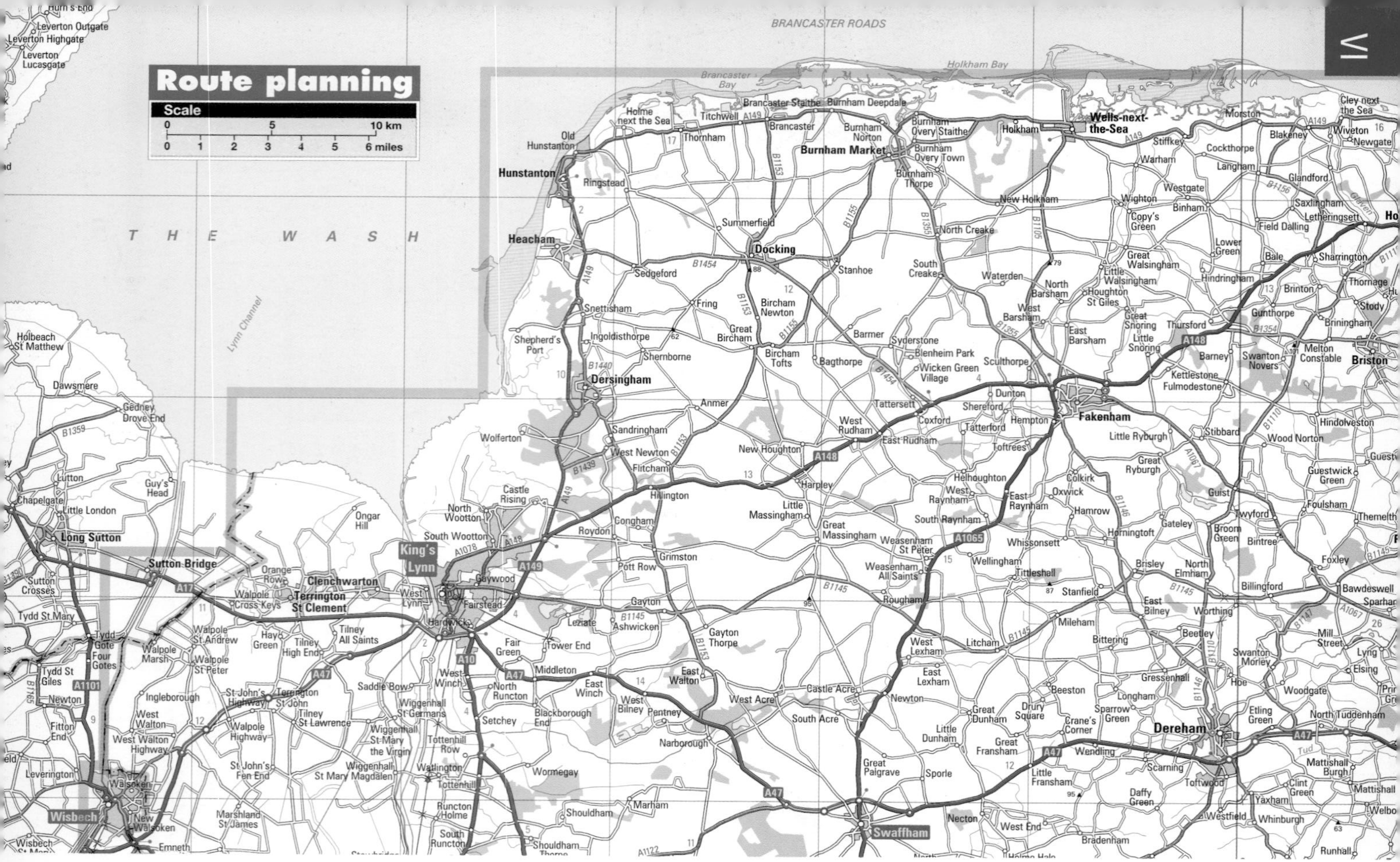

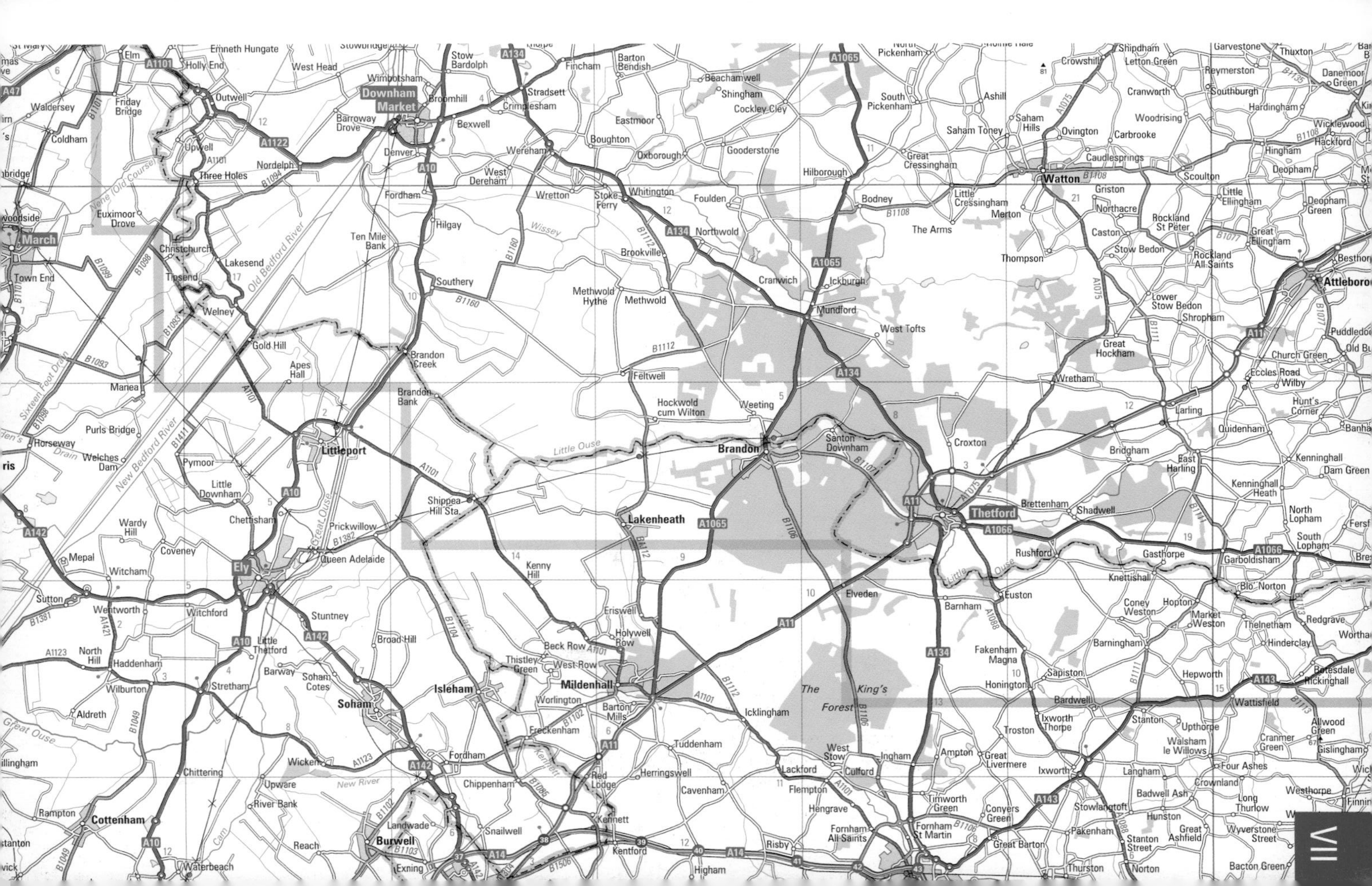

Attleborough
Watton
Thetford
Brandon
Lakenheath
Mildenhall
Isleham
Soham
Ely
Littleport
Downham Market
March
Cottenham
Burwell
Stoke Ferry
Hilborough
Mundford
Ickburgh
Cranwich
Weeting
Feltwell
Methwold
Methwold Hythe
Hockwold cum Wilton
Santon Downham
West Tofts
Croxton
Brettenham
Rushford
Euston
Barnham
Elveden
Icklingham
Tuddenham
Barton Mills
Worlington
Freckenham
West Row
Beck Row
Eriswell
Holywell Row
Kenny Hill
Shippea Hill Sta.
Prickwillow
Queen Adelaide
Stuntney
Fordham
Chippenham
Snailwell
Kentford
Red Lodge
Kennett
Higham
Risby
Lackford
Flempton
Hengrave
West Stow
Culford
Ingham
Ampton
Great Livermere
Troston
Honington
Ixworth
Ixworth Thorpe
Bardwell
Sapiston
Fakenham Magna
Barningham
Coney Weston
Hopton
Market Weston
Knettishall
Gasthorpe
Garboldisham
East Harling
Larling
Bridgham
Shadwell
Great Hockham
Wretham
Thompson
Merton
Caston
Griston
Stow Bedon
Little Cressingham
Great Cressingham
Saham Toney
Ashill
Ovington
Carbrooke
Scoulton
Hingham
Deopham
Little Ellingham
Great Ellingham
Rockland All Saints
Rockland St Peter
Quidenham
Kenninghall
North Lopham
South Lopham
Blo' Norton
Thelnetham
Hinderclay
Redgrave
Wattisfield
Hepworth
Walsham le Willows
Stanton
Bodney
Foulden
Gooderstone
Cockley Cley
Oxborough
Boughton
Eastmoor
Barton Bendish
Fincham
Stradsett
Crimplesham
Bexwell
Wereham
West Dereham
Wretton
Denver
Fordham
Hilgay
Southery
Brandon Creek
Brandon Bank
Ten Mile Bank
Stow Bardolph
Wimbotsham
Barroway Drove
Nordelph
Three Holes
Upwell
Outwell
Christchurch
Welney
Tipsend
Lakesend
Gold Hill
Apes Hall
Manea
Pymoor
Little Downham
Coveney
Chettisham
Witchford
Wardy Hill
Witcham
Mepal
Sutton
Wentworth
Haddenham
Wilburton
Stretham
Little Thetford
Barway
Soham Cotes
Wicken
Upware
Chittering
Waterbeach
Rampton
Aldreth
The King's Forest
Little Ouse
Great Ouse
Lark
Wissey
Old Bedford River
New Bedford River
Sixteen Foot Drain
A11
A10
A134
A1065
A1075
A1066
A1088
A142
A143
A1101
A1122
A14
B1106
B1112
B1160
B1111
B1077

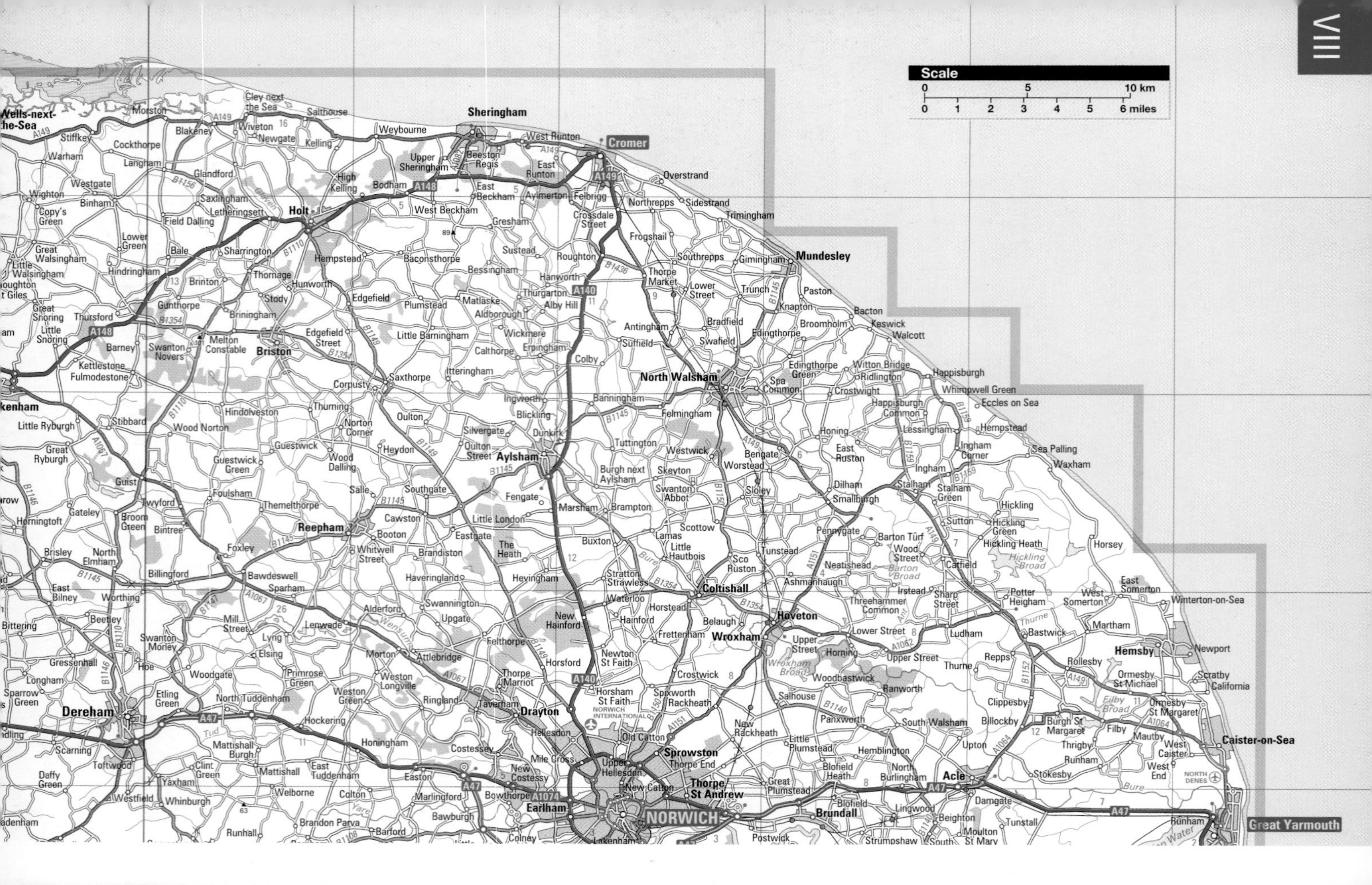
Scale
0 5 10 km
0 1 2 3 4 5 6 miles
Wells-next-the-Sea
Blakeney
Cley next the Sea
Salthouse
Weybourne
Sheringham
West Runton
Cromer
Overstrand
Sidestrand
Trimingham
Mundesley
Paston
Bacton
Keswick
Walcott
Happisburgh
Eccles on Sea
Sea Palling
Waxham
Horsey
Winterton-on-Sea
Hemsby
Newport
Scratby
California
Caister-on-Sea
Great Yarmouth
Holt
Briston
Aylsham
North Walsham
Reepham
Coltishall
Hoveton
Wroxham
Stalham
Ludham
Potter Heigham
Hickling
Martham
Acle
Brundall
Sprowston
Thorpe St Andrew
NORWICH
Drayton
Earlham
Dereham
Fakenham

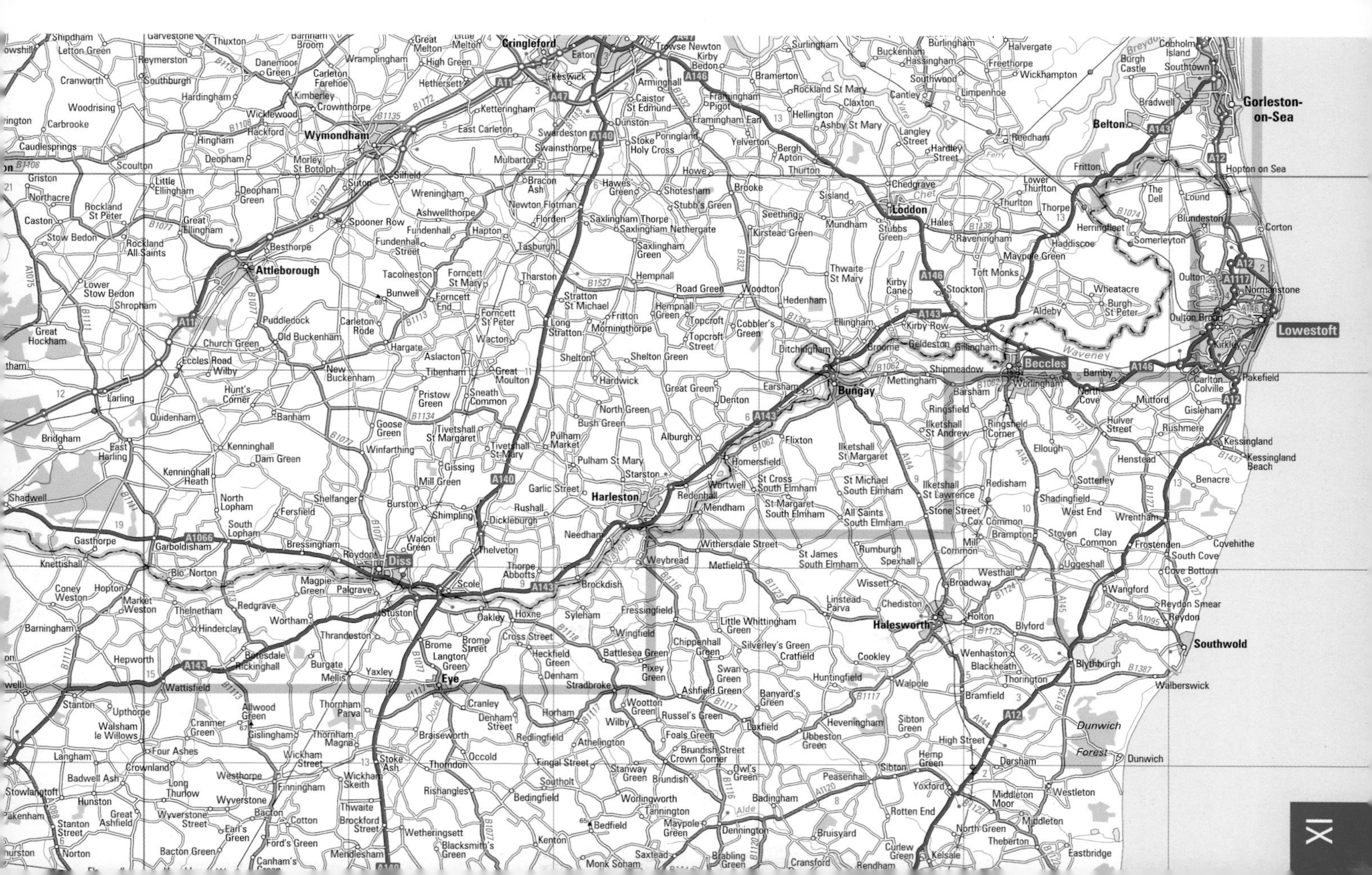
Cringleford
Wymondham
Attleborough
Loddon
Bungay
Beccles
Lowestoft
Gorleston-on-Sea
Belton
Hopton on Sea
Corton
Kessingland
Kessingland Beach
Pakefield
Harleston
Diss
Eye
Halesworth
Southwold
Walberswick
Blythburgh
Wrentham
Dunwich
Dunwich Forest
Waveney
Yare
Chet
Blyth
Alde
Dove
A11
A47
A12
A143
A146
A140
A144
A145
A1066
A1120
A1075

Administrative and Postcode boundaries

TF TG
TF TG

TF TL

TG
TM

TL TM

Lincolnshire

Cambridgeshire

Suffolk

Norfolk

North Norfolk

Broadland

Great Yarmouth

South Norfolk

Breckland

King's Lynn and West Norfolk

Scale

0	5	10	15	20	25	30km
0		5	10	15		20 miles

County and unitary authority boundaries
District boundaries
Postcode boundaries
Area covered by this atlas

Scale: 1⅓ inches to 1 mile

0	¼	½ mile
0	250m 500m 750m	1 km

2

8

45

7

44

6

43

BROADWATER RD

P
BEACH RD

Peddar's Way & Norfolk Coast Path

WESTGATE RD

BEACH ROAD

A149

132

CH Hotel

Old Hunstanton

P

GOLF COURSE ROAD

WODEHOUSE RD
MARSH RD
WATERS RD
PARKS RD

Motel

St Edmund's Point

P

OLD HUNSTANTON RD

PO

CHURCH ST

Chalkpit Wood

Birthday Wood

LIGHTHOUSE CL.

St Edmund's Chapel

B1161

CROMER ROAD

CLIFF PARADE

BERNARD CRESCENT

PEDDARS DR

CLARENCE RD

VICTORIA AVE

CHAPEL BANK

Hunstanton Hall

Deodara Wood

Ilex Wood

PE36

Kimberley Plantation

Ada Grove

Heart Plantation

Sensory Park

Glebe House Sch

HUNSTANTON

Hunstanton Park Earthwork

132

132

Cross

HARTLEY CL.

NURSERY

DOWNG RD

Lodge Farm

Oak Grove

Half Moon Plantation

41

Hunstanton Sea Life Sanctuary

SOUTHEND ROAD

SEAGATE ROAD

Liby

CRESCENT LA.

MELTON

OLD TOWN

KING'S LYNN RD

Smithdon High Sch

Cemy

WAY

Old Bank Wood

South Hill Wood

Larch Plantation

40

3

SOUTH BEACH RD

B1161 OASIS WAY

MANOR

BISHOP'S RD

WINDSOR RISE

PRINCESS DR

Sch

St Andrew's Chapel (remains of)

Downs Farm

Hill Wood

Ringstead Downs Nature Reserve

2

REDGATE HILL

The Firs

Redgate Hill

Ringstead Downs

RINGSTEAD ROAD

39

CH

Searles Golf Course

MYRTLE ROAD

Pit

PE31

MANOR RD

Manor Farm

HUNSTANTON RD

Long Wood

Little Wood

133

Whin Covert

1

Heacham Park

A149

CHURCH FARM RD

Church Farm

38

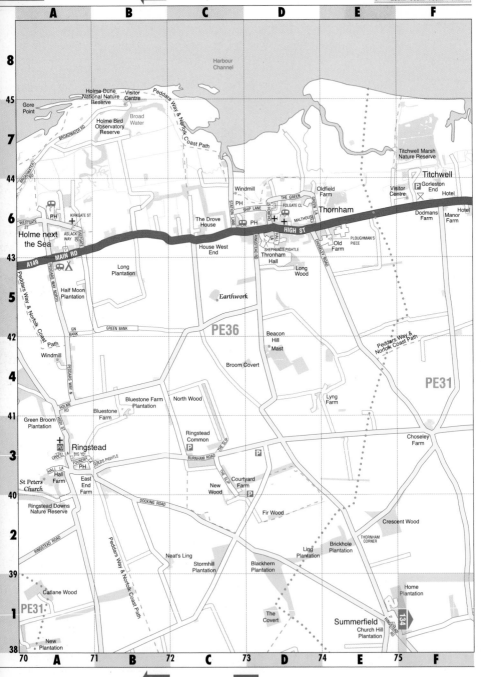

Scale: 1½ inches to 1 mile

0   ¼   ½ mile
0   250m 500m 750m 1 km

Harbour Channel

Gore Point

Holme Dune National Nature Reserve
Visitor Centre
BROADWATER RD
Broad Water
Holme Bird Observatory Reserve
Peddars Way & Norfolk Coast Path

Titchwell Marsh Nature Reserve

Titchwell
Gorleston End
Visitor Centre
Hotel
Windmill
Oldfield Farm
STATION LANE
SHIP LANE
THE GREEN
FOLGATE CL
GREEN LANE
Thornham
Dodmans Farm
Hotel
Manor Farm

WESTGATE ST
PH
KIRKGATE ST
The Drove House
PH
MALTHOUSE
HIGH ST

Holme next the Sea
ASLACK WAY
EASTGATE RD

PH
Old Farm
PLOUGHMAN'S PIECE
CHOSELEY ROAD

A149   MAIN RD
House West End
SHEPHERD'S PIGHTLE
Thornham Hall
KIRKGATE RD
Long Wood

PEDDARS WAY NORTH
Long Plantation
Half Moon Plantation
Earthwork

Peddars Way & Norfolk Coast Path
GN BANK
GREEN BANK
PE36
Beacon Hill
Mast

Windmill
PEDDARS WAY N
Broom Covert
Peddars Way & Norfolk Coast Path
PE31

Green Broom Plantation
Bluestone Farm Plantation
North Wood
Lyng Farm

Bluestone Farm
HOLME RD
Ringstead Common
P
Choseley Farm

Ringstead
CHAPEL LA
PO
BIG YD
FOUNDRY
GOLDS PIGHTLE
BURNHAM ROAD
THE SLIP
P
THE SLIP

St Peters Church
HALL LA
PH
Hall Farm
East End Farm
New Wood
Courtyard Farm
P

Ringstead Downs Nature Reserve
DOCKING ROAD
Fir Wood
Crescent Wood

RINGSTEAD ROAD
Peddars Way & Norfolk Coast Path

Catlane Wood
Neat's Ling
Stormhill Plantation
Blackhern Plantation
Ling Plantation
Brickhole Plantation
THORNHAM CORNER

PE31
The Covert
Home Plantation

New Plantation
Summerfield
Church Hill Plantation
RINGSTEAD RD
B1153

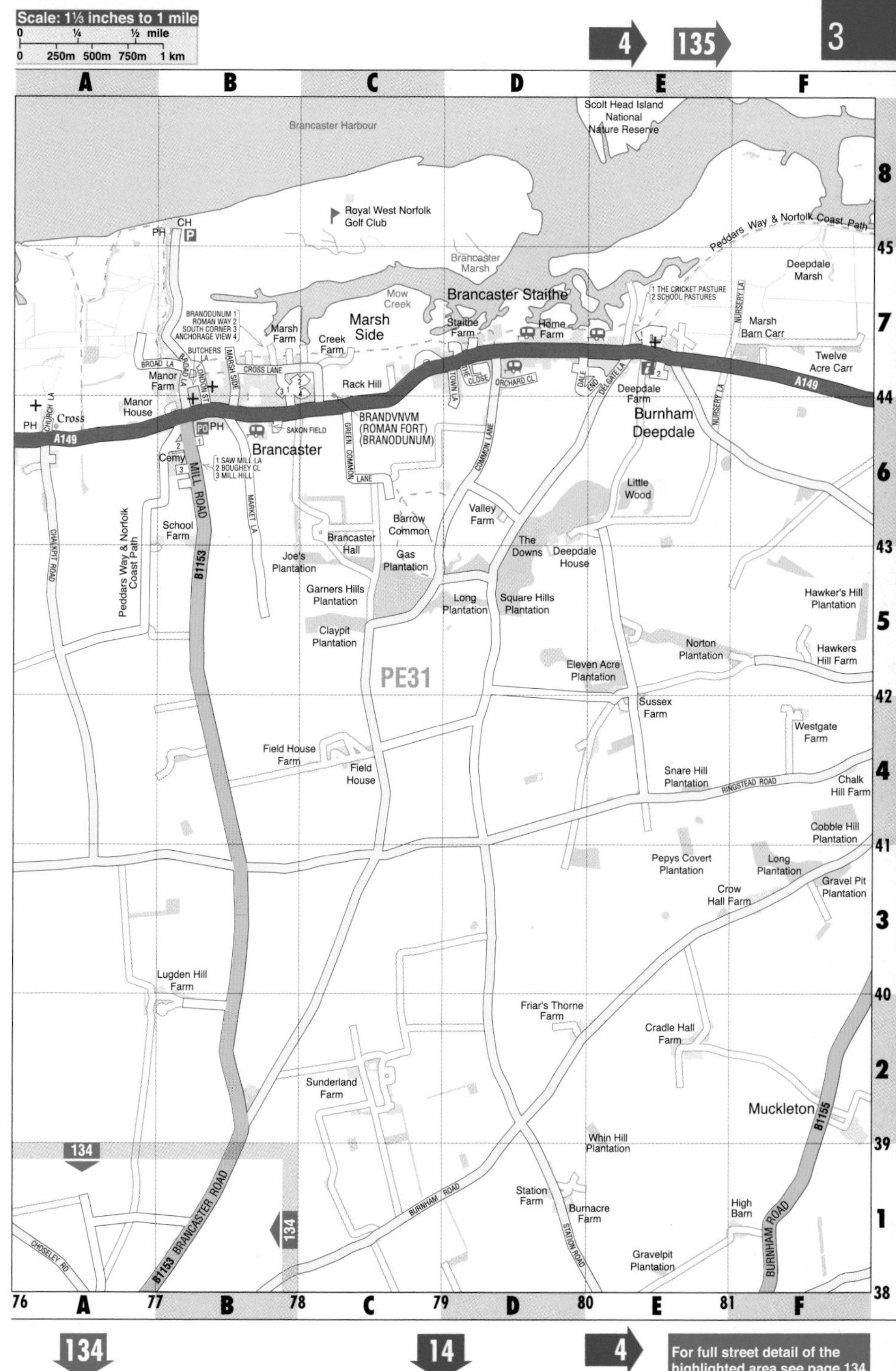

Scale: 1⅓ inches to 1 mile

0   ¼   ½ mile
0   250m 500m 750m 1 km

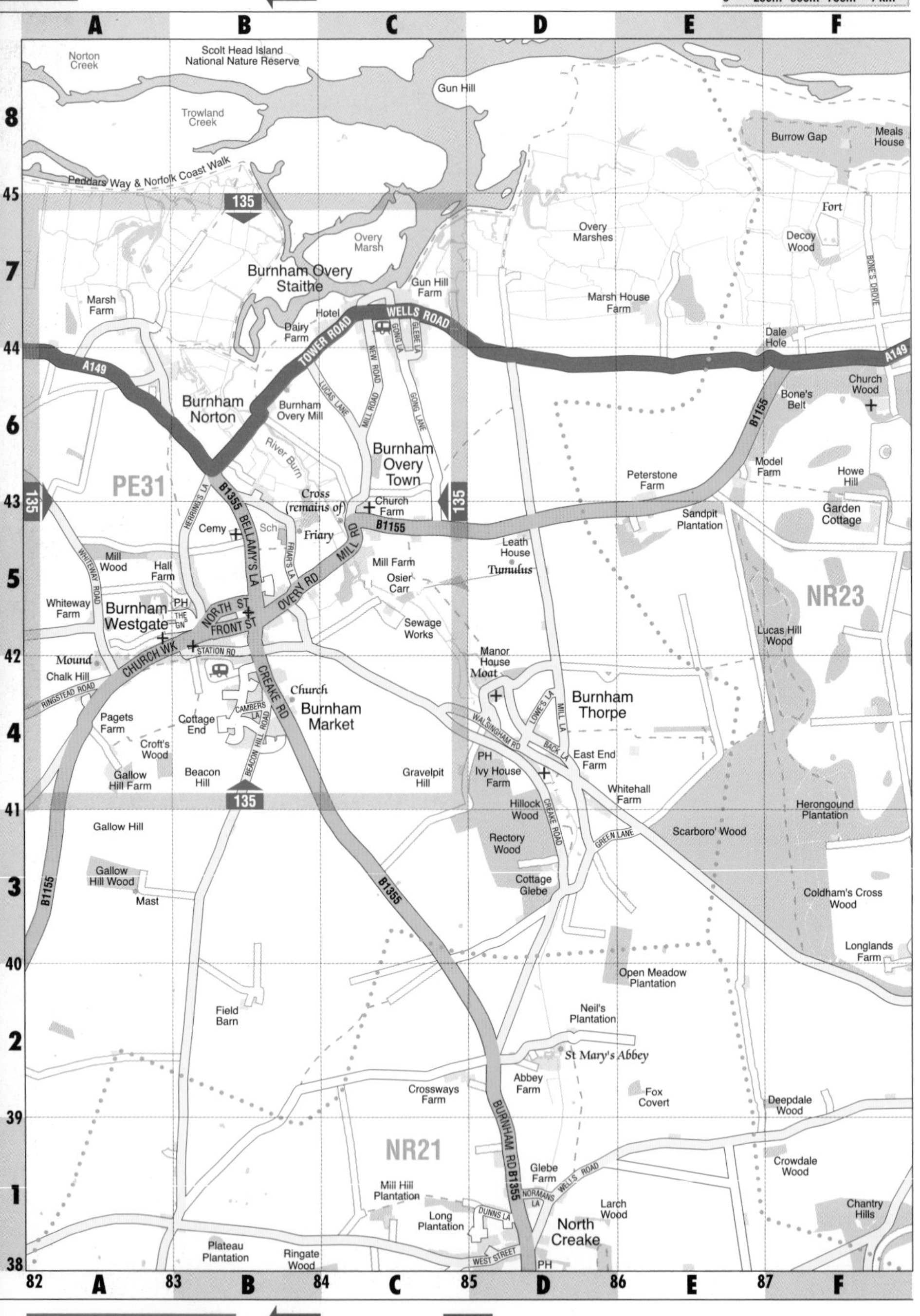

A   B   C   D   E   F

Norton Creek

Scolt Head Island National Nature Reserve

Gun Hill

Burrow Gap

Meals House

Trowland Creek

8

Peddars Way & Norfolk Coast Walk

45

135

Overy Marsh

Overy Marshes

Fort

Decoy Wood

7

Marsh Farm

Burnham Overy Staithe

Gun Hill Farm

Marsh House Farm

BONE'S DROVE

A149

44

A149

Hotel

Dairy Farm

WELLS ROAD

TOWER ROAD

GLEBE LA

NEW ROAD

Dale Hole

Church Wood

B1155

Bone's Belt

6

Burnham Norton

Burnham Overy Mill

Burnham Overy Town

LUCRE LANE

GONE LANE

Model Farm

Howe Hill

River Burn

Peterstone Farm

Garden Cottage

PE31

43

BELLAMY'S LA

B1355

Cross (remains of)

Church Farm

B1155

135

Leath House

Tumulus

Sandpit Plantation

NR23

5

Mill Wood

Hall Farm

Cemy

Sch

Friary

FRIAR'S LA

Mill Farm

Osier Carr

Lucas Hill Wood

Whiteway Farm

Burnham Westgate

PH THE LION

NORTH ST

FRONT ST

OVERY RD

Sewage Works

Manor House Moat

42

Mound

Chalk Hill

CHURCH WK

STATION RD

CAMBERS LA

CREAKE RD

RINGSTEAD ROAD

Church

Burnham Market

WALSINGHAM RD

CHAPEL LA

BACK LA

JOAN LA

MILL LA

Burnham Thorpe

4

Pagets Farm

Croft's Wood

Cottage End

BEACON HILL

Gravelpit Hill

PH Ivy House Farm

East End Farm

Whitehall Farm

Herongound Plantation

Gallow Hill Farm

Beacon Hill

135

Hillock Wood

CREAKE ROAD

GREEN LANE

Scarboro' Wood

Coldham's Cross Wood

41

Gallow Hill

Rectory Wood

Longlands Farm

3

B1155

Gallow Hill Wood

Mast

B1355

Cottage Glebe

Open Meadow Plantation

40

Field Barn

Neil's Plantation

2

St Mary's Abbey

Deepdale Wood

Crossways Farm

Abbey Farm

Fox Covert

Crowdale Wood

39

NR21

BURNHAM RD B1355

Glebe Farm

WELLS ROAD

Larch Wood

Chantry Hills

1

Mill Hill Plantation

Long Plantation

DUNNS LA

NORMANS LA

North Creake

Plateau Plantation

Ringate Wood

WEST STREET

PH

38

82   A   83   B   84   C   85   D   86   E   87   F

For full street detail of the highlighted area see page 135

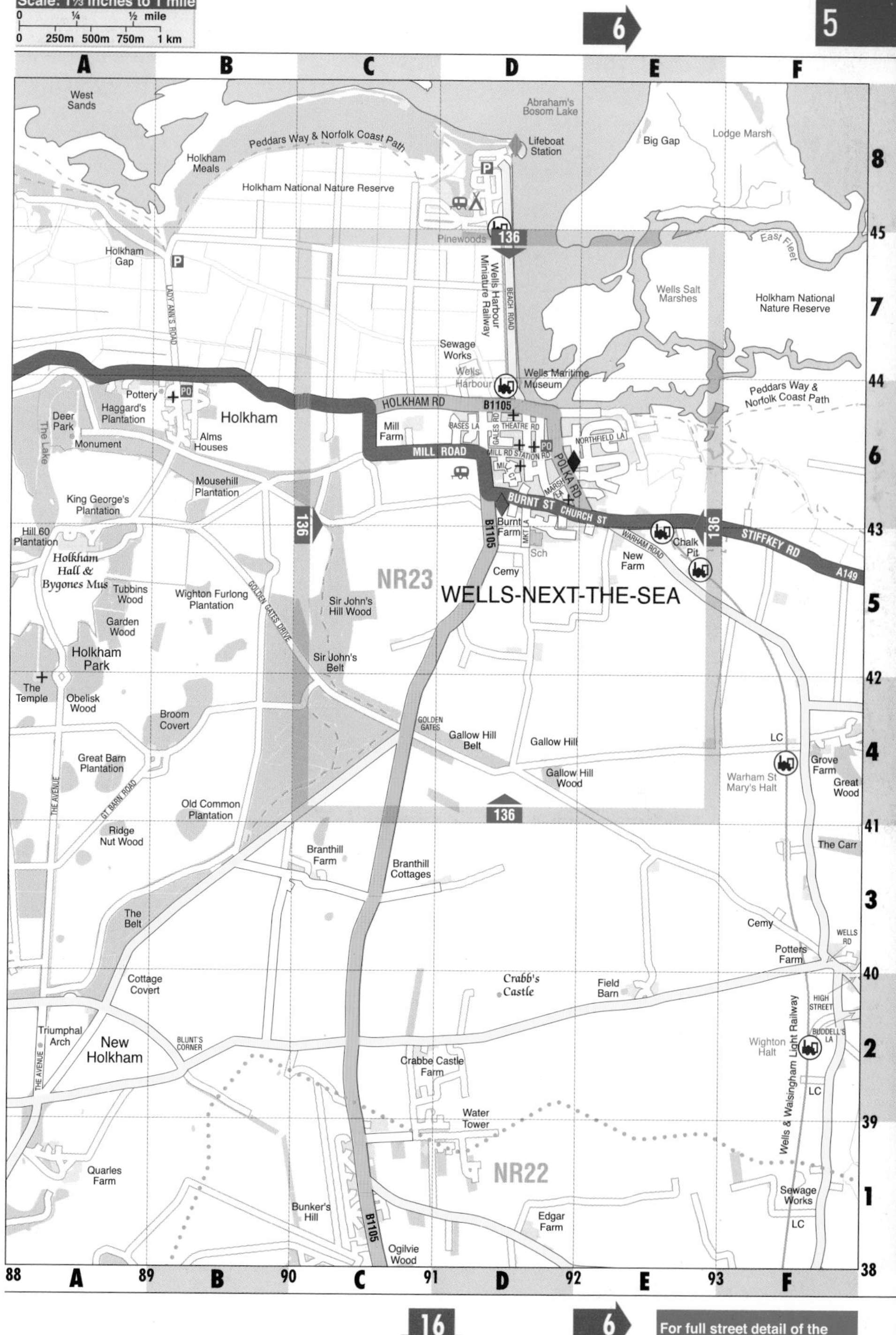

5

Scale: 1⅓ inches to 1 mile

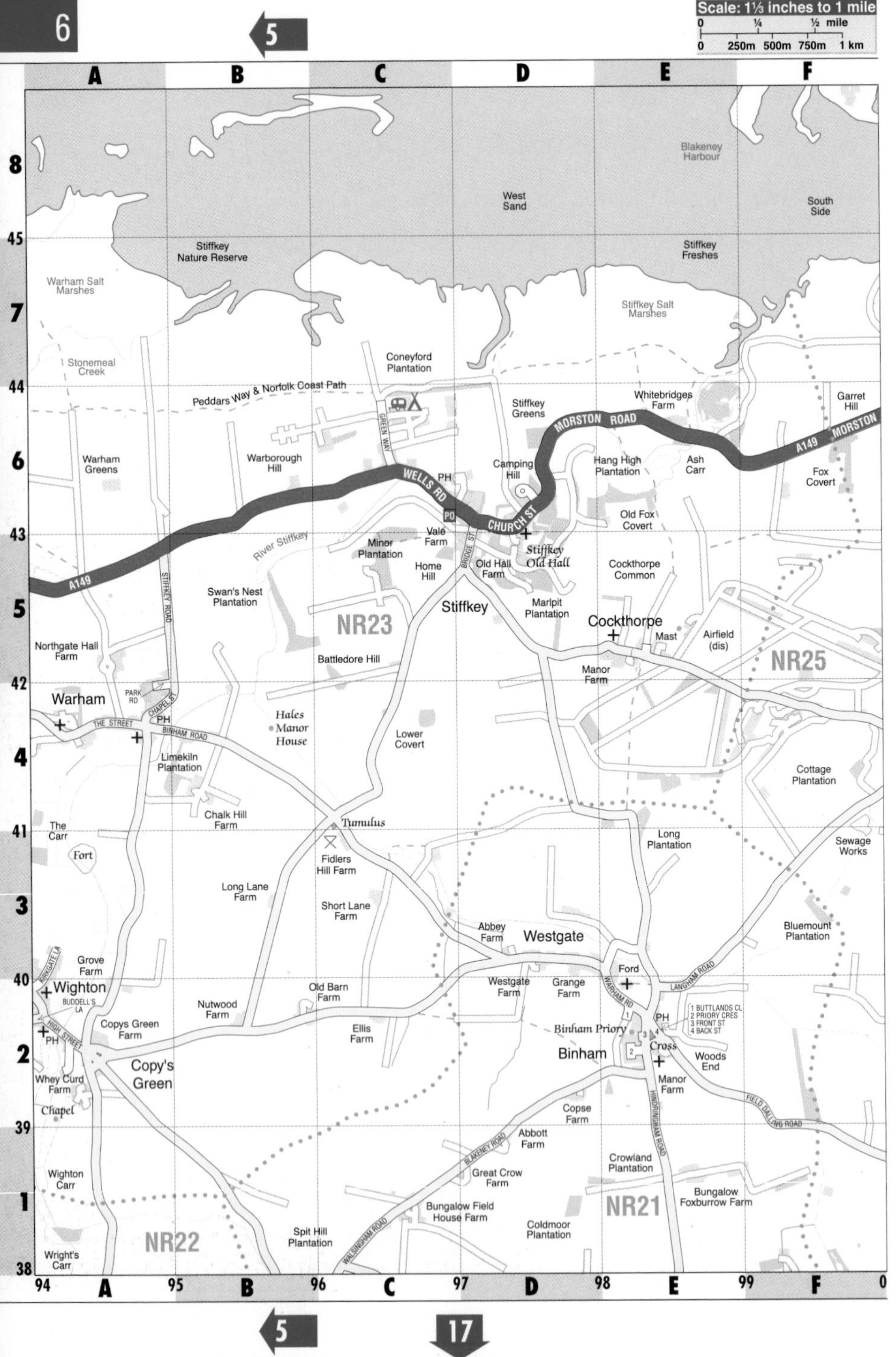

Blakeney Harbour
West Sand
South Side
Stiffkey Nature Reserve
Stiffkey Freshes
Warham Salt Marshes
Stiffkey Salt Marshes
Stonemeal Creek
Coneyford Plantation
Peddars Way & Norfolk Coast Path
Stiffkey Greens
Whitebridges Farm
Garret Hill
MORSTON ROAD
A149
Warham Greens
Warborough Hill
WELLS RD
Camping Hill
Hang High Plantation
Ash Carr
Fox Covert
CHURCH ST
Old Fox Covert
River Stiffkey
Minor Plantation
Vale Farm
Home Hill
Old Hall Farm
Stiffkey Old Hall
Cockthorpe Common
Swan's Nest Plantation
Stiffkey
Marlpit Plantation
Cockthorpe
Mast
Airfield (dis)
NR23
NR25
Northgate Hall Farm
Battledore Hill
Manor Farm
Warham
Hales Manor House
Lower Covert
THE STREET
BINHAM ROAD
Limekiln Plantation
Cottage Plantation
Chalk Hill Farm
Tumulus
The Carr
Fort
Fidlers Hill Farm
Long Plantation
Sewage Works
Long Lane Farm
Short Lane Farm
Abbey Farm
Westgate
Bluemount Plantation
Grove Farm
Wighton
Westgate Farm
Grange Farm
Ford
LANGHAM ROAD
Old Barn Farm
Nutwood Farm
Copys Green Farm
Ellis Farm
Binham Priory
Binham
Cross
Woods End
Copy's Green
Manor Farm
Whey Curd Farm
Chapel
Copse Farm
Abbott Farm
FIELD DALLING ROAD
Wighton Carr
Great Crow Farm
Crowland Plantation
Bungalow Field House Farm
Bungalow Foxburrow Farm
Spit Hill Plantation
Coldmoor Plantation
NR22
NR21
Wright's Carr
1 BUTTLANDS CL
2 PRIORY CRES
3 FRONT ST
4 BACK ST

5
17

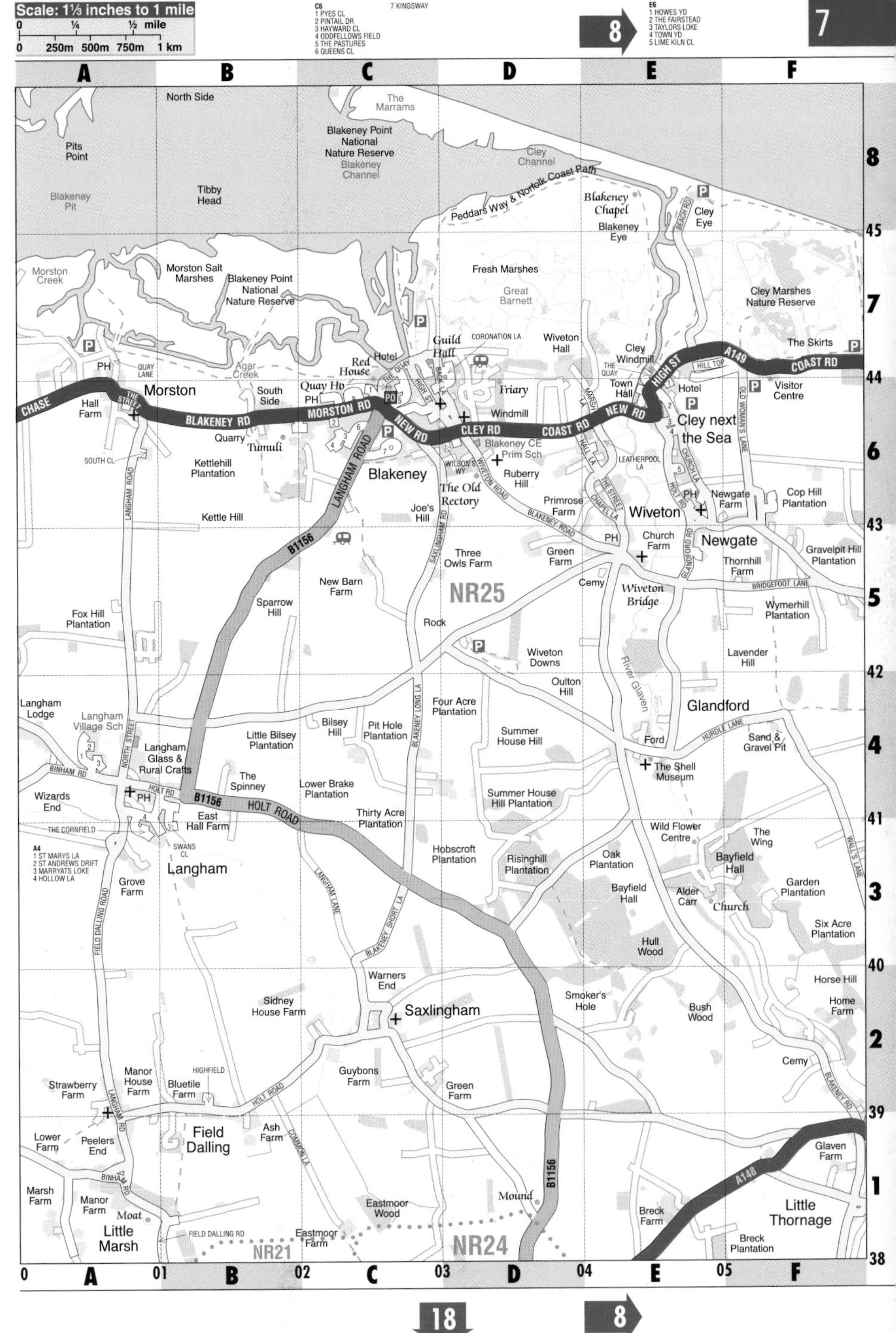

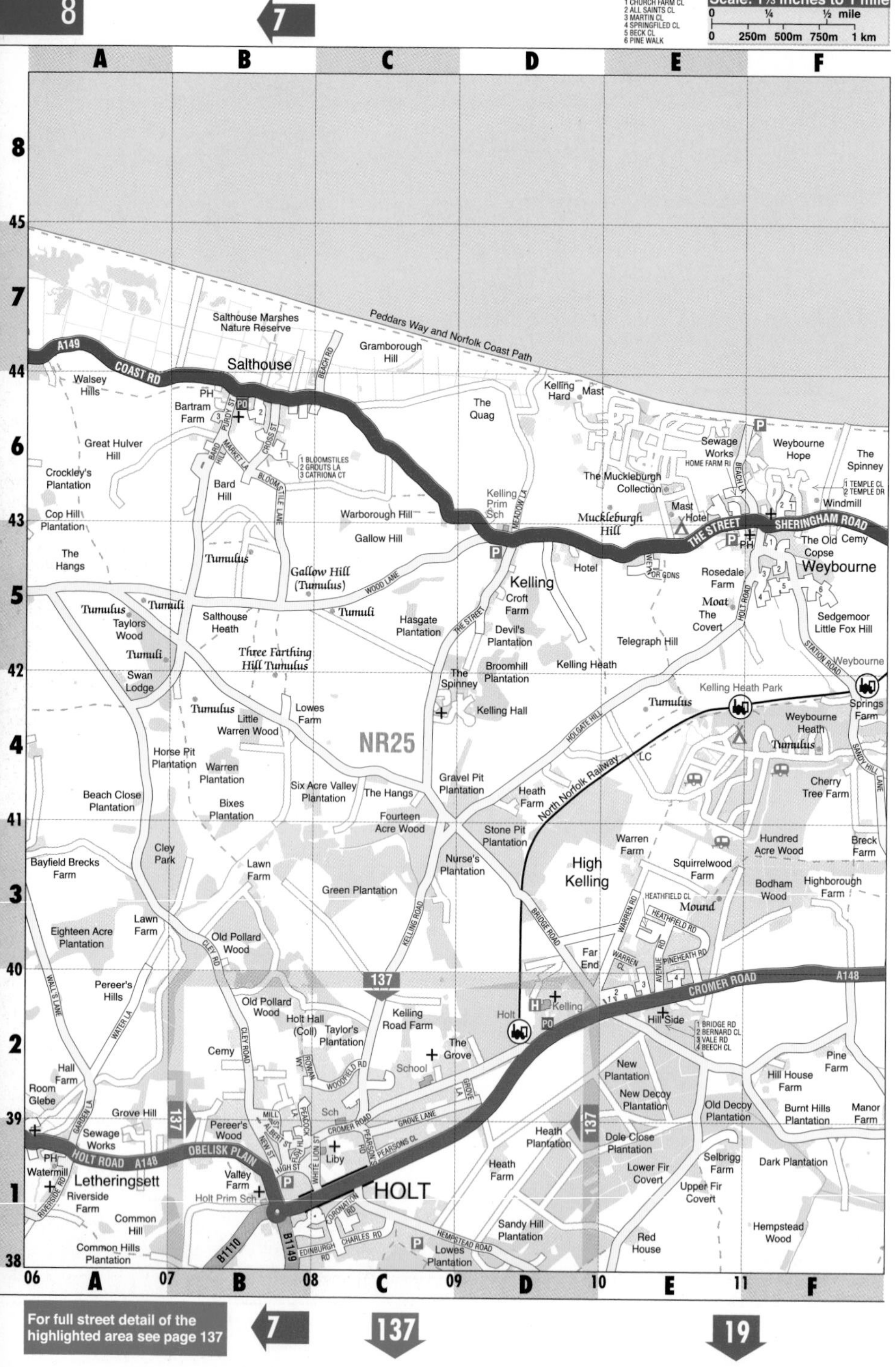

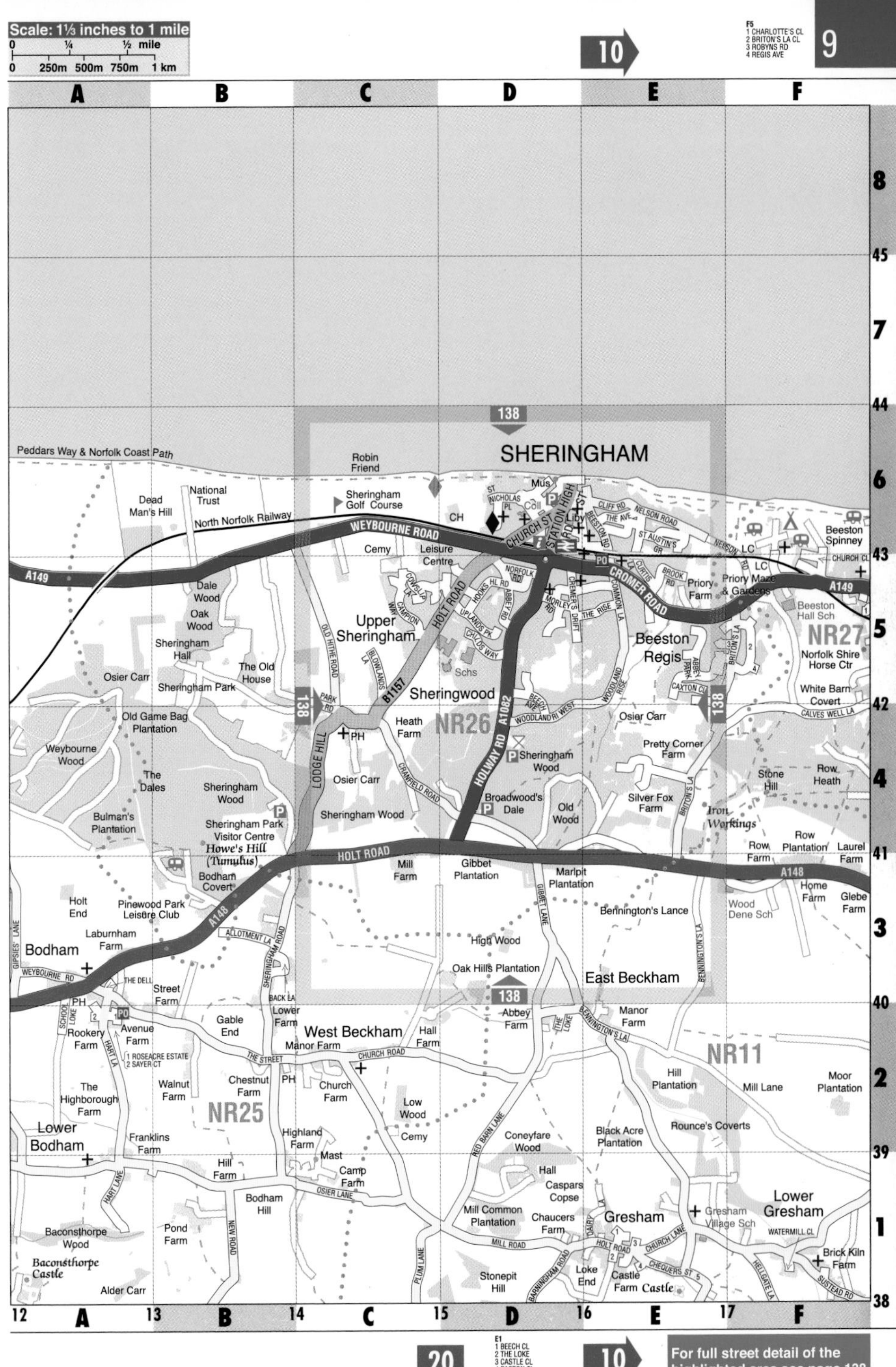

Scale: 1⅓ inches to 1 mile

0   ¼   ½ mile
0 250m 500m 750m 1 km

10

9

F5
1 CHARLOTTE'S CL
2 BRITON'S LA CL
3 ROBYNS RD
4 REGIS AVE

A   B   C   D   E   F

8

45

7

44

138

SHERINGHAM

6

Peddars Way & Norfolk Coast Path

Robin Friend

Dead Man's Hill

National Trust

Sheringham Golf Course

Mus

St NICHOLAS PL   Coll

CH

North Norfolk Railway

WEYBOURNE ROAD

Cemy

CLIFF RD

NELSON RD

ST AUSTIN'S GR

Beeston Spinney

43

A149

Dale Wood

Leisure Centre

NORFOLK

Priory Farm

Priory Mall & Gardens

A149

5

Oak Wood

Sheringham Hall

HOLT ROAD

UPLANDS RD

CROMER ROAD

Beeston Regis

Beeston Hall Sch

Norfolk Shire Horse Ctr

NR27

Osier Carr

The Old House

Upper Sheringham

LYNGS WAY

Schs

CAXTON CL

BRITON'S LA

White Barn Covert

CALVES WELL LA

42

Sheringham Park

LODGE HILL

PARK RD

B1157

Sheringwood

NR26

HOLWAY RD

A1082

WOODLAND WEST

Osier Carr

Pretty Corner Farm

Stone Hill

Row Heath

Old Game Bag Plantation

The Dales

Sheringham Wood

Heath Farm

Sheringham Wood

Broadwood's Dale

Old Wood

Silver Fox Farm

Iron Workings

Row Plantation

Laurel Wood

41

Weybourne Wood

Bulman's Plantation

Osier Carr

Sheringham Wood Visitor Centre

Howe's Hill (Tumulus)

A148

Sheringham Wood

P

Mill Farm

Gibbet Plantation

Marlpit Plantation

Bennington's Lance

Wood Dene Sch

Row Farm

Home Farm

Glebe Farm

A148

3

Holt End

Pinewood Park Leisure Club

Bodham Covert

A148

Laburnham Farm

ALLOTMENT LA

SHERINGHAM LA

High Wood

Oak Hills Plantation

East Beckham

NR11

40

Bodham

THE DELL

Street Farm

BACK LA

Lower Farm

138

Abbey Farm

Manor Farm

2

SCHOOL LOKE

PH

Rookery Farm

Avenue Farm

Gable End

THE STREET

West Beckham

Manor Farm

Hall Farm

RED BARN LANE

BENNINGTON'S LA

Hill Plantation

Mill Lane

Moor Plantation

39

The Highborough Farm

Walnut Farm

Chestnut Farm

PH

Church Farm

Low Wood

Coneyfare Wood

Black Acre Plantation

Rounce's Coverts

Lower Bodham

Franklins Farm

Highland Farm

Cemy

Hall Farm

Caspars Copse

Gresham

Gresham Village Sch

Lower Gresham

WATERMILL CL

1

Hill Farm

Mast

Camp Farm

OSIER LANE

Mill Common Plantation

Chaucers Farm

DAIRY

HOLT ROAD

CHEQUERS ST

Brick Kiln Farm

Baconsthorpe Wpod

Pond Farm

Bodham Hill

PLUM LANE

BARNINGHAM ROAD

Stonepit Hill

Loke End

Castle Farm   Castle

CHURCH ROAD

RELGATE LA

SUSTEAD RD

38

12   A   13   B   14   C   15   D   16   E   17   F

20

10

For full street detail of the highlighted area see page 138

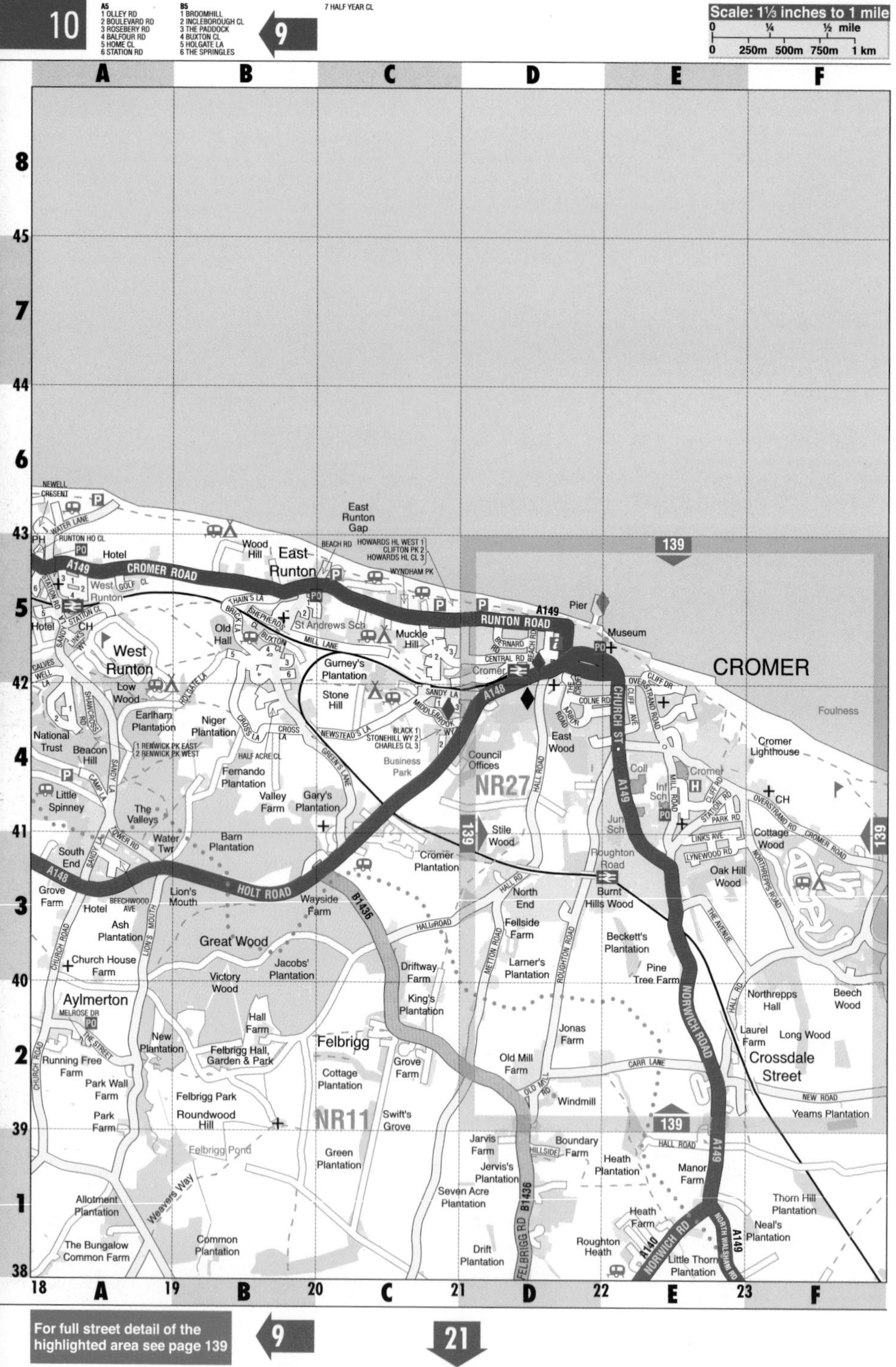

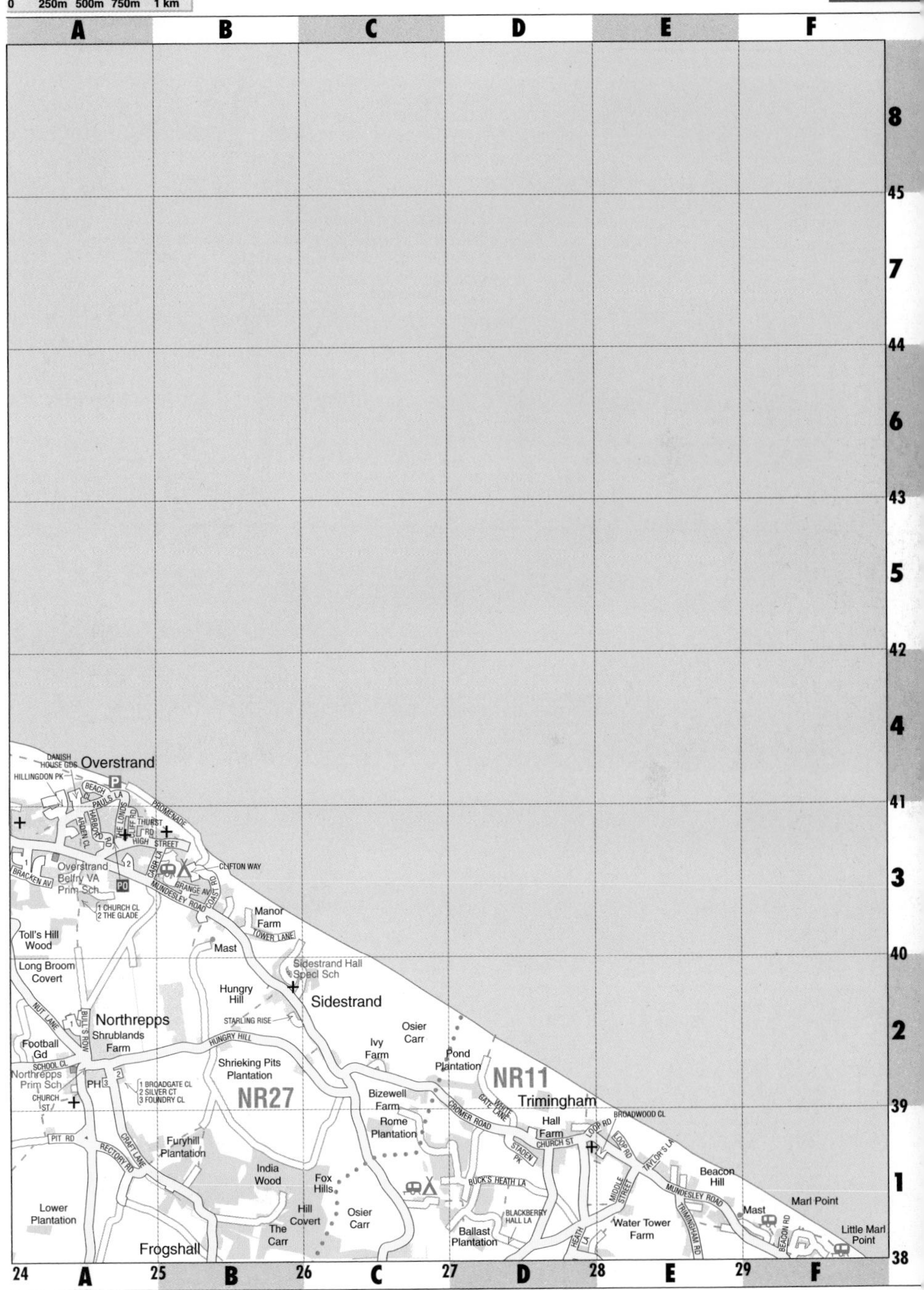

Scale: 1⅓ inches to 1 mile

| 0 | ¼ | ½ mile |
| 0 | 250m 500m 750m 1 km |

Overstrand

DANISH HOUSE GDNS
HILLINGDON PK

BEACH
PAULS LA
PROMENADE
THIRST
RD
HIGH STREET
CLIFTON WAY

Overstrand Belfry VA Prim Sch

BRACKEN AV
MUNDESLEY ROAD
GRANGE AV

1 CHURCH CL
2 THE GLADE

Toll's Hill Wood

Manor Farm

TOWER LANE

Long Broom Covert

Mast

Hungry Hill

Sidestrand Hall Specl Sch

Sidestrand

Northrepps

BULL LANE
BULLS HILL
Shrublands Farm

STARLING RISE

HUNGRY HILL

Osier Carr

Ivy Farm

Pond Plantation

NR11

Trimingham

Football Gd
SCHOOL CL
Northrepps Prim Sch
PH
CHURCH ST

Shrieking Pits Plantation

NR27

Bizewell Farm

Rome Plantation

RAIL PINE
CROMER ROAD

Hall Farm
CHURCH ST

BROADWOOD CL

LOOP RD

1 BROADGATE CL
2 SILVER CT
3 FOUNDRY CL

PIT RD
RECTORY RD
CRAFT LANE

Furyhill Plantation

India Wood

Fox Hills

BUCK'S HEATH LA

HELPS LA

STACK LA

MIDDLE STREET

PETCH'S LA

Beacon Hill

MUNDESLEY ROAD

Marl Point

Lower Plantation

The Carr

Hill Covert

Osier Carr

Ballast Plantation

BLACKBERRY HALL LA

ASH LA

Water Tower Farm

TRIMINGHAM RD

BEACON RD

Mast

Little Marl Point

Frogshall

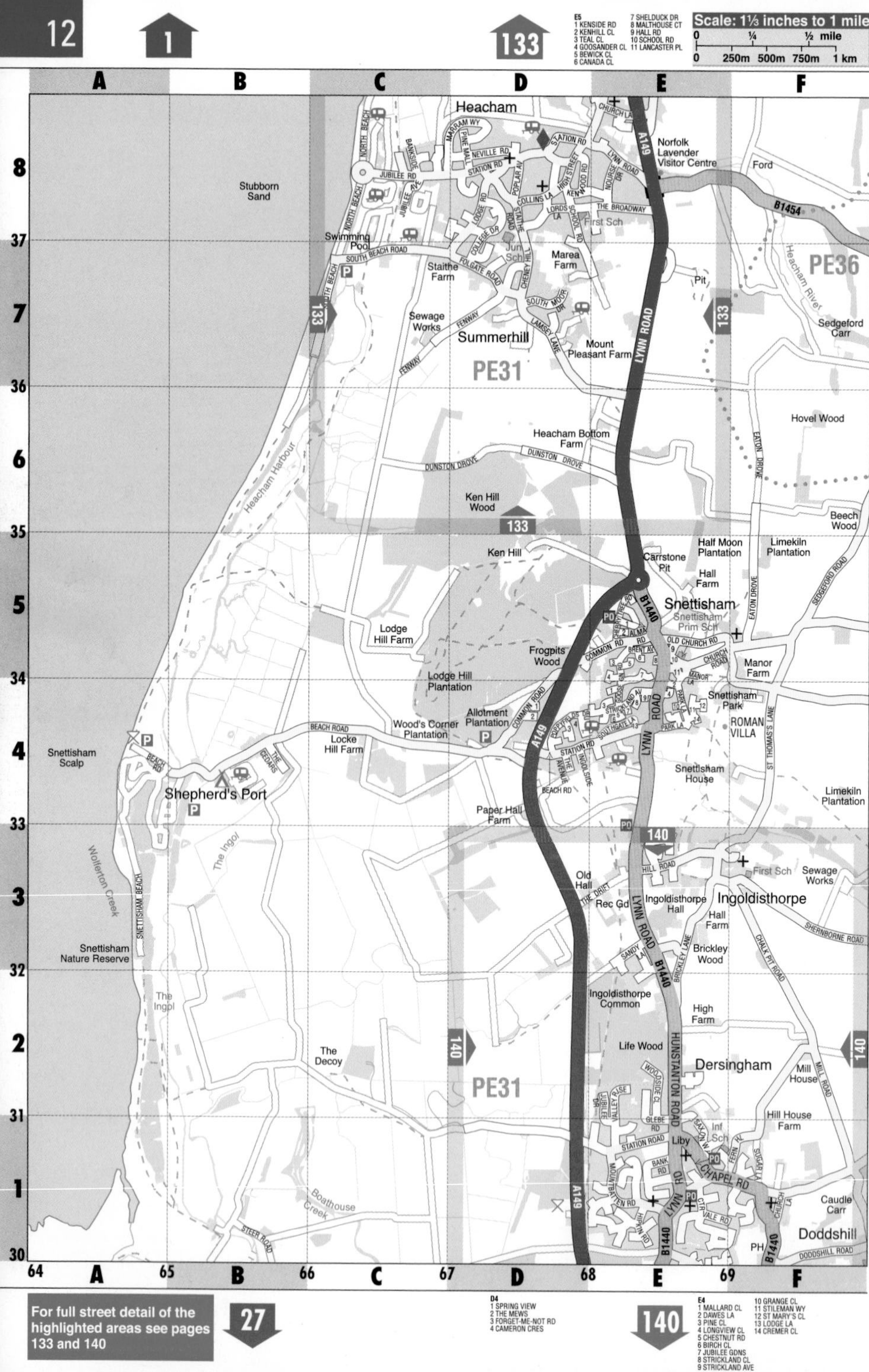
1
133
E5
1 KENSIDE RD
2 KENHILL CL
3 TEAL CL
4 GOOSANDER CL
5 BEWICK CL
6 CANADA CL
7 SHELDUCK DR
8 MALTHOUSE CT
9 HALL RD
10 SCHOOL RD
11 LANCASTER PL
Scale: 1⅓ inches to 1 mile
0 ¼ ½ mile
0 250m 500m 750m 1 km
A B C D E F
8
37
7
36
6
35
5
34
4
33
3
32
2
31
1
30
64 A 65 B 66 C 67 D 68 E 69 F
Heacham
Stubborn Sand
NORTH BEACH
JUBILEE RD
BANKSIDE
MARRAM WY
PINE MALL
NEVILLE RD
STATION RD
POPLAR AV
LODGE RD
COLLEGE DR
STATION RD
HIGH STREET
LYNN ROAD
COLLINS LA
LORDS LA
SCHOOL RD
THE BROADWAY
KENWOOD RD
NOURSE DR
CHURCH LA
First Sch
Jun Sch
Swimming Pool
SOUTH BEACH ROAD
FOLGATE ROAD
CHENEY HILL
STAITHE
Staithe Farm
Marea Farm
SOUTH MOOR DR
LAMSEY LANE
Sewage Works
FENWAY
Summerhill
Mount Pleasant Farm
PE31
A149
Norfolk Lavender Visitor Centre
Ford
B1454
Heacham River
PE36
Pit
Sedgeford Carr
LYNN ROAD
Hovel Wood
EATON DROVE
Heacham Bottom Farm
DUNSTON DROVE
Ken Hill Wood
Heacham Harbour
Beech Wood
Ken Hill
Carrstone Pit
Half Moon Plantation
Limekiln Plantation
Hall Farm
SEDGEFORD ROAD
B1440
Snettisham
Snettisham Prim Sch
OLD CHURCH RD
CHURCH ROAD
Manor Farm
COMMON RD
BRENT AV
ALMA RD
CHERRYTREE RD
Lodge Hill Farm
Frogpits Wood
Lodge Hill Plantation
MANOR RD
Snettisham Park
ROMAN VILLA
ST THOMAS'S LANE
COMMON ROAD
Allotment Plantation
Wood's Corner Plantation
BEACH ROAD
Locke Hill Farm
STRICKLAND AV
SOUTHGATE LA
PARK LA
STATION RD
INGOLDSIDE
THE AVENUE
BEACH RD
Snettisham Scalp
BEACH RD
THE CEDARS
Shepherd's Port
Snettisham House
Limekiln Plantation
Paper Hall Farm
140
HILL ROAD
Old Hall
THE DRIFT
Rec Gd
Ingoldisthorpe Hall
Ingoldisthorpe
First Sch
Sewage Works
SHERNBORNE ROAD
Hall Farm
CHALK PIT ROAD
The Ingol
Wolferton Creek
SNETTISHAM BEACH
Snettisham Nature Reserve
SANDY LA
BRICKLEY LANE
Brickley Wood
Ingoldisthorpe Common
The Ingol
High Farm
Life Wood
HUNSTANTON ROAD
The Decoy
Dersingham
Mill House
MILL ROAD
PE31
WOODSIDE CL
VALLEY RISE
JUBILEE DR
GLEBE RD
STATION ROAD
Inf Sch
SAXON WY
FERN HL
SUGAR LA
Hill House Farm
Liby
BANK RD
CHAPEL RD
MOUNTBATTEN RD
LYNN RD
CTR VALE RD
HIPKIN RD
CHURCH LA
Caudle Carr
Boathouse Creek
STEER ROAD
Doddshill
PH
DODDSHILL ROAD
For full street detail of the highlighted areas see pages 133 and 140
27
D4
1 SPRING VIEW
2 THE MEWS
3 FORGET-ME-NOT RD
4 CAMERON CRES
E4
1 MALLARD CL
2 DAWES LA
3 PINE CL
4 LONGVIEW CL
5 CHESTNUT RD
6 BIRCH CL
7 JUBILEE GDNS
8 STRICKLAND CL
9 STRICKLAND AVE
10 GRANGE CL
11 STILEMAN WY
12 ST MARY'S CL
13 LODGE LA
14 CREMER CL

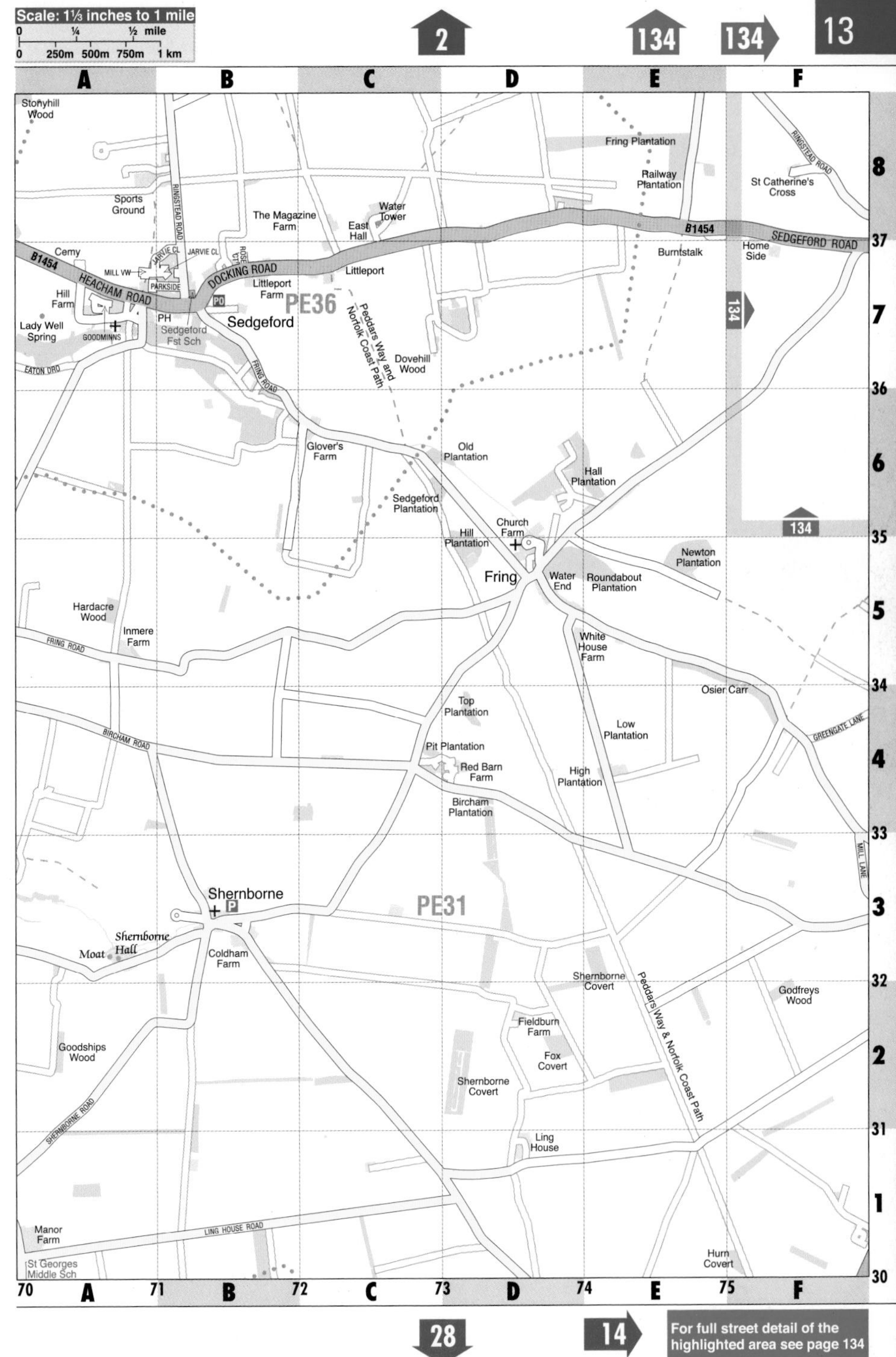

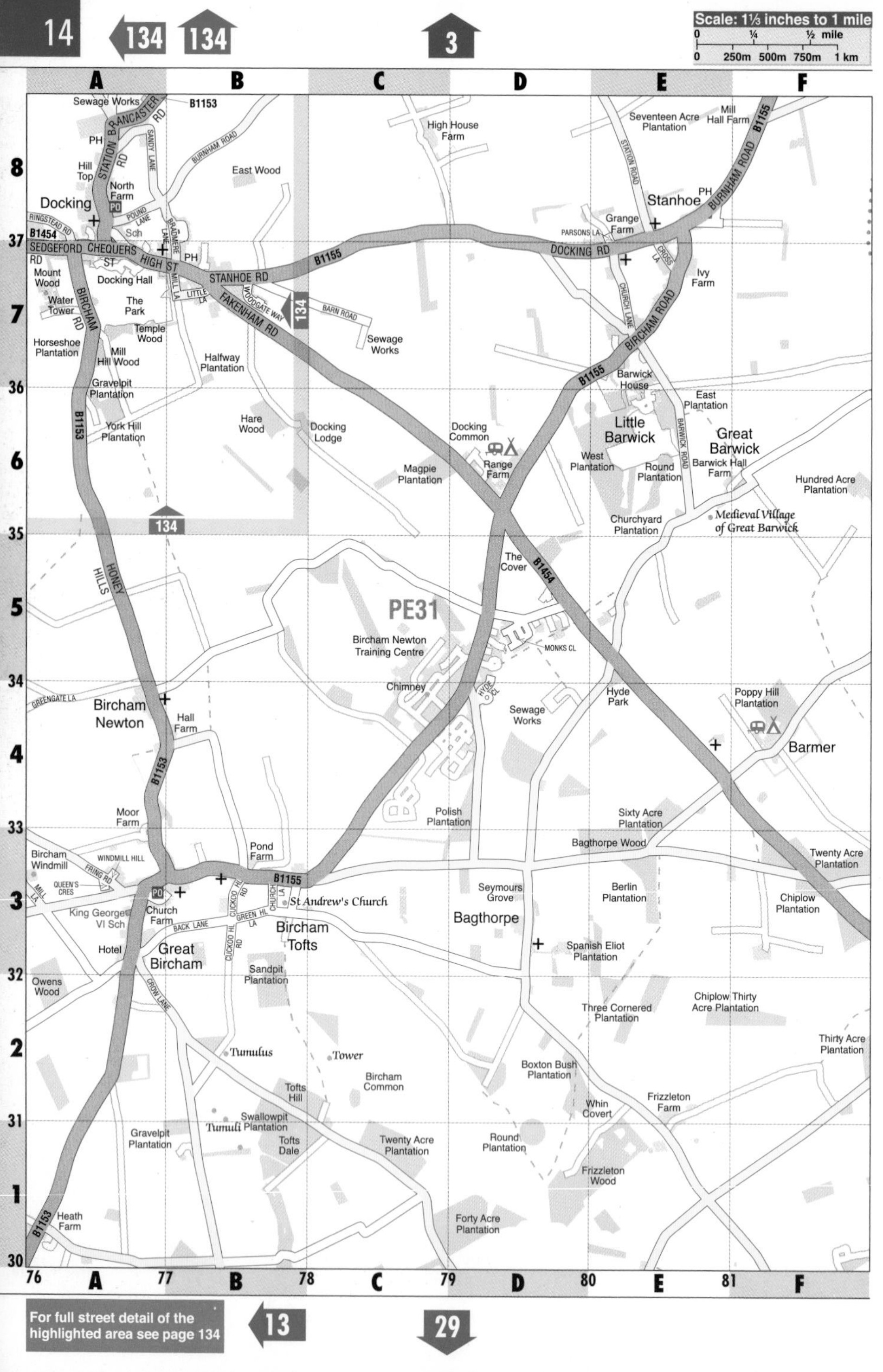

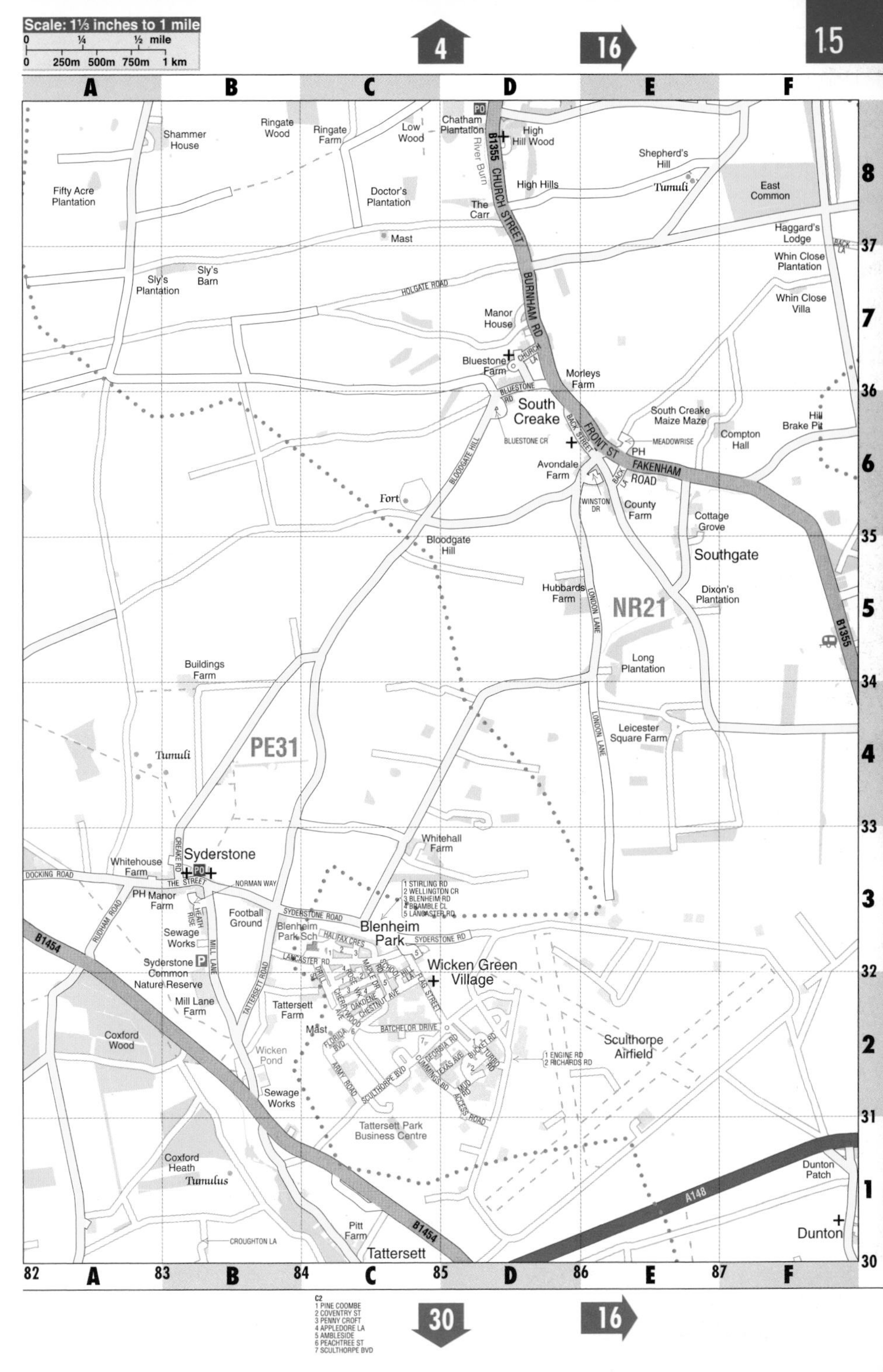

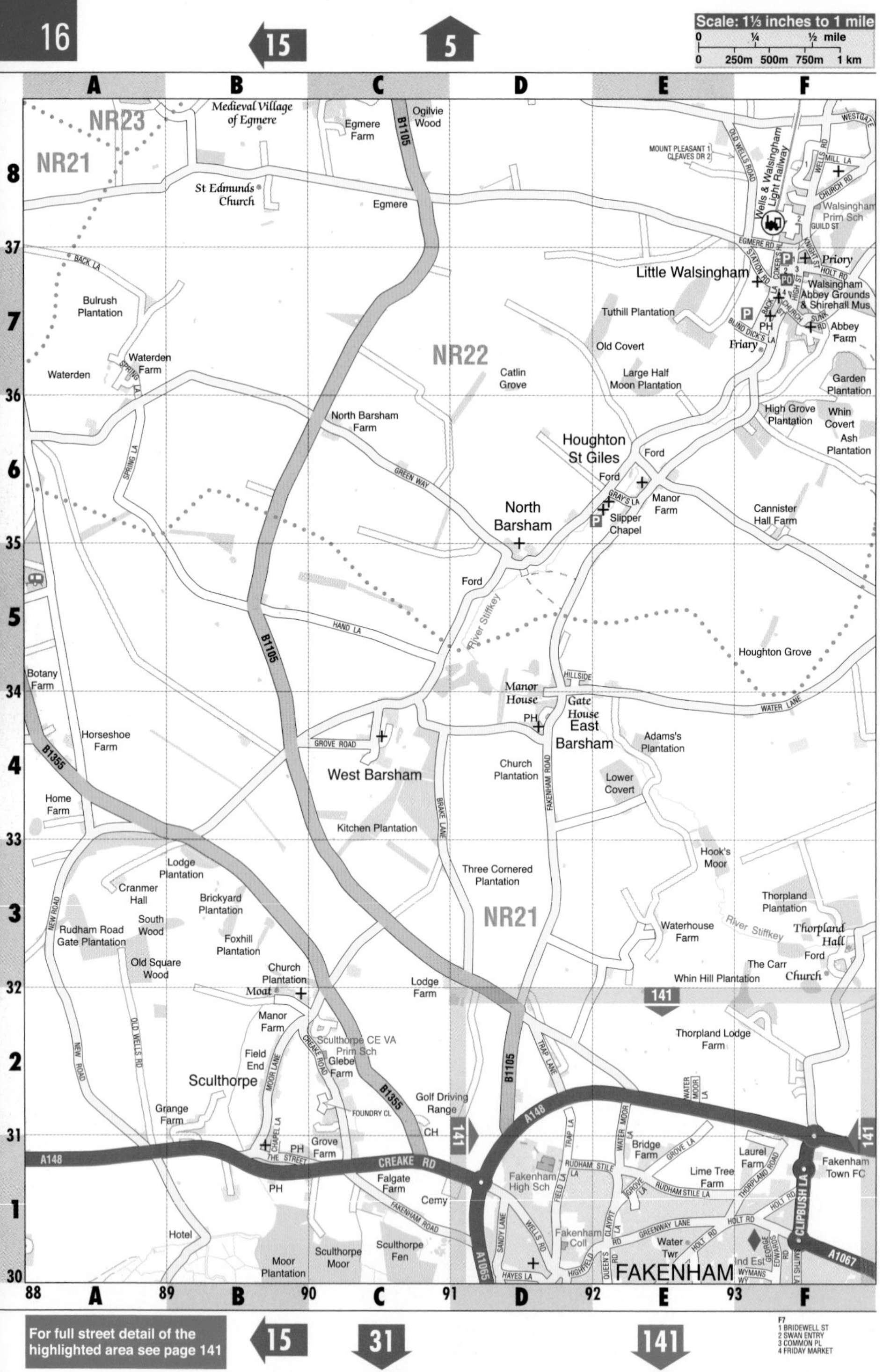

Scale: 1½ inches to 1 mile

F7
1 BRIDEWELL ST
2 SWAN ENTRY
3 COMMON PL
4 FRIDAY MARKET

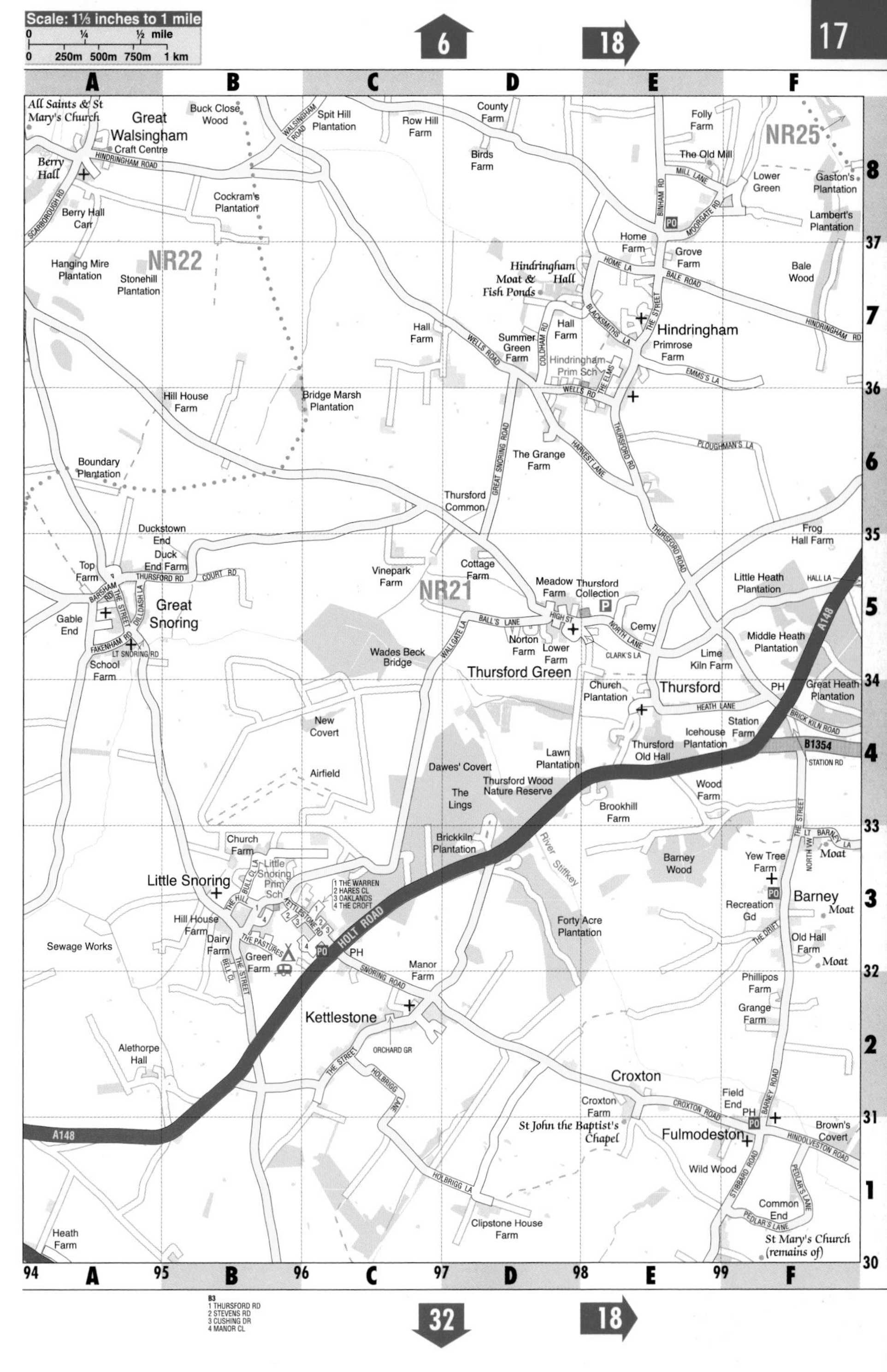
Scale: 1⅓ inches to 1 mile
0 ¼ ½ mile
0 250m 500m 750m 1 km
6
18
All Saints & St Mary's Church
Great Walsingham
Craft Centre
Berry Hall
Buck Close Wood
Spit Hill Plantation
Row Hill Farm
County Farm
Birds Farm
Folly Farm
The Old Mill
NR25
Lower Green
Gaston's Plantation
Lambert's Plantation
Cockram's Plantation
Berry Hall Carr
Hanging Mire Plantation
NR22
Stonehill Plantation
Home Farm
Grove Farm
Hindringham Moat & Fish Ponds
Hindringham Hall
Bale Wood
Hall Farm
Summer Green Farm
Hall Farm
Hindringham
Primrose Farm
Hindringham Prim Sch
Hill House Farm
Bridge Marsh Plantation
The Grange Farm
Boundary Plantation
Thursford Common
Duckstown End
Duck End Farm
Top Farm
Frog Hall Farm
Vinepark Farm
Cottage Farm
NR21
Meadow Farm
Thursford Collection
Little Heath Plantation
Great Snoring
Gable End
Norton Farm
Lower Farm
Cemy
Middle Heath Plantation
School Farm
Wades Beck Bridge
Thursford Green
Lime Kiln Farm
Church Plantation
Thursford
PH
Great Heath Plantation
New Covert
Station Farm
Icehouse Plantation
Thursford Old Hall
Lawn Plantation
Airfield
Dawes' Covert
Thursford Wood Nature Reserve
Wood Farm
The Lings
Brookhill Farm
Brickkiln Plantation
Church Farm
Little Snoring
Little Snoring Prim Sch
1 THE WARREN
2 HARES CL
3 OAKLANDS
4 THE CROFT
River Stiffkey
Barney Wood
Yew Tree Farm
Moat
Barney
Recreation Gd
Moat
Hill House Farm
Dairy Farm
Green Farm
PH
Forty Acre Plantation
Old Hall Farm
Moat
Sewage Works
Manor Farm
Phillipos Farm
Kettlestone
Grange Farm
Alethorpe Hall
Croxton
Croxton Farm
Field End
PH
St John the Baptist's Chapel
Fulmodeston
Brown's Covert
Wild Wood
Common End
Clipstone House Farm
Heath Farm
St Mary's Church (remains of)
A148
B1354
HOLT ROAD
HINDRINGHAM ROAD
SCARBOROUGH RD
WALSINGHAM ROAD
BINHAM RD
MILL LANE
MOORGATE RD
HOME LA
BALE ROAD
THE STREET
BLACKSMITHS LA
WELLS ROAD
COLDHAM RD
THE ELMS
WELLS RD
EMMS'S LA
HARVEST LANE
THURSFORD RD
PLOUGHMAN'S LA
GREAT SNORING ROAD
THURSFORD ROAD
THURSFORD RD
COURT RD
BARSHAM RD
DILLDASH LA
FAKENHAM RD
LT SNORING RD
BALL'S LANE
WALLGATE LA
HIGH ST
NORTH LANE
CLARK'S LA
HALL LA
HEATH LANE
BRICK KILN ROAD
STATION RD
THE STREET
LT BARNEY LA
NORTH VW
THE DRIFT
THE HILL
BULL CL
THE PASTURES
KETTLESTONE RD
BELL CL
SNORING ROAD
ORCHARD GR
HOLBRIGG LANE
HOLBRIGG LA
CROXTON ROAD
BARNEY ROAD
HINDOLVESTON ROAD
STIBBARD ROAD
PEDLAR'S LANE
A B C D E F
8 37 7 36 6 35 5 34 4 33 3 32 2 31 1 30
94 95 96 97 98 99
B3
1 THURSFORD RD
2 STEVENS RD
3 CUSHING DR
4 MANOR CL
32
18

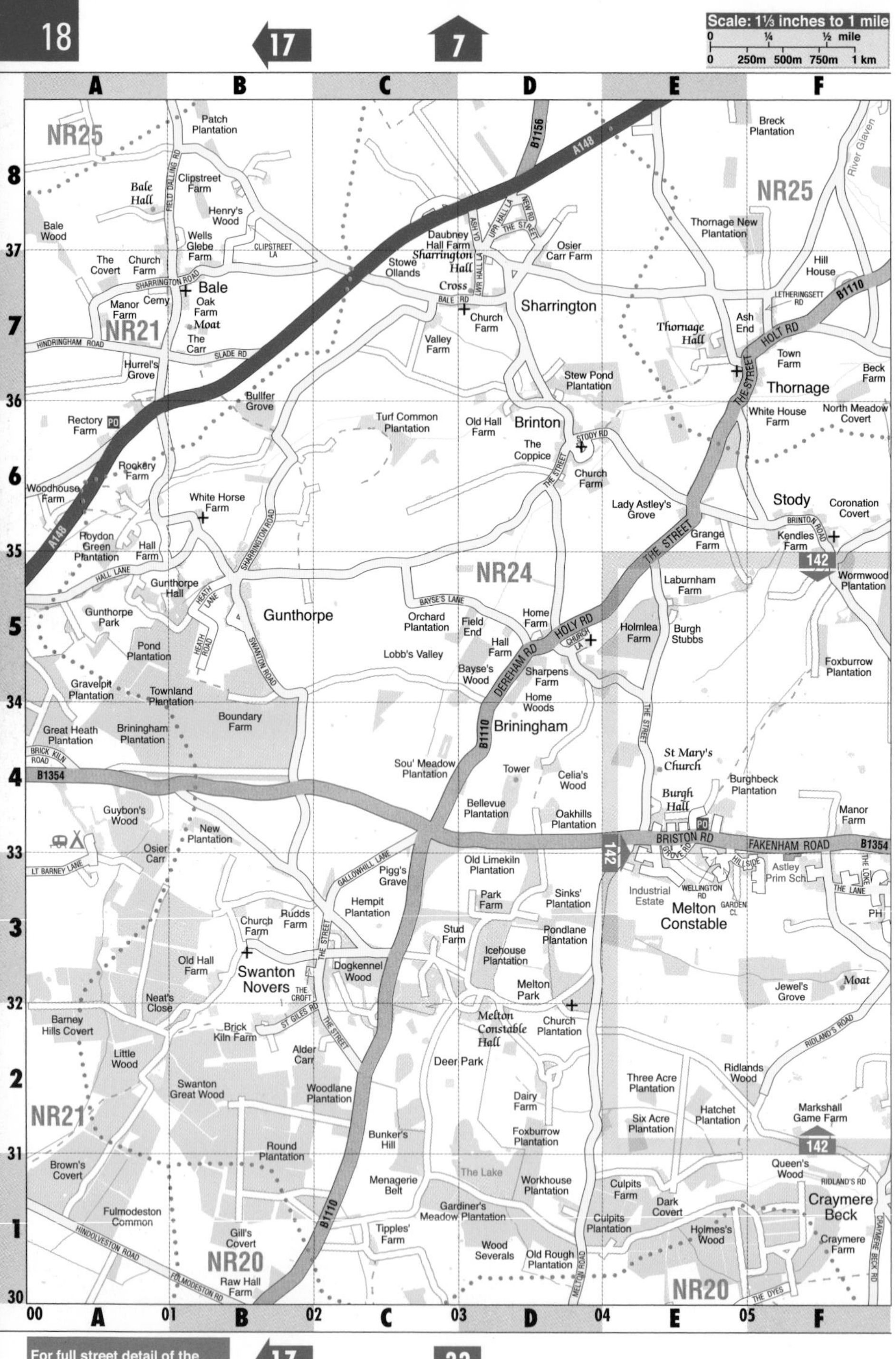

NR25

Patch Plantation

Clipstreet Farm

Bale Hall

Henry's Wood

Bale Wood

Wells Glebe Farm

The Covert   Church Farm

Clipstreet La

SHARRINGTON ROAD

Manor Farm   Cem'y

Bale
Oak Farm
Moat

Hurrel's Grove

The Carr

HINDRINGHAM ROAD

NR21

SLADE RD

Bulfer Grove

Rectory Farm

Rookery Farm

Woodhouse Farm

Royden Green Plantation

Hall Lane

HALL LANE

Gunthorpe Heath

Gunthorpe Park

HEATH ROAD

Pond Plantation

SHARRINGTON ROAD

BRETTON ROAD

White Horse Farm

Gunthorpe

NR24

Daubney Hall Farm
Sharrington Hall
Cross

Stow Ollands

KINGS HILL LA
NEW ROAD LA
THE STREET

B1156

A148

Church Farm

Valley Farm

Sharrington

Osier Carr Farm

Stew Pond Plantation

Turf Common Plantation

Old Hall Farm

Brinton

The Coppice

THE STREET

STODY RD

Church Farm

Lady Astley's Grove

THE STREET

Grange Farm

Breck Plantation

NR25

River Glaven

Thornage New Plantation

Hill House

Thornage Hall

Ash End

HOLT RD

LETHERINGSETT RD

B1110

Town Farm

Thornage

Beck Farm

White House Farm

North Meadow Covert

Stody

Coronation Covert

BRINTON RD

Kendles Farm

142

Wormwood Plantation

Bayse's Lane

Orchard Plantation

Field End

Home Farm

Laburnham Farm

Lobb's Valley

Hall Farm

HOLY RD

CHURCH

Holmlea Farm

Burgh Stubbs

Foxburrow Plantation

Gravelpit Plantation

Townland Plantation

Bayse's Wood

Sharpens Farm

DERGHAM RD

Home Woods

Great Heath Plantation

Briningham Plantation

Boundary Farm

BRICK KILN ROAD

B1354

Guybon's Wood

LT BARNEY LANE

Osier Carr

New Plantation

GALLOWHILL LANE

Sou' Meadow Plantation

B1110

Briningham

Tower

Bellevue Plantation

Celia's Wood

Oakhills Plantation

St Mary's Church

Burgh Hall

Burghbeck Plantation

PO

Manor Farm

142

BRISTON RD

FAKENHAM ROAD

B1354

WELLINGTON RD

Industrial Estate

HILLSIDE

GARDEN CL

Melton Constable

Astley Prim Sch

THE LANE

THE LOKE

PH

Pigg's Grave

Hempit Plantation

Old Limekiln Plantation

Park Farm

Sinks' Farm

Stud Farm

Pondlane Plantation

Church Farm

Rudds Farm

ST GILES LANE
THE STREET

Dogkennel Wood

Icehouse Plantation

Melton Park

Jewel's Grove

Moat

Old Hall Farm

Swanton Novers

THE CROFT

Church Plantation

RIDLANDS ROAD

Neat's Close

Barney Hills Covert

Brick Kiln Farm

Alder Carr

Melton Constable Hall

Deer Park

Dairy Farm

Three Acre Plantation

Ridlands Wood

Markshall Game Farm

142

Little Wood

NR21

Swanton Great Wood

Woodlane Plantation

Bunker's Hill

Foxburrow Plantation

Six Acre Plantation

Hatchet Plantation

Brown's Covert

Round Plantation

Menagerie Belt

The Lake

Workhouse Plantation

Culpits Farm

Dark Covert

Queen's Wood

RIDLAND'S RD

Fulmodeston Common

HINDOLVESTON ROAD

Gill's Covert

NR20

B1110

FULMODESTON RD

Tipples' Farm

Gardiner's Meadow Plantation

Wood Severals

Old Rough Plantation

Culpits Plantation

Holmes's Wood

HOLT ROAD

Craymere Beck

Craymere Farm

CRAYMERE BECK RD

NR20

THE DYES

Raw Hall Farm

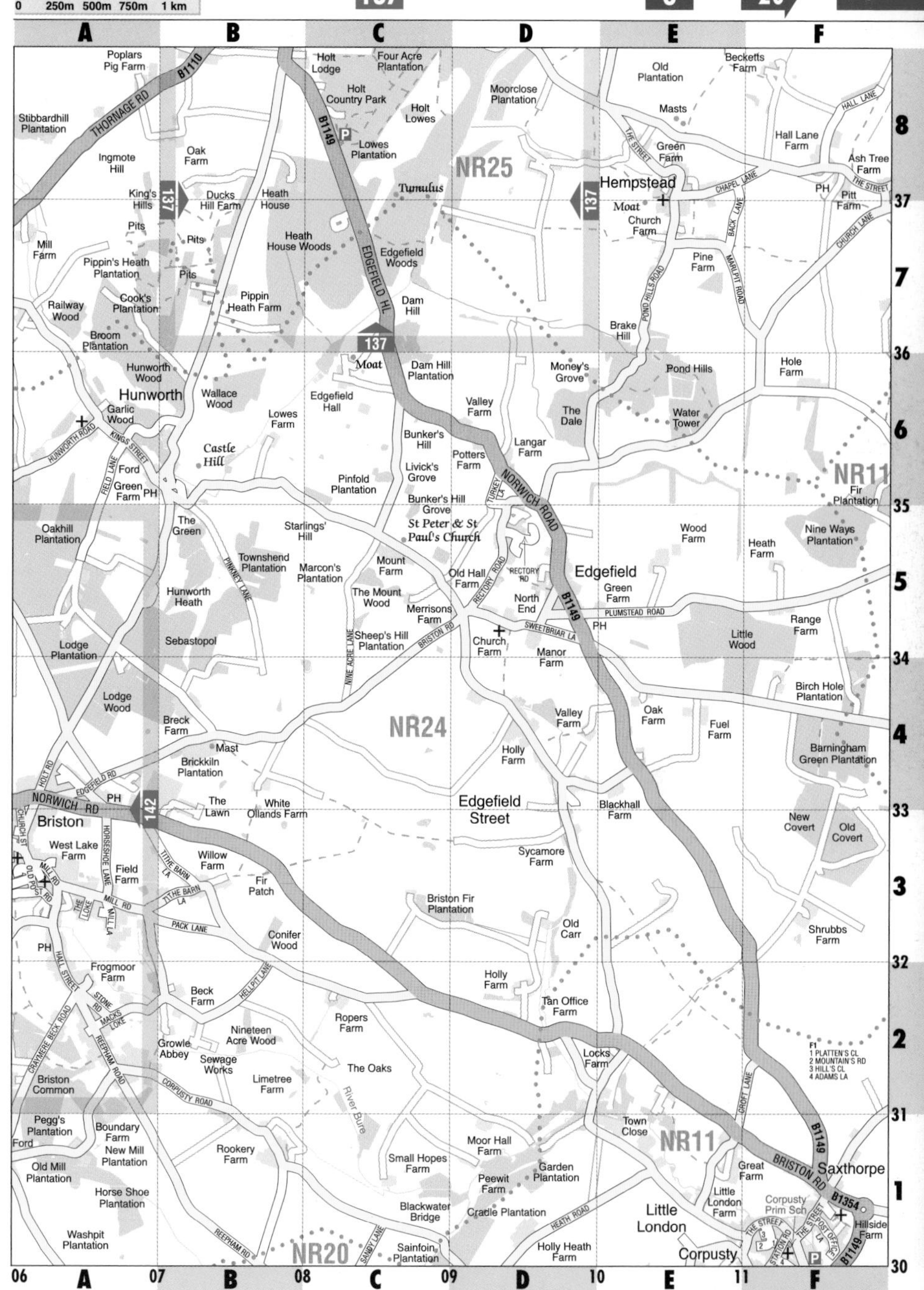

19
9

Scale: 1⅓ inches to 1 mile

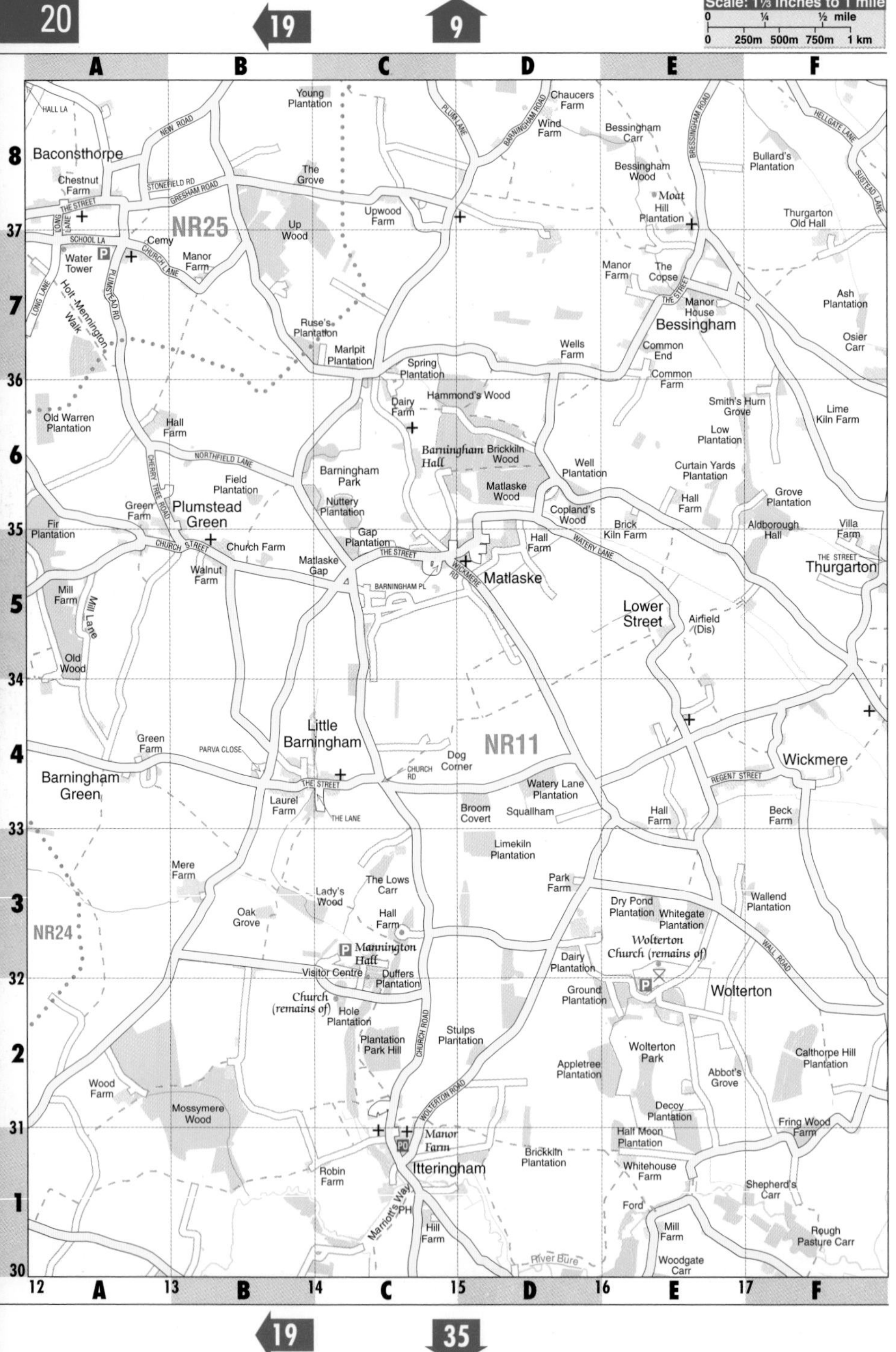
Baconsthorpe
Chestnut Farm
NR25
Water Tower
Cemy
Manor Farm
Holt-Mennington Walk
Young Plantation
The Grove
Up Wood
Upwood Farm
Ruse's Plantation
Marlpit Plantation
Chaucers Farm
Wind Farm
Bessingham Carr
Bessingham Wood
Moat Hill Plantation
Manor Farm
The Copse
Manor House
Bessingham
Common End
Common Farm
Wells Farm
Bullard's Plantation
Thurgarton Old Hall
Ash Plantation
Osier Carr
Old Warren Plantation
Hall Farm
Spring Plantation
Hammond's Wood
Dairy Farm
Barningham Hall
Brickkiln Wood
Matlaske Wood
Barningham Park
Nuttery Plantation
Gap Plantation
Field Plantation
Plumstead Green
Green Farm
Fir Plantation
Church Farm
Walnut Farm
Matlaske Gap
Matlaske
Hall Farm
Copland's Wood
Well Plantation
Brick Kiln Farm
Smith's Hurn Grove
Low Plantation
Curtain Yards Plantation
Hall Farm
Lime Kiln Farm
Grove Plantation
Aldborough Hall
Villa Farm
Thurgarton
Mill Farm
Mill Lane
Old Wood
Lower Street
Airfield (Dis)
Little Barningham
NR11
Dog Corner
Green Farm
Barningham Green
Laurel Farm
Watery Lane Plantation
Squallham
Broom Covert
Wickmere
Hall Farm
Beck Farm
Limekiln Plantation
Mere Farm
The Lows Carr
Lady's Wood
Oak Grove
Hall Farm
Park Farm
Dry Pond Plantation
Whitegate Plantation
Wallend Plantation
NR24
Mannington Hall
Visitor Centre
Duffers Plantation
Church (remains of)
Hole Plantation
Wolterton Church (remains of)
Dairy Plantation
Ground Plantation
Wolterton
Plantation Park Hill
Stulps Plantation
Appletree Plantation
Wolterton Park
Abbot's Grove
Calthorpe Hill Plantation
Wood Farm
Mossymere Wood
Decoy Plantation
Half Moon Plantation
Fring Wood Farm
Manor Farm
Itteringham
Brickkiln Plantation
Robin Farm
Whitehouse Farm
Shepherd's Carr
Ford
Mill Farm
Marriott's Way
PH
Hill Farm
Rough Pasture Carr
Woodgate Carr
River Bure

19
35

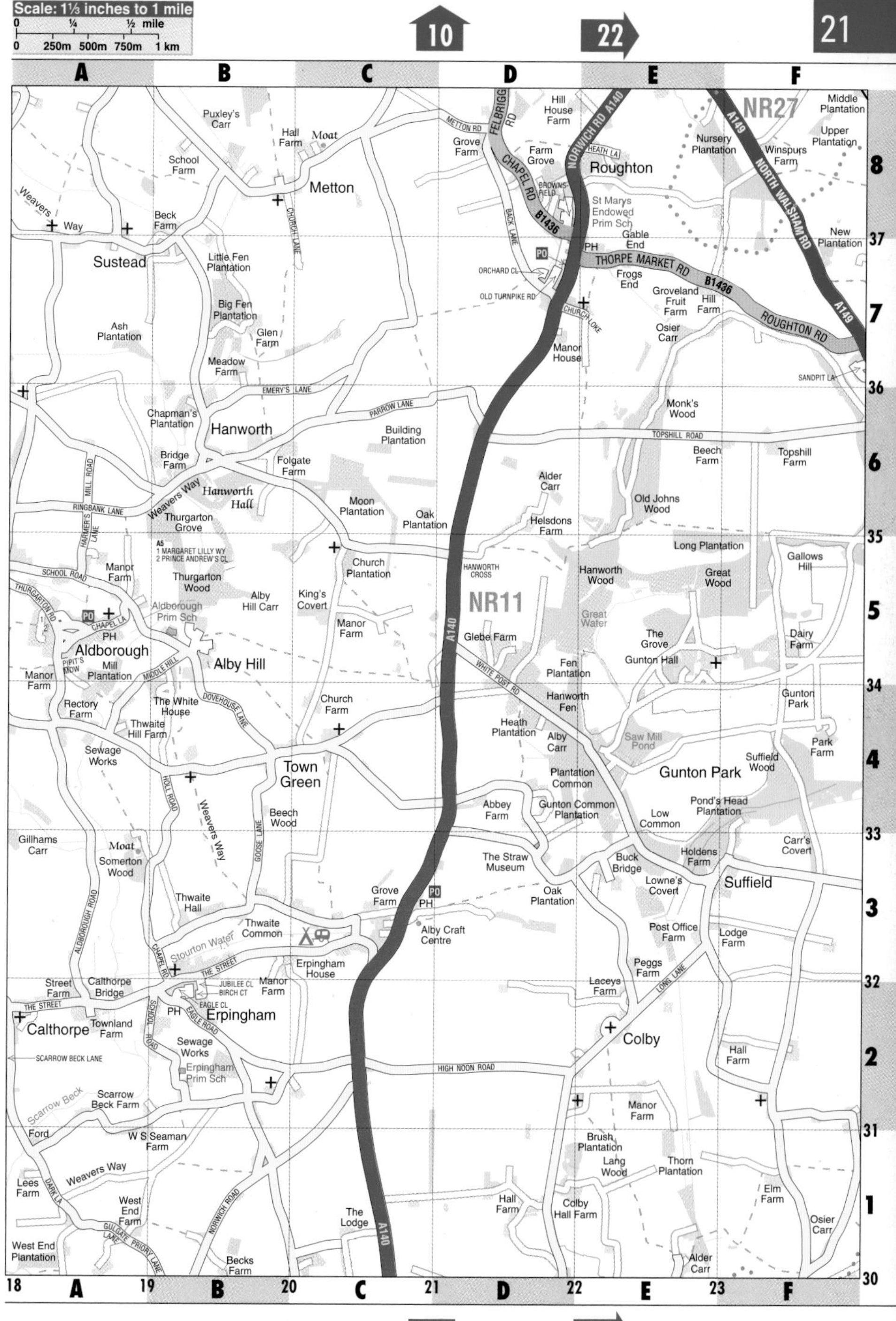

NR27

Middle Plantation

Upper Plantation

Nursery Plantation

Winspurs Farm

New Plantation

8

Hill House Farm

Farm Grove

Roughton

St Marys Endowed Prim Sch

Gable End

37

Grove Farm

BROWNS FIELD

PH

THORPE MARKET RD

PO

Frogs End

Groveland Fruit Farm

Hill Farm

B1436

7

ORCHARD CL

OLD TURNPIKE RD

Osier Carr

ROUGHTON RD

SANDPIT LA

36

Metton

METTON RD

CHAPEL RD

FELBRIGG RD

BACK LANE

B1436

CHURCH LANE

Manor House

HEATH LA

NORWICH RD   A140

A149

NORTH WALSHAM RD

A149

Puxley's Carr

Hall Farm

Moat

School Farm

Beck Farm

Weavers Way

Sustead

Little Fen Plantation

Big Fen Plantation

Glen Farm

Meadow Farm

Ash Plantation

EMERY'S LANE

CHURCH LANE

PARROW LANE

Monk's Wood

TOPSHILL ROAD

Beech Farm

Topshill Farm

36

Chapman's Plantation

Hanworth

Building Plantation

Alder Carr

6

Bridge Farm

Folgate Farm

Weavers Way

Hanworth Hall

Thurgarton Grove

RINGBANK LANE

HARMER'S LANE

MILL ROAD

Moon Plantation

Oak Plantation

Helsdons Farm

Old Johns Wood

Long Plantation

Gallows Hill

35

A5
1 MARGARET LILLY WY
2 PRINCE ANDREW'S CL.

Manor Farm

SCHOOL ROAD

THURGARTON ROAD

Thurgarton Wood

Church Plantation

Hanworth Cross

NR11

Hanworth Wood

Great Wood

Dairy Farm

5

PO

PH

Aldborough Prim Sch

Alby Hill Carr

King's Covert

Manor Farm

A140

Glebe Farm

Fen Plantation

Great Water

The Grove

Gunton Hall

CHAPEL LA

Aldborough

Mill Plantation

MIDDLE LANE

DOVEHOUSE LANE

Alby Hill

Church Farm

WHITE POST RD

Hanworth Fen

Gunton Park

Suffield Wood

Guntor Park

Park Farm

34

Manor Farm

Rectory Farm

The White House

Thwaite Hill Farm

Heath Plantation

Alby Carr

Saw Mill Pond

4

PIRT'S HOW

Sewage Works

HILL ROAD

Town Green

GOOSE LANE

Beech Wood

Plantation Common

Gunton Common Plantation

Low Common

Pond's Head Plantation

Carr's Covert

33

Gillhams Carr

Moat

Somerton Wood

Weavers Way

Thwaite Hall

Abbey Farm

The Straw Museum

Buck Bridge

Lowne's Covert

Holdens Farm

Suffield

3

ALDBOROUGH ROAD

Thwaite Common

Stourton Water

Grove Farm

PO

PH

Oak Plantation

Post Office Farm

Lodge Farm

Street Farm

Calthorpe Bridge

THE STREET

JUBILEE CL
BIRCH CT

Manor Farm

Alby Craft Centre

Peggs Farm

LONG LANE

32

THE STREET

CRAKE RD

EAGLE CL

PH

Erpingham House

Laceys Farm

Calthorpe

Townland Farm

Erpingham

Colby

Hall Farm

2

SCARROW BECK LANE

Sewage Works

Erpingham Prim Sch

HIGH NOON ROAD

Scarrow Beck

Scarrow Beck Farm

W S Seaman Farm

Manor Farm

31

Ford

DINN LA

WARWICK ROAD

Brush Plantation

Lang Wood

Thorn Plantation

Elm Farm

Lees Farm

Weavers Way

West End Farm

The Lodge

A140

Becks Farm

Hall Farm

Colby Hall Farm

Alder Carr

Osier Carr

1

West End Plantation

GUNGATE

PRIOST LANE

30

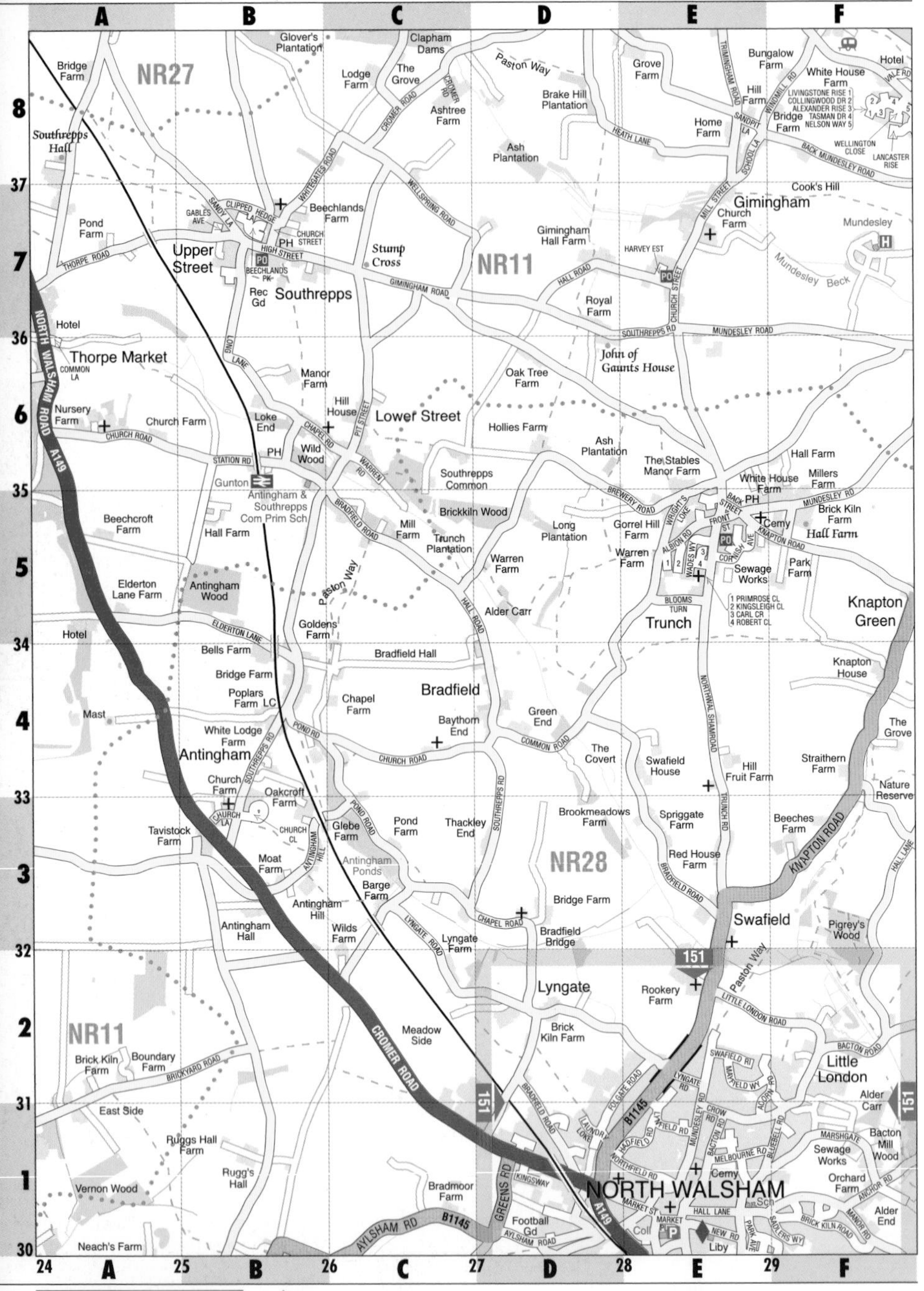

Scale: 1⅓ inches to 1 mile

0   ¼   ½ mile
0 250m 500m 750m 1 km

NR27

Bridge Farm

Southrepps Hall

Glover's Plantation

Clapham Dams

Paston Way

Grove Farm

Bungalow Farm

White House Farm

Hotel

Lodge Farm

The Grove

Brake Hill Plantation

Hill Farm

LIVINGSTONE RISE 1
COLLINGWOOD DR 2
ALEXANDER RISE 3
TASMAN DR 4
NELSON WAY 5

Bridge Farm

WELLINGTON CLOSE

LANCASTER RISE

Ashtree Farm

Ash Plantation

Home Farm

Pond Farm

Beechlands Farm

GABLES AVE

Stump Cross

Gimingham Hall Farm

NR11

Cook's Hill

Gimingham

Church Farm

Mundesley

Upper Street

PH

CHURCH STREET

High Street

Southrepps

HARVEY EST

Mundesley Beck

Rec Gd

Royal Farm

Hotel

Thorpe Market

COMMON LA

Manor Farm

Hill House

Lower Street

Oak Tree Farm

John of Gaunts House

Nursery Farm

Church Farm

Loke End

Wild Wood

Hollies Farm

Ash Plantation

The Stables

White House Farm

Hall Farm

Millers Farm

Beechcroft Farm

Hall Farm

Gunton

Antingham & Southrepps Com Prim Sch

Southrepps Common

Brickkiln Wood

Mill Farm

Trunch Plantation

Long Plantation

Gorrel Hill Farm

Manor Farm

PH

Brick Kiln Farm

Hall Farm

Elderton Lane Farm

Antingham Wood

Goldens Farm

Warren Farm

Alder Carr

Warren Farm

Sewage Works

1 PRIMROSE CL
2 KINGSLEIGH CL
3 CARL CR
4 ROBERT CL

Park Farm

Knapton Green

Hotel

Bells Farm

Bradfield Hall

BLOOMS TURN

Trunch

Knapton House

Mast

Bridge Farm

Poplars Farm LC

White Lodge Farm

Antingham

Chapel Farm

Bradfield

Baythorn End

Green End

The Covert

Swafield House

Hill Fruit Farm

Straithern Farm

The Grove

Nature Reserve

Tavistock Farm

Church Farm

Oakcroft Farm

CHURCH CL

Glebe Farm

Pond Farm

Thackley End

Brookmeadows Farm

Spriggate Farm

Red House Farm

Beeches Farm

Moat Farm

Antingham Ponds

Barge Farm

Bridge Farm

NR28

Swafield

Pigrey's Wood

Antingham Hall

Antingham Hill

Wilds Farm

Lyngate Farm

Chapel Road

Bradfield Bridge

151

NR11

Meadow Side

Lyngate

Brick Kiln Farm

Rookery Farm

Little London

Brick Kiln Farm

Boundary Farm

BRICKYARD ROAD

Alder Carr

Bacton Mill Wood

East Side

Sewage Works

Ruggs Hall Farm

Rugg's Hall

Bradmoor Farm

Football Gd

NORTH WALSHAM

Orchard Farm

Alder End

Vernon Wood

Neach's Farm

AYLSHAM RD

B1145

AYLSHAM RD

GREENS RD

CROMER ROAD

Liby

For full street detail of the highlighted area see page 151

21

37

151

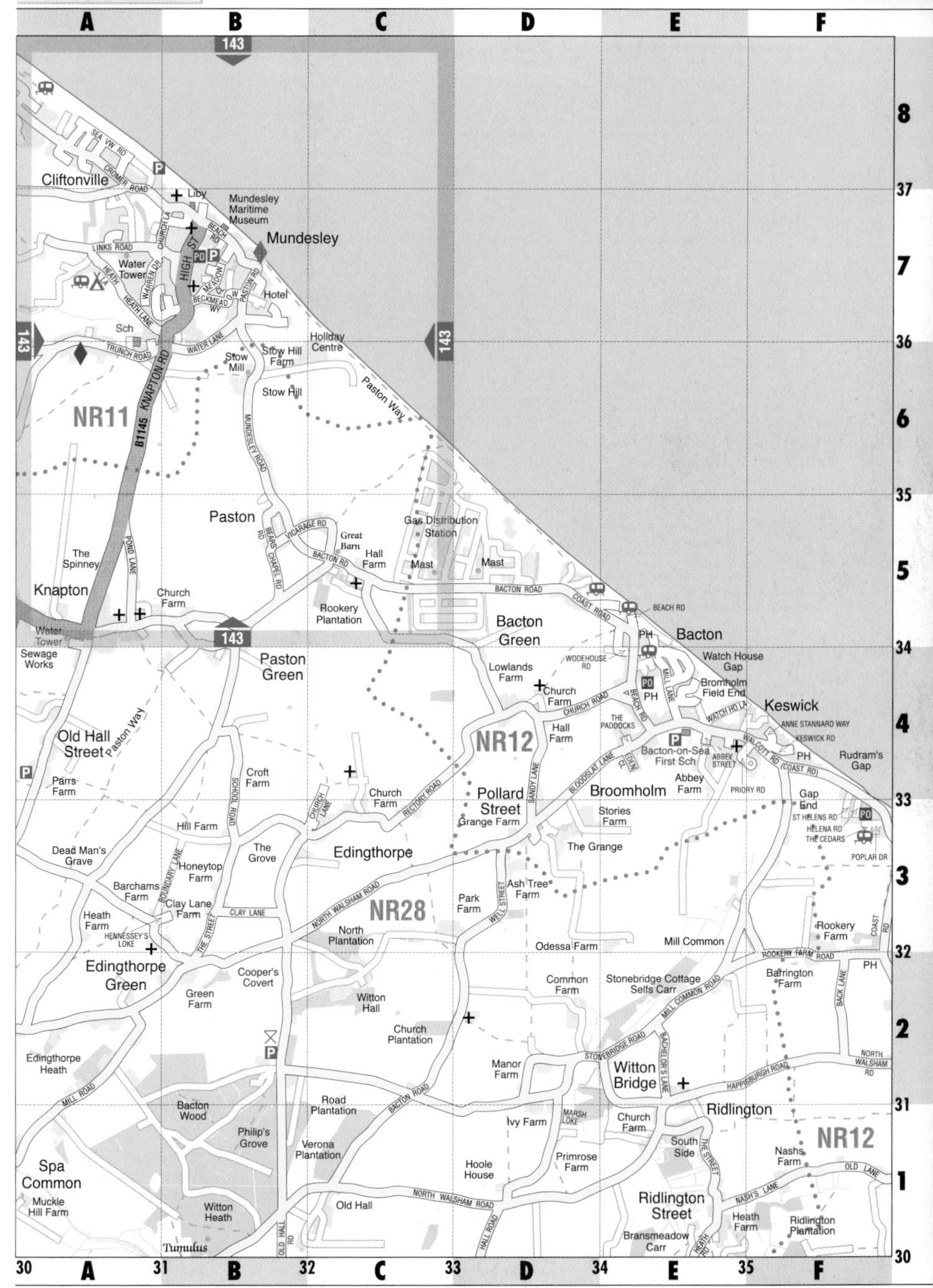

Scale: 1⅓ inches to 1 mile

0   ¼   ½   mile
0   250m 500m 750m 1 km

A **B** **C** **D** **E** **F**

143

Cliftonville

Liby

Mundesley
Maritime
Museum

Mundesley

LINKS ROAD

Water
Tower

SEA VW. RD

GRIMES ROAD

CHURCH LA.

HIGH ST.

BECKMEAD WAY

MUNDESLEY ROAD

WATER LANE

Sch

TRUNCH ROAD

Hotel

Holiday
Centre

Stow Hill
Farm

Stow Mill

Stow Hill

Paston Way

143

NR11

B1145 KNAPTON RD

POND LANE

BEARS CHAPEL RD.

VICARAGE RD.

BACTON RD.

Paston

The
Spinney

Knapton

Church
Farm

Great
Barn

Hall
Farm

Mast

Rookery
Plantation

Gas Distribution
Station

Mast

143

Water
Tower

Sewage
Works

Paston
Green

BACTON ROAD

COAST RD

Bacton
Green

WOODEHOUSE
RD.

Church
Farm

Lowlands
Farm

BEACH RD

Bacton

PH

P

Watch House
Gap

Bromholm
Field End

WITCH RD

Keswick

ANNE STANNARD WAY

KESWICK RD

Rudram's
Gap

Old Hall
Street

Paston Way

Parrs
Farm

P

Croft
Farm

Church
Farm

Hill Farm

NR12

Hall
Farm

CHURCH ROAD

THE
PADDOCKS

BLOODSLAT LANE

SANDY LANE

Bacton-on-Sea
First Sch

ABBEY
STREET

WALCOTT RD

BACTON RD

(COAST RD)

Abbey
Farm

PRIORY RD

Broomholm

Gap
End

P

ST HELENS RD

HELENA RD
THE CEDARS

POPLAR DR

Dead Man's
Grave

Honeytop
Farm

The
Grove

Edingthorpe

CHURCH LANE

RECTORY ROAD

Pollard
Street

Grange Farm

Stories
Farm

The Grange

Barchams
Farm

Clay Lane
Farm

Heath
Farm

HENNESSEY'S
LOKE

BOUNDARY LANE

THE STREET

CLAY LANE

SCHOOL ROAD

NORTH WALSHAM ROAD

WEST STREET

Ash Tree
Farm

NR28

Park
Farm

Odessa Farm

Mill Common

Rookery
Farm

ROOKERY FARM ROAD

COAST RD

PH

Edingthorpe
Green

North
Plantation

Green
Farm

Cooper's
Covert

P

Witton
Hall

Church
Plantation

Common
Farm

Stonebridge Cottage
Selfs Carr

STONEBRIDGE ROAD

RACHELDR'S LANE

BACK LANE

Barrington
Farm

NORTH
WALSHAM

PH

2

Edingthorpe
Heath

MILL ROAD

Bacton
Wood

Philip's
Grove

Road
Plantation

BACTON ROAD

Manor
Farm

MARSH
LOKE

Ivy Farm

Church
Farm

Witton
Bridge

HAPPISBURGH ROAD

Ridlington

THE STREET

NR12

Spa
Common

Muckle
Hill Farm

Witton
Heath

Tumulus

Verona
Plantation

Old Hall

NORTH WALSHAM ROAD

HALL RD

Hoole
House

Primrose
Farm

Ridlington
Street

Bransmeadow
Carr

South
Side

NASH'S LANE

Heath
Farm

Nashs
Farm

OLD LANE

Ridlington
Plantation

8

37

7

36

6

35

5

34

4

33

3

32

31

1

30

30   **A**   31   **B**   32   **C**   33   **D**   34   **E**   35   **F**

38

24

For full street detail of the
highlighted area see page 143

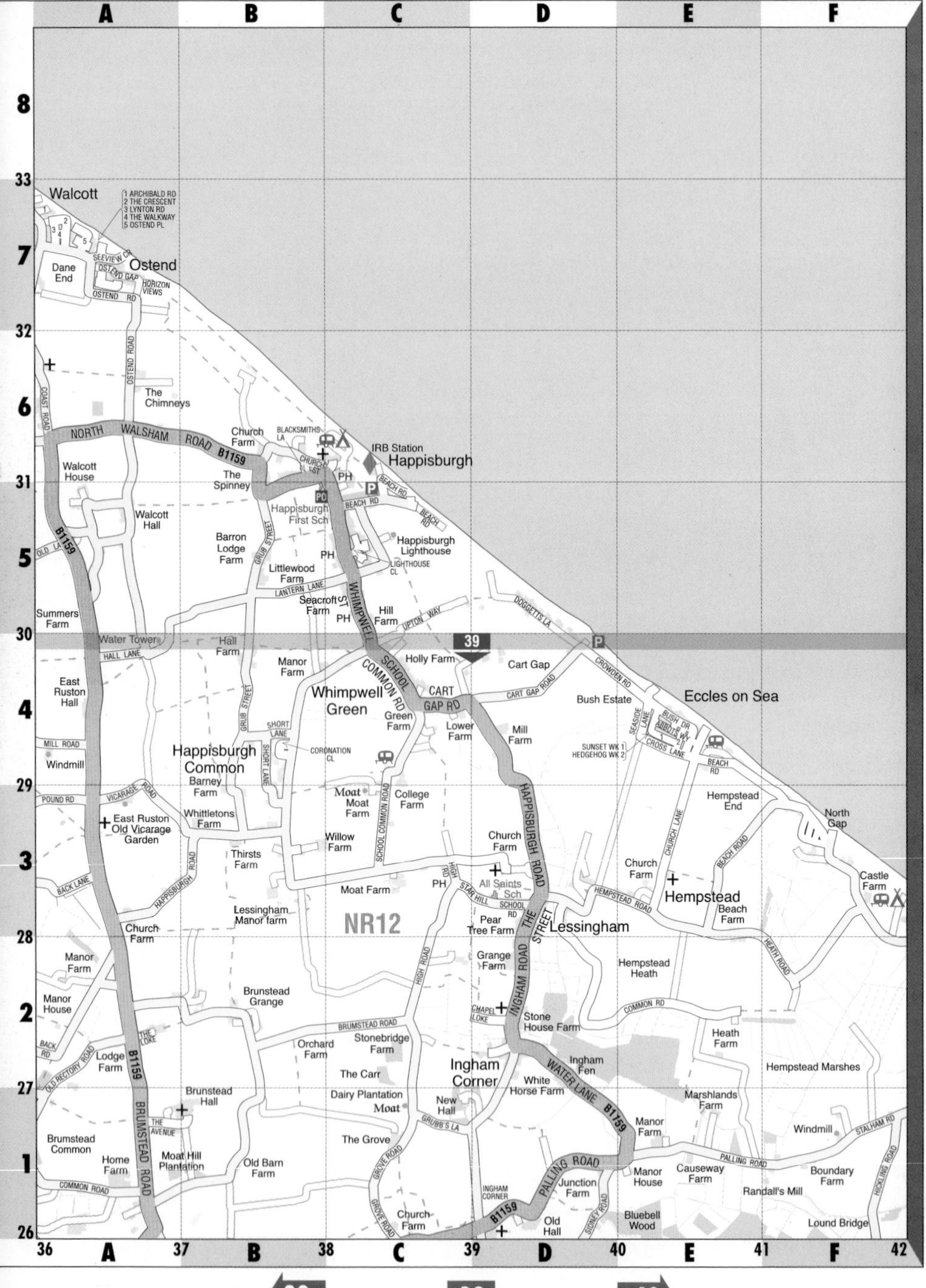

23

8

33

Walcott

1 ARCHIBALD RD
2 THE CRESCENT
3 LYNTON RD
4 THE WALKWAY
5 OSTEND PL

7

Dane
End

Ostend

SEEVIEW
OSTEND GAP
OSTEND RD

HORIZON
VIEWS

32

The
Chimneys

6

OSTEND ROAD

DUNE ROAD

NORTH WALSHAM ROAD

B1159

Church
Farm

BLACKSMITHS
LA

CHURCH GAP

IRB Station

Happisburgh

31

Walcott
House

The
Spinney

PH

P

Walcott
Hall

Barron
Lodge
Farm

Happisburgh
First Sch

PO

P

BEACH RD

BEACH RD

5

OLD LA

B1159

Summers
Farm

Littlewood
Farm

Seacroft
Farm

LANTERN LANE

GREEN STREET

PH

PH

Happisburgh
Lighthouse

HAPPISBURGH
LIGHTHOUSE
CL

Hill
Farm

UPTON WAY

DOGGETTS LA

30

Water Tower

HALL LANE

Hall
Farm

Holly Farm

39

Cart Gap

P

4

East
Ruston
Hall

Manor
Farm

Whimpwell
Green

SCHOOL COMMON RD

GRIN STREET

SHORT
LANE

CART
GAP RD

Green
Farm

CART GAP ROAD

Lower
Farm

Mill
Farm

Bush Estate

CROMER RD

Eccles on Sea

SEASIDE

BUSH DR
SUNSET VW

SUNSET WK 1
HEDGEHOG WK 2

CROSS LANE

CHURCH LANE

BEACH
RD

29

MILL ROAD

Windmill

VICARAGE ROAD

POUND RD

Happisburgh
Common

Barney
Farm

SHORT LANE

CORONATION
CL

Moat
Moat
Farm

College
Farm

Hempstead
End

North
Gap

3

BACK LANE

East Ruston
Old Vicarage
Garden

Whittletons
Farm

Thirsts
Farm

HAPPISBURGH ROAD

Willow
Farm

SCHOOL COMMON ROAD

Moat Farm

PH

STAR HILL

RED LA

Church
Farm

All Saints
Sch

SCHOOL
RD

THE STREET

INGHAM ROAD

Church
Farm

HEMPSTEAD ROAD

Hempstead

Beach
Farm

BEACH ROAD

HEATH ROAD

Castle
Farm

28

Church
Farm

HIGH ROAD

Lessingham
Manor farm

NR12

Pear
Tree Farm

Lessingham

Hempstead
Heath

COMMON RD

2

Manor
House

Manor
Farm

BACK
RD

THE LOKE

B1159

Brunstead
Grange

Orchard
Farm

Stonebridge
Farm

BRUMSTEAD ROAD

Grange
Farm

CHAPEL
LOKE

Stone
House Farm

Heath
Farm

Hempstead Marshes

27

OLD FACTORY ROAD

BRUMSTEAD ROAD

Lodge
Farm

THE AVENUE

Brunstead
Hall

The Carr

Dairy Plantation

GRUBB'S LA

Moat

New
Hall

Ingham
Corner

White
Horse Farm

WATER LANE

Ingham
Fen

B1159

Marshlands
Farm

Windmill

STALHAM RD

1

Brumstead
Common

Home
Farm

COMMON ROAD

BRUMSTEAD ROAD

THE
AVENUE

Moat Hill
Plantation

Old Barn
Farm

The Grove

GROVE ROAD

BROAD ROAD

Church
Farm

INGHAM RD

B1159

Old
Hall

PALLING ROAD

SIDNEY ROAD

Junction
Farm

Bluebell
Wood

Manor
House

Causeway
Farm

PALLING ROAD

Randall's Mill

Boundary
Farm

ROCKING ROAD

Lound Bridge

26

36   37   38   39   40   41   42

38

39

40

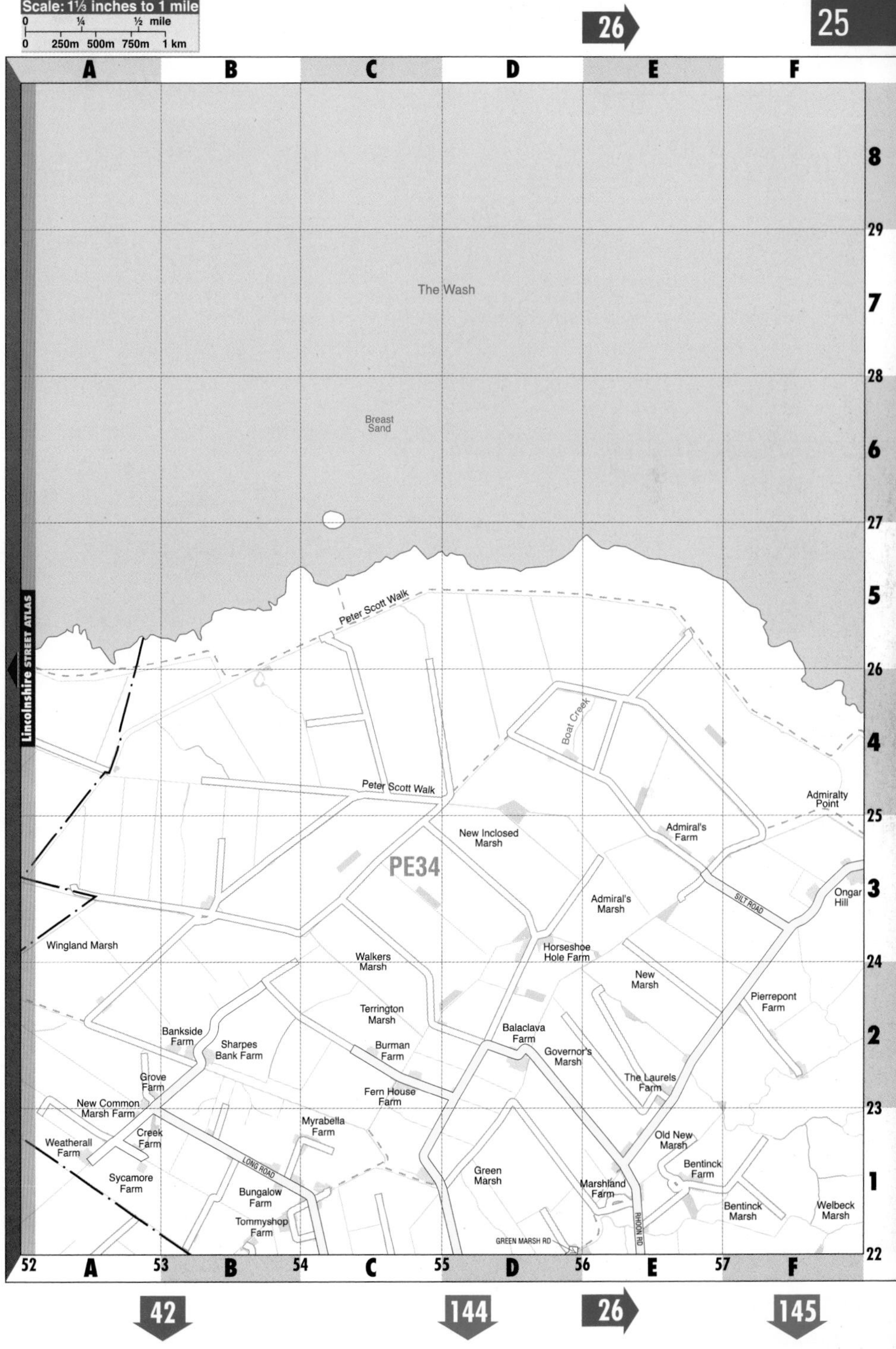

The Wash

Breast
Sand

Peter Scott Walk

Peter Scott Walk

Boat Creek

Admiralty
Point

New Inclosed
Marsh

PE34

Admiral's
Farm

Admiral's
Marsh

Ongar
Hill

SILT ROAD

Wingland Marsh

Horseshoe
Hole Farm

Walkers
Marsh

New
Marsh

Pierrepont
Farm

Terrington
Marsh

Bankside
Farm

Burman
Farm

Balaclava
Farm

Governor's
Marsh

The Laurels
Farm

Sharpes
Bank Farm

Grove
Farm

Fern House
Farm

New Common
Marsh Farm

Myrabella
Farm

Old New
Marsh

Bentinck
Farm

Weatherall
Farm

Creek
Farm

LONG ROAD

Green
Marsh

Marshland
Farm

Bentinck
Marsh

Welbeck
Marsh

Sycamore
Farm

RHODN RD

Bungalow
Farm

Tommyshop
Farm

GREEN MARSH RD

Lincolnshire STREET ATLAS

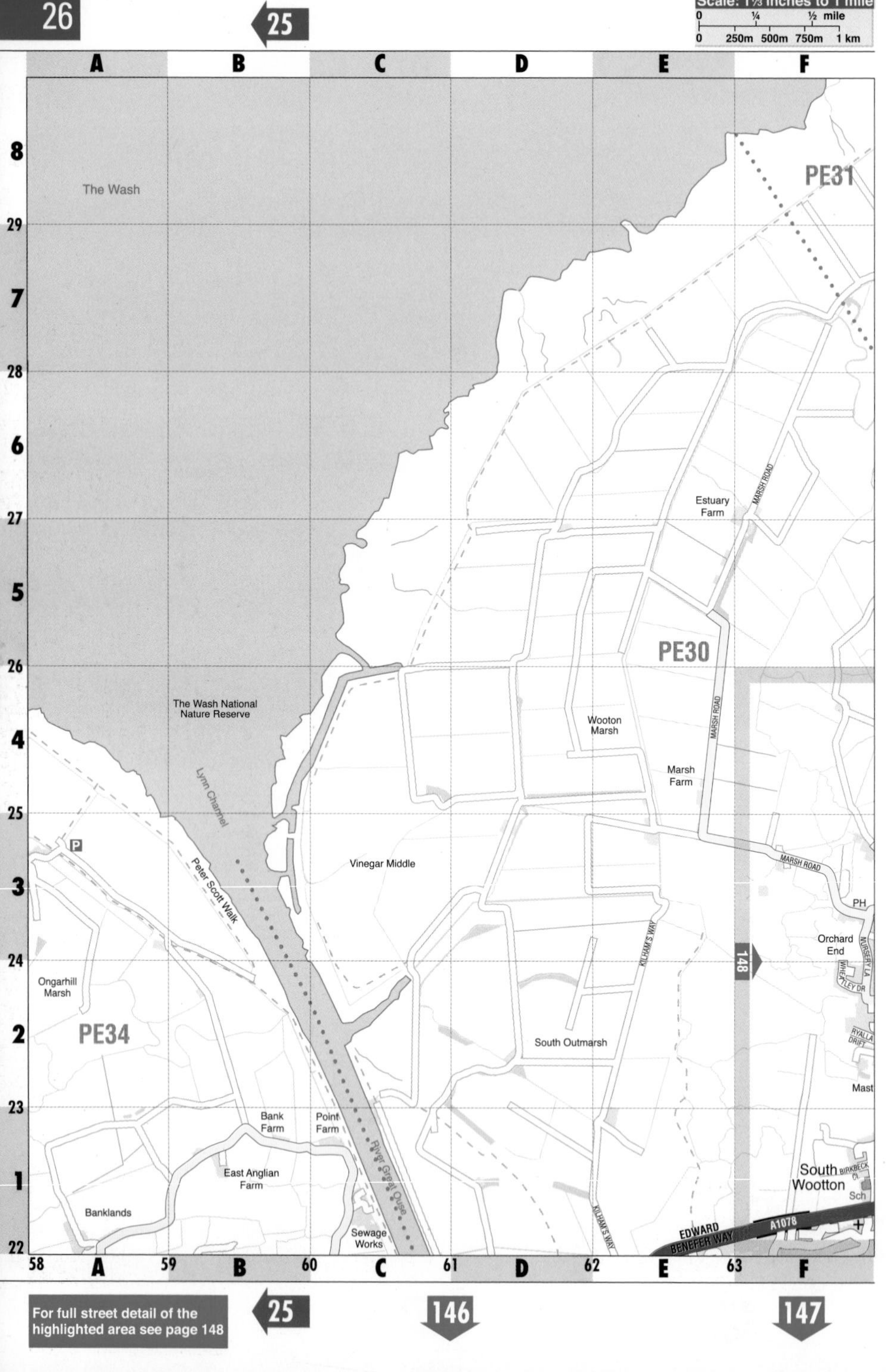

Scale: 1⅓ inches to 1 mile

0 ¼ ½ mile
0 250m 500m 750m 1 km

The Wash

PE31

PE30

The Wash National
Nature Reserve

Estuary
Farm

MARSH ROAD

Wooton
Marsh

Marsh
Farm

MARSH ROAD

MARSH ROAD

Lynn Channel

Peter Scott Walk

Vinegar Middle

PH

Orchard
End

148

KILHAM'S WAY

NURSERY LA

WHITLEY DR

Ongarhill
Marsh

PE34

South Outmarsh

RYALLA
DRIFT

Mast

Bank
Farm

Point
Farm

East Anglian
Farm

Banklands

KILHAM'S WAY

South
Wootton

BIRKBECK
PL

Sch

Sewage
Works

EDWARD
BENEFER WAY

A1078

For full street detail of the
highlighted area see page 148

25

146

147

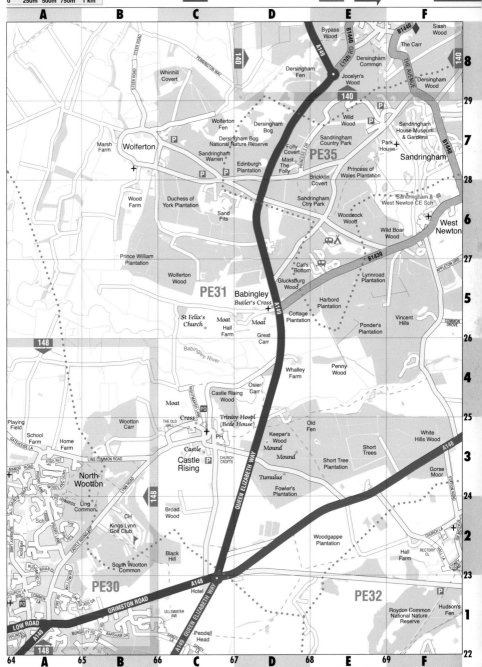

Scale: 1⅓ inches to 1 mile

0 ¼ ½ mile
0 250m 500m 750m 1 km

12
140 28

A B C D E F

8
Bypass Wood
B1440
Slash Wood
The Carr
THE AVENUE
Whinhill Covert
PENNINGTON WAY
Dersingham Fen
Jocelyn's Wood
Dersingham Common
Dersingham Wood
140

29
Wolferton Fen
Dersingham Bog
Wild Wood
Sandringham House Museum & Gardens
140

7
Marsh Farm
Wolferton
Dersingham Bog National Nature Reserve
Sandringham Warren
Edinburgh Plantation
Folly Covert
Mast The Folly
PE35
Sandringham Country Park
Park House
Sandringham
B1440

28
Wood Farm
Duchess of York Plantation
Sand Pits
Bricklin Covert
Sandringham Ctry Park
Princess of Wales Plantation
Sandringham & West Newton CE Sch

6
Prince William Plantation
Wolferton Wood
PE31
Woodcock Wood
Wild Boar Wood
West Newton

27
Babingley
Butler's Cross
Cat's Bottom
Glucksburg Wood
B1439
Lynnroad Plantation
COMMON DRIVE
APPLETON DRO

5
St Felix's Church
Moat Hall Farm
Moat
Cottage Plantation
Harbord Plantation
Ponder's Plantation
Vincent Hills

26
Great Carr
Babingley River
Whalley Farm
Penny Wood

4
Osier Carr
Castle Rising Wood
Moat
Wootton Carr
Cross
THE OLD HALL
Trinity Hospl (Bede House)
Old Fen
Keeper's Wood
Mound
Mound
Short Trees
Short Tree Plantation
White Hills Wood
A148

25
Playing Field
School Farm
Home Farm
GATEHOUSE LA
LING COMMON ROAD
PH
Castle
Castle Rising
CHURCH CROFTS
QUEEN ELIZABETH WAY
Tumulus
Fowler's Plantation
Gorse Moor

3
MANOR ROAD
North Wootton
Ling Common
148
Broad Wood
Woodgappe Plantation
CHURCH LA
RECTORY CL
Hall Farm

24

2
Sch
THE BIRCHES
Kings Lynn Golf Club
South Wootton Common
Black Hill
A148
Hotel
PE32
Roydon Common National Nature Reserve
Hudson's Fen

23

1
PE30
CHURCH LA
PO
GRIMSTON ROAD
QUEEN ELIZABETH WAY
ULLSWATER AVE
SANDY LA
Pendall Head
SANDY

22
LOW ROAD
A148
BURGHLEY RD
BARSHAM DR
A148

64 A 65 B 66 C 67 D 68 E 69 F

147 44 28

For full street detail of the highlighted area see page 140

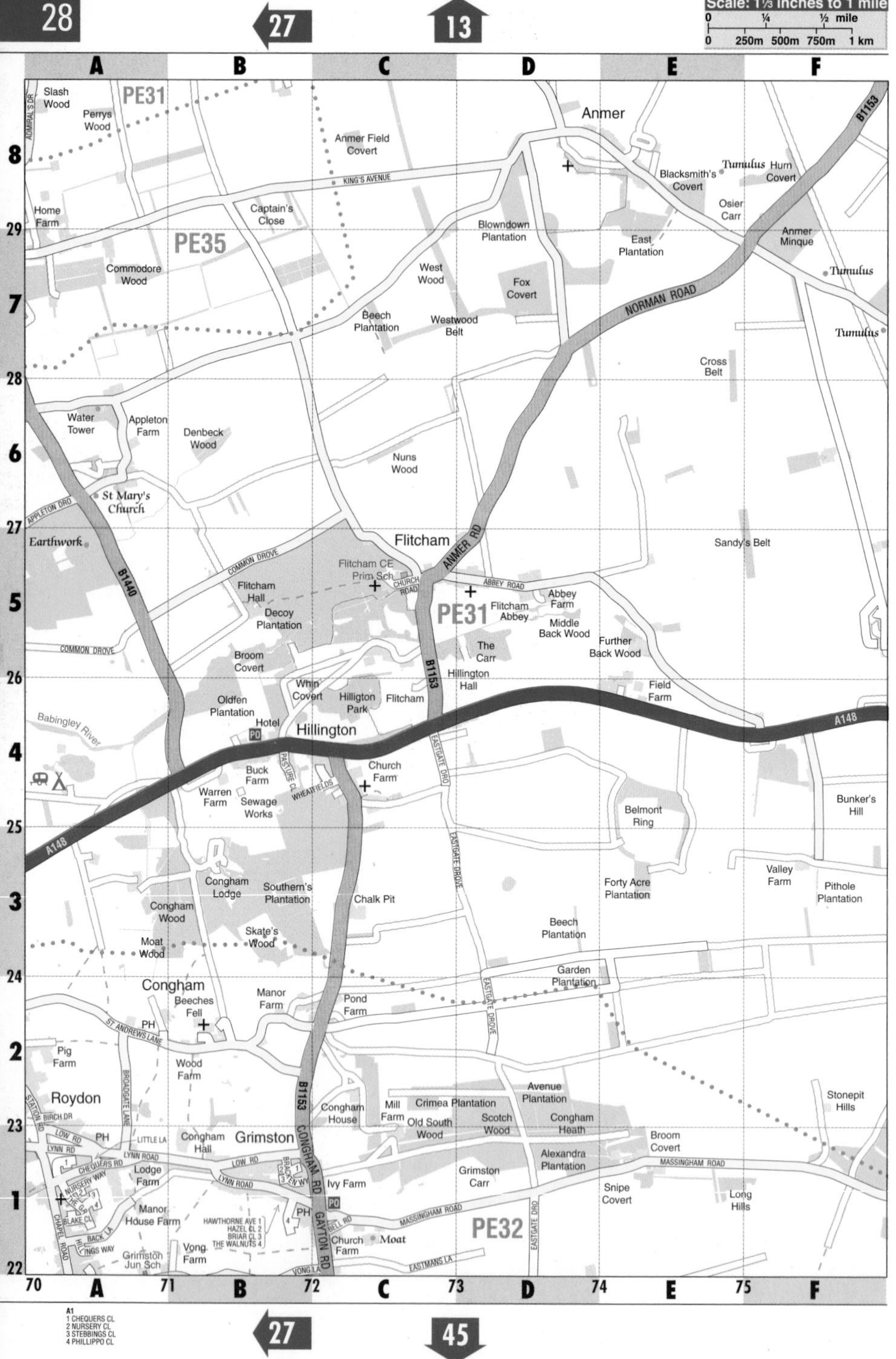

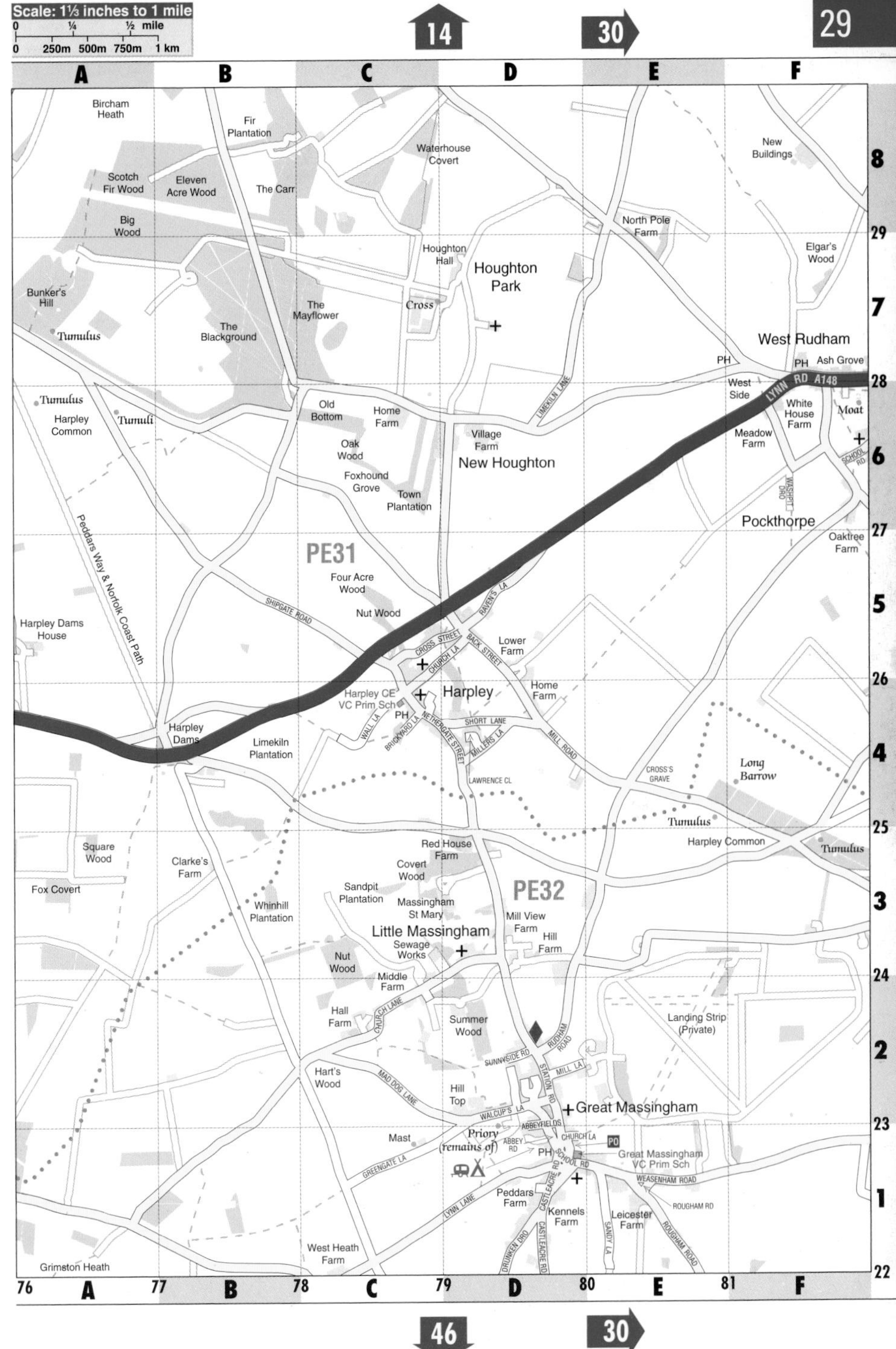
Scale: 1⅓ inches to 1 mile
14
30
Bircham Heath
Fir Plantation
Waterhouse Covert
New Buildings
Scotch Fir Wood
Eleven Acre Wood
The Carr
Big Wood
North Pole Farm
Houghton Hall
Houghton Park
Elgar's Wood
Bunker's Hill
The Mayflower
Cross
Tumulus
The Blackground
West Rudham
PH
Ash Grove
LYNN RD A148
West Side
Tumulus
Harpley Common
Tumuli
Old Bottom
Home Farm
LIMEKILN LANE
White House Farm
Moat
Oak Wood
Village Farm
Meadow Farm
SCHOOL RD
New Houghton
Foxhound Grove
Town Plantation
WASHPIT DRO
Pockthorpe
Peddars Way & Norfolk Coast Path
PE31
Oaktree Farm
Four Acre Wood
RAVEN'S LA
SHIPGATE ROAD
Nut Wood
Harpley Dams House
CROSS STREET
BACK STREET
Lower Farm
CHURCH LA
Harpley
Home Farm
Harpley CE VC Prim Sch
WALL LA
SHORT LANE
Harpley Dams
Limekiln Plantation
BRICKYARD LA
NETHERGATE STREET
MILLERS LA
MILL ROAD
Long Barrow
CROSS'S GRAVE
LAWRENCE CL
Tumulus
Red House Farm
Harpley Common
Tumulus
Square Wood
Clarke's Farm
Covert Wood
PE32
Fox Covert
Sandpit Plantation
Whinhill Plantation
Massingham St Mary
Mill View Farm
Little Massingham
Hill Farm
Sewage Works
Nut Wood
Middle Farm
Hall Farm
CHURCH LANE
Summer Wood
Landing Strip (Private)
RUDHAM ROAD
SUNNYSIDE RD
MILL LA
Hart's Wood
MAD DOG LANE
Hill Top
STATION RD
Great Massingham
WALCUP'S LA
ABBEYFIELDS
Priory (remains of)
ABBEY RD
CHURCH LA
PO
Mast
PH
SCHOOL RD
Great Massingham VC Prim Sch
GREENGATE LA
WEASENHAM ROAD
ROUGHAM RD
Peddars Farm
LYNN LANE
CASTLEACRE RD
Kennels Farm
Leicester Farm
SANDY LA
ROUGHAM ROAD
DRUNKEN DRO
West Heath Farm
Grimston Heath
46
30

29
15

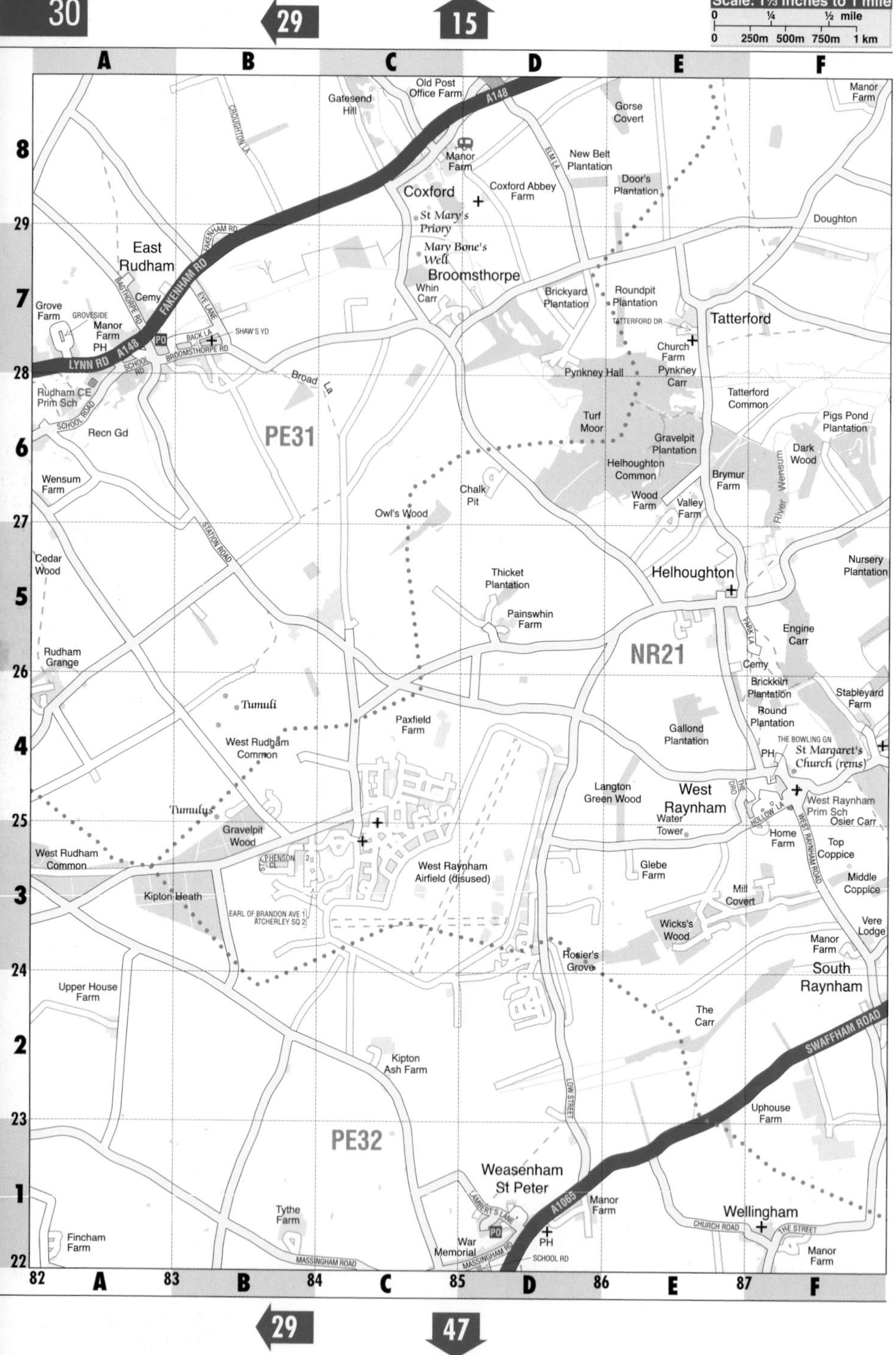
Scale: 1⅓ inches to 1 mile
0 ¼ ½ mile
0 250m 500m 750m 1 km
A B C D E F
8 29 7 28 6 27 5 26 4 25 3 24 2 23 1 22
82 83 84 85 86 87
Old Post Office Farm
Gatesend Hill
A148
Manor Farm
Gorse Covert
New Belt Plantation
Door's Plantation
Coxford
Coxford Abbey Farm
St Mary's Priory
Mary Bone's Well
Broomsthorpe
Whin Carr
Doughton
East Rudham
FAKENHAM RD
Cemy
Grove Farm
GROVESIDE
Manor Farm
PH
LYNN RD
SCHOOL RD
BACK LA
SHAW'S YD
BROOMSTHORPE RD
EYE LANE
Brickyard Plantation
Roundpit Plantation
TATTERFORD DR
Tatterford
Church Farm
Pynkney Carr
Pynkney Hall
Broad La
Rudham CE Prim Sch
SCHOOL ROAD
Recn Gd
PE31
Tatterford Common
Turf Moor
Gravelpit Plantation
Pigs Pond Plantation
Dark Wood
Helhoughton Common
Brymur Farm
River Wensum
Wensum Farm
Chalk Pit
Owl's Wood
Wood Farm
Valley Farm
STATION ROAD
Cedar Wood
Thicket Plantation
Helhoughton
Nursery Plantation
Painswhin Farm
Engine Carr
PARK LA
Rudham Grange
NR21
Cemy
Brickkiln Plantation
Stableyard Farm
Tumuli
Paxfield Farm
Round Plantation
Gallond Plantation
THE BOWLING GN
PH
St Margaret's Church (rems)
West Rudham Common
Langton Green Wood
West Raynham
THE DRO
HOLLOW LA
West Raynham Prim Sch
Osier Carr
Tumulus
Gravelpit Wood
Water Tower
Home Farm
Top Coppice
West Rudham Common
STEPHENSON CL
West Raynham Airfield (disused)
Glebe Farm
WEST RAYNHAM ROAD
Middle Coppice
Kipton Heath
EARL OF BRANDON AVE 1
ATCHERLEY SQ 2
Mill Covert
Wicks's Wood
Vere Lodge
Manor Farm
Rosier's Grove
South Raynham
Upper House Farm
The Carr
SWAFFHAM ROAD
Kipton Ash Farm
LOW STREET
Uphouse Farm
PE32
Weasenham St Peter
LAMBERT'S LANE
A1065
Manor Farm
Wellingham
Tythe Farm
Fincham Farm
War Memorial
PO
PH
SCHOOL RD
MASSINGHAM RD
MASSINGHAM ROAD
CHURCH ROAD
THE STREET
Manor Farm

29
47

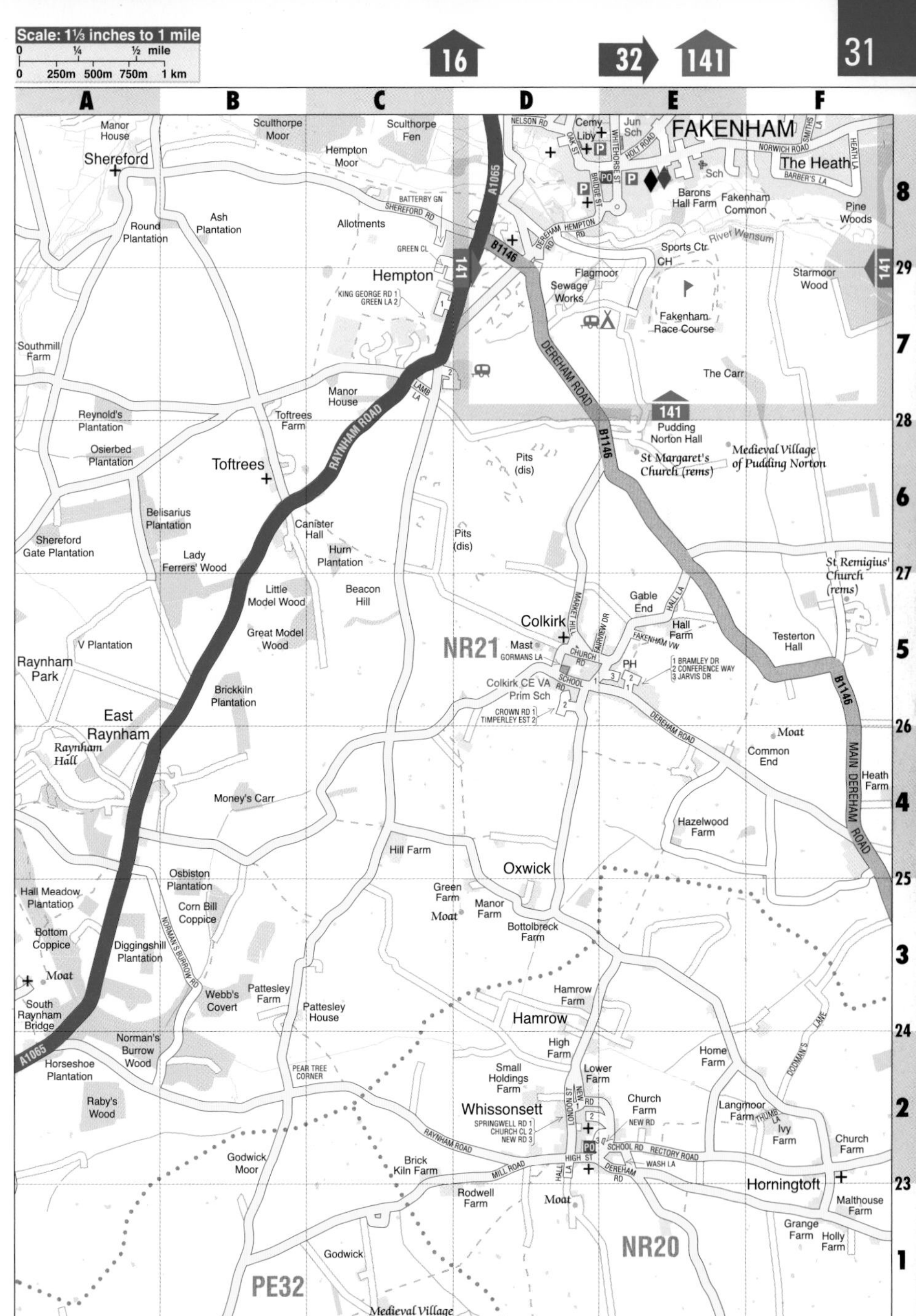

Scale: 1⅓ inches to 1 mile

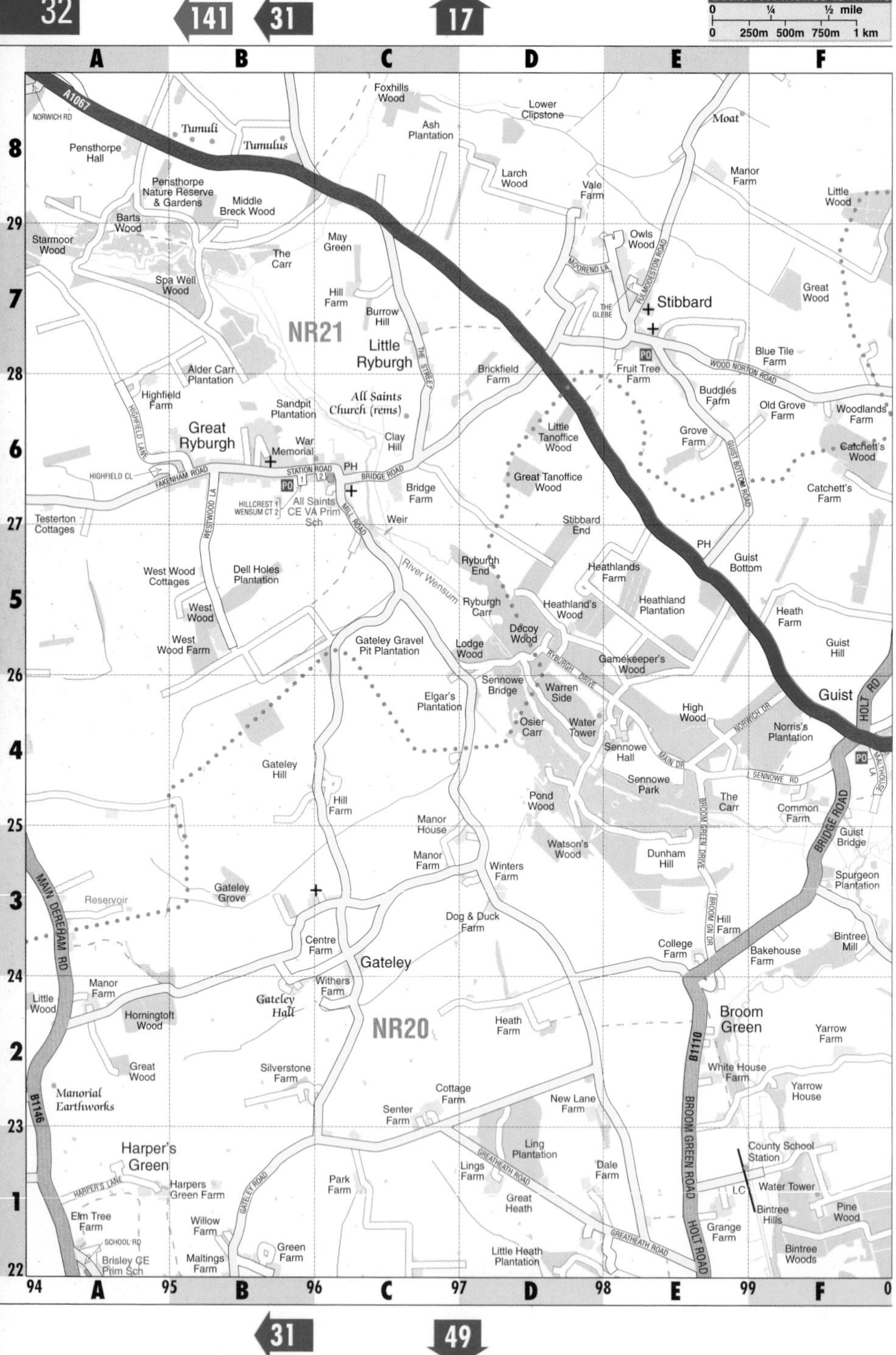
A1067
NORWICH RD
Pensthorpe Hall
Tumuli
Tumulus
Foxhills Wood
Ash Plantation
Lower Clipstone
Moat
Pensthorpe Nature Reserve & Gardens
Middle Breck Wood
Larch Wood
Vale Farm
Manor Farm
Little Wood
Barts Wood
Starmoor Wood
The Carr
May Green
Owls Wood
Spa Well Wood
Hill Farm
Burrow Hill
MOOREND LA
FULMODESTON ROAD
THE GLEBE
Stibbard
Great Wood
NR21
Little Ryburgh
THE STREET
Alder Carr Plantation
Brickfield Farm
Fruit Tree Farm
Blue Tile Farm
WOOD NORTON ROAD
Highfield Farm
HIGHFIELD LANE
Sandpit Plantation
All Saints Church (rems)
Buddles Farm
Old Grove Farm
Woodlands Farm
Great Ryburgh
War Memorial
Clay Hill
Little Tanoffice Wood
Grove Farm
Catchett's Wood
HIGHFIELD CL
FAKENHAM ROAD
STATION ROAD
PH
BRIDGE ROAD
Great Tanoffice Wood
GUIST BOTTOM ROAD
HILLCREST 1
WENSUM CT 2
All Saints CE VA Prim Sch
Bridge Farm
Catchett's Farm
Testerton Cottages
WESTWOOD LA
MILL ROAD
Weir
Stibbard End
PH
West Wood Cottages
Dell Holes Plantation
Ryburgh End
Heathlands Farm
Guist Bottom
River Wensum
West Wood
Ryburgh Carr
Heathland's Wood
Heathland Plantation
Heath Farm
West Wood Farm
Gateley Gravel Pit Plantation
Lodge Wood
Decoy Wood
Gamekeeper's Wood
Guist Hill
RYBURGH DRIVE
Sennowe Bridge
Warren Side
Guist
HOLT RD
Elgar's Plantation
High Wood
Osier Carr
Water Tower
NORWICH DR
Norris's Plantation
Sennowe Hall
MAIN DR
MALTHOUSE LA
Gateley Hill
SENNOWE RD
Sennowe Park
Hill Farm
Pond Wood
The Carr
Common Farm
BRIDGE ROAD
Manor House
BROOM GREEN DRIVE
Guist Bridge
Watson's Wood
Dunham Hill
Manor Farm
Winters Farm
Spurgeon Plantation
MAIN DEREHAM RD
Reservoir
Gateley Grove
Dog & Duck Farm
BROOM GN DR
Hill Farm
Bintree Mill
Centre Farm
College Farm
Bakehouse Farm
Gateley
Manor Farm
Withers Farm
Little Wood
Gateley Hall
Horningtoft Wood
Broom Green
Heath Farm
NR20
Yarrow Farm
B1110
Great Wood
Silverstone Farm
White House Farm
Manorial Earthworks
Cottage Farm
New Lane Farm
Yarrow House
B1146
Senter Farm
BROOM GREEN ROAD
Harper's Green
Ling Plantation
County School Station
Lings Farm
GREATHEATH ROAD
Dale Farm
HARPER'S LANE
Harpers Green Farm
GATELEY ROAD
Park Farm
Water Tower
LC
Great Heath
Elm Tree Farm
Willow Farm
Bintree Hills
Pine Wood
SCHOOL RD
Grange Farm
Brisley CE Prim Sch
Maltings Farm
Green Farm
Little Heath Plantation
GREATHEATH ROAD
HOLT ROAD
Bintree Woods
A B C D E F
8 29 7 28 6 27 5 26 4 25 3 24 2 23 1 22
94 95 96 97 98 99 0

Scale: 1⅓ inches to 1 mile

18
34

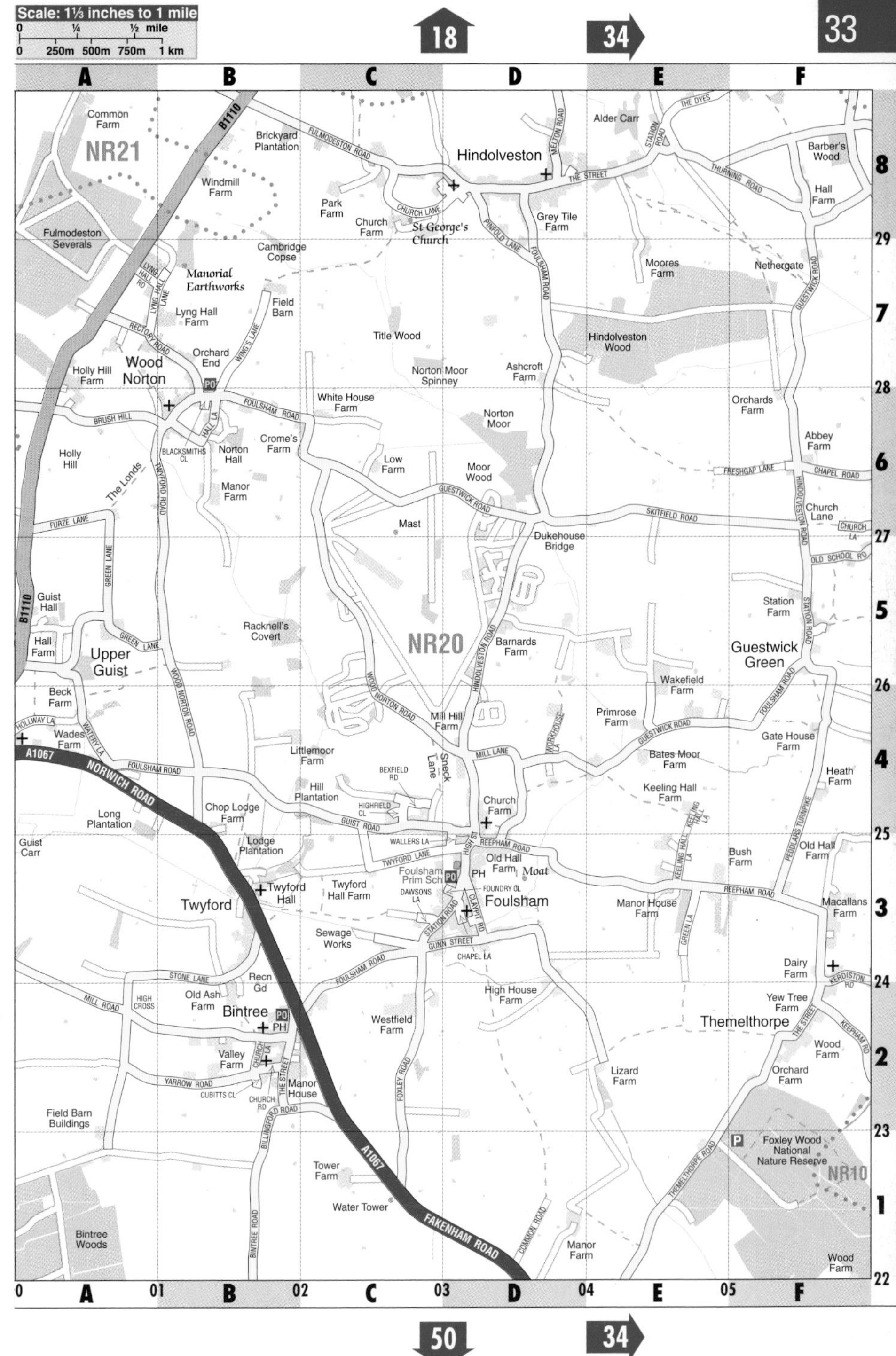

A B C D E F
Common Farm
NR21
B1110
Brickyard Plantation
Fulmodeston Road
Hindolveston
Melton Road
Alder Carr
Station Road
The Dyes
Barber's Wood
Windmill Farm
Park Farm
Church Lane
The Street
Thurning Road
Hall Farm
Fulmodeston Severals
Church Farm
St George's Church
Pinfold Lane
Grey Tile Farm
Cambridge Copse
Foulsham Road
Moores Farm
Nethergate
Guestwick Road
Manorial Earthworks
Lyng Hall Rd
Lyng Hall Lane
Field Barn
Lyng Hall Farm
Rectory Road
Wing's Lane
Title Wood
Hindolveston Wood
Orchard End
Wood Norton
Holly Hill Farm
Norton Moor Spinney
Ashcroft Farm
White House Farm
Orchards Farm
Brush Hill
Hall La
Norton Moor
Blacksmiths Cl
Norton Hall
Crome's Farm
Abbey Farm
Holly Hill
The Londs
Twyford Road
Low Farm
Moor Wood
Freshgap Lane
Chapel Road
Manor Farm
Guestwick Road
Hindolveston Road
Church Lane
Furze Lane
Mast
Skitfield Road
Church La
Dukehouse Bridge
Old School Rd
Green Lane
Guist Hall
Station Farm
Station Road
Racknell's Covert
NR20
Barnards Farm
Green Lane
Hall Farm
Upper Guist
Guestwick Green
Wood Norton Road
Beck Farm
Wakefield Farm
Foulsham Road
Mill Hill Farm
Primrose Farm
Hollway La
Wades Farm
Watery La
Workhouse La
Guestwick Road
Gate House Farm
Littlemoor Farm
Snack Lane
Mill Lane
Bates Moor Farm
A1067
Foulsham Road
Norwich Road
Bexfield Rd
Heath Farm
Hill Plantation
Keeling Hall Farm
Long Plantation
Chop Lodge Farm
Highfield Cl
Church Farm
Keeling Hall La
Guist Road
Guist Carr
Lodge Plantation
Wallers La
High St
Reepham Road
Pedlars Turnpike
Old Hall Farm
Twyford Lane
Bush Farm
Old Hall Farm
Moat
Foulsham Prim Sch
PO
PH
Twyford Hall
Twyford Hall Farm
Foundry Cl
Twyford
Dawsons La
Foulsham
Manor House Farm
Reepham Road
Macallans Farm
Station Road
Claypit Rd
Green La
Sewage Works
Gunn Street
Chapel La
Dairy Farm
Stone Lane
Foulsham Road
Kerdiston Rd
Recn Gd
Old Ash Farm
High House Farm
Mill Road
High Cross
Bintree
Yew Tree Farm
Westfield Farm
Themelthorpe
Keepham Rd
The Street
Valley Farm
Church La
Wood Farm
Foxley Road
Lizard Farm
Yarrow Road
Manor House
Orchard Farm
Cubitts Cl
Church Rd
Billingford Road
Field Barn Buildings
P
Foxley Wood National Nature Reserve
Themelthorpe Road
Tower Farm
NR10
A1067
Water Tower
Bintree Road
Common Road
Bintree Woods
Fakenham Road
Manor Farm
Wood Farm
0 01 02 03 04 05
29 28 27 26 25 24 23 22
8 7 6 5 4 3 2 1

50
34

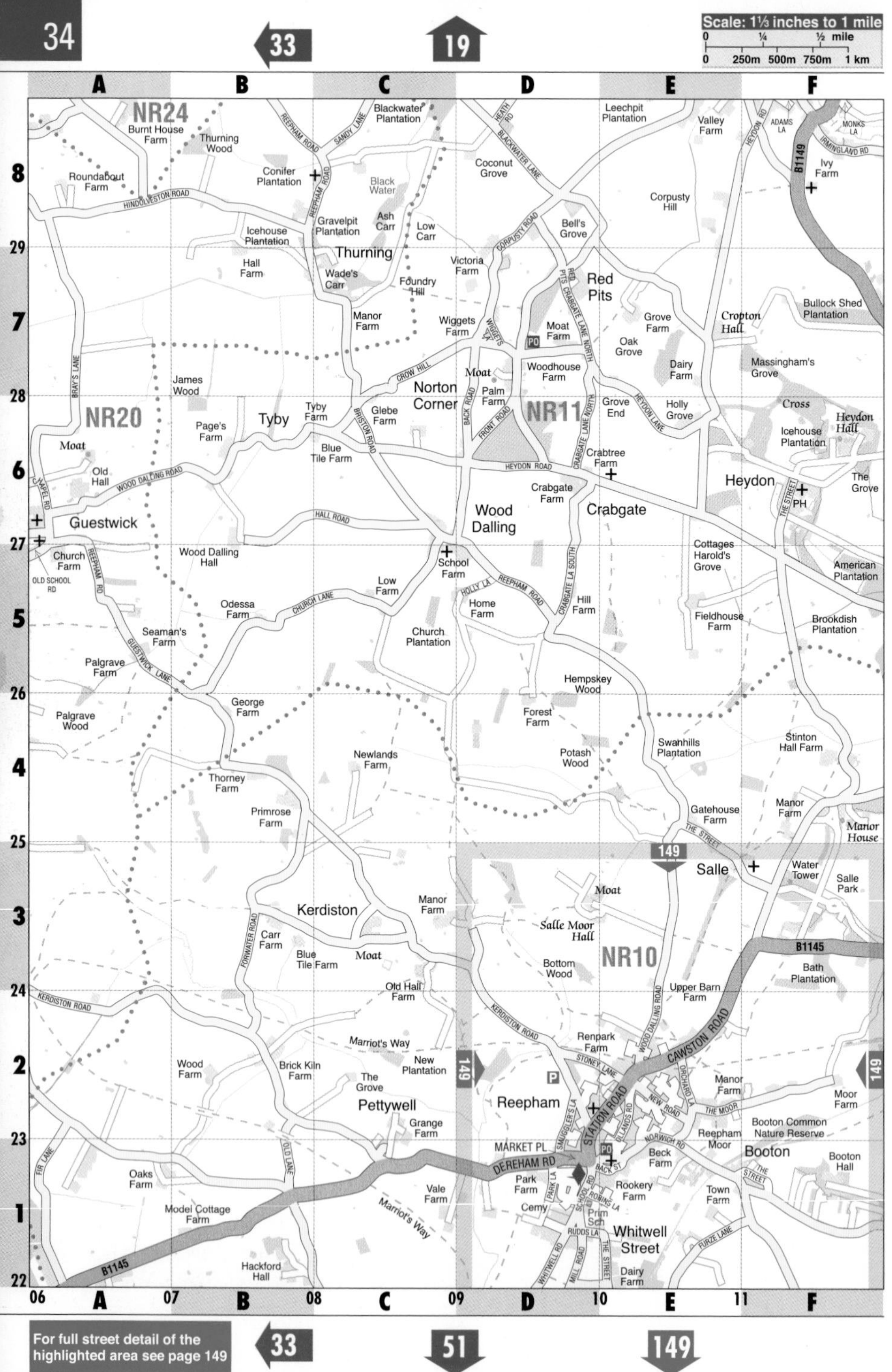

Scale: 1½ inches to 1 mile
0   ¼   ½ mile
0 250m 500m 750m 1 km

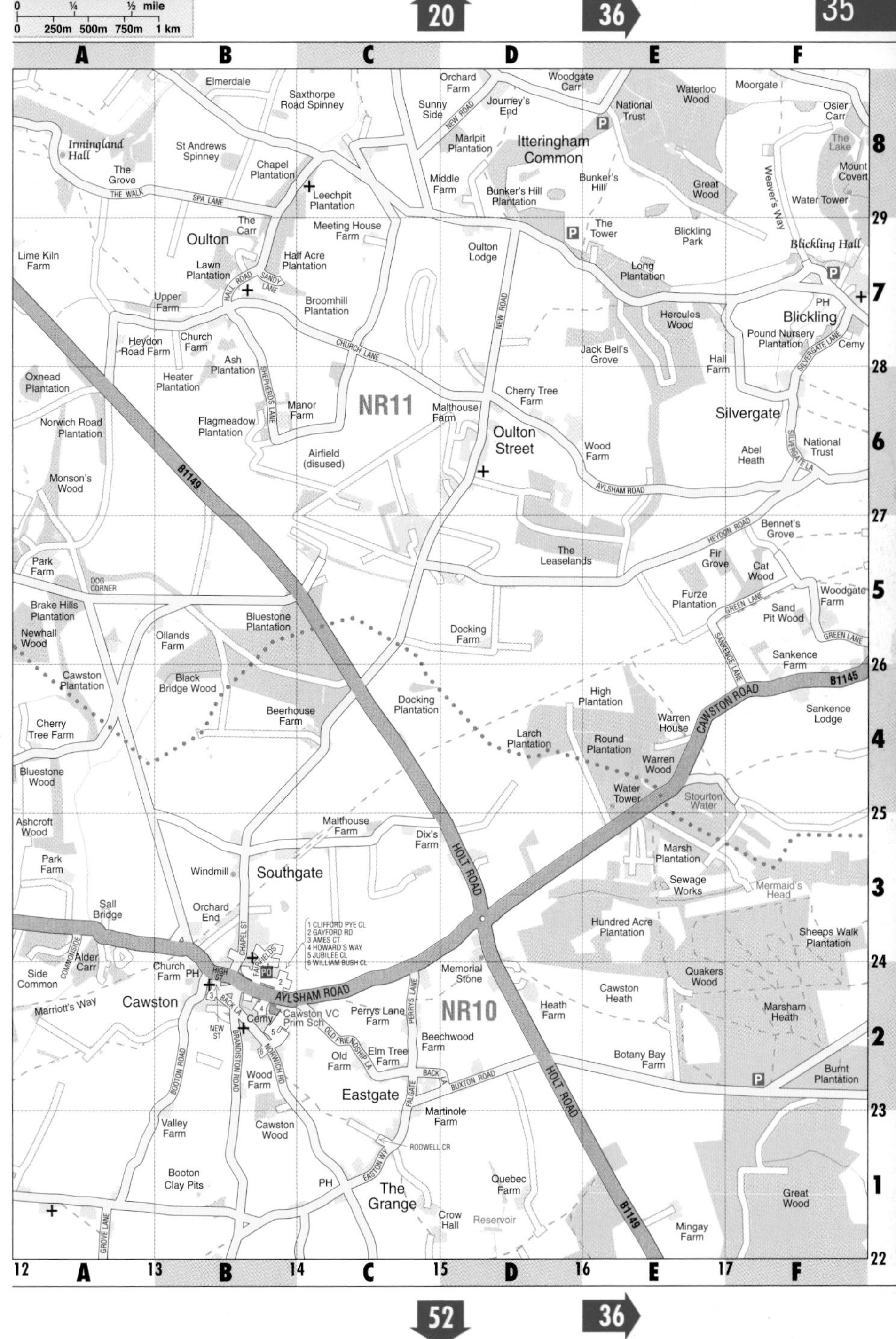

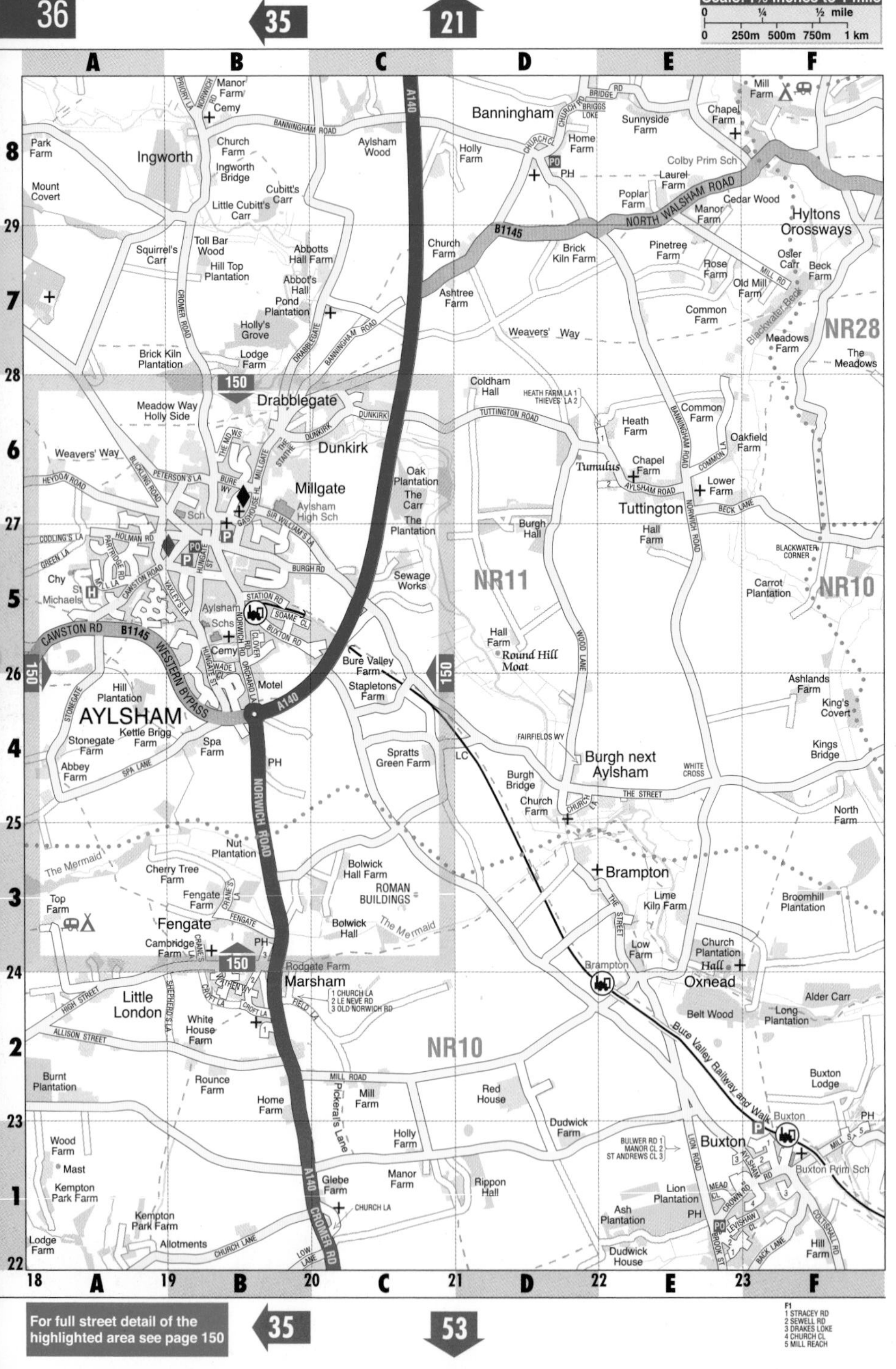

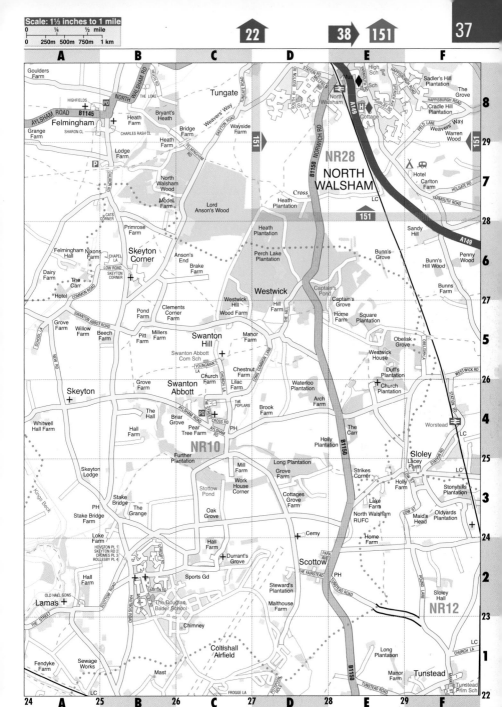
A
B
C
D
E
F
Goulders Farm
HEATH RD
NORTH WALSHAM RD
THE LOKE
Tungate
TUNGATE ROAD
STATION RD
BUXTON RD
MILLFIELD RD
SOUTH RD
Sch
North Walsham
Mus
High Sch
YARMOUTH RD
Sch
HAPPISBURGH ROAD
SPENSER AVE
Sadler's Hill Plantation
The Grove
HAPPISBURGH ROAD
THIRLBY RD
Cradle Hill Plantation
Cottage
A149
HIGHFIELDS
PO
AYLSHAM ROAD
B1145
Felmingham
Heath Farm
Bryant's Heath
Weavers' Way
SKEYTON ROAD
Wayside Farm
FIELD LANE
Weavers' Way
Warren Wood
8
Grange Farm
SHARON CL
CHARLES RASH CL
Bridge Farm
Heath Farm
FELMINGHAM RD
151
NORWICH RD
151
29
Lodge Farm
P
NR28
NORTH WALSHAM
Hotel
Carlton Farm
HOLGATE RD
7
CHURCH RD
North Walsham Wood
B1150
Cross
YARMOUTH ROAD
Model Farm
Lord Anson's Wood
Heath Plantation
LC
CATS CORNER
151
28
Primrose Farm
Heath Plantation
Sandy Hill
A149
Felmingham Hall
Nixons Farm
CHAPEL LA
Skeyton Corner
Anson's End
Perch Lake Plantation
Bunn's Grove
Penny Wood
6
LOW ROAD
SKEYTON CORNER
Brake Farm
Bunn's Hill Wood
Dairy Farm
The Carr
COMMON ROAD
Bunns Farm
Hotel
Westwick
Captain's Pond
Captain's Grove
27
Westwick Hill
Hill Farm
Wood Farm
THE HILL
Clements Corner Farm
Pond Farm
Home Farm
Square Plantation
SWANTON ABBOT ROAD
Grove Farm
Willow Farm
Beech Farm
Millers Farm
Pitt Farm
Swanton Hill
Manor Farm
Obelisk Grove
OBELISK LA
5
SCHOOL LA
Swanton Abbott Com Sch
LONG COMMON LANE
Westwick House
YOUNGMAN'S LA
Chestnut Farm
Duff's Plantation
NEW RD
Church Farm
CHURCH LA
WESTWICK RD
26
Grove Farm
Swanton Abbott
Lilac Farm
Waterloo Plantation
Church Plantation
Skeyton
THE STREET
THE POPLARS
Arch Farm
STATION RD
The Hall
AYLSHAM ROAD
Brook Farm
PO
CROSS RD
Briar Grove
Whitwell Hall Farm
Pear Tree Farm
AYLSHAM RD
PH
The Carr
Worstead
4
Hall Farm
LC
Holly Plantation
NR10
B1150
Further Plantation
Sloley
STATION RD
25
Lacey Farm
Mill Farm
Long Plantation
Skeyton Lodge
Grove Farm
Strikes Corner
LC
LOW ST
Work House Corner
Holly Farm
Stonyhills Plantation
Kings Beck
Stottow Pond
Cottages Grove Farm
Lake Farm
3
Stake Bridge
PH
The Grange
North Walsham RUFC
LOW ST
Maid's Head
Oldyards Plantation
Stake Bridge Farm
Oak Grove
Cemy
Loke Farm
Home Farm
24
HOVETON PL 1
SKEYTON RD 2
CROMES PL 3
ROLLESBY PL 4
GRIMESBY RD
Hall Farm
Durrant's Grove
PARK AVE
Scottow
Hall Farm
SCOTTOW ROAD
Sports Gd
THE FAIRSTEAD
PH
POUND LANE
2
OLD HALL GDNS
BARTON RD
Steward's Plantation
TUNSTEAD ROAD
Sloley Hall
Lamas
HAUTBOIS ROAD
FILBY RD
The Douglas Bader School
Malthouse Farm
NR12
THE STREET
23
Chimney
Coltishall Airfield
Long Plantation
LC
CHURCH LA
1
Fendyke Farm
Sewage Works
Mast
Manor Farm
Tunstead
MARKET ST
Tunstead Prim Sch
LC
POTSPOON HOLE
FROGGE LA
TUNSTEAD ROAD
22
24
25
26
27
28
29

151 37 23

Scale: 1⅓ inches to 1 mile

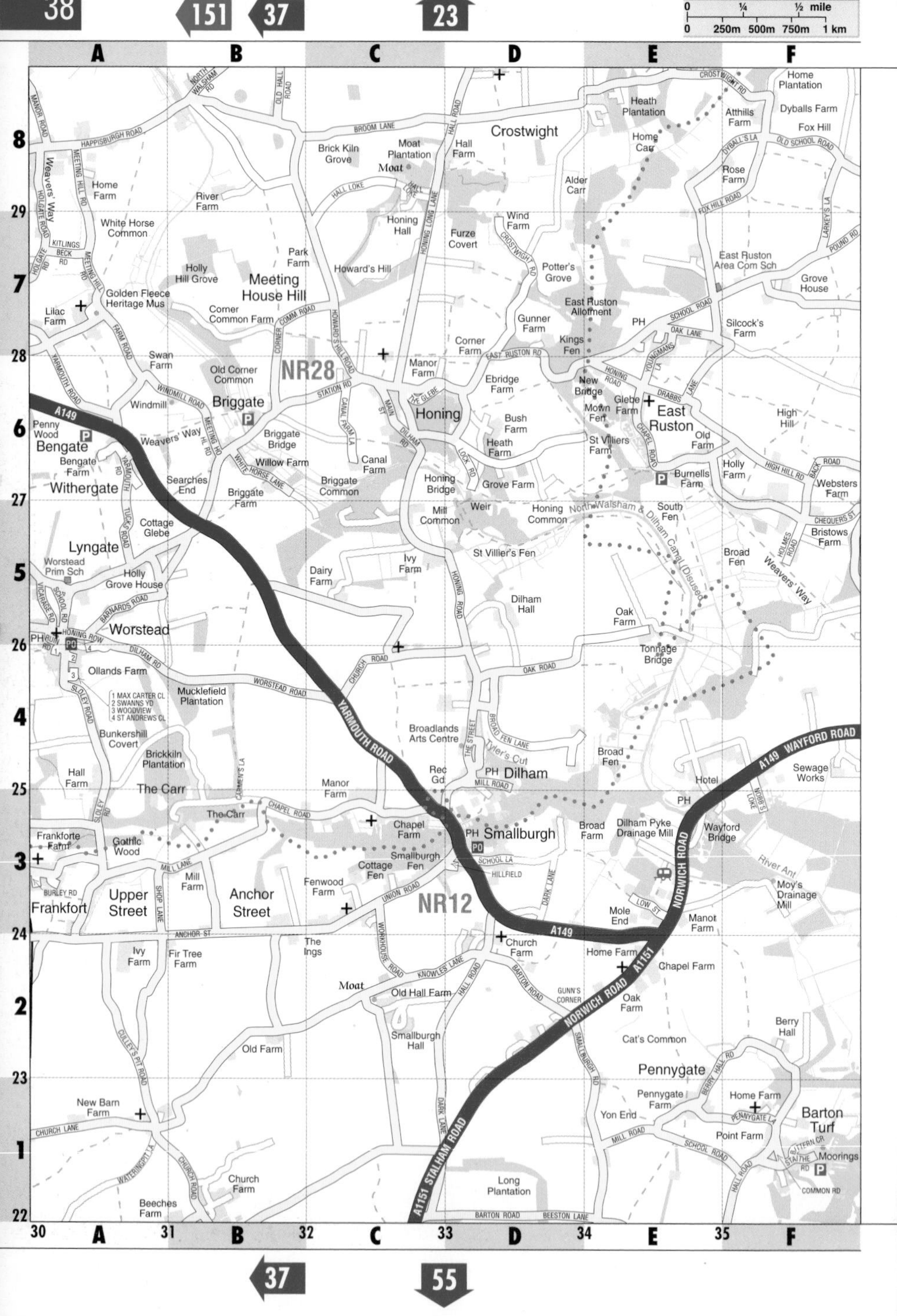

Crostwight
Honing
Briggate
Meeting House Hill
Bengate
Withergate
Lyngate
Worstead
East Ruston
Dilham
Smallburgh
Upper Street
Anchor Street
Frankfort
Pennygate
Barton Turf
NR28
NR12
A149
A1151
YARMOUTH ROAD
NORWICH ROAD
STALHAM ROAD
WAYFORD ROAD
North Walsham & Dilham Canal (Disused)
Weavers' Way
River Ant

37 55

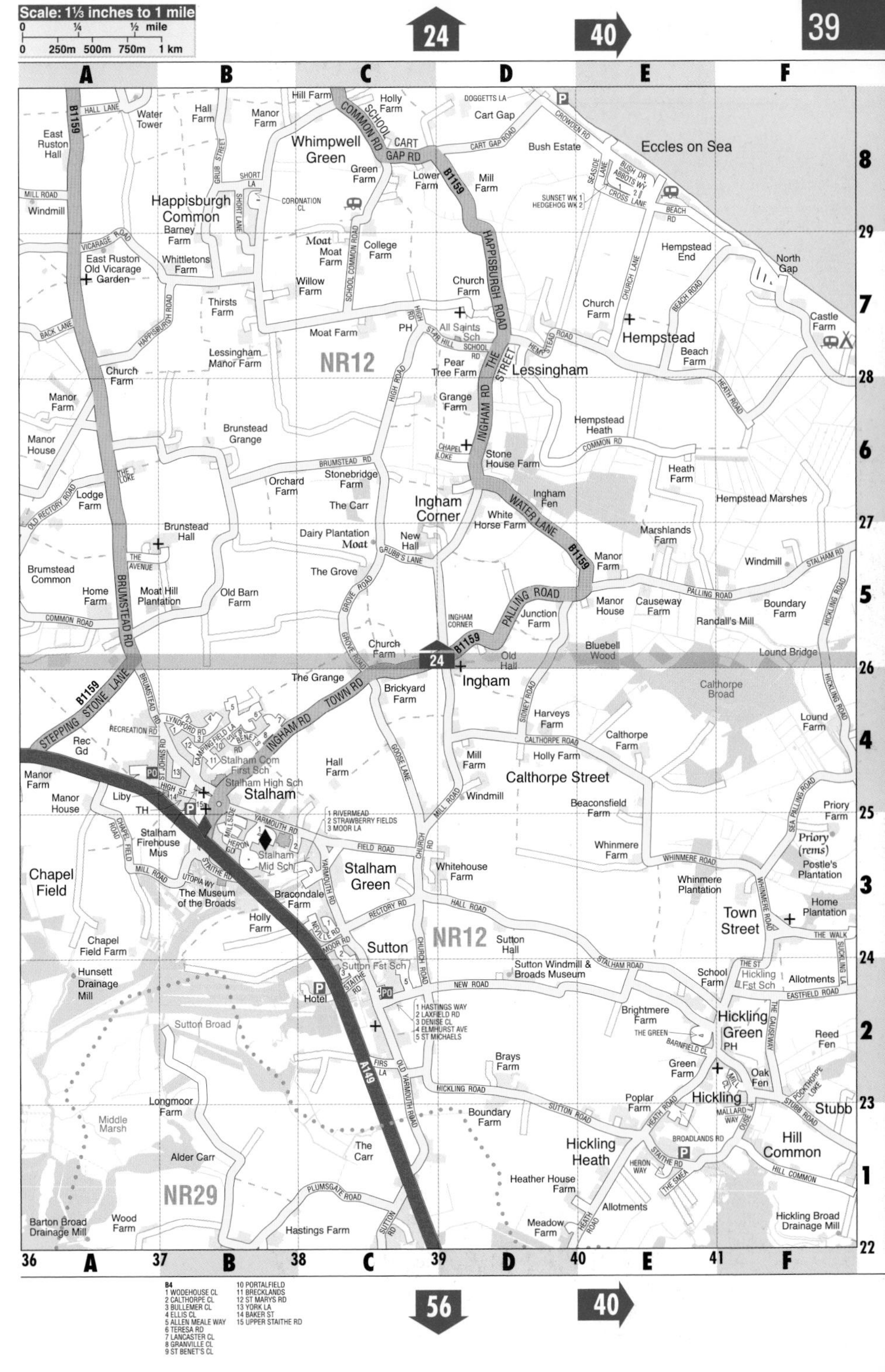
Scale: 1⅓ inches to 1 mile
0 ¼ ½ mile
0 250m 500m 750m 1 km
24
40
A B C D E F
Hill Farm
Holly Farm
SCHOOL COMMON RD
DOGGETTS LA
CROWDEN RD
Cart Gap
HALL LANE
Water Tower
Hall Farm
Manor Farm
East Ruston Hall
B1159
Whimpwell Green
CART GAP RD
CART GAP ROAD
Bush Estate
Eccles on Sea
GRUB STREET
SHORT LA
Green Farm
Lower Farm
Mill Farm
SEASIDE LANE
BUSH DR
ABBOTS WY
CROSS LANE
SUNSET WK
HEDGEHOG WK
BEACH RD
MILL ROAD
Windmill
Happisburgh Common
CORONATION CL
Moat
Moat Farm
College Farm
HAPPISBURGH ROAD
Barney Farm
VICARAGE ROAD
East Ruston Old Vicarage Garden
Whittletons Farm
SHORT LANE
Hempstead End
North Gap
Willow Farm
Church Farm
CHURCH LANE
BEACH ROAD
Thirsts Farm
HIGH RD
Church Farm
Hempstead
Castle Farm
BACK LANE
HAPPISBURGH ROAD
Moat Farm
PH
All Saints Sch
STAR HILL
SCHOOL RD
HEMPSTEAD ROAD
Beach Farm
Lessingham Manor Farm
NR12
Pear Tree Farm
THE STREET
Lessingham
Church Farm
HEATH ROAD
Manor Farm
HIGH ROAD
Grange Farm
INGHAM RD
Hempstead Heath
Brunstead Grange
COMMON RD
Manor House
CHAPEL LOKE
Stone House Farm
BRUMSTEAD RD
Stonebridge Farm
THE LOKE
Orchard Farm
Heath Farm
OLD RECTORY ROAD
Lodge Farm
The Carr
Ingham Corner
Ingham Fen
Hempstead Marshes
WATER LANE
White Horse Farm
Brunstead Hall
Dairy Plantation
Moat
New Hall
Marshlands Farm
GRUBB'S LANE
THE AVENUE
Manor Farm
Windmill
STALHAM RD
Brumstead Common
The Grove
Home Farm
Moat Hill Plantation
Old Barn Farm
GROVE ROAD
PALLING ROAD
Manor House
Causeway Farm
Boundary Farm
BRUMSTEAD RD
Junction Farm
Randall's Mill
HICKLING ROAD
COMMON ROAD
INGHAM CORNER
Bluebell Wood
Church Farm
Lound Bridge
Old Hall
Ingham
The Grange
Brickyard Farm
Calthorpe Broad
B1159
STEPPING STONE LANE
TOWN RD
INGHAM RD
SIDNEY ROAD
Harveys Farm
LYNDFORD RD
Calthorpe Farm
Lound Farm
RECREATION RD
CAMPING FIELD LA
CALTHORPE ROAD
Rec Gd
Stalham Com First Sch
Hall Farm
GOOSE LANE
Mill Farm
Holly Farm
Manor Farm
ST JOHNS RD
PO
Stalham High Sch
Calthorpe Street
SEA PALLING ROAD
Liby
HIGH ST
Stalham
Windmill
Manor House
TH
P
MILL ROAD
Beaconsfield Farm
Priory Farm
MILLSIDE
YARMOUTH RD
1 RIVERMEAD
2 STRAWBERRY FIELDS
3 MOOR LA
CHAPEL FIELD ROAD
Stalham Firehouse Mus
HERON GD
Stalham Mid Sch
FIELD ROAD
Priory (rems)
Whinmere Farm
CHURCH RD
Chapel Field
MILL ROAD
STAITHE RD
UTOPIA WY
Stalham Green
Whitehouse Farm
WHINMERE ROAD
Postle's Plantation
The Museum of the Broads
Bracondale Farm
YARMOUTH RD
HALL ROAD
Whinmere Plantation
WHINMERE ROAD
RECTORY RD
Holly Farm
Town Street
Home Plantation
NEVILLE RD
Chapel Field Farm
MOOR RD
Sutton
NR12
Sutton Hall
THE WALK
Sutton Fst Sch
CHURCH ROAD
Sutton Windmill & Broads Museum
STALHAM ROAD
THE ST
School Farm
Hickling Fst Sch
Allotments
SUCKLING LA
Hunsett Drainage Mill
STAITHE RD
P
Hotel
PO
NEW ROAD
EASTFIELD ROAD
1 HASTINGS WAY
2 LAXFIELD RD
3 DENISE CL
4 ELMHURST AVE
5 ST MICHAELS
Brightmere Farm
Hickling Green
THE CAUSEWAY
Reed Fen
Sutton Broad
THE GREEN
BARNFIELD CL
PH
Brays Farm
A149
FIRS LA
OLD YARMOUTH ROAD
Green Farm
MILL CL
Oak Fen
HICKLING ROAD
POCKTHORPE LOKE
Longmoor Farm
SUTTON ROAD
Poplar Farm
Hickling
Stubb
Middle Marsh
Boundary Farm
HEATH ROAD
MALLARD WAY
OUSE LA
STUBB ROAD
The Carr
Hickling Heath
BROADLANDS RD
Hill Common
Alder Carr
HERON WAY
STAITHE RD
P
THE SMEA
Heather House Farm
HILL COMMON
NR29
PLUMSGATE ROAD
Allotments
Barton Broad Drainage Mill
Wood Farm
Hastings Farm
SUTTON RD
Meadow Farm
HEATH ROAD
Hickling Broad Drainage Mill
8
29
7
28
6
27
5
26
4
25
3
24
2
23
1
22
36 A 37 B 38 C 39 D 40 E 41 F
B4
1 WODEHOUSE CL
2 CALTHORPE CL
3 BULLEMER CL
4 ELLIS CL
5 ALLEN MEALE WAY
6 TERESA RD
7 LANCASTER CL
8 GRANVILLE CL
9 ST BENET'S CL
10 PORTALFIELD
11 BRECKLANDS
12 ST MARYS RD
13 YORK LA
14 BAKER ST
15 UPPER STAITHE RD
56
40

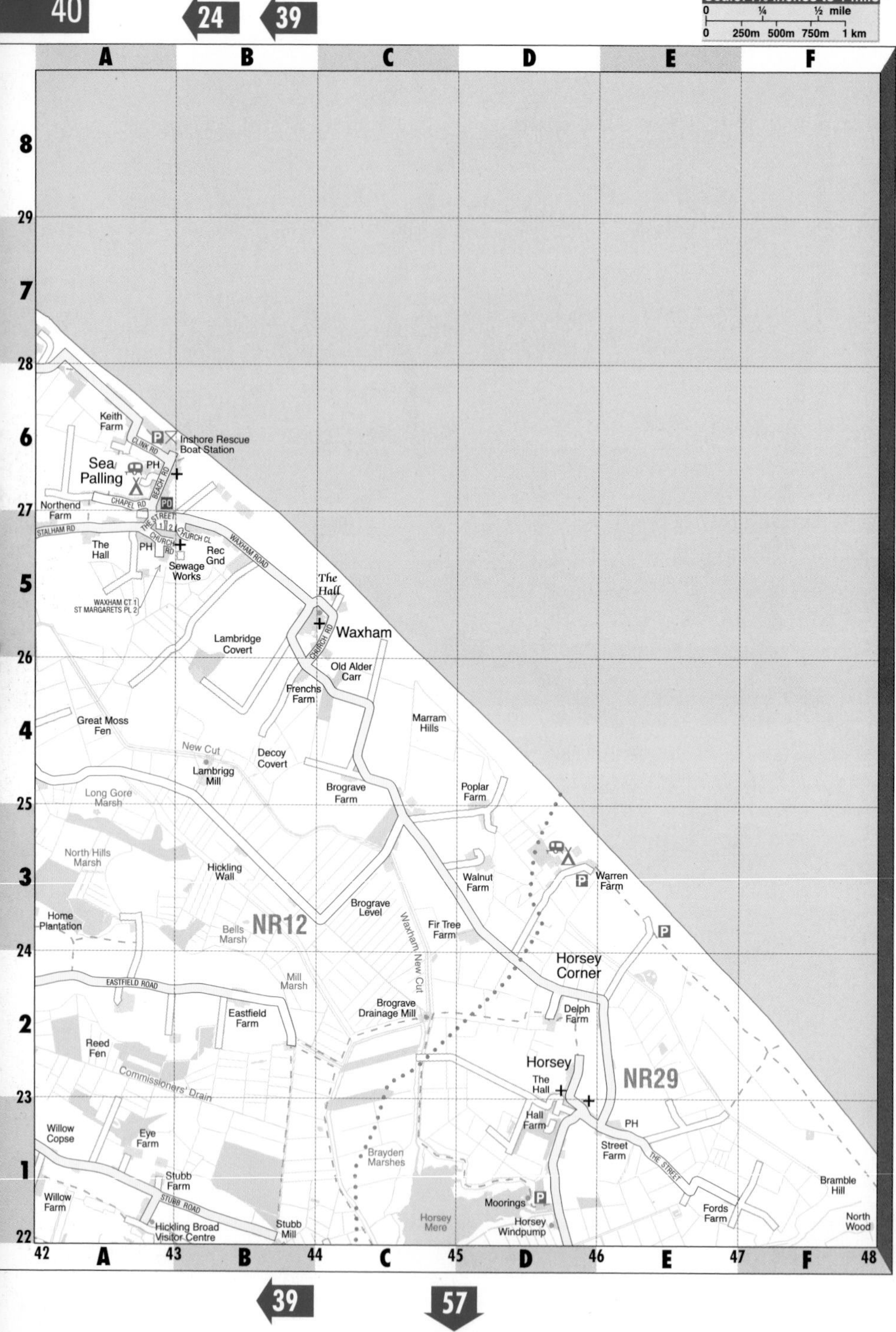

Scale: 1½ inches to 1 mile

0	¼	½ mile
0	250m	500m	750m	1 km

A   **B**   **C**   **D**   **E**   **F**

8

29

7

28

Keith Farm

6

P ✕ Inshore Rescue Boat Station

Sea Palling

LINK RD

PH

CHAPEL RD

PO

27

Northend Farm

STREET

STALHAM RD

CHURCH CL

CHURCH RD

WAXHAM ROAD

The Hall

PH

Rec Gnd

Sewage Works

5

The Hall

WAXHAM CT 1
ST MARGARETS PL 2

Waxham

26

Lambridge Covert

Old Alder Carr

Frenchs Farm

4

Great Moss Fen

New Cut

Decoy Covert

Marram Hills

CHURCH RD

Lambrigg Mill

Brograve Farm

Poplar Farm

25

Long Gore Marsh

North Hills Marsh

Hickling Wall

P ✕

3

Walnut Farm

P Warren Farm

Home Plantation

Bells Marsh

NR12

Brograve Level

Fir Tree Farm

P

24

EASTFIELD ROAD

Mill Marsh

Waxham New Cut

Horsey Corner

2

Reed Fen

Eastfield Farm

Brograve Drainage Mill

Delph Farm

23

Commissioners' Drain

Horsey

The Hall

NR29

Hall Farm

PH

Willow Copse

Eye Farm

Street Farm

THE STREET

Bramble Hill

1

Stubb Farm

Brayden Marshes

Moorings P

Fords Farm

North Wood

Willow Farm

STUBB ROAD

Hickling Broad Visitor Centre

Stubb Mill

Horsey Mere

Horsey Windpump

22

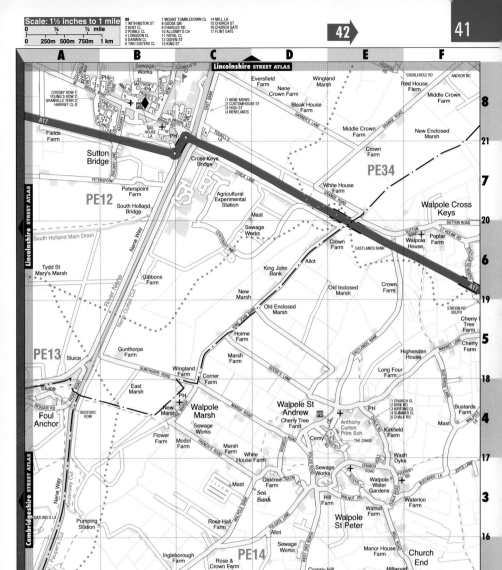

Scale: 1⅓ inches to 1 mile

0   ¼   ½ mile
0   250m   500m   750m   1 km

88
1 WITHINGTON ST
2 KENT CL
3 PEBBLE CL
4 LONGDON CL
5 DARWIN CL
6 TWO SISTERS CL

7 MOUNT TUMBLEDOWN CL
8 GOOSE GN
9 CHARLES RD
10 ALLENBY'S CH
11 ROYAL CL
12 QUEEN ST
13 KING ST

14 MILL LA
15 CHURCH ST
16 CHURCH GATE
17 FLINT GATE

Lincolnshire STREET ATLAS

1 NENE MDWS
2 CUSTOMHOUSE ST
3 HIGH ST
4 NENELANDS

Lincolnshire STREET ATLAS

Cambridgeshire STREET ATLAS

PE34

PE12

PE13

PE14

Walpole Cross Keys

Walpole Marsh

Walpole St Andrew

Walpole St Peter

Church End

Sutton Bridge

Foul Anchor

Ingleborough

Eversfield Farm

Wingland Marsh

Nene Crown Farm

Bleak House Farm

Red House Farm

Middle Crown Farm

New Enclosed Marsh

Middle Crown Farm

Crown Farm

White House Farm

Fields Farm

Crosby Row 1
Young's Row 2
Granville Terr 3
Harriet Cl 4

Cross Keys Bridge

Peterspoint Farm

South Holland Bridge

Agricultural Experimental Station

Mast

Sewage Works

Crown Farm

Poplar Farm

Walpole House

South Holland Main Drain

Tydd St Mary's Marsh

Gibbons Farm

King John Bank

Allot

Old Inclosed Marsh

Crown Farm

Station Rd South

Cherry Tree Farm

Cherry Farm

New Marsh

Old Enclosed Marsh

Highenden House

Long Four Farm

Sluice

Gunthorpe Farm

Holme Farm

Marsh Farm

Bustards Farm

Sluice

East Marsh

Wingland Farm

Corner Farm

New Marsh

1 CHURCH CL
2 KIRK RD
3 KIRTONS CL
4 SUMMER CL
5 CHALK RD

Mast

Kirkfield Farm

Cherry Tree Farm

Anthony Curton Prim Sch

Wash Dyke

Flower Farm

Model Farm

Marsh Farm

White House Farm

Mast

Oaktree Farm

Sewage Works

Walpole Water Gardens

Waterloo Farm

Hill Farm

Walnut Farm

Pumping Station

Sea Bank

Rose Hall Farm

Allot

Sewage Works

Manor House Farm

Millwood Farm

Trafford House Farm

Ivy Farm

Ingleborough Farm

Rose & Crown Farm

Thorn Moor

Cranny Hill Field

Nene Farm

The Salts

Thorn Moor Field

Crannifield Farm

Hill House Farm

Sebastopol Farm

Windmill

Long Swine Holme Field

Sea Bank

Mast

Honington House Farm

Grange Farm

Stratton's Farm

Mill House Peartree Farm

Sewage Works

The Old Grange Farm

Dixon's Dro

Moat

Five-Alls Rd

A17

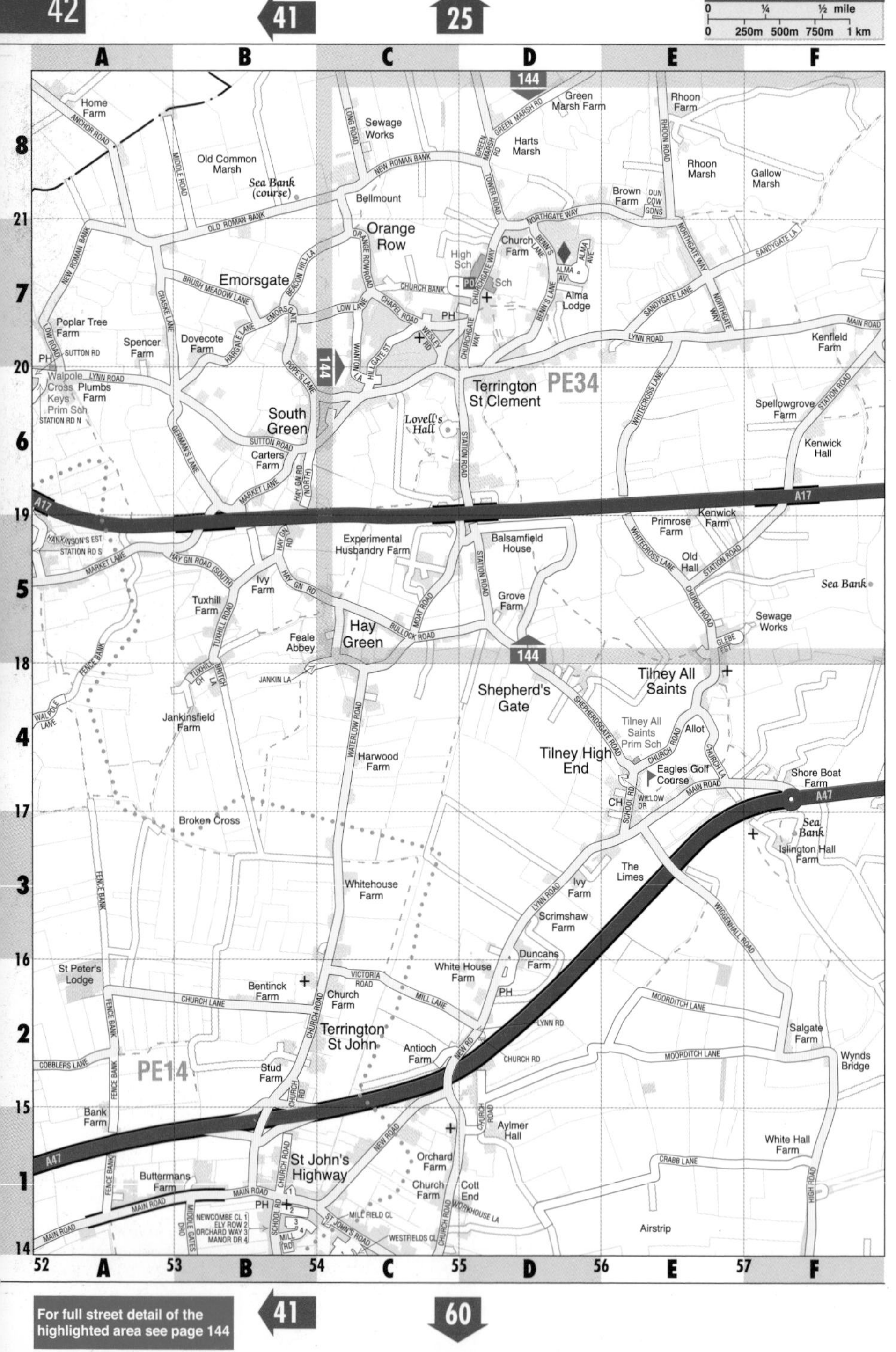

A   B   C   D   E   F

144

8

Home Farm
ANCHOR ROAD
Old Common Marsh
Sewage Works
Green Marsh Farm
Green Marsh Farm
Rhoon Farm

21

Sea Bank (course)
Bellmount
Harts Marsh
Rhoon Marsh
Gallow Marsh

7

Emorsgate
Orange Row
BRUSH MEADOW LANE
ORANGE ROW
LONG ROAD
NEW ROMAN BANK
High Sch
Church Farm
NORTHGATE WAY
ALMA AV.
Alma Lodge
Brown Farm
DUN COW GONS
SANDYGATE LA.

20

Poplar Tree Farm
Spencer Farm
Dovecote Farm
SUTTON RD
EMORSGATE
CHAPEL ROAD
LOW LANE
HILL GATE ST
PH
CHURCH WAY
PH
LYNN ROAD
SCHOOL LANE
NORTHGATE WAY
WHITE
Kenfield Farm
MAIN ROAD

PH
Walpole Cross Keys
Plumbs Farm
Prim Sch
STATION RD N
PH
LYNN ROAD
144
POPE'S LANE
WANTON LA.
CHURCH BANK
Terrington St Clement
PE34
Spellowgrove Farm
STATION ROAD

6

South Green
GRAHAM'S LANE
SUTTON ROAD
Carters Farm
TILNEY RD
Lovell's Hall
STATION ROAD
WHITECROSS LANE
Kenwick Hall

19

A17
WILKINSON'S EST
STATION RD S
MARKET LANE
A17

5

MARKET LANE
HAY GN ROAD (SOUTH)
Ivy Farm
HAY GN RD
Experimental Husbandry Farm
ROAD END
STATION ROAD
Balsamfield House
Grove Farm
Primrose Farm
Kenwick Farm
Old Hall
Sea Bank

Tuxhill Farm
TUXHILL ROAD
Feale Abbey
Hay Green
BULLOCK ROAD
GLEBE
Sewage Works

18

WALPOLE
BANK
FENCE BANK
LUDDS LA
JANKIN LA
144
Tilney All Saints

4

WALPOLE LANE
Jankinsfield Farm
WATERLOO RD
Harwood Farm
Shepherd's Gate
SHEPHERDSGATE ROAD
Tilney All Saints Prim Sch
Tilney High End
Allot
CHURCH LA.
CHURCH LA.
Shore Boat Farm

17

Broken Cross
CH
Eagles Golf Course
WILLOW DR
MAIN ROAD
A47
Sea Bank
Islington Hall Farm

3

Whitehouse Farm
LYNN ROAD
Ivy Farm
The Limes
WISBEACH ROAD

16

St Peter's Lodge
FENCE BANK
Bentinck Farm
CHURCH LANE
VICTORIA ROAD
Church Farm
White House Farm
PH
Scrimshaw Farm
Duncans Farm
MILL LANE
Moorditch Lane
Salgate Farm
Wynds Bridge

2

PE14
COBBLERS LANE
CHURCH LANE
Terrington St John
Antioch Farm
LYNN RD
CHURCH RD
MOORDITCH LANE
MOORDITCH LANE

15

Bank Farm
Stud Farm
CHURCH RD
NEW ROAD
Aylmer Hall
CRABB LANE
White Hall Farm

1

A47
Buttermans Farm
MAIN ROAD
St John's Highway
PH
NEWCOMBE CL
ELY ROW 2
ORCHARD WAY 3
MANOR DR 4
SCHOOL ROAD
MILE FIELD CL
Orchard Farm
Church Farm
Cott End
WINDHOUSE LA
WESTFIELDS CL
Airstrip
HIGH ROAD

14

MAIN ROAD
ST JOHN'S ROAD

52   A   53   B   54   C   55   D   56   E   57   F

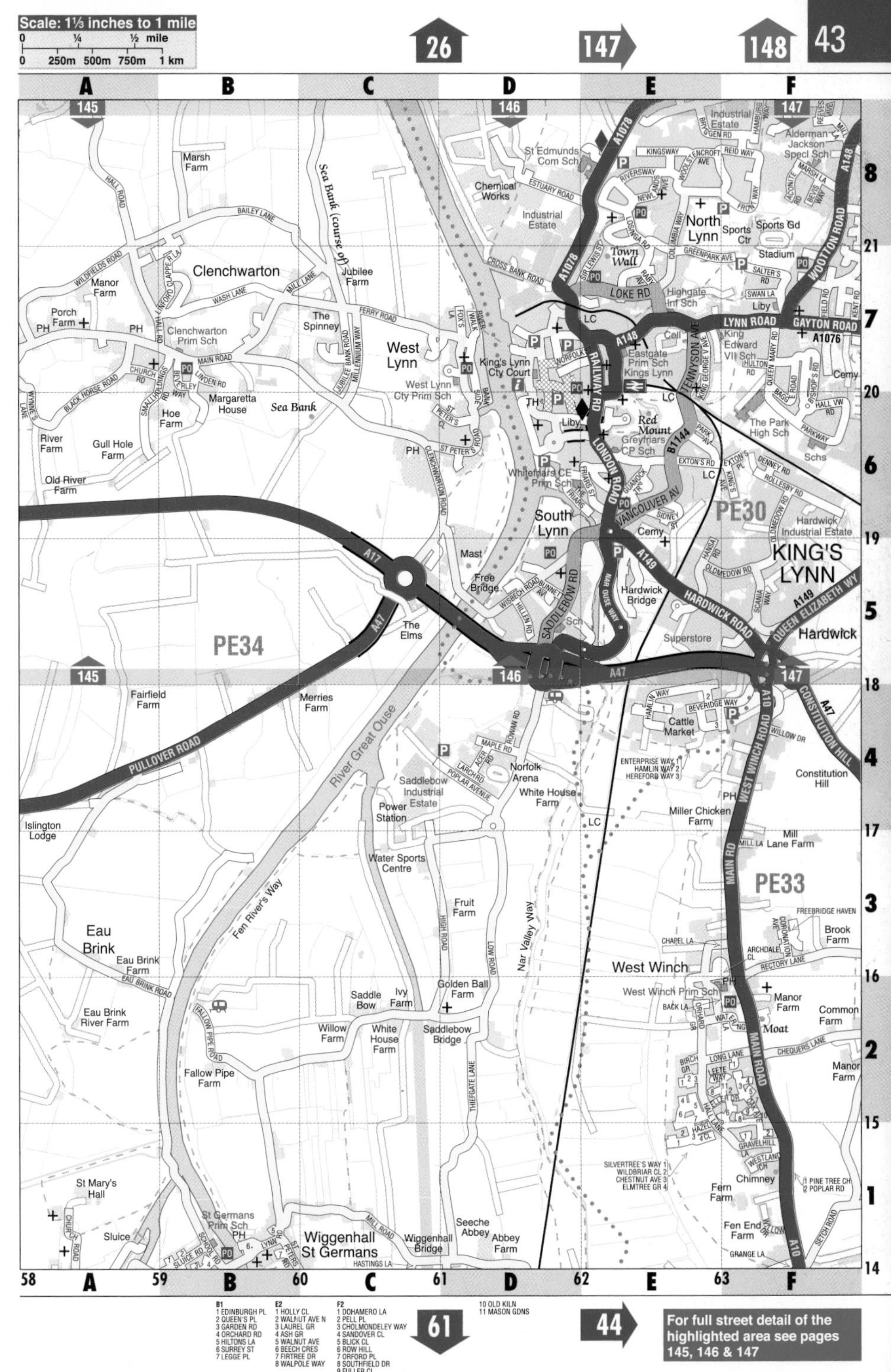

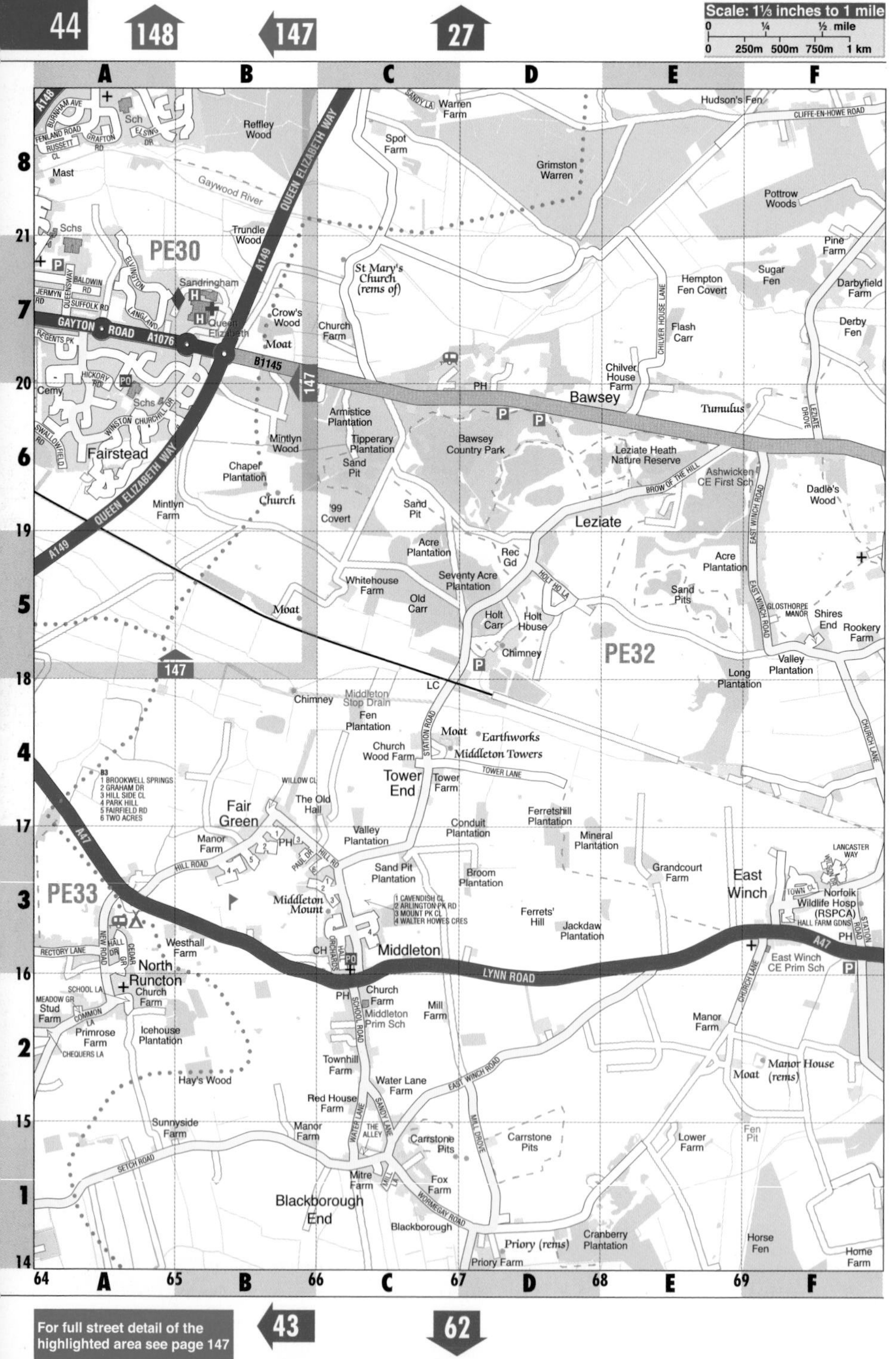

148
147
27
Scale: 1⅓ inches to 1 mile
0 ¼ ½ mile
0 250m 500m 750m 1 km
A B C D E F
8 21 7 20 6 19 5 18 4 17 3 16 2 15 1 14
64 65 66 67 68 69
Warren Farm
Hudson's Fen
CLIFFE-EN-HOWE ROAD
SANDY LA
Reffley Wood
Spot Farm
Grimston Warren
Pottrow Woods
Mast
Gaywood River
QUEEN ELIZABETH WAY
Schs
Trundle Wood
PE30
St Mary's Church (rems of)
Hempton Fen Covert
Sugar Fen
Pine Farm
Darbyfield Farm
Sandringham
Crow's Wood
Church Farm
CHILVER HOUSE LANE
Flash Carr
Derby Fen
GAYTON ROAD
A1076
Queen Elizabeth
Moat
B1145
A149
A148
Chilver House Farm
Bawsey
Tumulus
LEZIATE DROVE
Cemy
Armistice Plantation
Tipperary Plantation
Mintlyn Wood
Bawsey Country Park
Leziate Heath Nature Reserve
Ashwicken CE First Sch
Fairstead
Chapel Plantation
Sand Pit
BROW OF THE HILL
Dadle's Wood
Church
Mintlyn Farm
'99 Covert
Leziate
EAST WINCH ROAD
Acre Plantation
Rec Gd
Seventy Acre Plantation
Whitehouse Farm
Old Carr
HOLT HO LA
Sand Pits
Holt Carr
Holt House
GLOSTHORPE MANOR
Shires End
Rookery Farm
Chimney
PE32
Valley Plantation
Long Plantation
LC
Middleton Stop Drain
Fen Plantation
STATION ROAD
Earthworks
Middleton Towers
CHURCH LANE
Church Wood Farm
Tower End
Tower Farm
TOWER LANE
B3
1 BROOKWELL SPRINGS
2 GRAHAM DR
3 HILL SIDE CL
4 PARK HILL
5 FAIRFIELD RD
6 TWO ACRES
WILLOW CL
Fair Green
The Old Hall
Ferretshill Plantation
Manor Farm
Conduit Plantation
Mineral Plantation
LANCASTER WAY
A47
HILL ROAD
PAUL DR
HILL RD
Sand Pit Plantation
Broom Plantation
Grandcourt Farm
East Winch
PE33
Middleton Mount
1 CAVENDISH CL
2 ARLINGTON PK RD
3 MOUNT PK CL
4 WALTER HOWES CRES
Norfolk Wildlife Hosp (RSPCA)
Ferrets' Hill
Jackdaw Plantation
HALL FARM GDNS
STATION ROAD
Westhall Farm
RECTORY LANE
NEW ROAD
CEDAR GR
North Runcton
Middleton
LYNN ROAD
East Winch CE Prim Sch
SCHOOL LA
Church Farm
Middleton Prim Sch
SCHOOL ROAD
Mill Farm
Manor Farm
MEADOW GR
Stud Farm
COMMON LA
Primrose Farm
Icehouse Plantation
CHEQUERS LA
Townhill Farm
Manor House (rems)
Hay's Wood
Water Lane Farm
EAST WINCH ROAD
Red House Farm
Sunnyside Farm
Manor Farm
WATER LANE
SANDY LANE
THE ALLEY
Carrstone Pits
MILL DROVE
Lower Farm
Fen Pit
SETCH ROAD
Mitre Farm
MILL LA
Fox Farm
WORMEGAY ROAD
Blackborough End
Blackborough
Priory (rems)
Cranberry Plantation
Horse Fen
Home Farm
Priory Farm
For full street detail of the highlighted area see page 147
43
62

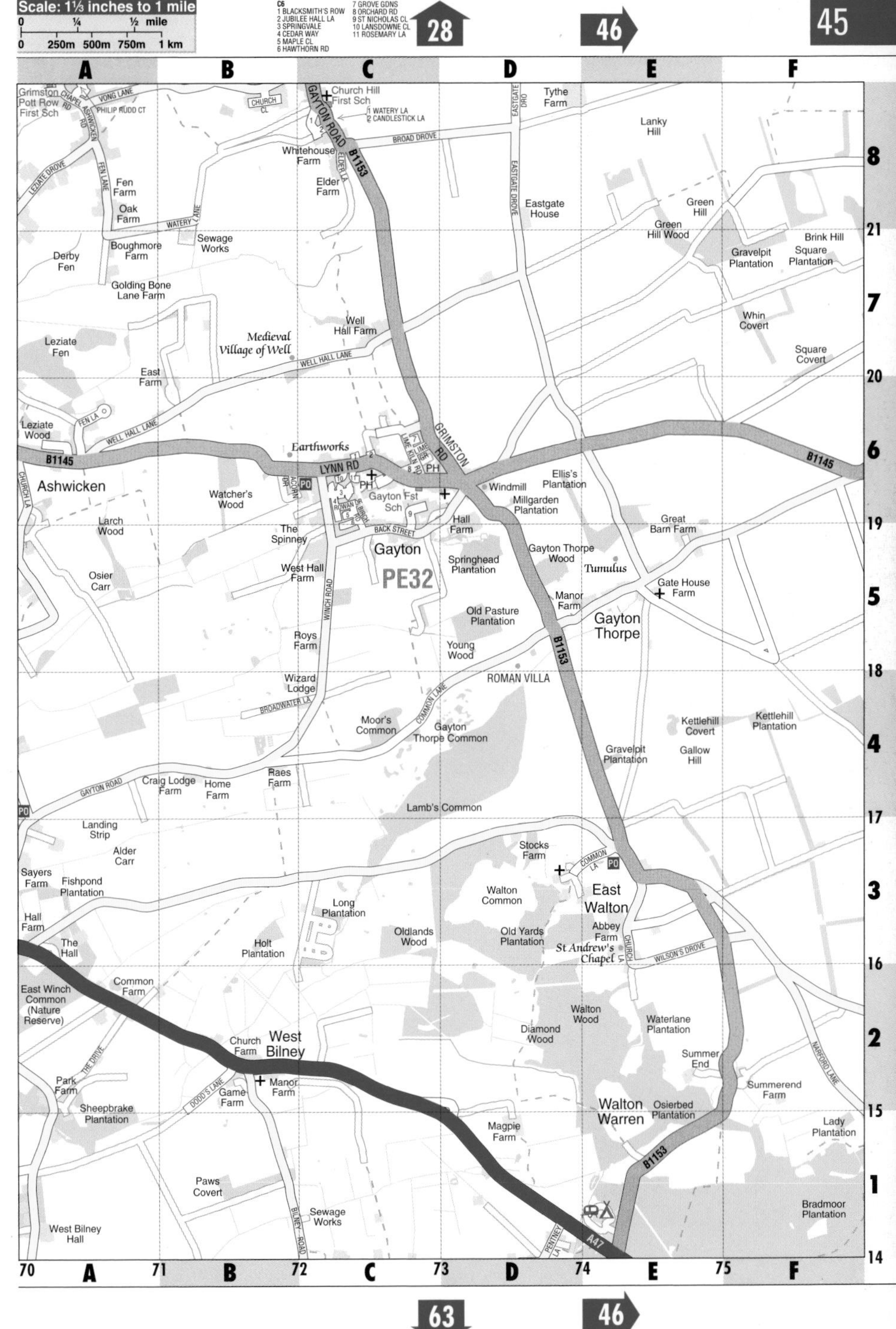
Scale: 1⅓ inches to 1 mile
0 ¼ ½ mile
0 250m 500m 750m 1 km
C6
1 BLACKSMITH'S ROW
2 JUBILEE HALL LA
3 SPRINGVALE
4 CEDAR WAY
5 MAPLE CL
6 HAWTHORN RD
7 GROVE GDNS
8 ORCHARD RD
9 ST NICHOLAS CL
10 LANSDOWNE CL
11 ROSEMARY LA
28
46
A
B
C
D
E
F
Grimston Pott Row First Sch
CHAPEL RD
VONG LANE
PHILIP RUDD CT
ASHWICKEN RD
CHURCH CL
Church Hill First Sch
GAYTON ROAD
B1153
1 WATERY LA
2 CANDLESTICK LA
EASTGATE DRO
Tythe Farm
Lanky Hill
BROAD DROVE
Whitehouse Farm
ELDER LA
LEZIATE DROVE
FEN LANE
Fen Farm
Elder Farm
EASTGATE DROVE
Eastgate House
Green Hill
Oak Farm
WATERY LANE
Green Hill Wood
Brink Hill
Sewage Works
Boughmore Farm
Derby Fen
Gravelpit Plantation
Square Plantation
Golding Bone Lane Farm
Well Hall Farm
Whin Covert
Leziate Fen
Medieval Village of Well
WELL HALL LANE
Square Covert
East Farm
FEN LA
GRIMSTON RD
Leziate Wood
WELL HALL LANE
LIME KILN RD
LIME GR
PH
Earthworks
B1145
LYNN RD
B1145
CHURCH LA
Ashwicken
ACORN DR
PO
PH
Windmill
Ellis's Plantation
Watcher's Wood
Gayton Fst Sch
Millgarden Plantation
Larch Wood
ROWAN DR
BIRCH RD
The Spinney
BACK STREET
Hall Farm
Great Barn Farm
Gayton
Gayton Thorpe Wood
Springhead Plantation
Osier Carr
West Hall Farm
Tumulus
WINCH ROAD
PE32
Gate House Farm
Manor Farm
Old Pasture Plantation
Gayton Thorpe
Roys Farm
Young Wood
B1153
ROMAN VILLA
Wizard Lodge
BROADWATER LA
COMMON LANE
Kettlehill Covert
Kettlehill Plantation
Moor's Common
Gayton Thorpe Common
Gravelpit Plantation
Gallow Hill
GAYTON ROAD
Craig Lodge Farm
Home Farm
Raes Farm
PO
Lamb's Common
Landing Strip
Alder Carr
Stocks Farm
COMMON LA
PO
Sayers Farm
Fishpond Plantation
East Walton
Walton Common
Long Plantation
Hall Farm
Abbey Farm
Oldlands Wood
Old Yards Plantation
The Hall
Holt Plantation
St Andrew's Chapel
CHURCH LA
WILSON'S DROVE
Common Farm
East Winch Common (Nature Reserve)
Walton Wood
Diamond Wood
Waterlane Plantation
Church Farm
West Bilney
Summer End
NARFORD LANE
Park Farm
THE DRIVE
DODD'S LANE
Manor Farm
Game Farm
Summerend Farm
Sheepbrake Plantation
Walton Warren
Osierbed Plantation
Magpie Farm
Lady Plantation
B1153
Paws Covert
Sewage Works
Bradmoor Plantation
West Bilney Hall
BILNEY ROAD
PENTNEY LA
A47
8
21
7
20
6
19
5
18
4
17
3
16
2
15
1
14
70
71
72
73
74
75
63
46

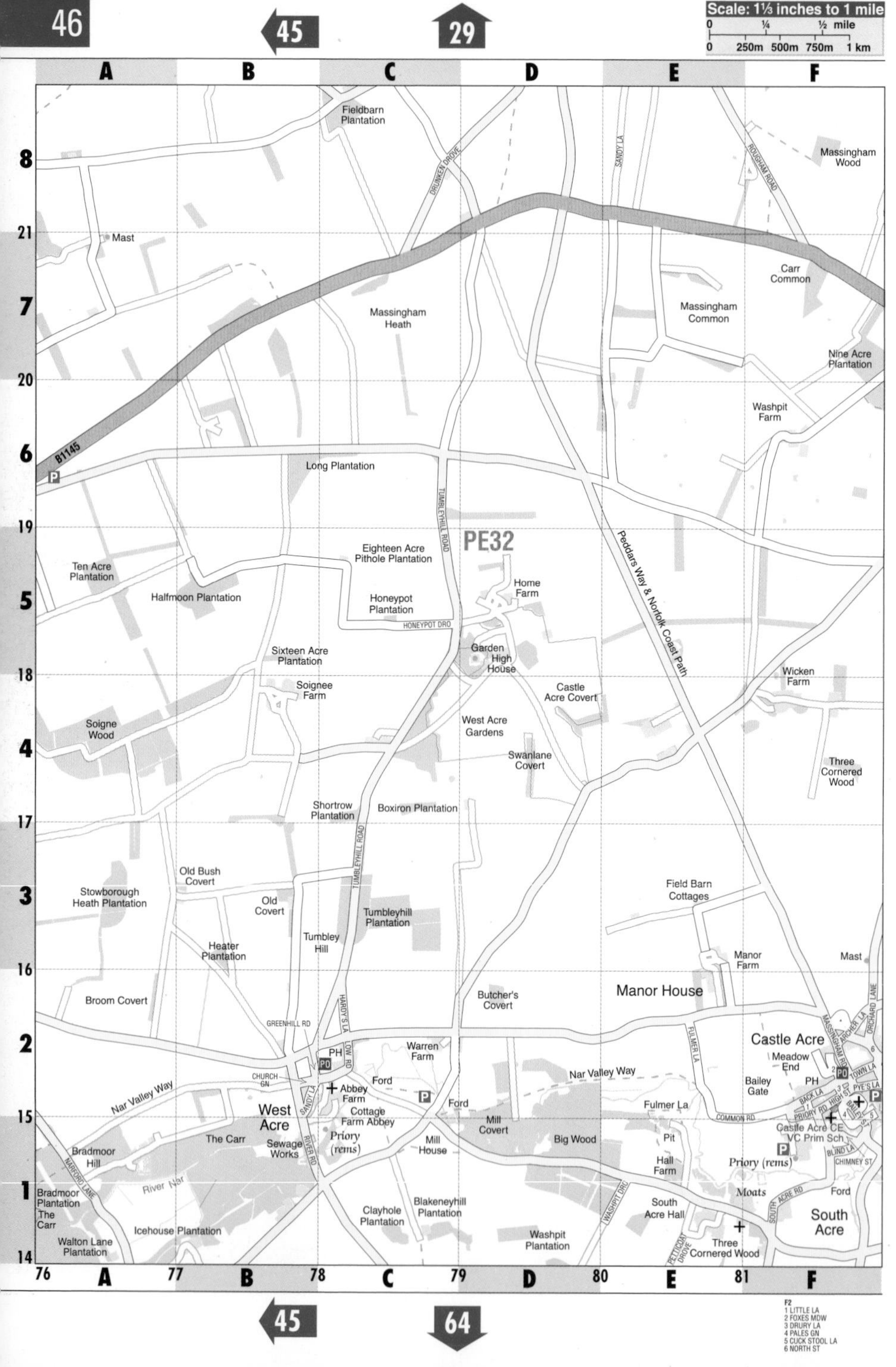

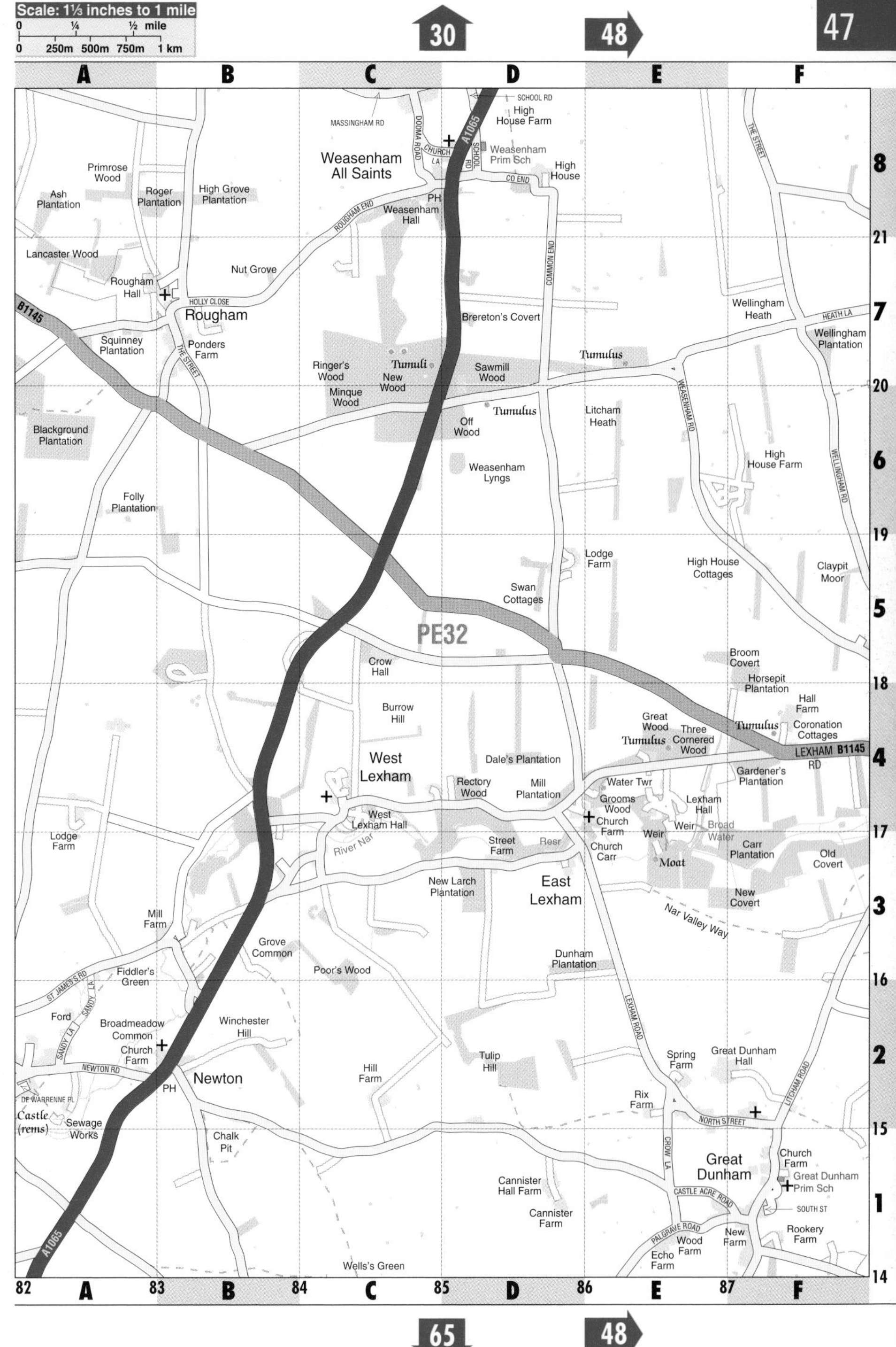

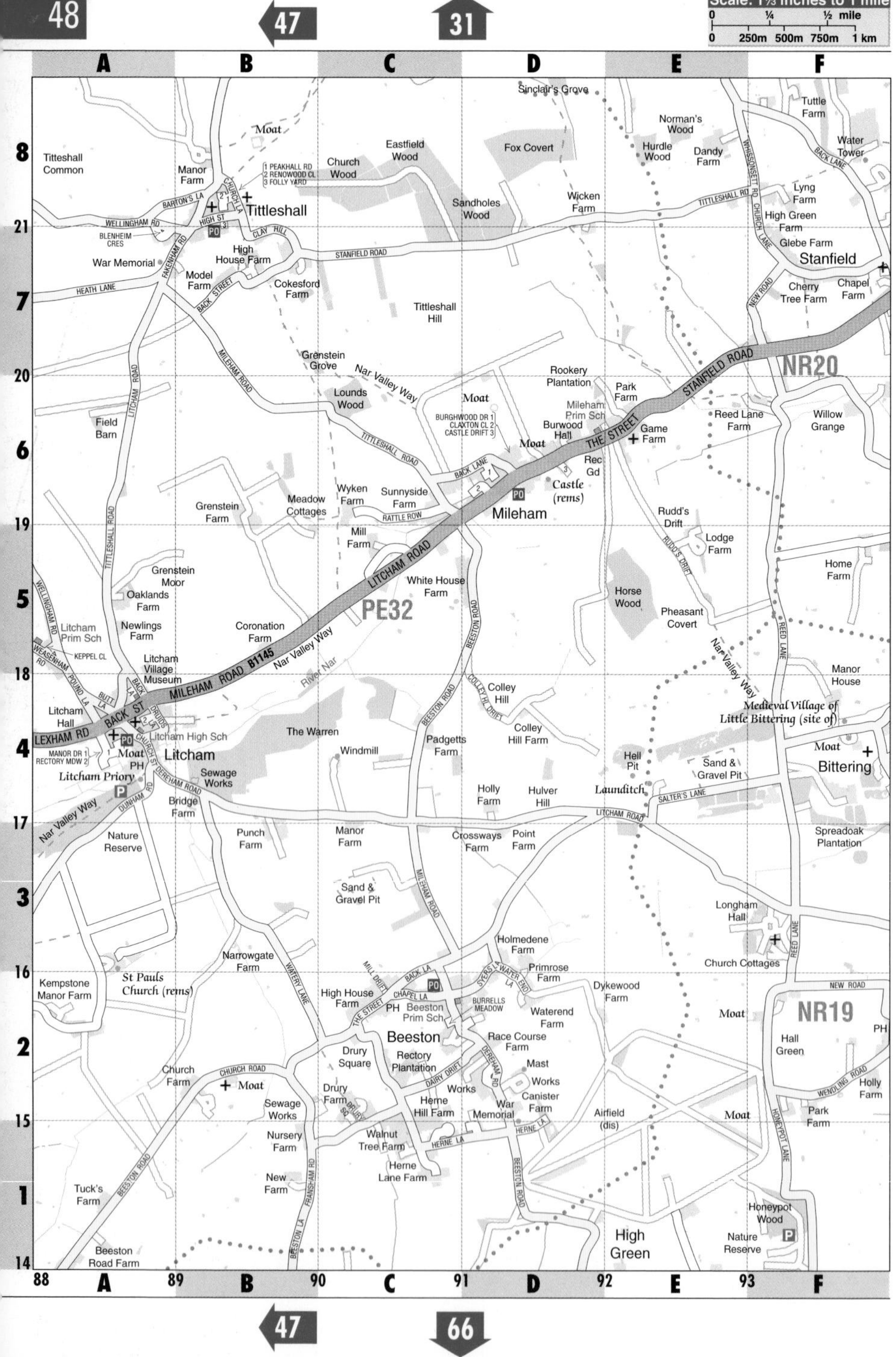

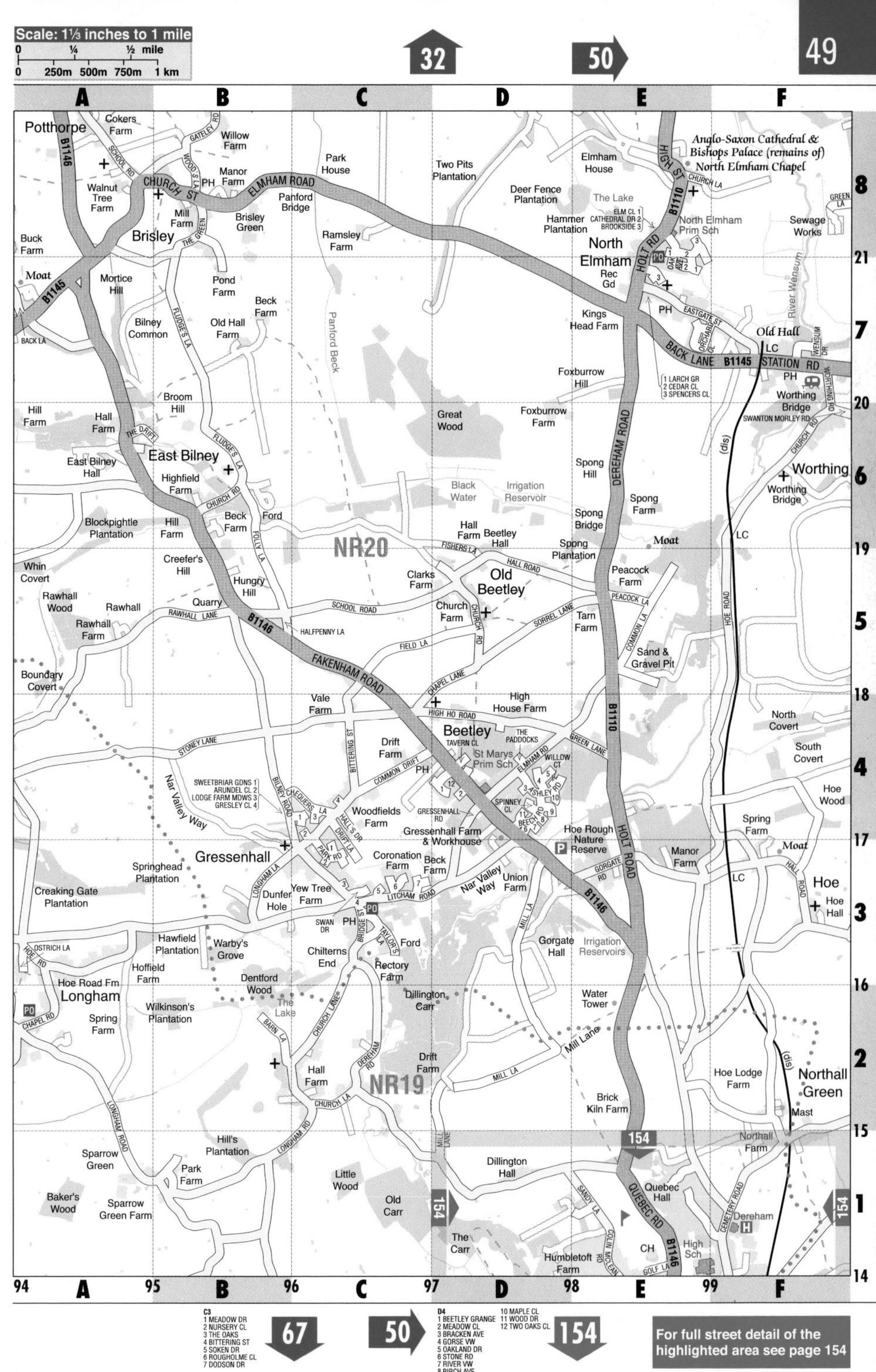

Scale: 1⅓ inches to 1 mile
0 ¼ ½ mile
0 250m 500m 750m 1 km
32
50
A B C D E F
Potthorpe
Cokers Farm
Willow Farm
Manor Farm
Park House
Two Pits Plantation
Elmham House
Anglo-Saxon Cathedral & Bishops Palace (remains of) North Elmham Chapel
Walnut Tree Farm
CHURCH ST
ELMHAM ROAD
Panford Bridge
Deer Fence Plantation
The Lake
Mill Farm
Brisley Green
Hammer Plantation
ELM CL 1
CATHEDRAL DR 2
BROOKSIDE 3
North Elmham Prim Sch
Sewage Works
Buck Farm
Brisley
Ramsley Farm
North Elmham
Rec Gd
Moat
Mortice Hill
Pond Farm
Beck Farm
Kings Head Farm
Bilney Common
Old Hall Farm
Panford Beck
River Wensum
Old Hall
BACK LA
BACK LANE
B1145
STATION RD
Foxburrow Hill
1 LARCH GR
2 CEDAR CL
3 SPENCERS CL
Worthing Bridge
Broom Hill
Hill Farm
Hall Farm
Great Wood
Foxburrow Farm
East Bilney
East Bilney Hall
Highfield Farm
Spong Hill
Worthing
Worthing Bridge
Black Water
Irrigation Reservoir
Blockpightle Plantation
Hill Farm
Beck Farm
Ford
Spong Farm
Spong Bridge
Hall Farm
Beetley Hall
NR20
Spong Plantation
Moat
Whin Covert
Creefer's Hill
Clarks Farm
Old Beetley
Peacock Farm
Rawhall Wood
Rawhall
Hungry Hill
Quarry
SCHOOL ROAD
Church Farm
Tarn Farm
Rawhall Farm
RAWHALL LANE
HALFPENNY LA
FIELD LA
FAKENHAM ROAD
Sand & Gravel Pit
Boundary Covert
Vale Farm
High House Farm
North Covert
STONEY LANE
Beetley
THE PADDOCKS
Drift Farm
St Marys Prim Sch
South Covert
Nar Valley Way
SWEETBRIAR GDNS 1
ARUNDEL CL 2
LODGE FARM MDWS 3
GRESLEY CL 4
Woodfields Farm
GRESSENHALL RD
Hoe Wood
Spring Farm
Gressenhall Farm & Workhouse
Hoe Rough Nature Reserve
Gressenhall
Springhead Plantation
Coronation Farm
Beck Farm
Manor Farm
Moat
Creaking Gate Plantation
Dunfer Hole
Yew Tree Farm
Union Farm
Hoe
Hoe Hall
LITCHAM ROAD
Hawfield Plantation
Warby's Grove
Chilterns End
Ford
Gorgate Hall
Irrigation Reservoirs
OSTRICH LA
Hoffield Farm
Rectory Farm
Hoe Road Fm
Longham
Dentford Wood
The Lake
Dillington Carr
Water Tower
Spring Farm
Wilkinson's Plantation
Mill Lane
Drift Farm
Hall Farm
NR19
Hoe Lodge Farm
Northall Green
Brick Kiln Farm
Mast
Sparrow Green
Hill's Plantation
Park Farm
154
Northall Farm
Dillington Hall
Little Wood
Quebec Hall
Baker's Wood
Sparrow Green Farm
Old Carr
The Carr
Dereham
CH
High Sch
Humbletoft Farm
94 95 96 97 98 99
C3
1 MEADOW DR
2 NURSERY CL
3 THE OAKS
4 BITTERING ST
5 SOKEN DR
6 ROUGHOLME CL
7 DODSON DR
D4
1 BEETLEY GRANGE
2 MEADOW CL
3 BRACKEN AVE
4 GORSE VW
5 OAKLAND DR
6 STONE RD
7 RIVER VW
8 BIRCH AVE
9 BEETLEY MDWS
10 MAPLE CL
11 WOOD DR
12 TWO OAKS CL
67
50
154
For full street detail of the highlighted area see page 154

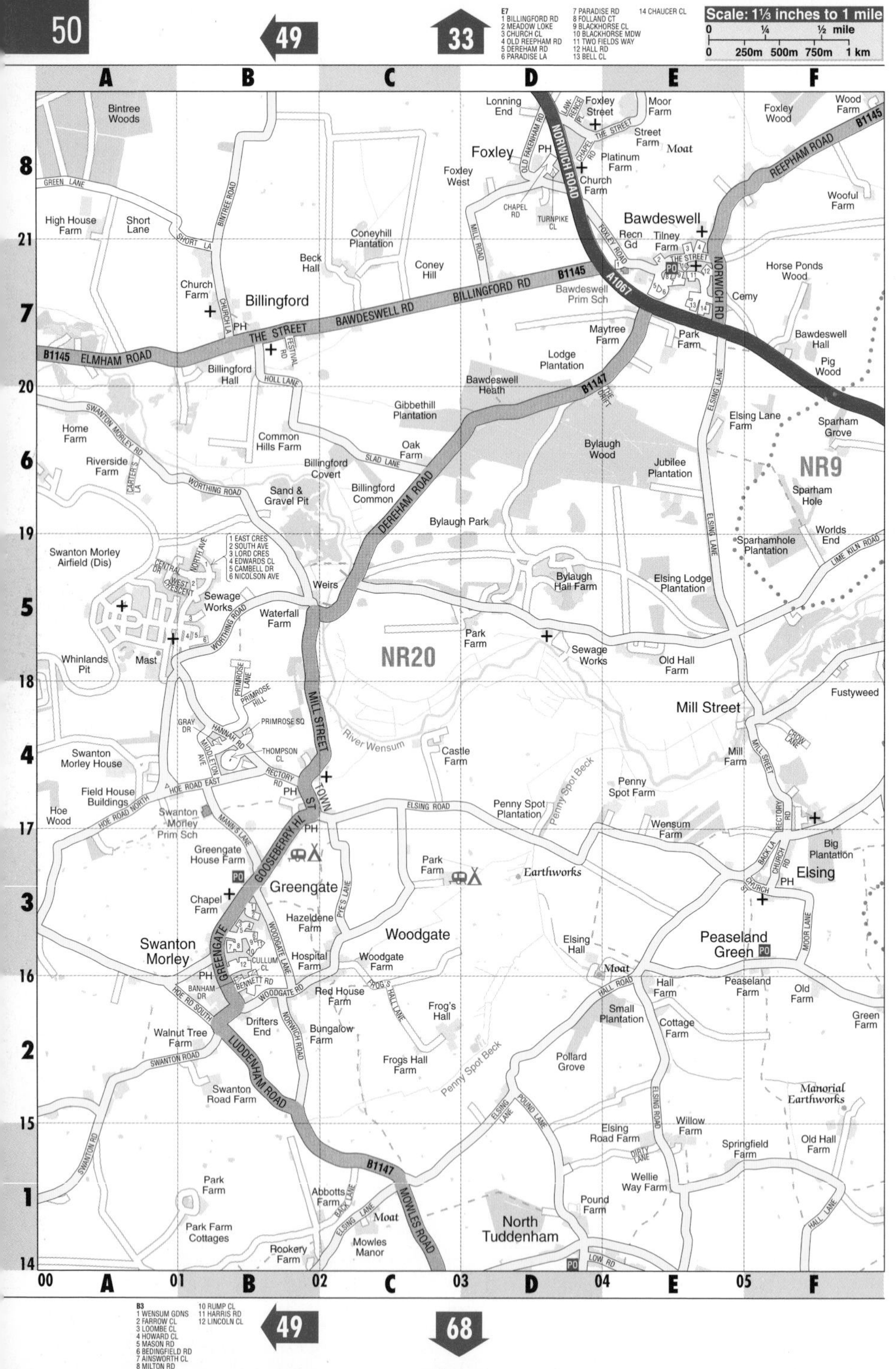

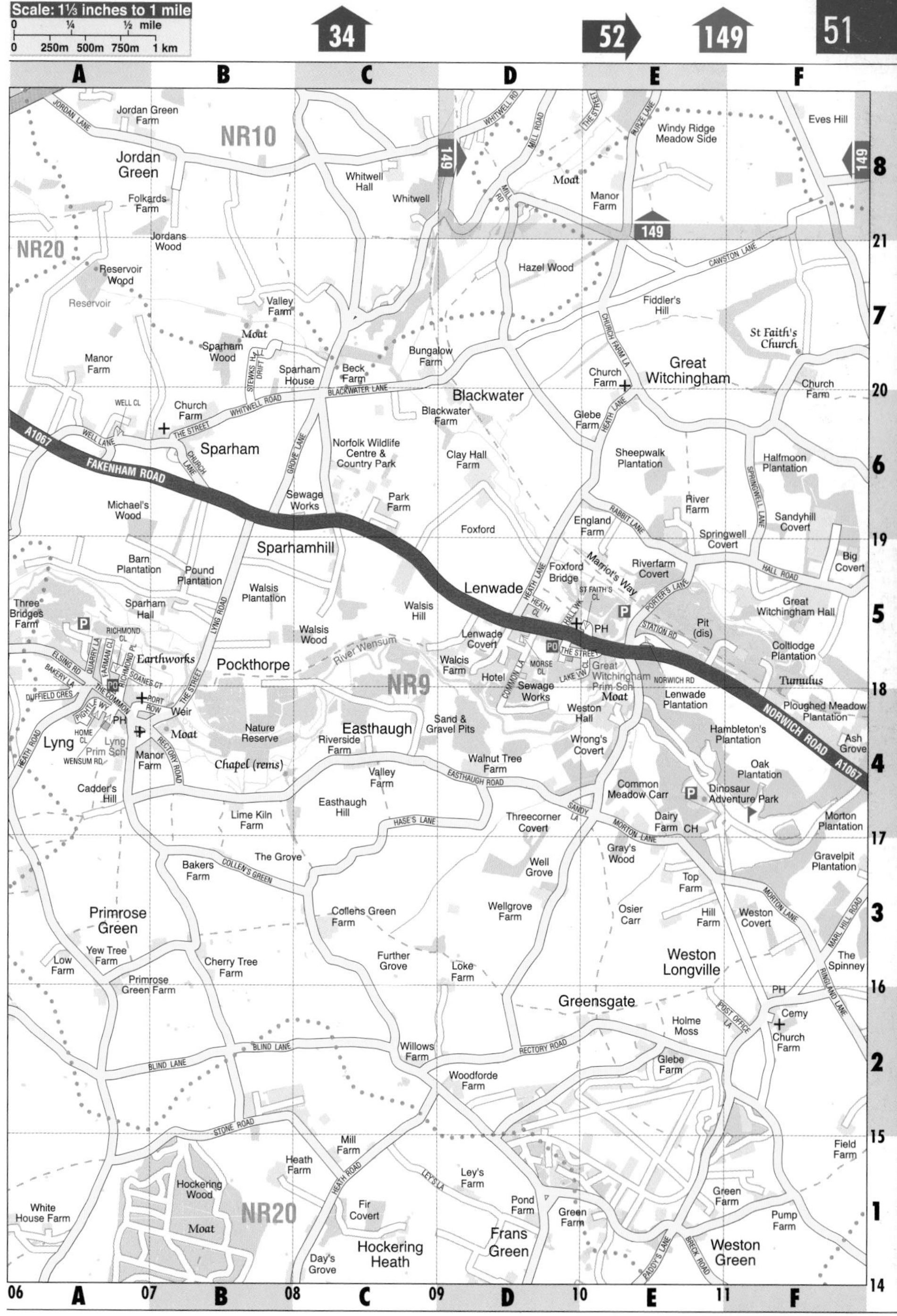

NR10

Jordan Green Farm
Jordan Green
Folkards Farm
Jordans Wood

Whitwell Hall
Whitwell

Windy Ridge
Meadow Side

Eves Hill

Moat
Manor Farm

149

NR20

Reservoir Wood
Reservoir

Valley Farm

Moat

Hazel Wood

Fiddler's Hill

St Faith's Church

Manor Farm

Sparham Wood

Sparham House
Beck Farm

Bungalow Farm

Church Farm

Great Witchingham

Church Farm

Church Farm
THE STREET
Sparham

Blackwater Farm

Blackwater

Glebe Farm

Sheepwalk Plantation

Halfmoon Plantation

A1067
FAKENHAM ROAD

Michael's Wood

Norfolk Wildlife Centre & Country Park

Clay Hall Farm

River Farm

Sandyhill Covert

Sewage Works

Park Farm

Foxford

England Farm

Springwell Covert

Big Covert

Barn Plantation
Pound Plantation

Sparhamhill

Walsis Plantation

Foxford Bridge

Riverfarm Covert

Great Witchingham Hall

Three Bridges Farm

Sparham Hall

Walsis Wood

Walsis Hill

Lenwade

St Faith's CL

PH

Pit (dis)

Coltlodge Plantation

Earthworks

Pockthorpe

NR9

Walcis Farm

Lenwade Covert

Hotel

Great Witchingham Prim Sch

Lenwade Plantation

Tumulus

Ploughed Meadow Plantation

NORWICH ROAD

Lyng

PH

Weir
Moat

Nature Reserve

Easthaugh

Riverside Farm

Sand & Gravel Pits

Sewage Works

Weston Hall

Wrong's Covert

Hambleton's Plantation

Oak Plantation

Ash Grove

A1067

Manor Farm

Chapel (rems)

Valley Farm

Walnut Tree Farm

Dinosaur Adventure Park

Morton Plantation

Cadder's Hill

Easthaugh Hill

EASTHAUGH ROAD

HASE'S LANE

Threecorner Covert

Gray's Wood

Common Meadow Carr

Dairy Farm

CH

Gravelpit Plantation

Lime Kiln Farm

The Grove

Well Grove

Top Farm

Bakers Farm

COLLEN'S GREEN

Coflehs Green Farm

Wellgrove Farm

Osier Carr

Hill Farm

Weston Covert

Primrose Green

Yew Tree Farm

Cherry Tree Farm

Further Grove

Loke Farm

Weston Longville

The Spinney

PH

Low Farm

Primrose Green Farm

Greensgate

Cemy

Church Farm

BLIND LANE

Willows Farm

RECTORY ROAD

Woodforde Farm

Holme Moss

Glebe Farm

Green Farm

STONE ROAD

Mill Farm

Heath Farm

LEY'S LA

Ley's Farm

Pond Farm

Green Farm

Field Farm

White House Farm

NR20

Hockering Wood

Moat

Fir Covert

Frans Green

Green Farm

Pump Farm

Weston Green

Day's Grove

Hockering Heath

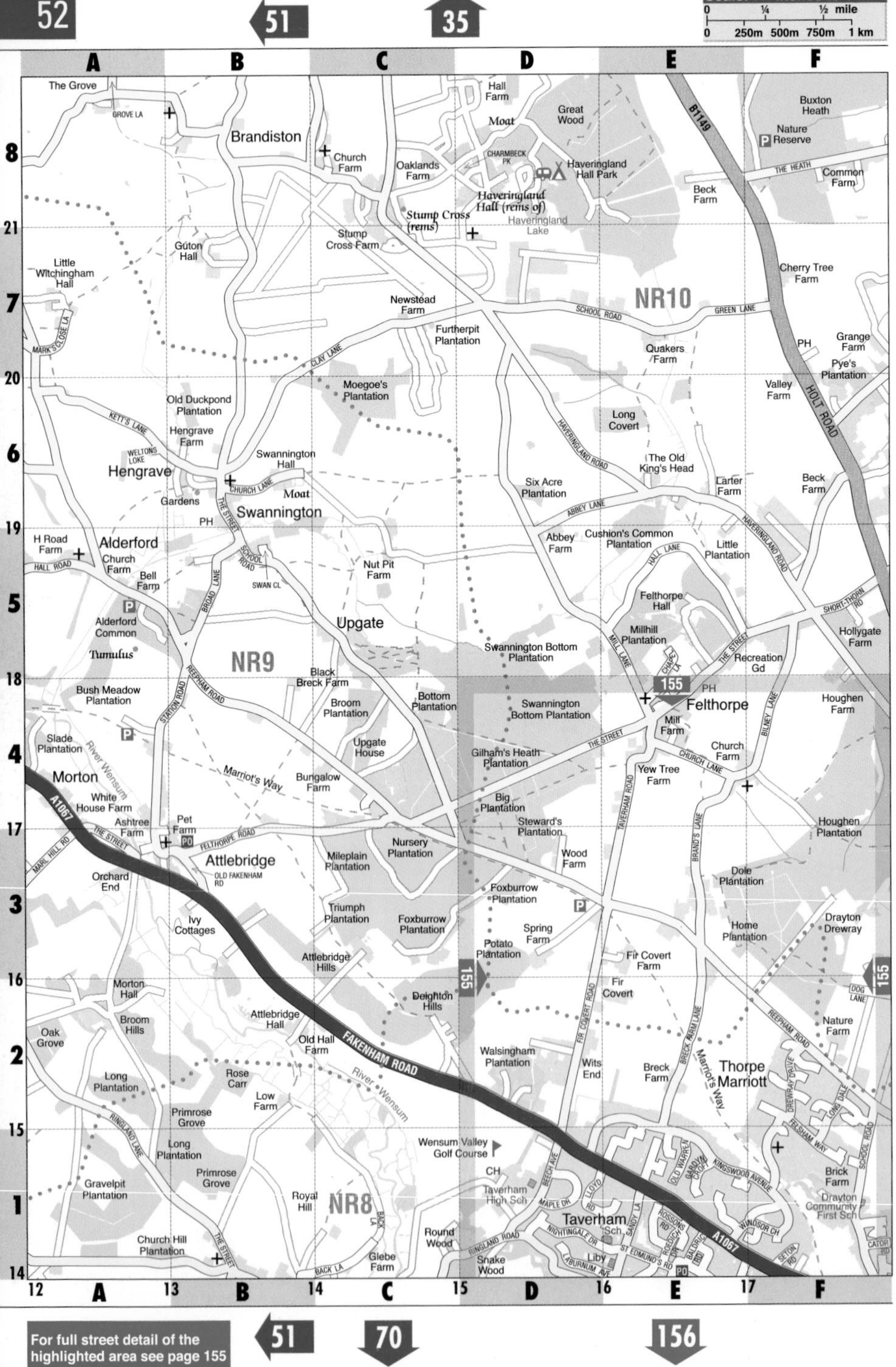

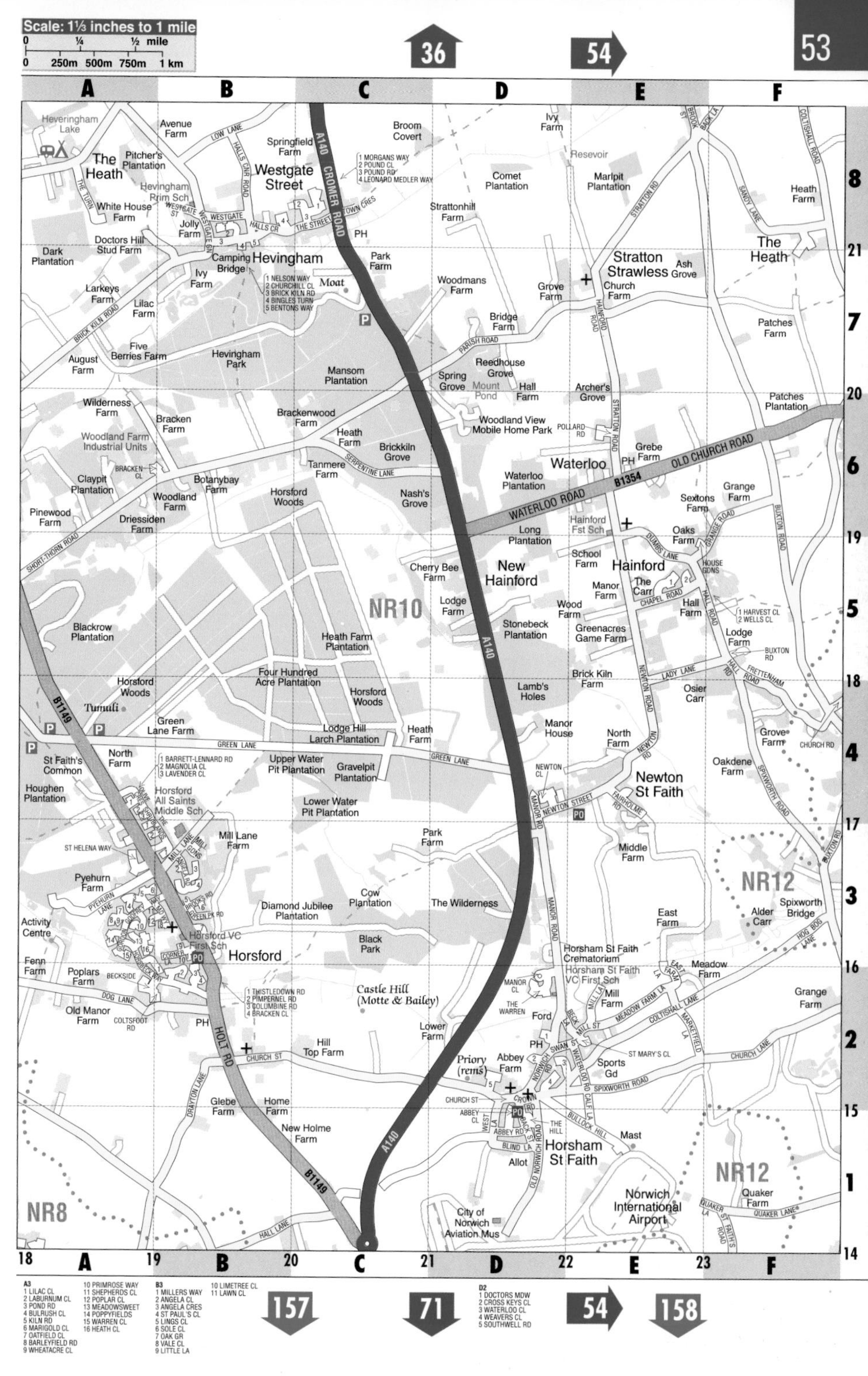

Scale: 1⅓ inches to 1 mile
0 ¼ ½ mile
0 250m 500m 750m 1 km
36
54
A B C D E F
8 21 7 20 6 19 5 18 4 17 3 16 2 15 1 14
18 19 20 21 22 23
Heveringham Lake
The Heath
Pitcher's Plantation
Avenue Farm
LOW LANE
HALLS CNR ROAD
Springfield Farm
Westgate Street
A140 CROMER ROAD
1 MORGANS WAY
2 POUND CL
3 POUND RD
4 LEONARD MEDLER WAY
Broom Covert
Ivy Farm
Resevoir
Comet Plantation
Marlpit Plantation
STRATTON RD
BROOK ST
BACK LA
COLTISHALL ROAD
SANDY LANE
Heath Farm
THE TURN
Hevingham Prim Sch
White House Farm
WESTGATE ST
WESTGATE
HALLS CR
THE STREET
TOWN CRES
Jolly Farm
PH
Strattonhill Farm
Doctors Hill Stud Farm
Dark Plantation
Camping Bridge
Hevingham
Park Farm
Stratton Strawless
Ash Grove
The Heath
Church Farm
1 NELSON WAY
2 CHURCHILL CL
3 BRICK KILN RD
4 BINGLES TURN
5 BENTONS WAY
Moat
Ivy Farm
Larkeys Farm
Lilac Farm
Woodmans Farm
Grove Farm
HAINFORD ROAD
BRICK KILN ROAD
Bridge Farm
Patches Farm
Five Berries Farm
Hevingham Park
PARISH ROAD
August Farm
Mansom Plantation
Reedhouse Grove
Spring Grove
Mount Pond
Hall Farm
Archer's Grove
Wilderness Farm
Brackenwood Farm
Woodland View Mobile Home Park
POLLARD RD
STRATTON ROAD
Patches Plantation
Bracken Farm
Woodland Farm Industrial Units
Heath Farm
Brickkiln Grove
Grebe Farm
OLD CHURCH ROAD
BRACKEN CL
SERPENTINE LANE
Waterloo
Tanmere Farm
Claypit Plantation
Botanybay Farm
Waterloo Plantation
WATERLOO ROAD
B1354
Grange Farm
Woodland Farm
Horsford Woods
Nash's Grove
Sextons Farm
Pinewood Farm
Driessiden Farm
Hainford Fst Sch
Oaks Farm
GRANGE ROAD
BUXTON ROAD
SHORT-THORN ROAD
Long Plantation
DUMBS LANE
School Farm
Hainford
HOUSE GDNS
Cherry Bee Farm
New Hainford
The Carr
Manor Farm
CHAPEL ROAD
NR10
Lodge Farm
Wood Farm
Hall Farm
HALL ROAD
1 HARVEST CL
2 WELLS CL
Blackrow Plantation
Stonebeck Plantation
Greenacres Game Farm
Lodge Farm
BUXTON RD
Heath Farm Plantation
A140
NEWTON ROAD
FRETTENHAM ROAD
Brick Kiln Farm
LADY LANE
Osier Carr
Four Hundred Acre Plantation
Horsford Woods
Lamb's Holes
Horsford Woods
B1149
Tumuli
Green Lane Farm
Lodge Hill Larch Plantation
Heath Farm
Manor House
North Farm
Grove Farm
CHURCH RD
GREEN LANE
NEWTON RD
St Faith's Common
North Farm
1 BARRETT-LENNARD RD
2 MAGNOLIA CL
3 LAVENDER CL
Upper Water Pit Plantation
Gravelpit Plantation
NEWTON CL
Newton St Faith
Oakdene Farm
SPIXWORTH ROAD
Houghen Plantation
Horsford All Saints Middle Sch
Lower Water Pit Plantation
NEWTON STREET
MANOR RD
FAIRHOLME RD
PO
ST HELENA WAY
Mill Lane Farm
Park Farm
Middle Farm
BUXTON RD
NR12
Pyehurn Farm
PYEHURN LANE
MILL LANE
MILL GDNS
Cow Plantation
Diamond Jubilee Plantation
The Wilderness
MANOR ROAD
East Farm
Alder Carr
Spixworth Bridge
Activity Centre
HOG BOG LANE
Horsford VC First Sch
Black Park
Horsford
Horsham St Faith Crematorium
Fenn Farm
Poplars Farm
BECKSIDE
Horsham St Faith VC First Sch
Meadow Farm
EAST FARM LA
DOG LANE
1 THISTLEDOWN RD
2 PIMPERNEL RD
3 COLUMBINE RD
4 BRACKEN CL
Castle Hill (Motte & Bailey)
MANOR CL
Mill Farm
MILL LA
Grange Farm
Old Manor Farm
COLTSFOOT RD
THE WARREN
Ford
MEADOW FARM LA
COLTISHALL LANE
PH
HOLT RD
Lower Farm
BECK LA
MILL ST
MARKETFIELD LA
Hill Top Farm
CHURCH ST
PH
SWAN ST
ST MARY'S CL
CHURCH LANE
Priory (rems)
Abbey Farm
NORWICH RD
WATERLOO RD
Sports Gd
DRAYTON LANE
CHURCH ST
CROWN RD
SPIXWORTH ROAD
CALF LA
Glebe Farm
Home Farm
ABBEY CL
WEST LA
ABBEY RD
BACK ST
THE HILL
BULLOCK HILL
Mast
New Holme Farm
BLIND LA
Horsham St Faith
Allot
OLD NORWICH ROAD
NR12
Norwich International Airport
Quaker Farm
QUAKER LA
QUAKER LANE
ST FAITH'S ROAD
NR8
City of Norwich Aviation Mus
HALL LANE
A3
1 LILAC CL
2 LABURNUM CL
3 POND RD
4 BULRUSH CL
5 KILN RD
6 MARIGOLD CL
7 OATFIELD CL
8 BARLEYFIELD RD
9 WHEATACRE CL
10 PRIMROSE WAY
11 SHEPHERDS CL
12 POPLAR CL
13 MEADOWSWEET
14 POPPYFIELDS
15 WARREN CL
16 HEATH CL
B3
1 MILLERS WAY
2 ANGELA CL
3 ANGELA CRES
4 ST PAUL'S CL
5 LINGS CL
6 SOLE CL
7 OAK GR
8 VALE CL
9 LITTLE LA
10 LIMETREE CL
11 LAWN CL
D2
1 DOCTORS MDW
2 CROSS KEYS CL
3 WATERLOO CL
4 WEAVERS CL
5 SOUTHWELL RD
157
71
54
158

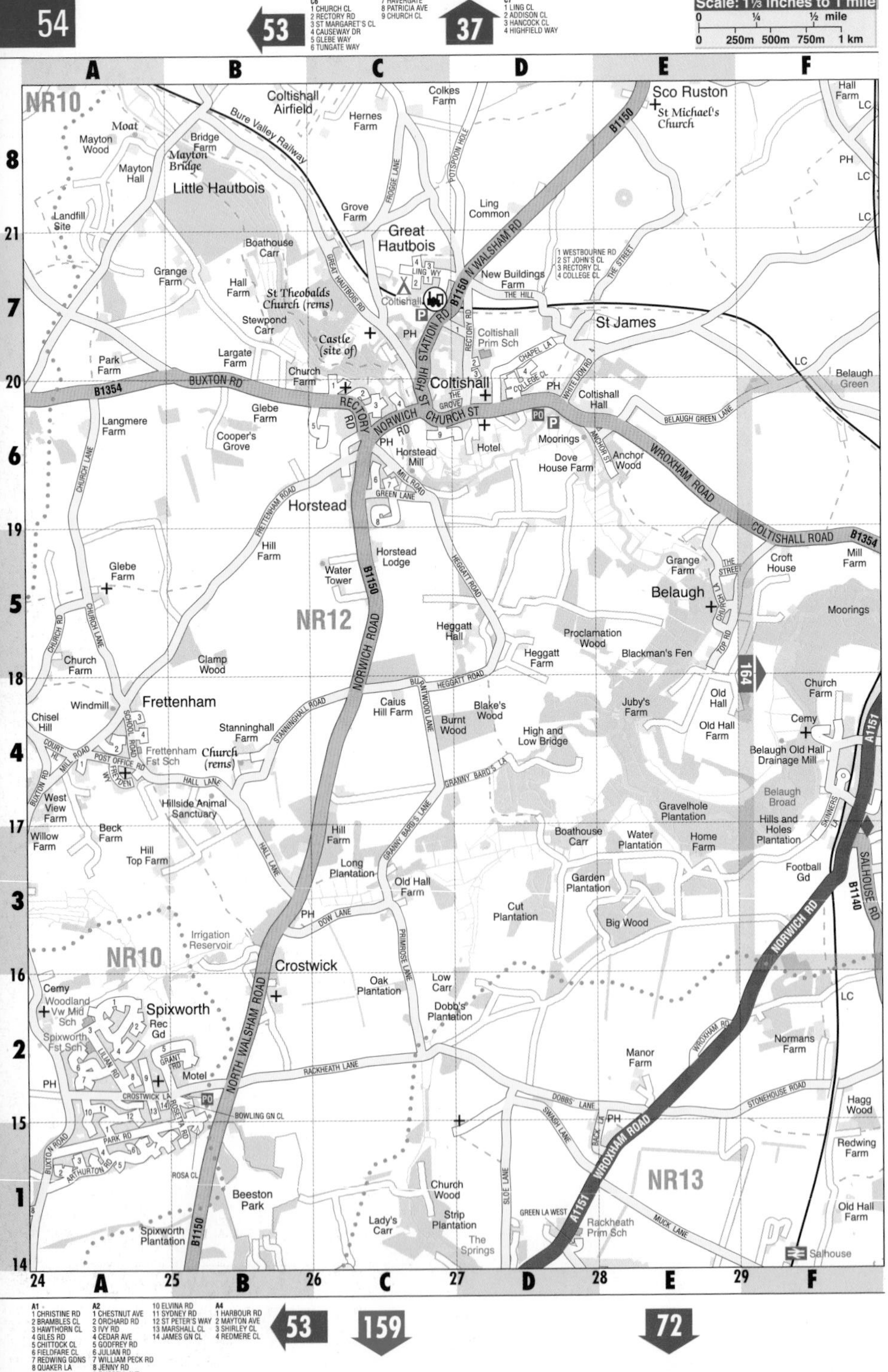
53
C6
1 CHURCH CL
2 RECTORY RD
3 ST MARGARET'S CL
4 CAUSEWAY DR
5 GLEBE WAY
6 TUNGATE WAY
7 HAVERGATE
8 PATRICIA AVE
9 CHURCH CL
37
C7
1 LING CL
2 ADDISON CL
3 HANCOCK CL
4 HIGHFIELD WAY
Scale: 1⅓ inches to 1 mile
0 ¼ ½ mile
0 250m 500m 750m 1 km
A B C D E F
NR10
Moat
Mayton Wood
Bridge Farm
Mayton Bridge
Mayton Hall
Little Hautbois
Bure Valley Railway
Coltishall Airfield
Colkes Farm
Hernes Farm
Sco Ruston
St Michael's Church
Hall Farm
LC
PH
FROGGE LANE
POTSPOON HOLE
B1150
Grove Farm
Ling Common
Landfill Site
Boathouse Carr
Great Hautbois
N WALSHAM RD
1 WESTBOURNE RD
2 ST JOHN'S CL
3 RECTORY CL
4 COLLEGE CL
THE STREET
Grange Farm
Hall Farm
St Theobalds Church (rems)
GREAT HAUTBOIS RD
LING WY
New Buildings Farm
THE HILL
Coltishall
Stewpond Carr
Castle (site of)
STATION RD
RECTORY RD
Coltishall Prim Sch
St James
Park Farm
Largate Farm
CHAPEL LA
WHITE LION RD
Church Farm
HIGH ST
Coltishall
COLLEGE CL
Belaugh Green
B1354
BUXTON RD
THE GROVE
Coltishall Hall
BELAUGH GREEN LANE
Langmere Farm
Glebe Farm
RECTORY RD
NORWICH RD
CHURCH ST
Cooper's Grove
Hotel
Moorings
Horstead Mill
Dove House Farm
ANCHOR ST
Anchor Wood
WROXHAM ROAD
CHURCH LANE
MILL ROAD
GREEN LANE
Horstead
FRETTENHAM ROAD
COLTISHALL ROAD
Hill Farm
Horstead Lodge
Grange Farm
THE STREET
Croft House
Mill Farm
Glebe Farm
Water Tower
B1150
HEGGATT ROAD
CHURCH LA
Belaugh
Moorings
NR12
NORWICH ROAD
Heggatt Hall
Proclamation Wood
CHURCH RD
CHURCH LANE
Heggatt Farm
Blackman's Fen
TOP RD
Church Farm
Clamp Wood
164
HEGGATT ROAD
Church Farm
Frettenham
Windmill
Caius Hill Farm
BUNTWOOD LANE
Blake's Wood
Juby's Farm
Old Hall
Chisel Hill
SCHOOL ROAD
STANNINGHALL ROAD
Stanninghall Farm
Burnt Wood
High and Low Bridge
Old Hall Farm
Cemy
A1151
COURT HL
MILL ROAD
POST OFFICE RD
Frettenham Fst Sch
Church (rems)
Belaugh Old Hall Drainage Mill
FREYDEN WY
GRANNY BARD'S LA
BUXTON RD
HALL LANE
West View Farm
Hillside Animal Sanctuary
Belaugh Broad
Gravelhole Plantation
Hills and Holes Plantation
SKINNERS LA
Willow Farm
Beck Farm
Hill Top Farm
HALL LANE
Hill Farm
GRANNY BARD'S LANE
Boathouse Carr
Water Plantation
Home Farm
SALHOUSE RD
Long Plantation
Old Hall Farm
Garden Plantation
Football Gd
B1140
Cut Plantation
PH
DOW LANE
Big Wood
Irrigation Reservoir
PRIMROSE LANE
NORWICH RD
NR10
Crostwick
Oak Plantation
Low Carr
Cemy
Woodland Vw Mid Sch
Spixworth
Rec Gd
Dobb's Plantation
LC
Spixworth Fst Sch
LILIAN RD
GRANT RD
NORTH WALSHAM ROAD
Manor Farm
WROXHAM RD
Normans Farm
PH
Motel
RACKHEATH LANE
CROSTWICK LA
PO
BOWLING GN CL
DOBBS' LANE
STONEHOUSE ROAD
Hagg Wood
ROSETTA RD
SWASH LANE
BACK LA
PH
WROXHAM ROAD
BUXTON ROAD
PARK RD
Redwing Farm
ARTHURTON RD
ROSA CL
NR13
A1151
Beeston Park
Church Wood
SLOE LANE
Old Hall Farm
Lady's Carr
Strip Plantation
GREEN LA WEST
Rackheath Prim Sch
MUCK LANE
Spixworth Plantation
B1150
The Springs
Salhouse
8
21
7
20
6
19
5
18
4
17
3
16
2
15
1
14
24
25
26
27
28
29
A1
1 CHRISTINE RD
2 BRAMBLES CL
3 HAWTHORN CL
4 GILES RD
5 CHITTOCK CL
6 FIELDFARE CL
7 REDWING GDNS
8 QUAKER LA
A2
1 CHESTNUT AVE
2 ORCHARD RD
3 IVY RD
4 CEDAR AVE
5 GODFREY RD
6 JULIAN RD
7 WILLIAM PECK RD
8 JENNY RD
9 RUSSELL AVE
10 ELVINA RD
11 SYDNEY RD
12 ST PETER'S WAY
13 MARSHALL CL
14 JAMES GN CL
A4
1 HARBOUR RD
2 MAYTON AVE
3 SHIRLEY CL
4 REDMERE CL
53
159
72

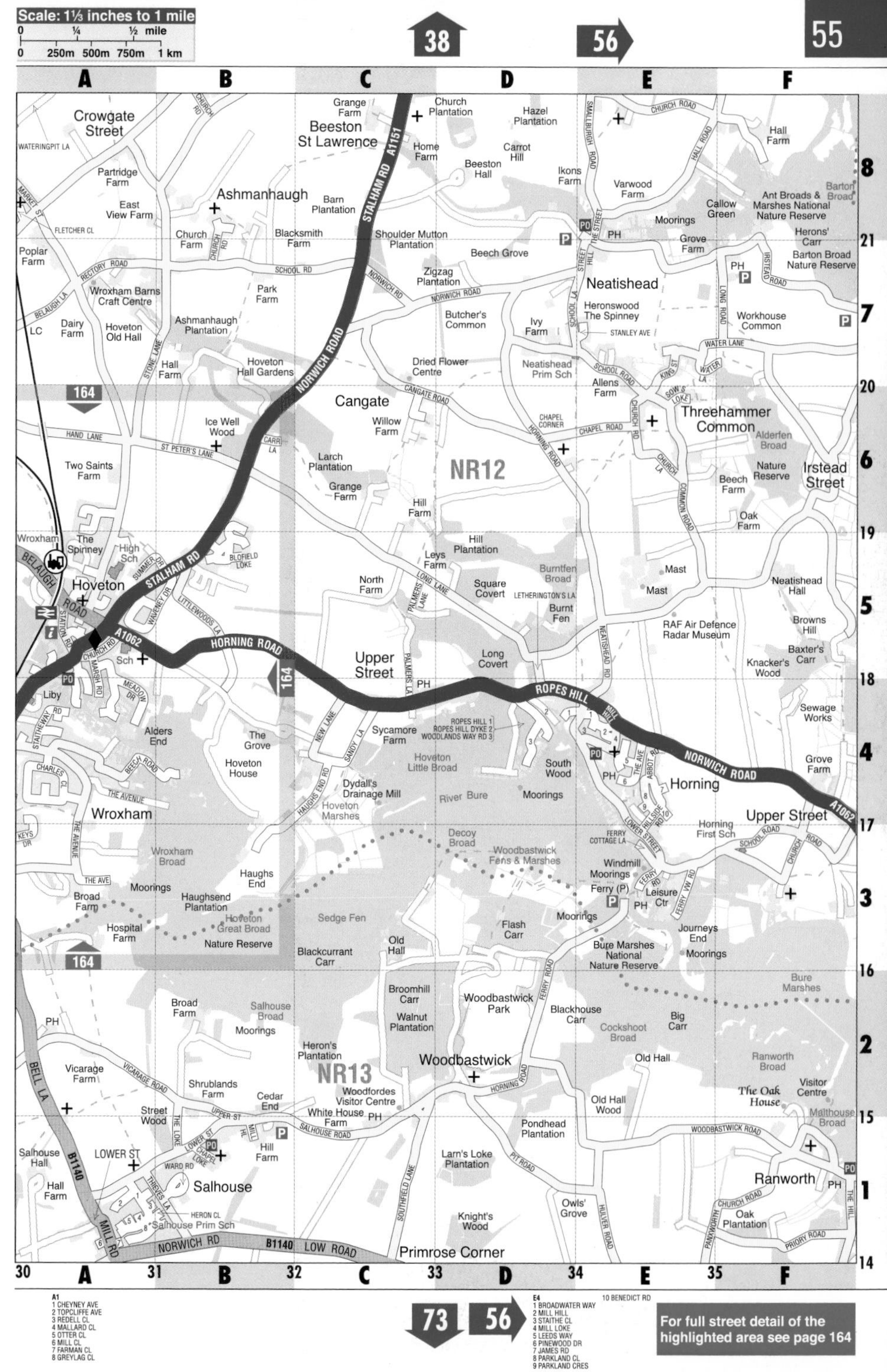

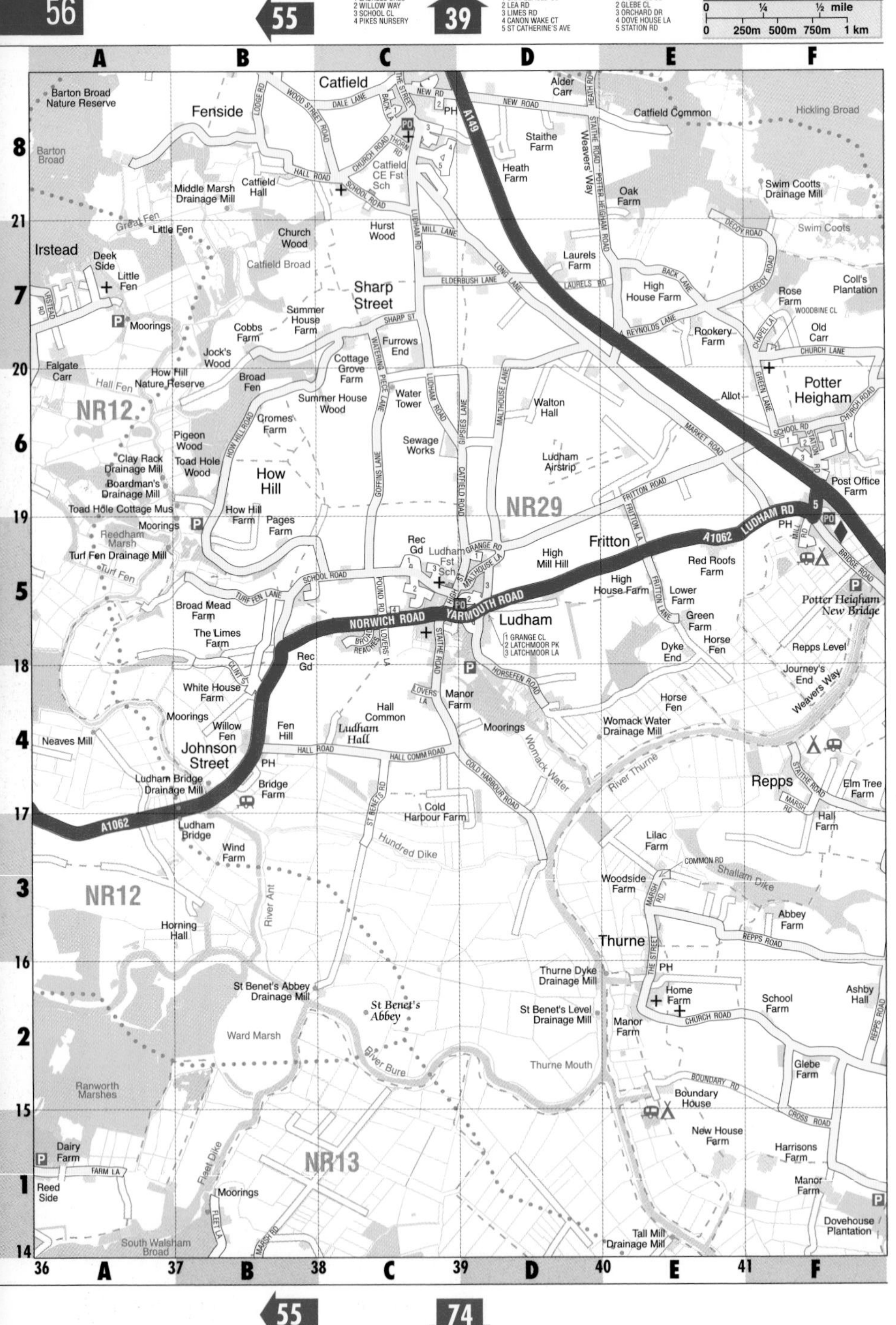

55

39

C5
1 LAURELS CRES
2 WILLOW WAY
3 SCHOOL CL
4 PIKES NURSERY

C8
1 CHAPELFIELD CL
2 LEA RD
3 LIMES RD
4 CANON WAKE CT
5 ST CATHERINE'S AVE

F6
1 VICARAGE CL
2 GLEBE CL
3 ORCHARD DR
4 DOVE HOUSE LA
5 STATION RD

Scale: 1½ inches to 1 mile

0   ¼   ½   mile
0   250m 500m 750m 1 km

| A | B | C | D | E | F |

8

Barton Broad
Nature Reserve

Barton
Broad

Catfield

Fenside

Alder
Carr

Catfield Common

Hickling Broad

21

Great Fen

Little Fen

Middle Marsh
Drainage Mill

Catfield
Hall

Catfield
CE Fst
Sch

New Rd
New Road

Staithe
Farm

Heath
Farm

Weavers Way

Oak
Farm

Swim Coutts
Drainage Mill

Swim Coutts

Irstead

Deek
Side
Little
Fen

Church
Wood

Hurst
Wood

Laurels
Farm

High
House Farm

Back Lane

Rose
Farm

Coll's
Plantation

WOODBINE CL

7

Moorings

Catfield Broad

Sharp
Street

Elderbush Lane

A Reynolds Lane

Rookery
Farm

Old
Carr

CHURCH LANE

20

Falgate
Carr

Hall Fen

How Hill
Nature Reserve

Cobbs
Farm

Jock's
Wood

Summer
House
Farm

Furrows
End

Cottage
Grove
Farm

Broad Fen

Water
Tower

Walton
Hall

Allot

Potter
Heigham

6

NR12

Pigeon
Wood

Gromes
Farm

Summer House
Wood

Sewage
Works

Ludham
Airstrip

NR29

Market Road

Post Office
Farm

Clay Rack
Drainage Mill

Boardman's
Drainage Mill

Toad Hole
Wood

How
Hill

Fritton Road

School Rd

19

Toad Hole Cottage Mus

Reedham
Marsh

Turf Fen Drainage Mill

Turf Fen

How Hill
Farm

Pages
Farm

Rec
Gd

Ludham
Fst
Sch

Grange Rd

High
Mill Hill

Fritton

High
House Farm

Red Roofs
Farm

Lower
Farm

A1062

Ludham Rd

Potter Heigham
New Bridge

5

Broad Mead
Farm

The Limes
Farm

Turf Fen Lane

School Road

Norwich Road

Yarmouth Road

Ludham

1 GRANGE CL
2 LATCHMOOR PK
3 LATCHMOOR LA

Green
Farm

Horse
Farm

Dyke
End

Repps Level

Journey's
End

Weavers Way

18

Rec
Gd

White House
Farm

Fen
Hill

Hall
Common

Manor
Farm

Moorings

Horse
Fen

Horse
Fen

4

Neaves Mill

Moorings

Willow
Fen

Johnson
Street

Ludham
Hall

Hall Road

Womack Water
Drainage Mill

Womack Water

River Thurne

Repps

Elm Tree
Farm

Hall
Farm

17

Ludham Bridge
Drainage Mill

A1062

PH

Bridge
Farm

Ludham
Bridge

Wind
Farm

Hall Comm Road

Cold Harbour Road

Cold
Harbour Farm

Hundred Dike

River Bure

Lilac
Farm

Shallam Dike

COMMON RD

3

NR12

Horning
Hall

River Ant

Woodside
Farm

REPPS ROAD

Abbey
Farm

Thurne

16

St Benet's Abbey
Drainage Mill

St Benet's
Abbey

Thurne Dyke
Drainage Mill

St Benet's Level
Drainage Mill

Manor
Farm

Home
Farm

PH

The Street

School
Farm

Ashby
Hall

2

Ward Marsh

River Bure

Thurne Mouth

BOUNDARY RD

CHURCH ROAD

Glebe
Farm

CROSS ROAD

15

Ranworth
Marshes

Boundary
House

New House
Farm

Harrisons
Farm

1

Dairy
Farm

FARM LA

Reed
Side

Moorings

NR13

Tall Mill
Drainage Mill

Manor
Farm

Dovehouse
Plantation

14

South Walsham
Broad

Feat Dike

| A | B | C | D | E | F |
| 36 | 37 | 38 | 39 | 40 | 41 |

55

74

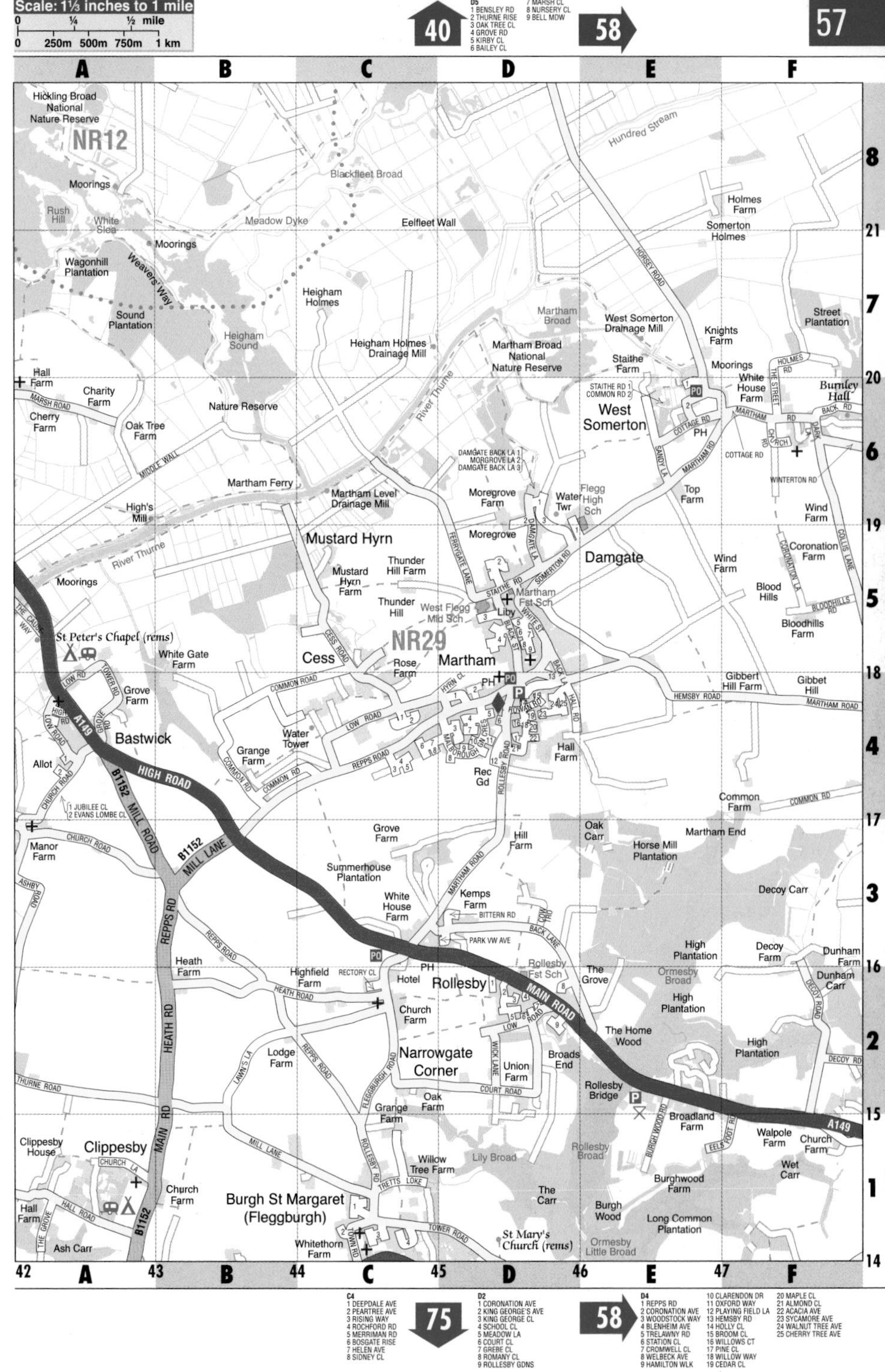
Scale: 1⅓ inches to 1 mile
0 ¼ ½ mile
0 250m 500m 750m 1 km
40
D5
1 BENSLEY RD
2 THURNE RISE
3 OAK TREE CL
4 GROVE RD
5 KIRBY CL
6 BAILEY CL
7 MARSH CL
8 NURSERY CL
9 BELL MDW
58
A
B
C
D
E
F
Hickling Broad National Nature Reserve
NR12
Moorings
Rush Hill
White Slea
Meadow Dyke
Blackfleet Broad
Eelfleet Wall
Hundred Stream
Holmes Farm
Somerton Holmes
Moorings
Wagonhill Plantation
Weavers' Way
Sound Plantation
Heigham Sound
Heigham Holmes
Heigham Holmes Drainage Mill
HORSEY ROAD
Martham Broad
Martham Broad National Nature Reserve
West Somerton Drainage Mill
Knights Farm
Street Plantation
Staithe Farm
Moorings
White House Farm
HOLMES RD
THE STREET
Burnley Hall
Hall Farm
MARSH ROAD
Charity Farm
Cherry Farm
Oak Tree Farm
Nature Reserve
River Thurne
STAITHE RD 1
COMMON RD 2
West Somerton
COTTAGE RD
PH
MARTHAM
RD
BACK RD
CHURCH RD
DARK
COTTAGE RD
MIDDLE WALL
DAMGATE BACK LA 1
MORGROVE LA 2
DAMGATE BACK LA 3
SANDY LA
MARTHAM RD
Martham Ferry
Martham Level Drainage Mill
Moregrove Farm
Water Twr
Flegg High Sch
Top Farm
WINTERTON RD
Wind Farm
High's Mill
Mustard Hyrn
Moregrove
DAMGATE LA
SOMERTON RD
Damgate
Wind Farm
CORONATION LA
Coronation Farm
COLLIS LANE
River Thurne
Thunder Hill Farm
FERRYGATE LANE
Moorings
Mustard Hyrn Farm
Thunder Hill
STAITHE RD
Martham Fst Sch
West Flegg Mid Sch
Liby
BLACK ST
WHITE ST
Blood Hills
BLOODHILLS RD
Bloodhills Farm
THE CAUSEWAY
St Peter's Chapel (rems)
White Gate Farm
NR29
CESS ROAD
Cess
Rose Farm
Martham
Gibbet Hill Farm
Gibbet Hill
LOW RD
TOWER RD
Grove Farm
COMMON ROAD
HYRN CL
PH
PO
P
BACK
HEMSBY ROAD
MARTHAM ROAD
HIGH RD
LOW ROAD
GROVE RD
A149
Bastwick
Water Tower
LOW ROAD
ROWAN RD
HALL RD
Grange Farm
MARLBOROUGH CRES
Hall Farm
Allot
REPPS ROAD
ROLLESBY ROAD
COMMON RD
Rec Gd
HIGH ROAD
CHURCH ROAD
COMMON RD
B1152 MILL ROAD
1 JUBILEE CL
2 EVANS LOMBE CL
Common Farm
COMMON RD
Oak Carr
Martham End
Manor Farm
CHURCH ROAD
Grove Farm
Hill Farm
Horse Mill Plantation
ASHBY ROAD
B1152 MILL LANE
Summerhouse Plantation
MARTHAM ROAD
Decoy Carr
Kemps Farm
White House Farm
BITTERN RD
BACK LANE
PARK VW AVE
REPPS RD
REPPS ROAD
High Plantation
Decoy Farm
Dunham Farm
Heath Farm
PO
PH
Rollesby Fst Sch
The Grove
Ormesby Broad
Dunham Carr
Highfield Farm
RECTORY CL
Hotel
Rollesby
MAIN ROAD
DECOY ROAD
HEATH ROAD
High Plantation
Church Farm
LOW ROAD
The Home Wood
HEATH RD
LAWN'S LA
Lodge Farm
REPPS ROAD
Narrowgate Corner
WICK LANE
Union Farm
Broads End
High Plantation
DECOY RD
FLEGGBURGH ROAD
THURNE ROAD
COURT ROAD
Rollesby Bridge
Oak Farm
Grange Farm
Broadland Farm
BURGH WOOD RD
MAIN RD
Clippesby House
Clippesby
MILL LANE
EELS FOOT RD
Walpole Farm
Church Farm
A149
CHURCH LA
ROLLESBY RD
Willow Tree Farm
Lily Broad
Rollesby Broad
Wet Carr
Church Farm
TRETTS LOKE
Burghwood Farm
Hall Farm
HALL ROAD
THE GROVE
Burgh St Margaret (Fleggburgh)
The Carr
Burgh Wood
Long Common Plantation
B1152
TOWER ROAD
TOWN RD
St Mary's Church (rems)
Ash Carr
Whitethorn Farm
Ormesby Little Broad
8
21
7
20
6
19
5
18
4
17
3
16
2
15
1
14
42
43
44
45
46
47
75
C4
1 DEEPDALE AVE
2 PEARTREE AVE
3 RISING WAY
4 ROCHFORD RD
5 MERRIMAN RD
6 BOSGATE RISE
7 HELEN AVE
8 SIDNEY CL
D2
1 CORONATION AVE
2 KING GEORGE'S AVE
3 KING GEORGE CL
4 SCHOOL CL
5 MEADOW LA
6 COURT CL
7 GREBE CL
8 ROMANY CL
9 ROLLESBY GDNS
58
D4
1 REPPS RD
2 CORONATION AVE
3 WOODSTOCK WAY
4 BLENHEIM AVE
5 TRELAWNY RD
6 STATION CL
7 CROMWELL CL
8 WELBECK AVE
9 HAMILTON WLK
10 CLARENDON DR
11 OXFORD WAY
12 PLAYING FIELD LA
13 HEMSBY RD
14 HOLLY CL
15 BROOM CL
16 WILLOWS CT
17 PINE CL
18 WILLOW WAY
19 CEDAR CL
20 MAPLE CL
21 ALMOND CL
22 ACACIA AVE
23 SYCAMORE AVE
24 WALNUT TREE AVE
25 CHERRY TREE AVE

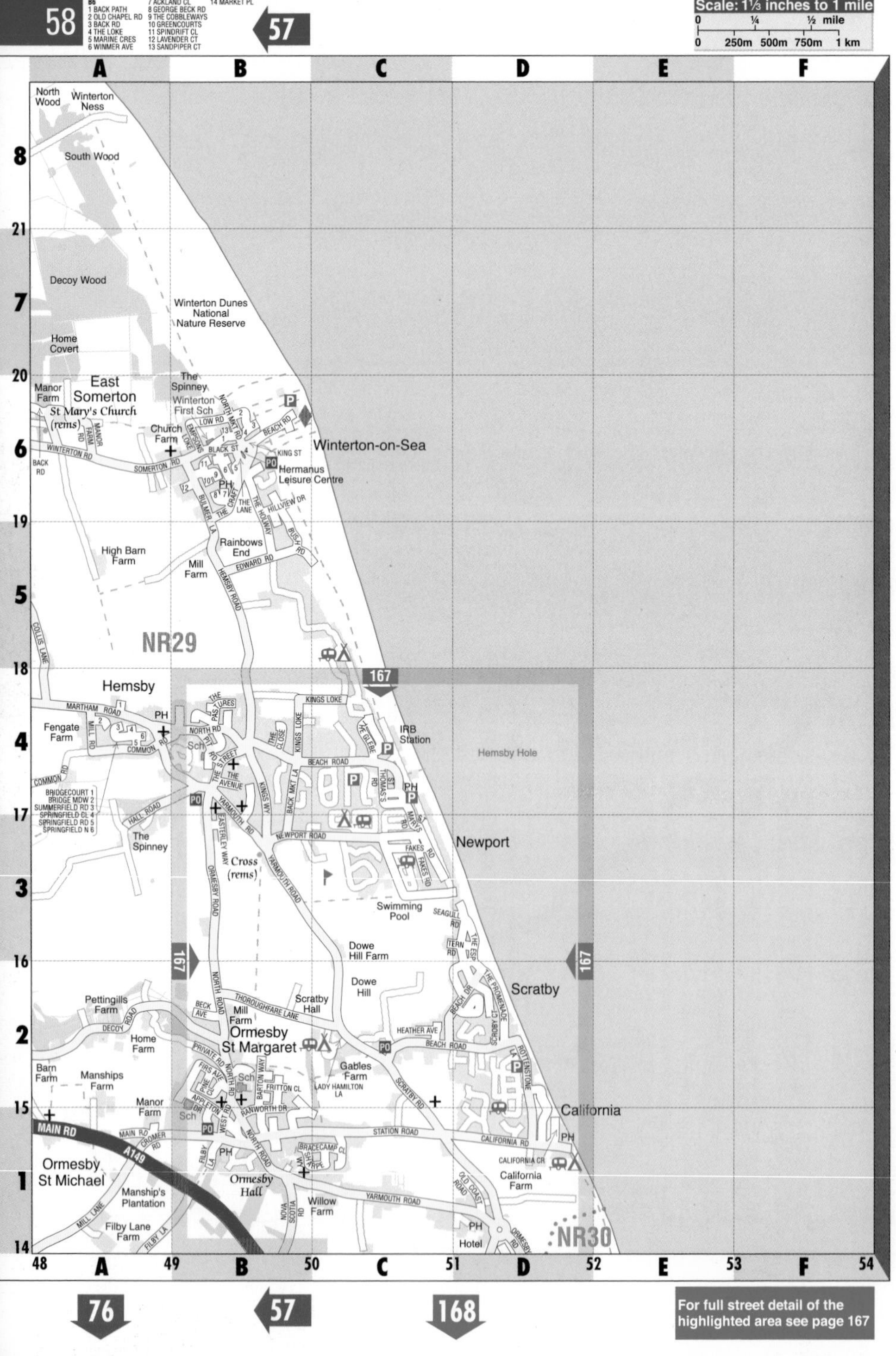
B6
1 BACK PATH
2 OLD CHAPEL RD
3 BACK RD
4 THE LOKE
5 MARINE CRES
6 WINMER AVE
7 ACKLAND CL
8 GEORGE BECK RD
9 THE COBBLEWAYS
10 GREENCOURTS
11 SPINDRIFT CL
12 LAVENDER CT
13 SANDPIPER CT
14 MARKET PL
57
Scale: 1⅓ inches to 1 mile
0 ¼ ½ mile
0 250m 500m 750m 1 km
A B C D E F
North Wood
Winterton Ness
South Wood
Decoy Wood
Winterton Dunes National Nature Reserve
Home Covert
Manor Farm
East Somerton
St Mary's Church (rems)
The Spinney
Winterton First Sch
Church Farm
WINTERTON RD
BACK RD
SOMERTON RD
LOW RD
BLACK ST
NORTH MKT RD
BEACH RD
KING ST
Winterton-on-Sea
Hermanus Leisure Centre
HILLVIEW DR
THE HOLWAY
THE LANE
THE CROFT
BULMER LA
BUSH RD
Rainbows End
EDWARD RD
Mill Farm
High Barn Farm
HEMSBY ROAD
NR29
COLLIS LANE
167
Hemsby
MARTHAM ROAD
Fengate Farm
MILL RD
COMMON RD
NORTH RD
THE PASTURES
KINGS LOKE
THE CLOSE
THE GLEBE
IRB Station
Hemsby Hole
BEACH ROAD
ST THOMAS'S RD
ST MARY'S RD
THE STREET
THE AVENUE
KINGS WAY
BACK MKT LA
BRIDGECOURT 1
BRIDGE MDW 2
SUMMERFIELD RD 3
SPRINGFIELD CL 4
SPRINGFIELD RD 5
SPRINGFIELD N 6
HALL ROAD
The Spinney
YARMOUTH RD
EASTERLEY WAY
NEWPORT ROAD
FAKES RD
Newport
Cross (rems)
ORMESBY ROAD
YARMOUTH ROAD
Swimming Pool
SEAGULL RD
TERN RD
THE ESP
THE PROMENADE
Dowe Hill Farm
Dowe Hill
Scratby
Pettingills Farm
BECK AVE
THOROUGHFARE LANE
Scratby Hall
Mill Farm
DECOY ROAD
Home Farm
Ormesby St Margaret
HEATHER AVE
BEACH DR
SCROBY CT
ROTTENSTONE LA
Barn Farm
Manships Farm
PRIVATE RD
FIRS AVE
PINE CL
BARTON WAY
FRITTON CL
LADY HAMILTON LA
Gables Farm
SCRATBY RD
Manor Farm
APPLETON DR
WEST RD
RANWORTH DR
California
MAIN RD
A149
CROMER RD
STATION ROAD
CALIFORNIA RD
CALIFORNIA CR
California Farm
Ormesby St Michael
FILBY LA
BRACECAMP CL
SHARPE WAY
Ormesby Hall
NOVA SCOTIA RD
Willow Farm
YARMOUTH ROAD
OLD COAST RD
Manship's Plantation
MILL LANE
Filby Lane Farm
Hotel
ORMESBY RD
NR30
48 49 50 51 52 53 54
76
57
168
For full street detail of the highlighted area see page 167

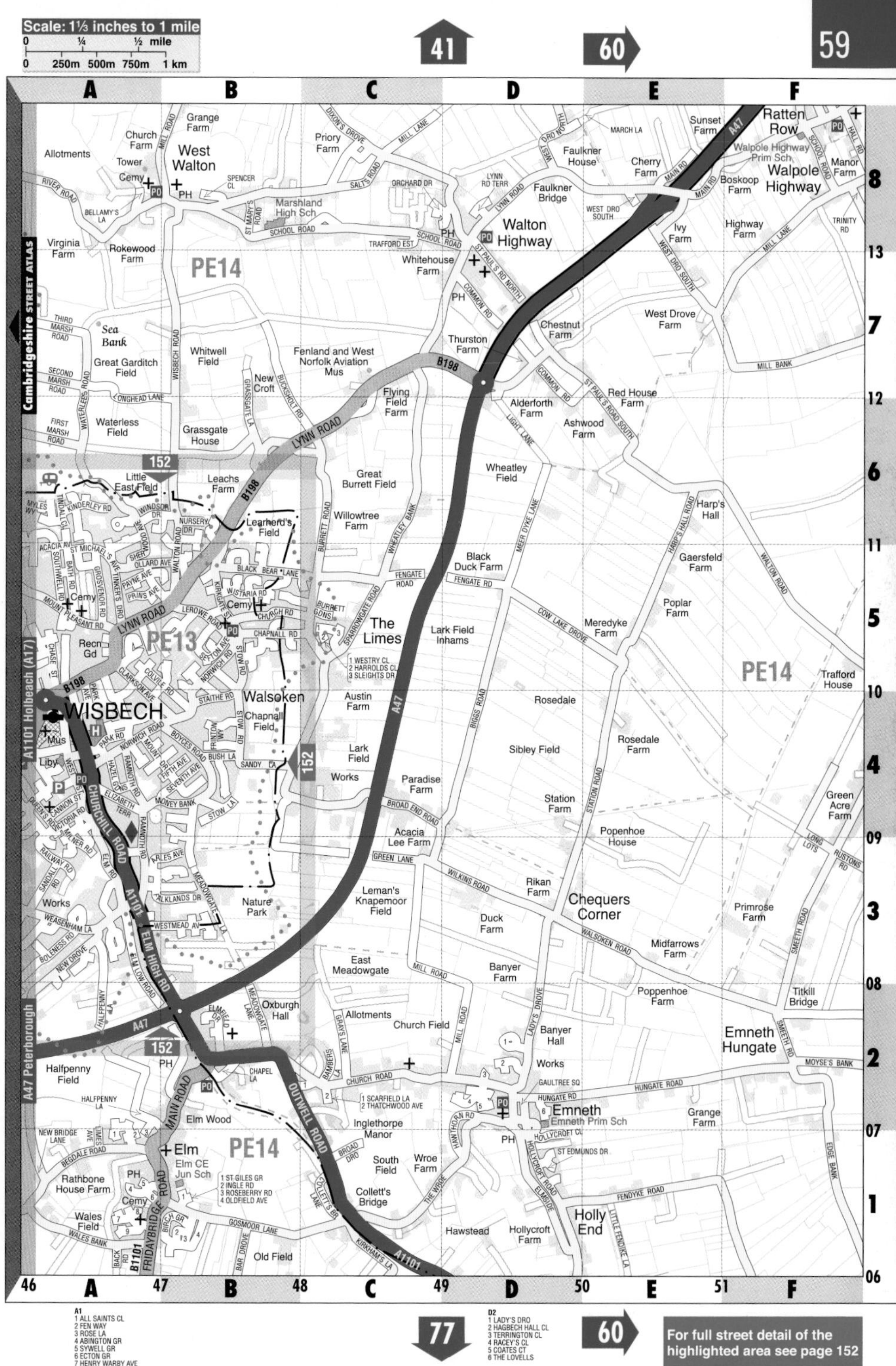

Cambridgeshire STREET ATLAS

Allotments

Church Farm

Grange Farm

West Walton

Tower Cemy

PH

Spencer CL

Priory Farm

Mill Lane

Faulkner House

MARCH LA

Sunset Farm

Ratten Row

Walpole Highway Prim Sch

Boskoop Farm

Walpole Highway

Manor Farm

8

13

Virginia Farm

Rokewood Farm

PE14

Marshland High Sch

SCHOOL ROAD

Whitehouse Farm

Walton Highway

Faulkner Bridge

WEST DRG SOUTH

Cherry Farm

Ivy Farm

Highway Farm

TRINITY RD

West Drove Farm

7

Sea Bank

Great Garditch Field

Whitwell Field

New Croft

Fenland and West Norfolk Aviation Mus

B198

Thurston Farm

Chestnut Farm

Alderforth Farm

Red House Farm

West Drove Farm

MILL BANK

12

Waterless Field

152

Grassgate House

LYNN ROAD

Flying Field Farm

Ashwood Farm

6

Little East Field

Leachs Farm

B198

Learherti's Field

Great Burrett Field

Willowtree Farm

Wheatley Field

Harp's Hall

Gaersfeld Farm

11

PE13

LYNN ROAD

Cemy

BLACK BEAR LANE

FENGATE ROAD

FENGATE RD

Black Duck Farm

Lark Field Inhams

COW LAKE DROVE

Meredyke Farm

Poplar Farm

PE14

Trafford House

5

WISBECH

Walsoken

The Limes

1 WESTRY CL
2 HARROLDS CL
3 SLEIGHTS DR

Austin Farm

Rosedale

Sibley Field

Rosedale Farm

Green Acre Farm

LONG LOTS

10

4

Works

Lark Field

Paradise Farm

BROAD END ROAD

Station Farm

Popenhoe House

Primrose Farm

09

3

Works

Nature Park

Acacia Lee Farm

GREEN LANE

Leman's Knapemoor Field

WILKINS ROAD

Rikan Farm

Chequers Corner

WALSOKEN ROAD

Midfarrows Farm

08

Halfpenny Field

A47

152

East Meadowgate

MILL ROAD

Allotments

Duck Farm

Banyer Farm

Poppenhoe Farm

Emneth Hungate

MOYSE'S BANK

2

Elm Wood

Oxburgh Hall

CHAPEL LA

Church Field

1 SCARFIELD LA
2 THATCHWOOD AVE

Works

GAULTREE SQ

HUNGATE ROAD

Banyer Hall

Emneth

Emneth Prim Sch

Grange Farm

07

Rathbone House Farm

Wales Field

Elm

Elm CE Jun Sch

1 ST GILES GR
2 INGLE RD
3 ROSEBERRY RD
4 OLDFIELD AVE

PE14

Inglethorpe Manor

South Field

Wroe Farm

Collett's Bridge

Hawstead

Hollycroft Farm

ST EDMUNDS DR

Holly End

LITTLE LONDON LA

FENDYKE ROAD

EDGE BANK

06

59
42

Scale: 1⅓ inches to 1 mile

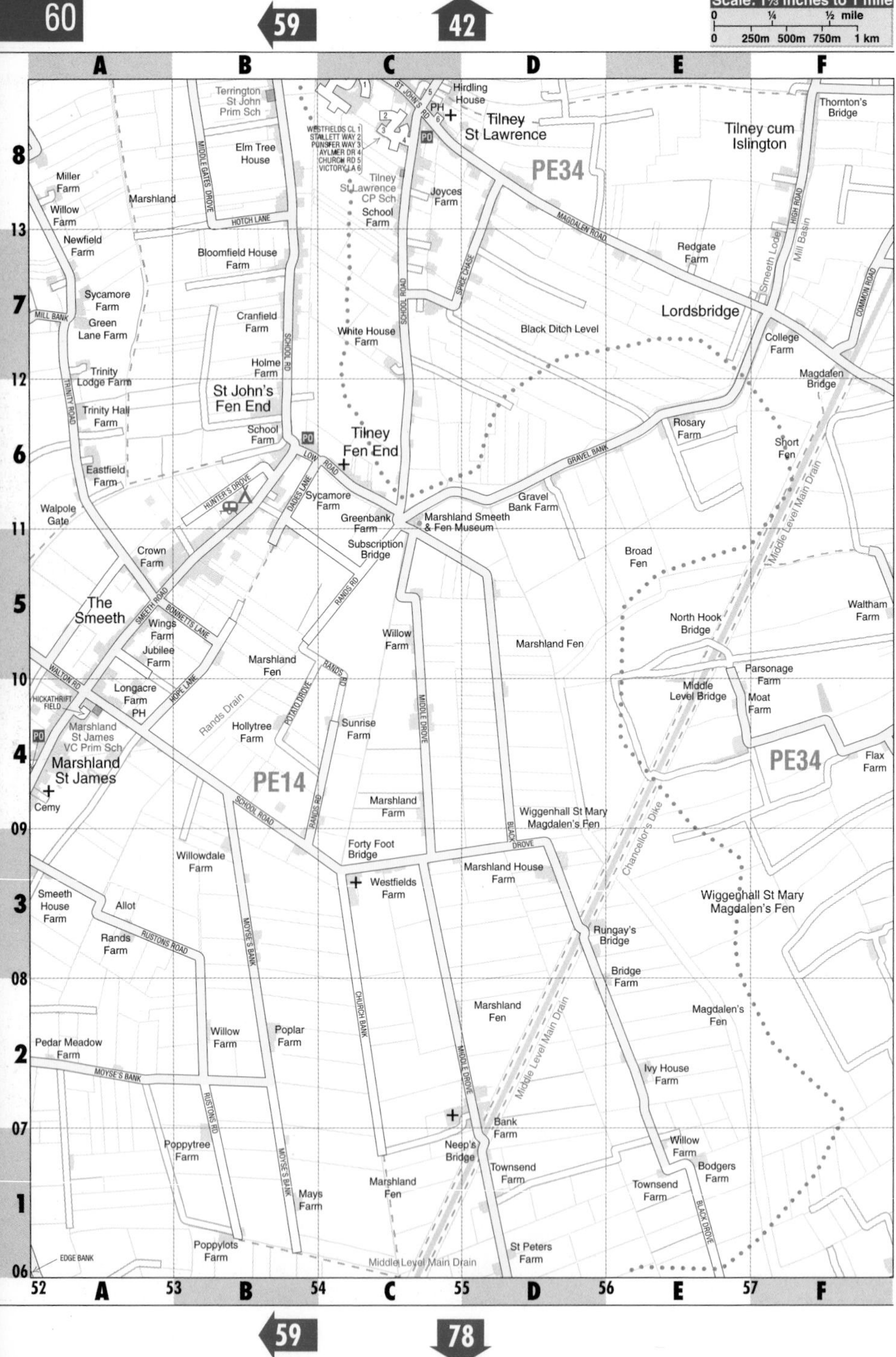

Tilney St Lawrence
Tilney cum Islington
Terrington St John Prim Sch
Elm Tree House
Hirdling House
Thornton's Bridge
PE34
Miller Farm
Marshland
Willow Farm
Newfield Farm
Tilney St Lawrence CP Sch
School Farm
Joyces Farm
WESTFIELDS CL 1
STALLETT WAY 2
PUNSFER WAY 3
AYLMER DR 4
CHURCH RD 5
VICTORY LA 6
MIDDLE GATES DROVE
HOTCH LANE
MAGDALEN ROAD
HIGH ROAD
Redgate Farm
Smeeth Lode
Mill Basin
Bloomfield House Farm
Sycamore Farm
Green Lane Farm
MILL BANK
Cranfield Farm
White House Farm
SPICE CHASE
SCHOOL ROAD
Black Ditch Level
Lordsbridge
COMMON ROAD
College Farm
Holme Farm
Trinity Lodge Farm
St John's Fen End
Magdalen Bridge
Trinity Hall Farm
TRINITY ROAD
School Farm
Tilney Fen End
Rosary Farm
Short Fen
Eastfield Farm
LOW ROAD
GRAVEL BANK
HUNTER'S DROVE
DADES LANE
Sycamore Farm
Gravel Bank Farm
Walpole Gate
Greenbank Farm
Marshland Smeeth & Fen Museum
Subscription Bridge
Crown Farm
Broad Fen
Middle Level Main Drain
RANDS RD
The Smeeth
SMEETH ROAD
BONNETTS LANE
Wings Farm
Jubilee Farm
Willow Farm
Marshland Fen
North Hook Bridge
Waltham Farm
Marshland Fen
WALTON RD
Longacre Farm
PH
HOPE LANE
POTATO DROVE
Parsonage Farm
Middle Level Bridge
Moat Farm
HICKATHRIFT FIELD
Marshland St James VC Prim Sch
Rands Drain
Hollytree Farm
Sunrise Farm
MIDDLE DROVE
Marshland St James
PE14
PE34
Flax Farm
Cemy
SCHOOL ROAD
Marshland Farm
Wiggenhall St Mary Magdalen's Fen
BLACK DROVE
Chancellor's Dike
Forty Foot Bridge
Willowdale Farm
Marshland House Farm
Westfields Farm
Smeeth House Farm
Allot
Wiggenhall St Mary Magdalen's Fen
Rands Farm
RUSTONS ROAD
Rungay's Bridge
MOYSE'S BANK
CHURCH BANK
Bridge Farm
Marshland Fen
Magdalen's Fen
Willow Farm
Poplar Farm
Pedar Meadow Farm
MOYSE'S BANK
Ivy House Farm
RUSTONS RD
Bank Farm
Neep's Bridge
Willow Farm
Poppytree Farm
Bodgers Farm
Townsend Farm
Townsend Farm
Marshland Fen
Mays Farm
BLACK DROVE
Poppylots Farm
St Peters Farm
EDGE BANK
Middle Level Main Drain

59
78

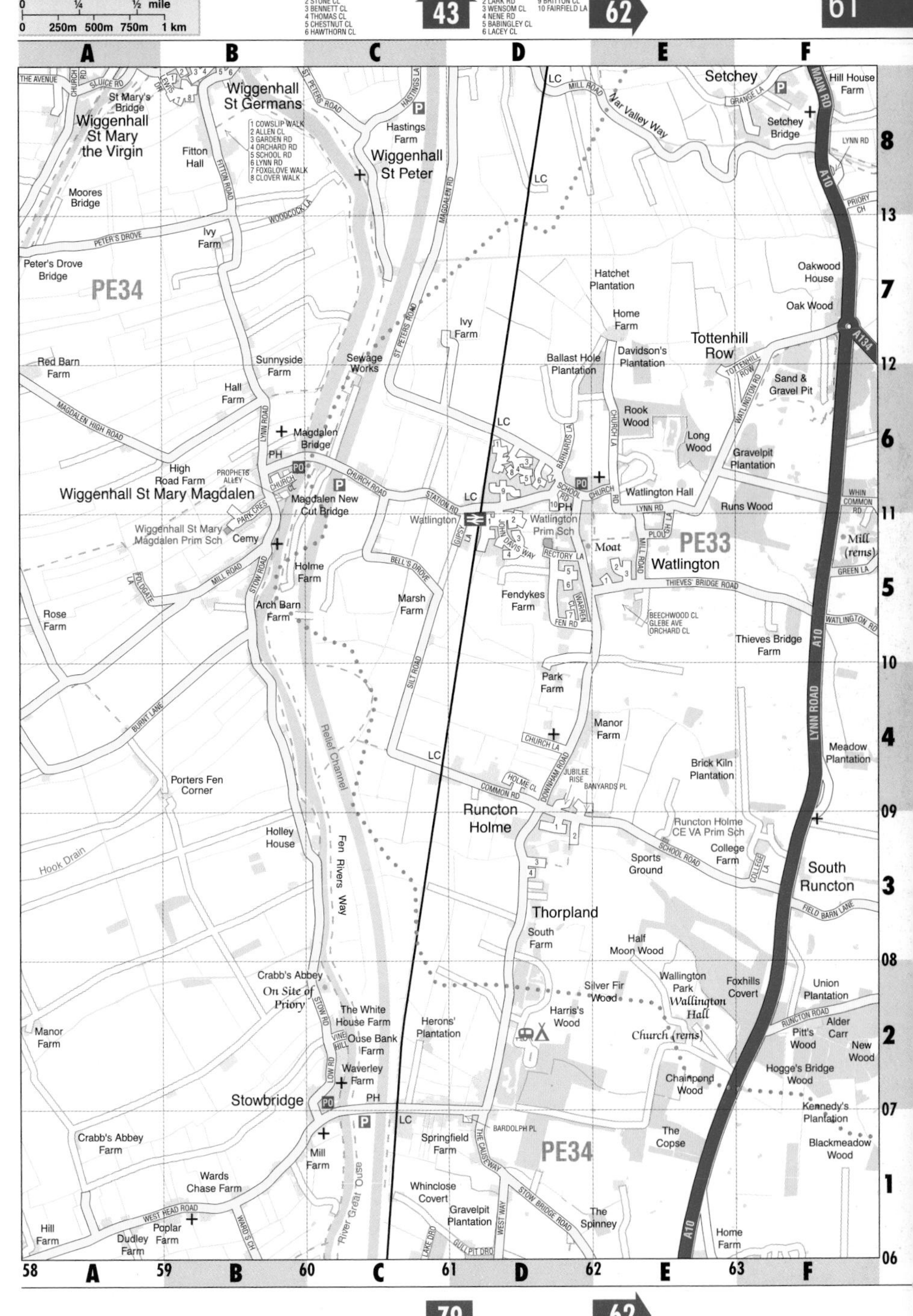

D5
1 PAIGE CL
2 STONE CL
3 BENNETT CL
4 THOMAS CL
5 CHESTNUT CL
6 HAWTHORN CL

7 ROWAN CL

D6
1 BURE CL
2 LARK RD
3 WENSOM CL
4 NENE RD
5 BABINGLEY CL
6 LACEY CL

7 CECIL CL
8 STIFFKEY CL
9 BRITTON CL
10 FAIRFIELD LA

THE AVENUE
St Mary's Bridge
Wiggenhall St Mary the Virgin
Fitton Hall
Moores Bridge
Peter's Drove Bridge
PE34
Red Barn Farm
Sunnyside Farm
Hall Farm
High Road Farm
Wiggenhall St Mary Magdalen
PROPHETS ALLEY
Magdalen Bridge
PH
Magdalen New Cut Bridge
Church Road
Wiggenhall St Mary Magdalen Prim Sch
Cemy
Holme Farm
Arch Barn Farm
Rose Farm
Porters Fen Corner
Holley House
Hook Drain
Crabb's Abbey On Site of Priory
The White House Farm
Ouse Bank Farm
Waverley Farm
PH
Stowbridge
Crabb's Abbey Farm
Mill Farm
Manor Farm
Wards Chase Farm
Hill Farm
Dudley Farm
Poplar Farm
WEST HEAD ROAD

Wiggenhall St Germans
Wiggenhall St Peter
Hastings Farm
1 COWSLIP WALK
2 ALLEN CL
3 GARDEN RD
4 ORCHARD RD
5 SCHOOL RD
6 LYNN RD
7 FOXGLOVE WALK
8 CLOVER WALK
Ivy Farm
Sewage Works
LC
LC
Watlington
LC
Watlington Prim Sch
PH
Marsh Farm
Fendykes Farm
DECTORY LA
FEN RD
BELL'S DROVE
Park Farm
LC
COMMON RD
Runcton Holme
JUBILEE RISE
BANYARDS PL
Thorpland
South Farm
Herons' Plantation
Harris's Wood
Springfield Farm
BARDOLPH PL
PE34
Whinclose Covert
Gravelpit Plantation
The Spinney

Setchey
Setchey Bridge
Hill House Farm
LYNN RD
PRIORY CH
A10
Hatchet Plantation
Home Farm
Ballast Hole Plantation
Davidson's Plantation
Rook Wood
Long Wood
Watlington Hall
LYNN RD
Runs Wood
PE33
Moat
Watlington
BEECHWOOD CL
GLEBE AVE
ORCHARD CL
Thieves Bridge Road
Thieves Bridge Farm
Manor Farm
CHURCH LA
Brick Kiln Plantation
Meadow Plantation
Sports Ground
Runcton Holme CE VA Prim Sch
College Farm
South Runcton
Half Moon Wood
Wallington Park
Silver Fir Wood
Wallington Hall
Foxhills Covert
Union Plantation
Church (rems)
Chainpond Wood
Pitt's Wood
Alder Carr
New Wood
Hogge's Bridge Wood
Kennedy's Plantation
The Copse
Blackmeadow Wood
Home Farm
A10
Oakwood House
Oak Wood
Tottenhill Row
Sand & Gravel Pit
Gravelpit Plantation
WHIN COMMON RD
Mill (rems)
GREEN LA
WATLINGTON RD

Var Valley Way
MILL ROAD
MAIN RD
ORANGE LA
A10
A134
LYNN ROAD
FIELD BARN LANE
RUNCTON ROAD
THE CAUSEWAY
STONE BRIDGE ROAD
PULL PIT DRO

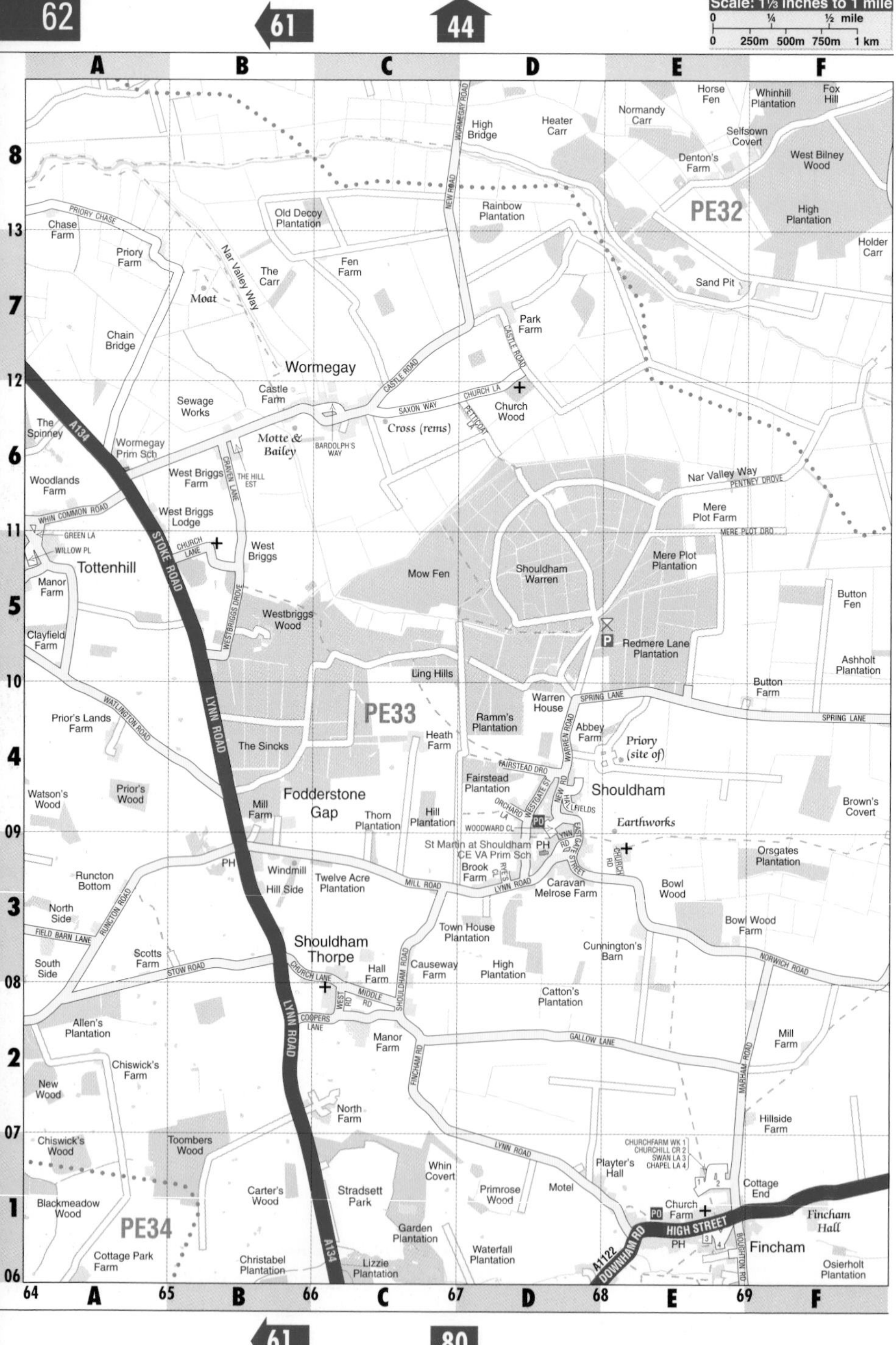

Scale: 1⅓ inches to 1 mile

| 0 | ¼ | ½ mile |
| 0 | 250m 500m 750m | 1 km |

A   B   C   D   E   F

8

13

7

12

6

11

5

10

4

09

3

08

2

07

1

06

64   A   65   B   66   C   67   D   68   E   69   F

Horse Fen
Whinhill Plantation
Fox Hill
Normandy Carr
Selfsown Covert
West Bilney Wood
Denton's Farm
PE32
High Bridge
Heater Carr
High Plantation
Holder Carr
Rainbow Plantation
Old Decoy Plantation
Fen Farm
Chase Farm
PRIORY CHASE
Priory Farm
The Carr
Nar Valley Way
NEW ROAD
WORMEGAY ROAD
Sand Pit
Moat
Chain Bridge
Park Farm
Wormegay
Castle Farm
Sewage Works
Church Wood
Cross (rems)
SAXON WAY
CASTLE ROAD
CHURCH LA
PETTOUR
The Spinney
A134
Wormegay Prim Sch
Motte & Bailey
BARDOLPH'S WAY
THE HILL EST
Nar Valley Way
PENTNEY DROVE
Mere Plot Farm
Woodlands Farm
West Briggs Farm
West Briggs Lodge
CHURCH LANE
Mere Plot Plantation
MERE PLOT DRO
WHIN COMMON ROAD
GREEN LA
WILLOW PL
West Briggs
Button Fen
Tottenhill
CHURCH LANE
Mow Fen
Shouldham Warren
STONE ROAD
SEDGEFORD LANE
Manor Farm
Westbriggs Wood
Ashholt Plantation
Clayfield Farm
Redmere Lane Plantation
Button Farm
Ling Hills
SPRING LANE
SPRING LANE
Prior's Lands Farm
PE33
Warren House
Ramm's Plantation
Abbey Farm
Priory (site of)
WATLINGTON ROAD
The Sincks
Heath Farm
WARREN ROAD
Brown's Covert
Watson's Wood
Prior's Wood
Mill Farm
Fodderstone Gap
Thorn Plantation
Hill Plantation
Fairstead Plantation
FAIRSTEAD DRO
ORCHARD CL
Shouldham
Earthworks
Orsgates Plantation
LYNN ROAD
PH
Runcton Bottom
RUNCTON ROAD
WOODWARD CL
St Martin at Shouldham CE VA Prim Sch
PO
PH
CHURCH LANE
FIELDS
North Side
FIELD BARN LANE
Windmill Hill Side
Twelve Acre Plantation
MILL ROAD
Brook Farm
Caravan
Bowl Wood
South Side
Scotts Farm
STOW ROAD
Melrose Farm
Bowl Wood Farm
Allen's Plantation
Shouldham Thorpe
Hall Farm
CHURCH LANE
MIDDLE RD
Town House Plantation
Causeway Farm
High Plantation
Cunnington's Barn
NORWICH ROAD
Mill Farm
Chiswick's Farm
COOPERS LANE
SHOULDHAM RD
Manor Farm
FINCHAM RD
Catton's Plantation
GALLOW LANE
New Wood
LYNN ROAD
North Farm
Hillside Farm
Chiswick's Wood
Toombers Wood
Whin Covert
LYNN ROAD
Primrose Wood
Motel
Player's Hall
CHURCHFARM WK 1
CHURCHILL CR 2
SWAN LA 3
CHAPEL LA 4
Cottage End
Fincham
Fincham Hall
Blackmeadow Wood
PE34
Carter's Wood
Stradsett Park
Garden Plantation
Waterfall Plantation
Church Farm
PO
HIGH STREET
PH
A1122
DOWNHAM RD
CRO PIGHTLE
Cottage Park Farm
Christabel Plantation
Lizzie Plantation
A134
Osierholt Plantation

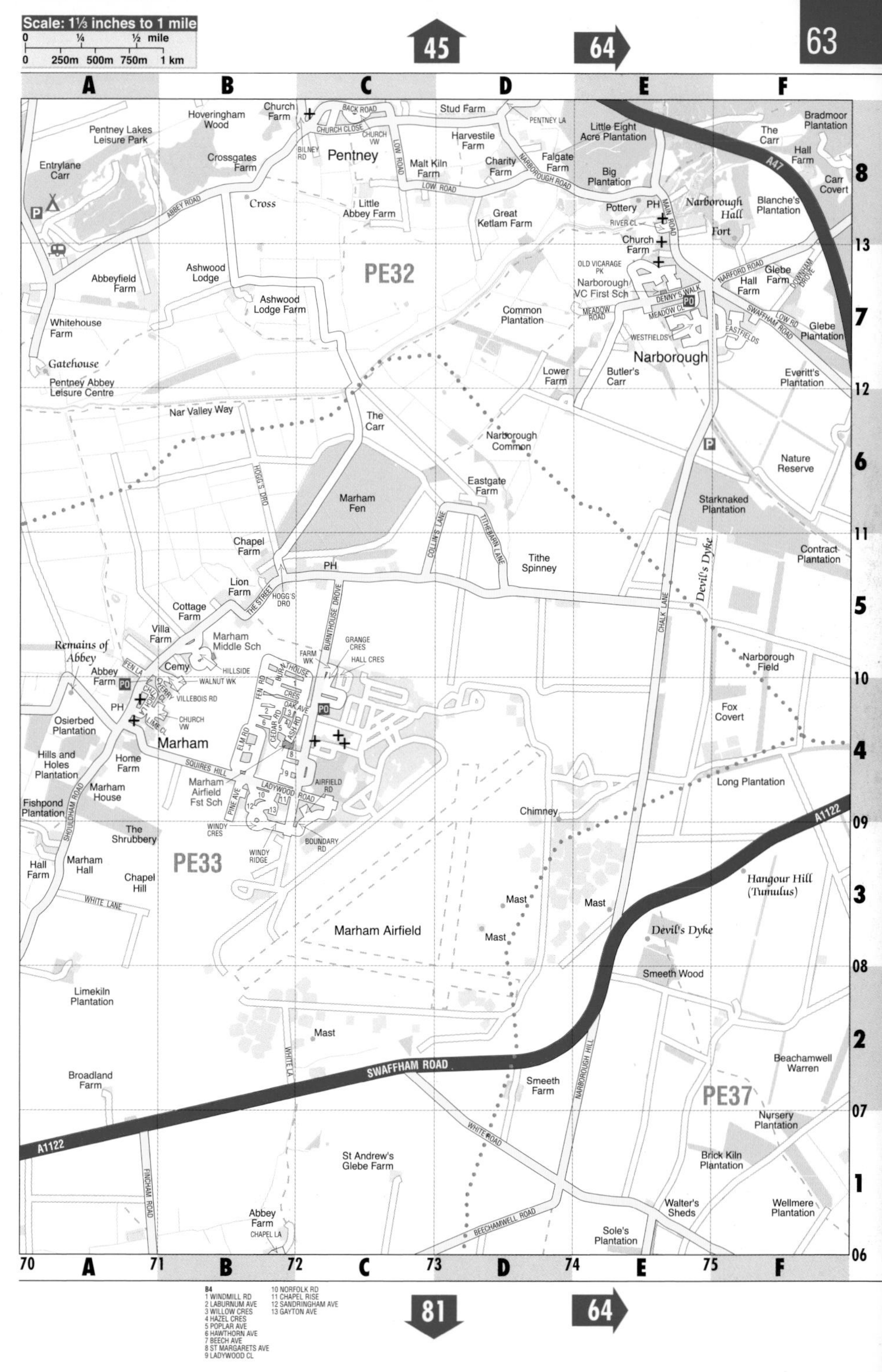

A   B   C   D   E   F

8
13
7
12
6
11
5
10
4
09
3
08
2
07
1
06

Pentney Lakes Leisure Park
Entrylane Carr
Hoveringham Wood
Church Farm
Back Road
Stud Farm
Little Eight Acre Plantation
The Carr
Bradmoor Plantation
Hall Farm
Carr Covert
Crossgates Farm
Pentney
CHURCH CLOSE
BILNEY RD
CHURCH VW
PENTNEY LA
A47
Cross
Little Abbey Farm
Malt Kiln Farm
Charity Farm
Falgate Farm
Big Plantation
Narborough Hall
Blanche's Plantation
Abbeyfield Farm
Ashwood Lodge
LOW ROAD
LOW ROAD
Great Ketlam Farm
Pottery
PH
Narborough Hall Fort
Whitehouse Farm
Ashwood Lodge Farm
PE32
RIVER CL
Church Farm
OLD VICARAGE PK
Glebe Farm
Hall Farm
Glebe Plantation
Gatehouse
Common Plantation
Narborough VC First Sch
MARFORD ROAD
DENNY'S WALK
PO
Pentney Abbey Leisure Centre
MEADOW RD
SWAFFHAM RD
LOW RD
Nar Valley Way
Lower Farm
Narborough
Butler's Carr
WESTFIELD'S
EASTFIELD'S
Everitt's Plantation
The Carr
Narborough Common
Nature Reserve
Marham Fen
Eastgate Farm
P
Starknaked Plantation
Chapel Farm
PH
COLLIN LANE
TITHE BARN LANE
Tithe Spinney
Devil's Dyke
Contract Plantation
Lion Farm
HOGG'S DRO
Cottage Farm
Villa Farm
THE STREET
Marham Middle Sch
GRANGE CRES
FARM WK
HALL CRES
CHALK WAY
Narborough Field
Remains of Abbey
Cemy
Abbey Farm
PO
HILLSIDE
WALNUT WK
VILLEBOIS RD
FERN LA
THE SPINNEY
CRES
PH
Marham
CHURCH VW
ELM RD
SQUIRES HILL
PO
Fox Covert
Osierbed Plantation
Hills and Holes Plantation
Home Farm
Marham Airfield Fst Sch
LADYWOOD RD
AIRFIELD RD
Long Plantation
A1122
Marham House
PINE RD
Chimney
Fishpond Plantation
WINDY CRES
The Shrubbery
WINDY RIDGE
BOUNDARY RD
Mast
Mast
Hangour Hill (Tumulus)
GREENHOW ROAD
Hall Farm
Marham Hall
Chapel Hill
PE33
Marham Airfield
Devil's Dyke
WHITE LANE
Mast
Smeeth Wood
Limekiln Plantation
WHITLEA
SWAFFHAM ROAD
NARBOROUGH HILL
Beachamwell Warren
Broadland Farm
Smeeth Farm
PE37
Nursery Plantation
A1122
FINCHAM ROAD
WHITE ROAD
St Andrew's Glebe Farm
Brick Kiln Plantation
Wellmere Plantation
Abbey Farm
CHAPEL LA
BEECHAMWELL ROAD
Sole's Plantation
Walter's Sheds

70   71   72   73   74   75

A   B   C   D   E   F

B4
1 WINDMILL RD
2 LABURNUM AVE
3 WILLOW CRES
4 HAZEL CRES
5 POPLAR AVE
6 HAWTHORN AVE
7 BEECH AVE
8 ST MARGARETS AVE
9 LADYWOOD CL
10 NORFOLK RD
11 CHAPEL RISE
12 SANDRINGHAM AVE
13 GAYTON AVE

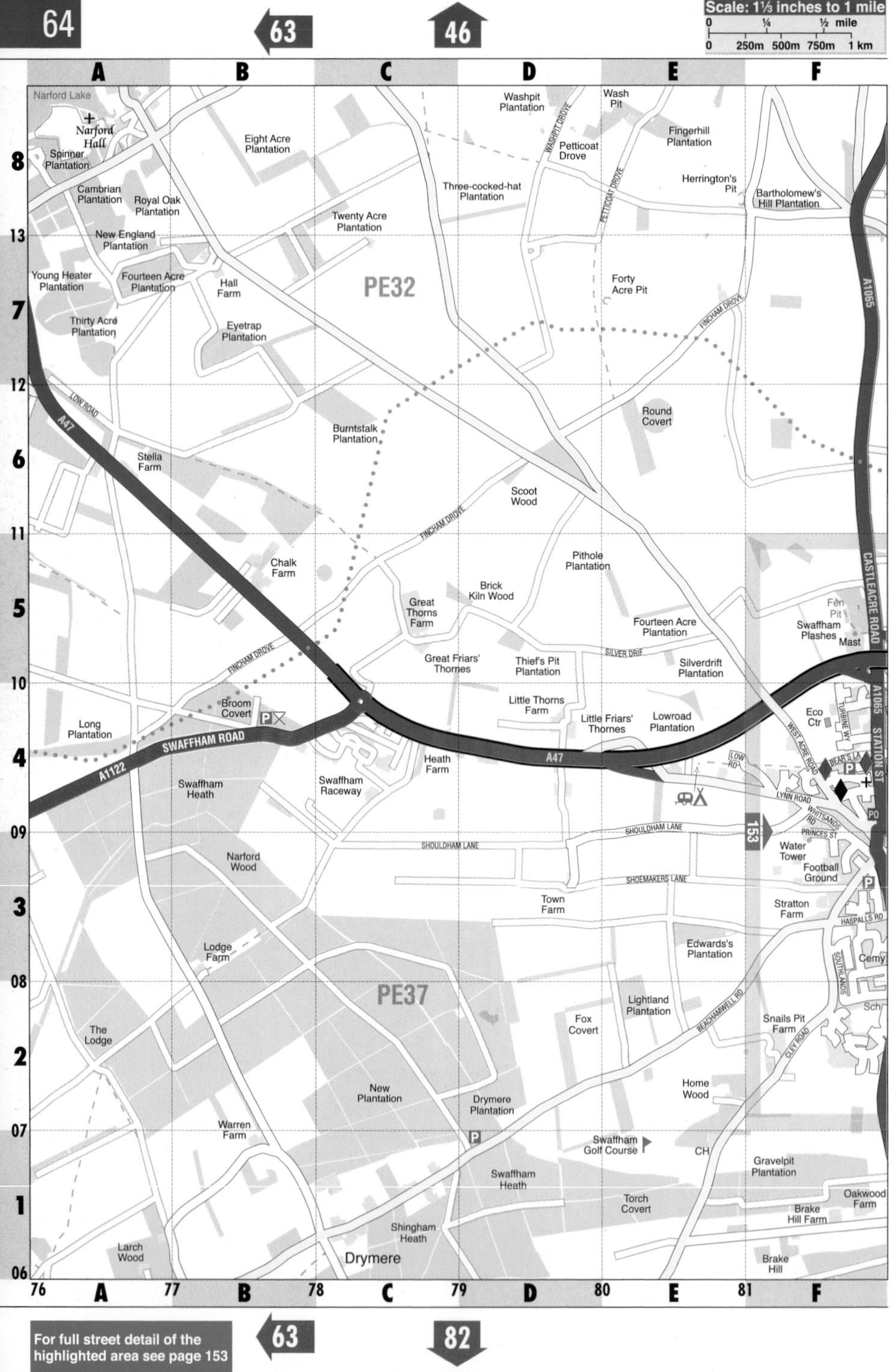

A   B   C   D   E   F

Narford Lake

Narford Hall

Spinner Plantation

8

Eight Acre Plantation

Washpit Plantation

Wash Pit

Fingerhill Plantation

Cambrian Plantation

Royal Oak Plantation

New England Plantation

Three-cocked-hat Plantation

Petticoat Drove

Herrington's Pit

Bartholomew's Hill Plantation

13

Twenty Acre Plantation

WASHPIT DROVE

PETTICOAT DROVE

Young Heater Plantation

Fourteen Acre Plantation

Hall Farm

PE32

7

Thirty Acre Plantation

Eyetrap Plantation

Forty Acre Pit

A1065

12

LOW ROAD

Stella Farm

Burntstalk Plantation

Round Covert

FINCHAM DROVE

6

A47

Scoot Wood

11

Chalk Farm

FINCHAM DROVE

Pithole Plantation

5

Great Thorns Farm

Brick Kiln Wood

Fourteen Acre Plantation

Fen Pit

Swaffham Plashes

Mast

CASTLEACRE ROAD

Long Plantation

FINCHAM DROVE

Great Friars' Thornes

Great Friars' Thornes

Thief's Pit Plantation

SILVER DROVE

Silverdrift Plantation

SILVER DROVE

Eco Ctr

A1065

10

Broom Covert

Little Thorns Farm

Little Friars' Thornes

Lowroad Plantation

THORNE PK

WEST ACRE ROAD

STATION ST

4

A1122

SWAFFHAM ROAD

A47

LOW RD

LYNN ROAD

PO

Swaffham Heath

Heath Farm

WHITTSANDS RD

PRINCES ST

Swaffham Raceway

153

Water Tower

HASPALLS RD

09

Narford Wood

SHOULDHAM LANE

SHOULDHAM LANE

Football Ground

Stratton Farm

SHOEMAKERS LANE

3

Town Farm

Edwards's Plantation

Cemy

SOUTH ANDS

Sch

08

Lodge Farm

PE37

Lightland Plantation

Snails Pit Farm

BLACKMARSH RD

2

The Lodge

Fox Covert

Home Wood

OLLY ROAD

Gravelpit Plantation

Oakwood Farm

New Plantation

Warren Farm

07

Drymere Plantation

Swaffham Golf Course

CH

Brake Hill Farm

1

Swaffham Heath

Torch Covert

Brake Hill

Larch Wood

Shingham Heath

Drymere

06

76   A   77   B   78   C   79   D   80   E   81   F

63

82

For full street detail of the highlighted area see page 153

Scale: 1⅓ inches to 1 mile

47
66

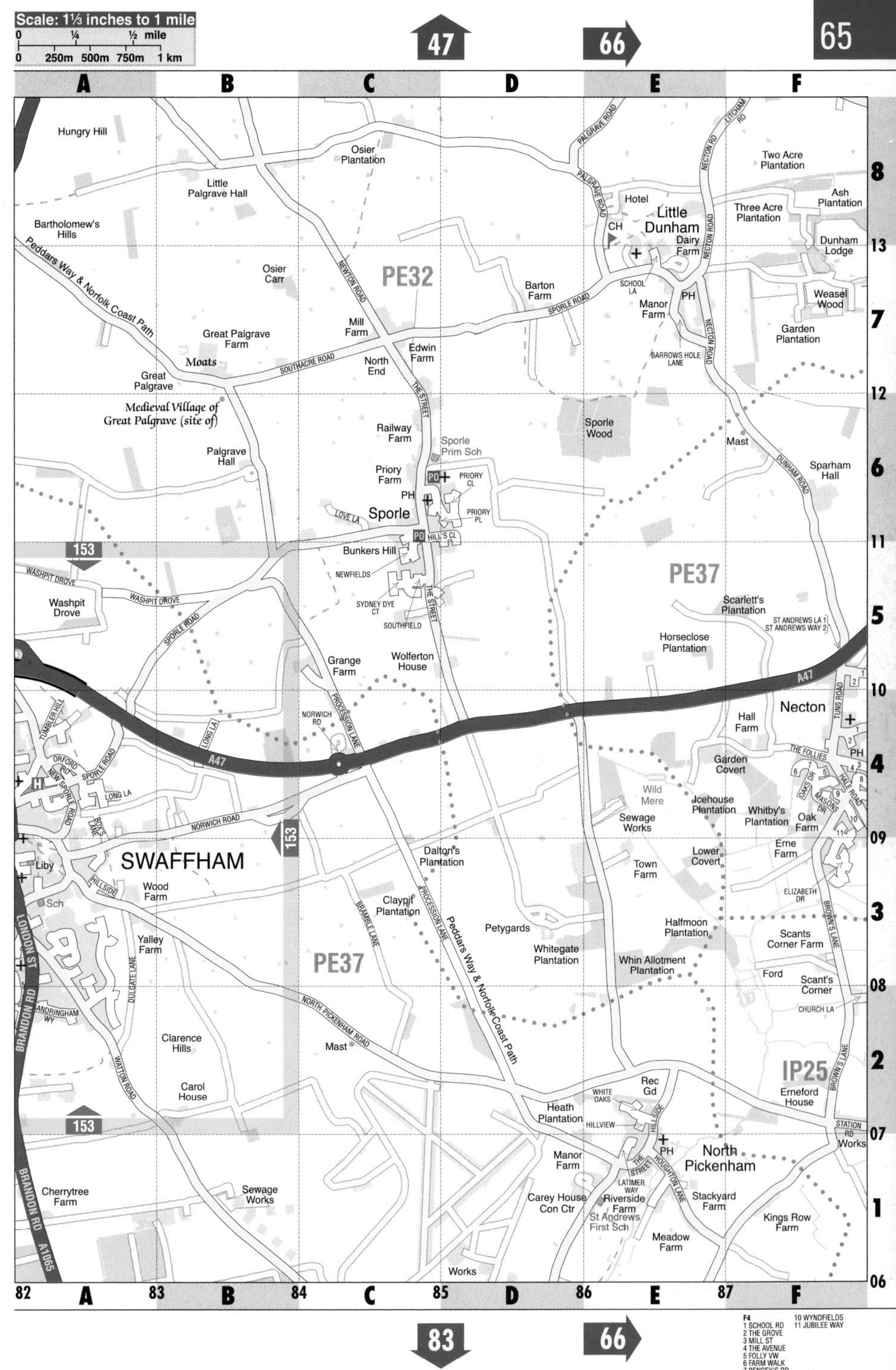
Hungry Hill
Osier Plantation
Little Palgrave Hall
Bartholomew's Hills
Peddars Way & Norfolk Coast Path
Osier Carr
PE32
Little Dunham
Hotel
CH
Dairy Farm
Two Acre Plantation
Three Acre Plantation
Ash Plantation
Dunham Lodge
Weasel Wood
Garden Plantation
Barton Farm
Manor Farm
PH
Great Palgrave Farm
Moats
Mill Farm
Edwin Farm
North End
Great Palgrave
Medieval Village of Great Palgrave (site of)
Railway Farm
Sporle Prim Sch
Sporle Wood
Mast
Sparham Hall
Palgrave Hall
Priory Farm
Sporle
Bunkers Hill
Washpit Drove
PE37
Scarlett's Plantation
Horseclose Plantation
Grange Farm
Wolferton House
Necton
Hall Farm
Garden Covert
Wild Mere
Sewage Works
Icehouse Plantation
Whitby's Plantation
Oak Farm
SWAFFHAM
Liby
Sch
Wood Farm
Dalton's Plantation
Town Farm
Lower Covert
Erne Farm
Yalley Farm
Claypit Plantation
Petygards
Halfmoon Plantation
Scants Corner Farm
Whitegate Plantation
Whin Allotment Plantation
Ford
Scant's Corner
Clarence Hills
Mast
IP25
Carol House
Rec Gd
Erneford House
Heath Plantation
Works
Manor Farm
North Pickenham
Cherrytree Farm
Sewage Works
Carey House Con Ctr
Riverside Farm
St Andrews First Sch
Stackyard Farm
Kings Row Farm
Meadow Farm
Works
153
A47
A1065
F4
1 SCHOOL RD
2 THE GROVE
3 MILL ST
4 THE AVENUE
5 FOLLY VW
6 FARM WALK
7 BENGEY'S RD
8 CHANTRY CT
9 BRIAR CL
10 WYNDFIELDS
11 JUBILEE WAY

83
66

65
48

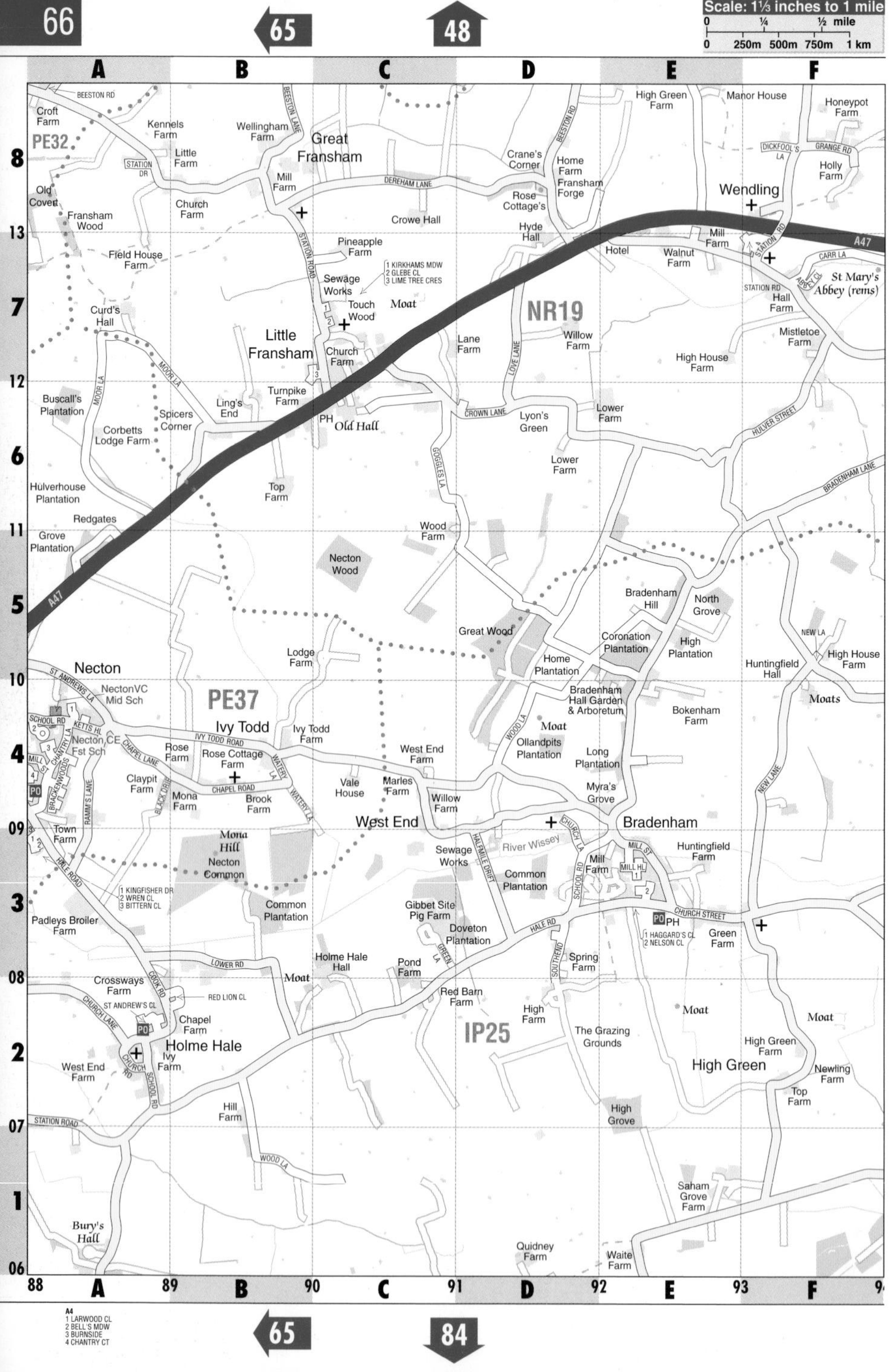
Scale: 1⅓ inches to 1 mile
0 ¼ ½ mile
0 250m 500m 750m 1 km
A B C D E F
Croft Farm
Kennels Farm
Wellingham Farm
Great Fransham
Crane's Corner
Home Farm
Fransham Forge
High Green Farm
Manor House
Honeypot Farm
Holly Farm
Wendling
PE32
Little Farm
Mill Farm
Rose Cottage's
Old Covert
Church Farm
Fransham Wood
Crowe Hall
Hyde Hall
Mill Farm
Hotel
Walnut Farm
Field House Farm
Pineapple Farm
Sewage Works
Touch Wood
Moat
NR19
St Mary's Abbey (rems)
Hall Farm
Curd's Hall
Little Fransham
Church Farm
Lane Farm
Willow Farm
Mistletoe Farm
High House Farm
Buscall's Plantation
Spicers Corner
Ling's End
Turnpike Farm
PH
Old Hall
Lyon's Green
Lower Farm
Corbetts Lodge Farm
Lower Farm
Hulverhouse Plantation
Top Farm
Redgates
Grove Plantation
Wood Farm
Necton Wood
A47
Bradenham Hill
North Grove
Great Wood
Coronation Plantation
High Plantation
Lodge Farm
Home Plantation
High House Farm
Huntingfield Hall
Necton
NectonVC Mid Sch
PE37
Bradenham Hall Garden & Arboretum
Moats
Bokenham Farm
Ivy Todd
Ivy Todd Farm
Moat
Necton CE Fst Sch
Rose Farm
Rose Cottage Farm
West End Farm
Ollandpits Plantation
Long Plantation
Claypit Farm
Mona Farm
Brook Farm
Vale House
Marles Farm
Willow Farm
Myra's Grove
Town Farm
West End
Bradenham
Mona Hill
Necton Common
Sewage Works
River Wissey
Mill Farm
Huntingfield Farm
Common Plantation
Padleys Broiler Farm
Common Plantation
Gibbet Site Pig Farm
Doveton Plantation
PO PH
Green Farm
Holme Hale Hall
Pond Farm
Spring Farm
Moat
Crossways Farm
Red Barn Farm
Moat
High Farm
Moat
Chapel Farm
IP25
The Grazing Grounds
Holme Hale
Ivy Farm
High Green Farm
West End Farm
High Green
Newling Farm
Top Farm
Hill Farm
High Grove
Saham Grove Farm
Bury's Hall
Quidney Farm
Waite Farm
BEESTON RD
STATION DR
DEREHAM LANE
STATION ROAD
MOOR LA
CROWN LANE
LOVE LANE
GOGGLES LA
HULVER STREET
BRADENHAM LANE
NEW LA
NEW LANE
IVY TODD ROAD
CHAPEL LANE
CHAPEL ROAD
WATERY LA
WOOD LA
CHURCH LA
MILL ST
MILL HL
SCHOOL RD
CHURCH STREET
HALE RD
HALF MILE DRIFT
GREEN LA
SOUTHEND
LOWER RD
HALE ROAD
COOK RD
CHURCH LANE
ST ANDREW'S CL
RED LION CL
CHURCH RD
SCHOOL RD
STATION ROAD
WOOD LA
ST ANDREWS LA
KETTS HL
CHANTRY LA
MILL ST
BRACKENWOODS
RAMM'S LANE
BLACK DRIF
DICKFOOL'S LA
GRANGE RD
CARR LA
ABBEY CL
STATION RD
1 KIRKHAMS MDW
2 GLEBE CL
3 LIME TREE CRES
1 KINGFISHER DR
2 WREN CL
3 BITTERN CL
1 HAGGARD'S CL
2 NELSON CL
8 13 7 12 6 11 5 10 4 09 3 08 2 07 1 06
88 89 90 91 92 93 94
A4
1 LARWOOD CL
2 BELL'S MDW
3 BURNSIDE
4 CHANTRY CT

65
84

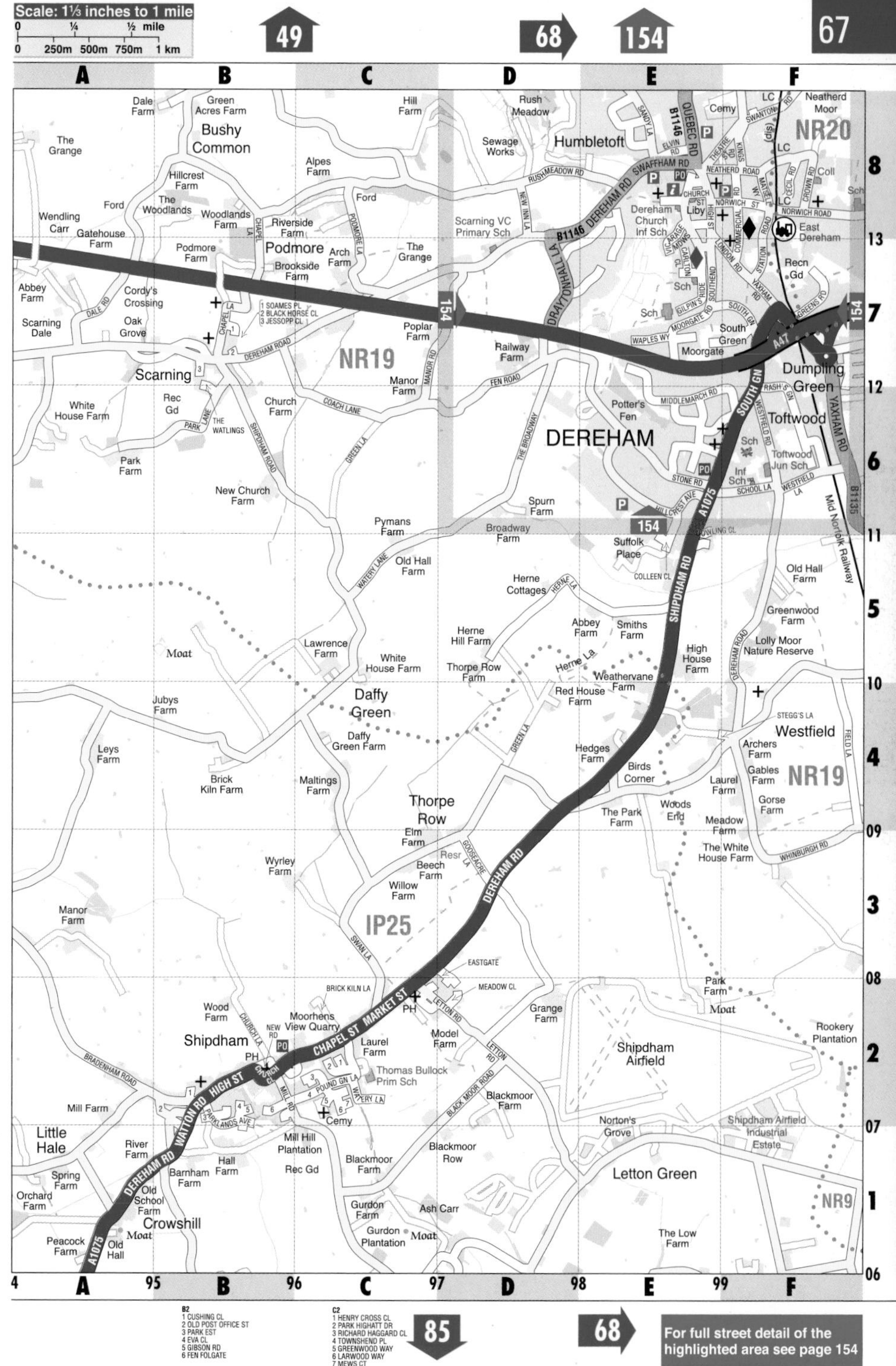

Scale: 1⅓ inches to 1 mile
0 ¼ ½ mile
0 250m 500m 750m 1 km
49
68
154
A B C D E F
Dale Farm
Green Acres Farm
Bushy Common
Hill Farm
Rush Meadow
Sewage Works
Humbletoft
Cemy
Neatherd Moor
NR20
The Grange
Hillcrest Farm
Alpes Farm
The Woodlands
Ford
Wendling Carr
Gatehouse Farm
Woodlands Farm
Riverside Farm
Podmore Farm
Podmore
Arch Farm
The Grange
Brookside Farm
Scarning VC Primary Sch
Dereham Church Inf Sch
Liby
East Dereham
Recn Gd
Abbey Farm
Cordy's Crossing
Scarning Dale
Oak Grove
1 SOAMES PL
2 BLACK HORSE CL
3 JESSOPP CL
Poplar Farm
NR19
Railway Farm
South Green
Moorgate
Dumpling Green
Scarning
White House Farm
Rec Gd
Church Farm
Manor Farm
Potter's Fen
DEREHAM
Toftwood
Park Farm
New Church Farm
Spurn Farm
Toftwood Jun Sch
Inf Sch
Pymans Farm
Broadway Farm
Suffolk Place
Old Hall Farm
Herne Cottages
Abbey Farm
Smiths Farm
Greenwood Farm
Herne Hill Farm
Lolly Moor Nature Reserve
Moat
Lawrence Farm
White House Farm
Thorpe Row Farm
High House Farm
Weathervane Farm
Red House Farm
Jubys Farm
Daffy Green
Daffy Green Farm
Westfield
Leys Farm
Hedges Farm
Archers Farm
Brick Kiln Farm
Maltings Farm
Birds Corner
Gables Farm
NR19
Thorpe Row
Laurel Farm
Gorse Farm
The Park Farm
Woods End
Meadow Farm
Elm Farm
Wyrley Farm
Beech Farm
The White House Farm
Willow Farm
Manor Farm
IP25
Park Farm
Wood Farm
Moorhens View Quarry
Grange Farm
Moat
Rookery Plantation
Shipdham
Laurel Farm
Model Farm
Shipdham Airfield
Thomas Bullock Prim Sch
Blackmoor Farm
Mill Farm
Cemy
Norton's Grove
Shipdham Airfield Industrial Estate
Little Hale
River Farm
Mill Hill Plantation
Blackmoor Row
Spring Farm
Barnham Farm
Hall Farm
Rec Gd
Blackmoor Farm
Letton Green
Orchard Farm
Old School Farm
NR9
Crowshill
Gurdon Farm
Ash Carr
Peacock Farm
Moat
Old Hall
Gurdon Plantation
Moat
The Low Farm
Mid Norfolk Railway
A47
A1075
B1146
B1135
DEREHAM RD
SHIPDHAM RD
CHAPEL ST
MARKET ST
HIGH ST
WATTON RD
4 95 96 97 98 99
13 12 11 10 09 08 07 06
8 7 6 5 4 3 2 1
B2
1 CUSHING CL
2 OLD POST OFFICE ST
3 PARK EST
4 EVA CL
5 GIBSON RD
6 FEN FOLGATE
C2
1 HENRY CROSS CL
2 PARK HIGHATT DR
3 RICHARD HAGGARD CL
4 TOWNSHEND PL
5 GREENWOOD WAY
6 LARWOOD WAY
7 MEWS CT
85
68
For full street detail of the highlighted area see page 154

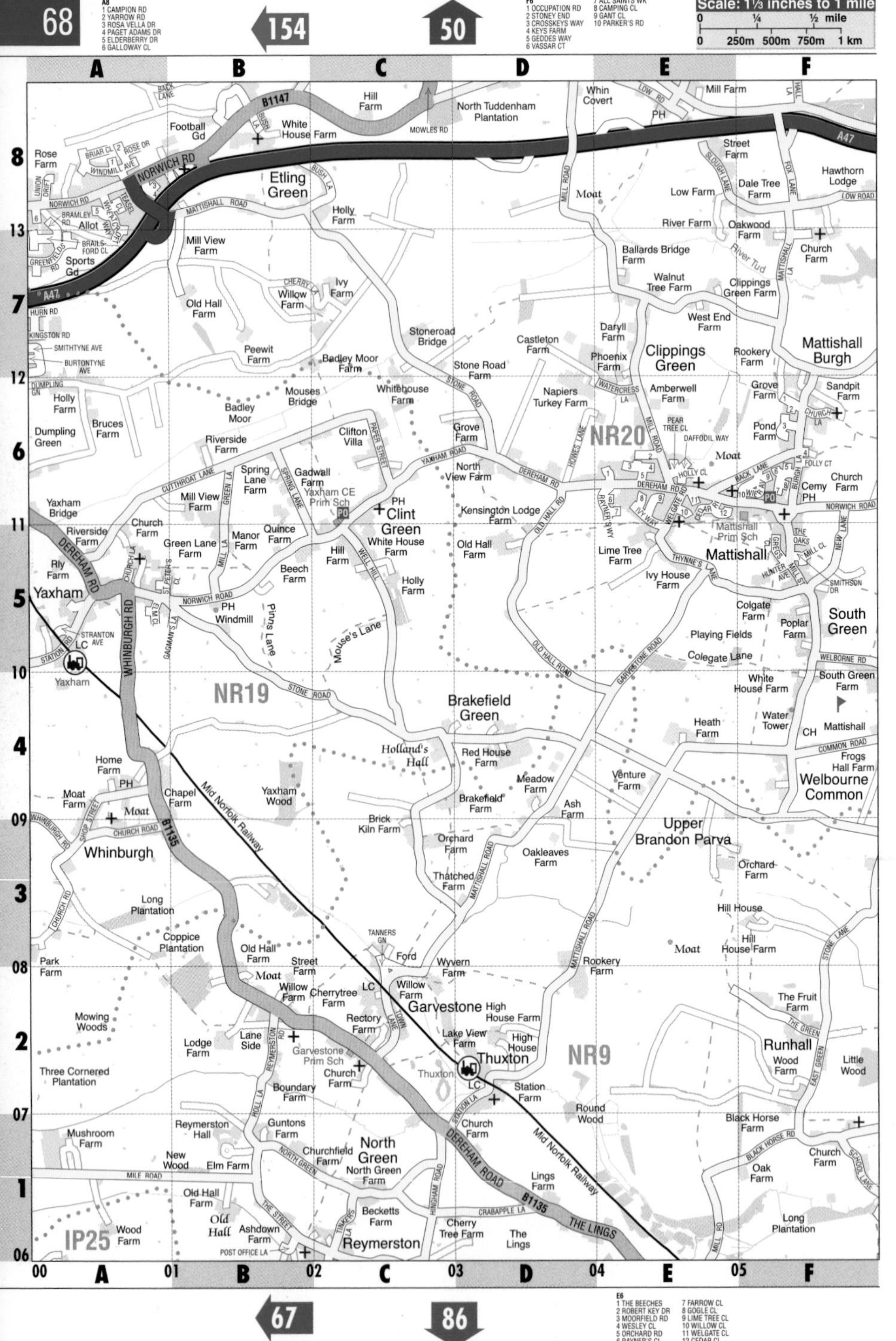

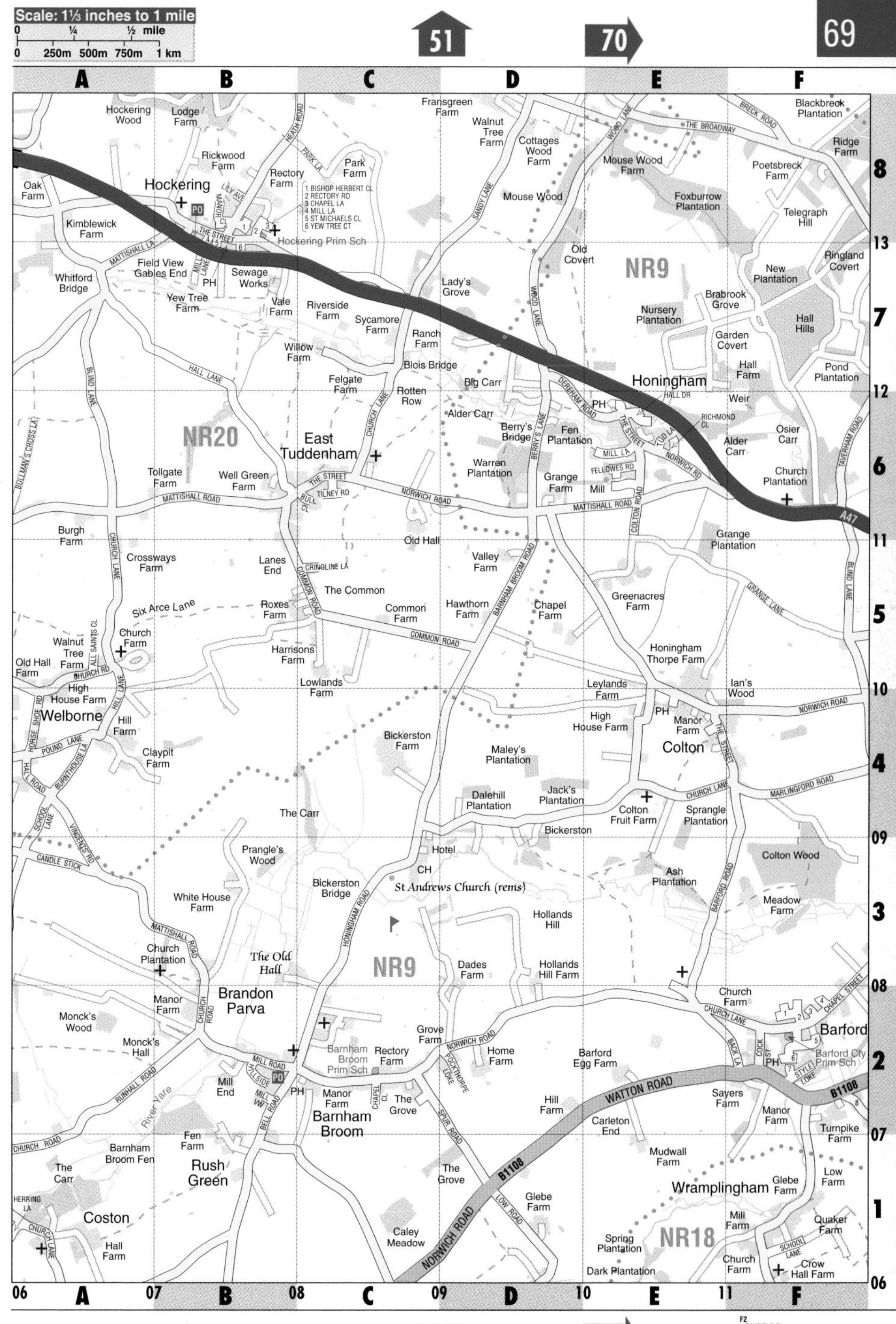

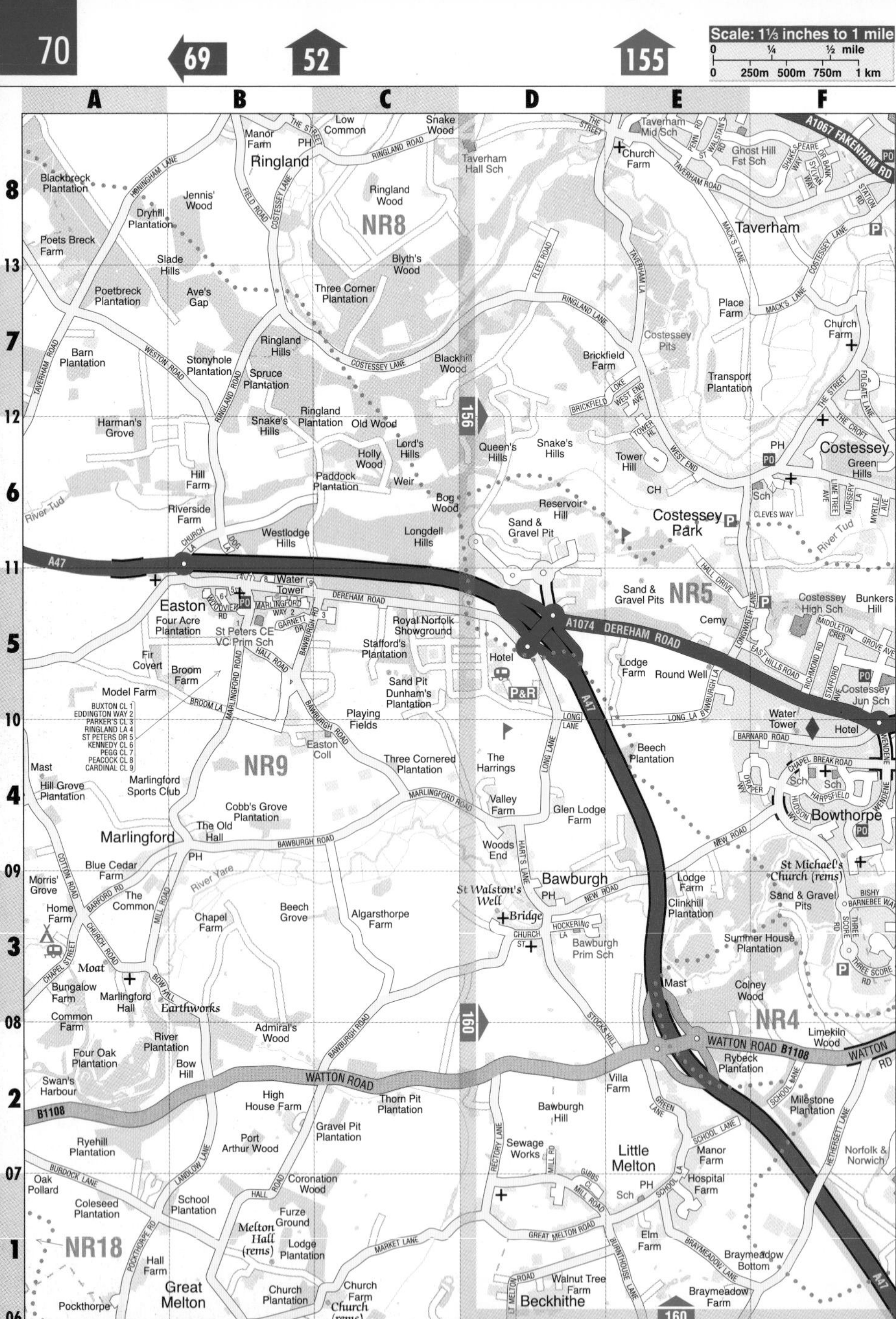

A　B　C　D　E　F

8

Blackbreck
Plantation

Poets Breck
Farm

13

Poetbreck
Plantation

7

Barn
Plantation

12

Harman's
Grove

6

Hill
Farm

Riverside
Farm

11

A47

Manor
Farm
PH

Ringland

THE STREET

Dryhill
Plantation

Jennis'
Wood

Slade
Hills

Ave's
Gap

Three Corner
Plantation

Ringland
Hills

Stonyhole
Plantation

Spruce
Plantation

Ringland
Plantation

Snake's
Hills

Westlodge
Hills

Low
Common

RINGLAND ROAD

Ringland
Wood

NR8

Blyth's
Wood

Old Wood

Holly
Wood

Paddock
Plantation

Weir

Longdell
Hills

Snake
Wood

Taverham
Hall Sch

Blackhill
Wood

COSTESSEY LANE

Lord's
Hills

Bog
Wood

Church
Farm

Taverham
Mid Sch

A1067 FAKENHAM RD

Ghost Hill
Fst Sch

Taverham

Place
Farm

Church
Farm

RINGLAND LANE

Brickfield
Farm

BRICKFIELD
LANE

WEST END

156

Queen's
Hills

Snake's
Hills

Reservoir
Hill

Sand &
Gravel Pit

Costessey
Pits

Tower
Hill

CH

Transport
Plantation

PH

Costessey
Park

Costessey
Green
Hills

Costessey

Sch

P&R

River Tud

5

Easton

Four Acre
Plantation

Fir
Covert

Model Farm

BUXTON CL 1
EDDINGTON WAY 2
PARKER S 3
RINGLAND LA 4
ST PETERS DR 5
KENNEDY CL 6
PEGGS CL 7
PEACOCK CL 8
CARDINAL CL 9

10

Mast

Hill Grove
Plantation

St Peters CE
VC Prim Sch

Broom
Farm

BROOM LA

NR9

Marlingford
Sports Club

DEREHAM ROAD

Royal Norfolk
Showground

Stafford's
Plantation

Sand Pit
Dunham's
Plantation

Playing
Fields

Easton
Coll

Three Cornered
Plantation

Cobb's Grove
Plantation

Sand &
Gravel Pits

A1074 DEREHAM ROAD

Hotel

LONG LANE

The
Harrings

Valley
Farm

NR5

Cerny

Lodge
Farm

Round Well

Beech
Plantation

Glen Lodge
Farm

Costessey
High Sch

Water
Tower

Bunkers
Hill

Costessey
Jun Sch

Hotel

Sch

Sch

Bowthorpe

4

Morris'
Grove

Home
Farm

Marlingford

Blue Cedar
Farm

The
Common

The Old
Hall

PH

09

River Yare

Chapel
Farm

Beech
Grove

Algarsthorpe
Farm

St Walston's
Well

Bridge

CHURCH
ST

Bawburgh

PH

NEW ROAD

Lodge
Farm

Bawburgh
Prim Sch

Clinkhill
Plantation

Summer House
Plantation

Colney
Wood

St Michael's
Church (rems)

Sand & Gravel
Pits

NR4

3

Moat

Bungalow
Farm

Marlingford
Hall

Earthworks

Admiral's
Wood

Mast

Limekiln
Wood

08

Common
Farm

Four Oak
Plantation

River
Plantation

Bow
Hill

BAWBURGH ROAD

160

WATTON ROAD B1108

Rybeck
Plantation

WATTON RD

2

Swan's
Harbour

B1108

Ryehill
Plantation

WATTON ROAD

High
House Farm

Thorn Pit
Plantation

Gravel Pit
Plantation

Port
Arthur Wood

Villa
Farm

Bawburgh
Hill

Manor
Farm

Milestone
Plantation

Norfolk &
Norwich

A47

07

Oak
Pollard

BURDOCK LANE

Coleseed
Plantation

School
Plantation

Coronation
Wood

Sewage
Works

Little
Melton

Hospital
Farm

PH
Sch

1

NR18

Hall
Farm

Great
Melton

Furze
Ground

Melton
Hall
(rems)

Lodge
Plantation

Church
Plantation

MARKET LANE

GREAT MELTON ROAD

Elm
Farm

Walnut Tree
Farm

Braymeadow
Bottom

Braymeadow
Farm

06

Pockthorpe

Church
Farm
Church
(rems)

Beckhithe

160

12　A　13　B　14　C　15　D　16　E　17　F

For full street detail of the
highlighted area see pages
156 and 160

69　88

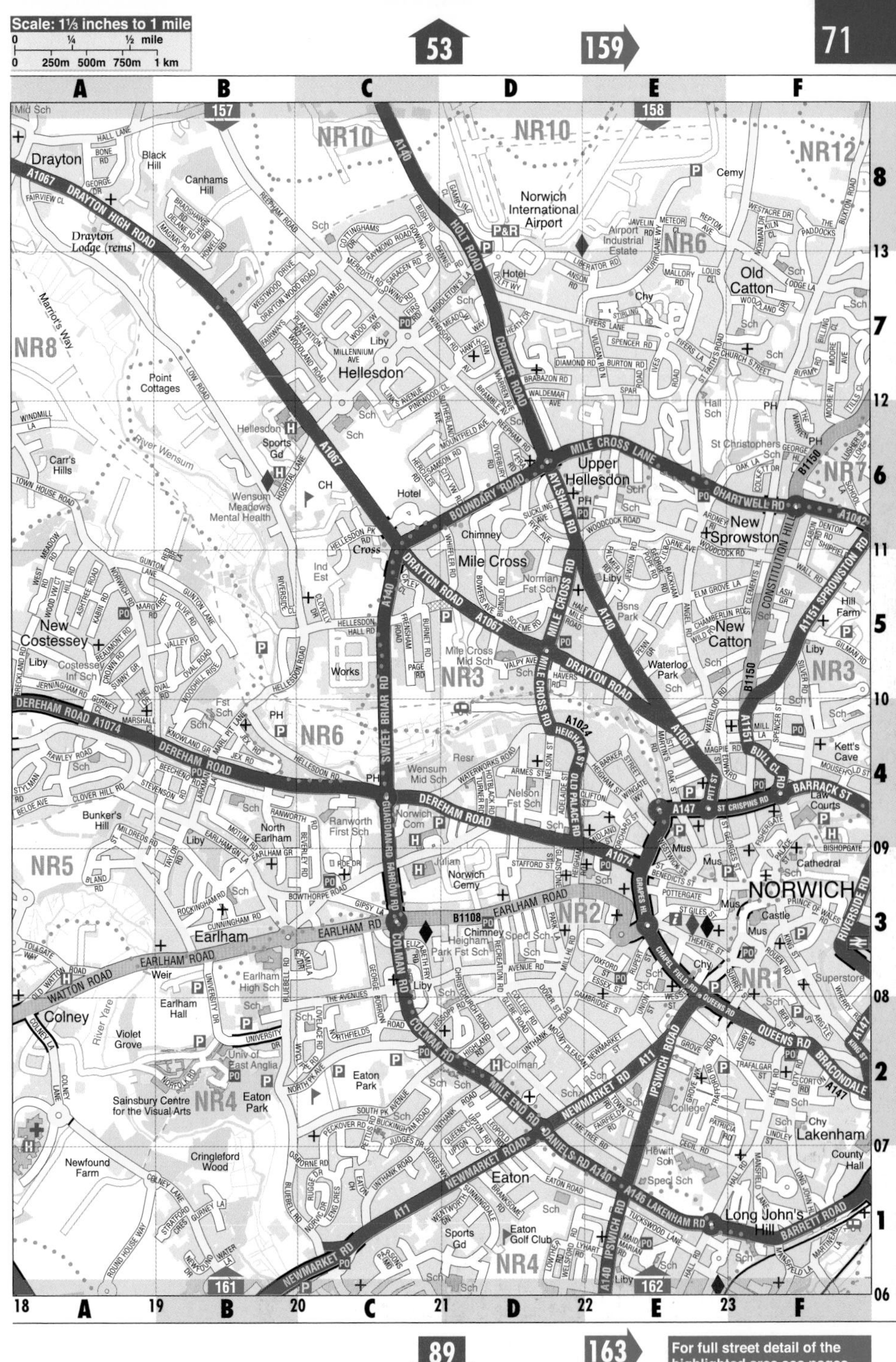

◀ 158   54

D6
1 ALTONGATE
2 HALLGATE
3 NORTHGATE
4 BROAD VW
5 BARKER WAY
6 BEECHBANK DR
7 HEATHERWOOD CL
8 ST DAVIDS DR
9 HEATH RD

D5
1 WOODLANDS CRES
2 LUCAS CT
3 GUNNER CL
4 FIENNES RD
5 DOWSING CT
6 FAIRFAX DR
7 LYNN CL
8 LEVEN CL
9 JOYCE WAY
10 MARVELL CL

Scale: 1⅓ inches to 1 mile
0   ¼   ½   mile
0   250m   500m   750m   1 km

E7
1 WILDE RD
2 FULLER CL
3 TAGG WAY
4 WEBB DR
5 WILLOUGHBY WAY
6 LUSCOMBE WAY
7 CANFOR RD
8 PALMER RD
9 BURTON DR
10 VERA CL
11 BERNARD CL
12 CORNWALL CL

Rackheath
1 BASEY RD
2 BIDWELL RD
3 LIBERATOR CL
4 MISSION RD
5 FITZMAURICE CT

New Rackheath

NR12 • NR6 • NR7 • NR13 • NR1 • NR14

Salhouse
Oak Tree Business Park
Mousehold Farm
Thorpe End
Great Plumstead

E4
1 MAIDENS CL
2 DALBIER CL
3 BUNYAN CL
4 EDGEHILL
5 PEACHMAN WAY

Thorpe St Andrew
Dussindale Park
Thorpe Hamlet
Postwick
Trowse Newton

D3
1 HIGHFIELD CL
2 PRIMROSE CRES
3 PRIMROSE CT
4 BIRCHWOOD
5 ST ANDREWS AVE

D4
1 MONTROSE CT
2 ASSOCIATION WAY
3 NEWCASTLE CL
4 FLEETWOOD DR
5 PARLIAMENT CT
6 HOPTON CL
7 MARSTON MOOR
8 MINION CL
9 CULVERIN CL
10 TURNHAM GN
11 SAKER CL
12 COMMONWEALTH WAY
13 DUSSINDALE DR
14 INDEPENDENT WAY
15 WINCEBY CL
16 ROWTON HEATH
17 ROUNDWAY DOWN
18 LENTHALL CL
19 HAMPDEN DR
20 NEWBURY WAY
21 WINSTANLEY RD
22 NEWARK CL
23 NASEBY WAY
24 LAUD CL
25 IRETON CL
26 ROUNDHEAD CT
27 DRAGOON CL
28 ROYALIST DR
29 MUSKETEER WAY
30 CAVALIER CL
31 MARY CHAPMAN CL
32 EASTERN CL

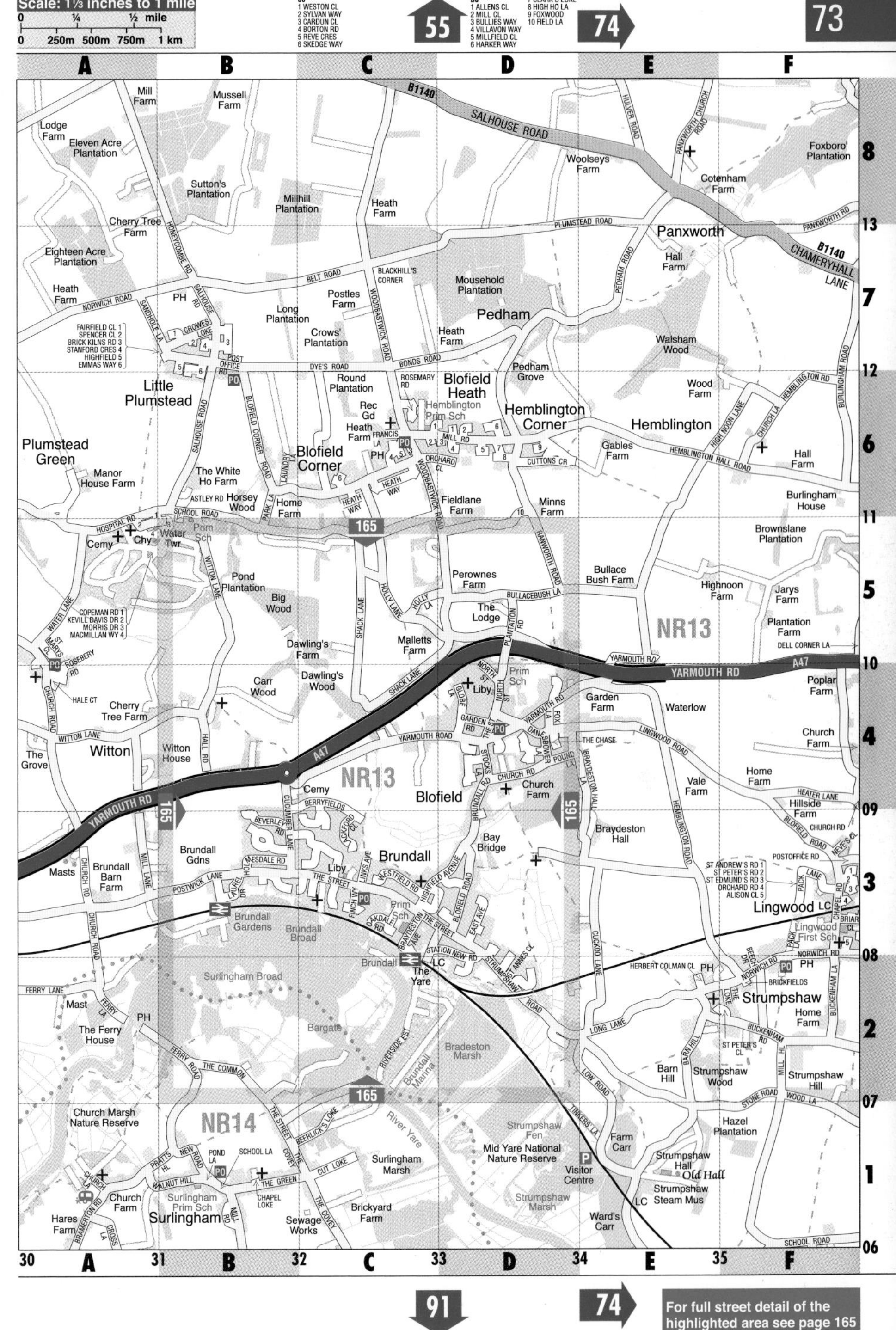

B8
1 HARROLD CL
2 PHEASANT WK
3 OAKFIELD DR
4 BROADACRES

73
56

Scale: 1⅓ inches to 1 mile

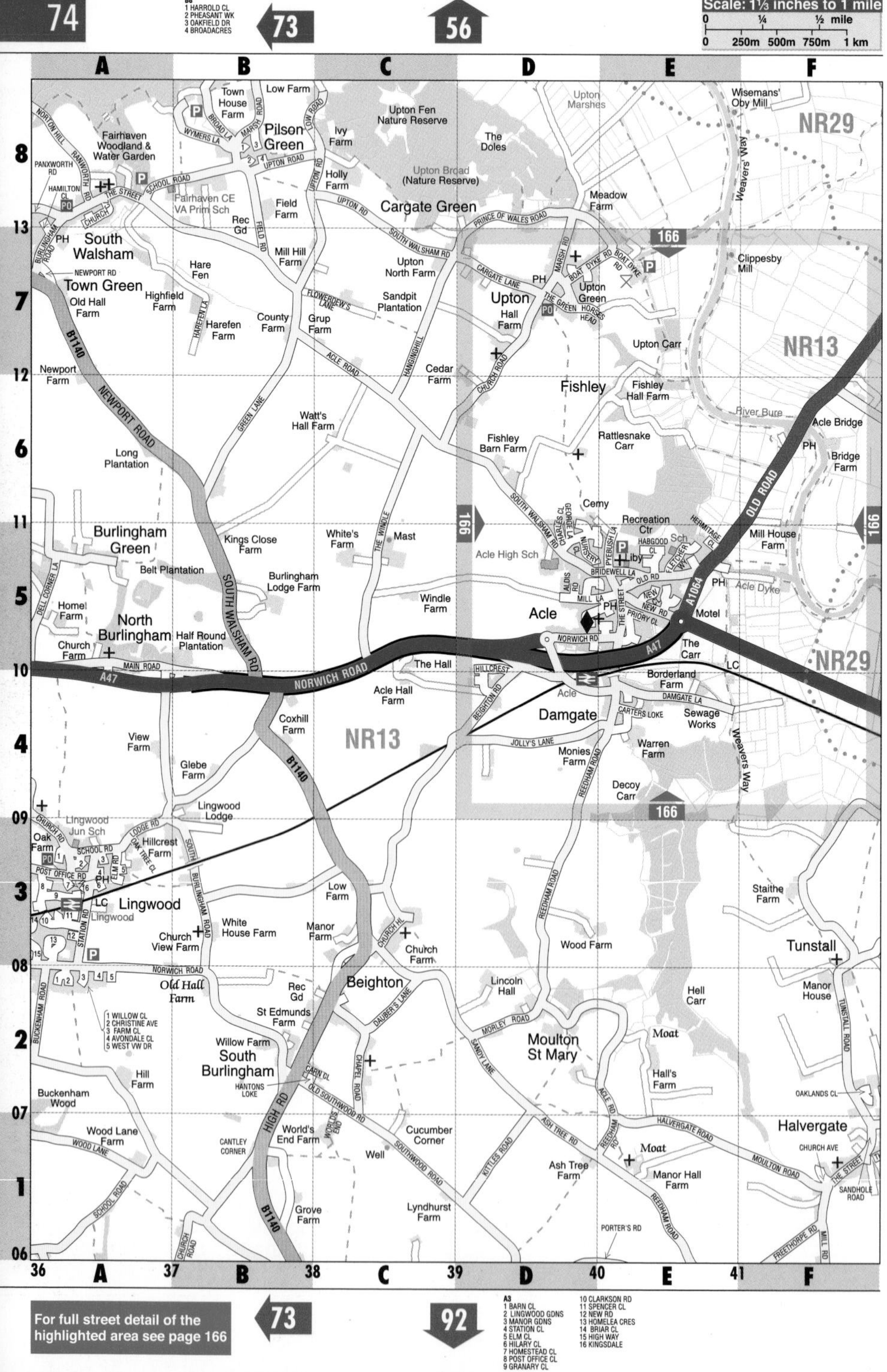
South Walsham
Pilson Green
Cargate Green
Upton
Fishley
Acle
Damgate
Burlingham Green
North Burlingham
Lingwood
Beighton
South Burlingham
Moulton St Mary
Tunstall
Halvergate
NR29
NR13
Upton Fen Nature Reserve
Upton Broad (Nature Reserve)
River Bure
Acle Bridge
NORWICH ROAD
NEWPORT ROAD
SOUTH WALSHAM RD
REEDHAM ROAD
OLD ROAD

For full street detail of the highlighted area see page 166

73
92

A3
1 BARN CL
2 LINGWOOD GDNS
3 MANOR GDNS
4 STATION CL
5 ELM CL
6 HILARY CL
7 HOMESTEAD CL
8 POST OFFICE CL
9 GRANARY CL
10 CLARKSON RD
11 SPENCER CL
12 NEW RD
13 HOMELEA CRES
14 BRIAR CL
15 HIGH WAY
16 KINGSDALE

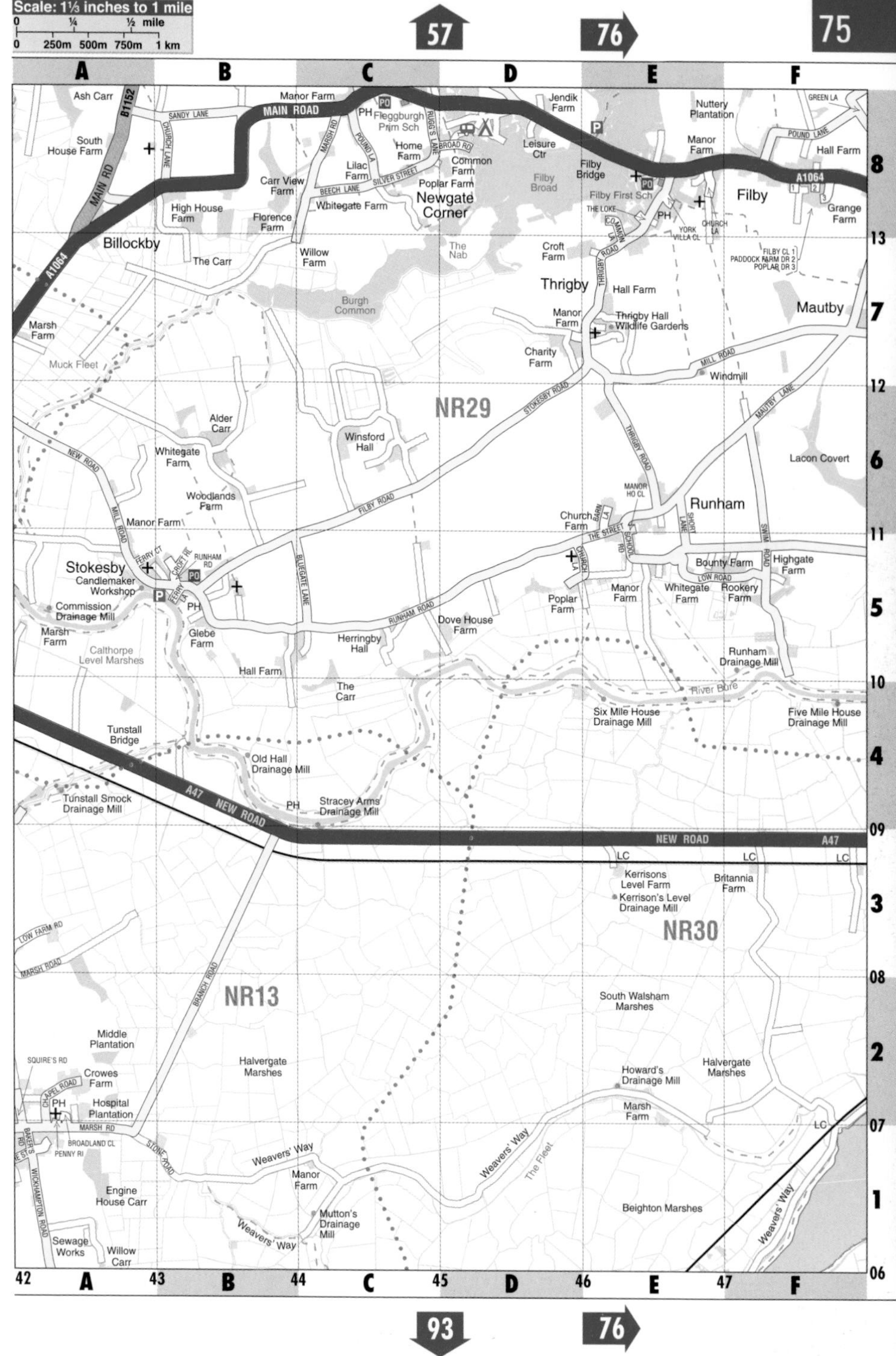
Scale: 1⅓ inches to 1 mile
0 ¼ ½ mile
0 250m 500m 750m 1 km
57
76
A B C D E F
Ash Carr
Manor Farm
MAIN ROAD
Flegg Burgh Prim Sch
Jendik Farm
Nuttery Plantation
GREEN LA
SANDY LANE
B1152
South House Farm
CHURCH LANE
MARSH RD
POUND LA
RUGG'S LANE
Home Farm
BROAD RD
Common Farm
Leisure Ctr
Manor Farm
POUND LANE
Hall Farm
Carr View Farm
Lilac Farm
SILVER STREET
Poplar Farm
Filby Broad
Filby Bridge
A1064
MAIN RD
BEECH LANE
Whitegate Farm
Newgate Corner
Filby First Sch
Filby
Grange Farm
High House Farm
Florence Farm
THE LOKE
COMMON LA
YORK VILLA CL
CHURCH LA
Billockby
The Carr
Willow Farm
The Nab
Croft Farm
FILBY CL 1
PADDOCK FARM DR 2
POPLAR DR 3
THRIGBY ROAD
Thrigby
Hall Farm
Burgh Common
Marsh Farm
Manor Farm
Thrigby Hall Wildlife Gardens
Mautby
Charity Farm
MILL ROAD
Muck Fleet
Windmill
STOKESBY ROAD
NR29
MAUTBY LANE
Alder Carr
Winsford Hall
Whitegate Farm
NEW ROAD
THRIGBY ROAD
Lacon Covert
Woodlands Farm
FILBY ROAD
MANOR HO CL
Runham
Manor Farm
MILL ROAD
Church Farm
BARN LA
SHORT LANE
THE STREET
SCHOOL RD
SWIM ROAD
FERRY CT
CROFT HL
RUNHAM RD
Stokesby
CHURCH LA
Bounty Farm
Highgate Farm
Candlemaker Workshop
BLUEGATE LANE
LOW ROAD
FERRY LA
Commission Drainage Mill
PH
Poplar Farm
Manor Farm
Whitegate Farm
Rookery Farm
RUNHAM ROAD
Dove House Farm
Marsh Farm
Glebe Farm
Calthorpe Level Marshes
Herringby Hall
Runham Drainage Mill
Hall Farm
The Carr
River Bure
Six Mile House Drainage Mill
Five Mile House Drainage Mill
Tunstall Bridge
Old Hall Drainage Mill
A47 NEW ROAD
Tunstall Smock Drainage Mill
Stracey Arms Drainage Mill
NEW ROAD A47
LC
Kerrisons Level Farm
Kerrison's Level Drainage Mill
Britannia Farm
LOW FARM RD
NR30
MARSH ROAD
BRANCH ROAD
NR13
South Walsham Marshes
Middle Plantation
SQUIRE'S RD
Halvergate Marshes
Crowes Farm
CHAPEL ROAD
Howard's Drainage Mill
Halvergate Marshes
Hospital Plantation
Marsh Farm
MARSH RD
BROADLAND CL
PENNY RI
BAKERS RD
STONE ROAD
Weavers' Way
Manor Farm
Weavers' Way
The Fleet
Engine House Carr
WICKHAMPTON ROAD
Mutton's Drainage Mill
Beighton Marshes
Weavers' Way
Sewage Works
Willow Carr
Weavers' Way
8 13 7 12 6 11 5 10 4 09 3 08 2 07 1 06
42 43 44 45 46 47
93
76

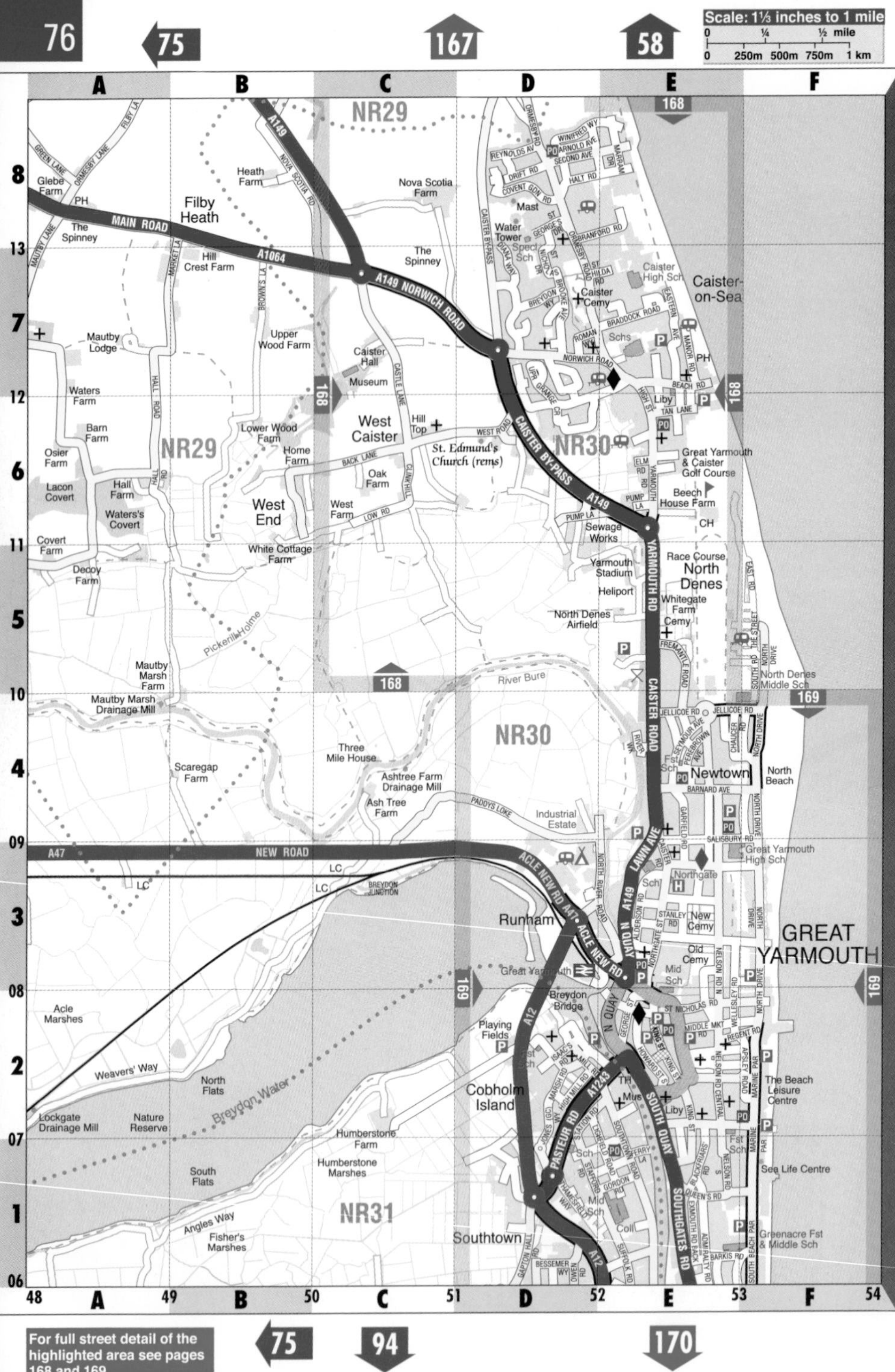

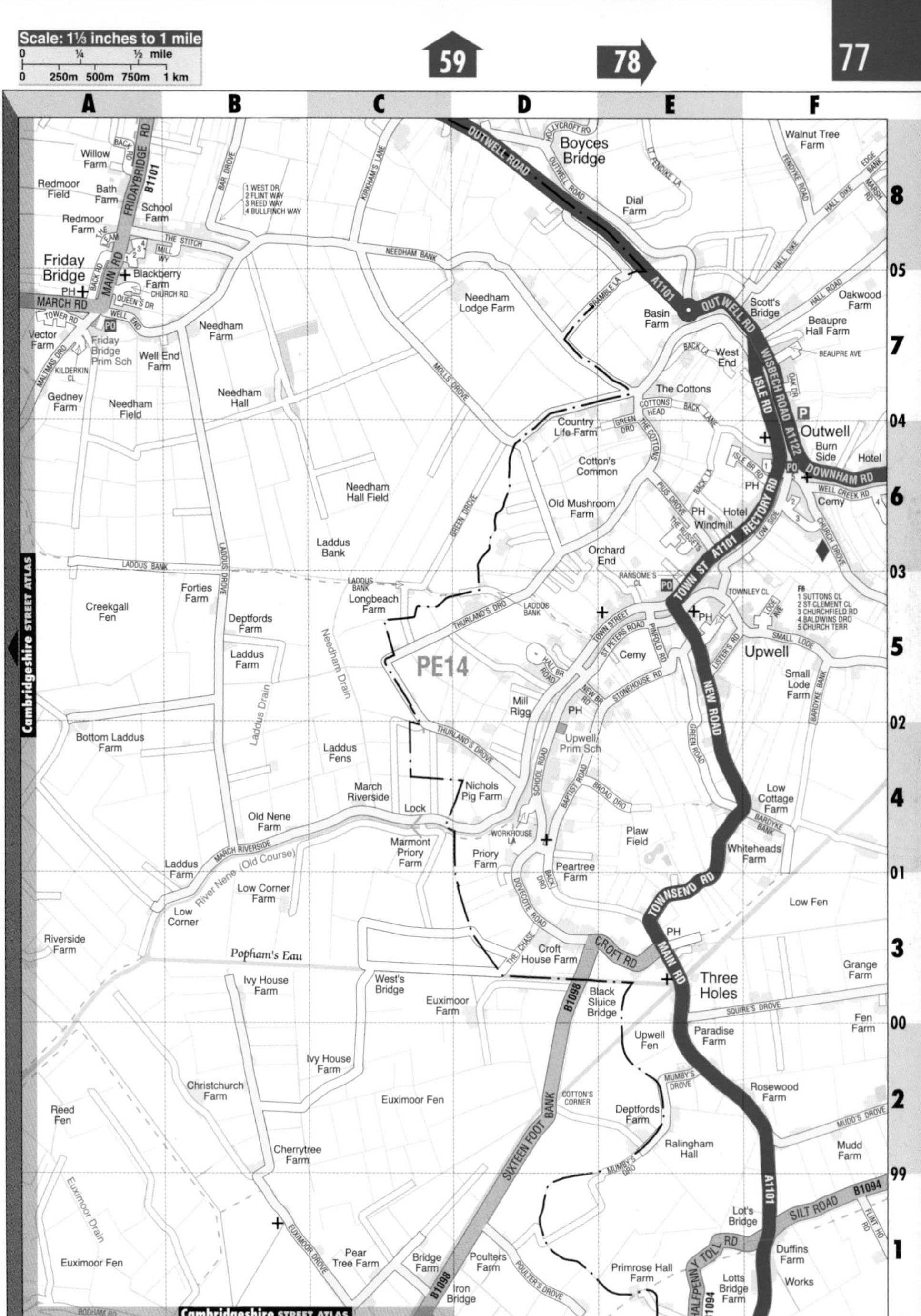

Scale: 1⅓ inches to 1 mile
0 ¼ ½ mile
0 250m 500m 750m 1 km
59
78
A B C D E F
8 05 7 04 6 03 5 02 4 01 3 00 2 99 1 98
46 47 48 49 50 51
Willow Farm
Redmoor Field
Bath Farm
Redmoor Farm
School Farm
Friday Bridge
Blackberry Farm
PH
MARCH RD
FRIDAYBRIDGE RD
B1101
MAIN RD
BACK RD
THE STITCH
MILL WY
CHURCH RD
QUEEN'S DR
WELL END
TOWER RD
PO
Vector Farm
Friday Bridge Prim Sch
Well End Farm
KILDERKIN CL
MALTMAS DRO
Gedney Farm
Needham Field
BAR DROVE
1 WEST DR
2 FLINT WAY
3 REED WAY
4 BULLFINCH WAY
Needham Farm
Needham Hall
KIRKHAM'S LANE
NEEDHAM BANK
Needham Lodge Farm
MOLLS DROVE
Needham Hall Field
GREEN DROVE
Laddus Bank
LADDUS BANK
LADDUS DROVE
Creekgall Fen
Forties Farm
Deptfords Farm
Laddus Farm
Laddus Drain
Needham Drain
Longbeach Farm
PE14
THURLAND'S DRO
Bottom Laddus Farm
Laddus Fens
THURLAND'S DROVE
March Riverside
Lock
Nichols Pig Farm
Old Nene Farm
MARCH RIVERSIDE
River Nene (Old Course)
Marmont Priory Farm
Laddus Farm
Low Corner Farm
Low Corner
Priory Farm
WORKHOUSE LA
Riverside Farm
Popham's Eau
Ivy House Farm
West's Bridge
Euximoor Farm
Ivy House Farm
Christchurch Farm
Euximoor Fen
Reed Fen
Cherrytree Farm
Euximoor Drain
Euximoor Fen
EUXIMOOR DROVE
Pear Tree Farm
Bridge Farm
Poulters Farm
POULTER'S DROVE
Iron Bridge
RODHAM RD
SIXTEEN FOOT BANK
B1098
COTTON'S CORNER
Cambridgeshire STREET ATLAS
OUTWELL ROAD
HOLLYCROFT RD
Boyces Bridge
OUTWELL ROAD
FENDIKE LA
Dial Farm
A1101
BRAMBLE LA
Basin Farm
OUT WELL RD
Scott's Bridge
West End
BACK LA
The Cottons
COTTONS HEAD
BACK LANE
Country Life Farm
GREEN DRO
THE COTTONS
Cotton's Common
Old Mushroom Farm
PIUS DROVE
THE RUSSETS
BACK LA
PH
Windmill
Hotel
Orchard End
RANSOME'S CL
PO
LADDUS BANK
TOWN STREET
ST PETERS ROAD
PINFOLD RD
Cemy
HALL BR ROAD
Mill Rigg
NEW BR RD
STONEHOUSE RD
PH
Upwell Prim Sch
SCHOOL ROAD
BAPTIST ROAD
BROAD DRO
GREEN ROAD
NEW ROAD
Plaw Field
Peartree Farm
BACK DRO
DOVECOTE ROAD
THE CHASE
Croft House Farm
CROFT RD
TOWNSEND RD
MAIN RD
PH
Three Holes
Black Sluice Bridge
Upwell Fen
MUMBY'S DROVE
Deptfords Farm
Ralingham Hall
MUMBY'S DRO
Primrose Hall Farm
Walnut Tree Farm
FENDYKE ROAD
EDGE BANK
MARSH RD
HALL DIKE
HALL ROAD
Oakwood Farm
Beaupre Hall Farm
BEAUPRE AVE
WISBECH ROAD
ISLE RD
A1122
OAK DR
P
Outwell
Burn Side
Hotel
ISLE BR RD
DOWNHAM RD
PO
PH
WELL CREEK RD
Cemy
CHURCH DROVE
LOW SIDE
RECTORY RD
TOWN ST
A1101
TOWNLEY CL
LODE AVE
F6
1 SUTTONS CL
2 ST CLEMENT CL
3 CHURCHFIELD RD
4 BALDWINS DRO
5 CHURCH TERR
PH
LISTER'S RD
SMALL LODE
Upwell
Small Lode Farm
BARDYKE BANK
Low Cottage Farm
BARDYKE BANK
Whiteheads Farm
Low Fen
Grange Farm
SQUIRE'S DROVE
Paradise Farm
Fen Farm
Rosewood Farm
MUDD'S DROVE
Mudd Farm
SILT ROAD
B1094
FLINT HO RD
Lot's Bridge
HALFPENNY TOLL RD
B1094
Duffins Farm
Lotts Bridge Farm
Works

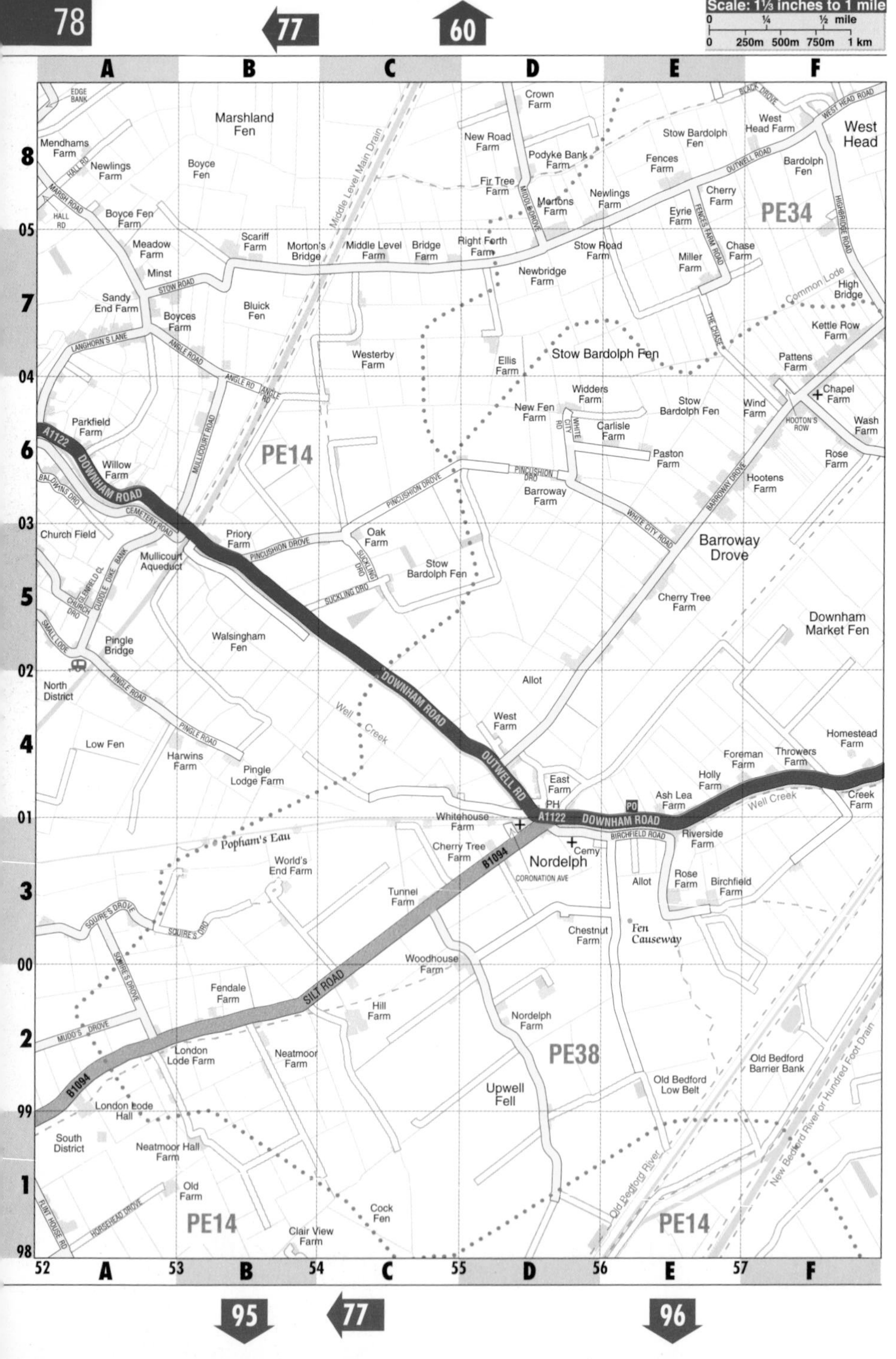
77
60
Scale: 1⅓ inches to 1 mile
0
¼
½ mile
250m
500m
750m
1 km
A
B
C
D
E
F
8
05
7
04
6
03
5
02
4
01
3
00
2
99
1
98
52
53
54
55
56
57
EDGE BANK
Marshland Fen
Crown Farm
New Road Farm
Podyke Bank Farm
Fir Tree Farm
Mortons Farm
Newlings Farm
Stow Bardolph Fen
Fences Farm
West Head Farm
West Head
Bardolph Fen
Cherry Farm
Eyrie Farm
PE34
Mendhams Farm
Newlings Farm
Boyce Fen
HALL RD
MARSH ROAD
Boyce Fen Farm
Meadow Farm
Minst
Scariff Farm
Morton's Bridge
Middle Level Farm
Bridge Farm
Right Forth Farm
Stow Road Farm
Newbridge Farm
Miller Farm
Chase Farm
Middle Level Main Drain
MIDDLE DROVE
FENCES FARM ROAD
HIGHBRIDGE ROAD
OUTWELL ROAD
WEST HEAD ROAD
BLACK DROVE
Sandy End Farm
Boyces Farm
STOW ROAD
Bluick Fen
Common Lode
High Bridge
Kettle Row Farm
THE CHASE
LANGHORN'S LANE
ANGLE ROAD
ANGLE RD
Westerby Farm
Ellis Farm
Stow Bardolph Fen
Pattens Farm
Widders Farm
Chapel Farm
New Fen Farm
Carlisle Farm
Stow Bardolph Fen
Wind Farm
HOOTON'S ROW
Wash Farm
Parkfield Farm
MULLICOURT ROAD
WHITE CITY RD
PE14
Paston Farm
Rose Farm
A1122
DOWNHAM ROAD
Willow Farm
PINCUSHION DROVE
PINCUSHION DRO
Barroway Farm
Hootens Farm
BARROWAY DROVE
BALDWINS DRO
CEMETERY ROAD
WHITE CITY ROAD
Church Field
Priory Farm
Oak Farm
Barroway Drove
Mullicourt Aqueduct
PINCUSHION DROVE
SUCKLING DRO
Stow Bardolph Fen
GLENFIELD CL
PUDDLE DIKE BANK
CHURCH DRO
SUCKLING DRO
Cherry Tree Farm
Downham Market Fen
SMALL LODE
Pingle Bridge
Walsingham Fen
North District
PINGLE ROAD
Allot
Well Creek
DOWNHAM ROAD
West Farm
Low Fen
PINGLE ROAD
Harwins Farm
Pingle Lodge Farm
OUTWELL RD
East Farm
Homestead Farm
Foreman Farm
Throwers Farm
Holly Farm
PH
Ash Lea Farm
Creek Farm
PO
Well Creek
Whitehouse Farm
A1122
DOWNHAM ROAD
Popham's Eau
Cherry Tree Farm
B1094
Cemy
BIRCHFIELD ROAD
Riverside Farm
Nordelph
World's End Farm
CORONATION AVE
Allot
Rose Farm
Birchfield Farm
Tunnel Farm
SQUIRE'S DROVE
SQUIRE'S DRO
Chestnut Farm
Fen Causeway
Woodhouse Farm
SQUIRE'S DROVE
Fendale Farm
SILT ROAD
Hill Farm
MUDD'S DROVE
Nordelph Farm
London Lode Farm
Neatmoor Farm
PE38
Old Bedford Barrier Bank
Old Bedford Low Belt
B1094
Upwell Fell
London Lode Hall
South District
Neatmoor Hall Farm
Old Bedford River
New Bedford River or Hundred Foot Drain
Old Farm
FLINT HOUSE RD
HORSEHEAD DROVE
PE14
Cock Fen
PE14
Clair View Farm
95
77
96

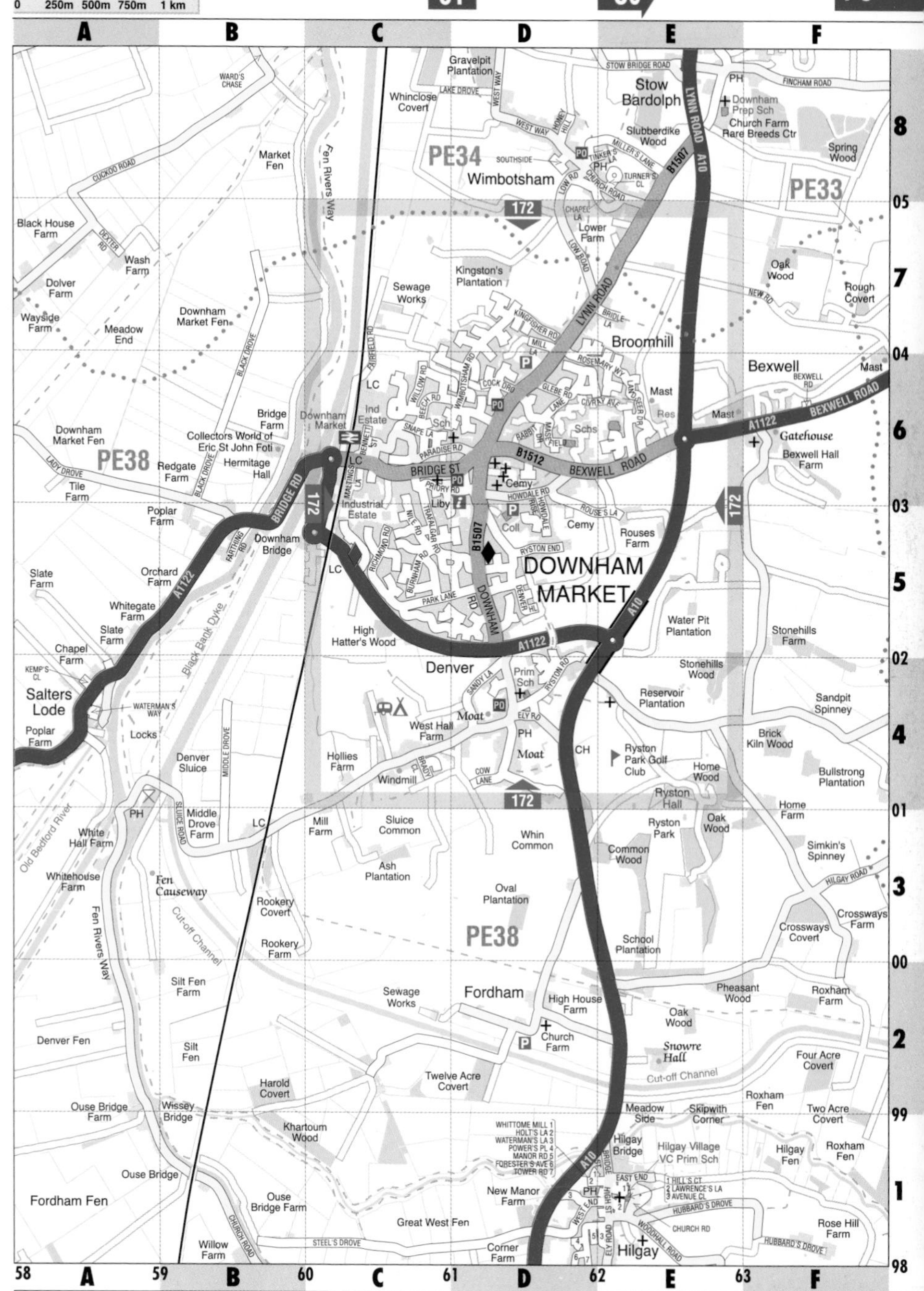

A B C D E F

8

WARD'S CHASE

Gravelpit Plantation

STOW BRIDGE ROAD

Whinclose Covert

Market Fen

LANE DROVE

WEST WAY

Stow Bardolph

FINCHAM ROAD

PH

+ Downham Prep Sch
Church Farm Rare Breeds Ctr

Spring Wood

PE34
Wimbotsham

SOUTHSIDE

Slubberdike Wood

MILLER'S LANE

PO

PE33

8

CUCKOO ROAD

Black House Farm

Wash Farm

DOVE RD

172

CHAPEL LA

Lower Farm

LOW ROAD

PH

HIGH
STREET
CHURCH
ROAD

TURNER'S CL

05

Oak Wood

7

Dolver Farm

Wayside Farm

Meadow End

Downham Market Fen

Kingston's Plantation

NEW RD

Rough Covert

7

BLACK DROVE

Sewage Works

KINGER RD

LYNN ROAD

A10

MILL RD

Broomhill

ROSEMARY RD

Bexwell

BEXWELL RD

Mast

04

Downham Market Fen

PE38

Redgate Farm

LANE DROVE

Bridge Farm

Collectors World of Eric St John Foti

Hermitage Hall

Downham Market

LC

Ind Estate

Sch

PARADISE RD

COCK RD

GLEB RD

PO

CEMY RD

LANCASTER RD

Schs

Mast
Res

Mast

A1122

BEXWELL ROAD

Gatehouse

Bexwell Hall Farm

6

Tile Farm

Poplar Farm

BRIDGE RD

172

LC

BRIDGE ST

B1512

Cemy

HOWDALE RD

ROUSE'S LA

03

172

6

Slate Farm

Whitegate Farm

Orchard Farm

RAFTING RD

Downham Bridge

Industrial Estate

RICHMOND RD

B1507

Liby

Coll

RYSTON END

Cemy

Rouses Plantation

5

A1122

Black Bank Dyke

LC

PARK LANE

DOWNHAM RD

DOWNHAM MARKET

A10

Water Pit Plantation

Stonehills Farm

02

Slate Farm

Chapel Farm

KEMP'S CL

Salters Lode

Poplar Farm

WATERMAN'S WAY

Locks

High Hatter's Wood

Denver

SANDY LA

Prim Sch

PO

ELY RD

Stonehills Wood

Reservoir Plantation

Sandpit Spinney

Brick Kiln Wood

4

SLUICE ROAD

MIDDLE DROVE

Denver Sluice

Hollies Farm

Windmill

West Hall Farm

Moat

COW LANE

PH

Moat

CH

Ryston Park Golf Club

Home Wood

Bullstrong Plantation

Old Bedford River

PH

White Hall Farm

Middle Drove Farm

LC

Mill Farm

Sluice Common

Ash Plantation

172

Whin Common

Ryston Park

Oak Wood

Ryston Hall

Common Wood

Home Farm

Simkin's Spinney

HILGAY ROAD

01

3

Whitehouse Farm

Fen Causeway

Cut-off Channel

Rookery Covert

Rookery Farm

Oval Plantation

PE38

School Plantation

Crossways Covert

Crossways Farm

00

Denver Fen

Silt Fen Farm

Sewage Works

Fordham

High House Farm

Oak Wood

Pheasant Wood

Roxham Farm

2

Silt Fen

PO

Church Farm

Snowre Hall

Cut-off Channel

Four Acre Covert

Ouse Bridge Farm

Wissey Bridge

Harold Covert

Khartoum Wood

Twelve Acre Covert

Meadow Side

Skipwith Corner

Roxham Fen

Two Acre Covert

99

Fordham Fen

Willow Farm

Ouse Bridge

Ouse Bridge Farm

STEEL'S DROVE

CHURCH ROAD

WHITTOME MILL 1
HOLT'S LA 2
WATERMAN'S LA 3
POWER'S PL 4
MANOR RD 5
FORESTER'S AVE 6
TOWER RD 7

Great West Fen

New Manor Farm

Corner Farm

A10

Hilgay Bridge

PH

EAST END

Hilgay Village VC Prim Sch

1 HILL'S CT.
2 LAWRENCE'S LA
3 AVENUE CL

HUBBARD'S DROVE

CHURCH RD

HUBBARD'S DROVE

Hilgay Fen

Roxham Fen

Rose Hill Farm

1

Hilgay

98

A B C D E F

58 59 60 61 62 63

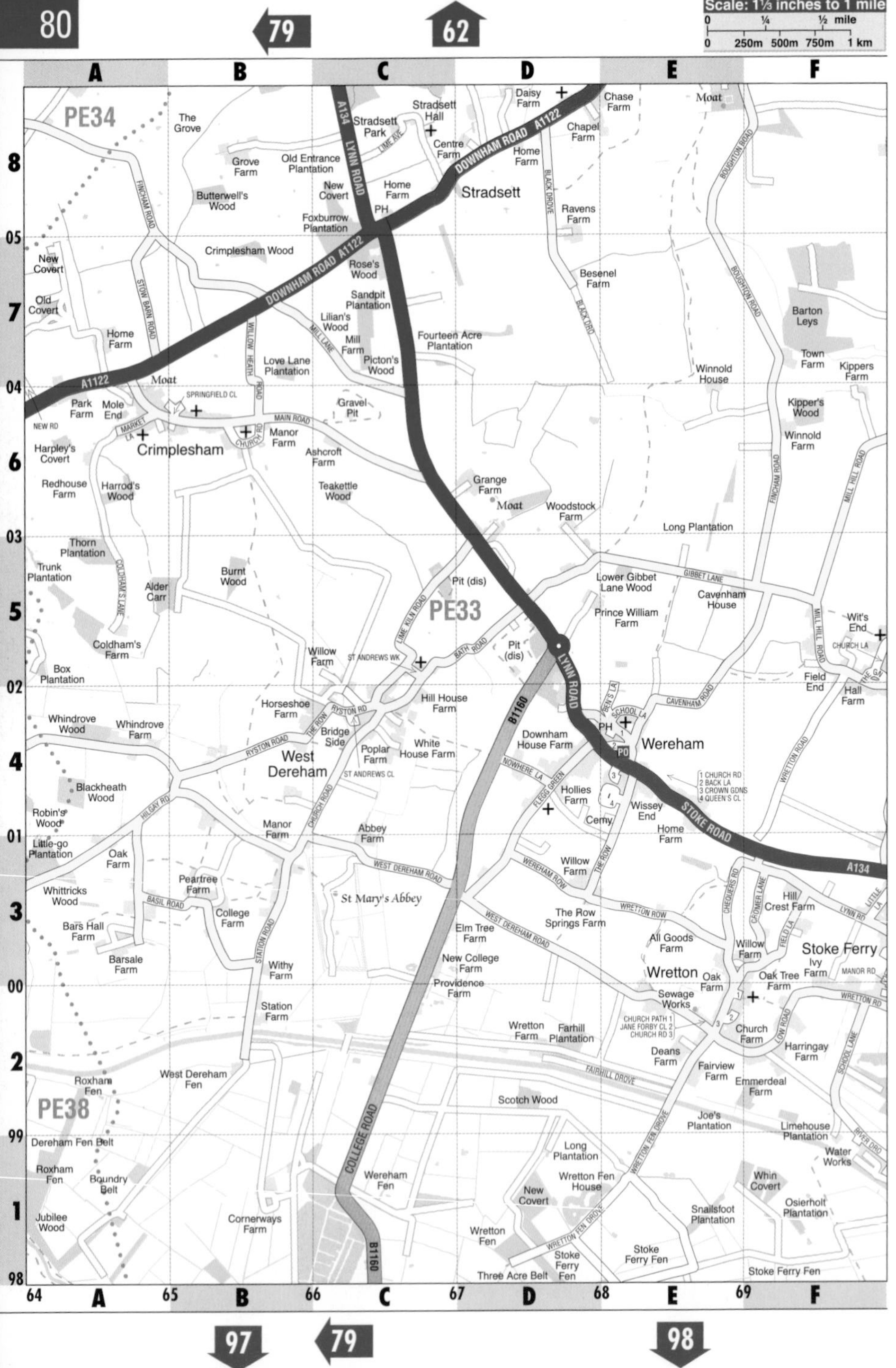
79
62
Scale: 1⅓ inches to 1 mile
0 ¼ ½ mile
0 250m 500m 750m 1 km
A B C D E F
PE34
The Grove
Grove Farm
Butterwell's Wood
Old Entrance Plantation
Stradsett Park
Stradsett Hall
LIME AVE
Centre Farm
Daisy Farm
Chase Farm
Moat
Chapel Farm
Home Farm
DOWNHAM ROAD A1122
A134 LYNN ROAD
New Covert
Home Farm
Stradsett
PH
Foxburrow Plantation
BLACK DROVE
Ravens Farm
BOUGHTON ROAD
FINCHAM ROAD
New Covert
Crimplesham Wood
Rose's Wood
Besenel Farm
Sandpit Plantation
Old Covert
STOW BARN ROAD
Lilian's Wood
MILL LANE
Mill Farm
Barton Leys
Home Farm
WILLOW HEATH ROAD
Love Lane Plantation
Picton's Wood
Fourteen Acre Plantation
BLACK DRO
Town Farm
Kippers Farm
Winnold House
A1122
Moat
SPRINGFIELD CL
Park Farm
Mole End
NEW RD
MARKET LA
Gravel Pit
MAIN ROAD
Kipper's Wood
Winnold Farm
CHURCH RD
Manor Farm
Harpley's Covert
Crimplesham
Ashcroft Farm
Redhouse Farm
Harrod's Wood
Teakettle Wood
Grange Farm
Moat
Woodstock Farm
MILL HILL ROAD
Long Plantation
Thorn Plantation
Trunk Plantation
COLDHAM'S LANE
Burnt Wood
Alder Carr
Pit (dis)
Lower Gibbet Lane Wood
GIBBET LANE
Cavenham House
LIME KILN ROAD
PE33
Prince William Farm
Wit's End
CHURCH LA
Coldham's Farm
Willow Farm
ST ANDREWS WK
BATH ROAD
Pit (dis)
LYNN ROAD
Box Plantation
Field End
Hall Farm
Horseshoe Farm
RYSTON RD
Hill House Farm
BEN'S LA
SCHOOL LA
CAVENHAM ROAD
Whindrove Wood
Whindrove Farm
THE ROW
Bridge Side
B1160
Downham House Farm
PH
Wereham
RYSTON ROAD
West Dereham
Poplar Farm
White House Farm
PO
NOWHERE LA
WRETTON ROAD
ST ANDREWS CL
FLEGG GREEN
1 CHURCH RD
2 BACK LA
3 CROWN GDNS
4 QUEEN'S CL
Blackheath Wood
Hollies Farm
Robin's Wood
HILGAY RD
CHURCH ROAD
Wissey End
STOKE ROAD
Cemy
Little-go Plantation
Manor Farm
Abbey Farm
Home Farm
Oak Farm
Willow Farm
WEST DEREHAM ROAD
WEREHAM ROW
THE ROW
A134
Whittricks Wood
Peartree Farm
BASIL ROAD
St Mary's Abbey
CHEQUERS RD
CROMER LANE
Hill Crest Farm
LYNN RD
LITTLE LA
College Farm
The Row Springs Farm
WRETTON ROW
Bars Hall Farm
WEST DEREHAM ROAD
Elm Tree Farm
All Goods Farm
FIELD LA
Willow Farm
Stoke Ferry
STATION ROAD
New College Farm
Barsale Farm
Withy Farm
Wretton
Oak Farm
Oak Tree Farm
Ivy Farm
MANOR RD
Providence Farm
Sewage Works
WRETTON RD
Station Farm
CHURCH PATH 1
JANE FORBY CL 2
CHURCH RD 3
Wretton Farm
Farhill Plantation
Church Farm
LOW ROAD
Harringay Farm
SCHOOL LANE
Deans Farm
West Dereham Fen
FAIRHILL DROVE
Fairview Farm
Emmerdeal Farm
Roxham Fen
PE38
Scotch Wood
WRETTON FEN DROVE
Joe's Plantation
Limehouse Plantation
RIVER DRO
Dereham Fen Belt
Long Plantation
Water Works
Roxham Fen
COLLEGE ROAD
Boundry Belt
Wereham Fen
Wretton Fen House
Whin Covert
New Covert
Snailsfoot Plantation
Osierholt Plantation
Jubilee Wood
Cornerways Farm
WRETTON FEN DROVE
Wretton Fen
Stoke Ferry Fen
B1160
Stoke Ferry Fen
Three Acre Belt
Stoke Ferry Fen
Stoke Ferry Fen
8
05
7
04
6
03
5
02
4
01
3
00
2
99
1
98
64 65 66 67 68 69
97
79
98

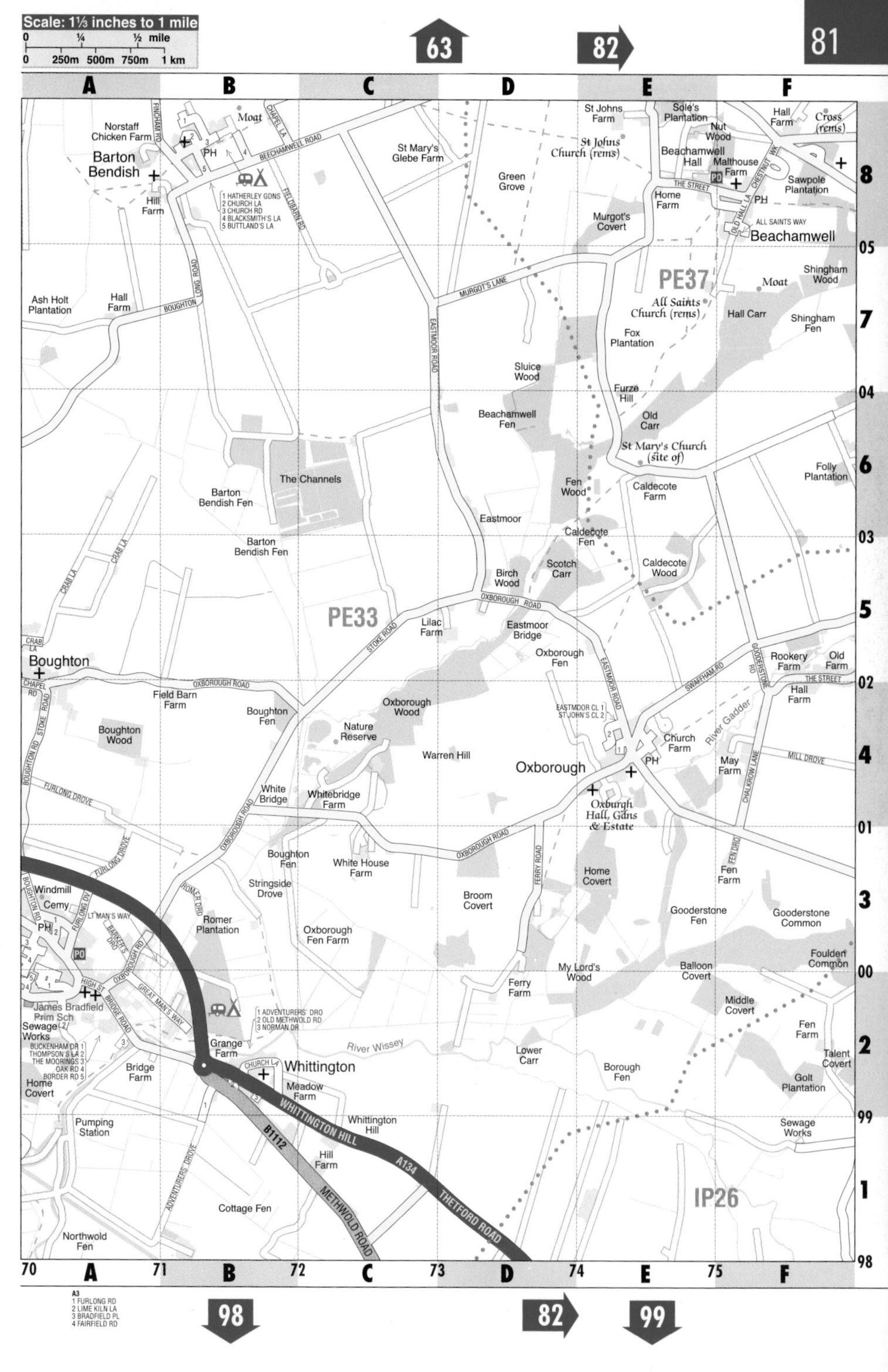
Scale: 1⅓ inches to 1 mile
0 ¼ ½ mile
0 250m 500m 750m 1 km
63
82
A B C D E F
8 05 7 04 6 03 5 02 4 01 3 00 2 99 1 98
70 71 72 73 74 75
Norstaff Chicken Farm
Barton Bendish
Moat
PH
Hill Farm
FINCHAM RD
CHAPEL LA
BEECHAMWELL ROAD
FIELDBARN RD
1 HATHERLEY GDNS
2 CHURCH LA
3 CHURCH RD
4 BLACKSMITH'S LA
5 BUTTLAND'S LA
St Mary's Glebe Farm
Green Grove
St Johns Farm
St Johns Church (rems)
Sole's Plantation
Nut Wood
Beachamwell Hall
Malthouse Farm
THE STREET
Home Farm
Hall Farm
Cross (rems)
Sawpole Plantation
CHESTNUT WK
OLD HALL LA
PH
ALL SAINTS WAY
Beachamwell
Murgot's Covert
PE37
Moat
Shingham Wood
All Saints Church (rems)
Hall Carr
Shingham Fen
Ash Holt Plantation
Hall Farm
BOUGHTON
LONG ROAD
MURGOT'S LANE
EASTMOOR ROAD
Fox Plantation
Sluice Wood
Furze Hill
Beachamwell Fen
Old Carr
St Mary's Church (site of)
Folly Plantation
The Channels
Barton Bendish Fen
Fen Wood
Caldecote Farm
Eastmoor
Caldecote Fen
Barton Bendish Fen
Scotch Carr
Caldecote Wood
Birch Wood
CRAB LA
OXBOROUGH ROAD
PE33
Lilac Farm
Eastmoor Bridge
STOKE ROAD
Oxborough Fen
Boughton
CHAPEL RD
OXBOROUGH ROAD
Field Barn Farm
Boughton Fen
Oxborough Wood
SWAFFHAM RD
Rookery Farm
Old Farm
GOODERSTONE RD
THE STREET
Hall Farm
EASTMOOR CL 1
ST JOHN'S CL 2
Boughton Wood
Nature Reserve
Warren Hill
Church Farm
River Gadder
MILL DROVE
PH
Oxborough
May Farm
BOUGHTON RD
STOKE ROAD
FURLONG DROVE
White Bridge
Whitebridge Farm
Oxburgh Hall, Gdns & Estate
CHALKROW LANE
OXBOROUGH RD
OXBOROUGH ROAD
Boughton Fen
White House Farm
FERRY ROAD
FEN DRO
Home Covert
Fen Farm
Windmill
Cemy
FURLONG DROVE
ROMER DRO
Stringside Drove
Broom Covert
Gooderstone Fen
Gooderstone Common
PH
LT MAN'S WAY
Romer Plantation
Oxborough Fen Farm
PO
OXBOROUGH RD
My Lord's Wood
Balloon Covert
Foulden Common
HIGH ST
GREAT MAN'S WAY
Ferry Farm
Middle Covert
James Bradfield Prim Sch
BRIDGE ROAD
1 ADVENTURERS' DRO
2 OLD METHWOLD RD
3 NORMAN DR
Fen Farm
Sewage Works
Grange Farm
River Wissey
Lower Carr
Talent Covert
BUCKENHAM DR 1
THOMPSON'S LA 2
THE MOORINGS 3
OAK RD 4
BORDER RD 5
Bridge Farm
CHURCH LA
Whittington
Borough Fen
Home Covert
Meadow Farm
Golt Plantation
WHITTINGTON HILL
Pumping Station
Whittington Hill
Sewage Works
B1112
A134
ADVENTURERS' DROVE
Hill Farm
METHWOLD ROAD
THETFORD ROAD
IP26
Cottage Fen
Northwold Fen
A3
1 FURLONG RD
2 LIME KILN LA
3 BRADFIELD PL
4 FAIRFIELD RD
98
82
99

81

64

Scale: 1½ inches to 1 mile

0   ¼   ½   mile
0   250m 500m 750m   1 km

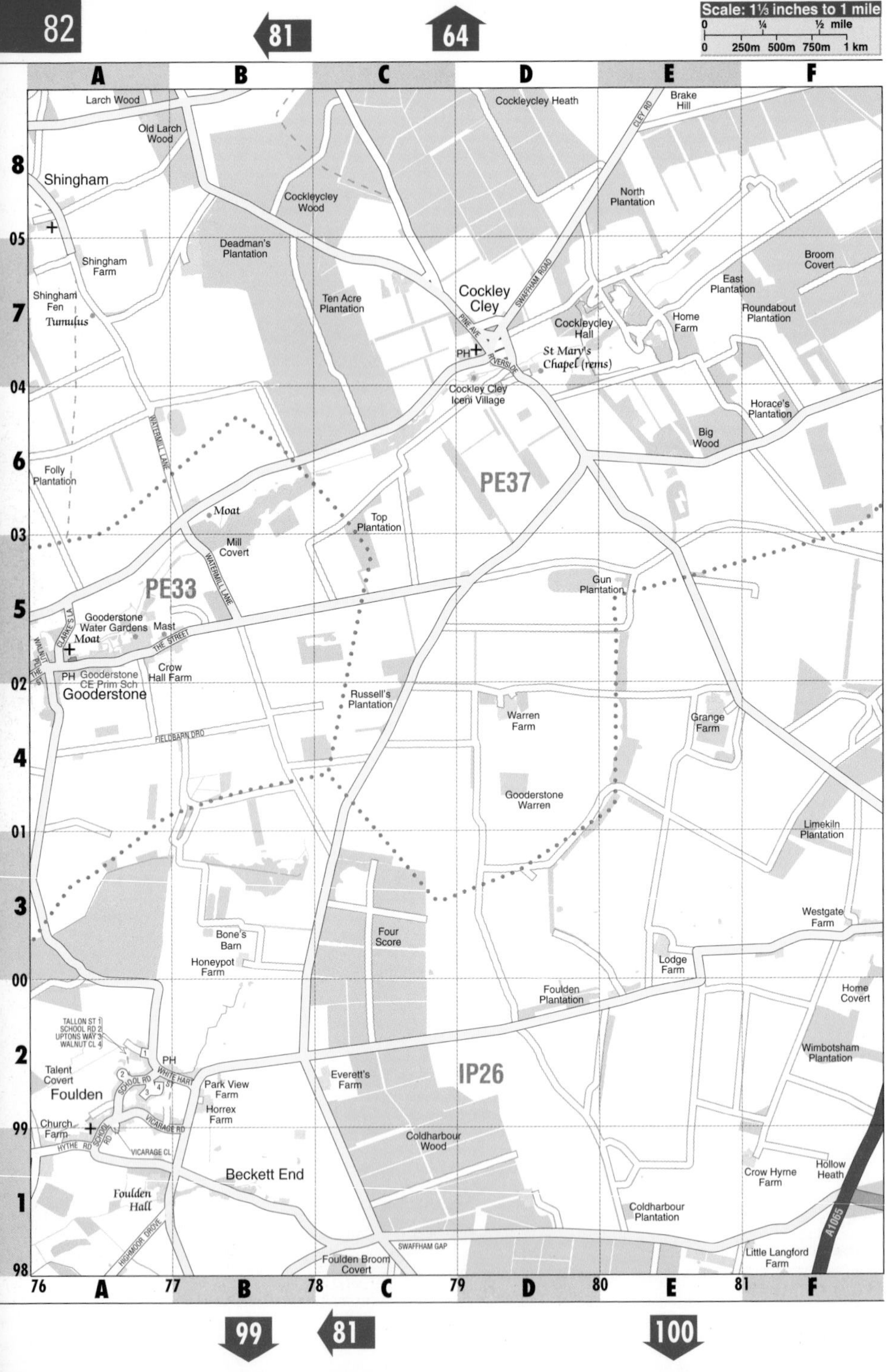

A   **B**   **C**   **D**   **E**   **F**

Larch Wood

Old Larch Wood

Cockleycley Heath

Brake Hill

8

Shingham

Cockleycley Wood

North Plantation

05

Deadman's Plantation

Shingham Farm

East Plantation

Broom Covert

7

Shingham Fen *Tumulus*

Ten Acre Plantation

Cockley Cley

Cockleycley Hall

Home Farm

Roundabout Plantation

PH

St Mary's Chapel (rems)

04

Cockley Cley Iceni Village

Horace's Plantation

6

Folly Plantation

Big Wood

WATERHALL LANE

PE37

Moat

Top Plantation

03

Mill Covert

Gun Plantation

PE33

WATERHALL LANE

5

Gooderstone Water Gardens Mast

THE STREET

Moat

CHURCH LA

02

PH Gooderstone CE Prim Sch

Crow Hall Farm

Russell's Plantation

Warren Farm

Grange Farm

Gooderstone

FIELDBARN DRO

4

Gooderstone Warren

Limekiln Plantation

01

3

Bone's Barn

Four Score

Westgate Farm

Honeypot Farm

Lodge Farm

00

Foulden Plantation

Home Covert

TALLON ST 1
SCHOOL RD 2
UPTONS WAY 3
WALNUT CL 4

2

Talent Covert

PH
WHITE HART

Park View Farm

Everett's Farm

IP26

Wimbotsham Plantation

Foulden

SCHOOL RD

Horrex Farm

99

Church Farm

VICARAGE RD

VICARAGE CL

Coldharbour Wood

Crow Hyrne Farm

Hollow Heath

A1065

1

Foulden Hall

Beckett End

Coldharbour Plantation

HIGHMOOR DROVE

98

Foulden Broom Covert

SWAFFHAM GAP

Little Langford Farm

76   **A**   **77**   **B**   **78**   **C**   **79**   **D**   **80**   **E**   **81**   **F**

99

81

100

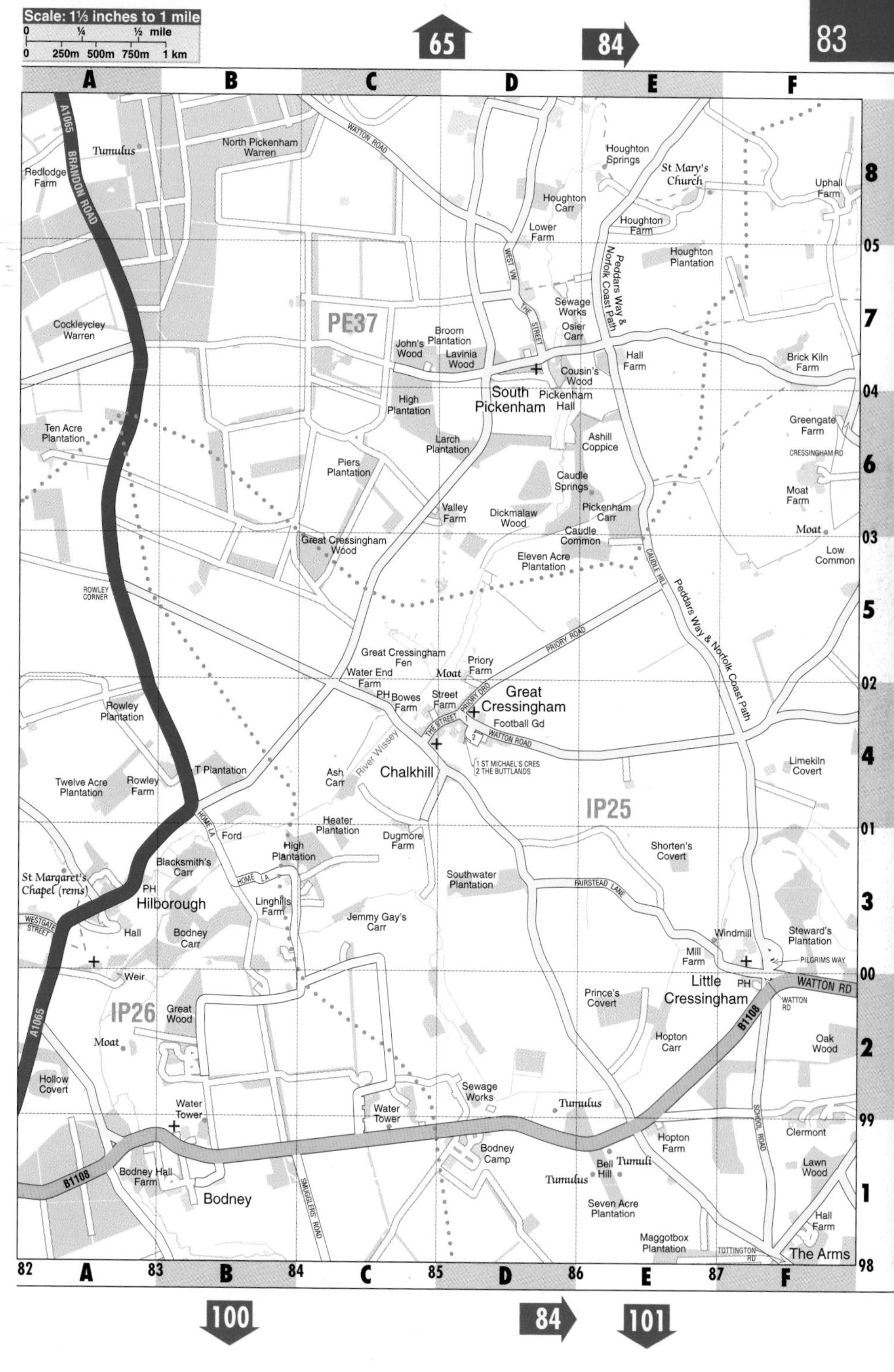
Scale: 1⅓ inches to 1 mile
0 ¼ ½ mile
0 250m 500m 750m 1 km
65
84
100
84
101
A B C D E F
8 05 7 04 6 03 5 02 4 01 3 00 2 99 1 98
82 83 84 85 86 87
PE37
IP25
IP26
A1065 BRANDON ROAD
Tumulus
North Pickenham Warren
Redlodge Farm
WATTON ROAD
Houghton Springs
St Mary's Church
Uphall Farm
Houghton Carr
Lower Farm
Houghton Farm
Houghton Plantation
WEST VW
Peddars Way & Norfolk Coast Path
Sewage Works
Osier Carr
THE STREET
Cockleycley Warren
Broom Plantation
John's Wood
Lavinia Wood
Cousin's Wood
Hall Farm
Brick Kiln Farm
South Pickenham
Pickenham Hall
High Plantation
Ten Acre Plantation
Larch Plantation
Ashill Coppice
Greengate Farm
CRESSINGHAM RD
Piers Plantation
Caudle Springs
Moat Farm
Valley Farm
Dickmalaw Wood
Pickenham Carr
Caudle Common
Moat
Great Cressingham Wood
Eleven Acre Plantation
Low Common
ROWLEY CORNER
CAUDLE HILL
PRIORY ROAD
Great Cressingham Fen
Priory Farm
Water End Farm
Moat
PH
Bowes Farm
Street Farm
PRIORY DRO
Great Cressingham
Rowley Plantation
THE STREET
Football Gd
WATTON ROAD
River Wissey
1 ST MICHAEL'S CRES
2 THE BUTTLANDS
Limekiln Covert
T Plantation
Ash Carr
Chalkhill
Twelve Acre Plantation
Rowley Farm
HOME LA
Ford
Heater Plantation
Dugmore Farm
High Plantation
Shorten's Covert
Blacksmith's Carr
St Margaret's Chapel (rems)
HOME LA
Southwater Plantation
FAIRSTEAD LANE
PH
Hilborough
Linghills Farm
Jemmy Gay's Carr
WESTGATE STREET
Hall
Bodney Carr
Windmill
Steward's Plantation
Mill Farm
PILGRIMS WAY
Weir
Little Cressingham
PH
WATTON RD
WATTON RD
Great Wood
Prince's Covert
B1108
Moat
Hopton Carr
Oak Wood
Hollow Covert
Sewage Works
Water Tower
Tumulus
Water Tower
SCHOOL ROAD
Hopton Farm
Clermont
Bodney Camp
Bell Hill
Tumuli
Bodney Hall Farm
Tumulus
Lawn Wood
B1108
SMUGGLERS' ROAD
Bodney
Seven Acre Plantation
Hall Farm
Maggotbox Plantation
TOTTINGTON RD
The Arms

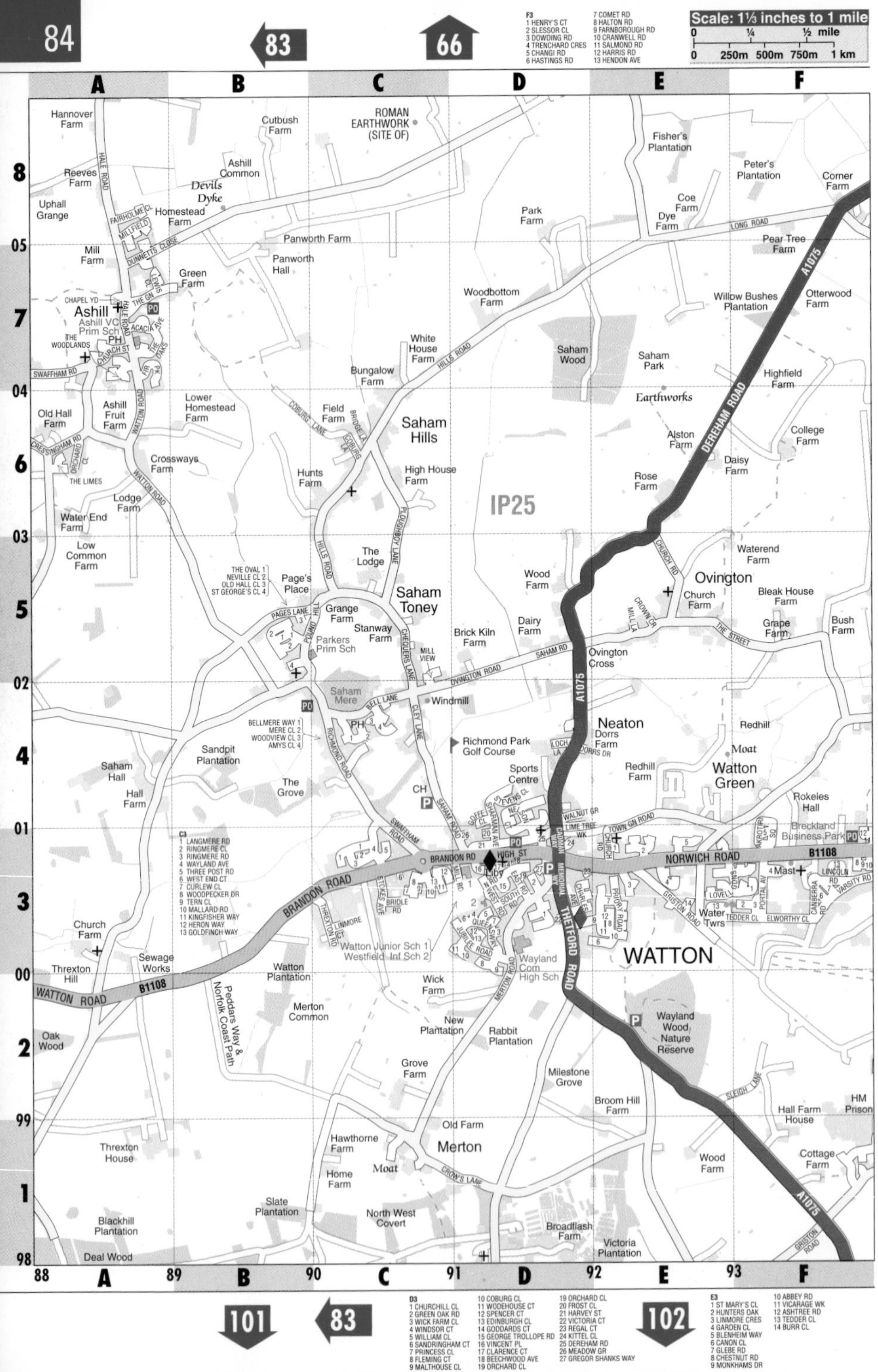

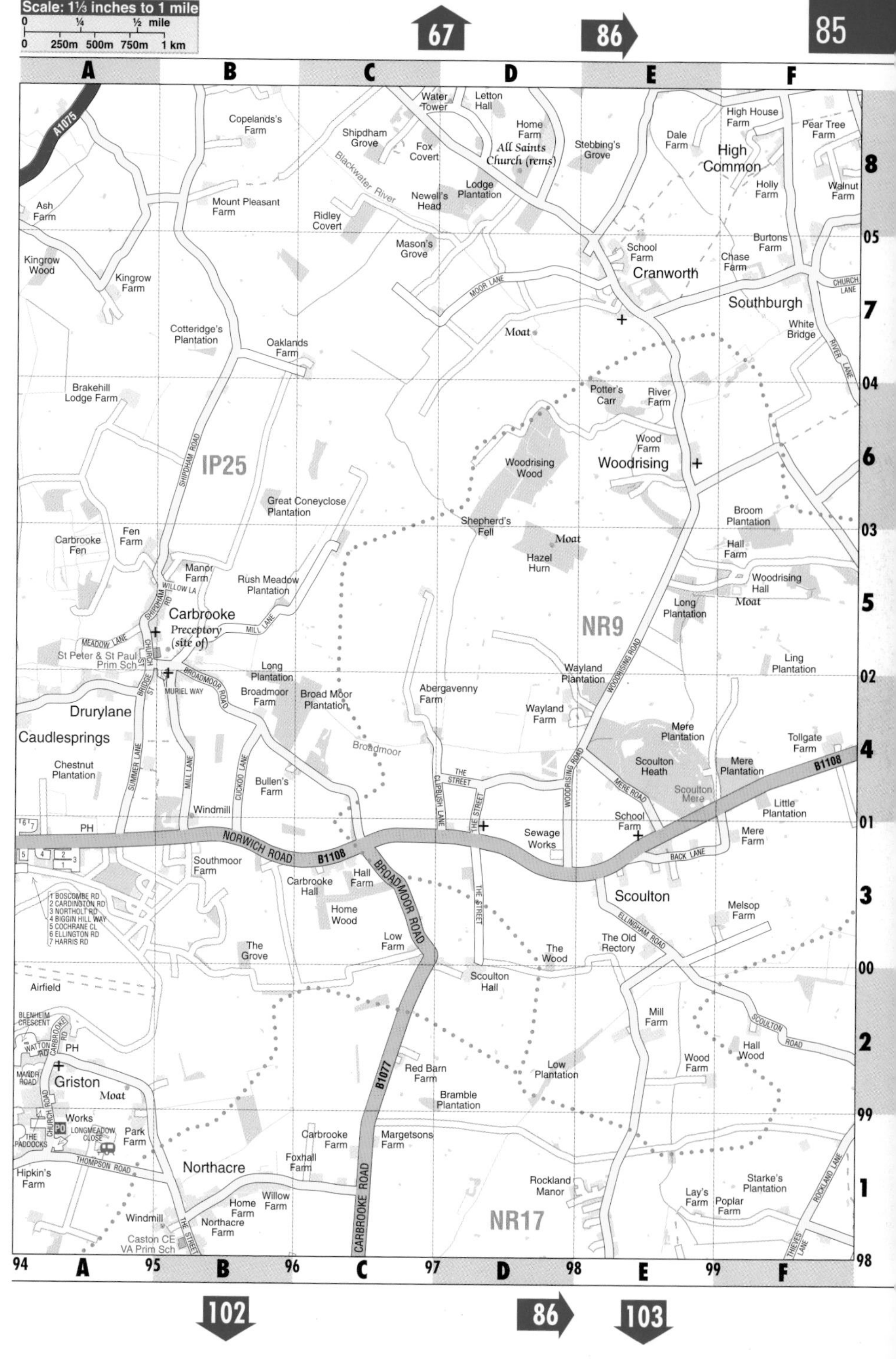

Scale: 1⅓ inches to 1 mile
0 ¼ ½ mile
0 250m 500m 750m 1 km
67
86
A B C D E F
Water Tower
Letton Hall
Copelands's Farm
Shipdham Grove
Fox Covert
Home Farm
All Saints Church (rems)
Stebbing's Grove
Dale Farm
High House Farm
Pear Tree Farm
High Common
Blackwater River
Lodge Plantation
Newell's Head
Mount Pleasant Farm
Ridley Covert
Ash Farm
Holly Farm
Walnut Farm
8
05
Mason's Grove
School Farm
Burtons Farm
Chase Farm
Cranworth
Kingrow Wood
Kingrow Farm
MOOR LANE
CHURCH LANE
Southburgh
7
Moat
White Bridge
Cotteridge's Plantation
Oaklands Farm
RIVER LANE
Brakehill Lodge Farm
04
Potter's Carr
River Farm
Wood Farm
SHIPDHAM ROAD
IP25
Woodrising Wood
Woodrising
6
Great Coneyclose Plantation
Shepherd's Fell
Broom Plantation
03
Carbrooke Fen
Fen Farm
Moat
Hazel Hurn
Hall Farm
Manor Farm
Rush Meadow Plantation
WILLOW LA
Woodrising Hall
Moat
SHIPDHAM RD
Carbrooke
Long Plantation
5
Preceptory (site of)
MILL LANE
NR9
MEADOW LANE
CHURCH ST
St Peter & St Paul Prim Sch
WOODRISING ROAD
Ling Plantation
02
Long Plantation
Wayland Plantation
BRIDGE ST
MURIEL WAY
BROADMOOR ROAD
Broadmoor Farm
Broad Moor Plantation
Abergavenny Farm
Wayland Farm
Drurylane
Mere Plantation
Tollgate Farm
Caudlesprings
4
Broadmoor
Scoulton Heath
Mere Plantation
B1108
Chestnut Plantation
SUMMER LANE
MILL LANE
CUCKOO LANE
Bullen's Farm
THE STREET
CLIPBUSH LANE
WOODRISING ROAD
MERE ROAD
Scoulton Mere
Little Plantation
Windmill
THE STREET
School Farm
PH
Sewage Works
Mere Farm
01
NORWICH ROAD
B1108
BACK LANE
Southmoor Farm
Hall Farm
BROADMOOR ROAD
Carbrooke Hall
Scoulton
3
1 BOSCOMBE RD
2 CARDINGTON RD
3 NORTHOLT RD
4 BIGGIN HILL WAY
5 COCHRANE CL
6 ELLINGTON RD
7 HARRIS RD
Home Wood
THE STREET
Melsop Farm
ELLINGHAM ROAD
The Grove
Low Farm
The Wood
The Old Rectory
00
Airfield
Scoulton Hall
BLENHEIM CRESCENT
CARBROOKE RD
Mill Farm
SCOULTON ROAD
WATTON RD
PH
2
Hall Wood
MANOR ROAD
Red Barn Farm
Low Plantation
Wood Farm
Griston
B1077
Moat
Bramble Plantation
99
CHURCH ROAD
Works
PO
THE PADDOCKS
LONGMEADOW CLOSE
Park Farm
Carbrooke Farm
Margetsons Farm
THOMPSON ROAD
Foxhall Farm
Starke's Plantation
Hipkin's Farm
Northacre
Rockland Manor
ROCKLAND LANE
1
CARBROOKE ROAD
Home Farm
Willow Farm
Lay's Farm
Poplar Farm
Windmill
Northacre Farm
NR17
THIEVES LANE
Caston CE VA Prim Sch
THE STREET
94 A 95 B 96 C 97 D 98 E 99 F 98
102
86
103

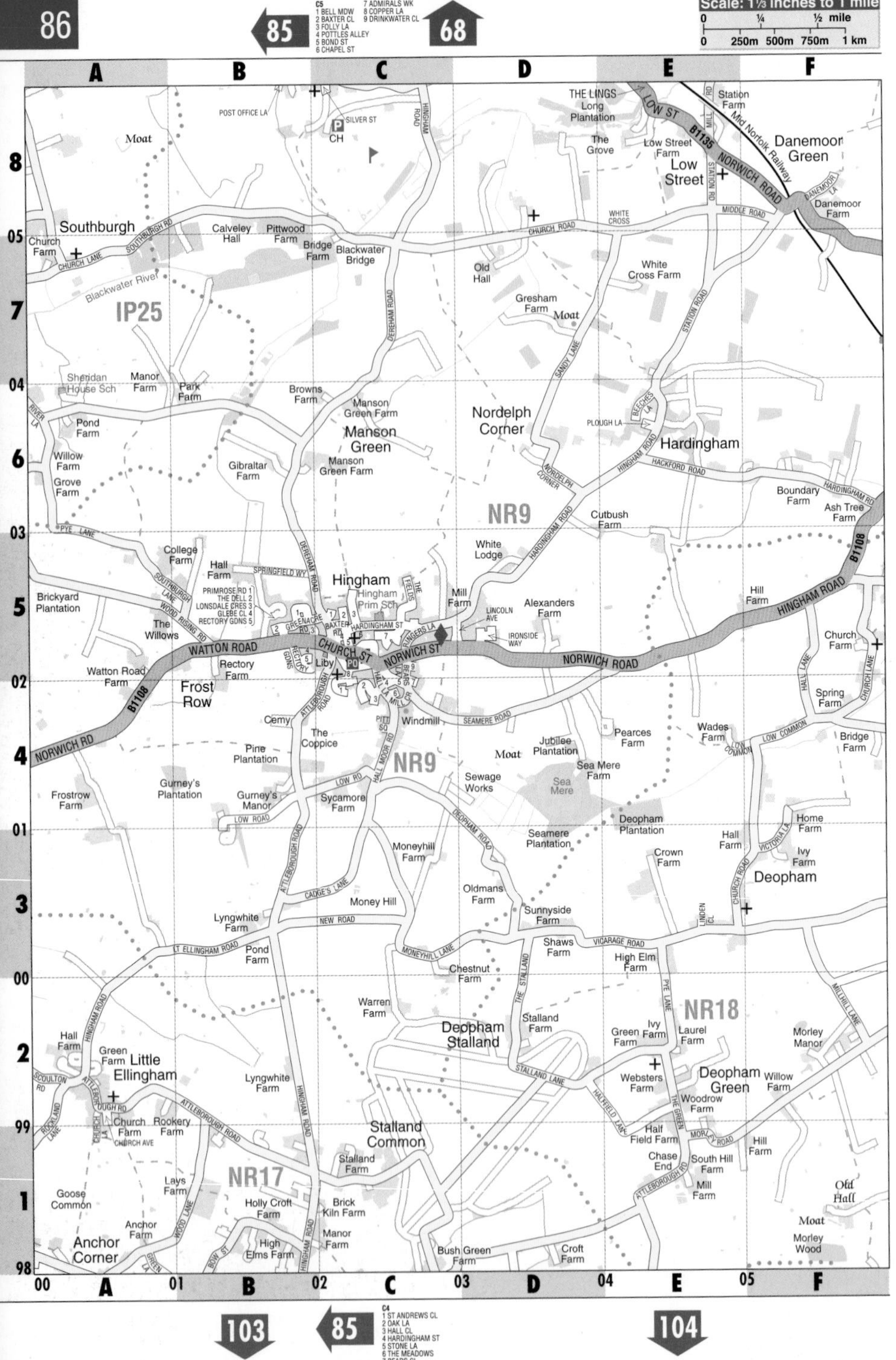

Scale: 1½ inches to 1 mile

0   ¼   ½ mile
0   250m 500m 750m 1 km

85
68
103
85
104

C5
1 BELL MDW
2 BAXTER CL
3 FOLLY LA
4 POTTLES ALLEY
5 BOND ST
6 CHAPEL ST
7 ADMIRALS WK
8 COPPER LA
9 DRINKWATER CL

C4
1 ST ANDREWS CL
2 OAK LA
3 HALL CL
4 HARDINGHAM ST
5 STONE LA
6 THE MEADOWS
7 BEARS CL

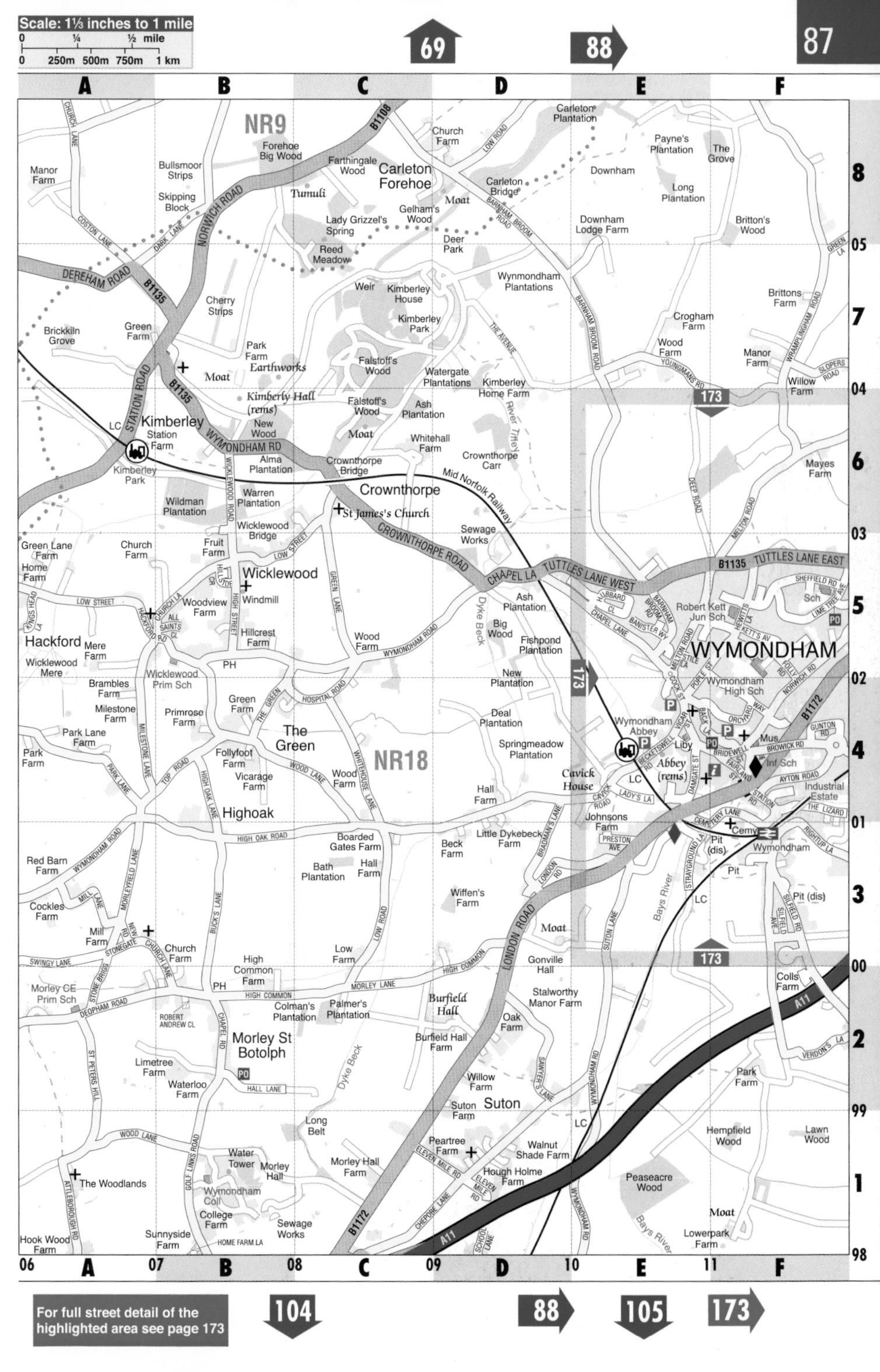

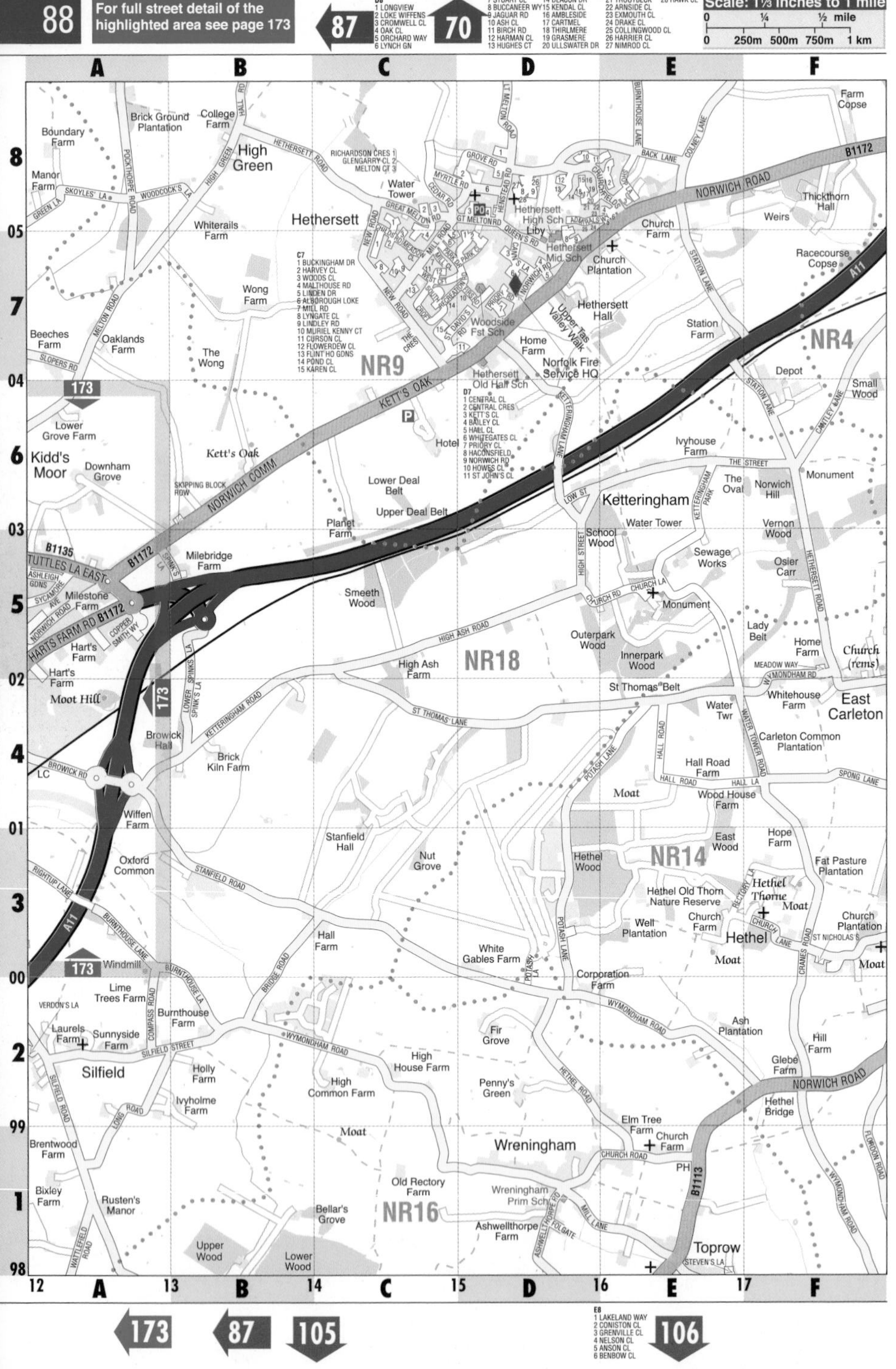

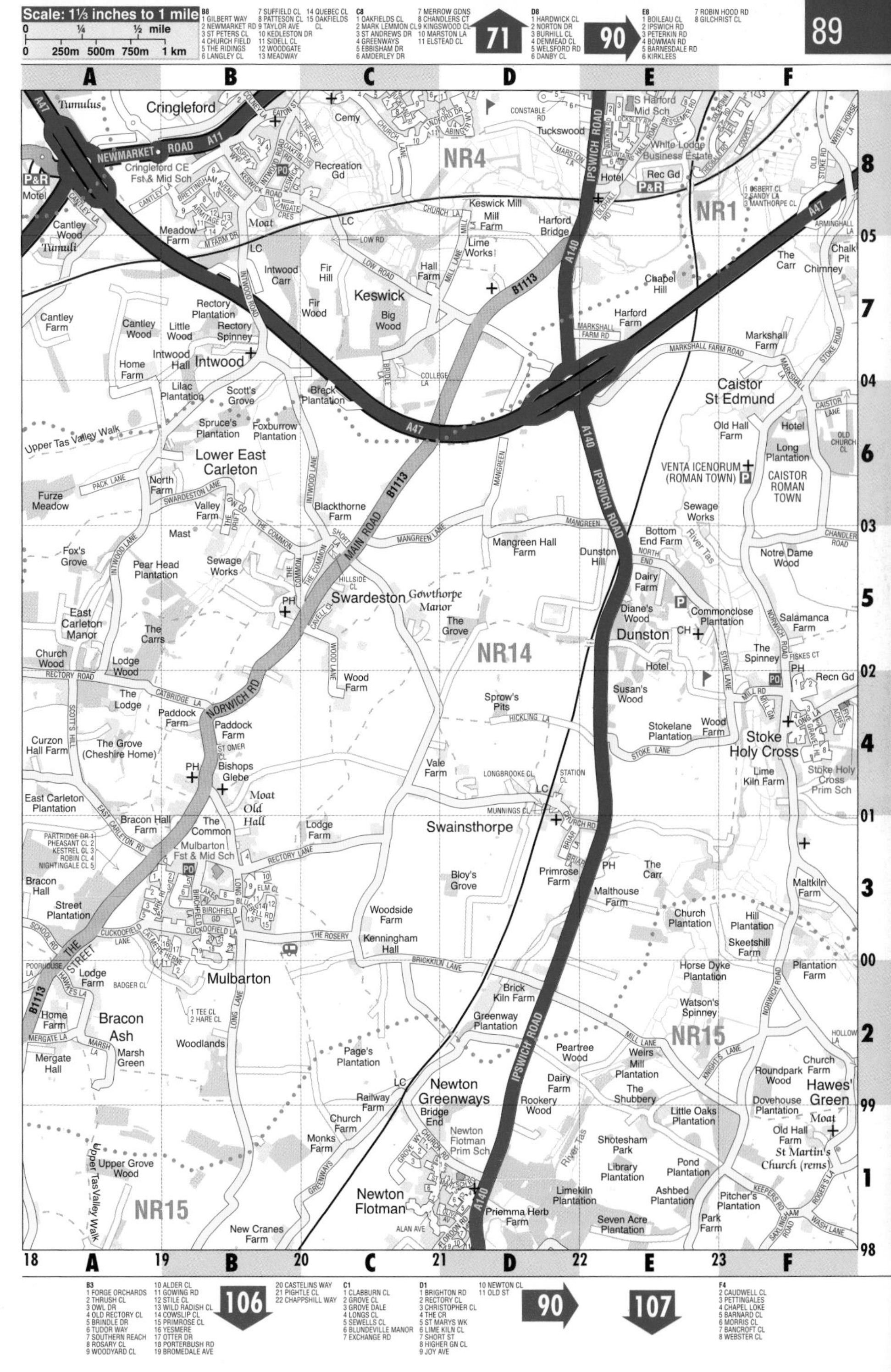
Scale: 1⅓ inches to 1 mile
0 ¼ ½ mile
0 250m 500m 750m 1 km
B8
1 GILBERT WAY
2 NEWMARKET RD
3 ST PETERS CL
4 CHURCH FIELD
5 THE RIDINGS
6 LANGLEY CL
7 SUFFIELD CL
8 PATTESON CL
9 TAYLOR AVE
10 KEDLESTON DR
11 SIDELL CL
12 WOODGATE
13 MEADWAY
14 QUEBEC CL
15 OAKFIELDS CL
C8
1 OAKFIELDS CL
2 MARK LEMMON CL
3 ST ANDREWS DR
4 GREENWAYS
5 EBBISHAM DR
6 AMDERLEY DR
7 MERROW GDNS
8 CHANDLERS CT
9 KINGSWOOD CL
10 MARSTON LA
11 ELSTEAD CL
71
D8
1 HARDWICK CL
2 NORTON DR
3 BURHILL CL
4 DENMEAD CL
5 WELSFORD RD
6 DANBY CL
90
E8
1 BOILEAU CL
2 IPSWICH RD
3 PETERKIN RD
4 BOWMAN RD
5 BARNESDALE RD
6 KIRKLEES
7 ROBIN HOOD RD
8 GILCHRIST CL
A B C D E F
Cringleford
Tumulus
NEWMARKET ROAD A11
A47
P&R
Motel
Cringleford CE Fst & Mid Sch
Cantley Wood
Tumuli
Meadow Farm
Moat
Recreation Gd
Cemy
NR4
Tuckswood
S Harford Mid Sch
White Lodge Business Estate
Rec Gd
Hotel
NR1
Keswick Mill
Mill Farm
Harford Bridge
Lime Works
Intwood Carr
Fir Hill
Hall Farm
Keswick
Chapel Hill
The Carr
Chalk Pit
Chimney
Cantley Farm
Cantley Wood
Little Wood
Rectory Plantation
Rectory Spinney
Fir Wood
Big Wood
Harford Farm
Markshall Farm
Home Farm
Intwood Hall
Intwood
Lilac Plantation
Scott's Grove
Breck Plantation
Caistor St Edmund
Old Hall Farm
Hotel
Upper Tas Valley Walk
Spruce's Plantation
Foxburrow Plantation
Lower East Carleton
Long Plantation
VENTA ICENORUM (ROMAN TOWN)
CAISTOR ROMAN TOWN
Furze Meadow
North Farm
Valley Farm
Blackthorne Farm
Sewage Works
Mast
Mangreen Hall Farm
Dunston Hill
Bottom End Farm
Notre Dame Wood
Fox's Grove
Pear Head Plantation
Sewage Works
Dairy Farm
Swardeston
Gowthorpe Manor
East Carleton Manor
The Carrs
The Grove
NR14
Diane's Wood
Commonclose Plantation
Dunston
Salamanca Farm
Church Wood
Lodge Wood
Hotel
The Spinney
Recn Gd
Wood Farm
Sprow's Pits
Susan's Wood
The Lodge
Paddock Farm
Curzon Hall Farm
The Grove (Cheshire Home)
Stokelane Plantation
Wood Farm
Stoke Holy Cross
Lime Kiln Farm
Stoke Holy Cross Prim Sch
Bishops Glebe
Vale Farm
East Carleton Plantation
Moat
Old Hall
Bracon Hall Farm
The Common
Lodge Farm
Swainsthorpe
Mulbarton Fst & Mid Sch
Bracon Hall
Bloy's Grove
Primrose Farm
The Carr
Malthouse Farm
Maltkiln Farm
Street Plantation
Woodside Farm
Church Plantation
Hill Plantation
Kenningham Hall
Skeetshill Farm
Lodge Farm
Mulbarton
Horse Dyke Plantation
Plantation Farm
Home Farm
Bracon Ash
Brick Kiln Farm
Greenway Plantation
Watson's Spinney
NR15
Mergate Hall
Marsh Green
Woodlands
Page's Plantation
Peartree Wood
Weirs Mill Plantation
Roundpark Wood
Church Farm
Hawes' Green
Railway Farm
Newton Greenways
Dairy Farm
Rookery Wood
The Shubbery
Little Oaks Plantation
Dovehouse Plantation
Moat
Old Hall Farm
Church Farm
Bridge End
Newton Flotman Prim Sch
Shotesham Park
St Martin's Church (rems)
Monks Farm
Upper Grove Wood
Library Plantation
Pond Plantation
Limekiln Plantation
Ashbed Plantation
Pitcher's Plantation
NR15
Newton Flotman
Priemma Herb Farm
Seven Acre Plantation
Park Farm
New Cranes Farm
IPSWICH ROAD A140
B1113
MAIN ROAD
NORWICH RD
THE STREET
18 19 20 21 22 23
8 05 7 04 6 03 5 02 4 01 3 00 2 99 1 98
B3
1 FORGE ORCHARDS
2 THRUSH CL
3 OWL DR
4 OLD RECTORY CL
5 BRINDLE DR
6 TUDOR WAY
7 SOUTHERN REACH
8 ROSARY CL
9 WOODYARD CL
10 ALDER CL
11 GOWING RD
12 STILE CL
13 WILD RADISH CL
14 COWSLIP CL
15 PRIMROSE CL
16 YESMERE
17 OTTER DR
18 PORTERBUSH RD
19 BROMEDALE AVE
106
20 CASTELINS WAY
21 PIGHTLE CL
22 CHAPPSHILL WAY
C1
1 CLABBURN CL
2 GROVE CL
3 GROVE DALE
4 LONGS CL
5 SEWELLS CL
6 BLUNDEVILLE MANOR
7 EXCHANGE RD
D1
1 BRIGHTON RD
2 RECTORY CL
3 CHRISTOPHER CL
4 THE CR
5 ST MARYS WK
6 LIME KILN CL
7 SHORT ST
8 HIGHER GN CL
9 JOY AVE
10 NEWTON CL
11 OLD ST
90
107
F4
2 CAUDWELL CL
3 PETTINGALES
4 CHAPEL LOKE
5 BARNARD CL
6 MORRIS CL
7 BANCROFT CL
8 WEBSTER CL

163
89
72

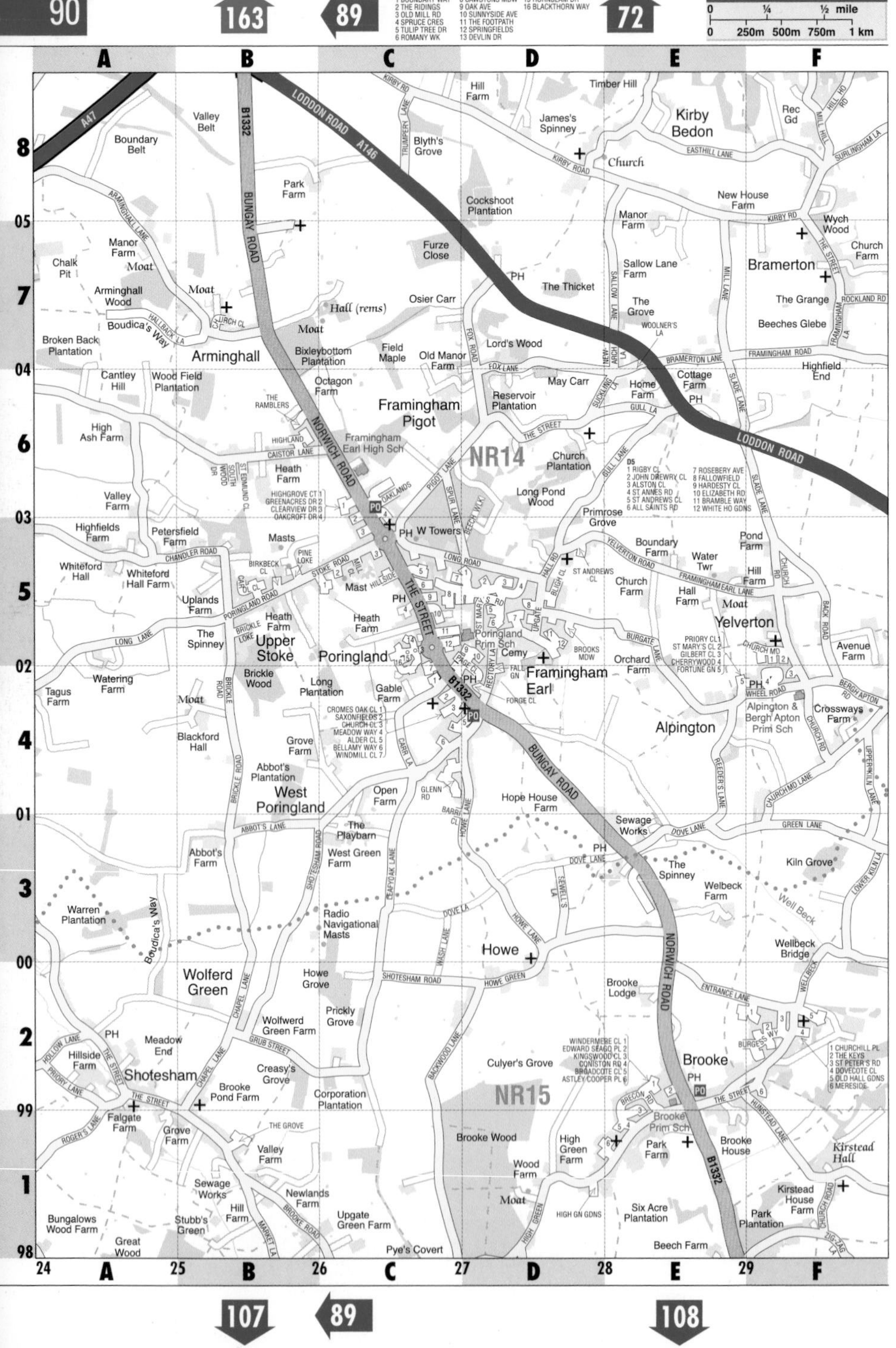
C5
1 BOUNDARY WAY
2 THE RIDINGS
3 OLD MILL RD
4 SPRUCE CRES
5 TULIP TREE DR
6 ROMANY WK
7 FITZGERALD RD
8 CAWSTONS MDW
9 OAK AVE
10 SUNNYSIDE AVE
11 THE FOOTPATH
12 SPRINGFIELDS
13 DEVLIN DR
14 OVERTONS WAY
15 HORNBEAM DR
16 BLACKTHORN WAY
Scale: 1⅓ inches to 1 mile
0 ¼ ½ mile
0 250m 500m 750m 1 km
A
B
C
D
E
F
8
05
7
04
6
03
5
02
4
01
3
00
2
99
1
98
24
25
26
27
28
29
A47
B1332
LODDON ROAD A146
Valley Belt
Boundary Belt
Hill Farm
Timber Hill
Kirby Bedon
Rec Gd
James's Spinney
Blyth's Grove
Church
KIRBY ROAD
EASTHILL LANE
SURLINGHAM LA
Park Farm
BUNGAY ROAD
Cockshoot Plantation
New House Farm
Manor Farm
KIRBY RD
Wych Wood
Chalk Pit
Manor Farm
Moat
Furze Close
Sallow Lane Farm
Bramerton
Church Farm
Arminghall Wood
Moat
PH
The Thicket
Osier Carr
Hall (rems)
The Grove
The Grange
ROCKLAND RD
Boudica's Way
Moat
Beeches Glebe
Broken Back Plantation
Arminghall
Bixleybottom Plantation
Field Maple
Old Manor Farm
Lord's Wood
BRAMERTON LANE
FRAMINGHAM ROAD
Cantley Hill
Wood Field Plantation
Octagon Farm
Framingham Pigot
Reservoir Plantation
May Carr
Home Farm
Cottage Farm
Highfield End
PH
High Ash Farm
Framingham Earl High Sch
NR14
THE STREET
GULL LA
LODDON ROAD
NORWICH ROAD
Heath Farm
Church Plantation
D5
1 RIGBY CL
2 JOHN DREWRY CL
3 ALSTON CL
4 ST ANNES RD
5 ST ANDREWS CL
6 ALL SAINTS RD
7 ROSEBERY AVE
8 FALLOWFIELD
9 HARDESTY CL
10 ELIZABETH RD
11 BRAMBLE WAY
12 WHITE HO GDNS
Valley Farm
HIGHGROVE CT 1
GREENACRES DR 2
CLEARVIEW DR 3
OAKCROFT DR 4
PO
Long Pond Wood
Primrose Grove
Highfields Farm
Petersfield Farm
Masts
PH
W Towers
Pond Farm
CHANDLER ROAD
LONG ROAD
Boundary Farm
Water Twr
Whiteford Hall
Whiteford Hall Farm
STOKE ROAD
YELVERTON ROAD
Hill Farm
Mast
Church Farm
FRAMINGHAM EARL LANE
Uplands Farm
PORINGLAND ROAD
PH
Hall Farm
Moat
Yelverton
Heath Farm
Heath Farm
THE STREET
The Spinney
Upper Stoke
Poringland
Poringland Prim Sch
BURGATE LANE
PRIORY CL 1
ST MARY'S CL 2
GILBERT CL 3
CHERRYWOOD 4
FORTUNE GN 5
Avenue Farm
LONG LANE
Cemy
Framingham Earl
Orchard Farm
Watering Farm
Brickle Wood
PH
Tagus Farm
Long Plantation
Gable Farm
WHEEL ROAD
Moat
CROMES OAK CL 1
SAXONFIELDS 2
CHURCH CL 3
MEADOW WAY 4
ALDER CL 5
BELLAMY WAY 6
WINDMILL CL 7
FORGE CL
PO
Alpington & Bergh Apton Prim Sch
Crossways Farm
Alpington
Blackford Hall
Grove Farm
BUNGAY ROAD
Abbot's Plantation
West Poringland
Open Farm
Hope House Farm
BRICKLE ROAD
ABBOT'S LANE
The Playbarn
Sewage Works
DOVE LANE
GREEN LANE
Abbot's Farm
West Green Farm
PH
DOVE LANE
The Spinney
Kiln Grove
Welbeck Farm
Well Beck
Warren Plantation
Radio Navigational Masts
DOVE LA
Boudica's Way
Wellbeck Bridge
Howe
Wolferd Green
Howe Grove
SHOTESHAM ROAD
HOWE GREEN
Brooke Lodge
NORWICH ROAD
ENTRANCE LANE
Wolfwerd Green Farm
Prickly Grove
PH
Meadow End
GRUB STREET
WINDERMERE CL 1
EDWARD SEAGO PL 2
KINGSWOOD CL 3
CONISTON RD 4
BROADCOTE CL 5
ASTLEY COOPER PL 6
1 CHURCHILL PL
2 THE KEYS
3 ST PETER'S RD
4 DOVECOTE CL
5 OLD HALL GDNS
6 MERESIDE
Hillside Farm
Shotesham
Creasy's Grove
Culyer's Grove
Brooke
PH
PO
Brooke Pond Farm
Corporation Plantation
NR15
THE STREET
Falgate Farm
Grove Farm
THE GROVE
Brooke Prim Sch
Brooke Wood
High Green Farm
Park Farm
Brooke House
Kirstead Hall
Valley Farm
Wood Farm
B1332
Sewage Works
Newlands Farm
Moat
Kirstead House Farm
Hill Farm
Six Acre Plantation
Park Plantation
Bungalows Wood Farm
Stubb's Green
Upgate Green Farm
HIGH GN GDNS
Great Wood
Pye's Covert
Beech Farm

107
89
108

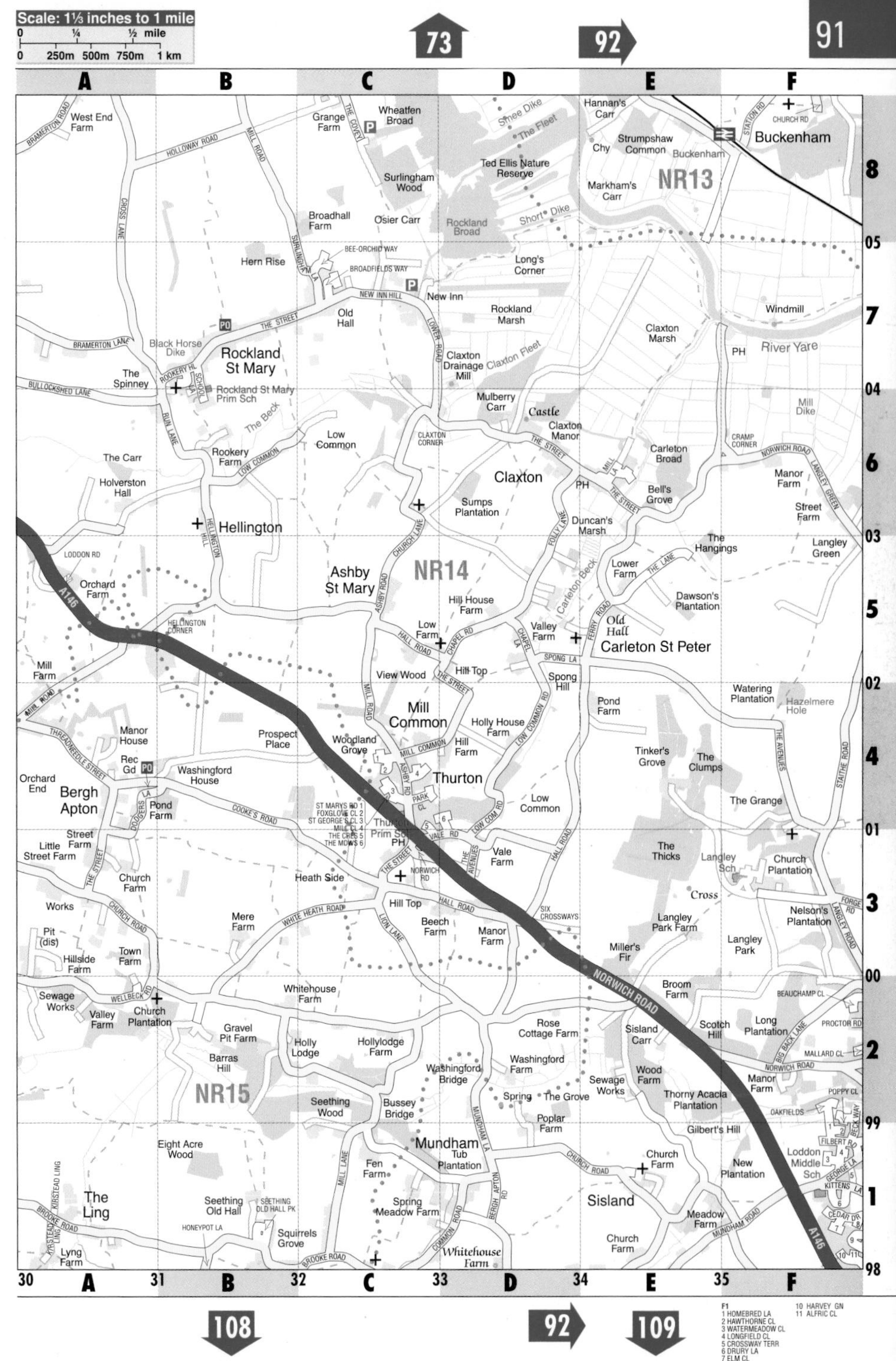
Scale: 1⅓ inches to 1 mile
0 ¼ ½ mile
0 250m 500m 750m 1 km
73
92
A B C D E F
West End Farm
Grange Farm
Wheatfen Broad
Hannan's Carr
Buckenham
Strumpshaw Common
Chy
Markham's Carr
NR13
Ted Ellis Nature Reserve
Surlingham Wood
Broadhall Farm
Osier Carr
Rockland Broad
Hern Rise
Long's Corner
New Inn
Rockland Marsh
Old Hall
Windmill
Claxton Marsh
River Yare
Rockland St Mary
Black Horse Dike
Claxton Drainage Mill
The Spinney
Rockland St Mary Prim Sch
Mulberry Carr
Castle
Claxton Manor
Low Common
The Carr
Rookery Farm
Carleton Broad
Manor Farm
Claxton
Holverston Hall
Sumps Plantation
Bell's Grove
Street Farm
Hellington
Duncan's Marsh
The Hangings
Langley Green
Ashby St Mary
NR14
Lower Farm
Orchard Farm
Hill House Farm
Dawson's Plantation
Low Farm
Valley Farm
Old Hall
Carleton St Peter
Mill Farm
Hill Top
View Wood
Spong Hill
Watering Plantation
Hazelmere Hole
Pond Farm
Mill Common
Holly House Farm
Manor House
Prospect Place
Woodland Grove
Hill Farm
Tinker's Grove
The Clumps
Rec Gd
Washingford House
Thurton
Orchard End
Bergh Apton
Pond Farm
Low Common
The Grange
Street Farm
Little Street Farm
Thurton Prim Sch
Vale Farm
The Thicks
Langley Sch
Church Plantation
Church Farm
Heath Side
Cross
Works
Hill Top
Nelson's Plantation
Mere Farm
Beech Farm
Manor Farm
Langley Park Farm
Pit (dis)
Langley Park
Hillside Farm
Town Farm
Miller's Fir
Whitehouse Farm
Broom Farm
Sewage Works
Valley Farm
Church Plantation
Gravel Pit Farm
Rose Cottage Farm
Sisland Carr
Scotch Hill
Long Plantation
Barras Hill
Holly Lodge
Hollylodge Farm
Washingford Farm
Wood Farm
Manor Farm
Washingford Bridge
Sewage Works
Thorny Acacia Plantation
NR15
Seething Wood
Bussey Bridge
Spring
The Grove
Poplar Farm
Gilbert's Hill
Eight Acre Wood
Mundham
Tub Plantation
Church Farm
Loddon Middle Sch
Fen Farm
New Plantation
The Ling
Seething Old Hall
Spring Meadow Farm
Sisland
Meadow Farm
Squirrels Grove
Church Farm
Lyng Farm
Whitehouse Farm
30 31 32 33 34 35
98 99 1 2 00 3 01 4 02 5 03 6 04 7 05 8
108
92
109
F1
1 HOMEBRED LA
2 HAWTHORNE CL
3 WATERMEADOW CL
4 LONGFIELD CL
5 CROSSWAY TERR
6 DRURY LA
7 ELM CL
8 SYCAMORE CL
9 LEMAN GR
10 HARVEY GN
11 ALFRIC CL

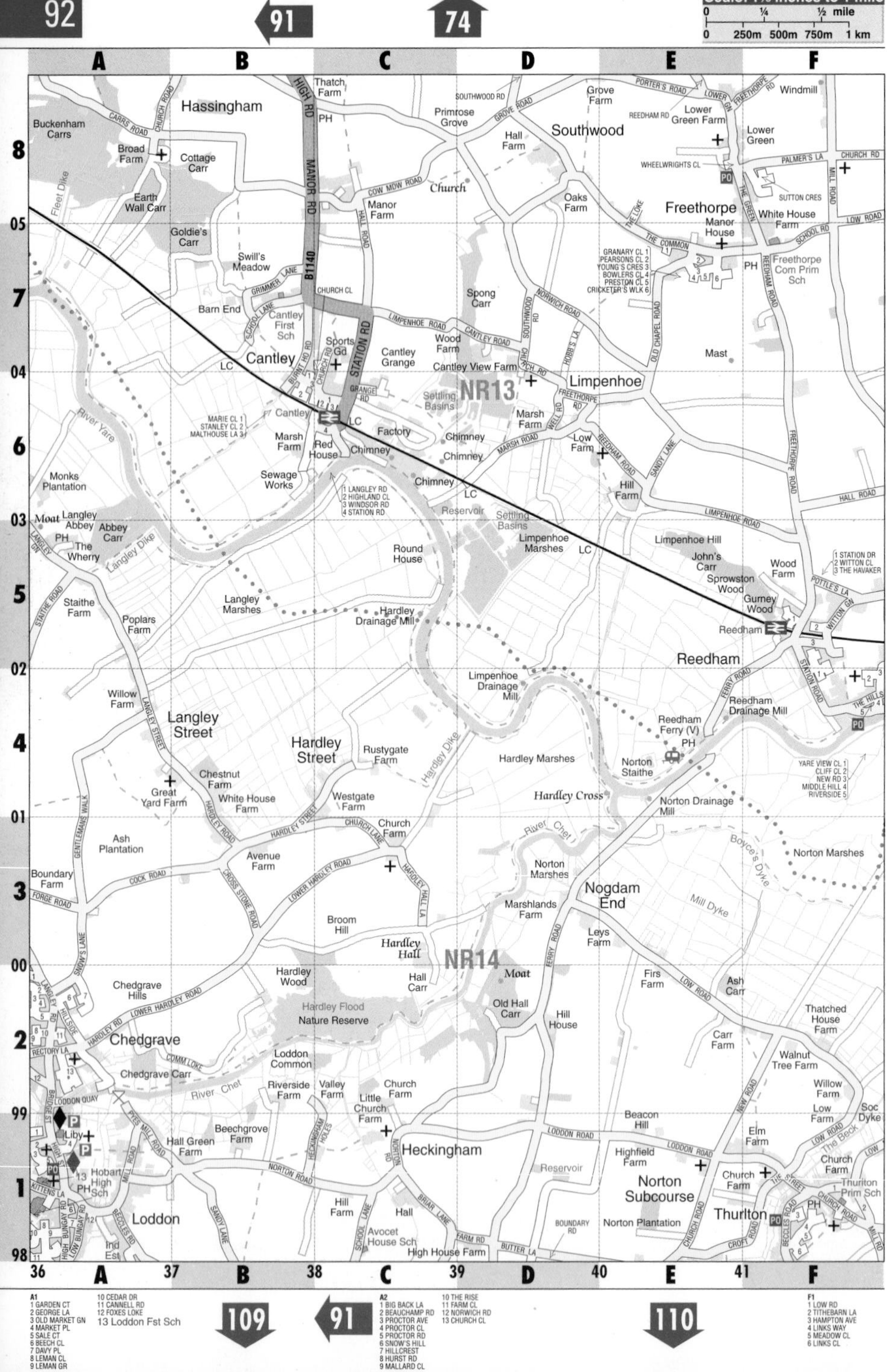

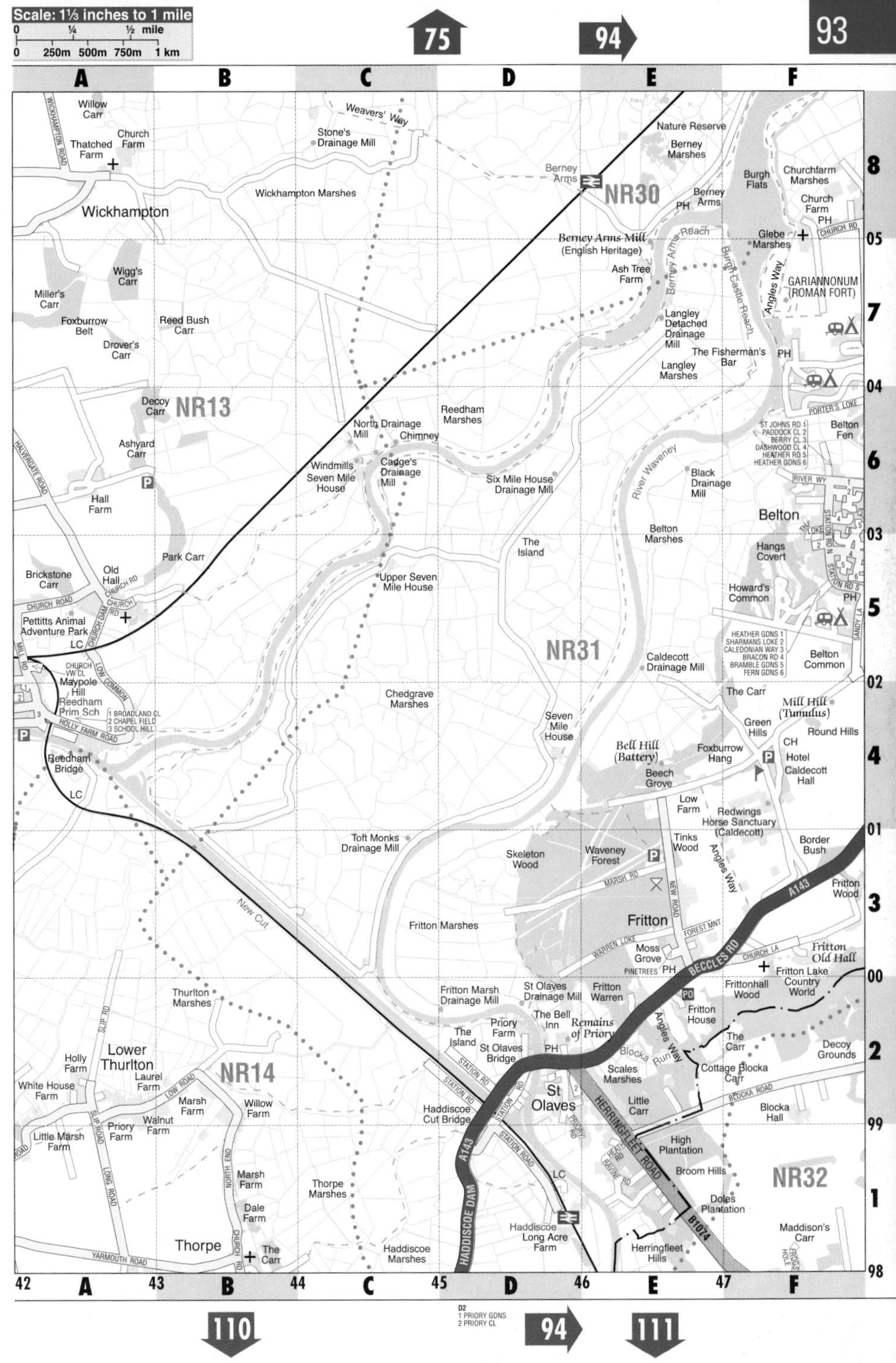
A
B
C
D
E
F
Willow Carr
Church Farm
Thatched Farm
WICKHAMPTON ROAD
Wickhampton
Weavers' Way
Stone's Drainage Mill
Wickhampton Marshes
Berney Arms
NR30
Nature Reserve
Berney Marshes
Burgh Flats
Churchfarm Marshes
Church Farm
PH
Berney Arms
CHURCH RD
Berney Arms Reach
Berney Arms Mill
(English Heritage)
Glebe Marshes
Ash Tree Farm
Burgh Castle Reach
Angles Way
GARIANNONUM (ROMAN FORT)
Wigg's Carr
Miller's Carr
Foxburrow Belt
Reed Bush Carr
Drover's Carr
Langley Detached Drainage Mill
The Fisherman's Bar
Langley Marshes
PORTER'S LOKE
Decoy Carr
NR13
Ashyard Carr
HALVERGATE ROAD
North Drainage Mill
Chimney
Reedham Marshes
Windmills
Seven Mile House
Cadge's Drainage Mill
Six Mile House Drainage Mill
River Waveney
Black Drainage Mill
ST JOHNS RD 1
PADDOCK CL 2
BERRY CL 3
DASHWOOD CL 4
HEATHER RD 5
HEATHER GDNS 6
Belton Fen
RIVER WY
Belton
Hall Farm
Park Carr
The Island
Belton Marshes
Hangs Covert
THE LOKE
STATION RD N
STATION RD S
Brickstone Carr
Old Hall
CHURCH RD
CHURCH ROAD
Upper Seven Mile House
Howard's Common
SANDY LA
Pettitts Animal Adventure Park
CHURCH DAM
LC
MILL RD
CHURCH VW CL
LOW COMMON
Maypole Hill
Reedham Prim Sch
1 BROADLAND CL
2 CHAPEL FIELD
3 SCHOOL HILL
HOLLY FARM ROAD
NR31
Caldecott Drainage Mill
HEATHER GDNS 1
SHARMANS LOKE 2
CALEDONIAN WAY 3
BRACON RD 4
BRAMBLE GDNS 5
FERN GDNS 6
Belton Common
Chedgrave Marshes
The Carr
Mill Hill (Tumulus)
Seven Mile House
Green Hills
Round Hills
Bell Hill (Battery)
Foxburrow Hang
CH
Hotel
Caldecott Hall
Reedham Bridge
Beech Grove
LC
Low Farm
Redwings Horse Sanctuary (Caldecott)
Toft Monks Drainage Mill
Tinks Wood
Border Bush
Skeleton Wood
Waveney Forest
MARSH RD
NEW ROAD
A143
Fritton Wood
New Cut
Fritton Marshes
Fritton
FOREST MNT
WARREN LOKE
Moss Grove
PINETREES
BECCLES RD
CHURCH LA
Fritton Old Hall
Fritton Lake Country World
Thurlton Marshes
Fritton Marsh Drainage Mill
St Olaves Drainage Mill
Fritton Warren
Fritton House
Fritonhall Wood
The Bell Inn
Remains of Priory
Priory Farm
The Island
St Olaves Bridge
PH
SLIP RD
Lower Thurlton
Holly Farm
Laurel Farm
LOW ROAD
NR14
Blocka Run
Scales Marshes
The Carr
Cottage Blocka Carr
Decoy Grounds
White House Farm
Marsh Farm
Willow Farm
STATION RD
St Olaves
HERRINGFLEET ROAD
Little Carr
BLOCKA ROAD
Blocka Hall
Priory Farm
Walnut Farm
Haddiscoe Cut Bridge
Little Marsh Farm
SLIP ROAD
NORTH END
STATION ROAD
PRIORY RD
HEATH RD
RAVINE RD
High Plantation
Broom Hills
NR32
LONG ROAD
Marsh Farm
Thorpe Marshes
HADDISCOE DAM
LC
Doles Plantation
B1074
Dale Farm
Haddiscoe Long Acre Farm
Herringfleet Hills
Maddison's Carr
FROGS HOLE
YARMOUTH ROAD
Thorpe
CHURCH RD
The Carr
Haddiscoe Marshes
8
05
7
04
6
03
5
02
4
01
3
00
2
99
1
98
42
43
44
45
46
47

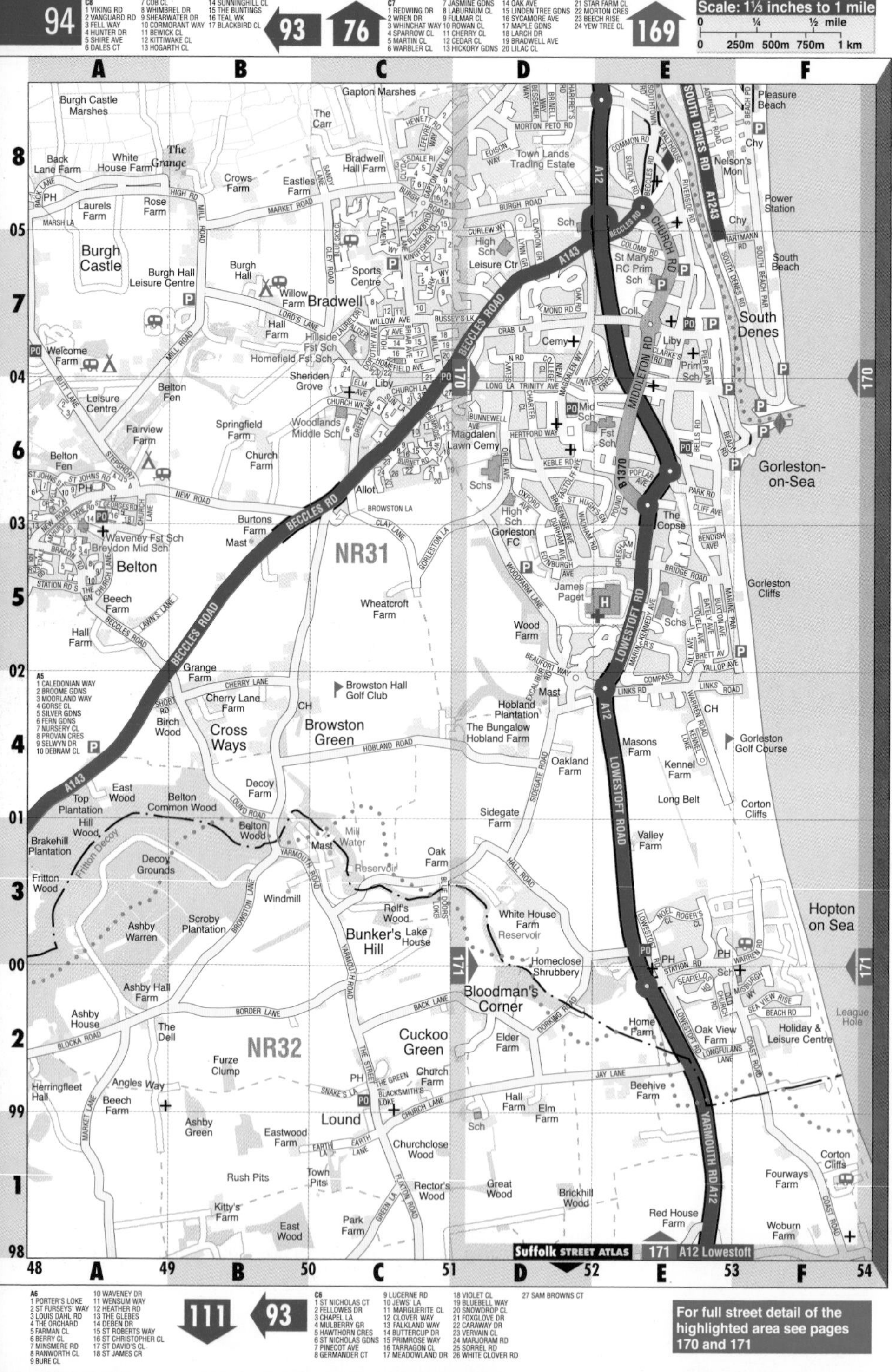

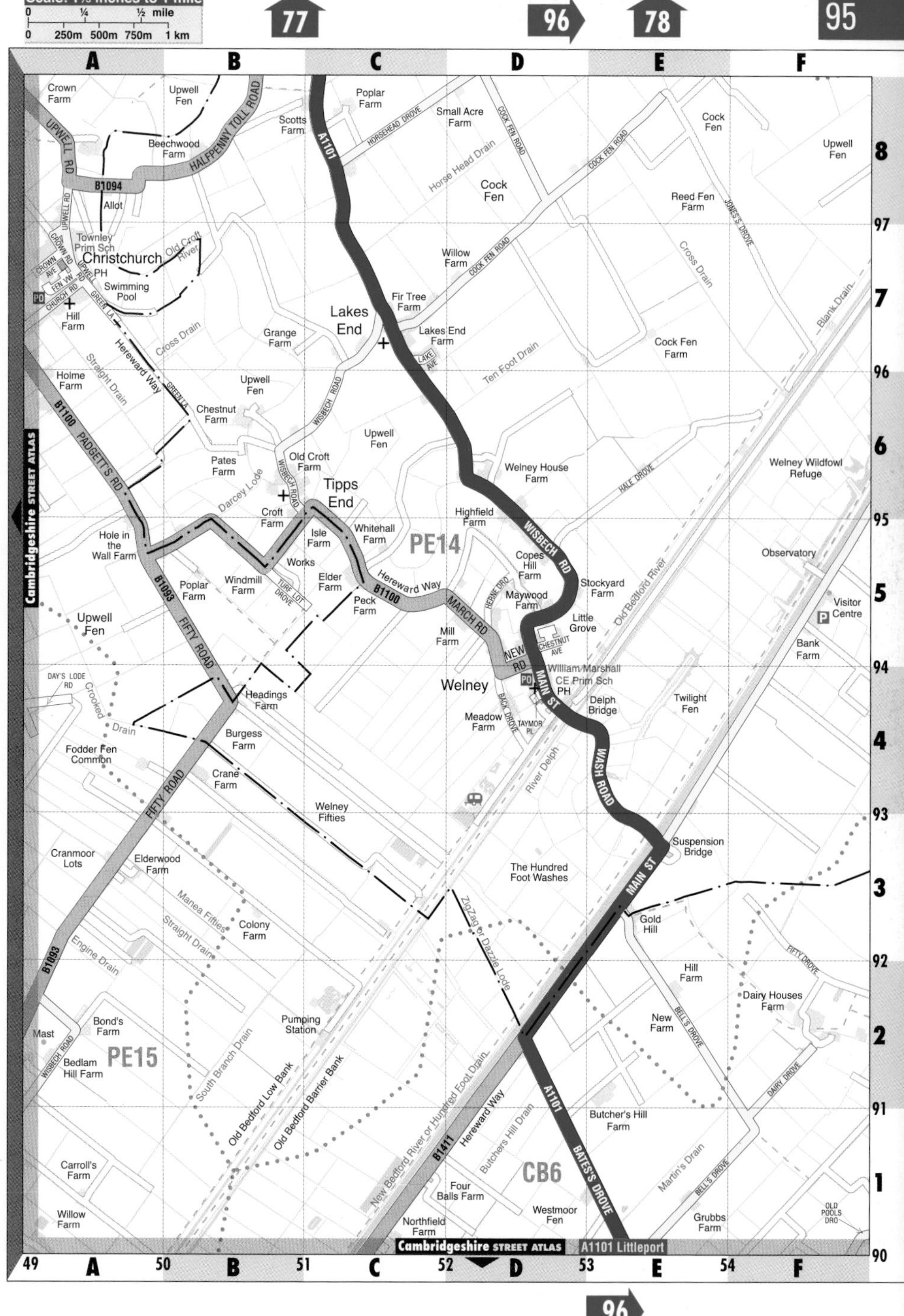

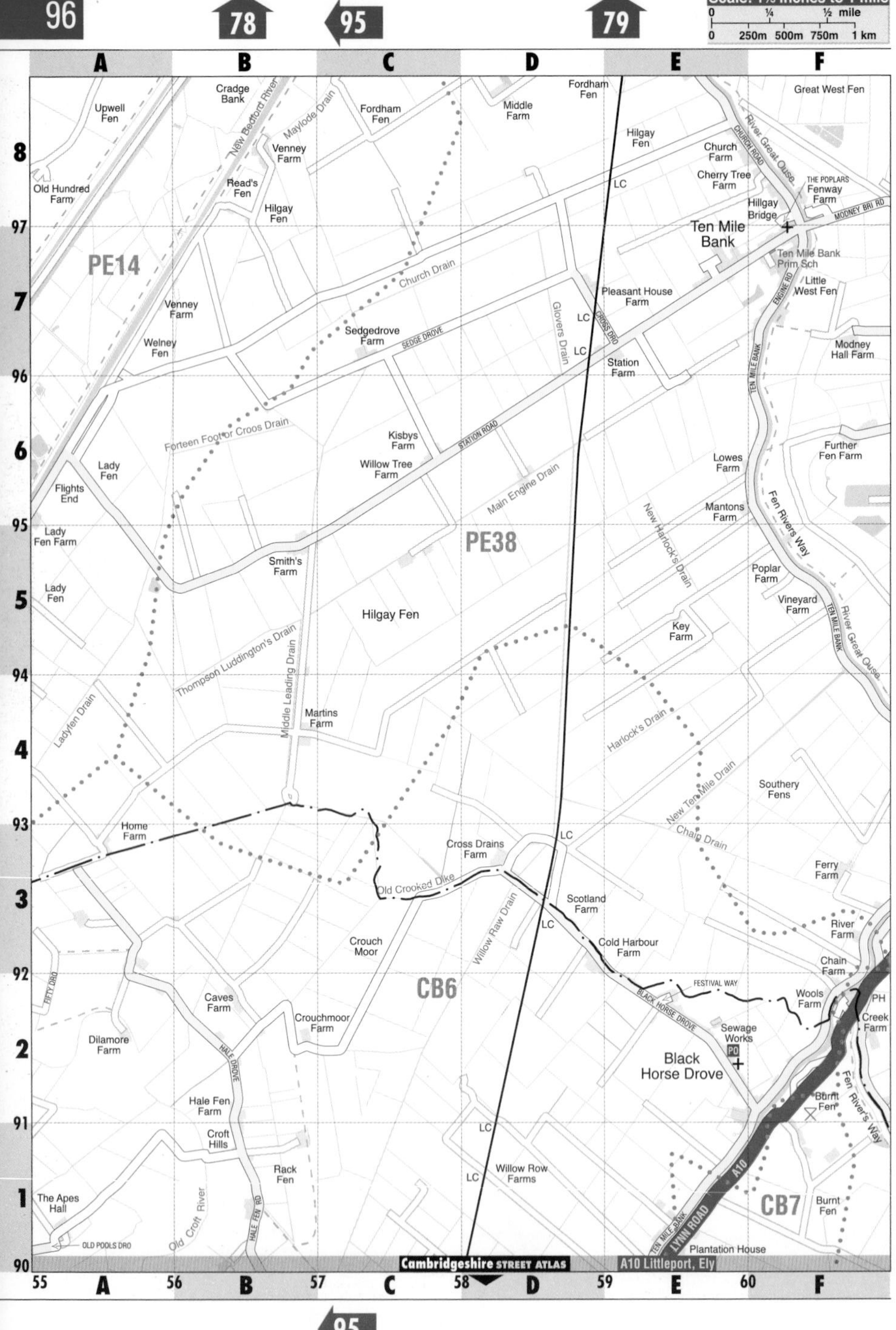

Scale: 1⅓ inches to 1 mile

A10 Littleport, Ely

Scale: 1⅓ inches to 1 mile

79 98 80

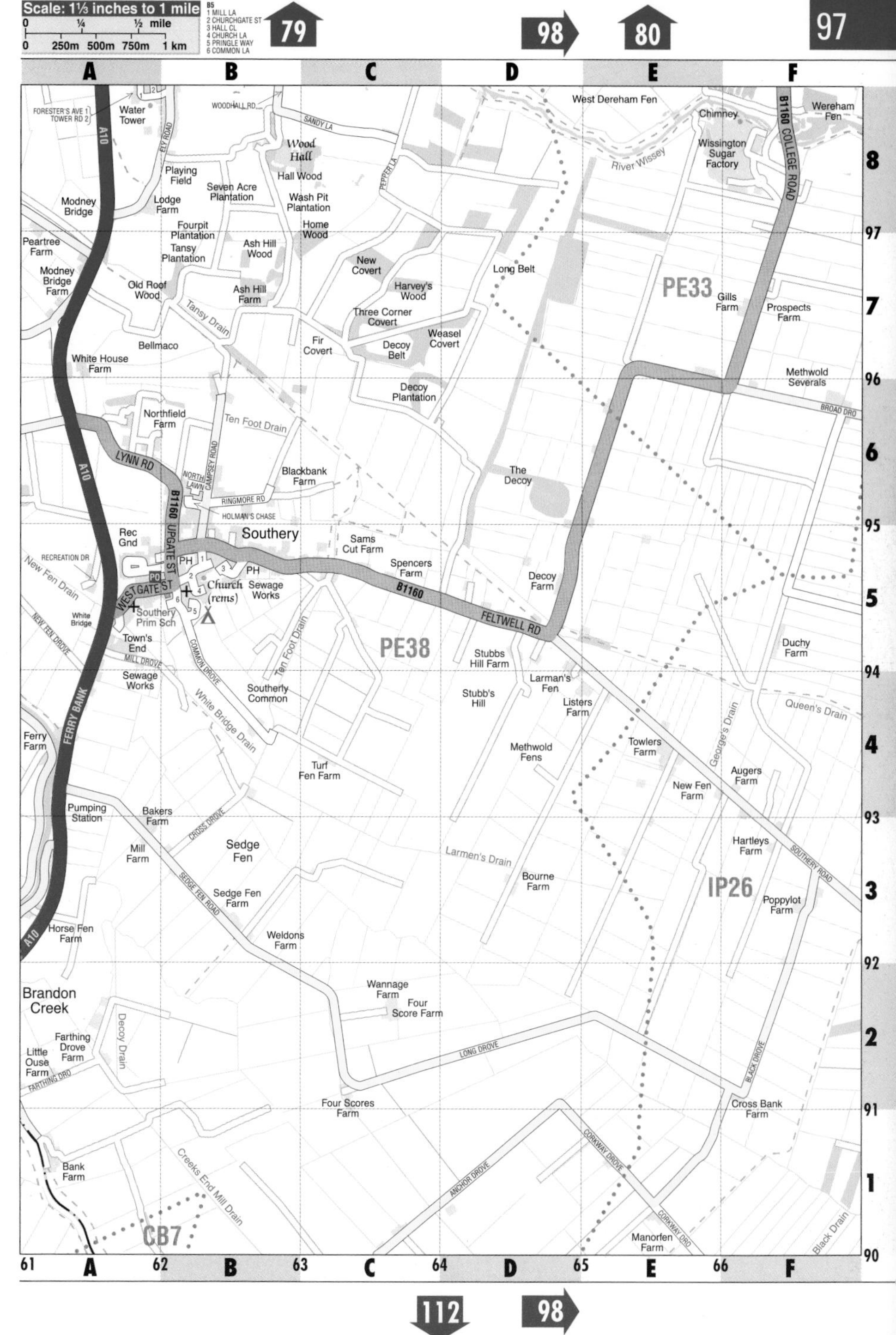

0 ¼ ½ mile
0 250m 500m 750m 1 km
B5
1 MILL LA
2 CHURCHGATE ST
3 HALL CL
4 CHURCH LA
5 PRINGLE WAY
6 COMMON LA
A B C D E F
West Dereham Fen
Wereham Fen
Chimney
Wissington Sugar Factory
B1160 COLLEGE ROAD
River Wissey
FORESTER'S AVE 1
TOWER RD 2
Water Tower
WOODHALL RD
SANDY LA
Wood Hall
Hall Wood
Wash Pit Plantation
Home Wood
PEPPER LA
ELY ROAD
Playing Field
Seven Acre Plantation
Lodge Farm
Modney Bridge
Fourpit Plantation
Tansy Plantation
Ash Hill Wood
Peartree Farm
Modney Bridge Farm
Old Roof Wood
Ash Hill Farm
New Covert
Harvey's Wood
Three Corner Covert
Long Belt
PE33
Gills Farm
Prospects Farm
Tansy Drain
Bellmaco
Fir Covert
Decoy Belt
Weasel Covert
White House Farm
Decoy Plantation
Methwold Severals
BROAD DRO
Northfield Farm
Ten Foot Drain
LYNN RD
CAMPSEY ROAD
NORTH LAWN
Blackbank Farm
The Decoy
RINGMORE RD
HOLMAN'S CHASE
B1160 UPGATE ST
Rec Gnd
Southery
RECREATION DR
PH
Sams Cut Farm
Spencers Farm
Decoy Farm
New Fen Drain
PO
WESTGATE ST
Church (rems)
PH
Sewage Works
B1160
FELTWELL RD
White Bridge
Southery Prim Sch
NEW FEN DROVE
Ten Foot Drain
PE38
Stubbs Hill Farm
Duchy Farm
Town's End
MILL DROVE
COMMON DROVE
Larman's Fen
Sewage Works
Stubb's Hill
Listers Farm
Southerly Common
Queen's Drain
White Bridge Drain
George's Drain
FERRY BANK
A10
Ferry Farm
Towlers Farm
Methwold Fens
Turf Fen Farm
Augers Farm
New Fen Farm
Pumping Station
Bakers Farm
CROSS DROVE
Sedge Fen
Hartleys Farm
Mill Farm
Larmen's Drain
SOUTHERY ROAD
SEDGE FEN ROAD
Bourne Farm
IP26
Sedge Fen Farm
Poppylot Farm
Horse Fen Farm
Weldons Farm
Brandon Creek
Wannage Farm
Four Score Farm
Decoy Drain
Farthing Drove Farm
Little Ouse Farm
FARTHING DRO
LONG DROVE
BLACK DROVE
Four Scores Farm
Cross Bank Farm
CORKWAY DROVE
Creeks End Mill Drain
Bank Farm
ANCHOR DROVE
CORKWAY DRO
CB7
Manorfen Farm
Black Drain
8 97 7 96 6 95 5 94 4 93 3 92 2 91 1 90
61 62 63 64 65 66

112 98

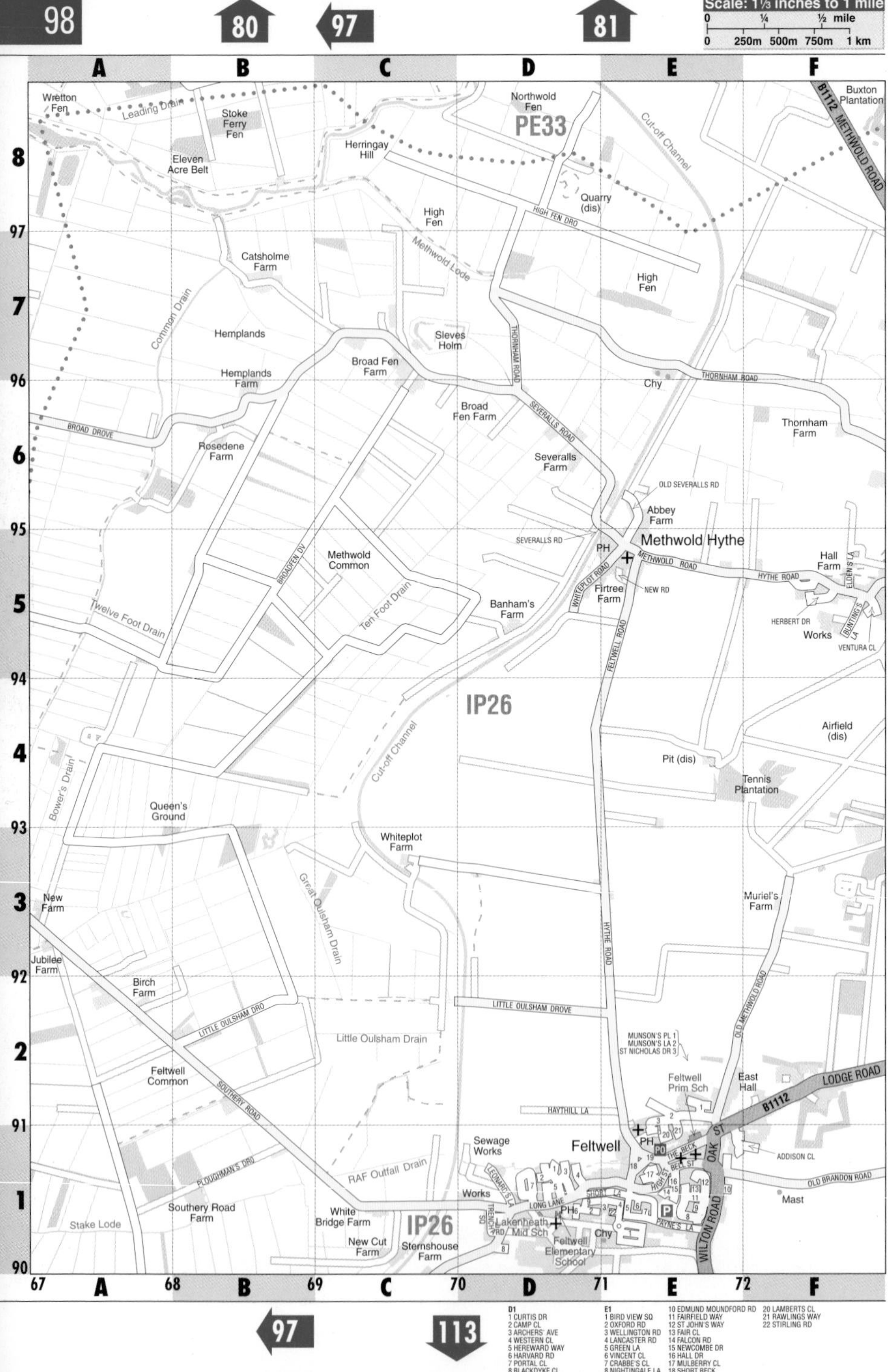

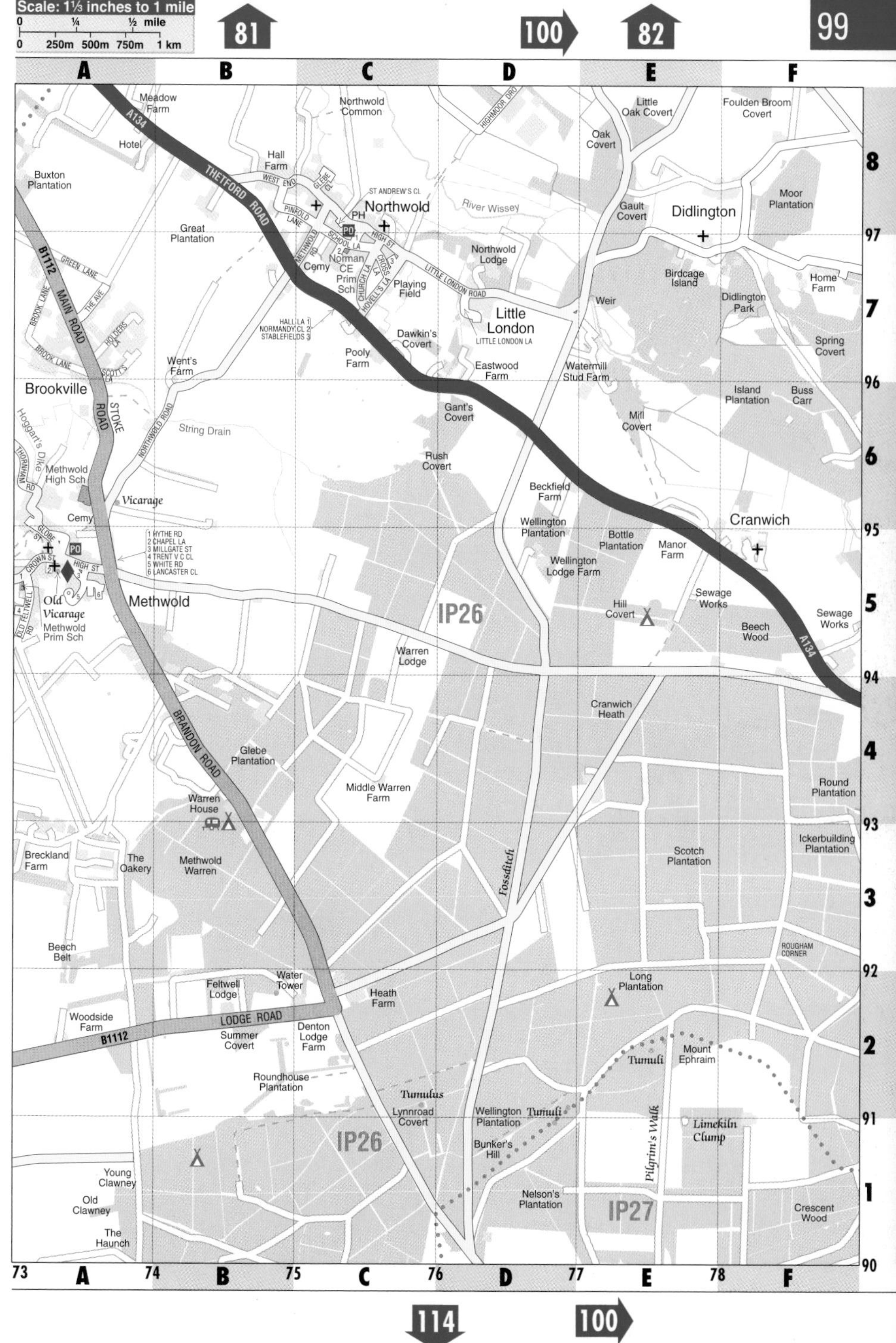

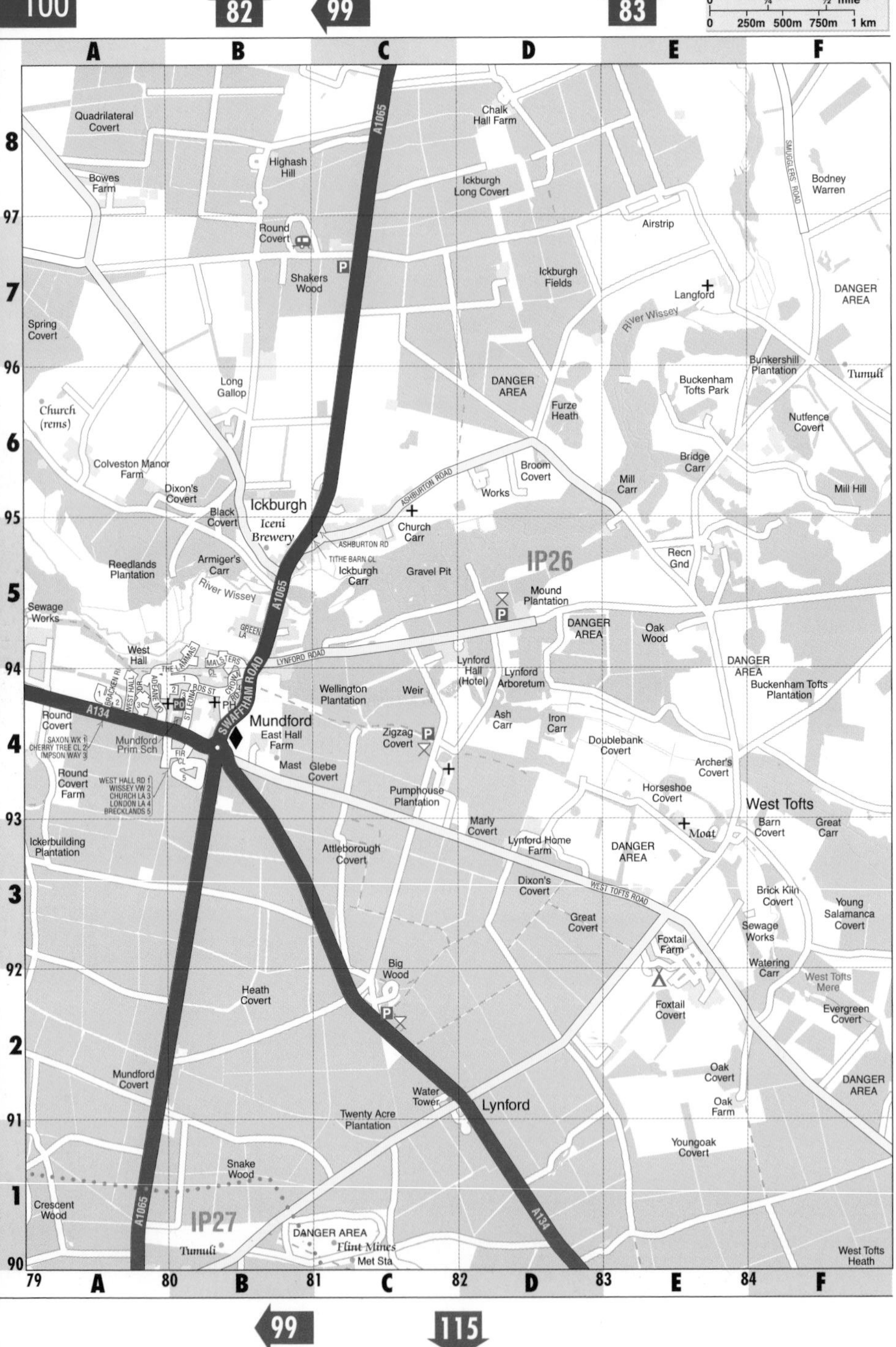

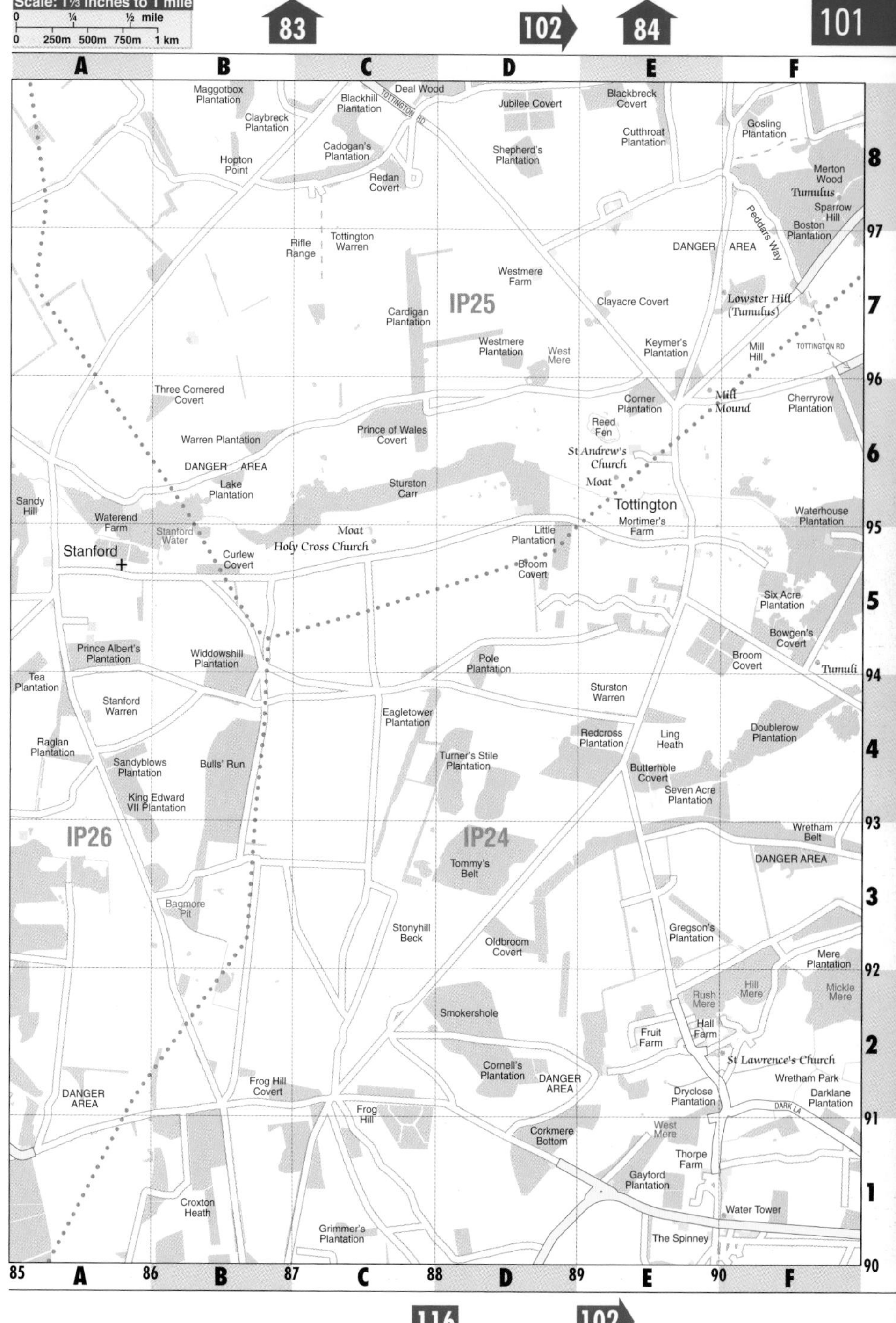

A   B   C   D   E   F

Maggotbox
Plantation

Claybreck
Plantation

Deal Wood

Blackhill
Plantation

Jubilee Covert

Blackbreck
Covert

Cutthroat
Plantation

Gosling
Plantation

Hopton
Point

Cadogan's
Plantation

Redan
Covert

Shepherd's
Plantation

Merton
Wood

8

Tumulus

Sparrow
Hill

Boston
Plantation

97

Rifle
Range

Tottington
Warren

Westmere
Farm

DANGER   AREA

Pedders Way

IP25

Cardigan
Plantation

Clayacre Covert

Lowster Hill
(*Tumulus*)

7

Westmere
Plantation

West
Mere

Keymer's
Plantation

Mill
Hill

Mill
Mound

TOTTINGTON RD

96

Three Cornered
Covert

Corner
Plantation

Cherryrow
Plantation

Warren Plantation

Prince of Wales
Covert

Reed
Fen

St Andrew's
Church

6

DANGER   AREA

Lake
Plantation

Sturston
Carr

Moat

Waterhouse
Plantation

Sandy
Hill

Waterend
Farm

Stanford
Water

Moat

Holy Cross Church

Little
Plantation

Tottington

Mortimer's
Farm

95

Stanford
✝

Curlew
Covert

Broom
Covert

Six Acre
Plantation

5

Prince Albert's
Plantation

Widdowshill
Plantation

Pole
Plantation

Bowgen's
Covert

Broom
Covert

Tumuli

94

Tea
Plantation

Stanford
Warren

Eagletower
Plantation

Sturston
Warren

Ling
Heath

Doublerow
Plantation

4

Raglan
Plantation

Sandyblows
Plantation

Bulls' Run

Turner's Stile
Plantation

Redcross
Plantation

Butterhole
Covert

Seven Acre
Plantation

Wretham
Belt

93

King Edward
VII Plantation

IP26

Tommy's
Belt

IP24

DANGER AREA

3

Bagmore
Pit

Stonyhill
Beck

Oldbroom
Covert

Gregson's
Plantation

Mere
Plantation

92

Smokershole

Rush
Mere

Hill
Mere

Mickle
Mere

2

Frog Hill
Covert

Frog
Hill

Cornell's
Plantation

DANGER
AREA

Fruit
Farm

Hall
Farm

St Lawrence's Church

Wretham Park

DANGER
AREA

Corkmere
Bottom

West
Mere

Dryclose
Plantation

DARK LA

Darklane
Plantation

91

Croxton
Heath

Grimmer's
Plantation

Gayford
Plantation

Thorpe
Farm

The Spinney

Water
Tower

1

85   A   86   B   87   C   88   D   89   E   90   F   90

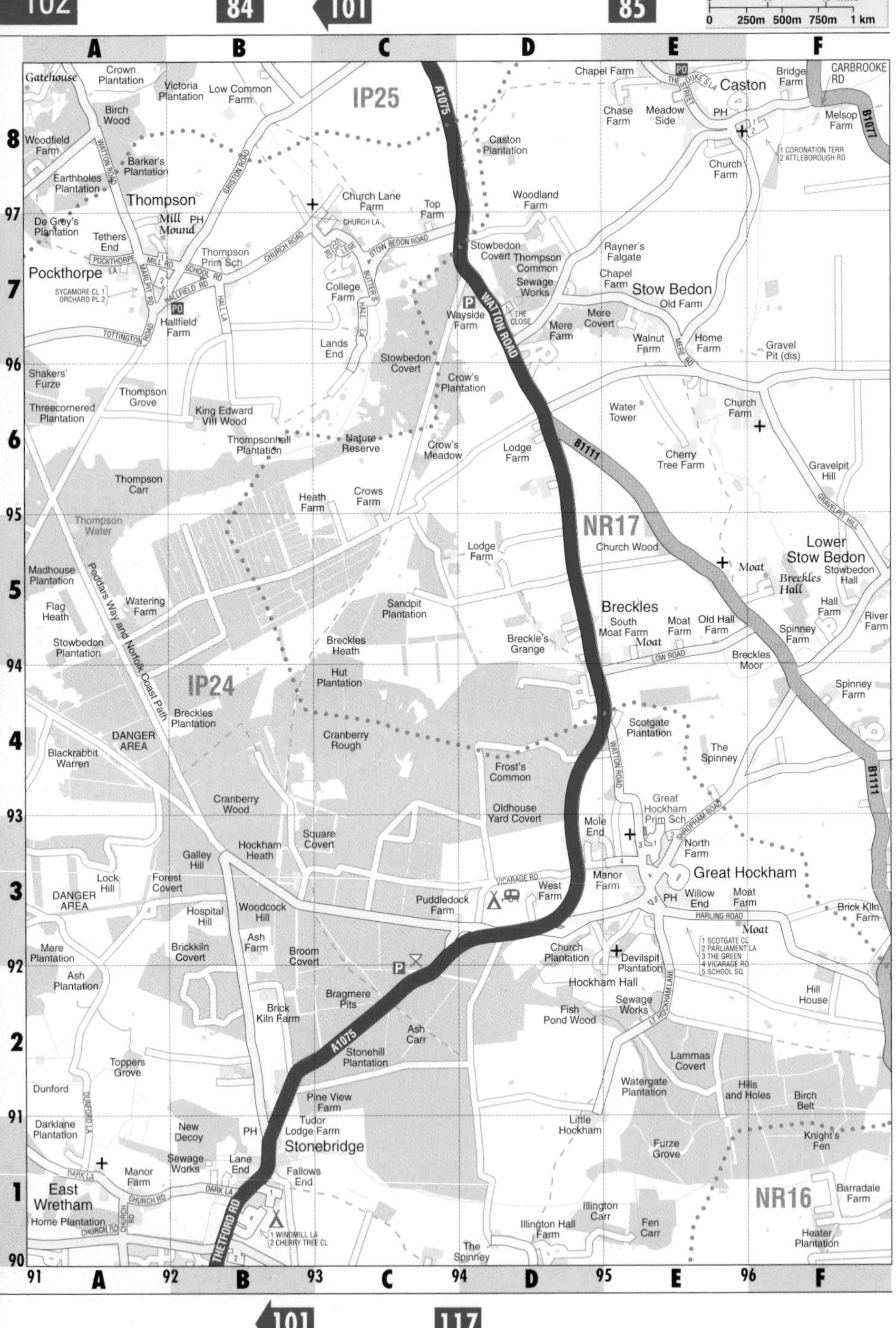

A   B   C   D   E   F

IP25

CARBROOKE RD

Gatehouse
Crown Plantation
Victoria Plantation
Low Common Farm
Chapel Farm
PO
Caston
Bridge Farm
Birch Wood
Chase Farm
Meadow Side
PH
Melsop Farm

8
Woodfield Farm
Barker's Plantation
Caston Plantation
1 CORONATION TERR
2 ATTLEBOROUGH RD
Earthholes Plantation
Woodland Farm
Church Farm

97
De Grey's Plantation
Thompson
Church Lane
Top Farm
Stowbedon Covert
Thompson Common
Rayner's Falgate
Stow Bedon
Tethers End
Mill Mound
PH
CHURCH LA
Sewage Works
Chapel Farm
Old Farm
Pockthorpe
Thompson Prim Sch
SYCAMORE CL 1
ORCHARD PL 2
College Farm
Wayside Farm
Mere Farm
Mere Covert
Walnut Farm
Home Farm
Gravel Pit (dis)
Hallfield Farm
Lands End
Stowbedon Covert

96
Shakers' Furze
Crow's Plantation
Water Tower
Church Farm
Threecornered Plantation
Thompson Grove
King Edward VIII Wood
Nature Reserve
Crow's Meadow
Lodge Farm
Cherry Tree Farm
Gravelpit Hill

6
Thompson Plantation
Thompsonhall Plantation
B1111
Lower Stow Bedon

Thompson Carr
Crows Farm
Heath Farm
NR17
Church Wood
Moat
Breckles Hall
Stowbedon Plantation
Hall Farm
Spinney Farm
River Farm

95
Thompson Water
Lodge Farm
Breckles
South Moat Farm
Moat Farm
Old Hall Farm

Madhouse Plantation
Sandpit Plantation
Breckle's Grange
Moat
Breckles Moor
Spinney Farm

5
Flag Heath
Watering Farm
Breckles Heath
LOW ROAD

Stowbedon Plantation
Hut Plantation
Scotgate Plantation

94
IP24
Breckles Plantation
Cranberry Rough
Frost's Common
The Spinney
Spinney Farm

4
DANGER AREA
Cranberry Wood
Oldhouse Yard Covert
Great Hockham Prim Sch
North Farm

Blackrabbit Warren
Square Covert
Mole End
Great Hockham

93
Lock Hill
Hockham Heath
Galley Hill
Willow End
Moat Farm
Brick Kiln Farm

3
DANGER AREA
Forest Covert
Woodcock Hill
Puddledock Farm
West Farm
Manor Farm
HARLING ROAD
Moat
Hill House

Mere Plantation
Hospital Hill
Ash Farm
Church Plantation
Devilspit Plantation
1 SCOTGATE CL
2 PARLIAMENT LA
3 THE GREEN
4 VICARAGE RD
5 SCHOOL SQ

92
Ash Plantation
Brickkiln Covert
Broom Covert
Hockham Hall Farm
Sewage Works
Fish Pond Wood
Lammas Covert

2
Toppers Grove
Brick Kiln Farm
Bragmere Pits
Ash Carr
A1075
Stonehill Plantation
Watergate Plantation
Hills and Holes
Birch Belt

Dunford
Pine View Farm
Little Hockham
Furze Grove
Knight's Fen

91
Darklane Plantation
New Decoy
PH
Tudor Lodge Farm
Stonebridge
NR16
Barradale Farm

1
East Wretham
Manor Farm
Sewage Works
Lane End
Fallows End
Illington Carr
Fen Carr
Heater Plantation

Home Plantation
1 WINDMILL LA
2 CHERRY TREE CL
Illington Hall Farm
The Spinney

90

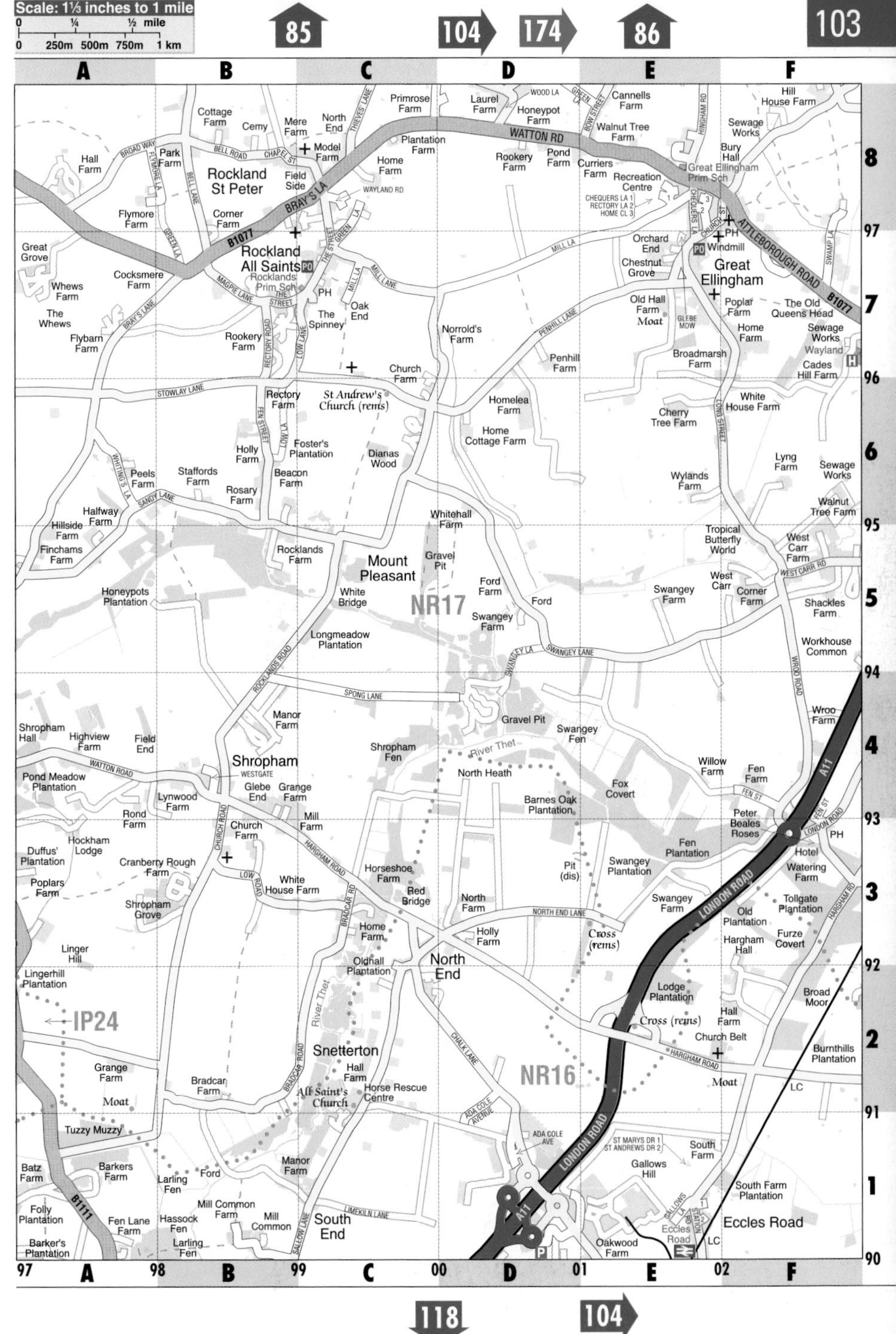

Scale: 1⅓ inches to 1 mile
85
104
174
86
Rockland St Peter
Rockland All Saints
Great Ellingham
Mount Pleasant
NR17
Shropham
Snetterton
North End
South End
NR16
IP24
Eccles Road
WATTON RD
ATTLEBOROUGH ROAD
B1077
LONDON ROAD
A11
B1111
Cottage Farm
Mere Farm
North End
Primrose Farm
Laurel Farm
Honeypot Farm
Cannells Farm
Walnut Tree Farm
Hill House Farm
Sewage Works
Bury Hall
Hall Farm
Park Farm
Model Farm
Plantation Farm
Home Farm
Rookery Farm
Pond Farm
Curriers Farm
Recreation Centre
Great Ellingham Prim Sch
Flymore Farm
Corner Farm
Field Side
Great Grove
Cocksmere Farm
Rocklands Prim Sch
Orchard End
Chestnut Grove
Windmill
Whews Farm
The Whews
Flybarn Farm
The Spinney
Oak End
Rookery Farm
Norrold's Farm
Old Hall Farm
Moat
Poplar Farm
The Old Queens Head
Sewage Works
Home Farm
Wayland
Broadmarsh Farm
Penhill Farm
Cades Hill Farm
Church Farm
Rectory Farm
St Andrew's Church (rems)
Homelea Farm
Home Cottage Farm
Cherry Tree Farm
White House Farm
Holly Farm
Foster's Plantation
Dianas Wood
Peels Farm
Staffords Farm
Beacon Farm
Rosary Farm
Lyng Farm
Wylands Farm
Halfway Farm
Hillside Farm
Finchams Farm
Whitehall Farm
Walnut Tree Farm
Tropical Butterfly World
Rocklands Farm
Gravel Pit
West Carr Farm
Honeypots Plantation
White Bridge
Ford Farm
Ford
West Carr
Swangey Farm
Corner Farm
Shackles Farm
Longmeadow Plantation
Swangey Farm
Workhouse Common
Manor Farm
Gravel Pit
Swangey Fen
Wroo Farm
Shropham Hall
Highview Farm
Field End
Shropham Fen
River Thet
North Heath
Willow Farm
Fen Farm
Pond Meadow Plantation
Glebe End
Grange Farm
Fox Covert
Barnes Oak Plantation
Lynwood Farm
Rond Farm
Mill Farm
Peter Beales Roses
Church Farm
Hockham Lodge
Fen Plantation
PH
Hotel
Duffus' Plantation
Cranberry Rough Farm
Horseshoe Farm
Pit (dis)
Swangey Plantation
Watering Farm
Poplars Farm
White House Farm
Red Bridge
North Farm
Swangey Farm
Tollgate Plantation
Shropham Grove
Home Farm
Holly Farm
Cross (rems)
Old Plantation
Hargham Hall
Furze Covert
Linger Hill
Oldhall Plantation
Lingerhill Plantation
Lodge Plantation
Broad Moor
Cross (rems)
Hall Farm
Church Belt
Grange Farm
Bradcar Farm
Hall Farm
All Saint's Church
Horse Rescue Centre
Burnthills Plantation
Moat
Tuzzy Muzzy
LC
Batz Farm
Barkers Farm
Larling Fen
Ford
Manor Farm
Gallows Hill
South Farm
South Farm Plantation
Folly Plantation
Fen Lane Farm
Hassock Fen
Mill Common Farm
Mill Common
Eccles Road
Oakwood Farm
Barker's Plantation
Larling Fen
118
104

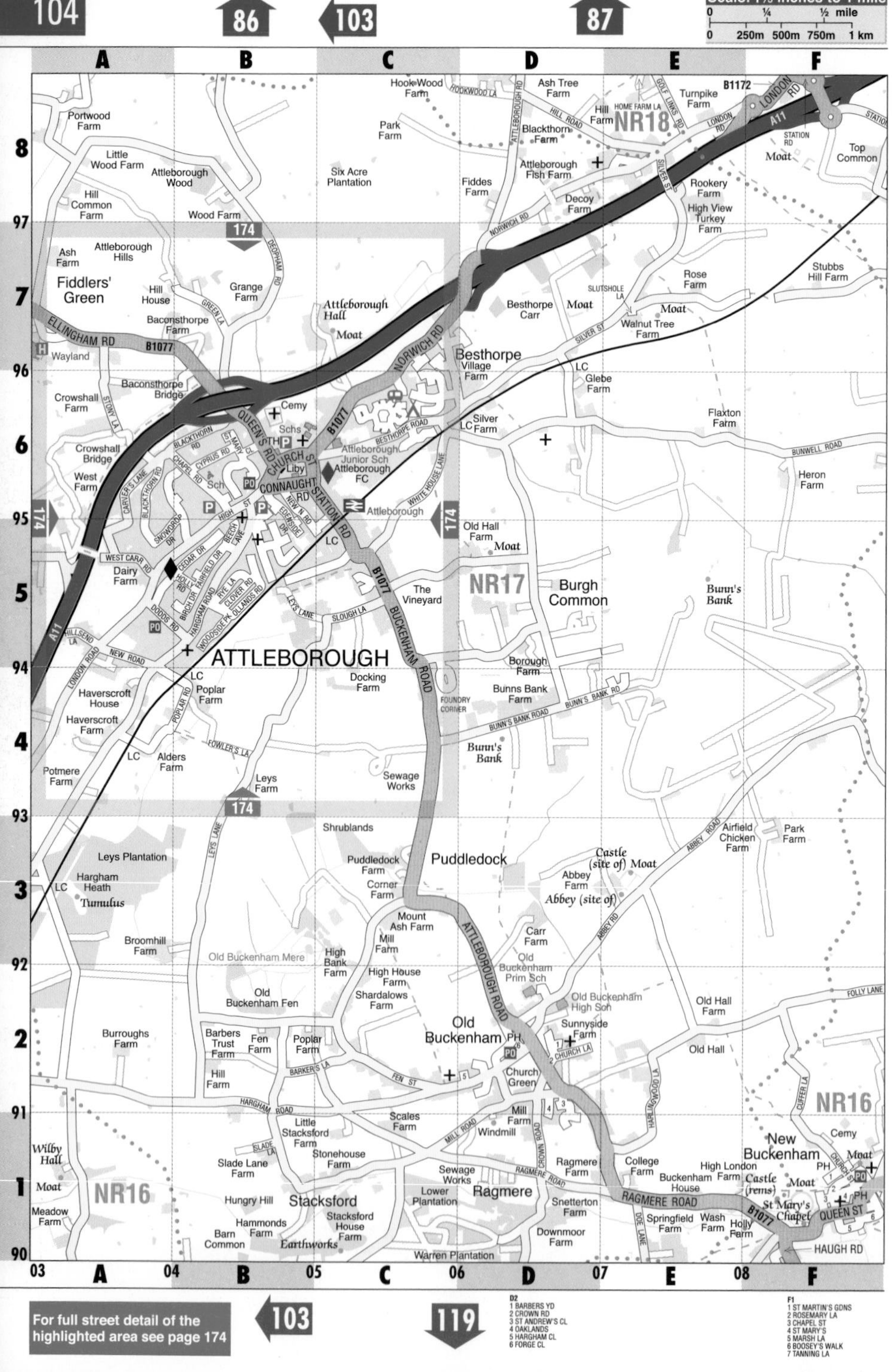

Scale: 1⅓ inches to 1 mile

0   ¼   ½   mile
0 250m 500m 750m 1 km

ATTLEBOROUGH

NR18

NR17

NR16

NR16

New
Buckenham

Old
Buckenham

Ragmere

Stacksford

Puddledock

Besthorpe

Fiddlers'
Green

For full street detail of the
highlighted area see page 174

D2
1 BARBERS YD
2 CROWN RD
3 ST ANDREW'S CL
4 OAKLANDS
5 HARGHAM CL
6 FORGE CL

F1
1 ST MARTIN'S GDNS
2 ROSEMARY LA
3 CHAPEL ST
4 ST MARY'S
5 MARSH LA
6 BOOSEY'S WALK
7 TANNING LA

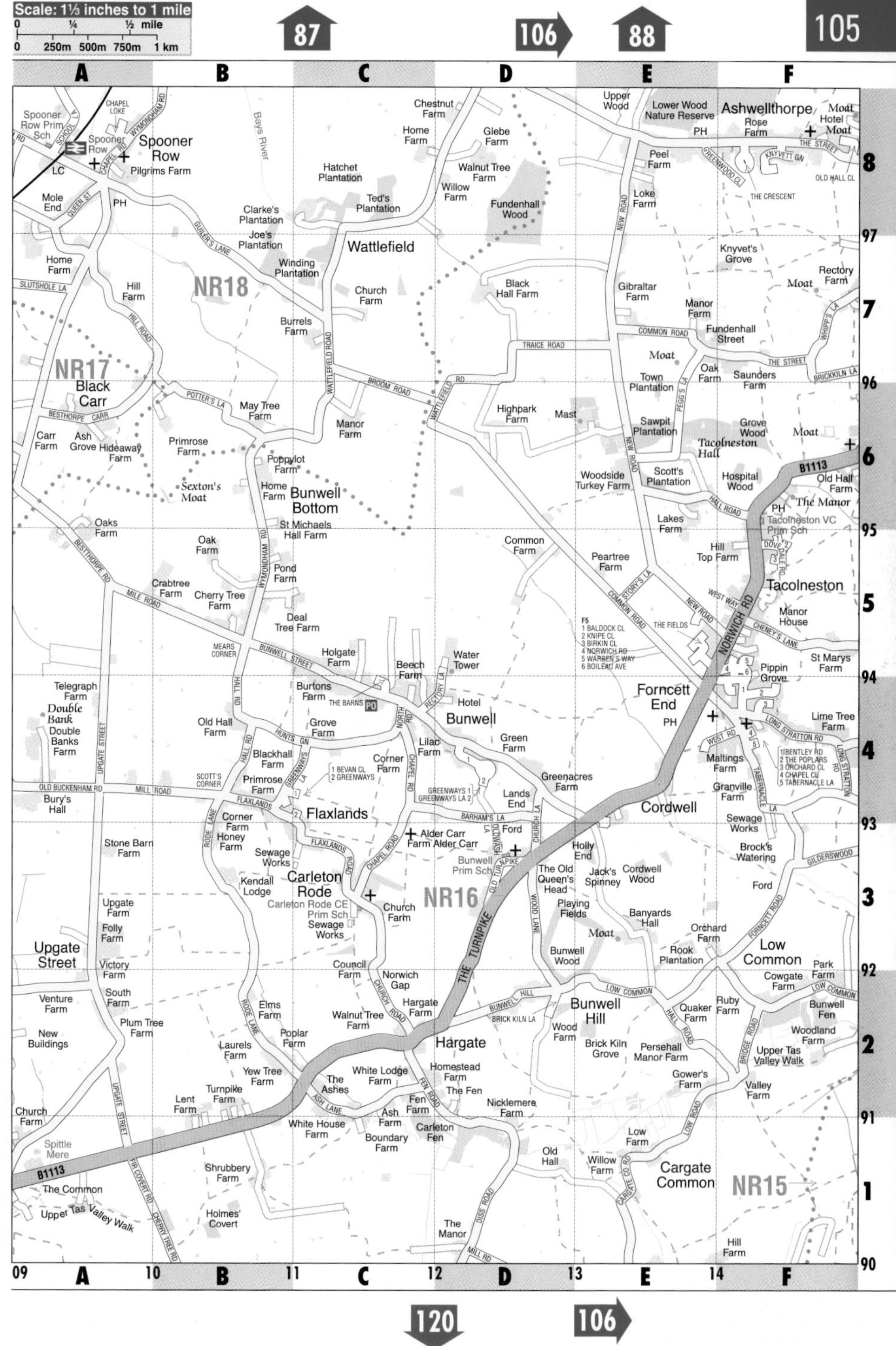

Scale: 1⅓ inches to 1 mile
0 ¼ ½ mile
0 250m 500m 750m 1 km
87
106
88
A B C D E F
Spooner Row
Wattlefield
Ashwellthorpe
NR18
NR17
Black Carr
Bunwell Bottom
Tacolneston
Forncett End
Bunwell
Flaxlands
Carleton Rode
NR16
Cordwell
Upgate Street
Low Common
Bunwell Hill
Hargate
Cargate Common
NR15
B1113
THE TURNPIKE
NORWICH RD
F5
1 BALDOCK CL
2 KNIPE CL
3 BIRKIN CL
4 NORWICH RD
5 WARREN'S WAY
6 BOILEAU AVE
1 BEVAN CL
2 GREENWAYS
1 BENTLEY RD
2 THE POPLARS
3 ORCHARD CL
4 CHAPEL CL
5 TABERNACLE LA
8 97 7 96 6 95 5 94 4 93 3 92 2 91 1 90
09 10 11 12 13 14
120
106

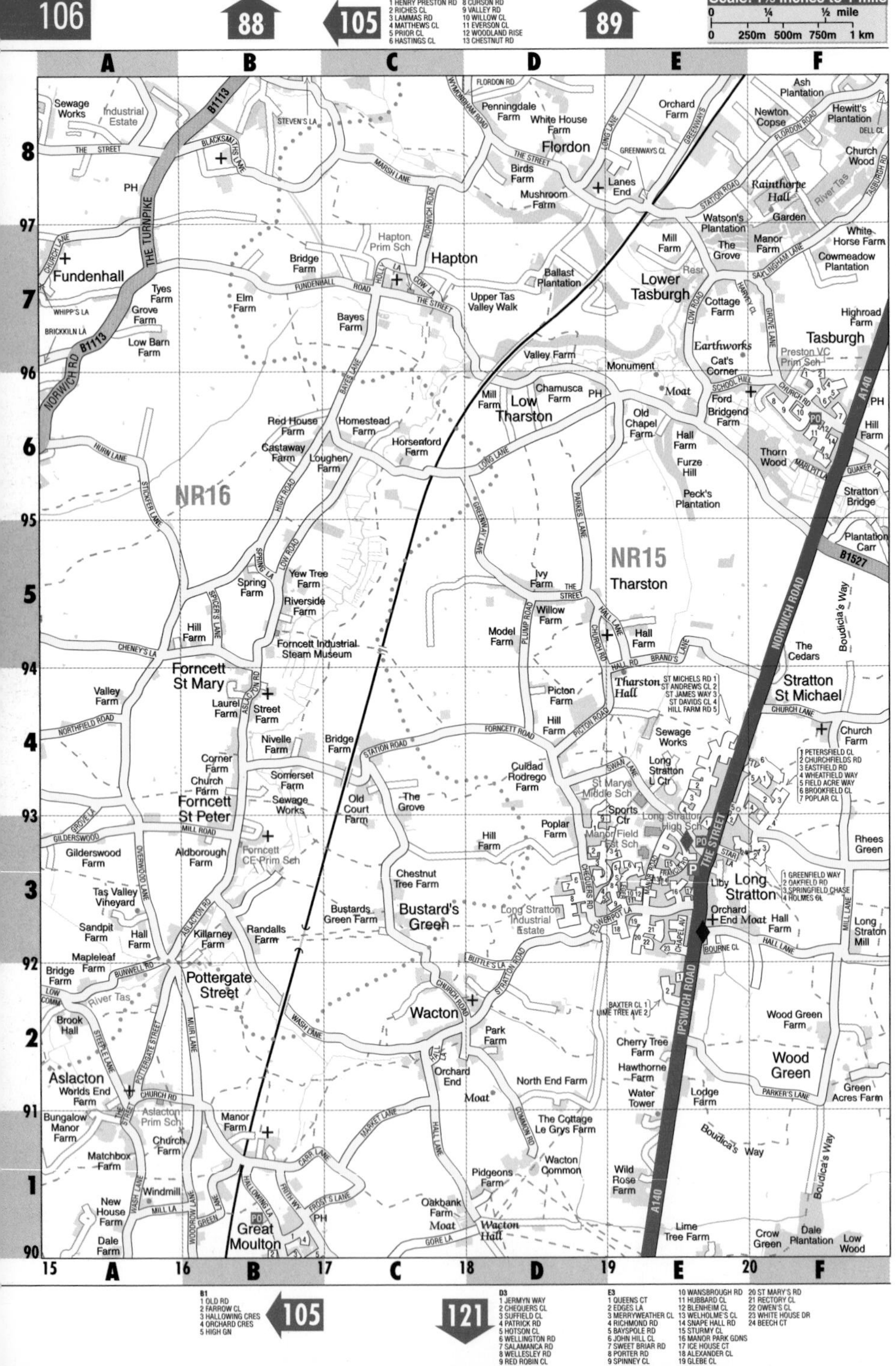

88
105
89
F6
1 HENRY PRESTON RD
2 RICHES CL
3 LAMMAS RD
4 MATTHEWS CL
5 PRIOR CL
6 HASTINGS CL
7 ORCHARD WAY
8 CURSON RD
9 VALLEY RD
10 WILLOW CL
11 EVERSON CL
12 WOODLAND RISE
13 CHESTNUT RD
14 OAK CL
Scale: 1⅓ inches to 1 mile
0 ¼ ½ mile
0 250m 500m 750m 1 km
A
B
C
D
E
F
Sewage Works
Industrial Estate
B1113
THE STREET
BLACKSMITHS LANE
STEVEN'S LA
FLORDON RD
WYMONDHAM ROAD
Penningdale Farm
White House Farm
Flordon
Orchard Farm
GREENWAYS
GREENWAYS CL
LONG LANE
Lanes End
Ash Plantation
Newton Copse
FLORDON ROAD
Hewitt's Plantation
DELL CL
Church Wood
TASBURGH RD
River Tas
Rainthorpe Hall
STATION ROAD
Garden
PH
THE TURNPIKE
MARSH LANE
NORWICH ROAD
Birds Farm
Mushroom Farm
CHURCH LANE
Fundenhall
Hapton Prim Sch
Hapton
Bridge Farm
HOLLY LA
COW LA
FUNDENHALL ROAD
THE STREET
Tyes Farm
Grove Farm
WHIPP'S LA
BRICKKILN LA
Low Barn Farm
NORWICH RD
Elm Farm
Bayes Farm
Upper Tas Valley Walk
Ballast Plantation
Mill Farm
Watson's Plantation
The Grove
Manor Farm
White Horse Farm
Cowmeadow Plantation
SAXLINGHAM LANE
Lower Tasburgh
Resr
LOW ROAD
HARVEY CL
Cottage Farm
GROVE LANE
Highroad Farm
Tasburgh
Earthworks
Preston VC Prim Sch
Valley Farm
Monument
Cat's Corner
SCHOOL HILL
CHURCH RD
BAYES LANE
Mill Farm
Low Tharston
Chamusca Farm
PH
Moat
Ford Bridgend Farm
A140
PH
Hill Farm
Red House Farm
Homestead Farm
Old Chapel Farm
Hall Farm
Castaway Farm
Loughen Farm
Horsenford Farm
LONG LANE
Furze Hill
Thorn Wood
MARLPIT LA
QUAKER LA
HURN LANE
STICKFER LANE
NR16
HIGH ROAD
GREENWAY LANE
PARKES LANE
Peck's Plantation
Stratton Bridge
Plantation Carr
B1527
SPRING LA
LOW ROAD
Yew Tree Farm
Spring Farm
Riverside Farm
Ivy Farm
THE STREET
NR15
Tharston
NORWICH ROAD
Boudicia's Way
SPICER'S LANE
Hill Farm
CHENEY'S LA
Forncett Industrial Steam Museum
Model Farm
PLUMP ROAD
Willow Farm
HALL LANE
CHURCH RD
Hall Farm
BRAND'S LANE
The Cedars
HALL RD
Forncett St Mary
ASLACTON RD
Laurel Farm
Street Farm
Valley Farm
Picton Farm
Tharston Hall
ST MICHELS RD 1
ST ANDREWS CL 2
ST JAMES WAY 3
ST DAVIDS CL 4
HILL FARM RD 5
Stratton St Michael
CHURCH LANE
Church Farm
NORTHFIELD ROAD
Nivelle Farm
Bridge Farm
STATION ROAD
FORNCETT ROAD
Hill Farm
PICTON ROAD
Sewage Works
1 PETERSFIELD CL
2 CHURCHFIELDS RD
3 EASTFIELD RD
4 WHEATFIELD WAY
5 FIELD ACRE WAY
6 BROOKFIELD CL
7 POPLAR CL
Corner Farm
Church Farm
Somerset Farm
Cuidad Rodrego Farm
SWAN LANE
Long Stratton L Ctr
St Marys Middle Sch
Forncett St Peter
Sewage Works
Old Court Farm
The Grove
Sports Ctr
Long Stratton High Sch
GROVE LA
GILDERSWOOD
MILL ROAD
Poplar Farm
Manor Field Fst Sch
THE STREET
Rhees Green
Gilderswood Farm
OVERWOOD LANE
Aldborough Farm
Forncett CE Prim Sch
Hill Farm
STAR LA
Chestnut Tree Farm
CHEQUERS RD
MANOR ROAD
FRANCIS RD
Lby
Long Stratton
1 GREENFIELD WAY
2 OAKFIELD RD
3 SPRINGFIELD CHASE
4 HOLMES CL
Tas Valley Vineyard
Bustards Green Farm
Bustard's Green
Long Stratton Industrial Estate
FLOWERPOT LA
CHAPEL AV
Orchard End
Moat
Hall Farm
MILL LANE
Long Stratton Mill
Sandpit Farm
ASLACTON RD
Randalls Farm
Hall Farm
Killarney Farm
HALL LANE
BOURNE CL
Mapleleaf Farm
BUNWELL RD
BUFFLE'S LA
STRATTON ROAD
Bridge Farm
Pottergate Street
LOW COMMON
River Tas
CHURCH ROAD
BAXTER CL 1
LIME TREE AVE 2
Brook Hall
STEEPLE LANE
POTTERGATE STREET
MUIR LANE
Wacton
IPSWICH ROAD
Wood Green Farm
WASH LANE
Park Farm
HALL LA
Cherry Tree Farm
Hawthorne Farm
Wood Green
Aslacton
Worlds End Farm
CHURCH RD
Orchard End
North End Farm
Water Tower
Lodge Farm
PARKER'S LANE
Green Acres Farm
Moat
Bungalow Manor Farm
THE STREET
Aslacton Prim Sch
Manor Farm
MARKET LANE
COMMON RD
The Cottage
Le Grys Farm
Boudica's Way
Church Farm
Matchbox Farm
CARR LANE
Wacton Common
Boudica's Way
Windmill
Pigeons Farm
Wild Rose Farm
New House Farm
WASH LANE
MILL LA
GREEN
HALLOWING LA
FRITH WY
FROST'S LANE
WOODROW LANE
Oakbank Farm
Moat
Wacton Hall
GORE LA
Great Moulton
PH
A140
Lime Tree Farm
Crow Green
Dale Plantation
Low Wood
Dale Farm
8
97
7
96
6
95
5
94
4
93
3
92
2
91
1
90
15
16
17
18
19
20
B1
1 OLD RD
2 FARROW CL
3 HALLOWING CRES
4 ORCHARD CRES
5 HIGH GN
105
121
D3
1 JERMYN WAY
2 CHEQUERS CL
3 SUFFIELD CL
4 PATRICK RD
5 HOTSON CL
6 WELLINGTON RD
7 SALAMANCA RD
8 WELLESLEY RD
9 RED ROBIN CL
E3
1 QUEENS CT
2 EDGES LA
3 MERRYWEATHER CL
4 RICHMOND RD
5 BAYSPOLE RD
6 JOHN HILL CL
7 SWEET BRIAR RD
8 PORTER RD
9 SPINNEY CL
10 WANSBROUGH RD
11 HUBBARD CL
12 BLENHEIM CL
13 WELHOLME'S CL
14 SNAPE HALL RD
15 STURMY CL
16 MANOR PARK GDNS
17 ICE HOUSE CT
18 ALEXANDER CL
19 GLEBE CL
20 ST MARY'S RD
21 RECTORY CL
22 OWEN'S CL
23 WHITE HOUSE DR
24 BEECH CT

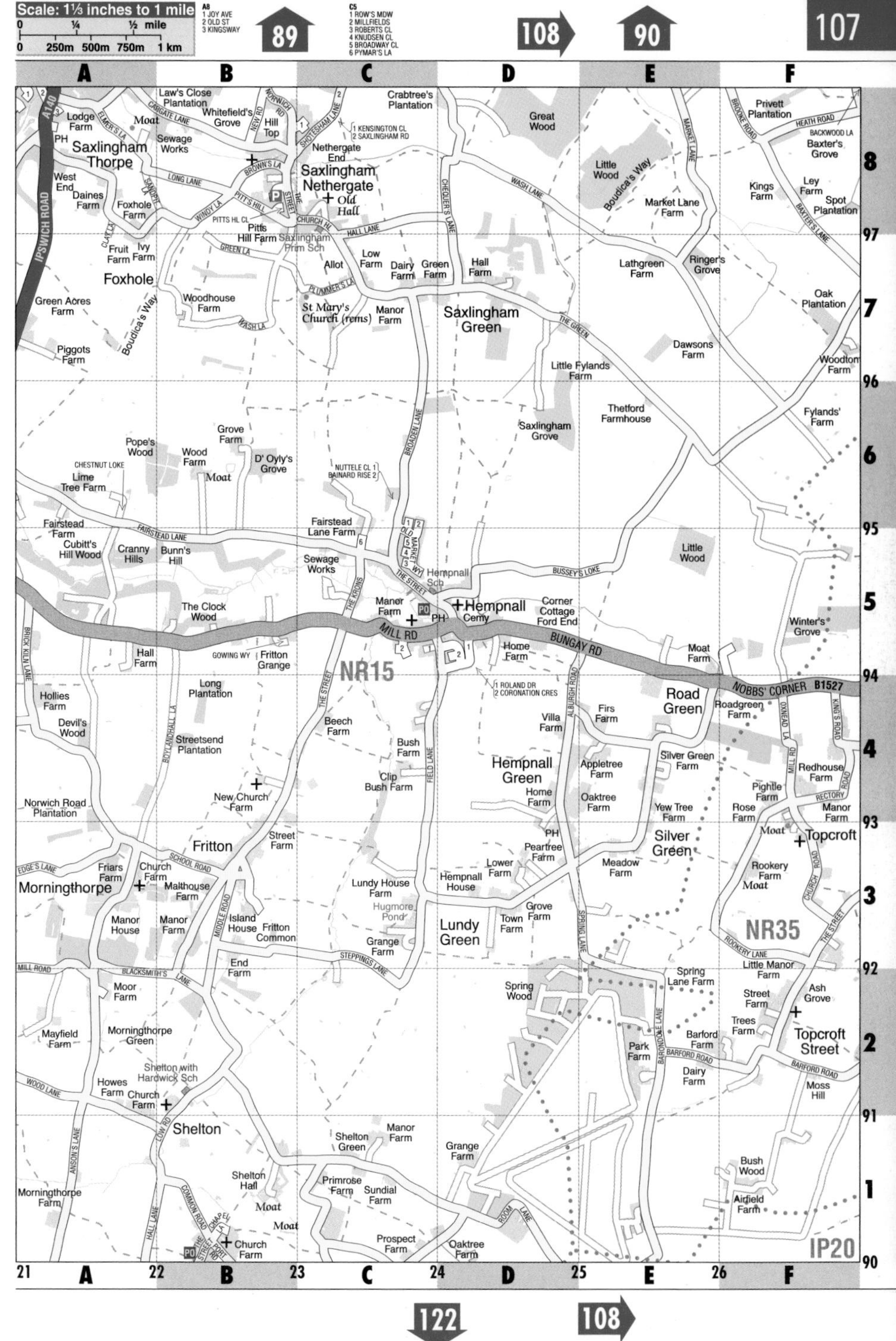
Scale: 1⅓ inches to 1 mile
0 ¼ ½ mile
0 250m 500m 750m 1 km
A8
1 JOY AVE
2 OLD ST
3 KINGSWAY
89
C5
1 ROW'S MDW
2 MILLFIELDS
3 ROBERTS CL
4 KNUDSEN CL
5 BROADWAY CL
6 PYMAR'S LA
108
90
107
A
B
C
D
E
F
Law's Close Plantation
Crabtree's Plantation
Great Wood
Privett Plantation
HEATH ROAD
BACKWOOD LA
Baxter's Grove
Lodge Farm
Moat
Whitefield's Grove
Hill Top
1 KENSINGTON CL
2 SAXLINGHAM RD
PH
Saxlingham Thorpe
Sewage Works
Nethergate End
Saxlingham Nethergate
Old Hall
Little Wood
Boudica's Way
Market Lane Farm
Kings Farm
Ley Farm
Spot Plantation
8
West End
Daines Farm
Foxhole Farm
LONG LANE
WINDY LA
PITT'S HILL
PITTS HL CL
Pitts Hill Farm
Saxlingham Prim Sch
CHURCH HL
HALL LANE
WASH LANE
CHEQUER'S LANE
MARKET LANE
BROOKE ROAD
BAXTER'S LANE
97
IPSWICH ROAD
A140
Fruit Farm
Ivy Farm
GREEN LA
Allot
Low Farm
Dairy Farm
Green Farm
Hall Farm
Lathgreen Farm
Ringer's Grove
Foxhole
PLUMMER'S LA
Green Acres Farm
Woodhouse Farm
St Mary's Church (rems)
Manor Farm
Saxlingham Green
THE GREEN
Oak Plantation
7
WASH LA
Piggots Farm
Dawsons Farm
Little Fylands Farm
Woodton Farm
96
Thetford Farmhouse
Fylands' Farm
Grove Farm
Pope's Wood
Wood Farm
D' Oyly's Grove
Saxlingham Grove
BROADEN LANE
6
CHESTNUT LOKE
Lime Tree Farm
Moat
NUTTELE CL 1
BAINARD RISE 2
Fairstead Farm
FAIRSTEAD LANE
Fairstead Lane Farm
95
Cubitt's Hill Wood
Cranny Hills
Bunn's Hill
Sewage Works
Little Wood
OLD MARKET WY
BUSSEY'S LOKE
Hempnall Sch
THE STREET
The Clock Wood
THE KRONS
Manor Farm
PO
PH
Hempnall
Cemy
Corner Cottage
Ford End
5
Winter's Grove
MILL RD
BUNGAY RD
BRICK KILN LANE
Hall Farm
GOWING WY
Fritton Grange
Home Farm
Moat Farm
NR15
1 ROLAND DR
2 CORONATION CRES
94
Hollies Farm
Long Plantation
ALBURGH ROAD
Road Green
NOBBS' CORNER
B1527
Roadgreen Farm
KING'S ROAD
Devil's Wood
THE STREET
BOYLANDHALL LA
Beech Farm
Villa Farm
Firs Farm
Streetsend Plantation
Bush Farm
OXHEAD LA
4
Silver Green Farm
Hempnall Green
Appletree Farm
Redhouse Farm
MILL RD
Clip Bush Farm
FIELD LANE
Pightle Farm
RECTORY
New Church Farm
Home Farm
Oaktree Farm
Norwich Road Plantation
Yew Tree Farm
Rose Farm
Manor Farm
93
PH
Moat
Topcroft
Street Farm
Silver Green
Fritton
Peartree Farm
EDGE'S LANE
SCHOOL ROAD
Friars Farm
Church Farm
Lower Farm
Meadow Farm
Rookery Farm
Morningthorpe
Malthouse Farm
Lundy House Farm
Hempnall House
Moat
CHURCH ROAD
3
Hugmore Pond
Grove Farm
Manor House
Manor Farm
Island House
Fritton Common
Lundy Green
Town Farm
MIDDLE ROAD
NR35
Grange Farm
SPRING LANE
THE STREET
ROOKERY LANE
End Farm
STEPPINGS LANE
MILL ROAD
BLACKSMITH'S LANE
Little Manor Farm
92
Spring Wood
Spring Lane Farm
Moor Farm
Street Farm
Ash Grove
Mayfield Farm
Morningthorpe Green
Trees Farm
Barford Farm
Topcroft Street
BARONDOLE LANE
Park Farm
BARFORD ROAD
2
Shelton with Hardwick Sch
Howes Farm
Church Farm
WOOD LANE
Dairy Farm
Moss Hill
91
Shelton
LOW RD
ANSON'S LANE
Shelton Green
Manor Farm
Grange Farm
Shelton Hall
Bush Wood
Primrose Farm
Sundial Farm
Morningthorpe Farm
COMMON ROAD
Moat
Airfield Farm
1
Moat
HALL LANE
CHAPEL
PO
Church Farm
Prospect Farm
Oaktree Farm
ROOM LANE
IP20
90
21
22
23
24
25
26
122
108

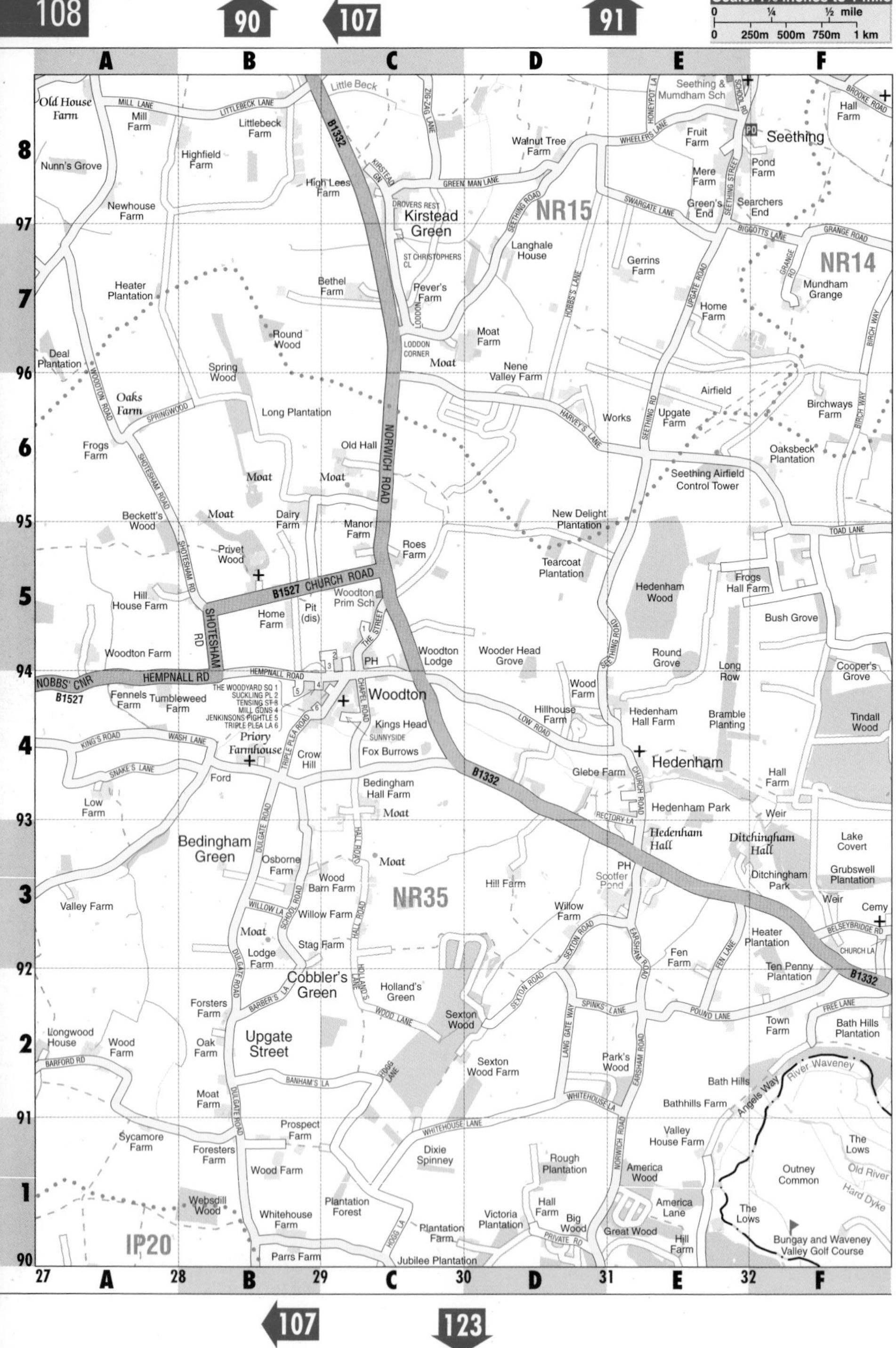

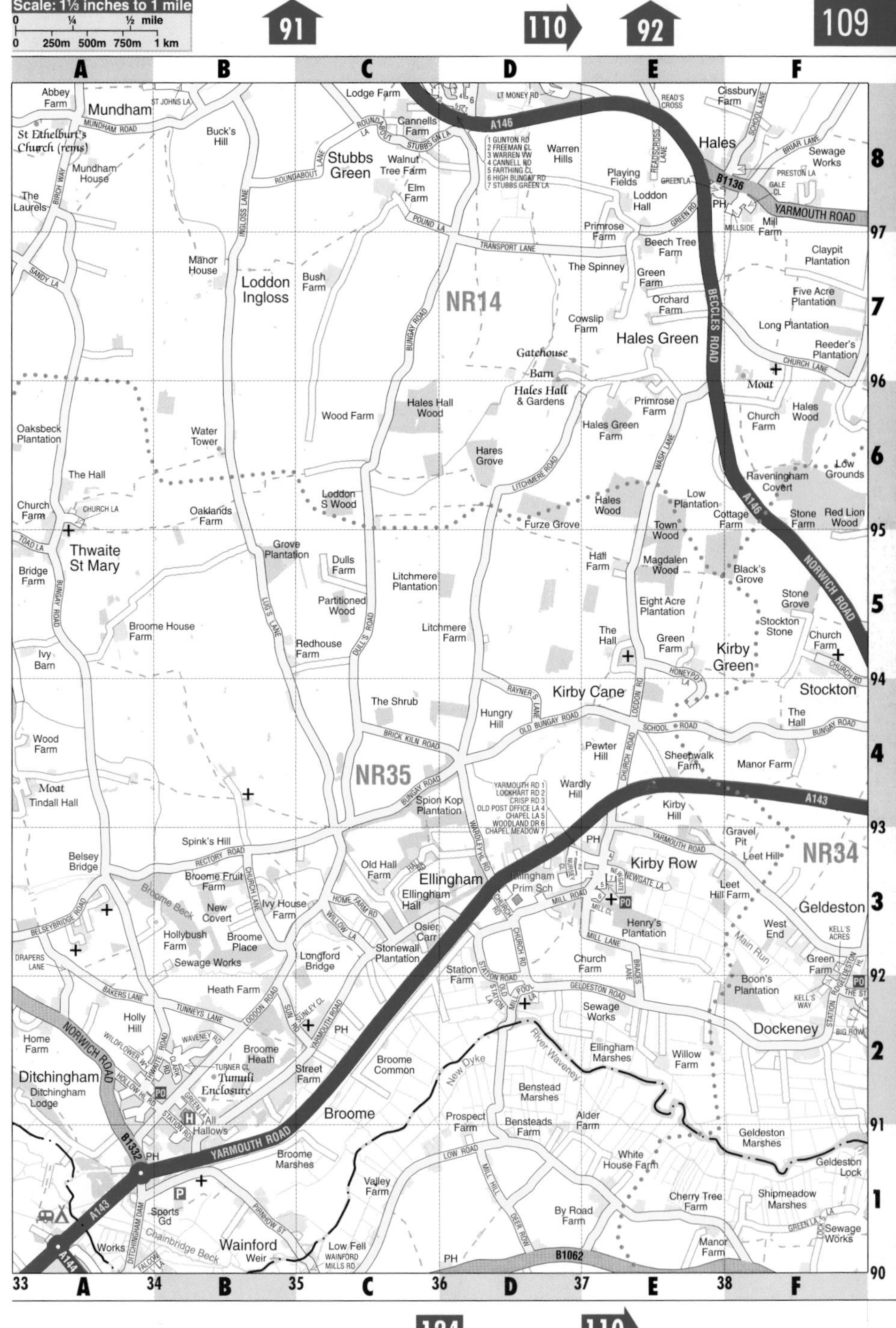
Scale: 1⅓ inches to 1 mile
0 ¼ ½ mile
0 250m 500m 750m 1 km
91
110
92
A B C D E F
Abbey Farm
Mundham
ST JOHNS LA
MUNDHAM ROAD
St Ethelburt's Church (rems)
Buck's Hill
Lodge Farm
Cannells Farm
ROUNDABOUT LA
STUBBS GN LA
LT MONEY RD
A146
1 GUNTON RD
2 FREEMAN CL
3 WARREN VW
4 CANNELL RD
5 FARTHING CL
6 HIGH BUNGAY RD
7 STUBBS GREEN LA
Warren Hills
READ'S CROSS
READSCROSS LANE
Cissbury Farm
SCHOOL LANE
Hales
BRIAR LANE
Sewage Works
PRESTON LA
GALE CL
B1136
YARMOUTH ROAD
PH
MILLSIDE
Mill Farm
Mundham House
BIRCH WAY
The Laurels
ROUNDABOUT LANE
Stubbs Green
Walnut Tree Farm
Elm Farm
Playing Fields
Loddon Hall
GREEN LA
GREEN RD
POUND LA
Primrose Farm
Beech Tree Farm
Claypit Plantation
TRANSPORT LANE
Manor House
INGLOSS LANE
Loddon Ingloss
Bush Farm
SANDY LA
NR14
The Spinney
Green Farm
Orchard Farm
BECCLES ROAD
Five Acre Plantation
Long Plantation
BUNGAY ROAD
Cowslip Farm
Hales Green
Reeder's Plantation
CHURCH LANE
Gatehouse Barn
Hales Hall & Gardens
Moat
Hales Hall Wood
Wood Farm
Primrose Farm
Church Farm
Hales Wood
Oaksbeck Plantation
Water Tower
Hales Green Farm
WASH LANE
Hares Grove
LITCHMERE ROAD
Low Grounds
Ravenningham Covert
The Hall
Loddon S Wood
Low Plantation
Hales Wood
A146
Church Farm
CHURCH LA
Oaklands Farm
Furze Grove
Cottage Farm
Stone Farm
Red Lion Wood
TOAD LA
Thwaite St Mary
Grove Plantation
Town Wood
Hall Farm
Magdalen Wood
Black's Grove
NORWICH ROAD
Bridge Farm
Dulls Farm
Litchmere Plantation
BUNGAY ROAD
Partitioned Wood
Eight Acre Plantation
Stone Grove
Broome House Farm
DULL'S ROAD
Stockton Stone
LUG'S LANE
Redhouse Farm
Litchmere Farm
The Hall
Green Farm
Kirby Green
Church Farm
Ivy Barn
HONEYPOT LA
CHURCH RD
RAYNER'S LANE
Kirby Cane
LODDON RD
Stockton
The Shrub
Hungry Hill
OLD BUNGAY ROAD
SCHOOL ROAD
The Hall
BUNGAY ROAD
Wood Farm
BRICK KILN ROAD
Pewter Hill
CHURCH ROAD
Sheepwalk Farm
Manor Farm
NR35
Moat
Tindall Hall
BUNGAY ROAD
Spion Kop Plantation
YARMOUTH RD 1
LOCKHART RD 2
CRISP RD 3
OLD POST OFFICE LA 4
CHAPEL LA 5
WOODLAND DR 6
CHAPEL MEADOW 7
Wardly Hill
Kirby Hill
A143
Gravel Pit
WARDLEY HILL RD
PH
YARMOUTH ROAD
Leet Hill
NR34
Spink's Hill
RECTORY ROAD
Belsey Bridge
Broome Fruit Farm
CHURCH LANE
Old Hall Farm
Ellingham
Ellingham Hall
Ellingham Prim Sch
NURSERY CL
NEWGATE LA
Kirby Row
Leet Hill Farm
Geldeston
Broome Beck
New Covert
Ivy House Farm
HOME FARM RD
MILL ROAD
MILL CL
PO
Henry's Plantation
West End
KELL'S ACRES
BELSEYBRIDGE ROAD
Hollybush Farm
Broome Place
WILLOW LA
Osier Carr
Stonewall Plantation
MILL LANE
Main Run
DRAPERS LANE
Sewage Works
Longford Bridge
Station Farm
STATION ROAD
CHURCH RD
Church Farm
BRACES LANE
Green Farm
Boon's Plantation
ROGELDESTON RD
PO
THE ST
BAKERS LANE
Heath Farm
LODDON ROAD
OLD STATION LA
MILL POOL LA
GELDESTON ROAD
KELL'S WAY
STATION ROAD
TUNNEYS LANE
SUN RD
SUNLEY CL
YARMOUTH ROAD
PH
Sewage Works
Dockeney
BIG ROW
Holly Hill
WAVENEY RD
Home Farm
NORWICH ROAD
WILDFLOWER WY
THWAITE ROAD
CLARK RD
TURNER CL
Broome Heath
River Waveney
Ellingham Marshes
Willow Farm
Tumuli Enclosure
Street Farm
Broome Common
New Dyke
Benstead Marshes
Ditchingham
Ditchingham Lodge
HOLLOW HL RD
PO
GREEN LA
All Hallows
H
STATION RD
Broome
Prospect Farm
Bensteads Farm
Alder Carr
B1332
YARMOUTH ROAD
Geldeston Marshes
PH
White House Farm
Broome Marshes
LOW ROAD
Geldeston Lock
P
A143
Valley Farm
MILL HILL
Cherry Tree Farm
Shipmeadow Marshes
Sports Gd
PIRNHOW ST
DEER ROW
By Road Farm
GREEN LA
LOCK LA
Sewage Works
Works
DITCHINGHAM DAM
Chainbridge Beck
Wainford Weir
Low Fell
WAINFORD MILLS RD
FALCON LA
PH
B1062
Manor Farm
A144
8 97 7 96 6 95 5 94 4 93 3 92 2 91 1 90
33 A 34 B 35 C 36 D 37 E 38 F
124
110

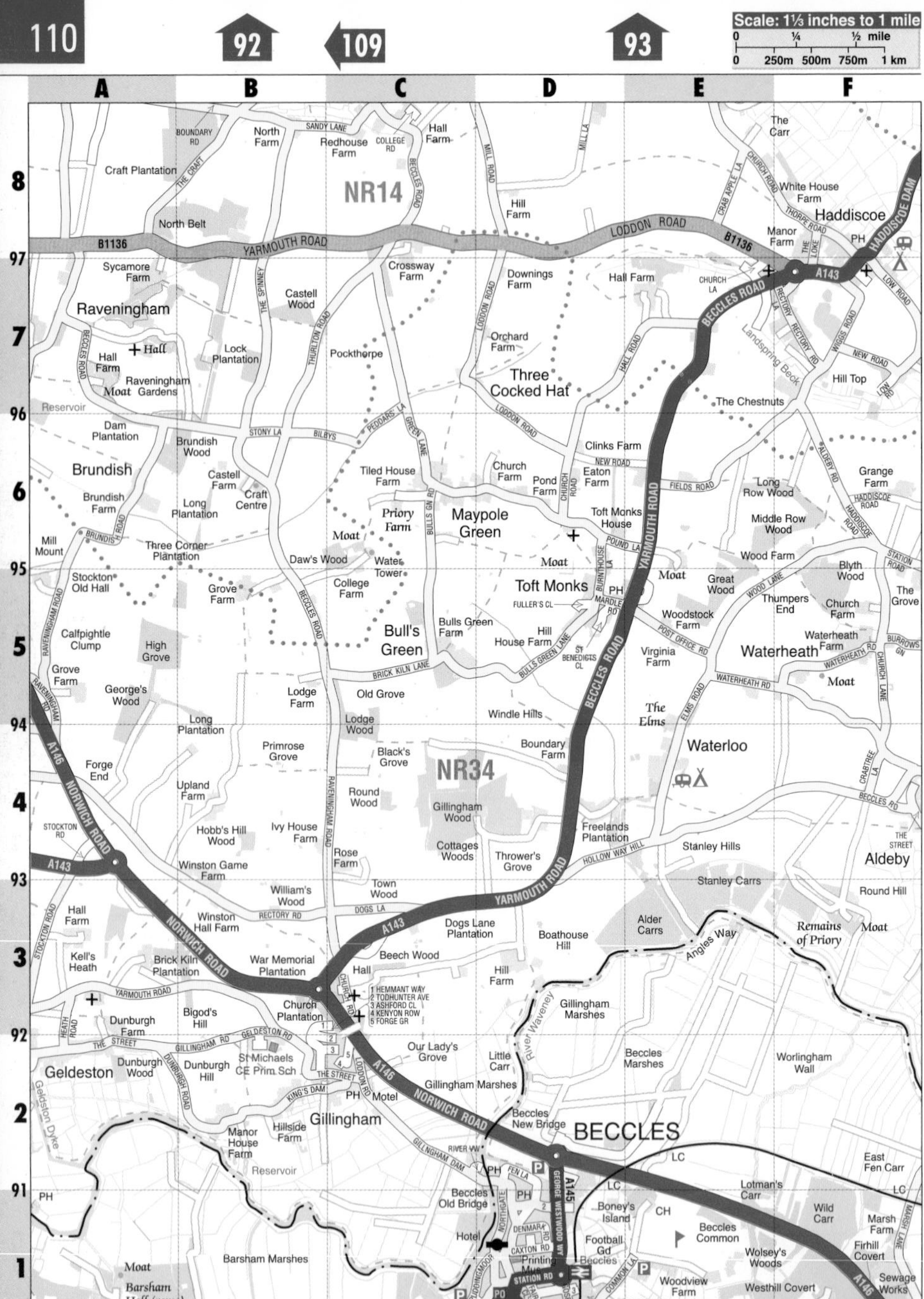

92 109 93

Scale: 1⅓ inches to 1 mile

0   ¼   ½ mile
0   250m 500m 750m 1 km

A   B   C   D   E   F

8

The Carr

BOUNDARY RD
North Farm
SANDY LANE
Redhouse Farm
COLLEGE RD
Hall Farm

White House Farm
Haddiscoe

Craft Plantation

NR14

Hill Farm

Manor Farm
PH

97
B1136   YARMOUTH ROAD   LODDON ROAD   B1136   A143
LOW ROAD

North Belt

Sycamore Farm

Crossway Farm

Downings Farm

Hall Farm

CHURCH LA

BECCLES ROAD

NEW ROAD

7

Raveningham

Castell Wood

Hall Farm
Hall

Lock Plantation

Pockthorpe

Orchard Farm

Three Cocked Hat

Hill Top

Raveningham Moat Gardens

Reservoir

The Chestnuts

96

Dam Plantation

Brundish Wood

STONY LA   BILEYS

PEDDARS LA

GREEN LANE

LODDON ROAD

Clinks Farm

NEW ROAD
Eaton Farm

FIELDS ROAD

Long Row Wood

Grange Farm

HADDISCOE ROAD

STATION ROAD

Brundish

Castell Farm

Tiled House Farm

Church Farm

Pond Farm

Toft Monks House

Middle Row Wood

6

Brundish Farm

Long Plantation

Craft Centre

Priory Farm

Maypole Green

Wood Farm

Blyth Wood

Mill Mount

Three Corner Plantation

Daw's Wood

Moat

Moat

Toft Monks

Moat

Great Wood

Woodstock Farm

Thumpers End

Church Farm

The Grove

95

Stockton Old Hall

Grove Farm

College Farm

Bulls Green Farm

Hill House Farm

FULLER'S CL
MARDLE RD

Virginia Farm

Woodstock Farm

Waterheath

WATERHEATH LANE

CHURCH LANE

BURROWS GN

5

Calfpightle Clump

High Grove

Bull's Green

BULL'S GREEN LANE

Moat

POST OFFICE RD

ELMS ROAD

WATERHEATH RD

Moat

Grove Farm

George's Wood

BRICK KILN LANE

Old Grove

Windle Hills

The Elms

Waterloo

94

Forge End

Long Plantation

Lodge Farm

Lodge Wood

Black's Grove

NR34

Boundary Farm

CRIMBLE LANE

THE STREET

4

Upland Farm

Primrose Grove

Hobb's Hill Wood

Ivy House Farm

Round Wood

Gillingham Wood

Cottages Woods

Thrower's Grove

Freelands Plantation

Stanley Hills

Aldeby

Round Hill

BECCLES ROAD

93
A143   Winston Game Farm

Rose Farm

Town Wood

YARMOUTH ROAD

HOLLOW WAY HILL

Stanley Carrs

Remains of Priory

Moat

STOCKTON RD

Hall Farm

William's Wood

DOGS LA

A143

Dogs Lane Plantation

Boathouse Hill

Alder Carrs

Angles Way

3

Kell's Heath

Brick Kiln Plantation

War Memorial Plantation

RECTORY RD

Beech Wood

Hill Farm

Gillingham Marshes

Beccles Marshes

Worlingham Wall

YARMOUTH ROAD

Bigod's Hill

GELDESTON RD

Church Plantation

1 HEMMANT WAY
2 TODHUNTER AVE
3 ASHFORD CL
4 KENYON ROW
5 FORGE GR

Our Lady's Grove

Little Carr

River Waveney

92

Dunburgh Farm

THE STREET

St Michaels CE Prim Sch

Gillingham Marshes

Beccles Marshes

Geldeston

Dunburgh Wood

Dunburgh Hill

KING'S DAM

Hillside Farm

Motel

NORWICH ROAD

A146

Beccles New Bridge

BECCLES

LC

2

Manor House Farm

Gillingham

PH

Reservoir

GILLINGHAM DAM

RIVER VW

PH

FEN LA

A145

GEORGE WESTWOOD WY

Boney's Island

CH

Lotman's Carr

East Fen Carr

LC

91
PH

Beccles Old Bridge

PH

DENMARK RD

Football Gd
Beccles

Beccles Common

Wild Carr

Marsh Farm

Firhill Covert

NORTHGATE

CAXTON RD

Hotel

STATION RD

Wolsey's Woods

Westhill Covert

A146

1

Moat

Barsham Marshes

P
PO
Printing

Lib

Woodview Farm

Beccles Carr

Horseshoe Covert

Worlingham Hall

Sewage Works

Barsham Hall (rems)

Beccles Mus

1 CLOWES CT
2 COMMON LA NTH
3 DOBSON WAY

90

39   A   40   B   41   C   42   D   43   E   44   F

109

For full street detail of Beccles see
Philip's STREET ATLAS of Suffolk

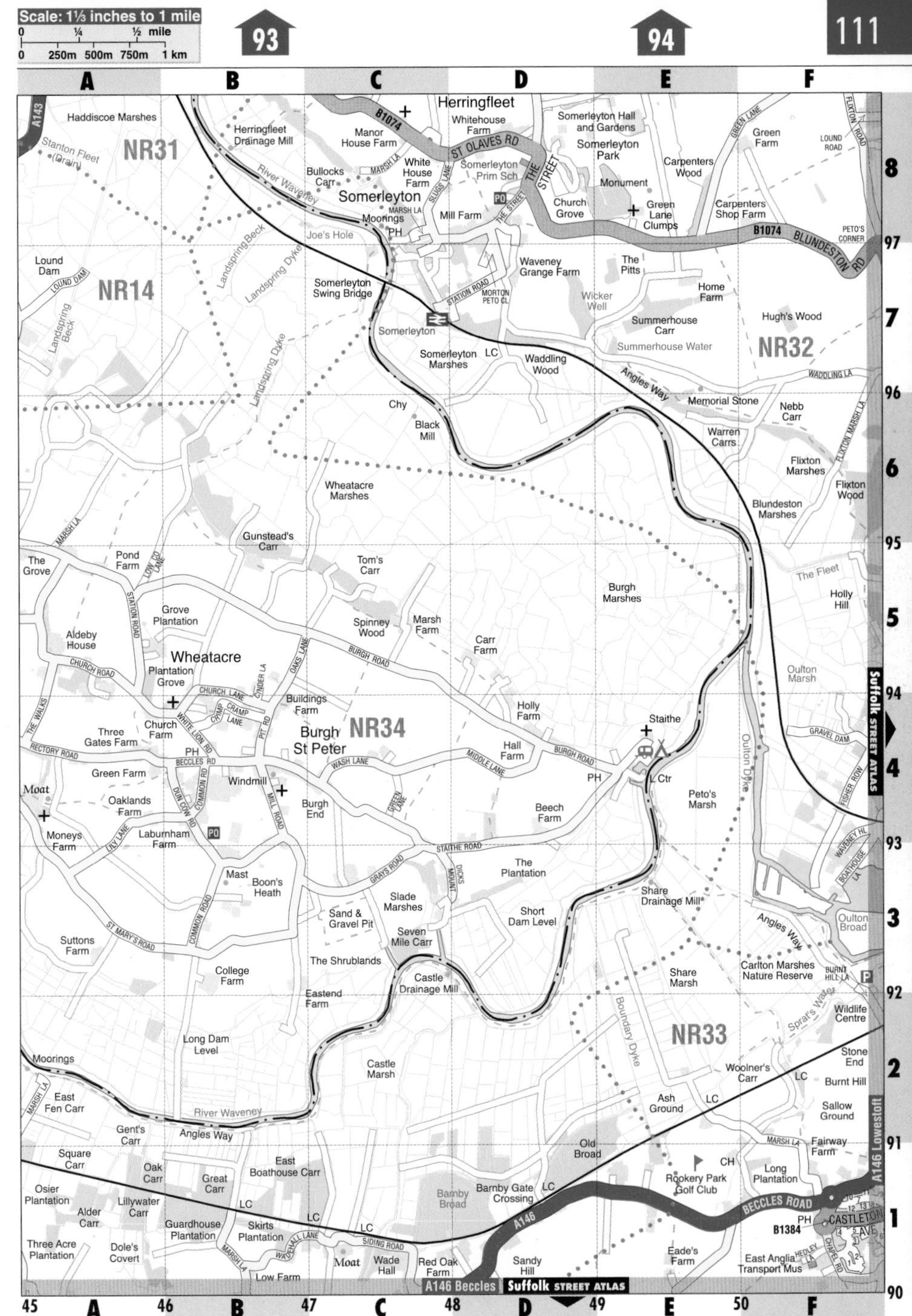

97

Scale: 1⅓ inches to 1 mile

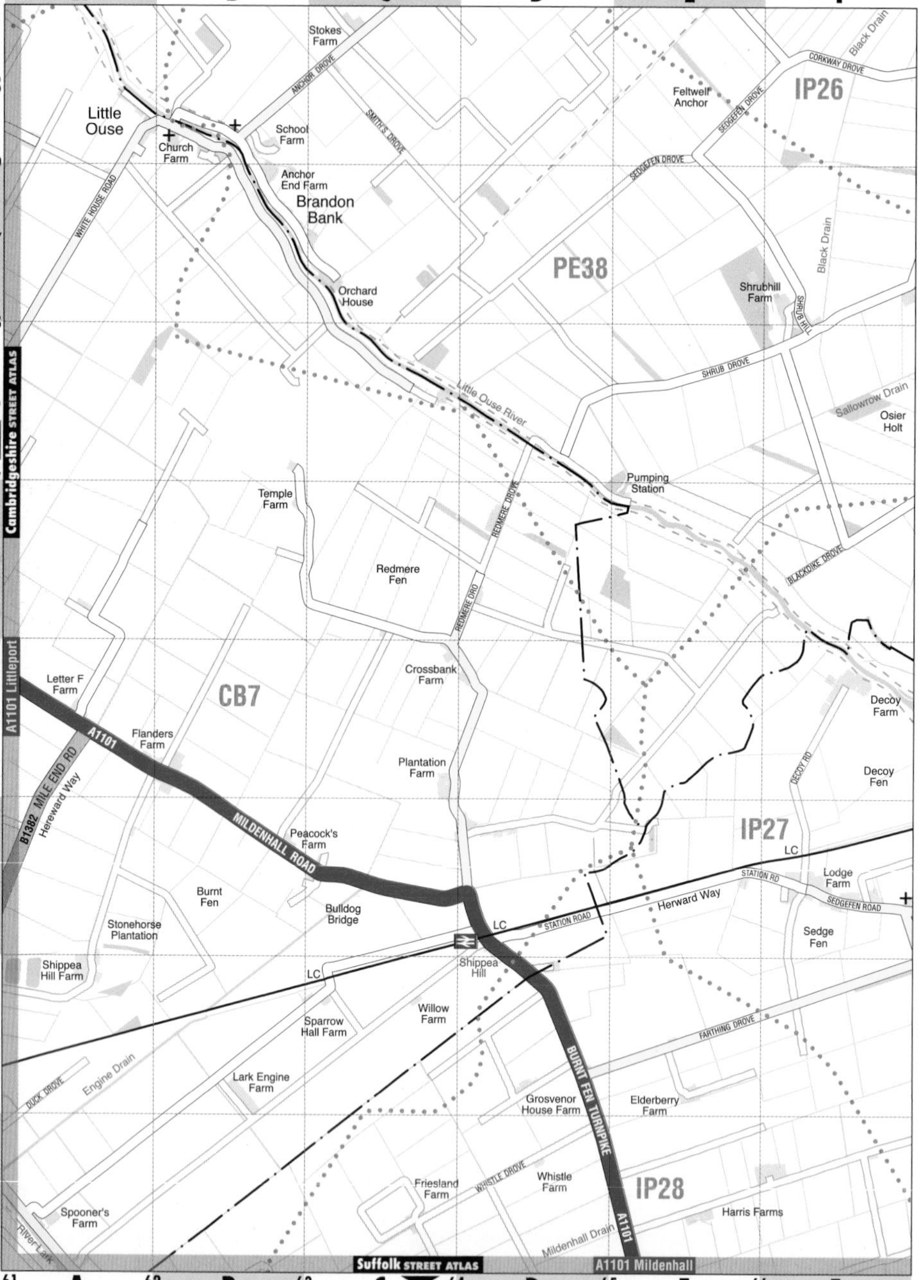

Cambridgeshire STREET ATLAS

A1101 Littleport

Suffolk STREET ATLAS

A1101 Mildenhall

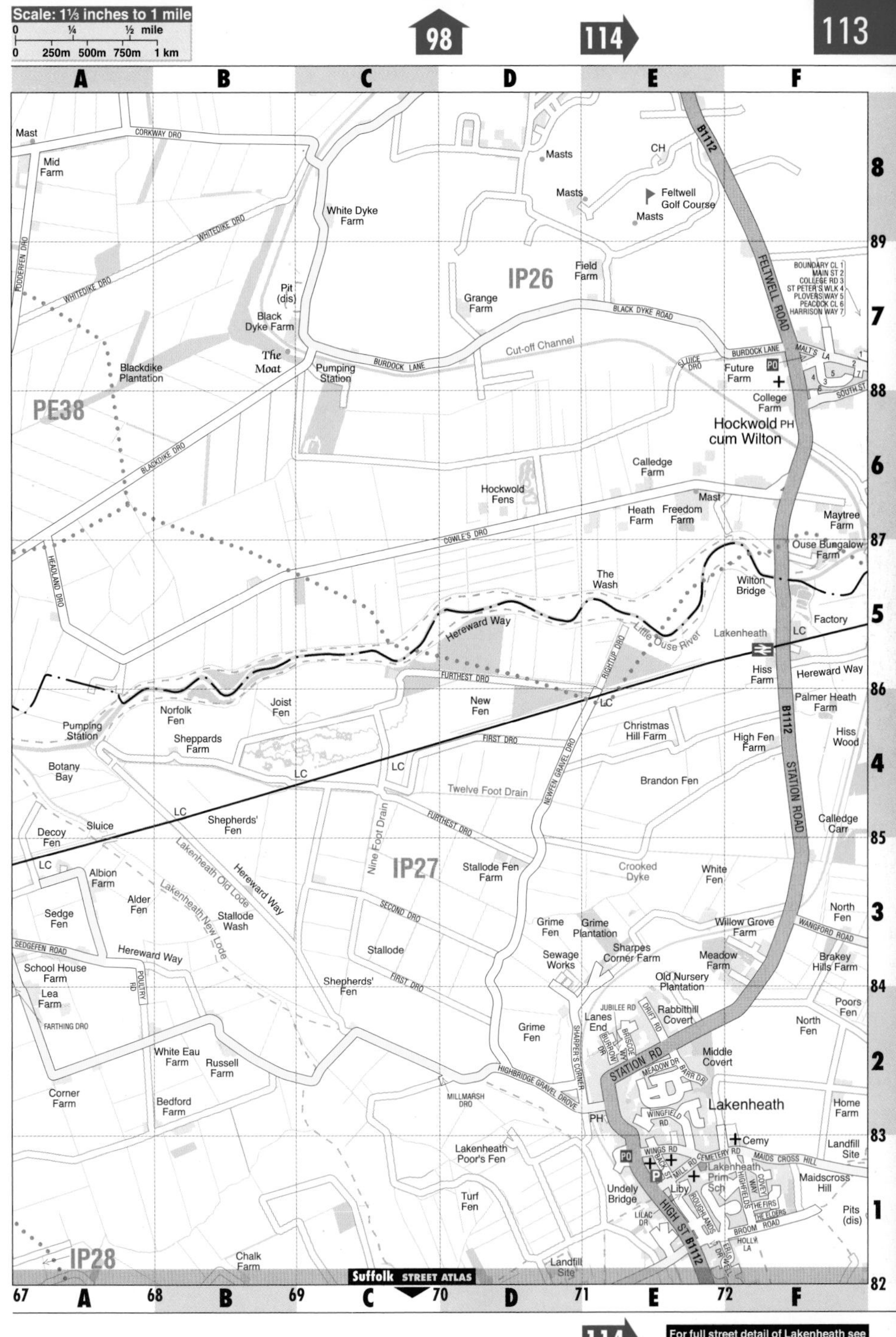

A   B   C   D   E   F

Mast

CORKWAY DRO

Mid
Farm

WHITEDIKE DRO

White Dyke
Farm

CH

Masts

Masts

Feltwell
Golf Course

Masts

8

B1112

FELTWELL ROAD

89

WHITEDIKE DRO

RODGEFEN DRO

Pit
(dis)

Black
Dyke Farm

IP26

Field
Farm

Grange
Farm

BLACK DYKE ROAD

BOUNDARY CL 1
MAIN ST 2
COLLEGE RD 3
ST PETER'S WLK 4
PLOVERS WAY 5
PEACOCK CL 6
HARRISON WAY 7

MALT 3

7

Blackdike
Plantation

The
Moat

BURDOCK LANE

Pumping
Station

Cut-off Channel

BURDOCK LANE

S LUICE
DRO

Future
Farm

PO

LA

1
2
4
5

SOUTH ST

88

PE38

BLACKDIKE DRO

College
Farm

Hockwold PH
cum Wilton

6

HEADLAND DRO

Calledge
Farm

Hockwold
Fens

Heath
Farm

Freedom
Farm

Mast

Maytree
Farm

COWLES DRO

Ouse Bungalow
Farm

87

The
Wash

Wilton
Bridge

Factory

5

Hereward Way

Little Ouse River

Lakenheath

LC

BUCKLH DRO

Hiss
Farm

Hereward Way

FURTHEST DRO

LC

Palmer Heath
Farm

86

Pumping
Station

Norfolk
Fen

Joist
Fen

New
Fen

Christmas
Hill Farm

High Fen
Farm

Hiss
Wood

Sheppards
Farm

LC

FIRST DRO

B1112

STATION ROAD

Botany
Bay

LC

LC

Twelve Foot Drain

Brandon Fen

Calledge
Carr

4

Decoy
Fen

Sluice

LC

FURTHEST DRO

NEWFEN GRAVEL DRO

NINE FOOT DRAIN

SECOND DRO

North
Fen

WANGFORD ROAD

85

LC

Shepherds'
Fen

Lakenheath Old Lode

Hereward Way

IP27

Stallode Fen
Farm

Crooked
Dyke

White
Fen

Willow Grove
Farm

Brakey
Hills Farm

3

Albion
Farm

Alder
Fen

Lakenheath New Lode

Stallode
Wash

Stallode

Grime
Fen

Grime
Plantation

Meadow
Farm

Poors
Fen

Sedge
Fen

SEDGEFEN ROAD

Hereward Way

POULTRY RD

FIRST DRO

Shepherds'
Fen

Sewage
Works

Sharpes
Corner Farm

Old Nursery
Plantation

North
Fen

84

School House
Farm

Lea
Farm

FARTHING DRO

Grime
Fen

Lanes
End

JUBILEE RD

Rabbithill
Covert

Middle
Covert

2

White Eau
Farm

Russell
Farm

HIGHBRIDGE GRAVEL DROVE

SHAPPER'S CORNER

STATION RD

MEADOW DR

PARK RD

Lakenheath

Home
Farm

Corner
Farm

Bedford
Farm

MILLMARSH
DRO

PH

WINGFIELD
RD

Cemy

WINGS RD

Landfill
Site

83

IP28

Chalk
Farm

Lakenheath
Poor's Fen

Turf
Fen

Undely
Bridge

LILAC DR

PO
P

Lakenheath

CEMETERY RD

Lakenheath
Prim Sch

Liby

MAIDS CROSS HILL

THE FIRS

BROOM ROAD

HIGH ST B1112

Maidscross
Hill

Pits
(dis)

1

Landfill
Site

67   68   69   70   71   72

82

A   B   C   D   E   F

114   For full street detail of Lakenheath see
Philip's STREET ATLAS of Suffolk

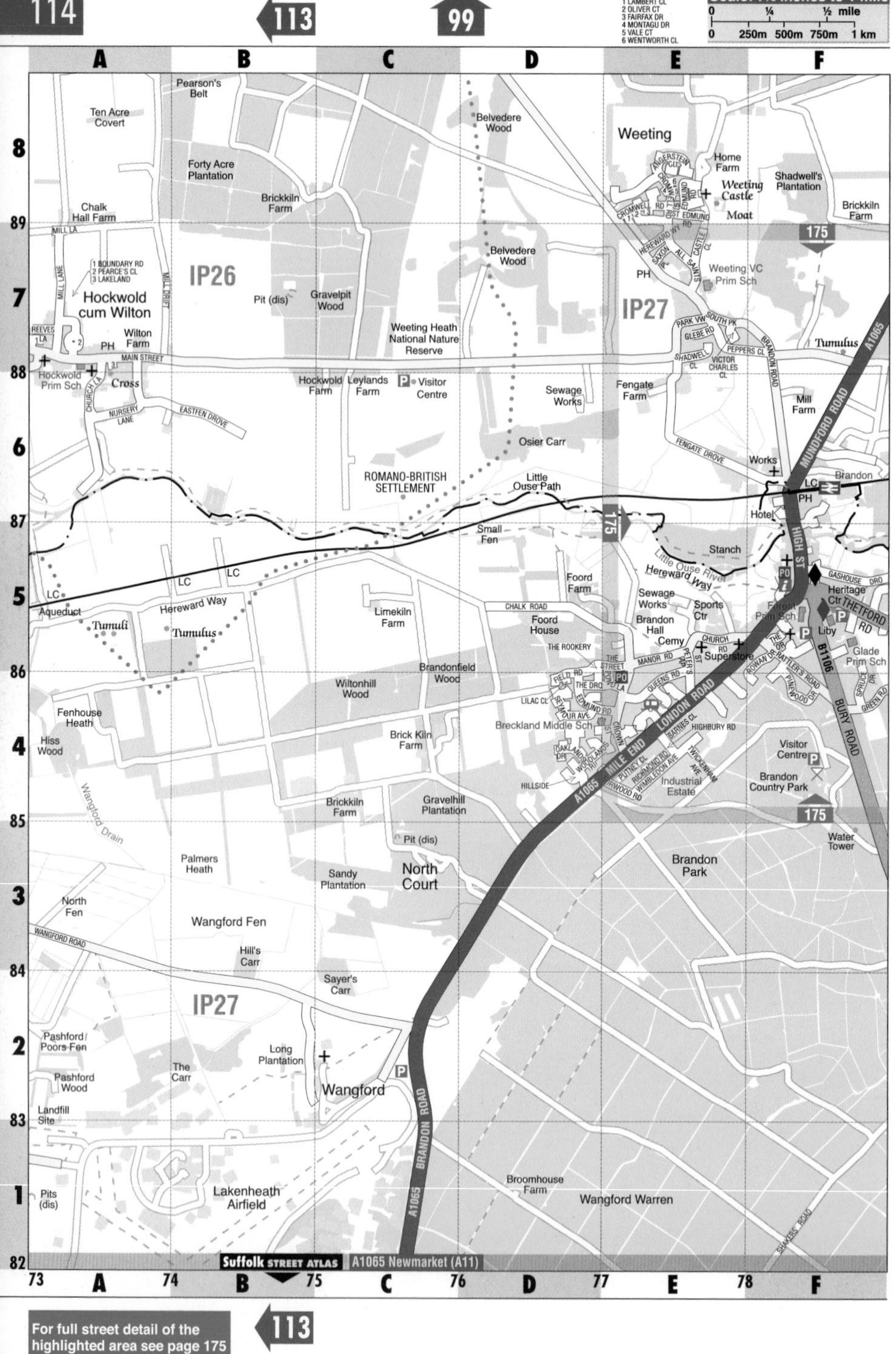

E8
1 LAMBERT CL
2 OLIVER CT
3 FAIRFAX DR
4 MONTAGU DR
5 VALE CT
6 WENTWORTH CL

Scale: 1⅓ inches to 1 mile

0   ¼   ½ mile

0 250m 500m 750m 1 km

Pearson's Belt

Ten Acre Covert

Forty Acre Plantation

Brickkiln Farm

Belvedere Wood

Weeting

Home Farm

Shadwell's Plantation

Brickkiln Farm

Weeting Castle

Chalk Hall Farm

1 BOUNDARY RD
2 PEARCE'S CL
3 LAKELAND

IP26

Pit (dis)

Gravelpit Wood

Belvedere Wood

Moat

175

Hockwold cum Wilton

Wilton Farm

Weeting Heath National Nature Reserve

Weeting VC Prim Sch

PH

IP27

Tumulus

A1065

REEVES CL
1A
2

Main Street

PH

Hockwold Prim Sch

Cross

NURSERY LANE

EASTERN DROVE

Hockwold Farm

Leylands Farm

Visitor Centre

Sewage Works

Fengate Farm

Mill Farm

Osier Carr

TENGATE DROVE

Works

Brandon

175

LC

ROMANO-BRITISH SETTLEMENT

Little Ouse Path

Hotel

PH

Aqueduct

LC

LC

Hereward Way

Tumuli

Tumulus

Small Fen

Hereward Way

Little Ouse River

Stanch

GASHOUSE DRO

THETFORD

B1106

Foord Farm

Sewage Works

Sports Ctr

Heritage Ctr

Liby

Foord House

Limekiln Farm

CHALK ROAD

THE ROOKERY

Brandon Hall

Cemy

Superstore

P

Glade Prim Sch

Fenhouse Heath

Hiss Wood

Wiltonhill Wood

Brandonfield Wood

MANOR RD

THE STREET

THE DRO

LILAC CL

Breckland Middle Sch

LONDON ROAD

Highbury Rd

BURY ROAD

Visitor Centre

Brandon Country Park

Brickkiln Farm

Gravelhill Plantation

HILLSIDE

MILE END

A1065

Industrial Estate

175

Water Tower

Palmers Heath

Pit (dis)

North Court

Brandon Park

North Fen

WANGFORD ROAD

Wangford Fen

Sandy Plantation

Hill's Carr

Sayer's Carr

IP27

The Carr

Long Plantation

P

Wangford

Pashford Poors Fen

Pashford Wood

Landfill Site

BRANDON ROAD

Broomhouse Farm

Wangford Warren

Pits (dis)

Lakenheath Airfield

SOMERS ROAD

A1065

A   74   B   75   C   76   D   77   E   78   F

For full street detail of the highlighted area see page 175

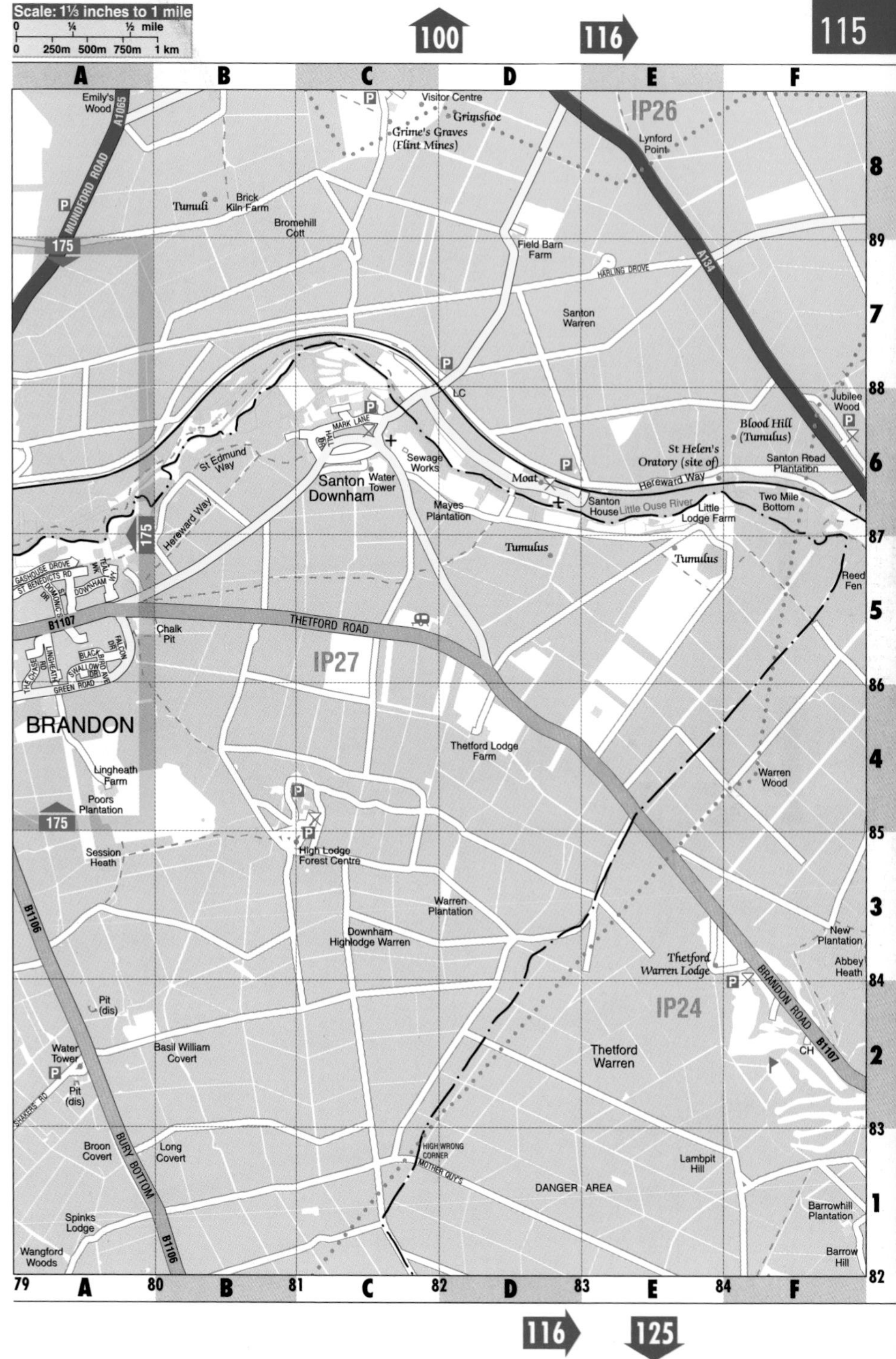
Scale: 1⅓ inches to 1 mile
0 ¼ ½ mile
0 250m 500m 750m 1 km
100
116
A B C D E F
Emily's Wood
A1065
MUNDFORD ROAD
Visitor Centre
Grimshoe
Grime's Graves (Flint Mines)
IP26
Lynford Point
Tumuli
Brick Kiln Farm
Bromehill Cott
175
Field Barn Farm
HARLING DROVE
A134
Santon Warren
LC
MARK LANE
Jubilee Wood
Blood Hill (Tumulus)
St Helen's Oratory (site of)
Santon Road Plantation
St Edmund Way
Sewage Works
Moat
Hereward Way
Santon Downham
Water Tower
Santon House
Little Ouse River
Little Lodge Farm
Two Mile Bottom
Mayes Plantation
Hereward Way
Tumulus
Tumulus
Reed Fen
GASHOUSE DROVE
ST BENEDICTS RD
DOWNHAM
B1107
THETFORD ROAD
Chalk Pit
IP27
THE CHASE
LINGHEATH RD
SWALLOW DR
BLACKBIRD AVE
FALCON DR
GREEN ROAD
BRANDON
Thetford Lodge Farm
Lingheath Farm
Poors Plantation
Warren Wood
High Lodge Forest Centre
Session Heath
Warren Plantation
B1106
Downham Highlodge Warren
New Plantation
Thetford Warren Lodge
Abbey Heath
BRANDON ROAD
IP24
Pit (dis)
Water Tower
Basil William Covert
Thetford Warren
CH
Pit (dis)
SHAKERS RD
HIGH WRONG CORNER
MOTHER DUY'S
Broon Covert
Long Covert
BURY BOTTOM
Lambpit Hill
DANGER AREA
Spinks Lodge
Barrowhill Plantation
Wangford Woods
Barrow Hill
8 89 7 88 6 87 5 86 4 85 3 84 2 83 1 82
79 80 81 82 83 84
116
125

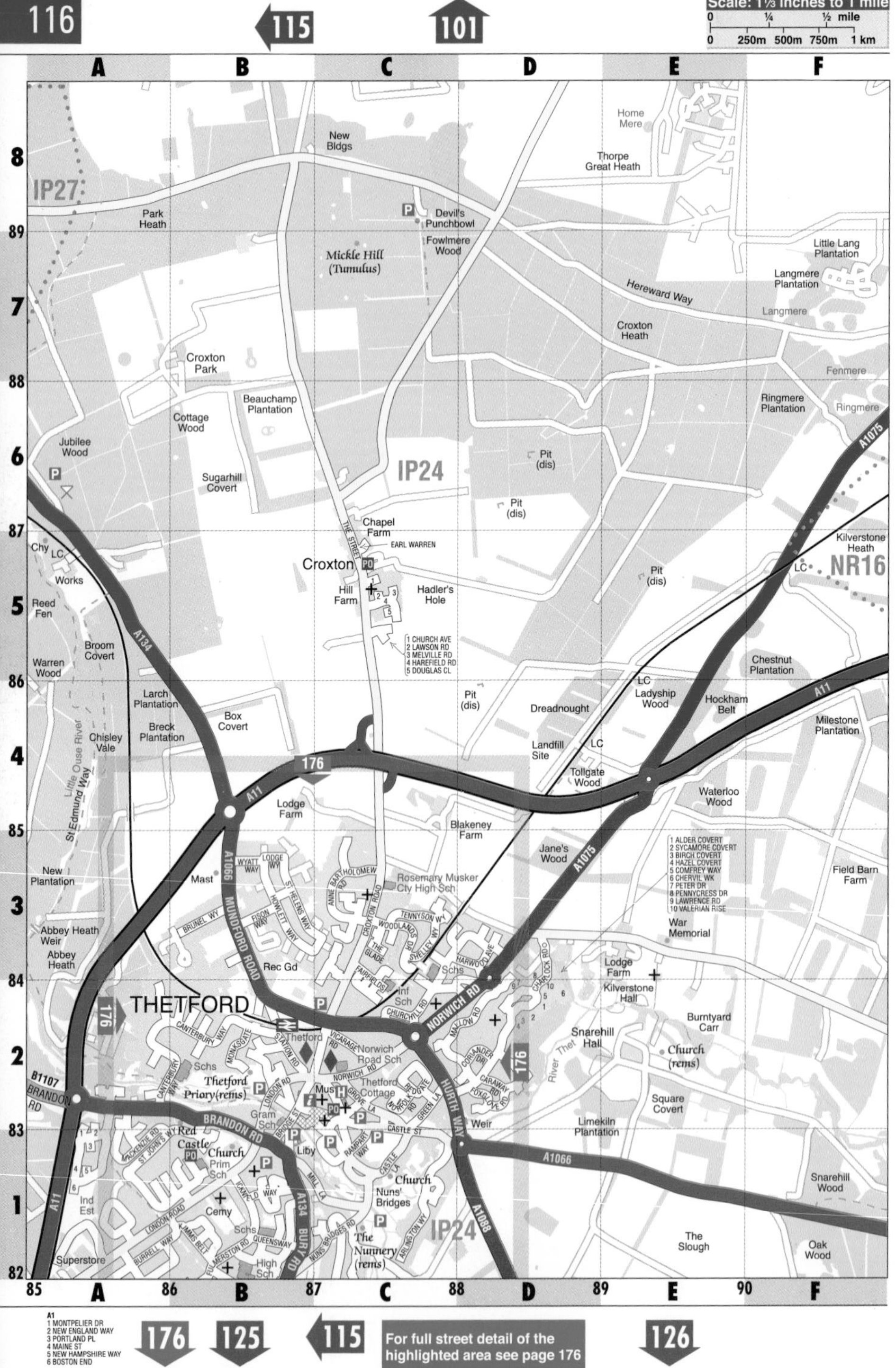

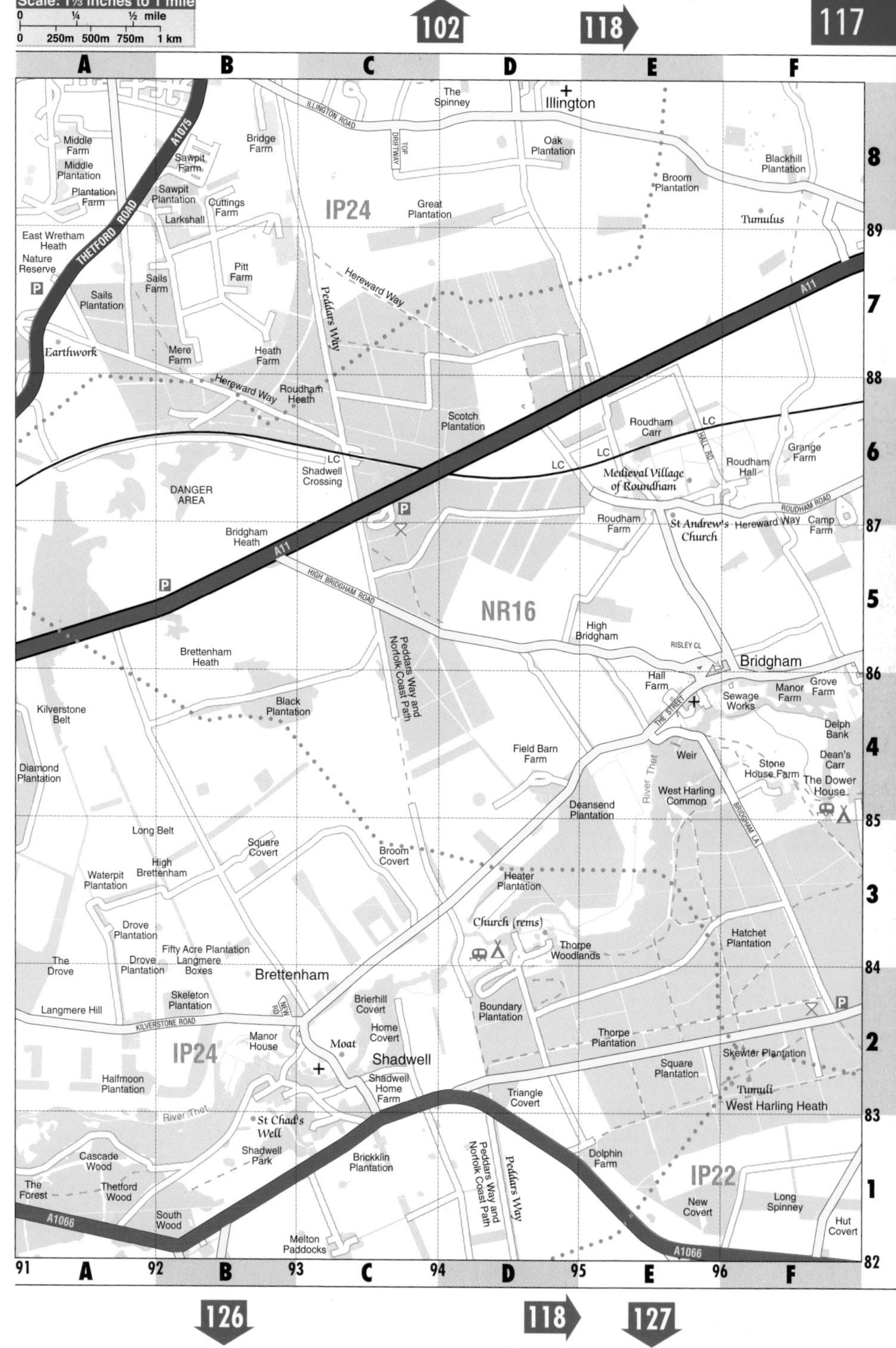

Scale: 1⅓ inches to 1 mile
0 ¼ ½ mile
0 250m 500m 750m 1 km
102
118
A B C D E F
The Spinney
Illington
ILLINGTON ROAD
Middle Farm
Middle Plantation
Plantation Farm
Sawpit Farm
Sawpit Plantation
Bridge Farm
TOP DRIFTWAY
Oak Plantation
Broom Plantation
Blackhill Plantation
A1075
THETFORD ROAD
Cuttings Farm
Larkshall
IP24
Great Plantation
Tumulus
East Wretham Heath
Nature Reserve
Pitt Farm
Sails Farm
Sails Plantation
Hereward Way
Peddars Way
A11
Earthwork
Mere Farm
Heath Farm
Roudham Heath
Scotch Plantation
Roudham Carr
LC
HALL RD
Grange Farm
Roudham Hall
Shadwell Crossing
DANGER AREA
Medieval Village of Roudham
ROUDHAM ROAD
Roudham Farm
St Andrew's Church
Camp Farm
Bridgham Heath
HIGH BRIDGHAM ROAD
NR16
High Bridgham
Brettenham Heath
Peddars Way and Norfolk Coast Path
RISLEY CL
Bridgham
Hall Farm
THE STREET
Sewage Works
Manor Farm
Grove Farm
Kilverstone Belt
Black Plantation
Delph Bank
Field Barn Farm
Weir
Stone House Farm
Dean's Carr
Diamond Plantation
River Thet
West Harling Common
The Dower House
Deansend Plantation
BRIDGHAM LA
Long Belt
Square Covert
Broom Covert
High Brettenham
Waterpit Plantation
Heater Plantation
Church (rems)
Hatchet Plantation
Drove Plantation
Thorpe Woodlands
Fifty Acre Plantation
Langmere Boxes
The Drove
Brettenham
Skeleton Plantation
Brierhill Covert
Boundary Plantation
Langmere Hill
KILVERSTONE ROAD
NEW RD
Home Covert
Thorpe Plantation
Manor House
Moat
Skewter Plantation
Shadwell
Square Plantation
Halfmoon Plantation
Shadwell Home Farm
Triangle Covert
Tumuli
West Harling Heath
St Chad's Well
Shadwell Park
Brickklin Plantation
Dolphin Farm
Cascade Wood
IP22
The Forest
Thetford Wood
New Covert
Long Spinney
A1066
South Wood
Melton Paddocks
Hut Covert
8 89 7 88 6 87 5 86 4 85 3 84 2 83 1 82
91 92 93 94 95 96
126
118
127

117 103

Scale: 1⅓ inches to 1 mile

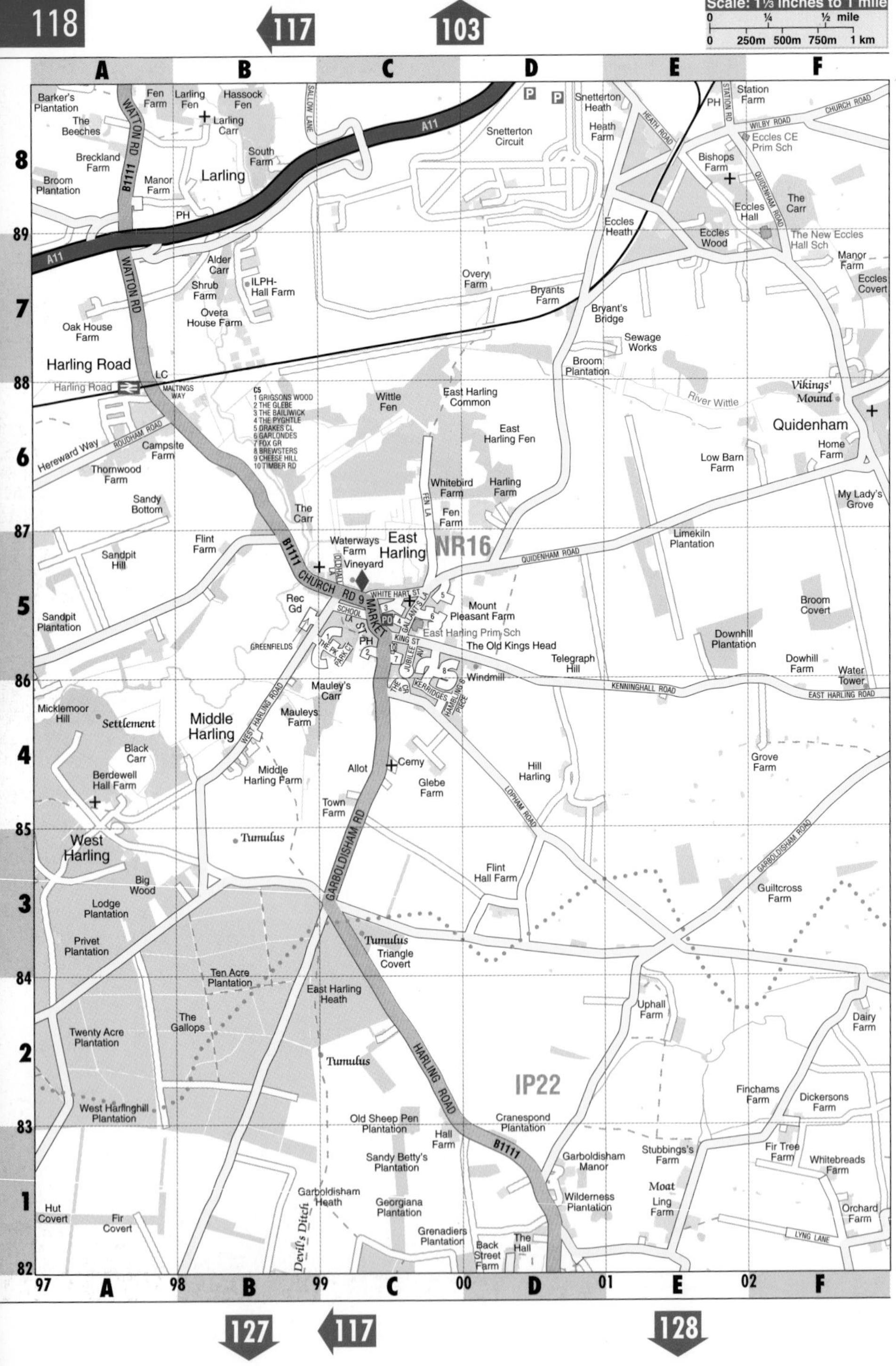

Larling
Snetterton Circuit
Harling Road
East Harling
NR16
Quidenham
Middle Harling
West Harling
IP22
Eccles Heath
Eccles Hall
Garboldisham Heath
Garboldisham Manor
Bryant's Bridge
River Wittle
Hereward Way
Vikings' Mound
Settlement
Tumulus
Devil's Ditch
Moat
CS
1 GRIGSONS WOOD
2 THE GLEBE
3 THE BAILIWICK
4 THE PYGHTLE
5 DRAKES CL
6 GARLONDES
7 FOX GR
8 BREWSTERS
9 CHEESE HILL
10 TIMBER RD

127 117 128

104
120

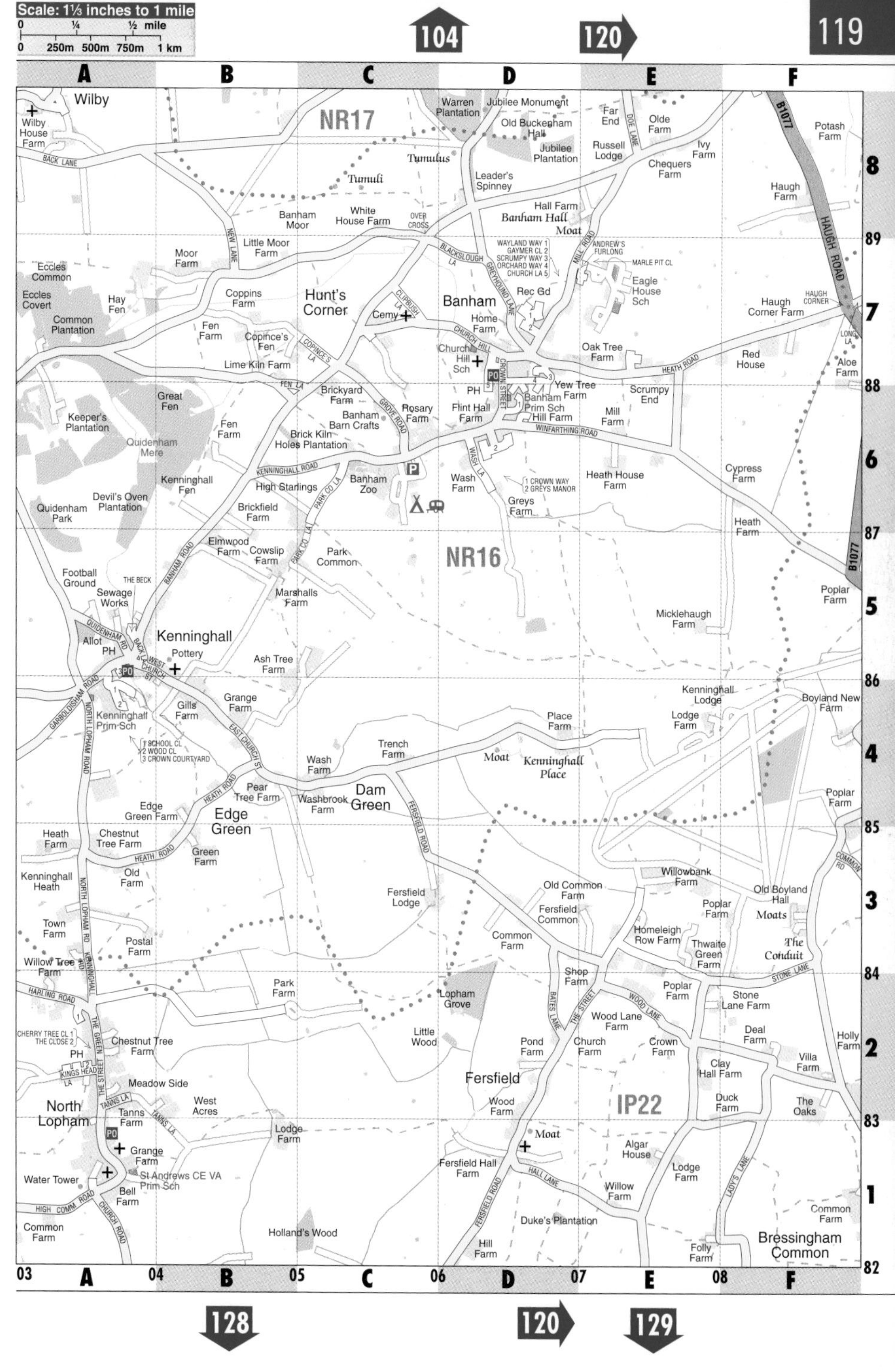
Scale: 1⅓ inches to 1 mile
0 ¼ ½ mile
0 250m 500m 750m 1 km
Wilby
Wilby House Farm
BACK LANE
NR17
Warren Plantation
Jubilee Monument
Old Buckenham Hall
Jubilee Plantation
Far End
Olde Farm
Russell Lodge
Ivy Farm
Chequers Farm
Potash Farm
Haugh Farm
HAUGH ROAD
B1077
Tumulus
Tumuli
Leader's Spinney
Banham Moor
White House Farm
OVER CROSS
Hall Farm
Banham Hall
Moat
Little Moor Farm
Moor Farm
NEW LANE
Eccles Common
Eccles Covert
Hay Fen
Common Plantation
Coppins Farm
Hunt's Corner
Banham
Rec Gd
Eagle House Sch
MARLE PIT CL
ANDREW'S FURLONG
WAYLAND WAY 1
GAYMER CL 2
SCRUMPY WAY 3
ORCHARD WAY 4
CHURCH LA 5
BLACKSLOUGH LA
GREYHOUND LANE
MILL ROAD
CLIPBUSH LA
Cemy
Home Farm
Haugh Corner Farm
HAUGH CORNER
Fen Farm
Copince's Fen
COPINCE'S LA
CHURCH HILL
Church Hill Sch
Oak Tree Farm
Red House
LONG LA
Aloe Farm
Lime Kiln Farm
FEN LA
HEATH ROAD
Great Fen
Keeper's Plantation
Quidenham Mere
Fen Farm
Brickyard Farm
Banham Barn Crafts
Rosary Farm
PH
Flint Hall Farm
CROWN STREET
Yew Tree Farm
Banham Prim Sch
Hill Farm
Scrumpy End
Mill Farm
WINFARTHING ROAD
Brick Kiln Holes Plantation
GROVE ROAD
KENNINGHALL ROAD
Kenninghall Fen
High Starlings
Banham Zoo
Wash Farm
WASH LA
1 CROWN WAY
2 GREYS MANOR
Heath House Farm
Cypress Farm
Devil's Oven Plantation
Quidenham Park
Brickfield Farm
PARK CO LA
Greys Farm
Heath Farm
Elmwood Farm
Cowslip Farm
Park Common
NR16
Football Ground
THE BECK
Sewage Works
BANHAM ROAD
Marshalls Farm
Micklehaugh Farm
Poplar Farm
Allot
PH
QUIDENHAM RD
BACK LA
Kenninghall
Pottery
WEST CHURCH ST
Ash Tree Farm
GARBOLDISHAM ROAD
Kenninghall Lodge
Boyland New Farm
Gills Farm
Grange Farm
Kenninghall Prim Sch
NORTH LOPHAM ROAD
1 SCHOOL CL
2 WOOD CL
3 CROWN COURTYARD
EAST CHURCH ST
Place Farm
Lodge Farm
Trench Farm
Wash Farm
Moat
Kenninghall Place
HEATH ROAD
Pear Tree Farm
Dam Green
Washbrook Farm
Edge Green Farm
Edge Green
FERSFIELD ROAD
Poplar Farm
Heath Farm
Chestnut Tree Farm
HEATH ROAD
Green Farm
COMMON RD
Kenninghall Heath
Old Farm
Willowbank Farm
Fersfield Lodge
Old Common Farm
Old Boyland Hall
Poplar Farm
Fersfield Common
Moats
Town Farm
Postal Farm
Common Farm
Homeleigh Row Farm
Thwaite Green Farm
The Conduit
Willow Tree Farm
KENNINGHALL
NORTH LOPHAM RD
Shop Farm
STONE LANE
HARLING ROAD
Park Farm
Lopham Grove
Poplar Farm
Stone Lane Farm
WOOD LANE
BATES LANE
THE STREET
Wood Lane Farm
THE GREEN
CHERRY TREE CL 1
THE CLOSE 2
Chestnut Tree Farm
Little Wood
Pond Farm
Church Farm
Crown Farm
Deal Farm
Holly Farm
PH
KINGS HEAD LA
THE STREET
Meadow Side
Fersfield
Clay Hall Farm
Villa Farm
North Lopham
TANNS LA
West Acres
Tanns Farm
Wood Farm
IP22
Duck Farm
The Oaks
Lodge Farm
PO
Grange Farm
Moat
Algar House
Water Tower
St Andrews CE VA Prim Sch
Fersfield Hall Farm
HALL LANE
Lodge Farm
LADY'S LANE
Bell Farm
Willow Farm
HIGH COMM ROAD
CHURCH ROAD
FERSFIELD ROAD
Duke's Plantation
Common Farm
Common Farm
Holland's Wood
Hill Farm
Folly Farm
Bressingham Common
A B C D E F
8 89 7 88 6 87 5 86 4 85 3 84 2 83 1 82
03 04 05 06 07 08

128
120
129

119
105

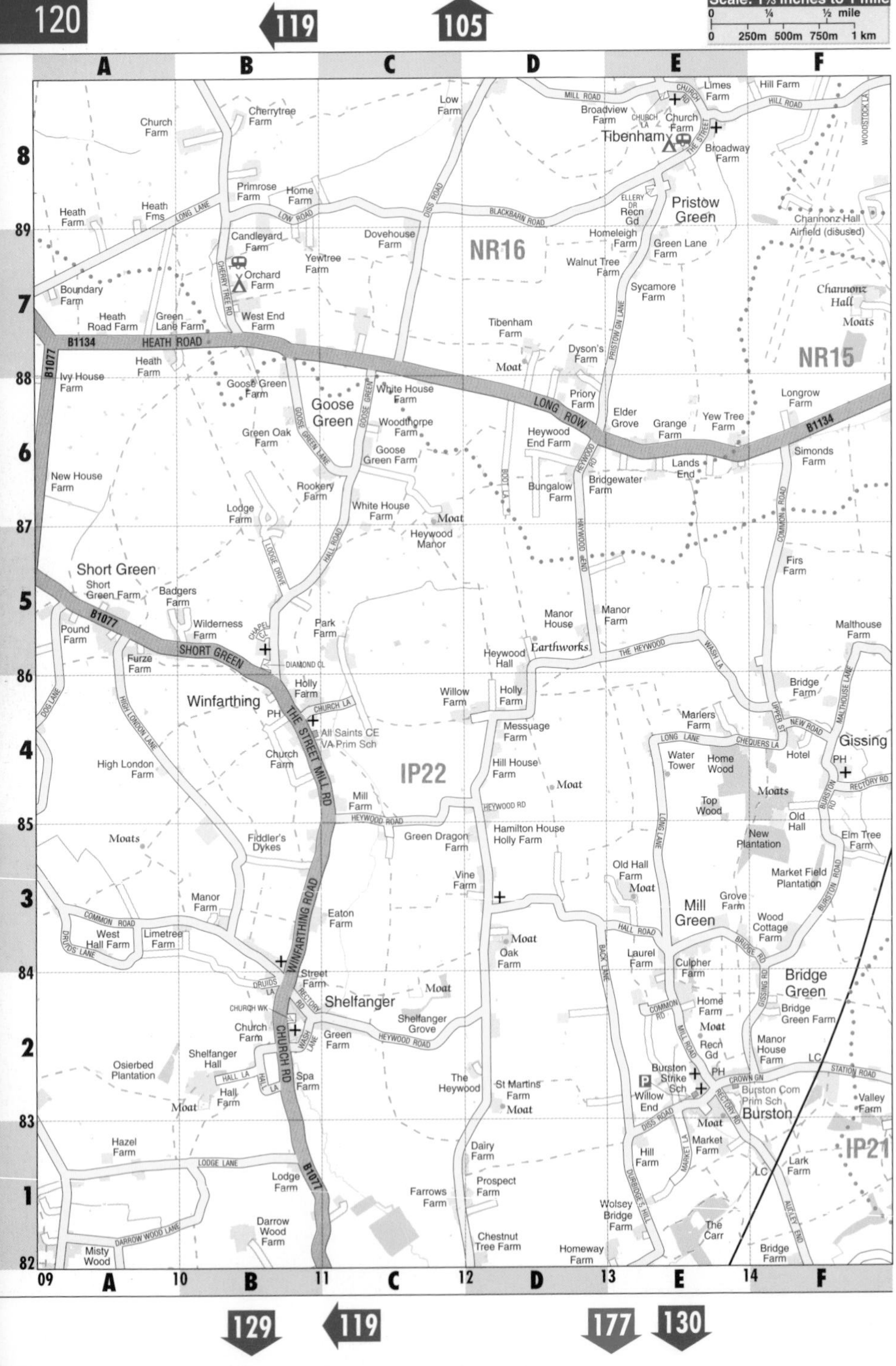
Scale: 1⅓ inches to 1 mile
0 ¼ ½ mile
0 250m 500m 750m 1 km
A
B
C
D
E
F
8
89
7
88
6
87
5
86
4
85
3
84
2
83
1
82
09
10
11
12
13
14
Church Farm
Cherrytree Farm
Low Farm
MILL ROAD
CHURCH RD
Limes Farm
Hill Farm
HILL ROAD
Broadview Farm
CHURCH LA
Church Farm
Tibenham
THE STREET
Broadway Farm
WOODSTOCK LA
Primrose Farm
Home Farm
DISS ROAD
ELLERY DR
Recn Gd
Pristow Green
Heath Farm
Heath Fms
LONG LANE
LOW ROAD
BLACKBARN ROAD
Channonz Hall Airfield (disused)
Candleyard Farm
Dovehouse Farm
NR16
Homeleigh Farm
Green Lane Farm
Yewtree Farm
Walnut Tree Farm
CHERRY TREE RD
Orchard Farm
Boundary Farm
Sycamore Farm
Channonz Hall
Moats
Heath Road Farm
Green Lane Farm
West End Farm
PRISTOW GN LANE
Tibenham Farm
B1134
HEATH ROAD
Dyson's Farm
NR15
B1077
Heath Farm
Moat
Ivy House Farm
Goose Green Farm
GOOSE GREEN
White House Farm
Priory Farm
Longrow Farm
LONG ROW
Goose Green
Elder Grove
Yew Tree Farm
Green Oak Farm
GOOSE GREEN LANE
Woodthorpe Farm
Heywood End Farm
Grange Farm
B1134
Goose Green Farm
HEYWOOD RD
Simonds Farm
Lands End
New House Farm
BOOT LA
Bridgewater Farm
Rookery Farm
Bungalow Farm
COMMON ROAD
Lodge Farm
White House Farm
Moat
HALL ROAD
Heywood Manor
HAYWOOD END
LODGE DRIVE
Firs Farm
Short Green
Short Green Farm
Badgers Farm
Manor House
Manor Farm
Pound Farm
B1077
Wilderness Farm
CHAPEL CL
Park Farm
Malthouse Farm
Furze Farm
SHORT GREEN
DIAMOND CL
Heywood Hall
Earthworks
THE HEYWOOD
WASH LA
Holly Farm
Holly Farm
Bridge Farm
DOG LANE
Winfarthing
Willow Farm
PH
CHURCH LA
MALTHOUSE LANE
HIGH LONDON LANE
All Saints CE VA Prim Sch
Messuage Farm
Marlers Farm
UPPER ST
NEW ROAD
THE STREET
MILL RD
LONG LANE
CHEQUERS LA
Gissing
Church Farm
Water Tower
Home Wood
Hotel
PH
High London Farm
IP22
Hill House Farm
Moat
Moats
RECTORY RD
Top Wood
BURSTON RD
Mill Farm
HEYWOOD RD
LONG LANE
Old Hall
HEYWOOD ROAD
Hamilton House Holly Farm
New Plantation
Elm Tree Farm
Moats
Fiddler's Dykes
Green Dragon Farm
Old Hall Farm
Market Field Plantation
WINFARTHING ROAD
Vine Farm
Moat
BURSTON ROAD
Manor Farm
Grove Farm
Mill Green
COMMON ROAD
Eaton Farm
HALL ROAD
Wood Cottage Farm
West Hall Farm
Limetree Farm
Moat
DRUIDS LANE
BACK LANE
BRIDGE RD
Oak Farm
Laurel Farm
Culpher Farm
GISSING RD
Bridge Green
Street Farm
DRUIDS LA
Moat
RECTORY RD
COMMON RD
Home Farm
CHURCH WK
Shelfanger
Bridge Green Farm
Shelfanger Grove
MILL ROAD
Moat
Church Farm
Green Farm
WASH LANE
HEYWOOD ROAD
Recn Gd
Manor House Farm
Osierbed Plantation
Shelfanger Hall
CHURCH RD
LC
HALL LA
Spa Farm
Burston Strike Sch
PH
STATION ROAD
HALL LA
The Heywood
St Martins Farm
Willow End
CROWN GN
Burston Com Prim Sch
Hall Farm
Moat
Moat
Valley Farm
RECTORY RD
DISS ROAD
Burston
Moat
Hazel Farm
Dairy Farm
Market Farm
IP21
Hill Farm
MARKET LA
LODGE LANE
Lodge Farm
B1077
Lark Farm
Prospect Farm
LC
Farrows Farm
DURBIDGES HILL
AUDLEY END
Wolsey Bridge Farm
Darrow Wood Farm
The Carr
DARROW WOOD LANE
Chestnut Tree Farm
Homeway Farm
Misty Wood
Bridge Farm

129
119
177
130

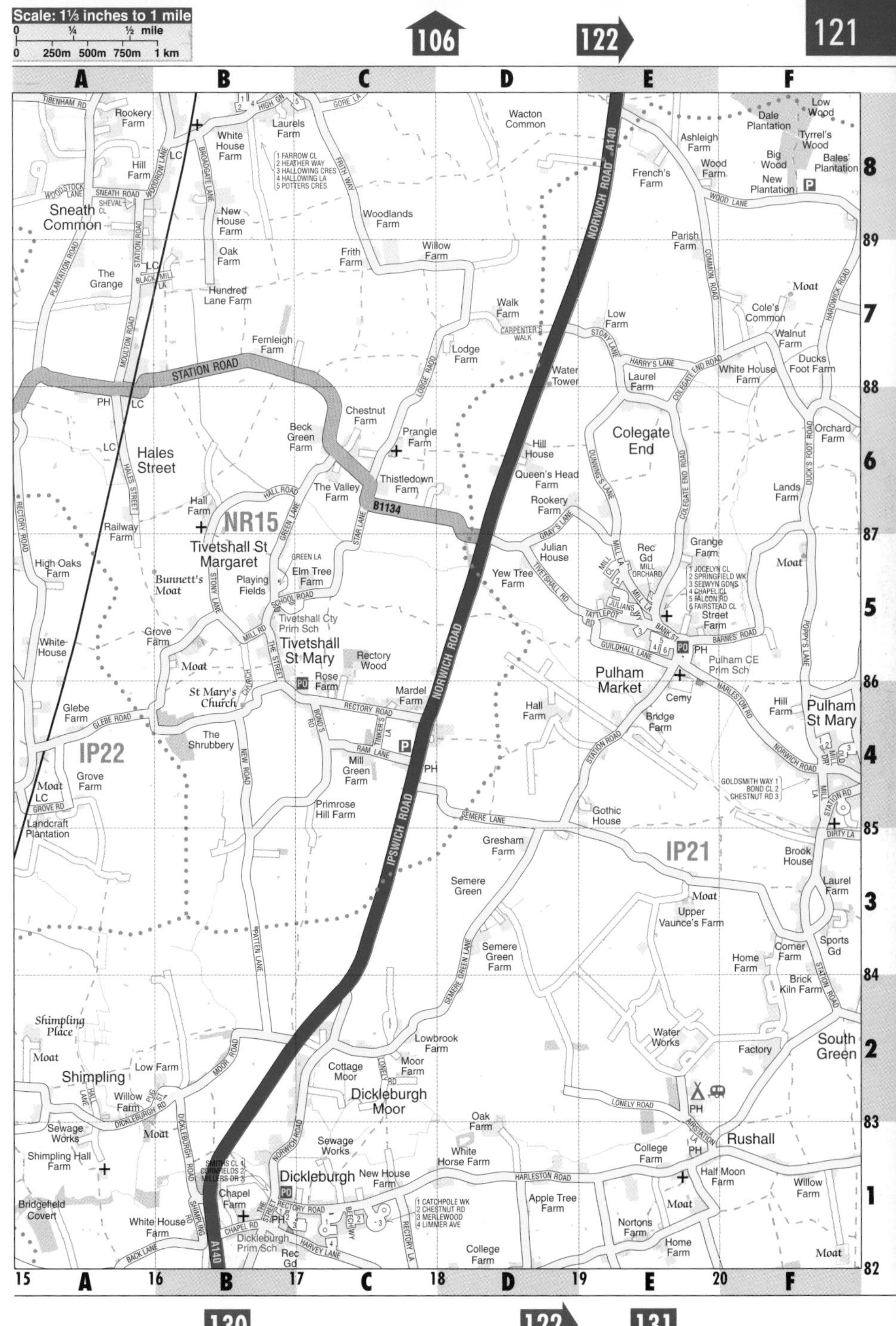

Scale: 1⅓ inches to 1 mile

0 ¼ ½ mile
0 250m 500m 750m 1 km

106   122

8
89
7
88
6
87
5
86
4
85
3
84
2
83
1
82

A   B   C   D   E   F

A TIBENHAM RD
Rookery Farm
White House Farm
Hill Farm
Sneath Common
The Grange
New House Farm
Oak Farm
Hundred Lane Farm
Fernleigh Farm
STATION ROAD
PH
LC
Hales Street
High Oaks Farm
Railway Farm
White House
Grove Farm
IP22
Glebe Farm
Moat
Grove Farm
Landcraft Plantation

B Laurels Farm
1 FARROW CL
2 HEATHER WAY
3 HALLOWING CRES
4 HALLOWING LA
5 POTTERS CRES
Beck Green Farm
The Valley Farm
NR15
Tivetshall St Margaret
Bunnett's Moat
Grove Farm
Playing Fields
Elm Tree Farm
Tivetshall Cty Prim Sch
Tivetshall St Mary
St Mary's Church
Rose Farm
The Shrubbery
Mill Green Farm
PH
Primrose Hill Farm

C HIGH LA
GORE LA
BIRCH WAY
Woodlands Farm
Frith Farm
Chestnut Farm
Prangle Farm
Thistledown Farm
GREEN LA
HALL ROAD
B1134
Rectory Wood
Mardel Farm
RECTORY ROAD
RAM LANE
SEMERE LANE

D Wacton Common
Willow Farm
Walk Farm
CARPENTER'S WALK
Lodge Farm
Hill House
Queen's Head Farm
Rookery Farm
Julian House
Yew Tree Farm
Hall Farm
Gothic House
Gresham Farm
Semere Green
Semere Green Farm
Lowbrook Farm
Moor Farm
Cottage Moor
Dickleburgh Moor
Sewage Works
Oak Farm
White Horse Farm

E NORWICH ROAD A140
French's Farm
Ashleigh Farm
Wood Farm
Parish Farm
Low Farm
Water Tower
Laurel Farm
Colegate End
Rec Gd MILL ORCHARD
1 JOCELYN CL
2 SPRINGFIELD WK
3 SEDWYN GDNS
4 CHAPEL RD
5 ALCON RD
6 FAIRSTEAD CL
Grange Farm
Pulham Market
Bridge Farm
IP21
Upper Vaunce's Farm
Home Farm
Water Works
Factory
College Farm
Apple Tree Farm
Nortons Farm
Home Farm

F Low Wood
Dale Plantation
Tyrrel's Wood
Big Wood
Bales' Plantation
New Plantation
P
Moat
Cole's Common
Walnut Farm
White House Farm
Ducks Foot Farm
Orchard Farm
Lands Farm
Moat
Pulham St Mary
Pulham CE Prim Sch
GOLDSMITH WAY 1
BOND CL 2
CHESTNUT RD 3
Brook House
Laurel Farm
Corner Farm
Sports Gd
Brick Kiln Farm
South Green
Rushall
Half Moon Farm
Willow Farm
Moat

Shimpling Place
Moat
Shimpling
Low Farm
Willow Farm
Moat
Sewage Works
Shimpling Hall Farm
Bridgefield Covert
White House Farm
Chapel Farm
Dickleburgh
Dickleburgh Prim Sch
Rec Gd
SMIPS CL 1
CANEFIELDS 2
HAVERS DR 3
New House Farm
1 CATCHPOLE WK
2 CHESTNUT RD
3 MERLEWOOD
4 LIMMER AVE
College Farm
HARLESTON ROAD
IPSWICH ROAD

15   16   17   18   19   20

130   122   131

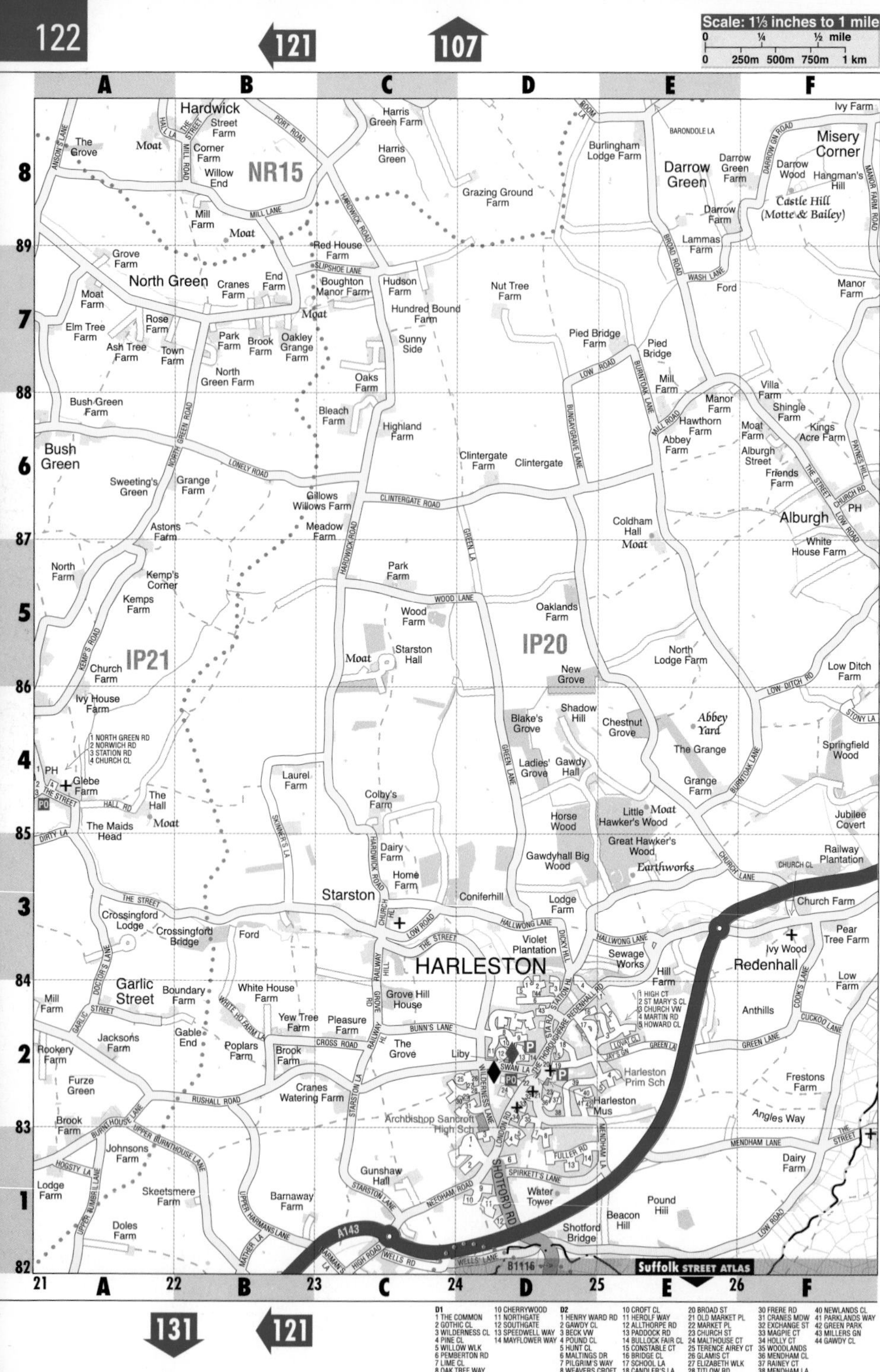

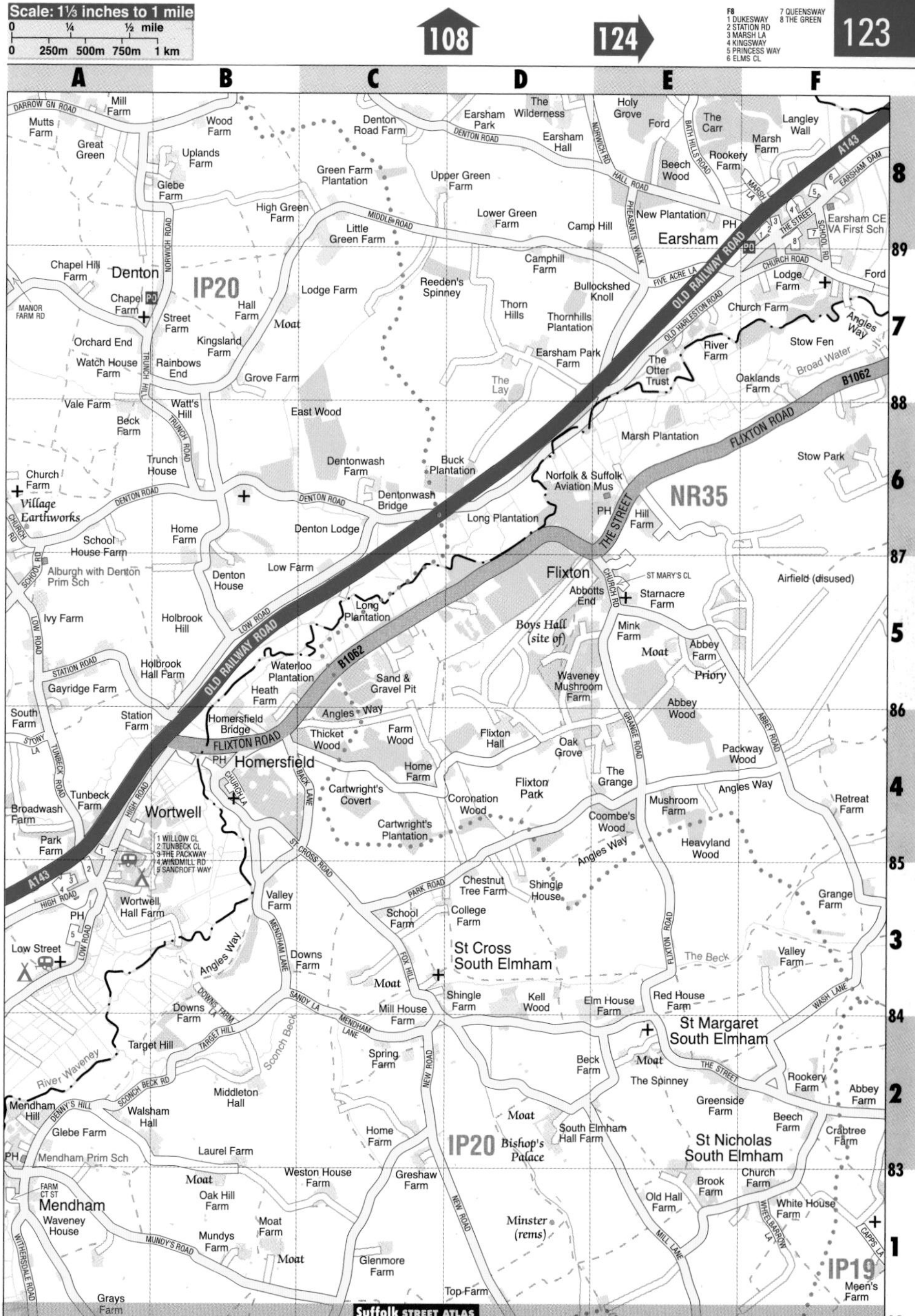

Scale: 1⅓ inches to 1 mile

0   ¼   ½ mile
0 250m 500m 750m 1 km

108   124

F8
1 DUKESWAY
2 STATION RD
3 MARSH LA
4 KINGSWAY
5 PRINCESS WAY
6 ELMS CL
7 QUEENSWAY
8 THE GREEN

123

A   B   C   D   E   F

DARROW GN ROAD
Mutts Farm
Mill Farm
Wood Farm
Denton Road Farm
Earsham Park
The Wilderness
Holy Grove
Ford
The Carr
Rookery Farm
Marsh Farm
Langley Wall
A143

Great Green
Uplands Farm
Green Farm Plantation
DENTON ROAD
Earsham Hall
NORWICH ROAD
Beech Wood
HALL ROAD
New Plantation
EARSHAM DAM

Glebe Farm
High Green Farm
Upper Green Farm
Lower Green Farm
Camp Hill
PLEASANTS WAY
PH
Earsham
THE STREET
8

Chapel Hill Farm
Denton
IP20
MIDDLE ROAD
Little Green Farm
Camphill Farm
Bullockshed Knoll
FIVE ACRE LA
OLD RAILWAY ROAD
CHURCH ROAD
Lodge Farm
Earsham CE VA First Sch
89

MANOR FARM RD
Chapel Farm
PH
Street Farm
Hall Farm
Lodge Farm
Reeden's Spinney
Thorn Hills
Thornhills Plantation
OLD HARLESTON ROAD
Church Farm
Ford
7

Orchard End
Kingsland Farm
Moat
Earsham Park Farm
River Farm
Stow Fen
Angles Way

Watch House Farm
Rainbows End
Grove Farm
The Lay
The Otter Trust
Oaklands Farm
Broad Water
B1062

Vale Farm
Watt's Hill
East Wood
Marsh Plantation
FLIXTON ROAD
Stow Park
88

Beck Farm
TRUNCH ROAD
Trunch House
Dentonwash Farm
Buck Plantation
Norfolk & Suffolk Aviation Mus
NR35
6

Church Farm
Village Earthworks
DENTON ROAD
Dentonwash Bridge
Long Plantation
PH
Hill Farm
THE STREET

School House Farm
Alburgh with Denton Prim Sch
Home Farm
Denton Lodge
Low Farm
Flixton
ST MARY'S CL
Airfield (disused)
87

Ivy Farm
LOW ROAD
Denton House
Long Plantation
Abbotts End
Starnacre Farm
CHURCH RD

STATION ROAD
Holbrook Hill
Waterloo Plantation
B1062
Sand & Gravel Pit
Boys Hall (site of)
Mink Farm
Moat
Abbey Farm
5

Gayridge Farm
Holbrook Hall Farm
Heath Farm
Angles Way
Farm Wood
Waveney Mushroom Farm
Priory
Abbey Wood
ABBEY ROAD

South Farm
SYONT LA
Station Farm
Homersfield Bridge
Thicket Wood
Home Farm
Flixton Hall
Oak Grove
GRANGE ROAD
Packway Wood
86

Broadwash Farm
TUNBECK ROAD
Tunbeck Farm
FLIXTON ROAD
PH
Homersfield
DUCK LANE
Cartwright's Covert
Coronation Wood
Flixton Park
The Grange
Mushroom Farm
Angles Way
Retreat Farm

Park Farm
A143
HIGH ROAD
Wortwell
1 WILLOW CL
2 TUNBECK CL
3 THE PACKWAY
4 WINDMILL RD
5 SANDCROFT WAY
Cartwright's Plantation
Coombe's Wood
Heavyland Wood
4

PH
Wortwell Hall Farm
Valley Farm
CROSS ROAD
PARK ROAD
Chestnut Tree Farm
Shingle House
Angles Way
Grange Farm
85

Low Street
Angles Way
DOWNS TROW
Downs Farm
SANDY LA
School Farm
College Farm
St Cross South Elmham
The Beck
Valley Farm
3

MENDHAM LANE
Downs Farm
Moat
Shingle Farm
Kell Wood
Elm House Farm
Red House Farm
St Margaret South Elmham
MARSH LANE

Target Hill
TARGET HILL
Mill House Farm
MENDHAM LANE
NEW ROAD
Beck Farm
Moat
THE STREET
84

River Waveney
SCONCH BECK RD
Middleton Hall
Spring Farm
The Spinney
Greenside Farm
Rookery Farm
Abbey Farm
2

Mendham Hill
DENNY'S HILL
Walsham Hall
Moat
Home Farm
Moat
South Elmham Hall Farm
St Nicholas South Elmham
Beech Farm
Crabtree Farm

Glebe Farm
Laurel Farm
Weston House Farm
Greshaw Farm
IP20
Bishop's Palace
Church Farm
Brook Farm
White House Farm
83

PH
Mendham Prim Sch
FARM CT ST
Moat
Oak Hill Farm
Moat
Minster (rems)
Old Hall Farm
MILL LANE
IP19
Meen's Farm
1

Mendham
Waveney House
MUNDY'S ROAD
Mundys Farm
Moat
Glenmore Farm
Top Farm
CAPPS LA

Grays Farm
WITHERSDALE ROAD

27   A   28   B   29   C   30   D   31   E   32   F

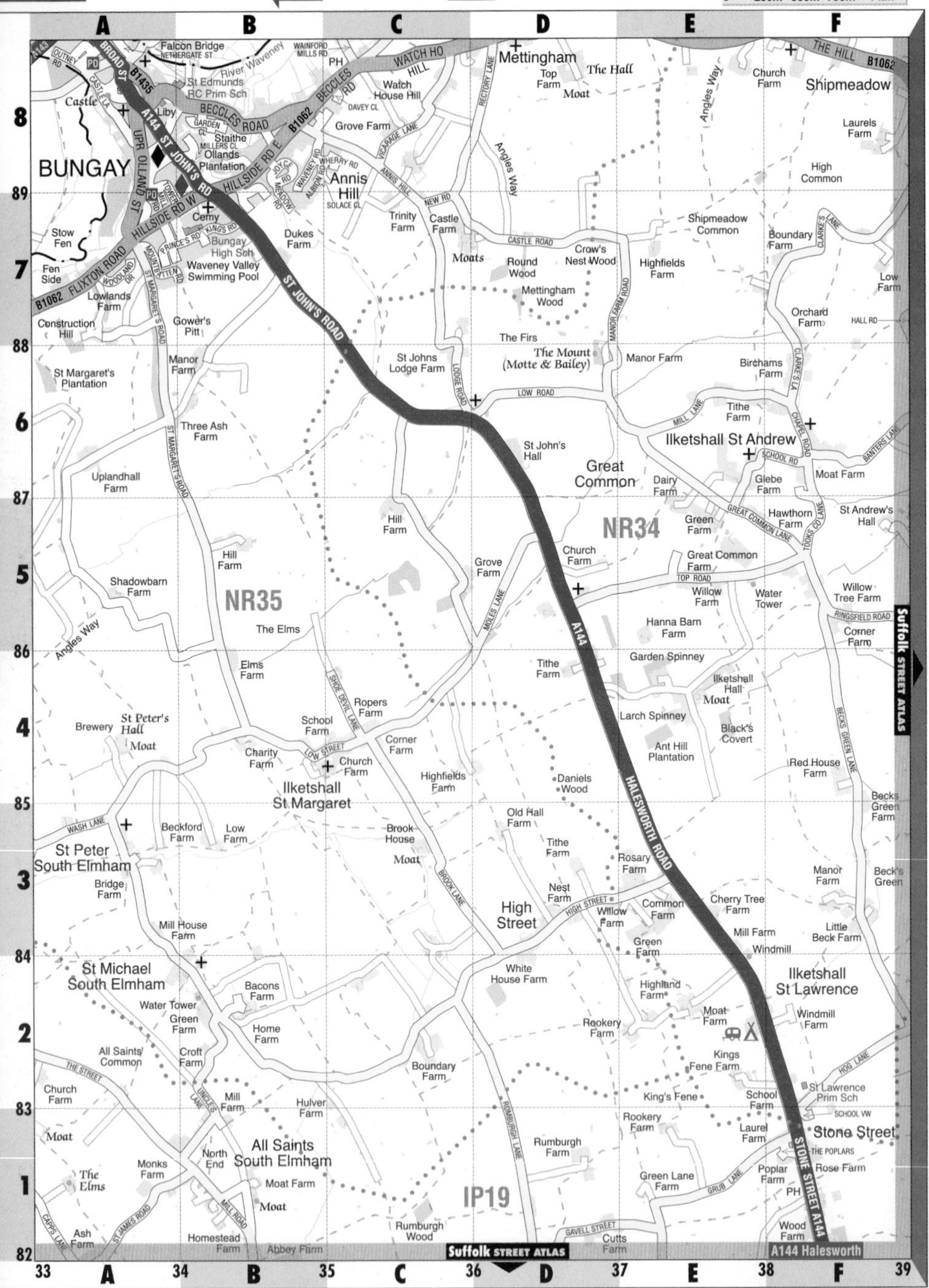

Scale: 1⅓ inches to 1 mile

0 ¼ ½ mile
0 250m 500m 750m 1 km

8

Castle

BUNGAY

89

Stow Fen

Fen Side

B1062

7

Construction Hill

88

St Margaret's Plantation

Upландhall Farm

6

Three Ash Farm

87

Shadowbarn Farm

Angles Way

NR35

5

Hill Farm

The Elms

86

Elms Farm

Brewery

St Peter's Hall

4

Moat

Charity Farm

School Farm

Ropers Farm

Corner Farm

85

Beckford Farm

Low Farm

Ilketshall St Margaret

Church Farm

Highfields Farm

St Peter South Elmham

3

Bridge Farm

Brook House

Moat

Nest Farm

High Street

Mill House Farm

84

St Michael South Elmham

Bacons Farm

Home Farm

White House Farm

All Saints' Common

Water Tower

Green Farm

2

Croft Farm

Boundary Farm

Church Farm

Mill Farm

Hulver Farm

North End

83

Moat

Monks Farm

All Saints South Elmham

Moat Farm

Moat

The Elms

IP19

Rumburgh Wood

1

Ash Farm

Homestead Farm

Abbey Farm

82

Falcon Bridge

NETHERGATE ST

St Edmunds RC Prim Sch

River Waveney

WAINFORD MILLS RD

WATCH HO HILL

Watch House Hill

PH

BECCLES ROAD

Grove Farm

Staithe MILLS Ollands Plantation

Annis Hill

Davey Cl

DAVEY CL

Trinity Farm

Castle Farm

Dukes Farm

Bungay High Sch

Waveney Valley Swimming Pool

Gower's Pitt

Manor Farm

St Johns Lodge Farm

Hill Farm

Grove Farm

The Firs

Moats

Round Wood

Crow's Nest Wood

Mettingham

Top Farm

Moat

The Hall

Shipmeadow

Church Farm

Laurels Farm

High Common

Shipmeadow Common

Boundary Farm

Low Farm

Orchard Farm

Highfields Farm

Mettingham Wood

The Mount (Motte & Bailey)

Manor Farm

Birchams Farm

Tithe Farm

Ilketshall St Andrew

St Andrew's Hall

St John's Hall

Great Common

Dairy Farm

Glebe Farm

Moat Farm

Green Farm

Great Common

Hawthorn Farm

NR34

Church Farm

Willow Farm

Willow Tree Farm

Water Tower

Corner Farm

Grove Farm

Hanna Barn Farm

Garden Spinney

Tithe Farm

Ilketshall Hall Moat

Black's Covert

Red House Farm

Becks Green Farm

Larch Spinney

Ant Hill Plantation

Daniels Wood

Old Hall Farm

Tithe Farm

Rosary Farm

Manor Farm

Beck's Green

Common Farm

Cherry Tree Farm

Mill Farm

Windmill

Willow Farm

Green Farm

Little Beck Farm

Highland Farm

Moat Farm

Ilketshall St Lawrence

Windmill Farm

Rookery Farm

Kings Fene Farm

King's Fene

School Farm

St Lawrence Prim Sch

SCHOOL VW

Rookery Farm

Laurel Farm

Stone Street

Rose Farm

Rumburgh Farm

Green Lane Farm

Poplar Farm

The Poplars

PH

Cutts Farm

Wood Farm

For full street detail of Bungay see Philip's STREET ATLAS of **Suffolk**

Suffolk STREET ATLAS

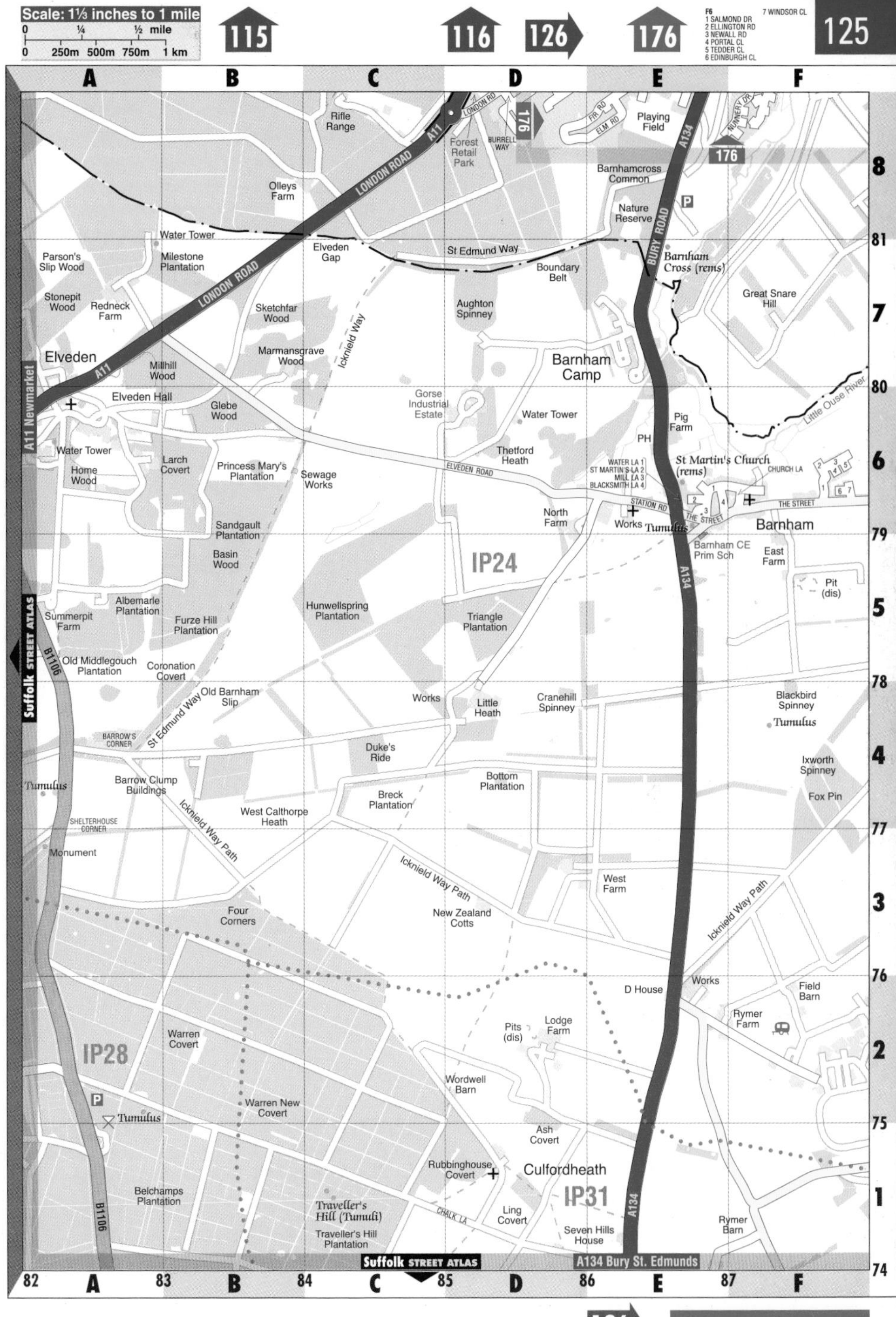

F6
1 SALMOND DR   7 WINDSOR CL
2 ELLINGTON RD
3 NEWALL RD
4 PORTAL CL
5 TEDDER CL
6 EDINBURGH CL

Rifle Range

Forest Retail Park

176

ELM RD

BURRELL WAY

LONDON RD

Playing Field

A134

176

Olleys Farm

LONDON ROAD

Barnhamcross Common

Water Tower

Elveden Gap

St Edmund Way

Nature Reserve

Boundary Belt

Barnham Cross (rems)

Parson's Slip Wood

Milestone Plantation

Stonepit Wood

Redneck Farm

Sketchfar Wood

Aughton Spinney

Great Snare Hill

Elveden

A11

Marmansgrave Wood

Ickneild Way

BURY ROAD

Barnham Camp

Little Ouse River

Millhill Wood

Elveden Hall

Glebe Wood

Gorse Industrial Estate

Water Tower

Pig Farm

St Martin's Church (rems)

CHURCH LA

Water Tower

Home Wood

Larch Covert

Princess Mary's Plantation

Sewage Works

ELVEDEN ROAD

Thetford Heath

PH

WATER LA 1
ST MARTIN'S-LA 2
MILL LA 3
BLACKSMITH LA 4

THE STREET

Barnham

A11 Newmarket

Sandgault Plantation

North Farm

STATION RD

Works   Tumulus

Barnham CE Prim Sch

East Farm

THE STREET

Basin Wood

IP24

Pit (dis)

Suffolk STREET ATLAS

Summerpit Farm

Albemarle Plantation

Furze Hill Plantation

Hunwellspring Plantation

Triangle Plantation

Old Middlegouch Plantation

Coronation Covert

Old Barnham Slip

St Edmund Way

Works

Little Heath

Cranehill Spinney

Blackbird Spinney

Tumulus

B1106

BARROW'S CORNER

Barrow Clump Buildings

Duke's Ride

Bottom Plantation

Ixworth Spinney

Fox Pin

Tumulus

Ickneild Way Path

West Calthorpe Heath

Breck Plantation

SHELTERHOUSE CORNER

Monument

Ickneild Way Path

West Farm

Ickneild Way Path

Four Corners

New Zealand Cotts

IP28

Works

D House

Field Barn

Warren Covert

Pits (dis)

Lodge Farm

Rymer Farm

P   Tumulus

Warren New Covert

Wordwell Barn

Ash Covert

Belchamps Plantation

Rubbinghouse Covert

Culfordheath

IP31

Rymer Barn

Traveller's Hill (Tumuli)

CHALK LA

Ling Covert

Seven Hills House

Traveller's Hill Plantation

A134

Suffolk STREET ATLAS ◀   A134 Bury St. Edmunds

B1106

126 ▶   For full street detail of the highlighted area see page 176

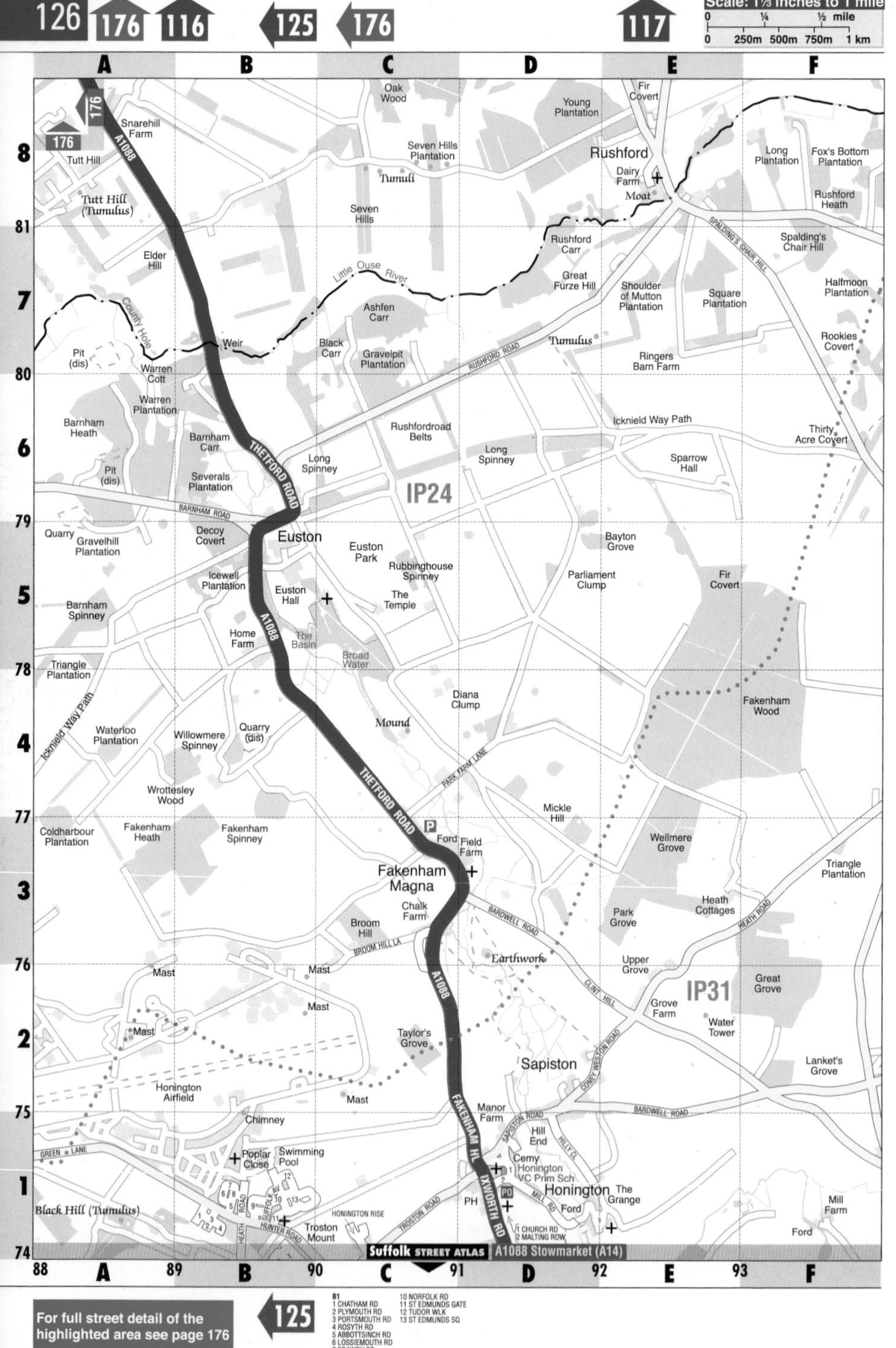

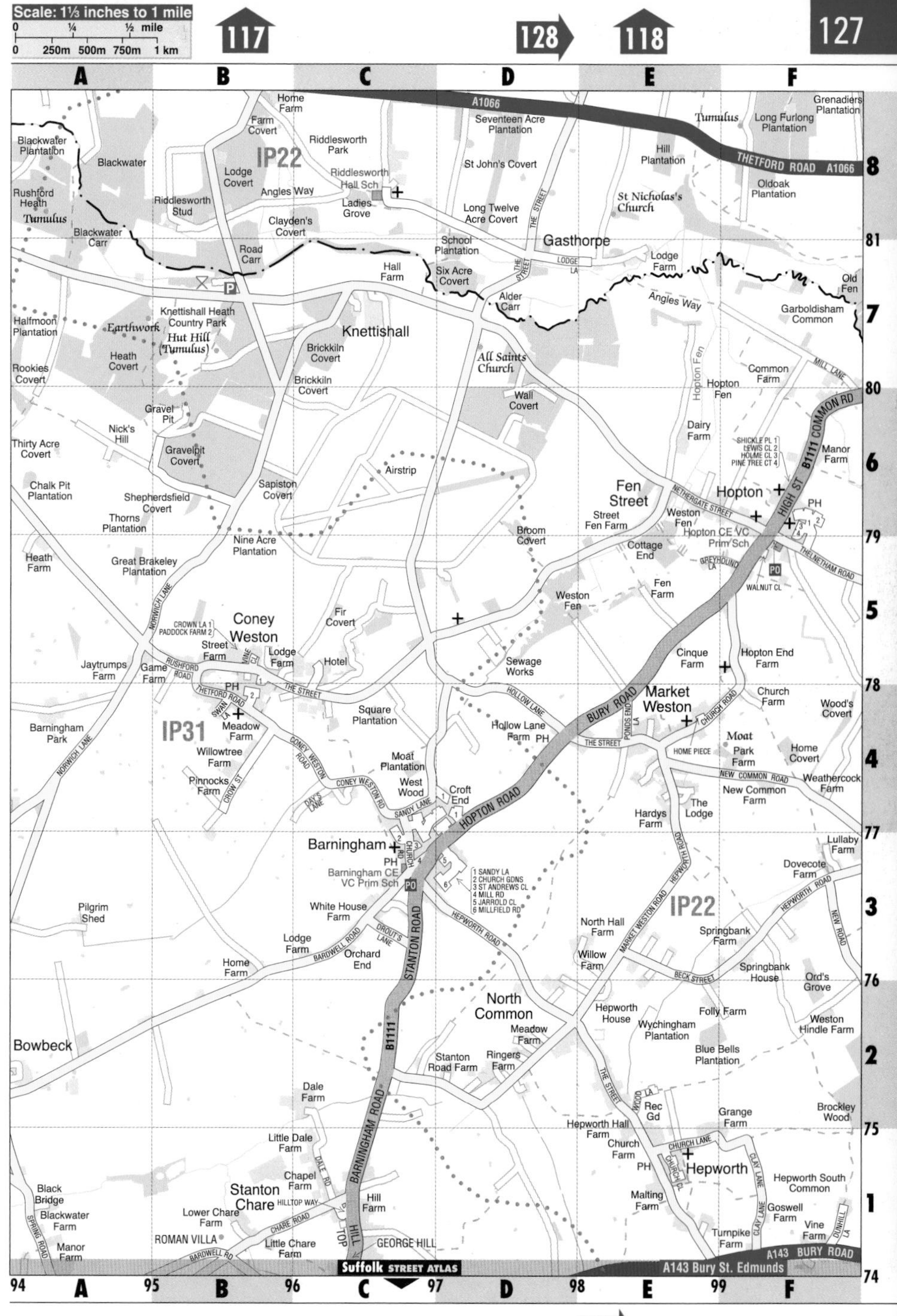

Scale: 1⅓ inches to 1 mile
0 ¼ ½ mile
0 250m 500m 750m 1 km
117
128
118
A B C D E F
A1066
THETFORD ROAD A1066
IP22
IP31
Home Farm
Farm Covert
Blackwater Plantation
Blackwater
Rushford Heath
Tumulus
Riddlesworth Park
Riddlesworth Hall Sch
Lodge Covert
Angles Way
Riddlesworth Stud
Ladies Grove
Clayden's Covert
Blackwater Carr
Road Carr
Seventeen Acre Plantation
St John's Covert
Long Twelve Acre Covert
School Plantation
Six Acre Covert
Hall Farm
THE STREET
Gasthorpe
LODGE LA
Lodge Farm
Alder Carr
Tumulus
Long Furlong Plantation
Grenadiers Plantation
Hill Plantation
St Nicholas's Church
Oldoak Plantation
Old Fen
Garboldisham Common
Knettishall Heath Country Park
Halfmoon Plantation
Earthwork
Hut Hill (Tumulus)
Heath Covert
Rookies Covert
Knettishall
Brickkiln Covert
Brickkiln Covert
All Saints Church
Wall Covert
Hopton Fen
MILL LANE
Common Farm
Hopton Fen
Gravel Pit
Nick's Hill
Thirty Acre Covert
Gravelpit Covert
Airstrip
Dairy Farm
B1111 COMMON RD
SHICKLE PL 1
LEWIS CL 2
HOLME CL 3
PINE TREE CT 4
Manor Farm
Chalk Pit Plantation
Shepherdsfield Covert
Sapiston Covert
Fen Street
Street Fen Farm
NETHERGATE STREET
Hopton
HIGH ST
PH
Weston Fen
Hopton CE VC Prim Sch
Thorns Plantation
Nine Acre Plantation
Broom Covert
Cottage End
GREYHOUND LA
THELNETHAM ROAD
PO
WALNUT CL
Heath Farm
Great Brakeley Plantation
Fen Farm
Weston Fen
NORWICH LANE
CROWN LA 1
PADDOCK FARM 2
Coney Weston
Street Farm
VINE CL
Lodge Farm
Fir Covert
Hotel
Jaytrumps Farm
Game Farm
RUSHFORD ROAD
THETFORD ROAD
SWAN LA
THE STREET
Sewage Works
Cinque Farm
Hopton End Farm
Church Farm
Wood's Covert
HOLLOW LANE
BURY ROAD
Market Weston
CHURCH ROAD
Square Plantation
Hollow Lane Farm
PH
PONDS END LA
THE STREET
HOME PIECE
Moat
Park Farm
Home Covert
Barningham Park
Meadow Farm
Willowtree Farm
CONEY WESTON ROAD
Moat Plantation
NORWICH LANE
HOPTON ROAD
NEW COMMON ROAD
New Common Farm
Weathercock Farm
Pinnocks Farm
CROW ST
CONEY WESTON RD
West Wood
Croft End
DAY'S LANE
SANDY LANE
The Lodge
Hardys Farm
Lullaby Farm
Barningham
CHURCH RD
PH
Barningham CE VC Prim Sch
1 SANDY LA
2 CHURCH GDNS
3 ST ANDREWS CL
4 MILL RD
5 JARROLD CL
6 MILLFIELD RD
Dovecote Farm
HEPWORTH ROAD
Pilgrim Shed
White House Farm
PO
MARKET WESTON ROAD
HEPWORTH ROAD
IP22
North Hall Farm
Springbank Farm
NEW ROAD
Lodge Farm
DROUT'S LANE
Orchard End
BARDWELL ROAD
Home Farm
HEPWORTH ROAD
Willow Farm
STANTON ROAD
BECK STREET
Springbank House
Ord's Grove
North Common
Hepworth House
Folly Farm
Wychingham Plantation
Weston Hindle Farm
Meadow Farm
Bowbeck
B1111
Stanton Road Farm
Ringers Farm
Blue Bells Plantation
THE STREET
Dale Farm
WOOD LA
Rec Gd
BARNINGHAM ROAD
Brockley Wood
Grange Farm
Little Dale Farm
Hepworth Hall Farm
Church Farm
CHURCH LANE
PH
CHURCH CL
Hepworth
CLAY LANE
Hepworth South Common
DALE RD
Chapel Farm
Black Bridge
Stanton Chare
HILLTOP WAY
Hill Farm
Malting Farm
Goswell Farm
Blackwater Farm
Lower Chare Farm
CHARE ROAD
CLAY LANE
Vine Farm
DUNHILL LA
SPRING ROAD
ROMAN VILLA
Little Chare Farm
TOP HILL
GEORGE HILL
Turnpike Farm
A143 BURY ROAD
Manor Farm
BARDWELL RD
Suffolk STREET ATLAS
A143 Bury St. Edmunds
8 81 7 80 6 79 5 78 4 77 3 76 2 75 1 74
94 95 96 97 98 99

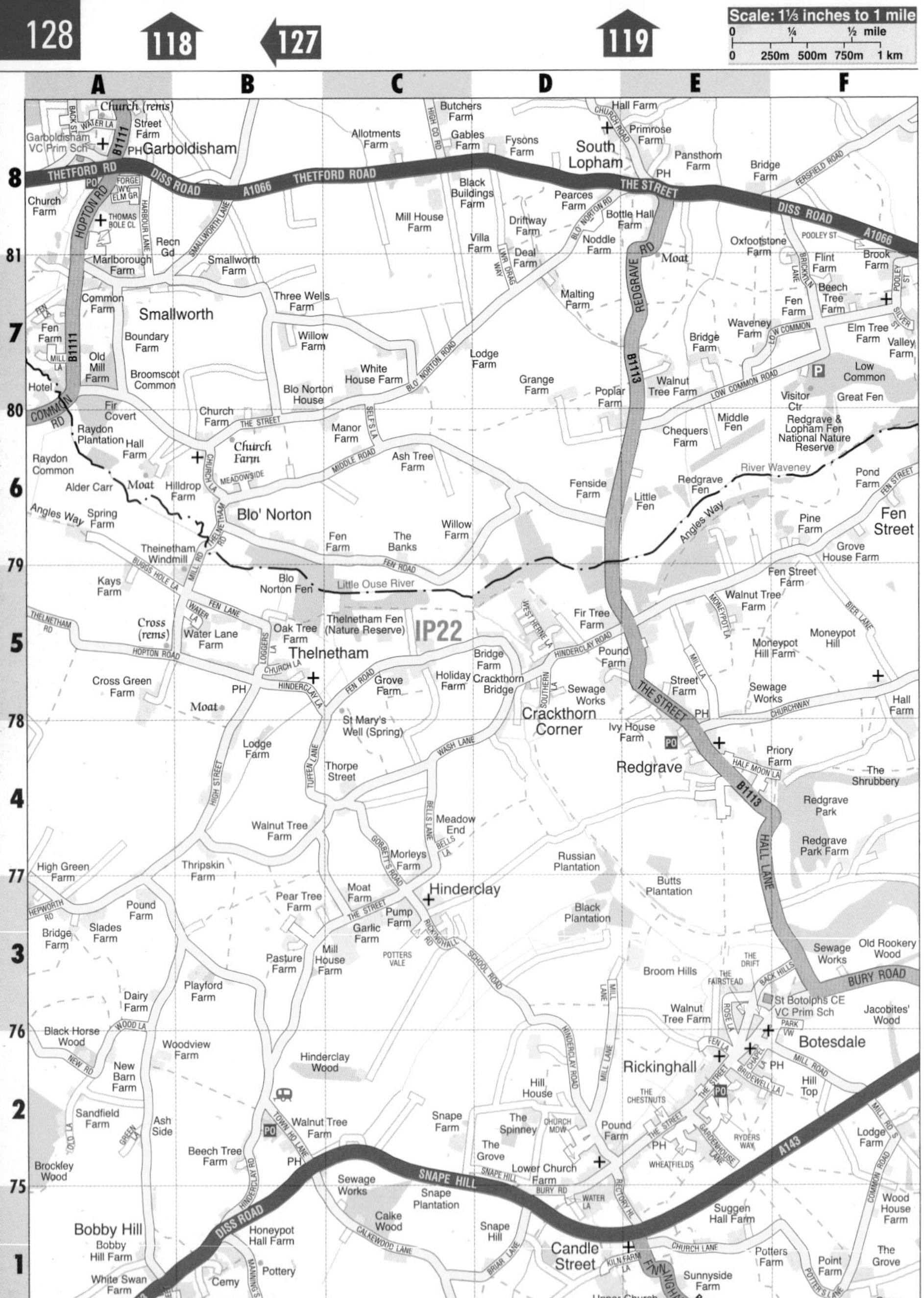

Scale: 1⅓ inches to 1 mile

0   ¼   ½ mile
0   250m 500m 750m 1 km

A   B   C   D   E   F

8
Church (rems)
Garboldisham
VC Prim Sch
Water La
B1111
Forge
Elm Ga
Thomas Bole Cl.
Street Farm
PH Garboldisham
DISS ROAD
A1066 THETFORD ROAD
Butchers Farm
Allotments Farm
Gables Farm
Fysons Farm
South Lopham
Primrose Farm
Hall Farm
PH
Pansthom Farm
Bridge Farm
FERFIELD ROAD
DISS ROAD
A1066

THETFORD ROAD
HOPTON RD
Church Farm

81
Marlborough Farm
Recn Gd
Smallworth Farm
Mill House Farm
Black Buildings Farm
Pearces Farm
Driftway Farm
Villa Farm
Bottle Hall Farm
Noddle Farm
Deal Farm
REDGRAVE RD
Moat
Oxfootstone Farm
POOLEY ST
Flint Farm
Beech Tree Farm
Brook Farm
A1066
POOLEY RD

7
Fen Farm
Common Farm
Smallworth
Three Wells Farm
Willow Farm
Lodge Farm
Malting Farm
Grange Farm
Waveney Farm
VW COMMON
Bridge Farm
Elm Tree Farm
Valley Farm
B1111
Old Mill La
Boundary Farm
White House Farm
Blo Norton House
Poplar Farm
Walnut Tree Farm
LOW COMMON ROAD
Low Common
Great Fen
Hotel
Broomscot Common
B1113

80
COMMON RD
Fir Covert
Church Farm
THE STREET
Manor Farm
Ash Tree Farm
Chequers Farm
Middle Fen
Visitor Ctr
Redgrave & Lopham Fen National Nature Reserve
P
Raydon Plantation
Hall Farm
Church Farm
MEADOWSIDE
MIDDLE ROAD
River Waveney
Pond Farm
IXER ST

6
Raydon Common
Alder Carr
Moat
Hilldrop Farm
Spring Farm
Blo' Norton
Fen Farm
The Banks
Willow Farm
Fenside Farm
Little Fen
Redgrave Fen
Angles Way
Pine Farm
Grove House Farm
Fen Street
Angles Way

79
Theinetham Windmill
BRIGGS HOLE LA
Kays Farm
Blo Norton Fen
Little Ouse River
FEN ROAD
Fir Tree Farm
Fen Street Farm
Walnut Tree Farm
BELL LANE
Moneypot Hill

5
Thelnetham Rd
Cross (rems)
HOPTON LANE
Water Lane Farm
Oak Tree Farm
COGGERS LA
Thelnetham
CHURCH LA
FEN ROAD
Thelnetham Fen (Nature Reserve)
IP22
WEST FEN LA
Bridge Farm
Crackthorn Bridge
Holiday Farm
Pound Farm
HINDERCLAY ROAD
Street Farm
PH
Sewage Works
THE STREET
Sewage Works
CHURCHWAY
Moneypot Hill Farm
Hall Farm

78
Cross Green Farm
PH
Moat
Grove Farm
HINDERCLAY LA
St Mary's Well (Spring)
Crackthorn Corner
Ivy House Farm
PO
Redgrave
B1113
Priory Farm
The Shrubbery

4
Lodge Farm
WOOD STREET
Thorpe Street
WASH LANE
TUFFEN LANE
BELL'S LANE
Meadow End Farm
WELLS LA
Russian Plantation
HALF MOON LA
HALL LANE
Redgrave Park
Redgrave Park Farm

77
High Green Farm
HEPWORTH RD
Thripskin Farm
Pound Farm
Walnut Tree Farm
Morleys Farm
BONDS STREET
Butts Plantation
Black Plantation
Broom Hills
Sewage Works
BURY ROAD
Old Rookery Wood
A143

3
Bridge Farm
Slades Farm
Pear Tree Farm
Moat Farm
Pump Farm
THE STREET
Garlic Farm
Mill House Farm
POTTERS VALE
Hinderclay
SCHOOL ROAD
MILL ROAD
THE FAIRSTEAD
THE DRIFT
BACK HILLS
St Botolphs CE VC Prim Sch
PARK
Jacobites' Wood

76
Dairy Farm
WOOD LA
Playford Farm
Pasture Farm
REDGRAVE ROAD
Hinderclay Wood
Hill House
Walnut Tree Farm
ROSE LA
VW
PH
Botesdale
MILL HILL
Hill Top

2
Black Horse Wood
NEW RD
New Barn Farm
GIPSY LA
Woodview Farm
Walnut Tree Farm
PO
PH
Snape Farm
The Spinney
CHURCH MDW
THE CHESTNUTS
Rickinghall
PO
BRIDEWELL LA
PH
RYDERS WAY
CANDLEWOOD LA
Lodge Farm
BACK HILLS

75
Sandfield Farm
Ash Side
Brockley Wood
Beech Tree Farm
PH
CALDWOOD LANE
SNAPE HILL
Sewage Works
Snape Plantation
Calke Wood
The Grove
Lower Church Farm
SNAPE HILL
BURY RD
Pound Farm
PH
WHEATFIELDS
Water Lane
A143
Suggen Hall Farm
Wood House Farm

1
Bobby Hill
Bobby Hill Farm
DISS ROAD
Honeypot Hall Farm
Pottery
Snape Hill
Candle Street
Sunnyside Farm
Potters Farm
Point Farm
The Grove
CHURCH LANE
TWINNIGHTAM RD
Upper Church Farm
B1113
POTTERS LANE
Grove Flock Farm

74
White Swan Farm
Cemy
A143
Wattisfield
HINNINGHAM LANE
KILNLANE

00   A   01   B   02   C   03   D   04   E   05   F   0

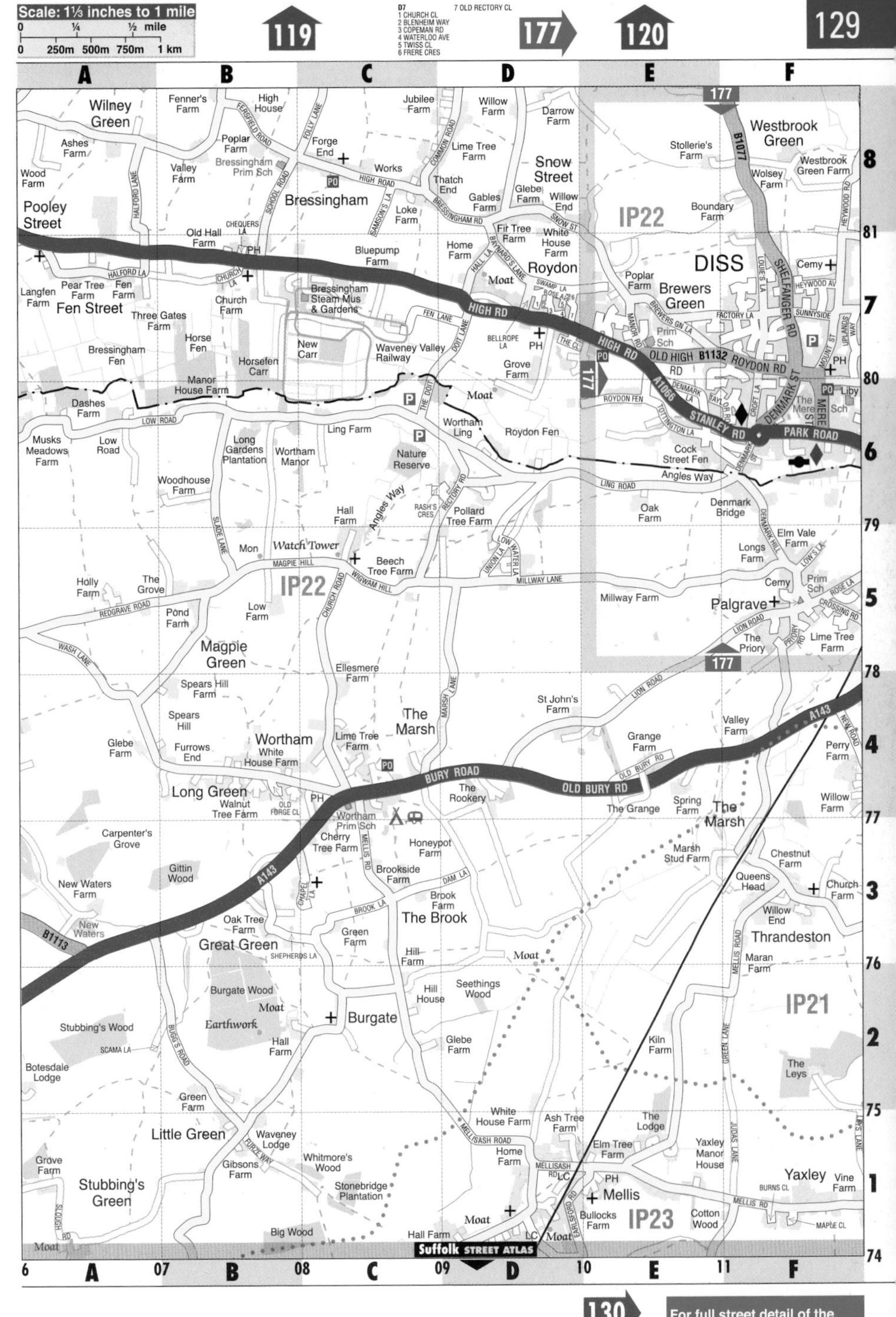

Scale: 1⅓ inches to 1 mile

0   ¼   ½ mile
0   250m 500m 750m 1 km

119

177

120

129

D7
1 CHURCH CL
2 BLENHEIM WAY
3 COPELAND RD
4 WATERLOO AVE
5 TWISS CL
6 FRERE CRES

7 OLD RECTORY CL

Wilney Green
Fenner's Farm
High House
Jubilee Farm
Willow Farm
Darrow Farm
Westbrook Green
Ashes Farm
Poplar Farm
Forge End
Lime Tree Farm
Stollerie's Farm
Westbrook Green
Wolsey Farm
Wood Farm
Valley Farm
Bressingham Prim Sch
Works
Thatch End
Snow Street
Boundary Farm
Pooley Street
Bressingham
Loke Lane
Gables Farm
Glebe Farm
IP22
Old Hall Farm
CHEQUERS LA PH
Bluepump Farm
Home Farm
Fit Tree Farm
Roydon
White House Farm
DISS
Langfen Farm
Pear Tree Farm
Fen Farm
Church Farm
Moat
Poplar Farm
Brewers Green
Cemy
Fen Street
Three Gates Farm
Bressingham Steam Mus & Gardens
HIGH RD
BELLROPE LA
PH
Prim Sch
SUNNYSIDE
Bressingham Fen
Horse Fen
New Carr
Waveney Valley Railway
FEN LANE
Grove Farm
OLD HIGH RD
B1132
ROYDON RD
P
PH
Liby
Horsefen Carr
Manor House Farm
Moat
Wortham Ling
Roydon Fen
Roydon Fen
STANLEY RD
PARK ROAD
Dashes Farm
Low Road
Ling Farm
P
Wortham Ling
Cock Street Fen
Musks Meadows Farm
Long Gardens Plantation
Nature Reserve
Angles Way
Oak Farm
Denmark Bridge
Woodhouse Farm
Wortham Manor
Hall Farm
Pollard Tree Farm
Millway Farm
Longs Farm
Elm Vale Farm
Holly Farm
The Grove
Watch Tower
MAGPIE HILL
Beech Tree Farm
RASH'S CRES
LOW AUTH LA
Millway Lane
Cemy
Prim Sch
IP22
Pond Farm
Low Farm
Palgrave
Lime Tree Farm
Magpie Green
WASH LANE
REDGRAVE ROAD
Ellesmere Farm
MARSH LANE
LION ROAD
The Priory
Spears Hill Farm
St John's Farm
177
Spears Hill
Wortham
The Marsh
Lime Tree Farm
Grange Farm
Valley Farm
A143
Perry Farm
Glebe Farm
Furrows End
White House Farm
PO
BURY ROAD
OLD BURY RD
The Marsh
Willow Farm
Long Green
Walnut Tree Farm
OLD FORGE LA
PH
Wortham Prim Sch
The Rookery
The Grange
Spring Farm
Chestnut Farm
Carpenter's Grove
Cherry Tree Farm
Honeypot Farm
Marsh Stud Farm
Queens Head
New Waters Farm
Gittin Wood
Brookside Farm
DAM LA
Willow End
Church Farm
New Waters
B1113
Oak Tree Farm
BROOK LA
Green Farm
Brook Farm
The Brook
Maran Farm
Thrandeston
Great Green
SHEPHERDS LA
Hill Farm
Hill Farm
Seethings Wood
Moat
Kiln Farm
IP21
Stubbing's Wood
SCAMA LA
Burgate Wood
Earthwork
Moat
Burgate
Glebe Farm
The Leys
Botesdale Lodge
Hall Farm
BUDS ROAD
Green Farm
White House Farm
Ash Tree Farm
The Lodge
Yaxley Manor House
Little Green
Waveney Lodge
Gibsons Farm
Whitmore's Wood
Home Farm
MELLISASH RD
Elm Tree Farm
Yaxley
Grove Farm
RIDGE WAY
Stonebridge Plantation
LC
PH
Mellis
Vine Farm
Stubbing's Green
Big Wood
Hall Farm
Moat
LC
Moat
Bullocks Farm
IP23
Cotton Wood
MELLIS RD
MAPLE CL

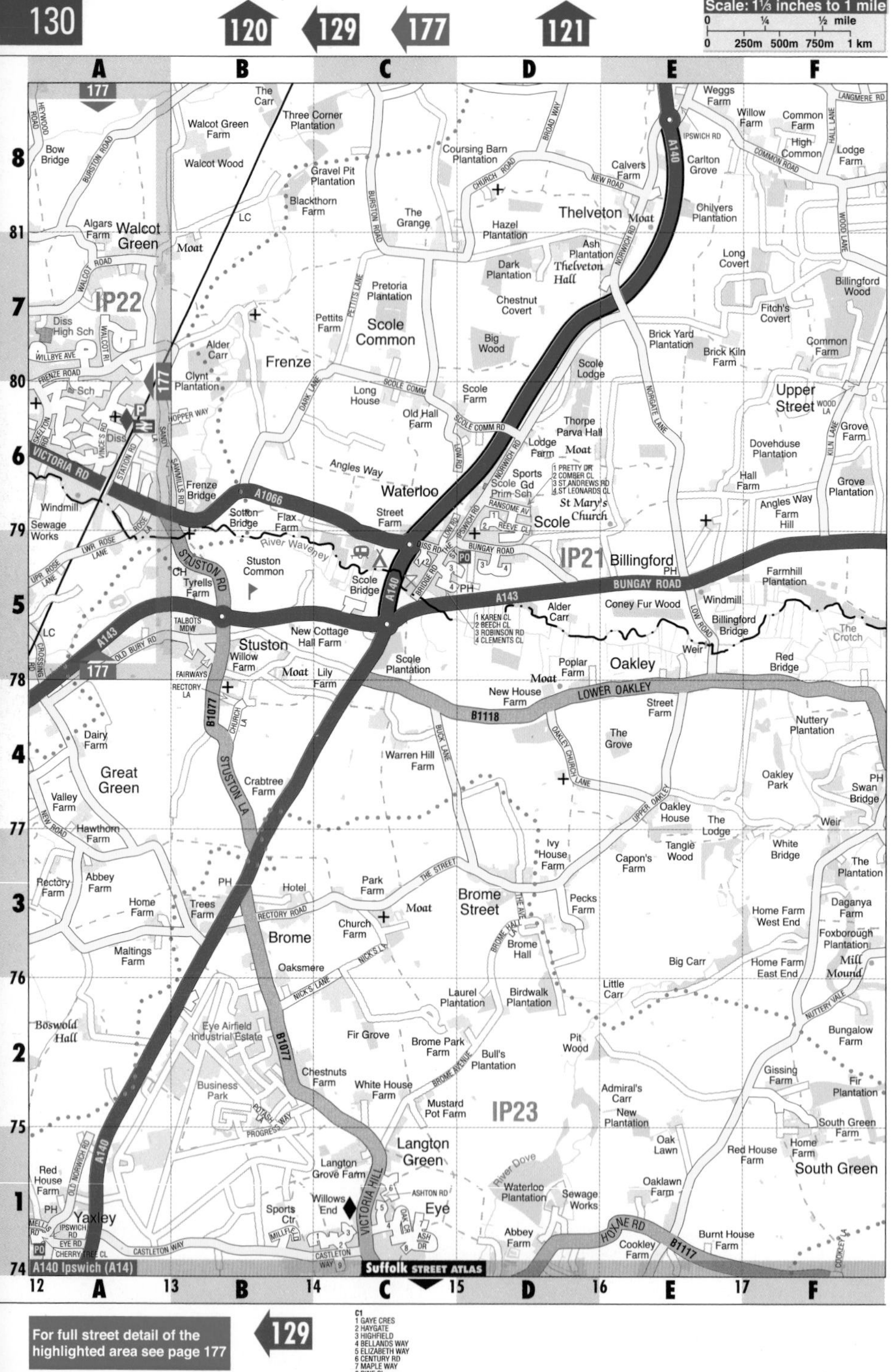

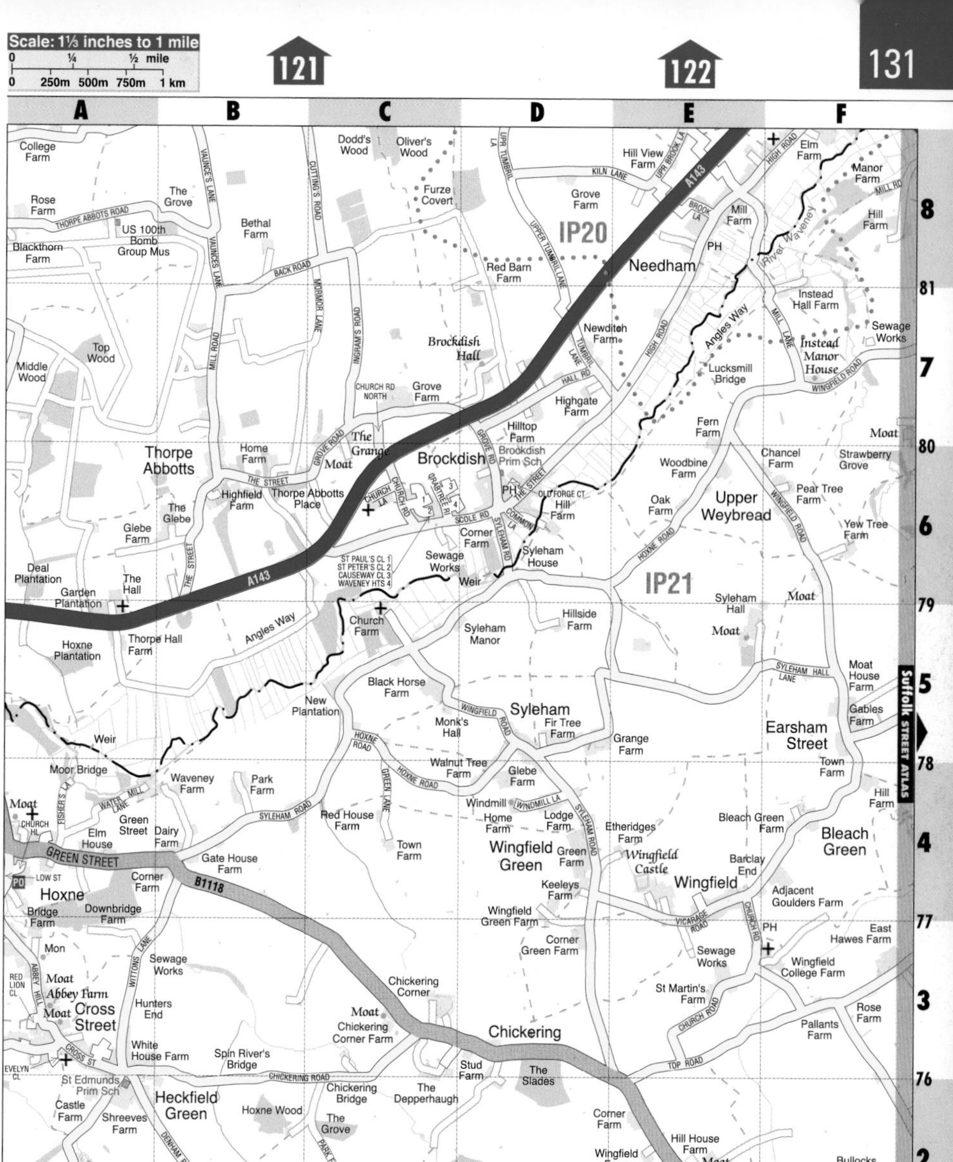

Scale: 1½ inches to 1 mile

0   ¼   ½ mile
0 250m 500m 750m 1 km

A   B   C   D   E   F

College Farm

Rose Farm

Blackthorn Farm

US 100th Bomb Group Mus

The Grove

Bethal Farm

Dodd's Wood

Oliver's Wood

Furze Covert

Red Barn Farm

Hill View Farm

Grove Farm

IP20

Elm Farm

Manor Farm

Hill Farm

Mill Farm

PH

Needham

Instead Hall Farm

Sewage Works

Instead Manor House

Middle Wood

Top Wood

Thorpe Abbotts

Home Farm

Brockdish Hall

Church Rd North

Grove Farm

Newditch Farm

Hilltop Farm

Highgate Farm

Angles Way

Lucksmill Bridge

Fern Farm

Chancel Farm

Woodbine Farm

Strawbery Grove

Moat

Glebe Farm

Highfield Farm

The Glebe

Thorpe Abbotts Place

The Grange

Moat

Brockdish

Brockdish Prim Sch

PH

Dufforge Ct

Hill Farm

Oak Farm

Upper Weybread

Pear Tree Farm

Yew Tree Farm

Deal Plantation

The Hall

Garden Plantation

Thorpe Hall Farm

Angles Way

A143

St Paul's Cl 1
St Peter's Cl 2
Causeway Cl 3
Waveney Hts 4

Church Farm

Corner Farm

Sewage Works

Siddle La

Common La

Syleham House

Weir

IP21

Syleham Hall

Moat

Moat

Hoxne Plantation

Church Farm

Syleham Manor

Hillside Farm

Syleham Hall Lane

Moat House Farm

Gables Farm

Weir

New Plantation

Black Horse Farm

Wingfield Road

Monk's Hall

Walnut Tree Farm

Syleham

Fir Tree Farm

Grange Farm

Town Farm

Earsham Street

Hill Farm

Moor Bridge

Waveney Farm

Park Farm

Red House Farm

Hoxne Road

Green Lane

Syleham Road

Home Farm

Windmill

Wyndmill La

Glebe Farm

Lodge Farm

Etheridges Farm

Bleach Green Farm

Bleach Green

Moat

Elm House

Water Mill La

Green Street

Dairy Farm

Gate House Farm

Town Farm

Wingfield Green

Green Farm

Wingfield Castle

Barclay End

Wingfield

Adjacent Goulders Farm

East Hawes Farm

Green Street

Hoxne

Bridge Farm

Corner Farm

B1118

Low St

Witting Lane

Downbridge Farm

Keeleys Farm

Wingfield Green Farm

Corner Green Farm

Vicarage Road

PH

Sewage Works

Wingfield College Farm

Mon

Abbey Farm

Sewage Works

Hunters End

Chickering Corner

St Martin's Farm

Church Rd

Rose Farm

Moat

Cross Street

White House Farm

Spin River's Bridge

Moat

Chickering Corner Farm

Chickering

Pallants Farm

St Edmunds Prim Sch

Castle Farm

Shreeves Farm

Heckfield Green

Denham Road

Chickering Road

Hoxne Wood

Chickering Bridge

The Grove

Park Farm Lane

The Depperhaugh

Stud Farm

The Slades

Corner Farm

Hill House Farm

Moat

Bullocks Hill Farm

Church Road

College Farm

Town Farm

Denham

Mill Farm

Broome Farm

Watering Road

Reading Green Farm

Reading Green

Depperhaugh Wood

Rookery Farm

Grove Wood

Barnes Farm

Wingfield Farm

Mill Mound

Moat

Tudor Farm

Battlesea Green

Mayhews Corner

White House

Battlesea Hill

Rattlerow Hill

Rattlerow Hill

Sewage Works

Standwell Farm

East Anglian Fruit Farm

Vicarage Farm

Cottage Grove

Westhall

Grove End

Stradbroke

Drapers Hill Farm

Grove Farm

Stradbroke CE Prim Sch

B1118

Queen St

8
81
7
80
6
79
5
78
4
77
3
76
2
75
1
74

Suffolk STREET ATLAS

1 1 1

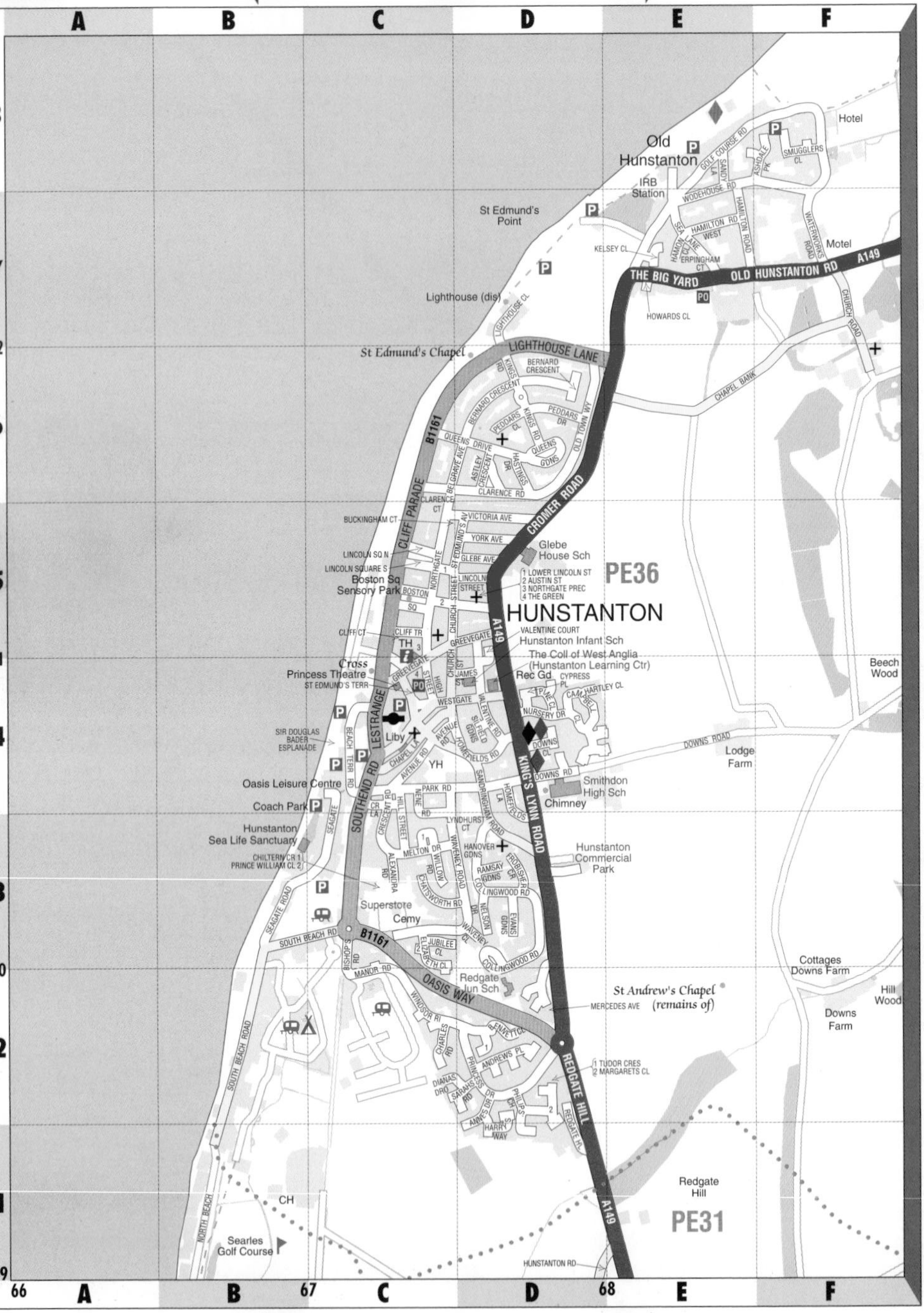
A
B
C
D
E
F
8
7
42
6
5
41
4
3
40
2
1
39
66
67
68
Hotel
Old Hunstanton
IRB Station
St Edmund's Point
GOLF COURSE RD
SANDY LA
ASHDALE PK
SMUGGLERS CL
WODEHOUSE RD
HAMILTON ROAD
HAMILTON RD WEST
SEA LANE
HAMON CL
ERPINGHAM CT
KELSEY CL
WATERWORKS ROAD
Motel
THE BIG YARD
OLD HUNSTANTON RD
A149
PO
HOWARDS CL
CHURCH ROAD
Lighthouse (dis)
LIGHTHOUSE CL
St Edmund's Chapel
LIGHTHOUSE LANE
BERNARD CRESCENT
KINGS RD
CHAPEL BANK
PEDDARS CL
PEDDARS DR
OLD TOWN WY
B1161
QUEENS DRIVE
QUEENS GDNS
HASTINGS DR
ASTLEY CRESCENT
BELGRAVE AVE
CLARENCE RD
CLARENCE CT
CLIFF PARADE
CROMER ROAD
BUCKINGHAM CT
VICTORIA AVE
ST EDMUND'S AV
YORK AVE
GLEBE AVE
Glebe House Sch
LINCOLN SQ N
LINCOLN SQUARE S
NORTHGATE
1 LOWER LINCOLN ST
2 AUSTIN ST
3 NORTHGATE PREC
4 THE GREEN
PE36
Boston Sq Sensory Park
BOSTON SQ
LINCOLN STREET
CHURCH STREET
HUNSTANTON
CLIFF CT
CLIFF TR
TH
GREEVEGATE
VALENTINE COURT
Hunstanton Infant Sch
The Coll of West Anglia (Hunstanton Learning Ctr)
Cross
Princess Theatre
ST EDMUND'S TERR
HIGH STREET
JAMES ST
Rec Gd
CYPRESS PL
PINE CL
HARTLEY CL
CAMPBELL CL
Beech Wood
WESTGATE
LESTRANGE
VALENTINE RD
NURSERY DR
SIR DOUGLAS BADER ESPLANADE
BEACH TERR RD
Liby
AVENUE RD
ST EDMUND'S GDNS
HOMEFIELDS RD
DOWNS CL
DOWNS ROAD
Lodge Farm
CHAPEL LA
YH
KING'S LYNN ROAD
DOWNS RD
Oasis Leisure Centre
SOUTHEND RD
PARK RD
Smithdon High Sch
Chimney
Coach Park
SEAGATE
CRESCENT RD
HILL STREET
CR LA
NENE RD
SANDRINGHAM ROAD
HOMEFIELDS LA
LYNDHURST CT
Hunstanton Sea Life Sanctuary
MELTON DR
WILLOW RD
WAVENEY ROAD
HANOVER GDNS
FROBISHER CR
Hunstanton Commercial Park
CHILTERN CR 1
PRINCE WILLIAM CL 2
ALEXANDRA RD
RAMSAY GDNS
COLLINGWOOD RD
CHATSWORTH RD
NELSON DR
EVANS GDNS
SEAGATE ROAD
Superstore
Cemy
SOUTH BEACH RD
BISHOP'S RD
JUBILEE CL
ELIZABETH CL
WAVENEY CL
COLLINGWOOD RD
Cottages
Downs Farm
MANOR RD
OASIS WAY
Redgate Jun Sch
St Andrew's Chapel (remains of)
MERCEDES AVE
Hill Wood
Downs Farm
WINDSOR RI
BENNETT CL
CHARLES RD
SOUTH BEACH ROAD
ANDREWS PL
REDGATE HILL
1 TUDOR CRES
2 MARGARETS CL
PRINCESS DR
DIANAS DRO
SARAHS RD
PHILIPS CR
ANNES DR
HARRY WAY
REDGATE HL
Redgate Hill
CH
PE31
NORTH BEACH
Searles Golf Course
HUNSTANTON RD

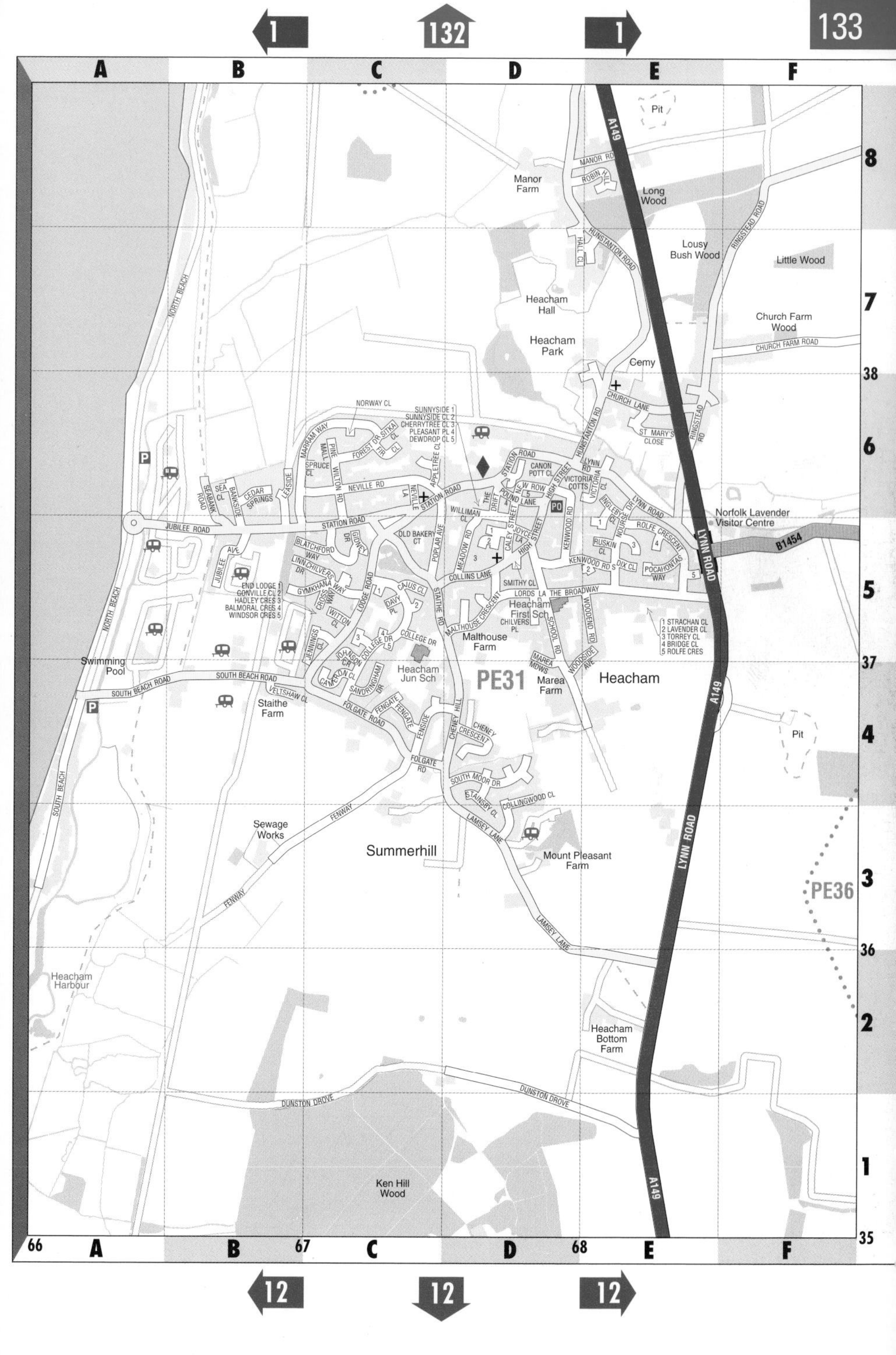
1
132
1
A
B
C
D
E
F
8
7
38
6
5
37
4
3
36
2
1
35
66
67
68
Pit
A149
MANOR RD
ROBIN HILL
Manor Farm
Long Wood
HALL CL
HUNSTANTON ROAD
Lousy Bush Wood
RINGSTEAD ROAD
Little Wood
NORTH BEACH
Heacham Hall
Church Farm Wood
Heacham Park
CHURCH FARM ROAD
Cemy
CHURCH LANE
ST MARY'S CLOSE
RINGSTEAD RD
HUNSTANTON RD
NORWAY CL
SUNNYSIDE 1
SUNNYSIDE CL 2
CHERRYTREE CL 3
PLEASANT PL 4
DEWDROP CL 5
MARRAM WAY
FOREST DR
SITKA CL
FIR CL
PINE MALL
SPRUCE CL
WILTON RD
APPLETREE CL
STATION ROAD
CANON POTT CL
LYNN RD
VICTORIA COTTS
VICTORIA CL
HIGH STREET
NEVILLE RD
NEVILLE LA
SEABANK ROAD
SEA CL
BANKSIDE
CEDAR SPRINGS
LEASIDE
THE DRIFT
POUND LANE
NEW ROW
WILLIMAN CL
PO
LYNN ROAD
INGLEBY CL
NOURSE DR
Norfolk Lavender Visitor Centre
ROLFE CRESCENT
B1454
JUBILEE ROAD
STATION ROAD
OLD BAKERY CT
BLATCHFORD WAY
GIDNEY DR
CALEY STREET
JOYCE LA
KENWOOD ROAD
RUSKIN CL
JUBILEE AVE
LINN CHILVERS DR
POPLAR AVE
MEADOW RD
HIGH STREET
KENWOOD RD S
DIX CL
POCAHONTAS WAY
END LODGE 1
GONVILLE CL 2
HADLEY CRES 3
BALMORAL CRES 4
WINDSOR CRES 5
GYMKHANA WAY
LODGE ROAD
CAIUS CL
COLLINS LANE
SMITHY CL
LORDS LA
THE BROADWAY
CROSS WAY
DAVY PL
STAITHE RD
MALTHOUSE CRESCENT
Heacham First Sch
WOODEND RD
NORTH BEACH
WITTON CL
CHILVERS PL
SCHOOL RD
1 STRACHAN CL
2 LAVENDER CL
3 TORREY CL
4 BRIDGE CL
5 ROLFE CRES
JENNINGS CL
COLLEGE DR
Malthouse Farm
Swimming Pool
JOHNSON CR
CAMERON CL
SANDRINGHAM DR
Heacham Jun Sch
PE31
MAREA MDWS
Marea Farm
WOODSIDE AVE
Heacham
SOUTH BEACH ROAD
SOUTH BEACH ROAD
VELTSHAW CL
Staithe Farm
FOLGATE ROAD
FENGATE
FENSIDE
CHENEY HILL
CHENEY CRESCENT
A149
Pit
FOLGATE RD
SOUTH MOOR DR
STAINSBY CL
COLLINGWOOD CL
SOUTH BEACH
Sewage Works
FENWAY
LAMSEY LANE
Summerhill
Mount Pleasant Farm
LYNN ROAD
PE36
FENWAY
LAMSEY LANE
Heacham Harbour
Heacham Bottom Farm
DUNSTON DROVE
DUNSTON DROVE
Ken Hill Wood
A149
12
12
12

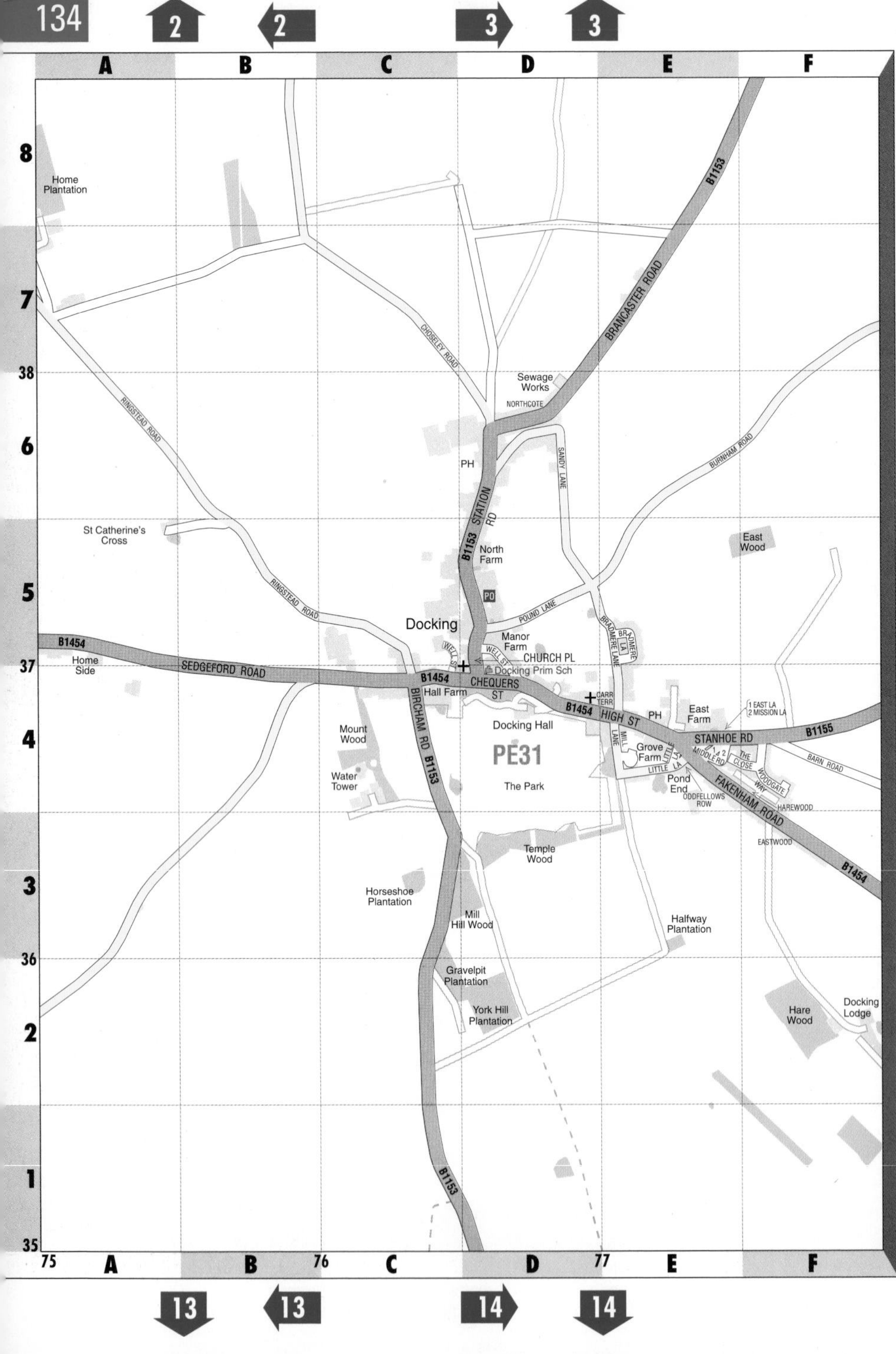

2 ← **2** → **3** **3**

A B C D E F

8

7

38

6

St Catherine's Cross

5

Docking

37 B1454
Home Side
SEDGEFORD ROAD
B1454

4

PE31

3

36

2

1

35
75 A B 76 C D 77 E F

Home Plantation

DUSELEY ROAD

Sewage Works
NORTHCOTE

BRANCASTER ROAD
B1153

B1153

BURNHAM ROAD

PH

STATION RD
B1153

North Farm

PO

POUND LANE
Manor Farm

East Wood

WELLS
Docking Prim Sch
CHURCH PL
WELL
SANDY LANE
BIRCHAM FIRE LANE

Hall Farm
CHEQUERS ST
B1454
HIGH ST
GARR TERR
MILL LANE
PH

Docking Hall

Grove Farm
LITTLE LA

East Farm
STANHOE RD
1 EAST LA
2 MISSION LA
THE CLOSE
MIDDLE RD
BARN ROAD
B1155

The Park

Pond End
ODDFELLOWS ROW
FAKENHAM ROAD
HAREWOOD
EASTWOOD
B1454

Mount Wood

Water Tower

BIRCHAM RD B1153

Temple Wood

Horseshoe Plantation

Mill Hill Wood

Halfway Plantation

Gravelpit Plantation

York Hill Plantation

Hare Wood

Docking Lodge

B1153

RINGSTEAD ROAD

RINGSTEAD ROAD

13 ← **13** → **14** **14**

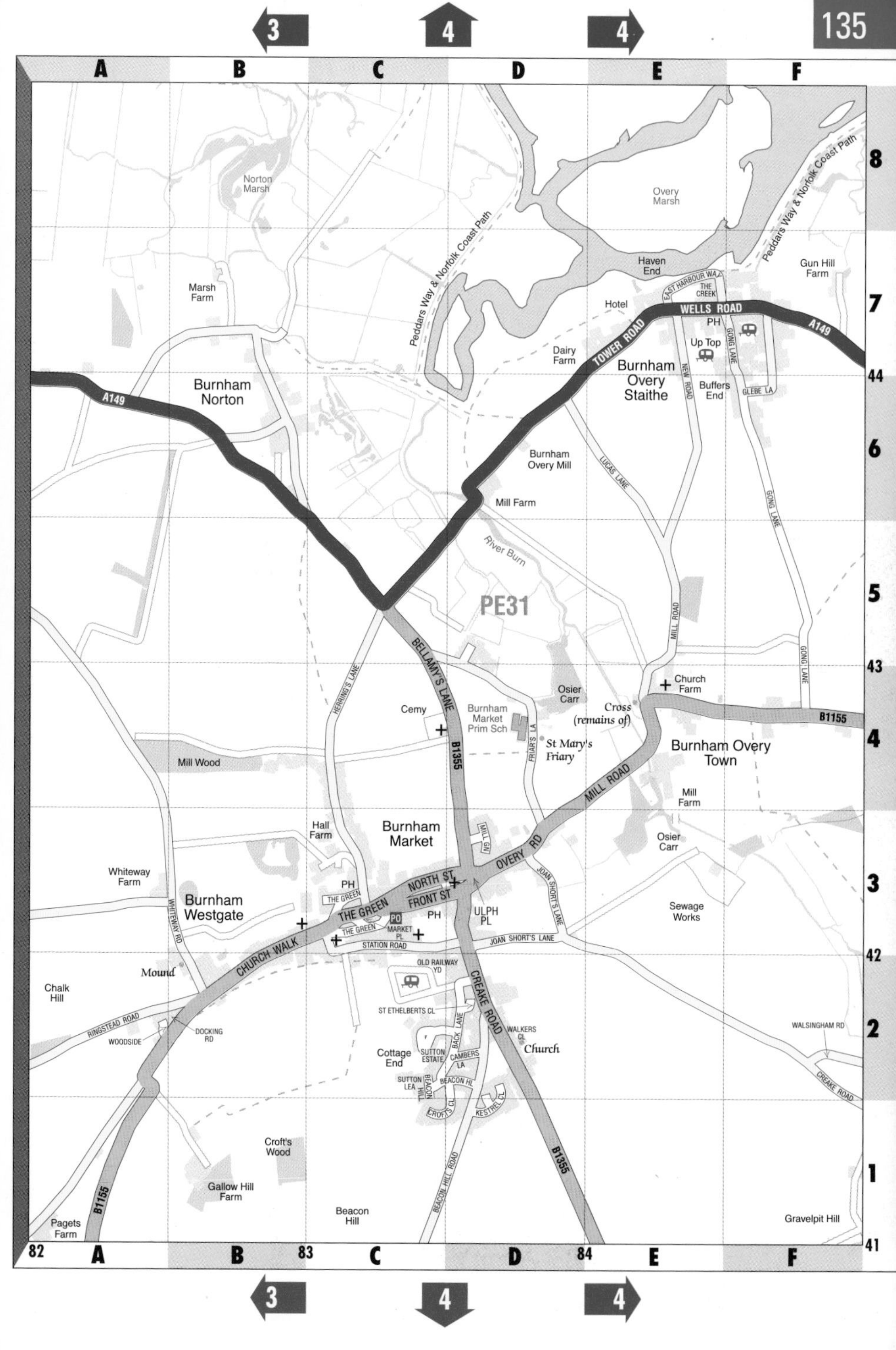
3
4
4
A
B
C
D
E
F
Norton
Marsh
Overy
Marsh
Peddars Way & Norfolk Coast Path
Peddars Way & Norfolk Coast Path
Haven
End
Gun Hill
Farm
Marsh
Farm
EAST HARBOUR WAY
THE
CREEK
Hotel
WELLS ROAD
A149
PH
Up Top
TOWER ROAD
Dairy
Farm
Burnham
Overy
Staithe
NEW ROAD
GONG LANE
Buffers
End
GLEBE LA
Burnham
Norton
A149
Burnham
Overy Mill
LUCAS LANE
GONG LANE
Mill Farm
River Burn
PE31
MILL ROAD
BELLAMY'S LANE
GONG LANE
HERRING'S LANE
Church
Farm
Osier
Carr
Cross
(remains of)
Cemy
Burnham
Market
Prim Sch
B1155
B1355
FRIAR'S LA
St Mary's
Friary
Burnham Overy
Town
Mill Wood
MILL ROAD
Mill
Farm
Hall
Farm
Burnham
Market
MILL GN
OVERY RD
Osier
Carr
Whiteway
Farm
PH
NORTH ST
JOAN SHORT'S LANE
Burnham
Westgate
THE GREEN
THE GREEN
FRONT ST
ULPH
PL
Sewage
Works
WHITEWAY RD
PO
PH
THE GREEN
MARKET
PL
STATION ROAD
JOAN SHORT'S LANE
CHURCH WALK
Mound
OLD RAILWAY
YD
Chalk
Hill
CREAKE ROAD
RINGSTEAD ROAD
ST ETHELBERTS CL
WOODSIDE
DOCKING
RD
BACK LANE
WALKERS
CL
Church
WALSINGHAM RD
Cottage
End
SUTTON
ESTATE
CAMBERS
LA
CREAKE ROAD
SUTTON
LEA
BEACON HILL
BEACON HL
CROFTS CL
KESTREL CL
Croft's
Wood
B1355
Gallow Hill
Farm
BEACON HILL ROAD
B1155
Beacon
Hill
Gravelpit Hill
Pagets
Farm
8
7
44
6
5
43
4
3
42
2
1
41
82
83
84
A
B
C
D
E
F
3
4
4

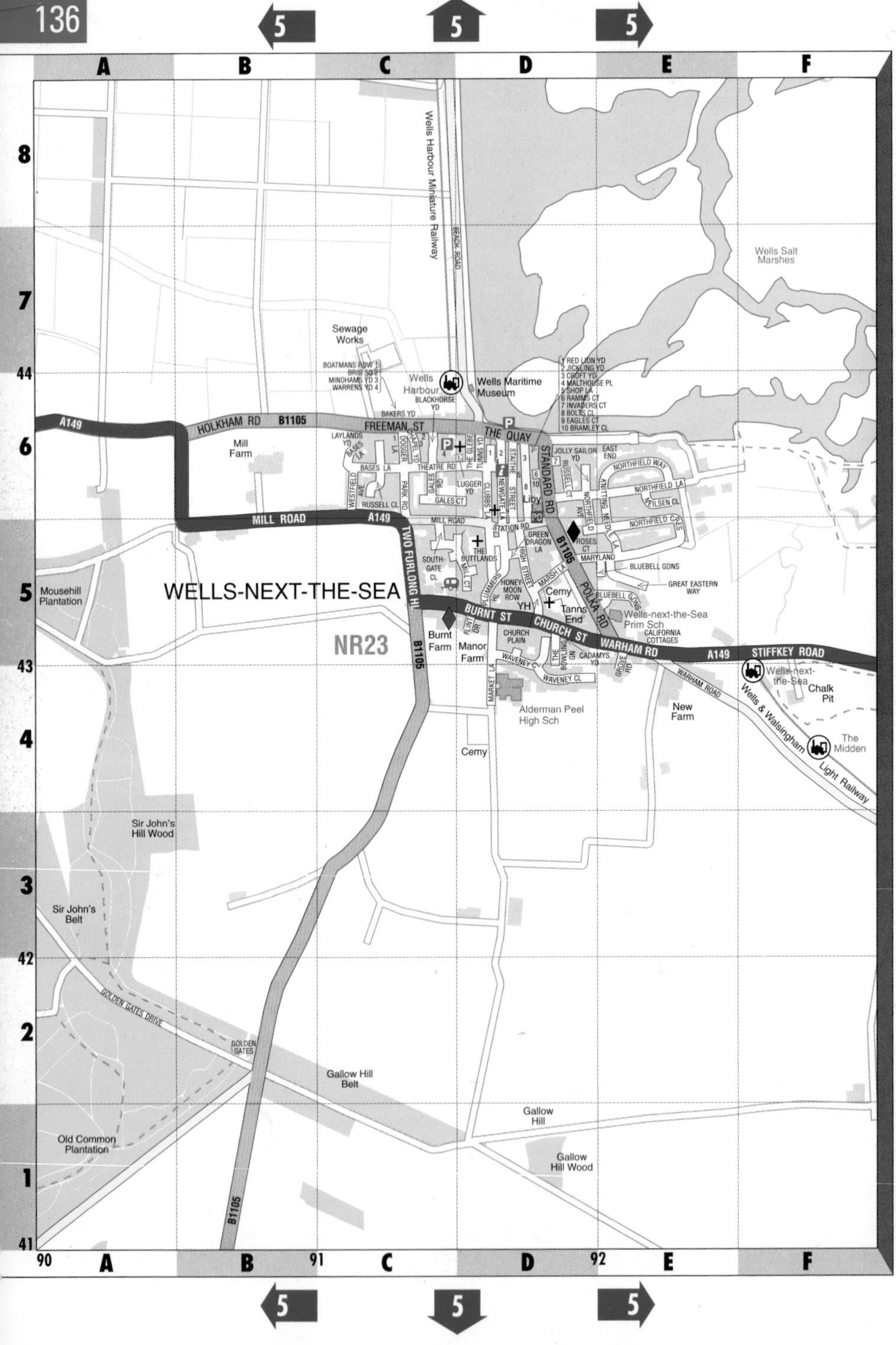
WELLS-NEXT-THE-SEA
NR23
Wells Harbour Miniature Railway
BEACH ROAD
Wells Salt Marshes
Sewage Works
Wells Harbour
Wells Maritime Museum
BOATMANS ROW 1
BRIG SQ 2
MINDHAMS YD 3
WARRENS YD 4
BLACKHORSE YD
BAKERS YD
1 RED LION YD
2 JICKLING YD
3 CROFT YD
4 MALTHOUSE PL
5 SHOP LA
6 RAMMS CT
7 INVADERS CT
8 BOLTS CL
9 EAGLES CT
10 BRAMLEY CL
A149
HOLKHAM RD
B1105
FREEMAN ST
THE QUAY
Mill Farm
LAYLANDS YD
BASES LA
DOGGER LA
CHAPEL YD
THEATRE RD
THE GLEBE
TUNNS YD
STAITHE STREET
STANDARD RD
JOLLY SAILOR YD
EAST END
NORTHFIELD WAY
NORTHFIELD LA
NILSEN CL
NORTHFIELD CRES
RUSSELL CT
NORTHFIELD AVE
KNITTING NEEDLE LA
WESTFIELD AVE
PARK RD
GALES RD
LUGGER YD
GALES CT
CLUBBS LA
NEWGATE LA
Liby
PO
RUSSELL CL
MILL ROAD
STATION RD
GREEN DRAGON LA
ROSES CT
MARYLAND
BLUEBELL GDNS
GREAT EASTERN WAY
TWO FURLONG HL
SOUTHGATE CL
THE BUTTLANDS
MILL CT
PLUMMERS HL
HONEYMOON ROW
HIGH STREET
MARSH LA
POLKA RD
Cemy
YH
Tanns End
Wells-next-the-Sea Prim Sch
CALIFORNIA COTTAGES
Mousehill Plantation
BURNT ST
CHURCH ST
WARHAM RD
STIFFKEY ROAD
Burnt Farm
Manor Farm
FLINT DR
CHURCH PLAIN
THE BOWLING GN
CADAMYS YD
GROVE RD
WAVENEY C
WAVENEY CL
MARKET LA
Alderman Peel High Sch
WARHAM ROAD
New Farm
Wells-next-the-Sea
Chalk Pit
Wells & Walsingham Light Railway
The Midden
Sir John's Hill Wood
Sir John's Belt
GOLDEN GATES DRIVE
GOLDEN GATES
Gallow Hill Belt
Gallow Hill
Gallow Hill Wood
Old Common Plantation

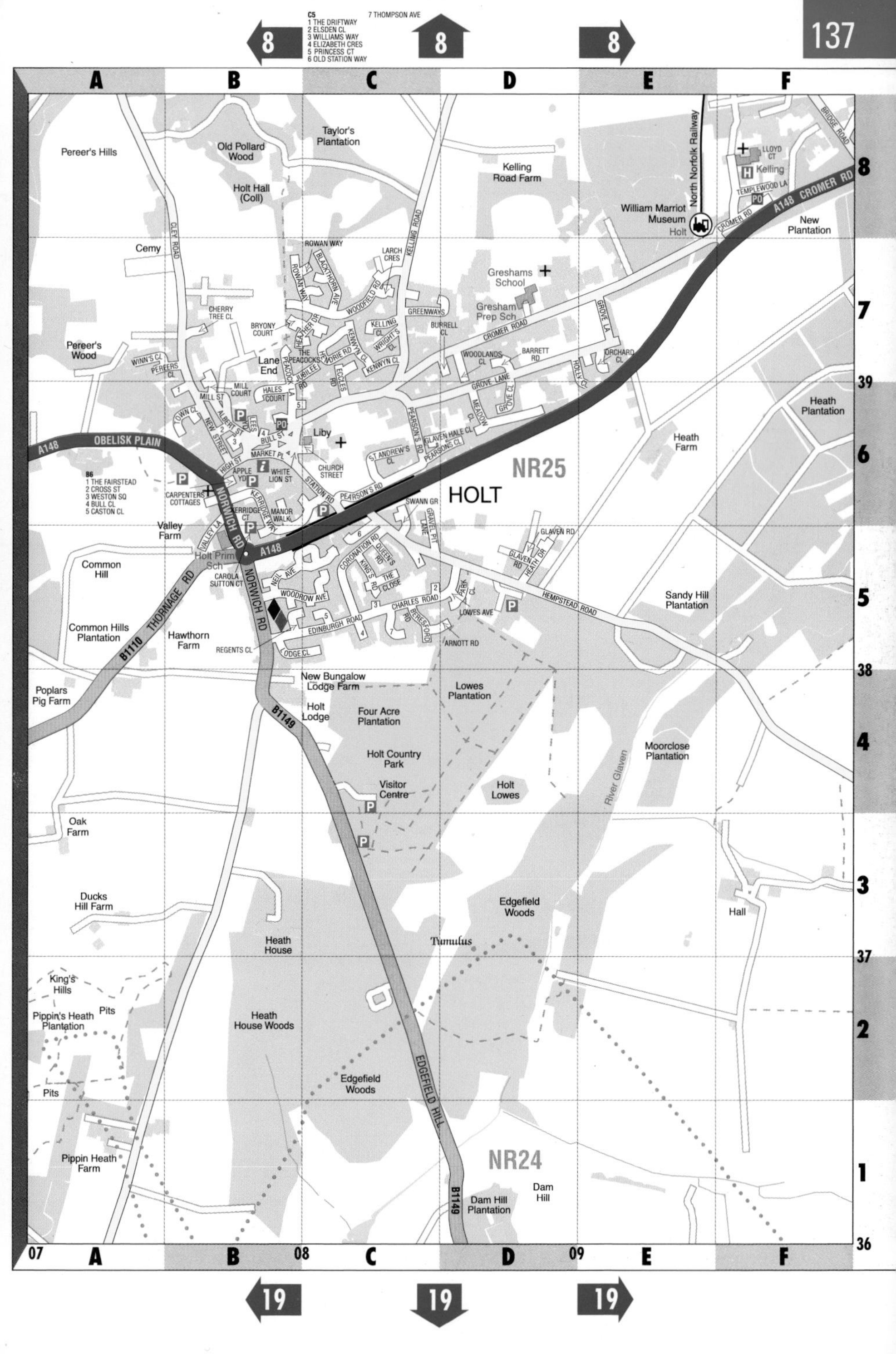
C5
1 THE DRIFTWAY
2 ELSDEN CL
3 WILLIAMS WAY
4 ELIZABETH CRES
5 PRINCESS CT
6 OLD STATION WAY
7 THOMPSON AVE
8
8
8
A
B
C
D
E
F
Pereer's Hills
Old Pollard Wood
Taylor's Plantation
Kelling Road Farm
North Norfolk Railway
BRIDGE ROAD
LLOYD CT
Kelling
TEMPLEWOOD LA
A148 CROMER RD
CROMER RD
William Marriot Museum
Holt
New Plantation
Holt Hall (Coll)
CLEY ROAD
KELLING ROAD
Cemy
ROWAN WAY
LARCH CRES
BLACKTHORN AVE
WOODFIELD RD
Greshams School
Gresham Prep Sch
CHERRY TREE CL
BRYONY COURT
HEATHER DR
KELLING CL
WRIGHT'S CL
GREENWAYS
BURRELL CL
CROMER ROAD
GROVE LA
KENWYN CL
THE PEACOCKS
Pereer's Wood
WINN'S CL
PEREERS CL
Lane End
WOODLANDS CL
BARRETT RD
ORCHARD CL
HOLLY CL
MILL COURT
HALES COURT
PEACOCK LA
JUBILEE
ECCLES
GROVE LANE
GROVE CL
MEADOW CL
MILL ST
TOWN CL
ALBERT ST
NEW STREET
LEES YD
BULL ST
Liby
PEARSON'S RD
GLAVEN HALE CL
PEARSONS CL
Heath Plantation
Heath Farm
A148
OBELISK PLAIN
HIGH ST
MARKET PL
ST ANDREW'S CL
CHURCH STREET
NR25
B6
1 THE FAIRSTEAD
2 CROSS ST
3 WESTON SQ
4 BULL CL
5 CASTON CL
APPLE YD
WHITE LION ST
STATION RD
PEARSON'S RD
HOLT
CARPENTERS COTTAGES
NORWICH RD
KERRIDGE WAY
MANOR WALK
SWANN GR
GRAVEL PIT LANE
Valley Farm
VALLEY LA
KERRIDGE CT
A148
GLAVEN RD
HEATH DR
Common Hill
Holt Prim Sch
CORONATION RD
QUEEN'S RD
KING'S RD
THE CLOSE
NEIL AVE
CAROLA SUTTON CT
HEMPSTEAD ROAD
Sandy Hill Plantation
PARK CL
WOODROW AVE
CHARLES ROAD
BERESFORD RD
LOWES AVE
B1110 THORNAGE RD
Common Hills Plantation
Hawthorn Farm
EDINBURGH ROAD
ARNOTT RD
REGENTS CL
LODGE CL
Poplars Pig Farm
New Bungalow Lodge Farm
Lowes Plantation
Holt Lodge
Four Acre Plantation
B1149
Holt Country Park
Moorclose Plantation
Visitor Centre
Holt Lowes
River Glaven
Oak Farm
Ducks Hill Farm
Edgefield Woods
Hall
Tumulus
Heath House
King's Hills
Pits
Pippin's Heath Plantation
Heath House Woods
EDGEFIELD HILL
Edgefield Woods
Pits
Pippin Heath Farm
NR24
Dam Hill
Dam Hill Plantation
B1149
8
7
39
6
5
38
4
3
37
2
1
36
07
08
09
19
19
19

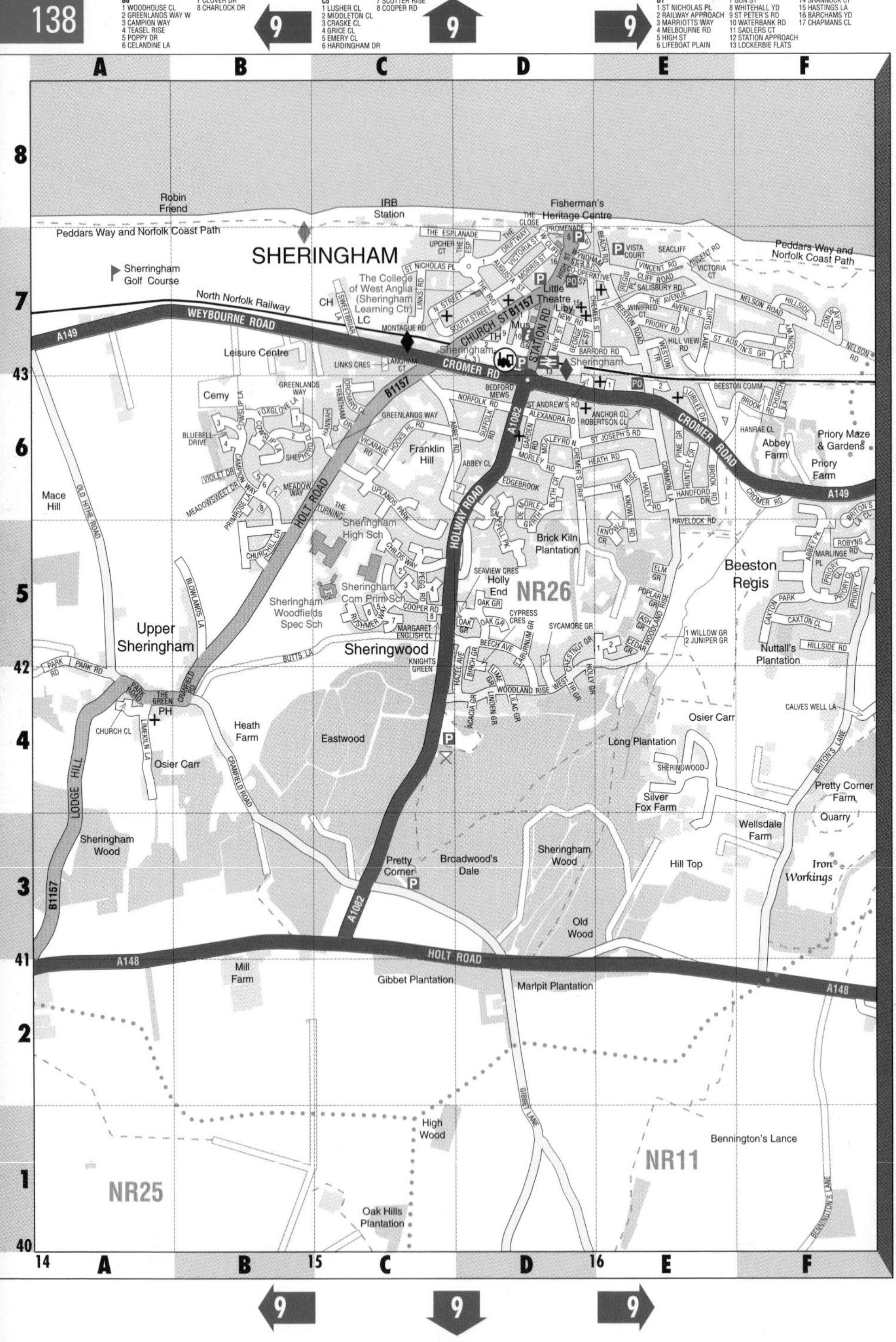

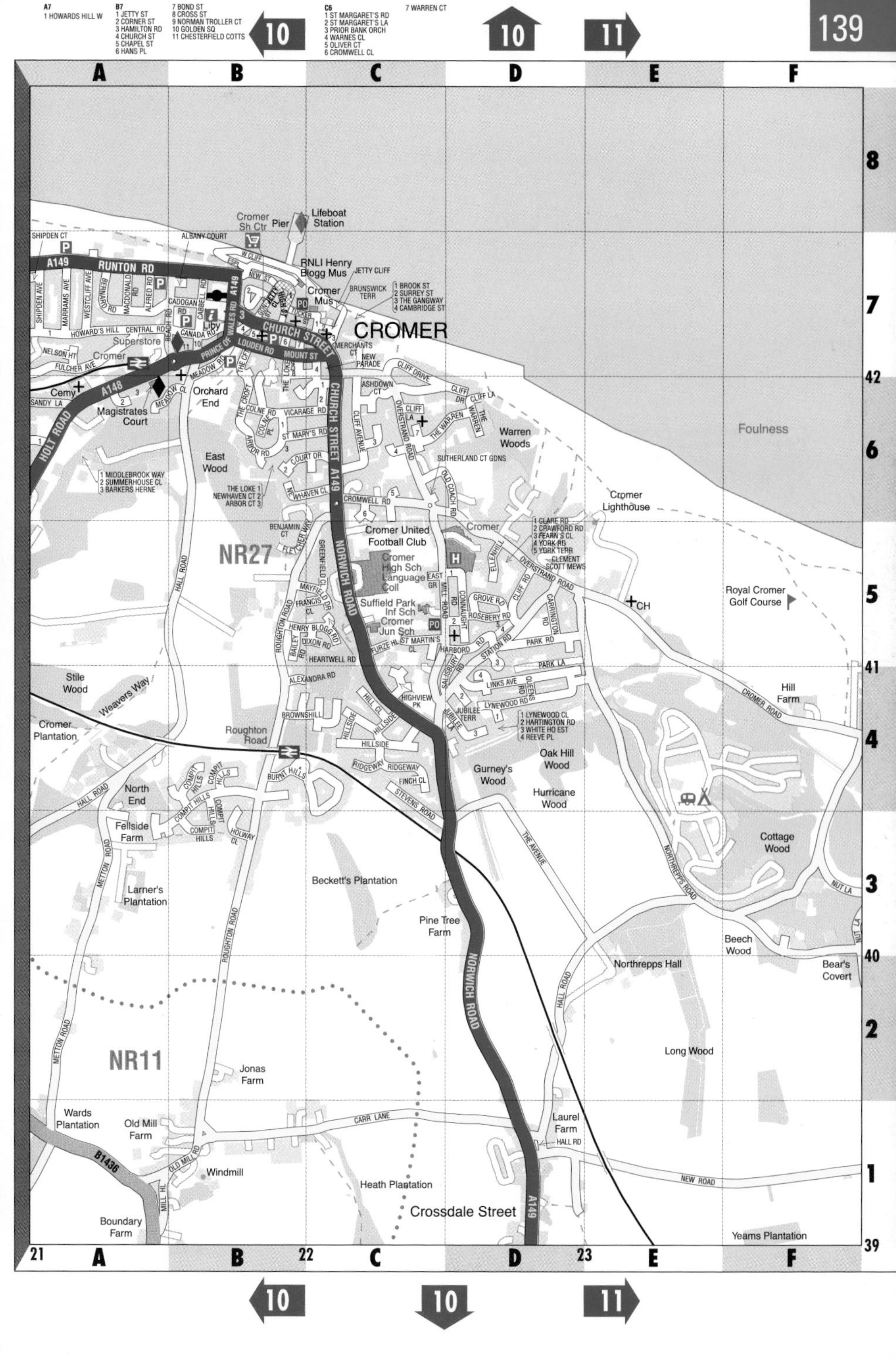

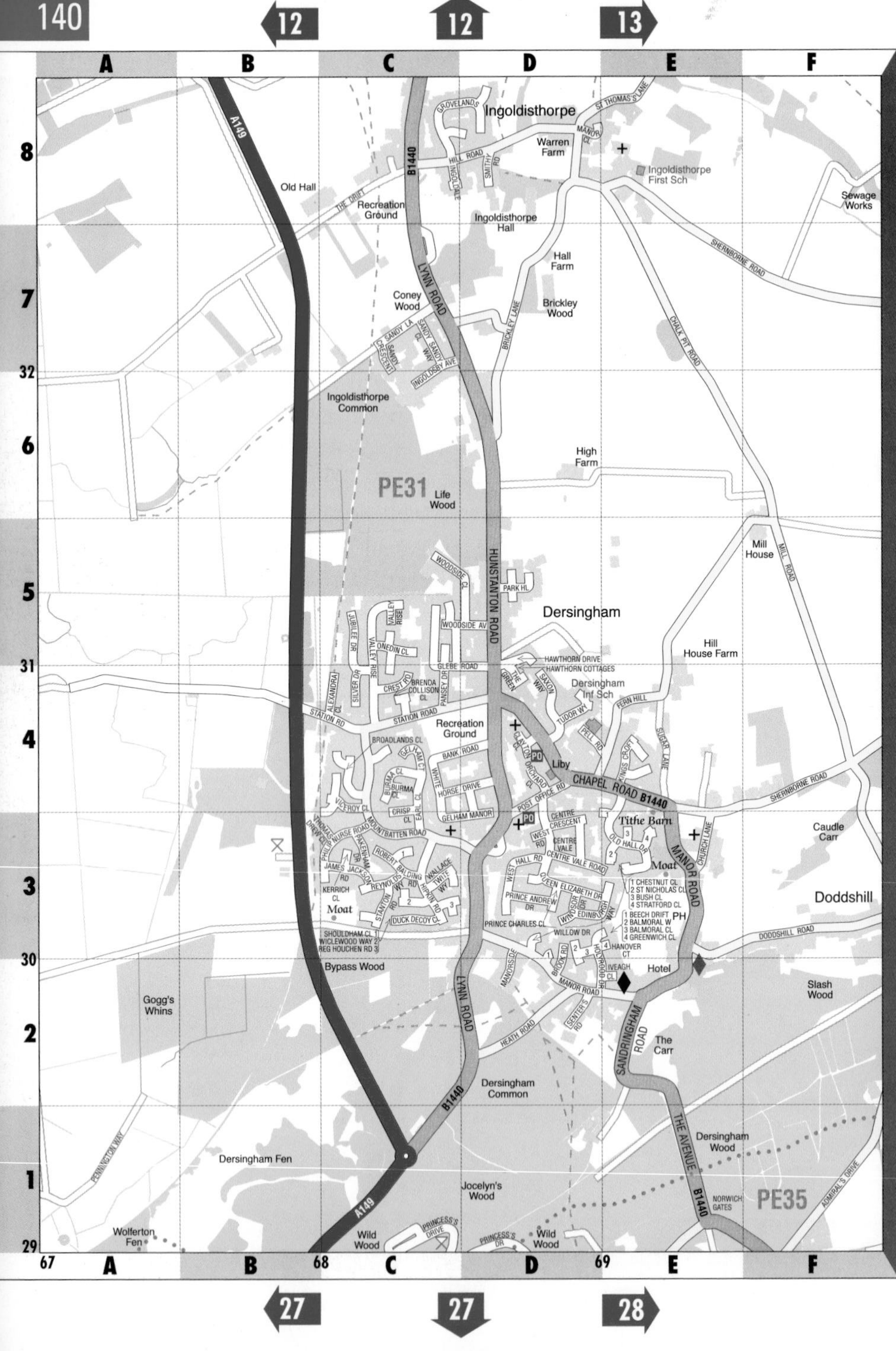

12
12
13
27
27
28
Ingoldisthorpe
Warren Farm
Ingoldisthorpe First Sch
Old Hall
Recreation Ground
Ingoldisthorpe Hall
Hall Farm
Sewage Works
Coney Wood
Brickley Wood
Ingoldisthorpe Common
High Farm
PE31
Life Wood
Mill House
Dersingham
Hill House Farm
Dersingham Inf Sch
Recreation Ground
Liby
Tithe Barn
Moat
Caudle Carr
Doddshill
Moat
Bypass Wood
Hotel
Slash Wood
Gogg's Whins
The Carr
Dersingham Common
Dersingham Wood
Dersingham Fen
Jocelyn's Wood
PE35
Wolferton Fen
Wild Wood
Wild Wood
NORWICH GATES
A149
B1440
LYNN ROAD
HUNSTANTON ROAD
CHAPEL ROAD
MANOR ROAD
SANDRINGHAM ROAD
THE AVENUE
SHERNBORNE ROAD
CHALK PIT ROAD
MILL ROAD
DODDSHILL ROAD
STATION ROAD
1 CHESTNUT CL
2 ST NICHOLAS CL
3 BUSH CL
4 STRATFORD CL
1 BEECH DRIFT
2 BALMORAL W
3 BALMORAL CL
4 GREENWICH CL
1 SHOULDHAM CL
2 WICLEWOOD WAY
3 REG HOUCHEN RD

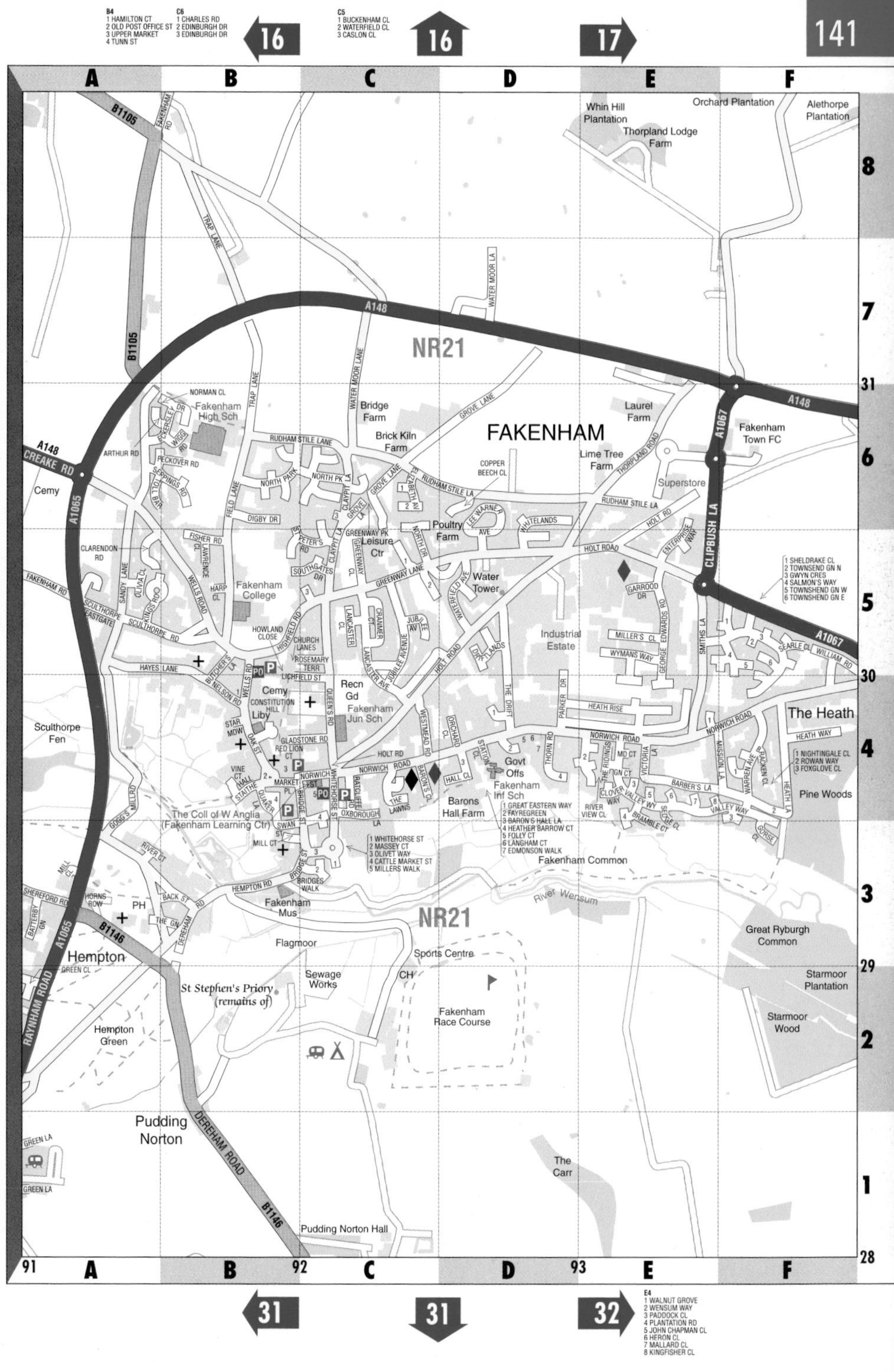
141
B4
1 HAMILTON CT
2 OLD POST OFFICE ST
3 UPPER MARKET
4 TUNN ST
C6
1 CHARLES RD
2 EDINBURGH DR
3 EDINBURGH DR
16
C5
1 BUCKENHAM CL
2 WATERFIELD CL
3 CASLON CL
16
17
A B C D E F
8
7
31
6
5
30
4
3
29
2
1
28
91 92 93
Whin Hill Plantation
Orchard Plantation
Alethorpe Plantation
Thorpland Lodge Farm
NR21
FAKENHAM
A148
B1105
B1105
A1065
A1067
CREAKE RD
Cemy
Fakenham High Sch
NORMAN CL
ARTHUR RD
PECKOVER RD
TRAP LANE
WATER MOOR LANE
WATER MOOR LA
Bridge Farm
Brick Kiln Farm
GROVE LANE
Laurel Farm
Fakenham Town FC
Lime Tree Farm
THORPLAND ROAD
Superstore
COPPER BEECH CL
RUDHAM STILE LANE
RUDHAM STILE LA
NORTH PARK
NORTH PK
Poultry Farm
Leisure Ctr
WHITELANDS
HOLT ROAD
HOLT RD
ENTERPRISE WAY
CLIPBUSH LA
1 SHELDRAKE CL
2 TOWNSEND GN N
3 GWYN CRES
4 SALMON'S WAY
5 TOWNSHEND GN W
6 TOWNSHEND GN E
FIELD LANE
DIGBY DR
FISHER RD
CLARENDON RD
SANDY LANE
WELLS ROAD
Fakenham College
GREENWAY LANE
Water Tower
GARROOD DR
FAKENHAM RD
SCULTHORPE RD
HOWLAND CLOSE
HIGHFIELD RD
CHURCH LANES
ROSEMARY TERR
LANCASTER CL
CRANMER CT
JUBILEE AV
JUBILEE AVENUE
Industrial Estate
MILLER'S CL
WYMANS WAY
GEORGE EDWARDS RD
SMITHS LA
SEARLE CL
WILLIAM RD
HAYES LANE
BUTCHER'S LA
NELSON RD
WELLS RD
LICHFIELD ST
Cemy
Recn Gd
Fakenham Jun Sch
QUEEN'S RD
DRIFTLANDS
THE DRIFT
PARKER DR
HEATH RISE
The Heath
NORWICH ROAD
HEATH WAY
Sculthorpe Fen
Liby
STAR MDW
OAK ST
GLADSTONE RD
RED LION CT
HOLT RD
WESTMEAD RD
ORCHARD CL
STATION RD
THORN RD
THE RIDINGS
VICTORIA LA
MISSION LA
WARREN AVE
BRACKEN CL
1 NIGHTINGALE CL
2 ROWAN WAY
3 FOXGLOVE CL
VINE CT
HALL STAITHE
MARKET PL
NORWICH RD
BRIDGE ST
WHITEHORSE ST
RATCLIFFE RD
OXBOROUGH LA
THE LAWNS
BARON'S CL
HALL CL
Govt Offs
Fakenham Inf Sch
Barons Hall Farm
1 GREAT EASTERN WAY
2 FAYREGREEN
3 BARON'S HALL LA
4 HEATHER BARROW CT
5 FOLLY CT
6 LANGHAM CT
7 EDMONSON WALK
RIVER VIEW CL
CLOVER WAY
VALLEY WAY
BRAMBLE CT
SEDGE CL
BARBER'S LA
GORSE CL
HEATH LA
Pine Woods
The Coll of W Anglia (Fakenham Learning Ctr)
GOGG'S MILL RD
SWAN ST
MILL CT
1 WHITEHORSE ST
2 MASSEY CT
3 OLIVET WAY
4 CATTLE MARKET ST
5 MILLERS WALK
Fakenham Common
RIVER CT
MILL CL
HEMPTON RD
BRIDGES WALK
BACK ST
SHEREFORD RD
HORNS ROW
PH
THE GN
DEREHAM RD
BATTERBY GN
Fakenham Mus
River Wensum
NR21
Great Ryburgh Common
B1146
Hempton
GREEN CL
Flagmoor
Sports Centre
CH
Sewage Works
St Stephen's Priory (remains of)
Starmoor Plantation
Starmoor Wood
RAYNHAM ROAD
Hempton Green
Fakenham Race Course
Pudding Norton
DEREHAM ROAD
GREEN LA
GREEN LA
The Carr
Pudding Norton Hall
31
31
32
E4
1 WALNUT GROVE
2 WENSUM WAY
3 PADDOCK CL
4 PLANTATION RD
5 JOHN CHAPMAN CL
6 HERON CL
7 MALLARD CL
8 KINGFISHER CL

18 18 19 19

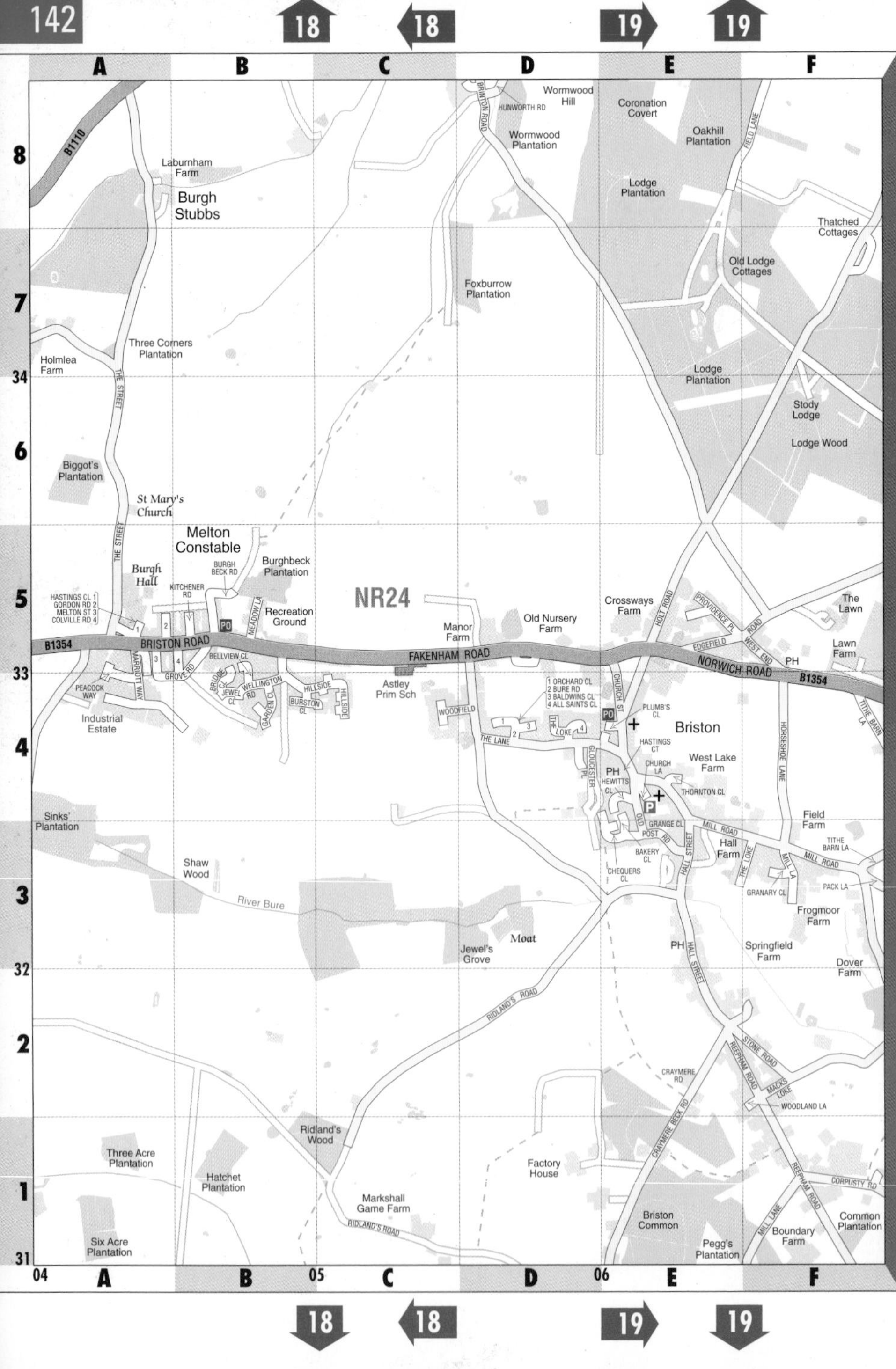

B1110
Laburnham Farm
Burgh Stubbs
Holmlea Farm
Three Corners Plantation
THE STREET
Biggot's Plantation
St Mary's Church
Melton Constable
Burgh Hall
BURGH BECK RD
KITCHENER RD
Burghbeck Plantation
MEADOW LA
Recreation Ground
HASTINGS CL 1
GORDON RD 2
MELTON ST 3
COLVILLE RD 4
B1354
BRISTON ROAD
MARRIOTT WAY
GROVE RD
BELLVIEW CL
BRIDGE CL
JEWEL RD
WELLINGTON RD
GARDEN CL
HILLSIDE
BURSTON CL
PEACOCK WAY
Industrial Estate
NR24
Manor Farm
FAKENHAM ROAD
Astley Prim Sch
WOODFIELD
THE LANE
Old Nursery Farm
1 ORCHARD CL
2 BURE RD
3 BALDWINS CL
4 ALL SAINTS CL
THE LOKE
CHURCH ST
GLOUCESTER PL
BRINTON ROAD
HUNWORTH RD
Wormwood Hill
Wormwood Plantation
Foxburrow Plantation
Coronation Covert
Oakhill Plantation
FIELD LANE
Lodge Plantation
Thatched Cottages
Old Lodge Cottages
Lodge Plantation
Stody Lodge
Lodge Wood
Crossways Farm
HOLT ROAD
PROVIDENCE PL
EDGEFIELD ROAD
WEST END
The Lawn
Lawn Farm
PH
NORWICH ROAD
B1354
TITHE BARN LA
PLUMB'S CL
Briston
HASTINGS CT
West Lake Farm
CHURCH LA
PH
HEWITTS CL
THORNTON CL
OLD POST RD
GRANGE CL
MILL ROAD
BAKERY CL
CHEQUERS CL
HALL STREET
Hall Farm
THE LOKE
MILL LA
Field Farm
TITHE BARN LA
MILL ROAD
PACK LA
GRANARY CL
HORSESHOE LANE
Frogmoor Farm
Sinks' Plantation
Shaw Wood
River Bure
Moat
Jewel's Grove
PH
Springfield Farm
Dover Farm
RIDLAND'S ROAD
STONE ROAD
REEPHAM ROAD
CRAYMERE RD
MACKS LOKE
WOODLAND LA
CRAYMERE BECK RD
Ridland's Wood
Three Acre Plantation
Hatchet Plantation
Factory House
Markshall Game Farm
RIDLAND'S ROAD
Six Acre Plantation
Briston Common
Pegg's Plantation
MILL LANE
Boundary Farm
CORPUSTY RD
Common Plantation

18 18 19 19

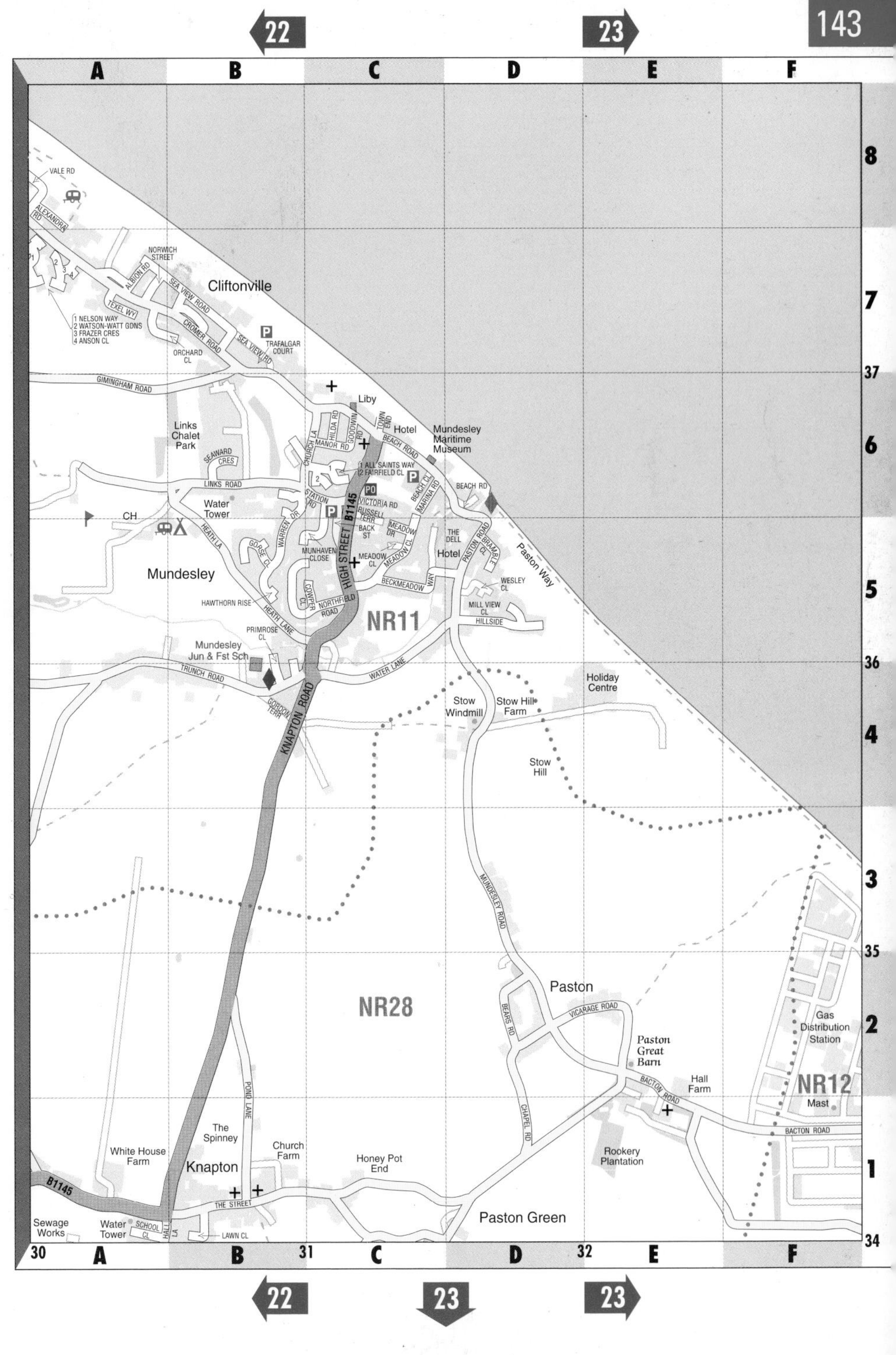

A   B   C   D   E   F

8

VALE RD

NORWICH
STREET

Cliftonville

1 NELSON WAY
2 WATSON-WATT GDNS
3 FRAZER CRES
4 ANSON CL

SEA VIEW ROAD

CROMER ROAD

ORCHARD
CL

TRAFALGAR
COURT

GIMINGHAM ROAD

7

37

Liby

Links
Chalet
Park

SKANARD
CRES

LINKS ROAD

MANOR RD

Hotel

Mundesley
Maritime
Museum

6

Water
Tower

HEATH LA

GOOSE CL

BECK ROAD

1 ALL SAINTS WAY
2 FAIRFIELD CL

BEACH ROAD

PO
VICTORIA RD

RUSSELL
TERR

BACK
ST

BEACH RD

CH

Mundesley

HAWTHORN RISE

MUNHAVEN
CLOSE

MEADOW
CL

WARREN RD

LOMPUR

NORTHFIELD
ROAD

THE
DELL

Hotel

BECKMEADOW
WAY

Paston Way

WESLEY
CL

MILL VIEW
CL

HILLSIDE

5

36

Mundesley
Jun & Fst Sch

PRIMROSE
CL

TRUNCH ROAD

GORDON TERR

KNAPTON ROAD

HIGH STREET B1145

WATER LANE

NR11

HEATH LANE

Stow
Windmill

Stow Hill
Farm

Stow
Hill

Holiday
Centre

4

3

35

NR28

MUNDESLEY ROAD

BEARS RD

CHAPEL RD

VICARAGE ROAD

Paston

Paston
Great
Barn

BACTON ROAD

Hall
Farm

Gas
Distribution
Station

NR12

Mast

BACTON ROAD

2

White House
Farm

The
Spinney

POND LANE

Church
Farm

Honey Pot
End

Rookery
Plantation

1

B1145

Sewage
Works

Water
Tower

SCHOOL
CL

Knapton

THE STREET

LAWN CL

Paston Green

34

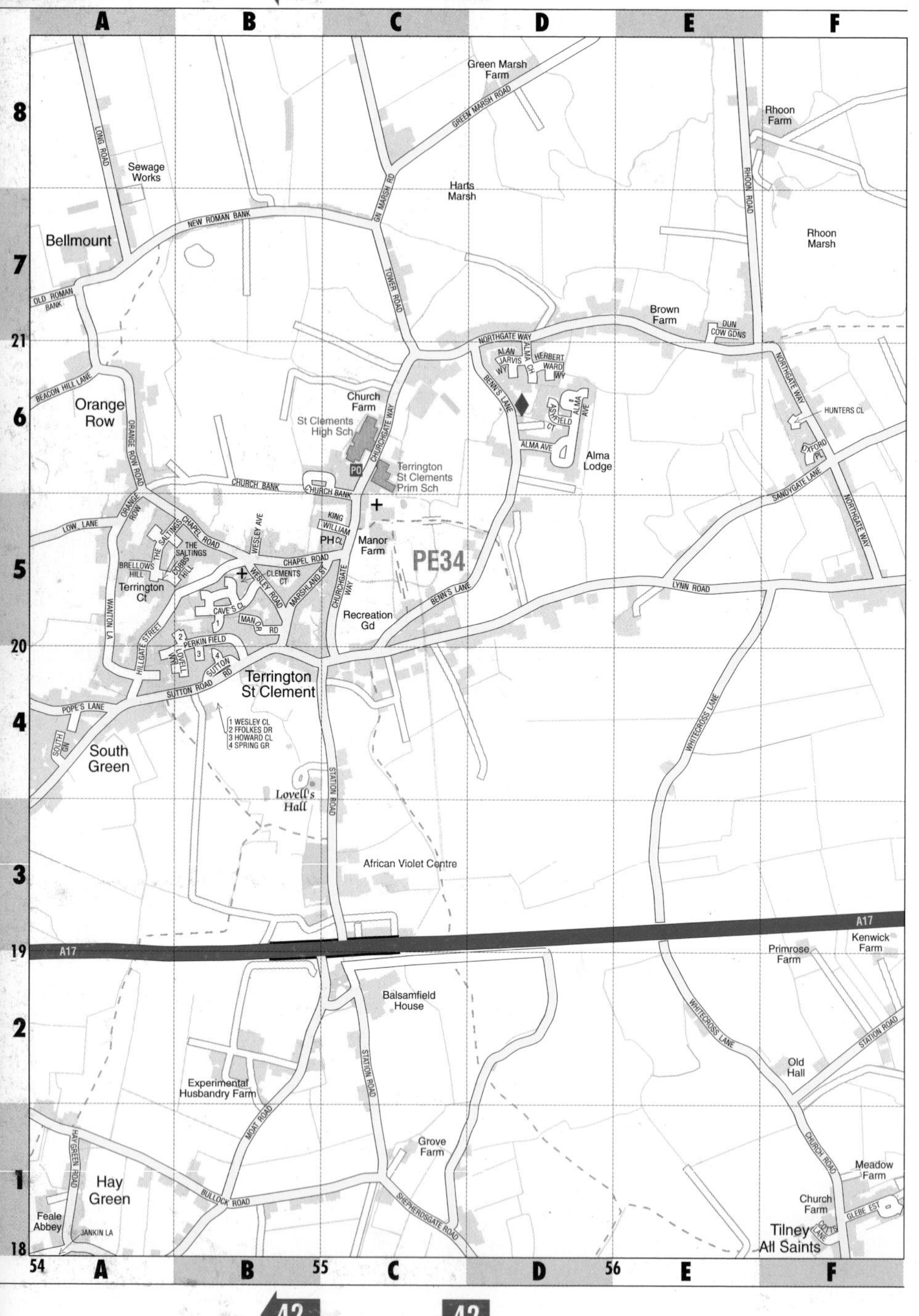

A B C D E F

8

Green Marsh Farm

GREEN MARSH ROAD

Rhoon Farm

Harts Marsh

Rhoon Marsh

7

Bellmount

New Roman Bank

OLD ROMAN BANK

21

BEACON HILL LANE

Brown Farm

DUN COW GDNS

NORTHGATE WAY

6

Orange Row

ORANGE ROW ROAD

Church Farm

St Clements High Sch

CHURCHGATE WAY

ALAN JARVIS WY

WERBERT WARD WY

HUNTERS CL

Terrington St Clements Prim Sch

Alma Lodge

ALMA AVE

SANDTGATE LANE

NORTHGATE WAY

LOW LANE

CHAPEL ROAD

THE SALTINGS

WESLEY AVE

KING WILLIAM CL PH CL

Manor Farm

PE34

BEIN'S LANE

5

BRELLOWS HILL

Terrington Ct

CHAPEL ROAD

ST CLEMENTS CT

CAVE'S CL

MARSHLAND ST

CHURCHGATE WAY

LYNN ROAD

MANNION LA

HILLGATE STREET

PERKIN FIELD

SUTTON RD

Recreation Gd

20

POPE'S LANE

SUTTON ROAD

1 WESLEY CL
2 FFOLKES DR
3 HOWARD CL
4 SPRING GR

WHITECROSS LANE

4

SOUTH GRN

South Green

Terrington St Clement

STATION ROAD

Lovell's Hall

African Violet Centre

3

A17

A17

19

A17

Primrose Farm

Kenwick Farm

2

MOR ROAD

Balsamfield House

STATION ROAD

WHITECROSS LANE

Old Hall

STATION ROAD

Experimental Husbandry Farm

Grove Farm

CHURCH ROAD

Meadow Farm

1

HALEGREEN ROAD

Hay Green

BULLOCK ROAD

SHEPHERDSGATE ROAD

Church Farm

GLEBE EST

Tilney All Saints

Feale Abbey

JANKIN LA

18

54 A 55 B C 56 D E F

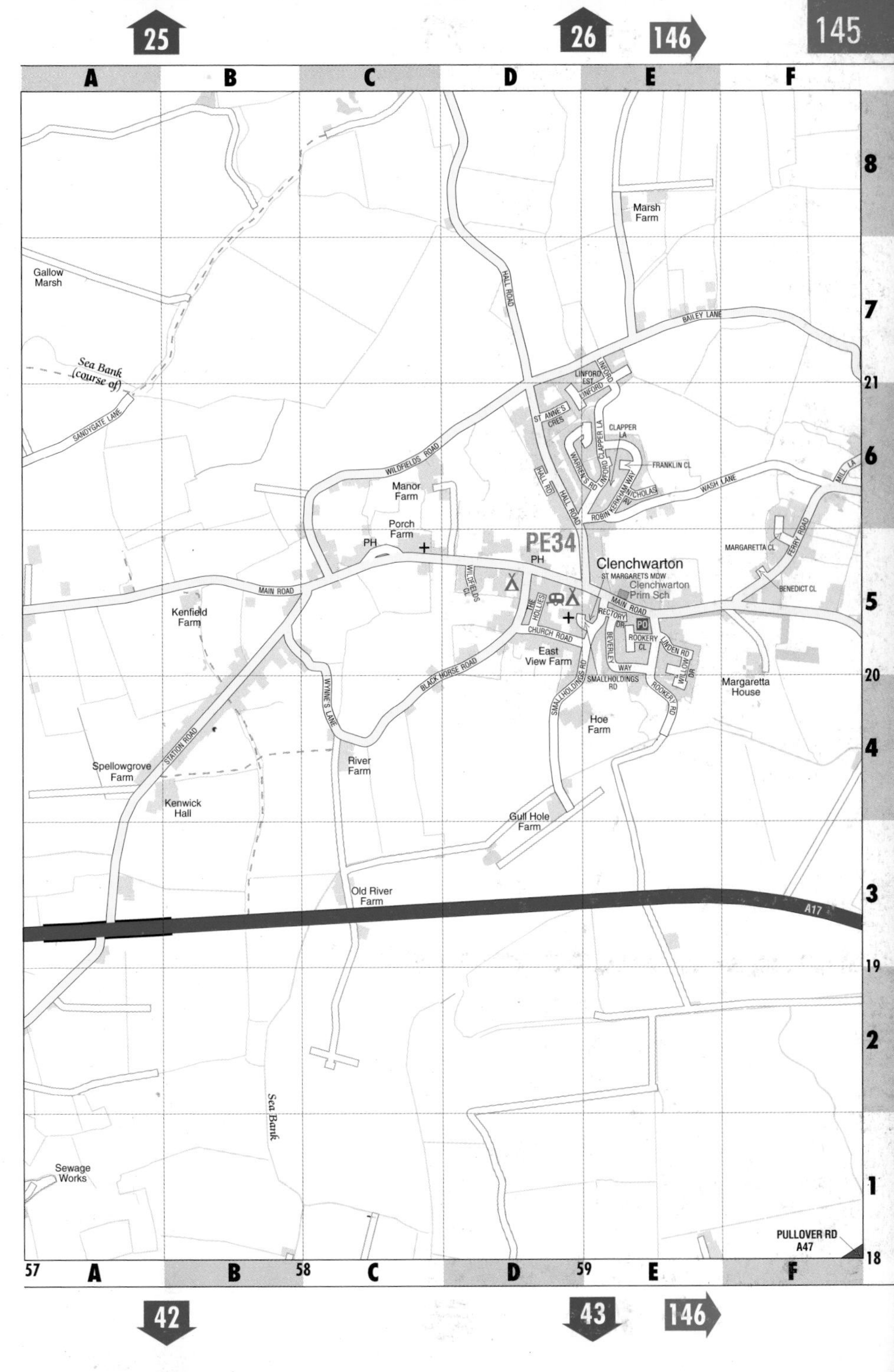

A   B   C   D   E   F

8

Marsh
Farm

Gallow
Marsh

7

BAILEY LANE

Sea Bank
(course of)

21

SANDTGATE LANE

LINFORD
LINFORD

ST ANNE'S
CRES

CLAPPER
LA

6

WILDFIELDS ROAD

Manor
Farm

FRANKLIN CL

WASH LANE

Porch
Farm

PH

PE34

MARGARETTA CL

Clenchwarton

BENEDICT CL

Main Road

ST MARGARETS MDW

PH

Clenchwarton
Prim Sch

Kenfield
Farm

WILDFIELDS

CHURCH ROAD

East
View Farm

RECTORY

PO

ROOKERY
CL

5

20

SMALLHOLDINGS

BLACK HORSE ROAD

SMALLHOLDINGS
RD

WAY

Margaretta
House

WYNNE'S LANE

Spellowgrove
Farm

River
Farm

Hoe
Farm

STATION ROAD

4

Kenwick
Hall

Gulf Hole
Farm

Old River
Farm

A17

3

19

Sea Bank

2

Sewage
Works

1

PULLOVER RD
A47

18

57   A   B   58   C   D   59   E   F

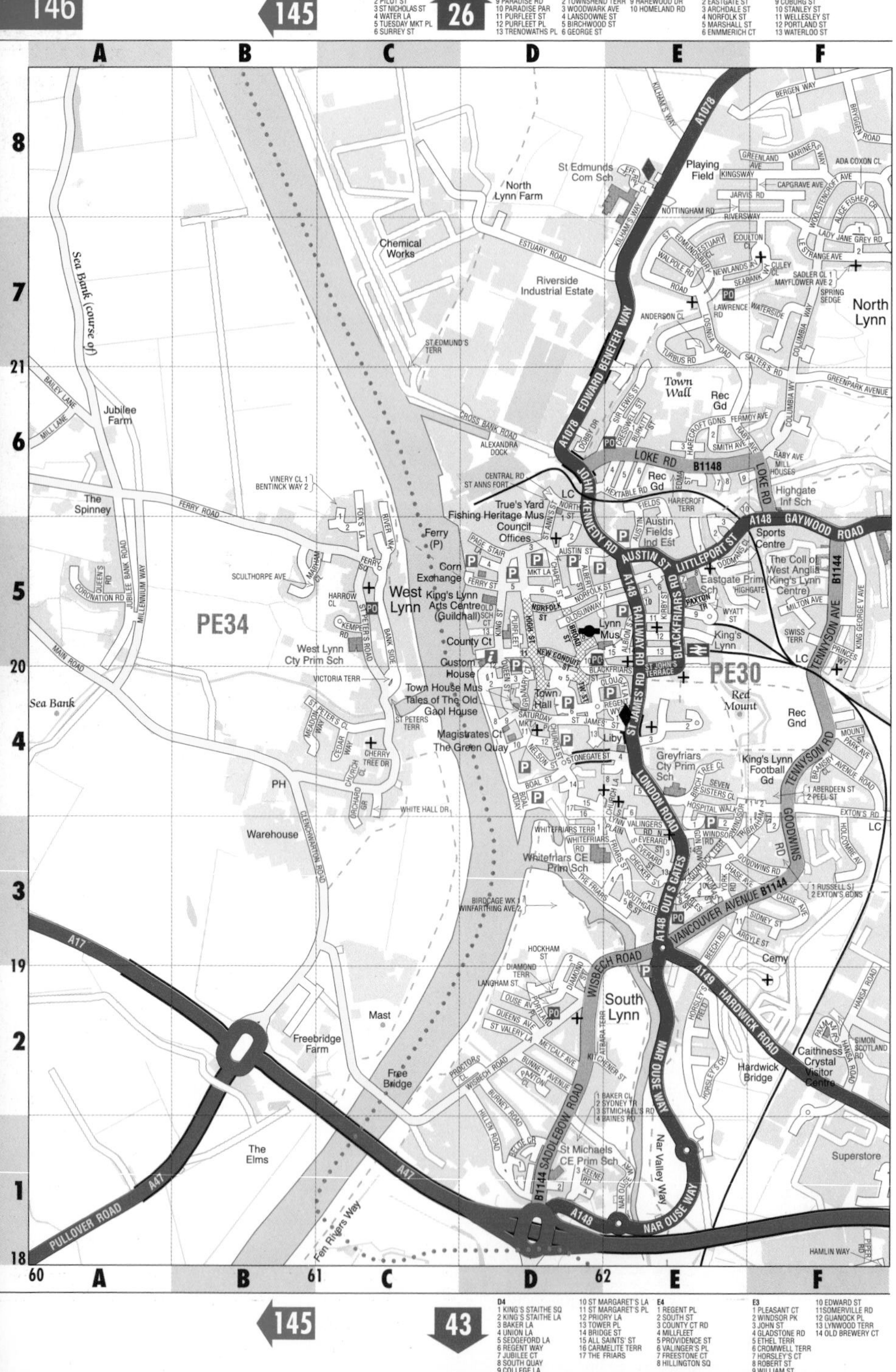

145
26

D5
1 ST NICHOLAS CL
2 PILOT ST
3 ST NICHOLAS ST
4 WATER LA
5 TUESDAY MKT PL
6 SURREY ST

7 PARADISE LA
8 ST DOMINIC SQ
9 PARADISE RD
10 PARADISE PAR
11 PURFLEET ST
12 PURFLEET PL
13 TRENOWATHS PL

E6
1 WALKER ST
2 TOWNSHEND TERR
3 WOODWARK AVE
4 LANSDOWNE ST
5 BIRCHWOOD ST
6 GEORGE ST

7 HARECROFT PAR
8 HARWOOD PAR
9 HARWOOD DR
10 HOMELAND RD

E5
1 KETTLEWELL LA
2 ESTUARY PL
3 NORFOLK ST
4 NORFOLK ST
5 MARSHALL ST
6 ENAMMERICH CT

7 EDINBURGH CT
8 LITTLEPORT TERR
9 COBURG ST
10 STANLEY ST
11 WELLESLEY ST
12 PORTLAND ST
13 WATERLOO ST

14 OLD MKT ST
15 MARKET ST

D4
1 KING'S STAITHE SQ
2 KING'S STAITHE LA
3 TOWER PL
4 UNION LA
5 SEDGEFORD LA
6 REGENT WAY
7 JUBILEE CT
8 SOUTH QUAY
9 COLLEGE LA

10 ST MARGARET'S LA
11 ST MARGARET'S PL
12 PRIORY LA
13 TOWER PL
14 BRIDGE ST
15 ALL SAINTS' ST
16 CARMELITE TERR
17 THE FRIARS

E4
1 REGENT PL
2 SOUTH ST
3 COUNTY CT RD
4 MILLFLEET
5 PROVIDENCE ST
6 VALINGER'S PL
7 FREESTONE CT
8 HILLINGTON SQ

E3
1 PLEASANT CT
2 WINDSOR PK
3 JOHN ST
4 GLADSTONE RD
5 ETHEL TERR
6 CROMWELL TERR
7 HORSLEY'S CT
8 ROBERT ST
9 WILLIAM ST

10 EDWARD ST
11 SOMERVILLE RD
12 QUANOCK PL
13 LYNWOOD TERR
14 OLD BREWERY CT

PE34

West
Lynn

PE30

North
Lynn

South
Lynn

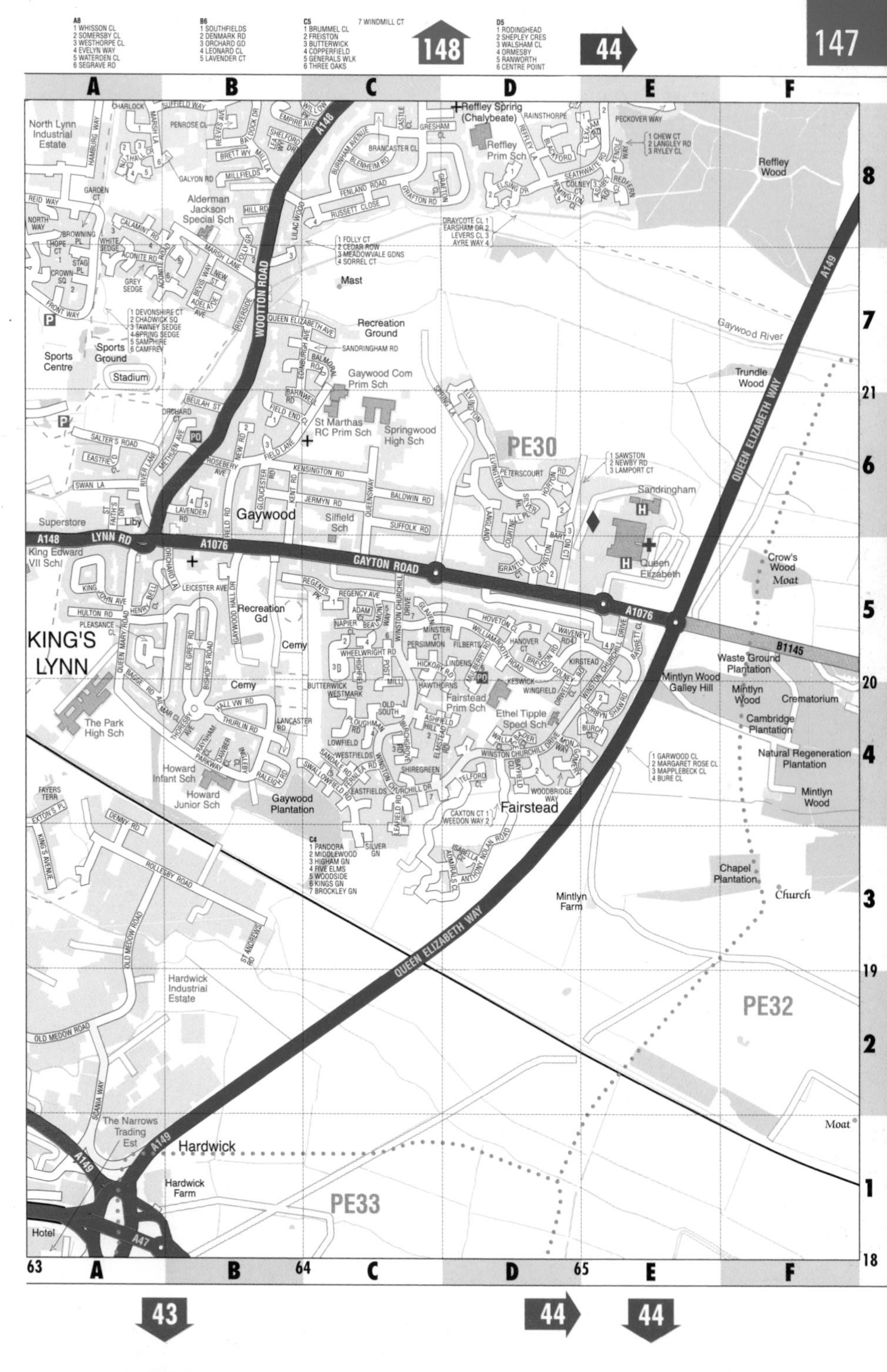

147
148
44
43
A8
1 WHISSON CL
2 SOMERSBY CL
3 WESTHORPE CL
4 EVELYN WAY
5 WATERDEN CL
6 SEGRAVE RD
B6
1 SOUTHFIELDS
2 DENMARK RD
3 ORCHARD GD
4 LEONARD CL
5 LAVENDER CT
C5
1 BRUMMEL CL
2 FREISTON
3 BUTTERWICK
4 COPPERFIELD
5 GENERALS WLK
6 THREE OAKS
7 WINDMILL CT
D5
1 RODINGHEAD
2 SHEPLEY CRES
3 WALSHAM CL
4 ORMESBY
5 RANWORTH
6 CENTRE POINT
A
B
C
D
E
F
8
7
21
6
5
20
4
3
19
2
1
18
63
64
65
North Lynn Industrial Estate
Reffley Spring (Chalybeate)
Reffley Prim Sch
Reffley Wood
1 CHEW CT
2 LANGLEY RD
3 RYLEY CL
Alderman Jackson Special Sch
1 FOLLY CT
2 CEDAR ROW
3 MEADOWVALE GDNS
4 SORREL CT
DRAYCOTE CL 1
EARSHAM DR 2
LEVERS CL 3
AYRE WAY 4
Mast
WOOTTON ROAD
A148
1 DEVONSHIRE CT
2 CHADWICK SQ
3 TAWNEY SEDGE
4 SPRING SEDGE
5 SAMPHIRE
6 CAMFREY
Recreation Ground
Sports Centre
Sports Ground
Stadium
Gaywood Com Prim Sch
St Marthas RC Prim Sch
Springwood High Sch
PE30
1 SAWSTON
2 NEWBY RD
3 LAMPORT CT
Sandringham
Queen Elizabeth
Gaywood River
Trundle Wood
A149
QUEEN ELIZABETH WAY
Superstore
Liby
Gaywood
Silfield Sch
LYNN RD
A1076
GAYTON ROAD
King Edward VII Sch
Crow's Wood
Moat
KING'S LYNN
Recreation Gd
Cemy
B1145
Waste Ground Plantation
Mintlyn Wood Galley Hill
Mintlyn Wood
Crematorium
Cambridge Plantation
Natural Regeneration Plantation
Fairstead Prim Sch
Ethel Tipple Specl Sch
The Park High Sch
Howard Infant Sch
Howard Junior Sch
Gaywood Plantation
Fairstead
1 GARWOOD CL
2 MARGARET ROSE CL
3 MAPPLEBECK CL
4 BURE CL
C4
1 PANDORA
2 MIDDLEWOOD
3 HIGHAM GN
4 FIVE ELMS
5 WOODSIDE
6 KINGS GN
7 BROCKLEY GN
CAXTON CT 1
WEEDON WAY 2
Chapel Plantation
Church
Mintlyn Farm
Hardwick Industrial Estate
PE32
Moat
The Narrows Trading Est
Hardwick
Hardwick Farm
PE33
Hotel
A47

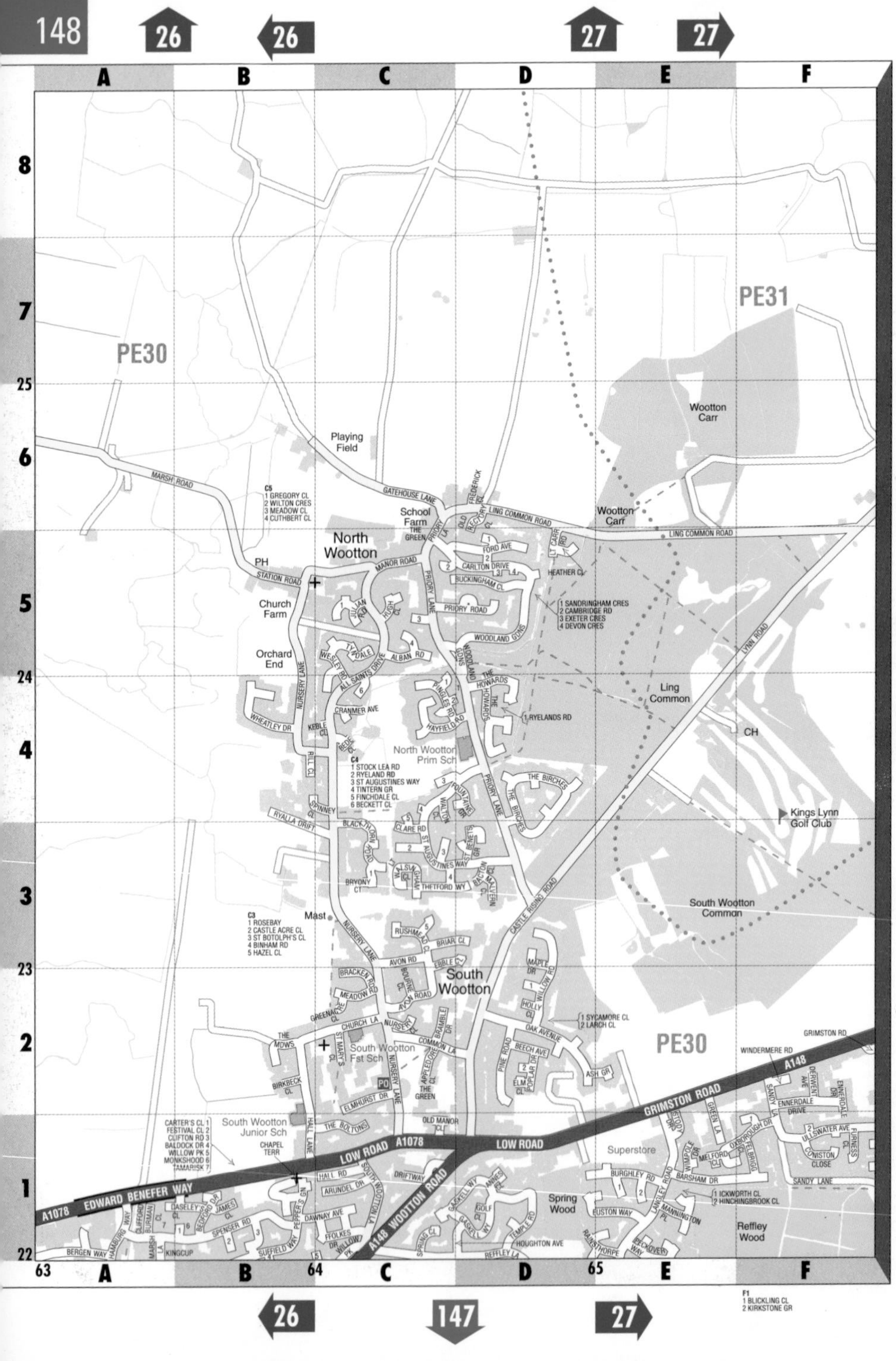
26
26
27
27
A
B
C
D
E
F
8
7
25
6
5
24
4
3
23
2
1
22
63
64
65
PE30
PE31
Wootton Carr
Playing Field
MARSH ROAD
GATEHOUSE LANE
FREDERICK CL
C5
1 GREGORY CL
2 WILTON CRES
3 MEADOW CL
4 CUTHBERT CL
School Farm
THE GREEN
North Wootton
LING COMMON ROAD
Wootton Carr
LING COMMON ROAD
PH
STATION ROAD
MANOR ROAD
PRIORY LA
OLD RECTORY CL
FORD AVE
CARLTON DRIVE
BUCKINGHAM CL
HEATHER CL
LT CARR RD
Church Farm
JULIAN RD
HUGH CL
PRIORY LANE
PRIORY ROAD
1 SANDRINGHAM CRES
2 CAMBRIDGE RD
3 EXETER CRES
4 DEVON CRES
WOODLAND GDNS
LYNN ROAD
Orchard End
TYNDALE
WESLEY RD
ALL SAINTS DRIVE
ALBAN RD
NURSERY LANE
THE HOWARDS
Ling Common
PINGLES RD
1 RYELANDS RD
WHEATLEY DR
KEBLE CL
CRANMER AVE
HAYFIELD RD
BEDE CL
CH
North Wootton Prim Sch
RILL CL
C4
1 STOCK LEA RD
2 RYELAND RD
3 ST AUGUSTINES WAY
4 TINTERN GR
5 FINCHDALE CL
6 BECKETT CL
THE BIRCHES
Kings Lynn Golf Club
SPINNEY CL
RYALLA DRIFT
FOUNTAINE GR
WALTON CL
BLACKTHORN ROAD
CLARE RD
ST AUGUSTINES WAY
ST BENETS GR
WALSINGHAM CL
THETFORD WY
BACTON CL
MALVERN CL
BRYONY CT
CASTLE RISING ROAD
South Wootton Common
C3
1 ROSEBAY
2 CASTLE ACRE CL
3 ST BOTOLPH'S CL
4 BINHAM RD
5 HAZEL CL
Mast
RUSHMEAD CL
BRIAR CL
AVON RD
EBBLE CL
MAPLE DR
BRACKEN RD
BOURNE CL
South Wootton
WILLOW RD
MEADOW RD
AVON ROAD
HOLLY CL
GREENACRE CL
CHURCH LA
NURSERY CL
BRAMBLE DR
1 SYCAMORE CL
2 LARCH CL
THE MDWS
ST MARY'S CL
South Wootton Fst Sch
COMMON LA
OAK AVENUE
PE30
GRIMSTON RD
WINDERMERE RD
A148
PINE ROAD
BEECH AVE
POPLAR DR
BIRKBECK CL
APPLEDORE CL
ELM CL
ASH GR
DERWENT AVE
ENNERDALE DR
PO
THE GREEN
NURSERY LANE
GRIMSTON ROAD
SANDY LA
ENNERDALE DRIVE
ELMHURST DR
HALL LANE
THE BOLTONS
South Wootton Junior Sch
OLD MANOR CL
KETSTOY DR
GREEN LA
OXBOROUGH DR
ULLSWATER AVE
FURNESS CL
CARTER'S CL 1
FESTIVAL CL 2
CLIFTON RD 3
BALDOCK DR 4
WILLOW PK 5
MONKSHOOD 6
TAMARISK 7
CHAPEL TERR
LOW ROAD
A1078
LOW ROAD
Superstore
WIMPOLE DR
MELFORD CL
FELBRIGG
CONISTON CLOSE
HALL RD
SOUTH WOOTTON LA
DRIFTWAY
BURGHLEY RD
BARSHAM DR
SANDY LANE
EDWARD BENEFER WAY
ARUNDEL DR
A148 WOOTTON ROAD
JANES PL
Spring Wood
LANGLEY ROAD
1 ICKWORTH CL
2 HINCHINGBROOK CL
A1078
DASELEY CL
BEDFORD DR
JAMES CL
DAWNAY AVE
GASKELL WY
GOLF CL
MANNINGTON PL
HAMBURG WAY
CLIFFORD BURMAN CL
SPENSER RD
FFOLKES DR
TEMPLE RD
EUSTON WAY
Reffley Wood
PEPPER'S GN
WILLOW PK
SPRING CL
RAINSTHORPE
BECKOVER WAY
BERGEN WAY
MARSH LA
KINGCUP
SUFFIELD WAY
HOUGHTON AVE
REFFLEY LA
A
B
C
D
E
F
26
147
27
F1
1 BLICKLING CL
2 KIRKSTONE GR

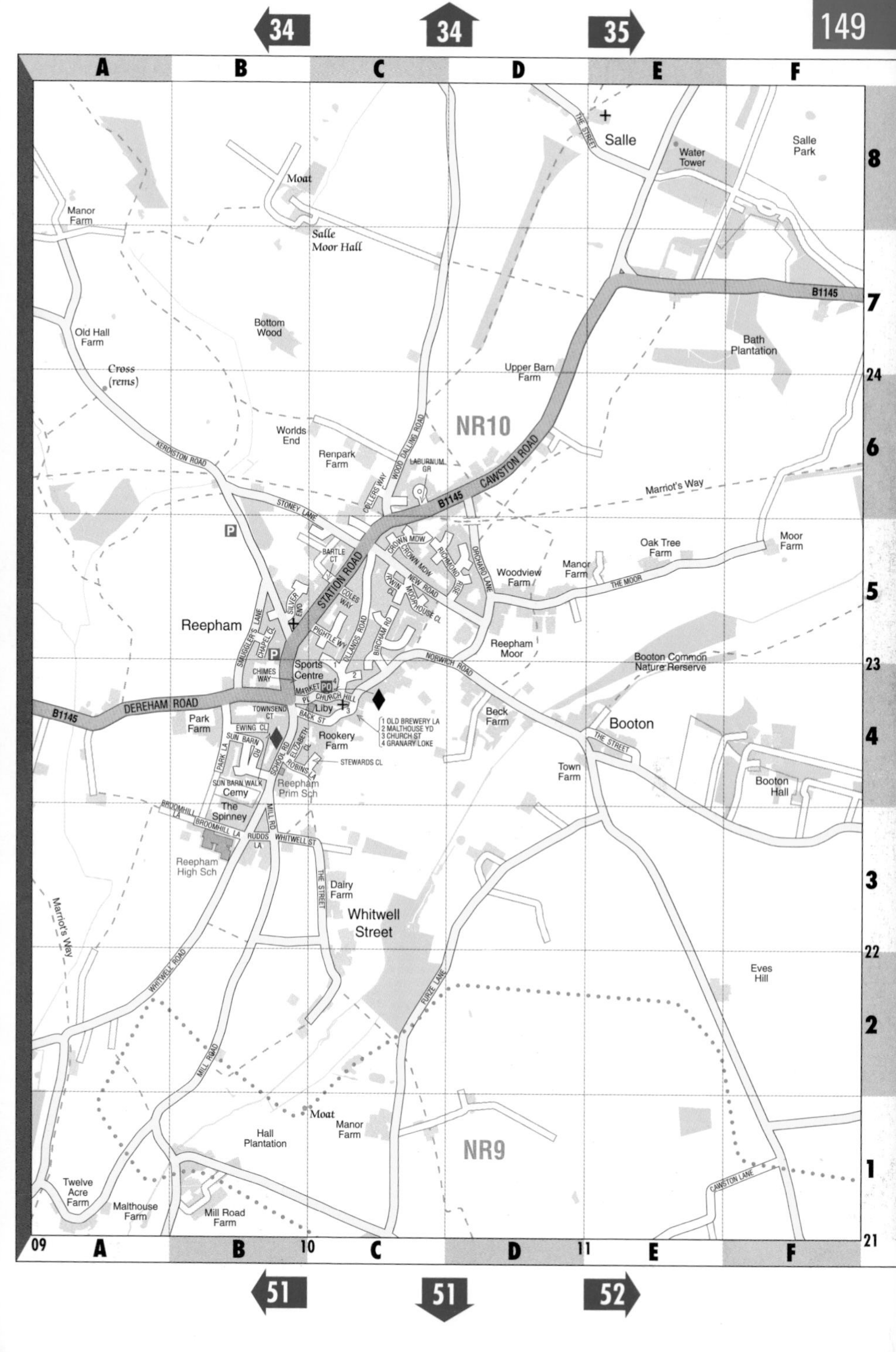
34
34
35
A
B
C
D
E
F
8
7
24
6
5
23
4
3
22
2
1
21
09
10
11
51
51
52
Salle
Salle Park
Water Tower
Moat
Manor Farm
Salle Moor Hall
B1145
Old Hall Farm
Bottom Wood
Bath Plantation
Cross (rems)
Upper Barn Farm
NR10
Worlds End
Renpark Farm
KERDISTON ROAD
WOOD DALLING ROAD
LABURNUM GR
CAWSTON ROAD
COLLERS WAY
Marriot's Way
STONEY LANE
Oak Tree Farm
Moor Farm
BARTLE CT
STATION ROAD
CROWN MDW
RICHMOND RISE
ORCHARD LANE
Woodview Farm
Manor Farm
THE MOOR
NEW ROAD
MOORHOUSE CL
COLES WAY
SILVER END
Reepham
SMUGGLER'S LANE
CHAPEL CL
PIGHTLE WY
OLLANDS ROAD
BIRCHAM RD
Reepham Moor
Booton Common Nature Rerserve
NORWICH ROAD
Sports Centre
CHIMES WAY
MARKET PL
CHURCH HILL
DEREHAM ROAD
TOWNSEND CT
Liby
BACK ST
1 OLD BREWERY LA
2 MALTHOUSE YD
3 CHURCH ST
4 GRANARY LOKE
Beck Farm
Booton
THE STREET
Park Farm
EWING CL
SUN BARN RD
PARK LA
SCHOOL RD
ELIZABETH CL
ROBINS LA
Rookery Farm
STEWARDS CL
Town Farm
Booton Hall
SUN BARN WALK
Reepham Prim Sch
Cemy
The Spinney
BROOMHILL LA
MILL RD
RUDDS LA
WHITWELL ST
Reepham High Sch
THE STREET
Dairy Farm
Whitwell Street
Marriot's Way
WHITWELL ROAD
Eves Hill
FURZE LANE
MILL ROAD
Moat
Manor Farm
Hall Plantation
NR9
CAWSTON LANE
Twelve Acre Farm
Malthouse Farm
Mill Road Farm

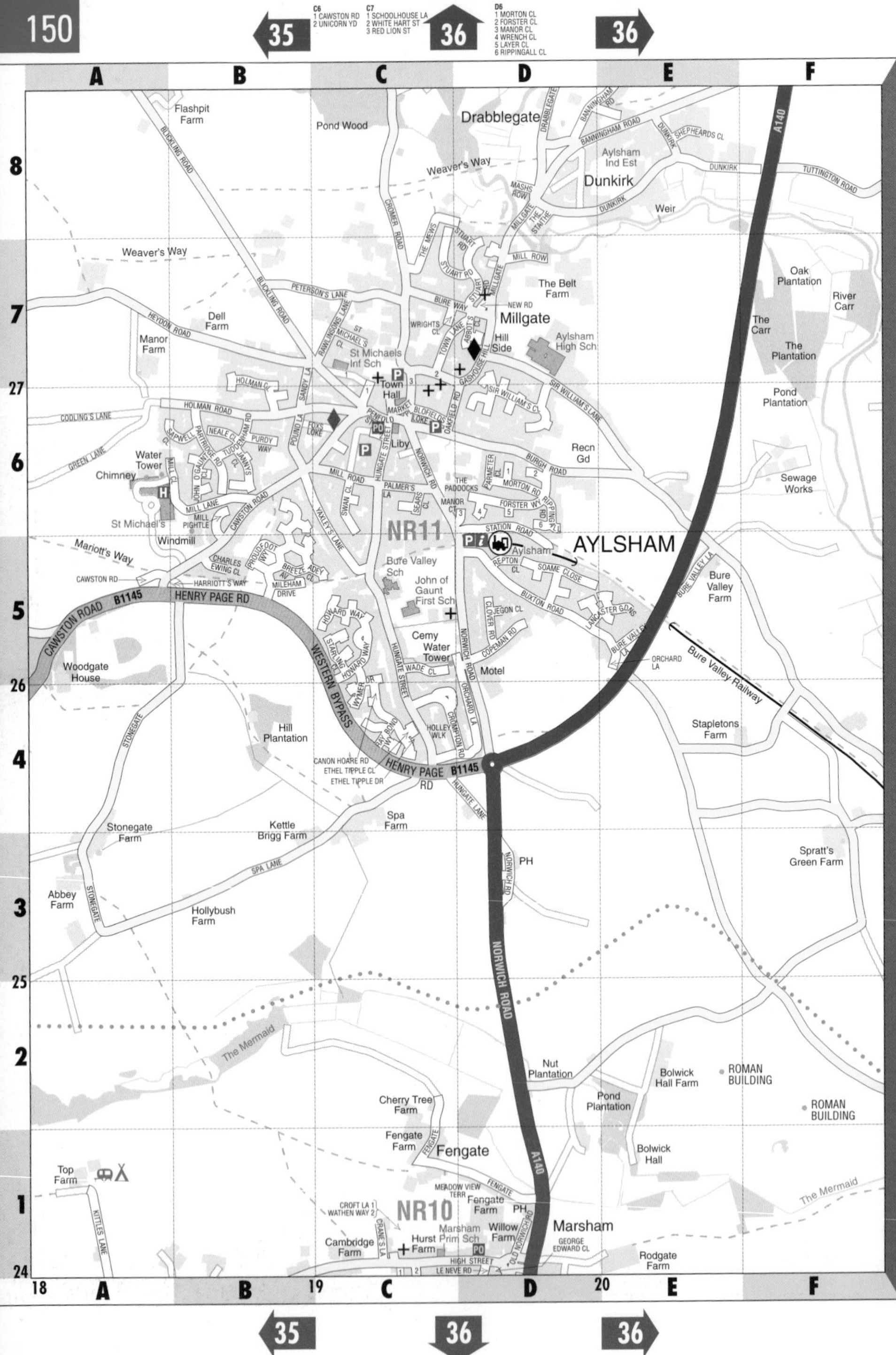

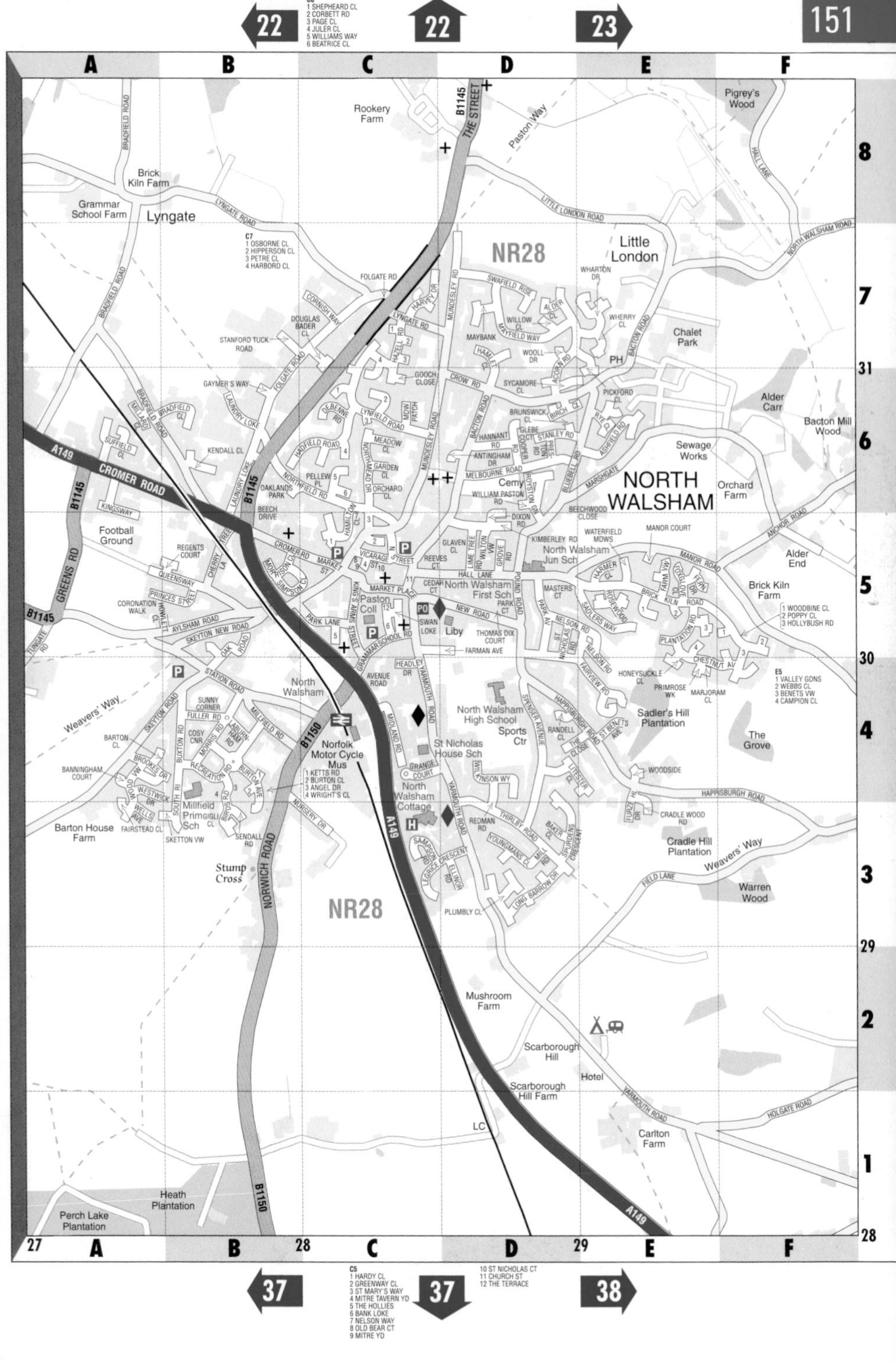

22 22 23

37 37 38

C6
1 SHEPHEARD CL
2 CORBETT RD
3 PAGE CL
4 JULER CL
5 WILLIAMS WAY
6 BEATRICE CL

C7
1 OSBORNE CL
2 HIPPERSON CL
3 PETRE CL
4 HARBORD CL

E5
1 WOODBINE CL
2 POPPY CL
3 HOLLYBUSH RD

E5
1 VALLEY GDNS
2 WEBBS CL
3 BENETS VW
4 CAMPION CL

C5
1 HARDY CL
2 GREENWAY CL
3 ST MARY'S WAY
4 MITRE TAVERN YD
5 THE HOLLIES
6 BANK CLOSE
7 NELSON WAY
8 OLD BEAR CT
9 MITRE YD
10 ST NICHOLAS CT
11 CHURCH ST
12 THE TERRACE

NR28

Little London

NORTH WALSHAM

59 **59**

A1101 Holbeach (A17)

PE14

SUTTON MDWS

SUTTON ROAD

Nene Way
River Nene

OSBORNE PARK

HEDGELANDS 1
RICHARD YOUNG CL 2
HENSON CL 3
HALEY CL 4

ADMIRALS DR
BUCKINGHAM WALK
WINDSOR DR
PRINCE OF WALES DR

NURSERY DRIVE

Leaherd's Field

CRAB MARSH
MYLES WY
CONFERENCE PL
KINDERLEY ROAD

ORCHARDS PRIM SCH

GORDON FENDICK SCH

WISBECH RD

LEBANON DR

OAKLANDS CL 2
LUCOMBE DR

BLACK BEAR LANE

KINGSWAY
PIPPIN GDNS
WISTARIA WOODLANDS COURT
ALL SAINTS AVE

LITTLE POSTGATE

A7

RIVER TERR
BANK DR
KEILLERS CT
PEATLINGS LANE

HORSE-SHOE CORNER

BANNISTER'S ROW

LYNN ROAD

OLD LYNN

JASMIN CL

CHURCH RD

B1169

THE CHASE
CL
THE CHASE

CHRISTOPHER DR

WESTON MILLER DR

Cemy

MOUNT PLEASANT ROAD

Football Ground
Sports Ground

CHURCH RD
CHAPNALL CL

CLAYTON CL
LEGGE CL
MUSTICOTT PL

PICKARDS WAY

LEVERINGTON ROAD

A1101

NORTH END

QUEEN ST
ALBANY RD
YORK TERR
OAKROYD CT
CLARKSON CR

KENLAN RD

The Clarkson Inf Sch

Walsoken

OCTAVIA CL

PEDLEY LA
SUMMERFIELD

Peckover Cty Prim Sch
The Lawns
Cemy

YORK GDNS

RECTORY GDNS

SEABANK RD

ROSE WK 1
SOVEREIGN CL 2
STRAWBERRY CL 3
OCTAGON DR 4

CRICKETERS WAY

Superstore

Yacht Harbour

OPPORTUNE

1 St Peters CE Jun Sch

E6
1 TRAFFORD PK
2 TURNPIKE CL
3 BAXTER CL
4 COUNCIL RD

WISBECH

Windmill

LYNN ROAD

PARK AVE

STAITHE ROAD

PE13

Hudson Leisure Centre

FREEDOM BRIDGE

B1198

Horse Fair Shop Cen
Park

North Cambs

E5
1 HAWKINS DR
2 HALSTEAD CL
3 ARDLEIGH CL
4 FRINTON WK
5 ROCHFORD WK

ASHDALE PK

Wisbech Gram Sch

EXCHANGE

NENE QUAY

Octavia Hill Birthplace Mus

Peckover House

CHAPEL

SOUTH BRINK

MARKET MWS

PARK AVE

COLVILE ROAD

NORWOOD ROAD

FELSTED CL

COCKETTS
COCKETTS ROAD

BUSH LA

PELDON

SANDY LANE

BARTON ROAD

PH

Castle

The Angles Theatre

The Old Castle Mus

Liby

The Nene Jun Sch

FIRST AVE

SECOND AVE

THIRD AVE

FOURTH AVE

FIFTH AVE

SIXTH AVE

MEDWAY

OAKLEY

BROAD END ROAD

BRAMPTON CL

MARLBOROUGH CT

Elgood's Brewery & Gdn

GREAT EASTERN ST

CANNON ST

CHURCHILL ROAD

Ramnoth Cty Jun Sch

MONEY BANK

ORCHARD

STOW GDNS

Windpump Hall Field

PURBECK
MAGAZINE LANE

RICHMOND

VICTORY RD

Elm Rd Primary Sch

PECKOVER DR

PENROSE GDNS

PE13

GREEN LANE

RIVERSIDE WY 1
RIGG CL 2

LONSDALE TERR

Larksfield

PROSPECT PL

KINGSWOOD PK

ARLES AVE

Meadowgate Sch

E3
1 MAYFLOWER RD
2 PROVENCE PL
3 RHONE PL
4 CAMARGUE PL
5 LES BAUX PL

Nene Way

CROMWELL ROAD

LC

WEASENHAM LANE

GORDON CL

MANSEL RD

The Queens Sch

Works

CORPORATION RD

QUEEN ELIZABETH DR

FALKLANDS DR

BOROUGH RD

The Coll of West Anglia (Isle Campus)

PIPPIN PL

WESTMEAD AVE

Allotments

Superstore

Industrial Estate

Great Boleness Field

EUROPA WY

BOLENESS RD

MIKANDA CL

The Coll of West Anglia (Wisbech Campus)

SUNSET GDNS
COPPINS CT
BLENHEIM WAY

A47

PE14

Stadium

B1198

CROMWELL ROAD

SALTERS WAY

ANGLIA WAY

NEW ROAD

HALFPENNY LANE

ELM HIGH ROAD

The Peel Centre

West Meadowgate

Oxburgh Hall

New Bridge Farm

New Bridge LC

NEW BRIDGE LANE

ELM HIGH ROAD

D2
1 WEABENHAM LA
2 KESTREL DR
3 NEW DR
4 ROBIN MEWS
5 REDWING DR
6 KINGFISHER DR

A1101

Town Field

A1122

ELMFIELD DRIVE

PE14

A47

A1122

59 **59**

Cambridgeshire STREET ATLAS

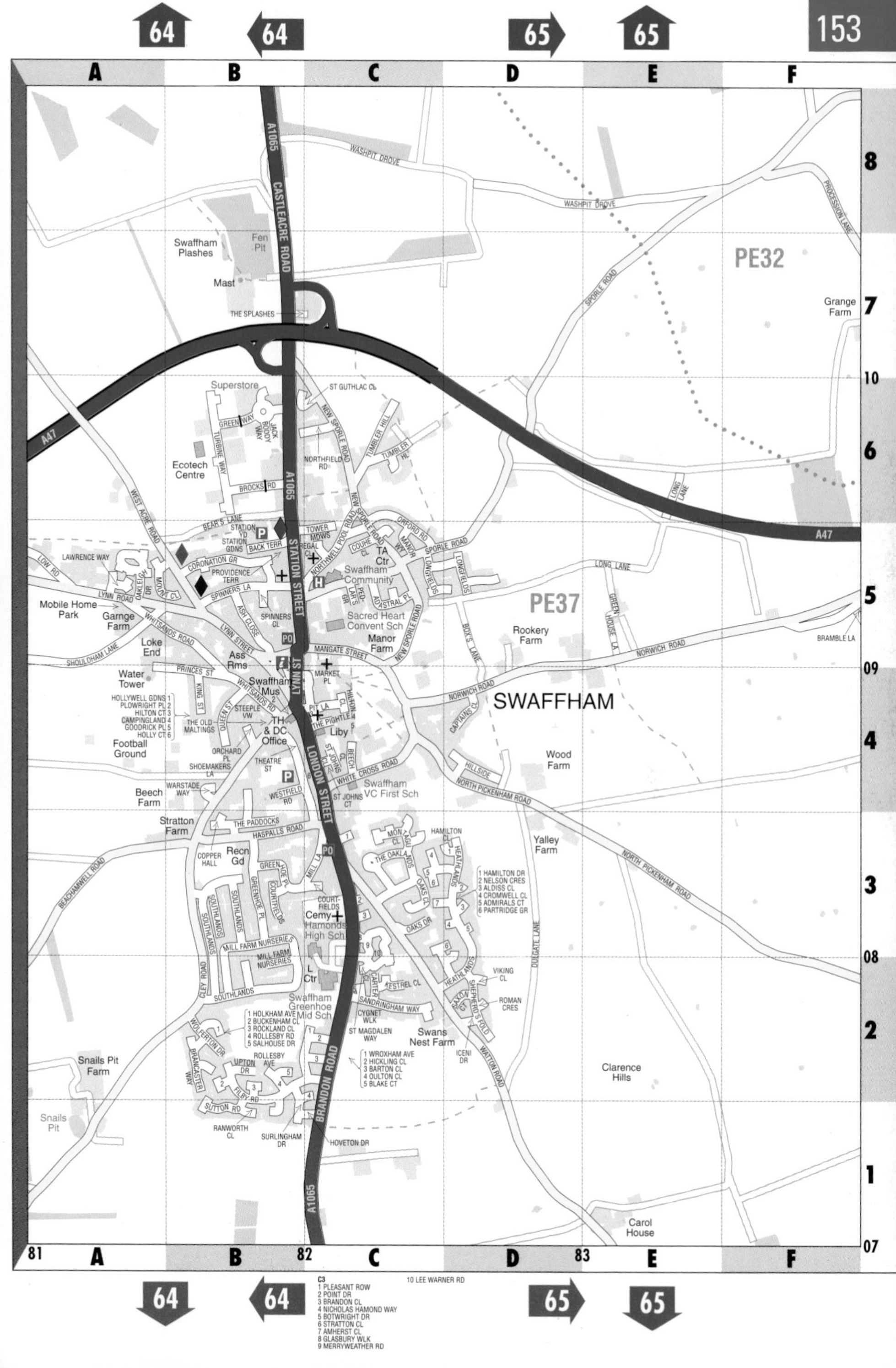
64
64
65
65
A
B
C
D
E
F
8
7
10
6
5
09
4
3
08
2
1
07
81
82
83
A47
A1065
CASTLEACRE ROAD
WASHPIT DROVE
PROCESSION LANE
PE32
SPORLE ROAD
Grange Farm
Swaffham Plashes
Fen Pit
Mast
THE SPLASHES
Superstore
ST GUTHLAC CL
GREEN WAY
JACK BODDY WAY
TURBINE WAY
NEW SPORLE ROAD
TUMBLER HILL
NORTHFIELD RD
Ecotech Centre
BROCKS RD
WEST ACRE ROAD
LONG LANE
BEAR'S LANE
STATION YD
STATION GDNS
BACK TERR
TOWER MDWS
REGAL CL
STATION STREET
NORTHWELL POOL ROAD
COUHE CL
TA Ctr
MANOR WY
ORFORD RD
SPORLE ROAD
LONGFIELDS
LAWRENCE WAY
LOW RD
CORONATION GR
PROVIDENCE TERR
Swaffham Community
OAKLEIGH DR
MOUNT CL
SPINNERS LA
LYNN ROAD
Mobile Home Park
Garnge Farm
WHITSANDS ROAD
ASH CLOSE
SPINNERS CL
Sacred Heart Convent Sch
ADVSTRAL PL
PE37
GREEN HOUSE LA
Rookery Farm
BRAMBLE LA
Loke End
LYNN STREET
MANGATE STREET
Manor Farm
BOX'S LANE
NORWICH ROAD
SHOULDHAM LANE
Ass Rms
LYNN ST
MARKET PL
Water Tower
PRINCES ST
Swaffham Mus
SWAFFHAM
1 HOLLYWELL GDNS
2 PLOWRIGHT PL
3 HILTON CT
4 CAMPINGLAND
5 GOODRICK PL
6 HOLLY CT
KING ST
QUEEN ST
STEEPLE VW
THE OLD MALTINGS
PIT LA
THE PIGHTLE
TH & DC Office
Liby
CAPTAINS CL
Football Ground
ORCHARD PL
SHOEMAKERS LA
THEATRE ST
LONDON STREET
ST JOHNS CL
BEECH CL
WHITE CROSS ROAD
Wood Farm
HILLSIDE
Beech Farm
WARSTADE WAY
WESTFIELD RD
Swaffham VC First Sch
ST JOHNS CT
NORTH PICKENHAM ROAD
Stratton Farm
THE PADDOCKS
HASPALLS ROAD
MONTAGU CL
HAMILTON CL
HEATHLANDS
Yalley Farm
COPPER HALL
Recn Gd
MILL LA
THE OAKLANDS
1 HAMILTON DR
2 NELSON CRES
3 ALDISS CL
4 CROMWELL CL
5 ADMIRALS CT
6 PARTRIDGE GR
BEACHAMWELL ROAD
GREENHOE PL
COURTFIELDS
SOUTHLANDS
OAKS CL
OAKS DR
Cemy
Hamonds High Sch
MILL FARM NURSERIES
L Ctr
DULGATE LANE
VIKING CL
CLEY ROAD
CARTER CL
ESTREL CL
ROMAN CRES
SAXON CT
SHEPHERD'S FOLD
Swaffham Greenhoe Mid Sch
SANDRINGHAM WAY
CYGNET WLK
1 HOLKHAM AVE
2 BUCKENHAM CL
3 ROCKLAND CL
4 ROLLESBY RD
5 SALHOUSE DR
WOLFERTON DR
ST MAGDALEN WAY
Swans Nest Farm
ICENI DR
WATTON ROAD
Snails Pit Farm
BRANCASTER WAY
ROLLESBY AVE
UPTON DR
1 WROXHAM AVE
2 HICKLING CL
3 BARTON CL
4 OULTON CL
5 BLAKE CT
Clarence Hills
FILBY RD
SUTTON RD
BRANDON ROAD
Snails Pit
RANWORTH CL
SURLINGHAM DR
HOVETON DR
Carol House
C3
1 PLEASANT ROW
2 POINT DR
3 BRANDON CL
4 NICHOLAS HAMOND WAY
5 BOTWRIGHT DR
6 STRATTON CL
7 AMHERST CL
8 GLASBURY WLK
9 MERRYWEATHER RD
10 LEE WARNER RD

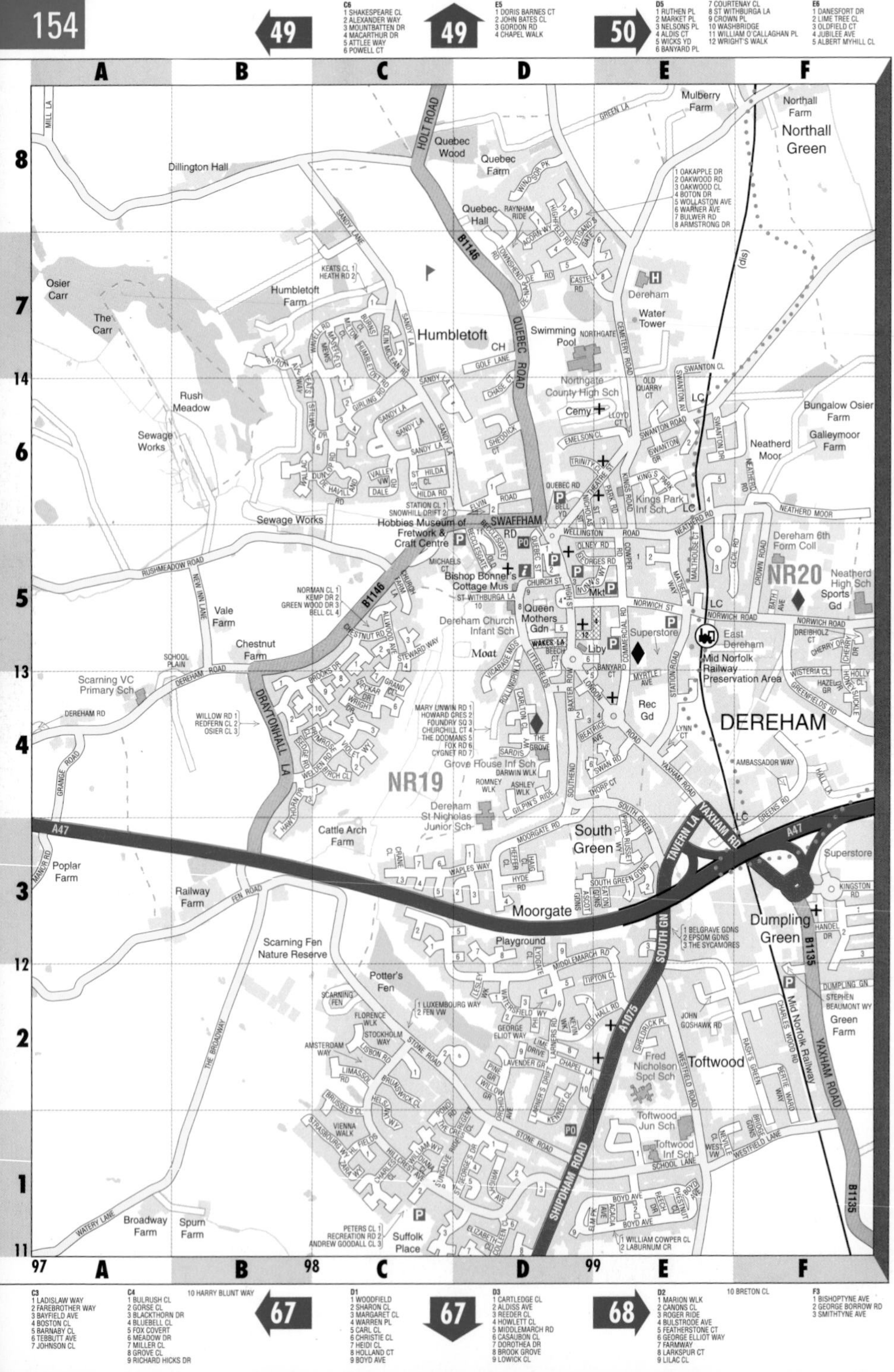

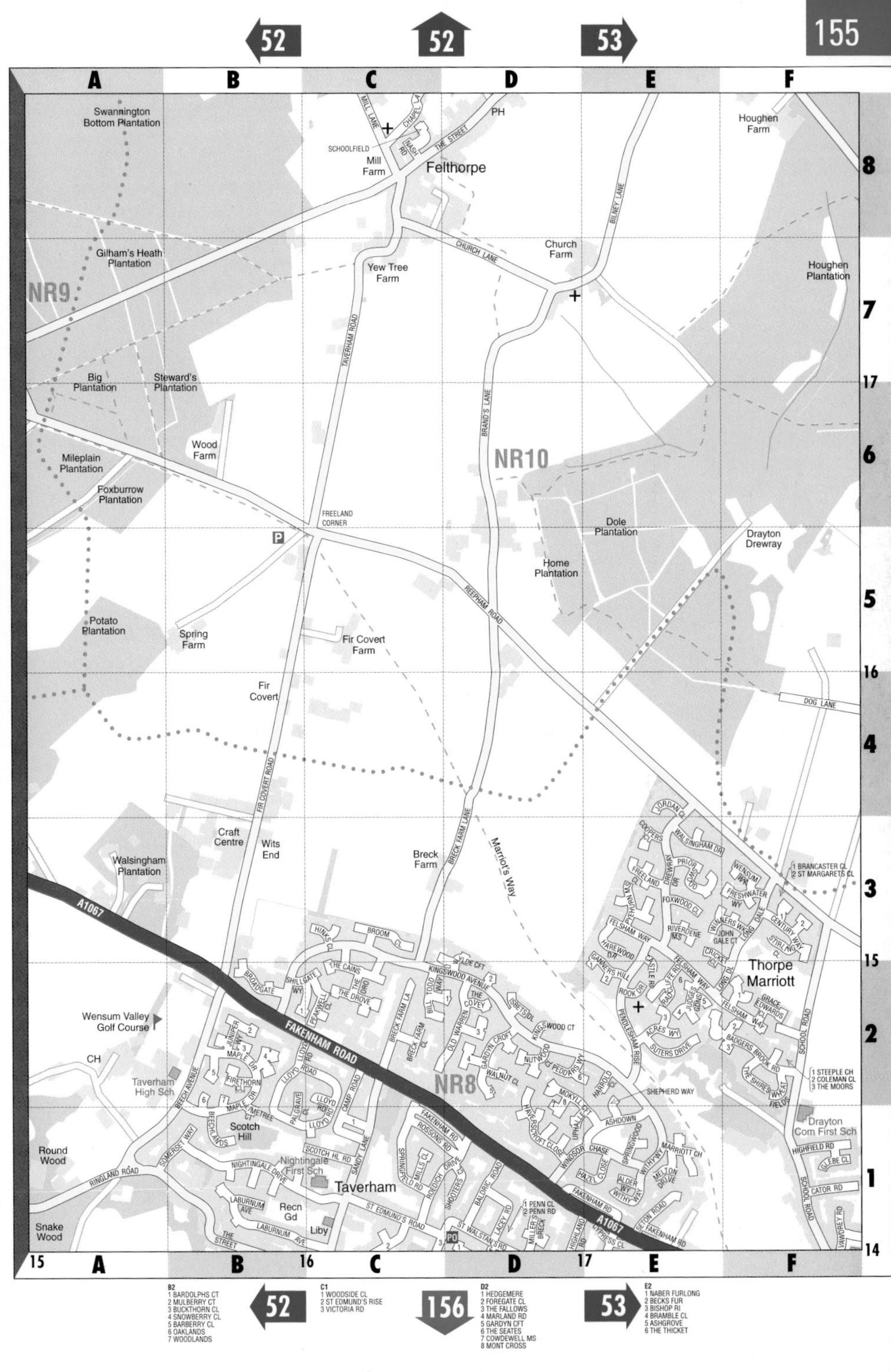
52
52
53
Swannington Bottom Plantation
Felthorpe
Mill Farm
Houghen Farm
Gilham's Heath Plantation
NR9
Yew Tree Farm
Church Farm
Houghen Plantation
Big Plantation
Steward's Plantation
Wood Farm
Mileplain Plantation
Foxburrow Plantation
NR10
Freeland Corner
Dole Plantation
Drayton Drewray
Home Plantation
Potato Plantation
Spring Farm
Fir Covert Farm
Fir Covert
Craft Centre
Wits End
Breck Farm
Marriot's Way
Walsingham Plantation
Wensum Valley Golf Course
Taverham High Sch
Scotch Hill
Round Wood
Nightingale First Sch
Taverham
Recn Gd
Liby
Snake Wood
NR8
Thorpe Marriott
Drayton Com First Sch
A1067
FAKENHAM ROAD
REEPHAM ROAD
TAVERHAM ROAD
BRAND'S LANE
CHURCH LANE
BILNEY LANE
FIR COVERT ROAD
BRECK FARM LANE
DOG LANE
SCHOOL ROAD
1 BRANCASTER CL
2 ST MARGARETS CL
1 STEEPLE CH
2 COLEMAN CL
3 THE MOORS
1 PENN CL
2 PENN RD
B2
1 BARDOLPHS CT
2 MULBERRY CT
3 BUCKTHORN CL
4 SNOWBERRY CL
5 BARBERRY CL
6 OAKLANDS
7 WOODLANDS
C1
1 WOODSIDE CL
2 ST EDMUND'S RISE
3 VICTORIA RD
D2
1 HEDGEMERE
2 FOREGATE CL
3 THE FALLOWS
4 MARLAND RD
5 GARDYN CFT
6 THE SEATES
7 COWDEWELL MS
8 MONT CROSS
E2
1 NABER FURLONG
2 BECKS FUR
3 BISHOP RI
4 BRAMBLE CL
5 ASHGROVE
6 THE THICKET
52
156
53

70
155

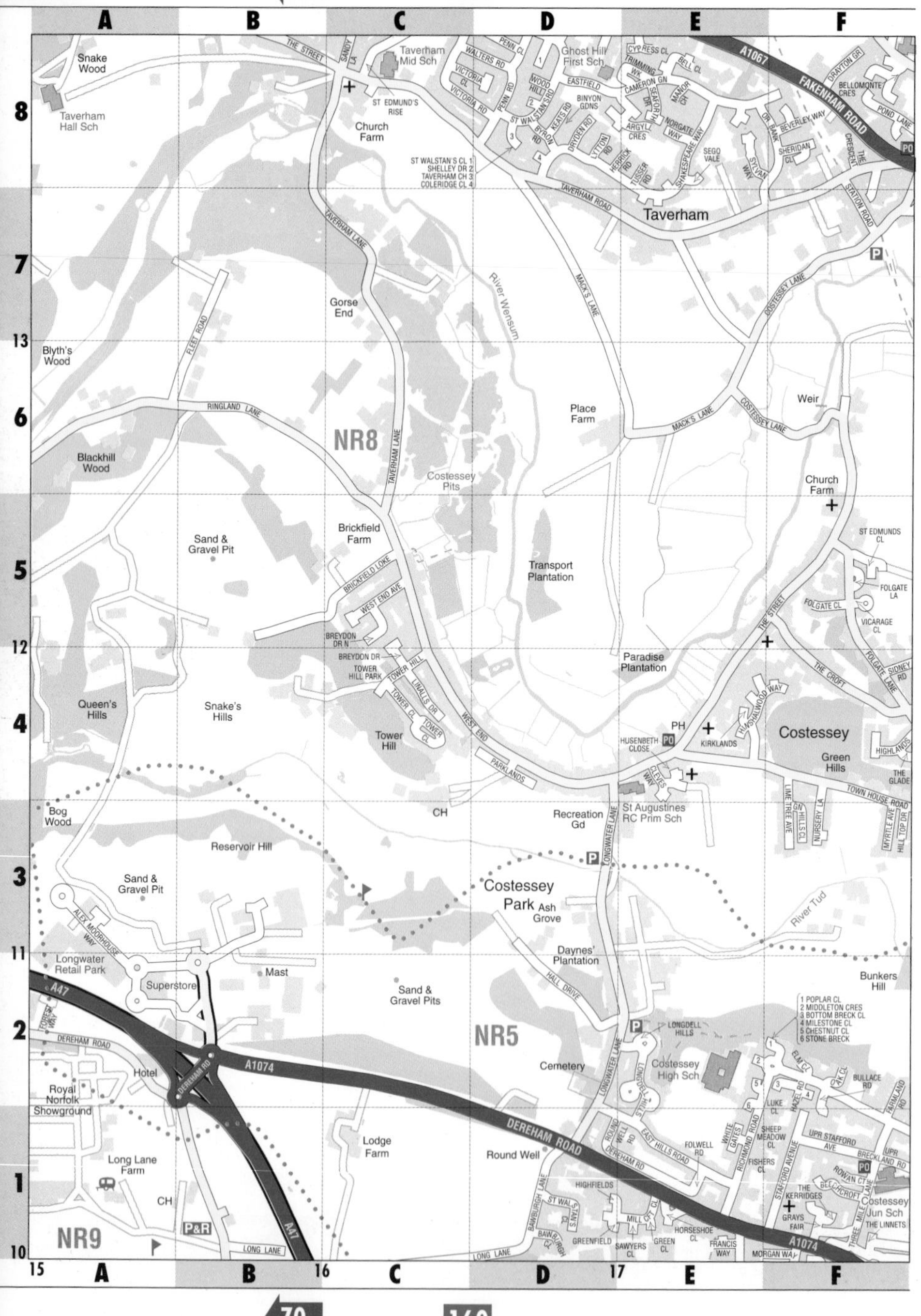
A
B
C
D
E
F
8
7
13
6
5
12
4
3
11
2
1
10
15
16
17
Snake Wood
Taverham Hall Sch
Taverham Mid Sch
Church Farm
Ghost Hill First Sch
Taverham
A1067
FAKENHAM ROAD
Gorse End
River Wensum
Blyth's Wood
Place Farm
Weir
NR8
Blackhill Wood
Costessey Pits
Church Farm
Brickfield Farm
Sand & Gravel Pit
Transport Plantation
Paradise Plantation
Queen's Hills
Snake's Hills
Tower Hill
Costessey
Green Hills
Bog Wood
CH
Recreation Gd
St Augustines RC Prim Sch
Reservoir Hill
Sand & Gravel Pit
Costessey Park
Ash Grove
River Tud
Longwater Retail Park
Daynes' Plantation
Bunkers Hill
Superstore
Mast
Sand & Gravel Pits
NR5
A47
A1074
Hotel
Cemetery
Costessey High Sch
Royal Norfolk Showground
Lodge Farm
Round Well
DEREHAM ROAD
Long Lane Farm
CH
NR9
Costessey Jun Sch
1 POPLAR CL
2 MIDDLETON CRES
3 BOTTOM BRECK CL
4 MILESTONE CL
5 CHESTNUT CL
6 STONE BRECK
ST WALSTAN'S CL 1
SHELLEY DR 2
TAVERHAM CH 3
COLERIDGE CL 4

A
B
C
D
E
F

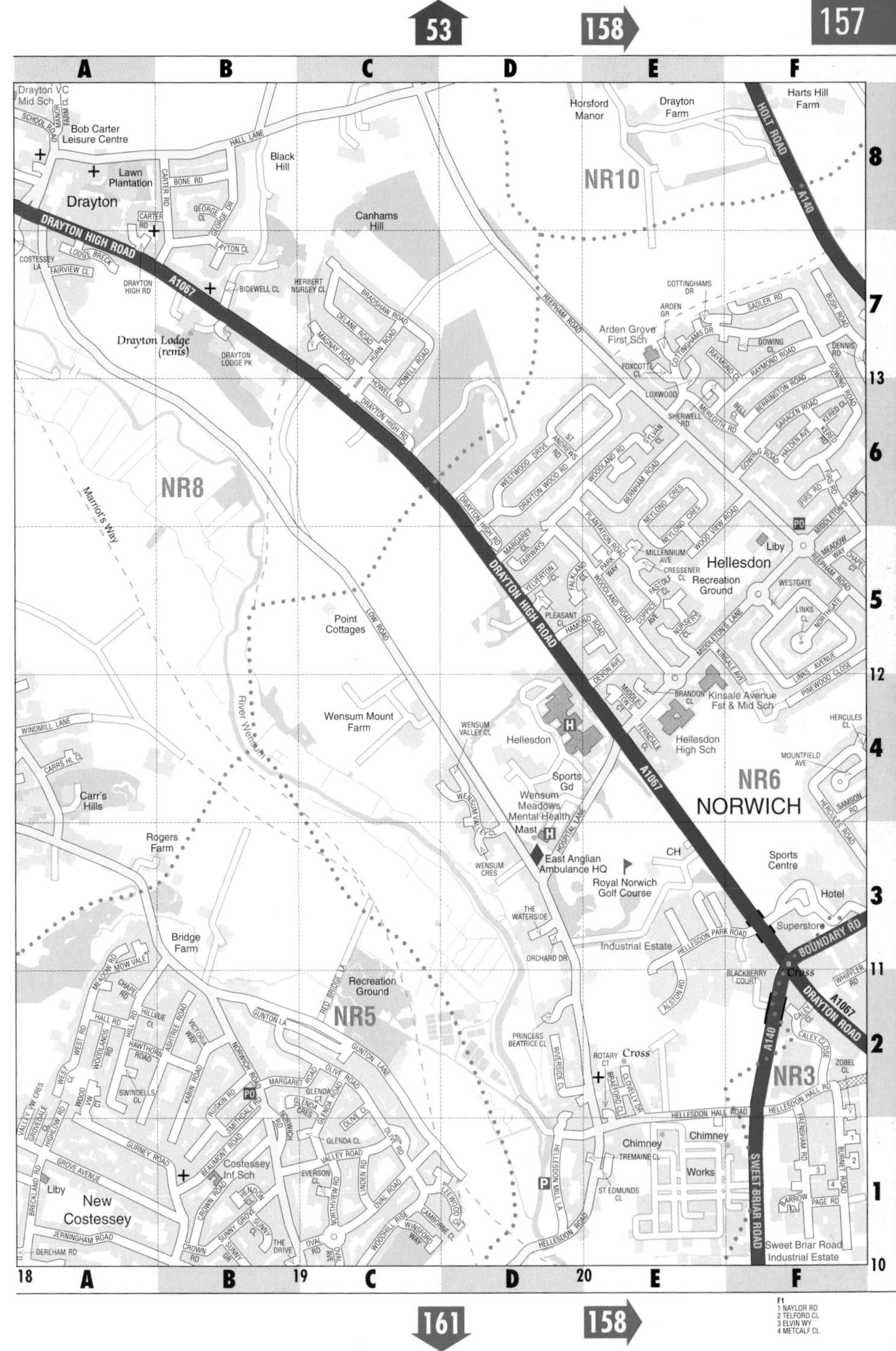

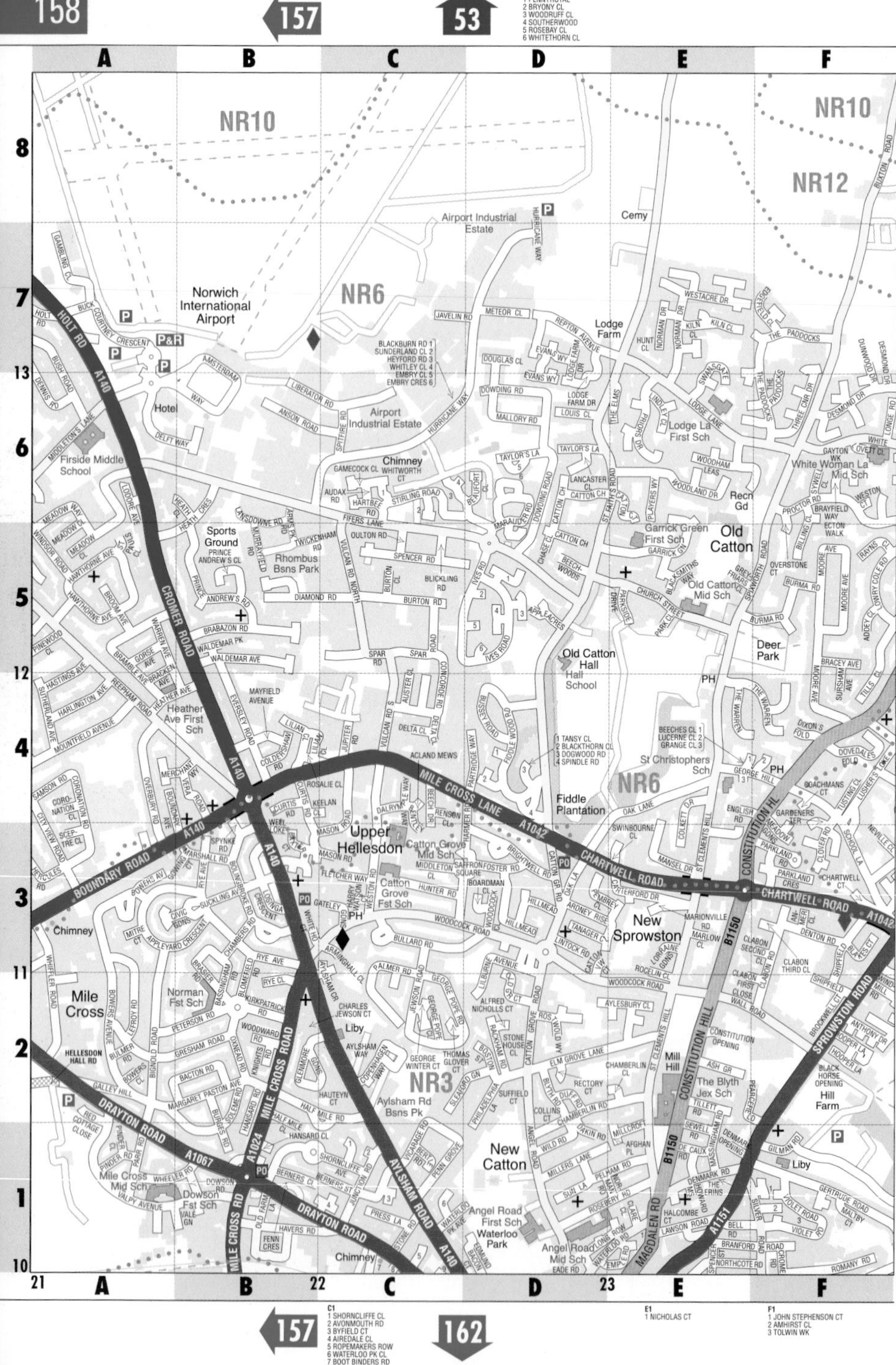

157

53

157

53

D5
1 PENNYROYAL
2 BRYONY CL
3 WOODRUFF CL
4 SOUTHERWOOD
5 ROSEBAY CL
6 WHITETHORN CL

NR10

NR10

NR12

8

Airport Industrial
Estate

Cemy

NR6

7

Norwich
International
Airport

P&R

Lodge
Farm

WESTACRE DR

THE PADDOCKS

13

Hotel

Airport
Industrial Estate

BLACKBURN RD 1
SUNDERLAND CL 2
HEYFORD RD 3
WHITLEY CL 4
EMBRY CL 5
EMBRY CRES 6

Lodge La
First Sch

White Woman La
Mid Sch

6

Firside Middle
School

Chimney
WHITWORTH
CT

Lancaster

Old
Catton

Sports
Ground
PRINCE
ANDREW'S CL

Rhombus
Bsns Park

Garrick Green
First Sch

Old Catton
Mid Sch

Deer
Park

5

12

Heather
Ave First
Sch

Old Catton
Hall
School

PH

4

MAYFIELD
AVENUE

1 TANSY CL
2 BLACKTHORN CL
3 DOGWOOD RD
4 SPINDLE RD

BEECHES CL 1
LUCERNE CL 2
GRANGE CL 3

St Christophers
Sch

NR6

PH

3

Chimney

BOUNDARY ROAD

A140

MILE CROSS LANE

Upper
Hellesdon

Catton Grove
Mid Sch

Catton
Grove
Fst Sch

Fiddle
Plantation

CHARTWELL ROAD

CHARTWELL ROAD

New
Sprowston

CONSTITUTION HL

11

Mile
Cross

Norman
Fst Sch

Liby

CHARLES
JEWSON CT

Alfred
Nicholls CT

Mill
Hill

The Blyth
Jex Sch

Hill
Farm

2

HELLESDON
HALL RD

Aylsham Rd
Bsns Pk

NR3

George
Glover
Sch

CONSTITUTION
OPENING

BLACK
HORSE
OPENING

1

DRAYTON ROAD

A1067

Mile Cross
Mid Sch

Dowson
Fst Sch

New
Catton

Angel Road
First Sch
Waterloo
Park

Angel Road
Mid Sch

Liby

10

21

A

B

22

C

D

23

E

F

DRAYTON ROAD

Chimney

157

162

157

162

C1
1 SHORNCLIFFE CL
2 AVONMOUTH RD
3 BYFIELD CT
4 AIREDALE CL
5 ROPEMAKERS ROW
6 WATERLOO PK CL
7 BOOT BINDERS RD
8 FINISHERS RD
9 LIME KILN MEWS

E1
1 NICHOLAS CT

F1
1 JOHN STEPHENSON CT
2 AMHIRST CL
3 TOLWIN WK

54
72

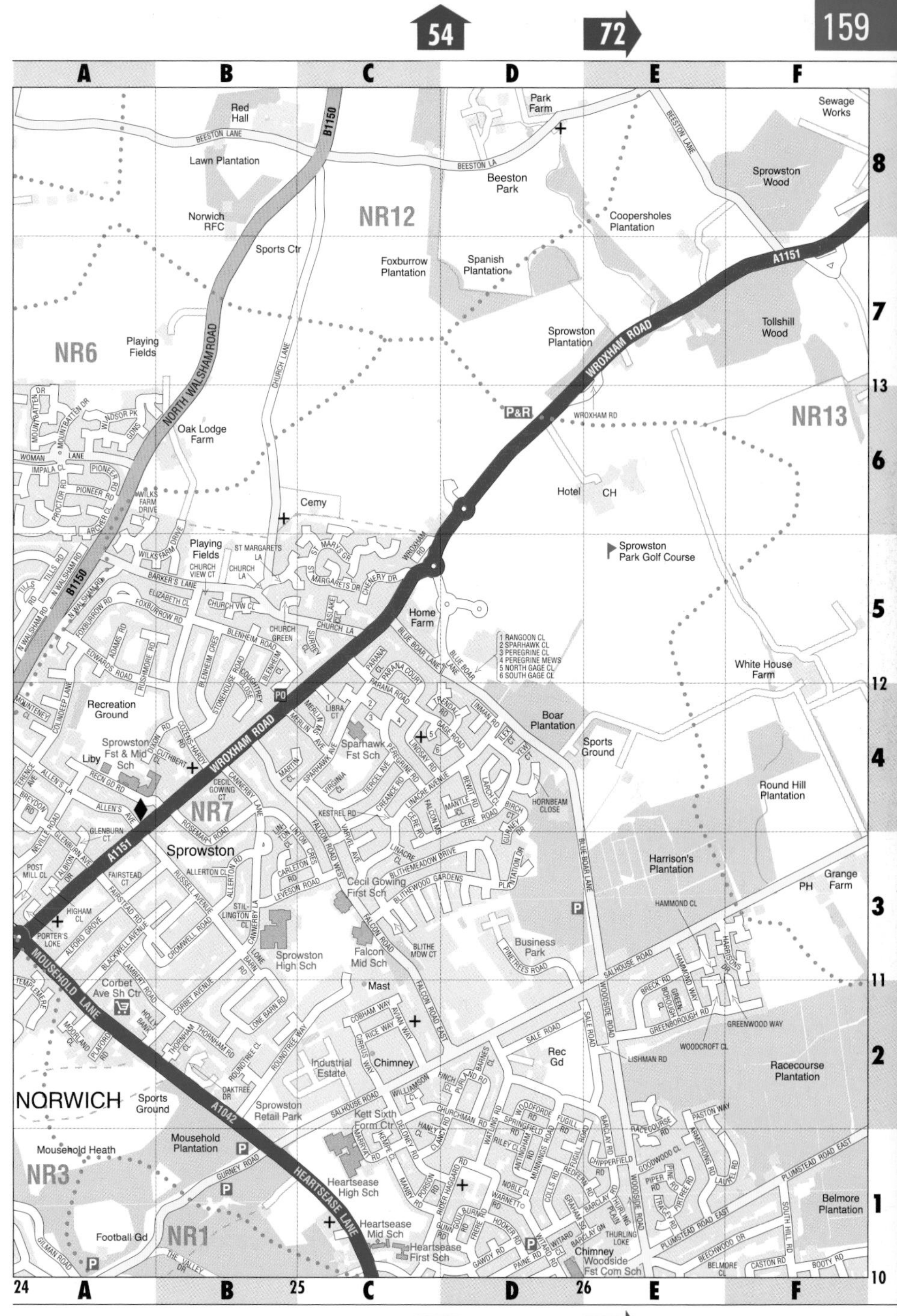
A
B
C
D
E
F
Red Hall
Lawn Plantation
Norwich RFC
Sports Ctr
B1150
BEESTON LANE
BEESTON LA
Park Farm
Beeston Park
NR12
Foxburrow Plantation
Spanish Plantation
Coopersholes Plantation
Sewage Works
Sprowston Wood
A1151
Tollshill Wood
Sprowston Plantation
WROXHAM ROAD
NR6
Playing Fields
NORTH WALSHAM ROAD
CHURCH LANE
P&R
WROXHAM RD
NR13
Oak Lodge Farm
MOUNTBATTEN DR
WINDSOR PK GDNS
WOMAN LANE
IMPALA CL
PIONEER RD
PROCTOR RD
ARCHER CL
WILKS FARM DRIVE
Cemy
Hotel
CH
Playing Fields
ST MARGARETS LA
CHURCH VIEW CT
CHURCH LA
BARKER'S LANE
ELIZABETH CL
CHURCH VW CL
FOXBURROW RD
ST MARYS GR
ST MARGARETS DR
CHENERY DR
Sprowston Park Golf Course
Home Farm
CHURCH GREEN
CHURCH LA
ASLAKE CL
SURREY CL
BLENHEIM ROAD
BLENHEIM CRES
BLUE BOAR LANE
1 RANGOON CL
2 SPARHAWK CL
3 PEREGRINE CL
4 PEREGRINE MEWS
5 NORTH GAGE CL
6 SOUTH GAGE CL
White House Farm
N WALSHAM RD
TILLS RD
EDWARDS ROAD
ADAMS RD
RUSHMORE RD
STONEHOUSE ROAD
COUGHTREY CLOSE
PO
PARANA CL
PARANA COURT
PARANA ROAD
TRENDALL RD
INMAN RD
Boar Plantation
Recreation Ground
COLINDEEP LANE
MOUNTENEY CL
DIXON RD
COZENS-HARDY RD
CUTHBERT CL
LIBRA CT
MERLIN MS
MERLIN AVE
Sparhawk Fst Sch
LINDSAY RD
GAGE ROAD
LEX CT
YEW CT
Sports Ground
Sprowston Fst & Mid Sch
Liby
RECN GD RD
ALLEN'S LA
ALLEN'S AVE
TERENCE AVE
BREYDON RD
CECIL GOWING CT
CANNERBY LANE
MARTIN CL
SPARHAWK AVE
VIRGINIA CL
TIERCEL AVE
CREANCE RD
PEREGRINE RD
LINACRE AVENUE
BEWIT RD
LARCH CL
MANTLE CL
FALCON MS
CERE RD
CERE ROAD
BIRCH CT
HORNBEAM CLOSE
Round Hill Plantation
NR7
ROSEMARY ROAD
KESTREL RD
JARVEL AVE
GURNEY DR
GLENBURN CT
NEVILLE RD
GLENBURN AVE
Sprowston
LINTON CL
LINTON CRES
FALCON ROAD WEST
LINACRE CL
BLITHEMEADOW DRIVE
PLANTATION DR
Harrison's Plantation
POST MILL CL
ALBION DR
FAIRSTEAD CT
ALLERTON CL
ALLERTON RD
RUSSELL AVENUE
CARLETON RD
LEVESON ROAD
Cecil Gowing First Sch
BLITHEWOOD GARDENS
Grange Farm
PH
HIGHAM CL
FAIRSTEAD RD
STILLINGTON CL
CANNERBY LA
HAMMOND CL
P
PORTER'S LOKE
ALFORD GROVE
BLACKWELL AVENUE
CROMWELL ROAD
Sprowston High Sch
FALCON ROAD
BLITHE MDW CT
Falcon Mid Sch
Business Park
PINETREES ROAD
SALHOUSE ROAD
HAMMOND WAY
HARRISONS DR
BRECK RD
GREENBOROUGH CL
TEMPLEMERE
MOUSEHOLD LANE
LAMBERT ROAD
Corbet Ave Sh Ctr
CORBET AVENUE
LONE BARN RD
Mast
FALCON ROAD EAST
WOODSIDE ROAD
GREENBOROUGH RD
GREENWOOD WAY
HOLLY BANK
THORNHAM CL
THORNHAM RD
ROUNDTREE CL
ROUNDTREE WAY
COBHAM WAY
RICE WAY
AVIAN WAY
CIRRUS WAY
SALE ROAD
SALE ROAD
WOODCROFT CL
MOORLAND CL
PLAYFORD RD
Industrial Estate
Chimney
Rec Gd
LISHMAN RD
Racecourse Plantation
NORWICH
Sports Ground
A1042
OAKTREE DR
Sprowston Retail Park
WILLIAMSON CL
FINCH CL
PURLAND RD
BARNES CL
Kett Sixth Form Ctr
CHURCHMAN RD
WATLING RD
WOODFORDE RD
SPRINGFIELD RD
FUGILL RD
BARCLAY RD
PASTON WAY
Mousehold Heath
Mousehold Plantation
HANLY CL
CLANCY RD
DELONEY RD
RILEY CL
RACECOURSE RD
GOODWOOD CL
ARMSTRONG RD
NR3
GURNEY ROAD
HEARTSEASE LANE
MARRYAT RD
KEMPE CL
ANTINGHAM RD
MUNNINGS ROAD
REDFERN RD
CHIPPERFIELD RD
PIPER RD
PINE RD
FIRTREE RD
LAVEN RD
PLUMSTEAD ROAD EAST
Heartsease High Sch
MANBY RD
PORSON RD
RIDER HAGGARD RD
NOBLE CL
WARNETT RD
COLLS RD
GRAHAM SQ
BARCLAY PLAIN
THURLING PLAIN
TRACEY RD
Belmore Plantation
SOUTH HILL RD
Football Gd
NR1
Heartsease Mid Sch
GUNN RD
GOULBURN RD
FRERE RD
HOOKER RD
WITARD RD
THURLING LOKE
BARCLAY GN
PLUMSTEAD ROAD EAST
GILMAN ROAD
THE VALLEY DR
Heartsease First Sch
GAWDY RD
PAINE RD
Chimney
Woodside Fst Com Sch
BEECHWOOD DR
BELMORE CL
CASTON RD
BOOTY RD
8
7
13
6
5
12
4
3
11
2
1
10
24
25
26

163
72

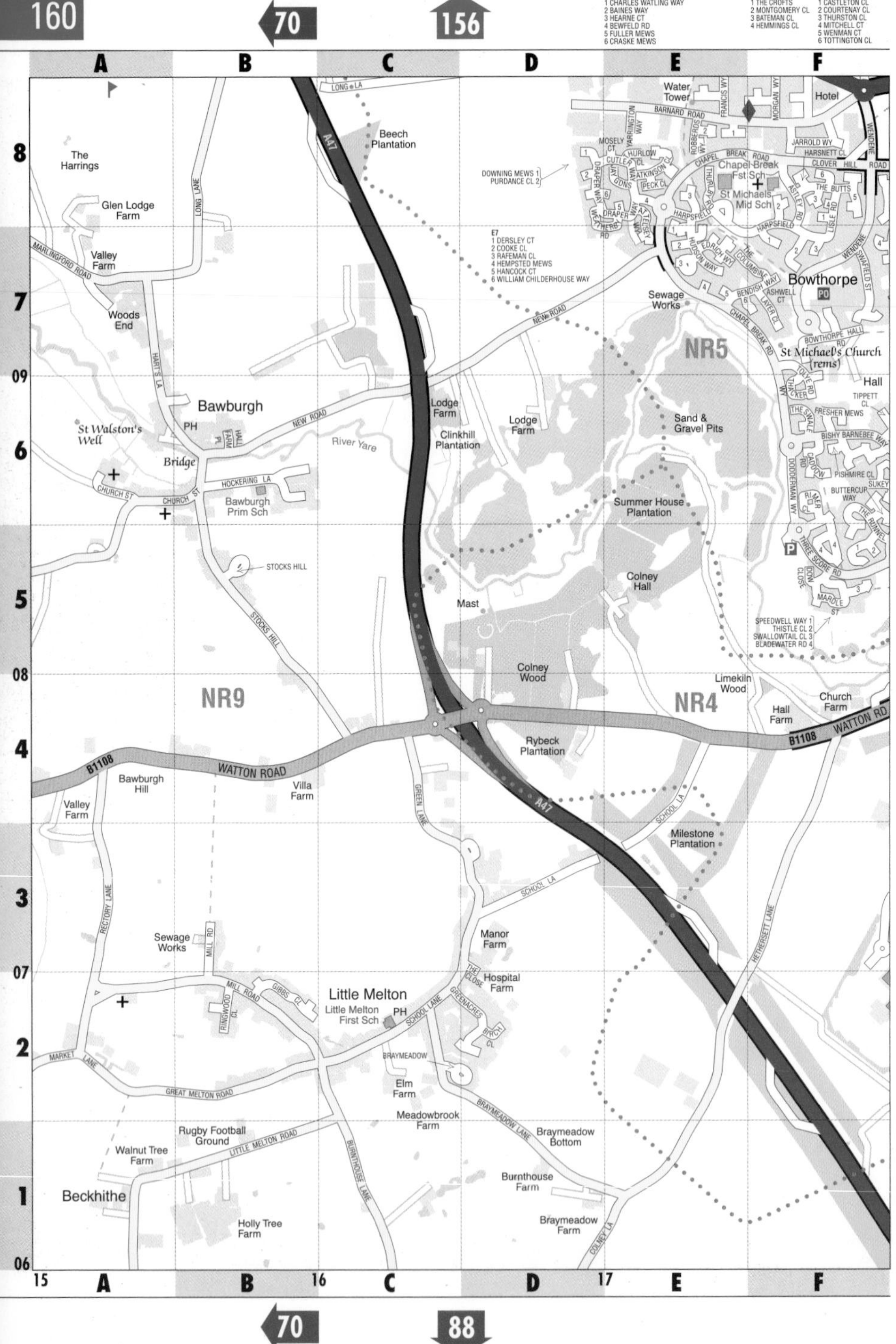
70
156
E8
1 CHARLES WATLING WAY
2 BAINES WAY
3 HEARNE CT
4 BEWFELD RD
5 FULLER MEWS
6 CRASKE MEWS
F7
1 THE CROFTS
2 MONTGOMERY CL
3 BATEMAN CL
4 HEMMINGS CL
F8
1 CASTLETON CL
2 COURTENAY CL
3 THURSTON CL
4 MITCHELL CT
5 WENMAN CT
6 TOTTINGTON CL
A
B
C
D
E
F
8
7
09
6
5
08
4
3
07
2
1
06
15
16
17
The Harrings
Glen Lodge Farm
Valley Farm
Woods End
MARLINGFORD ROAD
LONG LANE
LONG LA
HART'S LA
Beech Plantation
A47
Water Tower
Hotel
BARNARD ROAD
JARROLD WY
HARSNETT CL
CLOVER HILL ROAD
WENDENE
DOWNING MEWS 1
PURDANCE CL 2
Chapel Break Fst Sch
St Michaels Mid Sch
CHAPEL BREAK ROAD
HARPSFIELD
THE BUTTS
E7
1 DERSLEY CT
2 COOKE CL
3 RAFEMAN CL
4 HEMPSTED MEWS
5 HANCOCK CT
6 WILLIAM CHILDERHOUSE WAY
Bowthorpe
PO
Sewage Works
NEW ROAD
NR5
St Michael's Church (rems)
BOWTHORPE HALL RD
Hall
TIPPETT CL
FRESHER MEWS
BISHY BARNEBEE WAY
PISHMIRE CL
BUTTERCUP WAY
DODDERMAN WY
THREE SCORE RD
Bawburgh
PH
St Walston's Well
Bridge
River Yare
Lodge Farm
Clinkhill Plantation
Lodge Farm
Sand & Gravel Pits
HOCKERING LA
CHURCH ST
Bawburgh Prim Sch
Summer House Plantation
STOCKS HILL
Colney Hall
Mast
SPEEDWELL WAY 1
THISTLE CL 2
SWALLOWTAIL CL 3
BLADEWATER RD 4
Colney Wood
NR9
Limekiln Wood
NR4
Church Farm
Hall Farm
B1108
WATTON RD
Rybeck Plantation
WATTON ROAD
Bawburgh Hill
Valley Farm
Villa Farm
GREEN LANE
SCHOOL LA
Milestone Plantation
RECTORY LANE
SCHOOL LA
Manor Farm
Sewage Works
MILL RD
Hospital Farm
HETHERSETT LANE
MILL ROAD
GIBBS CL
RINGWOOD CL
Little Melton
Little Melton First Sch
SCHOOL LANE
GREENACRES
BIRCH CL
BRAYMEADOW
MARKET LANE
GREAT MELTON ROAD
Elm Farm
Meadowbrook Farm
BRAYMEADOW LANE
Braymeadow Bottom
Rugby Football Ground
LITTLE MELTON ROAD
Walnut Tree Farm
BURNTHOUSE LANE
Burnthouse Farm
Beckhithe
Holly Tree Farm
Braymeadow Farm
COLNEY LA

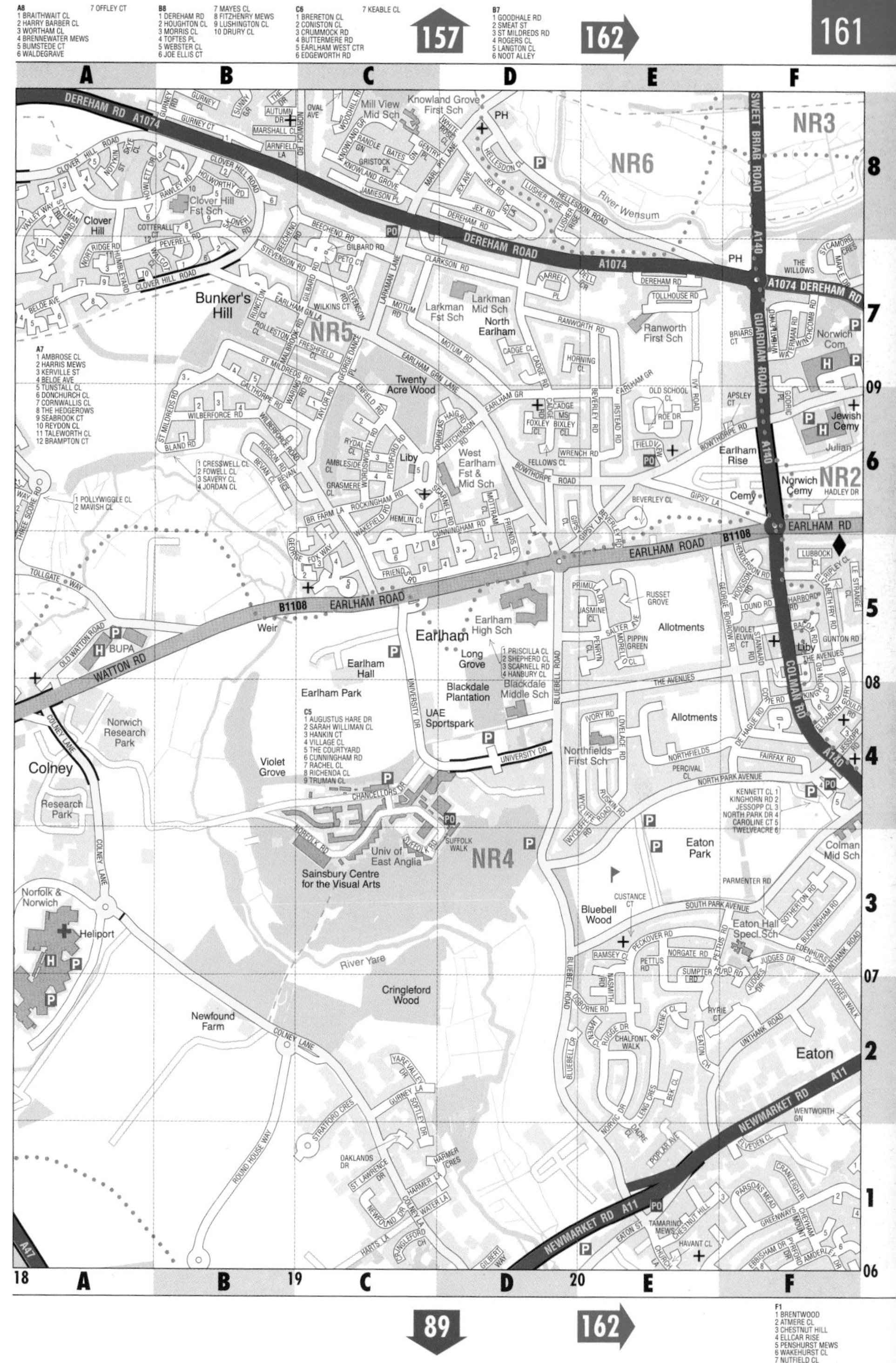

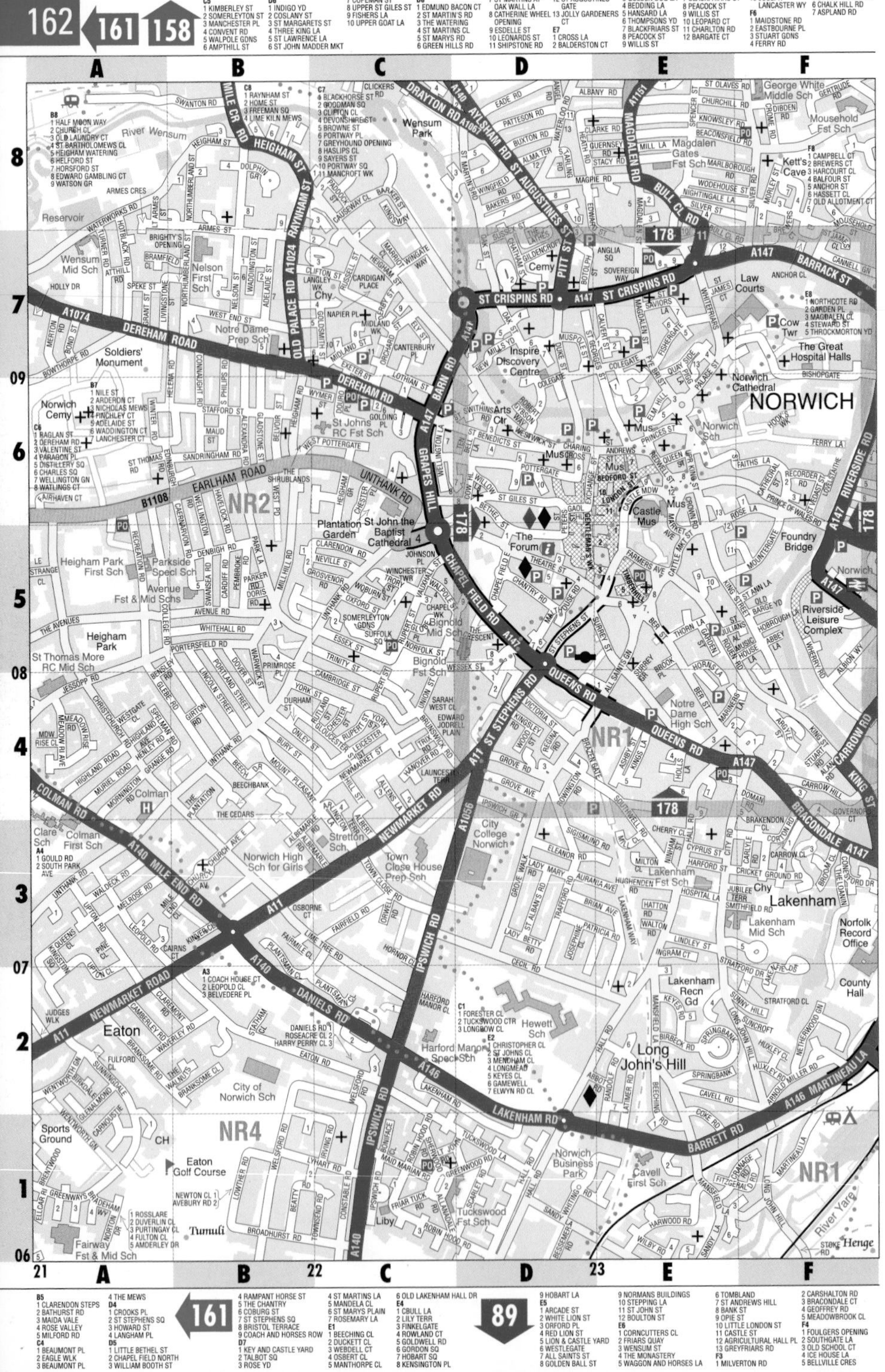

A6
1 LOLLARDS RD
2 GUELPH RD
3 MALVERN RD
4 TELEGRAPH LA W
5 ROSEDALE CRES
6 ST LEONARDS TERR
7 SAUNDERS CT
8 PROVIDENCE PL
9 ELMDON CT

B5
1 MATLOCK RD
2 ROSEVILLE CL
3 FROGS HALL LA
4 GLENDENNING RD
5 WILSON RD
6 BARTON WAY

B7
1 SAMUEL RD
2 HONEY CL
3 SIENNA MEWS
4 WELLESLEY AVE NORTH
5 WOMERSLEY CL
6 ABERDARE CT

C8
1 VALLEY SIDE RD
2 CROFTHOLME WAY
3 VANCOUVER RD
4 PLUMSTEAD RD

159

72

E7
1 BRENDA JAMES CL
2 LE TUNDER CL
3 LAUNDRY CL
4 BOULDERSIDE CL

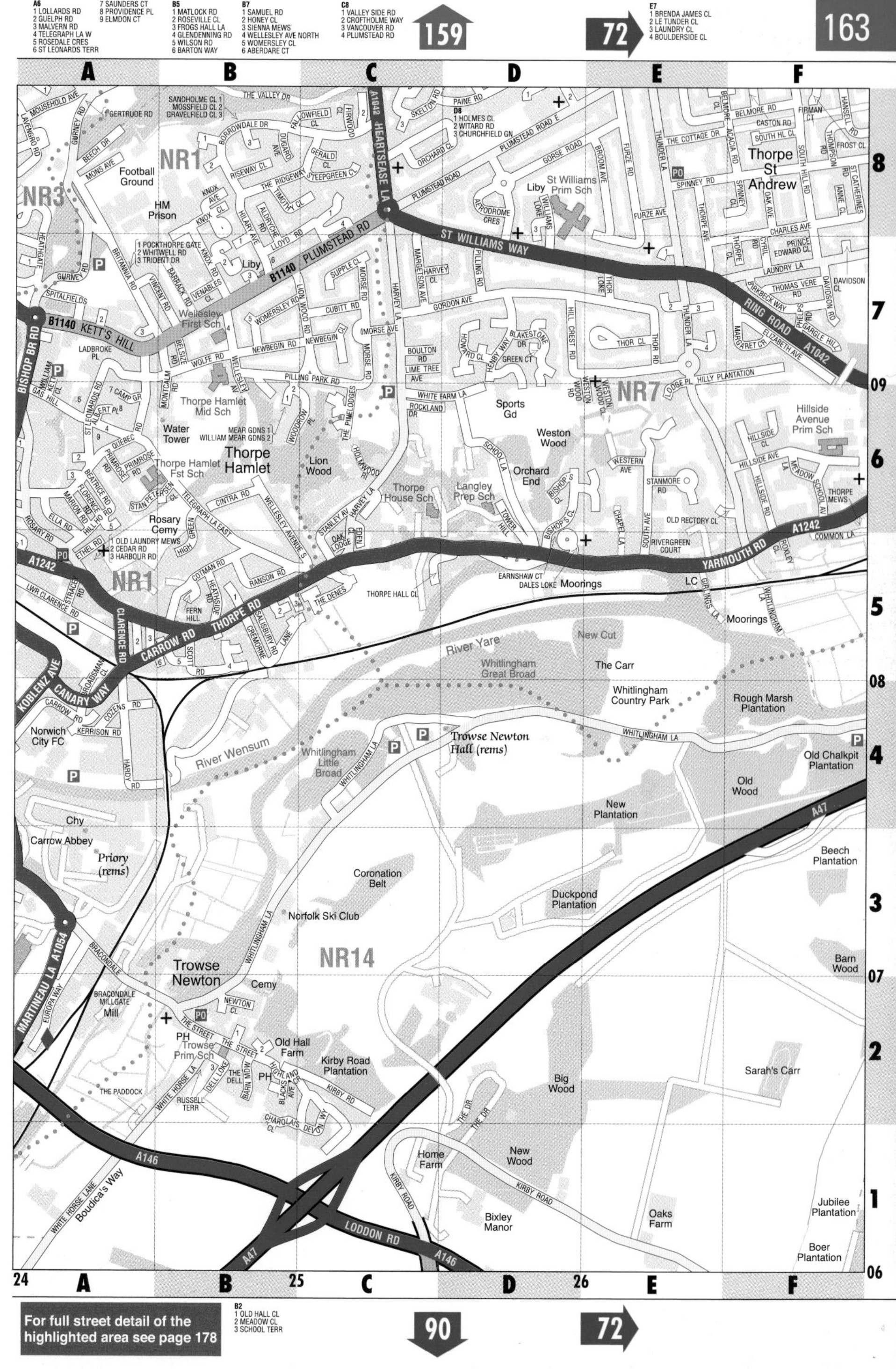

For full street detail of the highlighted area see page 178

B2
1 OLD HALL CL
2 MEADOW CL
3 SCHOOL TERR

90

72

54 54 55 55

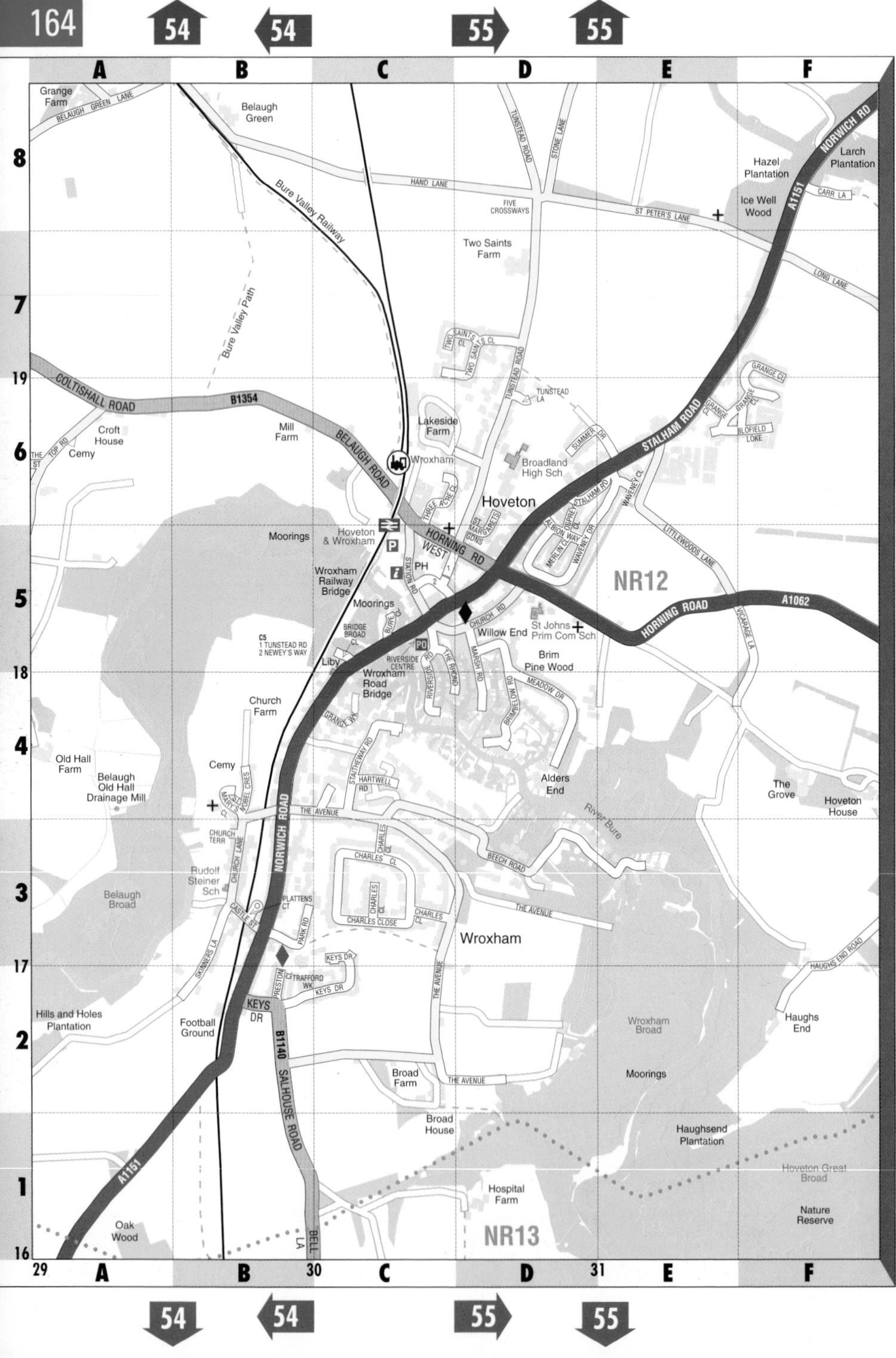

Grange Farm
BELAUGH GREEN LANE
Belaugh Green
Bure Valley Railway
HAND LANE
TUNSTEAD ROAD
STONE LANE
FIVE CROSSWAYS
ST PETER'S LANE
Hazel Plantation
Larch Plantation
NORWICH RD
A1151
CARR LA
Ice Well Wood
Two Saints Farm
LONG LANE
Bure Valley Path
TWO SAINTS CL
COLTISHALL ROAD
B1354
TUNSTEAD LA
GRANGE CL
STALHAM ROAD
BLOFIELD LOKE
Mill Farm
Croft House
Cemy
TOP RD
Lakeside Farm
BELAUGH ROAD
Wroxham
Broadland High Sch
SUMMER DR
Hoveton
THREE ACRE CL
ST MARGARETS GDNS
STALHAM RD
OSPREY CL
ALBION WAY
MERLIN CL
WAVENEY DR
WAVENEY CL
LITTLEWOODS LANE
Moorings
Hoveton & Wroxham
HORNING RD WEST
NR12
Wroxham Railway Bridge
STATION RD
PH
Moorings
CHURCH RD
HORNING ROAD
A1062
VICARAGE LA
Willow End
St Johns Prim Com Sch
C5
1 TUNSTEAD RD
2 NEWEY'S WAY
BRIDGE BROAD CL
BURE CL
Liby
RIVERSIDE CENTRE
Wroxham Road Bridge
RIVERSIDE RD
THE RHOND
MARSH RD
Brim Pine Wood
MEADOW DR
BRIMBELOW RD
Church Farm
GRANGE WK
STAITHEWAY RD
Old Hall Farm
Belaugh Old Hall Drainage Mill
Cemy
MARY'S CL
NOBEL CRES
HARTWELL RD
Alders End
The Grove
Hoveton House
THE AVENUE
River Bure
CHURCH TERR
CHURCH LANE
NORWICH ROAD
CHARLES CL
BEECH ROAD
Rudolf Steiner Sch
Belaugh Broad
CASTLE ST
PLATTENS CT
PARK RD
CHARLES CLOSE
CHARLES CL
THE AVENUE
Wroxham
SKINNERS LA
KEYS DR
PRESTON CL
TRAFFORD WK
KEYS DR
HAUGHS END ROAD
THE AVENUE
Hills and Holes Plantation
Football Ground
KEYS DR
B1140
SALHOUSE ROAD
Wroxham Broad
Haughs End
Broad Farm
THE AVENUE
Moorings
Broad House
Haughsend Plantation
A1151
Hoveton Great Broad
Hospital Farm
Nature Reserve
Oak Wood
NR13
BELL LA
A B C D E F
8 7 19 6 5 18 4 3 17 2 1 16
29 30 31

54 54 55 55

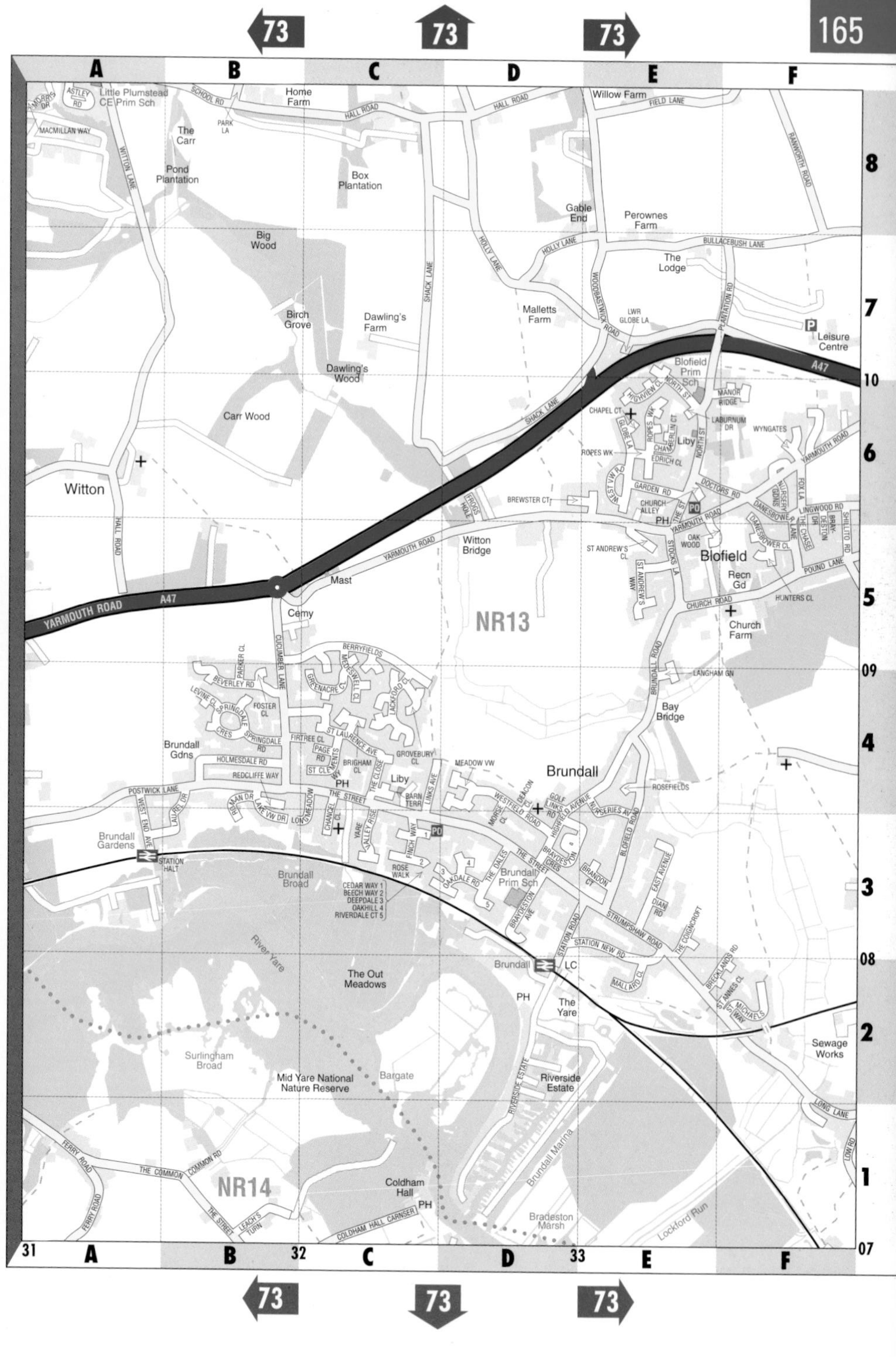

73
73
73
A
B
C
D
E
F
Little Plumstead CE Prim Sch
Home Farm
Willow Farm
HALL ROAD
FIELD LANE
SCHOOL RD
MACMILLAN WAY
The Carr
Pond Plantation
Box Plantation
WITTON LANE
RANWORTH ROAD
Gable End
Perownes Farm
Big Wood
HOLLY LANE
BULLACEBUSH LANE
The Lodge
SHACK LANE
Birch Grove
Dawling's Farm
Malletts Farm
WOODBASTWICK ROAD
LWR GLOBE LA
PLANTATION RD
Leisure Centre
A47
Dawling's Wood
Blofield Prim Sch
MANOR RIDGE
Carr Wood
CHAPEL CT
HIGHVIEW CL
NORTH ST
LABURNUM DR
WYNGATES
YARMOUTH ROAD
ROPES WK
EDRICH CL
Liby
Witton
GARDEN RD
DOCTORS RD
BREWSTER CT
CHURCH ALLEY
PO
PH
HALL ROAD
FROGS HOLE
Witton Bridge
ST ANDREW'S CL
OAK WOOD
DANESBOWER CL
LINGWOOD RD
SHILLITO RD
Blofield
STOCKS LA
ST ANDREW'S WAY
POUND LANE
Mast
Recn Gd
HUNTERS CL
YARMOUTH ROAD
A47
CHURCH ROAD
Cemy
NR13
Church Farm
BERRYFIELDS
PARKER CL
CUCUMBER LANE
BRUNDALL ROAD
BEVERLEY RD
LANGHAM GN
LEVINE CL
FOSTER CL
SPRINGDALE CRES
Bay Bridge
Brundall Gdns
FIRTREE CL
ST LAURENCE AVE
GROVEBURY CL
HOLMESDALE RD
PAGE RD
BRIGHAM CL
MEADOW VW
REDCLIFFE WAY
ST CLEMENTS WAY
PH
Liby
Brundall
POSTWICK LANE
THE STREET
BARN TERR
LINKS AVE
ROSEFIELDS
WEST END AVE
LAUREL DR
ROMAN DR
LAKE VW DR
LONGMEADOW
WESTFIELD ROAD
GOLF LINKS RD
HIGHFIELD AVENUE
NURSERIES AVE
Brundall Gardens
YARE VALLEY RISE
FINCH WAY
PO
STATION HALT
Brundall Broad
ROSE WALK
OAKDALE RD
THE DALES
Brundall Prim Sch
THE STREET
BRAYDESTON CRES
BRANDON CT
EAST AVENUE
CEDAR WAY 1
BEECH WAY 2
DEEPDALE 3
OAKHILL 4
RIVERDALE CT 5
STRUMPSHAW ROAD
DIAN RD
BRAYDESTON AVE
STATION ROAD
THE COIGNCROFT
River Yare
STATION NEW RD
Brundall
LC
MALLARD CL
BRECKLANDS RD
ST ANNES CL
ST MICHAELS WAY
The Out Meadows
PH
The Yare
Sewage Works
Surlingham Broad
Mid Yare National Nature Reserve
Bargate
Riverside Estate
RIVERSIDE ESTATE
LONG LANE
FERRY ROAD
THE COMMON
COMMON RD
Brundall Marina
LOW RD
NR14
Coldham Hall
PH
THE STREET
LEACH'S TURN
COLDHAM HALL CARNSER
Bradeston Marsh
Lockford Run
8
7
10
6
5
09
4
3
08
2
1
07
31
32
33
73
73
73

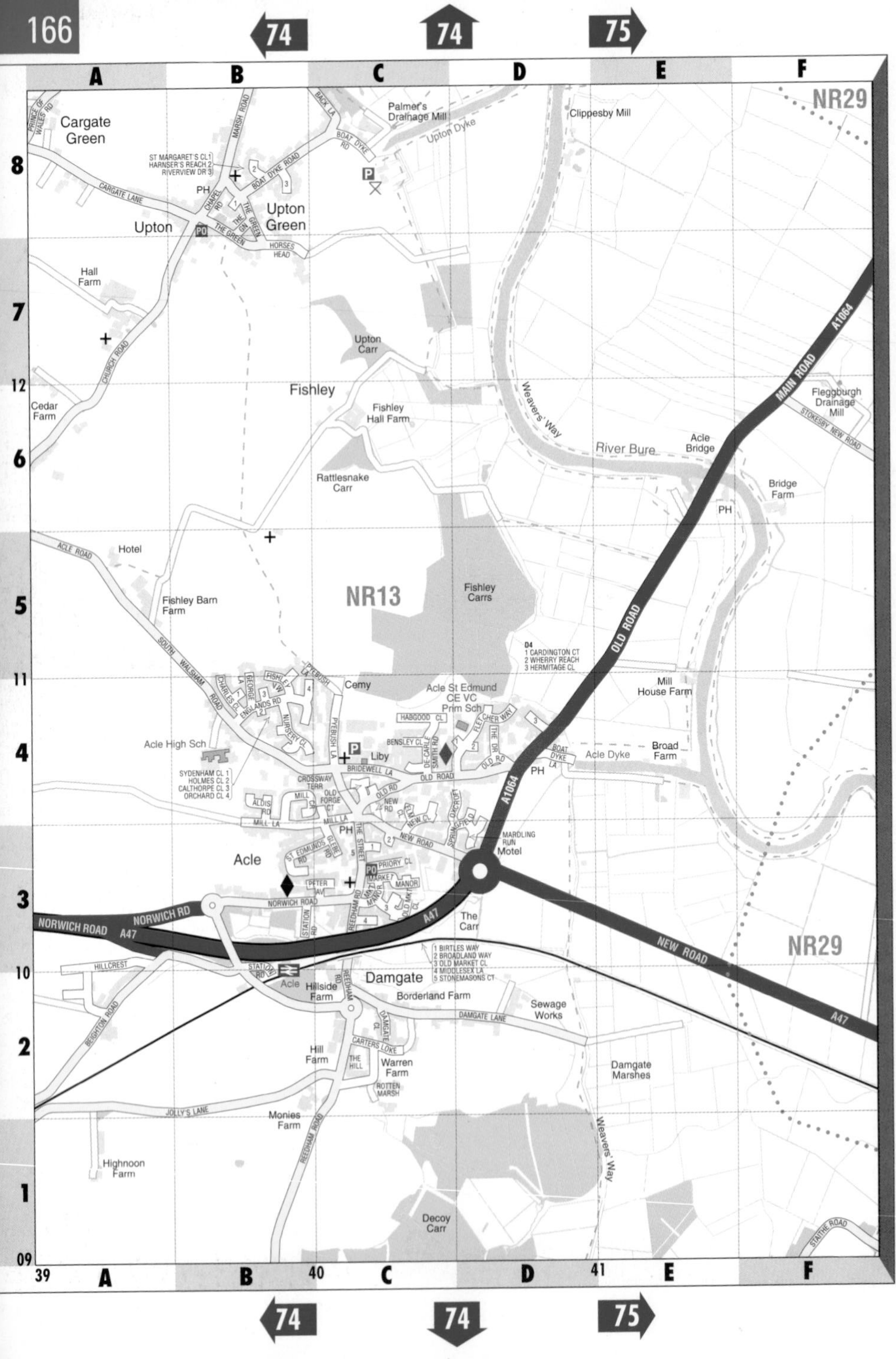
74
74
75
Cargate Green
Upton
Upton Green
Palmer's Drainage Mill
Upton Dyke
Clippesby Mill
NR29
ST MARGARET'S CL 1
HARNSER'S REACH 2
RIVERVIEW DR 3
CARGATE LANE
MARSH ROAD
BOAT DYKE ROAD
BACK LA
HORSES HEAD
Hall Farm
Upton Carr
CHURCH ROAD
Fishley
Fishley Hall Farm
Cedar Farm
Weavers' Way
River Bure
Acle Bridge
Fleggburgh Drainage Mill
MAIN ROAD
A1064
STOKESBY NEW ROAD
Bridge Farm
PH
Rattlesnake Carr
Hotel
ACLE ROAD
Fishley Barn Farm
NR13
Fishley Carrs
SOUTH WALSHAM ROAD
D4
1 CARDINGTON CT
2 WHERRY REACH
3 HERMITAGE CL
OLD ROAD
Mill House Farm
Cemy
Acle St Edmund CE VC Prim Sch
Acle High Sch
Liby
Acle Dyke
Broad Farm
SYDENHAM CL 1
HOLMES CL 2
CALTHORPE CL 3
ORCHARD CL 4
BRIDEWELL LA
MILL LA
Acle
PH
MARDLING RUN
Motel
NORWICH ROAD
NORWICH RD
A47
The Carr
NEW ROAD
NR29
1 BIRTLES WAY
2 BROADLAND WAY
3 OLD MARKET CL
4 MIDDLESEX LA
5 STONEMASONS CT
HILLCREST
Acle
Damgate
Hillside Farm
Borderland Farm
Sewage Works
DAMGATE LANE
BEIGHTON ROAD
Hill Farm
Warren Farm
Damgate Marshes
JOLLY'S LANE
Monies Farm
REEDHAM ROAD
Highnoon Farm
Decoy Carr
STAITHE ROAD
39
40
41
A
B
C
D
E
F
8
7
6
5
4
3
2
1
12
11
10
09
74
74
75

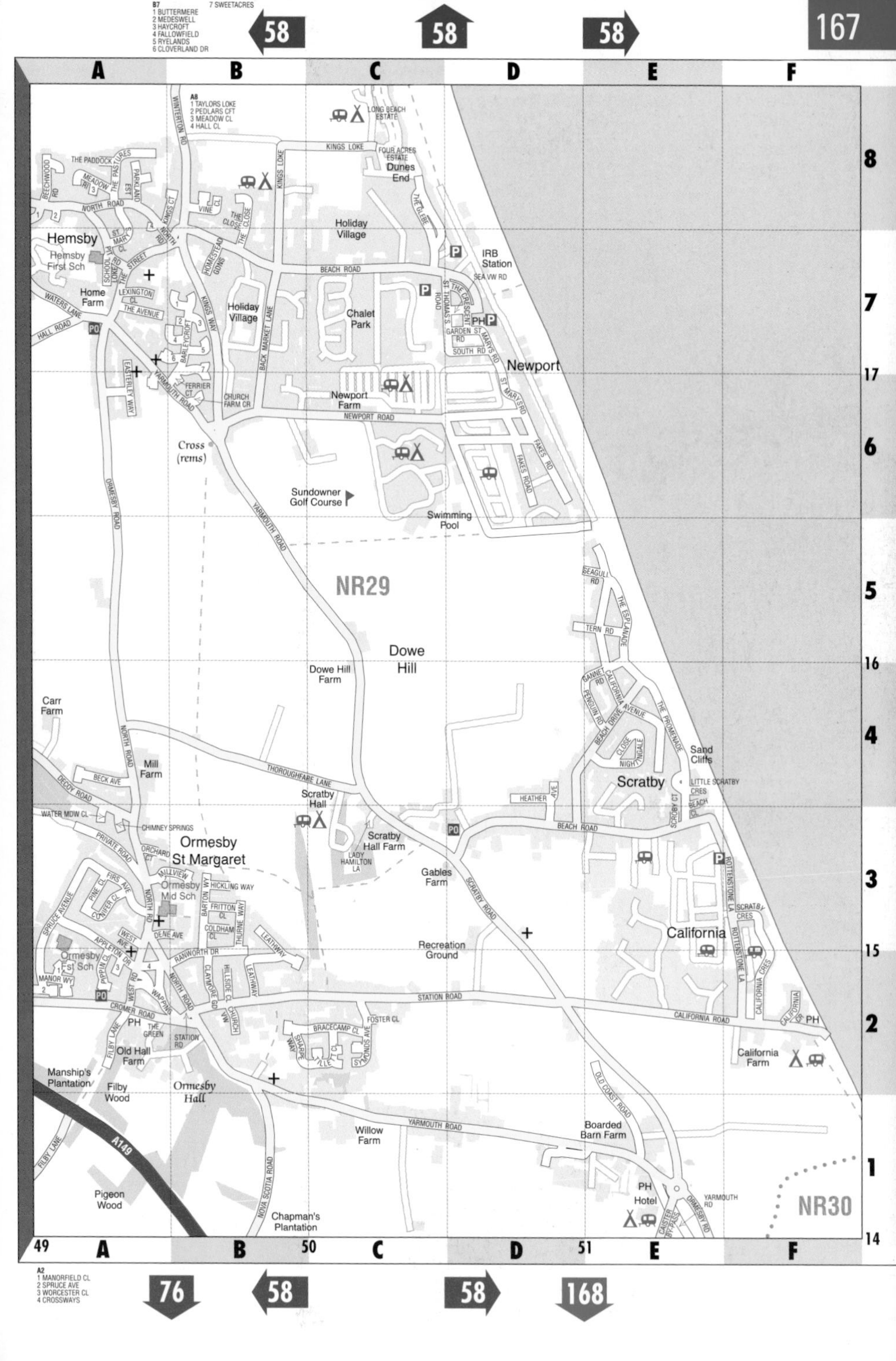

58 58 58

B7
1 BUTTERMERE
2 MEDESWELL
3 HAYCROFT
4 FALLOWFIELD
5 RYELANDS
6 CLOVERLAND DR

7 SWEETACRES

A
B
C
D
E
F

8
7
17
6
5
16
4
3
15
2
1
14

A8
1 TAYLORS LOKE
2 PEDLARS CFT
3 MEADOW CL
4 HALL CL

LONG BEACH
ESTATE

KINGS LOKE

FOUR ACRES
ESTATE
Dunes
End

Hemsby
Hemsby
First Sch

Home
Farm

Holiday
Village

BEACH ROAD

Holiday
Village

Chalet
Park

IRB
Station
SEA VW RD

PH

Newport

Newport
Farm

NEWPORT ROAD

Cross
(rems)

Sundowner
Golf Course

Swimming
Pool

NR29

Dowe
Hill

Dowe Hill
Farm

THE ESPLANADE

Carr
Farm

Mill
Farm

THOROUGHFARE LANE

Scratby
Hall

Sand
Cliffs

Scratby

LITTLE SCRATBY
CRES

HEATHER

BEACH ROAD

Ormesby
St Margaret

Ormesby
Mid Sch

Scratby
Hall Farm

Gables
Farm

Ormesby
Fst Sch

Recreation
Ground

California

Old Hall
Farm

THE GREEN

STATION ROAD

CALIFORNIA ROAD

California
Farm

Manship's
Plantation

Filby
Wood

Ormesby
Hall

YARMOUTH ROAD

Willow
Farm

Boarded
Barn Farm

PH
Hotel

A149

Pigeon
Wood

Chapman's
Plantation

NR30

49
A
B
50
C
D
51
E
F
14

A2
1 MANORFIELD CL
2 SPRUCE AVE
3 WORCESTER CL
4 CROSSWAYS

76 58 58 168

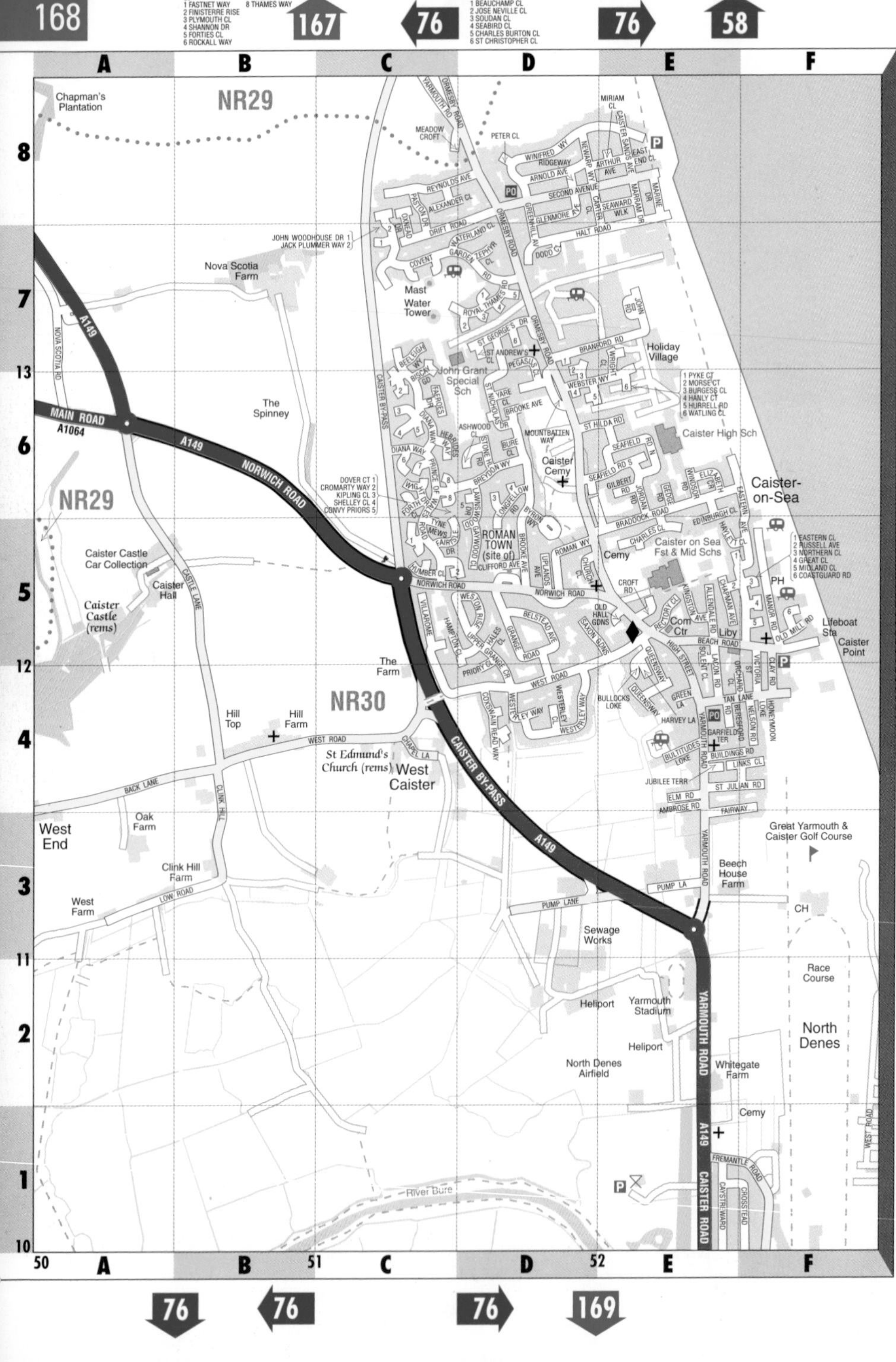

C6
1 FASTNET WAY
2 FINISTERRE RISE
3 PLYMOUTH CL
4 SHANNON DR
5 FORTIES CL
6 ROCKALL WAY
7 MALIN CT
8 THAMES WAY
167
76
D7
1 BEAUCHAMP CL
2 JOSE NEVILLE CL
3 SOUDAN CL
4 SEABIRD CL
5 CHARLES BURTON CL
6 ST CHRISTOPHER CL
76
58
NR29
Chapman's Plantation
Nova Scotia Farm
Mast
Water Tower
John Grant Special Sch
The Spinney
MAIN ROAD
A1064
A149
NORWICH ROAD
Caister Castle Car Collection
Caister Hall
Caister Castle (rems)
CASTLE LANE
The Farm
NR30
Hill Top
Hill Farm
WEST ROAD
St Edmund's Church (rems)
West Caister
BACK LANE
CLINK HILL
Oak Farm
West End
Clink Hill Farm
LOW ROAD
West Farm
CAISTER BY-PASS
PUMP LANE
PUMP LA
Sewage Works
Heliport
Yarmouth Stadium
North Denes Airfield
YARMOUTH ROAD
CAISTER ROAD
Whitegate Farm
Cemy
FREMANTLE ROAD
CROSSTEAD
CAYSTRI WARD
River Bure
Beech House Farm
Great Yarmouth & Caister Golf Course
CH
Race Course
North Denes
WEST ROAD
Holiday Village
1 PYKE CT
2 MORSE CT
3 BURGESS CL
4 HANLY CT
5 HURRELL RD
6 WATLING CL
Caister High Sch
Caister Cemy
Caister-on-Sea
ROMAN TOWN (site of)
Caister on Sea Fst & Mid Schs
1 EASTERN CL
2 RUSSELL AVE
3 NORTHERN CL
4 GREAT CL
5 MIDLAND CL
6 COASTGUARD RD
PH
Lifeboat Sta
Caister Point
Com Ctr
Liby
DOVER CT 1
CROMARTY WAY 2
KIPLING CL 3
SHELLEY CL 4
CONVY PRIORS 5
JOHN WOODHOUSE DR 1
JACK PLUMMER WAY 2
MEADOW CROFT
PETER CL
MIRIAM CL
WINIFRED WY
RIDGEWAY
ARNOLD AVE
SECOND AVENUE
REYNOLDS AVE
ALEXANDER CL
DRIFT ROAD
GLENMORE AVE
HALT ROAD
SEAWARD WLK
MARRAM DR
MARINE DR
ORMESBY ROAD
BRANFORD RD
WEBSTER WY
ST HILDA RD
SEAFIELD RD
GILBERT RD
BRADDOCK ROAD
EDINBURGH CL
CHARLES CL
ROMAN WY
NORWICH ROAD
BEACH ROAD
HIGH STREET
QUEENSWAY
BULLOCKS LOKE
HARVEY LA
GREEN LA
TAN LANE
BUILDINGS RD
LINKS CL
ST JULIAN RD
ELM RD
AMBROSE RD
FAIRWAY
JUBILEE TERR
BULTITUDES LOKE
GARFIELD TER
WEST ROAD
WESTERLEY WAY
COTSWAIN ROAD WAY
PRIORY CL
HAMPTON CL
VILLAROME
BELSTEAD AVE
OLD HALL GDNS
SAXON GDNS
CROFT RD
OLD MILL RD
MANOR RD
CLAY RD
HONEYMOON LOKE
50
51
52
A
B
C
D
E
F
8
7
13
6
5
12
4
3
11
2
1
10
76
76
76
169

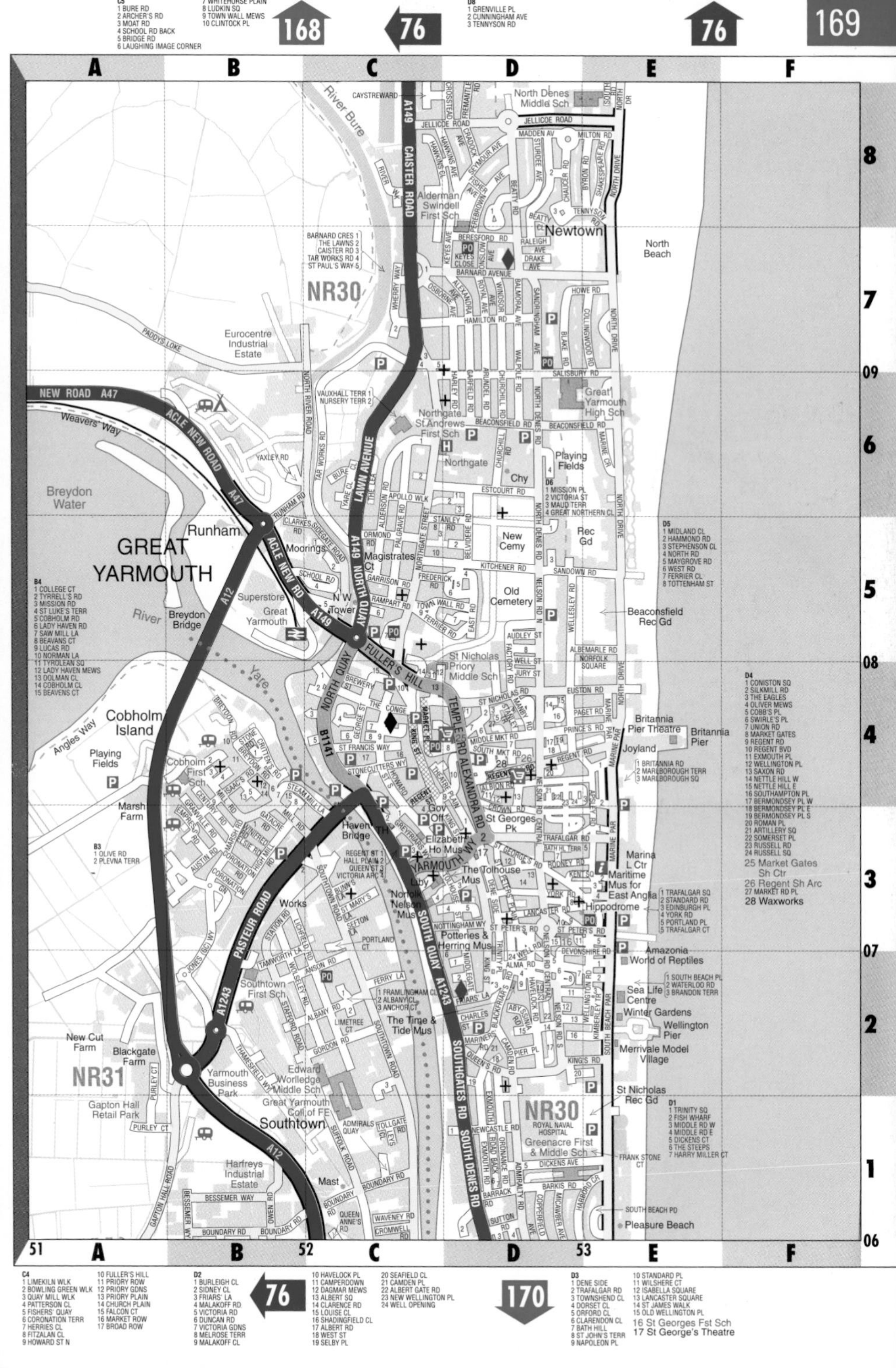
C5
1 BURE RD
2 ARCHER'S RD
3 MOAT RD
4 SCHOOL RD BACK
5 BRIDGE RD
6 LAUGHING IMAGE CORNER
7 WHITEHORSE PLAIN
8 LUDKIN SQ
9 TOWN WALL MEWS
10 CLINTOCK PL
168
76
D8
1 GRENVILLE PL
2 CUNNINGHAM AVE
3 TENNYSON RD
76
A
B
C
D
E
F
8
7
09
6
5
08
4
3
07
2
1
06
51
52
53
River Bure
CAYSTREWARD
CAISTER ROAD
A149
JELLICOE ROAD
North Denes Middle Sch
Alderman Swindell First Sch
Newtown
North Beach
BARNARD CRES 1
THE LAWNS 2
CAISTER RD 3
TAR WORKS RD 4
ST PAUL'S WAY 5
NR30
BARNARD AVENUE
HAMILTON RD
SALISBURY RD
PADDYS LOKE
Eurocentre Industrial Estate
NEW ROAD A47
ACLE NEW ROAD
Weavers' Way
Great Yarmouth High Sch
VAUXHALL TERR 1
NURSERY TERR 2
Northgate St Andrews First Sch
BEACONSFIELD RD
Northgate
Playing Fields
Chy
LAWN AVENUE
Breydon Water
Runham
GREAT YARMOUTH
Moorings
Magistrates Ct
New Cemy
Rec Gd
Old Cemetery
Superstore
Great Yarmouth
N W Tower
Breydon Bridge
River
Yare
A12
A149 NORTH QUAY
FULLER'S HILL
St Nicholas Priory Middle Sch
Beaconsfield Rec Gd
B4
1 COLLEGE CT
2 TYRRELL'S RD
3 MISSION RD
4 ST LUKE'S TERR
5 COBHOLM RD
6 LADY HAVEN RD
7 SAW MILL LA
8 BEAVANS CT
9 LUCAS RD
10 NORMAN LA
11 TYROLEAN SQ
12 LADY HAVEN MEWS
13 DOLMAN CL
14 COBHOLM CL
15 BEAVENS CT
D6
1 MISSION PL
2 VICTORIA ST
3 MAUD TERR
4 GREAT NORTHERN CL
D5
1 MIDLAND CL
2 HAMMOND RD
3 STEPHENSON CL
4 NORTH RD
5 MAYGROVE RD
6 WEST RD
7 FERRIER CL
8 TOTTENHAM ST
D4
1 CONISTON SQ
2 SILKMILL RD
3 THE EAGLES
4 OLIVER MEWS
5 COBB'S PL
6 SWIRLE'S PL
7 UNION RD
8 MARKET GATES
9 REGENT RD
10 REGENT BVD
11 EXMOUTH PL
12 WELLINGTON PL
13 SAXON RD
14 NETTLE HILL W
15 NETTLE HILL E
16 SOUTHAMPTON PL
17 BERMONDSEY PL W
18 BERMONDSEY PL E
19 BERMONDSEY PL S
20 ROMAN PL
21 ARTILLERY SQ
22 SOMERSET PL
23 RUSSELL RD
24 RUSSELL SQ
25 Market Gates Sh Ctr
26 Regent Sh Arc
27 MARKET RD PL
28 Waxworks
Cobholm Island
Angles Way
Playing Fields
Cobholm First Sch
Marsh Farm
B3
1 OLIVE RD
2 PLEVNA TERR
Britannia Pier Theatre
Britannia Pier
Joyland
1 BRITANNIA RD
2 MARLBOROUGH TERR
3 MARLBOROUGH SQ
B1141
TEMPLE RD
ALEXANDRA RD
St Georges Pk
Haven Bridge
Gov Off
Elizabeth Ho Mus
YARMOUTH WY
The Tolhouse Mus
Lby
Norfolk Nelson Mus
REGENT ST 1
HALL PLAIN 2
QUEEN ST 3
VICTORIA ARC 4
Marina L Ctr
Maritime Mus for East Anglia
Hippodrome
1 TRAFALGAR SQ
2 STANDARD RD
3 EDINBURGH PL
4 YORK RD
5 PORTLAND PL
6 TRAFALGAR CT
Works
PASTEUR ROAD
SOUTH QUAY
A1243
Potteries & Herring Mus
Amazonia World of Reptiles
Sea Life Centre
1 SOUTH BEACH PL
2 WATERLOO RD
3 BRANDON TERR
Winter Gardens
Wellington Pier
Southtown First Sch
1 FRAMLINGHAM CL
2 ALBANY CL
3 ANCHOR CT
The Time & Tide Mus
Merrivale Model Village
New Cut Farm
Blackgate Farm
NR31
Yarmouth Business Park
Edward Worlledge Middle Sch
Great Yarmouth Coll of FE
Southtown
Gapton Hall Retail Park
SOUTHGATES RD
SOUTH DENES RD
St Nicholas Rec Gd
NR30
ROYAL NAVAL HOSPITAL
Greenacre First & Middle Sch
FRANK STONE CT
D1
1 TRINITY SQ
2 FISH WHARF
3 MIDDLE RD W
4 MIDDLE RD E
5 DICKENS CT
6 THE STEEPS
7 HARRY MILLER CT
Harfreys Industrial Estate
Mast
BESSEMER WAY
BOUNDARY RD
SOUTH BEACH PD
Pleasure Beach
C4
1 LIMEKILN WLK
2 BOWLING GREEN WLK
3 QUAY MILL WLK
4 PATTERSON CL
5 FISHERS' QUAY
6 CORONATION TERR
7 HERRIES CL
8 FITZALAN CL
9 HOWARD ST N
10 FULLER'S HILL
11 PRIORY ROW
12 PRIORY GDNS
13 PRIORY PLAIN
14 CHURCH PLAIN
15 FALCON CT
16 MARKET ROW
17 BROAD ROW
D2
1 BURLEIGH CL
2 SIDNEY CL
3 FRIARS' LA
4 MALAKOFF RD
5 VICTORIA RD
6 DUNCAN RD
7 VICTORIA GDNS
8 MELROSE TERR
9 MALAKOFF CL
76
10 HAVELOCK PL
11 CAMPERDOWN
12 DAGMAR MEWS
13 ALBERT SQ
14 CLARENCE RD
15 LOUISE CL
16 SHADINGFIELD CL
17 ALBERT RD
18 WEST ST
19 SELBY PL
20 SEAFIELD CL
21 CAMDEN PL
22 ALBERT GATE RD
23 NEW WELLINGTON PL
24 WELL OPENING
170
D3
1 DENE SIDE
2 TRAFALGAR RD
3 TOWNSHEND CL
4 DORSET CL
5 ORFORD CL
6 CLARENDON CL
7 BATH HILL
8 ST JOHN'S TERR
9 NAPOLEON PL
10 STANDARD PL
11 WILSHERE CT
12 ISABELLA SQUARE
13 LANCASTER SQUARE
14 ST JAMES WALK
15 OLD WELLINGTON PL
16 St Georges Fst Sch
17 St George's Theatre

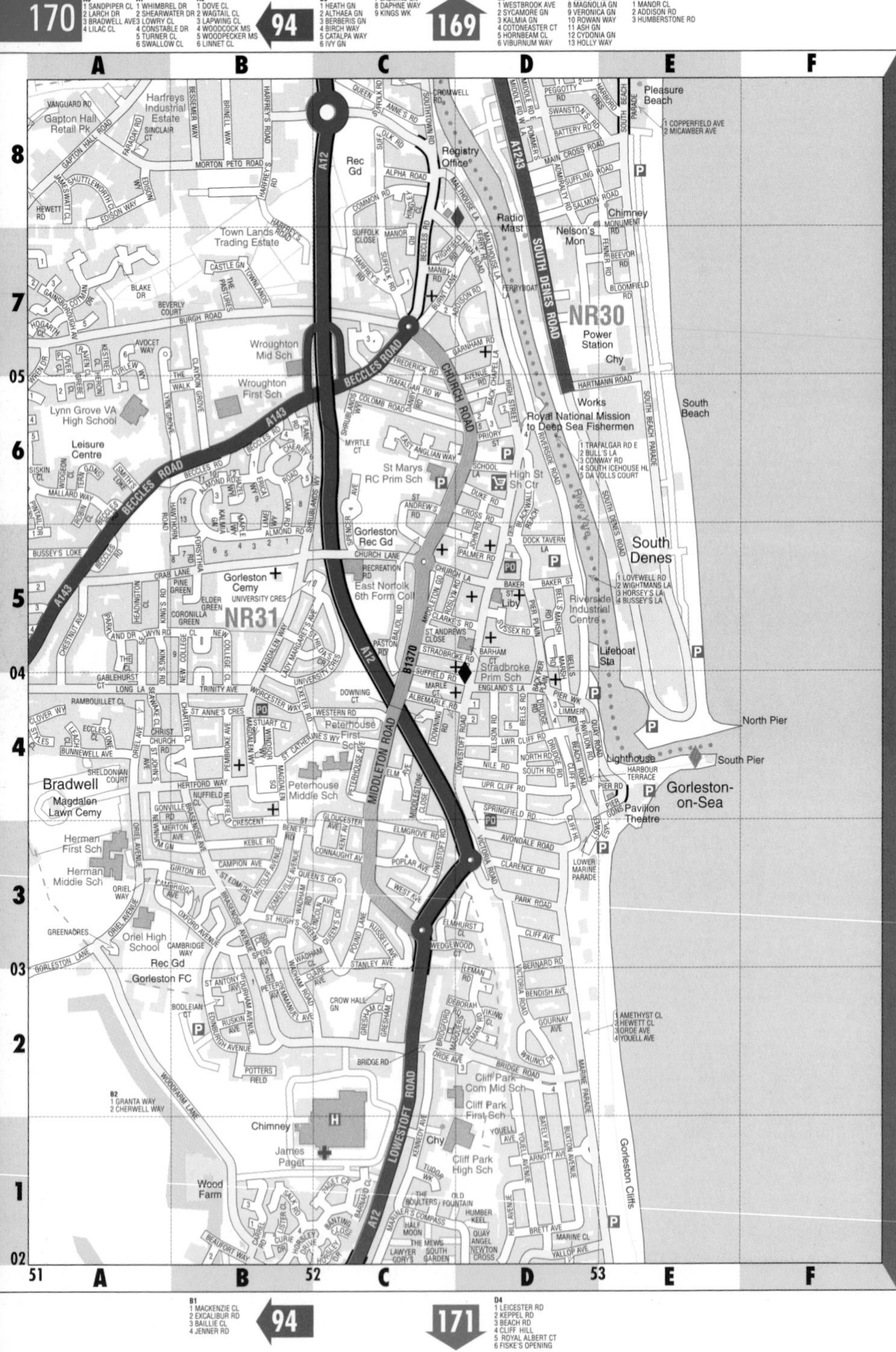

A   B   C   D   E   F

HORSLEY DR

Hobland
Plantation   Mast

The Bungalow
Hobland Farm

HOBLAND ROAD

Oakland
Farm

QUAY
OSTEND

MARINER'S COMP
MARINE CL
MARINE'S CL
VALLON
MARINE CL
CLIFF LA
LINKS
RD
MARINE
PARADE

LINKS ROAD

CH

WARREN LOW

Masons
Farm

Kennel
Farm

Gorleston
Golf Course

Sidegate
Farm

LOWESTOFT ROAD

A12

Long
Belt

Corton
Cliffs

Valley
Farm

NR31

01

DS
1 RANDALL CL
2 ST MARGARET'S WAY
3 ANGLIAN WAY
4 GROOMES CL
5 BISHOPS WK
6 ST CLARE CT
7 ST CLEMENT MEWS

Hopton
on Sea

HALL ROAD

Sawmill

White House
Farm

RACKHAM CL

LOWESTOFT ROAD

FLOWERDAY CL

ROGER'S CL

WHITTED

HOPTON DR

MARINER

ST VINCENT
WK

Holiday
Village

WARREN ROAD

Reservoir

PO
HALL
RD

A12

PH

STATION ROAD

Hopton First
Sch

ST ANDREW CL
BARN CL

PH

WARREN RD

Bloodman's
Corner

Homeclose
Shrubbery

IMPERIAL MEWS

SEAFIELDS DR

IVES

SEAVIEW DRIVE

Hopton First
Sch

CASTO
WAY

PEBBLE VW WK

DORMY ROAD

YARMOUTH ROAD

LOWESTOFT ROAD

St Margaret's
Church (rems)

OLD CHURCH RD

MANOR
RD

SEA NEW RISE

BEACH ROAD

League
Hole

BACK LANE

Home
Farm

Holiday & Leisure
Centre

Cuckoo
Green

Cuckoo Green
Farm

Elder
Farm

DORLING ROAD

Home
Farm

Oak View
Farm

LONG FULANS LANE

COAST ROAD

JAY LANE

Beehive
Farm

CHURCH LANE

Lothingland
Middle Sch

Hall
Farm

Elm
Farm

NR32

99

Fourways
Farm

Rector's
Wood

Great
Wood

Brickhill
Wood

Corton
Cliffs

YARMOUTH ROAD

A12

Red House
Farm

MARKET LANE

Woburn
Mast   Farm

COAST ROAD

CHURCH LA

STIRRUPS LANE

51   A   B   52   C   D   53   E   F   98

8   7   6   5   4   3   2   1

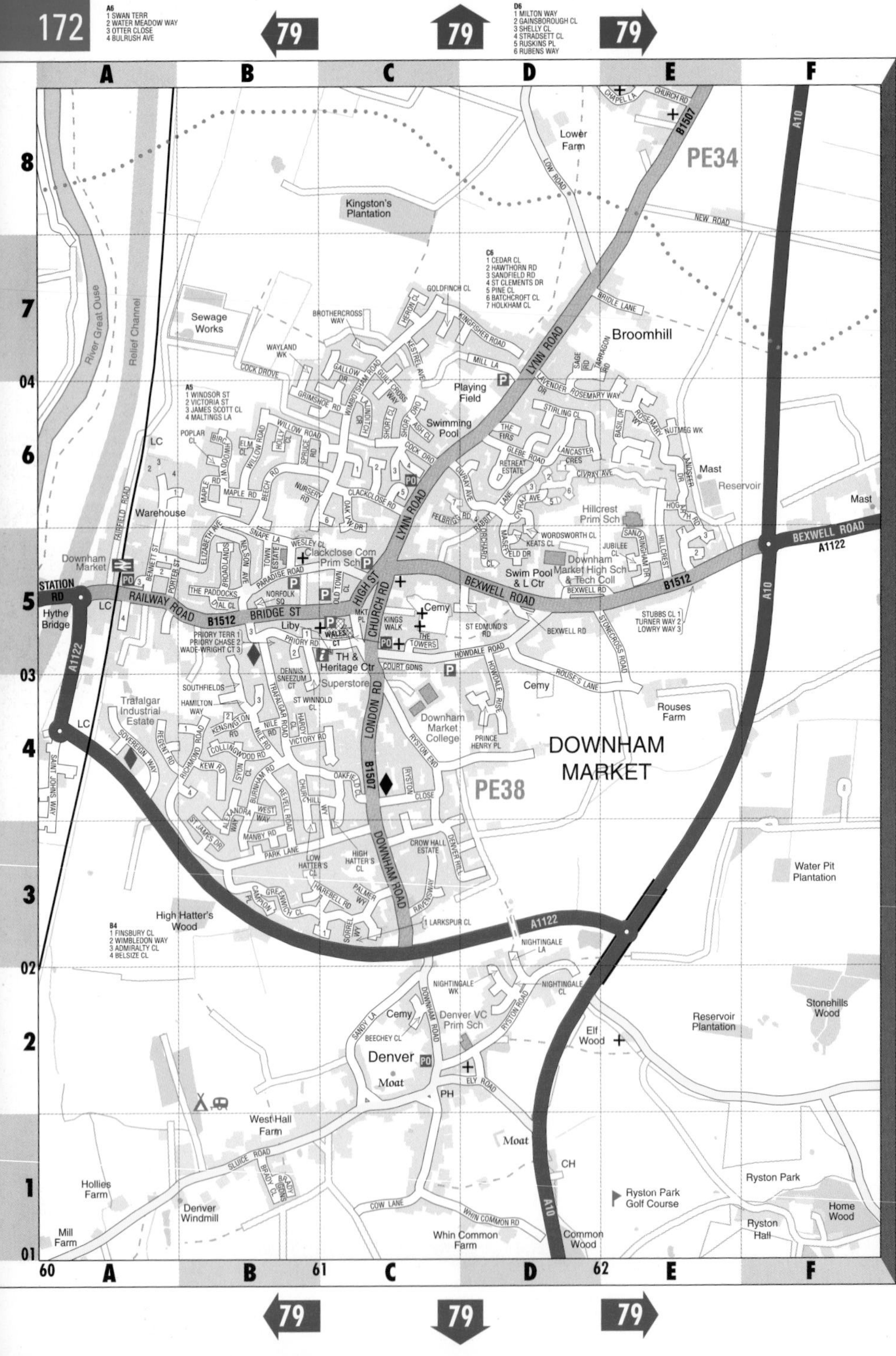
A6
1 SWAN TERR
2 WATER MEADOW WAY
3 OTTER CLOSE
4 BULRUSH AVE
79
79
D6
1 MILTON WAY
2 GAINSBOROUGH CL
3 SHELLY CL
4 STRADSETT CL
5 RUSKINS PL
6 RUBENS WAY
79
A
B
C
D
E
F
8
7
04
6
5
03
4
3
02
2
1
01
60
61
62
PE34
PE38
DOWNHAM MARKET
Lower Farm
Kingston's Plantation
NEW ROAD
LOW ROAD
CHAPEL LA
CHURCH RD
B1507
A10
C6
1 CEDAR CL
2 HAWTHORN RD
3 SANDFIELD RD
4 ST CLEMENTS DR
5 PINE CL
6 BATCHCROFT CL
7 HOLKHAM CL
River Great Ouse
Relief Channel
Sewage Works
GOLDFINCH CL
BROTHERCROSS WAY
HERON CL
KINGFISHER ROAD
BRIDLE LANE
Broomhill
WAYLAND WK
COCK DROVE
GALLOW DR
KESTREL AVE
MILL LA
LYNN ROAD
SAGE RD
TARRAGON RD
A5
1 WINDSOR ST
2 VICTORIA ST
3 JAMES SCOTT CL
4 MALTINGS LA
GRIMSHOE RD
WIMBOTSHAM ROAD
GUILDCROSS WAY
Playing Field
LAVENDER DR
ROSEMARY WAY
Swimming Pool
STIRLING CL
BASIL DR
NUTMEG WK
POPLAR CL
WILLOW ROAD
ELM CL
SPRUCE RD
SHORT CL
SHORT DRO
ASH CL
THE FIRS
GLEBE ROAD
LANCASTER CRES
LC
RETREAT ESTATE
COCK DRO
Mast
Reservoir
MAPLE RD
BEECH RD
NURSERY RD
CLACKCLOSE RD
CIVRAY AVE
LANDSEER DR
Warehouse
FAIRFIELD ROAD
OAK VW DR
FELBRIGG RD
RABBIT LANE
HOGARTH RD
Hillcrest Prim Sch
Mast
ELIZABETH AVE
SNAPE LA
WESLEY CL
WORDSWORTH CL
KEATS CL
JUBILEE CL
SANDRINGHAM DR
HILLCREST
BEXWELL ROAD
A1122
Downham Market
BENNETT ST
PORTER ST
BROADLANDS
NELSON AVE
TOWN ESTATE
Clackclose Com Prim Sch
ORCHARD CL
MASEFIELD DR
Downham Market High Sch & Tech Coll
Swim Pool & L Ctr
PARADISE ROAD
OLD TOWN CL
HIGH ST
CHURCH RD
STATION RD
THE PADDOCKS
NORFOLK SQ
BEXWELL RD
B1512
Hythe Bridge
RAILWAY ROAD
DIAL CL
BRIDGE ST
B1512
MKT PL
Cemy
STUBBS CL 1
TURNER WAY 2
LOWRY WAY 3
Liby
KINGS WALK
ST EDMUND'S RD
BEXWELL RD
PRIORY TERR 1
PRIORY CHASE 2
WADE-WRIGHT CT 3
PRIORY RD
WALES CT
THE TOWERS
HOWDALE ROAD
STONECROSS ROAD
TH & Heritage Ctr
COURT GDNS
ROUSE'S LANE
A1122
DENNIS SNEEZUM CT
Superstore
SOUTHFIELDS
Cemy
HOWDALE RISE
Rouses Farm
Trafalgar Industrial Estate
HAMILTON WAY
TRAFALGAR ROAD
ST WINNOLD CL
Downham Market College
LC
KENSINGTON RD
NILE RD
HARDY CL
VICTORY RD
LONDON RD
RYSTON END
PRINCE HENRY PL
SOVEREIGN WAY
REGENT RD
COLLINGWOOD RD
SAINT JOHNS WAY
RICHMOND ROAD
KEW RD
OAKFIELD CL
RYSTON CLOSE
BURNHAM RD
REVELL ROAD
CHURCH HILL WY
ALEXANDRA WAY
WEST WAY
ST JAMES DR
MANBY RD
PARK LANE
CROW HALL ESTATE
DENVER HILL
LOW HATTER'S CL
HIGH HATTER'S CL
DOWNHAM ROAD
Water Pit Plantation
High Hatter's Wood
CAMPION PL
GREENWICH CL
HAREBELL RD
PALMER WY
RAVENSWAY
1 LARKSPUR CL
SORREL WY
B4
1 FINSBURY CL
2 WIMBLEDON WAY
3 ADMIRALTY CL
4 BELSIZE CL
NIGHTINGALE LA
NIGHTINGALE WK
NIGHTINGALE CL
Stonehills Wood
Cemy
Denver VC Prim Sch
SANDY LA
RYSTON ROAD
Reservoir Plantation
BEECHEY CL
Elf Wood
Denver
Moat
ELY ROAD
PH
West Hall Farm
Moat
SLUICE ROAD
BRADY CL
BRADY GDNS
CH
Hollies Farm
Ryston Park
Ryston Park Golf Course
Denver Windmill
COW LANE
WHIN COMMON RD
Ryston Hall
Home Wood
Mill Farm
Whin Common Farm
Common Wood
79
79
79

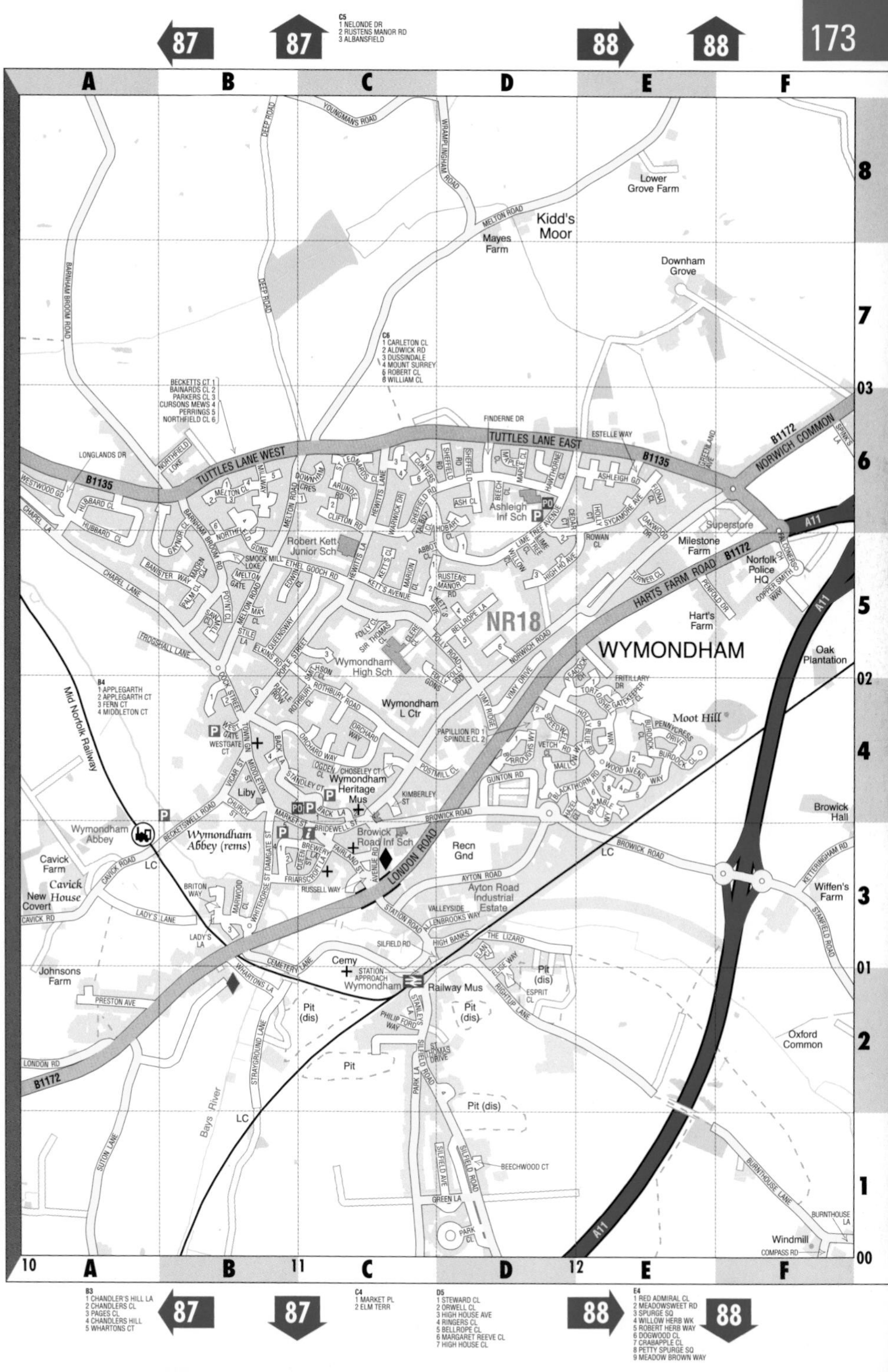
87
87
C5
1 NELONDE DR
2 RUSTENS MANOR RD
3 ALBANSFIELD
88
88
Lower Grove Farm
Kidd's Moor
Mayes Farm
Downham Grove
C6
1 CARLETON CL
2 ALDWICK RD
3 DUSSINDALE
4 MOUNT SURREY
6 ROBERT CL
8 WILLIAM CL
BECKETTS CT 1
BAINARDS CL 2
PARKERS CL 3
CURSONS MEWS 4
PERRINGS 5
NORTHFIELD CL 6
TUTTLES LANE WEST
TUTTLES LANE EAST
B1135
B1172
NORWICH COMMON
A11
Ashleigh Inf Sch
Robert Kett Junior Sch
Superstore
Milestone Farm
Norfolk Police HQ
HARTS FARM ROAD
Hart's Farm
NR18
WYMONDHAM
Oak Plantation
Wymondham High Sch
Wymondham L Ctr
B4
1 APPLEGARTH
2 APPLEGARTH CT
3 FERN CT
4 MIDDLETON CT
Mid Norfolk Railway
Moot Hill
Wymondham Heritage Mus
Liby
Browick Hall
Wymondham Abbey
Wymondham Abbey (rems)
Browick Road Inf Sch
Recn Gnd
Cavick Farm
Cavick House
New Covert
Ayton Road Industrial Estate
Wiffen's Farm
LONDON ROAD
Cemy
Wymondham
Railway Mus
Johnsons Farm
Pit (dis)
Pit
Oxford Common
Pit (dis)
Bays River
BEECHWOOD CT
Windmill
COMPASS RD
A
B
C
D
E
F
8
7
6
5
4
3
2
1
03
02
01
00
10
11
12
B3
1 CHANDLER'S HILL LA
2 CHANDLERS CL
3 PAGES CL
4 CHANDLERS HILL
5 WHARTONS CT
C4
1 MARKET PL
2 ELM TERR
D5
1 STEWARD CL
2 ORWELL CL
3 HIGH HOUSE AVE
4 RINGERS CL
5 BELLROPE CL
6 MARGARET REEVE CL
7 HIGH HOUSE CL
E4
1 RED ADMIRAL CL
2 MEADOWSWEET RD
3 SPURGE SQ
4 WILLOW HERB WK
5 ROBERT HERB WAY
6 DOGWOOD CL
7 CRABAPPLE CL
8 PETTY SPURGE SQ
9 MEADOW BROWN WAY
87
87
88
88

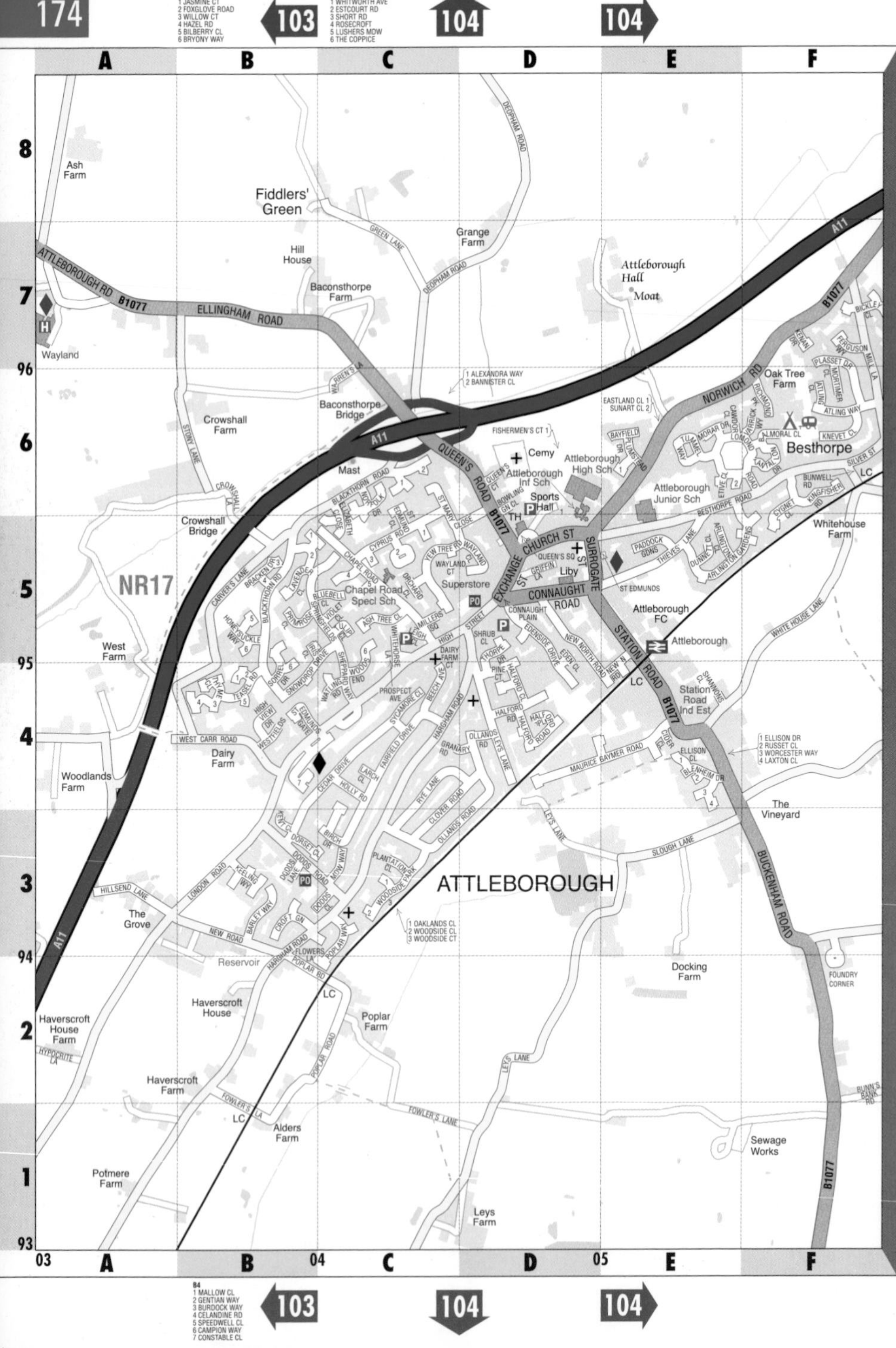

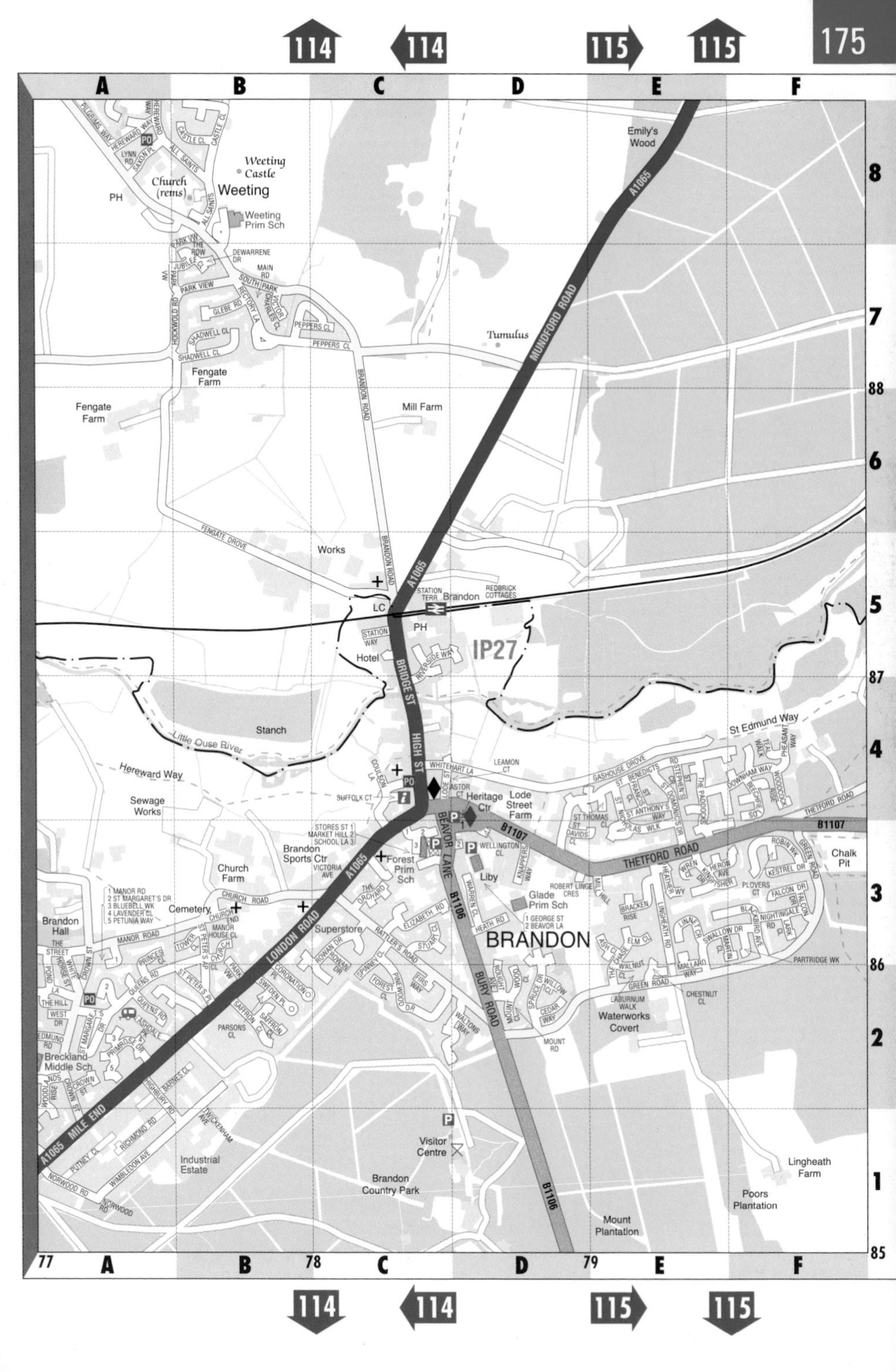
114
114
115
115
A
B
C
D
E
F
8
7
88
6
5
87
4
3
86
2
1
85
77
78
79
Weeting
Weeting Castle
Church (rems)
Weeting Prim Sch
PH
Emily's Wood
MUNDFORD ROAD
A1065
Tumulus
Fengate Farm
Mill Farm
Works
Brandon
LC
PH
Hotel
IP27
BRIDGE ST
HIGH ST
Stanch
Little Ouse River
Hereward Way
St Edmund Way
Sewage Works
Heritage Ctr
Lode Street Farm
THETFORD ROAD
B1107
Chalk Pit
Brandon Sports Ctr
Forest Prim Sch
Church Farm
Cemetery
Liby
Glade Prim Sch
BRANDON
Brandon Hall
Superstore
LONDON ROAD
BURY ROAD
B1106
Waterworks Covert
Breckland Middle Sch
Industrial Estate
Visitor Centre
Brandon Country Park
Mount Plantation
Poors Plantation
Lingheath Farm
A1065 MILE END
114
114
115
115

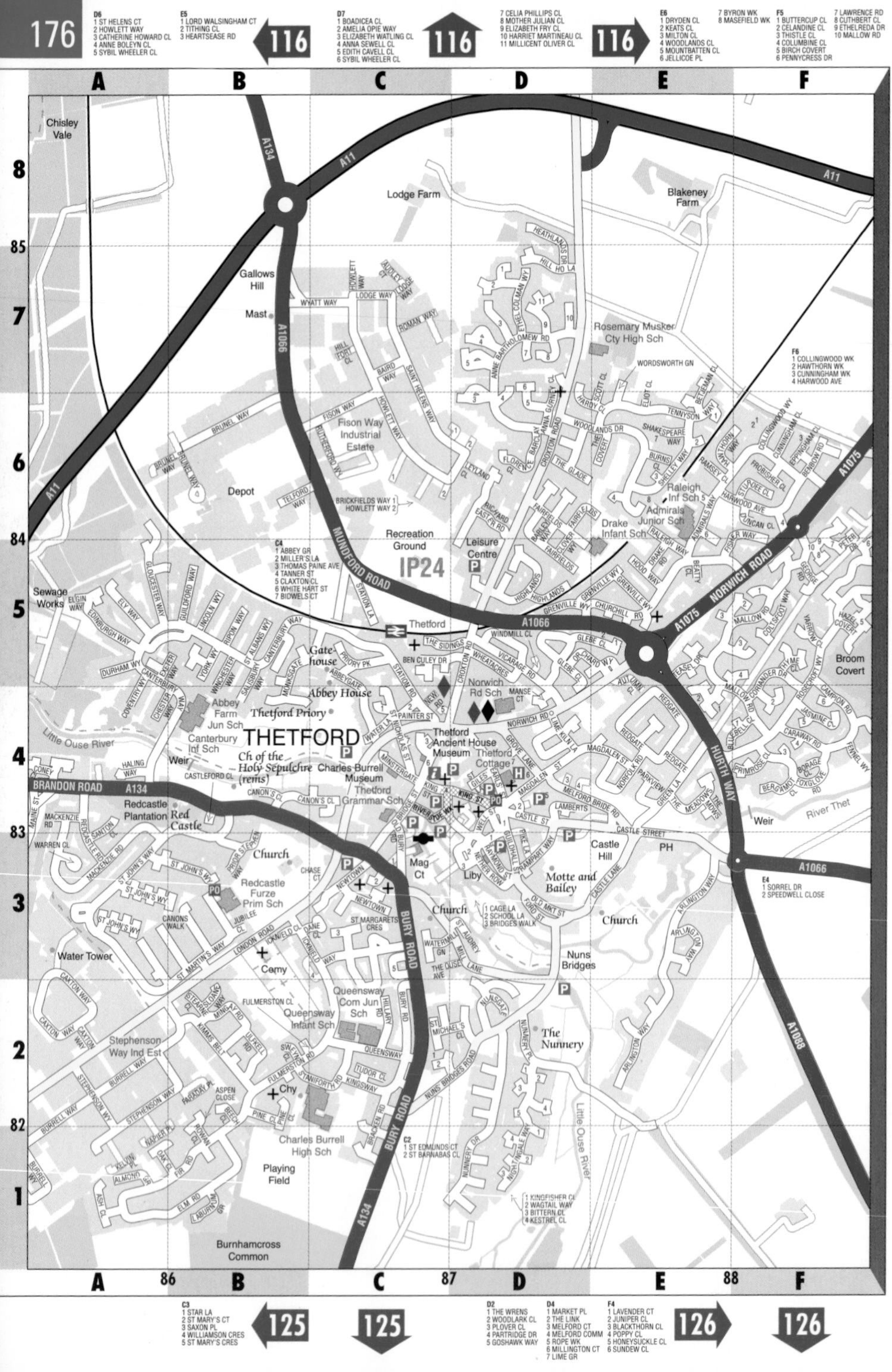

D6
1 ST HELENS CT
2 HOWLETT WAY
3 CATHERINE HOWARD CL
4 ANNE BOLEYN CL
5 SYBIL WHEELER CL

E5
1 LORD WALSINGHAM CT
2 TITHING CL
3 HEARTSEASE RD

116 ◄

D7
1 BOADICEA CL
2 AMELIA OPIE WAY
3 ELIZABETH WATLING CL
4 EDITH CAVELL CL
5 SYBIL WHEELER CL

116 ▲

7 CELIA PHILLIPS CL
8 MOTHER JULIAN CL
9 ELIZABETH FRY CL
10 HARRIET MARTINEAU CL
11 MILLICENT OLIVER CL

116 ▲

E6
1 DRYDEN CL
2 KEATS CL
3 MILTON CL
4 WOODLANDS CL
5 MOUNTBATTEN CL
6 JELLICOE PL

7 BYRON WK
8 MASEFIELD WK

F5
1 BUTTERCUP CL
2 CELANDINE CL
3 THISTLE CL
4 COLUMBINE CL
5 BIRCH COVERT
6 PENNYCRESS DR

7 LAWRENCE RD
8 CUTHBERT CL
9 ETHELREDA DR
10 MALLOW RD

C3
1 STAR LA
2 ST MARY'S CT
3 SAXON PL
4 WILLIAMSON CRES
5 ST MARY'S CRES

125 ▼   **125** ▼

D2
1 THE WRENS
2 WOODLARK CL
3 PLOVER CL
4 PARTRIDGE DR
5 GOSHAWK WAY

D4
1 MARKET PL
2 THE LINK
3 MELFORD CT
4 MELFORD COMM
5 ROPE WK
6 MILLINGTON CT
7 LIME GR

F4
1 LAVENDER CT
2 JUNIPER CL
3 BLACKTHORN CL
4 POPPY CL
5 HONEYSUCKLE CL
6 SUNDEW CL

126 ▼   **126** ▼

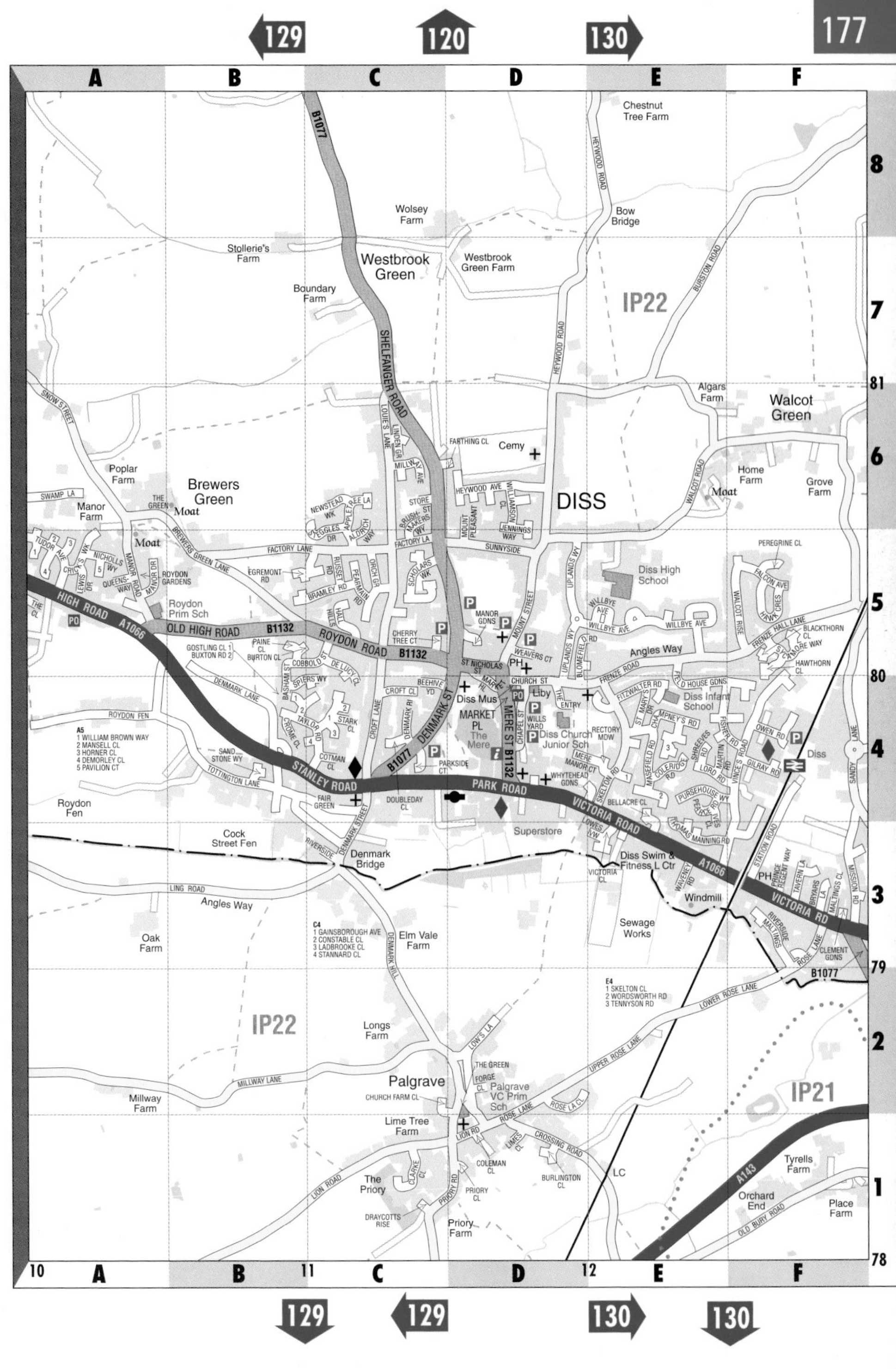

129
120
130
DISS
Westbrook Green
Brewers Green
Walcot Green
Palgrave
IP22
IP21
Chestnut Tree Farm
Wolsey Farm
Bow Bridge
Stollerie's Farm
Westbrook Green Farm
Boundary Farm
Algars Farm
Poplar Farm
Manor Farm
Home Farm
Grove Farm
Diss High School
Roydon Prim Sch
Diss Infant School
Diss Church Junior Sch
Diss Mus
MARKET PL
The Mere
Superstore
Diss Swim & Fitness L Ctr
Windmill
Sewage Works
Roydon Fen
Cock Street Fen
Denmark Bridge
Oak Farm
Elm Vale Farm
Longs Farm
Millway Farm
Lime Tree Farm
The Priory
Priory Farm
Palgrave VC Prim Sch
Tyrells Farm
Orchard End
Place Farm
A5
1 WILLIAM BROWN WAY
2 MANSELL CL
3 HORNER CL
4 DEMORLEY CL
5 PAVILION CT
C4
1 GAINSBOROUGH AVE
2 CONSTABLE CL
3 LADBROOKE CL
4 STANNARD CL
E4
1 SKELTON CL
2 WORDSWORTH RD
3 TENNYSON RD
HIGH ROAD A1066
OLD HIGH ROAD B1132
ROYDON ROAD B1132
STANLEY ROAD
PARK ROAD
VICTORIA ROAD
VICTORIA RD
SHELFANGER ROAD
DENMARK ST
MERE ST B1132
HEYWOOD ROAD
BURSTON ROAD
WALCOT ROAD
FRENZE ROAD
LOWER ROSE LANE
UPPER ROSE LANE
ROSE LANE
LION ROAD
CROSSING ROAD
MILLWAY LANE
LING ROAD
Angles Way
A143
B1077
10
11
12
78
79
80
81

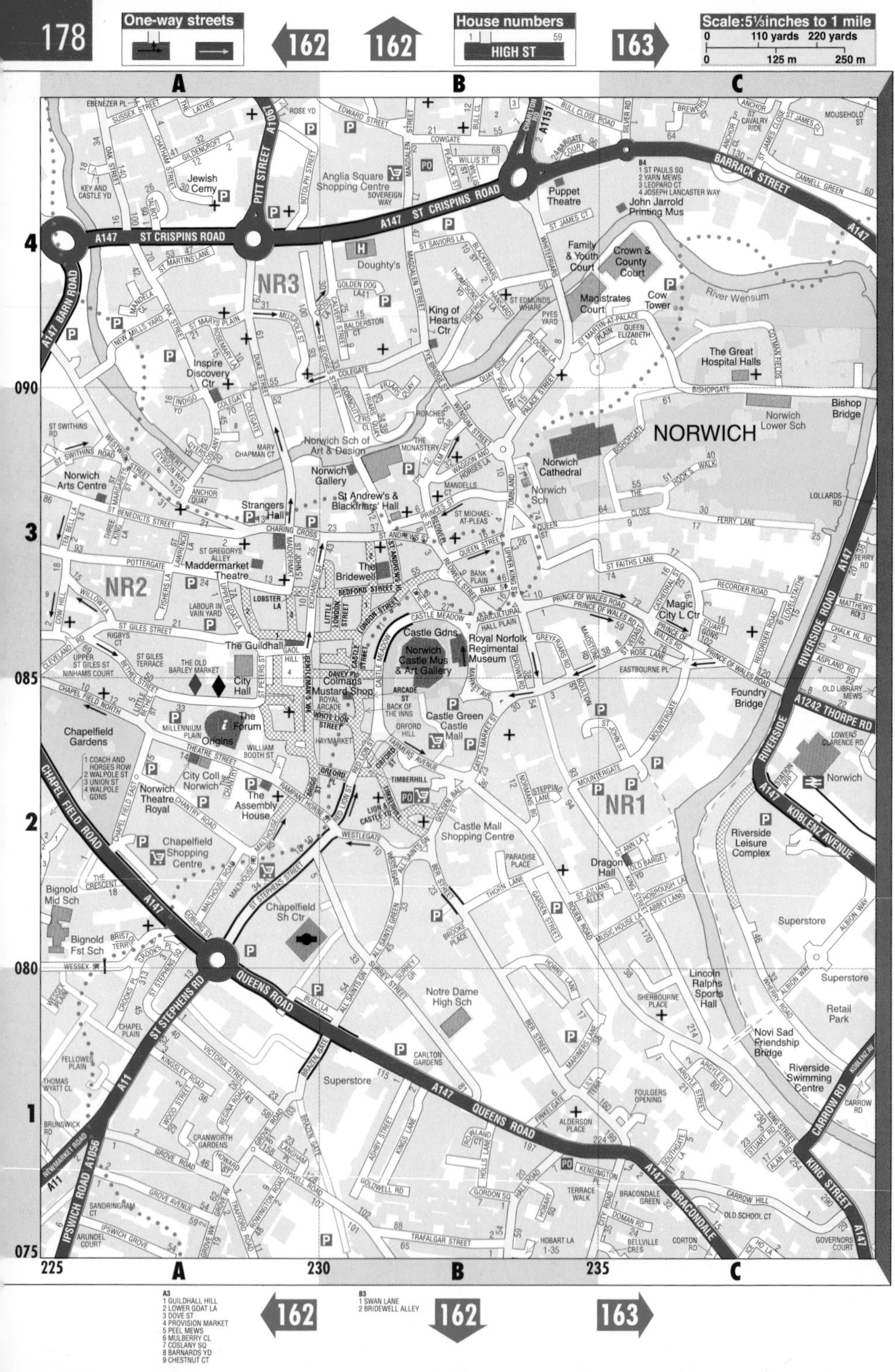

178
One-way streets
162
162
House numbers
HIGH ST
163
Scale: 5½ inches to 1 mile
110 yards
220 yards
125 m
250 m
A
B
C
NORWICH
NR1
NR2
NR3
A147 ST CRISPINS ROAD
PITT STREET
A1151
BARRACK STREET
A147 BARN ROAD
Jewish Cemy
Anglia Square Shopping Centre
Doughty's
Puppet Theatre
John Jarrold Printing Mus
Family & Youth Court
Crown & County Court
Magistrates Court
Cow Tower
River Wensum
King of Hearts Ctr
The Great Hospital Halls
Inspire Discovery Ctr
BISHOPGATE
Bishop Bridge
Norwich Lower Sch
Norwich Sch of Art & Design
Norwich Gallery
Norwich Cathedral
Norwich Sch
Norwich Arts Centre
Strangers Hall
St Andrew's & Blackfriars' Hall
Maddermarket Theatre
The Bridewell
Magic City L Ctr
PRINCE OF WALES ROAD
RIVERSIDE ROAD
Castle Gdns
Norwich Castle Mus & Art Gallery
Royal Norfolk Regimental Museum
The Guildhall
City Hall
Colmans Mustard Shop
Castle Green Castle Mall
Foundry Bridge
A1242 THORPE RD
Chapelfield Gardens
The Forum
Origins
City Coll Norwich
Norwich Theatre Royal
The Assembly House
Castle Mall Shopping Centre
Norwich
Chapelfield Shopping Centre
Riverside Leisure Complex
CHAPEL FIELD ROAD
A147 KOBLENZ AVENUE
Dragon Hall
Bignold Mid Sch
Bignold Fst Sch
Chapelfield Sh Ctr
Superstore
QUEENS ROAD
Notre Dame High Sch
Lincoln Ralphs Sports Hall
Retail Park
Novi Sad Friendship Bridge
Riverside Swimming Centre
CARROW RD
KING STREET
A147 BRACONDALE
A11 ST STEPHENS RD
IPSWICH ROAD A1056
NEWMARKET ROAD
225
230
235
090
085
080
075
4
3
2
1
A3
1 GUILDHALL HILL
2 LOWER GOAT LA
3 DOVE ST
4 PROVISION MARKET
5 PEEL MEWS
6 MULBERRY CL
7 COSLANY SQ
8 BARNARDS YD
9 CHESTNUT CT
B3
1 SWAN LANE
2 BRIDEWELL ALLEY
B4
1 ST PAULS SQ
2 YARN MEWS
3 LEOPARD CT
4 JOSEPH LANCASTER WAY
162
162
163

Index

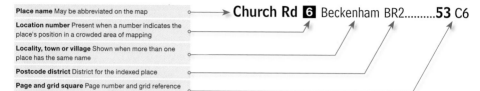

Place name May be abbreviated on the map

Location number Present when a number indicates the place's position in a crowded area of mapping

Locality, town or village Shown when more than one place has the same name

Postcode district District for the indexed place

Page and grid square Page number and grid reference for the standard mapping

Church Rd **6** Beckenham BR2........**53** C6

Public and commercial buildings are highlighted in magenta   Places of interest are highlighted in blue with a star★

Abbreviations used in the index

Acad	**Academy**	Comm	**Common**	Gd	**Ground**	L	**Leisure**
App	**Approach**	Cott	**Cottage**	Gdn	**Garden**	La	**Lane**
Arc	**Arcade**	Cres	**Crescent**	Gn	**Green**	Liby	**Library**
Ave	**Avenue**	Cswy	**Causeway**	Gr	**Grove**	Mdw	**Meadow**
Bglw	**Bungalow**	Ct	**Court**	H	**Hall**	Meml	**Memorial**
Bldg	**Building**	Ctr	**Centre**	Ho	**House**	Mkt	**Market**
Bsns, Bus	**Business**	Ctry	**Country**	Hospl	**Hospital**	Mus	**Museum**
Bvd	**Boulevard**	Cty	**County**	HQ	**Headquarters**	Orch	**Orchard**
Cath	**Cathedral**	Dr	**Drive**	Hts	**Heights**	Pal	**Palace**
Cir	**Circus**	Dro	**Drove**	Ind	**Industrial**	Par	**Parade**
Cl	**Close**	Ed	**Education**	Inst	**Institute**	Pas	**Passage**
Cnr	**Corner**	Emb	**Embankment**	Int	**International**	Pk	**Park**
Coll	**College**	Est	**Estate**	Intc	**Interchange**	Pl	**Place**
Com	**Community**	Ex	**Exhibition**	Junc	**Junction**	Prec	**Precinct**

Prom	**Promenade**		
Rd	**Road**		
Recn	**Recreation**		
Ret	**Retail**		
Sh	**Shopping**		
Sq	**Square**		
St	**Street**		
Sta	**Station**		
Terr	**Terrace**		
TH	**Town Hall**		
Univ	**University**		
Wk, Wlk	**Walk**		
Wr	**Water**		
Yd	**Yard**		

Index of localities, towns and villages

A

Acle 166 B3
Alburgh 122 F6
Alby Hill 21 B5
Aldborough 21 A5
Aldeby 110 F4
Alderford 52 A5
All Saints South
   Elmham 124 B1
Alpington 90 E4
Anchor Corner 86 A1
Anchor Street 38 B3
Anmer 28 E8
Annis Hill 124 C8
Antingham 22 B4
Arminghall 90 B7
Ashby St Mary 91 C5
Ashill 84 A7
Ashmanhaugh 55 B8
Ashwellthorpe 105 F8
Ashwicken 45 A6
Aslacton 106 A2
Attleborough 174 D3
Attlebridge 52 B3
Aylmerton 10 A2
Aylsham 150 B5

B

Babingley 27 D5
Baconsthorpe 20 A8
Bacton 23 E5
Bacton Green 23 D5
Bagthorpe 14 D3
Bale 18 B7
Banham 119 D7
Banningham 36 D8
Barford 69 F2
Barmer 14 F4
Barney 17 F3
Barnham 125 F6
Barnham Broom 69 C2
Barningham 127 C3
Barningham Green 20 A4
Barton Bendish 81 A8
Barton Turf 38 F1
Bastwick 57 A4
Battlesea Green 131 E2
Bawburgh 160 B6
Bawdeswell 50 E8
Bawsey 44 D6
Beachamwell 81 F8
Beccles 110 D2
Beckett End 82 B1

B (continued)

Beckhithe 160 A1
Bedingham Green 108 B3
Beeston 48 C2
Beeston Regis 138 F5
Beeston St Lawrence 55 C8
Beetley 49 D4
Beighton 74 C2
Belaugh 54 E5
Bellmount 144 A7
Belton 93 F6
Bengate 38 A6
Bergh Apton 91 A4
Bessingham 20 E7
Besthorpe 174 F6
Bexwell 79 F6
Billingford
   Bawdeswell 50 B7
   Diss 130 E5
Billockby 75 A7
Binham 6 E2
Bintree 33 B2
Bircham Newton 14 A4
Bircham Tofts 14 B3
Bittering 48 F4
Blackborough End 44 C1
Black Carr 105 A6
Blackwater 51 D6
Blakeney 7 C6
Bleach Green 131 F4
Blenheim Park 15 C3
Blickling 165 F5
Blofield 165 F5
Blofield Corner 73 C6
Blofield Heath 73 D6
Blo' Norton 128 B6
Bloodman's Corner 171 A4
Bobby Hill 128 A1
Bodham 9 A3
Bodney 83 B1
Booton 149 E4
Botesdale 128 F2
Boughton 81 A5
Bowbeck 127 A2
Bowthorpe 160 F7
Bracon Ash 89 A2
Bradenham 66 E4
Bradfield 22 C4
Bradwell 94 C7
Brakefield Green 68 D4
Bramerton 90 F7
Brampton 36 E3
Brancaster 3 B6
Brancaster Staithe 3 D7
Brandiston 52 B8
Brandon 175 D3
Brandon Bank 112 B7
Brandon Creek 97 A2

B (continued 2)

Brandon Parva 69 B2
Breckles 102 E5
Bressingham 129 C8
Bressingham Common . . . 119 F1
Brettenham 117 B2
Brewers Green 177 B6
Bridge Green 120 F2
Bridgham 117 F5
Briggate 38 B6
Briningham 18 D4
Brinton 18 D6
Brisley 49 A8
Briston 142 E4
Brockdish 131 C6
Brome 130 B3
Brome Street 130 D3
Brooke 90 E2
Brookville 99 A6
Broome 109 C2
Broom Green 32 E2
Broomhill 172 E7
Broomholm 23 E4
Broomsthorpe 30 C7
Browston Green 94 C4
Brundall 165 D4
Brundish 110 A6
Buckenham 91 F8
Bull's Green 110 C5
Bumwell Hill 105 E2
Bungay 124 A8
Bunker's Hill
   Lowestoft 94 C3
   Norwich 161 B7
Bunwell 105 D4
Bunwell Bottom 105 C6
Burgate 129 C2
Burgh Castle 94 A7
Burgh Common 104 D5
Burgh next Aylsham 36 D4
Burgh St Margaret
   (Fleggburgh) 57 C1
Burgh St Peter 111 C4
Burgh Stubbs 142 B8
Burlingham Green 74 A5
Burnham Deepdale 3 E6
Burnham Market 135 C3
Burnham Norton 135 B6
Burnham Overy Staithe . . 135 F6
Burnham Overy Town 135 E4
Burnham Thorpe 4 D4
Burnham Westgate 135 B3
Burston 120 F2
Bush Green 122 A6
Bushy Common 67 B8
Bustard's Green 106 C3
Buxton 36 E1

C

Caister-on-Sea 168 F6
Caistor St Edmund 89 F6
California 167 E3
Calthorpe 21 A2
Calthorpe Street 39 C4
Candle Street 128 D1
Cangate 55 C6
Cantley 92 B7
Carbrooke 85 B5
Cargate Common 105 E1
Cargate Green 166 A8
Carleton Forehoe 87 C8
Carleton Rode 105 C3
Carleton St Peter 91 E5
Castle Acre 46 F2
Castle Rising 27 C3
Caston 102 E8
Catfield 56 C8
Caudlesprings 85 A4
Cawston 35 B2
Cess 57 C5
Chalkhill 83 C4
Chapel Field 39 A3
Chedgrave 92 A2
Chickering 131 D3
Christchurch 95 A7
Church End 41 F7
Claxton 91 D6
Clenchwarton 145 E5
Cley next the Sea 7 E6
Cliftonville 143 B7
Clint Green 68 C6
Clippesby 57 A1
Clippings Green 68 E7
Cobbler's Green 108 B2
Cobholm Island 169 A4
Cockley Cley 82 D7
Colby 6 E5
Colby 21 C2
Colegate End 121 E6
Colkirk 31 D5
Colney 161 A4
Coltishall 54 C6
Colton 69 E4
Coney Weston 127 B5
Congham 28 B2
Copy's Green 6 A2
Cordwell 105 E4
Corpusty 19 E1
Costessey 156 F4
Costessey Park 156 D3
Coston 69 A1
Coxford 30 C8
Crabgate 34 D6

C (continued) / D

Crackthorn Corner 128 D5
Cranwich 99 F6
Cranworth 85 E7
Craymere Beck 18 F1
Crimplesham 80 B6
Cringleford 89 B8
Cromer 139 C7
Crossdale Street 139 D1
Cross Street 131 A3
Cross Ways 94 B4
Crostwick 54 B3
Crostwight 38 D8
Crowgate Street 55 A8
Crownthorpe 87 C6
Crowshill 67 A1
Croxton
   Fakenham 17 E2
   Thetford 116 C5
Cuckoo Green 171 A4
Culfordheath 125 D1

D

Daffy Green 67 C4
Damgate
   Acle 166 C2
   Martham 57 E5
Dam Green 119 C4
Danemoor Green 86 F8
Darrow Green 122 E8
Denham 131 B1
Denton 123 A7
Denver 172 C2
Deopham 86 F3
Deopham Green 86 E2
Deopham Stalland 86 D2
Dereham 154 F4
Dersingham 140 D5
Dickleburgh 121 C1
Dickleburgh Moor 121 C2
Diddington 99 E8
Dilham 38 D4
Diss 177 D6
Ditchingham 109 A2
Dockeney 109 F2
Docking 134 C5
Doddshill 140 F3
Dowe Hill 167 C5
Downham Market 176 D4
Drabblegate 150 D8
Drayton 157 A8
Drurylane 85 A4
Drymere 64 C1
Dumpling Green 154 F3
Dunkirk 150 E8
Dunston 89 D7

Dunton 15 F1
Dussindale Park 72 E4

E

Earlham 161 D5
Earsham 123 E8
Earsham Street 131 F5
East Barsham 16 D4
East Bilney 49 B6
East Carleton 88 F4
Eastgate 35 C2
East Harling 118 C5
Easthaugh 51 C4
East Lexham 47 D3
Easton 70 B5
East Raynham 31 A4
East Rudham 30 A7
East Runton 10 B5
East Ruston 38 E6
East Somerton 58 A6
East Tuddenham 69 C6
East Walton 45 E3
East Wretham 102 A1
East Winch 44 F3
Eaton 161 F2
Eau Brink 43 A3
Eccles on Sea 24 E4
Eccles Road 103 F1
Edgefield 19 D5
Edgefield Street 19 D4
Edge Green 119 B4
Edingthorpe 23 C3
Edingthorpe Green 23 C3
Ellingham 109 D3
Elm 59 B1
Elsing 50 F3
Elveden 125 A7
Emneth 59 D2
Emneth Hungate 59 F2
Emorsgate 42 B7
Erpingham 21 B2
Etling Green 68 B8
Euston 126 B5
Eye 130 C1

F

Fair Green 44 B4
Fairstead 147 D4
Fakenham 141 D6
Fakenham Magna 10 C2
Felbrigg 10 C2
Felmingham 37 A8
Felthorpe 155 C8
Feltwell 98 D1
Fengate 150 C1
Fenside 56 B8
Fen Street
  Hopton 127 E6
  Redgrave 128 F6
Fersfield 119 D2
Fiddlers' Green 174 B8
Field Dalling 7 B1
Filby 75 F8
Filby Heath 76 B8
Fincham 62 F1
Fishley 166 C6
Flaxlands 28 C5
Flitcham 28 C5
Flixton 123 D5
Flordon 106 D8
Fodderstone Gap 62 C4
Fordham 79 D2
Forncett End 105 E4
Forncett St Mary 106 B4
Forncett St Peter 106 B4
Foul Anchor 41 A4
Foulden 82 A2
Foulsham 33 D3
Foxhole 107 A7
Foxley 50 D8
Framingham Earl 90 D4
Framingham Pigot 90 C6
Frankfort 38 A3
Frans Green 51 D1
Freethorpe 92 E8
Frenze 130 B7
Frettenham 54 A4
Friday Bridge 77 A7
Fring 13 D5
Fritton
  Great Yarmouth 93 E3
  Long Stratton 107 B3
  Ludham 56 E5
Frogshall 11 B1
Frost Row 86 B4
Fulmodeston 17 F1
Fundenhall 106 A7

G

Garboldisham 128 A8
Garlic Street 122 A2
Garvestone 68 C2
Gasthorpe 127 D7
Gateley 32 C3
Gayton 45 C5
Gayton Thorpe 45 E5
Gaywood 147 B6
Geldeston 109 F3
Gillingham 110 B2
Gimingham 22 E7
Gissing 120 F4
Glandford 7 E4

Gooderstone 82 A4
Goose Green 120 C6
Gorleston-on-Sea 170 E4
Great Barwick 14 E6
Great Bircham 14 B3
Great Common 124 D6
Great Cressingham 83 D4
Great Dunham 47 E1
Great Ellingham 103 E7
Great Fransham 66 B8
Great Green
  Diss 130 A4
  Wortham 129 B3
Great Hautbois 54 C7
Great Hockham 102 E3
Great Massingham 29 D2
Great Melton 70 B1
Great Moulton 106 B1
Great Plumstead 72 F5
Great Ryburgh 32 B2
Great Snoring 17 A5
Great Walsingham 17 A8
Great Witchingham 51 E2
Great Yarmouth 169 A5
Greengate 50 B3
Greensgate 51 E2
Gresham 9 E3
Gressenhall 49 B3
Grimston 28 B1
Griston 85 A2
Guestwick 34 A6
Guestwick Green 33 F5
Guist 32 F4
Gunthorpe 18 B5

H

Hackford 87 A5
Haddiscoe 110 F8
Hainford 53 E5
Hales 109 F8
Hales Green 109 E7
Hales Street 121 A6
Halvergate 74 F1
Hamrow 31 D3
Hanworth 21 B6
Happisburgh 24 C4
Happisburgh Common 24 B4
Hapton 106 C7
Hardingham 86 F6
Hardley Street 92 C4
Hardwick
  King's Lynn 147 B1
  Long Stratton 122 B8
Hargate 105 D2
Harleston 122 D3
Harling Road 118 A7
Harper's Green 32 A1
Harpley 29 D4
Hassingham 92 A7
Hawes' Green 89 F2
Hay Green 144 A1
Heacham 133 E4
Heckfield Green 131 B2
Heckingham 92 C1
Hedenham 108 E4
Helhoughton 30 C5
Hellesdon 157 F5
Hellington 91 B6
Hemblington 73 E6
Hemblington Corner 73 D6
Hempnall 107 D5
Hempnall Green 107 D4
Hempstead
  Holt 19 E8
  Stalham 24 E3
Hempton 141 A3
Hemsby 167 A7
Hengrave 52 A6
Hepworth 127 E1
Herringfleet 111 D8
Hethel 88 F3
Hethersett 88 C8
Hevingham 53 B7
Heydon 34 F6
Hickling 39 E2
Hickling Green 39 F2
Hickling Heath 39 E1
High Common 85 F8
High Green
  Beeston 48 E1
  Bradenham 66 E2
  Hethersett 88 B8
High Kelling 8 E3
Highoak 87 B4
High Street 124 D3
Hilborough 83 A3
Hilgay 79 E1
Hill Common 39 F1
Hillington 28 B4
Hinderclay 128 C3
Hindolveston 33 D8
Hindringham 16 C5
Hingham 86 C5
Hockering 69 B8
Hockering Heath 51 C1
Hockwold cum Wilton 114 A7
Hoe 49 F3
Holkham 5 B6
Holly End 59 D1
Holme Hale 66 B2
Holme next the Sea 4 F2
Hole 137 D6
Homersfield 123 B4
Honing 38 C6
Honingham 69 E7
Honington 126 D1

Hopton 127 F6
Hopton on Sea 171 D6
Horning 55 E4
Horningtoft 31 F1
Horsey 40 D2
Horsey Corner 40 D2
Horsford 53 B3
Horsham St Faith 53 D1
Horstead 54 C6
Houghton St Giles 16 E6
Hoveton 164 D6
Howe 90 D3
How Hill 56 B6
Hoxne 131 A4
Humbletoft 154 C7
Hunstanton 132 D5
Hunt's Corner 119 C7
Hunworth 19 A6
Hyltons Crossways 36 F8

I

Ickburgh 100 B6
Ilketshall St Andrew 124 E6
Ilketshall St Lawrence 124 F2
Ilketshall St Margaret 124 B4
Illington 117 D8
Ingham 39 D4
Ingham Corner 24 D2
Ingleborough 41 B1
Ingoldisthorpe 140 D8
Ingworth 36 B8
Intwood 89 B7
Irstead 56 A7
Irstead Street 55 F6
Itteringham 20 C1
Itteringham Common 35 D8
Ivy Todd 66 B4

J

Johnson Street 56 B4
Jordan Green 51 A8

K

Kelling 8 D5
Kenninghall 119 B5
Kerdiston 34 C3
Keswick
  North Walsham 23 F4
  Norwich 89 C7
Ketteringham 88 E6
Kettlestone 17 C2
Kidd's Moor 173 D8
Kimberley 87 B6
King's Lynn 147 A5
Kirby Bedon 90 E8
Kirby Cane 109 E4
Kirby Green 109 F5
Kirby Row 109 E3
Kirstead Green 108 C8
Knapton 143 B1
Knapton Green 22 F5
Knettishall 127 C7

L

Lakenham 162 F3
Lakenheath 113 E2
Lakes End 95 C2
Lamas 37 A2
Langham 7 B3
Langley Street 92 B4
Langton Green 130 C1
Larling 118 B8
Lenwade 51 D5
Lessingham 24 D3
Letheringsett 8 A1
Letton Green 67 E1
Leziate 44 D6
Limpenhoe 92 D6
Lingwood 73 F3
Litcham 48 A4
Little Barningham 20 C4
Little Barwick 14 E6
Little Cressingham 83 E2
Little Dunham 65 E8
Little Ellingham 86 A2
Little Fransham 66 B7
Little Green 129 B1
Little Hale 67 A1
Little Hautbois 54 B8
Little London
  Aldborough 36 A2
  Corpusty 19 E1
  North Walsham 151 E7
  Northwold 99 D7
Little Marsh 8 A1
Little Massingham 29 C3
Little Melton 160 C2
Little Ouse 112 A8
Little Plumstead 73 B6
Little Ryburgh 32 C7
Little Snoring 17 B3
Little Thornage 7 F1
Little Walsingham 16 F7
Loddon 92 A1
Loddon Ingloss 109 B7
Long Green 129 B4
Longham 49 A2
Long John's Hill 162 E2
Long Stratton 106 E3
Lordsbridge 60 E7

Lound 94 C1
Low Common 105 F3
Lower Bodham 9 A2
Lower East Carleton 89 B6
Lower Gresham 9 F1
Lower Stow Bedon 102 F5
Lower Street
  Southrepps 22 C6
  Wickmere 20 E5
Lower Tasburgh 106 E7
Lower Thurlton 93 A2
Low Street 86 E8
Low Tharston 106 D6
Ludham 56 D5
Lundy Green 107 D3
Lynford 100 D2
Lyng 51 A4
Lyngate
  North Walsham 151 A8
  Worstead 38 A5

M

Magpie Green 129 B5
Manor House 46 E2
Manson Green 86 C6
Marham 63 B4
Market Weston 127 E4
Marlingford 70 A4
Marsham 150 D1
Marshland St James 60 A4
Marsh Side 3 C7
Martham 57 D5
Matlaske 20 D5
Mattishall 68 E5
Mattishall Burgh 68 F7
Mautby 75 F7
Maypole Green 110 C6
Meeting House Hill 38 B7
Mellis 129 E1
Melton Constable 142 B5
Mendham 123 A4
Merton 84 C1
Methwold 99 A5
Methwold Hythe 98 E5
Mettingham 124 E8
Metton 21 C8
Middle Harling 118 B4
Middleton 44 C3
Mile Cross 158 A2
Mileham 48 D6
Mill Common 91 C4
Millgate 150 D7
Mill Green 120 E3
Mill Street 50 E4
Misery Corner 122 F3
Moorgate 154 D3
Morley St Botolph 87 B2
Morningthorpe 107 A3
Morston 7 B6
Morton 52 A4
Moulton St Mary 74 D2
Mount Pleasant 103 C5
Muckleton 3 F2
Mulbarton 89 B3
Mundesley 143 B5
Mundford 100 B4
Mundham 91 C1
Mustard Hyrn 57 C5

N

Narborough 63 E7
Narrowgate Corner 57 C2
Neatishead 55 E8
Neaton 84 E4
Necton 65 F4
Needham 131 D8
New Buckenham 104 F8
New Catton 158 D1
New Costessey 157 A1
Newgate 7 E5
Newgate Corner 75 C8
New Holkham 5 A2
New Houghton 29 D6
New Rackheath 72 E7
New Sprowston 158 E3
Newton 47 B2
Newton Flotman 89 C1
Newton Greenways 89 D2
Newton St Faith 53 E4
Newtown 169 D7
Nogdam End 92 D3
Nordelph 78 D3
Nordelph Corner 86 D6
Northacre 85 B1
Northall Green 154 F8
North Barsham 16 D6
North Burlingham 74 A5
North Common 127 D2
North Court 114 C3
North Creake 4 D1
North Denes 168 F2
North Elmham 49 E8
North End 103 C3
North Green
  Harlestone 122 A4
  Reymerston 68 C1
North Lopham 119 A2
North Lynn 146 F7
North Pickenham 65 E1
Northrepps 11 A1
North Runcton 44 A2
North Tuddenham 50 D1
North Walsham 151 E6

Northwold 99 C8
North Wootton 148 C5
Norton Corner 34 C7
Norton Subcourse 92 E1
Norwich 178 A3

O

Oakley 130 E5
Old Beetley 49 D5
Old Buckenham 104 D2
Old Catton 158 E5
Old Hall Street 23 A4
Old Hunstanton 132 E8
Orange Row 144 A6
Ormesby St Margaret 167 B3
Ormesby St Michael 58 A1
Ostend 24 A7
Oulton 35 B7
Oulton Street 35 D6
Outwell 77 F6
Overstrand 11 A4
Ovington 84 E5
Oxborough 81 D4
Oxnead 36 E2
Oxwick 31 D4

P

Palgrave 177 C2
Panxworth 73 E7
Paston 143 D2
Paston Green 143 D1
Peaseland Green 50 F3
Pedham 73 D7
Pennygate 38 E2
Pentney 63 C8
Pettywell 34 C2
Pilson Green 74 B8
Plumstead Green
  Great and Little
    Plumstead 73 B6
  Holt 20 B6
Pockthorpe
  Lyng 51 B5
  Watton 102 A7
  West Rudham 29 F6
Podmore 67 B7
Pollard Street 23 D3
Pooley Street 129 A8
Poringland 90 C5
Postwick 72 F2
Pottergate Street 106 B2
Potter Heigham 56 F6
Potthorpe 49 A8
Primrose Corner 55 C1
Primrose Green 51 A3
Pristow Green 120 E8
Pudding Norton 141 B1
Puddledock 104 C3
Pulham Market 121 E5
Pulham St Mary 121 F4

Q

Quidenham 118 F6

R

Rackheath 72 E8
Ragmere 104 D1
Ranworth 55 F1
Ratten Row 110 A7
Raveningham 110 A2
Reading Green 131 C1
Redenhall 122 F3
Redgrave 128 E4
Red Pits 34 C7
Reedham 92 E5
Reepham 149 B5
Repps 56 C1
Reymerston 68 C1
Rickinghall 128 E2
Ridlington 23 E1
Ridlington Street 23 E1
Ringland 70 B8
Ringstead 2 A3
Road Green 107 E4
Rockland All Saints 103 B7
Rockland St Mary 91 B7
Rockland St Peter 103 B8
Rollesby 57 D2
Rougham 47 B7
Roughton 21 B8
Roydon
  Diss 129 D2
  King's Lynn 28 A2
Runcton Holme 61 D3
Runhall 68 F2
Runham
  Filby 75 E6
  Great Yarmouth 169 B5
Rushall 121 F1
Rushford 126 E8
Rush Green 69 E1

S

Saham Hills 84 C6
Saham Toney 84 C5
St Cross South Elmham . . . 123 D3
St James 54 E7
St John's Fen End 60 B6

St John's Highway 42 B1
St Margaret South Elmham 123 E2
St Michael South Elmham 124 A2
St Nicholas South Elmham 123 E2
St Olaves 93 D2
St Peter South Elmham 124 A3
Salhouse 55 B1
Salle 149 E8
Salters Lode 79 A4
Salthouse 8 B7
Sandringham 27 F7
Santon Downham 115 C6
Sapiston 126 D2
Saxlingham 7 C2
Saxlingham Green 107 D7
Saxlingham Nethergate 107 C8
Saxlingham Thorpe 107 A8
Saxthorpe 19 F1
Scarning 67 B7
Scole 130 D6
Scole Common 130 C7
Sco Ruston 54 E8
Scottow 37 D2
Scoulton 85 E3
Scratby 167 E4
Sculthorpe 16 B2
Sea Palling 40 A6
Sedgeford 13 B7
Seething 108 F8
Setchey 61 E8
Shadwell 117 C2
Sharp Street 56 C7
Sharrington 18 D7
Shelfanger 120 C2
Shelton 107 B1
Shepherd's Gate 42 D4
Shepherd's Port 12 B4
Shereford 31 A8
Sheringham 138 C7
Sheringwood 138 C5
Shernborne 13 B3
Shimpling 121 A2
Shingham 82 A8
Shipdham 67 B2
Shipmeadow 124 F8
Short Green 120 A5
Shotesham 90 A2
Shouldham 62 D4
Shouldham Thorpe 62 C3
Shropham 103 B4
Sidestrand 11 C2
Silfield 88 A2
Silvergate 35 F6
Silver Green 107 E3
Sisland 91 E1
Skeyton 37 A4
Skeyton Corner 37 B6
Sloley 37 F4
Smallburgh 38 D3
Smallworth 128 A7
Sneath Common 121 A8
Snetterton 103 C2
Snettisham 12 E5
Snow Street 129 D8
South Acre 46 F1
Southburgh 85 F7
South Burlingham 74 B2
South Creake 15 D6
South Denes 170 E5
South End 103 C1
Southery 97 B5
Southgate
Cawston 35 B3
South Creake 15 E5
South Green
Aylsham 154 E3
Hoxne 130 F1
Mattishall 68 F5
Pulham St Mary 121 F2
Terrington St Clement 42 B6
South Lopham 128 D8
South Lynn 146 E2
South Pickenham 83 D6
South Raynham 30 F3
Southrepps 22 B7
South Runcton 61 F3
Southtown 169 B1
South Walsham 74 A7
Southwood 92 D8
South Wootton 148 D2
Spa Common 23 A1
Sparham 51 B6
Sparhamhill 51 C5
Spixworth 54 A2
Spooner Row 105 A8
Sporle 65 C6
Sprowston 159 B3
Stacksford 104 C1
Stalham 39 B4
Stalham Green 39 C3
Stalland Common 86 C1
Stanfield 48 F7
Stanford 101 A5
Stanhoe 14 E8
Stanton Chare 127 B1
Starston 122 C3
Stibbard 32 E7
Stiffkey 6 D5
Stockton 109 F4
Stody 18 F6
Stoke Ferry 80 F3
Stoke Holy Cross 89 F4
Stokesby 75 A5
Stonebridge 102 B1
Stone Street 124 F1
Stow Bardolph 79 E8
Stow Bedon 102 E7
Stowbridge 61 B2
Stradbroke 131 E1
Stradsett 80 D8
Stratton St Michael 106 F4
Stratton Strawless 53 E7
Strumpshaw 73 F2
Stubb 39 F1
Stubbing's Green 129 A1
Stubbs Green 109 C8
Stuston 130 B5
Suffield 21 F3
Summerfield 2 E1
Summerhill 133 C3
Surlingham 73 B1
Sustead 21 A7
Suton 87 D2
Sutton 39 C3
Sutton Bridge 41 B7
Swaffham 153 D4
Swafield 22 E3
Swainsthorpe 89 D3
Swannington 52 B6
Swanton Abbott 37 C4
Swanton Hill 37 C5
Swanton Morley 50 B3
Swanton Novers 18 B3
Swardeston 89 C5
Syderstone 15 B3
Syleham 131 D5

T

Tacolneston 105 F5
Tasburgh 106 F7
Tatterford 30 E7
Tattersett 15 C1
Taverham 155 C1
Ten Mile Bank 96 E7
Terrington St Clement 144 B4
Terrington St John 42 C2
Tharston 106 E5
The Arms 83 F1
The Brook 129 C3
The Grange 35 C1
The Green 87 B4
The Heath
Fakenham 141 F4
Hevingham 53 A8
Stratton Strawless 53 F8
The Limes 59 C5
The Ling 91 A1
Thelnetham 128 B5
Thelveton 130 D8
The Marsh
Thrandeston 129 F3
Wortham 129 C4
Themelthorpe 33 F2
The Smeeth 60 A5
Thetford 176 B4
Thompson 102 A8
Thornage 18 F7
Thornham 2 D6
Thorpe 93 B1
Thorpe Abbotts 131 B6
Thorpe End 72 D6
Thorpe Hamlet 163 B6
Thorpe Market 22 A6
Thorpe Marriott 155 F2
Thorpe Row 67 C4
Thorpe St Andrew 163 F8
Thorpland 61 D3
Thrandeston 129 F3
Three Cocked Hat 110 D7
Threehammer Common 55 E6
Three Holes 77 E3
Thrigby 75 D7
Thurgarton 20 F5
Thurlton 92 F1
Thurne 56 E3
Thurning 34 C7
Thursford 17 E4
Thursford Green 17 D5
Thurton 91 D4
Thuxton 68 D2
Thwaite St Mary 109 A5
Tibenham 120 E8
Tilney All Saints 144 F1
Tilney cum Islington 60 F8
Tilney Fen End 60 C6
Tilney High End 42 D4
Tilney St Lawrence 60 D8
Tipps End 95 C6
Titchwell 2 F7
Tittleshall 48 B8
Tivetshall St Margaret 121 B5
Tivetshall St Mary 121 B5
Toft Monks 110 D5
Toftrees 31 B6
Toftwood 154 E2
Topcroft 107 F3
Topcroft Street 107 F2
Toprow 88 E1
Tottenhill 62 A5
Tottenhill Row 61 E7
Tottington 101 E6
Tower End 44 C4
Town Green
Aldborough 21 C4
South Walsham 74 A7
Town Street 39 F3
Trimingham 11 D2
Trowse Newton 163 B3
Trunch 22 E5
Tungate 37 C8
Tunstall 74 F3
Tunstead 37 F1
Tuttington 36 E6
Twyford 33 B3
Tyby 34 B6

U

Upgate 52 C5
Upgate Street
New Buckenham 105 A3
Woodton 108 B2
Upper Brandon Parva 68 E3
Upper Guist 33 A5
Upper Hellesdon 158 C3
Upper Sheringham 138 A5
Upper Stoke 90 B5
Upper Street
Horning 55 F4
Hoveton 55 C5
Scole 130 F6
Southrepps 22 B7
Worstead 38 A3
Upper Weybread 131 E6
Upton 166 A8
Upton Green 166 B8
Upwell 77 F5

W

Wacton 106 C2
Wainford 109 B1
Walcot Green 177 F6
Walcott 24 A7
Walpole Cross Keys 41 F7
Walpole Highway 59 F8
Walpole Marsh 41 C4
Walpole St Andrew 41 D4
Walpole St Peter 41 E3
Walsoken 152 F6
Walton Highway 59 D8
Walton Warren 45 E2
Wangford 114 C2
Warham 6 A4
Waterheath 110 E5
Waterloo
Beccles 110 E4
Coltishall 53 E6
Diss 130 C6
Watlington 61 E5
Wattisfield 128 B1
Wattlefield 105 C7
Watton 84 E3
Watton Green 84 E4
Waxham 40 C5
Weasenham All Saints 47 C8
Weasenham St Peter 30 D1
Weeting 175 B8
Welborne 69 A4
Welbourne Common 68 F4
Wellingham 30 F1
Wells-Next-The-Sea 136 C5
Welney 95 D4
Wendling 66 F8
Wereham 80 E4
West Acre 46 B2
West Barsham 16 C4
West Beckham 9 C2
West Bilney 45 B2
Westbrook Green 177 C7
West Caister 168 C4
West Dereham 80 B4
West End
Necton 66 C4
West Caister 76 B6
Westfield 67 F4
Westgate 6 D3
Westgate Street 53 B8
West Harling 118 A3
West Head 78 F8
West Lexham 47 C4
West Lynn 146 C5
West Newton 27 F6
Weston Green 51 E1
Weston Longville 51 E3
West Poringland 90 B4
West Raynham 30 E4
West Rudham 29 F7
West Runton 10 A5
West Somerton 57 E6
West Tofts 100 F4
West Walton 59 B8
Westwick 37 D6
West Winch 43 E3
Weybourne 8 F5
Wheatacre 111 B5
Whimpwell Green 24 C4
Whinburgh 68 A3
Whissonsett 31 D2
Whittington 81 B2
Whitwell Street 149 C3
Wicken Green Village 15 D2
Wickhampton 93 A8
Wicklewood 87 B5
Wickmere 20 F4
Wiggenhall St Germans 43 C1
Wiggenhall St Mary Magdalen 61 B6
Wiggenhall St Mary the Virgin 61 A8
Wiggenhall St Peter 61 C8
Wighton 6 A2
Wilby 119 A8
Wilney Green 129 A8
Wimbotsham 79 D8
Winfarthing 120 B4
Wingfield 131 E4
Wingfield Green 131 D4
Winterton-on-Sea 58 C6
Wisbech 152 A6
Withergate 38 A6
Witton 165 A6
Witton Bridge 23 E2
Wiveton 7 E6
Wolferd Green 90 B2
Wolferton 27 B7
Wolterton 20 E2
Woodbastwick 55 D2
Wood Dalling 34 D6
Woodgate 50 C3
Wood Green 106 F2
Wood Norton 33 A7
Woodrising 85 E6
Woodton 108 C4
Wormegay 62 C7
Worstead 38 A5
Wortham 129 B4
Worthing 49 F6
Wortwell 123 B4
Wramplingham 69 E1
Wreningham 88 D1
Wretton 80 E3
Wroxham 164 D3
Wymondham 173 E5

Y

Yaxham 68 A5
Yaxley 130 A1
Yelverton 90 E5

A

Abbey Cl
 Horsham St Faith & Newton St Faith NR10 53 D1
 Sheringham NR26 138 D6
 Wendling NR19 66 F7
Abbey Farm Mid Sch IP24 176 B4
Abbey Gn 1 IP24 176 C4
Abbey Hill IP21 131 A3
Abbey La
 Haveringland NR10 52 D6
 Norwich NR1 178 C2
Abbey Pk NR26 138 F5
Abbey Rd
 Flitcham with Appleton PE31 28 D5
 Flixton NR35 123 F4
 Great Massingham PE32 29 D1
 Horsham St Faith NR10 53 D1
 Old Buckenham NR17 104 D3
 Pentney PE32 63 B8
 Sheringham NR26 138 C6
 10 Watton IP25 84 E3
Abbey St NR12 23 E4
Abbeyfields PE32 29 D1
Abbeygate IP24 176 C5
Abbot Cl NR18 173 C5
Abbot Rd Horning NR12 55 E4
 Norwich NR1 162 D2
Abbot's Cl NR11 150 D7
Abbot's La NR14 90 B3
Abbots Way NR12 24 E4
Abbottsinch Rd 5 IP31 126 B1
Aberdare Ct 6 NR1 163 B7
Aberdeen St PE30 146 F4
Abinger Way NR4 89 D8
Abington Gr 4 PE14 59 A1
Abyssinia Rd NR30 169 D2
Acacia Ave Ashill IP25 84 A7
 East Dereham NR19 154 E1
 22 Martham NR29 57 D4
 Wisbech PE13 152 C8
Acacia Gr NR26 138 D4
Acacia Rd NR7 163 E8
Access Rd NR21 15 D2
Acer Rd PE34 43 D4
Ackland Cl 7 NR29 58 B6
Acland Mews NR6 158 C4
Acle High Sch NR13 166 B4
Acle New Rd NR30 169 B5
Acle Rd Beighton NR13 74 E2
 South Walsham NR13 74 C7
 Upton with Fishley NR13 166 A5
Acle St Edmund CE VC Prim Sch NR13 166 D4
Acle Sta NR13 166 B2
Aconite Rd PE30 147 B7
Acorn Dr PE32 45 B6
Acorn Rd NR28 151 D6
Acorn Way NR19 154 D7
Acres Way NR8 155 E2
Ada Cole Ave NR16 103 D1
Ada Coxon Cl PE30 146 F8
Adam Cl PE30 147 C5
Adams La 4 NR11 19 F1
Adams Rd NR7 159 A5
Adastral Pl PE37 153 C5
Addey Cl NR6 158 F5
Addison Cl
 2 Coltishall NR12 54 C7
 Feltwell IP26 98 F1
Addison Rd 2 NR31 170 C7
Adeane Mdw IP26 100 A4
Adelaide Ave PE30 147 B7
Adelaide St 5 NR2 162 B7
Adey Cl NR11 150 B5
Admiral's Dr PE35 140 F1
Admirals Cl PE30 147 D3
Admirals Ct PE37 153 D3
Admirals Dr PE13 152 D8
Admirals Jun Sch IP24 176 E6
Admirals Quay NR31 169 C1
Admirals Way
 Hethersett NR9 88 D8
 Thetford IP24 176 E5
Admirals Wlk 7 NR9 86 C5
Admiralty Cl 3 PE38 172 B4
Admiralty Rd NR30 169 D1
Adventurers' Dro PE33 81 B1
Aerodrome Cres NR7 163 D8
Afghan Pl NR3 158 E1
Agricultural Hall Plain NR1 178 B3
Ailmar Cl PE30 147 A4
Ainsworth Cl 7 NR20 50 B3
Airedale Cl 4 NR3 158 C1
Airfield Rd PE33 63 C4
Airport Ind Est NR6 158 C6
Airstation La IP21 121 E2
Akrotiri Sq IP25 84 F3
Alan Ave NR15 89 D1
Alan Jarvis Way PE34 144 D6
Alan Rd NR1 178 C1
Alban Rd PE30 148 C5
Albansfield 3 NR18 173 C5
Albany Cl NR31 169 C2
Albany Ct NR27 139 B7
Albany Rd
 Great Yarmouth NR31 169 C2
 Norwich NR3 162 D8
Albany Rd *continued*
 Wisbech PE13 152 C6
Albemarle Rd
 Great Yarmouth NR30 169 D5
 Norwich NR2 162 B3
Albert Ct 18 PE13 152 C4
Albert Gate Rd 22 NR30 169 D2
Albert Myhill Cl 5 NR20 154 E6
Albert Pl NR1 163 A6
Albert Rd 17 NR30 169 D2
Albert Sq 18 NR30 169 D2
Albert St Holt NR25 137 B6
 King's Lynn PE30 146 D5
Albert Terr NR2 162 C4
Albion Dr NR7 159 A3
Albion Rd Bungay NR35 124 B8
 Great Yarmouth NR30 169 D4
 Mundesley NR11 143 A7
 Trunch NR28 22 E5
Albion St PE30 146 E5
Albion Way
 Norwich NR1 178 C1
 Wroxham/Hoveton NR12 164 D6
Alborough Loke 6 NR9 88 C7
Alburgh Rd NR15 107 D4
Alburgh with Denton Fst Sch IP20 123 A5
Alby Craft Ctr* NR11 21 C3
Aldborough Prim Sch NR11 21 B5
Aldborough Rd NR11 21 A3
Aldeby Rd NR34 110 F6
Alder Cl
 Great Yarmouth NR31 94 C7
 10 Mulbarton NR14 89 B3
 North Walsham NR28 151 D7
 Poringland NR14 90 D4
Alder Covert IP24 116 D2
Alder Way NR8 155 E1
Alderman Jackson Specl Sch PE30 147 B8
Alderman Peel High Sch NR23 136 D4
Alderman Swindell Fst Sch NR30 169 D8
Alderson Pl NR1 178 B1
Alderson Rd NR30 169 C5
Aldis Ct NR19 154 D5
Aldis Rd NR13 166 B4
Aldiss Ave NR19 154 D3
Aldiss Cl PE37 153 D3
Aldiss Ct PE13 154 D6
Aldrich Way IP22 177 C5
Aldryche Rd NR1 163 B8
Aldwick Rd 2 NR18 173 C6
Alex Moorhouse Way NR5 156 A3
Alexander Cl
 Caister-on-Sea NR30 168 C8
 18 Long Stratton NR15 106 E3
Alexander Rise NR11 22 F8
Alexander Way 1 NR19 154 C6
Alexandra Ave NR30 169 D7
Alexandra Cl PE31 140 C4
Alexandra Rd
 Cromer NR27 139 B4
 Great Yarmouth NR30 169 D4
 Hunstanton PE36 132 C3
 Mundesley NR11 143 A8
 Norwich NR2 162 B6
 Sheringham NR26 138 D6
 Wisbech PE13 152 C5
Alexandra Way
 Attleborough NR17 174 C6
 Downham Market PE38 172 B3
Alford Gr NR7 159 A3
Alfred Nicholls Ct NR3 158 D2
Alfred Rd NR27 139 A7
Alfric Cl 11 NR14 91 F1
Algores Way PE13 152 B2
Alice Fisher Cres PE30 146 F7
Alison Cl NR13 73 F3
All Hallows' Hospl NR35 109 B2
All Saints IP27 175 B8
All Saints Ave PE13 152 F7
All Saints CE VA Prim Sch
 Ryburgh NR21 32 C6
 Winfarthing IP22 120 B4
All Saints Cl
 Briston NR24 142 D4
 Runhall NR20 69 A5
 2 Weybourne NR25 8 F5
 Wicklewood NR18 87 B5
 1 Wisbech PE14 59 A1
All Saints Dr PE30 148 C4
All Saints Gn NR1 178 B1
All Saints Rd 6 NR14 90 D5
All Saints Sch NR12 24 D3
All Saints' St 15 PE30 146 D4
All Saints Way
 Beachamwell PE37 81 F8
 Mundesley NR11 143 C6
All Saints Wlk 7 NR20 68 F6
Allanadale Rd NR4 162 C1
Allen Cl PE34 61 B8
Allen Meale Way 5 NR12 39 B4
Allen's Ave NR7 159 A4
Allen's La NR7 159 A4
Allenbrooks Way NR18 173 C3
Allenby's Chase 10 PE12 41 B8
Allendale Rd NR30 168 E5
Allens Cl 1 NR13 73 D6
Allens La NR2 162 C4
Allerton Cl NR7 159 B3
Allerton Rd NR7 159 B3
Alley The PE32 44 C1
Allison St NR10 36 A2
Allotment La NR25 9 B3
Allthorpe Rd 12 IP20 122 D2
Allwood Ave NR19 154 C5
Alma Ave PE34 144 D6
Alma Chase PE34 144 D6
Alma Rd
 Great Yarmouth NR30 169 D2
 Snettisham PE31 12 E5
Alma Terr NR3 162 D8
Almond Cl 21 NR29 57 D4
Almond Gr IP24 176 A1
Almond Rd NR31 170 B6
Alpha Rd NR31 170 C8
Alpington & Bergh Apton Prim Sch NR14 90 F4
Alston Cl 3 NR14 90 D5
Alston Rd NR6 157 E2
Althaea Gn 2 NR31 170 B5
Altongate 1 NR13 72 D6
Amazonia World of Reptiles* NR30 169 E2
Ambassador Way NR20 154 F4
Ambleside
 16 Hethersett NR9 88 D8
 5 Sculthorpe Airfield NR21 15 C2
Ambleside Cl NR5 161 C6
Ambrose Cl 1 NR5 161 A7
Ambrose Rd NR30 168 E3
Amderley Dr 6 NR4 89 C8
Amelia Opie Way 2 IP24 176 D7
Ames Ct NR10 35 B2
Amethyst Cl NR31 170 D2
Amherst Cl 7 PE37 153 C3
Amhirst Cl 2 NR6 158 F1
Amhurst Gdns NR31 94 A5
Amsterdam NR6 158 B6
Amsterdam Way PE13 154 C2
Amys Cl IP25 84 C4
Anchor Cl Norwich NR3 178 C4
 Sheringham NR26 138 E6
Anchor Ct NR31 169 C2
Anchor Dro PE38 112 B8
Anchor Quay NR2 178 A3
Anchor Rd
 North Walsham NR28 151 F5
 Sutton Bridge PE34 41 F8
Anchor St
 Coltishall NR12 54 D6
 5 Norwich NR3 162 F8
 Norwich NR3 178 C4
 Tunstead NR12 38 B2
Anchor Way 7 NR33 111 F1
Anchorage View PE31 3 B6
Anderson Cl
 King's Lynn PE30 146 E7
 Wisbech PE13 152 A7
Andrew Goodall Cl NR19 154 C1
Andrew's Furlong NR16 119 E7
Andrews Pl PE36 132 D2
Angel Dr NR28 151 B4
Angel Rd NR3 158 D1
Angel Rd Fst Sch NR3 158 D1
Angel Rd Mid Sch NR3 158 D1
Angela Cl 2 NR10 53 B3
Angela Cres 3 NR10 53 B3
Angela Rd NR10 53 B3
Angerstein Cl IP27 114 E8
Angle Rd PE14 78 A7
Anglia Sq NR3 178 B4
Anglia Way PE13 152 B2
Anglian Way 3 NR31 171 D5
Anglo-Saxon Cath & Bishops Pal (remains of)* NR20 49 F8
Anmer Cl NR13 158 F3
Anmer Rd PE31 28 C5
Anna Gurney Cl IP24 176 D6
Anna Sewell Cl 4 IP24 176 D7
Anne Bartholomew Rd IP24 176 D7
Anne Boleyn Cl 4 IP24 176 D6
Anne Cl NR7 163 F8
Anne Rd PE12 41 B8
Anne Stannard Way NR12 23 F4
Annes Cl PE30 148 D1
Annes Dr PE36 132 D1
Annis Hill NR35 124 C8
Anson Cl
 5 Hethersett NR9 88 E8
 Mundesley NR11 143 A7
Anson Rd
 Great Yarmouth NR31 169 C2
 Norwich NR6 158 B6
Anson's La NR15 122 A8
Ant Broads & Marshes National Nature Reserve* NR12 55 F8
Anthony Curton Prim Sch PE14 41 E4
Anthony Dr NR3 158 F2
Anthony Nolan Rd PE30 147 D3
Antingham & Southrepps Com Prim Sch NR11 22 B5
Antingham Dr NR28 151 D6
Antingham Hill NR28 22 B3
Antingham Rd NR7 159 D1
Apeldoorn Wlk PE13 152 D7
Apollo Wlk NR30 169 C6
Apple Yd NR25 137 B6
Appleacres NR6 158 D5
Appledore Cl PE30 148 C2
Appledore La 4 NR21 15 C2
Applegarth 1 NR18 173 B4
Applegarth Ct 2 NR18 173 B4
Appleton Dr NR29 167 A3
Appleton Dro PE31 27 F5
Appletree Cl PE31 133 C6
Appletree La IP22 177 C5
Appleyard Cres NR3 158 A3
Apsley Ct NR5 161 F6
Apsley Rd NR30 169 E3
Arbor Ct NR27 139 B6
Arbor Rd NR27 139 B6
Arcade St NR1 178 B2
Archbishop Sancroft High Sch IP20 122 D2
Archdale Cl PE33 43 F3
Archdale St 3 PE30 146 E5
Archer Cl NR6 159 A5
Archer La PE32 46 F2
Archer's Rd 2 NR30 169 C5
Archers' Ave 3 IP26 98 D1
Archibald Rd NR12 24 A7
Arden Cl NR27 11 A3
Arden Gr NR10 157 E7
Arden Gr Fst Sch NR10 157 E7
Arderon Ct 2 NR2 162 B7
Ardleigh Cl 3 PE13 152 E5
Ardney Rise NR3 158 D3
Argyle St
 King's Lynn PE30 146 E3
 Norwich NR1 178 C1
Argyll Cres NR8 156 E8
Arles Ave PE13 152 E3
Arlington Cl NR17 174 E5
Arlington Gdns NR17 174 E5
Arlington La NR2 162 C4
Arlington Pk Rd PE32 44 C3
Arlington Way IP24 176 E3
Armada Cl PE13 152 D8
Armes Cres NR2 162 A8
Armes St NR2 162 B7
Arminghall Cl NR3 158 C3
Arminghall La NR14 89 F8
Armitage Cl NR4 89 B8
Arms Pk Rd NR6 158 B6
Armstrong Dr NR19 154 E7
Armstrong Rd NR7 159 E2
Army Rd NR21 15 C2
Arnfield La NR5 161 B8
Arnold Ave NR30 168 D8
Arnold Miller Rd NR1 162 F2
Arnott Ave NR31 170 D1
Arnott Rd NR25 137 D5
Arnside Cl 22 NR9 88 D8
Arthur Ave NR30 168 E8
Arthur Rd NR21 141 A6
Arthurton Rd NR10 54 A1
Artillery Sq 21 NR30 169 D4
Artillery St 12 PE13 152 C4
Arundel Cl NR20 49 C4
Arundel Ct NR2 178 A1
Arundel Dr PE30 148 C1
Arundel Rd
 Great Yarmouth NR30 169 D7
 Wymondham NR18 173 C6
Ascot Gdns NR19 154 D3
Ash Cl Brandon IP27 175 E3
 Downham Market PE38 172 C6
 10 Hethersett NR9 88 D8
 Swaffham PE37 153 B5
 Thetford IP24 176 A1
 Wymondham NR18 173 D6
Ash Dr IP23 130 C1
Ash Gn 11 NR31 170 B6
Ash Gr King's Lynn PE30 148 D2
 Norwich NR3 158 E2
 Sheringham NR26 138 E5
 4 West Winch PE33 43 E2
Ash La NR16 105 C2
Ash Rd PE33 63 B4
Ash Tree Cl NR17 174 C5
Ash Tree Rd NR13 74 D1
Ash Yd NR24 18 D8
Ashbey Rd PE30 147 E8
Ashburton Rd IP26 100 C5
Ashby Rd
 Ashby St Mary NR14 91 C5
 Repps with Bastwick NR29 57 A3
 Thurton NR14 91 C4
Ashby St NR1 178 B1
Ashdale Pk
 Old Hunstanton PE36 132 F8
 Wisbech PE13 152 A5
Ashdown NR8 155 E1
Ashdown Ct NR27 139 C6
Ashfield Ct PE34 144 D6
Ashfield Hill PE30 147 C4
Ashfield Rd NR28 151 E6
Ashford Cl NR34 110 C2
Ashgrove 5 NR8 155 E2
Ashill VC Prim Sch IP25 84 A7
Ashleigh Gdns NR18 173 E6
Ashleigh Inf Sch NR18 173 D6
Ashley Rd NR20 49 D4
Ashley Wlk PE13 154 D4
Ashtree Rd
 Norwich NR5 157 B2
 12 Watton IP25 84 E3
Ashwell Ct NR5 160 F7
Ashwellthorpe Rd NR16 88 D1
Ashwicken CE Fst Sch PE32 44 F6
Ashwicken Rd PE32 45 A8
Ashwood Cl NR30 168 D6
Aslack Way PE36 2 A6
Aslacton Prim Sch NR15 106 A1
Aslacton Rd NR16 106 B3
Aslake Cl NR7 159 C5
Aspen Cl IP24 176 B2
Aspen Way NR4 89 B8
Aspland Rd NR1 178 C3
Assembly House The NR2 178 A2
Association Way 2 NR7 72 D4
Astell Rd NR1 89 F8
Astley Cooper Pl NR15 90 E1
Astley Cres PE36 132 D6
Astley Prim Sch NR24 142 C4
Astley Rd
 Great & Little Plumstead NR13 73 B6
 Little Plumpstead NR13 165 A8
 Norwich NR5 160 F8
Astor Ct IP27 175 D4
Atbara Terr PE30 146 E2
Atcherley Sq PE31 30 B3
Atkinson Cl NR5 160 E8
Atling Cl NR17 174 F6
Atling Way NR17 174 F6
Atmere Cl 2 NR4 161 F1
Attelsey Way NR5 160 E8
Atthill Rd NR2 162 A7
Attleborough High Sch NR17 174 D6
Attleborough Inf Sch NR17 174 D6
Attleborough Jun Sch NR17 174 E6
Attleborough Rd
 Attleborough NR17 174 A7
 Caston NR17 102 F8
 Deopham NR18 86 E1
 Great Ellingham NR17 103 F8
 Little Ellingham NR17 86 A2
 Morley NR18 87 A1
Attleborough Sta NR17 174 E5
Attlee Way 4 NR19 154 C6
Audax Rd NR6 158 C6
Audley Ct IP24 176 C7
Audley End IP21 120 F1
Audley St NR30 169 D5
Augusta St NR26 138 D7
Augustus Hare Dr 1 NR4 161 C5
Aurania Ave NR1 162 D3
Auster Cl NR6 158 C4
Austin Fields PE30 146 E5
Austin Fields Ind Est PE30 146 E5
Austin Rd NR31 169 B3
Austin St
 Hunstanton PE36 132 C5
 King's Lynn PE30 146 D5
Autumn Cl IP24 176 E4
Autumn Dr NR5 161 B8
Avenue The NR23 5 A2
Avebury Rd NR4 162 B1
Aveling Way 6 NR33 111 F1
Avenue Cl PE38 79 E1
Avenue Fst & Mid Schs NR2 162 B5
Avenue Rd
 Great Yarmouth NR31 170 D6
 High Kelling NR25 8 E2
 Hunstanton PE36 132 C4
 King's Lynn PE30 146 F4
 North Walsham NR28 151 C4
 Norwich NR2 162 B5
 Wymondham NR18 173 C3
Avenue S NR26 138 E7
Avenue The
 Brome & Oakley IP23 130 D3
 Brookville IP26 99 A7
 Brumstead NR12 24 A1
 Dersingham PE35 140 E1
 Hemsby NR29 167 A7
 Holkham NR23 5 A4
 Horning NR12 55 E4
 4 Necton PE37 65 F4
 Northrepps NR27 139 D3
 Sheringham NR26 138 E7
 Snettisham PE31 12 D4
 Wiggenhall St Germans PE34 61 A8
 Wroxham/Hoveton NR12 164 B4
 Wymondham NR18 87 D7
Avenues The
 Langley with Hardley NR14 91 F4
 Norwich NR4 161 E4
 Thurton NR14 91 D3
Avian Way NR7 159 C2
Avocet House Sch NR14 92 C1
Avon Rd PE30 148 C2
Avondale Cl NR13 74 A2
Avondale Rd NR31 170 D3
Avonmouth Rd 2 NR3 158 C1
Aylesbury Cl NR3 158 D2
Aylmer Dr PE34 60 C8
Aylsham Cres NR3 158 C3

Aylsham High Sch NR11 150 D7
Aylsham Ind Est NR11 150 E8
Aylsham Rd
Burgh & Tuttington NR11 36 E6
Cawston NR10 35 B2
Felmingham NR28 37 A8
North Walsham NR28 22 C1
Norwich NR3 158 C1
Oulton NR11 35 E6
Swanton Abbott NR10 37 C4
Aylsham Rd Bsns Pk NR6 158 C2
Aylsham Sta NR11 150 D5
Ayre Way PE30 147 D8
Ayton Rd NR18 173 D3
Ayton Rd Ind Est NR18 173 D3

B

Babingley Cl 5 PE33 61 D6
Bachelor's La NR28 23 E2
Back Chapel La NR31 170 D6
Back Dro Upwell PE14 77 D4
Welney PE14 95 D4
Back Hills IP22 128 E3
Back La Barford NR9 69 F2
Beeston with Bittering PE32 48 C2
Bircham PE31 14 B3
Blakeney NR25 7 C7
Burgh Castle NR31 94 A8
Burnham Market PE31 135 D2
Burnham Thorpe PE31 4 D4
Buxton with Lammas NR10 53 E8
Castle Acre PE32 46 F2
Catfield NR29 56 C8
Cawston NR10 35 B2
Dereham NR20 68 A8
Diss IP22 120 D3
East Rudham PE31 30 B7
East Ruston NR12 24 A3
Elsing NR20 50 F3
Happisburgh NR12 23 F2
Hempstead NR25 19 E7
Hethersett NR9 88 E8
Kenninghall NR16 119 A5
Litcham PE32 48 A4
Lound NR32 94 C2
Lyng NR9 51 A4
Marthan NR29 57 D5
Mattishall NR20 68 E6
Mileham PE32 48 C6
North Elmham NR20 49 E7
Outwell PE14 77 E7
Potter Heigham NR29 56 E7
Quidenham NR16 119 A8
Rackheath NR13 54 D1
Ringland NR8 52 C1
Rollesby NR29 57 D3
Roughton NR11 21 D8
Roydon PE32 28 A1
St Mary, South Elmham otherwise Homersfield IP20 123 B4
Scole IP21 121 A1
Scoulton NR9 85 E3
South Creake NR21 15 E6
Stanfield NR20 48 F8
Upton with Fishley NR13 166 C8
Walsingham NR22 16 F7
Wereham PE33 80 E4
West Beckham NR25 9 B3
West Caister NR30 168 A4
West Winch PE33 43 E2
Wymondham NR18 173 C4
Back Mkt La NR29 167 B7
Back Mundesley Rd NR11 22 F8
Back of the Inns NR1 178 B2
Back Path 1 NR29 58 B6
Back Pier Plain NR31 170 D4
Back Rd Brockdish IP21 131 B8
East Ruston NR12 38 F6
Elm PE14 77 A8
Pentney PE32 63 C8
Somerton NR29 57 F6
Wisbech PE14 77 A7
Wood Dalling NR11 34 D6
Yelverton NR14 90 F5
Back St Binham NR21 6 E2
Fakenham NR21 141 B3
Garboldisham IP22 128 A8
Gayton PE32 45 C5
Harpley PE31 29 D5
Horsham St Faith NR10 53 D1
Lakenheath IP27 113 E1
Litcham PE32 48 A4
Mundesley NR11 143 C5
Reepham NR10 149 B4
South Creake NR21 15 D6
Tittleshall PE32 48 B7
Trunch NR28 22 E5
Back Terr PE37 153 B5
Backwood La
Howe NR15 90 C2
Shotesham NR15 107 F8
Bacon Rd NR4 161 F5
Baconsthorpe Castle* NR25 9 A1
Bacton Cl PE30 148 D3
Bacton Rd Bacton NR12 23 D5
North Walsham NR28 151 D6
Norwich NR3 158 B2
Paston NR28 143 E2
Bacton Rd *continued*
Witton NR28 23 C1
Bacton-on-Sea Fst Sch NR12 23 E4
Bader Cl PE30 147 D4
Badger Cl NR14 89 A2
Badgers Brook Rd NR8 155 F2
Bagge Rd PE30 147 A5
Bagthorpe Rd PE31 30 A7
Bailey Cl
4 Hethersett NR9 88 D7
6 Marthan NR29 57 D5
Bailey La PE34 145 E7
Bailey Rd NR27 139 B5
Bailey St PE32 46 F2
Bailiwick The 3 NR16 118 C5
Baillie Cl 3 NR31 170 B1
Bainard Rise NR15 107 C6
Bainards Cl NR18 173 B6
Baines Rd 4 PE30 146 D1
Baines Way 2 NR5 160 E8
Baird Way IP24 176 C7
Baker Cl
King's Lynn PE30 146 D1
North Walsham NR28 151 D3
Baker La 3 PE30 146 D4
Baker St
Great Yarmouth NR31 170 D5
14 Stalham NR12 39 B4
Baker's Rd NR13 75 A1
Bakers La NR35 109 A2
Bakers Rd NR3 162 D8
Bakers Yd NR23 136 C6
Bakery Cl NR24 142 E3
Bakery La NR9 51 A5
Balderston Ct NR3 178 B4
Baldock Cl 1 NR16 105 F5
Baldock Dr PE30 147 B8
Baldric Rd NR8 155 D1
Baldwin Cl 5 PE13 152 D5
Baldwin Rd PE30 147 C6
Baldwins Cl NR24 142 D4
Baldwins Dro 4 PE14 77 F6
Bale Rd Brinton NR24 18 C7
Hindringham NR21 17 E7
Balfour Rd 4 NR27 10 A5
Balfour St 4 NR3 162 F8
Baliol Rd NR31 170 C5
Ball's La NR21 17 D5
Ballygate NR34 110 C1
Balmoral Ave NR30 169 D7
Balmoral Cl
Attleborough NR17 174 F6
Dersingham PE31 140 D3
Balmoral Cres PE31 133 C5
Balmoral Rd PE30 147 C7
Balmoral W PE31 140 D3
Bambers La PE14 59 C2
Bancroft Cl 7 NR14 89 F4
Banham Barn Craft* NR16 119 C6
Banham Dr NR20 50 B2
Banham Prim Sch NR16 119 D6
Banham Rd NR16 119 B5
Banham Zoo* NR16 119 C6
Banham's La NR35 108 B2
Banister Way NR18 173 A5
Bank Dr PE13 152 A7
Bank Loke 6 NR28 151 C5
Bank Plain NR3 178 B3
Bank Rd PE31 140 C4
Bank Side PE34 146 C5
Bank St Norwich NR2 178 B3
Pulham Market IP21 121 E5
Bankside PE31 133 B6
Banningham Ct NR28 151 A4
Banningham Rd NR11 150 D8
Bannister Cl NR17 174 C6
Bannister's Row PE13 152 B7
Banters La NR34 124 F6
Banting Cl NR31 170 C1
Banyard Ct PE13 154 E5
Banyard Pl 6 NR19 154 D5
Banyards Pl PE33 61 D4
Baptist Rd PE14 77 D4
Bar Dro PE14 77 B8
Barber's La
Bedingham NR35 108 B2
Fakenham NR21 141 E4
Barberry Cl 5 NR8 155 B2
Barbers Yd 1 NR17 104 D2
Barchams Yd 16 NR26 138 D7
Barclay Gn NR7 159 D1
Barclay Rd NR7 159 E1
Bard Hill NR25 8 B6
Bardolph Pl PE34 61 D1
Bardolph's Way PE33 62 C6
Bardolphs Ct 1 NR8 155 B2
Bardwell Rd
Barningham IP31 127 C3
Fakenham Magna IP24 126 D3
Stanton IP31 127 B1
Bardyke Bank PE14 77 F4
Barford Cty Prim Sch NR9 69 F2
Barford Rd
Marlingford NR9 69 E3
Sheringham NR26 138 D7
Topcroft NR35 107 E2
Bargate Ct NR3 178 B4
Barham Ct NR31 170 D5
Barham's La NR16 105 D4
Barker St NR2 162 C8
Barker Way 5 NR13 72 D6
Barker's Dro PE33 81 A3
Barker's La
Norwich NR7 159 A5
Old Buckenham NR17 104 B2
Barkers Herne NR27 139 A6
Barkis Rd NR30 169 D1
Barley Way
Attleborough NR17 174 B3
Thetford IP24 176 D6
Barleycroft NR29 167 B7
Barleyfield Rd 8 NR10 53 A3
Barn Cl
2 Hopton on Sea NR31 171 E5
1 Lingwood NR13 74 A3
Barn Hill NR13 73 E2
Barn La
Gressenhall NR19 49 B2
Mautby NR29 75 E6
Barn Mdw NR14 163 B2
Barn Rd Docking PE31 134 F4
Norwich NR2 178 A4
Barn Terr NR13 165 C4
Barnaby Cl 5 NR19 154 C3
Barnard Ave NR30 169 D7
Barnard Cl
Great Yarmouth NR31 170 C1
5 Stoke Holy Cross NR14 89 F4
Barnard Cres NR30 169 C7
Barnard Rd NR5 160 E8
Barnards La PE33 61 D6
Barnards Rd NR28 38 A5
Barnards Yd 8 NR3 178 A3
Barnby Rd NR10 37 B2
Barnes Cl
Brandon IP27 175 A2
Norwich NR7 159 D2
Barnes' Rd IP21 121 E5
Barnesdale Rd 5 NR4 89 E8
Barney Rd NR21 17 F2
Barnfield Cl NR12 39 E2
Barnham Broom Prim Sch NR9 69 C2
Barnham Broom Rd
East Tuddenham NR20 69 D5
Wymondham NR18 173 A7
Barnham CE Prim Sch IP24 125 E5
Barnham Rd IP24 126 B6
Barningham CE VC Prim Sch IP31 127 C3
Barningham Pl NR11 20 C5
Barningham Rd
Gresham NR11 20 D8
Stanton IP31 127 C1
Barns The NR16 105 C4
Barnwell Rd PE30 147 B6
Baron's Cl NR21 141 C4
Baron's Hall La NR21 141 D4
Barondole La
Alburgh IP20 122 E8
Topcroft NR35 107 E2
Barr Dr IP27 113 E2
Barrack Rd
Great Yarmouth NR30 169 D1
Norwich NR1 163 B7
Barrack St NR3 178 C4
Barrett Cl PE30 147 E5
Barrett Rd Holt NR25 137 D7
Norwich NR1 162 E1
Barrett-Lennard Rd NR10 53 A4
Barri Cl NR14 90 C3
Barrow Cl NR3 157 F1
Barrow's Cnr IP24 125 A4
Barroway Dro PE38 78 E6
Barrows Hole La PE32 65 E7
Barsham Dr PE30 148 E1
Barsham Rd NR21 17 A5
Bartle Ct NR10 149 C5
Barton Broad Nature Reserve* NR12 55 F7
Barton Cl
North Walsham NR28 151 A4
Swaffham PE37 153 C2
Barton Ct PE30 147 D5
Barton Rd
Ashmanhaugh NR12 38 D1
Coltishall NR10 37 B2
Wisbech PE13 152 A4
Barton Way
6 Norwich NR1 163 B5
Ormesby St Margaret NR29 167 B3
Barton's La PE32 48 A8
Barwick Rd PE31 14 E6
Bases La NR23 136 C6
Basey Rd NR13 72 E8
Basham St IP22 177 B4
Basil Dr PE38 172 E6
Basil Rd PE33 80 A3
Bassingham Rd NR3 158 B2
Batchcroft Cl 6 PE38 172 C6
Batchelor Dr NR21 15 C2
Bately Ave NR31 170 D1
Bateman Cl 3 NR5 160 F7
Bates Gn NR5 161 C8
Bates La IP22 119 D2
Bate's Dro CB6 95 D1
Bath Ave NR20 154 F5
Bath Hill 7 NR30 169 D3
Bath Hill Terr NR30 169 D3
Bath Hills Rd NR35 123 E8
Bath Rd
West Dereham PE33 80 D5
Wisbech PE13 152 C7
Bathurst Rd 2 NR2 162 B5
Batterby Gn
Fakenham NR21 141 A3
Hempton NR21 31 C8
Battery Rd NR30 170 D8
Battlesea Hill IP21 131 E2
Bawburgh Cl NR5 156 D1
Bawburgh La NR5 156 D1
Bawburgh Prim Sch NR9 160 B6
Bawburgh Rd NR9 70 B5
Bawdeswell Prim Sch NR20 50 E7
Bawdeswell Rd NR20 50 C7
Bawsey Ctry Pk* PE32 44 D6
Baxter Cl 2 Hingham NR9 86 C5
Long Stratton NR15 106 E2
3 Wisbech PE13 152 E6
Baxter Ct NR3 158 B3
Baxter Rd NR9 86 C5
Baxter Row NR19 154 D4
Baxter's La NR15 107 F8
Bayes La NR16 106 C6
Bayfield NR17 174 E6
Bayfield Ave 3 NR19 154 C3
Bayfield Cl
1 Ixworth NR9 69 F2
King's Lynn PE30 147 D4
Baynard's La IP22 129 D7
Bayse's La NR24 18 C5
Bayspole Rd 5 NR15 106 E3
Beach Cl Hemsby NR29 167 E3
Mundesley NR11 143 C6
Overstrand NR27 11 A4
Beach Dr NR29 167 E4
Beach La NR25 8 E6
Beach Rd Bacton NR12 23 E5
Caister-on-Sea NR30 168 E5
Cley next the Sea NR25 7 E8
Cromer NR27 139 B7
Eccles on Sea NR12 24 E4
3 Great Yarmouth NR31 170 D4
Happisburgh NR12 24 C5
Hemsby NR29 167 C7
Holme next the Sea PE36 1 F6
Hopton on Sea NR31 171 E4
Lessingham NR12 24 E3
Mundesley NR11 143 C6
Runton NR27 10 C5
Salthouse NR25 8 C6
Sea Palling NR12 40 A6
Sheringham NR26 138 E7
Snettisham PE31 12 A4
Wells-next-the-Sea NR23 136 C7
Winterton-on-Sea NR29 58 B6
Beach Terr Rd PE36 132 C4
Beachamwell Rd PE13 153 A3
Beacon Hill PE31 135 C2
Beacon Hill La PE34 144 A6
Beacon Hill Rd PE31 135 C1
Beacon Rd NR11 11 F1
Beaconsfield Rd
Great Yarmouth NR30 169 D6
Norwich NR3 162 E8
Bear's La PE37 153 B5
Bears Cl 7 NR9 86 C4
Bears La NR9 86 C5
Bears Rd NR28 143 D2
Beatrice Ave NR19 154 D4
Beatrice Cl 6 NR28 151 C6
Beatrice Rd
Norwich NR1 163 A6
Wisbech PE13 152 D7
Beatty Cl
Great Yarmouth NR30 169 D8
Thetford IP24 176 E5
Beatty Rd
Great Yarmouth NR30 169 D8
Norwich NR4 162 B1
Beauchamp Cl
1 Caister-on-Sea NR30 168 D7
Chedgrave NR14 91 F2
Beauchamp Rd 2 NR14 92 A2
Beaufort Cl NR6 158 D6
Beaufort Way
Great Yarmouth NR31 170 B1
Hopton on Sea NR31 171 B8
Beaumont Pl 1 NR2 162 C4
Beaumont Rd NR5 157 B1
Beaumont Way PE30 147 C5
Beaupre Ave PE14 77 F7
Beavans Ct 8 NR31 169 B4
Beavens Ct 15 NR31 169 B4
Beavor La IP27 175 C4
Beccles Mus* NR34 110 C1
Beccles Rd
Aldeby NR34 110 F4
Aldeby, Wheatacre, Burgh St Peter NR34 111 B4
Belton with Browston NR31 94 A5
Bungay NR35 124 B8
Carlton Colville NR33 111 F1
Fritton & St Olaves NR31 93 E3
Great Yarmouth NR31 170 A5
Haddiscoe NR14 110 E7
Hales NR14 109 E7
Loddon NR14 92 A1
Raveningham NR14 110 A7
Thurlton NR14 92 F1
Beccles Sta NR34 110 D1
Becclesgate NR19 154 D6
Beck Ave NR29 167 A4
Beck Cl 5 NR25 8 F5
Beck La
Burgh & Tuttington NR11 36 E6
Horsham St Faith & Newton St Faith NR10 53 D2
Beck St IP22 127 E3
Beck The Feltwell IP26 98 E1
Beck The *continued*
Kenninghall NR16 119 A5
Beck View 3 IP20 122 D2
Beck Way NR14 91 F1
Becketswell Rd NR18 173 B3
Beckett Cl 6 PE30 148 C4
Becketts Ct NR18 173 B6
Beckmeadow Way NR11 143 C5
Becks Fur 2 NR8 155 E2
Becks Gn La NR34 124 F4
Beckside NR10 53 A2
Bedding La NR3 178 B4
Bede Cl PE30 148 C4
Bedford Dr PE30 148 B1
Bedford Mews NR26 138 D6
Bedford Row PE14 41 A4
Bedford St
Norwich NR2 178 B3
Wisbech PE13 152 C6
Bedingfield Rd 6 NR20 50 B3
Beech Ave
Attleborough NR17 174 C4
King's Lynn PE30 148 D2
7 Marham PE33 63 B4
Sheringham NR26 138 D5
Taverham NR8 155 B1
Beech Cl 1 Gresham NR11 9 E1
High Kelling NR25 8 E2
6 Loddon NR14 92 A1
Scole IP21 130 C5
Swaffham PE37 153 C4
Thetford IP24 176 B2
Wymondham NR18 173 D6
Beech Cres 6 PE33 43 E2
Beech Ct
24 Long Stratton NR15 106 E3
Swaffham PE13 154 D5
Beech Dr
East Dereham NR19 154 E1
North Walsham NR28 151 B6
Norwich NR6 158 C4
Norwich NR2 162 B4
Norwich NR1 163 A8
Strumpshaw NR13 73 F3
Beech Drift PE31 140 D3
Beech La NR29 75 C8
Beech Rd Beetley NR20 49 D4
Downham Market PE38 172 B6
King's Lynn PE30 146 E3
Wroxham/Hoveton NR12 164 D3
Beech Rise 23 NR31 94 C7
Beech Way
Brundall NR13 165 C3
Dickleburgh IP21 121 C1
Beech Wlk NR14 90 D5
Beechamwell Rd PE33 81 B8
Beechbank NR2 162 B4
Beechbank Dr 6 NR13 72 D6
Beechcroft NR5 156 F1
Beecheno Rd NR5 161 C8
Beeches Cl NR6 158 E4
Beeches La NR9 86 E6
Beeches The 1 NR20 68 E6
Beechey Cl PE38 172 C2
Beechfields IP27 175 F4
Beeching Cl 1 NR1 162 E1
Beeching Rd NR1 162 E2
Beechlands NR8 155 B1
Beechlands Pk NR11 22 B7
Beechwood Ave
Aylmerton NR11 10 A3
18 Watton IP25 84 D3
Beechwood Cl
North Walsham NR28 151 D6
Watlington PE33 61 E5
Beechwood Ct NR18 173 D1
Beechwood Dr NR7 159 E1
Beechwood Rd
Hemsby NR29 167 A8
Wisbech PE13 152 D7
Beechwoods NR6 158 D5
Beehive Yd IP22 177 C4
Beeleigh Way NR30 168 C7
Bee-Orchid Way NR14 91 C7
Beerlick's Loke NR14 73 B1
Beeston Comm NR26 138 E6
Beeston Hall Sch NR27 9 F5
Beeston La
Barton Turf NR12 38 D1
Beeston St Andrew NR12 159 B8
Fransham NR19 66 B8
Beeston Prim Sch PE32 48 C2
Beeston Rd
Beeston with Bittering PE32 48 D1
Great Dunham PE32 66 A8
Mileham PE32 48 D5
Sheringham NR26 138 E7
Beetley Grange 1 NR20 49 D4
Beetley Mdws 9 NR20 49 D4
Beevor Rd NR30 170 E7
Begdale Rd PE14 59 A1
Beighton Rd NR13 166 A2
Bek Cl NR4 161 E2
Belaugh Gn La NR12 164 A8
Belaugh La NR12 55 A7
Belaugh Rd NR12 164 C6
Belgrave Ave PE36 132 C6
Belgrave Gdns NR19 154 E3
Bell Cl
13 Bawdeswell NR20 50 E7

Bell Cl *continued*
East Dereham NR19 154 C5
Little Snoring NR21 17 B3
Norwich NR6 157 F6
Taverham NR8 156 E8
Bell La Rocklands NR17 103 B8
Saham Toney IP25 84 C4
Salhouse NR13 164 B1
Bell Mdw 1 Hingham NR9 86 C5
9 Martham NR29 57 D5
Bell Rd
Barnham Broom NR9 69 B2
Grimston PE32 28 C1
Norwich NR3 158 E1
Rocklands NR17 103 B8
Bell St IP26 98 E1
Bellacre Cl IP22 177 E4
Bellamy Way NR14 90 C4
Bellamy's La
Burnham Norton PE31 135 C5
West Walton PE14 59 A8
Bellands Way 4 IP23 130 C1
Bell's Dro Littleport CB6 95 E2
Runcton Holme PE33 61 C5
Bell's Marsh Rd NR31 170 D5
Bell's Mdw 2 PE37 66 A4
Bellmere Way IP25 84 C4
Bellomonte Cres NR8 156 F8
Bellrope Cl 5 NR18 173 D5
Bellrope La
Roydon IP22 129 D7
Wymondham NR18 173 D5
Bells La IP22 128 C4
Bells Rd NR31 170 D4
Bellview Cl NR24 142 B4
Bellville Cres NR1 178 C1
Belmore Cl NR7 159 E1
Belmore Rd NR7 163 F8
Beloe Ave 4 NR5 161 A7
Beloe Cres PE30 146 D1
Belseybridge Rd NR35 108 F3
Belsize Cl 4 PE38 172 B4
Belsize Rd NR1 163 B7
Belstead Ave NR30 168 D5
Belt Rd NR13 73 C7
Belvedere Pl 3 NR4 162 A3
Belvidere Rd NR30 169 D5
Belvoir St NR2 162 B6
Ben Culey Dr IP24 176 C5
Ben's La PE33 80 E4
Benbow Cl 6 NR9 88 E8
Benbow Rd IP24 176 F6
Bendish Ave NR31 170 D2
Bendish Way NR5 160 E7
Benedict Cl PE34 145 F5
Benedict Rd 10 NR12 55 E4
Benets View 3 NR28 151 E5
Bengey's Rd 7 PE37 65 F4
Benjamin Ct NR27 139 B5
Benn's La PE34 144 C5
Bennett Cl
Hunstanton PE36 132 D2
3 Watlington PE33 61 D5
Bennett Rd NR20 50 B2
Bennett St PE38 172 A5
Bennington's La
Aylmerton NR11 138 F1
East Beckham NR11 9 D2
Bensley Cl NR13 166 C4
Bensley Rd
1 Martham NR29 57 D5
Norwich NR2 162 A4
Bentinck Way 2 PE34 146 C5
Bentley Rd NR16 105 F4
Bentley Way NR3 158 C4
Bentons Way NR10 53 B8
Ber St NR1 178 B1
Berberis Gn 3 NR31 170 B5
Beresford Rd
Caister-on-Sea NR30 168 E4
Great Yarmouth NR30 169 D7
Holt NR25 137 C5
Bergamot Cl IP24 176 F4
Bergen Way PE30 146 F8
Bergh Apton Rd
Alpington NR14 90 F4
Mundham NR14 91 D1
Bermondsey Pl E 19
NR30 169 D4
Bermondsey Pl S 18
NR30 169 D4
Bermondsey Pl W 17
NR30 169 D4
Bernard Cl
High Kelling NR25 8 E2
11 New Rackheath NR13 72 E7
Bernard Cres PE36 132 D6
Bernard Rd
Cromer NR27 139 A7
Great Yarmouth NR31 170 D2
Berners Cl NR3 158 B1
Berners St NR3 158 B1
Berney Arms Sta NR30 93 D8
Berney Arms Windmill*
NR30 93 E7
Bernham Rd NR6 157 E6
Berrington Rd NR6 157 F6
Berry Cl NR31 93 F6
Berry Hall Rd NR12 38 E1
Berry's La NR9 69 D6
Berryfields NR13 165 C5
Bertie Rd NR3 158 C1
Bertie Ward Way
NR19 154 F2
Bessemer Rd NR4 162 D1
Bessemer Way NR31 169 B1
Besthorpe Carr NR17 105 A6
Besthorpe Rd NR17 174 E5
Bestthorpe Rd NR16 105 A5
Bethel St NR2 178 A3
Betjeman Cl IP24 176 E6
Beulah St PE30 147 B6
Bevan Cl
Carleton Rode NR16 105 C4
Norwich NR5 161 B6
Beveridge Way PE33 43 E4
Beverley Cl NR5 161 E6
Beverley Rd
Brundall NR13 165 B4
Norwich NR5 161 E6
Beverley Way
Clenchwarton PE34 145 E5
Taverham NR8 156 F8
Beverly Ct NR31 170 A7
Bevis Way PE30 147 B7
Bewfeld Rd 4 NR5 160 E8
Bewick Cl
11 Great Yarmouth NR31 94 C8
5 Snettisham PE31 12 E5
Bewit Rd NR7 159 D4
Bexfield Rd NR20 33 C4
Bexwell Rd Bexwell PE38 79 F6
Downham Market PE38 172 D5
Bickley Cl NR17 174 F7
Bidewell Cl NR8 157 B7
Bidwell Rd NR13 72 E8
Bidwels ct IP24 176 C4
Bier La IP22 128 F5
Big Back La 1 NR14 92 A2
Big Row NR34 109 F2
Big Yard PE36 2 A3
Big Yard The PE36 132 E7
Biggin Hill Way IP25 85 A3
Biggotts La NR15 108 E7
Biggs Rd PE14 59 D4
Bignold Fst Sch NR2 178 A2
Bignold Mid Sch NR2 178 A2
Bignold Rd NR3 158 A2
Bilberry Cl 5 NR17 174 B5
Bilbys NR14 110 B6
Bill Todd Way NR8 155 C2
Billing Cl NR6 158 F5
Billingford Rd
1 Bawdeswell NR20 50 E7
Bintree NR20 33 B1
Bilney La NR10 155 E8
Bilney Rd Beetley NR20 49 B4
East Winch PE32 45 B1
Pentney PE32 63 C8
Bingles Turn NR10 53 B7
Binham Rd
Field Dalling NR25 7 A1
Hindringham NR21 17 E8
4 King's Lynn PE30 148 C3
Langham NR25 7 A4
Warham NR23 6 A4
Bintree Rd NR20 50 B8
Binyon Gdns NR8 156 D8
Birbeck Rd NR1 162 E2
Birch Ave 8 NR20 49 D4
Birch Cl
East Dereham NR19 154 C4
Little Melton NR9 160 D2
North Walsham NR28 151 D6
6 Snettisham PE31 12 E4
Birch Covert 5 IP24 176 F5
Birch Ct Erpingham NR11 21 B2
Norwich NR7 159 D4
Birch Dr
Attleborough NR17 174 C3
Roydon PE32 28 A2
Birch Gr
Sheringham NR26 138 D4
West Winch PE33 43 E2
Wisbech PE14 59 B1
Birch Rd Gayton PE32 45 C6
11 Hethersett NR9 88 D8
Birch Tree Cl PE30 146 E4
Birch Way
4 Great Yarmouth NR31 170 B5
Mundham NR14 108 F6
Bircham Rd
Docking PE31 134 C4
Reepham NR10 149 C5
Snettisham PE31 13 A4
Stanhoe PE31 14 E7
Bircham Windmill*
PE31 14 A3
Birches The PE30 148 D4
Birchfield Gdns NR14 89 B3
Birchfield La NR14 89 B3
Birchfield Rd PE38 78 E3
Birchgrove Rd PE30 147 C4
Birchwood 4 NR7 72 D3
Birchwood St 5 PE30 146 E6
Birchwood Way PE38 172 B6
Bird View Sq 1 IP26 98 E1
Birdcage Wlk PE30 146 D3
Birds Cnr IP25 67 E4
Birds Rd NR28 151 B3
Birkbeck Cl
King's Lynn PE30 148 B2
Stoke Holy Cross NR14 90 B5
Birkbeck Way NR7 163 F7
Birkdale NR4 162 A2
Birkin Cl 3 NR16 105 F5
Birtles Way NR13 166 C3
Biscay Gdns NR30 168 C6
Bishop Bonner's Cottage
Mus* NR19 154 D5
Bishop Bridge Rd
NR1 163 A6
Bishop Herbert Cl
NR20 69 B8
Bishop Rise 3 NR8 155 E2
Bishop's Cl NR7 163 D5
Bishop's Rd
Hunstanton PE36 132 C2
King's Lynn PE30 147 B4
Bishopgate NR1 178 C3
Bishops Wlk 5 NR31 171 D5
Bishoptyne Ave 1 NR19 154 F3
Bishy Barnebee Way
NR5 160 F6
Bittering St
4 Beetley NR20 49 C4
4 Gressenhall NR20 49 C3
Bittern Cl Necton PE37 66 A3
Thetford IP24 176 D1
Bittern Cres NR12 38 F1
Bittern Rd NR29 57 D3
Bixley Cl NR5 161 D6
Black Bear La PE13 152 F7
Black Drif PE37 66 A4
Black Dro
Downham West PE38 79 B6
Feltwell PE38 97 F2
Fincham PE33 80 D7
Marshland St James
PE14 60 D4
Stow Bardolph PE34 78 E8
Black Dyke Rd IP26 113 E7
Black Horse Cl NR19 67 B7
Black Horse Dro CB6 96 E2
Black Horse Opening
NR6 158 F2
Black Horse Rd
Clenchwarton PE34 145 C4
Runhall NR9 68 F1
Black Mill La NR15 121 A7
Black Moor Rd IP25 67 D2
Black St Hemsby NR29 58 B6
Martham NR29 57 D5
Blackbarn Rd NR16 120 D8
Blackberry Ct NR6 157 F2
Blackberry Gr NR27 10 C4
Blackberry Hall La
NR11 11 D1
Blackbird Ave IP27 175 F3
Blackbird Cl 17 NR31 94 C8
Blackburn Rd NR6 158 C6
Blackdale Mid Sch
NR4 161 D4
Blackdike Dro IP27 112 F5
Blackdyke Cl 8 IP26 98 D1
Blackford PE30 147 D8
Blackfriars' Rd NR30 169 D2
Blackfriars Rd
King's Lynn PE30 146 E5
8 Wisbech PE13 152 C5
Blackfriars St
King's Lynn PE30 146 D4
Norwich NR3 178 B4
Blackhills Cnr NR13 73 C7
Blackhorse Cl 9 NR20 50 E7
Blackhorse Mdw 10
NR20 50 E7
Blackhorse St 1 NR2 162 C7
Blackhorse Yd NR23 136 C6
Blackmoor Row IP25 67 D1
Blacks Ave NR14 163 B2
Blackslough La NR16 119 D7
Blacksmith La IP24 125 E6
Blacksmith's La
Barton Bendish PE33 81 B8
Morning Thorpe NR15 107 A2
Blacksmith's Loke
NR32 94 C2
Blacksmith's Row 1
PE32 45 C6
Blacksmiths Cl NR20 33 B6
Blacksmiths La
Ashwellthorpe NR16 106 B8
Happisburgh NR12 24 B6
Hindringham NR21 17 E7
Blacksmiths Way NR6 158 E5
Blackthorn Ave NR25 137 C7
Blackthorn Cl
Diss IP22 177 F5
Norwich NR6 158 D4
3 Thetford IP24 176 F4
Blackthorn Dr 3 NR19 154 C4
Blackthorn Rd
Attleborough NR17 174 B5
King's Lynn PE30 148 C3
Wymondham NR18 173 D4
Blackthorn Way 16 NR14 90 C5
Blackwall Reach
NR31 170 D5
Blackwater Cnr NR11 36 F5
Blackwater La
Great Witchingham NR9 51 C6
Heydon NR11 34 D8
Blackwell Ave NR7 159 A3
Bladewater Rd NR5 160 F5
Blake Cl PE32 28 A1
Blake Ct PE13 153 C2
Blake Dr NR31 170 A7
Blake Rd NR30 169 D7
Blakeney CE Prim Sch
NR25 7 D6
Blakeney Cl NR4 161 E2
Blakeney Long La NR25 7 C4
Blakeney Point National
Nature Reserve* NR25 7 C8
Blakeney Rd
Binham NR21 6 D1
Letheringsett with Glandford
NR25 7 F2
Morston NR25 7 B6
Blakeney Short La NR25 7 C3
Blakes Ct NR3 158 F3
Blakestone Dr NR7 163 D7
Bland Rd NR5 161 B6
Blatchford Way PE31 133 B5
Blencowe Terr 23 PE13 152 C5
Blenheim Ave 4 NR29 57 D4
Blenheim Cl
12 Long Stratton NR15 106 E3
Norwich NR7 159 B5
Blenheim Cres
Beeston with Bittering
PE32 48 D2
Griston IP25 85 A2
Norwich NR7 159 B5
Tittleshall PE32 48 A7
Blenheim Dr NR17 174 E4
Blenheim Pk Sch NR21 15 C3
Blenheim Rd
King's Lynn PE30 147 C8
Norwich NR7 159 B5
Sculthorpe Airfield NR21 15 C3
Blenheim Way
Emneth PE14 152 E2
2 Roydon IP22 129 D7
5 Watton IP25 84 E3
Blick Cl 5 PE33 43 F2
Blickling Cl 1 PE30 148 F1
Blickling Hall* NR11 35 F7
Blickling Rd
Blickling NR11 150 A8
Norwich NR6 158 C5
Bligh Cl NR14 90 D5
Blind Dick's La NR22 16 E7
Blind La
Castle Acre PE32 46 F1
Hockering NR9 51 A2
Honingham NR9 69 F5
Horsham St Faith NR10 53 D1
Mattishall NR20 69 A7
Blithe Mdw Ct NR7 159 C3
Blithemeadow Dr
NR7 159 C3
Blithewood Gdns NR7 159 C3
Blo' Norton Rd IP22 128 C7
Blocka Rd NR32 93 F2
Blofield Cnr Rd NR13 73 B6
Blofield Loke NR12 164 E6
Blofield Prim Sch
NR13 165 E7
Blofield Rd
Brundall NR13 165 E3
Lingwood & Burlingham
NR13 73 F3
Blofields Loke NR11 150 C6
Blomefield Rd
Diss IP22 177 D4
Norwich NR3 158 B2
Bloodgate Hill NR21 15 D6
Bloodhills Rd NR29 57 F5
Bloodslat La NR12 23 D4
Bloomfield Rd NR30 170 E7
Blooms Turn NR28 22 E5
Bloomstile La NR25 8 B6
Bloomstiles NR25 8 B6
Blowlands La NR26 138 B5
Blue Boar La NR7 159 D3
Blue Doors Loke NR31 94 C3
Blue Sky Cl NR31 94 C7
Bluebell Cl
Attleborough NR17 174 B5
4 East Dereham NR19 154 C4
Thetford IP24 176 F4
Bluebell Cres NR4 161 D2
Bluebell Dr NR26 138 B6
Bluebell Gdns NR23 136 E5
Bluebell Rd
Mulbarton NR14 89 B3
North Walsham NR28 151 D6
Norwich NR4 161 D3
Bluebell Way 18 NR31 94 C6
Bluebell Wlk IP27 175 A2
Bluestone Cres NR21 15 D6
Bluestone La NR21 15 D7
Bluestone Rd NR21 15 D6
Blundeston Rd NR32 111 F8
Blundeville Manor 6
NR15 89 C1
Blunt's Cnr NR23 5 B2
Blyth Cres NR26 138 D6
Blyth Jex Sch The
NR3 158 E2
Blyth Rd NR3 158 D2
Boadicea Cl 1 IP24 176 D7
Boal Quay PE30 146 D4
Boal St PE30 146 D4
Boardman Cl NR6 158 D3
Boat Dyke La NR13 166 D4
Boat Dyke Rd NR13 166 B8
Boathouse La NR32 111 F3
Boatmans Row NR23 136 C6
Bob Carter Leisure Ctr
NR8 157 A8
Bodleian Ct NR31 170 B2
Boileau Ave 6 NR16 105 F5
Boileau Cl 1 NR4 89 E8
Boleness Rd PE13 152 C2
Bolingbroke Rd NR3 158 B3
Boltons The PE30 148 C1
Bolts Cl NR23 136 D6
Bond Cl IP21 121 F4
Bond St 3 Cromer NR27 139 B7
5 Hingham NR9 86 C5
Norwich NR2 162 A7
Bond's Rd NR15 121 C4
Bonds Rd NR13 73 C7
Bone Rd NR8 157 B8
Bone's Dro NR23 4 F7
Boniface Cl NR4 162 C1
Bonnetts La PE14 60 B5
Boosey's Wlk 6 NR16 104 F1
Boot Binders Rd 7
NR6 158 C1
Boot La IP22 120 D6
Booton Comm Nature
Reserve* NR10 149 E5
Booton Rd NR10 35 B2
Booty Rd NR7 159 F1
Borage Cl IP24 176 F4
Border La NR32 94 B2
Border Rd PE33 81 A2
Borough Cl PE13 152 D3
Borrowdale Dr NR1 163 B8
Borton Rd 4 NR13 73 C6
Boscombe Rd IP25 85 A3
Bosgate Rise 6 NR29 57 C4
Boston Cl 4 NR19 154 C3
Boston End 6 IP24 116 A1
Boston Sq PE36 132 C5
Boston Sq Sensory Pk
PE36 132 C5
Boston St NR3 158 D2
Botolph St NR3 178 A4
Boton Dr NR19 154 D7
Bottom Breck Cl NR5 156 F2
Botwright Dr 5 PE37 153 C3
Boudica's Way NR14 163 A1
Boughey Cl PE31 3 B6
Boughton Long Rd
PE33 81 B7
Boughton Rd
Fincham PE33 62 E1
Stoke Ferry PE33 81 A3
Boulderside Cl 4 NR7 163 E7
Boulevard Rd 2 NR27 10 A5
Boulevard The
Sheringham NR26 138 D7
Thorpe End NR13 72 E6
Boulters The NR31 170 C1
Boulton Rd NR7 163 C7
Boulton St NR1 178 B2
Boundary Ave NR6 158 A4
Boundary Cl IP26 113 F7
Boundary La
Norwich NR7 72 E3
Paston NR28 23 B3
Boundary Rd
Ashby with Oby NR29 56 E2
Great Yarmouth NR31 169 B1
1 Hockwold cum Wilton
IP26 114 A7
Marham PE33 63 C3
Norton Subcourse NR14 92 D1
Norwich NR6 157 F3
Raveningham NR14 110 B8
Boundary Way 1 NR14 90 C5
Bourne Cl
King's Lynn PE30 148 C2
Long Stratton NR15 106 E3
Bow Hill NR9 70 A3
Bow St NR9 86 B1
Bowers Ave NR3 158 A2
Bowers Cl NR3 158 A2
Bowlers Cl NR13 92 E7
Bowling Gn Cl
Attleborough NR17 174 D6
Crostwick NR12 54 B2
Bowling Gn The
Raynham NR21 30 F4
Wells-next-the-Sea
NR23 136 D5
Bowling Gn Wlk 2
NR30 169 C4
Bowman Rd 4 NR4 89 E8
Bowthorpe Hall Gdns*
PE13 152 D5
Bowthorpe Hall Rd
NR5 160 F7
Bowthorpe Rd
Norwich NR5 161 D6
Wisbech PE13 152 D5
Box's La PE37 153 D5
Boyces Rd PE13 152 E5
Boyd Ave 9 NR19 154 D1
Boylandhall La NR15 107 B4
Brabazon Rd NR6 158 B5
Bracecamp Cl NR29 167 C2
Braces La NR35 109 E3
Bracey Ave NR6 158 F5
Bracken Ave
3 Beetley NR20 49 D4
Norwich NR6 158 A4
Overstrand NR27 11 A3
Bracken Cl
Fakenham NR21 141 F4
Horsford NR10 53 B2
Stratton Strawless NR10 53 A6
Bracken Dr NR17 174 B5
Bracken Rd
King's Lynn PE30 148 C2
Thetford IP24 176 C1
Bracken Rise
Brandon IP27 175 E3
Mundford IP26 100 A4
Bracken Way PE32 28 B1
Brackenwoods PE37 66 A4
Bracon Rd NR31 93 F5
Bracondale NR1 178 C1
Bracondale Ct 3 NR1 162 F3
Bracondale Gn NR1 178 C1
Bracondale Millgate
NR14 163 A2
Bradcar Rd NR17 103 B2
Braddock Rd NR30 168 E5
Bradeham Way NR4 162 A1

Bradenham Hall Gdn & Arboretum* IP25 ....66 E4
Bradenham La NR19 ....66 F6
Bradenham Rd IP25 ....67 A2
Bradfield Cl NR28 ....151 A6
Bradfield Pl 3 PE33 ....81 A3
Bradfield Rd
Antingham NR11 ....22 C5
North Walsham NR28 ....151 A6
Swafield NR28 ....22 E3
Bradman's La NR18 ....87 D3
Bradmere La PE31 ....134 E5
Bradshaw Rd NR8 ....157 C7
Bradwell Ave 3 NR31 ....170 A5
Brady Cl PE38 ....172 B1
Brady Gdns PE38 ....172 B1
Braeburn Ave PE13 ....152 C8
Braeford Cl NR6 ....157 E2
Brailsford Cl NR20 ....68 A7
Braithwait Cl 1 NR5 ....161 A8
Brake La NR21 ....16 C4
Bramble Ave NR6 ....158 A5
Bramble Cl
Mundesley NR11 ....143 D5
Sculthorpe Airfield NR21 ....15 C2
4 Taverham NR8 ....155 E2
Bramble Ct NR21 ....141 E4
Bramble Dr PE30 ....148 C2
Bramble Gdns NR31 ....93 F5
Bramble La
Outwell PE14 ....77 D7
Swaffham PE37 ....153 F5
Bramble Way
11 Poringland NR14 ....90 D5
Wymondham NR18 ....173 E4
Brambles Cl 2 NR10 ....54 A1
Bramerton La
Framingham Pigot NR14 ....90 E7
Rockland St Mary NR14 ....91 A7
Bramerton Rd NR14 ....91 A8
Bramfield Cl NR2 ....162 A7
Bramley Cl NR23 ....136 D6
Bramley Dr NR21 ....31 E5
Bramley Rd
Dereham NR20 ....68 A8
Diss IP22 ....177 C5
Wisbech PE13 ....152 C7
Brampton Cl PE13 ....152 A4
Brampton Ct 12 NR5 ....161 A7
Brampton Sta NR10 ....36 E3
Brancaster Cl
King's Lynn PE30 ....147 C8
1 Taverham NR8 ....155 F3
Brancaster Rd PE31 ....134 E7
Brancaster Way PE37 ....153 B2
Branch Rd NR13 ....75 B2
Brand's La
Felthorpe NR10 ....155 D6
Tharston & Hapton NR15 ....106 E5
Brandiston Rd NR10 ....35 B2
Brandon Cl
Norwich NR6 ....157 E4
3 Swaffham PE37 ....153 C3
Brandon Ct NR13 ....165 E3
Brandon Her Ctr* IP27 ....175 D4
Brandon Rd
Cockley Cley PE37 ....83 A8
Methwold IP26 ....99 B4
Saham Toney IP25 ....84 B3
Swaffham PE37 ....65 A1
Thetford IP24 ....176 A4
Wangford IP27 ....114 C1
Watton IP25 ....84 C3
Weeting-with-Broomhill IP27 ....175 C5
Brandon Sports Ctr IP27 ....175 B3
Brandon Sta IP27 ....175 C5
Brandon Terr NR30 ....169 E2
Brandvnvm (Roman Fort) (Branodunum)* PE31 ....3 C6
Branford Rd
Caister-on-Sea NR30 ....168 D7
Norwich NR3 ....158 E1
Branksome Cl NR4 ....162 B2
Branksome Rd NR4 ....162 A2
Branodunum PE31 ....3 B7
Bransby Cl PE30 ....146 F4
Brasenose Ave NR31 ....170 B3
Brasier Rd NR3 ....158 B2
Brawdy Rd 7 IP31 ....126 B1
Bray's La
Guestwick NR20 ....34 A6
Rocklands NR17 ....103 A7
Braydeston Ave NR13 ....165 D3
Braydeston Cres NR13 ....165 D3
Braydeston Dr NR13 ....165 F6
Braydeston Hall La NR13 ....73 E4
Brayfield Way NR6 ....158 F6
Braymeadow NR9 ....160 C2
Braymeadow La NR9 ....160 D2
Brazen Gate NR1 ....178 A1
Breck Farm Cl NR8 ....155 C2
Breck Farm La NR8 ....155 C2
Breck Rd Norwich NR7 ....159 E2
Weston Longville NR9 ....51 E1
Breckland Bsns Pk IP25 ....84 F3
Breckland Leisure Ctr & Waterworld IP24 ....176 D5
Breckland Mid Sch IP27 ....175 A2
Breckland Rd NR5 ....157 A1
Brecklands
Mundford IP26 ....100 B4
11 Stalham NR12 ....39 B4
Brecklands Rd NR13 ....165 E2
Brecon Rd NR15 ....90 E2
Breeze Ave NR11 ....150 B5
Brellows Hill PE34 ....144 A5
Brenda Collison Cl PE31 ....140 C4
Brenda James Cl 1 NR7 ....163 E7
Brennewater Mews 4 NR5 ....161 A8
Brent Ave PE31 ....12 E5
Brentwood 1 NR4 ....161 F1
Brereton Cl 1 NR5 ....161 C6
Bressingham Prim Sch IP22 ....129 B8
Bressingham Rd
5 Gresham NR11 ....9 E1
Roydon IP22 ....129 C8
Sustead NR11 ....20 E8
Bressingham Steam Mus & Gdns* IP22 ....129 C7
Breton Cl 10 NR19 ....154 D2
Brett Ave NR31 ....170 D1
Brett Way PE30 ....147 B8
Brettingham Ave NR4 ....89 B8
Brewers Ct NR3 ....178 C4
Brewers Gn La IP22 ....177 B6
Brewery La NR18 ....173 C3
Brewery Rd NR28 ....22 D5
Brewery St NR30 ....169 C4
Brewster Ct NR13 ....165 D6
Brewsters 8 NR16 ....118 C5
Breydon Dr NR8 ....156 C4
Breydon Dr N NR8 ....156 C5
Breydon Junc NR30 ....76 C3
Breydon Mid Sch NR31 ....94 A5
Breydon Rd
Great Yarmouth NR31 ....169 B4
King's Lynn PE30 ....147 D5
Norwich NR7 ....159 A4
Breydon Way NR30 ....168 D6
Brian Ave NR1 ....162 D3
Briar Ave NR31 ....94 C7
Briar Cl Dereham NR20 ....68 A8
Grimston PE32 ....28 B1
King's Lynn PE30 ....148 C3
14 Lingwood NR13 ....74 A3
9 Necton PE37 ....65 F4
Briar La
Heckingham NR14 ....109 F8
Rickinghall Inferior IP22 ....128 D1
Swainsthorpe NR14 ....89 D3
Briar Rd 39 IP20 ....122 D2
Briars Ct NR5 ....161 F7
Brick Kiln La
Bunwell NR16 ....105 D2
Gillingham NR34 ....110 C5
Long Stratton NR15 ....107 A5
Shipdham IP25 ....67 C2
Brick Kiln Rd
Ellingham NR35 ....109 C4
Hevingham NR10 ....53 A7
North Walsham NR28 ....151 E5
Thursford NR21 ....17 F4
Brick Kilns Rd NR13 ....73 B7
Brick La NR27 ....10 B5
Brickfield Loke NR8 ....156 C5
Brickfields NR13 ....73 F2
Brickfields Way IP24 ....176 C6
Brickkiln La
Ashwellthorpe NR16 ....105 F7
Mulbarton NR14 ....89 C2
South Lopham IP22 ....128 F7
Brickle Loke NR14 ....90 B5
Brickle Rd NR14 ....90 B4
Brickley La PE31 ....140 D7
Brickyard La PE31 ....29 C4
Brickyard Rd NR28 ....22 A2
Bridewell Alley 2 NR2 ....178 B3
Bridewell La
Acle NR13 ....166 C4
Botesdale IP22 ....128 E2
Bridewell Mus The* NR2 ....178 B3
Bridewell St
1 Little Walsingham NR22 ....16 F7
Wymondham NR18 ....173 C3
Bridge Broad Cl NR12 ....164 C5
Bridge Cl
16 Harleston IP20 ....122 D2
Heacham PE31 ....133 E5
Melton Constable NR24 ....142 B4
Bridge Farm La NR4 ....161 C6
Bridge Gdns NR19 ....154 F1
Bridge La IP25 ....84 C6
Bridge Mdw NR29 ....58 A4
Bridge Rd
Brome & Oakley IP21 ....130 C5
Bunwell NR16 ....105 F2
Burston & Shimpling IP22 ....120 E3
Colby NR11 ....36 D8
Downham West PE38 ....79 B5
Great Ryburgh NR21 ....32 C6
5 Great Yarmouth NR30 ....169 C5
High Kelling NR25 ....137 F8
North Elmham NR20 ....32 F3
Potter Heigham NR29 ....56 F5
Stoke Ferry PE33 ....81 A2
Sutton Bridge PE12 ....41 A8
Wymondham NR18 ....88 B2
Bridge St Brandon IP27 ....175 C4
Carbrooke IP25 ....85 A4
Downham Market PE38 ....172 B5
Bridge St *continued*
Fakenham NR21 ....141 B3
Gressenhall NR20 ....49 C3
Hilgay PE38 ....79 E1
14 King's Lynn PE30 ....146 D4
Loddon NR14 ....92 A2
Stiffkey NR23 ....6 D5
Thetford IP24 ....176 C4
14 Wisbech PE13 ....152 C5
Bridgecourt NR29 ....58 A4
Bridgefoot La NR25 ....7 F5
Bridges Wlk
Fakenham NR21 ....141 A3
Thetford IP24 ....176 D3
Bridgford Cl NR31 ....170 C2
Bridgham La NR16 ....117 F4
Bridle La
Downham Market PE38 ....172 D7
Keswick NR4 ....89 C7
Bridle Rd IP25 ....84 C3
Brig Sq NR23 ....136 C6
Brigg St NR1 ....178 A2
Briggs Loke NR11 ....36 D8
Brigham Cl NR13 ....165 C4
Brighton Rd 1 NR15 ....89 C1
Brightwell Rd NR3 ....158 D3
Brighty's Opening NR2 ....162 B7
Brigstock Rd PE13 ....152 B7
Brimbelow Rd NR12 ....164 D4
Brindle Dr 5 NR14 ....89 B3
Brinell Way NR31 ....170 B8
Brinton Rd NR24 ....142 D8
Briscoe Way IP27 ....113 E2
Brisley CE Prim Sch NR20 ....32 A1
Bristol Terr NR2 ....178 A2
Briston Rd
Briston NR24 ....142 A5
Corpusty NR11 ....19 F1
Edgefield NR24 ....19 C5
Wood Dalling NR11 ....34 C6
Britannia Pier Theatre NR30 ....169 E4
Britannia Rd
Great Yarmouth NR30 ....169 E4
Norwich NR1 ....163 A7
Britannia Way PE13 ....152 C2
Britch La PE34 ....42 B4
Briton Way NR18 ....173 B3
Briton's La
Beeston Regis NR26 ....138 F4
Sheringham NR26 ....9 F5
Briton's La Cl
2 Beeston Regis NR27 ....9 F5
Sheringham NR26 ....138 F5
Britton Cl 9 PE33 ....61 D6
Broad Dro Emneth PE14 ....59 C1
Grimston PE32 ....45 C8
Methwold IP26 ....97 F6
Upwell PE14 ....77 D4
Broad End La PE13 ....152 F4
Broad End Rd PE14 ....152 F4
Broad Fen La NR28 ....38 D4
Broad La Brancaster PE31 ....3 A7
Great & Little Plumstead NR13 ....72 F6
South Walsham NR13 ....74 B8
Swannington NR9 ....52 B5
Broad Rd Alburgh IP20 ....122 E8
Fleggburgh NR29 ....75 C8
Broad Reaches NR29 ....56 C5
Broad Row 17 NR30 ....169 C4
Broad St Bungay NR35 ....124 A8
20 Harleston IP20 ....122 D2
King's Lynn PE30 ....146 D5
Broad View 4 NR13 ....72 D6
Broad Way
Dickleburgh & Rushall IP21 ....130 D8
Rocklands NR17 ....103 A8
Broadacres 4 NR13 ....74 B8
Broadcote Cl NR15 ....90 E1
Broaden La NR15 ....107 C6
Broadfen Dro IP26 ....98 B5
Broadfields Way NR14 ....91 C7
Broadgate NR8 ....155 B2
Broadgate Cl NR27 ....11 A2
Broadgate La
Great Moulton NR15 ....121 B8
Roydon PE32 ....28 A2
Broadhurst Rd NR4 ....162 B1
Broadland Cl NR13 ....93 A4
Broadland Dr NR13 ....72 D6
Broadland High Sch NR12 ....164 D6
Broadland Sports Club NR29 ....75 D8
Broadland Way
Acle NR13 ....166 C3
Postwick with Witton NR7 ....72 E3
Broadlands PE38 ....172 B5
Broadlands Cl PE31 ....140 C4
Broadlands Rd NR12 ....39 E1
Broadmead Gn NR13 ....72 E6
Broadmoor Rd IP25 ....85 B4
Broadsman Cl NR1 ....163 A4
Broadwater La PE32 ....45 B4
Broadwater Rd PE36 ....1 F7
Broadwater Way 1 NR12 ....55 E4
Broadway Cl 5 NR15 ....107 C5
Broadway The
Heacham PE31 ....133 D5
Honingham NR9 ....69 E8
Scarning NR19 ....154 B2
Broadwood Cl NR11 ....11 E1
Brockdish Prim Sch IP21 ....131 D6
Brockley Gn 7 PE30 ....147 C4
Brocks Rd PE37 ....153 B6
Brockwell Ct NR3 ....158 F2
Brome Ave IP23 ....130 C2
Brome Hall La IP23 ....130 D3
Bromedale Ave 10 NR14 ....89 B3
Brook Gr 8 NR19 ....154 D3
Brook La Brookville IP26 ....99 A7
Burgate IP22 ....129 C3
Needham IP20 ....131 E8
St Margaret, Ilketshall NR35 ....124 C3
Brook Pl NR1 ....178 B2
Brook Rd
Dersingham PE31 ....140 D2
Sheringham NR26 ....138 E6
Brook St
Buxton with Lammas NR10 ....36 E1
Cromer NR27 ....139 C7
Lamas NR10 ....53 E8
Brooke Ave NR30 ....168 D5
Brooke Prim Sch NR15 ....90 E1
Brooke Rd
Kirstead NR15 ....91 A1
Mundham NR14 ....108 F8
Seething NR15 ....91 C1
Shotesham NR15 ....107 F8
Brookes Dr NR28 ....151 A4
Brookfield Cl NR15 ....106 F4
Brooks Dr NR19 ....154 B4
Brooks Mdw NR14 ....90 D5
Brooks Rd NR10 ....53 B3
Brookside NR20 ....49 E8
Brookwell Springs 1 PE32 ....44 B3
Broom Ave
Norwich NR6 ....158 A5
Norwich NR7 ....163 E8
Broom Cl
15 Marthan NR29 ....57 D4
Norwich NR1 ....162 F3
Taverham NR8 ....155 C3
Broom Gn Dr NR20 ....32 E4
Broom Gn Rd NR20 ....32 E2
Broom Hill La IP24 ....126 C3
Broom La Easton NR9 ....70 B5
Witton NR28 ....38 C8
Broom Rd
Lakenheath IP27 ....113 F1
Wymondham NR18 ....105 C6
Broome Gdns 2 NR31 ....94 A5
Broomhill 1 NR27 ....10 B5
Broomhill La NR10 ....149 B3
Broomsthorpe Rd PE31 ....30 A7
Brothercross Way PE38 ....172 C7
Brow of the Hill PE32 ....44 E6
Browick Rd NR18 ....173 C4
Browick Rd Inf Sch NR18 ....173 C3
Brown's La
Holme Hale IP25 ....65 F2
Mautby NR29 ....76 B7
Necton PE37 ....65 F3
Saxlingham Nethergate NR15 ....107 B8
Browne St 5 NR2 ....162 C7
Browning Pl PE30 ....147 A8
Brownsfield NR11 ....21 D8
Brownshill NR27 ....139 B4
Browston Hall Leisure Ctr NR31 ....94 C4
Browston La NR32 ....94 B3
Brummel Cl 1 PE30 ....147 C5
Brumstead Rd
Brumstead NR12 ....24 A1
Stalham NR12 ....39 A4
Brundall Gdns Sta NR13 ....165 A3
Brundall Low Rd NR13 ....72 F3
Brundall Prim Sch NR13 ....165 D3
Brundall Rd NR13 ....165 E4
Brundall Sta NR13 ....165 D2
Brundish Rd NR14 ....110 A6
Brunel Way IP24 ....176 B6
Brunswick Cl
Dereham NR19 ....154 C2
North Walsham NR28 ....151 D6
Brunswick Rd NR2 ....178 A1
Brunswick Terr NR27 ....139 C7
Brush Hill NR20 ....33 A6
Brush Mdw La PE34 ....42 B7
Brushmakers Way IP22 ....177 C6
Brussels Cl NR19 ....154 C2
Bryars La IP22 ....177 F3
Bryggen Rd PE30 ....146 F8
Bryony Cl 2 NR6 ....158 D5
Bryony Cour NR25 ....137 B7
Bryony Ct PE30 ....148 C3
Bryony Way 6 NR17 ....174 B5
Buccaneer Way 8 NR9 ....88 D8
Buck Courtney Cres NR6 ....158 A7
Buck La IP21 ....130 C4
Buck's Heath La NR11 ....11 D1
Buck's La NR18 ....87 B3
Buckenham Cl
1 Fakenham NR21 ....141 C5
Swaffham PE13 ....153 B2
Buckenham Dr PE33 ....81 A2
Buckenham La NR13 ....73 F2
Buckenham Rd
Attleborough NR17 ....174 F3
Lingwood & Burlingham NR13 ....74 A2
Buckenham Rd *continued*
Strumpshaw NR13 ....73 F2
Buckenham Sta NR13 ....91 F8
Bucket Rd NR21 ....15 D2
Buckingham Cl PE30 ....148 C5
Buckingham Ct PE36 ....132 C5
Buckingham Dr 1 NR9 ....88 C7
Buckingham Rd NR4 ....161 F3
Buckingham Wlk PE13 ....152 D8
Buckland Rise 8 NR4 ....161 F1
Bucksholt Rd PE14 ....59 B7
Buckthorn Cl 3 NR8 ....155 B2
Buddell's La NR23 ....5 F2
Bugg's Rd IP22 ....129 B2
Buggs Hole La IP22 ....128 A6
Buildings Rd NR30 ....168 E4
Bull Cl
East Tuddenham NR20 ....69 C6
4 Holt NR25 ....137 B6
Norwich NR3 ....178 B4
Bull Cl La NR21 ....17 B3
Bull Cl Rd NR3 ....178 B4
Bull La NR1 ....178 A1
Bull St NR25 ....137 B6
Bullace Rd NR5 ....156 F2
Bullacebush La NR13 ....165 E7
Bullard Rd NR3 ....158 C3
Bull's La NR31 ....170 D6
Bull's Row NR27 ....11 A2
Bullemer Cl 3 NR12 ....39 B4
Bullfinch Way 4 PE14 ....77 A8
Bullies Way 3 NR13 ....73 D6
Bullman's Cross La NR20 ....69 A6
Bullock Fair Cl 14 IP20 ....122 D2
Bullock Hill NR10 ....53 E1
Bullock Rd PE34 ....144 B1
Bullocks Loke NR30 ....168 E4
Bullockshed La NR14 ....91 A7
Bulls Gn La NR34 ....110 D5
Bulls Gn Rd NR34 ....110 C6
Bulmer La NR29 ....58 B6
Bulmer Rd NR3 ....158 A2
Bulrush Ave 4 PE38 ....172 A6
Bulrush Cl
1 East Dereham NR19 ....154 C4
4 Horsford NR10 ....53 A3
Bulstrode Ave 4 NR19 ....154 D2
Bultitudes Loke NR30 ....168 E4
Bulwer Rd
East Dereham NR19 ....154 E7
Lamas NR10 ....36 E1
Bumstede Ct 5 NR5 ....161 A8
Bungalow La NR7 ....72 D3
Bungay High Sch NR35 ....124 A7
Bungay Rd Bixley NR14 ....90 B8
Dickleburgh & Rushall IP21 ....130 E5
Ellingham NR35 ....109 C4
Hempnall NR15 ....107 D5
Loddon NR14 ....109 C7
Poringland NR14 ....90 D4
Scole IP21 ....130 D5
Stockton NR34 ....109 F4
Thwaite NR35 ....109 A5
Bungaygrave La IP20 ....122 D6
Bunkel Rd NR13 ....72 E8
Bunn's Bank Rd
Attleborough NR17 ....174 F2
Old Buckenham NR17 ....104 D4
Bunn's La
Great Yarmouth NR31 ....169 C3
Starston IP20 ....122 C2
Bunnett Ave PE30 ....146 D2
Bunnewell Ave NR31 ....170 A4
Bunting's La IP26 ....98 F5
Buntings The 15 NR31 ....94 C8
Bunwell Hill NR16 ....105 D2
Bunwell Prim Sch NR16 ....105 D3
Bunwell Rd
Aslacton NR16 ....106 A2
Attleborough NR17 ....174 F6
Besthorpe NR17 ....104 F6
Bunwell St NR16 ....105 B5
Bunyan Cl 3 NR13 ....72 E4
Burch Cl PE30 ....147 E4
Burcroft Rd PE13 ....152 B6
Burdett Rd PE13 ....152 B4
Burdock Cl NR18 ....173 E4
Burdock La
Hockwold cum Wilton IP26 ....113 C7
8 Wramplingham NR9 ....69 F2
Burdock Way 3 NR17 ....174 B4
Bure Cl 9 Belton NR31 ....94 A6
Caister-on-Sea NR30 ....168 D6
Great Yarmouth NR30 ....169 C6
4 King's Lynn PE30 ....147 E5
1 Watlington PE33 ....61 D6
Wroxham/Hoveton NR12 ....164 C5
Bure Marshes National Nature Reserve* NR13 ....55 E3
Bure Rd Briston NR24 ....142 D4
1 Great Yarmouth NR30 ....169 C5
Bure Valley La NR11 ....150 E5
Bure Valley Sch NR11 ....150 C5
Bure Way NR11 ....150 C7
Burgate La NR14 ....90 E5
Burgess Cl NR30 ....168 D6
Burgess Rd NR3 ....158 B2

Burgess Way NR15 90 E2
Burgh Beck Rd NR24 142 B5
Burgh Hall Leisure Ctr NR31 94 B7
Burgh La NR20 68 F6
Burgh Rd
Aylsham NR11 150 D6
Burgh St Peter NR34 111 C5
Great Yarmouth NR31 170 B7
Burgh Wood Rd NR29 57 E1
Burghley Rd PE30 148 E1
Burghwood Dr PE32 48 D6
Burhill Cl 3 NR4 89 D8
Burkitt St PE30 146 E6
Burleigh Cl 1 NR30 169 D2
Burley Rd NR12 38 A3
Burlingham Dr 2 NR33 111 F1
Burlingham Rd NR13 73 F6
Burlington Cl IP22 177 D1
Burma Cl PE31 140 C4
Burma Rd NR6 158 E5
Burnet Rd
Great Yarmouth NR31 94 C6
Norwich NR3 157 F1
Burney Rd PE30 146 D2
Burnham Ave PE30 147 C8
Burnham Mkt Prim Sch PE31 135 D4
Burnham Rd
Docking PE31 134 E6
Downham Market PE38 172 B4
North Creake NR21 4 D2
Ringstead PE36 2 C3
South Creake NR21 15 D7
Burns Cl
East Dereham NR19 154 C7
Thetford IP24 176 E6
Yaxley IP23 129 F1
Burnside 3 PE37 66 A4
Burnt Fen Turnpike IP28 112 D2
Burnt Hill La NR33 111 F3
Burnt Hills NR27 139 B4
Burnt House Rd NR13 92 B6
Burnt La
Great Yarmouth NR31 170 C7
Wiggenhall St Mary Magdalen PE34 61 A4
Burnt St NR23 136 D5
Burnthouse Cres PE33 63 B4
Burnthouse Dro PE33 63 C5
Burnthouse La
Hethersett NR9 160 C1
Runhall NR20 69 A4
Scole IP20 122 A1
Toft Monks NR34 110 D5
Wymondham NR18 173 F1
Burntoak La IP20 122 E4
Burntwood La NR12 54 C4
Burr Cl 14 IP25 84 E3
Burrell Cl NR25 137 D7
Burrell Way IP24 176 A1
Burrett Gdns PE13 59 C5
Burrett Rd PE13 59 C5
Burrettgate Rd PE13 152 F5
Burroughs Way NR18 173 D4
Burrow Dr IP27 113 E2
Burrows Gn NR34 110 F5
Burston Cl NR24 142 B4
Burston Com Prim Sch IP22 120 E2
Burston Rd
Dickleburgh & Rushall IP21 130 C8
Diss IP22 177 E7
Gissing IP22 120 F3
Burston Strike Sch* IP22 120 E2
Burton Ave NR28 151 B4
Burton Cl
North Walsham NR28 151 B4
Norwich NR6 158 C5
Roydon IP22 177 B5
Burton Dr 9 NR13 72 E7
Burton Rd NR6 158 C5
Burtontyne Ave NR19 68 A7
Bury Bottom IP27 115 A1
Bury Rd Botesdale IP22 128 F3
Brandon IP27 175 D2
Hepworth IP22 127 F1
Market Weston IP22 127 E4
Rickinghall Inferior IP22 128 D1
Thetford IP24 176 C1
Wortham IP22 129 C4
Bury St NR2 162 B4
Bush Cl PE31 140 E3
Bush Dr NR12 24 E4
Bush Est NR12 24 D4
Bush La Dereham NR20 68 B8
Wisbech PE13 152 E5
Bush Rd Hemsby NR29 58 B5
Norwich NR6 157 F7
Bussey Rd NR6 158 D4
Bussey's La NR31 170 D5
Bussey's Loke
Great Yarmouth NR31 170 A5
Hempnall NR15 107 D5
Bustards' La PE14 41 F3
Butcher's La NR21 141 B4
Butchers La PE31 3 B7
Butt La Belton NR31 94 A6
Litcham PE32 48 A4
Butter La NR14 92 D1
Butter's Hall La IP24 102 C7
Buttercup Cl 1 IP24 176 F5
Buttercup Dr 14 NR31 94 C6
Buttercup Way NR5 160 F6
Buttermere 1 NR29 167 B7
Buttermere Rd 4 NR5 161 C6
Butterwick 3 PE30 147 C5
Buttland's La PE33 81 B8
Buttlands Cl NR21 6 E2
Buttlands The
Great Cressingham IP25 83 D4
Wells-next-the-Sea NR23 136 D5
Buttle's La NR15 106 D3
Butts La NR26 138 B5
Butts The NR5 160 F8
Buxton Ave NR31 170 D1
Buxton Cl 4 Cromer NR27 10 B5
Easton NR9 70 B5
Buxton Prim Sch NR10 36 F1
Buxton Rd
Aylsham NR11 150 D5
Cawston NR10 35 D2
Diss IP22 177 B4
Frettenham NR12 53 F3
Hainford NR10 53 F5
Horstead with Stanninghall NR12 54 B6
North Walsham NR28 151 B4
Norwich NR3 162 D8
Spixworth NR10 158 F8
Buxton Sta NR10 36 F2
Byfield Ct 3 NR3 158 C1
Byron Ave PE13 154 B7
Byron Rd
Great Yarmouth NR30 169 E8
Taverham NR8 156 D8
Byron Way NR30 168 D6
Byron Wlk 7 IP24 176 E6

C

Cabbell Rd NR27 139 B7
Cabin Cl 11 NR33 111 F1
Cadamys Yd NR23 136 D5
Cadge Cl NR5 161 D7
Cadge Rd NR5 161 D6
Cadge's La NR9 86 B3
Cadiz Way NR31 171 E4
Cadman Way IP25 84 D3
Cadogan Rd NR27 139 B7
Caernarvon Rd NR2 162 B6
Cage La IP24 176 D3
Cains The NR8 155 C2
Cairns Ct NR4 162 A3
Caister By-pass NR30 168 C4
Caister Castle Car Collection* NR30 168 A5
Caister High Sch NR30 168 E6
Caister on Sea Fst & Mid Schs NR30 168 E5
Caister Rd NR30 169 C7
Caister Sands Ave NR29 168 E8
Caistor La
Caistor St Edmund NR14 89 F6
Poringland NR14 90 B6
Caistor Roman Town* NR14 89 F6
Caithness Crystal Visitor Ctr* PE30 146 F2
Caius Cl PE31 133 C5
Calamint Rd PE30 147 A8
Caledonian Way 1 NR31 94 A5
Caley Cl NR3 157 F2
Caley St PE31 133 D5
Calf La NR10 53 E2
California Ave NR29 167 E4
California Cotts NR23 136 E5
California Cres NR29 167 F2
California Rd NR29 167 E2
Calkewood La IP22 128 C1
Calthorpe Cl
Acle NR13 166 B4
2 Stalham NR12 39 B4
Calthorpe Rd
Ingham NR12 39 D4
Norwich NR5 161 B6
Calvert St NR3 178 B4
Calves Well La
Beeston Regis NR26 138 F4
Sheringham NR27 10 A5
Camargue Pl 4 PE13 152 E3
Cambell Dr NR20 50 B5
Camberley Rd NR4 162 A2
Cambers La PE31 135 D2
Camborne Cl NR5 157 C1
Cambridge Ave NR31 170 A3
Cambridge Dr PE13 152 A6
Cambridge Rd PE30 148 D5
Cambridge St
Cromer NR27 139 C7
Norwich NR2 162 C4
Cambridge Way NR31 170 B3
Camden Pl 21 NR30 169 D2
Camden Rd NR30 169 D2
Camelot Rd NR31 171 B8
Cameron Cl PE31 133 C4
Cameron Cres 4 PE31 12 D4
Cameron Gn NR8 156 E8
Camfrey 6 PE30 147 B7
Camp Cl 2 IP26 98 D1
Camp Gr NR1 163 A6
Camp La NR27 10 A4
Camp Rd NR8 155 C1
Campbell Cl PE36 132 D4
Campbell Ct 1 NR3 162 F8
Camperdown 11 NR30 169 D2
Camping Cl 8 NR20 68 F6
Camping Field La NR12 39 B4
Campingland PE13 153 C4
Campion Ave NR31 170 B3
Campion Cl 4 NR28 151 E5
Campion Pl PE38 172 B3
Campion Rd
1 Dereham NR20 68 A8
Thetford IP24 176 F4
Campion Way
6 Attleborough NR17 174 B4
3 Sheringham NR26 138 B6
Campsey Rd PE38 97 B6
Canada Cl 6 PE31 12 E5
Canada Rd NR27 139 B7
Canal Farm La NR28 38 C6
Canal St 6 PE13 152 C5
Canary Way NR1 163 A4
Canberra Rd IP25 84 F3
Candle Stick NR9 69 A3
Candlemaker Workshop* NR29 75 A5
Candler's La 18 IP20 122 D2
Candlestick La PE32 45 C8
Canfor Rd 7 NR13 72 E7
Cangate Rd NR12 55 C6
Cann's La NR9 88 D7
Cannell Gn NR3 178 C4
Cannell Rd 11 NR14 92 A1
Cannerby La NR7 159 B3
Cannon St PE13 152 C4
Cannon Terr 9 PE13 152 C4
Canon Cl 6 IP25 84 E3
Canon Hoare Rd NR11 150 C4
Canon Pickering VC Jun Sch IP20 122 D2
Canon Pott Cl PE31 133 D6
Canon Wake Ct 4 NR29 56 C8
Canon's Cl IP24 176 B4
Canons Cl 2 NR19 154 D2
Canons Wlk IP24 176 B3
Canterbury Inf Sch IP24 176 B4
Canterbury Pl NR2 162 C7
Canterbury Way IP24 176 B5
Cantley Cnr NR13 74 B1
Cantley Fst Sch NR13 92 B7
Cantley La
Cringleford NR4 89 A8
Ketteringham NR18 88 F6
Cantley Rd NR13 92 D7
Cantley Sta NR13 92 B6
Cants Cl 4 NR9 69 F2
Capgrave Ave PE30 146 F8
Capps La IP19 123 F1
Capstan Way 9 NR33 111 F1
Captains Cl PE13 153 D4
Caraway Dr 22 NR31 94 C6
Caraway Rd IP24 176 F4
Carbrooke Rd
Caston NR17 85 C1
Griston IP25 85 A2
Cardiff Rd NR2 162 B5
Cardigan Pl NR2 162 C7
Cardinal Cl NR9 70 B5
Cardington Ct 1 NR13 166 D4
Cardington Rd IP25 85 A3
Cardun Cl 3 NR13 73 C6
Carey House Con Ctr PE37 65 D1
Cargate Comm Rd NR16 105 E1
Cargate La
Saxlingham Nethergate NR15 107 A8
Upton with Fishley NR13 166 A8
Carl Cl 5 NR19 154 D1
Carl Cres NR28 22 E5
Carleton Cl 1 NR18 173 C6
Carleton Rd NR7 159 B3
Carleton Rode CE Prim Sch NR16 105 C3
Carlton Cl NR19 154 D4
Carlton Dr PE30 148 D5
Carlton Gdns NR1 178 B1
Carlton Marshes Nature Reserve* NR33 111 F3
Carlyle Rd NR1 162 F3
Carmelite Terr 16 PE30 146 D4
Carmen's La NR28 38 B3
Carn Cl NR13 74 B2
Carnoustie NR4 162 A1
Carnoustie Ct PE31 41 C8
Carol Cl NR14 90 B5
Carola Sutton Ct NR25 137 B5
Caroline Ct NR4 161 F4
Carpenter's Wlk NR15 121 D7
Carpenters Cotts NR25 137 B6
Carr La
Great Moulton NR15 106 B1
Hoveton NR12 164 F8
Northrepps NR27 139 C1
Overstrand NR27 11 A3
Poringland NR14 90 C4
Wendling NR19 66 F7
Carr Terr PE31 134 E5
Carrell Rd NR31 170 B1
Carrington Rd NR27 139 D5
Carrow Abbey NR1 163 A3
Carrow Cl NR1 162 F3
Carrow Hill NR1 178 C1
Carrow Rd NR1 178 C1
Carrs Hill Cl NR8 157 A4
Carrs Rd NR13 92 A8
Carshalton Rd 2 NR1 162 F3
Cart Gap Rd NR12 24 C4
Carter Cl
Caister-on-Sea NR30 168 D8
Swaffham PE37 153 C2
Carter Rd NR8 157 A8
Carter's Cl PE30 148 B1
Carter's La NR20 50 A6
Carterford Dr NR6 158 E3
Carters Loke NR13 166 C2
Cartledge Cl 1 NR19 154 D3
Cartmel 17 NR9 88 D8
Carver's La NR17 174 B5
Casaubon Cl 6 NR19 154 D3
Caslon Cl 3 NR21 141 C5
Castelins Way 20 NR14 89 B3
Castell Rd NR19 154 D7
Castle Acre Castle* PE32 47 A2
Castle Acre CE VC Fst Sch PE32 46 F1
Castle Acre Cl 2 PE30 148 C3
Castle Acre Rd PE32 47 E1
Castle Cl 3 Gresham NR11 9 E1
King's Lynn PE30 147 C8
Weeting IP27 175 B8
Castle Drift PE32 48 D6
Castle Gn NR31 170 B7
Castle La Bungay NR35 124 A8
Thetford IP24 176 E3
West Caister NR30 168 B5
Castle Mdw NR1 178 B2
Castle Mkt St NR1 178 B2
Castle Rd
Mettingham NR35 124 D7
Wormegay PE33 62 C6
Castle Rise NR8 155 E3
Castle Rising Castle* PE31 27 C3
Castle Rising Rd PE30 148 D3
Castle Sq 16 PE13 152 C5
Castle St Norwich NR2 178 B3
Thetford IP24 176 D4
Wroxham/Hoveton NR12 164 B3
Castleacre Rd
Great Massingham PE32 29 D1
Swaffham PE37 153 B8
Castleford Cl IP24 176 B4
Castleton Ave NR33 111 F1
Castleton Cl 1 NR5 160 F8
Castleton Way IP23 130 A1
Caston CE VA Prim Sch NR17 85 B1
Caston Cl 5 NR25 137 B6
Caston Rd NR7 163 F8
Catalpa Way 5 NR31 170 B5
Catbridge La NR14 89 A4
Catchpole Wlk IP21 121 C1
Catfield CE Fst Sch NR29 56 C8
Catfield Rd NR29 56 D6
Cathedral Dr NR20 49 E8
Cathedral St NR1 178 C3
Catherine Howard Cl 3 IP24 176 D6
Catherine Wheel Opening 8 NR3 162 D8
Catling's La PE13 41 A3
Catmere Herne NR14 89 A3
Cator Rd NR8 155 F1
Catriona Ct NR25 8 B6
Cats Cnr NR10 37 B7
Cattle Mkt St 4 NR21 141 C4
Catton Chase NR6 158 D5
Catton Ct NR6 158 E6
Catton Gr Fst Sch NR3 158 C3
Catton Gr Mid Sch NR3 158 C3
Catton Gr Rd NR3 158 D2
Catton View Ct NR3 158 D3
Caudle Hill IP25 83 E5
Caudwell Cl 2 NR14 89 F4
Causeway Cl
Brockdish IP21 131 C6
Norwich NR2 162 C8
Causeway Dr 4 NR12 54 C6
Causeway The
Heigham Bridge NR29 57 A5
Hickling NR12 39 F2
Stow Bardolph PE34 61 D1
Cavalier Cl 30 NR7 72 D4
Cave's Cl PE34 144 B5
Cavell Cl NR14 89 C5
Cavell Fst Sch NR1 162 E1
Cavell Rd NR1 162 E2
Cavendish Cl PE32 44 C3
Cavenham Rd PE33 80 E4
Cavick Rd NR18 173 A3
Cawdor Cl NR17 174 E6
Cawston La
Great Witchingham NR9 51 E7
Little Witchingham NR9 149 E1
Cawston Rd
Aylsham NR11 150 A5
Reepham NR10 149 D6
Cawston VC Prim Sch NR10 35 B2
Cawstons Mdw 8 NR14 90 C5
Caxton Cl NR26 138 F5
Caxton Ct PE30 147 D4
Caxton Pk NR26 138 F5
Caxton Rd NR34 110 D1
Caxton Way IP24 176 A2
Caystreward NR30 168 E1
Cecil Cl 7 PE33 61 D6
Cecil Gowing Ct NR7 159 B4
Cecil Gowing Fst Sch NR7 159 C3
Cecil Rd
East Dereham NR20 154 F5
Norwich NR1 162 D3
Cedar Ave 4 NR10 54 A2
Cedar Cl
1 Downham Market PE38 172 C6
12 Great Yarmouth NR31 94 C7
19 Martham NR29 57 D4
12 Mattishall NR20 68 E6
North Elmham NR20 49 E7
Cedar Ct
North Walsham NR28 151 C5
Wymondham NR18 173 D6
Cedar Dr
Attleborough NR17 174 C4
10 Loddon NR14 92 A1
Cedar Gr
North Runcton PE33 44 A3
Sheringham NR26 138 E5
Cedar Rd
Hethersett NR9 88 C8
Marham PE33 63 B4
Norwich NR1 163 A5
Cedar Rise NR20 68 E6
Cedar Row PE30 147 B7
Cedar Springs PE31 133 B6
Cedar Way
Brandon IP27 175 D2
Brundall NR13 165 C3
4 Gayton PE32 45 C6
King's Lynn PE34 146 C4
Cedars The Keswick NR12 23 F3
Norwich NR2 162 B4
Shepherd's Port PE31 12 B4
Celandine Cl 2 IP24 176 F5
Celandine La 6 NR26 138 B6
Celandine Rd 4 NR17 174 B4
Celia Phillips Cl 7 IP24 176 D7
Cemetery La NR18 173 B3
Cemetery Rd
East Dereham NR19 154 E7
Lakenheath IP27 113 E1
Outwell PE14 78 A6
Centenary Way PE12 41 C6
Central Ave NR7 72 D3
Central Cl 1 NR9 88 D7
Central Cres 2 NR9 88 D7
Central Dr NR20 50 A5
Central Rd
Cromer NR27 139 A7
King's Lynn PE30 146 D6
Centre Cres PE31 140 D3
Centre Point 6 PE30 147 D5
Centre Vale PE31 140 D3
Centre Vale Rd PE31 140 D3
Century Rd 6 Eye IP23 130 C1
Great Yarmouth NR31 169 B3
Century Way NR8 155 F3
Cere Rd NR7 159 C4
Cess Rd NR29 57 C5
Chadwick Sq 2 PE30 147 A7
Chalfont Wlk NR4 161 E2
Chalk Hill Rd NR1 178 C3
Chalk La Culford IP31 125 C1
Narborough PE32 63 E5
North End NR16 106 D2
Sutton Bridge PE12 41 C7
Chalk Pit Rd PE31 140 E7
Chalk Rd Brandon IP27 114 D5
5 Walpole St Andrew PE14 41 E4
Chalkpit Rd PE31 3 A6
Chalkrow La PE33 81 F4
Chamberlin Cl NR3 158 E2
Chamberlin Ct NR13 165 E6
Chamberlin Rd NR3 158 D1
Chambers Rd NR3 158 B3
Chameryhall La NR13 73 F7
Champney's Rd IP22 177 E4
Chancel Cl NR13 165 C3
Chancellors Dr NR4 161 C4
Chandler Rd NR14 89 F5
Chandler's Hill La 1 NR18 173 B3
Chandlers Cl 2 NR18 173 B3
Chandlers Ct 8 NR4 89 C8
Chandlers Hill 4 NR18 173 B3
Changi Rd 5 IP25 84 F3
Chantry Ct 8 PE37 65 F4
Chantry La PE37 66 A4
Chantry Rd NR2 178 A2
Chantry The NR2 178 A2
Chapel Ave NR15 106 E3
Chapel Bank PE36 132 E6
Chapel Break Fst Sch NR5 160 F8
Chapel Break Rd NR5 160 E7
Chapel Cl
Barnham Broom NR9 69 C2
Pulham Market IP21 121 E5
Reepham NR10 149 B5
Tacolneston NR16 105 F4
Winfarthing IP22 120 B5
Chapel Cnr NR12 55 D6
Chapel Ct Blofield NR13 165 E6
Norwich NR6 157 F5
Chapel Field NR13 93 A4
Chapel Field E NR2 178 A2
Chapel Field N NR2 178 A2
Chapel Field Rd
Norwich NR2 178 A2
Stalham NR12 39 A3
Chapel La
Aldborough NR11 21 A5
Ashby St Mary NR14 91 D5

Chapel La *continued*
Barton Bendish PE33 81 B8
Beeston with Bittering PE32 48 C2
Beetley NR20 49 C4
Botesdale IP22 128 E2
Burgate IP22 129 C3
Coltishall NR12 54 D7
East Dereham NR19 154 D2
Emneth PE14 59 B2
Felthorpe NR10 155 C8
Fincham PE33 62 E1
Foulsham NR20 33 D3
3 Great Yarmouth NR31 94 C6
Hempstead NR25 19 E8
Hockering NR20 69 B8
Hunstanton PE36 132 C4
Kirby Row NR35 109 E3
Methwold IP26 99 A5
Necton PE37 66 A4
Norwich NR7 163 E6
Potter Heigham NR29 56 F7
Ringstead PE36 2 A3
Scarning NR19 67 B7
Sculthorpe NR21 16 B1
Shelton NR15 107 B1
Shotesham NR15 90 B2
Skeyton NR10 37 B6
West Caister NR30 168 C4
West Winch PE33 43 E3
Wimbotsham PE34 172 E8
Wiveton NR25 7 E6
Wymondham NR18 173 A5
Chapel Loke
Lessingham NR12 24 C2
Salhouse NR13 55 B1
4 Stoke Holy Cross NR14 89 F4
Surlingham NR14 73 B1
Wymondham NR18 105 A8
Chapel Mdw NR35 109 E3
Chapel Rd
Alby with Thwaite NR11 21 B3
Ashby St Mary NR14 91 D5
Attleborough NR17 174 C5
Beighton NR13 74 C2
Boughton PE33 81 A4
Carleton Rode NR16 105 C3
Dersingham PE31 140 D4
Dilham NR28 38 B3
East Ruston NR12 38 E6
Foxley NR20 50 D8
Grimston PE32 28 A1
Guestwick NR20 33 F6
Hainford NR10 53 E5
Halvergate NR13 75 A2
Lingwood NR13 73 F3
Longham NR19 49 A2
Lowestoft NR33 111 F1
Morley NR18 87 B2
Neatishead NR12 55 E6
Necton PE37 66 B4
Norwich NR5 157 A2
Paston NR28 143 D1
Roughton NR11 21 D8
Roydon PE32 45 A8
St Andrew, Ilketshall NR34 124 F6
Scole IP21 121 B1
Sea Palling NR12 40 A6
Southrepps NR11 22 B6
Swafield NR28 22 D3
Terrington St Clement PE34 144 B5
Upton with Fishley NR13 166 B8
Wisbech PE13 152 B5
Woodton NR35 108 C4
Wymondham NR18 105 A8
Chapel Rd Specl Sch NR17 174 C5
Chapel Rise 11 PE33 63 B4
Chapel St Barford NR9 70 A3
Cawston NR10 35 B3
3 Cromer NR27 139 B7
Diss IP22 177 D4
6 Hingham NR9 86 C5
Ixworth NR9 69 F2
King's Lynn PE30 146 D5
3 Old Buckenham NR16 104 F1
Rocklands NR17 103 B8
Shipdham IP25 67 C2
Warham NR23 6 A4
14 Wisbech PE13 152 C4
Chapel Terr PE30 148 B1
Chapel Wlk 4 NR19 154 E5
Chapel Yd Ashill IP25 84 A7
Wells-next-the-Sea NR23 136 C6
Chapelfield Cl 1 NR29 56 C8
Chapman Ave NR30 168 E5
Chapmans Cl 17 NR26 138 D7
Chapnall Cl PE13 152 F6
Chapnall Rd PE13 152 F6
Chappshill Way 22 NR14 89 B3
Chare Rd IP31 127 B1
Charing Cross NR2 178 A3
Charles Ave
Norwich NR7 163 F8
Watton IP25 84 D3
Charles Burrell High Sch IP24 176 C1
Charles Burrell Mus* IP24 176 C4
Charles Burton Cl 5 NR30 168 D7
Charles Cl Acle NR13 166 B4
Caister-on-Sea NR30 168 E5
Cromer NR27 10 C4
Dereham NR19 154 C1
Charles Cl *continued*
Wroxham/Hoveton NR12 164 C3
Charles Ewing Cl NR11 150 B5
Charles Jewson Ct NR6 158 B2
Charles Rash Cl NR28 37 B8
Charles Rd
Fakenham NR21 141 C6
Holt NR25 137 C5
Hunstanton PE36 132 C2
9 Sutton Bridge PE12 41 B8
Charles Sq 6 NR2 162 C6
Charles St
Great Yarmouth NR30 169 D2
King's Lynn PE30 146 E3
11 Wisbech PE13 152 C4
Charles Watling Way 1 NR5 160 E8
Charles Wood Rd NR19 154 F2
Charlock PE30 147 A8
Charlock Dr 8 NR26 138 B6
Charlotte's Cl 1 NR27 9 F5
Charlton Rd NR3 178 B4
Charmbeck Pk NR10 52 D8
Charolais Cl NR14 163 B2
Charter Cl NR31 170 B4
Chartwell Ct NR7 158 F3
Chartwell Rd NR6 158 D3
Chase Ave PE30 146 E3
Chase Cl NR6 158 D5
Chase Ct
East Dereham NR19 154 D6
Thetford IP24 176 B3
Chase St PE13 152 C6
Chase The
Brandon IP27 175 E2
Brundall NR13 165 F6
Stow Bardolph PE34 78 E7
Upwell PE14 77 D3
Walpole St Andrew PE14 41 E4
Wisbech PE13 152 A7
Chatham Rd 1 IP31 126 B1
Chatham St NR3 178 A4
Chatsworth Rd PE36 132 C3
Chaucer Cl 14 NR20 50 E7
Chaucer Rd NR30 169 D8
Checker St PE30 146 E3
Cheese Hill 9 NR16 118 C5
Chenery Dr NR7 159 C5
Cheney Cres PE31 133 D4
Cheney Hill PE31 133 D4
Cheney's La NR16 105 F5
Chepore La NR18 87 C1
Chequer's La NR15 107 D8
Chequers Cl
Briston NR24 142 E3
2 Long Stratton NR15 106 D3
1 Roydon PE32 28 A1
Chequers La
Bressingham IP22 129 B7
Burston & Shimpling IP22 120 E4
Great Ellingham NR17 103 E8
Gressenhall NR20 49 B4
North Runcton PE33 44 A2
Saham Toney IP25 84 C5
West Winch PE33 43 F2
Chequers Rd
Roydon PE32 28 A1
Tharston & Hapton NR15 106 D3
Wretton PE33 80 E3
Chequers St
Docking PE31 134 D4
East Ruston NR12 38 F5
Gresham NR11 9 E1
Cherry Cl
11 Great Yarmouth NR31 94 C7
Marham PE33 63 A4
Norwich NR1 162 E3
Cherry Dr NR19 154 F5
Cherry Drift NR19 154 E6
Cherry La
Belton with Browston NR31 94 B4
Dereham NR20 68 B7
Cherry Orch NR20 154 F5
Cherry Rd
Great Yarmouth NR31 170 B6
Wisbech PE13 152 C8
Cherry Tree Ave 25 NR29 57 D4
Cherry Tree Cl
Holt NR25 137 B7
Mundford IP26 100 A4
North Lopham IP22 119 A2
Wretham IP24 102 B1
Cherry Tree Ct IP22 177 C5
Cherry Tree Dr PE34 146 C4
Cherry Tree La NR28 151 B5
Cherry Tree Rd
Carleton Rode NR16 105 A1
Plumstead NR11 20 A6
Snettisham PE31 12 E5
Tibenham NR16 120 B7
Cherrytree Cl PE31 133 D6
Cherrywood
Alpington NR14 90 F4
10 Redenhall with Harleston IP20 122 D1
Cherrywood Ave NR21 15 C2
Chervil Wlk IP24 116 D2
Cherwell Way 2 NR31 170 B2
Chester Pl NR2 162 C6
Chester St NR2 162 C4
Chester Way IP24 176 A4
Chesterfield Cotts 11 NR27 139 B7
Chestnut Ave
Great Yarmouth NR31 170 A5
North Walsham NR28 151 E4
Sculthorpe Airfield NR21 15 C2
1 Spixworth NR10 54 A2
Welney PE14 95 D5
West Winch PE33 43 E1
Chestnut Cl
Brandon IP27 175 E2
Dersingham PE31 140 E3
East Dereham NR19 154 E1
Norwich NR5 156 E2
5 Watlington PE33 61 D5
Chestnut Ct 9 NR2 178 A3
Chestnut Gr NR26 138 D4
Chestnut Hill 3 NR4 161 F1
Chestnut Loke NR15 107 A6
Chestnut Rd
Dickleburgh IP21 121 C1
East Dereham NR19 154 C5
Pulham St Mary IP21 121 F4
5 Snettisham PE31 12 E4
13 Tasburgh NR15 106 F6
8 Watton IP25 84 E3
8 Wisbech PE13 152 C4
Chestnut Terr PE12 41 B8
Chestnut Wlk PE37 81 F8
Chestnuts The IP22 128 E2
Chew Ct PE30 147 E8
Cheyham Mount NR4 161 F1
Cheyney Ave 1 NR13 55 A1
Chickering Rd IP21 131 B2
Childs Rd NR9 88 C8
Childs Way NR26 138 C5
Chiltern Cres PE36 132 C3
Chilver House La PE32 44 E7
Chilvers Pl PE31 133 D5
Chimes Way NR10 149 B4
Chimney Springs NR29 167 A3
Chimney St PE32 46 F1
Chipperfield Rd NR7 159 E1
Chittock Cl 5 NR10 54 A1
Cholmondeley Way 3 PE33 43 F2
Choseley Ct NR18 173 C4
Choseley Rd
Docking PE31 134 C7
Thornham PE36 2 D6
Christ Church Rd NR31 170 A4
Christchurch Rd NR2 162 A4
Christie Cl 6 NR19 154 D1
Christine Ave NR13 74 A2
Christine Rd 1 NR10 54 A1
Christopher Cl
3 Newton Flotman NR15 89 D1
1 Norwich NR1 162 E2
Christopher Dr PE13 152 A7
Church Alley NR13 165 E6
Church Ave
Croxton IP24 116 C5
Halvergate NR13 74 F1
Little Ellingham NR17 86 A1
Norwich NR4 162 B3
Church Ave E NR2 162 B3
Church Bank
Marshland St James PE14 60 C2
Terrington St Clement PE34 144 B6
Church Cl
Antingham NR28 22 B3
3 Bawdeswell NR20 50 E7
Beeston Regis NR27 9 F5
Bixley NR14 90 B7
Brandon IP27 175 B3
Caister-on-Sea NR30 168 D5
Cantley NR13 92 C7
Colby NR11 36 D8
9 Coltishall NR12 54 C6
Grimston PE32 45 B8
Hepworth IP22 127 E1
1 Horstead with Stanninghall NR12 54 C6
King's Lynn PE34 146 C4
Lamas NR10 36 F1
13 Loddon NR14 92 A2
2 Norwich NR2 162 B8
Overstrand NR27 11 A3
Pentney PE32 63 C8
Poringland NR14 90 C4
Pulham St Mary IP21 122 A4
1 Roydon IP22 129 D7
Sea Palling NR12 40 B5
Shipdham IP25 67 B2
South Walsham NR13 74 A8
Upper Sheringham NR26 138 A4
Walpole St Andrew PE14 41 E4
Whissonsett NR20 31 D2
Wiggenhall St Mary Magdalen PE34 61 B6
Wortwell IP20 122 F3
Church Cotts NR19 48 E3
Church Crofts PE31 27 C3
Church Dam NR13 93 A5
Church Dro PE14 77 F6
Church End IP27 175 B3
Church Farm Cl
Palgrave IP22 177 C2
1 Weybourne NR25 8 F5
Church Farm Cres NR29 167 B6
Church Farm La NR19 154 C5
Church Farm Rare Breeds Ctr* PE34 79 F8
Church Farm Rd PE31 133 F7
Church Field 4 NR4 89 B8
Church Gate 16 PE12 41 B8
Church Gdns IP31 127 C3
Church Gn
Norwich NR7 159 B5
West Acre PE32 46 B2
Church Hill
Banham NR16 119 D7
Beighton NR13 74 C3
Hoxne IP21 131 A4
Reepham NR10 149 C4
Saxlingham Nethergate NR15 107 B8
Starston IP20 122 C3
Church Hill Fst Sch PE32 45 C8
Church Hill Sch NR16 119 D7
Church La Aldeby NR34 110 F5
Aldeby, Wheatacre, Burgh St Peter NR34 111 B5
Antingham NR28 22 B3
Ashwellthorpe NR16 106 A7
Baconsthorpe NR25 19 F7
Bacton NR28 23 C3
Banham NR16 119 D7
Barnham IP24 125 F6
Barton Bendish PE33 81 B8
Belaugh NR12 54 E5
Belton with Browston NR31 94 A5
Billingford NR20 50 B7
Bintree NR20 33 B2
Bircham PE31 14 B3
Blo' Norton IP22 128 B6
Boughton PE33 80 F5
Bracon Ash NR14 88 F3
Bradenham IP25 66 D4
Bressingham IP22 129 B7
Brininghan NR24 18 D5
Briston NR24 142 E4
Brockdish IP21 131 C6
Broome NR35 109 B3
Bunwell NR16 105 D3
Burgh & Tuttington NR11 36 D4
Claxton NR14 91 C5
Cley next the Sea NR25 7 E6
Corton NR32 171 F1
Cranworth IP25 85 F7
Deopham NR18 86 F4
Dersingham PE31 140 E3
Ditchingham NR35 108 F3
East Tuddenham NR20 69 C6
East Walton PE32 45 E3
East Winch PE32 44 F2
Easton NR9 70 B6
Felthorpe NR10 155 D7
Filby NR29 75 E8
Fleggburgh NR29 57 A1
Frettenham NR12 54 A5
Fritton & St Olaves NR31 93 F3
Great Massingham PE32 29 D1
Great Yarmouth NR31 170 C5
Gresham NR11 9 E1
Gressenhall NR19 49 C2
Guestwick NR20 33 F6
Haddiscoe NR14 110 E7
Hales NR14 109 F7
Harpley PE31 29 C5
Heacham PE31 133 E6
Heckingham NR14 92 C1
Hemblington NR13 73 F6
Hepworth IP22 127 E1
Hevingham NR10 36 B1
Hindolveston NR20 33 C8
Hockwold cum Wilton IP26 114 A6
Holme Hale PE37 65 F2
Ixworth NR9 69 E2
Ketteringham NR18 88 E5
King's Lynn PE30 146 E4
Langley with Hardley NR14 92 C3
Lessingham NR12 24 E3
Leziate PE32 44 F4
Little Ellingham NR17 86 A1
Little Massingham PE32 29 C2
Long Stratton NR15 106 F4
Lound NR32 171 A3
Marham PE33 63 A4
Marlingford NR9 69 E4
Marsham NR10 36 B2
Mattishall NR20 68 F6
Mautby NR29 75 D5
Morley NR18 87 A3
Mundesley NR11 143 C6
Mundford IP26 100 B4
Neatishead NR12 55 E6
North Elmham NR20 49 E8
Northwold PE33 81 B2
Norwich NR7 159 C5
Norwich NR4 161 E1
Old Buckenham NR17 104 D2
Oulton NR11 35 C7
Potter Heigham NR29 56 F7
Redenhall with Harleston IP20 122 E3
Rickinghall Superior IP22 128 E1
Roydon PE32 27 F2
Runcton Holme PE33 61 D4
Runhall NR20 69 A6
Runhall NR9 87 A8
St Mary, South Elmham otherwise Homersfield IP20 123 B4
Sheringham NR26 138 F6
Shipdham IP25 67 B2
Church La *continued*
Shouldham Thorpe PE33 62 B3
South Creake NR21 14 D7
4 Southery PE38 97 B5
Sparham NR9 51 B6
Spixworth NR10 53 F2
Sprowston NR7 159 B5
Stanfield NR20 48 F8
Stanhoe PE31 14 E7
Stuston IP21 130 B4
Surlingham NR14 73 A1
Sustead NR11 21 B8
Swannington NR9 52 B6
Swanton Abbott NR10 37 C5
Terrington St John PE14 42 B2
Thelnetham IP22 128 B5
Thompson IP24 102 C7
Thwaite NR35 109 A6
Tibenham NR16 120 E8
Tilney All Saints PE34 42 E4
Tittleshall PE32 48 B8
Tivetshall St Mary NR15 121 B4
Tunstead NR12 37 F1
Watlington PE33 61 E6
Weasenham All Saints PE32 47 C8
Wicklewood NR18 87 B5
Winfarthing IP22 120 B4
Wood Dalling NR11 34 B5
Wormegay PE33 62 D6
Wroxham/Hoveton NR12 164 B3
Yaxham NR19 68 A5
Church Lanes NR21 141 B5
Church Loke NR11 21 D7
Church Marsh Nature Reserve* NR14 73 A1
Church Mdw
Rickinghall Inferior IP22 128 D2
Yelverton NR14 90 E5
Church Mdw La NR14 90 F4
Church Mews PE13 152 C5
Church of the Holy Sepulchre (rems)* IP24 176 B4
Church Path PE33 80 E2
Church Pl PE31 134 D5
Church Plain
14 Great Yarmouth NR30 169 C4
Wells-next-the-Sea NR23 136 D5
Church Rd
Alburgh IP20 122 F6
Alpington NR14 90 F4
Aslacton NR15 106 A2
Aylmerton NR11 10 A3
Bacton NR12 23 D4
Barningham IP31 127 C3
Barton Bendish PE33 81 B8
Barton Turf NR12 55 E8
Beeston with Bittering PE32 48 B2
Beetley NR20 49 B6
Bergh Apton NR15 91 A3
Bintree NR20 33 B2
Brandon IP27 175 B3
Bridgham NR16 118 B5
Brockdish IP21 131 C6
Brundall NR13 165 E5
Burgh Castle NR31 93 F8
Cantley NR13 92 D7
Carleton Rode NR16 105 C2
Catfield NR29 56 C8
Christchurch PE14 95 A7
Clenchwarton PE34 145 D5
Colby NR11 36 D8
Colkirk NR21 31 D5
Crimplesham PE33 80 B6
Denham IP21 131 A1
Deopham NR18 86 E3
Dickleburgh & Rushall IP21 130 D8
Dilham NR28 38 C4
Downham Market PE38 172 C5
Earsham NR35 123 F7
Ellingham NR35 109 D3
Elm PE14 77 B7
Elsing NR20 50 F3
Felmingham NR28 37 B7
Flitcahm PE31 28 C5
Flixton NR35 123 E5
Fordham PE38 79 B1
Freethorpe NR13 92 F8
Frettenham NR10 53 F4
Garboldisham IP22 128 A8
Gillingham NR34 110 C3
Great & Little Plumstead NR13 73 A4
Great Yarmouth NR31 170 C7
Griston IP25 85 A1
Haddiscoe NR14 110 E8
Hardingham NR9 86 D7
Hedenham NR35 108 E4
Hilgay PE38 79 E1
Hoe NR20 49 F6
Holme Hale IP25 66 A2
Honington IP31 126 D1
Horning NR12 55 F3
Hunstanton PE36 132 F7
Itteringham NR11 20 C2
Ketteringham NR18 88 D5
Kirby Cane NR35 109 E4
Kirstead NR15 90 F1
Leverington PE13 152 F7

Church Rd *continued*
Lingwood & Burlingham NR13 73 F3
Little Barningham NR11 20 C4
Market Weston IP22 127 E4
Marlingford NR9 70 A3
Neatishead NR12 55 E6
Newton Flotman NR15 89 C1
North Lopham IP22 119 A1
Norton Subcourse NR14 92 E1
Ovington IP25 84 E5
Postwick with Witton NR13 72 F3
Potter Heigham NR29 56 F6
Quidenham NR16 118 F8
Reedham NR13 93 A5
Repps with Bastwick NR29 57 A4
Runhall NR9 69 A1
Sea Palling NR12 40 A5
Shelfanger IP22 120 B2
Shouldham PE33 62 E3
Shropham NR17 103 B3
Sisland NR14 91 D1
Snettisham PE31 12 E5
Somerton NR29 57 F6
South Lopham IP22 128 D8
Stockton NR34 109 F5
Stoke Ferry PE33 80 E2
Strumpshaw NR13 91 F8
Sutton NR12 39 C3
Swafield NR28 22 C4
Swainsthorpe NR14 89 D4
Tasburgh NR15 106 F6
Terrington St John PE14 42 B1
Tharston & Hapton NR15 106 D5
Thompson IP24 102 B7
Thurlton NR14 92 F1
Thurne NR29 56 E2
Tibenham NR16 120 E8
Tilney All Saints PE34 144 F1
Tilney St Lawrence PE34 42 D2
Toft Monks NR34 110 D6
Topcroft NR35 107 F3
Tunstead NR12 55 B8
Upton with Fishley NR13 166 A6
Wacton NR15 106 C2
Walpole St Andrew PE14 41 E3
Walsingham NR22 16 F8
Watlington PE34 61 C6
Watton IP25 84 E3
Wellingham PE32 30 E1
Wereham PE33 80 E4
West Beckham NR25 9 C2
West Dereham PE33 80 B4
Wheatacre NR34 111 A5
Whinburgh & Westfield NR19 68 A3
Wiggenhall St Germans PE34 61 A8
Wimbotsham PE34 172 E8
Wingfield IP21 131 E3
Woodton NR35 108 B5
Wortham IP22 129 C5
Wreningham NR16 88 E1
Wroxham/Hoveton NR12 164 D5
Yelverton NR14 90 F5
Church Rd N IP21 131 C7
Church St Ashill IP25 84 A7
Attleborough NR17 174 D5
Bawburgh NR9 160 A6
Bradenham IP25 66 E3
Brisley NR20 49 A8
Briston NR24 142 E4
Carbrooke IP25 85 A5
Coltishall NR12 54 C6
Cromer NR27 139 C6
Diss IP22 177 D4
East Dereham NR19 154 D5
Elsing NR20 50 F3
Gimingham NR11 22 E7
Great Ellingham NR17 103 E7
23 Harleston IP20 122 D2
Hingham NR9 86 C5
Holt NR25 137 C6
Horsford NR10 53 B2
Hunstanton PE36 132 C4
Kenninghall NR16 119 B4
King's Lynn PE30 146 D4
Litcham PE32 48 A4
Little Walsingham NR22 16 F7
New Buckenham NR16 104 F1
North Creake NR21 15 D8
11 North Walsham NR28 151 D5
Northrepps NR27 11 A2
Norwich NR6 158 E5
Plumstead NR11 20 A5
Reepham NR10 149 C4
Sheringham NR26 138 D7
Southrepps NR11 22 B7
Stiffkey NR23 6 D6
15 Sutton Bridge PE12 41 B8
Thornham PE36 2 D6
Trimingham NR11 11 D1
Wells-next-the-Sea NR23 136 D5
Wymondham NR18 173 B4
Church Terr
5 Outwell PE14 77 F6
21 Wisbech PE13 152 C5
Wroxham NR12 164 B3
Church View
Harleston IP20 122 E2
Church View *continued*
Marham PE33 63 B4
Ormesby St Margaret NR29 167 B2
Pentney PE32 63 C8
Church View Cl
Norwich NR7 159 B5
Reedham NR13 93 A5
Church View Ct NR7 159 B5
Church Wlk
Burnham Market PE31 135 B2
Great Yarmouth NR31 94 C6
Shelfanger IP22 120 B2
Churchfarm Wlk PE33 62 E1
Churchfield Gn 3 NR7 163 D8
Churchfield Rd 3 PE14 77 F6
Churchfields NR9 88 D8
Churchfields Rd NR15 106 F4
Churchgate St 2 PE38 97 B5
Churchgate Way PE34 144 C5
Churchill Cl
Hevingham NR10 53 B8
1 Watton IP25 84 D3
Churchill Cres
Fincham PE33 62 E1
Sheringham NR26 138 B5
Churchill Ct NR19 154 D4
Churchill Pl NR15 90 F2
Churchill Rd
Great Yarmouth NR30 169 D6
Norwich NR3 162 E8
Thetford IP24 176 E5
Wisbech PE13 152 D4
Churchill Way PE38 172 B4
Churchman Rd NR7 159 C2
Churchway IP22 128 F5
Cider Cl NR17 174 E4
Cinder La NR34 111 B4
Cintra Rd NR1 163 B6
Cirrus Way NR7 159 C2
City Coll Norwich NR2 178 A2
City of Norwich Aviation Mus* NR6 53 D1
City of Norwich Sch NR4 162 B2
City Rd NR1 178 C1
City View Rd NR6 158 A4
Civic Gdns NR3 158 B3
Civray Ave PE38 172 C6
Clabburn Cl 1 NR15 89 C1
Clabon Fst Cl NR3 158 F2
Clabon Rd NR3 158 F2
Clabon Second Cl NR3 158 F3
Clabon Third Cl NR3 158 F3
Clackclose Com Prim Sch PE38 172 B5
Clackclose Rd PE38 172 C6
Clancy Rd NR7 159 C1
Clapper La PE34 145 E5
Clare Ave NR31 170 B2
Clare Cl NR3 158 E1
Clare Rd Cromer NR27 139 D5
King's Lynn PE30 148 C3
Clare Sch NR4 162 A3
Claremont Rd
Norwich NR4 162 A2
Wisbech PE13 152 E5
Clarence Ct
Hunstanton PE36 132 C6
17 Watton IP25 84 D3
Clarence Rd
14 Great Yarmouth NR30 169 D2
Hunstanton PE36 132 D6
Norwich NR1 163 A5
Wisbech PE13 152 D6
Clarendon Cl 6 NR30 169 D2
Clarendon Dr 10 NR29 57 D4
Clarendon Rd
Norwich NR2 162 C5
Sculthorpe NR21 141 A5
Clarendon Stps 1 NR2 162 B5
Clark Rd NR35 109 B2
Clark's La NR21 17 E5
Clark's Loke 7 NR13 73 D6
Clarke Cl IP22 177 C1
Clarke Rd NR3 162 D8
Clarke's Cl 2 NR9 69 F2
Clarke's La
Barsham NR34 124 F7
Gooderstone PE33 82 A5
Clarke's Rd NR31 170 C5
Clarkes Rd NR30 169 B5
Clarkson Ave PE13 152 D5
Clarkson Ct PE13 152 D6
Clarkson Inf Sch The PE13 152 E6
Clarkson Rd
10 Lingwood NR13 74 A3
Norwich NR5 161 C7
Claxton Cl Mileham PE32 48 D6
5 Thetford IP24 176 C4
Claxton Cnr NR14 91 C6
Clay Hill PE32 48 B7
Clay La Bacton NR28 23 B3
Bradwell NR31 94 C5
Hepworth IP22 127 F1
Saxlingham Nethergate NR15 107 A7
Swannington NR9 52 C7
Clay Rd NR30 168 F5
Claydon Gr NR31 170 B7
Claymore Gdns NR29 167 B2
Claypit La NR21 141 C5
Claypit Rd NR20 33 D3
Clayton Cl
Dersingham PE31 140 D4
Clayton Cl *continued*
Wisbech PE13 152 F6
Clearview Dr NR14 90 C5
Cleaves Dr NR22 16 F8
Clement Gdns IP22 177 F3
Clement Scott Mews NR27 139 D5
Clements Cl IP21 130 C5
Clements Ct PE34 144 B5
Clenchwarton Prim Sch PE34 145 E5
Clenchwarton Rd PE34 146 B4
Clere Cl NR18 173 C5
Cleveland Rd NR2 178 A3
Cleves Way NR8 156 E4
Cley La IP25 84 C4
Cley Marshes Nature Reserve* NR25 7 F7
Cley Rd Blakeney NR25 7 D6
Bradwell NR31 94 C7
Cockley Cley PE37 82 E8
Holt NR25 137 B8
Swaffham PE37 153 B2
Clickers Rd NR3 162 C8
Cliff Ave Cromer NR27 139 C6
Great Yarmouth NR31 170 D3
Cliff Cl NR13 92 F4
Cliff Ct PE36 132 C6
Cliff Dr NR27 139 C7
Cliff Hill 4 NR31 170 D4
Cliff La Cromer NR27 139 C6
Great Yarmouth NR31 171 D8
Cliff Par PE36 132 C5
Cliff Pk Com Mid Sch NR31 170 D2
Cliff Pk Fst Sch NR31 170 D2
Cliff Pk High Sch NR31 170 D1
Cliff Rd Cromer NR27 139 D5
Overstrand NR27 11 A3
Sheringham NR26 138 E7
Cliff Terr PE36 132 C5
Cliffe-en-Howe Rd PE32 44 F8
Clifford Ave NR30 168 D5
Clifford Burman Cl PE30 148 A1
Clifford Pye Cl NR10 35 B2
Clifton Cl 3 NR2 162 C7
Clifton Pk NR27 10 C5
Clifton Rd
King's Lynn PE30 148 B1
Wymondham NR18 173 C6
Clifton St NR2 162 B7
Clifton Way NR27 11 B3
Clink Hill NR30 168 B4
Clink Rd NR12 40 A6
Clint Hill IP31 126 D2
Clint St NR29 56 B5
Clintergate Rd IP20 122 C6
Clintock Pl 10 NR30 169 C5
Clipbush La
Banham NR16 119 C7
Fakenham NR21 141 E5
Scoulton NR9 85 C4
Clipped Hedge La NR11 22 B7
Clipstreet La NR21 18 B8
Close The
Brancaster PE31 3 D7
Brundall NR13 165 C4
Docking PE31 134 E4
Great Yarmouth NR31 170 A5
Hemsby NR29 167 B7
Holt NR25 137 C5
Little Melton NR9 160 D2
North Lopham IP22 119 A2
North Walsham NR28 151 D4
Norwich NR1 178 C3
Rackheath NR13 72 D8
Roydon IP22 177 A5
Sheringham NR26 138 D8
Stow Bedon NR17 102 D7
Clough Dr 9 IP26 98 E1
Clough La PE30 146 D4
Clovelly Dr NR6 157 E2
Clover Dr 7 NR26 138 B6
Clover Hill Fst Sch NR5 161 B8
Clover Hill Rd NR5 160 F8
Clover Rd
Attleborough NR17 174 C3
Aylsham NR11 150 D5
Norwich NR7 158 F3
Clover Way
Fakenham NR21 141 E4
Great Yarmouth NR31 170 A4
Thetford IP24 176 D5
Clover Wlk PE34 61 B8
Cloverland Dr 6 NR29 167 B7
Clowes Ct NR34 110 D1
Clubbs La NR23 136 D6
Clydesdale Rise NR31 94 C8
Coach & Horses Row NR2 178 A2
Coach House Ct 1 NR4 162 A3
Coach La NR19 67 C6
Coachmans Ct NR7 158 F4
Coalwharf Rd PE13 152 B4
Coast Rd Bacton NR12 23 F4
Cley next the Sea NR25 7 F7
Corton NR32 171 F1
Happisburgh NR12 23 F3
Hopton on Sea NR31 171 D4
Overstrand NR27 11 B3
Salthouse NR25 8 A7
Wiveton NR25 7 D6
Coastguard Rd NR30 168 F5
Coates Ct 5 PE14 59 D2
Cob Cl 7 NR31 94 C8
Cobb's Pl 5 NR30 169 D4
Cobblers La PE14 41 F2
Cobbleways The 9 NR29 58 B6
Cobbold St IP22 177 B5
Cobbs Hill PE34 144 B5
Cobham Way NR7 159 C2
Cobholm Cl 14 NR31 169 B4
Cobholm Fst Sch NR31 169 B4
Cobholm Rd 5 NR31 169 B4
Coburg Cl 10 IP25 84 D3
Coburg La IP25 84 B6
Coburg St
9 King's Lynn PE30 146 E5
Norwich NR2 178 A2
Cochrane Cl IP25 85 A3
Cock Dro PE38 172 B7
Cock Fen Rd PE14 95 D7
Cock Rd NR14 92 A3
Cock St Ixworth NR9 69 F2
Wymondham NR18 173 B5
Cocketts Dr PE13 152 E5
Cocklehole Rd PE34 41 F8
Codling's La NR11 150 A6
Coigncroft The NR13 165 E3
Coke Rd NR1 162 E1
Coker's Hill NR22 16 F7
Colby Prim Sch NR11 36 E8
Cold Harbour Rd NR29 56 D4
Coldershaw Rd NR6 158 B4
Coldham Cl NR29 167 B3
Coldham Hall Carnser NR14 165 C1
Coldham Rd NR21 17 D7
Coldham's La PE33 80 A5
Coldhorn Cres PE13 152 D7
Coleburn Rd NR1 89 E8
Colegate NR3 178 A3
Colegate End Rd IP21 121 E6
Coleman Cl
Palgrave IP22 177 D1
Taverham NR8 155 F2
Coleridge Cl NR8 156 D8
Coleridge Rd IP22 177 E4
Coles Way NR10 149 C5
Colin Mclean Rd NR19 154 C7
Colindeep La NR7 159 A4
Colkett Dr NR6 158 E3
Colkirk CE VA Prim Sch NR21 31 D5
Coll of W Anglia (Fakenham Learning Ctr) The NR21 141 B4
Coll of W Anglia (Hunstanton Learning Ctr) The PE36 132 D4
Coll of W Anglia (Isle Campus) The PE13 152 E2
Coll of W Anglia (King's Lynn Ctr) The PE30 146 F5
Coll of W Anglia (Sheringham Centre) The NR26 138 C7
Coll of W Anglia (Wispech Campus) The PE13 152 E2
Collectors World of Eric St John Foti* PE38 79 B6
Colleen Cl
Dereham NR19 67 E5
East Dereham NR19 154 D1
College Cl NR12 54 D7
College Ct 1 NR31 169 B4
College Dr PE31 133 C4
College La Keswick NR4 89 C7
9 King's Lynn PE30 146 D4
Runcton Holme PE33 61 F3
College Rd
Hockwold cum Wilton IP26 113 F7
Norwich NR2 162 A5
Thompson IP24 102 C7
Thurlton NR14 110 C8
Wereham PE33 97 F8
Collen's Gn NR9 51 B3
Collers Way NR10 149 C6
Collett's Bridge La PE14 59 C1
Colley Hill Drift PE32 48 D4
Collin's La PE33 63 C5
Collingwood Cl
Heacham PE31 133 D3
25 Hethersett NR9 88 D7
Collingwood Dr NR11 22 F8
Collingwood Rd
Downham Market PE38 172 B4
Great Yarmouth NR30 169 E7
Hunstanton PE36 132 D3
Collingwood Way IP24 176 F6
Collingwood Wlk 1 IP24 176 F6
Collins Ct NR6 158 D2
Collins La PE31 133 D5
Collis La NR29 57 F5
Colls Rd NR7 159 D1
Colman Ave 1 NR14 89 F4
Colman Fst Sch NR4 162 A3
Colman Hospl NR2 162 A4
Colman Mid Sch NR4 161 F3
Colman Rd NR4 161 F5
Colmans Mustard Shop* NR1 178 B2
Colne Pl NR27 139 B6
Colne Rd NR27 139 B6
Colney La Colney NR4 161 A3
Colney La *continued*
Hethersett NR9 160 D1
Colney Rd PE30 147 D5
Colomb Rd NR31 170 C6
Coltishall Airfield NR10 54 B8
Coltishall La NR10 53 E2
Coltishall Prim Sch NR12 54 D7
Coltishall Rd
Belaugh NR12 164 A6
Buxton with Lammas NR10 53 F8
Coltishall Sta NR12 54 C7
Colton Rd NR9 69 E6
Coltsfoot Rd NR10 53 A7
Coltsfoot Way IP24 176 F5
Columbia Way PE30 146 F6
Columbine Cl 4 IP24 176 F5
Columbine Rd NR10 53 B2
Columbine The NR5 160 E7
Colvile Rd PE13 152 E5
Colville Rd NR24 142 B5
Comber Cl IP21 130 D6
Comet Rd 7 IP25 84 F3
Comfrey Way IP24 116 D2
Commercial Rd NR19 154 E5
Common Drift NR20 49 C4
Common Dro
Flitcham with Appleton PE31 27 F5
Southery PE38 97 B5
Common End PE32 47 D8
Common La
Beccles NR34 110 D1
Beetley NR20 49 E5
Brancaster PE31 3 D6
Brockdish IP21 131 D6
Burgh & Tuttington NR11 36 E6
East Walton PE32 45 E3
Field Dalling NR25 7 B1
Filby NR29 75 E8
Gayton PE32 45 C4
Great Witchingham NR9 51 D4
King's Lynn PE30 148 C2
North Runcton PE33 44 A2
Norwich NR7 163 F5
Sheringham NR26 138 E6
6 Southery PE38 97 B5
Thorpe Market NR11 22 A6
Common La N NR34 110 D1
Common Loke NR14 92 A2
Common Pl 3 NR22 16 F7
Common Rd
Aldeby NR34 111 B3
Ashwellthorpe NR16 105 E7
Barton Turf NR12 38 F1
Botesdale IP22 128 F1
Bressingham IP22 129 C8
Brumstead NR12 24 A1
Burston & Shimpling IP22 120 E2
Castle Acre PE32 46 E1
East Tuddenham NR20 69 B5
Forncett NR16 105 E5
Foxley NR20 33 D1
Gissing NR15 120 F5
Great Yarmouth NR31 170 C8
Hemsby NR29 57 F4
Hopton IP22 127 F6
Lessingham NR12 24 E2
Martham NR29 57 B4
Mundham NR14 91 C1
Neatishead NR12 55 E6
Pulham Market IP21 121 E7
Runcton Holme PE33 61 D4
Runhall NR20 68 F4
Scole IP21 130 F8
Shelfanger IP22 119 F3
Shelton NR15 107 B1
Skeyton NR10 37 A6
Snettisham PE31 12 D4
Somerton NR29 57 E6
Surlingham NR14 165 B1
Swafield NR28 22 D4
Thurne NR29 56 E3
Wacton NR15 106 D2
West Walton PE14 59 D7
Wiggenhall St Germans PE34 60 F7
Common The
Freethorpe NR13 92 E7
1 Harleston IP20 122 D1
Lyng NR9 51 A4
Surlingham NR14 165 A1
Swardeston NR14 89 B6
Commonside NR10 35 A2
Commonwealth Way 12 NR7 72 D4
Compass Rd NR18 173 F1
Compit Hills NR27 139 B3
Concorde Rd NR6 158 C5
Conesford Dr NR1 162 F3
Coney Weston Rd
Barningham IP31 127 C4
Sapiston IP31 126 D2
Conference Way
Colkirk NR21 31 E5
Wisbech PE13 152 C8
Conge The NR30 169 C4
Congham Rd PE32 28 B1
Conifer Cl NR29 167 A3
Coniston Cl
2 Hethersett NR9 88 E8
King's Lynn PE30 148 F1
2 Norwich NR5 161 C6
Coniston Rd NR15 90 E1
Coniston Sq 1 NR30 169 D4
Connaught Ave NR31 170 C3

Connaught Plain
NR17 174 D5
Connaught Rd
Attleborough NR17 174 D5
Cromer NR27 139 D5
Norwich NR2 162 B7
Constable Cl
7 Attleborough NR17 174 B4
2 Diss IP22 177 C4
Constable Ct 15 IP20 122 D2
Constable Dr 4 NR31 170 A7
Constable Rd NR4 162 C1
Constitution Hill
Fakenham NR21 141 B4
North Runcton PE33 43 F4
Norwich NR6 158 E3
Constitution Opening
NR3 158 E2
Convent Rd 4 NR2 162 C5
Convy Priors NR30 168 C6
Conway Rd
Great Yarmouth NR31 170 D6
Sheringham NR26 138 F7
Conyers NR18 173 C6
Cook Rd IP25 66 A3
Cook's La IP20 122 F2
Cooke Cl NR5 160 E7
Cooke's Rd NR15 91 B4
Cookley La IP23 130 F1
Cooper La NR1 89 F8
Cooper Rd
North Walsham NR28 151 D6
8 Sheringham NR26 138 C5
Co-operative St NR26 138 D7
Coopers Cl NR8 155 E3
Coopers La PE33 62 B2
Copeman Rd
Aylsham NR11 150 D5
Great & Little Plumstead
NR13 73 A6
3 Roydon IP22 129 D7
Copenhagen Way
NR6 158 C2
Copince's La NR16 119 C7
Copper Beech Cl
NR21 141 D6
Copper Hall PE37 153 B3
Copper La 8 NR9 86 C5
Copper Smith Way
NR18 173 F5
Copperfield 4 PE30 147 C5
Copperfield Ave 1
NR30 170 D8
Coppice Ave NR6 157 E5
Coppice The 6 NR17 174 C5
Coppins Ct PE14 152 E2
Corbet Ave NR7 159 B2
Corbett Rd 2 NR28 151 C6
Corbyn Shaw Rd PE30 147 E4
Cordon St PE13 152 C4
Coriander Dr IP24 176 F4
Corie Rd NR4 161 F4
Corkway Dro PE38 97 E1
Cormorant Way 10 NR31 94 C8
Corncutters Cl NR3 178 B3
Corner Comm Rd NR28 38 B7
Corner La NR10 53 B3
Corner St 2 NR27 139 B7
Cornfield The NR25 7 A3
Cornfields IP21 121 B1
Cornish Ave NR28 22 E5
Cornish Way NR28 151 C7
Cornwallis Cl 7 NR5 161 A7
Coronation Ave
2 Marthan NR29 57 D4
Nordelph PE38 78 D3
1 Rollesby NR29 57 D2
West Winch PE33 43 F3
Coronation Cl NR6 158 A4
Coronation Cotts PE32 47 F4
Coronation Cres
NR15 107 D5
Coronation Gn NR31 169 B3
Coronation Gr PE37 153 B5
Coronation La
Blakeney NR25 7 D7
Somerton NR29 57 F5
Coronation Pl IP27 175 B2
Coronation Rd
Clenchwarton PE34 146 A5
Great Yarmouth NR31 169 B3
Holt NR25 137 C5
Norwich NR6 158 A4
Coronation Terr
Caston NR17 102 F8
6 Great Yarmouth NR30 169 C4
Coronation Wlk NR28 151 A5
Coronilla Gn NR31 170 B5
Corporation Rd PE13 152 D3
Corpusty Prim Sch
NR11 19 F1
Corpusty Rd
Briston NR24 142 F1
Thurning NR24 19 B2
Wood Dalling NR11 34 D7
Corton Rd NR1 178 C1
Coslany Sq NR3 178 C4
Coslany St NR3 178 A3
Costessey High Sch
NR5 156 E2
Costessey Inf Sch
NR5 157 B1
Costessey Jun Sch
NR5 156 F1
Costessey La
Drayton NR8 156 E6
Ringland NR8 70 B8
Taverham NR8 157 A7
Coston La NR18 87 A8
Cosy Cnr NR28 151 B4
Cotman Cl IP22 177 C4
Cotman Dr NR31 170 A7
Cotman Fields NR1 178 C4
Cotman Rd NR1 163 B5
Cotoneaster Ct 4 NR31 170 B6
Cottage Dr The NR7 163 E8
Cottage Farm Abbey
PE32 46 C2
Cottage Rd NR29 57 E6
Cotterall Ct NR5 161 A8
Cottinghams Dr NR10 157 E7
Cotton Rd NR9 70 A4
Cotton's Cnr PE14 77 D2
Cottons Head PE14 77 E7
Cotts La PE34 144 F1
Coughtrey Cl NR7 159 B5
Couhe Cl PE37 153 C5
Coulson La IP27 175 C4
Coulton Cl PE30 146 E7
Council Rd 4 PE13 152 E6
County Ct Rd 3 PE30 146 E4
Court Cl 6 NR29 57 D2
Court Dr NR27 139 B6
Court Gdns PE38 172 C5
Court Hill NR12 54 A4
Court Rd
Great Snoring NR21 17 B5
Rollesby NR29 57 D2
Courtenay Cl
4 East Dereham NR19 154 D5
2 Norwich NR5 160 F8
Courtfields PE37 153 B3
Courtnell Pl PE30 147 D5
Courtney Cl 7 NR19 154 D5
Courtyard The 5 NR4 161 C5
Covent Gdn Rd NR30 168 C7
Coventry St 2 NR21 15 C2
Coventry Way IP24 176 A4
Covert Sycamore
IP24 176 A4
Covert The IP24 176 E6
Covey The
Surlingham NR14 91 C8
Taverham NR8 155 D2
Covey Way IP27 113 F1
Cow Hill NR2 178 A3
Cow La Denver PE38 172 C1
Tharston & Hapton
NR15 106 C7
Cow Lake Dro PE14 59 D5
Cow Mdw Rd NR13 92 C8
Cow Tro NR29 57 D3
Cow Twr* NR3 178 C4
Cowdewell Mews 7
NR8 155 D1
Cowgate NR3 178 B4
Cowle's Dro IP26 113 D5
Cowper Cl NR11 143 C5
Cowper Rd NR19 154 E5
Cowslip Cl 14 NR14 89 B3
Cowslip La NR26 138 B6
Cowslip Wlk PE34 61 B8
Cox's La PE13 152 A3
Coxswain Read Way
NR30 168 D4
Cozens Rd NR1 163 A4
Cozens-Hardy Rd NR7 159 B4
Crab Apple La NR14 110 E8
Crab La Boughton PE33 81 A5
Great Yarmouth NR31 170 A5
Crab Marsh PE13 152 B8
Crabapple Cl 7 NR18 173 E4
Crabapple La NR9 68 D1
Crabb La PE34 42 E1
Crabb's Abbey PE34 61 B2
Crabbe's Cl 7 IP26 98 E1
Crabgate La N NR11 34 D6
Crabgate La S NR11 34 D5
Crabtree La NR34 110 D1
Crabtree Rise IP21 131 C6
Cradle Wood Rd NR28 151 E3
Cradock Ave NR30 169 D8
Craft La NR27 11 A1
Craft The
Raveningham NR14 110 B8
Winterton-on-Sea NR29 58 B6
Cramp Cnr NR14 91 F6
Cranage Rd NR1 162 E1
Crane Cl NR19 154 C3
Crane's La NR10 150 C1
Cranes Mdw 31 IP20 122 D2
Cranes Rd NR14 88 F3
Cranfield Rd NR26 138 A4
Cranleigh Rise NR4 161 F1
Cranley Rd NR7 72 E4
Cranmer Ave PE30 148 C4
Cranmer Ct NR21 141 C5
Cranny Field Chase
PE14 41 E1
Cranwell Rd 10 IP25 84 F3
Cranworth Gdns NR1 178 A1
Craske Cl 3 NR26 138 C5
Craske Dr NR13 72 E7
Craske La PE34 42 A7
Craske Mews 6 NR5 160 E8
Craven La PE33 62 B6
Crawford Rd NR27 139 D5
Craymere Beck Rd
Briston NR24 142 E1
Hindolveston NR24 18 F1
Craymere Rd NR24 142 E2
Creake Rd
Burnham Market PE31 135 D2
Sculthorpe NR21 141 A6
Sculthorpe Airfield PE31 15 B3
Creance Rd NR7 159 C4
Crecen La PE36 132 C4
Creek The PE31 135 E7
Cremer Cl 14 PE31 12 E4
Cremer St NR26 138 D7
Cremer's Drift NR26 138 D6
Cremorne La NR1 163 B5
Crescent Pas PE13 152 C5
Crescent Rd PE36 132 C3
Crescent The
Ashwellthorpe NR16 105 F8
Bacton/Walcott NR12 24 A7
East Dereham NR19 154 C1
East Harling NR16 118 C4
Hemsby NR29 167 D7
Hethersett NR9 88 C7
4 Newton Flotman NR15 89 D1
Norwich NR2 178 A2
Taverham NR8 156 F8
Thurton NR14 91 C4
Wisbech PE13 152 C4
Cressener Cl NR6 157 E5
Cressingham Rd IP25 83 F6
Cresswell Cl NR5 161 B6
Cresswell St PE30 146 E6
Crest Rd PE31 140 C4
Crick's Wlk IP22 177 A5
Cricket Cl NR8 155 E3
Cricket Gd Rd NR1 162 E3
Cricket Pasture The
PE31 3 E7
Cricketer's Wlk NR13 92 E7
Cricketers Way PE13 152 A6
Crimp Cramp La NR34 111 B4
Cringleford CE Fst & Mid Sch
NR4 89 B8
Cringleford Chase
NR4 161 C1
Crinoline La NR20 69 C5
Crisp Cl PE31 140 C3
Crisp Rd NR35 109 E3
Critten's Rd NR31 169 B4
Croft Cl Diss IP22 177 C4
10 Harleston IP20 122 D2
Croft Gn NR17 174 B3
Croft Hill NR29 75 B5
Croft La Corpusty NR11 19 F2
Diss IP22 177 C4
Marsham NR10 150 C1
Croft Rd
Caister-on-Sea NR30 168 E5
Norton Subcourse NR14 92 E1
Upwell PE14 77 D3
Croft The
Costessey NR8 156 F4
Cromer NR27 139 B6
Little Snoring NR21 17 C3
Swanton Novers NR24 18 B3
Croft Yd NR23 136 D6
Croftholme Way 2 NR7 163 C8
Crofts Cl PE31 135 C1
Crofts The 1 NR5 160 F7
Cromarty Way NR30 168 D5
Crome Cl IP22 177 B4
Crome Rd NR3 162 F8
Cromer High Sch Language
Coll NR27 139 C5
Cromer Hospl NR27 139 D6
Cromer Jun Sch NR27 139 C5
Cromer La PE33 80 F3
Cromer Mus* NR27 139 C7
Cromer Rd
Aylsham NR11 150 C8
Blickling NR11 36 B7
Hevingham NR10 36 B1
Holt NR25 137 D7
Hunstanton PE36 132 D5
Mundesley NR11 143 B7
North Walsham NR28 151 A6
Norwich NR6 158 A5
Ormesby St Margaret
with Scratby NR29 167 A2
Overstrand NR27 139 F4
Runton NR27 10 A5
Sheringham NR26 138 E6
Southrepps NR11 22 C8
Trimingham NR11 11 C2
Cromer Sta NR27 139 A7
Cromes Oak Cl NR14 90 C4
Cromes Pl NR10 37 B2
Crompton Rd NR11 150 C4
Cromwell Cl
6 Cromer NR27 139 C6
3 Hethersett NR9 88 D8
7 Marthan NR29 57 D4
Swaffham PE37 153 D3
Cromwell Rd
Cromer NR27 139 C6
Great Yarmouth NR31 169 C1
Norwich NR7 159 B3
Weeting-with-Broomhill
IP27 114 E8
Wisbech PE13 152 A2
Cromwell Terr 6 PE30 146 E3
Crooks Pl NR1 178 A1
Crosby Row PE12 41 A8
Cross Bank Rd PE30 146 C6
Cross Dro Hilgay PE38 96 D7
Southery PE38 97 B3
Cross Keys Cl 2 NR10 53 D2
Cross La Brancaster PE31 3 B7
Lessingham NR12 24 E4
Northwold IP26 99 C7
Norwich NR3 178 A4
Runton NR27 10 B4
Stanhoe PE31 14 E7
Surlingham NR14 91 A8
Cross Rd
Ashby with Oby NR29 56 F1
Cross Rd *continued*
Great Yarmouth NR31 170 D6
Starston IP20 122 C2
Cross St 6 Cromer NR27 139 B6
Harpley PE31 29 C5
2 Holt NR25 137 B6
Hoxne IP21 131 A3
Salthouse NR25 8 B6
Cross Stone Rd NR14 92 B3
Cross Way PE31 133 C5
Cross's Grave PE31 29 E4
Crossing Rd
Great Green IP21 130 A5
Palgrave IP22 177 D1
Crosskeys Way 3 NR20 68 F6
Crossroad NR10 37 C4
Crosstead NR30 169 D8
Crossway Terr
Acle NR13 166 B4
5 Loddon NR14 91 F1
Crossways 4 NR29 167 A2
Crostwick La NR10 54 A2
Crostwight Rd NR28 38 D7
Croughton La PE31 30 B8
Crow Hall Est PE38 172 C3
Crow Hall Gn NR31 170 C2
Crow Hill NR11 34 C7
Crow La Bircham PE31 14 A2
Elsing NR20 50 F4
Great Dunham PE32 47 E1
Crow Rd NR28 151 D6
Crow St IP31 127 B4
Crow's La IP25 84 C1
Crowden Rd NR12 24 D4
Crowes Loke NR13 73 B7
Crown Ave PE14 95 A7
Crown Cres IP25 84 E5
Crown Ctyd NR16 119 A4
Crown Gdns PE33 80 E4
Crown Gn IP22 120 E2
Crown La
Coney Weston IP31 127 B4
Fransham NR19 66 D6
Crown Mdw NR10 149 C5
Crown Pl 9 NR19 154 D5
Crown Rd
Christchurch PE14 95 A7
Colkirk NR21 31 D5
East Dereham NR20 154 F5
Great Yarmouth NR30 169 D3
Horsham St Faith NR10 53 D2
Lamas NR10 36 E1
Mundford IP26 100 B4
Norwich NR1 178 B3
2 Old Buckenham NR17 104 D2
Crown Sq PE30 147 A7
Crown St
Banham NR16 119 D7
Brandon IP27 175 A2
Methwold IP26 99 A5
Crown Way NR16 119 D6
Crownthorpe Rd NR18 87 C6
Crowshall La NR17 174 B5
Croxton Rd
Fulmodeston NR21 17 E2
Thetford IP24 176 D4
Crummock Rd 3 NR5 161 C6
Cubitt Rd NR1 163 C7
Cubitts Cl NR20 33 B2
Cuck Stool La 5 PE32 46 F2
Cuckoo Hill Rd PE31 14 B3
Cuckoo La
Brundall NR13 73 E3
Carbrooke IP25 85 B4
Redenhall with Harleston
IP20 122 F2
Cuckoo Rd PE34 79 A8
Cuckoofield La NR14 89 A3
Cucumber La NR13 165 B5
Cuddle Dike Bank PE14 78 A5
Cuffer La NR16 104 F2
Culey Cl PE30 146 F7
Culley's Pit Rd NR12 38 A2
Culling's Hill NR13 72 F2
Cullum Cl NR20 50 B3
Culverin Cl 9 NR7 72 D4
Cummings Bvd NR21 15 C2
Cunningham Ave 2
NR30 169 D8
Cunningham Cl IP24 176 F6
Cunningham Rd 6 NR5 161 C5
Cunningham Wlk 3
IP24 176 F6
Curd's Hall NR19 66 A7
Curie Dr NR31 170 B1
Curlew Cl 7 IP25 84 C3
Curlew Way NR31 170 A6
Curson Cl 11 NR9 88 C7
Curson Rd 8 NR15 106 F6
Cursons Mews NR18 173 B6
Curtis Dr 1 IP26 98 D1
Curtis La NR26 138 E7
Curtis Rd NR3 158 B4
Cushing Cl 1 IP25 67 B2
Cushing Dr 3 NR21 17 B3
Custance Ct NR4 161 E3
Customhouse St PE12 41 C8
Cut Loke NR14 73 C1
Cuthbert Cl
4 King's Lynn PE30 148 C5
Norwich NR7 159 B4
8 Thetford IP24 176 F5
Cutler Way
Bowthorpe NR5 160 F6
Norwich NR5 160 E8
Cutthroat La NR19 68 A6
Cutting's Rd IP21 131 C8
Cuttons Cnr NR13 73 D6
Cydonia Gn 12 NR31 170 B6
Cygnet Cl NR17 174 F6
Cygnet Rd NR19 154 E4
Cygnet Wlk PE13 153 C2
Cypress Cl NR8 156 E8
Cypress Cres NR26 138 D5
Cypress Pl PE36 132 D4
Cyprus Rd NR17 174 C5
Cyprus St NR1 162 E3
Cyril Rd NR7 163 F7

D

Da Volls Ct NR31 170 D6
Dacre Cl NR4 161 E1
Dades La PE14 60 B6
Daffodil Way NR20 68 E6
Dagmar Mews 12 NR30 169 D2
Dairy Drift PE32 48 C2
Dairy Dro CB6 95 F2
Dairy Farm Cl NR21 141 C6
Dairy Farm Ct NR17 174 C5
Dairy La NR11 9 E1
Dakenham Cl NR13 72 F8
Dakin Rd NR3 158 D1
Dalbier Cl 2 NR13 72 E4
Dale End PE31 3 D7
Dale La NR29 56 C8
Dale Rd
East Dereham NR19 154 C6
Scarning NR19 67 A7
Stanton IP31 127 C1
Dales Ct 6 NR31 94 C8
Dales Loke NR14 163 D5
Dales The NR13 165 D3
Dalrymple Way NR3 158 C4
Dam La IP22 129 D3
Damgate Back La NR29 57 D6
Damgate Cl NR13 166 C2
Damgate La Acle NR13 166 D2
Marthan NR29 57 D6
Damgate St NR18 173 B3
Danby Cl 6 NR4 89 D8
Danby Rd NR31 170 C6
Dane Cl IP24 176 B3
Danemoor La NR9 86 F8
Danesbower Cl NR13 165 F6
Danesbower La NR13 165 F6
Danesfort Dr 1 NR19 154 E6
Daniels Rd NR4 162 B2
Danish House Gdns
NR27 11 A4
Daphne Way 8 NR31 170 B5
Dark La
Ashmanhaugh NR12 38 C1
Dickleburgh & Rushall
IP21 130 B6
Erpingham NR11 21 A1
Kimberley NR18 87 B7
Smallburgh NR12 38 D3
Somerton NR29 57 F6
Wretham IP24 101 F2
Darrell Pl NR5 161 D7
Darrow Gn Rd IP20 122 F8
Darrow Wood* IP20 122 F8
Darrow Wood La IP22 120 A1
Darwin Cl 5 PE12 41 B8
Darwin Wlk NR19 154 D4
Daseley's Cl PE30 148 A1
Dashwood Cl NR31 93 F6
Dauber's La NR13 74 C2
Davey Cl NR35 124 C8
Davey Pl NR2 178 B3
Davidson Cl NR7 163 F7
Davidson Rd NR7 163 F7
Davy Pl Heacham PE31 133 C5
7 Loddon NR14 92 A1
Dawber Cl PE30 147 B4
Dawes La 2 PE31 12 E4
Dawnay Ave PE30 148 B1
Dawsons La NR20 33 C3
Day's La IP31 127 C4
Day's Lode Rd PE14 95 A4
De Caux Rd NR3 158 E1
De Grey Rd PE30 147 B5
De Hague Rd NR4 161 F4
De Havilland Rd
Dereham NR19 154 C6
Wisbech PE13 152 C6
De Lucy Cl IP22 177 C5
De Morley Cl 4 IP22 177 A5
De Morley Garth
NR26 138 D6
De Warrenne Pl PE32 47 A2
Deacon Cl NR13 165 D4
Deacon Dr 14 NR9 88 D8
Deben Dr 14 NR31 94 A6
Debenne Rd NR28 151 C6
Debnam Cl 10 NR31 94 A5
Deborah Rd NR31 170 C2
De-Carle Smith Rd
NR13 166 C4
Decoy Rd
Lakenheath IP27 112 F4
Ormesby St Margaret
with Scratby NR29 167 A4
Ormesby St Michael NR29 57 F2
Potter Heigham NR29 56 F7
Deep Rd NR18 173 B8
Deepdale NR13 165 D3
Deepdale Ave 1 NR29 57 C4
Deer Row NR35 109 D1
Delane Rd NR8 157 C7
Delft Way NR6 158 A6

Delgate La PE31 ... 3 E7
Dell Cl NR15 ... 106 F8
Dell Cnr La NR13 ... 73 F5
Dell Cres NR5 ... 161 D7
Dell Loke NR14 ... 163 B2
Dell The Bodham NR25 ... 9 A3
Hingham NR9 ... 86 B5
Mundesley NR11 ... 143 D5
Trowse Newton NR14 ... 163 B2
Deloney Rd NR7 ... 159 C2
Delta Cl NR6 ... 158 C4
De-Narde Rd NR19 ... 154 D7
Denbigh Rd NR2 ... 162 B5
Dene Ave NR29 ... 167 A3
Dene Side 1 NR30 ... 169 D3
Denes The NR1 ... 163 C5
Denham Low Rd IP21 ... 131 A1
Denham Rd IP21 ... 131 B2
Denmark Hill IP22 ... 177 C3
Denmark La IP22 ... 177 B4
Denmark Opening NR3 ... 158 E1
Denmark Rd
Beccles NR34 ... 110 D1
2 King's Lynn PE30 ... 147 B6
Norwich NR3 ... 158 E1
Denmark Rise IP22 ... 177 C4
Denmark St IP22 ... 177 C3
Denmead Cl 4 NR4 ... 89 D8
Dennis Rd NR6 ... 157 F7
Dennis Sneezum Ct PE38 ... 172 B4
Denny Rd PE30 ... 147 A4
Denny's Hill IP20 ... 123 A2
Denny's Wlk PE32 ... 63 E7
Denton Rd
Denton IP20 ... 123 C6
Norwich NR3 ... 158 F3
Denver Hill PE38 ... 172 C3
Denver VC Prim Sch PE38 ... 172 D2
Denver Windmill* PE38 ... 172 B1
Deopham Rd
Attleborough NR17 ... 174 C7
Hingham NR9 ... 86 C4
Morley NR18 ... 87 A2
Derby St NR2 ... 162 C7
Dereham 6th Form Coll NR20 ... 154 F5
Dereham Church Inf Sch NR19 ... 154 D5
Dereham Hospl NR19 ... 154 E7
Dereham La NR19 ... 66 C8
Dereham Rd
5 Bawdeswell NR20 ... 50 E7
Beeston with Bittering PE32 ... 48 D2
Briningham NR24 ... 18 D5
Bylaugh NR20 ... 50 C5
Colkirk NR21 ... 31 E5
Costessey NR5 ... 156 D1
Dereham NR20 ... 50 B2
East Dereham NR19 ... 154 B5
Easton NR9 ... 70 C5
Garvestone NR9 ... 68 C1
Gressenhall NR19 ... 49 C2
Hempton NR21 ... 141 B2
Hingham NR9 ... 86 B5
Honingham NR9 ... 69 D7
Kimberley NR18 ... 87 A7
Litcham PE32 ... 48 A4
Mattishall NR20 ... 68 D6
North Elmham NR20 ... 49 E6
1 Norwich NR5 ... 161 B8
Ovington IP25 ... 84 E6
Pudding Norton NR21 ... 141 B1
Reepham NR10 ... 149 A4
Scarning NR19 ... 154 A4
Shipdham IP25 ... 67 A1
25 Watton IP25 ... 84 D3
Whinburgh & Westfield NR19 ... 67 F5
Whissonsett NR20 ... 31 E2
Yaxham NR19 ... 68 A5
Dereham St Nicholas Jun Sch NR19 ... 154 D4
Dersingham Bog National Nature Reserve* PE31 ... 27 D7
Dersingham Inf Sch PE31 ... 140 D4
Dersley Ct NR5 ... 160 E7
Derwent Ave PE30 ... 148 F2
Desborough Way NR13 ... 72 D4
Desmond Dr NR6 ... 158 F6
Devlin Dr 18 NR14 ... 90 C5
Devon Ave NR6 ... 157 E4
Devon Cres PE30 ... 148 D5
Devon Way NR14 ... 163 C1
Devonshire Ct 1 PE30 ... 147 A7
Devonshire Rd NR30 ... 169 D2
Devonshire St 4 NR2 ... 162 C7
Dewarrene Dr IP27 ... 175 B7
Dewdrop Cl PE31 ... 133 D6
Dewing Rd NR13 ... 72 E8
Dexter Rd PE34 ... 79 A7
Dial Cl PE38 ... 172 B5
Diamond Cl IP22 ... 120 B5
Diamond Rd NR6 ... 158 B5
Diamond St PE30 ... 146 D2
Diamond Terr PE30 ... 146 D2
Dian Rd NR13 ... 165 E3
Diana Cl NR19 ... 154 C1
Diana Way NR30 ... 168 C6
Dianas Dro PE36 ... 132 C2
Dibden Rd NR3 ... 162 F8
Dickens Ave NR30 ... 169 D1
Dickens Ct 5 NR30 ... 169 D1
Dickfool's La NR19 ... 66 F8
Dickleburgh Prim Sch IP21 ... 121 B1
Dickleburgh Rd IP21 ... 121 A1
Dicks Mount NR34 ... 111 D3
Dicky Hill IP20 ... 122 D3
Digby Dr NR21 ... 141 B6
Dilham Arts Ctr* NR28 ... 38 C4
Dilham Rd Honing NR28 ... 38 C6
Worstead NR28 ... 38 A4
Dilldash La NR21 ... 17 A5
Dinosaur Adventure Pk* NR9 ... 51 E4
Dirty La
North Tuddenham NR20 ... 50 E1
Pulham St Mary IP21 ... 121 F3
Diss Church Jun Sch IP22 ... 177 D4
Diss High Sch IP22 ... 177 E5
Diss Inf Sch IP22 ... 177 E4
Diss Mus* IP22 ... 177 D4
Diss Rd
Burston & Shimpling IP22 ... 120 E1
Garboldisham IP22 ... 128 A8
Scole IP21 ... 130 C5
South Lopham IP22 ... 128 F8
Tibenham NR16 ... 120 C8
Wattisfield IP22 ... 128 B1
Diss Sta IP22 ... 177 F4
Diss Swimming & Fitness Ctr IP22 ... 177 E3
Distillery Sq 5 NR2 ... 162 C6
Ditchingham Dam NR35 ... 109 A1
Dix Cl PE31 ... 133 E5
Dixon Rd Cromer NR27 ... 139 B5
North Walsham NR28 ... 151 D5
Norwich NR7 ... 159 A4
Dixon's Dro PE14 ... 59 C8
Dixon's Fold NR6 ... 158 F4
Dobbs' La NR13 ... 54 D2
Dobby Dr PE30 ... 146 D6
Dobson Way NR34 ... 110 D1
Dock Tavern La NR31 ... 170 D5
Docking Prim Sch PE31 ... 134 D4
Docking Rd
Burnham Westgate PE31 ... 135 B2
Ringstead PE36 ... 2 B2
Sedgeford PE36 ... 13 B7
Stanhoe PE31 ... 14 D7
Syderstone PE31 ... 15 A3
Doctor's La IP21 ... 122 A2
Doctors Mdw 1 NR10 ... 53 D2
Doctors Rd NR13 ... 165 E6
Dodd Cl NR30 ... 168 D7
Dodd's La PE32 ... 45 B2
Dodderman Way NR5 ... 160 F6
Dodds Cl NR17 ... 174 B3
Dodds La NR17 ... 174 B3
Dodds Rd NR17 ... 174 B3
Doddshill Rd PE31 ... 140 F3
Dodgers La NR15 ... 91 A3
Dodma Rd PE32 ... 47 C8
Dodman's La NR20 ... 31 F2
Dodmans Cl PE30 ... 146 E5
Dodmans The NR19 ... 154 D4
Dodson Dr
7 Beetley NR19 ... 49 C3
7 Gressenhall NR20 ... 49 C3
Doe La Banham NR16 ... 119 E8
Old Buckenham NR17 ... 104 E1
Dog Cnr NR11 ... 35 A5
Dog La Easton NR9 ... 70 B6
Horsford NR10 ... 155 F4
Shelfanger IP22 ... 120 A4
Dogger La NR23 ... 136 C6
Doggetts La NR12 ... 24 D4
Dogs La NR34 ... 110 C3
Dogwood Cl 6 NR18 ... 173 E4
Dogwood Rd NR6 ... 158 D4
Dohamero La 1 PE33 ... 43 F2
Doit La IP22 ... 129 D7
Doit The IP22 ... 129 C6
Dolman Cl 13 NR31 ... 169 B4
Dolphin Gr NR2 ... 162 B8
Doman Rd NR1 ... 178 C1
Donchurch Cl 6 NR5 ... 161 A7
Doris Barnes Ct 1 NR19 ... 154 E5
Doris Rd NR2 ... 162 B5
Dorking Rd NR31 ... 171 B4
Dorothea Dr 7 NR19 ... 154 D3
Dorothy Ave NR31 ... 94 C7
Dorrs Dr IP25 ... 84 D4
Dorset Cl
Attleborough NR17 ... 174 B3
4 Great Yarmouth NR30 ... 169 D3
Doubleday Cl IP22 ... 177 C4
Doughty's Hospl NR3 ... 178 B4
Douglas Bader Cl NR28 ... 151 C7
Douglas Bader Sch The NR10 ... 37 B2
Douglas Cl
Croxton IP24 ... 116 C5
Norwich NR6 ... 158 D7
Douglas Haig Rd NR5 ... 161 D6
Doune Way 9 IP20 ... 122 D2
Douro Pl NR2 ... 162 C6
Dove Cl
1 Great Yarmouth NR31 ... 170 A6
Dove Cl *continued*
9 Harleston IP20 ... 122 D1
Dove House La 4 NR29 ... 56 F6
Dove La NR15 ... 90 C3
Dove St 3 NR2 ... 178 A3
Dovecote Cl NR15 ... 90 F2
Dovecote Rd PE14 ... 77 D3
Dovedale Rd NR16 ... 105 F5
Dovedales Fold NR7 ... 158 F4
Dovehouse La NR11 ... 21 B4
Dover Ct NR30 ... 168 C5
Dover St NR2 ... 162 B5
Dow Cl NR5 ... 160 F5
Dow La NR12 ... 54 C3
Dowding Rd
Norwich NR6 ... 158 D6
3 Watton IP25 ... 84 F3
Downham Cres NR18 ... 173 B6
Downham Dro PE32 ... 63 F7
Downham Mkt Coll PE38 ... 172 C4
Downham Mkt High Sch & Tech Coll PE38 ... 172 D5
Downham Mkt Sta PE38 ... 172 A5
Downham Prep Sch PE34 ... 79 E8
Downham Rd
Crimplesham PE33 ... 80 B7
Denver PE38 ... 172 C2
Fincham PE33 ... 62 E1
Nordelph PE38 ... 78 D3
Outwell PE14 ... 77 F6
Runcton Holme PE33 ... 61 D4
Stradsett PE33 ... 80 D8
Downham Way IP27 ... 175 F4
Downing Ct NR31 ... 170 C4
Downing Mews NR5 ... 160 D8
Downing Rd NR31 ... 170 C4
Downs Cl PE36 ... 132 D4
Downs Farm La IP20 ... 123 B3
Downs Rd PE36 ... 132 D4
Dowsing Ct 5 NR13 ... 72 D5
Dowson Fst Sch NR3 ... 158 A1
Dowson Rd NR3 ... 158 B1
Drabblegate NR11 ... 150 D8
Drabbs La NR12 ... 38 E6
Dragon Hall* NR1 ... 178 C2
Dragoon Cl 27 NR7 ... 72 D4
Drake Ave NR30 ... 169 D7
Drake Cl 24 NR9 ... 88 D8
Drake Inf Sch IP24 ... 176 E6
Drake Rd IP24 ... 176 E5
Drakes Cl 5 NR16 ... 118 C5
Drakes Loke NR10 ... 36 F1
Draper Way NR5 ... 160 D8
Drapers La NR35 ... 109 A3
Draycote Cl PE30 ... 147 D8
Draycotts Rise IP22 ... 177 C1
Drayton Com Fst Sch NR8 ... 155 F1
Drayton Gr NR8 ... 156 F8
Drayton High Rd NR8 ... 157 A8
Drayton La NR10 ... 53 B1
Drayton Lodge Pk NR8 ... 157 B7
Drayton Rd NR3 ... 157 F2
Drayton Wood Rd NR6 ... 157 D6
Draytonhall La NR19 ... 154 B3
Dreibholz Ct NR20 ... 154 F5
Drewray Dr NR8 ... 155 E3
Dried Flower Ctr* NR12 ... 55 C7
Drift La NR20 ... 49 C3
Drift Rd
Caister-on-Sea NR30 ... 168 C7
Lakenheath IP27 ... 113 E2
Drift The
Bawdeswell NR20 ... 50 E6
Beetley NR20 ... 49 A6
Botesdale IP22 ... 128 E3
Fakenham NR21 ... 141 D4
Fulmodeston NR21 ... 17 F3
Heacham PE31 ... 133 D6
Ingoldisthorpe PE31 ... 140 C8
Swardeston NR14 ... 89 B5
Driftlands NR21 ... 141 D5
Driftway PE30 ... 148 C1
Driftway The
1 Holt NR25 ... 137 C5
Sheringham NR26 ... 138 D8
Drill St NR21 ... 15 C3
Drinkwater Cl 9 NR9 ... 86 C5
Drive The Acle NR13 ... 166 D4
East Winch PE32 ... 45 A2
Norwich NR5 ... 161 B8
Trowse with Newton NR14 ... 163 D1
Drout's La IP31 ... 127 C3
Drove The
Brandon IP27 ... 114 D4
Raynham NR21 ... 30 E4
Taverham NR8 ... 155 C2
Drovers Rest NR15 ... 108 C8
Drudge Rd NR31 ... 170 D4
Druids La Litcham PE32 ... 48 A4
Shelfanger IP22 ... 120 B2
Druids' La IP22 ... 120 A3
Drunken Dro PE32 ... 46 C8
Drury Cl 12 NR5 ... 161 B8
Drury La
3 Castle Acre PE32 ... 46 F2
6 Loddon NR14 ... 91 F1
Dryden Cl 1 IP24 ... 176 E6
Dryden Rd NR8 ... 156 D8
Duck Decoy Cl PE31 ... 140 C3
Duck Dro CB7 ... 112 A2
Duck's Foot Rd IP21 ... 121 F6
Duckett Cl 2 NR1 ... 162 E1
Duff Rd NR3 ... 158 D2
Duffield Cres NR9 ... 51 A4
Dugard Ave NR1 ... 163 B8
Duke Rd NR31 ... 170 D6
Duke St Norwich NR3 ... 178 A4
Wisbech PE13 ... 152 D4
Duke's La NR17 ... 102 E8
Dukesway 1 NR35 ... 123 F8
Dulgate La PE37 ... 153 D2
Dulgate Rd NR35 ... 108 B3
Dull's Rd NR35 ... 109 C5
Dumbs La NR10 ... 53 E5
Dumpling Gn
Dereham NR19 ... 68 A6
East Dereham NR19 ... 154 F2
Dun Cow Gdns PE34 ... 144 E7
Dun Cow Rd NR34 ... 111 B4
Dunburgh Rd NR34 ... 110 A2
Duncan Cl IP24 ... 176 F6
Duncan Rd 6 NR30 ... 169 D2
Dunford La IP24 ... 102 A2
Dunham Rd
Litcham PE32 ... 48 A4
Necton PE37 ... 65 F6
Dunhill La IP22 ... 127 F1
Dunkirk NR11 ... 150 E8
Dunlop Rd NR19 ... 154 B6
Dunnett Cl NR17 ... 174 E5
Dunnetts Cl IP25 ... 84 A7
Dunning's La IP21 ... 121 E6
Dunns La NR21 ... 4 D1
Dunston Dro PE31 ... 133 B1
Dunwood Dr NR6 ... 158 F7
Durbidge's Hill IP22 ... 120 E1
Durham Ave NR31 ... 170 B2
Durham St NR2 ... 162 B4
Durham Way IP24 ... 176 A5
Dussindale 3 NR18 ... 173 C6
Dussindale Dr 18 NR7 ... 72 D4
Duverlin Cl 2 NR4 ... 162 A1
Dyball's La NR12 ... 38 F8
Dye's Rd NR13 ... 73 C7
Dyers Yd NR3 ... 178 A3
Dyes The NR20 ... 33 E8

E

Eade Rd NR3 ... 162 D8
Eagle Cl NR11 ... 21 B2
Eagle House Sch NR16 ... 119 E7
Eagle Rd NR11 ... 21 B2
Eagle Wlk 2 NR2 ... 162 C4
Eagles Ct NR23 ... 136 E6
Eagles The 3 NR30 ... 169 D4
Earl Cl PE31 ... 140 C3
Earl of Brandon Ave PE31 ... 30 B3
Earl Rd NR13 ... 72 E8
Earl Warren IP24 ... 116 C5
Earlham Gn La NR5 ... 161 B7
Earlham Gr NR5 ... 161 D6
Earlham High Sch NR4 ... 161 D5
Earlham Rd NR4 ... 161 C5
Earlham W Ctr 5 NR5 ... 161 C6
Earls' St IP24 ... 176 D4
Earlsford Rd IP23 ... 129 D1
Earnshaw Ct NR1 ... 163 D5
Earsham CE VA Fst Sch NR35 ... 123 F8
Earsham Dam NR35 ... 123 F8
Earsham Dr PE30 ... 147 D8
Earsham Rd NR35 ... 108 E2
Earth La NR32 ... 94 C1
East Anglia Transport Mus* NR33 ... 111 F1
East Anglian Way NR31 ... 170 C6
East Ave NR13 ... 165 E3
East Bank PE12 ... 41 C8
East Bilney Hall NR20 ... 49 A6
East Carleton Rd NR14 ... 89 A4
East Cres NR20 ... 50 B5
East Dereham Sta NR20 ... 154 E5
East End PE38 ... 79 E1
East End Cl NR30 ... 168 E8
East Farm La NR10 ... 53 E3
East Gn NR9 ... 68 F2
East Gr NR27 ... 139 C5
East Harbour Way PE31 ... 135 E7
East Harling Prim Sch NR16 ... 118 C5
East Harling Rd NR16 ... 118 F4
East Hills Rd NR5 ... 156 E1
East La PE31 ... 134 E4
East Norfolk 6th Form Coll NR31 ... 170 C5
East Rd
Great Yarmouth NR30 ... 169 D5
Watton IP25 ... 84 D3
East Ruston Area Com Sch NR12 ... 38 F7
East Ruston Old Vicarage Gdn* NR12 ... 24 A3
East Ruston Rd NR28 ... 38 D6
East Winch CE Prim Sch PE32 ... 44 F3
East Winch Rd
Leziate PE32 ... 44 F5
Middleton PE32 ... 44 C2
East Winchcommon (Nature Reserve)* PE32 ... 45 A2
Eastbourne Pl NR1 ... 178 C3
Easterley Way NR29 ... 167 A7
Eastern Ave
Caister-on-Sea NR30 ... 168 E6
Norwich NR7 ... 72 D4
Eastern Cl
Caister-on-Sea NR30 ... 168 E5
32 Norwich NR7 ... 72 D4
Eastern Cres NR7 ... 72 D4
Eastern Rd NR7 ... 72 D4
Eastfen Dro IP26 ... 114 B6
Eastfield NR8 ... 156 D8
Eastfield Cl PE30 ... 147 A6
Eastfield Rd
Hickling NR12 ... 39 F2
Long Stratton NR15 ... 106 F4
1 Wisbech PE13 ... 152 E7
Eastfield Way PE13 ... 152 C6
Eastfields
King's Lynn PE30 ... 147 C4
Narborough PE32 ... 63 F7
Eastgate IP25 ... 67 D3
Eastgate Dro
Congham PE31 ... 28 D2
Grimston PE32 ... 45 D8
Hillington PE31 ... 28 C3
Eastgate Prim Sch PE30 ... 146 E5
Eastgate Rd PE36 ... 2 A6
Eastgate St
2 King's Lynn PE30 ... 146 E5
North Elmham NR20 ... 49 E7
Shouldham PE33 ... 62 D4
Easthaugh Rd NR9 ... 51 D4
Easthill La NR14 ... 90 E8
Eastland Cl NR17 ... 174 E6
Eastlands Bank PE14 ... 41 E5
Eastleigh Gdns 6 NR9 ... 69 F2
Eastmans La PE32 ... 28 C1
Eastmoor Cl PE33 ... 81 E4
Eastmoor Rd PE33 ... 81 C7
Easton Coll NR9 ... 70 C4
Easton Way NR10 ... 35 C1
Eastwood PE31 ... 134 F3
Eaton Chase NR4 ... 161 E2
Eaton Dro
Sedgeford PE36 ... 13 A7
Snettisham PE31 ... 12 F5
Eaton Gdns NR19 ... 154 E3
Eaton Hall Specl Sch NR4 ... 161 F3
Eaton Rd NR4 ... 162 B2
Eaton St Cringleford NR4 ... 89 B8
Norwich NR4 ... 161 E1
Eau Brink Rd PE34 ... 43 A2
Ebbisham Dr NR4 ... 161 F1
Ebble Cl PE30 ... 148 C2
Ebenezer Pl NR3 ... 178 A4
Eccles CE Prim Sch NR16 ... 118 F8
Eccles Rd NR25 ... 137 C7
Eccles Rd Sta NR16 ... 103 E1
Ecclestone Cl NR31 ... 170 A4
Eckersley Dr NR21 ... 141 A6
Ecotech Ctr* PE37 ... 153 B6
Ecton Gr 6 PE14 ... 59 A1
Ecton Wlk NR6 ... 158 F5
Eddington Way NR9 ... 70 B5
Eden Cl
Bacton/Walcott NR12 ... 23 E4
Norwich NR7 ... 163 C6
Eden La NR17 ... 174 D5
Edenhurst Cl NR4 ... 161 F3
Edenside Dr NR17 ... 174 D5
Edge Bank PE14 ... 77 F8
Edge's La NR15 ... 107 A3
Edgebrook NR26 ... 138 D6
Edgefield Cl NR6 ... 158 F7
Edgefield Hill NR25 ... 137 C2
Edgefield Rd NR24 ... 142 E5
Edgehill 4 NR7 ... 72 E4
Edges La 2 NR15 ... 106 E3
Edgeworth Rd 6 NR5 ... 161 C6
Edinburgh Ave
Great Yarmouth NR31 ... 170 B2
King's Lynn PE30 ... 147 C7
Edinburgh Cl
6 Barnham IP24 ... 125 F6
Caister-on-Sea NR30 ... 168 E5
13 Watton IP25 ... 84 D3
Edinburgh Ct 7 PE30 ... 146 E5
Edinburgh Dr
Fakenham NR21 ... 141 C6
Wisbech PE13 ... 152 C8
Edinburgh Pl
Great Yarmouth NR30 ... 169 E3
1 Wiggenhall St Germans PE34 ... 43 B1
Edinburgh Rd
Holt NR25 ... 137 C5
Norwich NR2 ... 162 A6
Edinburgh Way
Dersingham PE31 ... 140 D3
Thetford IP24 ... 176 A5
Edison Way NR31 ... 170 A8
Edith Cavell Cl 5 IP24 ... 176 D7
Edma St PE30 ... 146 E6
Edmondson Wlk NR21 ... 141 D4
Edmund Bacon Ct 1 NR3 ... 162 D8
Edmund Moundford Rd 10 IP26 ... 98 E1
Edmund Rd IP27 ... 175 A2
Edrich Cl NR13 ... 165 E6
Edrich Way NR5 ... 160 E7
Edward Benefer Way
King's Lynn PE30 ... 146 D6
North Wootton PE30 ... 26 E1

Edward Gambling Ct 8 NR2 162 B8
Edward Rd NR29 58 B5
Edward Seago Pl NR15 90 E2
Edward St
10 King's Lynn PE30 146 E3
Norwich NR3 178 B4
Edward Worlledge Mid Sch NR31 169 C2
Edwards Cl NR20 50 B5
Edwards Rd NR7 159 A5
Edwin Cl NR18 173 B5
Eels Foot Rd NR29 57 E1
Egmere Medieval Village of* NR22 16 B8
Egmere Rd NR22 16 F8
Egremont Rd IP22 177 B5
Eighth Ave PE13 152 E4
El Alamein Way NR31 94 C8
Elan Cl NR18 173 D3
Elden's La IP26 98 F5
Elder Gn NR31 170 B5
Elder La PE32 45 C8
Elderberry Dr 5 NR20 68 A8
Elderbush La NR29 56 C7
Elders The IP27 113 F1
Elderton La NR28 22 B5
Eleanor Rd NR1 162 D3
Eleven Mile Rd NR18 87 C1
Elgin IP24 176 A5
Elgood's Brewery & Gdn* PE13 152 A4
Eliot Cl IP24 176 E6
Elise Way NR18 173 D2
Elizabeth Ave
Downham Market PE38 172 B5
Fakenham NR21 141 C6
Norwich NR7 163 F7
Elizabeth Cl
Attleborough NR17 174 C6
East Dereham NR19 154 D1
Hunstanton PE36 132 C3
Norwich NR7 159 A5
Reepham NR10 149 B4
Elizabeth Cres
Caister-on-Sea NR30 168 E6
4 Holt NR25 137 C5
Elizabeth Dr PE37 65 F3
Elizabeth Fry Cl 9 IP24 176 D7
Elizabeth Fry Rd NR2 161 F4
Elizabeth Rd
Brandon IP27 175 C3
10 Poringland NR14 90 D5
Elizabeth Terr PE13 152 D4
Elizabeth Watling Cl 3 IP24 176 D7
Elizabeth Way 5 IP23 130 C1
Elizabeth Wlk 27 IP20 122 D2
Elizabethan House Mus* NR30 169 C3
Elkins Rd NR18 173 B5
Ella Rd NR1 163 A6
Ellcar Rise 4 NR4 161 F1
Ellenhill NR27 139 D5
Eller Dr PE33 43 E2
Ellingham Prim Sch NR35 109 D3
Ellingham Rd
Attleborough NR17 174 B7
Scoulton NR9 85 E3
Ellington Rd
2 Barnham IP24 125 F6
Watton IP25 85 A3
Ellinor Rd NR28 151 D3
Ellis Cl 4 NR12 39 B4
Ellison Cl NR17 174 E4
Ellison Dr NR17 174 E4
Elm Ave NR31 170 C4
Elm CE Jun Sch PE14 59 B1
Elm Cl Acle NR13 166 C4
Brandon IP27 175 E3
Downham Market PE38 172 B6
King's Lynn PE30 148 D2
5 Lingwood NR13 74 A3
7 Loddon NR14 91 F1
Mulbarton NR14 89 B3
North Elmham NR20 49 E8
Norwich NR5 156 F2
Yaxham NR19 68 A5
Elm Gr
Garboldisham IP22 128 A8
Sheringham NR26 138 E5
Elm Gr La NR3 158 D2
Elm High Rd PE14 152 E1
Elm Hill NR3 178 B3
Elm La PE31 30 D8
Elm Low Rd PE14 152 D2
Elm Pk NR19 154 E1
Elm Rd
Caister-on-Sea NR30 168 E4
Lingwood NR13 74 A3
Marham PE33 63 B4
Thetford IP24 176 B1
Wisbech PE13 152 D3
Elm Rd Prim Sch PE13 152 D4
Elm Terr 2 NR18 173 C4
Elmdon Ct 9 NR1 163 A6
Elmer's La NR15 107 A8
Elmfield Dr PE14 152 E1
Elmgrove Rd NR31 170 C3
Elmham Rd
Beetley NR20 49 D4
North Elmham NR20 50 A7
Elmhurst Ave NR12 39 C2
Elmhurst Cl NR31 170 C3
Elmhurst Dr PE30 148 C2
Elms Cl 6 NR35 123 F8
Elms Rd NR34 110 E5
Elms The
Hindringham NR21 17 E6
Norwich NR6 158 E6
Elmside PE14 59 D1
Elmstead Rd PE30 147 C4
Elmtree Gr PE33 43 E1
Elsden Cl 2 NR25 137 C5
Elsie Rd NR31 169 B3
Elsing Dr PE30 147 D8
Elsing La
Bawdeswell NR20 50 E6
Dereham NR20 50 C1
Elsing Rd Lyng NR9 51 A5
North Tuddenham NR20 50 E2
Swanton Morley NR20 50 C4
Elstead Cl 11 NR4 89 C8
Elveden Cl NR4 161 F1
Elveden Rd IP24 125 D6
Elvin Rd NR19 154 D6
Elvin Way 3 NR3 157 F1
Elvina Rd 10 NR10 54 A2
Elvington PE30 147 D5
Elworthy Cl IP25 84 F3
Elwyn Rd 7 NR1 162 E2
Ely Pl 19 PE13 152 C5
Ely Rd Denver PE38 172 D2
Hilgay PE38 97 B8
Ely Row PE14 42 B1
Ely St NR2 162 C7
Ely Way IP24 176 A5
Embry Cl NR6 158 D6
Embry Cres NR6 158 C6
Emelson Cl NR19 154 D6
Emery Cl 5 NR26 138 C5
Emery's La NR11 21 B6
Emmanuel Ave NR31 170 B2
Emmas Way NR13 73 B6
Emmerich Ct 6 PE30 146 E5
Emms's La NR21 17 E7
Emneth Prim Sch PE14 59 D2
Emorsgate PE34 42 B7
Empire Ave PE30 147 B8
Empress Rd NR31 169 B3
Empsons Loke NR29 58 B6
End Lodge PE31 133 C5
Enfield Rd NR5 161 C6
Engine Rd Hilgay PE38 96 F7
Sculthorpe Airfield NR21 15 D2
England's La NR31 170 D4
Englands Rd NR13 166 B4
English Rd NR6 158 E4
Ennerdale Dr PE30 148 F2
Enterprise Way
Fakenham NR21 141 E5
King's Lynn PE33 43 E4
Wisbech PE13 152 A2
Entrance La NR15 90 E2
Entry The IP22 177 D4
Enue 13 PE33 63 B4
Eppingham Cl IP24 176 F6
Epsom Gdns NR19 154 E3
Erica Way NR31 170 B6
Erins The 1 NR6 158 E1
Eriswell Dr IP27 113 E1
Erpingham Ct PE36 132 E7
Erpingham Prim Sch NR11 21 B2
Esdelle St 9 NR3 162 D8
Esplanade NR27 139 B7
Esplanade The
Hemsby NR29 167 E5
Sheringham NR26 138 C7
Esprit Cl NR18 173 D2
Essex St NR2 162 C5
Estcourt Rd
2 Attleborough NR17 174 C5
Great Yarmouth NR30 169 D6
Estelle Way NR18 173 E6
Estuary Cl PE30 146 E7
Estuary Rd PE30 146 D7
Ethel Colman Way IP24 176 D7
Ethel Gooch Rd NR18 173 B5
Ethel Rd NR1 163 A5
Ethel Terr 5 PE30 146 E3
Ethel Tipple Cl NR11 150 C4
Ethel Tipple Dr NR11 150 C4
Ethel Tipple Specl Sch PO30 147 D4
Eurocentre Ind Est NR30 169 B7
Europa Way
Norwich NR1 163 A2
Wisbech PE13 152 B2
Euston Hall* IP24 126 B5
Euston Rd NR30 169 D4
Euston Way PE30 148 D1
Euximoor Dro PE14 77 B1
Eva Cl 4 IP25 67 B2
Eva Rd NR13 72 E7
Evans Gdns PE36 132 D3
Evans Lombe Cl NR29 57 A4
Evans Way NR6 158 D6
Evelyn Cl IP21 131 A3
Evelyn Way 4 PE30 147 A8
Eversley Rd NR6 158 B4
Everson Cl
Norwich NR5 157 C1
11 Tasburgh NR15 106 F6
Ewing Cl NR10 149 B4
Excalibur Rd 2 NR31 170 B1
Exchange Rd 7 NR15 89 C1
Exchange Sq PE13 152 B5
Exchange St
Attleborough NR17 174 D5
32 Harleston IP20 122 D2
Exchange St *continued*
Norwich NR2 178 A3
Exeter Cres PE30 148 D5
Exeter Rd NR31 170 B4
Exeter St NR2 162 C7
Exeter Way 9 IP24 176 F5
Exmouth Cl 23 NR9 88 D8
Exmouth Pl 11 NR30 169 D4
Exmouth Rd NR30 169 D1
Exton's Gdns PE30 146 F3
Exton's Pl PE30 147 A3
Exton's Rd PE30 146 F4
Eye Airfield Ind Est IP23 130 B2
Eye La PE31 30 B7
Eye Rd IP23 130 A1

F

Factory La IP22 177 B5
Factory Rd NR30 169 D5
Faeroes Dr NR30 168 C6
Fair Cl Beccles NR34 110 D1
13 Feltwell IP26 98 E1
Fair Gn IP22 177 C4
Fairfax Dr 6 Norwich NR7 72 D4
3 Weeting IP27 114 E1
Fairfax Rd NR4 161 F4
Fairfield Cl
Great & Little Plumstead NR13 73 B7
Mundesley NR11 143 C6
Fairfield Dr NR17 174 C4
Fairfield La 10 PE33 61 D6
Fairfield Rd
Downham Market PE38 172 A5
5 Middleton PE32 44 B3
Norwich NR2 162 C3
4 Stoke Ferry PE33 81 A3
Fairfield Way 11 IP26 98 E1
Fairfields Cawston NR10 35 B2
Thetford IP24 176 D5
Fairfields Way NR11 36 D4
Fairhaven CE VA Prim Sch NR13 74 B8
Fairhaven Ct NR2 162 A6
Fairhaven Woodland & Water Gdn* NR13 74 A8
Fairhill Dro PE33 80 E2
Fairholme Cl IP25 84 A8
Fairholme Rd NR10 53 E4
Fairisle Dr NR30 168 C5
Fairland St NR18 173 C3
Fairmile Cl NR2 162 B3
Fairstead Cl
North Walsham NR28 151 A3
Pulham Market IP21 121 E5
Fairstead Ct NR7 159 A3
Fairstead Dro PE33 62 D4
Fairstead La
Hempnall NR15 107 A5
Little Cressingham IP25 83 D3
Fairstead Prim Sch PE30 147 D4
Fairstead Rd NR7 159 A3
Fairstead The
Botesdale IP22 128 E3
2 Cley next the Sea NR25 7 E6
1 Holt NR25 137 B6
Scottow NR10 37 D2
Fairview Cl NR8 157 A7
Fairview Dr NR21 31 E5
Fairview Rd NR28 151 E4
Fairway NR30 168 E3
Fairway Fst Sch NR4 162 A1
Fairway Mid Sch NR4 162 A1
Fairway The NR31 171 D8
Fairways Norwich NR6 157 D5
Stuston IP21 130 B5
Fakenham Coll NR21 141 B5
Fakenham High Sch NR21 141 B6
Fakenham Hill IP31 126 C2
Fakenham Jun Sch NR21 141 C4
Fakenham Mus* NR21 141 B3
Fakenham Race Course NR21 141 D2
Fakenham Rd
Attlebridge NR9 52 C2
Beetley NR20 49 C5
Briston NR24 142 C5
Docking PE31 134 E4
East Rudham PE31 30 A7
Foxley NR20 33 C1
Great Snoring NR21 17 A5
Ryburgh NR21 32 A6
Sculthorpe NR21 141 A5
South Creake NR21 15 E6
Sparham NR9 51 A6
Taverham NR8 155 B2
Tittleshall PE32 48 A7
Fakenham View NR21 31 E5
Fakes Rd NR29 167 D6
Falcon Ave IP22 177 F5
Falcon Ct 15 NR30 169 C4
Falcon Dr IP27 175 F3
Falcon La Bungay NR35 109 A1
24 Wisbech PE13 152 C5
Falcon Mews NR7 159 C4
Falcon Mid Sch NR7 159 C3
Falcon Rd 14 Feltwell IP26 98 E1
Norwich NR7 159 C3
Pulham Market IP21 121 E5
7 Wisbech PE13 152 C5
Falcon Rd E NR7 159 C2
Falcon Rd W NR7 159 C4
Falconers Chase NR18 173 F5
Falgate NR10 35 C2
Falkland Cl NR6 157 D5
Falkland Way 13 NR31 94 C6
Falklands Dr PE13 152 E3
Falklands Rd PE12 41 A8
Fall Gn NR14 90 D4
Fallow Pipe Rd PE34 43 B2
Fallowfield
4 Hemsby NR29 167 B7
8 Poringland NR14 90 D5
Fallowfield Cl NR1 163 B8
Fallows The 3 NR8 155 D2
Faraday Pl IP24 176 B2
Faraday Rd NR31 170 A8
Fardell Rd 7 PE13 152 C4
Farebrother Way 2 NR19 154 C3
Farm Cl Lingwood NR13 74 A2
11 Loddon NR14 92 A2
Farm Ct St IP20 123 A1
Farm La NR13 56 A1
Farm Rd
Heckingham NR14 92 D1
Worstead NR28 38 A7
Farm View NR28 151 E5
Farm Wlk Marham PE33 63 C5
6 Necton PE37 65 F4
Farman Ave NR28 151 D5
Farman Cl 5 Belton NR31 94 A6
Lyng NR9 51 A5
7 Salhouse NR13 55 A1
Farmers Ave NR1 178 B2
Farmland Rd NR5 156 F1
Farmway 7 NR19 154 D2
Farnborough Rd 9 IP25 84 F3
Farrow Cl
2 Great Moulton NR15 106 B1
7 Mattishall NR20 68 E6
2 Swanton Morley NR20 50 B3
Farthing Cl Diss IP22 177 D6
Loddon NR14 109 D8
Farthing Dro
Beck Row, Holywell Row & Kenny Hill IP27 112 E2
Lakenheath IP27 113 A2
Southery PE38 97 A2
Farthing Rd PE38 79 B5
Fastnet Way 1 NR30 168 C6
Fastolf Cl NR6 157 E5
Fastolff Ave NR31 170 B3
Fayers Terr PE30 147 A4
Fayregreen NR21 141 D4
Feale Abbey PE34 144 A1
Fearn's Cl NR27 139 D5
Featherstone Ct 5 NR19 154 D2
Felbrigg Cl PE30 148 F1
Felbrigg Hall Garden & Park* NR11 10 B2
Felbrigg Rd
Downham Market PE38 172 C6
Roughton NR11 21 D8
Fell Way 3 NR31 94 C8
Fellowes Dr 2 NR31 94 C6
Fellowes Rd NR9 69 E6
Fellows Cl NR5 161 D6
Felmingham Rd NR28 37 C7
Felsham Way NR8 155 E2
Felsted Ave PE13 152 E5
Felthorpe Rd NR9 52 B3
Feltwell Elementary Sch IP26 98 D1
Feltwell Prim Sch IP26 98 E2
Feltwell Rd
Hockwold cum Wilton IP26 113 F7
Methwold IP26 98 E5
Southery PE38 97 D5
Fen Cl PE13 152 E6
Fen Dro PE33 81 F3
Fen Folgate 6 IP25 67 B2
Fen La Banham NR16 119 B6
Beccles NR34 110 D2
Ditchingham NR35 108 E3
Garboldisham IP22 128 A7
Grimston PE32 45 A7
Harling NR16 118 C6
Leziate PE32 45 A6
Marham PE33 63 A5
Rickinghall Inferior IP22 128 E2
Roydon IP22 129 C7
Thelnetham IP22 128 B5
Fen Rd Blo' Norton IP22 128 C6
Carleton Rode NR16 105 C2
Hinderclay IP22 128 C5
Marham PE33 63 B4
Scarning NR19 154 B3
Watlington PE33 61 D5
Fen St
Attleborough NR17 103 F3
Old Buckenham NR17 104 C2
Redgrave IP22 128 F6
Rocklands NR17 103 B6
Fen View
Christchurch PE14 95 A7
East Dereham NR19 154 C2
Fen Way 2 PE14 59 A1
Fence Bank PE14 42 A1
Fences Farm Rd PE34 78 E8
Fendyke Rd PE14 59 E1
Fengate Heacham PE31 133 C4
Marsham NR10 150 D1
Fengate Dro IP27 175 B6
Fengate Rd PE14 59 C5
Fenland & W Norfolk Aviation Mus* PE14 59 C7
Fenland Rd
King's Lynn PE30 147 C8
Wisbech PE13 152 E6
Fenn Cres NR3 158 B1
Fennel Way IP24 176 F4
Fenner Rd NR30 170 E7
Fenside PE31 133 C4
Fenway PE31 133 B3
Ferguson Way NR17 174 F7
Fermoy Ave PE30 146 E6
Fern Ct 3 NR18 173 B4
Fern Dr NR28 151 E5
Fern Gdns NR31 93 F5
Fern Hill
Dersingham PE31 140 E4
Norwich NR1 163 B5
Ferndale Cl NR6 157 E4
Fernlea Rd PE30 147 C4
Ferrier Cl 7 NR30 169 D5
Ferrier Ct NR29 167 B6
Ferrier Rd NR30 169 C5
Ferry Bank PE38 97 A4
Ferry Ct NR29 75 A5
Ferry Hill NR31 170 D7
Ferry La
Great Yarmouth NR31 169 C2
Norwich NR1 178 C3
Postwick with Witton NR13 73 A2
Stokesby with Herringby NR29 75 B5
Ferry Rd
Carleton St Peter NR14 91 E5
Clenchwarton PE34 145 F5
Horning NR12 55 E3
King's Lynn PE34 146 B6
Norton Subcourse NR14 92 D2
Norwich NR1 178 C3
Oxborough PE33 81 D3
Reedham NR13 92 E4
Surlingham NR14 165 A1
Woodbastwick NR13 55 D2
Ferry Sq PE34 146 C5
Ferry St PE30 146 D5
Ferry View Rd NR12 55 E3
Ferryboat La NR31 170 D7
Ferrygate La NR29 57 D5
Fersfield Rd
Bressingham IP22 129 B8
Kenninghall NR16 119 C4
South Lopham IP22 128 F8
Festival Cl PE30 148 B1
Festival Rd NR20 50 B7
Festival Way CB6 96 E2
Ffolkes Dr
King's Lynn PE30 148 C1
Terrington St Clement PE34 144 B5
Ffolkes Pl 1 PE33 61 D3
Fiddle Wood Rd NR6 158 D4
Field Acre Way NR15 106 E4
Field Barn Cotts PE32 46 E3
Field Barn La PE33 61 F3
Field Dalling Rd
Field Dalling NR25 7 A3
Gunthorpe NR21 18 B8
Field End Cl PE30 147 B6
Field House Gdns IP22 177 E5
Field La Beetley NR20 49 C5
10 Blofield NR13 73 D6
Blofield NR13 165 E8
Fakenham NR21 141 B6
Hempnall NR15 107 C4
King's Lynn PE30 147 B6
Marsham NR10 36 B2
North Walsham NR28 151 E3
Stody NR24 142 F8
Whinburgh & Westfield NR19 67 F4
Wretton PE33 80 F3
Field Rd Brandon IP27 114 D4
King's Lynn PE30 147 B5
Ringland NR8 70 B8
South Walsham NR13 74 B8
Stalham NR12 39 C3
Fieldbarn Dro PE33 82 A4
Fieldbarn Rd PE33 81 B8
Fieldfare Cl 6 NR12 54 A1
Fields Rd NR34 110 E6
Fields The
Forncett NR16 105 E5
Hingham NR9 86 C5
Fieldview NR5 161 E6
Fiennes Rd 4 NR7 72 D5
Fifers La NR6 158 C6
Fifth Ave PE13 152 E4
Fifty Dro CB6 95 F3
Fifty Rd PE14 95 A3
Filbert Rd NR14 91 F1
Filberts PE30 147 D5
Filby Cl NR29 75 F8
Filby Fst Sch NR29 75 E8
Filby La NR29 167 A1
Filby Rd Coltishall NR10 37 B2
Stokesby with Herringby NR29 75 C6
Swaffham PE37 153 B2
Finch Cl Cromer NR27 139 C4
Norwich NR7 159 D2
Finch Way NR13 165 C3
Fincham Dro PE32 64 B5
Fincham Rd
Barton Bendish PE33 81 A8
Crimplesham PE33 80 A8

Fincham Rd *continued*
Fincham PE33 63 A1
Shouldham Thorpe PE33 62 C2
Stow Bardolph PE34 79 F8
Wereham PE33 80 F6
Finchdale Cl 5 PE30 148 C4
Finchley Ct 4 NR2 162 B7
Finderne Dr NR18 173 D6
Finishers Rd 8 NR6 158 C1
Finisterre Rise 2 NR30 168 C6
Finkelgate NR1 178 B1
Finningham Rd IP22 128 E1
Finsbury Cl 1 PE38 172 B4
Fiona Cl NR18 173 E6
Fir Cl Heacham PE31 133 C6
Mundford IP26 100 B4
Fir Covert Rd
Carleton Rode NR16 105 A1
Taverham NR10 155 B4
Fir Gr NR26 138 D4
Fir La NR10 34 A1
Fir Pk IP25 84 A7
Fir Rd IP24 176 B1
Fir Tree Dr 7 PE33 43 E2
Firethorn Cl NR8 155 B2
Firman Ct NR7 163 F8
Firs Ave NR29 167 A3
Firs La NR12 39 C2
Firs Rd Hethersett NR9 88 D7
Norwich NR6 157 F6
Firs The
Downham Market PE38 172 D6
Lakenheath IP27 113 F1
Firs Way IP27 175 C2
Firside Mid Sch NR6 158 A6
First Ave PE13 152 D5
First Dro IP27 113 C3
First Marsh Rd PE13 59 A6
Firtree Cl NR13 165 B4
Firtree Rd NR7 159 E1
Firwood Cl NR1 163 C8
Fish Wharf 2 NR30 169 D1
Fisher Ave NR30 169 D8
Fisher Rd Diss IP22 177 E4
Fakenham NR21 141 B5
Fisher Row NR32 111 F4
Fisher Way IP24 176 E5
Fisher's La IP21 131 A4
Fishergate NR3 178 B4
Fisherman's Her Ctr*
NR26 138 D8
Fishermen's Ct NR17 174 D6
Fishers Cl NR5 156 E1
Fishers La Beetley NR20 49 D6
Norwich NR2 178 A3
Fishers' Quay 5 NR30 169 C4
Fishley View NR13 166 B4
Fiske's Opening 6
NR31 170 D4
Fiskes Ct NR14 89 F5
Fison Way IP24 176 C6
Fison Way Ind Est
IP24 176 C6
Fitton Rd PE34 61 B8
Fitzalan Cl 8 NR30 169 C4
Fitzgerald Rd
Norwich NR1 162 E1
7 Poringland NR14 90 C5
Fitzhenry Mews 8 NR5 161 B8
Fitzwalter Rd IP22 177 E4
Five Acre La NR35 123 E7
Five Acres NR14 89 F4
Five Alls Rd PE14 41 F1
Five Crossways NR12 164 D8
Five Elms 4 PE30 147 C4
Flag St NR21 15 C2
Flaxlands NR16 105 B4
Flaxlands Rd NR16 105 C3
Fleet La NR13 56 B1
Fleet Rd NR8 156 B6
Fleetwood Dr 4 NR13 72 D4
Flegg Gn PE33 80 D4
Flegg High Sch NR29 57 E6
Fleggburgh Prim Sch
NR29 75 C8
Fleggburgh Rd NR29 57 C2
Fleming Ct 8 IP25 84 D3
Fletcher Cl NR12 55 A8
Fletcher Way
Acle NR13 166 D4
Cromer NR27 139 B5
Norwich NR3 158 C3
Flint Dr NR23 136 D5
Flint Gate 17 PE12 41 B8
Flint House Gdns 13 NR9 88 C7
Flint House Rd PE14 77 F1
Flint Way 2 PE14 77 A8
Flitcham Abbey PE31 28 D5
Flitcham CE Prim Sch
PE31 28 C5
Flixton Marsh La
NR32 111 F6
Flixton Rd
Bungay NR35 124 A7
Flixton NR35 123 E6
Lound NR32 94 C1
St Margaret, South Elmham
IP20 123 E3
Somerleyton, Ashby &
Herringfleet NR32 111 F8
Flordon Rd
Bracon Ash NR14 88 F1
Flordon NR15 106 D8
Florence Barclay Cl
IP24 176 D6
Florence Rd NR1 163 A6
Florence Wlk NR19 154 C2
Florida Bvd NR21 15 C2
Flowerday Cl NR31 171 D5
Flowerdew Cl 12 NR9 88 C7
Flowerdew's La NR13 74 B7
Flowerpot La NR15 106 D3
Flowers La NR17 174 B3
Fludge's La NR20 49 B6
Flymore La NR17 103 A8
Fodderfen Dro PE38 113 A7
Foldgate La PE34 61 A5
Folgate NR16 88 D1
Folgate Cl
Costessey NR8 156 F5
Thornham PE36 2 D6
Folgate La
Costessey NR8 156 F4
Walpole PE14 41 D3
Folgate Rd
Heacham PE31 133 C4
North Walsham NR28 151 B6
Folland Ct 8 NR20 50 E7
Follies The PE37 65 F4
Folly Cl NR18 173 C5
Folly Ct
Fakenham NR21 141 D4
King's Lynn PE30 147 B7
Mattishall NR20 68 F6
Folly Gdns NR18 173 C5
Folly Gr PE30 147 B7
Folly La Beetley NR20 49 B6
Bressingham IP22 129 C8
Claxton NR14 91 D5
3 Hingham NR9 86 C5
Old Buckenham NR17 104 F2
Folly Rd NR18 173 C5
Folly View 5 PE37 65 F4
Folly Yd PE32 48 B7
Folwell Rd NR5 156 E1
Footpath The 11 NR14 90 C5
Ford Ave PE30 148 D5
Ford St IP24 176 D3
Foregate Cl 2 NR8 155 D2
Forest Cl IP27 175 C2
Forest Dr PE31 133 C6
Forest Mount NR31 93 E3
Forest Prim Sch IP27 175 C3
Forest Ret Pk IP24 125 D8
Forester Cl 1 NR4 162 C1
Forester's Ave PE38 97 A8
Forge Cl
Old Buckenham NR17 104 D2
Palgrave IP22 177 D2
Poringland NR14 90 D4
Forge Gr NR34 110 C2
Forge Orchards 1 NR14 89 B3
Forge Rd NR14 91 F3
Forge Way IP22 128 A8
Forget-Me-Not Rd 3
PE31 12 D4
Forncett CE Prim Sch
NR16 106 B3
Forncett Ind Steam Mus*
NR16 106 B5
Forncett Rd
Bunwell NR16 105 F3
Tharston & Hapton
NR15 106 D4
Forster Cl 2 NR11 150 D6
Forster Way NR11 150 D6
Forsythia Rd NR31 170 B5
Forth Cl NR30 168 C5
Forties Cl 5 NR30 168 C6
Fortune Gn NR14 90 E4
Forum The* NR2 178 A2
Forwater Rd NR10 34 B3
Foster Cl Brundall NR13 165 B4
Ormesby St Margaret
NR29 167 C2
Foster Rd NR3 158 D3
Foulgers Opening
NR1 178 C1
Foulsham Prim Sch
NR20 33 D3
Foulsham Rd
Bintree NR20 33 C2
Guestwick NR20 33 F4
Guist NR20 33 A4
Hindolveston NR20 33 D7
Wood Norton NR20 33 B6
Foundry Cl
Foulsham NR20 33 D3
Northrepps NR27 11 A2
Sculthorpe NR21 16 C2
Foundry Cnr NR17 174 F2
Foundry La PE36 2 A3
Foundry Sq NR19 154 D4
Fountaine Gr PE30 148 C4
Fountains Rd NR4 89 E8
Four Acres Est NR29 167 C8
Fourth Ave PE13 152 E4
Fowell Cl NR5 161 B6
Fowler's La NR17 174 B2
Fox Covert 5 NR19 154 C4
Fox Gr 7 NR16 118 C5
Fox Hill IP20 123 C3
Fox Hill Rd NR12 38 E7
Fox La Brundall NR13 165 F6
Framingham Pigot NR14 90 D6
North Tuddenham NR20 68 F8
Fox Rd Dereham NR19 154 D4
Framingham Pigot NR14 90 D7
Fox's La PE34 146 C6
Foxburrow Rd NR7 159 A5
Foxcotte Cl NR6 157 E7
Foxes Loke 12 NR14 92 A1
Foxes Mdw 2 PE32 46 F2
Foxglove Cl
Fakenham NR21 141 F4
North Walsham NR28 151 E5
Thurton NR14 91 C4
Foxglove Dr 21 NR31 94 C6
Foxglove La NR26 138 B6
Foxglove Rd
2 Attleborough NR17 174 B5
Thetford IP24 176 F4
Foxglove Wlk PE34 61 B8
Foxley Cl NR5 161 D6
Foxley Rd
Bawdeswell NR20 50 D8
Foulsham NR20 33 C2
Foxley Wood National Nature
Reserve* NR10 33 F1
Foxs Loke NR11 150 B6
Foxwood 9 NR13 73 D6
Foxwood Cl NR8 155 E3
Framingham Earl High Sch
NR14 90 C6
Framingham Earl La
NR14 90 E5
Framingham La NR14 90 F7
Framingham Rd NR14 90 F7
Framlingham Cl NR31 169 C2
Francis Cl NR27 139 C5
Francis La NR13 73 C6
Francis Rd NR15 106 E3
Francis Stone Ct NR7 72 D3
Francis Way NR5 160 E8
Frank Stone Ct NR30 169 E1
Franklin Cl PE34 145 E6
Fransham Forge*
NR19 66 D8
Fransham Rd PE32 48 B1
Frazer Cres NR11 143 A7
Fred Nicholson Specl Sch
NR19 154 E2
Frederick Cl PE30 148 D6
Frederick Rd NR30 169 C5
Free La NR35 108 F2
Freebridge Haven PE33 43 F3
Freedom Bridge PE13 152 B6
Freeland Cl NR8 155 E3
Freeland Cnr NR10 155 C6
Freeman Cl NR14 109 D8
Freeman Sq NR2 162 C8
Freeman St NR23 136 C6
Freestone Ct 7 PE30 146 E4
Freethorpe Com Prim Sch
NR13 92 F7
Freethorpe Rd
Cantley NR13 92 D6
Freethorpe NR13 74 F1
Freiston 2 PE30 147 C5
Fremantle Rd NR30 168 E1
French's Rd PE14 41 C4
Frensham Rd NR3 157 F2
Frenze Hall La IP22 177 F5
Frenze Rd IP22 177 E4
Frere Cnr 6 IP22 129 D7
Frere Rd
30 Harleston IP20 122 D2
Norwich NR7 159 D1
Fresher Mews NR5 160 F6
Freshfield Cl NR5 161 C7
Freshgap La NR20 33 E6
Freshwater Way NR8 155 F3
Frettenham Fst Sch
NR12 54 A4
Frettenham Rd
Hainford NR10 53 F5
Horstead with Stanninghall
NR12 54 B5
Freyden Way NR12 54 A4
Friar Tuck Rd NR4 162 C1
Friar's La PE31 135 D4
Friars' La 3 NR30 169 D2
Friars Quay NR3 178 B3
Friars St PE30 146 E3
Friars The 17 PE30 146 D4
Friarscroft La NR18 173 B3
Friday Bridge Prim Sch
PE14 77 A7
Friday Mkt 4 NR22 16 F7
Fridaybridge Rd
Elm PE14 77 A8
Wisbech PE14 59 A1
Friends Cl NR5 161 D6
Friends Rd NR4 161 C5
Fring Rd Bircham PE31 14 A3
Snettisham PE31 13 A5
Frinton Way 4 PE13 152 E5
Frith Way NR15 106 B1
Fritillary Dr NR18 173 E4
Fritton Cl NR29 167 B3
Fritton La NR29 56 E6
Fritton Lake Ctry World*
NR31 93 F2
Fritton Rd NR29 56 E6
Frobisher Cl IP24 176 F6
Frobisher Cres PE36 132 D3
Frog's Hall La NR20 50 C2
Frogge La
Coltishall NR12 54 C8
Scottow NR12 37 C1
Frogs Hall La 3 NR1 163 B5
Frogs Hole
Blofield NR13 165 D6
Somerleyton, Ashby &
Herringfleet NR32 93 F1
Frogshall La NR18 173 A5
Front Rd
Tydd St Giles PE13 41 A4
Wood Dalling NR11 34 D6
Front St Binham NR21 6 E2
Burnham Market PE31 135 C3
Front St *continued*
Trunch NR28 22 E5
Front Way PE30 147 A7
Frost Cl Norwich NR7 163 F8
20 Watton IP25 84 D3
Frost's La NR15 106 B1
Fugill Rd NR7 159 D1
Fulcher Ave NR27 139 A7
Fulford Cl NR4 162 A2
Fuller Cl
2 Rackheath NR13 72 E7
9 West Winch PE33 43 F2
Fuller Mews 5 NR5 160 E8
Fuller Rd
North Walsham NR28 151 B4
Redenhall with Harleston
IP20 122 D1
Fuller's Cl NR34 110 D5
Fuller's Hill 10 NR30 169 C4
Fulmar Cl 9 NR31 94 C7
Fulmer La PE32 46 E2
Fulmerston Cl IP24 176 B2
Fulmerston Rd IP24 176 B2
Fulmodeston Rd
Fulmodeston NR21 18 B1
Hindolveston NR20 33 C8
Stibbard NR21 32 E7
Fulton Cl 4 NR4 162 A1
Fundenhall Rd NR15 106 B7
Fundrey Rd PE13 152 F6
Furlong Dro PE33 81 A3
Furlong Rd 1 PE33 81 A3
Furness Cl PE30 148 F1
Furthest Dro IP27 113 C4
Furze Ave NR7 163 E8
Furze Hill NR27 139 C5
Furze Hill Dr NR28 151 E3
Furze La
Great Witchingham NR9 149 C2
Guist NR20 33 A6
Furze Rd NR7 163 E8
Furze Way IP22 129 B1
Fye Bridge St NR3 178 B4

G

Gablehurst Ct NR31 170 A4
Gables Ave NR11 22 B7
Gage Rd NR7 159 C4
Gagman's La NR19 68 A5
Gainsborough Ave
1 Diss IP22 177 C4
Great Yarmouth NR31 170 A7
Gainsborough Cl 2
PE38 172 D6
Gale Cl NR14 109 F8
Gales Ct NR23 136 D6
Gales Rd NR23 136 C6
Gallant's La NR16 118 C5
Galley Cl 8 NR33 111 F1
Galley Hill NR3 158 A2
Gallow Dr PE38 172 C7
Gallow Hill (Tumulus)*
NR25 8 B5
Gallow La PE33 62 D2
Galloway Cl 6 NR20 68 A8
Gallowhill La NR24 18 C3
Gallows La NR16 103 E1
Galyon Rd PE30 147 B8
Gambling Cl NR6 158 A7
Gamecock Cl NR6 158 C6
Gamewell Cl 6 NR1 162 E2
Gangway The NR27 139 C7
Ganners Hill NR8 155 E3
Gannet Rd NR29 167 E4
Gant Cl 9 NR20 68 F6
Gaol Hill NR2 178 A3
Gaol St 13 PE13 152 C4
Gapton Hall Ind Est
NR31 170 A8
Gapton Hall Rd NR31 170 A8
Gapton Hall Ret Pk
NR31 169 A1
Garboldisham Rd
Harling NR16 118 C3
Kenninghall NR16 118 F3
Garboldisham VC Prim Sch
IP22 128 A8
Garden Cl Briston NR24 142 B4
Bungay NR35 124 B8
North Walsham NR28 151 C6
4 Watton IP25 84 E3
Garden Ct
King's Lynn PE30 147 A8
1 Loddon NR14 92 A1
Garden La NR25 8 A1
Garden Pl 2 NR3 162 E8
Garden Rd
Brundall NR13 165 E6
Hemsby NR29 167 D7
Sheringham NR26 138 D6
3 Wiggenhall St Germans
PE34 43 B1
Garden Row PE30 146 E3
Garden St
Cromer NR27 139 B7
Norwich NR1 178 B2
Gardeners Terr NR7 158 F4
Gardenhouse La IP22 128 E2
Gardyn Croft 5 NR8 155 D2
Garfield Rd NR30 169 D7
Garfield Terr NR30 168 E4
Gargle Hill NR7 163 F7
Gariannonum (Roman Fort)*
NR31 93 F7
Garlic St IP21 122 A2
Garlondes 6 NR16 118 C5
Garner's La PE34 41 D8
Garnham Rd NR31 170 C7
Garrett Cl NR3 158 F1
Garrick Gn NR6 158 E5
Garrick Gn Fst Sch
NR6 158 E5
Garrison Rd NR30 169 C5
Garrood Dr NR21 141 E5
Garvestone Prim Sch
NR9 68 C2
Garvestone Rd NR20 68 E4
Garwood Cl PE30 147 E4
Gas Hill NR1 163 A6
Gas House La PE12 41 B8
Gashouse Dro IP27 175 E4
Gashouse Hill NR11 150 D6
Gaskell Way PE30 148 C1
Gatacre Rd NR31 169 B3
Gatehouse La PE30 148 C6
Gatekeeper Cl NR18 173 E4
Gateley Gdns NR3 158 B3
Gateley Rd NR20 49 B8
Gaultree Sq PE14 59 D2
Gavell St IP19 124 D1
Gawdy Cl 2 IP20 122 D2
Gawdy Rd NR7 159 D1
Gaye Cres 1 IP23 130 C1
Gayford Rd NR10 35 B2
Gaymer Cl NR16 119 D7
Gaymer's Way NR28 151 B6
Gaynor Cl NR18 173 B5
Gayton Fst Sch PE32 45 C6
Gayton Rd
East Winch PE32 45 A4
Grimston PE32 45 C8
King's Lynn PE30 147 C5
Gayton Wlk NR6 158 F6
Gaywood Cl NR30 168 D5
Gaywood Com Prim Sch
PE30 147 C7
Gaywood Hall Dr
PE30 147 B5
Gaywood Rd PE30 146 F5
Geddes Way 5 NR20 68 F6
Gedge Rd NR30 168 E6
Geldeston Hill NR34 109 F2
Geldeston Rd
Ellingham NR35 109 D2
Geldeston NR34 110 B2
Gelham Manor PE31 140 C3
Generals Wlk 5 PE30 147 C5
Geneva Gdns NR31 171 E4
Genista Gr 7 NR31 170 B6
Gentian Way 2 NR17 174 B4
Gentleman's Wlk NR2 178 A3
Gentlemans Wlk NR14 92 A3
Gentry Pl NR5 161 C8
Geoffrey Rd 4 NR1 162 F3
George Beck Rd 8 NR29 58 B6
George Borrow Rd
2 East Dereham NR19 154 F3
Norwich NR4 161 E5
George Cl NR8 157 B8
George Dance Pl NR5 161 C7
George Dr NR8 157 B7
George Edwards Rd
NR21 141 E5
George Elliot Way 6
NR19 154 D2
George Fox Way NR5 161 B5
George Hill
Norwich NR6 158 E4
Stanton IP31 127 C1
George La Acle NR13 166 B4
2 Loddon NR14 92 A1
George Pope Cl NR3 158 C2
George Pope Rd NR3 158 C2
George Rd IP24 176 F5
George St
Brandon IP27 175 D3
Great Yarmouth NR30 169 C4
6 King's Lynn PE30 146 E6
Sheringham NR26 138 D7
George Trollope Rd 15
IP25 84 D3
George Westwood Way
NR34 110 D2
George White Mid Sch
NR3 162 F8
George Winter Ct
NR3 158 C2
Georges Rd NR19 154 D5
Georgia Rd NR21 15 C2
Gerald Cl NR1 163 C8
German's La PE34 42 A6
Germander Ct 8 NR31 94 C6
Gertrude Rd NR3 158 F1
Ghost Hill Fst Sch
NR8 156 D8
Gibbet La
East Beckham NR11 138 D2
Wereham PE33 80 E5
Gibbs Cl NR9 160 B2
Gibson Rd 5 IP25 67 B2
Gidney Dr PE31 133 C5
Gigli Cl NR28 151 B3
Gilbard Rd NR5 161 C7
Gilbert Cl NR14 90 F4
Gilbert Rd NR30 168 E6
Gilbert Way NR4 161 D1
Gilchrist Cl 8 NR4 89 E8
Gildencroft NR3 178 A4
Gilderswood NR16 105 F3
Giles Rd NR10 54 A1
Gillingham Rd NR34 110 A2
Gillngham Dam NR34 110 C2
Gilman Rd NR3 158 F1
Gilpin's Ride NR19 154 D4

Gilray Rd IP22 177 F4
Gimingham Rd
Mundesley NR11 143 A6
Southrepps NR11 22 C7
Gipsies' La NR25 9 A3
Gipsies La NR29 56 D6
Gipsy Cl NR5 161 D6
Gipsy La Norwich NR5 161 E5
Watlington PE33 61 D5
Girling Rd NR19 154 C6
Girlings La NR7 163 E5
Girton Rd
Great Yarmouth NR31 170 A3
Norwich NR2 162 B4
Gissing Rd IP22 120 F2
Glade Prim Sch IP27 175 D3
Glade The
Costessey NR8 156 F4
Overstrand NR27 11 A3
Thetford IP24 176 D6
Gladstone Rd
Fakenham NR21 141 B4
4 King's Lynn PE30 146 E3
Gladstone St NR2 162 B6
Glamis Ct 26 IP20 122 D2
Glandford Rd NR25 7 E5
Glasbury Wlk PE13 153 C3
Glaven PE30 147 C5
Glaven Cl NR28 151 D5
Glaven Hale Cl NR25 137 C6
Glaven Rd NR25 137 D5
Glebe Ave
Hunstanton PE36 132 D5
Watlington PE33 61 E5
Glebe Cl Fransham NR19 66 C7
Hingham NR9 86 B5
19 Long Stratton NR15 106 E3
Northwold IP26 99 C8
2 Potter Heigham NR29 56 F6
Taverham NR8 155 F1
Thetford IP24 176 D5
Glebe Ct NR28 151 D6
Glebe Est PE34 144 F1
Glebe House Sch
PE36 132 D5
Glebe La PE31 135 F6
Glebe Mdw NR17 103 E7
Glebe Rd Acle NR13 166 C3
Dersingham PE31 140 C4
Downham Market PE38 172 D6
Gissing IP21 121 A4
Norwich NR2 162 A4
7 Watton IP25 84 E3
Weeting IP27 175 B7
Glebe The
2 Harling NR16 118 C5
Hemsby NR29 167 C8
Honing NR28 38 C6
Stibbard NR21 32 E7
Wells-next-the-Sea
NR23 136 D6
Glebe Way 5 NR12 54 C6
Glebes The 13 NR31 94 A5
Glenalmond NR4 162 A1
Glenburn Ave NR7 159 A3
Glenburn Ct NR7 159 A3
Glenda Cl NR5 157 C1
Glenda Cres NR5 157 B2
Glenda Ct NR5 157 B1
Glenda Rd NR5 157 C1
Glendenning Rd 4 NR1 163 B5
Glenfield Cl PE14 78 A5
Glengarry Cl NR9 88 C8
Glenham Ct PE31 140 C4
Glenmore Ave NR30 168 D7
Glenmore Gdns NR3 158 B2
Glenn Rd NR14 90 C4
Globe La NR13 165 E6
Globe Pl NR2 162 C5
Globe St IP26 99 A5
Glosthorpe Manor
PE32 44 F5
Gloucester Ave NR31 170 C4
Gloucester Ct PE13 152 D7
Gloucester Pl NR24 142 D4
Gloucester Rd PE30 147 B6
Gloucester St NR2 162 C4
Gloucester Way IP24 176 A5
Gobbett's Rd IP22 128 C4
Goddard Cres 1 PE13 152 D7
Goddards Ct 14 IP25 84 D3
Godfrey Rd 5 NR10 54 A2
Godric Pl NR2 161 F6
Godwick Medieval Village
of* PE32 31 C1
Godwin Rd PE13 152 D7
Goffe Cl IP25 84 D4
Goffins La NR29 56 C6
Gogg's Mill Rd NR21 141 A3
Goggles La NR19 66 C6
Gogle Cl 8 NR20 68 E6
Golden Ball St NR1 178 B2
Golden Dog La NR3 178 B4
Golden Fleece Heritage
Mus* NR28 38 A7
Golden Gates NR23 136 B2
Golden Gates Dr
NR23 136 A2
Golden Pightle 7 NR9 69 F2
Golden Sq 10 NR27 139 B7
Goldfinch Cl PE38 172 C7
Goldfinch Way 13 IP25 84 C3
Golding Pl
Norwich NR2 162 C6
16 Wisbech PE13 152 C4
Golds Pightle PE36 2 B3
Goldsmith St NR2 162 C7
Goldsmith Way IP21 121 F4
Goldwell Rd NR1 178 B1
Golf Cl King's Lynn PE30 148 D1
Runton NR27 10 A5
Golf Course Rd PE36 132 E8
Golf La NR19 154 D7
Golf Links Rd
Brundall NR13 165 D4
Wymondham College
NR18 104 E8
Gong La PE31 135 F6
Gonville Cl PE31 133 C5
Gonville Rd NR31 170 A4
Gooch Cl NR28 151 C6
Gooderstone CE Prim Sch
PE33 82 A5
Gooderstone Rd PE33 81 F5
Gooderstone Water Gdns*
PE33 82 A5
Goodhale Rd 1 NR5 161 B7
Goodman Sq 2 NR2 162 C7
Goodminns PE36 13 A7
Goodrick Pl PE13 153 C4
Goodwin Rd NR11 143 C6
Goodwins Rd PE30 146 E3
Goodwood Cl NR7 159 E1
Goosander Cl 4 PE31 12 E5
Goose Gn
8 Sutton Bridge PE12 41 B8
Winfarthing IP22 120 C6
Goose Gn La IP22 120 B6
Goose Gn Rd PE31 12 E4
Goose La
Alby with Thwaite NR11 21 B3
Stalham NR12 39 C4
Gooseacre La IP25 67 D3
Goose's La PE14 41 D5
Gooseberry Hill NR20 50 B3
Gordon Ave NR7 163 C7
Gordon Ct PE13 152 C3
Gordon Fendick Sch
PE13 152 D8
Gordon Godfrey Way
NR10 53 A3
Gordon Rd
Briston NR24 142 A5
3 East Dereham NR20 154 E5
Great Yarmouth NR31 169 C2
Gordon Sq NR1 178 B1
Gordon Terr NR11 143 B4
Gore La NR15 121 C8
Gorgate Rd NR20 49 E3
Gorleston La NR31 170 A2
Gormans La NR21 31 D5
Gorse Ave NR6 158 A5
Gorse Cl 4 Belton NR31 94 A5
2 East Dereham NR19 154 C4
Fakenham NR21 141 F3
Mundesley NR11 143 B5
Gorse Ind Est IP24 125 C6
Gorse Rd NR7 163 D8
Gorse View 4 NR20 49 D4
Gorse Vw 4 NR20 49 D4
Goshawk Way 5 IP24 176 D2
Gosmoor La PE14 59 B1
Gostling Cl IP22 177 B4
Gothic Cl 2 IP20 122 D1
Goulburn Rd NR7 159 D1
Gould Rd 1 NR2 162 A4
Gournay Ave NR31 170 D2
Governors Ct NR1 178 C1
Gowing Cl NR6 157 F7
Gowing Ct NR3 158 B3
Gowing Rd
11 Mulbarton NR14 89 B3
Norwich NR6 157 F6
Gowing Way NR15 107 B5
Grace Edwards Cl
NR8 155 F2
Grafton Cl PE30 147 C8
Grafton Rd PE30 147 C8
Graham Dr 2 PE32 44 B3
Graham Sq NR7 159 D1
Graham St PE30 146 E3
Grammar Sch Rd
NR28 151 C4
Granary Cl
Briston NR24 142 F3
Freethorpe NR13 92 E7
9 Lingwood NR13 74 A3
Granary Ct PE30 146 D4
Granary Loke NR10 149 C4
Granary Rd NR17 174 C4
Grand Cl NR19 154 C4
Grange Ave NR27 11 B3
Grange Cl Briston NR24 142 E3
Ludham NR29 56 D5
Norwich NR6 158 E4
10 Snettisham PE31 12 E4
Wroxham/Hoveton
NR12 164 E6
Grange Cres PE33 63 C5
Grange Ct NR28 151 C4
Grange La
Honingham NR9 69 F5
West Winch PE33 61 E8
Grange Rd
Caister-on-Sea NR30 168 D5
Cantley NR13 92 C6
Flixton NR35 123 E4
Hainford NR10 53 F5
Ludham NR29 56 D5
Mundham NR14 108 F7
Norwich NR2 162 A4
Scarning NR19 154 A4
Sutton Bridge PE34 41 E8
Wendling NR19 66 F8
Wisbech PE13 152 A7
Grange Wlk NR12 164 C4
Granny Bard's La NR12 54 C3
Grant Rd NR10 54 A2
Grant St NR2 162 A7
Granta Way 1 NR31 170 B2
Grantly Ct PE30 147 D5
Granville Cl 8 NR12 39 B4
Granville Rd NR31 169 B4
Granville Terr PE12 41 A8
Grapes Hill NR2 162 C6
Grasmere 19 NR9 88 D8
Grasmere Cl NR5 161 C6
Grassgate La PE14 59 B7
Gravel Bank PE14 60 D6
Gravel Dam NR32 111 F4
Gravel Hill NR14 89 F4
Gravel Pit La NR25 137 C5
Gravelfield Cl NR1 163 B8
Gravelhill La PE33 43 F1
Gravelpit Hill NR17 102 F6
Gray Dr NR20 50 B4
Gray's La Barsham NR22 16 E6
Pulham Market IP21 121 D5
Grays Fair NR5 156 F1
Grays La PE14 59 C2
Grays Rd NR34 111 C3
Great Barn Rd NR23 5 A4
Great Barwick Medieval
Village of* PE31 14 E6
Great Cl NR30 168 F5
Great Comm La NR34 124 E5
Great Dunham Prim Sch
PE32 47 F1
Great Eastern Rd
PE13 152 B4
Great Eastern Way
Fakenham NR21 141 D4
Wells-next-the-Sea
NR23 136 E5
Great Ellingham Prim Sch
NR17 103 E8
Great Hautbois Rd
NR12 54 C7
Great Hockham Prim Sch
IP24 102 E4
Great Hospl NR1 178 C4
Great Man's Way PE33 81 A2
Great Massingham VC Prim
Sch PE32 29 E1
Great Melton Rd
Hethersett NR9 88 C8
Little Melton NR9 160 A2
Great Northern Cl
NR30 169 D6
Great Palgrave Medieval
Village of* PE32 65 B6
Great Snoring Rd NR21 17 D6
Great Witchingham Prim Sch
NR9 51 E5
Great Yarmouth Coll
NR31 169 C1
Great Yarmouth High Sch
NR30 169 E6
Great Yarmouth Race Course
NR30 168 F2
Great Yarmouth Sea Life
Ctr* NR30 169 E2
Great Yarmouth Sta
NR30 169 B5
Greatheath Rd NR20 32 D1
Grebe Cl
Great Yarmouth NR31 170 A7
7 Rollesby NR29 57 D2
Green Bank PE36 2 A5
Green Cl
Hempton NR21 141 A2
Norwich NR5 156 E1
Green Comm La PE31 3 C6
Green Ct
Fakenham NR21 141 E4
Norwich NR7 163 D7
Green Dragon La
NR23 136 D5
Green Dro PE14 77 D6
Green Gr PE33 81 D8
Green Hill La PE31 14 B3
Green Hills Cl NR8 156 F3
Green Hills Rd 6 NR3 162 D8
Green House La PE37 153 E5
Green La Alpington NR14 90 F3
Attleborough NR17 174 C7
Aylsham NR11 150 A6
Bawburgh NR9 160 C4
Beetley NR20 49 D4
Billingford NR20 49 F8
Burgh St Peter NR34 111 C4
Burnham Thorpe PE31 4 D3
Caister-on-Sea NR30 168 E4
Christchurch PE14 95 A7
Coltishall NR12 54 C6
Dereham NR19 154 E8
Ditchingham NR35 109 B2
Earsham NR35 108 E2
5 Feltwell IP26 98 E1
Filby NR29 75 F8
Foulsham NR20 33 E3
Great & Little Plumstead
NR13 72 E5
Great Ellingham NR17 103 E8
Great Moulton NR15 106 B1
Great Yarmouth NR31 94 C6
Guist NR20 33 A5
Hales NR14 109 E8
Haveringland NR10 52 E7
Horsford NR10 53 B4
King's Lynn PE30 148 E2
Little Ellingham NR17 86 A1
Methwold IP26 99 A7
Mundford IP26 100 B5
Green La *continued*
Postwick with Witton NR7 72 E4
Potter Heigham NR29 56 F6
Pudding Norton NR21 141 A1
Redenhall with Harleston
IP20 122 E2
Rocklands NR17 103 C7
Saxlingham Nethergate
NR15 107 B7
Shipdham IP25 67 D4
Shipmeadow NR34 109 F1
Somerleyton, Ashby &
Herringfleet NR32 111 E8
South Walsham NR13 74 B6
Starston IP20 122 D4
Stow Bedon NR17 103 B8
Syleham IP21 131 C4
Thelnetham IP22 128 A2
Thetford IP24 176 E4
Thornham PE36 2 D6
Thrandeston IP21 129 F2
Tivetshall St Margaret
NR15 121 B5
Toft Monks NR34 110 C6
Tottenhill PE33 61 F5
Troston IP31 126 A1
Upwell PE14 95 B6
Walsoken PE14 152 F4
Wicklewood NR18 87 C5
Wramplingham NR18 87 F7
Wymondham NR18 173 D1
Yaxham NR19 68 B6
Green La E NR13 72 E7
Green La N NR13 72 D5
Green La W
Horsham St Faith NR13 53 D1
Rackheath NR13 72 D8
Green Man La NR15 108 C8
Green Marsh Rd PE34 144 C7
Green Oak Rd 2 IP25 84 D3
Green Pk 42 IP20 122 D2
Green Pk Rd NR10 53 B3
Green Quay The*
PE30 146 D4
Green Rd Brandon IP27 175 E2
Hales NR14 109 E8
Upwell PE14 77 E4
Green St IP21 131 A4
Green The Ashill IP25 84 A7
Belton with Browston
NR31 94 A5
Boughton PE33 80 F4
Brisley NR20 49 B8
Burnham Market PE31 135 C3
Deopham NR18 86 E2
Dersingham PE31 140 D4
Diss IP22 177 A6
8 Earsham NR35 123 F8
Fakenham NR21 141 A3
Freethorpe NR13 92 E8
Hickling NR12 39 E2
Hockham IP24 102 E3
Hunstanton PE36 132 C4
Lound NR32 94 C2
North Lopham IP22 119 A2
North Wootton PE30 148 C5
Norwich NR2 178 D2
Ormesby St Margaret
NR29 167 A2
Runhall NR9 68 F2
Saxlingham Nethergate
NR15 107 D7
South Wootton PE30 149 C2
Surlingham NR14 73 B1
Thornham PE36 2 D6
Upton with Fishley NR13 166 B8
Wicklewood NR18 87 B4
Green Way
Barsham NR22 16 C6
Stiffkey NR23 6 C6
Swaffham PE37 153 B6
Green Wood Dr NR19 154 C5
Greenacre Cl
Brundall NR13 165 C4
King's Lynn PE30 148 B2
Greenacre Fst & Mid Sch
NR30 169 D1
Greenacre Rd NR9 86 B5
Greenacres
Bradwell NR31 170 A3
Little Melton NR9 160 C2
Greenacres Dr NR14 90 C5
Green's La NR27 10 C4
Greenborough Cl NR7 159 E2
Greenborough Rd
NR7 159 E2
Greencourts 10 NR29 58 B6
Greenfield NR5 156 D1
Greenfield Cl NR27 139 C5
Greenfields NR16 118 B5
Greenfields Rd NR20 154 F4
Greengate NR20 50 B2
Greengate La
Bircham PE31 13 F4
Great Massingham PE32 29 C1
Greenhill Ave NR30 168 D8
Greenhill Rd PE32 46 B2
Greenhoe Pl PE37 153 B3
Greenland Ave
King's Lynn PE30 146 E8
Wymondham NR18 173 E6
Greenlands Way NR26 138 C6
Greenlands Way W 2
NR26 138 B6
Greenpark Ave PE30 146 F6
Greens Rd
East Dereham NR20 154 F3
North Walsham NR28 151 A5
Greenway Cl
Fakenham NR21 141 C5
2 North Walsham NR28 151 C5
Greenway La
Fakenham NR21 141 C5
Tharston & Hapton
NR15 106 D6
Greenway Pk NR21 141 C6
Greenways
Bunwell NR16 105 D4
Flordon NR15 106 E8
Holt NR25 137 C7
Newton Flotman NR15 89 C1
Norwich NR4 161 F1
Greenways Cl NR15 106 E8
Greenways La
Bunwell NR16 105 D4
Carleton Rode NR16 105 B4
Greenwich Cl
Dersingham PE31 140 E3
Downham Market PE38 172 B3
Greenwood Cl NR16 105 E8
Greenwood Rd NR4 162 C1
Greenwood Way
5 Shipdham IP25 67 C2
Thorpe St Andrew NR7 159 F2
Greevegate PE36 132 C4
Gregor Shanks Way 27
IP25 84 D3
Gregory Cl 1 PE30 148 C5
Gregs Cl NR20 68 F5
Grenville Cl 3 NR9 88 E8
Grenville Pl 1 NR30 169 D8
Grenville Way IP24 176 D5
Gresham Cl
Great Yarmouth NR31 170 C2
King's Lynn PE30 147 C8
Gresham Rd
Baconsthorpe NR25 20 B8
Norwich NR3 158 B2
Gresham Village Sch
NR11 9 E1
Greshams Prep Sch
NR25 137 D7
Greshams Sch NR25 137 D7
Gresley Cl NR20 49 C4
Gressenhall Farm &
Workhouse* NR20 49 D4
Gressenhall Rd NR20 49 D4
Grey Sedge PE30 147 A7
Greyfriars Cl NR6 158 E5
Greyfriars Cty Prim Sch
PE30 146 E4
Greyfriars Rd NR1 178 B3
Greyfriars Way NR30 169 C3
Greyhound La
Banham NR16 119 D7
Hopton IP22 127 E5
Greyhound Opening 7
NR2 162 C7
Greylag Cl 8 NR13 55 A1
Greys Manor NR16 119 D6
Grice Cl 4 NR26 138 C5
Griffin La
Attleborough NR17 174 D5
Thorpe St Andrew NR7 72 D3
Grigsons Wood 1
NR16 118 C5
Grime's Graves* IP27 115 C8
Grimmer La NR13 92 B7
Grimmer's Rd 6 PE13 152 E7
Grimshoe Rd PE38 172 B6
Grimston Jun Sch PE32 28 B1
Grimston Pott Row Fst Sch
PE32 45 A8
Grimston Rd
Gayton PE32 45 C6
King's Lynn PE30 148 E1
Gristock Pl NR5 161 C8
Griston Rd
Thompson IP24 102 B8
Watton IP25 84 E3
Groomes Cl 4 NR31 171 D5
Grosvenor Rd
Norwich NR2 162 B5
Wisbech PE13 152 D7
Grouts La NR25 8 B6
Grove Ave
Norwich NR5 157 A1
Norwich NR1 178 A1
Grove Cl
8 East Dereham NR19 154 C4
Holt NR25 137 D6
2 Newton Flotman NR15 89 C1
Grove Dale 3 NR15 89 C1
Grove End IP21 131 F1
Grove Gdns 7 PE32 45 C6
Grove House Inf Sch
NR19 154 D4
Grove La Booton NR10 52 A8
Fakenham NR21 141 C6
Forncett NR16 106 A3
Holt NR25 137 D6
Sparham NR9 51 B6
Tasburgh NR15 106 F7
Thetford IP24 176 D4
Grove Rd
Banham NR16 119 C6
Barsham NR21 16 C4
Brockdish IP21 131 C6
Cantley NR13 92 D8
Cromer NR27 139 D5
Gissing IP21 121 A4
Hethersett NR9 88 D8
Ingham NR12 24 C1

Grove Rd *continued*
4 Marthan NR29 57 D5
Melton Constable NR24 142 A4
North Walsham NR28 151 D5
Norwich NR1 178 A1
Repps with Bastwick NR29 57 A4
Starston IP20 122 C2
Wells-next-the-Sea NR23 136 E4
Grove The
Coltishall NR12 54 D6
East Dereham NR19 154 D4
Fleggburgh NR29 57 A1
2 Necton PE37 65 F4
Roydon PE32 28 A1
Shotesham NR15 90 B1
Grove Way NR15 89 C1
Grove Wlk NR1 178 A1
Grovebury Cl NR13 165 C4
Grovedale Cl NR5 157 A1
Grovelands PE31 140 D8
Groveside PE31 30 A7
Growle Abbey NR24 19 B2
Grub La IP19 124 E1
Grub St
Happisburgh NR12 24 B4
Shotesham NR15 90 B2
Grubb's La NR12 24 C1
Guanock Pl 12 PE30 146 E3
Guanock Terr PE30 146 E3
Guardian Rd NR5 161 F7
Guelph Rd 2 NR1 163 A6
Guernsey Rd NR3 162 E8
Guestwick Rd
Foulsham NR20 33 E4
Hindolveston NR20 33 F7
Wood Norton NR20 33 C6
Guild Rd PE13 152 E6
Guild St NR22 16 F8
Guildford Way IP24 176 B5
Guildhall Hill 1 NR2 178 A3
Guildhall La IP21 121 E5
Guildhall St IP24 176 D3
Guiler's La NR18 105 B8
Guilt Cross Way PE38 172 C6
Guist Bottom Rd NR21 32 E6
Guist Rd NR20 33 C4
Gulgate La NR11 21 A1
Gull La NR14 90 E6
Gullpit Dro PE34 61 D1
Gun St 7 NR26 138 D7
Gunn Rd NR7 159 D1
Gunn St NR20 33 C3
Gunn's Cnr NR12 38 D2
Gunner Cl 3 NR7 72 D5
Gunthorpe Rd PE14 41 B5
Gunton La NR5 157 B2
Gunton Rd
Loddon NR14 109 C8
Norwich NR2 161 F5
Wymondham NR18 173 D4
Gunton Sta NR11 22 B6
Gurney Cl NR5 161 B8
Gurney Ct NR5 161 B8
Gurney Dr NR7 159 D3
Gurney La NR4 161 C2
Gurney Rd
Norwich NR5 157 A1
Norwich NR1 163 A7
Gwyn Cres NR21 141 F5
Gymkhana Way PE31 133 B5

H

Habgood Cl NR13 166 C4
Hackford Rd
Hardingham NR9 86 E6
Wicklewood NR18 87 A5
Haconsfield 8 NR9 88 D7
Haddiscoe Dam NR14 110 F8
Haddiscoe Rd NR34 110 F6
Haddiscoe Sta NR31 93 D1
Hadfield Rd NR28 151 B6
Hadley Cres PE31 133 C5
Hadley Dr NR2 161 F6
Hadley Rd NR26 138 E6
Hagbech Hall Cl 2 PE14 59 D2
Haggard's Cl IP25 66 E3
Haig Cl NR19 154 D3
Hainford Fst Sch NR10 53 E6
Hainford Rd NR10 53 E7
Halcombe Ct NR3 158 E1
Halden Ave NR6 157 F6
Hale Ct NR13 73 A4
Hale Dro Littleport CB6 96 B2
Welney PE14 95 E6
Hale Fen Rd CB6 96 B1
Hale Rd Ashill IP25 84 A7
Bradenham IP25 66 D3
Necton PE37 65 F4
Hales Cl NR30 168 D5
Hales Ct NR25 137 B6
Hales Hall & Gdns* NR14 109 D6
Hales St NR15 121 A6
Halesworth Rd NR34 124 E4
Haley Cl 4 PE13 152 C8
Half Acre Cl NR27 10 B4
Half Mile Cl NR3 158 B2
Half Mile Rd NR3 158 B2
Half Moon NR31 170 C1
Half Moon La IP22 128 E4
Half Moon Way 1 NR2 162 B8
Half Year Cl 7 NR27 10 B5
Halfar Rd 8 IP31 126 B1
Halffield La NR18 86 D2
Halfmile Drift IP25 66 D3
Halford Cl NR17 174 D4
Halford La IP22 129 A7
Halford Pl NR17 174 D4
Halford Rd NR17 174 D4
Halfpenny La
Beetley NR20 49 C5
Elm PE14 59 A2
Wisbech PE14 152 D1
Halfpenny Toll Rd PE14 95 B8
Halifax Cres NR21 15 C3
Haling Way IP24 176 A4
Hall Bridge Rd PE14 77 D5
Hall Cl Fakenham NR21 141 D4
Heacham PE31 133 D7
4 Hemsby NR29 167 A7
5 Hethersett NR9 88 D7
3 Hingham NR9 86 C4
3 Southery PE38 97 B5
Hall Comm Rd NR29 56 C4
Hall Cres PE33 63 C5
Hall Dike PE14 77 F7
Hall Dr Costessey NR5 156 D2
16 Feltwell IP26 98 E1
Honingham NR9 69 E6
North Runcton PE33 44 A3
Santon Downham IP27 115 C6
Hall Farm Gdns PE32 44 F3
Hall Farm Pl NR9 160 B6
Hall Hills IP22 177 C5
Hall La
Baconsthorpe NR25 19 F8
Bressingham IP22 119 D1
Burston & Shimpling IP21 121 A2
Colkirk NR21 31 E5
Deopham NR18 86 F4
East Carleton NR14 88 E4
East Dereham NR20 154 F4
East Ruston NR12 24 A4
East Tuddenham NR20 69 B6
Felthorpe NR10 52 E5
Frettenham NR12 54 B3
Gunthorpe NR24 18 A5
Hingham NR9 86 C5
Horsford NR10 53 B1
King's Lynn PE30 148 B1
Knapton NR28 143 B1
Long Stratton NR15 106 F3
Morley NR18 87 B2
North Tuddenham NR20 68 F8
North Walsham NR28 151 D5
Northwold IP26 99 C7
Postwick with Witton NR13 72 F2
Redgrave IP22 128 E4
Ringstead PE36 2 A3
Roydon IP22 129 D7
Saxlingham Nethergate NR15 107 C7
Scole IP21 130 F8
Shelfanger IP22 120 B2
Shelton NR15 122 A8
Taverham NR8 157 B8
Tharston & Hapton NR15 106 D5
Thompson IP24 102 B7
Thornham PE36 2 D6
Thursford NR21 17 F5
Wacton NR15 106 C1
West Winch PE33 43 E2
Whissonsett NR20 31 D2
Wiveton NR25 7 D6
Wood Norton NR20 33 B6
Hall Loke NR28 38 C8
Hall Moor Rd NR9 86 C4
Hall Orchards PE32 44 C3
Hall Plain NR30 169 C3
Hall Rd Alderford NR9 52 A5
Barsham NR34 124 F7
Barton Turf NR12 55 E8
12 Bawdeswell NR20 50 E7
Bedingham NR35 108 C3
Beetley NR20 49 D5
Blofield NR13 165 C8
Bracon Ash NR14 88 E4
Brockdish IP21 131 D7
Bunwell NR16 105 E2
Burston & Shimpling IP22 120 E3
Cantley NR13 92 C8
Carleton Rode NR16 105 B4
Catfield NR29 56 B8
Clenchwarton PE34 145 D6
Cromer NR27 139 B5
Earsham NR35 123 E8
Easton NR9 70 B5
Ellingham NR35 109 C3
Elsing NR20 50 D2
Felbrigg NR27 139 A4
Fleggburgh NR29 57 A1
Framingham Earl NR14 90 D5
Gimingham NR11 22 D7
Great Melton NR9 88 B8
Great Witchingham NR9 51 F5
Hainford NR10 53 E5
Hemsby NR29 167 A7
Hoe NR20 49 F3
Honing NR28 38 D8
Hopton on Sea NR31 171 B6
King's Lynn PE30 148 C1
Ludham NR29 56 B4
Marthan NR29 57 D4
Mautby NR29 76 A6
Northrepps NR27 139 D2
Hall Rd *continued*
Norwich NR5 157 A2
Norwich NR1 178 B1
Oulton NR11 35 B7
Outwell PE14 77 F7
Postwick with Witton NR13 165 A5
Pulham St Mary IP21 122 A4
Reedham NR13 92 F6
Roudham NR16 117 E6
Runhall NR20 69 A4
Smallburgh NR12 38 D2
9 Snettisham PE31 12 E5
Sutton NR12 39 D3
Swafield NR28 22 C5
Tacolneston NR16 105 E6
Tharston & Hapton NR15 106 E5
Thurton NR14 91 C3
Tivetshall St Margaret NR15 121 B6
Toft Monks NR14 110 D7
Walpole Highway PE14 59 F8
Winfarthing IP22 120 C5
Wood Dalling NR11 34 C6
Hall Sch NR6 158 D5
Hall St NR24 142 E3
Hall Staithe NR21 141 B4
Hall View Rd PE30 147 B4
Hall Wlk NR9 51 D5
Hall's Dr NR20 49 C4
Hallback La NR14 90 A7
Hallfield Rd IP24 102 A7
Hallfields PE33 62 D4
Hallgate 2 NR13 72 D6
Hallowing Cres 3 NR15 106 B1
Hallowing La NR15 121 B8
Halls Cnr NR10 53 B8
Halls Cnr Rd NR10 53 B8
Hallwong La IP20 122 D3
Halstead Cl 2 PE13 152 E5
Halt Rd NR30 168 D7
Halton Rd 8 IP25 84 F3
Halvergate Rd
Beighton NR13 74 E1
Reedham NR13 93 A6
Hambling's Piece NR16 118 C4
Hamburg Way PE30 147 A8
Hamilton Cl
North Walsham NR28 151 C5
South Walsham NR13 74 A8
Hamilton Ct 1 NR21 141 B4
Hamilton Dr PE37 153 D3
Hamilton Rd
3 Cromer NR27 139 B7
Great Yarmouth NR30 169 D7
Old Hunstanton PE36 132 E7
Hamilton Rd W PE36 132 E7
Hamilton Way PE38 172 B5
Hamilton Wlk 9 NR29 57 D4
Hamlet Cl NR28 151 D7
Hamlin Way PE30 146 F1
Hammond Cl NR7 159 E3
Hammond Rd 2 NR30 169 D5
Hammond Way NR7 159 E3
Hamon Cl PE36 132 E7
Hamond Rd NR6 157 D5
Hamonds High Sch PE37 153 C3
Hampden Dr 10 NR7 72 D4
Hampden Rd 2 PE13 152 D5
Hampton Ave 3 NR14 92 F1
Hampton Cl NR30 168 C5
Hanbury Cl 4 NR5 161 D5
Hancock Cl 3 NR12 54 C7
Hancock Ct NR5 160 E7
Hand La Barsham NR21 16 C5
Hoveton NR12 164 C8
Handel Dr NR19 154 F3
Handford Dr NR26 138 E6
Hanginghill NR13 74 C6
Hankin Ct 3 NR4 161 C5
Hankinson's Est PE34 42 A5
Hanly Cl NR7 159 C2
Hanly Ct NR30 168 D6
Hannah Cl NR26 138 C6
Hannah Rd NR20 50 B4
Hannant Rd NR28 151 D6
Hanover Ct
Dersingham PE31 140 E3
King's Lynn PE30 147 D5
Hanover Gdns PE36 132 D3
Hanover Rd NR2 162 C4
Hanrae Cl NR26 138 F6
Hans Pl 4 NR27 139 B7
Hansa Rd PE30 146 F2
Hansard Cl NR3 158 B1
Hansard La NR3 178 B4
Hansard Rd NR3 158 B1
Hansell Rd NR7 163 F8
Hantons Loke NR13 74 B2
Hanworth Cross NR11 21 D5
Happisburgh Fst Sch NR12 24 C5
Happisburgh Rd
East Ruston NR12 24 A3
Lessingham NR12 24 D4
North Walsham NR28 151 D4
Witton NR28 23 E2
Hapton Prim Sch NR15 106 C7
Harbord Cl 4 NR28 151 C7
Harbord Cres NR30 170 D8
Harbord Rd
Cromer NR27 139 C5
Norwich NR4 161 F5
Overstrand NR27 11 A3
Harbour La IP22 128 A7
Harbour Rd
1 Frettenham NR12 54 A4
Norwich NR1 163 A5
Harbour Terr NR31 170 E4
Harcourt Cl 3 NR3 162 F8
Hardesty Cl 9 NR14 90 D5
Hardingham Dr 6 NR26 138 C5
Hardingham Rd NR9 86 D5
Hardingham St 4 NR9 86 C4
Hardley Cross* NR14 92 E4
Hardley Hall La NR14 92 C3
Hardley Rd NR14 92 A2
Hardley St NR14 92 B3
Hardwick Cl 1 NR4 89 D8
Hardwick Ind Est PE30 147 B2
Hardwick Rd
King's Lynn PE30 146 E2
Pulham Market IP21 121 F7
Shelton NR15 122 C8
Hardy Cl
Downham Market PE38 172 B4
1 North Walsham NR28 151 C5
Thetford IP24 176 D6
Hardy Rd NR1 163 A4
Hardy's La PE32 46 C2
Hare Cl 2 NR14 89 B2
Hare Rd NR13 72 F5
Harebell Rd PE38 172 B3
Harecroft Gdns PE30 146 E6
Harecroft Par 7 PE30 146 E6
Harecroft Rd PE13 152 B5
Harecroft Terr PE30 146 E6
Harefen La NR13 74 B7
Harefield Rd IP24 116 C5
Hares Cl NR21 17 C3
Harewood PE31 134 F4
Harewood Dr
9 King's Lynn PE30 146 E6
Taverham NR8 155 E3
Harewood Par 8 PE30 146 E6
Harford Manor Cl NR2 162 C2
Harford Manor Specl Sch NR4 162 C2
Harford St NR1 162 E3
Harfrey's Rd NR31 170 B8
Harfreys Ind Est
Gorleston-on-Sea NR31 170 A8
Great Yarmouth NR31 169 B1
Hargate La PE34 42 B7
Hargham Cl 5 NR17 104 D2
Hargham Rd
Attleborough NR17 174 B2
Old Buckenham NR17 104 B2
Shropham NR17 103 C3
Harker Way 6 NR13 73 D6
Harleston Mus* IP20 122 D2
Harleston Prim Sch IP20 122 E2
Harleston Rd
Pulham Market IP21 121 E4
Scole IP21 121 D1
Harley Rd NR30 169 D6
Harling Dro IP27 115 E7
Harling Rd
Garboldisham IP22 118 C2
Hockham IP24 102 E3
North Lopham IP22 119 A2
Harling Rd Sta NR16 118 A6
Harlington Ave NR6 158 A4
Harlingwood La NR17 104 E1
Harman Cl 12 NR9 88 D8
Harman's La IP20 122 C1
Harmer Cl NR28 151 E5
Harmer Cres NR4 161 C1
Harmer La NR4 161 C1
Harmer Rd NR3 158 D3
Harmer's La NR11 21 A5
Harnser's Reach NR13 166 B8
Harp Cl NR21 141 B5
Harp's Hall Rd PE14 59 E5
Harper's La NR20 32 A1
Harpley CE VC Prim Sch PE31 29 C4
Harpsfield NR5 160 E8
Harrier Cl 26 NR9 88 D8
Harriet Cl PE12 41 A8
Harriet Martineau Cl 10 IP24 176 D7
Harriott's Way NR11 150 B5
Harris Mews 2 NR5 161 A7
Harris Rd
11 Swanton Morley NR20 50 B3
12 Watton IP25 84 F3
Harrisons Dr NR7 159 E3
Harrold Cl
1 South Walsham NR13 74 B8
Taverham NR8 155 E2
Harrolds Cl PE13 59 C5
Harrow Cl PE34 146 C5
Harry Barber Cl 2 NR5 161 A8
Harry Blunt Way 10 NR19 154 C4
Harry Miller Ct 7 NR30 169 D1
Harry Perry Cl NR4 162 C2
Harry Watson Ct NR6 158 C3
Harry's La IP21 121 E7
Harrys Way
Hunstanton PE36 132 D1
Wisbech PE13 152 C2
Harsnett Cl NR5 160 F8
Hart La NR25 9 A2
Hart's La NR9 160 A7
Hartbee Rd NR6 158 C6
Hartington Rd NR27 139 D4
Hartley Cl PE36 132 D4
Hartmann Rd NR30 170 E6
Harts Farm Rd NR18 173 E5
Harts La NR4 161 C1
Hartwell Rd NR12 164 C4
Harvard Rd 6 IP26 98 D1
Harvest Cl 1 NR10 53 E5
Harvest La NR21 17 D6
Harvey Cl
2 Hethersett NR9 88 C7
Norwich NR7 163 C7
Tasburgh NR15 106 E7
Harvey Dr NR28 151 C7
Harvey Est NR11 22 E7
Harvey Gn 10 NR14 91 F1
Harvey La
Caister-on-Sea NR30 168 E4
Dickleburgh IP21 121 C1
Norwich NR7 163 C6
Harvey St 21 IP25 84 D3
Harvey's La NR15 108 D6
Harwood Ave 4 IP24 176 E6
Harwood Rd NR1 162 E1
Hase's La NR9 51 C4
Haslips Cl 8 NR2 162 C7
Haspalls Rd PE37 153 B3
Hassett Cl 6 NR3 162 F8
Hastings Ave NR6 158 A4
Hastings Cl
Briston NR24 142 A5
6 Tasburgh NR15 106 F6
Hastings Ct NR24 142 E4
Hastings Dr PE36 132 D6
Hastings La
15 Sheringham NR26 138 D7
Wiggenhall St Germans PE34 61 C8
Hastings Rd 6 IP25 84 F3
Hastings Way NR12 39 C3
Hatherley Gdns PE33 81 B8
Hatton Rd NR1 162 E3
Haugh Cnr NR16 119 F7
Haugh Rd NR16 119 F8
Haughs End Rd NR12 164 F2
Hautbois Rd NR10 37 B2
Hauteyn Ct NR6 158 C2
Havaker The NR13 92 F5
Havant Cl NR4 161 E1
Havelock Pl 10 NR30 169 D2
Havelock Rd
Great Yarmouth NR30 169 D2
Norwich NR2 162 B6
Sheringham NR26 138 E5
Havergate 7 NR12 54 C6
Haveringland Rd NR10 52 E6
Havers Rd NR3 158 B1
Haverscroft Cl NR8 155 D2
Hawk Cres IP22 177 F5
Hawkes La NR14 89 A2
Hawkins Ave NR30 169 C8
Hawkins Cl NR30 169 C8
Hawkins Dr 1 PE13 152 E5
Hawthorn Ave 6 PE33 63 B4
Hawthorn Cl Diss IP22 177 F5
3 Spixworth NR10 54 A1
6 Watlington PE33 61 D5
Hawthorn Cotts PE31 140 D4
Hawthorn Cres NR31 94 C6
Hawthorn Dr
Dersingham PE31 140 D5
East Dereham NR19 154 B3
Hawthorn Rd
2 Downham Market PE38 172 C6
Emneth PE14 59 D1
6 Gayton PE32 45 C5
Great Yarmouth NR31 170 B6
Norwich NR5 157 A2
Hawthorn Rise NR11 143 B5
Hawthorn Way IP24 176 E6
Hawthorn Wlk 2 IP24 176 F6
Hawthorne Ave
Grimston PE32 28 B1
Hellesdon NR6 158 A5
Wisbech PE13 152 C8
Hawthorne Cl
2 Loddon NR14 91 F1
Wymondham NR18 173 D6
Hawthorns PE30 147 C4
Hay Gn Rd PE34 144 A1
Hay Gn Rd N PE34 42 B6
Hay Gn Rd S PE34 42 A5
Haycroft 3 NR29 167 B7
Hayes La NR21 141 A5
Hayfield Rd PE30 148 C4
Haygate 2 IP23 130 C1
Haylett Cl NR30 168 E5
Haymarket NR2 178 B2
Haythill La IP26 98 D2
Hayward Cl 3 NR25 7 C6
Haywood End IP22 120 D6
Hazel Ave NR26 138 D4
Hazel Cl Grimston PE32 28 B1
5 King's Lynn PE30 148 C3
Taverham NR8 155 D1
West Winch PE33 43 E1
Wymondham NR18 173 D4
Hazel Covert IP24 176 F5
Hazel Cres 4 PE33 63 B4
Hazel Gdns 1 PE13 152 D4
Hazel Gr NR19 154 F4
Hazel Rd
4 Attleborough NR17 174 B5
Norwich NR5 156 F1
Hazel Way NR31 170 B6
Hazell Rd NR28 151 C7
Heacham Fst Sch PE31 133 D5

Heacham Jun Sch
PE31 ... 133 C4
Heacham Rd PE36 ... 13 A7
Headington Cl NR31 ... 170 A5
Headland Dro IP26 ... 113 A5
Headley Dr NR28 ... 151 C4
Hearne Ct 3 NR5 ... 160 E8
Heartsease Fst & Mid Sch
NR7 ... 159 C1
Heartsease High Sch
NR7 ... 159 C1
Heartsease La NR7 ... 159 B1
Heartsease Mid Sch
NR7 ... 159 C1
Heartsease Rd 3 IP24 ... 176 E5
Heartwell Rd NR27 ... 139 C5
Heater La NR13 ... 73 F4
Heath Cl 16 Horsford NR10 ... 53 A3
Lenwade NR9 ... 51 D5
Norwich NR6 ... 158 A6
Heath Cres NR6 ... 158 B5
Heath Dr NR25 ... 137 D5
Heath Farm La NR11 ... 36 E6
Heath Gn 1 NR31 ... 170 B5
Heath La
Fakenham NR21 ... 141 F4
Gimingham NR11 ... 22 D8
Great Witchingham NR9 ... 51 E6
Gunthorpe NR24 ... 18 B5
Lenwade NR9 ... 51 D5
Mundesley NR11 ... 143 B5
Roughton NR11 ... 21 E8
Thursford NR21 ... 17 E4
Tittleshall PE32 ... 47 F7
Heath Rd
Ashby with Oby NR29 ... 57 B2
Banham NR16 ... 119 E7
Brandon IP27 ... 175 D3
Catfield NR29 ... 56 D8
Corpusty NR11 ... 19 D1
Dersingham PE31 ... 140 D2
East Dereham NR19 ... 154 C7
Felmingham NR28 ... 37 B8
Fritton & St Olaves NR31 ... 93 E1
Geldeston NR34 ... 110 A3
Gunthorpe NR24 ... 18 B5
Heydon NR11 ... 34 D8
Hickling NR12 ... 39 E1
Hockering NR20 ... 69 B8
Honing NR28 ... 23 E1
Kenninghall NR16 ... 119 A3
Lessingham NR12 ... 24 F2
Lyng NR9 ... 51 A4
Norwich NR3 ... 162 D8
Quidenham NR16 ... 118 E8
Rollesby NR29 ... 57 B2
Sapiston IP31 ... 126 E3
Sheringham NR26 ... 138 D6
Shotesham NR15 ... 107 F8
9 Thorpe End NR13 ... 72 D6
Troston IP31 ... 126 B1
Winfarthing IP22 ... 120 A7
Heath Rise
Fakenham NR21 ... 141 E4
Sculthorpe Airfield PE31 ... 15 B3
Heath The NR10 ... 52 F8
Heath Way Blofield NR13 ... 73 C6
Fakenham NR21 ... 141 F4
Heather Ave
Hemsby NR29 ... 167 D4
Norwich NR6 ... 158 A4
Heather Ave Fst Sch
NR6 ... 158 B4
Heather Barrow Ct
NR21 ... 141 D4
Heather Cl PE30 ... 148 D5
Heather Dr NR25 ... 137 B7
Heather Gdns NR31 ... 93 F6
Heather Rd 12 NR31 ... 94 A6
Heather Way
Brandon IP27 ... 175 E3
Great Moulton NR15 ... 121 B8
Heatherwood Cl 7 NR13 ... 72 D6
Heathfield Cl NR25 ... 8 E3
Heathfield Rd NR25 ... 8 E3
Heathgate NR3 ... 163 A8
Heathlands PE37 ... 153 D2
Heathlands Dr IP24 ... 176 D8
Heathside Rd NR1 ... 163 B5
Hebrides Way NR30 ... 168 C6
Heckingham Holes
NR14 ... 92 B1
Hedgehog Wlk NR12 ... 24 E4
Hedgelands 1 PE13 ... 152 C8
Hedgemere 1 NR8 ... 155 D2
Hedgerows The 8 NR5 ... 161 A7
Hedley La NR33 ... 111 F1
Heffer Cl NR19 ... 154 D3
Heggatt Rd NR12 ... 54 C5
Heidi Cl 7 NR19 ... 154 D1
Heigham Gr NR2 ... 162 C6
Heigham Pk Fst Sch
NR2 ... 162 A5
Heigham Rd NR2 ... 162 B6
Heigham St NR2 ... 162 B8
Heigham Watering 5
NR2 ... 162 B8
Helen Ave 7 NR29 ... 57 C4
Helena Rd
Norwich NR2 ... 162 B6
Witton NR12 ... 23 F3
Helford St 6 NR2 ... 162 B8
Hellesdon Cl NR5 ... 161 D8
Hellesdon Hall Rd
NR6 ... 157 E1
Hellesdon High Sch
NR6 ... 157 E4
Hellesdon Hospl NR6 ... 157 D4
Hellesdon Mill La
NR6 ... 157 D1
Hellesdon Pk Rd NR6 ... 157 E3
Hellesdon Rd NR6 ... 161 D8
Hellgate La NR11 ... 20 F8
Hellington Cnr NR14 ... 91 B5
Hellington Hill NR14 ... 91 B6
Hellpit La NR24 ... 19 B2
Helsinki Way NR19 ... 154 C2
Helska Leisure Ctr
NR12 ... 55 E3
Hemblington Hall Rd
NR13 ... 73 E6
Hemblington Prim Sch
NR13 ... 73 C6
Hemblington Rd NR13 ... 73 E4
Hemington Cl PE30 ... 147 D8
Hemlin Cl NR5 ... 161 C6
Hemmant Way NR34 ... 110 B3
Hemmings Cl 4 NR5 ... 160 F7
Hempnall Rd NR35 ... 108 A4
Hempnall Sch NR15 ... 107 C5
Hempstead Rd
Holt NR25 ... 137 D5
Lessingham NR12 ... 24 D3
Hempsted Mews NR5 ... 160 E7
Hempton Rd NR21 ... 141 B3
Hemsby Fst Sch NR29 ... 167 A7
Hemsby Rd
13 Martham NR29 ... 57 D4
Winterton-on-Sea NR29 ... 58 B5
Henby Way NR7 ... 163 D7
Henderson Rd NR4 ... 161 F5
Hendon Ave 13 IP25 ... 84 F3
Hendon Cl NR5 ... 157 B1
Hendrie Rd NR25 ... 137 C7
Henley Rd NR2 ... 162 A4
Hennessey's Loke NR28 ... 23 A3
Henry Bell Cl PE30 ... 147 A5
Henry Blogg Rd NR27 ... 139 B5
Henry Cross Cl 1 IP25 ... 67 C2
Henry Page Rd NR11 ... 150 B5
Henry Preston Rd 1
NR15 ... 106 F6
Henry St PE13 ... 152 C5
Henry Warby Ave 7
PE14 ... 59 A1
Henry Ward Rd 1 IP20 ... 122 D2
Henry's Ct 1 IP25 ... 84 F3
Henson Cl 3 PE13 ... 152 C8
Henstead Rd NR9 ... 88 D8
Hepworth Rd IP31 ... 127 D3
Herbert Colman Cl
NR13 ... 73 E2
Herbert Dr IP26 ... 98 F5
Herbert Nursey Cl
NR8 ... 157 C7
Herbert Ward Way
PE34 ... 144 D6
Hercules Cl NR6 ... 157 F4
Hercules Rd NR6 ... 157 F4
Hereford Way PE33 ... 43 E4
Hereward Rd 1 PE13 ... 152 D5
Hereward Way
5 Feltwell IP26 ... 98 D1
Weeting IP27 ... 175 A8
Weeting-with-Broomhill
IP27 ... 114 E8
Herman Fst Sch NR31 ... 170 A3
Herman Mid Sch
NR31 ... 170 A3
Hermanus Leisure Ctr
NR29 ... 58 B6
Hermitage Cl 3 NR13 ... 166 D4
Herne Cotts NR19 ... 67 D5
Herne Dro PE14 ... 95 D5
Herne La
Beeston with Bittering
PE32 ... 48 C1
Shipdham NR19 ... 67 D5
Herolf Way 11 IP20 ... 122 D2
Heron Ave IP27 ... 175 E3
Heron Cl
Downham Market PE38 ... 172 C7
6 Fakenham NR21 ... 141 E4
Great Yarmouth NR31 ... 170 A7
Salhouse NR13 ... 55 B1
Heron Gdns NR12 ... 39 B3
Heron Rd PE13 ... 152 D2
Heron Way
Hickling NR12 ... 39 E1
12 Watton IP25 ... 84 C3
Herrick Rd NR8 ... 156 E8
Herries Cl 7 NR30 ... 169 C4
Herring La NR9 ... 69 A1
Herring's La PE31 ... 135 C4
Herringfleet Rd NR31 ... 93 E2
Hertford Way NR31 ... 170 B4
Hethel Old Thorn Nature
Reserve* NR14 ... 88 E3
Hethel Rd NR16 ... 88 D2
Hethersett High Sch
NR9 ... 88 D7
Hethersett La NR4 ... 160 F3
Hethersett Old Hall Sch
NR9 ... 88 D7
Hethersett Rd
East Carleton NR14 ... 88 F5
Great Melton NR9 ... 88 B8
Hevingham Prim Sch
NR10 ... 53 B8
Hewett Cl NR31 ... 170 D2
Hewett Rd NR31 ... 170 A8
Hewett Sch NR1 ... 162 D2
Hewitts Cl NR24 ... 142 E4
Hewitts La NR18 ... 173 C5
Hextable Rd PE30 ... 146 E6
Heydon Hall* NR11 ... 34 F6
Heydon La NR11 ... 34 E7
Heydon Rd
Aylsham NR11 ... 150 A7
Corpusty NR11 ... 34 F8
Wood Dalling NR11 ... 34 D6
Heyford Rd NR6 ... 158 C6
Heywood Ave IP22 ... 177 D6
Heywood Rd Diss IP22 ... 177 E8
Shelfanger IP22 ... 120 C2
Tibenham NR16 ... 120 D6
Winfarthing IP22 ... 120 C4
Heywood The IP22 ... 120 E5
Hickathrift Field PE14 ... 61 A4
Hickling Broad National
Nature Reserve*
NR12 ... 57 A8
Hickling Broad Visitor Ctr*
NR12 ... 40 A1
Hickling Cl PE37 ... 153 C2
Hickling Fst Sch NR12 ... 39 F2
Hickling La NR14 ... 89 D4
Hickling Rd
Sea Palling NR12 ... 24 F1
Sutton NR12 ... 39 C2
Hickling Way NR29 ... 167 B3
Hickory Gdns 18 NR31 ... 94 C7
Hickory Rd PE30 ... 147 C5
High Ash Rd NR18 ... 88 C5
High Banks NR18 ... 173 C3
High Bridgham Rd
NR16 ... 117 C5
High Bungay Rd NR14 ... 109 D8
High Comm NR18 ... 87 D2
High Comm Rd IP22 ... 128 C8
High Cross NR20 ... 33 A2
High Ct IP20 ... 122 E2
High Fen Dro IP26 ... 98 D8
High Gn Brooke NR15 ... 90 D1
Great Melton NR9 ... 88 B8
5 Great Moulton NR15 ... 106 B1
Great Moulton NR15 ... 121 B8
Norwich NR1 ... 163 B5
High Gn Gdns NR15 ... 90 D1
High Hatter's Cl PE38 ... 172 C3
High Hill Rd NR12 ... 38 F6
High House Ave
7 Wymondham NR18 ... 173 D5
3 Wymondham NR18 ... 173 D5
High House Cotts PE32 ... 47 E5
High House La 8 NR13 ... 73 D6
High House Rd NR20 ... 49 C4
High Lodge Forest Ctr*
IP27 ... 115 C3
High London La IP22 ... 120 A4
High Mill Rd NR31 ... 169 B3
High Noon La NR13 ... 73 E6
High Noon Rd NR11 ... 21 D2
High Oak La NR18 ... 87 B4
High Oak Rd NR18 ... 87 B3
High Rd Beighton NR13 ... 74 B1
Bressingham IP22 ... 129 C8
Burgh Castle NR31 ... 94 B8
Cantley NR13 ... 92 B8
Forncett NR16 ... 106 B6
Great Yarmouth NR31 ... 170 D7
Lessingham NR12 ... 24 C2
Needham IP20 ... 131 E7
Repps with Bastwick
NR29 ... 57 A4
Roydon IP22 ... 177 A5
Tilney St Lawrence PE34 ... 60 F8
Wiggenhall St Germans
PE34 ... 42 F1
Wortwell IP20 ... 123 A3
High St
Attleborough NR17 ... 174 D5
Blakeney NR25 ... 7 C6
Brandon IP27 ... 175 C5
Caister-on-Sea NR30 ... 168 E5
Castle Acre PE32 ... 46 F2
Cawston NR10 ... 35 B3
Cley next the Sea NR25 ... 7 E6
Coltishall NR12 ... 54 C7
Cromer NR27 ... 139 B7
Docking PE31 ... 134 E4
Downham Market PE38 ... 172 C5
East Dereham NR19 ... 154 D5
Feltwell IP26 ... 98 E1
Fincham PE33 ... 62 E1
Foulsham NR20 ... 33 D3
Great Yarmouth NR31 ... 170 D6
Heacham PE31 ... 133 D5
Hilgay PE38 ... 79 E1
Holt NR25 ... 137 B6
Hopton IP22 ... 127 F6
Hunstanton PE36 ... 132 C4
Ketteringham NR18 ... 88 D5
King's Lynn PE30 ... 146 D5
Lakenheath IP27 ... 113 E1
Loddon NR14 ... 92 A1
Ludham NR29 ... 56 C5
Marsham NR10 ... 150 C1
Methwold IP26 ... 99 A5
Mundesley NR11 ... 143 C5
North Elmham NR20 ... 49 E8
Northwold IP26 ... 99 C7
Overstrand NR27 ... 11 A3
Ringstead PE36 ... 2 A3
St Margaret, Ilketshall
NR35 ... 124 D3
5 Sheringham NR26 ... 138 D7
Shipdham IP25 ... 67 B2
Southrepps NR11 ... 22 B7
Stalham NR12 ... 39 B4
Stoke Ferry PE33 ... 81 A2
Sutton Bridge PE12 ... 41 C8
Thelnetham IP22 ... 128 B4
Thornham PE36 ... 2 D6
High St continued
Thursford NR21 ... 17 D5
Tittleshall PE32 ... 48 B8
Walsingham NR22 ... 16 F7
Watton IP25 ... 84 D3
Wells-next-the-Sea
NR23 ... 136 D5
Whissonsett NR20 ... 31 D2
Wicklewood NR18 ... 87 B5
Wighton NR23 ... 5 F2
Wisbech PE13 ... 152 C5
High View Dr NR17 ... 174 B4
High Way 15 NR13 ... 74 A3
High Wrong Cnr IP24 ... 115 C1
Higham Cl NR7 ... 159 A3
Higham Gn 3 PE30 ... 147 C4
Highbridge Gravel Dro
IP27 ... 113 D2
Highbridge Rd PE34 ... 78 F8
Highbury Rd IP27 ... 175 A2
Higher Gn Cl 7 NR15 ... 89 D1
Highfield 3 Eye IP23 ... 130 C1
Field Dalling NR25 ... 7 B2
Great & Little Plumstead
NR13 ... 73 B7
King's Lynn PE30 ... 147 C5
Highfield Ave NR13 ... 165 D3
Highfield Cl
Foulsham NR20 ... 33 C4
1 Norwich NR7 ... 72 D3
Ryburgh NR21 ... 32 A6
Highfield La NR21 ... 32 A6
Highfield Rd
East Dereham NR19 ... 154 D8
Fakenham NR21 ... 141 B5
Great Yarmouth NR31 ... 170 C7
Taverham NR8 ... 155 F1
Highfield Way 4 NR12 ... 54 C7
Highfields
Felmingham NR28 ... 37 A8
Lakenheath IP27 ... 113 F1
Norwich NR5 ... 156 D1
Highgate PE30 ... 146 E5
Highgate Inf Sch
PO30 ... 146 F6
Highgrove Ct NR14 ... 90 C6
Highland NR14 ... 90 B6
Highland Ave NR2 ... 162 A4
Highland Cl NR13 ... 92 C6
Highland Cres NR14 ... 163 B2
Highland Rd
Norwich NR2 ... 162 A4
Taverham NR8 ... 155 D1
Highlands
Costessey NR8 ... 156 F4
Thetford IP24 ... 176 D5
Highlow Rd NR5 ... 157 A1
Highmoor Dro IP26 ... 99 D8
Highview Cl NR13 ... 165 E6
Highview Pk NR27 ... 139 C4
Hilary Ave NR1 ... 163 B8
Hilary Cl 6 NR13 ... 74 A3
Hilda Rd NR11 ... 143 C6
Hilgay Rd Ryston PE38 ... 79 F3
West Dereham PE33 ... 80 A4
Hilgay Village Prim Sch
PE38 ... 79 E1
Hill Ave NR31 ... 170 D1
Hill Cl NR27 ... 139 C4
Hill Comm NR12 ... 39 F1
Hill Crest Rd NR7 ... 163 D7
Hill Est The PE33 ... 62 B6
Hill Farm Rd NR15 ... 106 F3
Hill Fields NR19 ... 154 C1
Hill Fort Cl IP24 ... 176 C7
Hill House La IP24 ... 176 D7
Hill House Rd
Bramerton NR14 ... 90 F8
Norwich NR1 ... 163 A5
Hill La Runhall NR20 ... 69 A4
Sculthorpe Airfield NR21 ... 15 C2
Hill Rd
Ingoldisthorpe PE31 ... 140 C8
King's Lynn PE30 ... 147 B8
Middleton PE33 ... 44 B3
Morley NR18 ... 104 D8
Norwich NR5 ... 157 A2
Tibenham NR16 ... 120 F8
Wymondham NR18 ... 105 A7
Hill Side Cl 3 PE32 ... 44 B3
Hill St 19 Feltwell IP26 ... 98 E1
Hunstanton PE36 ... 132 C4
Norwich NR2 ... 162 C4
5 Wisbech PE13 ... 152 C5
Hill The Brandon IP27 ... 175 A2
Coltishall NR12 ... 54 D7
Damgate NR13 ... 166 C2
Horsham St Faith NR10 ... 53 D1
Little Snoring NR21 ... 17 B3
Shipmeadow NR34 ... 124 F8
Westwick NR10 ... 37 D5
Woodbastwick NR13 ... 55 F1
Hill Top
Cley next the Sea NR25 ... 7 E7
Stanton IP31 ... 127 C1
Hill Top Dr NR8 ... 156 F3
Hill View Rd NR26 ... 138 E7
Hillary Rd IP24 ... 176 C2
Hill's Cl 3 Corpusty NR11 ... 19 F1
Sporle PE32 ... 65 C6
Hill's Ct PE38 ... 79 E1
Hillburn Rd PE13 ... 152 B4
Hillcrest Acle NR13 ... 166 A3
Downham Market PE38 ... 172 E5
Great Ryburgh NR21 ... 32 B6
7 Loddon NR14 ... 92 A2
Hillcrest Ave NR19 ... 154 C1
Hillcrest Prim Sch
PE38 ... 172 E6
Hillen Rd PE30 ... 146 D2
Hillfield NR12 ... 38 D3
Hillgate St PE34 ... 144 A4
Hillingdon Pk NR27 ... 11 A4
Hillings Way PE32 ... 28 A1
Hillington Sq PE30 ... 146 E4
Hillmead NR3 ... 158 D3
Hills Rd IP25 ... 84 C5
Hills The NR13 ... 92 F4
Hillsend La NR17 ... 174 A3
Hillside
Barnham Broom NR9 ... 69 B2
Barsham NR21 ... 16 D5
Brandon IP27 ... 114 D4
Briston NR24 ... 142 B4
Cromer NR27 ... 139 C4
Loddon NR14 ... 92 A2
Marham PE33 ... 63 B5
Mundesley NR11 ... 143 D5
North Pickenham PE37 ... 65 E2
Poringland NR14 ... 90 C5
Roughton NR11 ... 10 D1
Sheringham NR26 ... 138 F7
Swaffham PE37 ... 153 D4
Hillside Animal Sanctuary*
NR12 ... 54 B4
Hillside Ave NR7 ... 163 F6
Hillside Ave Prim Sch
NR7 ... 163 F6
Hillside Cl
Norwich NR7 ... 163 F6
Ormesby St Margaret
NR29 ... 167 B2
Swardeston NR14 ... 89 C5
Hillside Cres NR18 ... 87 B5
Hillside Fst Sch NR31 ... 94 C7
Hillside Rd
Horning NR12 ... 55 E3
Norwich NR7 ... 163 F6
Sheringham NR26 ... 138 F5
Hillside Rd E NR35 ... 124 B7
Hillside Rd W NR35 ... 124 A7
Hilltop Way IP31 ... 127 C1
Hillview PE37 ... 65 E2
Hillview Dr NR29 ... 58 B6
Hillvue Cl NR5 ... 157 A2
Hilly Cl IP31 ... 126 D1
Hilly Plantation NR7 ... 163 E7
Hilton Cl PE37 ... 153 C4
Hilton Ct PE13 ... 153 D4
Hiltons La 5 PE34 ... 43 B1
Hinchingbrook Cl
PE30 ... 148 E1
Hinderclay La IP22 ... 128 B5
Hinderclay Rd
Redgrave IP22 ... 128 D5
Rickinghall Inferior
IP22 ... 128 D3
Wattisfield IP22 ... 128 B1
Hindolveston Rd
Foulsham NR20 ... 33 D4
Fulmodeston NR21 ... 17 F1
Guestwick NR20 ... 33 F6
Thurning NR20 ... 34 A8
Hindringham Prim Sch
NR21 ... 17 D7
Hindringham Rd
Binham NR21 ... 6 E2
Gunthorpe NR21 ... 18 A7
Hindringham NR21 ... 17 F7
Walsingham NR22 ... 17 A8
Hingham Prim Sch
NR9 ... 86 C5
Hingham Rd
Deopham NR18 ... 86 F5
Garvestone NR9 ... 86 C8
Great Ellingham NR17 ... 103 E8
Hardingham NR9 ... 86 E6
Little Ellingham NR17 ... 86 A2
Hingley Cl NR31 ... 170 C8
Hinks Cl NR10 ... 155 C3
Hinshalwood Way
NR8 ... 156 E4
Hipkin Rd PE31 ... 140 C3
Hipperson Cl 2 NR28 ... 151 C7
Hippodrome* NR30 ... 169 E3
Hobart Cl NR18 ... 173 C6
Hobart High Sch NR14 ... 92 A1
Hobart La NR1 ... 178 B1
Hobart Sq NR1 ... 178 B1
Hobb's La NR13 ... 92 D7
Hobbies Mus of Fretwork &
Craft Ctr* NR19 ... 154 C5
Hobbs's La NR15 ... 108 D7
Hobland Rd
Belton with Browston
NR31 ... 94 C4
Bradwell NR31 ... 171 A7
Hobrough La NR1 ... 178 C2
Hockering La NR9 ... 160 B6
Hockering Prim Sch
NR20 ... 69 B8
Hockham St PE30 ... 146 D2
Hockwold Prim Sch
IP26 ... 114 A6
Hockwold Rd IP27 ... 175 B7
Hodgson Rd NR4 ... 161 F5
Hoe Hall NR20 ... 49 F3
Hoe Rd Hoe NR20 ... 49 F5
Longham NR19 ... 49 A3
Hoe Rd E NR20 ... 50 A4
Hoe Rd N NR20 ... 50 A3
Hoe Rd S NR20 ... 50 A2

Hoe Rough Nature Reserve*
NR20 .....49 E4
Hog Bog La NR10 .....53 F3
Hog La NR34 .....124 F2
Hogarth Cl 13 NR31 .....94 C8
Hogarth Rd PE38 .....172 E6
Hogg La NR35 .....108 C1
Hogg's Dro PE33 .....63 B5
Hogherd's La 9 PE13 .....152 C5
Hogsty La IP21 .....122 A1
Holbrigg La NR21 .....17 C1
Holcombe Ave PE30 .....146 F3
Holders La IP26 .....99 A7
Holgate Hill NR25 .....8 D4
Holgate La 5 NR27 .....10 B5
Holgate Rd
North Walsham NR28 .....151 F1
South Creake NR21 .....15 C7
Holkham Ave PE37 .....153 B2
Holkham Cl 7 PE38 .....172 C6
Holkham Hall & Bygones Mus* NR23 .....5 A5
Holkham National Nature Reserve* NR23 .....5 B8
Holkham Rd NR23 .....136 B6
Holl La Billingford NR20 .....50 B7
Garvestone NR9 .....68 B1
Holl Rd NR11 .....21 B4
Holland Ct 8 NR19 .....154 D1
Holland's La NR35 .....108 C3
Holley Wlk NR11 .....150 C4
Hollies The
Clenchwarton PE34 .....145 D5
5 North Walsham NR28 .....151 C5
Hollow Hill Rd NR35 .....109 A2
Hollow La
Barningham IP31 .....127 D4
4 Langham NR25 .....7 A4
Raynham NR21 .....30 F3
Shotesham NR15 .....89 F2
Hollow Way Hill NR34 .....110 D4
Holloway Rd NR14 .....91 B8
Holls La NR1 .....178 B1
Hollway La NR20 .....33 A4
Holly Ave NR31 .....94 C7
Holly Bank NR7 .....159 A2
Holly Blue Rd NR18 .....173 E4
Holly Cl Dereham NR19 .....154 F4
Downham Market PE38 .....172 B6
Holt NR25 .....137 D7
King's Lynn PE30 .....148 D2
14 Marthan NR29 .....57 D4
Mattishall NR20 .....68 E6
Rougham PE32 .....47 B7
1 West Winch PE33 .....43 E2
Holly Ct
34 Harleston IP20 .....122 D2
Swaffham PE13 .....153 C4
Wymondham NR18 .....173 E6
Holly Dr NR2 .....162 A7
Holly Farm Rd NR13 .....93 A4
Holly Gr NR26 .....138 D5
Holly La Blofield NR13 .....165 D7
Lackenheath IP27 .....113 E1
9 Tharston & Hapton NR15 .....106 D3
Wood Dalling NR11 .....34 D5
Holly Rd NR17 .....174 C4
Holly Way 13 NR31 .....170 B6
Hollybush Rd NR28 .....151 F5
Hollycroft Cl PE14 .....59 D1
Hollycroft Rd PE14 .....77 D8
Hollywell Gdns PE13 .....153 B4
Holman Cl NR11 .....150 B7
Holman Rd NR11 .....150 B6
Holman's Chase PE38 .....97 B6
Holme Cl Hopton IP22 .....127 F6
Runcton Holme PE33 .....61 D4
Holme Dunes National Nature Reserve* PE36 .....2 A8
Holme Rd PE36 .....2 A4
Holmes Cl Acle NR13 .....166 B4
Norwich NR7 .....163 D8
Holmes Dr PE13 .....152 E5
Holmes Rd
East Ruston NR12 .....38 F5
Somerton NR29 .....57 F7
Holmesdale Rd NR13 .....165 B4
Holmwood Rise NR7 .....163 C6
Holt Ct PE14 .....41 E3
Holt Ctry Pk* NR25 .....137 C4
Holt House La PE32 .....44 D5
Holt Prim Sch NR25 .....137 B5
Holt Rd Aylmerton NR11 .....10 B3
Briston NR24 .....142 E5
Cawston NR10 .....35 D2
Cley next the Sea NR25 .....7 E6
Cromer NR27 .....139 A6
Fakenham NR21 .....141 C4
Felthorpe NR10 .....52 F6
Field Dalling NR25 .....7 B2
Gresham NR11 .....9 E1
Guist NR20 .....32 F4
Hoe NR19 .....154 C8
Langham NR25 .....7 A4
Letheringsett with Glandford NR25 .....8 A1
Little Snoring NR21 .....17 C3
North Elmham NR20 .....49 E7
Norwich NR10 .....157 F8
Sheringham NR26 .....138 B5
Thornage NR25 .....18 F7
Upper Sheringham NR26 .....138 C3
Walsingham NR22 .....16 F7
Holt Rd *continued*
Weybourne NR25 .....8 E5
Holt Sta NR25 .....137 E8
Holt's La PE38 .....79 D1
Holway Cl NR27 .....139 B3
Holway Rd NR26 .....138 D5
Holway The NR29 .....58 B6
Holworthy Rd NR5 .....161 B8
Holy Rd NR24 .....18 D5
Holyrood Dr PE31 .....140 D3
Home Cl
Great Ellingham NR17 .....103 E8
Lyng NR9 .....51 A4
5 Sheringham NR27 .....10 A5
Home Farm La NR18 .....104 E8
Home Farm Rd NR35 .....109 C3
Home Farm Rise NR25 .....8 E6
Home La
Hilborough IP25 .....83 B4
Hindringham NR21 .....17 E7
Home Piece IP22 .....127 E4
Home St NR2 .....162 C8
Homebred La 1 NR14 .....91 F1
Homefield Ave NR31 .....94 C7
Homefield Fst Sch NR31 .....94 C7
Homefields La PE36 .....132 D4
Homeland Rd 10 PE30 .....146 E6
Homelea Cres 13 NR13 .....74 A3
Homestead Cl 7 NR13 .....74 A3
Homestead Gdns NR29 .....167 B7
Honey Cl 2 NR1 .....163 B7
Honey Dro PE33 .....80 B1
Honey Hill PE34 .....79 D8
Honey Hills PE31 .....14 A5
Honeycombe Rd NR13 .....73 B8
Honeymoon Loke NR30 .....168 F4
Honeymoon Row NR23 .....136 D5
Honeypot Dro PE32 .....46 C5
Honeypot La
Kirby Cane NR35 .....109 E5
Longham NR19 .....48 F2
Seething NR15 .....108 E8
Honeysuckle Cl
North Walsham NR28 .....151 E4
5 Thetford IP24 .....176 F4
Honeysuckle Dr NR20 .....154 F4
Honeysuckle Way NR17 .....174 B5
Honing Long La NR28 .....38 C7
Honing Rd NR28 .....38 D5
Honing Row NR28 .....38 A5
Honingham La NR8 .....70 A8
Honingham Rd NR9 .....69 C3
Honington Airfield IP31 .....126 A2
Honington Rise IP31 .....126 C1
Honington VC Prim Sch IP31 .....126 D1
Hood Way IP24 .....176 E5
Hook's Wlk NR1 .....178 C3
Hooker Rd NR7 .....159 D1
Hooks Hill Rd NR26 .....138 C6
Hookwood La NR18 .....104 C8
Hooper La NR3 .....158 F2
Hooton's Row PE38 .....78 F6
Hope Ct PE30 .....147 A8
Hope La PE14 .....60 A4
Hopton CE VC Prim Sch IP22 .....127 F5
Hopton Cl 6 NR7 .....72 D4
Hopton Fst Sch NR31 .....171 E4
Hopton Gdns NR31 .....171 D5
Hopton Rd
Barningham IP31 .....127 D4
Garboldisham IP22 .....128 A8
Thelnetham IP22 .....128 A5
Horizon Views NR12 .....24 A7
Hornbeam Cl
5 Great Yarmouth NR31 .....170 B6
Norwich NR7 .....159 D4
Hornbeam Dr 15 NR14 .....90 C5
Horner Cl 3 IP22 .....177 A5
Horning Cl NR5 .....161 D7
Horning Fst Sch NR12 .....55 F3
Horning Rd
Hoveton NR12 .....164 E5
Neatishead NR12 .....55 D6
Woodbastwick NR13 .....55 D2
Horning Rd W NR12 .....164 C5
Hornor Cl NR2 .....162 C3
Horns La NR1 .....178 B2
Horns Row NR21 .....141 A3
Horsbeck Way NR10 .....53 A3
Horse Fair 2 PE13 .....152 C5
Horse Rescue Ctr* NR16 .....103 C2
Horse Shoe Rd NR20 .....69 A4
Horsefen Rd NR29 .....56 D4
Horsehead Dro PE14 .....95 C8
Horses Head NR13 .....166 B7
Horseshoe Cl NR5 .....156 E1
Horse-Shoe Cnr PE13 .....152 B7
Horseshoe La NR24 .....142 F4
Horseshoe Terr PE13 .....152 B7
Horsey Rd NR29 .....57 E7
Horsey Windpump* NR29 .....40 D1
Horsey's La NR31 .....170 D5
Horsford All Saints Mid Sch NR10 .....53 B4
Horsford St 7 NR2 .....162 B8
Horsford VC Fst Sch NR10 .....53 B3
Horsham St Faith VC Fst Sch NR10 .....53 E2
Horsley Dr
Great Yarmouth NR31 .....170 B1
Hopton on Sea NR31 .....171 D4
Horsley's Chase PE30 .....146 E2
Horsley's Ct 7 PE30 .....146 E3
Horsley's Field PE30 .....146 E2
Horton Rd PE30 .....147 D6
Hospital La
Hellesdon NR6 .....157 D3
Norwich NR1 .....162 E3
Hospital Rd
Great & Little Plumstead NR13 .....73 A5
Sutton Bridge PE12 .....41 E8
Wicklewood NR18 .....87 C4
Hospital Wlk PE30 .....146 E4
Hotblack Rd NR2 .....162 A8
Hotch La PE14 .....60 B8
Hotson Cl 5 NR15 .....106 D3
Houghton Ave PE30 .....148 D1
Houghton Cl 2 NR5 .....161 B8
Houghton Hall* PE31 .....29 C7
Houghton La PE37 .....65 E1
House Gdns NR10 .....53 E5
Hovell's La IP26 .....99 C7
Hoveton & Wroxham Sta NR12 .....164 C5
Hoveton Cl PE30 .....147 D5
Hoveton Dr PE37 .....153 C1
Hoveton Hall Gdns* NR12 .....55 B7
Hoveton Pl NR10 .....37 B2
How Hill Nature Reserve* NR29 .....56 A6
How Hill Rd NR29 .....56 B6
Howard Cl
Harleston IP20 .....122 E2
Norwich NR7 .....163 D7
4 Swanton Morley NR20 .....50 B3
Terrington St Clement PE34 .....144 B4
Howard Cres NR19 .....154 D4
Howard Inf Sch PE30 .....147 B4
Howard Jun Sch PE30 .....147 B4
Howard Mews NR3 .....158 E1
Howard St NR1 .....178 A1
Howard St N 9 NR30 .....169 C4
Howard St S NR30 .....169 C4
Howard Way NR11 .....150 C5
Howard's Hill NR27 .....139 A7
Howard's Hill Rd NR28 .....38 C7
Howard's Way NR10 .....35 B2
Howards Cl PE36 .....132 E7
Howards Hill Cl NR27 .....10 C5
Howards Hill W 1 NR27 .....139 A7
Howards The PE30 .....148 D4
Howdale Rd PE38 .....172 C5
Howdale Rise PE38 .....172 D5
Howe Gn NR15 .....90 D2
Howe La NR15 .....90 D3
Howe Rd NR30 .....169 D7
Howell Rd NR8 .....157 C6
Howes Cl 10 NR9 .....88 D7
Howes La NR20 .....68 D6
Howes Yd 1 NR25 .....7 E6
Howland Cl NR21 .....141 B5
Howlett Cl
4 East Dereham NR19 .....154 D3
North Walsham NR28 .....151 A5
Howlett Dr NR5 .....161 A8
Howlett Way 2 IP24 .....176 D6
Howletts Hill PE13 .....152 C4
Hoxne Rd Denham IP21 .....131 B1
Eye IP23 .....130 E1
Syleham IP21 .....131 C4
Upper Weybread IP21 .....131 E6
Hubbard Cl
11 Long Stratton NR15 .....106 E3
Wymondham NR18 .....173 A6
Hubbard's Dro PE38 .....79 E1
Hudson Leisure Ctr PE13 .....152 A5
Hudson Way NR5 .....160 E7
Hugh Cl PE30 .....148 C5
Hughenden Rd NR1 .....162 E3
Hughes Ct 13 NR9 .....88 D8
Hulton Rd PE30 .....147 A5
Hulver Rd NR13 .....73 E8
Hulver St NR19 .....66 F6
Humber Cl NR30 .....168 C5
Humber Keel NR31 .....170 D1
Humberstone Rd 3 NR31 .....170 C7
Humbletoft Rd NR19 .....154 C7
Humbleyard NR5 .....161 A7
Hungate La NR11 .....150 C4
Hungate Rd PE14 .....59 E2
Hungate St NR11 .....150 C5
Hungry Hill NR27 .....11 B2
Hunstanton Commercial Pk PE36 .....132 D3
Hunstanton Inf Sch PE36 .....132 D4
Hunstanton Rd
Dersingham PE31 .....140 D5
Heacham PE31 .....132 D1
Hunstanton Sea Life Sanctuary* PE36 .....132 B3
Hunstead La NR15 .....90 F2
Hunt Cl Old Catton NR6 .....158 E7
5 Redenhall with Harleston IP20 .....122 D2
Hunter Ave NR20 .....68 F5
Hunter Dr 4 NR31 .....94 C8
Hunter Rd
Norwich NR3 .....158 C3
Troston IP31 .....126 B1
Hunter's Dro PE14 .....60 B6
Hunters Cl
Brundall NR13 .....165 F5
Terrington St Clement PE34 .....144 F6
Hunters Oak 2 IP25 .....84 E3
Huntley Cres NR26 .....138 E6
Hunts Gn NR16 .....105 B4
Hunworth Rd NR24 .....142 D8
Hurd Rd NR4 .....161 E3
Hurdle La NR25 .....7 E4
Hurn La NR16 .....106 A6
Hurn Rd Dereham NR20 .....68 A7
Taverham NR8 .....157 C7
Hurrell Rd NR30 .....168 D6
Hurricane Way NR6 .....158 C6
Hurst Rd 8 NR14 .....92 A2
Hurth Way IP24 .....176 E4
Husenbeth Cl NR8 .....156 E4
Hutchinson Rd NR5 .....161 D6
Huxley Cl NR1 .....162 F2
Huxley Rd NR1 .....162 F2
Hyde Cl PE31 .....14 D4
Hyde Ct NR13 .....72 E5
Hyde Rd NR19 .....154 D3
Hypocrite La NR17 .....174 A2
Hyrn Cl NR29 .....57 D4
Hythe Rd Feltwell IP26 .....98 E3
Foulden IP26 .....82 A1
Methwold IP26 .....98 F5

I

Ice House Ct 17 NR15 .....106 E3
Ice House La NR1 .....178 C1
Iceni Dr PE37 .....153 D2
Icknield Cl IP24 .....176 B3
Icknield Way IP24 .....176 B3
Ickworth Cl PE30 .....148 E1
Ilex Ct NR7 .....159 D4
Illington Rd IP24 .....117 C8
ILPH Hall Farm* NR16 .....118 B7
Impala Cl NR6 .....159 A6
Imperial Mews NR31 .....171 C4
Impson Way IP26 .....100 A4
Incleborough Cl 2 NR27 .....10 B5
Independent Way 14 NR7 .....72 D4
Indigo Yd NR3 .....178 A3
Ingham Cnr NR12 .....24 D1
Ingham Rd
Lessingham NR12 .....24 D2
Stalham NR12 .....39 B4
Ingle Rd PE14 .....59 B1
Ingleby Cl
Heacham PE31 .....133 E6
King's Lynn PE30 .....147 B4
Ingloss La NR14 .....109 B7
Ingoldale PE31 .....140 C8
Ingoldisthorpe Fst Sch PE31 .....140 E8
Ingoldsby Ave PE31 .....140 C6
Ingolside PE31 .....12 D4
Ingram Ct NR1 .....162 E3
Ingram's Rd IP21 .....131 C7
Inman Rd NR7 .....159 D4
Inspire Discovery Ctr* NR3 .....178 A4
Intwood La
East Carleton NR14 .....89 A5
Swardeston NR14 .....89 C6
Intwood Rd NR4 .....89 B8
Invaders Ct NR23 .....136 D6
Ipswich Gr NR2 .....178 A1
Ipswich Rd
2 Norwich NR4 .....89 E8
Norwich NR2 .....178 A1
Pulham Market NR15 .....121 E8
Saxlingham Nethergate NR15 .....107 A7
Scole IP21 .....130 D5
Yaxley IP23 .....130 A1
Ireton Cl 25 NR7 .....72 D4
Iris Cl NR17 .....174 B5
Irmingland Rd NR11 .....34 F8
Ironside Way NR9 .....86 D5
Irstead Rd
Barton Turf NR12 .....55 F7
Norwich NR5 .....161 E6
Irving Rd NR4 .....162 C1
Irwin Cl NR10 .....149 C5
Isaac's Rd NR31 .....169 B4
Isabella Cl PE30 .....147 D3
Isabella Sq 12 NR30 .....169 D3
Isbets Dale NR8 .....155 D2
Isis Cl NR31 .....170 B3
Isle Bridge Rd PE14 .....77 E6
Isle Rd PE14 .....77 F7
Iveagh Cl PE31 .....140 E2
Ives Cl IP22 .....177 E4
Ives Rd NR6 .....158 D5
Ivory Rd NR4 .....161 E4
Ivy Gn 6 NR31 .....170 B5
Ivy Rd Earlham NR5 .....161 E7
3 Spixworth NR10 .....54 A2
Ivy Todd Rd PE37 .....66 B4
Ivy Way NR20 .....68 E6
Ixworth Rd IP31 .....126 D1

J

Jack Plummer Way NR30 .....168 C7
Jaguar Rd 9 NR9 .....88 D8
James Bradfield Prim Sch PE33 .....81 A2
James Cl PE30 .....148 B1
James Gn Cl 14 NR10 .....54 A2
James Jackson Rd PE31 .....140 C3
James Paget Hospl NR31 .....170 B1
James Rd 7 NR12 .....55 E4
James Scott Cl 3 PE38 .....172 A5
James St PE36 .....132 D4
James Watt Cl NR31 .....170 A8
Jamieson Pl NR5 .....161 C8
Jane Forby Cl PE33 .....80 E2
Jankin La PE34 .....144 A1
Jannys Cl NR11 .....150 B6
Jarrold Cl IP31 .....127 D3
Jarrold Way NR5 .....160 F8
Jarvie Cl PE36 .....13 A7
Jarvis Dr NR21 .....31 E5
Jarvis Rd PE30 .....146 E8
Jasmin Cl PE13 .....152 F7
Jasmine Cl
Earlham NR4 .....161 E5
Thetford IP24 .....176 F4
Jasmine Ct 1 NR17 .....174 B5
Jasmine Gdns 7 NR31 .....94 C7
Jasmine Gn 7 NR31 .....170 B5
Javelin Rd NR6 .....158 C7
Jay Gdns NR5 .....160 E8
Jay La NR32 .....171 C3
Jay's Gn IP20 .....122 E2
Jefferey Ave 4 PE13 .....152 E7
Jeffery Cl PE30 .....146 E8
Jegon Cl NR11 .....150 D5
Jellicoe Pl 6 IP24 .....176 E5
Jellicoe Rd NR30 .....169 C8
Jenkinsons Pightle NR35 .....108 B4
Jenner Rd 4 NR31 .....170 B1
Jennings Cl PE31 .....133 C5
Jennings Way IP22 .....177 D5
Jenny Rd 8 NR10 .....54 A2
Jermyn Rd PE30 .....147 C6
Jermyn Way 1 NR15 .....106 D3
Jerningham Rd NR5 .....157 A1
Jessopp Cl
Norwich NR2 .....161 F4
Scarning NR19 .....67 B7
Jessopp Rd NR4 .....161 F4
Jetty Cl NR27 .....139 B7
Jetty Cliff NR27 .....139 C7
Jetty St 2 NR27 .....139 B7
Jewel Cl NR24 .....142 B4
Jews' La 10 NR31 .....94 C6
Jewson Rd NR3 .....158 C2
Jex Ave NR5 .....161 D8
Jex La NR5 .....161 D8
Jex Rd NR5 .....161 D8
Jickling Yd NR23 .....136 D6
Joan Short's La PE31 .....135 D3
Jocelyn Cl IP21 .....121 E5
Joe Ellis Ct 6 NR5 .....161 B8
John Bates Cl 2 NR19 .....154 E5
John Chapman Cl 5 NR21 .....141 E4
John Davis Way PE33 .....61 D5
John Drewry Cl 2 NR14 .....90 D5
John F Kennedy Ct 2 PE13 .....152 D4
John Gale Ct NR8 .....155 E3
John Goshawk Rd NR19 .....154 E2
John Grant Specl Sch NR30 .....168 D6
John Hill Cl 6 NR15 .....106 E3
John Jarrod Printing Mus* NR1 .....178 C4
John Kennedy Rd PE30 .....146 D6
John of Gaunt Fst Sch NR11 .....150 C5
John O'Gaunt Cl NR11 .....150 B6
John Rd
Caister-on-Sea NR30 .....168 E7
Great Yarmouth NR31 .....170 D5
John St 3 PE30 .....146 E3
John Stephenson Ct 1 NR6 .....158 F1
John Thompson Rd 3 PE13 .....152 D4
John Woodhouse Dr NR30 .....168 C7
Johnson Cl 7 NR19 .....154 C3
Johnson Cres PE31 .....133 C4
Johnson Pl NR2 .....162 C5
Jolly Gardeners Ct 13 NR3 .....162 D8
Jolly Sailor Yd NR23 .....136 D6
Jolly's La NR13 .....166 A2
Jones (GC) Way NR31 .....169 B2
Jones's Dro PE14 .....95 E8
Jordan Cl Norwich NR5 .....161 B6
Taverham NR8 .....155 E4
Jordan La NR10 .....51 A8
Jordan Rd NR30 .....168 E6
Jose Neville Cl 2 NR30 .....168 D7
Joseph Lancaster Way 4 NR3 .....178 B4
Josephine Cl NR1 .....162 D3
Joshua Ct NR31 .....171 D8
Joy Ave 1 NR15 .....107 A8

Joy - Law 197

Joyce La
Heacham PE31 ...133 D5
Walpole PE14 ...41 F3
Joyce Rd NR35 ...124 B8
Joyce Way 9 NR7 ...72 D5
Joyland* NR30 ...169 E4
Jubilee Ave
4 East Dereham NR20 ...154 E6
East Harling NR16 ...118 C5
Fakenham NR21 ...141 C4
Heacham PE31 ...133 B5
Jubilee Bank Rd PE34 ...146 A5
Jubilee Cl Cawston NR10 ...35 B2
Downham Market PE38 ...172 E5
Erpingham NR11 ...21 B2
Hunstanton PE36 ...132 C3
Repps with Bastwick NR29 ...57 A4
Thetford IP24 ...176 B3
Weeting IP27 ...175 B7
Jubilee Ct 7 PE30 ...146 D4
Jubilee Dr
Dersingham PE31 ...140 C5
Sheringham NR26 ...138 E6
Jubilee Gdns 7 PE31 ...12 E4
Jubilee Hall La 2 PE32 ...45 C6
Jubilee La NR27 ...139 C4
Jubilee Rd
Heacham PE31 ...133 A5
Holt NR25 ...137 B6
Lackenheath IP27 ...113 E2
Watton IP25 ...84 D3
Jubilee Rise PE33 ...61 D3
Jubilee Terr
Caister-on-Sea NR30 ...168 E4
Cromer NR27 ...139 D4
Norwich NR1 ...162 F3
Jubilee Way 11 PE37 ...65 F4
Jubilee Wlk PE13 ...152 D8
Judas La IP23 ...129 F1
Judges Dr NR4 ...161 F2
Judges Gdns NR8 ...155 E2
Judges Wlk NR4 ...161 F2
Juler Cl 4 NR28 ...151 C6
Julian Hospl NR2 ...161 F6
Julian Rd
King's Lynn PE30 ...148 C5
6 Spixworth NR10 ...54 A2
Julian Way NR31 ...171 D5
Julians Way IP21 ...121 E5
Junction Rd NR3 ...158 C1
Juniper Cl 2 IP24 ...176 F4
Juniper Gr NR26 ...138 E5
Juniper Way NR8 ...155 B2
Jupiter Rd NR6 ...158 C4
Jury St NR30 ...169 D4

K

Kabin Rd NR5 ...157 B2
Kalmia Gn 3 NR31 ...170 B6
Karen Cl
15 Hethersett NR9 ...88 C7
Scole IP21 ...130 C5
Keable Cl 7 NR5 ...161 C6
Keats Cl
Downham Market PE38 ...172 D5
East Dereham NR19 ...154 C7
2 Thetford IP24 ...176 E6
Keats Rd NR8 ...156 D8
Keble Cl PE30 ...148 B4
Keble Rd NR31 ...170 B3
Kedleston Dr 10 NR4 ...89 B8
Keel Cl 12 NR33 ...111 F1
Keelan Cl NR6 ...158 B4
Keeling Hall La NR20 ...33 E3
Keeling Way NR17 ...174 B3
Keene Rd PE30 ...146 D1
Keepers Rd NR15 ...89 F1
Keepham Rd NR20 ...33 F2
Keillers Cl PE13 ...152 A7
Keith Rd 9 NR20 ...50 B3
Kell's Acres NR34 ...109 F3
Kell's Way NR34 ...109 F2
Kelling Cl NR25 ...137 C7
Kelling Heath Pk Sta NR25 ...8 E4
Kelling Hospl NR25 ...137 F8
Kelling Prim Sch NR25 ...8 D6
Kelling Rd NR25 ...137 C7
Kelsey Cl PE36 ...132 D7
Kelvin Pl IP24 ...176 A1
Kemp Dr NR19 ...154 C5
Kemp's Cl PE38 ...79 A4
Kemp's Rd IP21 ...122 A5
Kempe Cl NR7 ...159 C1
Kempe Rd PE34 ...146 C5
Kenan Dr NR17 ...174 F7
Kendal Cl 15 NR9 ...88 D8
Kendall Cl NR28 ...151 B6
Kendle Way PE30 ...147 E8
Kenhill Cl 2 PE31 ...12 E5
Kenlan Rd PE13 ...152 D6
Kennedy Ave NR31 ...170 C1
Kennedy Cl
East Dereham NR19 ...154 D1
Easton NR9 ...70 B5
Kennel Loke NR31 ...171 D8
Kennett Cl NR4 ...161 F4
Kenninghall Prim Sch NR16 ...119 A4
Kenninghall Rd
Banham NR16 ...119 B6
Harling NR16 ...118 E4
Kenninghall NR16 ...119 A3
Kenside Rd 1 PE31 ...12 E5
Kensington Cl NR15 ...107 C8
Kensington Pl NR1 ...178 B1
Kensington Rd
Downham Market PE38 ...172 B4
King's Lynn PE30 ...147 B6
Kent Ave NR31 ...170 C3
Kent Cl
Attleborough NR17 ...174 B3
2 Sutton Bridge PE12 ...41 B8
Kent Rd PE30 ...147 B6
Kent Sq NR30 ...169 D3
Kenwood Rd PE31 ...133 D5
Kenwood Rd S PE31 ...133 D5
Kenwyn Cl NR25 ...137 C7
Kenyon Row NR34 ...110 C2
Keppel Cl PE32 ...48 A5
Keppel Rd 2 NR31 ...170 D4
Kerdiston Rd
Reepham NR10 ...149 A6
Themelthorpe NR20 ...33 F2
Kered Cl NR6 ...157 F6
Kered Rd NR6 ...157 F6
Kerrich Cl PE31 ...140 C3
Kerridge Ct NR25 ...137 B6
Kerridge Way
29 Harleston IP20 ...122 D2
Holt NR25 ...137 B6
Kerridges NR16 ...118 C4
Kerridges The NR5 ...156 F1
Kerrison Rd NR1 ...163 A4
Kerville St 3 NR5 ...161 A7
Kestrel Ave PE38 ...172 C7
Kestrel Cl
Burnham Market PE31 ...135 D1
Great Yarmouth NR31 ...170 A7
Mulbarton NR14 ...89 A3
Swaffham PE37 ...153 C2
Thetford IP24 ...176 D1
Kestrel Dr
Brandon IP27 ...175 F3
2 Wisbech PE14 ...152 D2
Kestrel Rd NR7 ...159 C4
Keswick PE30 ...147 D5
Keswick Cl NR4 ...89 B8
Keswick Rd Bacton NR12 ...23 F4
Cringleford NR4 ...89 B8
Kett Sixth Form Ctr NR7 ...159 C2
Kett's Ave NR18 ...173 C5
Kett's Cl
3 Hethersett NR9 ...88 D7
Wymondham NR18 ...173 C5
Kett's Hill NR1 ...163 A7
Kett's La NR9 ...52 A6
Kett's Oak NR9 ...88 C6
Ketteringham La NR9 ...88 D6
Ketteringham Pk NR18 ...88 E6
Ketteringham Rd NR18 ...173 F3
Kettlestone Rd NR21 ...17 B3
Kettlewell La 1 PE30 ...146 E5
Ketts Hill PE37 ...66 A4
Ketts Rd NR28 ...151 B4
Kevill Davis Dr NR13 ...73 A5
Kevin Wlk NR19 ...154 D2
Kew Rd PE38 ...172 B4
Key & Castle Yd NR3 ...178 A4
Keyes Ave NR30 ...169 D7
Keyes Cl 5 NR1 ...162 E2
Keyes Rd NR1 ...162 E2
Keys Dr NR12 ...164 B2
Keys Farm 4 NR20 ...68 F6
Keys The NR15 ...90 F2
Kilderkin Cl PE14 ...77 A7
Kilham's Way
King's Lynn PE30 ...146 E7
North Wootton PE30 ...26 E1
Kiln Cl NR6 ...158 E7
Kiln Farm La IP22 ...128 E1
Kiln La
Dickleburgh & Rushall IP21 ...130 F6
Needham IP20 ...131 D8
Kiln Rd 5 NR10 ...53 A3
Kilverstone Rd IP24 ...117 A2
Kimberley Pk Sta NR18 ...87 A6
Kimberley Rd NR28 ...151 D5
Kimberley St
1 Norwich NR2 ...162 C5
Wymondham NR18 ...173 C4
Kimberley Terr NR30 ...169 E2
Kimms Belt IP24 ...176 B2
Kinderley Rd PE13 ...152 C8
King Edward VII Sch PE30 ...147 A5
King George Cl 3 NR29 ...57 D2
King George Rd NR21 ...31 C7
King George V Ave PE30 ...146 F5
King George VI Sch PE31 ...14 A3
King George's Ave 2 NR29 ...57 D2
King John Ave PE30 ...147 A5
King John Bank PE14 ...41 C5
King of Hearts Ctr* NR1 ...178 B4
King St
East Harling NR16 ...118 C5
Great Yarmouth NR30 ...169 C4
King's Lynn PE30 ...146 D5
Neatishead NR12 ...55 E7
Norwich NR1 ...178 C1
13 Sutton Bridge PE12 ...41 B8
Swaffham PE37 ...153 B4
Thetford IP24 ...176 C4
Winterton-on-Sea NR29 ...58 B6
Wisbech PE13 ...152 C5
King William Cl PE34 ...144 C5
Kingcup PE30 ...148 A1
Kingfisher Cl
8 Fakenham NR21 ...141 E4
7 Fakenham NR21 ...141 E4
Great Yarmouth NR31 ...94 C7
Thetford IP24 ...176 D1
Kingfisher Dr
Brandon IP27 ...175 E3
Necton PE37 ...66 A3
6 Wisbech PE14 ...152 D2
Kingfisher Rd
Attleborough NR17 ...174 F6
Downham Market PE38 ...172 C7
Kingfisher Way 11 IP25 ...84 C3
Kinghorn Rd NR2 ...161 F4
King's Arms St NR28 ...151 C5
King's Ave Anmer PE31 ...28 C8
King's Lynn PE30 ...147 A3
Kings Croft PE31 ...140 E4
Kings Ct NR29 ...167 A8
King's Dam NR34 ...110 B2
Kings Gn 6 PE30 ...147 C4
Kings Head La
Deopham NR18 ...87 A5
North Lopham IP22 ...119 A2
Kings La NR1 ...178 B1
Kings Loke NR29 ...167 B8
King's Lynn Arts Ctr (Guildhall)* PE30 ...146 D5
King's Lynn Rd PE36 ...132 D4
King's Lynn Sports Ctr PE30 ...146 F5
King's Lynn Sta PE30 ...146 E5
King's Pk NR19 ...154 E6
Kings Pk Fst Sch NR19 ...154 E6
Kings Rd Bungay NR35 ...124 B7
East Dereham NR19 ...154 E6
Fakenham NR21 ...141 A5
King's Rd
Great Yarmouth NR30 ...169 D2
Holt NR25 ...137 C5
Kings Rd PE36 ...132 D6
King's Rd NR35 ...108 A4
Kings Rd PE13 ...152 C4
Kings St NR24 ...19 A6
King's Staithe La 2 PE30 ...146 D4
King's Staithe Sq 1 PE30 ...146 D4
Kings Way NR29 ...167 B7
King's Wk 4 PE13 ...152 C4
Kings Wlk
Downham Market PE38 ...172 C5
9 Great Yarmouth NR31 ...170 B5
Kingsdale 16 NR13 ...74 A3
Kingsleigh Cl NR28 ...22 E5
Kingsley Ave PE13 ...152 B4
Kingsley Rd NR1 ...178 A1
Kingston Ave NR30 ...168 E5
Kingston Rd NR19 ...154 F3
Kingston Sq NR4 ...162 A3
Kingsway 7 Blakeney NR25 ...7 C6
4 Earsham NR35 ...123 F8
King's Lynn PE30 ...146 E8
Leverington PE13 ...152 F7
3 Newton Flotman NR15 ...107 A8
North Walsham NR28 ...151 A6
Norwich NR2 ...162 C8
Thetford IP24 ...176 C2
Kingswood Ave NR8 ...155 C2
Kingswood Cl
Brooke NR15 ...90 E1
9 Norwich NR4 ...89 C8
Kingswood Ct NR8 ...155 D2
Kingswood Pk PE13 ...152 D3
Kinsale Ave NR6 ...157 E5
Kinsale Ave Fst & Mid Sch NR6 ...157 E4
Kinver Cl NR4 ...162 B3
Kipling Cl NR30 ...168 D6
Kirby Cl 5 NR29 ...57 D5
Kirby Rd Bixley NR14 ...90 C8
Norwich NR14 ...163 C2
Kirby St PE30 ...146 E5
Kirk Rd 2 PE14 ...41 D4
Kirkgate La NR23 ...6 A2
Kirkgate St
Holme next the Sea PE36 ...2 A6
Wisbech PE13 ...152 E7
Kirkham's La PE14 ...77 C8
Kirkhams Mdw NR19 ...66 C7
Kirklands NR8 ...156 E4
Kirklees 6 NR4 ...89 E8
Kirkpatrick Rd NR3 ...158 B2
Kirkstone Gr 2 PE30 ...148 F1
Kirkstead PE30 ...147 D5
Kirkstead Gn NR15 ...108 C8
Kirkstead Ling NR15 ...91 A1
Kirtons Cl 3 PE14 ...41 E4
Kitchener Rd
Great Yarmouth NR30 ...169 D5
Melton Constable NR24 ...142 B5
Kitchener St PE30 ...146 D2
Kitlings Beck Rd NR28 ...38 A7
Kittel Cl 24 IP25 ...84 D3
Kittens La NR14 ...91 F1
Kittiwake Cl 12 NR31 ...94 C8
Kittles La NR10 ...150 A1
Kittles Rd NR13 ...74 D1
Knappers Way IP27 ...175 D3
Knapton Rd
Knapton NR28 ...22 F3
Mundesley NR11 ...143 B4
Trunch NR28 ...22 E5
Knevet Cl NR17 ...174 F6
Knight St NR22 ...16 F7
Knight's La NR15 ...89 E2
Knights Gn NR26 ...138 C5
Knights Rd NR3 ...158 B2
Knipe Cl 2 NR16 ...105 F5
Knitting Needle La NR23 ...136 E6
Knowland Gr NR5 ...161 C8
Knowland Gr Fst Sch NR5 ...161 C8
Knowle Cres NR26 ...138 E5
Knowle Rd NR26 ...138 E6
Knowles' La NR12 ...38 C2
Knowsley Rd NR3 ...162 E8
Knox Ave NR1 ...163 B8
Knox Cl NR1 ...163 B8
Knox Rd NR1 ...163 B7
Knudsen Cl 4 NR15 ...107 C5
Knyvett Gn NR16 ...105 F8
Koblenz Ave NR1 ...178 C1
Kooreman Ave PE13 ...152 D7
Krons The NR15 ...107 C5

L

Laburnum Rd NR28 ...151 B4
Laburnum Ave
2 Marham PE33 ...63 B4
Taverham NR8 ...155 B1
Laburnum Cl
8 Great Yarmouth NR31 ...94 C7
2 Horsford NR10 ...53 A3
5 Wisbech PE13 ...152 E7
Laburnum Cres NR19 ...154 E1
Laburnum Dr NR13 ...165 F6
Laburnum Gr
Reepham NR10 ...149 C6
Sheringham NR26 ...138 D4
Thetford IP24 ...176 B1
Laburnum Wlk IP27 ...175 E2
Lacey Cl 6 PE33 ...61 D6
Lacey Rd NR8 ...155 D1
Lackford Cl NR13 ...165 C4
Lacon Rd NR30 ...168 E5
Ladbroke Pl NR1 ...163 A7
Ladbrooke Cl 3 IP22 ...177 C4
Laddus Bank PE14 ...77 A6
Laddus Dro PE14 ...77 B6
Ladislaw Way 1 NR19 ...154 C3
Lady Ann's Rd NR23 ...5 B7
Lady Betty Rd NR1 ...162 D3
Lady Dro PE38 ...79 A6
Lady Hamilton La NR29 ...167 C6
Lady Haven Mews 12 NR31 ...169 C5
Lady Haven Rd 6 NR31 ...169 B4
Lady Jane Grey Rd PE30 ...146 F7
Lady La NR10 ...53 E5
Lady Margaret's Ave NR31 ...170 B4
Lady Mary Rd NR1 ...162 D3
Lady's Dro 1 PE14 ...59 D2
Lady's La
Bressingham IP22 ...119 F1
Wymondham NR18 ...173 A3
Ladywood Cl 9 PE33 ...63 B4
Ladywood Rd PE33 ...63 B4
Lake Ave PE14 ...95 C7
Lake Ct PE13 ...152 D4
Lake Dro PE34 ...61 C1
Lake View Cl NR9 ...51 D5
Lake View Dr NR13 ...165 B4
Lakeland 3 IP26 ...114 A7
Lakeland Way 1 NR9 ...88 E8
Lakenfields NR1 ...162 F2
Lakenham Fst Sch NR1 ...162 E3
Lakenham Mid Sch NR1 ...162 F3
Lakenham Rd NR4 ...162 C2
Lakenham Way NR1 ...162 E3
Lakenheath Airfield IP27 ...114 B1
Lakenheath Prim Sch IP27 ...113 E1
Lakenheath Sta IP27 ...113 F5
Lakes Ave NR14 ...89 B3
Lamb La NR21 ...31 C7
Lambert Cl 1 IP27 ...114 E1
Lambert Rd NR7 ...159 A3
Lambert's La PE32 ...30 D1
Lamberts Cl 20 IP26 ...98 E1
Lammas Rd 3 NR15 ...106 F6
Lammas The IP26 ...100 A4
Lamport Ct 3 PE30 ...147 D6
Lamsey La PE31 ...133 D3
Lancaster Ave NR21 ...141 C5
Lancaster Cl
Fakenham NR21 ...141 C5
Methwold IP26 ...99 A5
Norwich NR6 ...158 D6
7 Stalham NR12 ...39 B4
Lancaster Cres PE38 ...172 D6
Lancaster Gdns NR11 ...150 D5
Lancaster Pl 11 PE31 ...12 E5
Lancaster Rd
4 Feltwell IP26 ...98 E1
Great Yarmouth NR30 ...169 D3
King's Lynn PE30 ...147 B4
Sculthorpe Airfield NR21 ...15 C3
Lancaster Rise NR11 ...22 F8
Lancaster Sq 13 NR30 ...169 D3
Lancaster Way PE32 ...44 F3
Lanchester Ct 7 NR2 ...162 B7
Landlow La NR9 ...70 B1
Lane The Briston NR24 ...142 D4
Carleton St Peter NR14 ...91 E5
Lane The *continued*
Little Barningham NR11 ...20 C4
Winterton-on-Sea NR29 ...58 B6
Lang Gate Way NR35 ...108 D2
Langham Ct
Fakenham NR21 ...141 D4
Sheringham NR26 ...138 C7
Langham Glass & Rural Crafts* NR25 ...7 A4
Langham Gn NR13 ...165 E4
Langham La NR25 ...7 C3
Langham Pl NR1 ...178 A1
Langham Rd
Binham NR21 ...6 E2
Blakeney NR25 ...7 C6
Field Dalling NR25 ...7 A2
Morston NR25 ...7 A6
Langham St PE30 ...146 D2
Langhorn's La PE14 ...78 A7
Langland PE30 ...147 D6
Langley Abbey NR14 ...92 A6
Langley Cl 6 NR4 ...89 B8
Langley Gn NR14 ...91 F6
Langley Prep Sch NR7 ...163 D6
Langley Rd
Cantley NR13 ...92 C6
Chedgrave NR14 ...91 F3
King's Lynn PE30 ...147 E8
Loddon NR14 ...92 A2
Langley Sch NR14 ...91 F3
Langley St NR14 ...92 A4
Langley Wlk NR2 ...162 C7
Langmere Rd
Scole IP21 ...130 F8
1 Watton IP25 ...84 C3
Langton Cl 5 NR5 ...161 B7
Lansdowne Cl 10 PE32 ...45 C6
Lansdowne Rd NR6 ...158 B6
Lansdowne St 4 PE30 ...146 E6
Lantern La NR12 ...24 B5
Lapwing Cl 3 NR31 ...170 A6
Larch Cl
Attleborough NR17 ...174 C4
King's Lynn PE30 ...148 D2
Norwich NR7 ...159 D4
Larch Cres NR25 ...137 C7
Larch Dr
18 Great Yarmouth NR31 ...94 C7
2 Great Yarmouth NR31 ...170 A5
Larch Gr NR20 ...49 E7
Larch Rd PE34 ...43 D4
Lark Cl IP27 ...175 F3
Lark Rd 2 PE33 ...61 D6
Lark Rise NR14 ...89 A3
Lark Way NR31 ...94 C7
Larkey's La NR12 ...38 F7
Larkman Fst Sch NR5 ...161 D7
Larkman La NR5 ...161 C7
Larkman Mid Sch NR5 ...161 D7
Larksfield PE13 ...152 C3
Larkspur Cl PE38 ...172 C3
Larkspur Ct 8 NR19 ...154 D2
Larner's Drift NR19 ...154 D1
Larners Rd NR19 ...154 D2
Larwood Cl 1 PE37 ...66 A4
Larwood Way 6 IP25 ...67 C2
Latchmoor La NR29 ...56 D5
Latchmoor Pk NR29 ...56 D5
Lathes The NR3 ...178 A4
Latimer Rd NR1 ...162 E1
Latimer Way PE37 ...65 E1
Laud Cl 24 NR7 ...72 D4
Laughing Image Cnr 6 NR30 ...169 C5
Launditch Cres PE38 ...172 C6
Laundry Cl 3 NR7 ...163 E7
Laundry La Blofield NR13 ...73 B6
Norwich NR7 ...163 F7
Laundry Loke NR28 ...151 B6
Laurel Dr
Brundall NR13 ...165 B3
Great Yarmouth NR31 ...94 C7
Laurel Gr 3 PE33 ...43 E2
Laurel Rd NR7 ...159 E1
Laurels Cres 1 NR29 ...56 C5
Laurels Rd NR29 ...56 D7
Laurels The NR31 ...171 D5
Lavender Cl
Attleborough NR17 ...174 B5
Brandon IP27 ...175 A2
Heacham PE31 ...133 E5
Horsford NR10 ...53 A4
Lavender Ct
12 Hemsby NR29 ...58 B6
5 King's Lynn PE30 ...147 B6
1 Thetford IP24 ...176 F4
Lavender Dr PE38 ...172 D6
Lavender Gr NR19 ...154 D2
Lavender Rd PE30 ...147 B6
Lavengro Rd NR3 ...163 A8
Lawn Ave NR30 ...169 C6
Lawn Cl 11 Horsford NR10 ...53 B3
Knapton NR28 ...143 B1
Lawn Cres 6 NR13 ...72 E6
Lawn's La
Belton with Browston NR31 ...94 A5
Fleggburgh NR29 ...57 B2
Lawns The
Fakenham NR21 ...141 C4
Great Yarmouth NR30 ...169 C7
Wisbech PE13 ...152 B6
Lawnswood Dr NR30 ...168 D6

Lawrence Cl
Fakenham NR21 141 B5
Harpley PE31 29 D4
Lawrence Pl NR20 50 D8
Lawrence Rd
King's Lynn PE30 146 E7
7 Thetford IP24 176 F5
Lawrence Way PE37 153 A5
Lawrence's La PE38 79 E1
Lawson Rd
Croxton IP24 116 C5
Norwich NR3 158 E1
Lawson Way NR26 138 F7
Lawyer Corys NR31 170 C1
Laxfield Rd NR12 39 C3
Laxton Cl NR17 174 E4
Layer Cl
5 Aylsham NR11 150 D6
Norwich NR5 160 F7
Laylands Yd NR23 136 C6
Layton Cl NR8 157 B7
Le Neve Rd NR10 150 D1
Le Strange Ave PE30 146 F7
Le Strange Cl NR2 161 F5
Le Tunder Cl 2 NR7 163 E7
Lea Rd 2 NR29 56 C8
Lea The NR30 169 C6
Lea Way PE30 147 B8
Leach Cl
Great Yarmouth NR31 170 A4
Wisbech PE13 152 C2
Leach's Turn NR14 165 B1
Leafield Rd PE30 147 C3
Leafyoak La NR14 90 C3
Leamon Ct IP27 175 D4
Leaside PE31 133 B6
Leatherpool La NR25 7 E6
Leathway NR29 167 B2
Lebanon Dr PE13 152 F7
Lee Warner Ave NR21 141 D6
Lee Warner Rd 10 PE13 153 C3
Leeder Hill NR13 72 F2
Leeds Way 5 NR12 55 E4
Lees Yd NR25 137 B6
Leete Way PE33 43 E2
Leewood Cres NR5 157 C1
Lefevre Way NR31 94 C8
Lefroy Rd NR3 158 A2
Legge Pl 7 PE34 43 B1
Legge-Bourke Ct
PE13 152 F6
Legrice Cres NR28 151 C3
Leicester Ave PE30 147 B5
Leicester Rd 1 NR31 170 D4
Leicester St NR2 162 C4
Leigh Cl NR17 174 C5
Leman Gr 8 NR14 92 A1
Leman Gr 9 NR14 91 F1
Leman Rd NR31 170 D2
Leng Cres NR4 161 E2
Lenthall Cl 18 NR7 72 D4
Leonard Cl 4 PE30 147 B6
Leonard Medler Way
NR10 53 B8
Leonard's La IP26 98 D1
Leonards St 10 NR3 162 D8
Leopard Ct 3 NR3 178 B4
Leopold Cl 2 NR4 162 A3
Leopold Rd NR4 162 A3
Lerowe Rd PE13 152 E7
Les Baux Pl 5 PE13 152 E3
Lesley Wlk NR19 154 D2
Lestrange PE36 132 C4
Letheringsett Rd NR25 18 F7
Letherington's La NR12 55 D5
Letton Rd IP25 67 C2
Leven Cl 8 NR7 72 D5
Leverington Rd PE13 152 A6
Levers Cl PE30 147 D8
Leveson Rd NR7 159 B3
Levine Cl NR13 165 B4
Levishaw Cl NR10 36 E1
Lewis Cl Ashill IP25 84 A7
Hopton IP22 127 F6
Lewis Dr Roydon IP22 177 A5
Wiggenhall St Germans
PE34 61 A8
Lexham Rd
Great Dunham PE32 47 E2
King's Lynn PE30 147 E8
Litcham PE32 47 F4
Lexington Cl NR29 167 A7
Ley's La NR20 51 C1
Leyland Cl IP24 176 D6
Leys Cl NR31 169 C1
Leys La
Attleborough NR17 174 D2
Old Buckenham NR17 104 B3
Yaxley IP23 129 F1
Leziate Dro
Grimston PE32 45 A8
Leziate PE32 44 F6
Leziate Heath Nature
Reserve* PE32 44 E6
Liberator Cl NR13 72 E8
Liberator Rd NR6 158 B6
Libra Ct NR7 159 C4
Lichfield Rd NR31 169 B3
Lichfield St NR21 141 B4
Licking's Dro PE13 152 A2
Lifeboat Plain 6 NR26 138 D7
Light La PE14 59 D6
Lighthouse Cl
Happisburgh NR12 24 C5
Hunstanton PE36 132 D7
Lighthouse La PE36 132 D6
Lilac Cl Brandon IP27 114 D4
9 East Dereham NR19 154 D2
20 Great Yarmouth NR31 94 C7
4 Great Yarmouth NR31 170 A5
1 Horsford NR10 53 A3
Wisbech PE13 152 F7
Lilac Dr IP27 113 E1
Lilac Gr NR26 138 D4
Lilac Wood PE30 147 B8
Lilburne Ave NR3 158 D2
Lilian Cl NR6 158 B4
Lilian Rd NR10 54 A2
Lily Ave NR20 69 B8
Lily La NR34 111 A3
Lily Terr NR1 178 B1
Limassol Rd NR19 154 C2
Lime Ave Stradsett PE33 80 C8
Wisbech PE13 152 C7
Lime Cl
7 Harleston IP20 122 D1
Marham PE33 63 A4
Lime Dr NR19 154 D2
Lime Gr Gayton PE32 45 C6
Sheringham NR26 138 D4
7 Thetford IP24 176 D4
Lime Kiln Cl
5 Cley next the Sea NR25 7 E6
6 Newton Flotman NR15 89 D1
Lime Kiln La
2 Stoke Ferry PE33 81 A3
Thetford IP24 176 D4
Lime Kiln Mews
9 New Catton NR6 158 C1
Norwich NR3 162 C8
Lime Kiln Rd
Gayton PE32 45 C6
Sparham NR9 50 F5
West Dereham PE33 80 C5
Lime St PE12 41 C8
Lime Tree Ave
Costessey NR8 156 F4
Long Stratton NR15 106 E2
Norwich NR7 163 C7
Wymondham NR18 173 D6
Lime Tree Cl
2 East Dereham NR19 154 E6
9 Mattishall NR20 68 E6
Wymondham NR18 173 D5
Lime Tree Cres NR19 66 C7
Lime Tree Rd
North Walsham NR28 151 D5
Norwich NR2 162 B3
Lime Tree Wlk IP25 84 D3
Lime Way NR31 170 B5
Limekiln La
Houghton PE31 29 D6
South End NR16 106 C1
Upper Sheringham
NR26 138 A4
Limekiln Wlk 1 NR30 169 C4
Limes Ave PE14 59 A1
Limes Cl IP22 177 D1
Limes Rd 3 NR29 56 C8
Limes The IP25 84 A6
Limetree Cl 10 NR10 53 B3
Limetree Ct
Great Yarmouth NR31 169 C2
Taverham NR8 155 B2
Limmer Ave IP21 121 C1
Limmer Rd NR31 170 D4
Limpenhoe Rd
Cantley NR13 92 C7
Reedham NR13 92 E6
Linacre Ave NR7 159 C4
Linacre Cl NR7 159 C3
Linalls Dr NR8 156 C4
Lincoln Ave
Great Yarmouth NR31 170 C3
Hingham NR9 86 D5
Lincoln Cl 12 NR20 50 B3
Lincoln Ralphs Sports Hall
NR1 178 C1
Lincoln Rd IP25 84 F3
Lincoln Sq N PE36 132 C5
Lincoln Sq S PE36 132 C5
Lincoln St
Hunstanton PE36 132 D5
Norwich NR2 162 B5
Lincoln Way IP24 176 B5
Linden Cl NR18 86 E3
Linden Dr 5 NR9 88 C7
Linden Gr Diss IP22 177 C6
Sheringham NR26 138 D4
Linden Rd
Clenchwarton PE34 145 E5
Norwich NR5 157 C1
Linden Tree Gdns 15
NR31 94 C7
Lindford Dr NR4 89 C8
Lindley Cl NR6 158 E6
Lindley Rd 9 NR9 88 C7
Lindley St NR1 162 E3
Lindsay Rd NR7 159 C4
Linford PE34 145 D6
Linford Clapper La
PE34 145 E6
Linford Est PE34 145 E5
Ling Cl 1 NR12 54 C7
Ling Comm Rd PE30 148 D6
Ling House Rd PE31 13 B1
Ling Rd IP22 177 B3
Ling Way NR12 54 C7
Lingheath Rd IP27 175 E3
Lings Cl 5 NR10 53 B3
Lings The NR9 86 D8
Lingwood Fst Sch NR13 73 F3
Lingwood Gdns 2 NR13 74 A3
Lingwood Jun Sch
NR13 74 A3
Lingwood Rd
Blofield NR13 73 E4
Brundall NR13 165 F6
Lingwood Sta NR13 74 A3
Link The 2 IP24 176 D4
Links Ave
Brundall NR13 165 C4
Cromer NR27 139 D4
Norwich NR6 157 F4
Links Cl
Caister-on-Sea NR30 168 E4
Norwich NR6 157 F5
6 Thurlton NR14 92 F1
Links Cres NR26 138 C7
Links Rd
Great Yarmouth NR31 171 D8
Mundesley NR11 143 B6
Sheringham NR26 138 C7
Links Way
Sheringham NR27 10 A5
4 Thurlton NR14 92 F1
Linmore Cres 3 IP25 84 E3
Linmore Ct IP25 84 C3
Linn Chilvers Dr PE31 133 B5
Linnet Cl 6 NR31 170 A6
Linnet Cres IP27 175 E3
Linnets The NR5 156 F1
Lintock Rd NR3 158 D3
Linton Cl NR7 159 B3
Linton Cres NR7 159 B4
Lion & Castle Yd NR1 178 B2
Lion La NR14 91 C3
Lion Rd
Buxton with Lammas
NR10 36 E1
Palgrave IP22 177 C1
Lion Wood Rd NR1 163 B7
Lion's Mouth NR11 10 A3
Lisbon Rd NR19 154 C2
Lishman Rd NR7 159 E2
Lisle Rd NR5 160 F7
Lister Cl NR31 170 B1
Lister's Rd PE14 77 E5
Litcham Hall PE32 48 A4
Litcham High Sch PE32 48 A4
Litcham Prim Sch PE32 48 A5
Litcham Rd
Beeston with Bittering
PE32 48 D4
Great Dunham PE32 47 F2
Gressenhall NR20 49 C3
Little Dunham PE32 65 F8
Mileham PE32 48 C5
Tittleshall PE32 48 A6
Litcham Village Mus*
PE32 48 A4
Litchmere Rd NR14 109 D6
Litester Cl NR28 151 D4
Little Armes St NR2 162 A8
Little Barney La NR21 17 F3
Little Bethel St NR2 178 A2
Little Bittering Medieval
Village of* NR19 48 F4
Little Carr Rd PE30 148 D5
Little Church St PE13 152 C5
Little Dowgate PE13 152 A7
Little Ellingham Rd
NR9 86 A3
Little Fendike La PE14 77 E8
Little Hockham La
IP24 102 E2
Little Holme Rd PE34 41 F6
Little John Rd NR4 162 C1
Little La
1 Castle Acre PE32 46 F2
Docking PE31 134 E4
9 Horsford NR10 53 B3
Roydon PE32 28 A1
Stoke Ferry PE33 80 F3
Little London Rd
North Walsham NR28 151 D8
Northwold IP26 99 C7
Little London St NR2 178 B3
Little Man's Way PE33 81 A3
Little Melton Fst Sch
NR9 160 C2
Little Melton Rd NR9 160 B1
Little Money Rd NR14 109 D8
Little Oulsham Dro
IP26 98 B2
Little Plumstead CE Prim Sch
NR13 165 A8
Little Scratby Cres
NR29 167 E4
Little Snoring Prim Sch
NR21 17 B3
Little Snoring Rd NR21 17 A5
Little Walsingham Cl
PE30 148 C3
Littlebeck La NR15 108 B8
Littlefields NR19 154 D5
Littleport St PE30 146 E5
Littleport Terr 8 PE30 146 E5
Littlewoods La NR12 164 E5
Livingstone Rise NR11 22 F8
Livingstone St NR2 162 A7
Lizard The NR18 173 D3
Lloyd Ct NR25 137 F8
Lloyd Rd Norwich NR1 163 B7
Taverham NR8 155 B2
Loanin The NR1 162 F3
Lobster La NR2 178 A3
Loch La IP25 84 D4
Lock Rd NR28 38 D6
Lock's La NR34 109 F1
Lockerbie Flats 13
NR26 138 D7
Lockhart Rd NR35 109 D3
Locksley Rd NR4 89 E8
Loddon NR15 108 C7
Loddon Cnr NR15 108 C7
Loddon Fst Sch 18 NR14 92 A1
Loddon Mid Sch NR14 91 F1
Loddon Rd
Ditchingham NR35 109 B2
Gillingham NR34 110 C2
Haddiscoe NR14 110 D8
Heckingham NR14 92 D1
Holverston NR14 91 A5
Kirby Cane NR35 109 E4
Norton Subcourse NR14 92 E1
Toft Monks NR34 110 D7
Trowse with Newton
NR14 163 C1
Yelverton NR14 90 E6
Lode Ave PE14 77 F5
Lode St IP27 175 C4
Lodge Breck NR8 157 A7
Lodge Cl NR25 137 B5
Lodge Dr IP22 120 B5
Lodge Farm Dr NR6 158 D6
Lodge Farm Mdws
NR20 49 C4
Lodge Hill NR26 138 A3
Lodge La Norwich NR6 158 E6
Riddlesworth IP22 127 D7
Shelfanger IP22 120 B1
13 Snettisham PE31 12 E4
Lodge La Fst Sch NR6 158 E6
Lodge Pl NR7 163 E6
Lodge Rd Catfield NR29 56 B8
Feltwell IP26 98 F2
Heacham PE31 133 C5
Lingwood & Burlingham
NR13 74 A3
St John, Ilketshall
NR34 124 C6
Tivetshall St Margaret
NR15 121 C6
Lodge Way IP24 176 C7
Lodore Ave NR6 158 A6
Loggers La IP22 128 B5
Loke Rd PE30 146 E6
Loke The
Belton with Browston
NR31 93 F6
Briston NR24 142 D4
Brumstead NR12 24 A2
Cringleford NR4 89 C8
Cromer NR27 139 B6
East Beckham NR11 9 D2
Felmingham NR28 37 B8
Filby NR29 75 E8
Freethorpe NR13 92 E7
2 Gresham NR11 9 E1
Haddiscoe NR14 110 F8
4 Hemsby NR29 58 B6
Salhouse NR13 55 B2
Strumpshaw NR13 73 F2
Loke Wiffens 2 NR9 88 D8
Lollards Rd
1 Norwich NR1 163 A6
Norwich NR1 178 C3
Lolly Moor Nature Reserve*
NR19 67 F5
Lomond Rd NR17 174 F6
London La
Mundford IP26 100 B4
South Creake NR21 15 E5
London Rd
Attleborough NR17 174 B3
Brandon IP27 175 B3
Downham Market PE38 172 C4
East Dereham NR19 154 E4
Elveden IP24 125 B7
Harleston IP20 122 D1
King's Lynn PE30 146 E4
Snetterton NR16 103 D1
Thetford IP24 176 B3
Wymondham NR18 173 A2
London St
Brancaster PE31 3 B7
Norwich NR2 178 B3
Swaffham PE37 153 C4
Whissonsett NR20 31 D2
Londs The NR27 11 A3
Lone Barn Rd NR7 159 B2
Lonely Rd
Pulham St Mary IP21 122 B6
Scole IP21 121 C2
Long Barrow Dr NR28 151 D3
Long Beach Est NR29 167 C8
Long Comm La NR10 37 D4
Long Dale NR8 155 E2
Long Dro PE38 97 D2
Long John Hill NR1 162 E2
Long La
Baconsthorpe NR25 20 A7
Bawburgh NR9 160 B8
Burston & Shimpling
IP22 120 E4
Catfield NR29 56 D7
Feltwell IP26 98 D1
Flordon NR15 106 E8
Great Yarmouth NR31 170 A4
Hoveton NR12 164 F7
Mulbarton NR14 89 B2
Saxlingham Nethergate
NR15 107 B8
Southrepps NR11 22 B7
Stoke Holy Cross NR14 89 F4
Strumpshaw NR13 165 F2
Swaffham PE37 153 E5
Long La *continued*
Tharston & Hapton
NR15 106 D6
West Winch PE33 43 E2
Winfarthing IP22 119 F7
Long Lots PE14 59 F3
Long Rd
Barton Turf NR12 55 F7
Poringland NR14 90 C5
Saham Toney IP25 84 F8
Terrington St Clement
PE34 144 A8
Thurlton NR14 93 A1
Wymondham NR18 88 A1
Long Row Norwich NR3 158 D1
Tibenham NR16 120 D6
Long St NR17 103 E6
Long Straton Mill*
NR15 106 F3
Long Stratton High Sch
NR15 106 E3
Long Stratton Ind Est
NR15 106 D3
Long Stratton Leisure Ctr
NR15 106 E4
Long Stratton Rd
NR16 105 F4
Long's Cres NR13 72 D7
Longbow Cl 3 NR4 162 C1
Longbrooke Cl NR14 89 D4
Longdell Hills NR5 156 E2
Longdon Cl 4 PE12 41 B8
Longe Rd NR6 158 F6
Longfellow Rd NR30 168 D5
Longfield Cl 4 NR14 91 F1
Longfields PE37 153 C5
Longfields Rd NR7 72 D5
Longfulans La NR31 171 D3
Longham La NR20 49 B3
Longham Rd NR19 49 A2
Longhead La PE14 59 A6
Longlands Dr NR18 173 A6
Longmead 4 NR1 162 E2
Longmeadow NR13 165 B3
Longmeadow Cl IP25 85 A1
Longs Cl 4 NR15 89 C1
Longview 1 NR9 88 D8
Longview Cl 4 PE31 12 E4
Longwater La NR8 156 D3
Longwater Ret Pk
NR5 156 A2
Lonsdale Cres NR9 86 B5
Lonsdale Rd NR13 72 E7
Lonsdale Terr PE13 152 C3
Loombe Cl 3 NR20 50 B3
Loop Rd NR11 11 D1
Lopham Rd NR16 118 D4
Lord Cres NR20 50 B5
Lord Rd IP22 177 E4
Lord Walsingham Ct 1
IP24 176 E5
Lord's La NR31 94 B7
Lords La PE31 133 D5
Lorraine Gdns NR3 158 E3
Losinga Cres NR3 158 B3
Losinga Rd PE30 146 E7
Lossiemouth Rd 6
IP31 126 B1
Lothian St NR2 162 C6
Lothingland Mid Sch
NR32 171 A3
Louden Rd NR27 139 B7
Louie's La IP22 177 C6
Louis Cl NR6 158 D6
Louis Dahl Rd 3 NR31 94 A6
Louise Cl 15 NR30 169 D2
Lound Dam NR14 111 A7
Lound Rd
Belton with Browston
NR31 94 B4
Norwich NR4 161 F5
Somerleyton, Ashby &
Herringfleet NR32 111 F8
Lovat Cl IP20 122 E2
Love La Fransham NR19 66 D7
Sporle with Palgrave
PE32 65 C6
Wisbech PE13 152 C4
Lovelace Rd NR4 161 E4
Lovell Gdns IP25 84 E3
Lovell Way PE34 144 B4
Lovells The 6 PE14 59 D2
Lovelstaithe NR1 178 C3
Lovers' La NR29 56 C4
Lovett Cl NR6 158 F6
Lovewell Rd NR31 170 D5
Low Bungay Rd NR14 92 A1
Low Comm
Aslacton NR16 106 A2
Bunwell NR16 105 E2
Deopham NR18 86 E4
Hellington NR14 91 B6
Reedham NR13 93 A5
South Lopham IP22 128 F7
Swardeston NR14 89 B6
Low Comm La NR34 111 A5
Low Comm Rd
South Lopham IP22 128 E7
Thurton NR14 91 D3
Low Ditch Rd IP20 122 F4
Low Farm Rd NR13 75 A3
Low Hatter's Cl PE38 172 B3
Low La Hevingham NR10 53 B8
Rocklands NR17 103 B6
Terrington St Clement
PE34 144 A5
Low Rd Alburgh IP20 122 F6
Bunwell NR16 105 E1

Low Rd continued
Denton IP20 ...123 B5
Dickleburgh & Rushall
  IP21 ...130 E5
Forncett NR16 ...106 B5
Freethorpe NR13 ...92 F7
Great & Little Plumstead
  NR13 ...72 E5
Grimston PE32 ...28 B1
Haddiscoe NR14 ...110 F7
Hedenham NR35 ...108 D4
Hellesdon NR6 ...157 C5
Hingham NR9 ...86 B4
Keswick NR4 ...89 C7
Kimberley NR9 ...87 D8
King's Lynn PE30 ...148 C1
Mautby NR29 ...75 E5
Mettingham NR35 ...109 D1
Narborough PE32 ...63 F7
North Tuddenham NR20 ...68 E8
Norton Subcourse NR14 ...92 E2
Pentney PE32 ...63 C8
Redenhall with Harleston
  IP20 ...122 F1
Repps with Bastwick
  NR29 ...57 A4
Rollesby NR29 ...57 D2
Roydon PE32 ...28 A1
St John, Iketshall
  NR34 ...124 D6
St John's Fen End PE14 ...60 B6
Scole IP21 ...130 C5
Shelton NR15 ...107 B1
Shropham NR17 ...103 B3
Skeyton Corner NR10 ...37 B6
South Walsham NR13 ...74 B8
Starston IP20 ...122 C3
Stoke Ferry PE33 ...80 F2
Stow Bardolph PE34 ...61 C2
Stow Bedon NR17 ...102 E5
Strumpshaw NR13 ...165 F1
Swaffham PE37 ...153 A5
Tasburgh NR15 ...106 E7
[1] Thurlton NR14 ...92 F1
Thurlton NR14 ...93 B2
Tibenham NR16 ...120 B8
Walpole Cross Keys PE34 ...42 A7
West Acre PE32 ...46 C2
West Caister NR30 ...168 A3
Wicklewood NR18 ...87 C3
Wiggenhall St Germans
  PE34 ...43 D3
Wimbotsham PE34 ...172 D8
Winterton-on-Sea NR29 ...58 B6
Wisbech PE14 ...152 C1
Woodbastwick NR13 ...55 C1
Wortham IP22 ...129 A6
Wortwell IP20 ...123 A3
Low Side PE14 ...77 F7
Low St Hardingham NR9 ...86 E8
Hoxne IP21 ...131 A4
Ketteringham NR18 ...88 D6
St Margaret, Iketshall
  NR35 ...124 B4
Sloley NR12 ...37 E3
Smallburgh NR12 ...38 E3
Weasenham St Peter
  PE32 ...30 D2
Wicklewood NR18 ...87 A5
Low Wr La IP22 ...129 D5
Low's La IP22 ...177 D2
Lowe's La PE31 ...4 D4
Lower Clarence Rd
  NR1 ...178 C2
Lower Cliff Rd NR31 ...170 D4
Lower Drag Way IP22 ...128 D8
Lower Espl NR31 ...170 D3
Lower Globe La NR31 ...165 E7
Lower Gn NR31 ...92 E8
Lower Goat La [2] NR2 ...178 A3
Lower Hall La NR14 ...18 D7
Lower Hardley Rd
  NR14 ...92 A2
Lower Kiln La NR15 ...90 F3
Lower Lincoln St
  PE36 ...132 C5
Lower Marine Par
  NR31 ...170 D3
Lower Oakley IP21 ...130 D4
Lower Rd
Holme Hale IP25 ...66 B3
Rockland St Mary NR14 ...91 C7
Lower Rose La IP21 ...177 E2
Lower Spink's La NR18 ...88 B4
Lower St Horning NR12 ...55 A1
Salhouse NR13 ...55 A1
Lower Wood Nature
  Reserve* NR9 ...105 E8
Lowes Ave NR25 ...137 D5
Lowes View IP22 ...177 E3
Lowestoft Rd NR31 ...170 C1
Lowfield PE30 ...147 E4
Lowick Cl [3] NR19 ...154 D3
Lowry Cl [4] NR3 ...170 A7
Lowry Cole Rd NR6 ...158 F5
Lowry Way PE38 ...172 E5
Lowther Rd NR4 ...162 B1
Loxwood NR6 ...157 E6
Lubbock Cl NR2 ...161 F5
Lucas Cl [2] NR7 ...72 D5
Lucas La PE31 ...135 E6
Lucas Rd PE30 ...169 B4
Lucerne Cl NR6 ...158 F4
Lucerne Rd [5] NR31 ...94 C6
Lucombe Dr PE13 ...152 F7
Luddenham Rd NR20 ...50 B2
Ludham Airstrip NR29 ...56 D6
Ludham Fst Sch NR29 ...56 C5

Ludham Rd
Catfield NR29 ...56 C6
Potter Heigham NR29 ...56 F5
Ludkin Sq [4] NR30 ...169 C5
Lug's La NR35 ...109 B5
Lugger Yd NR23 ...136 D6
Luke Cl NR5 ...156 F2
Luscombe Way [6] NR13 ...72 E7
Lusher Cl [1] NR26 ...138 C5
Lusher Rise NR5 ...161 D8
Lusher's Loke NR7 ...158 F4
Lushers Mdw [5] NR17 ...174 C5
Lushington Cl [9] NR5 ...161 B8
Luxembourg Way
  NR19 ...154 C2
Lydgate Cl NR20 ...154 D3
Lyhart Rd NR4 ...162 B1
Lynch Gn [6] NR9 ...88 D8
Lyndford Rd NR12 ...39 B4
Lyndhurst Ct PE36 ...132 D3
Lynewood Cl NR27 ...139 D4
Lynewood Rd NR27 ...139 D4
Lynfield Rd NR28 ...151 C6
Lynford Rd IP26 ...100 B5
Lyng Hall La NR20 ...33 A7
Lyng Hall Rd NR20 ...33 A7
Lyng La IP22 ...118 F1
Lyng Prim Sch NR9 ...51 A4
Lyng Rd NR9 ...51 B5
Lyngate Cl [8] NR9 ...88 C7
Lyngate Rd NR28 ...151 B8
Lynn Cl [7] NR7 ...72 D5
Lynn Ct NR19 ...154 E4
Lynn Gr NR31 ...170 A6
Lynn Gr High Sch
  NR31 ...170 A6
Lynn La PE32 ...29 D1
Lynn Mus* PE30 ...146 E5
Lynn Rd
Castle Rising PE30 ...148 F5
Clenchwarton PE34 ...144 E5
Dersingham PE31 ...140 C2
Downham Market PE38 ...172 C6
East Rudham PE31 ...30 A7
Gayton PE32 ...45 C6
Grimston PE32 ...28 B1
Ingoldisthorpe PE31 ...140 C7
King's Lynn PE30 ...147 A5
Littleport CB7 ...96 E1
Middleton PE32 ...44 D2
Roydon PE32 ...28 A1
Runcton Holme PE33 ...61 F4
Shouldham PE33 ...62 D3
Shouldham Thorpe PE33 ...62 B2
Southery PE38 ...97 A6
Stow Bardolph PE34 ...79 E8
Stradsett PE33 ...80 C8
Swaffham PE37 ...153 A5
Terrington St Clement
  PE34 ...42 A6
Tilney St Lawrence PE34 ...42 D2
Walpole Cross Keys PE34 ...41 F6
Walsoken PE14 ...59 B6
Watlington PE33 ...61 E6
Weeting IP27 ...175 A8
Wereham PE33 ...80 D5
West Rudham PE31 ...29 F6
West Walton PE14 ...59 D8
West Winch PE33 ...61 F8
Wiggenhall St Mary Magdalen
  PE34 ...61 B6
Wisbech PE13 ...152 C6
Wretton PE33 ...80 F3
Lynn Rd Terr PE14 ...59 D8
Lynn St PE37 ...153 B4
Lynton Rd NR12 ...24 A7
Lynwood Terr [13] PE30 ...146 E3
Lytton Rd NR8 ...156 D8

M

MacArthur Dr [3] NR19 ...154 C6
MacDonald Rd NR27 ...139 A7
Mack's La NR8 ...156 D7
MacKenzie Cl [1] NR31 ...170 B1
MacKenzie Rd IP24 ...176 A3
Mackintosh Rd NR11 ...72 E8
Macks Loke NR24 ...142 F2
Macmillan Way NR11 ...165 A8
Mad Dog La PE32 ...29 C2
Madden Ave NR30 ...169 D8
Maddermarket Theatre
  NR2 ...178 A3
Maden Cl NR8 ...173 B5
Magazine Cl PE13 ...152 A4
Magazine La PE13 ...152 A4
Magdalen Cl [3] NR3 ...162 E8
Magdalen Gates Fst Sch
  NR3 ...162 E8
Magdalen High Rd
  PE34 ...61 A6
Magdalen Rd
Norwich NR3 ...162 E8
Tilney St Lawrence PE34 ...60 D8
Wiggenhall St Germans
  PE34 ...61 C7
Magdalen Sq NR31 ...170 B4
Magdalen St
Norwich NR3 ...178 A4
Thetford IP24 ...176 D4
Magdalen Way NR31 ...170 B4
Magic City Leisure Ctr
  NR1 ...178 C3
Magnay Rd NR3 ...157 C2
Magnolia Cl NR10 ...53 A4
Magnolia Gn [8] NR31 ...170 B6

Magpie Ct [35] IP20 ...122 D2
Magpie Hill IP22 ...129 B5
Magpie La NR17 ...103 B7
Magpie Rd NR3 ...162 D8
Maid Marian Rd NR4 ...162 C1
Maida Vale [5] IP22 ...177 E3
Maidens Cl [1] NR13 ...72 E4
Maids Cross Hill IP27 ...113 F1
Maidstone Rd NR1 ...178 B3
Main Cross Rd NR30 ...170 D8
Main Dereham Rd
  NR21 ...31 F4
Main Dr NR20 ...50 E7
Main Rd
Clenchwarton PE34 ...145 B5
Crimplesham PE33 ...80 B6
Filby NR29 ...76 A8
Fleggburgh NR13 ...166 F6
Holme next the Sea PE36 ...2 A5
Lingwood & Burlingham
  NR13 ...74 A5
Methwold IP26 ...99 A7
Narborough PE32 ...63 E8
Ormesby St Michael NR29 ...58 A1
Rollesby NR29 ...57 D2
Swardeston NR14 ...89 C5
Tilney All Saints PE34 ...42 E4
Upwell PE14 ...77 E3
Walpole Highway PE14 ...59 E8
Weeting IP27 ...175 B7
West Caister NR30 ...168 A4
West Winch PE33 ...61 F8
Wisbech PE14 ...77 A7
Main St
Hockwold cum Wilton
  IP26 ...113 F7
Honing NR28 ...38 C6
Welney PE14 ...95 D4
Maine St
[26] Thetford IP24 ...116 A1
Thetford IP24 ...176 D4
Malakoff Cl [9] NR30 ...169 D2
Malakoff Rd [8] NR30 ...169 D2
Malborough Gn Cres
  NR29 ...57 D4
Malbrook Rd NR5 ...161 B7
Maldon Rd PE13 ...152 E5
Malin Cl [7] NR30 ...168 C6
Mallard Cl
Brundall NR13 ...165 E2
Chedgrave NR14 ...91 F2
[7] Fakenham NR21 ...141 E4
[9] Loddon NR14 ...92 A2
[4] Salhouse NR13 ...55 A1
[3] Snettisham PE31 ...12 E4
Mallard Rd [2] NR13 ...165 E2
Mallard Way
Brandon IP27 ...175 E2
Great Yarmouth NR31 ...170 A6
Hickling NR12 ...39 F1
Mallory Rd NR6 ...158 D6
Mallow Cl [1] NR17 ...174 B4
Mallow Rd [4] IP24 ...176 F5
Mallow Way NR18 ...173 D4
Malsters Cl IP26 ...100 B5
Malt Dr NR13 ...152 B3
Malt's La IP26 ...113 F7
Malthouse Cl [9] NR25 ...84 D2
Malthouse Cres PE31 ...133 D5
Malthouse Ct
East Dereham NR20 ...154 E5
[8] Redenhall with Harleston
  IP20 ...122 D2
[8] Snettisham PE31 ...12 E5
Thornham PE36 ...2 D6
Malthouse La
Cantley NR13 ...92 B6
Gissing IP22 ...120 F4
Great Yarmouth NR31 ...170 C8
Guist NR20 ...32 F4
Ludham NR29 ...56 D5
Malthouse Pl NR23 ...136 D6
[4] Hethersett NR9 ...88 C7
Norwich NR2 ...178 A2
Malthouse Yd NR10 ...149 C4
Malting Row IP31 ...126 D1
Maltings Cl IP22 ...177 F3
Maltings Dr [6] IP20 ...122 D2
Maltings La [4] PE38 ...172 A5
Maltings Way NR16 ...119 B6
Maltmas Dro PE14 ...77 A7
Malvern Cl NR8 ...161 A4
Malvern Rd [3] NR1 ...163 A6
Manby Rd
Downham Market PE38 ...172 B3
Great Yarmouth NR30 ...169 D4
Norwich NR7 ...157 D5
Manchester Pl [3] NR2 ...162 C5
Mancroft Wlk [11] NR2 ...162 C7
Mandela Cl NR3 ...178 A4
Mandells St NR3 ...178 A4
Mangate St PE37 ...153 C5
Mangreen NR14 ...89 D6
Mangreen La NR14 ...89 C5
Mann's La NR20 ...50 B4
Manning's La IP22 ...128 B1
Mannington Hall*
  NR11 ...20 C3
Mannington Pl PE30 ...148 E1
Manor Chase NR18 ...173 C6
Manor Cl
[3] Aylsham NR11 ...150 D6
[1] Great Yarmouth NR31 ...170 C7
Hockering NR20 ...69 B8
Horsham St Faith &
  Newton St Faith NR10 ...53 D2
Ingoldisthorpe PE31 ...140 D8

Manor Cl continued
Lamas NR10 ...36 E1
[4] Little Snoring NR21 ...17 B3
Tunstead NR12 ...37 F1
Manor Ct
Aylsham NR11 ...150 C6
North Walsham NR28 ...151 E5
Manor Dr Urcham PE32 ...48 A4
Roydon IP22 ...177 E3
Terrington St John PE14 ...42 B1
Manor Farm Cl NR8 ...157 A8
Manor Farm Rd
Denton IP20 ...122 F8
St John, Iketshall
  NR34 ...124 D7
Reepham NR20 ...58 A6
Manor Field Fst Sch
  NR15 ...106 E3
Manor Gdns Diss IP22 ...177 D5
Hopton on Sea NR31 ...171 E4
[3] Lingwood NR13 ...74 A3
Wisbech PE13 ...152 A4
Manor House Cl
Brandon IP27 ...175 B3
Mautby NR29 ...75 E6
Manor La PE31 ...12 E5
Manor Pk Gdns [18]
  NR15 ...106 E3
Manor Rd
Brandon IP27 ...175 A3
Caister-on-Sea NR30 ...168 E4
Cantley NR13 ...92 B8
Dersingham PE31 ...140 D2
Great Yarmouth NR31 ...170 C7
Griston IP25 ...85 A2
Heacham PE31 ...133 D8
Hilgay PE38 ...79 D1
Hopton on Sea NR31 ...171 E4
Horsham St Faith &
  Newton St Faith NR10 ...53 D3
Hunstanton PE36 ...132 C2
King's Lynn PE30 ...148 C5
Long Stratton NR15 ...106 E3
Mundesley NR11 ...143 C6
Newton St Faith NR10 ...53 D4
North Walsham NR28 ...151 E5
Potington IP22 ...177 A5
Scarning NR19 ...154 A3
Stoke Ferry PE33 ...80 F2
Terrington St Clement
  PE34 ...144 B5
Manor Ridge NR13 ...165 E6
Manor Way
Ormesby St Margaret
  NR29 ...167 A2
Swaffham PE37 ...153 C5
Manor Wlk PE31 ...133 C4
Manorfield Cl [1] NR29 ...167 A2
Manorside PE31 ...140 D2
Manse Ct IP24 ...176 D4
Mansel Dr NR6 ...158 E3
Mansell Cl [2] IP22 ...177 A5
Mansell Rd PE13 ...152 D3
Mansfield La NR1 ...162 E1
Manthorpe Cl [6] NR1 ...162 E1
Mantle Cl NR7 ...159 D4
Maple Ave PE13 ...152 C7
Maple Cl [10] Beetley NR20 ...49 D4
[1] Beetley NR20 ...49 D4
[5] Gayton PE32 ...45 C6
[20] Martham NR29 ...57 D4
Wymondham NR18 ...173 D6
Yaxley IP23 ...129 F1
Maple Dr
King's Lynn PE30 ...148 D3
Norwich NR7 ...161 F7
Sculthorpe Airfield NR21 ...15 C3
Taverham NR8 ...155 B1
Maple Rd
Downham Market PE38 ...172 B6
King's Lynn PE30 ...148 D3
Maple Way [7] Eye IP23 ...130 C1
Great Yarmouth NR31 ...170 B6
Mapplebeck Cl PE30 ...147 E4
Marauder Rd NR6 ...158 D6
March Cl PE13 ...152 E5
March Rd Elm PE14 ...77 A7
Welney PE14 ...95 C5
March Riverside PE14 ...59 E8
Mardle Rd NR4 ...110 D5
Mardle St NR5 ...160 F5
Mardling Run NR13 ...166 B2
Marea Mdws PE31 ...133 D5
Margaret Cl
[8] East Dereham NR19 ...154 D3
Norwich NR6 ...157 D5
Margaret Cres NR7 ...163 F7
Margaret English Cl
  NR26 ...138 C5
Margaret Lilly Way [1]
  NR11 ...21 A5
Margaret Paston Ave
  NR3 ...158 A2
Margaret Rd NR5 ...157 B2
Margaret Reeve Cl [6]
  NR18 ...173 D5
Margaret Rose Cl
  PE30 ...147 E4
Margaretta Cl PE36 ...132 D2
Margaretts Cl NR14 ...145 F5
Margetson Ave NR7 ...163 F7
Marguerite Cl [11] NR31 ...94 C5
Marham Airfield PE33 ...63 C3
Marham Airfield Fst Sch
  PE33 ...63 B5
Marham Cl PE34 ...146 B5
Marham Mid Sch PE33 ...63 B5

Marham Rd PE33 ...62 E2
Marie Cl NR13 ...92 B6
Marigold Cl [6] NR10 ...53 A3
Marina Leisure Ctr
  NR30 ...169 E3
Marina Rd NR11 ...143 C6
Marina St NR31 ...170 D1
Marine Cres
Great Yarmouth NR30 ...169 E6
[5] Hemsby NR29 ...58 B6
Marine Dr NR30 ...168 E8
Marine Par NR31 ...170 D2
Mariner's Cl NR31 ...171 D8
Mariner's Compass
  NR3 ...171 C8
Mariners La NR1 ...178 B3
Mariners Pk Cl NR1 ...171 D5
Mariners' Rd NR30 ...169 D2
Mariners Way PE30 ...146 F8
Marion Cl NR13 ...173 C5
Marion Rd NR1 ...163 A6
Marion Wlk [1] NR1 ...154 D2
Marionville Rd NR3 ...158 C3
Maritime Mus for E Anglia*
  NR30 ...169 E3
Marjoram Rd NR1 ...151 E4
Marjoram Rd [2] NR1 ...94 C6
Mark Cl NR1 ...72 D5
Mark Lemmon Cl [2] NR6 ...158 A3
Mark's Cl La NR9 ...52 A7
Market Ave NR1 ...178 B3
Market Gates [6] NR30 ...169 D4
Market Hill
Brandon IP27 ...175 D3
Colkirk NR21 ...31 D5
Diss IP22 ...177 D4
Market La
Blundeston NR32 ...171 D1
Brancaster PE31 ...3 B6
Burston & Shimpling
  IP22 ...120 E1
Crimplesham PE33 ...80 A6
Filby NR29 ...76 B7
Great Moulton NR15 ...70 C1
Great Moulton NR15 ...106 D3
King's Lynn PE30 ...146 D5
Little Melton NR9 ...160 A2
Salthouse NR25 ...8 B6
Shotesham NR15 ...107 B8
Market Manor NR13 ...166 C3
Market Mews PE13 ...152 C5
Market Pl
Aylsham NR11 ...150 C6
Burnham Westgate
  NR31 ...135 C3
Diss IP22 ...177 D4
Downham Market PE38 ...172 C5
[2] East Dereham NR19 ...154 D5
Fakenham NR21 ...141 B4
Great Yarmouth NR30 ...169 C4
[2] Harleston IP20 ...122 D2
Holt NR25 ...137 B6
[4] Loddon NR14 ...92 A1
North Walsham NR28 ...151 C5
Reepham NR10 ...149 B4
Swaffham PE13 ...153 C4
[1] Thetford IP24 ...176 D4
[14] Winterton-on-Sea NR29 ...58 B6
Wisbech PE13 ...152 C5
[1] Wymondham NR18 ...173 C4
Market Rd
Burgh Castle NR31 ...94 B8
Potter Heigham NR29 ...56 F5
Market Row [16] NR30 ...169 C4
Market St
East Harling NR16 ...118 C5
[8] King's Lynn PE30 ...146 E5
North Walsham NR28 ...151 C5
Shipdham IP25 ...67 C2
Tunstead NR12 ...37 F1
[19] Wisbech PE13 ...152 C5
Wymondham NR18 ...173 B4
Market Weston Rd
  IP22 ...127 C3
Marketfield La NR10 ...53 E2
Markshall Farm Rd
  NR14 ...89 F7
Markshall La NR14 ...89 F7
Marl Hill Rd NR9 ...51 F3
Marl Pit La NR5 ...161 C8
Marland Rd NR8 ...155 D2
Marlborough Rd PE13 ...152 A4
Marlborough Rd NR1 ...163 A6
Marlborough Sq NR30 ...169 E4
Marlborough Terr
  NR30 ...169 E4
Marle Ct NR1 ...170 C4
Marle Pit NR16 ...119 E7
Marlingford Pl PE30 ...138 F5
Marlingford Rd
Easton NR9 ...160 A7
Marlingford Way NR9 ...69 F4
Marlingford Sports Club
  NR9 ...70 B4
Marlow Cl NR3 ...158 E3
Marlpit La NR15 ...106 F6

Marlpit Rd
Hempstead NR25 19 E7
Thompson IP24 102 A7
Marram Dr NR30 168 E8
Marram Way PE31 133 B6
Marrams Ave NR27 139 A7
Marriot Cl NR2 162 C7
Marriott Chase NR8 155 E1
Marriott Way NR24 142 A5
Marriotts Way 3 NR26 138 D7
Marryat Rd NR7 159 C1
Marryats Loke 3 NR25 7 A4
Marsh Cl 7 NR29 57 D5
Marsh La Aldeby NR34 111 A6
Bracon Ash NR14 89 A2
Burgh Castle NR31 94 A8
Carlton Colville NR33 111 F2
3 Earsham NR35 123 F8
King's Lynn PE30 148 A1
5 New Buckenham NR16 104 F1
North Cove NR34 111 B1
Somerleyton, Ashby & Herringfleet NR32 111 C8
Tharston & Hapton NR15 106 C8
Wells-next-the-Sea NR23 136 D5
Wiveton NR25 7 E6
Worlingham NR34 110 F1
Wortham IP22 129 D4
Marsh Loke NR28 23 D1
Marsh Rd Cantley NR13 92 D6
Fleggburgh NR29 75 C8
Fritton & St Olaves NR31 93 E3
Great Yarmouth NR31 169 B3
Halvergate NR13 75 A1
North Wootton PE30 148 A6
Outwell PE14 77 F8
Potter Heigham NR29 57 A6
Repps with Bastwick NR29 56 F4
South Walsham NR13 74 B8
Thurne NR29 56 E3
Upton with Fishley NR13 166 B8
Walpole PE14 41 C4
Wroxham/Hoveton NR12 164 D5
Marsh Side PE31 3 B7
Marsh The PE14 41 C4
Marsh Wlk PE13 152 D5
Marshall Cl
Norwich NR5 161 B8
13 Spixworth NR10 54 A2
Marshall Rd NR3 158 B3
Marshall St 5 PE30 146 E5
Marsham Prim Sch NR10 150 C1
Marshgate NR28 151 E6
Marshland High Sch PE14 59 B8
Marshland Smeeth & Fen Mus* PE14 60 C6
Marshland St PE34 144 B5
Marshland St James VC Prim Sch PE14 60 A4
Marston La 10 NR4 89 C8
Marston Moor 7 NR7 72 D4
Martham Broad National Nature Resrve* NR29 57 D7
Martham Fst Sch NR29 57 D5
Martham Rd
Martham NR29 57 F4
Rollesby NR29 57 D3
Somerton NR29 57 E6
Martin Cl Brandon IP27 175 E3
5 Great Yarmouth NR31 94 C7
Norwich NR7 159 B4
3 Weybourne NR25 8 F5
Martin Rd Diss IP22 177 E4
Harleston IP20 122 E2
Martineau La NR1 162 F1
Marvell Gn 10 NR7 72 D5
Marwood Cl NR18 173 B3
Mary Chapman Cl 31 NR7 72 D4
Mary Chapman Ct NR3 178 A3
Mary Unwin Rd NR19 154 D4
Maryland NR23 136 D5
Masefield Dr PE38 172 D5
Masefield Mews NR19 154 C7
Masefield Rd IP22 177 E4
Masefield Wlk 8 IP24 176 E6
Mashs Row NR11 150 D8
Mason Gdns 11 PE33 43 F2
Mason Rd Norwich NR6 158 B3
5 Swanton Morley NR20 50 B3
Masons Dr PE37 65 F4
Masquers Cl NR31 170 C2
Massey Ct 2 NR21 141 C3
Massingham Rd
Castle Acre PE32 46 F2
Grimston PE31 28 C1
Norwich NR3 158 E1
Weasenham All Saints PE32 30 B1
Mast Cl 18 NR33 111 F1
Masters Ct NR28 151 D5
Mather La IP20 122 B1
Matlock Rd 1 NR1 163 B5
Matsell Way NR19 154 E5
Matthews Cl 4 NR15 106 F6
Mattishall La
Hockering NR20 69 A7
Mattishall NR20 68 F7
Mattishall Prim Sch NR20 68 F5
Mattishall Rd
Dereham NR20 68 B8
East Tuddenham NR20 69 B6
Garvestone NR9 68 D2
Honingham NR9 69 D6
Runhall NR9 69 A3
Maud St NR2 162 B6
Maud Terr NR30 169 D6
Maurice Gaymer Rd NR17 174 D4
Mautby La NR29 75 F6
Mavish Cl NR5 161 A6
Max Carter Cl NR28 38 A4
May Cl NR18 173 B5
Maybank NR28 151 D7
Mayes Cl 7 NR5 161 B8
Mayfield Ave NR6 158 B4
Mayfield Dr NR27 139 B5
Mayfield Way NR28 151 D7
Mayflower Ave PE30 146 F7
Mayflower Rd 1 PE13 152 E3
Mayflower Way 14 IP20 122 D1
Maygrove Rd 5 NR30 169 D5
Mayton Ave 2 NR12 54 A4
Mdws The 2 PE31 12 D4
Mead Cl NR10 36 E1
Meadon Way PE34 146 B4
Meadow Brown Way 9 NR18 173 E4
Meadow Cl
2 Beetley NR20 49 D4
Cromer NR27 139 A6
3 Hemsby NR29 167 A8
Hethersett NR9 88 C7
Holt NR25 137 D6
3 King's Lynn PE30 148 C5
Mundesley NR11 143 C5
Narborough PE32 63 E7
North Walsham NR28 151 C6
2 Norwich NR14 163 B2
Shipdham IP25 67 D2
5 Thurlton NR14 92 F1
Meadow Cotts PE32 48 B6
Meadow Ct
Fakenham NR21 141 E4
Great Yarmouth NR31 171 C8
Meadow Dr
1 Beetley NR19 49 C3
6 East Dereham NR19 154 C4
1 Gressenhall NR20 49 C3
Lackenheath IP27 113 E2
Mundesley NR11 143 C5
Wroxham/Hoveton NR12 164 D4
Meadow Farm Dr NR4 89 B7
Meadow Farm La NR10 53 E2
Meadow Gdns NR6 158 F4
Meadow Gr
North Runcton PE33 44 A2
26 Watton IP25 84 D3
Meadow La
Briston NR24 142 B5
Carbrooke IP25 85 A5
Kelling NR25 8 D5
Norwich NR7 163 F6
5 Rollesby NR29 57 D2
Meadow Loke 2 NR20 50 E7
Meadow Patch NR28 151 C6
Meadow Rd
Bungay NR35 124 B8
Cromer NR27 139 B6
Heacham PE31 133 D5
King's Lynn PE30 148 C2
Narborough PE32 63 E7
Norwich NR5 157 A2
Meadow Rise NR29 167 A8
Meadow Rise Ave NR2 162 A4
Meadow Rise Cl NR2 162 A4
Meadow Rise Rd NR2 162 A4
Meadow Vale NR5 157 A3
Meadow View NR13 165 D4
Meadow View Terr NR11 150 B5
Meadow Way
Attleborough NR17 174 C3
East Carleton NR14 88 F5
Horsford NR10 53 B3
Norwich NR6 157 F5
Poringland NR14 90 C4
Sheringham NR26 138 B6
Meadowbrook Cl 5 NR1 162 F3
Meadowcroft NR29 168 C8
Meadowgate La PE14 152 E2
Meadowgate Sch PE13 152 E3
Meadowland Dr 17 NR31 94 C6
Meadowrise NR21 15 E6
Meadows The
Aylsham NR11 150 C7
6 Hingham NR9 86 C4
South Wootton PE30 148 B2
Thetford IP24 176 E4
Thurton NR14 91 D4
Meadowside IP22 128 B6
Meadowsweet 18 NR10 53 A3
Meadowsweet Dr NR26 138 B6
Meadowsweet Rd 2 NR18 173 E4
Meadowvale Gdns PE30 147 B7
Meadway 18 NR4 89 B8
Mear Gdns NR1 163 B6
Mears Cnr NR16 105 B5
Medeswell 2 NR29 167 B7
Medeswell Cl NR13 165 C5
Medway Cl PE13 152 E4
Meer Dyke La PE14 59 D5
Meeting Hill Rd NR28 38 A7
Meeting House Hill Rd NR28 38 B6
Melbourne Rd
North Walsham NR28 151 D6
4 Sheringham NR26 138 D7
Melford Bride Rd IP24 176 D4
Melford Cl PE30 148 E1
Melford Comm 4 IP24 176 D4
Melford Ct 3 IP24 176 D4
Mellis Rd
Thrandeston IP21 129 F2
Wortham IP22 129 C3
Yaxley IP23 130 A1
Mellisash Rd IP23 129 D1
Melrose Dr NR11 10 A2
Melrose Rd NR4 162 A3
Melrose Terr 8 NR30 169 D2
Melton Cl NR18 173 B6
Melton Constable Hall* NR24 18 D2
Melton Ct NR9 88 C8
Melton Dr
Hunstanton PE36 132 C3
Taverham NR8 155 E1
Melton Gate NR18 173 B5
Melton Rd
Hindolveston NR20 33 D8
Wymondham NR18 173 B5
Melton St NR24 142 A5
Melville Rd IP24 116 C5
Memorial Way
Thorpe St Andrew NR7 72 E4
Watton IP25 84 D4
Mendham Cl
36 Harleston IP20 122 D2
3 Norwich NR1 162 E2
Mendham La
38 Harleston IP20 122 D2
St Mary, South Elmham otherwise Homersfield IP20 123 B3
Mendham Prim Sch IP20 123 A2
Mercedes Ave PE36 132 D2
Merchant Way NR6 158 A4
Merchants Ct NR27 139 C7
Mere Cl IP25 84 C4
Mere Manor Ct IP22 177 D4
Mere Plot Dro PE33 62 E5
Mere Rd Scoulton NR9 85 E4
Stow Bedon NR17 102 E7
Mere St IP22 177 D4
Meredith Rd NR6 157 E6
Mereside NR15 90 F2
Mergate La NR14 89 A2
Meridian Way NR7 72 E3
Merlewood IP21 121 C1
Merlin Ave NR7 159 B4
Merlin Cl NR12 164 D5
Merlin Mews NR7 159 C4
Merriman Rd 5 NR29 57 C4
Merrivale Model Village* NR30 169 E2
Merrow Gdns 7 NR4 89 C8
Merryweather Cl 3 NR15 106 E3
Merryweather Rd 9 PE13 153 C3
Merton Ave NR31 170 A3
Merton Rd
Norwich NR2 162 A7
Watton IP25 84 D2
Metcalf Ave PE30 146 D2
Metcalf Cl 4 NR3 157 F1
Meteor Cl NR6 158 D7
Methuen Ave PE30 147 A6
Methwold High Sch IP26 99 A6
Methwold Prim Sch IP26 99 A5
Methwold Rd
Methwold IP26 98 E5
Northwold IP26 99 C7
Metton Rd
Felbrigg NR11 139 A2
Roughton NR11 21 D8
Mews Ct 7 IP25 67 C2
Mews The
Great Yarmouth NR31 170 C1
4 Norwich NR2 162 C4
Micawber Ave 2 NR30 170 D8
Michaels Ct NR19 154 C5
Mid Norfolk Rly* NR19 154 E5
Mid Yare National Nature Reserve* NR13 165 D1
Midden Sta The NR23 136 F4
Middle Dro Denver PE38 79 B4
Marshland St James PE14 60 C2
Stow Bardolph PE14 78 D8
Middle Gates Dro PE14 60 B8
Middle Hill
Alby with Thwaite NR11 21 A5
Reedham NR13 92 F4
Middle La NR34 111 D4
Middle Mkt Rd NR30 169 D4
Middle Rd
Blo' Norton IP22 128 C6
Docking PE31 134 E4
Earsham IP20 123 C8
Great & Little Plumstead NR13 72 F5
Middle Rd *continued*
Hardingham NR9 86 E8
Morning Thorpe NR15 107 B3
Shouldham Thorpe PE33 62 C2
Terrington St Clement PE34 42 B8
Middle Rd E 4 NR30 169 D1
Middle Rd W 3 NR30 169 D1
Middle St NR11 11 E1
Middle Wall NR29 57 A6
Middlebrook Way
Cromer NR27 139 A6
Runton NR27 10 C4
Middlegate NR30 169 D2
Middlemarch Rd 5 NR19 154 D3
Middlesex La NR13 166 C3
Middlestone Cl NR31 170 C4
Middleton Ave NR20 50 B4
Middleton Cl
Norwich NR3 158 C3
2 Sheringham NR26 138 C5
Middleton Cres NR5 156 E2
Middleton Ct 4 NR18 173 B4
Middleton Gdns NR31 170 C5
Middleton Prim Sch PE32 44 C2
Middleton Rd NR31 170 C4
Middleton St NR18 173 B4
Middleton's Ct NR6 157 E4
Middleton's La NR6 157 F5
Middlewood 2 PE30 147 C4
Midland Cl
Caister-on-Sea NR30 168 F5
1 Great Yarmouth NR30 169 D5
Midland Rd NR28 151 C4
Midland St NR2 162 C7
Midland Wlk NR2 162 C7
Mikanda Cl PE14 152 C2
Mildenhall Rd CB7 112 B3
Mile Cross La NR6 158 C4
Mile Cross Mid Sch NR3 158 B1
Mile Cross Rd NR3 162 B8
Mile End IP27 175 A1
Mile End Cl NR4 162 A3
Mile End Rd
Littleport CB7 112 A3
Norwich NR4 162 A3
Mile Rd
Carleton Rode NR16 105 A5
Garvestone NR9 68 A1
Mileham Prim Sch PE32 48 D6
Mileham Rd
Beeston with Bittering PE32 48 C3
Litcham PE32 48 A4
Milestone Cl NR5 156 F2
Milestone La NR18 87 A4
Milford Rd 5 NR2 162 B5
Mill Bank PE14 59 F7
Mill Cl Aylsham NR11 150 A6
2 Blofield Heath NR13 73 D6
Hempton NR21 141 A3
Hethersett NR9 88 C7
Hickling NR12 39 F2
Kirby Row NR35 109 E3
Mattishall NR20 68 F5
Norwich NR1 162 E3
Poringland NR14 90 C5
Pulham Market IP21 121 E5
6 Salhouse NR13 55 A1
Thurton NR14 91 C4
Wisbech PE13 152 C6
Mill Cnr NR9 86 C4
Mill Comm NR14 91 C4
Mill Comm Rd NR28 23 E2
Mill Cres NR13 166 B4
Mill Croft Cl NR5 156 E1
Mill Ct Fakenham NR21 141 B3
Holt NR25 137 B6
Wells-next-the-Sea NR23 136 D5
Mill Drift
Beeston with Bittering PE32 48 C3
Hockwold cum Wilton IP26 114 A7
Mill Dro
Gooderstone PE33 81 F4
Middleton PE32 44 D2
Southery PE38 97 A5
Mill Farm Nurseries PE37 153 B2
Mill Field Cl PE14 42 C1
Mill Gdns
Bedingham NR35 108 B4
Horsford NR10 53 B3
Mill Gn
Burnham Market PE31 135 D3
Stoke Holy Cross NR14 89 F4
Mill Hill Bradenham IP25 66 E3
Bramerton NR14 90 F8
Brancaster PE31 3 B6
Brandon IP27 175 E3
2 Horning NR12 55 E4
Mettingham NR35 109 D1
Norwich NR3 158 E2
Roughton NR11 139 A1
Salhouse NR13 55 B1
Strumpshaw NR13 73 F2
Mill Hill Rd
Boughton PE33 80 F5
Norwich NR2 162 B5
Mill Houses PE30 146 F6
Mill La Acle NR13 166 C3
Mill La *continued*
All Saints & St Nicholas, South Elmham IP20 123 E1
Aslacton NR15 106 A1
Attleborough NR17 174 F7
Aylsham NR11 150 B6
Bacton/Walcott NR12 23 E4
Barnham IP24 125 E6
Bircham PE31 13 F3
Blackborough End PE32 44 C1
Briston NR24 142 F3
Brooke NR15 108 A8
Burnham Thorpe PE31 4 D4
Carbrooke IP25 85 B4
Catfield NR29 56 C7
Claxton NR14 91 E6
Clenchwarton PE34 145 F6
Crimplesham PE33 80 B7
Cromer NR27 10 B5
Dereham NR19 154 A8
Docking PE31 134 E4
Downham Market PE38 172 D7
Ellingham NR35 109 E3
Felthorpe NR10 155 C8
Fleggburgh NR29 57 B1
Foulsham NR20 33 D4
Garboldisham IP22 128 A7
Great Ellingham NR17 103 D7
Great Massingham PE32 29 D2
Great Yarmouth NR31 94 C7
Haddiscoe NR14 110 D8
Hindringham NR21 17 E8
Hockering NR20 69 B7
Hockwold cum Wilton IP26 114 A7
Hoe NR20 49 D3
Honingham NR9 69 E6
Hopton IP22 127 F7
Horsford NR10 53 B3
Horsham St Faith & Newton St Faith NR10 53 E2
Keswick NR4 89 D7
King's Lynn PE30 147 B8
Kirby Bedon NR14 90 E7
Long Stratton NR15 106 F3
Morley NR18 87 A3
Newton Flotman NR15 89 E2
Norwich NR3 162 E8
Ormesby St Margaret with Scratby NR29 58 A1
Ovington IP25 84 E5
Postwick with Witton NR13 73 A3
Pulham Market IP21 121 E5
Redgrave IP22 128 E5
Repps with Bastwick NR29 57 B3
Rickinghall Inferior IP22 128 D2
Rocklands NR17 103 C7
St John, Ilketshall NR34 124 E6
Seething NR15 91 C1
Shelton NR15 122 B8
1 Southery PE38 97 B5
14 Sutton Bridge PE12 41 B8
Swaffham PE37 153 C3
Syderstone PE31 15 B3
Thetford IP24 176 D3
Tilney St Lawrence PE34 42 C2
Tunstead NR12 38 A3
Walpole Highway PE14 59 F7
Walsingham NR22 16 F8
West Walton PE14 59 C8
Weybread IP21 131 F7
Wreningham NR16 88 D1
Yaxham NR19 68 B5
Mill Loke 4 NR12 55 E4
Mill Orch IP21 121 E5
Mill Pightle NR11 150 B6
Mill Pool La NR35 109 D2
Mill Rd Alburgh IP20 122 E6
Aldborough NR11 21 A6
All Saints South Elmham IP19 124 B1
Ashby St Mary NR14 91 C4
Aylsham NR11 150 C6
Bacton NR28 23 A1
Banham NR16 119 D7
Barnham Broom NR9 69 B2
Barningham IP31 127 C3
Barton Turf NR12 38 E1
Bergh Apton NR14 91 A4
Bintree NR20 33 A2
Blofield Heath NR13 73 D6
Botesdale IP22 128 F2
Brancaster PE31 3 B6
Briston NR24 142 F3
Brockdish IP21 131 B7
Burgh Castle NR31 94 A7
Burgh St Peter NR34 111 B4
Burnham Market PE31 135 E4
Burston & Shimpling IP22 120 E2
Carleton Rode NR16 105 A4
Colby NR11 36 F7
Coltishall NR12 54 C6
Cromer NR27 139 C5
Dersingham PE31 140 F5
Dilham NR28 38 D4
East Ruston NR12 24 A4
Emneth PE14 59 D2
Forncett NR16 106 B3
Foxley NR20 50 D8
Freethorpe NR13 92 F8
Frettenham NR12 54 A4
Great Yarmouth NR31 169 B3

Mill Rd *continued*
Gresham NR11 9 D1
Halvergate NR13 74 F1
Hardingham NR9 86 E8
Harpley PE31 29 D4
Hempnall NR15 107 C5
Hemsby NR29 58 A4
7 Hethersett NR9 88 C7
Honington IP31 126 D1
Kirby Row NR35 109 D3
Lakenheath IP27 113 E1
Little Melton NR9 160 B2
Loddon NR14 92 A1
Long Stratton NR15 107 A2
Marlingford NR9 70 A3
Marsham NR10 36 C2
Mattishall NR20 68 E6
Mautby NR29 75 E7
North Walsham NR28 151 D3
Old Buckenham NR17 104 C1
Potter Heigham NR29 56 F5
Reedham NR13 93 A5
Reepham NR10 149 B2
Repps with Bastwick NR29 57 A4
Ryburgh NR21 32 C6
Salhouse NR13 55 A1
Shelton NR15 122 B8
Shipdham IP25 67 B2
Shouldham Thorpe PE33 62 C3
Stalham NR12 39 A3
Stoke Holy Cross NR14 89 F4
Stokesby with Herringby NR29 75 A6
Surlingham NR14 91 B8
Sutton NR12 39 C3
Terrington St John PE14 42 B1
Thelnetham IP22 128 B5
Thompson IP24 102 A7
Thurlton NR14 110 D8
Tibenham NR16 120 D8
Tivetshall St Mary NR15 121 B5
Topcroft NR35 107 F4
Walpole St Andrew PE14 41 E3
Watlington PE34 61 D8
Watton IP25 84 D3
Wells-next-the-Sea NR23 136 B5
West Walton PE14 59 B8
Weybread IP21 131 F8
Whissonsett NR20 31 D2
Wiggenhall St Germans PE34 43 C1
Wiggenhall St Mary Magdalen PE34 61 B5
Winfarthing IP22 120 B4
Mill Rd S IP22 128 F2
Mill Reach NR10 36 F1
Mill Row NR11 150 D7
Mill St Bradenham IP25 66 E3
Elsing NR20 50 F4
Gimingham NR11 22 E7
Holt NR25 137 B6
Horsham St Faith NR10 53 E2
Lamas NR10 36 F1
Mattishall NR20 68 F5
3 Necton PE37 65 F4
Swanton Morley NR20 50 B4
Mill View
Barnham Broom NR9 69 B2
Saham Toney IP25 84 C5
Sedgeford PE36 13 A7
Mill View Cl NR11 143 D5
Mill View Mid Sch NR5 161 C8
Mill Way PE14 77 B8
Millard Cl NR28 151 A6
Millcroft NR3 158 E1
Millennium Plain NR2 178 A2
Millennium Way PE34 146 A5
Miller Cl 7 NR19 154 C4
Miller's Breck NR8 155 D1
Miller's La
2 Thetford IP24 176 C4
Wimbotsham PE34 79 E8
Millers Cl NR35 124 B8
Millers Dr IP21 121 B1
Millers Gn 43 IP20 122 D2
Millers La Harpley PE31 29 D4
Norwich NR3 158 D1
Millers Sq NR17 174 C5
Millers Way 1 NR10 53 B3
Millers Wlk NR21 141 C3
Millfield Ashill IP25 84 A8
Eye IP23 130 B1
Millfield Cl 5 NR13 73 D6
Millfield La PE33 43 F3
Millfield Prim Sch NR28 151 B3
Millfield Rd
Barningham IP31 127 D3
North Walsham NR28 151 B4
Millfields 2 NR15 107 C5
Millfleet 4 PE30 146 E4
Millgate NR11 150 D7
Millgate St IP26 99 A5
Millhill La NR18 86 F2
Millicent Oliver Cl 11 IP24 176 D7
Millington Ct 6 IP24 176 D4
Millmarsh Dro IP27 113 D2
Mills Cl NR8 155 C1
Millside Hales NR14 109 F8
Stalham NR12 39 B3
Millview NR29 167 A3
Millway NR18 173 B6
Millway Ave IP22 177 C6
Millway La
Palgrave IP22 177 B2
Wortham IP22 129 D5
Milner Rd PE13 152 C4
Milnes Way 3 NR33 111 F1
Milton Ave PE30 146 F5
Milton Cl
East Dereham NR19 154 C7
Norwich NR1 162 E3
3 Thetford IP24 176 E6
Milton Rd
Great Yarmouth NR30 169 D8
8 Swanton Morley NR20 50 B3
Milton Way 1 PE38 172 D6
Milverton Rd 1 NR1 162 F3
Mindhams Yd NR23 136 C6
Mingay Rd IP24 176 B2
Minion Cl 8 NR7 72 D4
Minsmere Rd 7 NR31 94 A6
Minster Ct PE30 147 C5
Minstergate IP24 176 C4
Miriam Cl NR29 168 E8
Misburgh Way NR31 171 E4
Mission La
Docking PE31 134 E4
Fakenham NR21 141 E4
Mission Pl NR30 169 D6
Mission Rd Diss IP22 177 F3
3 Great Yarmouth NR31 169 B4
Rackheath NR13 72 E8
Mitchell Ct 4 NR5 160 F8
Mitre Ct NR3 158 A3
Mitre Tavern Yd 4 NR28 151 C5
Mitre Yd 9 NR28 151 C5
Moat Rd
3 Great Yarmouth NR30 169 C5
Terrington St Clement PE34 144 B1
Modney Bridge Rd PE38 96 F8
Mokyll Croft NR8 155 D2
Moles La NR34 124 D5
Molls Dro PE14 77 C7
Monastery The NR3 178 B3
Money Bank PE13 152 E4
Moneyhill La NR9 86 C3
Moneypot La IP22 128 E5
Monkhams Dr 9 IP25 84 E3
Monks Cl PE31 14 D5
Monksgate IP24 176 B4
Mons Ave NR1 163 A8
Mont Cross 8 NR8 155 D2
Montagu Cl PE37 153 C3
Montagu Dr 4 IP27 114 E1
Montague Rd NR26 138 C7
Montcalm Rd NR1 163 B6
Montgomery Cl 2 NR5 160 F7
Montgomery Way PE30 147 D4
Montpelier Dr 1 IP24 116 A1
Montrose Ct 1 NR7 72 D4
Monument Rd NR30 170 E7
Moor La Cranworth IP25 85 D7
Elsing NR20 50 F3
Fransham NR19 66 A7
Sculthorpe NR21 16 B2
Stalham NR12 39 C3
Moor Rd
Burston & Shimpling IP21 121 B2
Stalham NR12 39 C3
Moor The NR10 149 E5
Moorditch La PE34 42 E2
Moore Ave NR6 158 F5
Moorend La NR21 32 D7
Moorfield Rd 3 NR20 68 E6
Moorgate Rd
East Dereham NR19 154 D3
Hindringham NR21 17 E8
Moorhouse Cl NR10 149 C5
Moorings The PE33 81 A2
Moorland Cl NR7 159 A2
Moorland Way 3 NR31 94 A5
Moors The NR8 155 F2
Morar Dr NR17 174 E6
Morello Cl NR4 161 E5
Morgan Way NR5 160 F8
Morgans Way NR10 53 C8
Morgrove La NR29 57 D6
Morley CE Prim Sch NR18 87 A2
Morley La NR18 87 C2
Morley Rd
Beighton NR13 74 D2
Deopham NR18 86 E1
Sheringham NR26 138 D6
Morley Rd N NR26 138 D6
Morley St NR3 162 F8
Morleyfield La NR18 87 A3
Mormor La IP21 131 C8
Mornington Rd NR2 162 A4
Morris Cl
3 Norwich NR5 161 B8
6 Stoke Holy Cross NR14 89 F4
Morris Dr NR13 165 A8
Morris Rd NR28 151 B4
Morris St NR26 138 D7
Morrison Cl NR28 151 B5
Morse Ave NR1 163 C7
Morse Cl
Brundall NR13 165 D3
Great Witchingham NR9 51 D5
Morse Ct NR30 168 D6
Morse Rd NR1 163 C7
Morston Chase NR25 6 F6
Morston Rd
Blakeney NR25 7 C6
Morston Rd *continued*
Stiffkey NR23 6 D6
Mortimer Cl NR17 174 F6
Morton Cl 1 NR11 150 D6
Morton Cres 22 NR31 94 C7
Morton La NR9 51 F3
Morton Peto Cl NR32 111 D7
Morton Peto Rd NR31 170 B8
Morton Rd NR11 150 D6
Mosely Ct NR5 160 E8
Mossfield Cl NR1 163 B8
Mother Julian Cl 8 IP24 176 D7
Mother Quy's IP24 115 C1
Mottram Cl NR5 161 D6
Motum Rd NR5 161 C7
Moulton Rd
Halvergate NR13 74 F1
Tivetshall St Margaret NR15 121 A7
Mount Cl Brandon IP27 175 D2
Swaffham PE37 153 A5
Mount Dr PE13 152 E4
Mount Pk Cl PE32 44 C3
Mount Pleasant
Diss IP22 177 D5
Little Walsingham NR22 16 F8
Norwich NR2 162 B4
Mount Pleasant Rd PE13 152 C7
Mount Rd IP27 175 D2
Mount St Cromer NR27 139 B7
Diss IP22 177 D5
King's Lynn PE30 146 F4
Mount Surrey 4 NR18 173 C6
Mount Tumbledown Cl 7 PE12 41 B8
Mountain's Rd 2 NR11 19 F1
Mountbatten Cl 5 IP24 176 E6
Mountbatten Dr
2 East Dereham NR19 154 C6
Old Catton NR6 159 A6
Wisbech PE13 152 A7
Mountbatten Rd
Bungay NR35 124 A7
Dersingham PE31 140 C3
Mountbatten Way NR30 168 D6
Mounteney Cl NR7 159 A4
Mountergate NR1 178 B2
Mountfield Ave
Hellesdon NR6 157 F4
Norwich NR6 158 A4
Mousehold Ave NR3 163 A8
Mousehold Fst Sch NR3 162 F8
Mousehold La NR7 159 A3
Mousehold St NR3 178 C4
Mowles Rd NR20 68 C8
Moyse's Bank
Emneth Hungate PE14 59 F2
Marshland St James PE14 60 A2
Muck La NR13 72 F8
Muckleburgh Collection The* NR25 8 E6
Mud Rd NR21 15 D2
Mudd's Dro PE14 77 F2
Muir La NR15 106 B2
Mulbarton Fst Sch NR14 89 B3
Mulbarton Mid Sch NR14 89 B3
Mulberry Cl
17 Feltwell IP26 98 E1
6 Norwich NR3 178 A3
Mulberry Ct 2 NR8 155 B2
Mulberry Gr 4 NR31 94 C6
Mulberry La NR15 107 A3
Mulberry Rd PE30 147 D4
Mullicourt Rd PE14 78 B6
Mumby's Dro PE14 77 E1
Mundesley Hospl NR11 22 F7
Mundesley Jun & Fst Sch NR11 143 B5
Mundesley Maritime Mus* NR11 143 C6
Mundesley Rd
Gimingham NR11 22 E7
North Walsham NR28 151 C6
Overstrand NR27 11 A3
Paston NR28 143 D3
Trimingham NR11 11 E1
Trunch NR28 22 F5
Mundford Prim Sch IP26 100 B4
Mundford Rd
Thetford IP24 176 C6
Weeting-with-Broomhill IP27 175 D7
Mundham La NR14 91 D2
Mundham Rd
Loddon NR14 91 E1
Mundham NR14 109 A8
Mundy's Rd IP20 123 A1
Munhaven Cl NR11 143 C5
Munnings Cl NR14 89 D4
Munnings Rd NR7 159 D1
Munson's La IP26 98 E2
Munson's Pl IP26 98 E2
Murgot's La PE33 81 D7
Muriel Kenny Ct 10 NR9 88 C7
Muriel Rd NR2 162 A4
Muriel Way IP25 85 B4
Murrayfield Rd NR6 158 B5
Mus of the Broads The* NR12 39 B3
Museum Sq PE13 152 C5
Music House La NR1 178 B2
Musketeer Way 29 NR7 72 D4
Muspole St NR3 178 A4
Musticott Pl PE13 152 F6
Myles Way PE13 152 C8
Myrtle Ave
Costessey NR8 156 F3
East Dereham NR19 154 E4
Myrtle Ct NR31 170 C6
Myrtle Rd NR9 88 C8

N

Naber Furlong 1 NR8 155 E2
Napier Cl PE30 147 C5
Napier Pl Norwich NR2 162 C7
Thetford IP24 176 A1
Naples Cl NR31 171 E4
Napoleon Pl 9 NR30 169 D3
Narborough Hill PE33 63 E2
Narborough Rd PE32 63 D8
Narborough VC Fst Sch PE32 63 E7
Narford La PE32 45 F2
Narford Rd PE32 63 F7
Narrows Trading Est The PE30 147 A1
Naseby Way 23 NR7 72 D4
Nash Rd NR10 155 C8
Nash's La NR28 23 E1
Nasmith Rd NR4 161 E3
Naylor Rd 1 NR3 157 F1
Neale Cl NR11 150 B6
Neatherd High Sch NR20 154 F5
Neatherd Moor NR20 154 F6
Neatherd Rd NR19 154 E5
Neatishead Prim Sch NR12 55 D7
Neatishead Rd NR12 55 E5
Necton CE Fst Sch PE37 66 A4
Necton Mid Sch PE37 66 A4
Necton Rd PE32 65 E7
Needham Bank PE14 77 C8
Needham Rd IP20 122 C1
Neil Ave NR25 137 B5
Neilsen Cl NR23 136 E6
Nelonde Dr 1 NR18 173 C5
Nelson Ave PE38 172 B5
Nelson Cl
Bradenham IP25 66 E3
4 Hethersett NR9 88 E8
Nelson Cres PE37 153 D3
Nelson Ct IP25 84 D4
Nelson Dr PE36 132 D3
Nelson Fst Sch NR2 162 B7
Nelson Gdns PE13 152 D6
Nelson Hts NR27 139 A7
Nelson Pl 3 NR19 154 D5
Nelson Rd
Caister-on-Sea NR30 168 F4
Fakenham NR21 141 B4
Great Yarmouth NR31 170 D4
North Walsham NR28 151 D5
Sheringham NR26 138 F7
Nelson Rd Central NR30 169 D3
Nelson Rd N NR30 169 D5
Nelson Rd S NR30 169 D2
Nelson St
King's Lynn PE30 146 D4
Norwich NR2 162 B7
Nelson Way
Hevingham NR10 53 B8
Mundesley NR11 143 A7
7 North Walsham NR28 151 C5
Nene Mdws PE12 41 C8
Nene Par PE13 152 B6
Nene Quay PE13 152 C5
Nene Rd
Hunstanton PE36 132 C4
4 Watlington PE33 61 D6
Nene Sch The PE13 152 D4
Nenelands PE12 41 C8
Nether Row IP24 176 D3
Nethergate St
Ditchingham NR35 124 A8
Harpley PE31 29 C4
Hopton IP22 127 E6
Netherwood Gn NR1 162 F2
Nettle Hill E 15 NR30 169 D4
Nettle Hill W NR30 169 D4
Neve's Cl NR13 73 F3
Neville Cl
East Dereham NR19 154 E1
Norwich NR7 158 F3
Saham Toney IP25 84 B5
Neville La PE31 133 C6
Neville Rd
Heacham PE31 133 C6
Norwich NR7 159 A3
Stalham NR12 39 C3
Neville St NR2 162 C5
New Bridge La
Elm PE14 59 A1
Wisbech PE14 152 A1
New Bridge Rd PE14 77 D5
New Cl NR13 166 C3
New Coll Cl NR31 170 B5
New Comm Rd IP22 127 F4
New Conduit St PE30 146 D5
New Dro 3 PE13 152 D2
New Eccles Hall Sch The NR16 118 F7
New England Way 2 IP24 116 A1
New Fen Dro PE38 97 A5
New Hampshire Way 5 IP24 116 A1
New Inn Hill NR14 91 C7
New Inn La NR19 154 B5
New La Banham NR16 119 B8
Bradenham IP25 66 F4
Hoveton NR12 55 C4
Mattishall NR20 68 F5
New Mills Yd NR3 178 A4
New N Rd NR17 174 D5
New Par NR27 139 C7
New Rd Acle NR13 166 C3
Attleborough NR17 174 B3
Aylsham NR11 150 D7
Baconsthorpe NR25 20 A8
Bawburgh NR9 160 B6
Belton NR31 94 A5
Blakeney NR25 7 C6
Bodham NR25 9 B1
Brettenham IP24 117 B2
Brinton NR24 18 D8
Burnham Overy Staithe PE31 135 E7
Catfield NR29 56 C8
Crimplesham PE33 80 A6
Dickleburgh & Rushall IP21 130 D8
Dunton NR21 16 A2
Fritton & St Olaves NR31 93 E3
Gissing IP22 120 F4
Great Yarmouth NR30 169 A6
Haddiscoe NR14 110 F7
Halvergate NR13 75 B4
Hethersett NR9 88 C7
Hingham NR9 86 C3
Itteringham NR11 35 D8
King's Lynn PE30 147 B6
12 Lingwood NR13 74 A3
Longham NR19 48 F2
Methwold IP26 98 E5
Mettingham NR35 124 C7
Morley NR18 87 A3
North Runcton PE33 44 A3
North Walsham NR28 151 D5
Northrepps NR27 139 E1
Norton Subcourse NR14 92 E1
Oulton NR11 35 D7
Outwell PE14 77 E5
Palgrave IP22 129 F4
Reedham NR13 92 F4
Reepham NR10 149 C5
St Cross, South Elmham IP20 123 D1
Saxlingham Nethergate NR15 107 B8
Sculthorpe NR21 16 A3
Sheringham NR26 138 D7
Shipdham IP25 67 B2
Shouldham PE33 62 D4
Skeyton NR10 37 A5
South Creake NR21 15 D7
Stanfield NR20 48 F7
Stokesby with Herringby NR29 75 A6
Surlingham NR14 73 B1
Sutton NR12 39 D2
Sutton Bridge PE12 41 B8
Tacolneston NR16 105 E5
Thelnetham IP22 127 F3
Thetford IP24 176 C4
Thrandeston IP21 130 A4
Tilney St Lawrence PE34 42 C1
Tivetshall St Mary NR15 121 B4
Toft Monks NR34 110 D6
Welney PE14 95 D5
Whissonsett NR20 31 D2
Wimbotsham PE34 172 E8
Wiveton NR25 7 E6
Wormegay PE33 62 C8
New Roman Bank PE34 144 B7
New Row PE31 133 D6
New Sporle Rd PE37 153 C5
New St Cawston NR10 35 B2
Cromer NR27 139 B7
Holt NR25 137 B6
King's Lynn PE30 147 B7
Sheringham NR26 138 D7
New Wellington Pl 23 NR30 169 D2
Newall Rd 3 IP24 125 F6
Newarch La NR14 90 E7
Newark Cl 22 NR7 72 D4
Newarp Way NR30 168 D8
Newbegin Cl NR1 163 C7
Newbegin Rd NR1 163 B7
Newbury Way 20 NR7 72 D4
Newby Rd 2 PE30 147 D6
Newcastle Cl 3 NR7 72 D4
Newcastle Rd NR30 169 D1
Newcombe Cl PE14 42 B1
Newcombe Dr 15 IP26 98 E1
Newell Cresent NR27 10 A6
Newey's Way 2 NR12 164 C5
Newfen Gravel Dro IP27 113 D4
Newfields PE32 65 C5
Newfound Dr NR4 161 C1
Newgate NR35 109 E3
Newgate La
Kirby Cane NR35 109 E3
Wells-next-the-Sea NR23 136 D6
Newhaven Cl NR27 139 B6
Newhaven Ct NR27 139 B6

Newlands Ave PE30 ....146 E7
Newlands Cl 40 IP20 ....122 D2
Newman Rd NR13 ....72 D7
Newmarket Rd
2 Cringleford NR4 ....89 B8
Norwich NR2 ....178 A1
Newmarket St NR2 .....162 C4
Newnham Gn NR31 .....170 A4
Newport NR29 ....167 D6
Newport Rd
Hemsby NR29 ....167 C6
South Walsham NR13 ......74 A6
Newstead Wlk IP22 ....177 C6
Newstead's La NR27 .....10 C4
Newton Cl
Horsham St Faith & Newton St Faith NR10 ......53 D4
10 Newton Flotman NR15 ...89 D1
Norwich NR4 ....162 B1
Newton Cross NR31 ....170 D1
Newton Flotman Prim Sch NR15 ....89 D1
Newton Rd
Hainford NR10 ....53 E5
Newton by Castle Acre PE32 ....47 A2
Sporle with Palgrave PE32 ....65 C7
Newton St NR10 ....53 D4
Newtown IP24 ....176 C3
Neylond Cres NR6 ......157 E6
Nicholas Ave PE34 .....145 E6
Nicholas Hamond Way 4 PE37 ....153 C3
Nicholas Mews 3 NR2 ...162 B7
Nicholls Way IP22 .....177 A5
Nick's La IP23 ....130 B2
Nicolson Ave NR20 ......50 B5
Nightingale Cl
Denver PE38 ....172 D2
Fakenham NR21 ....141 F4
Hemsby NR29 ....167 E4
Mulbarton NR14 ....89 A3
Nightingale Dr NR8 ....155 B1
Nightingale Fst Sch NR8 ....155 B1
Nightingale La
Denver PE38 ....172 D3
8 Feltwell IP26 ....98 E1
3 Feltwell IP26 ....98 E1
Norwich NR3 ....162 E8
Nightingale Rd IP27 ....175 F3
Nightingale Way IP24 ..176 D1
Nightingale Wlk PE38 ..172 C2
Nightmarsh La PE31 .....27 C4
Nile Rd
Downham Market PE38 ...172 B4
Great Yarmouth NR31 .....170 D4
Nile St 1 NR2 ....162 B7
Nimrod Cl 27 NR9 ....88 D8
Nine Acre La NR24 ......19 C4
Ninham St NR1 ....162 E3
Ninhams Ct NR2 ....178 A3
Nobb's Loke NR12 ....38 F4
Nobbs' Cnr NR35 ....108 A4
Nobel Cres NR12 ....164 B4
Noble Cl NR7 ....159 D1
Noel Cl NR31 ....171 C5
Noot Alley 6 NR5 ....161 B7
Nordelph Cnr NR9 ....86 D6
Norfolk & Norwich Univ Hospl NR4 ....161 A3
Norfolk & Suffolk Aviation Mus* NR35 ....123 D6
Norfolk Arena PE34 .....168 F2
Norfolk Dr NR17 ....174 C6
Norfolk Lavender Visitor Ctr* PE31 ....133 E6
Norfolk Motor Cycle Mus* NR28 ....151 C4
Norfolk Nelson Mus* NR30 ....169 C3
Norfolk Rd
10 Honington IP31 ....126 B1
10 Marham PE33 ....63 B4
Norwich NR4 ....161 B3
Sheringham NR26 ....138 D6
Thetford IP24 ....176 E4
Norfolk Record Office NR1 ....162 F3
Norfolk Shire Horse Ctr* NR27 ....9 F5
Norfolk Sq
Downham Market PE38 ...172 B5
Great Yarmouth NR30 .....169 E5
Norfolk St
4 King's Lynn PE30 ......146 E5
Norwich NR2 ....162 C5
Wisbech PE13 ....152 C4
Norfolk Wildlife Ctr & Country Pk* NR9 ....51 C6
Norfolk Wildlife Hospl (RSPCA)* PE32 ....44 F3
Norgate La IP21 ....130 E6
Norgate Rd NR4 ....161 E3
Norgate Way NR8 ......156 E8
Norman CE Prim Sch IP26 ....99 C7
Norman Cl
East Dereham NR19 ......154 C5
Fakenham NR21 ....141 B6
Norman Dr
Northwold PE33 ....81 B2
Norwich NR6 ....158 E7
Norman Fst Sch NR3 ...158 B2
Norman La 10 NR31 .....169 B4
Norman Rd
Flitcham with Appleton PE31 ....28 E7
Norwich NR3 ....158 E1
Norman Troller Ct 9 NR27 ....139 B7
Norman Way PE31 ....15 B3
Norman's Burrow Rd NR21 ....31 B3
Normandy Cl IP26 ....99 C7
Normans Bldgs NR1 ....178 B2
Normans La NR21 ....4 D1
North Ave NR20 ....50 B5
North Beach PE36 ......132 B1
North Brink PE13 ......152 A4
North Cambridgeshire Hospl PE13 ....152 D5
North Denes Airfield NR30 ....168 D2
North Denes Mid Sch NR30 ....169 D8
North Denes Rd NR30 ..169 D6
North Dr
Fakenham NR21 ....141 C5
Great Yarmouth NR30 ....169 E4
North Elmham Chapel* NR20 ....49 F8
North Elmham Prim Sch NR20 ....49 E8
North End
Haddiscoe NR14 ....93 B1
Stoke Holy Cross NR14 .....89 E5
Wisbech PE13 ....152 B6
North End La NR16 .....106 D3
North Everard St PE30 ....146 E3
North Gage Cl NR7 .....159 C4
North Gn NR9 ....68 B1
North Gn Rd IP21 ......122 A4
North La NR21 ....17 E5
North Lawn PE38 ....97 B6
North Lopham Rd NR16 ....119 A3
North Lynn Ind Est PE30 ....147 A8
North Mkt Rd
7 Great Yarmouth NR30 ..169 D4
Winterton-on-Sea NR29 ....58 B6
North Norfolk Rly* NR26 ....9 B6
North Pickenham Rd PE37 ....153 D4
North Pk NR21 ....141 B6
North Pk Ave NR4 ......161 E4
North Pk Dr NR4 ....161 F4
North Quay NR30 ......169 C4
North Rd Bunwell NR16 ..105 C4
4 Great Yarmouth NR30 ..169 D5
Great Yarmouth NR31 .....170 D4
Hemsby NR29 ....167 A7
Ormesby St Margaret with Scratby NR29 ....167 A4
Watton IP25 ....84 D3
North River Rd NR30 ...169 C6
North St Brundall NR13 ..165 E6
Burnham Market PE31 ....135 C3
6 Castle Acre PE32 ....46 F2
Great Dunham PE32 ....47 E2
King's Lynn PE30 ....146 D6
Langham NR25 ....7 A4
North Walsham NR28 .....151 C5
Sheringham NR26 ....138 C7
Wisbech PE13 ....152 C5
North View NR21 ....17 F3
North Walsham Cottage Hospl NR28 ....151 C4
North Walsham Fst Sch NR28 ....151 D5
North Walsham High Sch NR28 ....151 D4
North Walsham Jun Sch NR28 ....151 D5
North Walsham Rd
Bacton NR28 ....23 C3
Coltishall NR12 ....54 D7
Crostwick NR12 ....54 B2
Felmingham NR28 ....37 B8
Happisburgh NR12 ....23 F2
Northrepps NR27 ....10 E1
Norwich NR6 ....159 A5
Paston NR28 ....151 F7
Sprowston NR6 ....159 B6
Swafield NR28 ....22 E4
Thorpe Market NR11 ....22 A7
Witton NR28 ....38 B8
North Walsham Sta NR28 ....151 C4
North Way PE30 ....147 A8
North Wootton Prim Sch PE30 ....148 D4
Northcote PE31 ....134 D6
Northcote Rd 1 NR3 ....162 E8
Northern Cl NR30 ....168 F5
Northfield Ave NR23 ...136 D6
Northfield Cl NR18 .....173 B6
Northfield Cres NR23 ...136 E5
Northfield Gdns NR18 ..173 B5
Northfield La
Plumstead NR11 ....20 B6
Wells-next-the-Sea NR23 ....136 E6
Northfield Loke NR18 ...173 B6
Northfield Rd
Forncett NR16 ....106 A4
Mundesley NR11 ....143 C5
North Walsham NR28 .....151 B6
Swaffham PE37 ....153 C6
Northfield Way NR23 ...136 E6
Northfields NR4 ....161 E4
Northfields Fst Sch NR4 ....161 E4
Northgate
Beccles NR34 ....110 D1
Dereham NR19 ....154 C7
11 Harleston IP20 ....122 D1
Hunstanton PE36 ....132 C5
Norwich NR6 ....157 F5
3 Thorpe End NR13 ....72 D6
Northgate Cty High Sch NR19 ....154 D6
Northgate Hospl NR30 ....169 D6
Northgate Prec PE36 ...132 C6
Northgate St NR30 .....169 C5
Northgate St Andrews Fst Sch NR30 ....169 C6
Northgate Way PE34 ...144 D6
Northmead Dr NR28 ....151 C6
Northolt Rd IP25 ....85 A3
Northrepps Prim Sch NR27 ....11 A2
Northrepps Rd NR27 ....139 E3
Northside NR7 ....72 E3
Northumberland St NR2 ....162 B7
Northview Rd NR5 ......157 C1
Northwell Pool Rd PE37 ....153 C5
North-West Twr* NR30 ....169 C5
Northwold Rd IP26 ......99 A6
Norton Dr 2 Norwich NR4 .89 D8
Norwich NR4 ....162 A1
Norton Hill NR13 ....74 A8
Norton Rd NR14 ....92 B1
Nortridge Rd NR5 ......161 A7
Norvic Dr NR4 ....161 E1
Norway Cl PE31 ....133 C6
Norwich Arts Ctr* NR2 ....178 A3
Norwich Bsns Pk NR4 ..162 D1
Norwich Castle Mus & Art Gall* NR1 ....178 B3
Norwich Cath* NR1 .....178 B3
Norwich City FC NR1 ...163 A4
Norwich Com Hospl NR2 ....161 F7
Norwich Comm NR18 ...173 F6
Norwich Dr NR20 ....32 E4
Norwich Gall* NR1 ......178 B3
Norwich Gates PE35 ....140 E1
Norwich High Sch for Girls NR2 ....162 B3
Norwich Int Airport NR6 ....158 B7
Norwich La IP31 ....127 A4
Norwich Lower Sch NR1 ....178 C3
Norwich Puppet Theatre NR1 ....178 B4
Norwich Rd Acle NR13 ..166 A3
Ashmanhaugh NR12 ....55 C7
Attleborough NR17 ....174 E6
Aylsham NR11 ....150 C6
Barnham Broom NR9 ......69 D2
Bawdeswell NR20 ....50 E7
Bracon Ash NR14 ....88 F2
Briston NR24 ....142 E5
Brooke NR15 ....90 E3
Burgh & Tuttington NR11 ....36 E6
Caister-on-Sea NR30 .....168 C5
Cantley NR13 ....92 D7
Carbrooke IP25 ....85 B3
Cawston NR10 ....35 B2
Chedgrave NR14 ....91 F2
Cromer NR27 ....139 C5
Denton IP20 ....123 B7
Dickleburgh & Rushall IP21 ....130 D6
Ditchingham NR35 ....109 A2
Earsham NR35 ....108 E1
East Dereham NR20 ......154 F5
East Tuddenham NR20 .....69 C6
Edgefield NR24 ....19 D6
Fakenham NR21 ....141 C4
Foxley NR20 ....50 D8
Gillingham NR34 ....110 C2
Great & Little Plumstead NR13 ....73 A7
Guist NR20 ....33 A4
Hardingham NR9 ....86 E8
9 Hethersett NR9 ....88 D7
Hingham NR9 ....86 D5
Holt NR25 ....137 B5
Horning NR12 ....55 E4
Horsham St Faith NR10 ....53 D2
Horstead with Stanninghall NR12 ....54 C4
Ingworth NR11 ....36 B8
Kimberley NR18 ....87 B7
Langley with Hardley NR14 ....91 F6
Lingwood & Burlingham NR13 ....74 A2
12 Loddon NR14 ....92 A2
Long Stratton NR15 ......106 F5
Ludham NR29 ....56 C5
Marlingford NR9 ....69 F4
Mattishall NR20 ....68 F6
Mulbarton NR14 ....89 B4
Neatishead NR12 ....164 F8
North Walsham NR28 .....151 B3
Norwich NR5 ....157 B2
Poringland NR14 ....90 B6
Pulham St Mary IP21 .....121 F4
Norwich Rd *continued*
Rackheath NR13 ....72 F8
Reepham NR10 ....149 C5
Roughton NR11 ....21 D8
Salhouse NR13 ....55 B1
Saxlingham Nethergate NR15 ....107 B8
Scole IP21 ....121 B1
Shotesham NR15 ....89 F2
Shouldham PE33 ....62 F3
Smallburgh NR12 ....38 D2
Stockton NR34 ....109 F5
Strumpshaw NR13 ....73 F2
Swaffham PE37 ....153 D4
Swanton Morley NR20 ......50 B2
4 Tacolneston NR16 .....105 F5
Tacolneston NR16 ....106 A6
Tharston & Hapton NR15 ....106 C7
Thetford IP24 ....176 D4
Thurton NR14 ....91 C3
Tivetshall St Mary NR15 ...121 D4
West Caister NR30 ......168 B6
Weston Longville NR9 ......51 E5
Wisbech PE13 ....152 E5
Woodton NR35 ....108 C6
Wroxham/Hoveton NR12 ....164 B3
Wymondham NR18 ....173 D5
Yaxham NR19 ....68 B5
Norwich Rd Sch IP24 ..176 D4
Norwich Research Pk NR4 ....161 A4
Norwich Riverside NR1 ....178 C2
Norwich Sch NR1 ......178 B3
Norwich Sch of Art & Design NR3 ....178 B3
Norwich St
East Dereham NR19 ......154 E5
Fakenham NR21 ....141 B4
Hingham NR9 ....86 C5
Mundesley NR11 ....143 A7
Norwich Sta NR1 ......178 C2
Norwich Theatre Royal NR2 ....178 A2
Norwood Rd IP27 ....175 A1
Notre Dame High Sch NR1 ....178 B1
Notre Dame Prep Sch NR2 ....162 B7
Nottingham Rd PE30 ...146 E8
Nottingham Way NR30 ....169 C3
Notykin St NR5 ....161 A8
Nourse Dr PE31 ....133 E5
Nova Scotia Rd
Filby NR30 ....168 A7
Ormesby St Margaret with Scratby NR29 ....167 B1
Nowhere La PE33 ....80 D4
Nuffield Cl NR31 ....170 B4
Nuffield Cres NR31 .....170 B4
Nunn's Way NR19 ......154 D5
Nunnery Dr IP24 ....176 D1
Nunnery Pl IP24 ....176 D2
Nunnery The* IP24 .....176 D2
Nuns' Bridges Rd IP24 ....176 C2
Nunsgate IP24 ....176 D2
Nurseries Ave NR13 ....165 E4
Nursery Cl Acle NR13 ...166 B4
2 Beetley NR19 ....49 C3
7 Belton NR31 ....94 A5
2 Gressenhall NR20 ....49 C3
King's Lynn PE30 ....148 C2
8 Marthan NR29 ....57 D5
Norwich NR6 ....157 E5
2 Roydon PE32 ....28 A1
Nursery Dr
Hunstanton PE36 ....132 D4
North Walsham NR28 .....151 B3
Wisbech PE13 ....152 E8
Nursery Gdns NR13 ....165 F6
Nursery La
Brancaster PE31 ....3 E6
Costessey NR8 ....156 F3
Hockwold cum Wilton IP26 ....114 A6
King's Lynn PE30 ....148 C3
Nursery Rd PE38 ....172 C6
Nursery Terr NR30 .....169 C6
Nursery Way PE32 ....28 A1
Nursey Cl NR35 ....109 D3
Nut La NR27 ....139 F3
Nutfield Cl 7 NR4 ......161 F1
Nuthall Cres PE30 .....147 A8
Nutmeg Wlk PE38 ......172 E6
Nuttele Cl NR15 ....107 C6
Nuttery Vale IP23 ......130 F2
Nutwood Cl NR8 ....155 D2

O

Oak Ave
14 Great Yarmouth NR31 ...94 C7
King's Lynn PE30 ....148 D2
Marham PE33 ....63 B4
North Elmham NR20 ....49 E7
Norwich NR7 ....163 F8
9 Poringland NR14 ....90 C5
West Winch PE33 ....43 F2
Oak Cl 4 Hethersett NR9 ..88 D8
Norwich NR5 ....156 F2
14 Tasburgh NR15 ....106 F6
Thetford IP24 ....176 A1
Oak Cres IP23 ....130 C1
Oak Dr PE14 ....77 F7
Oak Gr 7 Horsford NR10 ..53 B3
Sheringham NR26 ....138 D5
Oak La East Ruston NR12 ..38 E7
2 Hingham NR9 ....86 C4
Norwich NR3 ....158 D3
Oak Lodge NR7 ....163 C5
Oak Rd Dilham NR28 ......38 D4
Great Yarmouth NR31 .....170 B6
North Walsham NR28 .....151 B4
Stoke Ferry PE33 ....81 A2
Oak St Fakenham NR21 ...141 B4
Feltwell IP26 ....98 E1
Norwich NR3 ....178 A4
Oak Tree Bsns Pk NR13 ..72 E8
Oak Tree Cl 3 NR29 ......57 D5
Oak Tree Way 8 IP20 ...122 D1
Oak View Dr PE38 ......172 C6
Oak Wood NR13 ....165 E5
Oakapple Dr NR19 ......154 D8
Oak's La NR13 ....72 F2
Oakcroft Dr NR14 ....90 C5
Oakdale Rd NR13 ....165 D3
Oakdene NR21 ....15 C2
Oakfield Cl PE38 ....172 C4
Oakfield Dr 3 NR13 ......74 B8
Oakfield Rd
Aylsham NR11 ....150 C6
Long Stratton NR15 ......106 F3
Oakfields NR14 ....91 F2
Oakfields Cl 1 NR4 ......89 C8
Oakfields Rd NR4 ....89 B8
Oakhill NR13 ....165 D3
Oakland Dr 5 NR20 ......49 D4
Oaklands
Little Snoring NR21 ....17 C3
4 Old Buckenham NR17 ...104 D2
Poringland NR14 ....90 C6
6 Taverham NR8 ....155 B2
Oaklands Cl
Attleborough NR17 ....174 C3
Halvergate NR13 ....74 F2
Oaklands Dr
Brandon IP27 ....114 D4
Cringleford NR4 ....161 C1
Walsoken PE13 ....152 F7
Oaklands La 2 PE33 .....61 D3
Oaklands Pk NR28 ......151 B6
Oaklands The PE37 .....153 C3
Oakleigh Dr PE13 ......153 A5
Oakley Church La IP21 ....130 D4
Oakley Cl PE13 ....152 E4
Oakroyd Cres PE13 .....152 C6
Oaks Cl PE37 ....153 C3
Oaks Dr Necton PE37 .....65 F4
Swaffham PE37 ....153 C3
Oaks La NR34 ....111 B5
Oaks The Ashill IP25 .....84 A7
3 Beetley NR19 ....49 C3
3 Gressenhall NR20 ....49 C3
Mattishall NR20 ....68 F5
Oaktree Dr NR7 ....159 B2
Oakwood Cl NR19 ......154 D8
Oakwood Dr NR18 ......173 E6
Oakwood Rd NR19 ......154 D8
Oasis Leisure Ctr PE36 ....132 C4
Oasis Sport & Leisure Ctr NR7 ....72 D5
Oasis Way PE36 ....132 C2
Oatfield Cl 7 NR10 ....53 A3
Obelisk La NR28 ....37 F5
Obelisk Plain NR25 .....137 A6
Occupation Rd 1 NR20 ...68 F6
Octagon Dr 4 PE13 .....152 A6
Octavia Cl PE13 ....152 F6
Octavia Hill Birthplace Mus* PE13 ....152 C5
Oddfellows Field 4 NR25 ..7 C6
Oddfellows Row PE31 ..134 E4
Offley Ct 7 NR5 ....161 A8
Ogden Cl NR18 ....173 C4
Oil Mill La PE13 ....152 B5
Old Allotment Ct 7 NR3 ....162 F8
Old Bakery Ct PE31 .....133 C5
Old Barge Yd NR1 ......178 C2
Old Barley Mkt The NR2 ....178 A3
Old Bear Ct NR28 ......151 C5
Old Becclesgate NR19 ..154 D5
Old Brandon Rd IP26 ....98 F1
Old Brewery Ct 14 PE30 ...146 E3
Old Brewery La NR10 ...149 C4
Old Buckenham High Sch NR17 ....104 D2
Old Buckenham Prim Sch NR17 ....104 D3
Old Buckenham Rd NR16 ....105 A4
Old Bungay Rd NR35 ...109 D4
Old Bury Rd
Palgrave IP22 ....129 E4
Stuston IP21 ....177 F1
Thetford IP24 ....176 C4
Wortham IP22 ....129 D4
Old Catton Mid Sch NR6 ....158 E5
Old Chapel Rd
Cantley NR13 ....92 E7
2 Hemsby NR29 ....58 B6
Old Chapel Way NR7 .....72 E3
Old Church Cl NR14 ......89 F6
Old Church Rd
Hainford NR10 ....53 E6
Hopton on Sea NR31 .....171 D4
Snettisham PE31 ....12 E5

Old - Pec 203

Old Coach Rd NR27 ....139 C6
Old Coast Rd NR29 .....167 E2
Old Fakenham Rd
Attlebridge NR9 ....52 B3
Foxley NR20 ....50 D8
Old Farm La NR3 ....158 B1
Old Feltwell Rd IP26 ....99 A5
Old Forge Cl IP22 ......129 B4
Old Forge Ct
Acle NR13 ....166 C4
Brockdish IP21 ....131 D6
Old Fountain NR31 .....170 C1
Old Friendship La
NR10 ....35 C2
Old Gr Ct NR3 ....158 D2
Old Hall Cl
Ashwellthorpe NR16 ......105 F8
1 Norwich NR14 ....163 B2
Saham Toney IP25 ....84 B5
Old Hall Dr PE31 ....140 E3
Old Hall Gdns
Brooke NR15 ....90 F2
Buxton with Lammas
NR10 ....37 A2
Caister-on-Sea NR30 .....168 E5
Old Hall La PE37 ....81 F8
Old Hall Rd
East Dereham NR19 ......154 D2
Mattishall NR20 ....68 D5
Witton NR28 ....38 B8
Old Hall The PE31 ....27 C3
Old Harleston Rd
NR35 ....123 E7
Old High Rd IP22 ......177 A5
Old Hithe Rd NR26 .....138 A6
Old Hunstanton Rd
PE36 ....132 E7
Old Kiln 10 PE33 ....43 F2
Old La East Ruston NR12 ...24 A5
Happisburgh NR12 ....23 F1
Reepham NR10 ....34 B1
Thelnetham IP22 ....128 A2
Old Lakenham Hall Dr 6
NR1 ....162 E1
Old Laundry Ct 3 NR2 ..162 B8
Old Laundry Mews
NR1 ....163 A5
Old Liby Mews NR1 ....178 C2
Old Lynn Rd PE13 ......152 E7
Old Maltings The
PE13 ....153 B4
Old Manor Cl PE30 .....148 C1
Old Methwold Rd
Feltwell IP26 ....98 E2
Northwold PE33 ....81 B2
Old Mill Dr IP21 ....121 F4
Old Mill Rd
Caister-on-Sea NR30 .....168 F5
3 Poringland NR14 ....90 C5
Roughton NR11 ....139 B1
Old Mkt PE13 ....152 C5
Old Mkt Cl NR13 ....166 C3
Old Mkt Gn 3 NR14 .....92 A1
Old Mkt Pl 21 IP20 ......122 D2
Old Mkt St
14 King's Lynn PE30 ......146 E5
Thetford IP24 ....176 D3
Old Mkt Way NR15 .....107 C5
Old Norwich Rd
Horsham St Faith &
Newton St Faith NR10 ......53 D1
Yaxley IP23 ....130 A1
Old Pal Rd NR2 ....162 B7
Old Pools Dro CB6 ....95 F1
Old Post Office La
NR35 ....109 E3
Old Post Office St
2 Fakenham NR21 ....141 B4
2 Shipdham IP25 ....67 B2
Old Post Rd NR24 ......142 E4
Old Quarry Ct NR19 ....154 E6
Old Rd Acle NR13 ....166 E5
1 Great Moulton NR15 ...106 B1
Old Rectory Cl
King's Lynn PE30 ....148 D5
4 Mulbarton NR14 ....89 B3
Norwich NR7 ....163 E6
7 Roydon IP22 ....129 D7
South Wootton PE30 ......148 B1
Old Rectory Rd NR12 ....24 A1
Old Reepham Rd 4
NR20 ....50 E7
Old Rly Rd IP20 ....123 B5
Old Rly Yd PE31 ....135 C2
Old Roman Bank
PE34 ....144 A7
Old Sch Cl NR5 ....161 E5
Old Sch Ct NR1 ....178 C1
Old Sch Rd
East Ruston NR12 ....38 F8
Guestwick NR20 ....33 F5
Old Severalls Rd IP26 ...98 E6
Old South PE30 ....147 C4
Old Southwood Rd
NR13 ....74 B2
Old St 2 NR15 ....107 A8
Old Sta La NR35 ....109 D2
Old Sta Way 6 NR25 ...137 C5
Old Stoke Rd NR14 ......89 F8
Old Town Way PE36 ....132 D6
Old Turnpike Rd NR11 ...21 D7
Old Vicarage Pk PE32 ....63 E7
Old Warren NR8 ....155 D2
Old Watton Rd NR4 ....161 A5
Old Wellington Pl 15
NR30 ....169 D3
Old Wells Rd
Sculthorpe NR21 ....16 A2
Old Wells Rd *continued*
Walsingham NR22 ....16 E8
Old Woman's La NR25 ....7 F6
Old Yarmouth Rd NR12 ..39 C2
Oldfield Ave PE14 ....59 B1
Oldfield Ct 3 NR19 .....154 E6
Oldfield La PE13 ....152 B3
Oldhall La NR16 ....118 C5
Oldhall Rd NR4 ....89 E8
Oldmedow Rd PE30 ....147 A2
Oldsunway PE30 ....146 D5
Oldwash La NR16 ......105 D3
Olive Ave NR15 ....89 D1
Olive Cl NR5 ....157 C1
Olive Cres NR10 ....53 A4
Olive Rd
Great Yarmouth NR31 .....169 B3
Norwich NR5 ....157 C1
Oliver Ct
5 Cromer NR27 ....139 C6
2 Weeting IP27 ....114 E1
Oliver Mews 4 NR30 ...169 D4
Olivet Way NR21 ....141 C3
Olivia Cl NR21 ....141 A5
Ollands Rd
Attleborough NR17 ....174 C3
Reepham NR10 ....149 C4
Ollard Ave PE13 ....152 D7
Olley Rd 1 NR27 ....10 A5
Olney Rd NR19 ....154 D5
Onedin Cl PE31 ....140 C5
Onley St NR2 ....162 B4
Onslow Ave NR30 ......169 D7
Onyx Ct 10 PE13 ....152 C4
Opie St NR2 ....178 B3
Opportune Rd PE13 ....152 C6
Orange Gr 3 PE13 ......152 C4
Orange Row PE34 ......144 A5
Orange Row Rd PE34 ...144 A6
Orchard Bank NR8 .....155 E8
Orchard Cl Acle NR13 ...166 B4
Ashill IP25 ....84 A6
Attleborough NR17 ....174 C5
Blofield Heath NR13 ....73 C6
Brancaster Staithe PE31 .....3 D7
Briston NR24 ....142 D4
Caister-on-Sea NR30 .....168 E4
Dersingham PE31 ....140 D4
Downham Market PE38 ...172 D5
Fakenham NR21 ....141 D4
Holt NR25 ....137 E7
3 Ixworth NR9 ....69 F2
Mundesley NR11 ....143 B7
North Elmham NR20 ....49 E7
North Walsham NR28 .....151 C6
Norwich NR7 ....163 C8
Roughton NR11 ....21 D7
Sheringham NR26 ....138 C6
Tacolneston NR16 ....105 F4
Watlington PE33 ....61 E5
19 Watton IP25 ....84 D3
8 Wisbech PE14 ....59 A1
Orchard Cres 4 NR15 ...106 B1
Orchard Ct
King's Lynn PE30 ....147 B6
Ormesby St Margaret
NR29 ....167 A3
Orchard Dr
Hellesdon NR6 ....157 D3
3 Potter Heigham NR29 ...56 F6
West Walton PE14 ....59 C8
Wisbech PE13 ....152 E4
Orchard Gdns 3 PE30 ...147 B6
Orchard Gr Diss IP22 ...177 C5
Kettlestone NR21 ....17 C2
King's Lynn PE34 ....146 C3
Orchard La
Aylsham NR11 ....150 D4
Castle Acre PE32 ....46 F2
King's Lynn PE30 ....147 B5
Reepham NR10 ....149 D5
Shouldham PE33 ....62 D4
Orchard Pl
Swaffham PE37 ....153 B4
Thompson IP24 ....102 A7
Orchard Rd
8 Gayton PE32 ....45 C6
Lingwood NR13 ....73 F3
5 Mattishall NR20 ....68 E6
2 Spixworth NR10 ....54 A2
4 Wiggenhall St Germans
PE34 ....43 B1
Orchard St NR2 ....162 C7
Orchard The
4 Belton NR31 ....94 A6
Brandon IP27 ....175 C3
Orchard Way
Banham NR16 ....119 D7
4 Burgh St Margaret
(Fleggburgh) NR29 ....57 C1
5 Hethersett NR9 ....88 D8
7 Tasburgh NR15 ....106 F6
Terrington St John PE14 ....42 B1
Thetford IP24 ....176 D5
Wymondham NR18 ....173 C4
Orchards Prim Ssh
PE13 ....152 D8
Orchid Ave NR19 ......154 D1
Orde Ave NR31 ....170 C2
Ordnance Rd NR30 .....169 D1
Orford Cl 5 NR30 ......169 D3
Orford Hill NR1 ....178 B2
Orford Pl Norwich NR1 ...178 B2
7 West Winch PE33 ....43 F2
Orford Rd PE37 ....153 C6
Orford St NR1 ....178 B2
Orhard Gr PE33 ....43 E2
Oriel Ave NR31 ....170 A3
Oriel High Sch NR31 ...170 A3
Origins* NR2 ....178 A2
Ormesby 4 PE30 ....147 D5
Ormesby Fst Sch
NR29 ....167 A2
Ormesby La NR29 ....76 A8
Ormesby Mid Sch
NR29 ....167 A3
Ormesby Rd
Caister-on-Sea NR30 .....168 D7
Hemsby NR29 ....167 A6
Ormesby St Margaret
with Scratby NR29 ....168 C8
Scottow NR10 ....37 B2
Ormond Rd NR30 ......169 C5
Orwell Cl
King's Lynn PE30 ....147 D4
2 Wymondham NR18 ....173 D5
Orwell Cres NR31 ....94 A6
Orwell Rd NR2 ....162 C3
Osbert Cl 4 NR1 ....162 E1
Osborne Ave NR30 .....169 C7
Osborne Cl 1 NR28 ....151 C7
Osborne Ct NR4 ....162 B3
Osborne Pk PE13 ......152 C8
Osborne Rd
Norwich NR4 ....161 D2
Wisbech PE13 ....152 B7
Osier Cl NR19 ....154 B4
Osier La NR25 ....9 C1
Osprey Cl NR12 ....164 D5
Ostend Gap NR12 ....24 A7
Ostend Pl NR12 ....24 A7
Ostend Rd NR12 ....24 A6
Ostrich La NR19 ....49 A3
Otter Cl
3 Downham Market
PE38 ....172 A6
5 Salhouse NR13 ....55 A1
Otter Dr 17 NR14 ....89 B3
Otter Trust The*
NR35 ....123 E7
Oulton Cl PE37 ....153 C2
Oulton Rd NR6 ....158 C5
Ouse Ave PE30 ....146 D2
Ouse Ave The IP24 .....176 C3
Ouse La NR12 ....39 F1
Out S Gates PE30 ......146 E3
Outney Rd NR35 ....124 A8
Outwell Rd Emneth PE14 ..59 B2
Stow Bardolph PE34 ....78 E8
Oval Ave NR5 ....161 C8
Oval Rd NR5 ....157 C1
Oval The IP25 ....84 B5
Over Cross NR16 ......119 C8
Overbury Rd NR6 ......158 A4
Overstone Ct NR6 ......158 F5
Overstrand Belfry VA Prim
Sch NR27 ....11 A3
Overstrand Rd NR27 ....139 C6
Overstrand Sports Club
NR27 ....11 A3
Overtons Way 14 NR14 ...90 C5
Overwood La NR16 .....106 A3
Overy Rd PE31 ....135 D3
Ovington Rd IP25 ....84 C4
Owen Rd Diss IP22 ......177 F4
Great Yarmouth NR31 .....169 B1
Owen's Cl 22 NR15 .....106 E3
Owl Dr 3 NR14 ....89 B3
Oxborough Dr PE30 ....148 E1
Oxborough La NR21 ....141 C4
Oxborough Rd
Oxborough PE33 ....81 D3
Stoke Ferry PE33 ....81 A2
Oxburgh Cl 1 PE13 .....152 A7
Oxburgh Hall Gdns & Estate*
PE33 ....81 E4
Oxcroft NR13 ....166 C4
Oxford Ave NR31 ....170 B3
Oxford Pl PE34 ....144 F6
Oxford Rd 2 Feltwell IP26 .98 E1
2 Feltwell IP26 ....98 E1
Oxford St NR2 ....162 C5
Oxford Way 11 NR29 .....57 D4
Oxnead Dr NR30 ....168 C7
Oxnead La NR35 ....107 F4
Oxnead Rd NR3 ....158 B2

P

Pack La Briston NR24 ....142 F3
East Carleton NR14 ....89 A6
Strumpshaw NR13 ....73 F3
Packway The IP20 ......123 A3
Paddock Cl Belton NR31 ..93 F6
3 Fakenham NR21 ....141 E4
Paddock Farm IP31 .....127 B4
Paddock Farm Dr NR29 ..75 F8
Paddock Gdns NR17 ....174 E5
Paddock Rd 13 IP20 ....122 D2
Paddock St NR2 ....162 C8
Paddock The
3 Cromer NR27 ....10 B5
Hemsby NR29 ....167 A8
Trowse with Newton
NR14 ....163 A2
Paddocks The
Aylsham NR11 ....150 C6
Bacton/Walcott NR12 ......23 E4
Beetley NR20 ....49 D4
Brandon IP27 ....175 E4
Downham Market PE38 ...172 B5
Griston IP25 ....85 A1
Norwich NR6 ....158 F6
Swaffham PE37 ....153 B3
Paddy's La NR9 ....51 E1
Paddys Loke NR30 .....169 A7
Padgate NR13 ....72 D6
Padgett's Rd PE14 ....95 A6
Page Cl
3 North Walsham NR28 ..151 C6
Poringland NR14 ....90 C5
Page Rd Brundall NR13 ..165 C4
Norwich NR3 ....157 F1
Page Stair La PE30 .....146 D5
Pages Cl 3 NR18 ....173 B3
Pages La IP25 ....84 B5
Paget Adams Dr 4 NR20 .68 A8
Paget Cres NR31 ....170 C1
Paget Rd NR30 ....169 D4
Paige Cl 1 PE33 ....61 D5
Paine Cl IP22 ....177 B5
Paine Rd NR7 ....163 D8
Painter St IP24 ....176 C4
Pakenham Dr PE31 .....140 C3
Palace St NR1 ....178 B3
Pales Gn 4 PE32 ....46 F2
Palgrave Cl NR8 ....155 B1
Palgrave Rd
Great Dunham PE32 ....47 E1
Great Yarmouth NR30 .....169 C5
Little Dunham PE32 ....65 D8
Palgrave VC Prim Sch
IP22 ....177 D2
Palling Rd NR12 ....24 D1
Palm Cl NR18 ....173 B5
Palmer Rd
Great Yarmouth NR31 .....170 D5
8 New Rackheath NR13 ...72 E7
Norwich NR3 ....158 C3
Palmer Way PE38 ......172 C3
Palmer's La
Aylsham NR11 ....150 C6
Freethorpe NR13 ....92 F8
Palmers La NR12 ....55 C5
Pandora 1 PE30 ....147 C4
Pansey Dr PE31 ....140 C4
Panton Cl PE30 ....146 D2
Panxworth Church Rd
NR13 ....73 E8
Panxworth Rd NR13 .....73 F7
Paper St NR19 ....68 C6
Papillion Rd NR18 ......173 D4
Paradise La
6 Bawdeswell NR20 ....50 E7
7 King's Lynn PE30 ......146 D5
Paradise Par 10 PE30 ...146 D5
Paradise Pl NR1 ....178 B2
Paradise Rd
7 Bawdeswell NR20 ....50 E7
Downham Market PE38 ...172 B5
9 King's Lynn PE30 ......146 D5
Paragon Pl 4 NR2 ......162 C6
Parana Cl NR7 ....159 C5
Parana Ct NR7 ....159 C5
Parana Rd NR7 ....159 C5
Parish Rd NR10 ....53 D7
Park Ave 5 Barford NR9 ...69 F2
King's Lynn PE30 ....146 F4
North Walsham NR28 .....151 D5
Scottow NR10 ....37 D2
Wisbech PE13 ....152 C6
Park Cl Hethersett NR9 ...88 D7
Holt NR25 ....137 D5
Norwich NR6 ....158 E5
Thurton NR14 ....91 C4
Wymondham NR18 ....173 D1
Park Comm La NR16 ...119 B5
Park Cres PE34 ....61 B5
Park Ct Harling NR16 ....118 C5
North Walsham NR28 .....151 D5
Park Dr NR9 ....88 C7
Park Est 3 IP25 ....67 B2
Park Farm La
Euston IP24 ....126 C4
Hoxne IP21 ....131 C2
Park High Sch PE30 ....147 A4
Park Highatt Dr 2 IP25 ..67 C2
Park Hill PE31 ....140 D5
Park La Blofield NR13 ....165 B8
Cromer NR27 ....139 D4
Deopham NR18 ....87 A4
Downham Market PE38 ...172 B3
Helhoughton NR21 ....30 E5
Hockering NR20 ....69 C8
North Walsham NR28 .....151 C5
Norwich NR2 ....162 B5
Reepham NR10 ....149 B4
Scarning NR19 ....67 B6
Snettisham PE31 ....12 E4
Wymondham NR18 ....173 C2
Park Rd Cromer NR27 ...139 D5
Diss IP22 ....177 D4
East Dereham NR19 ......154 E6
Great Yarmouth NR31 .....170 D3
Gressenhall NR20 ....49 C3
Hunstanton PE36 ....132 C4
St Cross, South Elmham
IP20 ....123 C3
Spixworth NR10 ....54 A1
Upper Sheringham
NR26 ....138 A4
Warham NR23 ....6 A4
Wells-next-the-Sea
NR23 ....136 C6
Wisbech PE13 ....152 D5
Wroxham/Hoveton
NR12 ....164 B3
Park St 4 PE13 ....152 D5
Park The NR16 ....118 B5
Park View
Botesdale IP22 ....128 F3
Brandon IP27 ....175 B2
Weeting IP27 ....175 A7
Park View Ave NR29 .....57 D3
Park Way NR6 ....157 E5
Parker Cl NR13 ....165 B4
Parker Dr NR21 ....141 D4
Parker Rd NR2 ....162 B5
Parker's La NR15 ......106 F2
Parker's Rd 10 NR20 .....68 F6
Parker's Cl NR9 ....70 C5
Parkers Cl NR18 ....173 B6
Parkers Prim Sch IP25 ..84 C5
Parkes La NR15 ....106 D6
Parkhill 4 PE32 ....44 B3
Parkland Cl 8 NR12 .....55 E4
Parkland Cres
9 Horning NR12 ....55 E4
Norwich NR6 ....158 F3
Parkland Dr NR31 ......170 A5
Parkland Est NR29 .....167 A8
Parkland Rd NR6 ....158 F3
Parklands NR8 ....156 D4
Parklands Ave IP25 ......67 B2
Parklands Way 41 IP20 ..122 D2
Parkside PE36 ....13 A7
Parkside Ct IP22 ....177 C4
Parkside Dr NR6 ....158 E5
Parkside Specl Sch
NR2 ....162 A5
Parkview IP24 ....176 E4
Parkway PE30 ....147 B4
Parliament Ct 5 NR7 ....72 D4
Parliament La IP24 .....102 E3
Parmenter Rd NR4 .....161 F3
Parmeter Cl NR11 ......150 D6
Parr Rd NR3 ....158 A1
Parrow La NR11 ....21 C6
Parsons Cl IP27 ....175 B2
Parsons La PE31 ....14 D8
Parsons Mead NR4 .....161 F1
Partridge Dr
Mulbarton NR14 ....89 A3
4 Thetford IP24 ....176 D2
Partridge Gr PE37 ......153 D3
Partridge Rd NR11 .....150 B6
Partridge Way NR6 ....158 D4
Partridge Wlk IP27 .....175 F3
Parva Cl NR11 ....20 B4
Pasteur Rd NR31 ....169 B2
Paston Cl 4 NR11 ....9 E1
Paston Coll NR28 ......151 C5
Paston Dr NR30 ....168 C8
Paston Great Barn*
NR28 ....143 E2
Paston Rd
Great Yarmouth NR31 .....170 C5
Mundesley NR11 ....143 D5
Paston Way NR7 ....159 E2
Pasture Cl PE31 ....28 B4
Pastures The
5 Blakeney NR25 ....7 C6
Great Yarmouth NR31 .....170 B7
Hemsby NR29 ....167 A8
Little Snoring NR21 ....17 B3
Patricia Ave NR12 ....54 C6
Patricia Rd NR1 ....162 D3
Patrick Rd 4 NR15 .....106 D3
Patten La NR15 ....121 B3
Patterson Cl 4 NR30 ...169 C4
Patteson Cl 8 NR4 ....89 B8
Patteson Rd NR3 ......162 D8
Paul Dr PE32 ....44 B3
Pauls La NR27 ....11 A3
Pavilion Cl 5 IP22 .....177 A5
Pavilion Rd NR31 ......170 D4
Pavilion Theatre NR31 ..170 E4
Paxman Rd PE30 ......146 F2
Paxton Terr PE30 ......146 E5
Payne Ave PE13 ....152 D7
Payne's La IP26 ....98 E1
Paynes Hill IP20 ....122 F6
Peachman Way 5 NR7 ....72 E4
Peachtree St 6 NR21 ....15 C2
Peacock Chase NR18 ...173 D4
Peacock Cl Easton NR9 ...70 B5
Hockwold cum Wilton
IP26 ....113 F6
Peacock La
Beetley NR20 ....49 E5
Holt NR25 ....137 B7
Peacock St NR3 ....178 B4
Peacock Way NR24 .....142 A4
Peacocks The NR25 ....137 C7
Peakhall Rd PE32 ....48 B8
Peakwell Cl NR8 ....155 C2
Pear Tree Cl NR20 ....68 E6
Pear Tree Cnr NR21 .....31 C2
Pearce Rd IP22 ....177 E4
Pearce's Cl 2 IP26 .....114 A7
Pearcefield NR3 ....158 E2
Pearmain Rd IP22 ......177 C5
Pearson's Rd NR25 .....137 C6
Pearsons Cl
Freethorpe NR13 ....92 E7
Holt NR25 ....137 C6
Peartree Ave 2 NR29 ....57 C4
Peartree Way 9 PE14 ....59 A1
Peatlings La PE13 ......152 A7
Pebble Cl 3 PE12 ....41 B8
Pebble View Wlk
NR31 ....171 E4
Peck Cl NR5 ....160 E8
Peckover Cty Prim Sch
PE13 ....152 B6
Peckover Dr PE13 ......152 E4
Peckover House*
PE13 ....152 B5

Peckover Rd
Fakenham NR21 141 A6
Norwich NR4 161 E3
Peckover Way PE30 147 E8
Peddars Cl PE36 132 D6
Peddars Dr PE36 132 D6
Peddars' La NR34 110 C6
Peddars Way NR8 155 D2
Peddars Way N PE36 2 A4
Peddlars Turnpike
NR20 33 F3
Pedham Rd NR13 73 E7
Pedlar's Gr PE37 153 C5
Pedlar's La NR21 17 F1
Pedlars Croft [2] NR29 167 A8
Pedley La PE13 152 A6
Peel Mews [5] NR3 178 A3
Peel St PE30 146 F4
Pegasus Cl NR30 168 D7
Pegg Cl NR9 70 B5
Pegg Rd NR26 138 C5
Pegg's La NR16 105 E6
Peggotty Rd NR30 170 D8
Peldon Dr PE13 152 E5
Pelham Rd NR3 158 D1
Pell Pl [2] PE33 43 F2
Pell Rd PE31 140 D4
Pellew Pl NR28 151 C6
Pemberton Rd [6] IP20 122 D1
Pembrey Cl NR3 158 D3
Pembroke Ave NR31 170 B4
Pembroke Rd NR2 162 B5
Pendlesham Rise NR8 155 E2
Pendula Rd PE13 152 E7
Penfold Dr NR18 173 E5
Penfold St NR11 150 C6
Penguin Rd NR29 167 D7
Penhill La NR17 103 D7
Penn Cl NR8 156 D8
Penn Gr NR3 158 C1
Penn Rd NR8 156 D8
Pennington Way PE31 140 A1
Penny Croft [3] NR21 15 C2
Pennycress Dr
[6] Thetford IP24 176 F5
Wymondham NR18 173 E4
Pennygate La NR12 38 F1
Pennyroyal [1] NR6 158 D5
Penrose Cl PE30 147 B8
Penrose Gdns PE13 152 E4
Penryn Cl NR4 161 E5
Penshurst Mews [5]
NR4 161 F1
Pensthorpe Nature Reserve &
Gdns* NR21 32 B8
Pentney Abbey Leisure Ctr
PE32 63 A7
Pentney Dro PE33 62 E6
Pentney La PE32 63 D8
Pepper La PE38 97 C8
Pepper's Gn PE30 148 B1
Peppers Cl IP27 175 B7
Percival Cl NR4 161 E4
Perebrown Ave NR30 169 D7
Pereers Cl NR25 137 A7
Peregrine Cl Diss IP22 177 F5
Norwich NR7 159 C4
Peregrine Mews NR7 159 C4
Peregrine Rd NR7 159 C4
Perkin Field PE34 144 B4
Perrings NR18 173 B6
Perrys La NR10 35 C2
Persimmon PE30 147 C5
Peter Ave NR13 166 B3
Peter Beales Roses*
NR17 103 F3
Peter Cl NR29 168 D8
Peter Dr IP24 176 F5
Peter's Dro PE34 61 A7
Peterhouse Ave NR31 170 C4
Peterhouse Fst Sch
NR31 170 C4
Peterhouse Mid Sch
NR31 170 B4
Peterkin Rd [3] NR4 89 E8
Peters Cl NR19 154 C1
Peterscourt PE30 147 D6
Petersfield Cl NR15 106 F4
Peterson Rd NR3 158 A2
Peterson's La NR11 150 B7
Peterspoint PE12 41 A7
Peto Ct NR5 161 C7
Peto's Cnr NR32 111 F8
Petre Cl [3] NR28 151 C7
Petticoat Dro PE32 64 E8
Petticoat La PE33 62 D6
Pettingales [3] NR14 89 F4
Pettits La IP21 130 C7
Pettitts Animal Adventure
Pk* NR13 93 A5
Petts Cl [3] PE13 152 E7
Pettus Rd NR4 161 E3
Petunia Way IP27 175 A2
Peverell Rd NR5 161 B7
Pheasant Cl NR14 89 A3
Pheasant Way IP27 175 F4
Pheasant Wlk [2] NR13 74 B8
Pheasants Wlk NR35 123 E8
Phelps Rd NR7 163 F7
Philadelphia La NR3 158 D2
Philip Ford Way NR18 173 C2
Philip Nurse Rd PE31 140 B3
Philip Pl NR19 154 D2
Philip Rudd Ct PE32 45 A8
Philips' Chase PE36 132 D2
Phillippo Cl [4] PE32 28 A1
Pickards Way PE13 152 A6
Pickford Cl NR28 151 E6
Picton Rd NR15 106 D4
Pier Gdns NR31 170 E4
Pier Pl NR30 169 D2
Pier Plain NR31 170 D5
Pier Rd NR31 170 E4
Pier Wlk NR31 170 D4
Pigeon St PE14 41 D3
Pigg La NR3 178 B4
Pightle Cl [21] NR14 89 B3
Pightle The PE37 153 C4
Pightle Way Lyng NR9 51 A4
Reepham NR10 149 C5
Pigot La NR14 90 C6
Pike La IP24 176 D3
Pikeman Pl NR13 72 E5
Pikes Nursery [4] NR29 56 C5
Pilgrim's Way [7] IP20 122 D2
Pilgrims Way
Little Cressingham IP25 83 F3
Weeting IP27 175 A8
Pilling Pk Rd NR1 163 B7
Pilling Rd NR7 163 D7
Pilot St [2] PE30 146 D5
Pimpernel Rd NR10 53 B2
Pincushion Dro PE14 78 B5
Pinder Cl NR3 158 A1
Pinder Rd NR3 158 A1
Pine Ave
Cockley Cley PE37 82 D7
Marham PE33 63 B4
Pine Cl
[5] Downham Market
PE38 172 C6
[8] Eye IP23 130 C1
[4] Harleston IP20 122 D1
Hunstanton PE36 132 D4
[17] Marthan NR29 57 D4
Norwich NR4 162 A3
Ormesby St Margaret
NR29 167 A3
[3] Snettisham PE31 12 E4
Thetford IP24 176 B1
Pine Coombe [1] NR21 15 C2
Pine Ct NR17 174 D4
Pine Gn NR31 170 B5
Pine Gr
East Dereham NR19 154 D2
Sheringham NR26 138 E6
Pine Loke NR14 90 B5
Pine Mall PE31 133 C6
Pine Rd
King's Lynn PE30 148 D2
Norwich NR7 159 E1
Pine Tree Chase PE33 43 F1
Pine Tree Ct IP22 127 F5
Pine Trees Bsns Pk
NR7 159 D3
Pine Wlk [6] NR25 8 F5
Pinecot Ave [7] NR31 94 C6
Pineheath Rd NR25 8 E3
Pinelodges The NR7 163 C6
Pinetrees NR31 93 E3
Pinetrees Rd NR7 159 D3
Pinewood Cl NR6 157 F4
Pinewood Dr
Brandon IP27 175 C2
[6] Horning NR12 55 E4
Pinewood Leisure Ctr
NR25 9 B3
Pinfold La
Hindolveston NR20 33 D8
Northwold IP26 99 B8
Pinfold Rd PE14 77 E5
Pingle Rd PE14 78 A4
Pingles Rd PE30 148 C4
Pinkney La NR24 19 B5
Pintail Dr [2] Blakeney NR25 7 C6
Great Yarmouth NR31 170 A6
Pioneer Rd NR6 159 A6
Piper Rd
King's Lynn PE30 146 F1
Norwich NR7 159 E1
Pipit's Mdw NR11 21 A5
Pippin Cl
Dereham NR19 154 E3
Ormesby St Margaret
NR29 167 A2
Pippin Gdns PE13 152 F7
Pippin Gn NR4 161 E5
Pippin Pl PE13 152 E2
Pirnhow St NR35 109 B1
Pishmire Cl NR5 160 F6
Pit La PE37 153 C4
Pit Rd
Aldeby, Wheatacre,
Burgh St Peter NR34 111 B4
Hemsby NR29 167 A7
Northrepps NR27 11 A1
Woodbastwick NR13 55 D1
Pit St NR11 22 C6
Pitchford Rd NR5 161 C6
Pitt Sq NR9 86 C4
Pitt St NR3 178 A4
Pitt's Hill NR15 107 B8
Pitts Hill Cl NR15 107 B8
Pius Dro PE14 77 E6
Plaford Rd NR7 159 A2
Plane Rd NR31 170 B6
Plantation Cl NR17 174 C3
Plantation Dr NR7 159 D3
Plantation Gdn The*
NR2 162 C5
Plantation Rd
Aslacton NR15 121 A7
Blofield NR13 165 F7
Plantation Rd *continued*
[4] Fakenham NR21 141 E4
North Walsham NR28 151 E5
Norwich NR6 157 E6
Plantation The NR2 162 B4
Plantsman Cl NR2 162 B3
Plasset Dr NR17 174 F7
Platten's Cl [1] NR11 19 F1
Plattens Ct NR12 164 B3
Playbarn The* NR15 90 C3
Players Way NR6 158 E6
Playing Field La [12] NR29 57 D4
Pleasance Cl PE30 147 A5
Pleasant Cl NR6 157 D5
Pleasant Ct [1] PE30 146 E3
Pleasant Pl PE31 133 D6
Pleasant Row [1] PE37 153 C3
Pleasure Beach*
NR30 169 E1
Plevna Terr NR31 169 B3
Plough La
Hardingham NR9 86 D6
Watlington PE33 61 E5
Ploughboy La IP25 84 C6
Ploughman Rd PE30 147 C4
Ploughman's Dro IP26 98 B1
Ploughman's La NR21 17 E6
Ploughman's Piece PE36 2 E6
Plover Cl
Great Yarmouth NR31 170 A7
[3] Thetford IP24 176 D2
Plovers Ct IP27 175 F3
Plovers Way IP26 113 F7
Plowright Pl PE13 153 B4
Plum La NR11 20 C8
Plumb's Cl NR24 142 E4
Plumbly Cl NR28 151 D3
Plummer's La NR15 107 C7
Plummers Hill NR23 136 D5
Plump Rd NR15 106 D5
Plumsgate Rd NR12 39 C1
Plumstead Dr NR17 174 E6
Plumstead Rd
Baconsthorpe NR25 20 A7
Edgefield NR24 19 E5
Great & Little Plumstead
NR13 72 E6
[4] Norwich NR1 163 C8
Thorpe End NR13 72 E6
Woodbastwick NR13 73 D7
Plumstead Rd E NR7 163 D8
Plymouth Cl [3] NR30 168 C6
Plymouth Rd [2] IP31 126 B1
Pocahontas Way PE31 133 E5
Pockthorpe Gate NR3 163 A7
Pockthorpe La IP24 102 A7
Pockthorpe Loke
Barnham Broom NR9 69 D2
Hickling NR12 39 F2
Pockthorpe Rd NR9 88 A8
Podmore La NR19 67 C8
Point Dr [2] PE37 153 C3
Police Rd PE14 41 D4
Polka Rd NR23 136 D5
Pollard Rd NR10 53 E6
Pollywiggle Cl NR5 161 A6
Pommer's La NR30 170 D8
Pond Cl [14] NR9 88 C7
Pond Hills Rd NR25 19 E7
Pond La Brandon IP27 175 A2
Knapton NR28 143 B2
Surlingham NR14 73 B1
Taverham NR8 156 F8
Pond Rd
Antingham NR28 22 B4
East Dereham NR19 154 C2
[3] Horsford NR10 53 A3
Swafield NR28 22 C3
Ponds End La IP22 127 E4
Pooley St IP22 128 F7
Poorhouse La NR14 89 A2
Pope's La PE34 144 A4
Poplar Ave
Great Yarmouth NR31 170 C3
Heacham PE31 133 C5
King's Lynn PE34 43 D4
[5] Marham PE33 63 B4
Norwich NR4 161 E1
Poplar Cl
Downham Market PE38 172 B6
Honington IP31 126 B1
[12] Horsford NR10 53 A3
Long Stratton NR15 106 F4
Norwich NR5 156 F2
Poplar Dr Filby NR29 75 F8
Happisburgh NR12 23 F3
King's Lynn PE30 148 D2
Poplar Gr NR26 138 E5
Poplar Rd
Attleborough NR17 174 B2
West Winch PE33 43 F1
Poplar Way NR17 174 C2
Poplars The Hilgay PE38 96 F8
Spexhall IP19 124 F1
Swanton Abbott NR10 37 C4
Tacolneston NR16 105 F4
Pople St NR18 173 B4
Poppy Cl
Chedgrave NR14 91 F2
North Walsham NR28 151 F5
[4] Thetford IP24 176 F4
Poppy Dr [5] NR26 138 B6
Poppy's La IP21 121 F5
Poppyfields [14] NR10 53 A3
Poringland Prim Sch
NR14 90 D5
Poringland Rd NR14 90 B5
Porson Rd NR7 159 C1
Port Rd NR15 122 B8
Port Row NR9 51 B4
Portal Ave IP25 84 F3
Portal Cl
[4] Barnham IP24 125 F6
[7] Feltwell IP26 98 D1
Portalfield [10] NR12 39 B4
Porter Rd [8] NR15 106 E3
Porter St PE38 172 A5
Porter's La NR9 51 E5
Porter's Loke
[1] Belton NR31 94 A6
Burgh Castle NR31 93 F6
Norwich NR7 159 A3
Porter's Rd
Beighton NR13 74 E1
Freethorpe NR13 92 E8
Porterbush Rd [18] NR14 89 B3
Portersfield Rd NR2 162 B5
Porthole Cl [10] NR33 111 F1
Portland Ct NR31 169 C3
Portland Pl
Great Yarmouth NR30 169 E3
King's Lynn PE30 146 D2
[3] Thetford IP24 116 A1
Portland St
[12] King's Lynn PE30 146 E5
Norwich NR2 162 B5
Portsmouth Rd [3] IP31 126 B1
Portway Pl [6] NR2 162 C7
Portway Sq [10] NR2 162 C7
Post Mill PE30 147 C5
Post Mill Cl NR7 159 A3
Post Office Cl [8] NR13 74 A3
Post Office La
Corpusty NR11 34 F8
Garvestone NR9 86 B8
Weston Longville NR9 51 E2
[12] Wisbech PE13 152 C5
Post Office Rd
Dersingham PE31 140 D3
Frettenham NR12 54 A4
Great & Little Plumstead
NR13 73 B7
Lingwood NR13 74 A3
Lingwood & Burlingham
NR13 73 F3
Toft Monks NR34 110 E5
Postmill Cl NR18 173 C4
Postwick La NR13 165 A4
Postwick Sta NR7 72 E3
Potash La
Bracon Ash NR16 88 D2
Eye IP23 130 B2
Potato Dro PE14 60 B4
Potspoon Hole
Coltishall NR12 54 D8
Tunstead NR12 37 D1
Potter Heigham Rd
NR29 56 D8
Potter's La
Rickinghall Superior
IP22 128 F1
Wymondham NR18 105 B6
Pottergate NR2 178 A3
Pottergate St NR15 106 A2
Potters Cres NR15 121 C8
Potters Dr NR31 171 D5
Potters Vale IP22 128 C3
Pottle's La NR13 92 F5
Pottles Alley [4] NR9 86 C5
Poulter's Dro PE14 77 D1
Poultry Rd IP27 113 A3
Pound Cl
[4] Harleston IP20 122 D2
Hevingham NR10 53 C8
Pound Gn La IP25 67 C2
Pound Hill IP25 84 B5
Pound La
Aylsham NR11 150 B6
Brundall NR13 165 F5
Burgh St Margaret (Fleggburgh)
NR29 75 C8
Ditchingham NR35 108 E2
Docking PE31 134 D5
Filby NR29 75 F8
Great Yarmouth NR31 170 C3
Heacham PE31 133 D6
Litcham PE32 48 A4
Loddon NR14 109 C8
North Tuddenham NR20 50 D2
Norwich NR7 72 D4
Runhall NR20 69 A4
Sloley NR12 37 F2
Toft Monks NR34 110 D6
Pound Rd
East Ruston NR12 38 F7
Hevingham NR10 53 C8
Ludham NR29 56 C5
North Walsham NR28 151 D5
Powell Ct [5] NR19 154 C6
Power's Pl PE38 79 D1
Poynt Cl NR18 173 B5
Pratts Hill NR14 73 A1
Press La NR3 158 C1
Preston Ave NR18 173 A2
Preston Cl
Freethorpe NR13 92 E7
Wroxham/Hoveton
NR12 164 B2
Preston La NR14 109 F8
Preston Rd NR28 151 D6
Preston VC Prim Sch
NR15 106 F7
Pretty Dr IP21 130 D6
Pride Way NR13 72 E5
Primrose Cl
Attleborough NR17 174 B5
Primrose Cl *continued*
East Dereham NR19 154 B4
[15] Mulbarton NR14 89 B3
Mundesley NR11 143 B5
Thetford IP24 176 F4
Trunch NR28 22 E5
Primrose Cres [2] NR7 72 D3
Primrose Ct [3] NR7 72 D3
Primrose Dr IP27 175 A2
Primrose Hill NR20 50 B4
Primrose La
Crostwick NR12 54 C3
Sheringham NR26 138 B5
Swanton Morley NR20 50 B4
Primrose Pl NR2 162 B5
Primrose Rd
Hingham NR9 86 B5
Norwich NR1 163 A6
Primrose Sq NR20 50 B4
Primrose Way
[15] Great Yarmouth NR31 94 C6
[10] Horsford NR10 53 A3
Primrose Wlk NR28 151 E4
Primula Dr NR4 161 D5
Prince Andrew Dr
PE31 140 D3
Prince Andrew's Cl
[2] Aldborough NR11 21 A5
Norwich NR6 158 B5
Prince Andrew's Rd
NR6 158 B5
Prince Charles Cl
PE31 140 D3
Prince Edward Cl NR7 163 F7
Prince Henry Pl PE38 172 D4
Prince of Wales Cl
PE13 152 D8
Prince of Wales Rd
Caister-on-Sea NR30 168 C6
Cromer NR27 139 B7
Norwich NR1 178 B3
Upton with Fishley NR13 166 A8
Prince Regent Way
IP22 177 F3
Prince Rupert Way
NR13 72 D5
Prince St PE13 152 D5
Prince William Cl
PE36 132 C3
Prince's Rd
Bungay NR35 124 A7
Great Yarmouth NR30 169 D4
Prince's St PE12 41 B8
Princes Cl IP27 175 A2
Princes Rd PE13 152 C4
Princes St
North Walsham NR28 151 A5
Norwich NR3 178 B3
Swaffham PE37 153 B4
Princes Way PE30 146 F5
Princess Beatrice Cl
NR6 157 D2
Princess Cl [7] IP25 84 D3
Princess Ct [5] NR25 137 C5
Princess Dr PE36 132 D2
Princess Theatre
PE36 132 C4
Princess Way [5] NR35 123 F8
Princess's Dr
Dersingham PE35 140 C1
Sandringham PE35 27 D7
Pringle Way [5] PE38 97 B5
Prins Ave PE13 152 D7
Prins Ct [3] PE13 152 D7
Printing Mus* NR34 110 D1
Prior Bank Orch [3]
NR27 139 C6
Prior Cl [5] NR15 106 F6
Prior Rd NR7 72 D5
Prior Stephen Way
IP24 176 B3
Priors Dr NR6 158 E6
Priorswood NR8 155 E3
Priory Chase
Downham Market PE38 172 B5
Wormegay PE33 61 F8
Priory Cl Acle NR13 166 C3
Alpington NR14 90 F5
Caister-on-Sea NR30 168 D4
[2] Fritton & St Olaves
NR31 93 D2
[7] Hethersett NR9 88 D7
Palgrave IP22 177 D1
Sheringham NR26 138 F5
Sporle with Palgrave
PE32 65 D6
Priory Cres NR21 6 E2
Priory Dro IP25 83 D4
Priory Gdns
[1] Fritton & St Olaves
NR31 93 D2
[12] Great Yarmouth NR30 169 C4
Priory La Ingworth NR11 21 A1
[12] King's Lynn PE30 146 D4
Shotesham NR15 90 A2
Priory Maze & Gdns*
NR26 138 F6
Priory Pk IP24 176 C5
Priory Pl PE32 65 D6
Priory Plain [13] NR30 169 C4
Priory Rd Bacton NR12 23 E4
Castle Acre PE32 46 F1
Downham Market PE38 172 B5
Fritton & St Olaves NR31 93 D2
Great Cressingham IP25 83 D5
Hethersett NR9 88 D7
King's Lynn PE30 148 C5
Palgrave IP22 177 C1

Priory Rd *continued*
Sheringham NR26 138 E7
Watton IP25 84 E3
Woodbastwick NR13 55 F1
Priory Row 11 NR30 169 C4
Priory St NR31 170 D6
Priory Terr PE38 172 B5
Priscilla Cl 1 NR5 161 D5
Pristow Gn La NR16 120 E7
Private Rd
Earsham NR35 123 D8
Ormesby St Margaret NR29 167 A3
Procession La PE32 153 F8
Proctor Ave 3 NR14 92 A2
Proctor Cl 4 NR14 92 A2
Proctor Rd
Chedgrave NR14 91 F2
5 Loddon NR14 92 A2
Norwich NR6 158 F6
Proctors Cl PE30 146 C2
Progress Way IP23 130 B1
Prom The NR29 167 E4
Promenade
Overstrand NR27 11 A4
Sheringham NR26 138 D7
Prophets Alley PE34 61 B6
Prospect Pl PE13 152 C3
Proudfoot Way NR11 150 B5
Provan Cres 8 NR31 94 A5
Provence Pl 2 PE13 152 E3
Providence Pl
Briston NR24 142 E5
8 Thorpe Hamlet NR1 163 A6
Providence St 5 PE30 146 E4
Providence Terr PE13 153 A5
Provision Mkt NR2 178 A3
Provost Rd IP26 98 D1
Pudding Norton Medieval Village of* NR21 31 E6
Puddingmoor NR34 110 C1
Pug St IP21 121 B2
Pulham CE Prim Sch IP21 121 E5
Pullover Rd PE34 146 A1
Pump La NR30 168 D3
Punsfer Way PE34 60 C8
Purbeck Cl PE13 152 A4
Purdance Cl NR5 160 D8
Purdy St NR25 8 B6
Purdy Way NR11 150 B6
Purfleet PE30 146 D5
Purfleet St
11 King's Lynn PE30 146 D5
8 King's Lynn PE30 146 D5
Purland Rd NR7 159 D2
Purley Ct NR31 169 A1
Pursehouse Way IP22 177 E4
Purtingay Cl 3 NR4 162 A1
Putney Cl IP27 175 A1
Pye La Cranworth IP25 86 A6
Deopham NR18 86 E2
Pye's La Castle Acre PE32 46 F2
Swanton Morley NR20 50 C3
Pyebush La NR13 166 B5
Pyecroft Rd PE14 41 E3
Pyehurn La NR10 53 A3
Pyehurn Mews NR8 155 E3
Pyes Cl 1 NR25 7 C6
Pyes Mill Rd NR14 92 A1
Pyes Yd NR3 178 B4
Pyghtle The 4 NR16 118 C5
Pyke Ct NR30 168 D7
Pym Cl NR13 72 E5
Pymar's La 6 NR15 107 C5
Pyrford Dr NR4 161 F1

Q

Quaker La
Fakenham NR21 141 B4
Norwich NR6 53 E1
8 Spixworth NR12 54 A1
Tasburgh NR15 106 F6
Wisbech PE13 152 E3
Quarry La NR9 51 A5
Quay Angel NR31 170 D1
Quay La NR25 7 A7
Quay Mill Wlk 3 NR30 169 C4
Quay Ostend NR31 171 C8
Quay Rd NR31 170 D4
Quay Side NR3 178 B4
Quay The Blakeney NR25 7 C6
Wells-next-the-Sea NR23 136 D6
Wiveton NR25 7 E7
Quebec Cl 14 NR4 89 B8
Quebec Rd
Dereham NR19 154 D7
Norwich NR1 163 A6
Quebec St NR19 154 D5
Queen Anne's Rd NR31 170 C8
Queen Elizabeth Ave PE30 147 B7
Queen Elizabeth Cl NR3 178 C4
Queen Elizabeth Dr
Dersingham PE31 140 D3
Wisbech PE13 152 D3
Queen Elizabeth Hospl PE30 147 E5
Queen Elizabeth Way
Bawsey PE30 147 F6
Castle Rising PE30 27 C1
Queen Mary Rd PE30 147 A5
Queen St
Great Yarmouth NR30 169 C3
King's Lynn PE30 146 D5
New Buckenham NR16 104 F1
Norwich NR1 178 B3
Stradbroke IP21 131 E1
12 Sutton Bridge PE12 41 B8
Swaffham PE37 153 B4
Wisbech PE13 152 C6
Wymondham NR18 173 C3
Queen's Cl PE33 80 E4
Queen's Cres
Bircham PE31 14 A3
Great Yarmouth NR31 170 B3
Queen's Ct NR17 174 D6
Queen's Dr PE14 77 A7
Queen's Pl 2 PE34 43 B1
Queen's Rd
Attleborough NR17 174 C6
Clenchwarton PE34 146 A5
Fakenham NR21 141 C4
Great Yarmouth NR30 169 D2
Hethersett NR9 88 D8
Holt NR25 137 C5
Queen's Sq NR17 174 D5
Queens Ave PE30 146 D2
Queens Cl
6 Blakeney NR25 7 C6
Norwich NR4 162 A3
Queens Ct 1 NR15 106 E3
Queens Dr PE36 132 C6
Queens Gdns PE36 132 D6
Queens Rd
Brandon IP27 175 A2
Cromer NR27 139 D4
Norwich NR1 178 A1
Wisbech PE13 152 C4
Queens Sch The PE13 152 D3
Queensway
Caister-on-Sea NR30 168 E4
7 Earsham NR35 123 F8
King's Lynn PE30 147 C6
North Walsham NR28 151 A5
Roydon IP22 177 A5
Thetford IP24 176 C2
Watton IP25 84 D3
Wymondham NR18 173 B5
Queensway Com Jun Sch IP24 176 C2
Queensway Inf Sch IP24 176 C2
Quidenham Rd
Harling NR16 118 D5
Kenninghall NR16 119 A5
Quidenham NR16 118 F8

R

Rabbit La
Downham Market PE38 172 D6
Great Witchingham NR9 51 E6
Raby Ave PE30 146 E6
Racecourse Rd NR7 159 E1
Raceys Cl 4 PE14 59 D2
Rachel Cl 7 NR5 161 C5
Rackham Cl NR31 171 C5
Rackham Rd NR3 158 D2
Rackheath La NR12 54 B2
Rackheath Prim Sch NR13 54 D1
Radcliffe Rd NR8 155 E2
RAF Air Defence Radar Mus* NR12 55 E5
Rafeman Cl NR5 160 E7
Raglan St 1 NR2 162 C6
Ragmere Rd NR17 104 D1
Railway App 2 NR26 138 D7
Railway Hill IP20 122 C2
Railway La PE12 41 B7
Railway Mus* NR18 173 D2
Railway Rd
Downham Market PE38 172 A5
King's Lynn PE30 146 E5
Wisbech PE13 152 C3
Rainey Ct 37 IP20 122 D2
Rainsborough Rise NR13 72 D5
Rainsthorpe PE30 147 D8
Rainthorpe Hall* NR15 106 F8
Raleigh Ave NR30 169 D7
Raleigh Inf Sch IP24 176 E6
Raleigh Rd PE30 147 B4
Raleigh Way IP24 176 E6
Ram La NR15 121 C4
Ramblers The NR14 90 B6
Rambouillet Cl NR31 170 A4
Ramm's La PE37 66 A4
Ramms Ct NR23 136 D6
Ramnoth Cty Jun Sch PE13 152 D4
Ramnoth Rd PE13 152 D4
Rampant Horse St NR2 178 A2
Rampart Rd NR30 169 C5
Rampart Way IP24 176 D3
Ramsay Gdns PE36 132 D3
Ramsey Cl
Norwich NR4 161 E3
Thetford IP24 176 E6
Randall Cl 1 NR31 171 D5
Randell Cl NR28 151 D4
Randle Gn NR5 161 C8
Randolf Rd NR1 162 E2
Rands Rd PE14 60 C5
Rangoon Cl NR7 159 C4
Ransome Ave IP21 130 D6
Ransome's Cl PE14 77 E5
Ranson Rd NR1 163 B5
Ranworth 5 PE30 147 D5
Ranworth Cl
8 Belton NR31 94 A6
Swaffham PE37 153 B1
Ranworth Dr NR29 167 B2
Ranworth Fst Sch NR5 161 E7
Ranworth Rd
Blofield NR13 165 F8
Norwich NR5 161 D7
South Walsham NR13 74 A8
Rash's Cres IP22 129 C6
Rash's Gn NR19 154 F2
Ratcliffe Rd NR21 141 C4
Rattle Row
Mileham PE32 48 C6
Wymondham NR18 173 B4
Rattler's Rd IP27 175 C3
Rattlerow Hill IP21 131 F2
Raven Cl NR31 170 A7
Raven's La PE31 29 D5
Raveningham Gdns* NR14 110 A7
Raveningham Rd
Gillingham NR34 110 C4
Stockton NR34 110 A5
Ravensway PE38 172 C3
Ravine Rd NR31 93 E1
Rawhall La NR20 49 B5
Rawley Rd NR5 161 B8
Rawlings Way 21 IP26 98 E1
Rawlinsons La NR11 150 C7
Ray Bond Way NR11 150 C4
Raymond Cl NR6 157 E7
Raymond Rd NR6 157 F7
Raymond St
Thetford IP24 176 D3
15 Wisbech PE13 152 C4
Rayner's Cl 6 NR20 68 E6
Rayner's La NR35 109 D4
Rayner's Way NR20 68 E6
Raynham Cl PE30 147 B4
Raynham Rd
Dunton NR21 31 C6
Hempton NR21 141 A2
Whissonsett NR20 31 C2
Raynham Ride NR19 154 D7
Raynham St NR2 162 B7
Rayns Cl NR6 158 F5
Read's Cross NR14 109 E8
Readscross La NR14 109 E8
Recorder Rd NR1 178 C3
Recreation Dr PE38 97 A5
Recreation Gd Rd NR7 159 A4
Recreation Rd
East Dereham NR19 154 C1
Great Yarmouth NR31 170 C5
Hethersett NR9 88 C7
North Walsham NR28 151 B4
Norwich NR2 162 A5
Stalham NR12 39 A4
Rectory Cl
Caister-on-Sea NR30 168 E5
Coltishall NR12 54 D7
21 Long Stratton NR15 106 E3
2 Newton Flotman NR15 89 D1
Rollesby NR29 57 C2
Roydon PE32 27 F2
Rectory Ct NR3 158 D2
Rectory Dr PE34 145 E5
Rectory Gdns
Hingham NR9 86 B5
Wisbech PE13 152 E6
Rectory Hill IP22 128 D2
Rectory La
Bracon Ash NR14 88 E3
Bunwell NR16 105 C4
Great Ellingham NR17 103 E8
Haddiscoe NR14 110 F7
Hedenham NR35 108 D4
Little Melton NR9 160 A3
Loddon NR14 92 A2
Mettingham NR35 124 D8
Mulbarton NR14 89 B3
North Runcton PE33 44 A3
Poringland NR14 90 D5
Scole IP21 121 C1
Stuston IP21 130 B4
Watlington PE33 61 D5
Weeting IP27 175 B7
West Winch PE33 43 F3
Rectory Mdw
Diss IP22 177 E4
Litcham PE32 48 A4
Rectory Rd
Aldeby, Wheatacre, Burgh St Peter NR34 111 A4
Bacton NR28 23 C3
Brome & Oakley IP23 130 B3
Broome NR35 109 B3
Burston & Shimpling IP22 120 E2
2 Coltishall NR12 54 C6
Dickleburgh IP21 121 B1
East Carleton NR14 89 A4
Edgefield NR24 19 D5
Elsing NR20 50 F4
Gillingham NR34 110 B3
Gissing IP22 120 F4
Haddiscoe NR14 110 F7
Hockering NR20 69 B8
Hoveton NR12 55 A7
Lyng NR9 51 B4
Northrepps NR27 11 A1
Outwell PE14 77 F6
Rectory Rd *continued*
Rocklands NR17 103 B7
Shelfanger IP22 120 B2
Sutton NR12 39 C3
Swanton Morley NR20 50 B4
Tivetshall St Mary NR15 121 C4
Topcroft NR35 107 F4
Weston Longville NR9 51 D2
Whissonsett NR20 31 E2
Wood Norton NR20 33 A7
Wortham IP22 129 D6
Red Admiral Cl 1 NR18 173 E4
Red Barn La NR11 9 D1
Red Bridge La NR5 157 C2
Red Cottage Cl NR3 158 A2
Red Lion Cl
Holme Hale IP25 66 B2
Hoxne IP21 131 A3
Red Lion St
3 Aylsham NR11 150 C7
Norwich NR1 178 B2
Red Lion Yd NR23 136 D6
Red Robin Cl 9 NR15 106 D3
Redbrick Cotts IP27 175 D5
Redcastle Furze Prim Sch IP24 176 B3
Redcastle Rd IP24 176 A4
Redcliffe Way NR13 165 B4
Redell Cl 3 NR13 55 A1
Redenhall Rd IP20 122 D2
Redfern Cl
East Dereham NR19 154 B4
King's Lynn PE30 147 E8
Redfern Rd NR7 159 D1
Redgate IP24 176 E4
Redgate Hill PE36 132 D2
Redgate Jun Sch PE36 132 D2
Redgate Rd PE13 41 A4
Redgrave & Lopham Fen National Nature Reserve* IP22 128 F6
Redgrave Rd
South Lopham IP22 128 E7
Wortham IP22 129 A5
Redman Rd NR28 151 D3
Redmere Cl 4 NR12 54 A4
Redmere Dro CB7 112 D5
Redwell St NR2 178 B3
Redwing Dr
1 Great Yarmouth NR31 94 C7
5 Wisbech PE14 152 D2
Redwing Gdns 7 NR10 54 A1
Redwings Horse Sanctuary (Caldecott)* NR31 93 F4
Reed La NR19 48 F3
Reed Way 3 PE14 77 A8
Reeder Cl NR19 154 D3
Reeder's La NR14 90 E4
Reedham Prim Sch NR13 93 A4
Reedham Rd
Acle NR13 166 B1
Beighton NR13 74 E1
Cantley NR13 92 D6
Reedham Sta NR13 92 F5
Reepham High Sch NR10 149 B3
Reepham Prim Sch NR10 149 B4
Reepham Rd
Bawdeswell NR20 50 F8
Briston NR24 142 E2
Felthorpe NR10 155 D5
Foulsham NR20 33 D3
Guestwick NR20 34 A5
Horsford NR10 157 D7
Norwich NR6 157 E2
Swannington NR9 52 B5
Thurning NR20 34 B8
Wood Dalling NR11 34 D5
Reeve Cl IP21 130 D6
Reeve Pl NR27 139 D4
Reeves Ave PE30 147 B8
Reeves Ct NR28 151 C5
Reeves La IP26 114 A7
Reffley La PE30 147 D8
Reffley Prim Sch PE30 147 D8
Reg Houchen Rd PE31 140 C3
Regal Ct 28 IP25 84 D3
Regal Rd PE13 152 B2
Regency Ave PE30 147 C5
Regent Bvd 10 NR30 169 D4
Regent Cl NR19 154 D1
Regent Pl 1 PE30 146 E4
Regent Rd
Downham Market PE38 172 A4
9 Great Yarmouth NR30 169 D4
Regent St
Great Yarmouth NR30 169 C3
Wickmere NR11 20 E4
Regent Way 6 PE30 146 D4
Regents Cl NR25 137 B5
Regents Ct NR28 151 B5
Regents Pk PE30 147 C5
Regina Rd NR1 178 A1
Regis Ave 4 NR27 9 F5
Regis Pl NR26 138 E7
Reid Way PE30 147 A8
Renowood Cl PE32 48 B8
Renson Cl NR3 158 C4
Renwick Pk E NR27 10 A4
Renwick Pk W NR27 10 A4
Repps Rd
Ashby with Oby NR29 57 B3
1 Martham NR29 57 D4
Repps Rd *continued*
Thurne NR29 56 E3
Repton Ave NR6 158 D7
Repton Cl NR11 150 D5
Retreat Est PE38 172 D6
Reve Cres 5 NR13 73 C6
Revell Rd PE38 172 B4
Reydon Cl 10 NR5 161 A7
Reymerston Rd NR9 68 B2
Reynolds Ave NR30 168 C8
Reynolds La NR29 56 E7
Reynolds Way PE31 140 C3
Rhombus Bsns Pk NR6 158 B5
Rhond The NR12 164 C5
Rhone Pl 3 PE13 152 E3
Rhoon Rd PE34 144 E8
Rice Way NR7 159 C2
Richard Easter Rd IP24 176 D6
Richard Haggard Cl 3 IP25 67 C2
Richard Hicks Dr 9 NR19 154 C4
Richard Young Cl 2 PE13 152 C8
Richards Rd NR21 15 D2
Richardson Cres NR9 88 C8
Richenda Cl 8 NR5 161 C5
Riches Cl 2 NR15 106 F6
Richmond Cl
Honingham NR9 69 E6
Lyng NR9 51 A5
Richmond Ct PE13 152 A4
Richmond Pk NR17 174 F6
Richmond Pl NR9 51 A4
Richmond Rd
Brandon IP27 175 A1
Downham Market PE38 172 B4
4 Long Stratton NR15 106 E3
Norwich NR5 156 E1
Saham Toney IP25 84 C4
Richmond Rise NR10 149 C5
Rickinghall Rd IP22 128 C3
Riddlesworth Hall Sch IP22 127 C8
Rider Haggard Rd NR7 159 D1
Ridgeway
Caister-on-Sea NR30 168 D8
Cromer NR27 139 C4
Ridgeway The NR1 163 B8
Ridings The
5 Cringleford NR4 89 B8
Fakenham NR21 141 E4
2 Poringland NR14 90 C5
Ridland's Rd NR24 142 C1
Rigby Cl 1 NR14 90 D5
Rigbys Ct NR2 178 A3
Rigg Cl 2 PE13 152 B3
Rightup Dro IP27 113 E5
Rightup La NR18 173 D2
Riley Cl NR7 159 D1
Rill Cl PE30 148 B4
Rimer Cl NR5 160 F6
Ring Rd NR7 163 F7
Ringbank La NR11 21 A6
Ringers Cl 4 NR18 173 D5
Ringers La NR9 86 C5
Ringland La
Costessey NR8 156 B6
Easton NR9 70 B5
Morton on the Hill NR9 52 A2
Weston Longville NR9 51 F3
Ringland Rd NR8 155 A1
Ringmere Cl 2 IP25 84 C3
Ringmere Rd 3 IP25 84 C3
Ringmore Rd PE38 97 B6
Ringsfield Rd NR34 124 F5
Ringstead Downs Nature Reserve* PE36 1 F2
Ringstead Rd
Burnham Market PE31 135 A2
Docking PE31 134 A6
Heacham PE31 133 E6
Ringstead PE36 2 A2
Sedgeford PE36 13 B8
Thornham PE36 2 D6
Ringwood Cl NR9 160 B2
Ripley Cl NR2 161 F5
Ripon Way IP24 176 B5
Rippingall Cl 6 NR11 150 D6
Rippingall Rd NR11 150 D6
Rise The 10 Loddon NR14 92 A2
Sheringham NR26 138 E6
Riseway Cl NR1 163 B8
Rising Way 3 NR29 57 C4
Risley Cl NR16 117 E5
River Cl PE32 63 E8
River Ct NR21 141 A3
River Dro PE33 80 F2
River La Cranworth IP25 85 F7
King's Lynn PE30 147 A6
River Rd West Acre PE32 46 B1
West Walton PE14 59 A8
River Terr PE13 152 A8
River View
Beccles NR34 110 C2
7 Beetley NR20 49 D4
River View Cl NR21 141 E4
River Vw 7 NR20 49 D4
River Way NR31 93 F6
River Wlk
Great Yarmouth NR30 169 C8
King's Lynn PE34 146 C6

Riverdale Ct NR13 .....165 D3
Riverdene Mews NR8 ...155 E3
Rivergreen Ct NR1 .....163 E6
Rivermead NR12 ....39 B3
Riverside
Cockley Cley PE37 ....82 D7
Diss IP22 ....177 B3
King's Lynn PE30 ....147 B7
Norwich NR1 ....178 C2
Reedham NR13 ....92 F4
Riverside Cl NR6 ....157 D2
Riverside Ctr NR12 .....164 C5
Riverside Est NR13 .....165 D1
Riverside Ind Ctr
NR31 ....170 D5
Riverside Ind Est
PE30 ....146 D7
Riverside Maltings
IP22 ....177 F3
Riverside Rd
Great Yarmouth NR31 .....170 D6
Holt NR25 ....8 A1
Norwich NR1 ....178 C3
Wroxham/Hoveton
NR12 ....164 C4
Riverside Swimming Ctr
NR1 ....178 C1
Riverside Way
Brandon IP27 ....175 C5
1 Wisbech PE13 ....152 B3
Riverside Wlk IP24 .....176 C4
Riversway PE30 ....146 E7
Riverview Dr NR13 .....166 B8
RNLI Henry Blogg Mus*
NR27 ....139 B7
Roaches Ct NR3 ....178 B3
Robberds Way NR5 .....160 E8
Robert Andrew Cl
NR18 ....87 B2
Robert Balding Rd
PE31 ....140 C3
Robert Cl Trunch NR28 ....22 E5
5 Wymondham NR18 ....173 C6
Robert Gybson Way
NR2 ....178 A3
Robert Herb Way 5
NR18 ....173 E4
Robert Kett Jun Sch
NR18 ....173 C5
Robert Key Dr 2 NR20 ...68 E6
Robert Linge Cres
IP27 ....175 D3
Robert St 8 PE30 ....146 E3
Roberts Cl 3 NR15 .....107 C5
Robertson Cl NR26 .....138 E6
Robin Cl
Great Yarmouth NR31 .....170 A5
Mulbarton NR14 ....89 A3
Robin Hill PE31 ....133 D8
Robin Hood Rd NR4 .....162 C1
Robin Kerkham Way
PE34 ....145 E6
Robin Mews 4 PE14 ....152 D2
Robin Wlk IP27 ....175 F3
Robins La NR10 ....149 B4
Robinson Rd IP21 ......130 C5
Robson Rd NR5 ....161 B6
Robyns Rd
3 Sheringham NR26 ....9 F5
Sheringham NR26 ....138 F5
Rocelin Cl NR3 ....158 E3
Rochford Rd 4 NR29 ....57 C4
Rochford Wlk 5 PE13 ...152 E5
Rockall Way 6 NR30 ...168 C6
Rockingham Rd NR5 ...161 C6
Rockland Cl PE13 ......153 B2
Rockland Dr NR7 ....163 C6
Rockland La NR17 ....85 F1
Rockland Rd NR14 ....90 F7
Rockland St Mary Prim Sch
NR14 ....91 B6
Rocklands Prim Sch
NR17 ....103 B7
Rocklands Rd NR17 ....103 B4
Rode La NR16 ....105 B3
Rodham Rd PE15 ....77 A1
Rodinghead 1 PE30 ....147 D5
Rodney Rd NR30 ....169 D3
Rodwell Cnr NR10 ....35 C1
Roe Dr NR5 ....161 E5
Roedich Dr NR8 ....155 C1
Roger Ride 3 NR19 ....154 D2
Roger's Cl NR31 ....171 D5
Roger's La NR15 ....89 F1
Rogers Cl 4 NR5 ......161 B7
Roland Dr NR15 ....107 D5
Rolfe Cres PE31 ....133 E5
Rollesby Ave PE13 .....153 B2
Rollesby Fst Sch NR29 ...57 D3
Rollesby Gdns 9 NR29 ...57 D2
Rollesby Pl NR10 ....37 B2
Rollesby Rd
Fleggburgh NR29 ....57 C1
King's Lynn PE30 ....147 A3
Martham NR29 ....57 D4
Swaffham PE37 ....153 B2
Rolleston Cl NR5 ....161 B7
Rollingpin La NR19 ....154 D4
Roman Cres PE37 ......153 D2
Roman Dr NR13 ....165 B3
Roman Pl 20 NR30 .....169 D4
Roman Way
Brancaster PE31 ....3 B7
Caister-on-Sea NR30 .....168 D5
Thetford IP24 ....176 C7
Romany Cl 8 NR29 ......57 D2
Romany Rd NR3 ....158 F1
Romany Wlk 6 NR14 .....90 C5
Romer Dro PE33 ....81 B3
Romney Wlk NR19 ......154 D4
Rook Dr NR8 ....155 E2
Rookery Cl PE34 ....145 E5
Rookery Farm Rd NR28 ..23 F2
Rookery Hill NR14 ....91 B7
Rookery La NR35 ......107 F3
Rookery Rd PE34 ......145 E4
Rookery The IP27 ......114 D5
Room La NR15 ....122 D8
Rope Wlk 5 IP24 ....176 D4
Ropemakers Row 5
NR3 ....158 C1
Ropes Hill NR12 ....55 D4
Ropes Hill Dyke NR12 ...55 D4
Ropes Wlk NR13 ....165 E6
Rosa Cl NR12 ....54 B1
Rosa Vella Dr 3 NR20 ....68 A8
Rosalie Cl NR6 ....158 B4
Rosary Cl 8 NR14 ....89 B3
Rosary Rd NR1 ....163 A6
Rose Ave IP22 ....129 D7
Rose Cottage's NR19 ....66 D8
Rose Dr NR20 ....68 A8
Rose La Botesdale IP22 ..128 E3
Diss IP22 ....177 F3
3 Elm PE14 ....59 A1
Norwich NR1 ....178 C3
Palgrave IP22 ....177 D1
Rose La Cl IP22 ....177 D2
Rose Valley 4 NR2 .....162 B5
Rose Wlk
Brundall NR13 ....165 C3
Sculthorpe Airfield NR21 ...15 C2
1 Wisbech PE13 ....152 A6
Rose Yd NR3 ....178 A4
Roseacre Cl NR2 ....162 C2
Roseacre Est NR25 ....9 A2
Rosebay 1 PE30 ....148 C3
Rosebay Cl 5 NR6 .....158 D5
Roseberry Rd PE14 ......59 B1
Rosebery Ave
King's Lynn PE30 ....147 B6
7 Poringland NR14 ....90 D5
Rosebery Rd
Cromer NR27 ....139 D5
Great & Little Plumstead
NR13 ....73 A4
Norwich NR3 ....158 D1
3 Sheringham NR27 ....10 A5
Rosecroft 4 NR17 ......174 C5
Rosecroft Way IP24 ....176 F4
Rosedale Cres 5 NR1 ...163 A6
Rosedale Gdns NR31 ....94 A5
Rosefields NR13 ....165 E4
Rosemary La
11 Gayton PE32 ....45 C6
2 New Buckenham NR16 .104 F1
Norwich NR3 ....178 A4
Rosemary Musker Cty High
Sch IP24 ....176 E7
Rosemary Rd
Blofield NR13 ....73 C6
Norwich NR7 ....159 B4
Rosemary Terr NR21 ....141 B5
Rosemary Way PE38 ...172 D6
Rosery The NR14 ....89 C3
Roses Ct NR23 ....136 D5
Rosetta Rd NR10 ....54 A2
Roseville Cl 2 NR1 .....163 B5
Rosewood NR28 ....151 E5
Roslyn Rd NR31 ....170 C5
Rosslare 1 NR4 ....162 A1
Rossons Rd NR8 ....155 C1
Rostwold Way NR3 .....158 D2
Rosyth Rd 4 IP31 ......126 B1
Rothbury Cl NR18 ......173 B4
Rothbury Rd NR18 .....173 C4
Rotten Marsh NR13 ....166 C2
Rottenstone La NR29 ...167 F3
Roudham Rd NR16 .....117 F6
Rouen Rd NR1 ....178 B2
Rougham Cnr IP26 ....99 F3
Rougham End PE32 ......47 C8
Rougham Hall PE32 .....47 A7
Rougham Rd PE32 ....29 E1
Roughlands IP27 ....113 E1
Rougholme Cl
6 Beetley NR19 ....49 C3
6 Gressenhall NR20 ....49 C3
Rought Ave IP27 ....175 D2
Roughton Rd
Roughton NR27 ....139 B2
Thorpe Market NR11 ....21 F7
Roughton Rd Sta
NR27 ....139 B4
Round House Way
NR4 ....161 B1
Round Well Rd NR5 ....156 D1
Roundabout La NR14 ...109 B8
Roundham Medieval Village
of* NR16 ....117 E6
Roundhead Ct 26 NR7 ...72 D4
Roundtree Cl NR7 ......159 B2
Roundtree Way NR7 ....159 B2
Roundway Down 17 NR7 .72 D4
Rouse's La PE38 ....172 D4
Row Hill 6 PE33 ....43 F2
Row The Weeting IP27 ..175 A7
Wereham PE33 ....80 D3
West Dereham PE33 ....80 B4
Rowan Cl
10 Great Yarmouth NR31 ...94 C7
Thetford IP24 ....176 B1
7 Watlington PE33 ....61 D5
Rowan Cl *continued*
Wisbech PE13 ....152 F7
Rowan Ct NR5 ....156 F1
Rowan Dr
Brandon IP27 ....175 C3
Gayton PE32 ....45 C6
Rowan Rd
King's Lynn PE34 ....43 D4
Martham NR29 ....57 D4
Rowan Way
Fakenham NR21 ....141 F4
10 Great Yarmouth NR31 ..170 B6
Holt NR25 ....137 B7
Row's Mdw 1 NR15 ....107 C5
Rowington Rd NR1 .....178 A1
Rowland Ct NR1 ....178 B1
Rowley Cnr IP26 ....83 A5
Rowton Heath 18 NR7 ....72 D4
Roxley Cl NR7 ....163 F5
Royal Albert Ct 5 NR31 .170 D4
Royal Arcade NR2 ......178 B2
Royal Ave NR30 ....169 D7
Royal Cl 11 PE12 ....41 B8
Royal Norfolk Regimental
Mus* NR1 ....178 B3
Royal Pl 2 PE13 ....152 C4
Royal Thames Rd
NR30 ....168 D7
Royalist Dr 28 NR7 ......72 D4
Royden Way 3 NR29 .....57 C1
Roydon Comm National
Nature Reserve*
PE32 ....27 F1
Roydon Fen IP22 ......177 A4
Roydon Gdns IP22 .....177 A5
Roydon Prim Sch
IP22 ....177 B5
Roydon Rd IP22 ....177 C5
Royston Gn NR28 ......151 D6
Rubens Way 6 PE38 ...172 D6
Rudd's Drift PE32 ....48 E5
Rudds La NR10 ....149 B3
Rudham CE Prim Sch
PE31 ....30 A6
Rudham Rd
Great Massingham PE32 ...29 D2
Syderstone PE31 ....15 A3
Rudham Stile La NR21 ..141 B6
Rudolf Steiner Sch
NR12 ....164 B3
Rugg's La NR29 ....75 C8
Rugge Dr NR4 ....161 E2
Ruin Rd NR28 ....38 A5
Rumburgh La NR35 ....124 D2
Rump Cl 10 NR20 ....50 B3
Run La NR14 ....91 B6
Runcton Cl NR5 ....161 B7
Runcton Holme CE VA Prim
Sch PE33 ....61 E3
Runcton Rd PE33 ....61 F2
Runhall Rd NR9 ....69 A2
Runham Rd
Great Yarmouth NR30 .....169 B5
Stokesby NR29 ....75 B5
Runnel The NR5 ....160 F6
Runton House Cl NR27 ..10 A5
Runton Rd NR27 ....139 A7
Rupert St NR2 ....162 C4
Rushall Rd IP20 ....122 B2
Rushford Rd
Coney Weston IP31 ....127 B5
Euston IP24 ....126 D7
Rushmead Cl PE30 .....148 C3
Rushmeadow Rd
NR19 ....154 A5
Rushmer Way NR26 ....138 C5
Rushmore Rd NR7 ......159 A4
Ruskin Ave NR31 ......170 B2
Ruskin Cl PE31 ....133 E5
Ruskin Pl 5 PE38 ......172 D6
Ruskin Rd NR4 ....161 E4
Russell Ave
Caister-on-Sea NR30 .....168 E5
Great Yarmouth NR31 .....170 C3
Norwich NR7 ....159 B3
9 Spixworth NR10 ....54 A2
Russell Cl NR23 ....136 C6
Russell Ct NR23 ....136 D6
Russell Rd NR30 ....169 D4
Russell Sq 24 NR30 ....169 D4
Russell St
King's Lynn PE30 ....146 F3
Norwich NR2 ....162 C7
Wisbech PE13 ....152 C6
Russell Terr
Mundesley NR11 ....143 C6
Trowse Newton NR14 .....163 B2
Russell Way NR18 .....173 C3
Russet Cl NR17 ....174 E4
Russet Gr NR4 ....161 E5
Russet Rd IP22 ....177 C5
Russet Way NR19 ......154 E3
Russets The PE14 ....77 E6
Russett Cl PE30 ....147 C8
Rustens Manor Rd 2
NR18 ....173 C5
Rustons Rd PE14 ....59 F3
Ruthen Pl 1 NR19 .....154 D5
Rutherford Way IP24 ...176 C6
Rutland St NR2 ....162 C4
Ryalla Drift PE30 ......148 B4
Ryburgh Dr NR20 ....32 D5
Rydal Cl NR5 ....161 C6
Ryders Way IP22 ....128 E2
Rye Ave NR3 ....158 B3
Rye Cl
North Walsham NR28 .....151 E6
Norwich NR3 ....158 B2
Rye La NR17 ....174 C4
Rye's Cl PE33 ....62 D3
Ryeland Rd 2 PE30 ....148 C4
Ryelands 5 NR29 ......167 B7
Ryelands Rd PE30 .....148 D4
Ryley Cl PE30 ....147 E8
Ryrie Ct NR4 ....161 E2
Ryston Cl PE38 ....172 C4
Ryston End PE38 ......172 C4
Ryston Pk PE38 ....172 F1
Ryston Rd Denver PE38 ..172 D2
West Dereham PE33 ....80 B4

S

Sackville Cl 4 NR30 ....169 C3
Sacred Heart Convent Sch
PE37 ....153 C5
Saddlebow Ind Est
PE34 ....43 C4
Saddlebow Rd PE30 ....146 D1
Sadler Cl PE30 ....146 F7
Sadler Rd NR6 ....157 F7
Sadlers Ct 11 NR26 ....138 D7
Sadlers Way NR28 .....151 E5
Saffron Cl IP27 ....175 B2
Saffron Sq NR6 ....158 C3
Sage Rd PE38 ....172 D7
Saham Rd IP25 ....84 C4
Sainsbury Ctr for the Visual
Arts* NR4 ....161 C3
St Alban's Rd NR1 .....162 D3
St Albans Way IP24 ...176 B5
St Andrew Cl 1 NR31 ...171 E5
St Andrew's & Blackfriars
Halls* NR1 ....178 B3
St Andrew's Cl
Blofield NR13 ....165 E5
Caister-on-Sea NR30 .....168 D7
Holme Hale IP25 ....66 A2
Holt NR25 ....137 C6
Northwold IP26 ....99 C8
3 Old Buckenham NR17 ..104 D2
St Andrew's Rd
Great Yarmouth NR31 .....170 C6
Lingwood NR13 ....73 F3
Sheringham NR26 ....138 D6
St Andrew's Way
NR13 ....165 E5
St Andrews Ave 5 NR7 ...72 D3
St Andrews CE VA Prim Sch
IP22 ....119 A1
St Andrews Cl
Barningham IP31 ....127 C3
Buxton with Lammas
NR10 ....36 E1
Framingham Earl NR14 .....90 D5
Great Yarmouth NR31 .....170 C5
1 Hingham NR9 ....86 C4
Long Stratton NR15 ......106 E4
Poringland NR14 ....90 D5
West Dereham PE33 ....80 C4
Worstead NR28 ....38 A4
St Andrews Dr
3 Norwich NR4 ....89 C8
Quidenham NR16 ....103 E1
St Andrews Drift 2 NR25 ..7 A4
St Andrews Hill NR2 ...178 B3
St Andrews La
Necton PE37 ....65 F5
Roydon PE32 ....28 A2
St Andrews Rd
North Runcton PE30 ......147 B3
Norwich NR6 ....157 D6
Scole IP21 ....130 D5
St Andrews Sch NR27 ...10 B5
St Andrews St NR2 ....178 B3
St Andrews Way PE37 ....65 F5
St Andrews Wlk PE33 ....80 C5
St Ann La NR1 ....178 C2
St Ann's St PE30 ....146 D5
St Anne's Cres
Clenchwarton PE34 ....145 D6
Great Yarmouth NR31 .....170 B4
St Annes Rd 4 NR14 .....90 D5
St Anns Fort PE30 .....146 D6
St Anthony's Way
IP27 ....175 E4
St Antony's Ave NR31 ..170 B2
St Audreys IP24 ....176 D3
St Augustines Gate 12
NR3 ....162 D8
St Augustines RC Prim Sch
NR8 ....156 E3
St Augustines Rd
PE13 ....152 C5
St Augustines St NR3 ..162 D8
St Augustines Way 3
PE30 ....148 C4
St Austin's Gr NR26 ...138 E7
St Barnabas Cl 2 IP24 ..176 C1
St Bartholomews Cl 4
NR2 ....162 B8
St Benedicts Cl NR34 ..110 D5
St Benedicts Rd IP27 ...175 E4
St Benedicts St NR2 ...178 A3
St Benet's Abbey*
NR12 ....56 C2
St Benet's Cl 9 NR12 ....39 B4
St Benet's Rd
Great Yarmouth NR31 .....170 B3
Stalham NR12 ....39 B4
St Benets Ave NR28 ....151 E4
St Benets Gr PE30 .....148 D3
St Benets Rd NR29 ......56 C3
St Botolph's Cl 3 PE30 .148 C3
St Botolphs CE VC Prim Sch
IP22 ....128 F3
St Catherine's Ave 5
NR29 ....56 C8
St Catherine's Way
NR31 ....170 B4
St Catherines Rd NR7 ..163 F8
St Christopher Cl
16 Belton NR31 ....94 A6
6 Caister-on-Sea NR30 ...168 D7
St Christophers Cl
NR15 ....108 C7
St Christophers Sch
NR6 ....158 E4
St Clare Ct 6 NR31 ....171 D5
St Clement Cl 2 PE14 ....77 F6
St Clement Mews 7
NR31 ....171 D5
St Clements Dr 4 PE38 .172 C6
St Clements High Sch
PE34 ....144 C6
St Clements Hill NR3 ...158 E2
St Clements Way
NR13 ....165 C4
St Crispins Rd NR3 ....178 A4
St Cross Rd IP20 ....123 B4
St David's Cl 17 NR31 ...94 A6
St David's Rd NR9 ....88 C7
St Davids Cl
Brandon IP27 ....175 D3
Long Stratton NR15 ......106 E4
St Davids Dr 8 NR13 ....72 D6
St Dominic Sq 8 PE30 ..146 D5
St Domonic's Dr IP27 ..175 E4
St Edmund Cl
Attleborough NR17 ....174 C5
Great Yarmouth NR31 .....170 B3
Poringland NR14 ....90 B6
St Edmund Rd IP27 ....114 E8
St Edmund's Ave
PE36 ....132 D5
St Edmund's Rd
Downham Market PE38 ...172 D5
Lingwood NR13 ....73 F3
Taverham NR8 ....155 C1
St Edmund's Rise 2
NR8 ....155 C1
St Edmund's Terr
Hunstanton PE36 ....132 C4
King's Lynn PE30 ....146 C7
St Edmunds NR17 .....174 E5
St Edmunds Cl
Costessey NR8 ....156 F5
Norwich NR6 ....157 E1
St Edmunds Com Sch
PE30 ....146 E8
St Edmunds Ct 1 IP24 ..176 C1
St Edmunds Dr PE14 ....59 D1
St Edmunds Gate
Attleborough NR17 ....174 B4
11 Honington IP31 ....126 B1
St Edmunds Prim Sch
IP21 ....131 A2
St Edmunds RC Prim Sch
NR35 ....124 B8
St Edmunds Rd NR13 ..166 B3
St Edmunds Sq 13 IP31 .126 B1
St Edmunds Wharf
NR3 ....178 B4
St Edmundsbury Rd
PE30 ....146 E7
St Ethelberts Cl PE31 ..135 C2
St Faith's Church*
NR9 ....51 F7
St Faith's Cl NR9 ....51 E5
St Faith's Dr PE30 .....147 A6
St Faith's Rd NR6 .....158 D6
St Faiths La NR1 ....178 C3
St Francis Cl IP27 ......175 E4
St Francis Way NR30 ..169 C4
St Furseys' Way 2 NR31 .94 A6
St George's Cl
Saham Toney IP25 ....84 B5
Thurton NR14 ....91 C4
St George's Dr
Caister-on-Sea NR30 .....168 D7
East Dereham NR19 ....154 D1
St George's Rd NR30 ...169 D3
St George's Theatre 16
NR30 ....169 D3
St Georges Fst Sch 16
NR30 ....169 D3
St Georges Mid Sch
PE31 ....13 A1
St Georges Rd NR31 .....94 A6
St Georges St NR3 .....178 A4
St Germans Prim Sch
PE34 ....43 B1
St Giles Gr PE14 ....59 B1
St Giles' La IP24 ....176 D4
St Giles Rd NR24 ....18 B2
St Giles St NR2 ....178 A3
St Giles Terr NR2 ......178 A3
St Gregorys Alley NR2 ..178 A3
St Guthlac Cl PE37 ....153 C6
St Helena Way NR10 ....53 A3
St Helens Ct 1 IP24 ...176 D6
St Helens Rd NR12 ......23 F3
St Helens Way IP24 ....176 C7
St Hilda Cl NR19 ......154 C6
St Hilda Rd
Caister-on-Sea NR30 .....168 D6
East Dereham NR19 ....154 C6
St Hilda's Cres NR31 ...170 B5
St Hugh's Gn NR31 ....170 B3
St James Cl NR3 ......178 C4
St James Cres 18 NR31 ...94 A6
St James Ct NR3 ......178 B4

St James Dr PE38 172 B4
St James Rd IP19 124 A1
St James' Rd PE30 146 E4
St James St PE30 146 D4
St James Way NR15 106 E4
St James Wlk 14 NR30 169 D3
St James's Rd PE32 47 A2
St John Maddermarket NR2 178 A3
St John St NR1 178 C2
St John the Baptist Cath* NR2 162 C5
St John's Ave NR31 170 A4
St John's Cl
Coltishall NR12 54 D7
11 Hethersett NR9 88 D7
Oxborough PE33 81 E4
St John's Rd
Bungay NR35 124 A8
Terrington St John PE34 60 C8
St John's Terr
8 Great Yarmouth NR30 169 D3
King's Lynn PE30 146 E4
St John's Way 12 IP26 98 E1
St Johns Cl
2 Norwich NR1 162 E2
Swaffham PE37 153 C4
St Johns Ct PE13 153 C4
St Johns La NR14 109 A8
St Johns Prim Sch NR12 164 D5
St Johns RC Fst Sch NR2 162 C6
St Johns Rd Belton NR31 93 F6
Stalham NR12 39 B4
St Johns Way PE38 172 A4
St Joseph's Rd NR26 138 D6
St Julian Rd NR30 168 E4
St Julians Alley NR1 178 B2
St Laurence Ave NR13 165 C4
St Lawrence Dr NR4 161 C1
St Lawrence La NR2 178 A3
St Lawrence Prim Sch NR34 124 F2
St Leger NR15 106 E3
St Leonards Cl
Scole IP21 130 D5
Wymondham NR18 173 C6
St Leonards Rd NR1 163 A6
St Leonards St IP26 100 B4
St Leonards Terr 6 NR1 163 A6
St Luke's Terr 4 NR31 169 B4
St Magdalen Way PE13 153 C2
St Margaret's Cl
3 Coltishall NR12 54 C6
Upton with Fishley NR13 166 B8
St Margaret's Cres IP24 176 C3
St Margaret's Dr IP27 175 A2
St Margaret's La
2 Cromer NR27 139 C6
10 King's Lynn PE30 146 D4
St Margaret's Pl 11 PE30 146 D4
St Margaret's Rd
Bungay NR35 124 A6
1 Cromer NR27 139 C6
St Margaret's Way
1 Burgh St Margaret (Fleggburgh) NR29 57 C1
2 Hopton on Sea NR31 171 D5
St Margarets Ave 8 PE33 63 B4
St Margarets Cl 2 NR10 155 F3
St Margarets Dr NR7 159 C5
St Margarets Gdns NR12 164 D6
St Margarets La NR7 159 B5
St Margarets Mdw PE34 145 E5
St Margarets Pl NR12 40 A5
St Margarets St NR2 178 A3
St Marthas RC Prim Sch PE30 147 C6
St Martin's Cl NR27 139 C5
St Martin's Gdns 1 NR16 104 F1
St Martin's La IP24 125 E6
St Martin's Rd
2 Norwich NR3 162 D8
Wisbech PE13 152 E7
St Martin's Way IP24 176 B2
St Martin-at-Palace Plain NR3 178 B4
St Martins at Oak Wall La 7 NR3 162 D8
St Martins Cl 4 NR3 162 D8
St Martins La NR3 178 A4
St Mary Cl NR17 174 C6
St Mary's 4 NR16 104 F1
St Mary's Cl
Alpington NR14 90 F5
Flixton NR35 123 E5
Harleston IP20 122 E2
Heacham PE31 133 E6
Hemsby NR29 167 A7
Horsham St Faith & Newton St Faith NR10 53 E2
King's Lynn PE30 148 C2
Newton Flotman NR15 89 C1
12 Snettisham PE31 12 E4
1 Watton IP25 84 E3
Wroxham/Hoveton NR12 164 B4
St Mary's Cres 5 IP24 176 C3
St Mary's Ct 2 IP24 176 C3
St Mary's Dr IP22 177 E4
St Mary's La NR31 169 C3
St Mary's Rd
Aldeby NR34 111 A3
Cromer NR27 139 B6
20 Long Stratton NR15 106 E3
Poringland NR14 90 D5
West Walton PE14 59 B8
St Mary's Way 3 NR28 151 C5
St Marys Cl NR13 73 A5
St Marys Dr NR16 103 E1
St Marys Endowed Prim Sch NR11 21 E8
St Marys Gr NR7 159 C5
St Marys La 1 NR25 7 A4
St Marys Mid Sch NR15 106 E4
St Marys Plain NR3 178 A4
St Marys Prim Sch NR20 49 D4
St Marys RC Prim Sch NR31 170 C6
St Marys Rd
Ashby St Mary NR14 91 C4
Hemsby NR29 167 D6
5 Norwich NR3 162 D8
12 Stalham NR12 39 B4
St Marys Wlk 5 NR15 89 D1
St Matthew's Dr PE12 41 B8
St Matthews Rd NR1 178 C3
St Michael's Ave PE13 152 C7
St Michael's Cl
Aylsham NR11 150 C7
Thetford IP24 176 C2
St Michael's Cres IP25 83 D4
St Michael's Hospl NR11 150 A6
St Michael's Rd PE30 146 D1
St Michael-at-Pleas NR3 178 B3
St Michaels NR12 39 C2
St Michaels CE Prim Sch
Gillingham NR34 110 B2
King's Lynn PE30 146 D1
St Michaels Cl NR20 69 B7
St Michaels Inf Sch NR11 150 C7
St Michaels Mid Sch NR5 160 F8
St Michaels Way NR13 165 F2
St Michels Rd NR15 106 E4
St Mildreds Rd 3 NR5 161 B7
St Nicholas Cl
Dersingham PE31 140 E3
9 Gayton PE32 45 C6
1 King's Lynn PE30 146 D5
St Nicholas Ct
1 Great Yarmouth NR31 94 C6
10 North Walsham NR28 151 C5
St Nicholas Dr
Caister-on-Sea NR30 168 D6
Feltwell IP26 98 E2
St Nicholas Gdns 6 NR31 94 C6
St Nicholas House Sch NR28 151 D4
St Nicholas Pl 1 NR26 138 D7
St Nicholas Priory Mid Sch NR30 169 D5
St Nicholas Rd
Great Yarmouth NR30 169 D4
North Walsham NR28 151 D5
St Nicholas St
Diss IP22 177 D5
East Dereham NR19 154 D6
3 King's Lynn PE30 146 D5
Thetford IP24 176 C4
St Nicholas Wlk IP27 175 E4
St Nicholas's NR14 88 F3
St Olaves Rd
Herringfleet NR32 111 D8
Norwich NR3 162 E8
St Omer Cl NR14 89 B4
St Paul's Cl
Brockdish IP21 131 C6
4 Horsford NR10 53 B3
6 Wisbech PE13 152 C4
St Paul's Rd N PE14 59 D7
St Paul's Rd S PE14 59 E7
St Paul's Way NR30 169 C7
St Pauls Cl NR6 158 A5
St Pauls Sq 1 NR3 178 B4
St Peter & St Paul Prim Sch IP25 85 A5
St Peter's App IP27 175 B3
St Peter's Cl
Brockdish IP21 131 C6
King's Lynn PE34 146 B4
Strumpshaw NR13 73 F2
Yaxham NR19 68 A5
St Peter's La NR12 164 E8
St Peter's Pl IP27 175 B2
St Peter's Rd
Brooke NR15 90 F2
Fakenham NR21 141 B6
Great Yarmouth NR30 169 D3
King's Lynn PE34 146 C5
Lingwood NR13 73 F3
9 Sheringham NR26 138 D7
5 Wisbech PE13 152 C4
St Peter's Way 12 NR10 54 A2
St Peter's Wlk IP26 113 F7
St Peters Ave NR31 170 B2
St Peters CE Jun Sch PE13 152 E6
St Peters CE VC Prim Sch NR9 70 B5
St Peters Cl 3 NR4 89 B8
St Peters Dr NR9 70 B5
St Peters Hill NR18 87 A2
St Peters' Plain NR30 169 D3
St Peters Rd
Outwell PE14 77 E5
Watlington PE34 61 C7
Wiggenhall St Germans PE34 61 B8
St Peters St NR2 178 A2
St Peters Terr PE34 146 C4
St Philips Rd NR2 162 B6
St Roberts Way 15 NR31 94 A6
St Saviors La NR3 178 B4
St Stephen's Cres IP27 175 E4
St Stephens Rd NR1 178 A1
St Stephens Sq NR1 178 A1
St Stephens St NR1 178 A2
St Swithins Rd NR2 178 A3
St Thomas Cl IP27 175 E4
St Thomas Dr NR18 173 C2
St Thomas' La NR18 88 C4
St Thomas More RC Mid Sch NR2 162 A5
St Thomas Rd NR2 162 A6
St Thomas's La
Ingoldisthorpe PE31 140 D8
Snettisham PE31 12 F4
St Thomas's Rd NR29 167 C7
St Valery La PE30 146 D2
St Vedast St NR1 178 C3
St Vincent Wlk NR31 171 E5
St Walstan's Cl
Norwich NR5 156 D1
Taverham NR8 156 D8
St Walstan's Rd NR8 156 D8
St Williams Prim Sch NR7 163 D8
St Williams Way NR7 163 C7
St Winnold Cl PE38 172 B4
St Withburga La 8 NR19 154 D5
Saker Cl 11 NR7 72 D4
Salamanca Rd 7 NR15 106 D3
Salcott Dr PE13 152 E5
Sale Ct 5 NR14 92 A1
Sale Rd NR7 159 D2
Salhouse Dr PE37 153 B2
Salhouse Prim Sch NR13 55 B1
Salhouse Rd
Great & Little Plumstead NR13 73 B6
New Rackheath NR13 72 E7
Norwich NR7 159 C2
Sprowston NR13 72 D6
Woodbastwick NR13 55 C1
Wroxham NR12 164 B2
Salhouse Sta NR13 54 F1
Salisbury Rd
Cromer NR27 139 D4
Great Yarmouth NR30 169 D6
Norwich NR1 163 B5
Sheringham NR26 138 E7
Salisbury Way IP24 176 B4
Sallow La
Framingham Pigot NR14 90 E7
Snetterton NR16 118 B8
Salmon Rd NR30 170 D8
Salmon's Way NR21 141 F5
Salmond Dr 1 IP24 125 F6
Salmond Rd 11 IP25 84 F3
Salter Ave NR4 161 E5
Salter's La PE32 48 E4
Salter's Rd PE30 146 F7
Salters Way PE13 152 A2
Salthouse Marshes Nature Reserve* NR25 8 B7
Saltings The PE34 144 A5
Salts Rd PE14 59 C8
Samphire 5 PE30 147 B7
Sampson Rd NR28 151 C3
Samson Rd NR6 157 F4
Samson's La IP22 129 C7
Samuel Rd 1 NR1 163 B7
Sancroft Way IP20 123 A3
Sand Stone Way IP22 177 B4
Sandale Rd PE30 147 C4
Sandall Rd PE13 152 C3
Sandfield Rd 3 PE38 172 C6
Sandhole La NR13 73 A7
Sandhole Rd NR13 74 F1
Sandholme Cl NR1 163 B8
Sandover Cl 4 PE33 43 F2
Sandown Rd
Great Yarmouth NR30 169 D5
Wisbech PE13 152 A2
Sandpiper Cl 1 NR31 170 A5
Sandpiper Ct 13 NR39 58 B6
Sandpit La
Gimingham NR11 22 E8
Saxlingham Nethergate NR15 107 A8
Thorpe Market NR11 21 F7
Sandringham & W Newton CE Prim Sch PE31 27 F6
Sandringham Ave
Great Yarmouth NR30 169 D7
12 Marham PE33 63 B4
Wisbech PE13 152 D6
Sandringham Cres PE30 148 D5
Sandringham Ct
Norwich NR2 178 A1
6 Watton IP25 84 D3
Sandringham Ctry Pk* PE35 27 E7
Sandringham Dr
Downham Market PE38 172 E5
Heacham PE31 133 C4
Sandringham House Mus & Gdns* PE35 27 F7
Sandringham Private Hospl PE30 147 E6
Sandringham Rd
Dersingham PE31 140 E2
Hunstanton PE36 132 D4
King's Lynn PE30 147 C7
Norwich NR2 162 B6
Sandringham Way PE37 153 C2
Sands Cl NR31 171 E4
Sandy Cl PE31 140 C7
Sandy Cres PE31 140 C7
Sandy Hill La NR25 8 F4
Sandy La Aylsham NR11 150 B6
Bacton NR12 23 D3
Barningham IP31 127 C4
Beighton NR13 74 D2
Belton with Browston NR31 93 F5
Blackborough End PE32 44 C2
Bradwell NR31 94 C8
Buxton with Lammas NR10 53 F8
Canadas NR11 10 A3
Cantley NR13 92 E6
Castle Acre PE32 47 A2
Cromer NR27 139 A6
Denver PE38 172 C2
Dereham NR19 154 C8
Diss IP22 177 F4
Docking PE31 134 D6
East Dereham NR19 154 C6
East Tuddenham NR20 69 D8
Fakenham NR21 141 A5
Fleggburgh NR29 75 B8
Great Massingham PE32 46 E8
Grimston PE32 44 C8
Hardingham NR9 86 D7
Hilgay PE38 97 C8
Hoveton NR12 55 C4
Ingoldisthorpe PE31 140 C7
King's Lynn PE30 148 F1
Loddon NR14 92 B1
Mundham NR14 109 A7
Norwich NR4 162 D1
Old Hunstanton PE36 132 E8
Oulton NR11 35 B7
Raveningham NR14 110 B8
Rocklands NR17 103 A6
Runton NR27 10 C4
St Mary, South Elmham otherwise Homersfield IP20 123 B3
Sheringham NR27 10 A5
Somerton NR29 57 E6
South Wootton PE30 27 C1
Southrepps NR11 22 B7
Taverham NR8 156 C8
Thurning NR20 34 C8
West Acre PE32 46 B2
Weston Longville NR9 51 D4
Wisbech PE13 152 F4
Sandy La E NR19 154 C6
Sandy Way PE31 140 C7
Sandygate La PE34 144 F5
Sandyland PE13 152 B5
Sankence La NR11 35 E5
Santon Cl IP24 176 A3
Sapiston Rd IP31 126 D1
Sapwell Cl NR11 150 A6
Saracen Rd NR6 157 F6
Sarah W Cl NR2 162 C4
Sarah Williman Cl 2 NR4 161 C5
Sarahs Rd PE36 132 C2
Sardis Way NR19 154 D4
Saturday Mkt Pl PE30 146 D4
Saunders Ct 7 NR1 163 A6
Savery Cl NR5 161 B6
Savory Rd PE13 152 B7
Saw Mill La
Brancaster PE31 3 B6
7 Great Yarmouth NR31 169 B4
Sawmill Cl NR18 173 B5
Sawston 1 PE30 147 D6
Sawyer's La NR18 87 D2
Sawyers Cl NR5 156 E1
Saxlingham La NR15 106 F7
Saxlingham Prim Sch NR15 107 B7
Saxlingham Rd
Blakeney NR25 7 C5
Saxlingham Nethergate NR15 107 C8
Shotesham NR15 89 F1
Saxon Cres 9 IP31 126 B1
Saxon Ct PE37 153 D2
Saxon Field PE31 3 B6
Saxon Gdns NR30 168 D5
Saxon Pl
3 Thetford IP24 176 C3
Weeting IP27 175 A8
Saxon Rd NR30 169 D4
Saxon Way
Dersingham PE31 140 D4
Wormegay PE33 62 C6
Saxon Wlk IP26 100 A4
Saxonfields NR14 90 C4
Sayer Ct NR25 9 A2
Sayers St 9 NR2 162 C7
Scama La IP22 129 A2
Scania Way PE30 147 A1
Scarborough Rd NR22 17 A8
Scarfield La PE14 59 C2
Scarlet Rd NR4 162 D1
Scarnell Rd NR5 161 C6
Scarning Fen NR19 154 C2
Scarning VC Prim Sch NR19 154 A4
Scarrow Beck La NR11 21 A2
Sceptre Cl NR6 158 A3
Scholars Wlk IP22 177 C5
School Ave NR7 163 F6
School Cl
Kenninghall NR16 119 A4
Knapton NR28 143 A1
3 Ludham NR29 56 C5
Northrepps NR27 11 A2
4 Rollesby NR29 57 D2
School Comm Rd NR12 24 C3
School Hill
Reedham NR13 93 A4
Tasburgh NR15 106 E6
School La
Brandon IP27 175 C3
Cantley NR13 92 B7
Colney NR4 160 E3
East Dereham NR19 154 E1
East Harling NR16 118 C5
Gimingham NR11 22 E8
Great Yarmouth NR31 170 D6
17 Harleston IP20 122 D2
Heckingham NR14 109 F8
Little Dunham PE32 65 E7
Little Melton NR9 160 C2
Neatishead NR12 55 D7
North Runcton PE33 44 A2
Northwold IP26 99 C7
Norwich NR7 158 F3
Rockland St Mary NR14 91 B7
Runhall NR9 68 F1
Skeyton NR10 37 A5
Smallburgh NR12 38 D3
Stoke Ferry PE33 80 F2
Surlingham NR14 73 B1
Thetford IP24 176 D3
Walpole St Andrew PE14 41 E3
Wereham PE33 80 E4
1 Wisbech PE13 152 C5
Wramplingham NR18 69 F1
Wymondham NR18 105 A8
School Loke
Bodham NR25 9 A2
Hemsby NR29 167 A7
School Pastures PE31 3 E7
School Plain NR19 154 B5
School Rd
Alburgh IP20 123 A5
Aldborough NR11 21 A5
Ashmanhaugh NR12 55 B7
Bacton NR28 23 B4
Barton Turf NR12 38 E1
Bedingham NR35 108 B3
Beetley NR20 49 C5
Blofield NR13 165 B8
Bracon Ash NR14 89 A3
Bradenham IP25 66 D3
Bressingham IP22 129 B8
Brisley NR20 49 A8
Catfield NR29 56 C8
Colkirk NR21 31 D5
Earsham NR35 123 F8
East Ruston NR12 38 E7
Erpingham NR11 21 B2
Foulden IP26 82 A1
Freethorpe NR13 92 F7
Frettenham NR12 54 A4
Great Massingham PE32 29 D1
Great Yarmouth NR30 169 B5
Haveringland NR10 52 D7
Heacham PE31 133 D5
Hinderclay IP22 128 C3
Holme Hale IP25 66 A2
Horning NR12 55 F3
Kirby Cane NR35 109 E4
Lessingham NR12 24 D3
Lingwood NR13 74 A3
Little Cressingham IP25 83 F2
Little Plumpstead NR13 73 B6
Ludham NR29 56 B5
Marshland St James PE14 60 B4
Mautby NR29 75 E5
Middleton PE32 44 C2
Morning Thorpe NR15 107 B3
Neatishead NR12 55 E7
1 Necton PE37 65 F4
Newton Flotman NR15 89 D1
Outwell PE14 77 D4
Potter Heigham NR29 56 F6
Reepham NR10 149 B4
Runcton Holme PE33 61 E3
St Andrew, Ilketshall NR34 124 E6
Sculthorpe Airfield NR21 15 C3
Seething NR15 108 E8
10 Snettisham PE31 12 E5
South Walsham NR13 74 A8
Strumpshaw NR13 73 F1
Swannington NR9 52 B5
Taverham NR8 155 F1
Terrington St John PE14 60 B7
Thompson IP24 102 B7
Tilney All Saints PE34 42 E4
Tilney St Lawrence PE34 60 C7
Tivetshall St Mary NR15 121 B5
Walpole Highway PE14 59 F8
Walton Highway PE14 59 C8
Watlington PE33 61 D6

School Rd *continued*
Weasenham All Saints PE32 47 D8
Weasenham St Peter PE32 30 D1
West Rudham PE31 29 F6
West Walton PE14 59 B8
Whissonsett NR20 31 E2
Wiggenhall St Germans PE34 61 B8
Worstead NR28 38 A5
School Rd Back 4 NR30 169 C5
School Sq IP24 102 E3
School Terr 3 NR14 163 B2
School View NR34 124 F1
Schoolfield NR10 155 C8
Schoolhouse La 1 NR11 150 C7
Scole Comm IP21 130 C6
Scole Comm Rd IP21 130 D6
Scole Prim Sch IP21 130 D6
Scole Rd IP21 131 C6
Scolt Head Island National Nature Reserve* PE31 3 E8
Sconch Beck Rd IP20 123 A2
Scotch Hill Rd NR8 155 B1
Scotgate Cl IP24 102 E3
Scott Cl IP24 176 E6
Scott Rd NR1 163 B5
Scott's Cnr NR16 105 B4
Scott's Hill NR14 89 A4
Scott's La IP26 99 A7
Scotter Rise 7 NR26 138 C5
Scottow Rd NR10 37 B2
Scoulton Rd NR17 85 F2
Scratby Cres NR29 167 F3
Scratby Rd NR29 167 D3
Scroby Ct NR29 167 E3
Scrumpy Way NR16 119 D7
Sculthorpe Airfield NR21 15 E2
Sculthorpe Ave PE34 146 B5
Sculthorpe Bvd 7 NR21 15 C2
Sculthorpe CE VA Prim Sch NR21 16 C2
Sculthorpe Eastgate NR21 141 A5
Sculthorpe Rd NR21 141 A5
Sea Cl PE31 133 B6
Sea La PE36 132 E7
Sea Palling Rd NR12 39 F3
Sea View Rd
Hemsby NR29 167 D7
Mundesley NR11 143 B7
Sea View Rise NR31 171 E4
Seabank Rd
Heacham PE31 133 B6
Wisbech PE13 152 F6
Seabank Way PE30 146 E7
Seabird Cl 4 NR30 168 D7
Seabrook Ct 9 NR5 161 A7
Seacliff NR26 138 E7
Seafield Cl 20 NR30 169 D2
Seafield Rd N NR30 168 E6
Seafield Rd S NR30 168 D6
Seafields Dr NR31 171 D4
Seaforth Dr NR8 156 E8
Seagate PE36 132 C3
Seagate Rd PE36 132 B3
Seagull Rd NR29 167 E5
Seamere Rd NR9 86 D4
Searle Cl NR21 141 F5
Sears Cl NR11 150 C6
Seaside La NR12 24 E4
Seates The 6 NR8 155 D2
Seathwaite Rd PE30 147 D8
Seaview Cres NR26 138 D5
Seawake Cl NR31 170 A4
Seaward Cres NR11 143 B6
Seaward Wlk NR30 168 E8
Seckar Dr NR19 154 C4
Second Ave
Caister-on-Sea NR30 168 D8
Wisbech PE13 152 D4
Second Dro IP27 113 C3
Second Marsh Rd PE14 59 A7
Sedge Cl NR21 141 E4
Sedge Dro PE38 96 C7
Sedge Fen Rd PE38 97 B3
Sedge Rd NR19 154 B4
Sedgefen Dro PE38 112 E7
Sedgefen Rd IP27 112 F3
Sedgeford Fst Sch PE36 13 B7
Sedgeford La 5 PE30 146 D4
Sedgeford Rd
Docking PE31 134 B4
Snettisham PE31 12 F5
Seeche Abbey PE34 43 D1
Seething & Mumdham Sch NR15 108 E8
Seething Old Hall Pk NR15 91 B1
Seething Rd NR35 108 D5
Seething St NR15 108 E8
Seeview Cres NR12 24 A7
Sefton Ave PE13 152 E6
Sefton La NR31 169 C3
Sego Vale NR8 156 E8
Segrave Rd 6 PE30 147 A8
Selby Pl 19 NR30 169 D2
Self's La IP22 128 C7
Selwyn Dr 9 NR31 94 A5
Selwyn Gdns IP21 121 E5
Selwyn Rd NR31 170 A5
Semere Gn La IP21 121 D2
Semere La IP21 121 D4
Sendall Rd NR28 151 B3
Sennowe Rd NR20 32 F4
Senter's Rd PE31 140 D2
Seppings Rd NR21 141 A6
Seppings Way NR13 72 E6
Serpentine La NR10 53 C6
Setch Rd Middleton PE33 44 A1
West Winch PE33 43 F1
Seton Rd NR8 155 E1
Setons Halt Sta NR23 5 F2
Seven Sisters Cl PE30 146 D4
Seventh Ave PE13 152 E4
Severalls Rd IP26 98 D5
Sewell Rd Lamas NR10 36 F1
Norwich NR3 158 E1
Sewell's La NR15 90 D3
Sewells Cl 5 NR15 89 C1
Sexton Rd NR35 108 D2
Seymour Ave
Brandon IP27 114 D4
Great Yarmouth NR30 169 D8
Shack La NR13 165 D6
Shadingfield Cl 16 NR30 169 D2
Shakers' Rd
Brandon IP27 115 A1
Wangford IP27 114 F1
Shakespeare Rd NR30 169 E8
Shakespeare Way
Taverham NR8 156 E8
Thetford IP24 176 E6
Shannock Ct 14 NR26 138 D7
Shannon Dr 4 NR30 168 C6
Shannons Cl NR17 174 E4
Sharman Ave IP25 84 D4
Sharmans Loke NR31 93 F5
Sharon Cl
2 East Dereham NR19 154 D1
Felmingham NR28 37 A8
Sharp St NR29 56 C7
Sharpe Way NR29 167 B2
Sharper's Cnr IP27 113 D2
Sharrington Rd NR24 18 B5
Shaw's Yd PE31 30 B7
Shawcross Rd NR27 10 A4
Shearwater Dr 2 NR31 170 A7
Sheddick Ct NR19 154 D6
Sheep Mdw Cl NR5 156 E1
Sheffield Rd NR18 173 C5
Sheldonian Ct NR31 170 A4
Sheldrake Cl NR21 141 F5
Sheldrick Pl NR19 154 E2
Shelduck Dr 7 PE31 12 E5
Shelfanger Rd IP22 177 C7
Shelford Dr PE30 147 B8
Shell Mus The* NR25 7 E4
Shelley Cl NR30 168 D6
Shelley Dr NR8 156 D8
Shelley Way IP24 176 E6
Shelly Cl 3 PE38 172 D6
Shelterhouse Cnr IP24 125 A4
Shelton with Hardwick Sch NR15 107 B2
Shepheard Cl 1 NR28 151 C6
Shepheards Cl NR11 150 E8
Shepherd Cl
2 Norwich NR4 161 D5
Sheringham NR26 138 B6
Shepherd Way NR8 155 E2
Shepherd's Fold PE37 153 D2
Shepherd's La NR10 36 A2
Shepherds Cl
Cromer NR27 10 B5
11 Horsford NR10 53 A3
Runton NR27 10 B5
Shepherds La
Burgate IP22 129 B3
Oulton NR11 35 B6
Shepherds Pightle PE36 2 D6
Shepherdsgate Rd PE34 144 C1
Shepley Cres 2 PE30 147 D5
Sheppard Way NR17 174 C5
Sherbourne Pl NR1 178 C1
Shereford Rd
Fakenham NR21 141 A3
Hempton NR21 31 C8
Sheridan Cl NR8 156 F8
Sheridan House Sch IP25 86 A7
Sheringham Com Prim Sch NR26 138 C5
Sheringham High Sch NR26 138 C5
Sheringham Little Theatre NR26 138 D7
Sheringham Mus* NR26 138 D7
Sheringham Pk* NR26 9 B6
Sheringham Pk Visitor Ctr* NR26 9 B4
Sheringham Rd
West Beckham NR25 9 B3
Weybourne NR25 8 F5
Sheringham Sta NR26 138 C7
Sheringham Woodfields Spec Sch NR26 138 C5
Sheringwood NR26 138 E4
Shernborne Rd PE31 140 E7
Sherwell Rd NR6 157 E6
Sherwood Ave PE13 152 D7
Sherwood Rd NR4 162 C1
Sheval Cl NR15 121 A8
Shickle Pl IP22 127 F6
Shillgate Way NR8 155 B2
Shillito Rd NR13 165 F6
Shimpling Rd IP21 121 B1
Ship La PE36 2 C6
Shipden Ave NR27 139 A7
Shipden Ct NR27 139 A7
Shipdham Airfield IP25 67 E2
Shipdham Airfield Ind Est IP25 67 F2
Shipdham Rd
Carbrooke IP25 85 A5
East Dereham NR19 154 D1
Scarning NR19 67 B6
Shipdham NR19 67 E5
Shipfield NR3 158 F2
Shipgate Rd PE31 29 B5
Shippea Hill Sta CB7 112 C3
Shipstone Rd 11 NR3 162 D8
Shire Ave 5 NR31 94 C8
Shiregreen PE30 147 C4
Shires The NR8 155 F2
Shirley Cl 3 NR12 54 A4
Shoe Devil La NR35 124 C4
Shoemakers La PE37 64 E3
Shooters Cl NR8 155 D1
Shop La Hethersett NR9 88 E8
Tunstead NR12 38 A3
Wells-next-the-Sea NR23 136 D6
Shop St NR19 68 A3
Shorncliffe Ave NR3 158 C1
Shorncliffe Cl 1 NR3 158 C1
Short Beck 18 IP26 98 E1
Short Cl PE38 172 C6
Short Dro PE38 172 C6
Short Gn IP22 120 B5
Short La Billingford NR20 50 A8
Feltwell IP26 98 D1
Happisburgh NR12 24 B3
Harpley PE31 29 D4
Mautby NR29 75 E6
Swardeston NR14 89 C5
Short Rd
3 Attleborough NR17 174 C5
Belton with Browston NR31 94 A4
Short St 8 NR15 89 D1
Short-thorn Rd NR10 52 F5
Shotesham La NR15 107 C8
Shotesham Rd
Howe NR15 90 C2
Poringland NR14 90 B3
Woodton NR35 108 A6
Shotford Rd IP20 122 D1
Shouldham Cl PE31 140 C3
Shouldham La PE37 153 A4
Shouldham Rd
Marham PE33 63 A3
Shouldham Thorpe PE33 62 C2
Shreeves Rd IP22 177 E4
Shropham Rd IP24 102 E3
Shrub Cl NR17 174 D5
Shrub Dro PE38 112 E6
Shrub Hill PE38 112 F7
Shrublands The
Horsford NR10 53 B4
Norwich NR2 162 B6
Shrublands Way NR31 170 B5
Shuttleworth Cl NR31 170 A8
Sidegate Rd
Great Yarmouth NR30 169 C5
Hopton on Sea NR31 171 B7
Sidell Cl 11 NR4 89 B8
Sidestrand Hall Specl Sch NR27 11 B2
Siding Rd NR34 111 C1
Sidings The IP24 176 C5
Sidney Cl
2 Great Yarmouth NR30 169 D2
8 Martham NR29 57 C4
Sidney Rd
Costessey NR8 156 F4
Ingham NR12 39 D4
Sidney St PE30 146 F3
Sienna Mews 3 NR1 163 B7
Sigismund Rd NR1 162 D3
Silfield Ave NR18 173 D1
Silfield Gdn PE36 132 D4
Silfield Rd NR18 173 C2
Silfield Sch PE30 147 C6
Silfield St NR18 88 A2
Silkmill Rd 2 NR30 169 D4
Silt Rd Nordelph PE38 78 B2
Runcton Holme PE33 61 C4
Terrington St Clement PE34 25 F3
Upwell PE14 77 F1
Silver Cour NR27 11 A2
Silver Dr PE31 140 C4
Silver Drif PE37 64 E5
Silver End NR10 149 B5
Silver Gdns 5 NR31 94 A5
Silver Hill PE30 147 D6
Silver Rd NR3 178 C4
Silver St
Attleborough NR17 174 F6
Besthorpe NR17 104 D7
Fleggburgh NR29 75 C8
Garvestone NR9 86 C8
Norwich NR3 162 E8
South Lopham IP22 128 F7
Wisbech PE13 152 C6
Silvergate La NR11 35 F6
Silvertree's Way PE33 43 E1
Simon Scotland Rd PE30 146 F2
Simpson Cl NR28 151 B5
Sinclair Ct NR31 170 A8
Sir Douglas Bader Espl PE36 132 C4
Sir Edward Stracey Rd NR13 72 D8
Sir Lewis St PE30 146 E6
Sir Thomas Cl NR18 173 C5
Sir William's Cl NR11 150 D6
Sir William's La NR11 150 D7
Siskin Cl NR31 170 A6
Sitka Cl PE31 133 C6
Six Crossways NR14 91 D3
Sixteen Foot Bank PE14 77 D1
Sixth Ave PE13 152 E4
Skedge Way 6 NR13 73 C6
Skelton Cl 1 IP22 177 E4
Skelton Rd Diss IP22 177 E4
Norwich NR7 163 C8
Sketton View NR28 151 B3
Skeyton Cnr NR10 37 B6
Skeyton New Rd NR28 151 B5
Skeyton Rd
Coltishall NR10 37 B2
North Walsham NR28 151 A4
Skinner's La IP20 122 B4
Skinners La NR12 164 B2
Skipping Block Row NR18 88 B6
Skippon Way NR13 72 D5
Skitfield Rd NR20 33 E6
Skoner Rd NR5 161 B8
Skoyles' La NR9 88 A8
Skye Cl NR5 161 A8
Slad La NR20 50 C6
Slade La
Framingham Pigot NR14 90 E6
Old Buckenham NR17 104 B1
Wortham IP22 129 B6
Yelverton NR14 90 F6
Slade Rd NR21 18 B7
Sleaford Gn NR3 158 C2
Sleigh La IP25 84 E2
Sleights Dr PE14 59 C5
Slessor Cl 2 IP25 84 F3
Slip Rd NR14 93 A1
Slip The PE36 2 C3
Slipshoe La NR15 122 B7
Sloane Way IP24 176 B2
Sloe La NR13 72 D8
Sloley Rd NR28 38 A3
Slopers Rd NR18 87 F7
Slough La
Attleborough NR17 174 E3
North Tuddenham NR20 68 E8
Slough Rd IP22 129 A1
Slugs La NR32 111 C8
Sluice Dro IP26 113 E7
Sluice Rd Denver PE38 172 B1
Wiggenhall St Germans PE34 61 A8
Slutshole La
Besthorpe NR17 104 D7
Wymondham NR17 105 A7
Small Lode PE14 77 F5
Smallburgh Rd
Barton Turf NR12 55 E8
Smallburgh NR12 38 D2
Smallholdings Rd PE34 145 D4
Smallworth La IP22 128 B7
Smea The NR12 39 E1
Smeat St 2 NR5 161 B7
Smee La NR13 72 E4
Smee Rd NR13 72 F4
Smeeth Rd Emneth PE14 59 F2
St John's Fen End PE14 60 A5
Smith Ave PE30 146 E6
Smith's Dro PE38 112 C8
Smith's Loke NR31 170 A6
Smithdale Rd NR5 157 B1
Smithdon High Sch PE36 132 D4
Smithfield Rd NR1 162 E3
Smiths Dr IP21 121 B1
Smiths La NR21 141 E5
Smithson Cl NR18 173 C4
Smithson Dr NR20 68 F5
Smithtyne Ave
Dereham NR19 68 A7
3 East Dereham NR19 154 F3
Smithy Cl PE31 133 D5
Smithy Rd PE31 140 D8
Smock Mill Loke NR18 173 B5
Smuggler's La NR10 149 B4
Smugglers Cl PE36 132 F8
Smugglers' Rd IP26 100 F8
Snaefell Pk NR26 138 D6
Snake's La Lound NR32 94 C2
Topcroft NR35 108 A4
Snape Hall Rd 14 NR15 106 E3
Snape Hill IP22 128 C2
Snape La PE38 172 B5
Sneath Rd NR15 121 A8
Snetterton Circuit NR16 118 D8
Snettisham Beach PE31 12 A3
Snettisham Nature Reserve* PE31 12 A3
Snettisham Pk* PE31 12 E4
Snettisham Prim Sch PE31 12 E5
Snoring Rd NR21 17 C3
Snow St IP22 177 A6
Snow's Hill 6 NR14 92 A2
Snow's La NR14 92 A2
Snowberry Cl 4 NR8 155 B2
Snowdrop Cl 20 NR31 94 C6
Snowdrop Dr NR17 174 B4
Snowhill Drift NR19 154 D6
Soame Cl NR11 150 D5
Soames Pl NR19 67 B7
Soanes Ct NR9 51 A5
Softley Dr NR4 161 C2
Soken Dr 5 Beetley NR19 49 C3
5 Gressenhall NR20 49 C3
Solace Cl NR35 124 C8
Sole Cl 6 NR10 53 B3
Soleme Rd NR3 158 B1
Solent Cl NR30 168 E5
Somerleyton Gdns NR2 162 C5
Somerleyton Hall & Gdns* NR32 111 E8
Somerleyton Prim Sch NR32 111 D8
Somerleyton St 2 NR2 162 C5
Somerleyton Sta NR32 111 C7
Somers Rd PE13 152 B4
Somersby Cl 2 PE30 147 A8
Somerset Pl 22 NR30 169 D4
Somerset Way NR8 155 A1
Somerton Rd
Martham NR29 57 D5
Somerton NR29 58 A6
Somerville Ave NR31 170 B3
Somerville Rd 11 PE30 146 E3
Sorrel Ct PE30 147 C8
Sorrel Dr
Attleborough NR17 174 B4
1 Thetford IP24 176 E4
Sorrel La NR20 49 D5
Sorrel Rd 25 NR31 94 C6
Sorrel Way PE38 172 C3
Sotherton Rd NR4 161 F3
Soudan Cl 3 NR30 168 D7
South Acre Hall PE32 46 E1
South Acre Rd PE32 46 F1
South Ave Norwich NR7 163 E5
Swanton Morley Airfield NR20 50 B5
South Beach PE31 133 A3
South Beach Par NR30 170 E6
South Beach Pl NR30 169 E2
South Beach Rd
Heacham PE31 133 A4
Hunstanton PE36 132 B3
South Brink PE13 152 A3
South Burlingham Rd NR13 74 B3
South Cl NR25 7 A6
South Cnr PE31 3 B7
South Creake Maize Maze* NR21 15 E6
South Croft NR9 88 C7
South Denes Rd NR30 169 D1
South Everard St PE30 146 E3
South Gage Cl NR7 159 C4
South Gdn NR31 170 C1
South Gn
East Dereham NR19 154 E3
Terrington St Clement PE34 144 B5
South Gn Gdns NR19 154 E3
South Harford Mid Sch NR4 89 E8
South Hill Cl NR7 163 F8
South Hill Rd NR7 163 F8
South Icehouse Hill NR31 170 D6
South Lynn Plain PE30 146 E4
South Mkt Rd NR30 169 D4
South Moor Dr PE31 133 D4
South Pk IP27 175 B7
South Pk Ave 2 NR4 162 A4
South Quay
Great Yarmouth NR30 169 C3
8 King's Lynn PE30 146 D4
South Rd
Great Yarmouth NR30 169 E8
Hemsby NR29 167 D7
Watton IP25 84 D3
South Rise NR28 151 B3
South St
Great Dunham PE32 47 F1
Hockwold cum Wilton IP26 113 F6
2 King's Lynn PE30 146 E4
Sheringham NR26 138 C7
South Walsham Rd
Acle NR13 166 A5
South Walsham NR13 74 B5
South Wlk NR13 72 E5
South Wood Dr NR14 90 B6
South Wootton Fst Sch PE30 148 C2
South Wootton Jun Sch PE30 148 B1
South Wootton La PE30 148 C1
Southacre Rd PE32 65 C7
Southampton Pl 16 NR30 169 D4
Southburgh La NR9 86 A5
Southburgh Rd NR9 86 A7
Southend
Bradenham IP25 66 D3
East Dereham NR19 154 D4
Southend Rd PE36 132 C3
Southern La IP22 128 D5

Southern Reach 7 NR14 .89 B3
Southerwood 4 NR6 ...158 D5
Southery Prim Sch
PE38 ...97 A5
Southery Rd
Feltwell IP26 ...98 B2
Methwold IP26 ...97 F3
Southfield PE32 ...65 C5
Southfield Dr 8 PE33 ...43 F2
Southfield La NR13 ...55 C1
Southfields
Downham Market PE38 ...172 B4
1 King's Lynn PE30 ...147 B6
Southgate 12 IP20 ...122 D1
Southgate Cl NR23 ...136 C5
Southgate La
Norwich NR1 ...178 C1
Snettisham PE31 ...12 E4
Southgate St PE30 ...146 E3
Southgates Dr NR21 ...141 B5
Southgates Rd NR30 ...169 D2
Southlands PE37 ...153 B2
Southrepps Rd
Antingham NR28 ...22 B4
Gimingham NR11 ...22 E6
Southside PE34 ...79 D8
Southtown Fst Sch
NR31 ...169 B2
Southtown Rd NR31 ...169 C2
Southwell Rd
5 Horsham St Faith &
Newton St Faith NR10 ...53 D2
Norwich NR1 ...178 A1
Wisbech PE13 ...152 C7
Southwood Rd
Beighton NR13 ...74 C1
Cantley NR13 ...92 C8
Sovereign Cl 2 PE13 ...152 A6
Sovereign Way PE38 ...172 A4
Sow's Loke NR12 ...55 E6
Spa La Aylsham NR11 ...150 B3
Oulton NR11 ...35 B8
Spalding's Chair Hill
IP24 ...126 E8
Spar Rd NR6 ...158 C5
Sparhawk Ave NR7 ...159 C4
Sparhawk Cl NR7 ...159 C4
Sparhawk Fst Sch
NR7 ...159 C4
Sparrow Cl 4 NR31 ...94 C7
Sparrowgate Rd PE14 ...59 C5
Speedwell Cl
5 Attleborough NR17 ...174 B4
2 Thetford IP24 ...176 E4
Speedwell Rd NR18 ...173 D4
Speedwell Way
Norwich NR5 ...160 F5
13 Redenhall with Harleston
IP20 ...122 D1
Speke St NR2 ...162 A7
Spelman Rd NR2 ...162 A4
Spencer Ave NR31 ...170 C6
Spencer Cl
Great & Little Plumstead
NR13 ...73 B7
11 Lingwood NR13 ...74 A3
West Walton PE14 ...59 B8
Spencer Ct 12 IP25 ...84 D3
Spencer Rd NR6 ...158 C5
Spencer St NR3 ...162 E8
Spencers Cl NR20 ...49 E7
Spens Ave NR31 ...170 B3
Spenser Ave NR28 ...151 D4
Spenser Rd PE30 ...148 B1
Spice Chase PE34 ...60 C7
Spicer's La NR16 ...106 B5
Spiers Way IP22 ...177 B4
Spindle Cl NR18 ...173 D4
Spindle Rd NR6 ...158 D4
Spindrift Cl 11 NR29 ...58 B6
Spink's La NR18 ...173 F6
Spinks' La NR35 ...108 D2
Spinks La NR18 ...88 B4
Spinners Cl PE37 ...153 B5
Spinners La PE37 ...153 B5
Spinney Cl Beetley NR20 ..49 D4
Brandon IP27 ...175 C2
King's Lynn PE30 ...148 B4
9 Long Stratton NR15 ...106 E3
Norwich NR7 ...163 F8
Spinney Rd NR7 ...163 E8
Spinney The NR14 ...110 B7
Spirkett's La IP20 ...122 D1
Spitalfields NR1 ...163 A7
Spitfire Rd NR6 ...158 C6
Spixworth Fst Sch
NR10 ...54 A2
Spixworth Rd
Hainford NR10 ...53 F4
Horsham St Faith &
Newton St Faith NR10 ...53 E2
Norwich NR6 ...158 E5
Splash Leisure Complex
NR26 ...138 B7
Splashes The PE37 ...153 B7
Spong La
Carleton St Peter NR14 ...91 D5
East Carleton NR14 ...88 F4
Shropham NR17 ...103 C4
Spooner Row Prim Sch
NR18 ...105 A8
Spooner Row Sta
NR18 ...105 A8
Sporle Fst Sch PE32 ...65 D6
Sporle Rd
Little Dunham PE32 ...65 D7
Swaffham PE37 ...153 C5
Spring Cl PE30 ...148 C1
Spring Gr PE34 ...144 B4
Spring La
Forncett NR16 ...106 B5
Hempnall NR15 ...107 E3
King's Lynn PE30 ...147 C7
North Barsham NR22 ...16 A7
Shouldham PE33 ...62 D4
South Creake NR22 ...16 A6
Yaxham NR19 ...68 B6
Spring Rd IP31 ...127 A1
Spring Sedge 4 PE30 ...147 A8
Spring View 1 PE31 ...12 D4
Springbank NR1 ...162 E2
Springdale Cres NR13 ...165 B4
Springdale Rd NR13 ...165 B4
Springfield NR13 ...166 C3
Springfield Cl
Crimplesham PE33 ...80 B6
Hemsby NR29 ...58 A4
Springfield N NR29 ...58 A4
Springfield Rd
Great Yarmouth NR31 ...170 D4
Hemsby NR29 ...58 A4
Norwich NR7 ...159 D2
Taverham NR8 ...155 C1
Walpole St Andrew PE14 ...41 D4
Springfield Way NR9 ...86 B5
Springfield Wlk IP21 ...121 E5
Springfields
Attleborough NR17 ...174 B5
12 Poringland NR14 ...90 C5
Springfiled Cl 4 NR25 ...8 F5
Springles The 6 NR27 ...10 B5
Springvale 3 PE32 ...45 C6
Springwell La NR9 ...51 F6
Springwell Rd NR20 ...31 D2
Springwood
Taverham NR8 ...155 E1
Woodton NR35 ...108 A6
Springwood High Sch
PE30 ...147 C6
Sprowston Fst & Mid Sch
NR7 ...159 A4
Sprowston High Sch
NR7 ...159 B3
Sprowston Rd NR3 ...158 F2
Sprowston Ret Pk
NR7 ...159 C2
Spruce Ave 2 NR29 ...167 A2
Spruce Cl PE31 ...133 B6
Spruce Cres 4 NR14 ...90 C5
Spruce Dr IP27 ...175 D2
Spruce Rd PE38 ...172 B6
Spur La NR14 ...90 C6
Spur Rd NR9 ...69 C2
Spurdens Cres NR28 ...151 D3
Spurge Sq 3 NR18 ...173 E4
Spynke Rd NR3 ...158 B3
Squire's Dr PE14 ...77 E3
Squire's Dro PE14 ...78 A3
Squire's Rd NR13 ...75 A2
Squires Hill PE33 ...63 B4
Stablefields IP26 ...99 C7
Stacy Rd NR3 ...162 E8
Staden Pk NR11 ...11 D1
Stafford Ave NR5 ...156 F1
Stafford Rd NR31 ...169 B2
Stafford St NR2 ...162 B6
Stag Pl PE30 ...147 A7
Stainsby Cl PE31 ...133 D4
Staithe Cl 3 NR12 ...55 E4
Staithe La PE36 ...2 C7
Staithe Rd
Barton Turf NR12 ...38 F1
Burgh St Peter NR34 ...111 C3
Catfield NR29 ...56 D8
Halvergate NR13 ...166 F1
Heacham PE31 ...133 C5
Hickling NR12 ...39 E1
Langley with Hardley
NR14 ...91 F4
Ludham NR29 ...56 C5
Martham NR29 ...57 D5
Repps with Bastwick
NR29 ...56 F4
Somerton NR29 ...57 E6
Stalham NR12 ...39 B3
Wisbech PE13 ...152 E5
Staithe Stree NR23 ...136 D6
Staithe The NR11 ...150 D8
Staitheway Rd NR12 ...164 C4
Stalham Firehouse Mus*
NR12 ...39 B3
Stalham High Sch
NR12 ...39 B4
Stalham Mid Sch NR12 ..39 B3
Stalham Rd
Ashmanhaugh NR12 ...55 C8
Hickling NR12 ...39 E2
Sea Palling NR12 ...24 F1
Wroxham/Hoveton
NR12 ...164 D6
Stalland La NR18 ...86 D2
Stalland The NR18 ...86 D2
Stallett Way PE34 ...60 C8
Stan Petersen Cl NR1 ...163 A6
Standard Pl 10 NR30 ...169 D3
Standard Rd
Great Yarmouth NR30 ...169 E3
Wells-next-the-Sea
NR23 ...136 D6
Standley Ct NR18 ...173 B4
Stanfield Rd
Mileham PE32 ...48 E6
Tittleshall PE32 ...48 C7
Wymondham NR18 ...173 F3
Stanford Cres NR13 ...73 B7
Stanford Tuck Rd
NR28 ...151 B7
Stanhoe Rd PE31 ...134 E4
Staniforth Rd IP24 ...176 B2
Stanley Ave
Great Yarmouth NR31 ...170 C3
Neatishead NR12 ...55 E7
Norwich NR7 ...163 C5
Stanley Cl NR13 ...92 B6
Stanley Dr PE12 ...41 A8
Stanley Rd Diss IP22 ...177 B4
Great Yarmouth NR30 ...169 C5
North Walsham NR28 ...151 D6
Stanley St 10 PE30 ...146 E5
Stanley Terr NR30 ...169 D4
Stanleys La NR18 ...173 C2
Stanmore Rd NR7 ...163 E6
Stannard Cl 4 IP22 ...177 C4
Stannard Rd NR4 ...161 F5
Stanninghall Rd NR12 ...54 B4
Stanton Rd
Barningham IP31 ...127 C2
Dersingham PE31 ...140 C3
Star Farm Cl 21 NR31 ...94 C6
Star Hill NR12 ...24 C3
Star La
Long Stratton NR15 ...106 E3
1 Thetford IP24 ...176 C3
Tivetshall St Margaret
NR15 ...121 C5
Star Mdw NR21 ...141 B4
Stark Cl IP22 ...177 C4
Starling Cl NR11 ...150 C5
Starling Rd NR3 ...162 D8
Starling Rise NR27 ...11 B2
Starston La IP20 ...122 C1
Statham Cl NR4 ...162 B2
Station App
Norwich NR1 ...178 C2
12 Sheringham NR26 ...138 D7
Wymondham NR18 ...173 C2
Station Cl
East Dereham NR19 ...154 D6
4 Lingwood NR13 ...74 A3
6 Martham NR29 ...57 D4
Sheringham NR27 ...10 A5
Swainsthorpe NR14 ...89 D4
Station Dr
Fransham NR19 ...66 A8
Reedham NR13 ...92 F5
Wisbech PE13 ...152 C4
Station Gdns PE13 ...153 B5
Station Halt NR13 ...165 B3
Station Hill IP20 ...122 D2
Station La
Garvestone NR9 ...68 D1
Hethersett NR9 ...88 E7
Thetford IP24 ...176 C5
Thornham PE36 ...2 C6
Station New Rd NR13 ...165 D3
Station Rd Acle NR13 ...166 B2
Alburgh IP20 ...123 A5
Aldeby NR34 ...110 F6
Attleborough NR17 ...174 E5
Attlebridge NR9 ...52 A4
Aylsham NR11 ...150 D6
Barnham IP24 ...125 E6
Beccles NR34 ...110 D1
Brundall NR13 ...165 D2
Burnham Market PE31 ...135 C3
Burston & Shimpling
IP21 ...120 F2
Cantley NR13 ...92 C6
Clenchwarton PE34 ...145 B4
Coltishall NR12 ...54 C7
Congham PE32 ...27 F3
Corpusty NR11 ...19 F1
Cromer NR27 ...139 D5
Dersingham PE31 ...140 B4
Diss IP22 ...177 F3
Ditchingham NR35 ...109 B2
Docking PE31 ...134 D5
Downham Market PE38 ...172 A5
2 Earsham NR35 ...123 F8
East Dereham NR19 ...154 E4
East Rudham PE31 ...30 B5
East Winch PE32 ...44 F3
Ellingham NR35 ...109 D3
Flordon NR15 ...106 E8
Forncett NR16 ...106 C4
Foulsham NR20 ...33 C3
Fransham NR19 ...66 B7
Fulmodeston NR21 ...17 F4
Geldeston NR34 ...109 F2
Great Moulton NR15 ...121 A7
Great Ryburgh NR21 ...32 B6
Great Yarmouth NR31 ...169 B3
Guestwick NR20 ...33 F5
Haddiscoe NR31 ...93 D1
Hardingham NR9 ...86 E8
Harleston IP20 ...122 D2
Heacham PE31 ...133 D6
Hilgay PE38 ...96 C6
Hindolveston NR20 ...33 E8
Holme Hale IP25 ...65 F2
Holt NR25 ...137 C6
Honing NR28 ...38 C6
Hopton on Sea NR31 ...171 D4
Kimberley NR18 ...87 A6
King's Lynn PE30 ...148 B5
Lakenheath IP27 ...112 E3
Lenwade NR9 ...51 E5
Lingwood & Burlingham
NR13 ...74 A3
Middleton PE32 ...44 C4
Mundesley NR11 ...143 B6
North Elmham NR20 ...49 F7
North Walsham NR28 ...151 B4
Station Rd *continued*
Ormesby St Margaret
with Scratby NR29 ...167 B2
5 Potter Heigham NR29 ...56 F6
Pulham Market IP21 ...121 E4
Pulham St Mary IP21 ...122 A4
Quidenham NR16 ...118 E8
Rackheath/Salhouse
NR13 ...72 F8
Reedham NR13 ...92 F5
Reepham NR10 ...149 C5
Roydon PE32 ...28 A2
6 Sheringham NR27 ...10 A5
Sheringham NR26 ...138 D7
Snettisham PE31 ...12 D4
Somerleyton, Ashby &
Herringfleet NR32 ...111 C7
South Wootton PE31 ...149 C5
Stanhoe PE31 ...14 E8
Strumpshaw NR13 ...91 F8
Taverham NR8 ...156 F8
Terrington St Clement
PE34 ...144 C2
Thetford IP24 ...176 C5
Thorpe Market NR11 ...22 A6
Tilney All Saints PE34 ...144 F2
Tivetshall St Margaret
NR15 ...121 B7
Walsingham NR22 ...16 F7
Walsoken PE14 ...59 E4
Watlington PE33 ...61 C6
Wells-next-the-Sea
NR23 ...136 D5
Wendling NR19 ...66 F7
West Dereham PE33 ...80 B3
Weybourne NR25 ...8 F5
Whinburgh & Westfield
NR19 ...68 A5
Worstead NR28 ...37 F3
Wroxham/Hoveton
NR12 ...164 C5
Wymondham NR18 ...173 C3
Station Rd Ind Est
NR17 ...174 E4
Station Rd N
Belton NR31 ...93 F6
Walpole Cross Keys PE14 ...41 F5
Station Rd S
Belton NR31 ...93 F5
Walpole Cross Keys PE14 ...41 F5
Station St PE37 ...153 B5
Station Terr IP27 ...175 C5
Station Way IP27 ...175 C5
Station Yd PE13 ...153 B5
Steam Mill La NR31 ...169 B4
Stearne Cl IP24 ...176 B2
Stebbings Cl 3 PE32 ...28 A1
Steel's Dro PE38 ...79 C1
Steepgreen Cl NR1 ...163 C8
Steeple Chase NR8 ...155 F2
Steeple La NR15 ...106 A2
Steeple View PE13 ...153 B4
Steeps The 6 NR30 ...169 D1
Steer Rd PE31 ...27 B8
Stegg's La NR19 ...67 F4
Steggles Dr IP22 ...177 C5
Stephen Beaumont Way
NR19 ...154 F2
Stephenson Cl
3 Great Yarmouth NR30 ..169 D5
West Raynham Airfield
PE31 ...30 B3
Stephenson Way IP24 ..176 A2
Stephenson Way Ind Est
IP24 ...176 A2
Stepping La NR1 ...178 B2
Stepping Stone La
NR12 ...39 A4
Steppings La NR15 ...107 C3
Stepshort NR31 ...94 A6
Stermyn St 22 PE13 ...152 C5
Steven's La
Ashwellthorpe NR16 ...106 B8
Wreningham NR16 ...88 E1
Stevens Cl IP25 ...84 D4
Stevens Rd
Cromer NR27 ...139 C4
2 Little Snoring NR21 ...17 B3
Stevenson Rd NR5 ...161 B7
Steward Cl 1 NR18 ...173 D5
Steward St 4 NR3 ...162 E8
Steward Way NR19 ...154 C5
Stewards Cl NR10 ...149 C4
Stewks Hall Drift NR9 ...51 B6
Stibbard Rd NR21 ...17 F1
Stickfer La NR16 ...106 A6
Stiffkey Cl 8 PE33 ...61 D6
Stiffkey Rd Warham NR23 ..5 F5
Wells-next-the-Sea
NR23 ...136 F5
Stigand's Gate NR19 ...154 D7
Stile Cl 12 NR14 ...89 B3
Stile La NR18 ...173 B5
Stileman Way 11 PE31 ...12 E4
Stillington Cl NR7 ...159 B3
Stilwell Dr NR19 ...154 B6
Stirling Cl
Downham Market PE38 ...172 D6
Taverham NR8 ...155 F3
Stirling Rd
Old Catton NR6 ...158 C6
Sculthorpe Airfield NR21 ...15 C3
Stirrups La NR32 ...171 E1
Stitch The PE14 ...77 B8
Stock Lea Rd 1 PE30 ...148 C4
Stockholm Way NR19 ...154 C2
Stocks Hill NR9 ...160 B5
Stocks La NR13 ...165 E5
Stockton Rd NR34 ...110 A3
Stody Dr PE30 ...148 E1
Stody Rd NR24 ...18 D6
Stoke Holy Cross Prim Sch
NR14 ...89 F4
Stoke La NR14 ...89 F5
Stoke Rd
Barton Bendish PE33 ...81 C5
Bixley NR14 ...162 F1
Boughton PE33 ...81 A4
Caistor St Edmund NR14 ...89 F7
Methwold IP26 ...99 A6
Poringland NR14 ...90 B5
Wereham PE33 ...80 E4
Wormegay PE33 ...62 A5
Stokes Ave IP25 ...84 C3
Stokesby New Rd
NR13 ...166 F6
Stokesby Rd NR29 ...75 D6
Stone Breck NR5 ...156 E2
Stone Brigg NR18 ...87 A7
Stone Cl 2 PE33 ...61 D5
Stone Hill Rd NR30 ...168 D6
Stone House Cl NR6 ...158 D2
Stone La Bintree NR20 ...33 B3
Bressingham IP22 ...119 F2
5 Hingham NR9 ...86 C4
Hoveton NR12 ...164 D8
Runhall NR9 ...68 F3
Stone Rd 6 Beetley NR20 .49 D4
6 Beetley NR20 ...49 D5
Briston NR24 ...142 E2
East Dereham NR19 ...154 C2
Great Yarmouth NR31 ...169 B4
Halvergate NR13 ...75 A1
Hockering NR20 ...51 B1
Mattishall NR20 ...68 C6
Norwich NR3 ...158 C1
Strumpshaw NR13 ...73 F1
Yaxham NR19 ...68 B4
Stone St IP19 ...124 F1
Stonebridge Rd NR28 ...23 D2
Stonecross Rd PE38 ...172 D5
Stonecutters Way
NR30 ...169 C4
Stonefield Rd NR25 ...20 A8
Stonegate
Aylsham NR11 ...150 A3
Morley NR18 ...87 A3
Stonegate St PE30 ...146 D4
Stonehill Way NR27 ...10 C4
Stonehouse Rd
Norwich NR7 ...159 B4
Salhouse NR13 ...54 F2
Upwell PE14 ...77 E5
Stonemasons Ct NR13 ...166 C3
Stoney End 2 NR20 ...68 F6
Stoney La Beetley NR20 ...49 B4
Reepham NR10 ...149 B6
Stoney Rd PE32 ...27 F2
Stony La
Attleborough NR17 ...174 B6
Pulham Market IP21 ...121 E7
Raveningham NR14 ...110 B6
Tivetshall St Margaret
NR15 ...121 B5
Wortwell IP20 ...122 F4
Storbeck Rd 2 PE13 ...152 D7
Stores St IP27 ...175 C3
Story's La NR16 ...105 E5
Stow Barn Rd PE33 ...80 A7
Stow Bedon Rd IP24 ...102 C7
Stow Bridge Rd
Stow Bardolph PE34 ...61 D1
Wimbotsham PE34 ...79 E8
Stow Gdns PE13 ...152 E4
Stow La PE13 ...152 E4
Stow Rd Outwell PE14 ...78 A7
Runcton Holme PE33 ...62 B3
Wiggenhall St Mary Magdalen
PE34 ...61 B5
Wisbech PE13 ...152 F5
Stow Windmill*
NR28 ...143 D4
Stowlay La NR17 ...103 B6
Stracey Rd Lamas NR10 ...36 F1
Norwich NR1 ...163 A5
Strachan Cl PE31 ...133 E5
Stradbroke CE Prim Sch
IP21 ...131 E1
Stradbroke Prim Sch
NR31 ...170 D5
Stradbroke Rd NR31 ...170 C5
Stradsett Cl 4 PE38 ...172 D6
Straight La 10 IP20 ...122 D2
Strangers Hall* NR2 ...178 A3
Stranton Ave NR19 ...68 A5
Strasbourg Way NR19 ...154 B1
Stratford Cl
Dersingham PE31 ...140 E3
Norwich NR1 ...162 F2
Stratford Cres NR4 ...161 C1
Stratford Dr NR1 ...162 E3
Stratton Cl 6 PE37 ...153 C3
Stratton Rd
Hainford NR10 ...53 E6
Stratton Strawless NR10 ...53 E8
Wacton NR15 ...106 D2
Straw Mus The* NR11 ...21 D3
Strawberry Cl 3 PE13 ...152 A6
Strawberry Fields NR12 ..39 B3
Strayground La NR18 ...173 B2
Street Hill NR12 ...55 E7
Street The Acle NR13 ...166 C3
Alburgh IP20 ...122 F6

Street The *continued*
Aldborough NR11 ....20 F5
Aldeby NR34 ....110 F4
Ashby St Mary NR14 ....91 C5
Ashwellthorpe NR16 ....106 A8
Aslacton NR15 ....106 A1
Aylmerton NR11 ....10 A2
Baconsthorpe NR25 ....19 F8
Bacton NR28 ....23 B2
Barnham IP24 ....125 E6
Barton Turf NR12 ....55 E8
Bawdeswell NR20 ....50 E7
Beachamwell PE37 ....81 E8
Beeston with Bittering PE32 ....48 C2
Belaugh NR12 ....164 A6
Bergh Apton NR15 ....91 A3
Billingford NR20 ....50 B7
Bintree NR20 ....33 B2
Blo' Norton IP22 ....128 B6
Booton NR10 ....149 E4
Botesdale IP22 ....128 E2
Bracon Ash NR14 ....89 A3
Bramerton NR14 ....90 F7
Brampton NR10 ....36 E3
Brandon IP27 ....175 A3
Bressingham IP22 ....119 D2
Bridgham NR16 ....117 E4
Brinton NR24 ....18 D6
Brockdish IP21 ....131 D6
Brome & Oakley IP23 ....130 C3
Brooke NR15 ....90 E2
Brundall NR13 ....165 E5
Burgh & Tuttington NR11 ....36 E4
Caston NR17 ....102 E8
Catfield NR29 ....56 C8
Claxton NR14 ....91 D6
Coltishall NR12 ....54 E7
Coney Weston IP31 ....127 B4
Corpusty NR11 ....19 F1
Costessey NR8 ....156 E5
Croxton IP24 ....116 C6
Dickleburgh IP21 ....121 B1
Dilham NR28 ....38 D4
Earsham NR35 ....123 F8
East Tuddenham NR20 ....69 C6
Erpingham NR11 ....21 A2
Felthorpe NR10 ....155 C8
Flixton NR35 ....123 E6
Flordon NR15 ....106 D8
Foxley NR20 ....50 D8
Framingham Pigot NR14 ....90 D6
Fulmodeston NR21 ....17 F3
Garvestone NR9 ....68 B1
Geldeston NR34 ....109 F2
Gooderstone PE33 ....81 F5
Great Cressingham IP25 ....83 C4
Great Snoring NR21 ....17 A5
Great Yarmouth NR30 ....76 F5
Halvergate NR13 ....74 F1
Hempnall NR15 ....107 C5
Hemsby NR29 ....167 A7
Hevingham NR10 ....53 C8
Heydon NR11 ....34 F6
Hickling NR12 ....39 F2
Hinderclay IP22 ....128 C3
Hindolveston NR20 ....33 D8
Hindringham NR21 ....17 E7
Hockering NR20 ....69 B8
Honingham NR9 ....69 E6
Horsey NR29 ....40 E1
Kelling NR25 ....8 C5
Ketteringham NR18 ....88 E6
Kettlestone NR21 ....17 C2
Knapton NR28 ....143 B1
Lamas NR10 ....37 A1
Lenwade NR9 ....51 D5
Lessingham NR12 ....24 D3
Little Barningham NR11 ....20 B4
Little Snoring NR21 ....17 B3
Long Stratton NR15 ....106 E3
Lound NR32 ....94 C2
Marham PE33 ....63 B5
Market Weston IP22 ....127 E4
Marlingford NR9 ....69 E4
Mautby NR29 ....75 E5
Melton Constable NR24 ....142 A5
Mileham PE32 ....48 D6
Morning Thorpe NR15 ....107 C4
Morston NR25 ....7 A6
Morton on the Hill NR9 ....52 A3
North Lopham IP22 ....119 A2
North Pickenham PE37 ....65 E1
Norwich NR14 ....163 B2
Ovington IP25 ....84 E5
Poringland NR14 ....90 C5
Pulham St Mary IP21 ....122 A3
Redenhall with Harleston IP20 ....122 F1
Redgrave IP22 ....128 E5
Reepham NR10 ....149 C3
Riddlesworth IP22 ....127 D7
Ringland NR8 ....70 B8
Rockland St Mary NR14 ....91 B7
Rocklands NR17 ....103 C7
Rougham PE32 ....47 B7
Ryburgh NR21 ....32 C7
St Margaret, South Elmham IP20 ....123 E2
St Michael South Elmham IP19 ....124 A2
Salle NR10 ....149 D8
Saxlingham Nethergate NR15 ....107 B8
Scoulton NR9 ....85 D3

Street The *continued*
Sculthorpe NR21 ....16 B1
Sculthorpe Airfield PE31 ....15 B3
Sea Palling NR12 ....40 A5
Shelton NR15 ....122 B8
Shotesham NR15 ....90 A2
Somerleyton, Ashby & Herringfleet NR32 ....111 D8
Somerton NR29 ....57 F6
South Lopham IP22 ....128 D8
South Pickenham PE37 ....83 D7
South Walsham NR13 ....74 A8
Sparham NR9 ....51 B4
Sporle with Palgrave PE32 ....65 C7
Starston IP20 ....122 C3
Surlingham NR14 ....165 B1
Sustead NR11 ....20 E7
Swafield NR28 ....151 D8
Swanton Abbott NR10 ....37 C4
Swanton Novers NR24 ....18 C2
Taverham NR8 ....156 B8
Tharston & Hapton NR15 ....106 C7
Themelthorpe NR20 ....33 F2
Thornage NR25 ....18 E6
Thurlton NR14 ....92 F1
Thurne NR29 ....56 E2
Thurton NR14 ....91 C3
Tibenham NR16 ....120 E8
Tivetshall St Mary NR15 ....121 B5
Topcroft NR35 ....107 F3
Warham NR23 ....6 A4
Waterloo IP21 ....130 C5
Wattisfield IP22 ....128 A1
Wellingham PE32 ....47 F8
West Beckham NR25 ....9 B2
Weybourne NR25 ....8 E5
Winfarthing IP22 ....120 B4
Witton NR28 ....23 E1
Wiveton NR25 ....7 E6
Woodton NR35 ....108 C5
Stretton Sch NR2 ....162 C3
Strickland Ave 9 PE31 ....12 E4
Strickland Cl 8 PE31 ....12 E4
Stringside Dro PE33 ....81 B3
Strumpshaw Rd NR13 ....165 E3
Strumpshaw Steam Mus* NR13 ....73 E1
Stuart Cl Brandon IP27 ....175 C3
Great Yarmouth NR31 ....170 B4
7 Hethersett NR9 ....88 D8
Stuart Gdns NR1 ....178 C3
Stuart Rd
Aylsham NR11 ....150 C7
Norwich NR1 ....178 C1
Stubb Rd NR12 ....39 F2
Stubbs Cl PE38 ....172 E5
Stubbs Gn La NR14 ....109 C8
Sturdee Ave NR30 ....169 D8
Sturdee Cl IP24 ....176 F6
Sturmy Cl 15 NR15 ....106 E3
Stuston La IP21 ....130 B4
Stuston Rd IP21 ....130 B5
Style Loke NR9 ....69 F2
Styles Cl NR31 ....170 A4
Stylman Rd NR5 ....161 A7
Suckling Ave NR3 ....158 B3
Suckling Dro PE14 ....78 C5
Suckling La
Framingham Pigot NR14 ....90 D6
Hickling NR12 ....39 F3
Suckling Pl NR35 ....108 C5
Suffield Cl
7 Cringleford NR4 ....89 B8
3 Long Stratton NR15 ....106 D3
North Walsham NR28 ....151 A6
Suffield Ct NR6 ....158 D2
Suffield Pk Inf Sch NR27 ....139 C5
Suffield Rd NR31 ....170 C4
Suffield Way PE30 ....147 B8
Suffling Rd NR30 ....170 D8
Suffolk Ave IP31 ....126 B1
Suffolk Cl NR31 ....170 C7
Suffolk Ct IP27 ....175 C4
Suffolk Pl NR19 ....154 C1
Suffolk Rd
Great Yarmouth NR31 ....170 C8
King's Lynn PE30 ....147 C6
Norwich NR4 ....161 C3
Sheringham NR26 ....138 D6
Suffolk Sq NR2 ....162 C5
Suffolk Wlk NR4 ....161 D3
Sugar La PE31 ....140 E4
Sukey Way NR5 ....160 F6
Summer Cl 4 PE14 ....41 E4
Summer Dr NR12 ....164 D6
Summer La IP25 ....85 A4
Summerfield Cl PE13 ....152 A6
Summerfield Rd NR29 ....58 A4
Summerhouse Cl NR27 ....139 A6
Sumpter Rd NR4 ....161 E3
Sun Barn Rd NR10 ....149 B4
Sun Barn Wlk NR10 ....149 B4
Sun La
Great Yarmouth NR31 ....94 C6
Norwich NR3 ....158 D1
Sun Rd NR35 ....109 B2
Sunart Cl NR17 ....174 E6
Suncroft NR1 ....162 F2
Sunderland Cl NR6 ....158 C6
Sundew Cl 6 IP24 ....176 F4
Sunk Rd NR22 ....16 F7
Sunley Cl NR35 ....109 C2
Sunningdale NR4 ....162 A2
Sunninghill Cl 14 NR31 ....94 C8

Sunny Cl NR5 ....157 B1
Sunny Cnr NR28 ....151 B4
Sunny Gr NR5 ....161 B8
Sunny Hill NR1 ....162 E2
Sunnyside
Bedingham NR35 ....108 C4
Diss IP22 ....177 D5
Heacham PE31 ....133 D5
Sunnyside Ave 10 NR14 ....90 C5
Sunnyside Cl PE31 ....133 D5
Sunnyside Rd PE32 ....29 D2
Sunsalve Ride NR19 ....154 C1
Sunset Gdns PE13 ....152 E2
Sunset Wlk NR12 ....24 E4
Supple Cl NR1 ....163 C7
Surlingham Dr PE37 ....153 B1
Surlingham La
Bramerton NR14 ....90 F8
Rockland St Mary NR14 ....91 B8
Surlingham Prim Sch NR14 ....73 B1
Surrey Cl NR7 ....159 C5
Surrey Gr NR1 ....178 B1
Surrey St Cromer NR27 ....139 C7
6 King's Lynn PE30 ....146 D5
Norwich NR1 ....178 B2
6 Wiggenhall St Germans PE34 ....43 B1
Surrogate St NR17 ....174 D5
Sursham Ave NR6 ....158 F4
Sussex Rd NR31 ....170 D5
Sussex St NR3 ....178 A4
Sustead La NR11 ....20 F8
Sustead Rd NR11 ....9 F1
Suters Dr NR8 ....155 E2
Sutherland Ave NR6 ....158 A4
Sutherland Ct Gdns NR27 ....139 C6
Suton La NR18 ....173 A1
Sutton Cres NR13 ....92 F8
Sutton Est PE31 ....135 C2
Sutton Fst Sch NR12 ....39 C2
Sutton Lea PE31 ....135 C2
Sutton Mdws PE13 ....152 A8
Sutton Rd Catfield NR29 ....39 C1
Great Yarmouth NR30 ....169 D1
Hickling NR12 ....39 D1
Swaffham PE37 ....153 B1
Terrington St Clement PE34 ....144 A4
Walpole Cross Keys PE34 ....42 A7
Wisbech PE13 ....152 A7
Sutton Windmill & Broads Mus* NR12 ....39 D2
Suttons Cl 1 PE14 ....77 F6
Swaffham Com Hospl PE37 ....153 C5
Swaffham Gap IP26 ....82 C1
Swaffham Greenhoe Mid Sch PE37 ....153 B2
Swaffham Leisure Ctr PE37 ....153 C2
Swaffham Mus* PE37 ....153 B4
Swaffham Raceway PE37 ....64 C4
Swaffham Rd
Ashill IP25 ....84 A7
Barton Bendish PE33 ....63 C2
Cockley Cley PE37 ....82 D7
East Dereham NR19 ....154 D6
Mundford IP26 ....100 B4
Narborough PE32 ....63 F7
Oxborough PE33 ....81 E4
Raynham NR21 ....30 F2
Swaffham PE37 ....64 A4
Watton IP25 ....84 C4
Swaffham VC Fst Sch PE37 ....153 C4
Swafield Rise NR28 ....151 D7
Swafield St NR5 ....160 F7
Swale The NR5 ....160 F6
Swallow Cl 6 NR31 ....170 A7
Swallow Dr IP27 ....175 E3
Swallowfield Rd PE30 ....147 C4
Swallowtail Cl NR5 ....160 F5
Swamp La
Great Ellingham NR17 ....103 F7
Roydon IP22 ....177 A6
Swan Cl Aylsham NR11 ....150 C6
Swannington NR9 ....52 B5
Swan Cotts PE32 ....47 D5
Swan Dr NR20 ....49 C3
Swan Entry 2 NR22 ....16 F7
Swan La
Coney Weston IP31 ....127 B4
Fincham PE33 ....62 E1
King's Lynn PE30 ....147 A6
1 Norwich NR2 ....178 B3
Redenhall with Harleston IP20 ....122 D2
Shipdham IP25 ....67 C3
Tharston & Hapton NR15 ....106 E4
Swan Loke NR28 ....151 C5
Swan Rd NR19 ....154 E4
Swan St
Fakenham NR21 ....141 B3
Horsham St Faith NR10 ....53 D2
Swan Terr 1 PE38 ....172 A6
Swangey La NR17 ....103 D4
Swann Gr NR25 ....137 C6
Swanns Yd NR28 ....38 A4
Swans Cl NR25 ....7 B3
Swansea Rd NR2 ....162 B5
Swansgate NR6 ....158 E6
Swanston's Rd NR30 ....170 D8
Swanton Abbot Rd NR10 ....37 A5

Swanton Abbott Com Sch NR10 ....37 B5
Swanton Ave NR19 ....154 E7
Swanton Cl NR19 ....154 E7
Swanton Dr NR20 ....154 E6
Swanton Gr NR19 ....154 E6
Swanton Morley Prim Sch NR20 ....50 B4
Swanton Morley Rd
Hoe NR20 ....50 A6
North Elmham NR20 ....49 F6
Swanton Rd
Dereham NR20 ....50 A1
East Dereham NR19 ....154 E6
Gunthorpe NR24 ....18 B5
Norwich NR3 ....162 B8
Swardeston La NR14 ....89 B6
Swargate La NR15 ....108 E8
Swash La NR13 ....54 D2
Sweden Pl IP27 ....175 B2
Sweet Briar Rd
7 Long Stratton NR15 ....106 E3
Norwich NR6 ....161 F8
Sweet Briar Rd Ind Est NR3 ....157 F1
Sweetacres 7 NR29 ....167 B6
Sweetbriar Gdns NR20 ....49 C4
Sweetbriar La
Edgefield NR24 ....19 D5
Sheringham NR26 ....138 C7
Sweyn Cl IP24 ....176 B2
Swim Rd NR29 ....75 F6
Swinbourne Cl NR6 ....158 E3
Swindells Cl NR5 ....157 A2
Swingy La NR18 ....87 A3
Swirle's Pl 6 NR30 ....169 D4
Swiss Terr PE30 ....146 F5
Sybil Rd PE13 ....152 C6
Sybil Wheeler Cl 5 IP24 ....176 D6
Sycamore Ave
16 Great Yarmouth NR31 ....94 C7
23 Martham NR29 ....57 D4
Wymondham NR18 ....173 E6
Sycamore Cl
Attleborough NR17 ....174 C4
King's Lynn PE30 ....148 D2
8 Loddon NR14 ....91 F1
North Walsham NR28 ....151 D6
Thompson IP24 ....102 A7
Sycamore Covert IP24 ....116 D2
Sycamore Cres NR2 ....161 F7
Sycamore Gn 2 NR31 ....170 B6
Sycamore Gr NR26 ....138 D5
Sycamore Way IP22 ....177 F5
Sycamores The NR19 ....154 E3
Sydenham Cl NR13 ....166 B4
Syderstone Comm Nature Reserve* PE31 ....15 A3
Syderstone Rd NR21 ....15 B3
Sydney Dye Ct PE32 ....65 C5
Sydney Rd 11 NR10 ....54 A2
Sydney Terr 2 PE30 ....146 D1
Syers La PE32 ....48 D2
Syleham Hall La IP21 ....131 F5
Syleham Rd IP21 ....131 B4
Sylvan Cl NR6 ....157 E6
Sylvan Way
2 Blofield Heath NR13 ....73 C6
Taverham NR8 ....156 E8
Sylvden Dr PE13 ....152 F6
Symonds Ave NR29 ....167 C2
Syon Cl PE38 ....172 B4
Sywell Cl NR6 ....158 F6
Sywell Gr 5 PE14 ....59 A1

T

Tabernacle La NR16 ....105 F4
Tacolneston VC Prim Sch NR16 ....105 F6
Tagg Way 3 NR13 ....72 E7
Talbot Cl NR18 ....173 C5
Talbot Sq NR3 ....178 A4
Talbots Mdw IP21 ....130 B5
Tales of the Old Gaol House* PE30 ....146 D4
Taleworth Cl NR5 ....161 A7
Tallon St IP26 ....82 A2
Tamarind Mews NR4 ....161 E1
Tamarisk PE30 ....148 B1
Tamworth La NR31 ....169 B2
Tan La NR30 ....168 E4
Tanager Cl NR3 ....158 D3
Tanner St 4 IP24 ....176 C4
Tanners Gn NR9 ....68 C3
Tanning La 7 NR16 ....104 F1
Tanns La IP22 ....119 A2
Tansy Cl NR6 ....158 D4
Tantallon Dr NR17 ....174 F6
Tar Works Rd NR30 ....169 C6
Target Hill IP20 ....123 B2
Tarragon Cl 16 NR31 ....94 C6
Tarragon Rd PE38 ....172 D7
Tas Valley Vineyard* NR16 ....106 A3
Tasburgh Rd NR15 ....106 F8
Tasman Dr NR11 ....22 F8
Tatterford Dr PE31 ....30 E7
Tattersett Pk Bsns Ctr NR21 ....15 C1
Tattersett Rd PE31 ....15 B2
Tattlepot Rd IP21 ....121 E5
Taverham Chase NR8 ....156 D8
Taverham Hall Sch NR8 ....156 A8

Taverham High Sch NR8 ....155 B2
Taverham La NR8 ....156 C6
Taverham Mid Sch NR8 ....156 C8
Taverham Rd
Felthorpe NR10 ....155 C7
Honingham NR9 ....69 F6
Taverham NR8 ....156 D8
Tavern Cl NR20 ....49 D4
Tavern La Diss IP22 ....177 F3
East Dereham NR19 ....154 E3
Tavistock Rd PE13 ....152 D5
Tawny Sedge 3 PE30 ....147 A8
Taylor Ave 9 NR4 ....89 B8
Taylor Rd Diss IP22 ....177 B4
Norwich NR5 ....161 C6
Taylor's La
Gressenhall NR20 ....49 C3
Norwich NR6 ....158 D6
Trimingham NR11 ....11 E1
Taylors Loke
3 Cley next the Sea NR25 ....7 E6
1 Hemsby NR29 ....167 A8
Taymor Pl PE14 ....95 D4
Teal Cl 3 PE31 ....12 E5
Teal Wlk Brandon IP27 ....175 F4
18 Great Yarmouth NR31 ....94 C8
Teasel Cl NR20 ....68 A8
Teasel Dr IP24 ....176 E5
Teasel Rd NR17 ....174 B4
Teasel Rise 4 NR26 ....138 B6
Tebbutt Ave 6 NR19 ....154 C3
Ted Ellis Nature Reserve* NR14 ....91 D8
Tedder Cl
5 Barnham IP24 ....125 F6
13 Watton IP25 ....84 E3
Tee Cl 1 NR14 ....89 B2
Telegraph La E NR1 ....163 B6
Telegraph La W 4 NR1 ....163 A6
Telford Cl
King's Lynn PE30 ....147 D4
2 Norwich NR3 ....157 F1
Telford Way IP24 ....176 B6
Temple Cl NR25 ....8 F6
Temple Dr NR25 ....8 F6
Temple Rd
Great Yarmouth NR30 ....169 D4
King's Lynn PE30 ....148 D1
Norwich NR3 ....158 D1
Templemere NR3 ....159 A2
Templewood La NR25 ....137 F8
Ten Bell La NR2 ....178 A3
Ten Mile Bank
Hilgay PE38 ....96 F6
Littleport CB6 ....96 E1
Ten Mile Bank Prim Sch PE38 ....96 F7
Tennyson Ave PE30 ....146 F4
Tennyson Rd
3 Diss IP22 ....177 E4
3 Great Yarmouth NR30 ....169 D8
King's Lynn PE30 ....146 F4
Tennyson Way IP24 ....176 E6
Tensing St NR35 ....108 C5
Terence Airey Ct 25 IP20 ....122 D2
Terence Ave NR7 ....159 A4
Teresa Rd 6 NR12 ....39 B4
Tern Cl 9 IP25 ....84 C3
Tern Gdns NR31 ....170 A6
Tern Rd NR29 ....167 E5
Terr The 12 NR28 ....151 C5
Terrace Wlk NR1 ....178 B1
Terrington Cl 3 PE14 ....59 D2
Terrington St Clements Sch PE34 ....144 C6
Terrington St John Prim Sch PE14 ....60 B8
Testerton Cotts NR21 ....32 A6
Texas Ave NR21 ....15 C2
Texel Way NR11 ....143 A7
Thacker Way NR5 ....160 F6
Thain's La NR27 ....10 B5
Thames Way 8 NR30 ....168 C6
Thamesfield Way NR31 ....169 B2
Thatchwood Ave PE14 ....59 C2
Theatre Plain NR30 ....169 C4
Theatre Rd NR23 ....136 C6
Theatre St
East Dereham NR19 ....154 D6
Norwich NR2 ....178 A2
Swaffham PE37 ....153 B4
Thelnetham Rd
Blo' Norton IP22 ....128 B6
Hopton IP22 ....127 F5
Themelthorpe Rd NR20 ....33 E1
Theobald Rd NR1 ....89 E8
Thetford Ancient House Mus* IP24 ....176 C4
Thetford Cottage Hospl IP24 ....176 D4
Thetford Gram Sch IP24 ....176 C4
Thetford Priory* IP24 ....176 C4
Thetford Rd
Brandon IP27 ....175 E3
Coney Weston IP31 ....127 B4
Euston IP24 ....126 B6
Garboldisham IP22 ....127 F8
Northwold IP26 ....99 B8
Santon Downham IP27 ....115 B5
Watton IP25 ....84 D3
Wretham IP24 ....117 A7
Thetford Sta IP24 ....176 C5

Thetford Warren Lodge*
IP24 . . . . .115 E3
Thetford Way PE30 . . . . .148 C3
Thicket The 6 NR8 . . . . .155 E2
Thiefgate La PE34 . . . . . . .43 D2
Thieves' Bridge Rd
PE33 . . . . .61 E5
Thieves' La
Attleborough NR17 . . . . . . .174 E5
Burgh & Tuttington NR11 . . . .36 E6
Little Ellingham NR17 . . . . . .103 C8
Thieves La NR13 . . . . .55 A1
Third Ave PE13 . . . . .152 E5
Third Marsh Rd PE14 . . . .59 A7
Thirlby Rd NR28 . . . . . . .151 D3
Thirlmere 18 NR9 . . . . .88 D8
Thistle Cl Norwich NR5 . .160 F5
3 Thetford IP24 . . . . .176 F5
Thistledown Rd NR10 . . . .53 B2
Thomas Bole Cl IP22 . . .128 A8
Thomas Bullock Prim Sch
IP25 . . . . .67 C2
Thomas Cl 4 PE33 . . . . . . .61 D5
Thomas Dix Ct NR28 . . .151 D5
Thomas Drew Cl PE31 . .140 C3
Thomas Glover Ct
NR6 . . . . .158 C2
Thomas Manning Rd
IP22 . . . . .177 E4
Thomas Paine Ave 3
IP24 . . . . .176 C4
Thomas St PE30 . . . . .146 E3
Thomas Vere Rd NR7 . . .163 F7
Thomas Way NR30 . . . . .168 C6
Thomas Wyatt Cl NR2 . .178 A1
Thompson Ave 7 NR25 .137 C5
Thompson Cl NR20 . . . . . .50 B4
Thompson Prim Sch
IP24 . . . . .102 B7
Thompson Rd
Griston IP25 . . . . .85 A1
Norwich NR7 . . . . .163 F8
Thompson's La PE33 . . . .81 A2
Thompsons Yd NR3 . . . .178 B4
Thor Cl NR7 . . . . .163 E7
Thor Loke NR7 . . . . .163 E7
Thor Rd NR7 . . . . .163 E7
Thoresby Ave PE30 . . . . .147 B4
Thoresby Coll PE30 . . . . .146 D4
Thorn La NR1 . . . . .178 B2
Thorn Rd Catfield NR29 . . .56 C8
Fakenham NR21 . . . . .141 D4
Thornage Rd NR25 . . . . .137 A5
Thornham Cl NR7 . . . . . .159 B2
Thornham Cnr PE36 . . . . . .2 E2
Thornham Rd
Methwold IP26 . . . . .99 A6
Norwich NR7 . . . . .159 B2
Thornton Cl NR24 . . . . . .142 E4
Thornycroft Gdns 1
NR33 . . . . .111 F1
Thoroughfare La
NR29 . . . . .167 B4
Thoroughfare The
IP20 . . . . .122 D2
Thorp Ct NR19 . . . . .154 D4
Thorpe Abbots Rd
IP21 . . . . .131 A8
Thorpe Ave NR7 . . . . .163 E8
Thorpe Cl NR7 . . . . .163 F7
Thorpe Dr NR17 . . . . .174 D4
Thorpe Hall Cl NR7 . . . .163 C5
Thorpe Hamlet Fst Sch
NR1 . . . . .163 B6
Thorpe Hamlet Mid Sch
NR1 . . . . .163 B6
Thorpe House Sch
NR7 . . . . .163 C6
Thorpe Mews NR7 . . . . . .163 F6
Thorpe Mkt Rd NR11 . . . .21 E7
Thorpe Rd
Haddiscoe NR14 . . . . .110 F8
Norwich NR1 . . . . .178 C2
Southrepps NR11 . . . . .22 A7
Thorpe St Andrew Sch
NR7 . . . . .72 D4
Thorpeland Cl 4 PE33 . . .61 D3
Thorpeland La 3 PE33 . . .61 D3
Thorpland Rd NR21 . . . .141 E6
Threadneedle St NR15 . . .91 A4
Three Acre Cl NR12 . . . .164 C6
Three Cnr Dr NR6 . . . . . .158 F6
Three King La NR2 . . . . .178 A3
Three Mile La NR5 . . . . .156 F1
Three Oaks 6 PE30 . . . . .147 C5
Three Post Rd 5 IP25 . . .84 C3
Three Score Rd
Colney NR5 . . . . .161 A5
Norwich NR5 . . . . .160 F5
Threxton Rd IP25 . . . . . . .84 C3
Thrigby Hall Wildlife Gdns*
NR29 . . . . .75 E7
Thrigby Rd NR29 . . . . .75 E6
Throckmorton Yd 5
NR3 . . . . .162 E8
Thrush Cl 2 NR14 . . . . . . .89 B3
Thumb La NR20 . . . . .31 F2
Thunder La NR7 . . . . . . .163 E7
Thurgarton Rd NR11 . . . . .21 A5
Thurland's Dro PE14 . . . . .77 D5
Thurlby Rd NR5 . . . . .160 E8
Thurlin Rd PE30 . . . . . . .147 B4
Thurling Loke NR7 . . . . . .159 E1
Thurling Plain NR7 . . . . .159 E1
Thurloe Cl PE13 . . . . .152 C2
Thurlow Cl NR5 . . . . .160 E8
Thurlton Prim Sch
NR14 . . . . .92 F1
Thurlton Rd NR14 . . . . . .110 B7
Thurne Rd NR29 . . . . .57 A2
Thurne Rise 2 NR29 . . . . .57 D5
Thurne Way NR29 . . . . . .167 B3
Thurning Rd NR20 . . . . . . .33 E8
Thursford Collection*
NR21 . . . . .17 D5
Thursford Rd
Great Snoring NR21 . . . . . . .17 A5
Hindringham NR21 . . . . .17 E6
1 Little Snoring NR21 . . . . .17 B3
Thursford Wood Nature
Reserve* NR21 . . . . .17 D4
Thurst Rd NR27 . . . . .11 A3
Thurston Cl 3 NR5 . . . . .160 F8
Thurton Prim Sch
NR14 . . . . .91 D4
Thuxton Sta NR9 . . . . .68 C2
Thwaite Rd NR35 . . . . . .109 A2
Thyme Cl
Attleborough NR17 . . . . . . .174 B4
Thetford IP24 . . . . .176 F5
Thynne's La NR20 . . . . . . .68 E5
Tibenham Rd NR15 . . . . .121 A8
Tiercel Ave NR7 . . . . . . .159 C4
Tillett Cl NR29 . . . . .167 C2
Tillett Rd NR3 . . . . .158 E2
Tills Cl NR6 . . . . .158 F4
Tills Rd NR6 . . . . .159 A5
Tilney All Saints Prim Sch
PE34 . . . . .42 E4
Tilney Rd NR20 . . . . .69 C6
Tilney St Lawrence CP Sch
PE34 . . . . .60 C8
Timber Rd NR16 . . . . . . .118 C5
Timberhill NR1 . . . . .178 B2
Time & Tide Mus*
NR30 . . . . .169 D2
Timothy Cl NR1 . . . . .163 B8
Timperley Est NR21 . . . . .31 D5
Tindall Cl PE13 . . . . .152 C8
Tinker's Dro PE13 . . . . . .152 D7
Tinker's La NR15 . . . . . .121 C4
Tinkers' La
Garvestone NR9 . . . . .68 C1
Strumpshaw NR13 . . . . .73 D1
Tintern Gr 4 PE30 . . . . . .148 C4
Tippett Cl NR5 . . . . .160 F6
Tipton Cl NR19 . . . . .154 D2
Titchwell Marsh Nature
Reserve* PE31 . . . . .2 F7
Tithe Barn Cl IP26 . . . . . .100 C5
Tithe Barn La NR24 . . . . .142 F3
Tithebarn La
Marham PE33 . . . . .63 D6
2 Thurlton NR14 . . . . .92 F1
Tithing Cl 2 IP24 . . . . . .176 E5
Titlow Rd 28 IP20 . . . . . .122 D2
Tittleshall Rd
Litcham PE32 . . . . .48 A5
Mileham NR20 . . . . .48 E8
Tittleshall PE32 . . . . .48 C6
Tivetshall Cty Prim Sch
NR15 . . . . .121 B5
Tivetshall Rd IP21 . . . . .121 D5
Toad Hole Cottage Mus*
NR29 . . . . .56 A6
Toad La
Ditchingham NR35 . . . . . . .108 F5
Great & Little Plumstead
NR13 . . . . .72 F5
Thwaite NR35 . . . . .109 A5
Todhunter Ave NR34 . . .110 C2
Todkill's La PE12 . . . . . . .41 C8
Toftes Pl 4 NR5 . . . . .161 B8
Toftwood Inf Sch
NR19 . . . . .154 E1
Toftwood Jun Sch
NR19 . . . . .154 E2
Tolhouse Mus* NR30 . . .169 C3
Tolhouse St NR30 . . . . . .169 C3
Toll Bar NR21 . . . . .141 A6
Tollgate Rd NR31 . . . . . .169 C1
Tollgate Way NR5 . . . . . .161 A5
Tollhouse Rd NR5 . . . . . .161 E7
Tolwin Wlk 3 NR6 . . . . . .158 F1
Tolye Rd NR5 . . . . .160 F7
Tombland NR1 . . . . .178 B3
Tooks Comm La NR34 . .124 F5
Top Driftway IP24 . . . . . .117 C8
Top Rd Belaugh NR12 . . . .164 A6
St Andrew, Ilketshall
NR34 . . . . .124 E5
Wicklewood NR18 . . . . .87 B4
Wingfield IP21 . . . . .131 E3
Topcliffe Ave 2 NR13 . . . .55 A1
Topshill Rd NR11 . . . . .21 E6
Torrey Cl PE31 . . . . .133 E5
Tortoishell Way NR18 . . .173 E4
Tottenham St 8 NR30 . . .169 D5
Tottenhill Row PE33 . . . . .61 F6
Tottington Cl 6 NR5 . . . .160 F8
Tottington La IP22 . . . . .177 B4
Tottington Rd
Little Cressingham IP25 . . .101 C8
Thompson IP24 . . . . .102 A7
Tottington IP24 . . . . .101 F7
Tower Cl Brandon IP27 . .175 B3
Costessey NR8 . . . . .156 C4
Tower Hill
Costessey NR8 . . . . .156 C4
Norwich NR7 . . . . .163 D6
Tower Hill Pk NR8 . . . . . .156 C4
Tower La
Middleton PE32 . . . . .44 D4
Sidestrand NR27 . . . . .11 B3
Tower Mdws PE37 . . . . . .153 C5
Tower Mill Rd NR35 . . . .124 A8
Tower Pl 13 PE30 . . . . . . .146 D4
Tower Rd
Burgh St Margaret (Fleggburgh)
NR29 . . . . .57 C1
Burnham Overy PE31 . . . . .135 E7
Canadas NR11 . . . . .10 A4
Elm PE14 . . . . .77 A7
Hilgay PE38 . . . . .97 A8
Repps with Bastwick
NR29 . . . . .57 A5
Terrington St Clement
PE34 . . . . .144 C7
Tower St PE30 . . . . .146 D4
Town Bridge 25 PE13 . . . .152 B5
Town Cl Corpusty NR11 . . . .19 E1
East Winch PE32 . . . . .44 F3
Holt NR25 . . . . .137 B6
Town Cl House Prep Sch
NR2 . . . . .162 C3
Town Cl Rd NR2 . . . . . . .162 C3
Town Cnr NR10 . . . . .53 C8
Town End NR11 . . . . .143 C6
Town Est PE38 . . . . .172 B5
Town Gn NR18 . . . . .173 B4
Town Gn Rd IP25 . . . . .84 E3
Town House La IP22 . . .128 B2
Town House Mus*
PE30 . . . . .146 D4
Town House Rd NR8 . . . .156 F4
Town La Aylsham NR11 . .150 C7
Brancaster Staithe PE31 . . . . .3 D7
Castle Acre PE32 . . . . .46 F2
Garvestone NR9 . . . . .68 C2
Town Lands Trading Est
NR31 . . . . .170 B7
Town Rd
Burgh St Margaret (Fleggburgh)
NR29 . . . . .57 C1
Ingham NR12 . . . . .39 C4
Town St Outwell PE14 . . . . .77 D5
Swanton Morley NR20 . . . . .50 B4
Town Wall Mews 9
NR30 . . . . .169 C5
Town Wall Rd NR30 . . . .169 C5
Town Yd 4 NR25 . . . . .7 E6
Townlands NR31 . . . . . . .170 B7
Townley Cl PE14 . . . . .77 E5
Townley Prim Sch
PE14 . . . . .95 A7
Townsend Gn N NR21 . . .141 F5
Townsend Rd
Norwich NR4 . . . . .162 C1
Upwell PE14 . . . . .77 E3
Townshend Cl 3 NR30 . .169 D3
Townshend Gn E
NR21 . . . . .141 F5
Townshend Gn W
NR21 . . . . .141 F5
Townshend Pl 4 IP25 . . . .67 C2
Townshend Rd
Dereham NR19 . . . . .154 D7
Wisbech PE13 . . . . .152 D6
Townshend Terr 2
PE30 . . . . .146 E6
Tracey Rd NR7 . . . . .159 E1
Trafalgar Ct
Cliftonville NR11 . . . . .143 B7
Great Yarmouth NR30 . . . . .169 E3
Trafalgar Ind Est
PE38 . . . . .172 A4
Trafalgar Rd
Downham Market PE38 . . .172 B4
2 Great Yarmouth NR30 . . .169 D3
Trafalgar Rd E NR31 . . . .170 D6
Trafalgar Rd W NR31 . . .170 C6
Trafalgar Sq NR30 . . . . . .169 E3
Trafalgar St NR1 . . . . . . .178 B1
Trafford Est PE14 . . . . . . .59 C8
Trafford Pk 1 PE13 . . . . .152 E6
Trafford Rd
Norwich NR1 . . . . .178 A1
Wisbech PE13 . . . . .152 D5
Trafford Wlk NR12 . . . . . .164 B2
Traice Rd NR16 . . . . .105 D7
Transport La NR14 . . . . .109 D7
Trap La NR21 . . . . .141 B6
Trelawny Rd 5 NR29 . . . . .57 D4
Tremaine Cl NR6 . . . . . . .157 E1
Trenchard Cres 4 IP25 . . .84 F3
Trenchard Sq IP26 . . . . . . .98 D1
Trendall Rd NR7 . . . . . . .159 C4
Trenowaths Pl 13 PE30 . .146 D5
Trent V C Cl IP26 . . . . . . .99 A5
Tretts Loke NR29 . . . . .57 C1
Trident Dr NR1 . . . . .163 A7
Trimingham Rd
Gimingham NR11 . . . . .22 E8
Trimingham NR11 . . . . .11 E1
Trimming Wlk NR8 . . . . .156 E8
Trinity Ave NR31 . . . . . . .170 B4
Trinity Cl NR19 . . . . .154 D6
Trinity Hospl (Bede House)*
PE31 . . . . .27 C3
Trinity Pl NR30 . . . . .169 D3
Trinity Rd
Walpole Highway PE14 . . . . .59 F8
Wisbech PE13 . . . . .152 E6
Trinity Sq 1 NR30 . . . . . .169 D1
Trinity St NR2 . . . . .162 C5
Triple Plea La NR35 . . . .108 B4
Triple Plea Rd NR35 . . . .108 B4
Trix Rd NR2 . . . . .162 C4
Tropical Butterfly World*
NR17 . . . . .103 F5
Trory St NR2 . . . . .162 C5
Troston Rd IP31 . . . . . . .126 C1
Troutbeck 21 NR9 . . . . . . .88 D8
Trowse Prim Sch
NR14 . . . . .163 B2
True's Yd Fishing Heritage
Mus* PE30 . . . . .146 D6
Truman Cl
9 Norwich NR4 . . . . .161 C5
Rackheath/Salhouse
NR13 . . . . .72 F8
Trumpery La NR14 . . . . . . .90 C8
Trunch Hill IP20 . . . . . . .123 A7
Trunch Rd Denton IP20 . .123 B6
Mundesley NR11 . . . . .143 B4
Swafield NR28 . . . . .22 E4
Tucker St NR27 . . . . .139 B7
Tucks Rd NR28 . . . . .38 A5
Tuckswood Ctr 2 NR4 . .162 C1
Tuckswood Fst Sch
NR4 . . . . .162 D1
Tuckswood La NR4 . . . . .162 D1
Tud La NR9 . . . . .69 E6
Tuddenham Rd NR11 . . .150 B6
Tudor Ave IP22 . . . . .177 A5
Tudor Cl IP24 . . . . .176 C2
Tudor Cres PE36 . . . . . . .132 D2
Tudor Way
Dersingham PE31 . . . . .140 D4
6 Mulbarton NR14 . . . . .89 B3
Tudor Wlk
Great Yarmouth NR31 . . . . .170 C1
12 Honington IP31 . . . . . . .126 B1
Tuesday Mkt Pl 5 PE30 .146 D5
Tuffen La IP22 . . . . .128 B4
Tulip Cl NR17 . . . . .174 C5
Tulip Tree Dr 5 NR14 . . . .90 C5
Tumbler Hill PE37 . . . . . .153 C6
Tumbleyhill Rd PE32 . . . . .46 C3
Tumbril La IP21 . . . . .131 D7
Tummel Way NR17 . . . . . .174 E6
Tunbeck Cl IP20 . . . . . . .123 A3
Tunbeck Rd IP20 . . . . . . .123 A4
Tungate Cres NR4 . . . . . . .89 B8
Tungate Rd NR28 . . . . . .151 A5
Tungate Way 6 NR12 . . . . .54 C6
Tunn St 4 NR21 . . . . .141 B4
Tunneys La NR35 . . . . . .109 B2
Tunns Yd NR23 . . . . .136 D6
Tuns Rd PE37 . . . . .65 F4
Tunstall Cl 5 NR5 . . . . . .161 A7
Tunstall Rd NR13 . . . . . . .74 F2
Tunstead La NR12 . . . . . .164 D6
Tunstead Prim Sch
NR12 . . . . .37 F1
Tunstead Rd
Tunstead NR12 . . . . .37 E1
1 Wroxham/Hoveton
NR12 . . . . .164 C5
Turbine Way PE37 . . . . . .153 B6
Turbo Rd NR21 . . . . .15 D2
Turbus Rd PE30 . . . . .146 E7
Turf Fen La NR29 . . . . . . .56 B5
Turf Lot Dro PE14 . . . . . . .95 B5
Turin Way NR31 . . . . . . .171 E4
Turkey La NR24 . . . . .19 D6
Turn The NR10 . . . . .53 A8
Turner Cl
Ditchingham NR35 . . . . . . .109 B2
5 Great Yarmouth NR31 . . .170 A7
Wymondham NR18 . . . . . . .173 E5
Turner Rd NR2 . . . . .162 A7
Turner Way PE38 . . . . . . .172 E5
Turner's Cl PE34 . . . . .79 E8
Turnham Gn 10 NR7 . . . . . .72 D4
Turning The NR26 . . . . . .138 C6
Turnpike Cl Foxley NR20 . . .50 D8
2 Wisbech PE13 . . . . .152 E6
Turnpike The
Ashwellthorpe NR16 . . . . . .106 A7
Carleton Rode NR16 . . . . . .105 D2
Tusser Rd NR8 . . . . .156 E8
Tusting Cl NR7 . . . . .158 F4
Tuttington Rd NR11 . . . .150 F8
Tuttles La E NR18 . . . . . .173 D6
Tuttles La W NR18 . . . . .173 B6
Tuxhill Chase PE34 . . . . . .42 B4
Tuxhill Rd PE34 . . . . .42 B5
Twelveacre NR4 . . . . .161 F4
Twickenham Ave IP27 . .175 B1
Twickenham Rd NR6 . . .158 B5
Twiss Cl 5 IP22 . . . . .129 D7
Two Acres 6 PE32 . . . . . . .44 B3
Two Fields Way 11 NR20 . .50 E7
Two Furlong Hill
NR23 . . . . .136 C5
Two Saints Cl NR12 . . . .164 D7
Two Sisters Cl 6 PE12 . . .41 B8
Twrs The PE38 . . . . .172 C5
Twyford La NR20 . . . . .33 C3
Twyford Rd NR20 . . . . . . .33 A6
Tyndale PE30 . . . . .148 C5
Tyne Mews NR30 . . . . . . .168 C5
Tyrolean Sq NR31 . . . . . .169 B4
Tyrrell's Rd 2 NR31 . . . . .169 B4

U

UEA Sportspark NR4 . . .161 D4
Ulfkell Rd IP24 . . . . .176 B2
Ullswater Ave
Castle Rising PE30 . . . . .27 C1
King's Lynn PE30 . . . . .148 F1
Ullswater Dr 20 NR9 . . . . .88 D8
Ulph Pl PE31 . . . . .135 D3
Uncle's La IP19 . . . . .124 B2
Unicorn Yd 2 NR11 . . . . .150 C6
Union Drift NR20 . . . . .68 A8
Union La
4 King's Lynn PE30 . . . . . .146 D4
Union La continued
Wortham IP22 . . . . .129 D5
Union Pl 17 PE13 . . . . . . .152 C5
Union Rd
7 Great Yarmouth NR30 . .169 D4
Smallburgh NR12 . . . . .38 C3
Union St Norwich NR2 . . .178 A2
4 Wisbech PE13 . . . . .152 C5
University Cres NR31 . . .170 B4
University Dr NR4 . . . . . .161 C5
University of E Anglia
Norwich NR6 . . . . .157 D4
Norwich NR4 . . . . .161 C3
Unthank Rd NR4 . . . . . . .161 F2
Upgate NR14 . . . . .90 D5
Upgate Rd NR15 . . . . . . .108 E7
Upgate St
Carleton Rode NR16 . . . . . .105 A4
Southery PE38 . . . . .97 B5
Uphalle NR8 . . . . .155 D1
Uplands Ave NR30 . . . . .168 D5
Uplands Pk NR26 . . . . . .138 C6
Uplands Way IP22 . . . . .177 D5
Upper Breckland Rd
NR5 . . . . .156 F1
Upper Brook La IP20 . . .131 E8
Upper Burnthouse La
IP20 . . . . .131 E8
Upper Cliff Rd NR31 . . . .170 D4
Upper Goat La NR2 . . . . .178 A3
Upper Grange Cres
NR30 . . . . .168 D5
Upper Hall La NR24 . . . . .18 D8
Upper Harmans La
IP20 . . . . .122 B1
Upper Kiln La NR15 . . . . . .90 F4
Upper King St NR2 . . . . .178 B3
Upper Mkt 3 NR21 . . . . .141 B4
Upper Oakley IP21 . . . . .130 E4
Upper Olland St NR35 . .124 A8
Upper Rose La IP22 . . . .177 E2
Upper St Gissing IP22 . . .120 F4
Salhouse NR13 . . . . .55 B2
Upper St Giles St NR2 . .178 A3
Upper Stafford Ave
NR5 . . . . .156 F1
Upper Staithe Rd 15
NR12 . . . . .38 B4
Upper Tumbril La
Brockdish IP20 . . . . .131 D8
Needham IP20 . . . . .122 A1
Scole IP20 . . . . .131 D8
Upton Broad Nature
Reserve* NR13 . . . . .74 C8
Upton Cl NR4 . . . . .162 A3
Upton Dr PE37 . . . . .153 B2
Upton Rd Norwich NR4 . .162 A3
South Walsham NR13 . . . . . .74 B8
Upton Way NR12 . . . . .24 C5
Uptons Way IP26 . . . . .82 A2
Upwell Prim Sch PE14 . . .77 D4
Upwell Rd PE14 . . . . .95 A7
Utopia Way NR12 . . . . .39 B3

V

Vale Cl 8 NR10 . . . . .53 B3
Vale Ct 5 IP27 . . . . .114 E1
Vale Gn NR6 . . . . .158 B1
Vale Rd High Kelling NR25 . . .8 E2
Mundesley NR11 . . . . .143 A8
Thurton NR14 . . . . .91 C3
Valentine Ct PE36 . . . . . .132 D5
Valentine Rd PE36 . . . . . .132 D4
Valentine St 3 NR2 . . . . .162 C6
Valerian Rise IP24 . . . . .116 D2
Valinger's Pl 6 PE30 . . . .146 E4
Valingers Rd PE30 . . . . . .146 E3
Valley Dr The NR1 . . . . . .163 B8
Valley Gdns 1 NR28 . . . . .151 E5
Valley La NR25 . . . . .137 B5
Valley Rd Norwich NR5 . . .157 C1
9 Tasburgh NR15 . . . . . . .106 F6
Valley Rise PE31 . . . . . . .140 C4
Valley Side Rd 1 NR1 . . .163 C8
Valley View NR19 . . . . . .154 C6
Valley View Cres NR5 . . .157 A1
Valley Way NR21 . . . . . . .141 E4
Valleyside NR18 . . . . . . .173 C3
Valpy Ave NR3 . . . . .158 A1
Vancouver Ave PE30 . . . .146 E3
Vancouver Rd 3 NR7 . . . .163 C8
Vane Cl NR7 . . . . .72 D4
Vanguard Rd
2 Great Yarmouth NR31 . . . .94 C8
Great Yarmouth NR31 . . . . .170 A8
Varsity Rd IP25 . . . . .84 F3
Varvel Ave NR7 . . . . .159 C4
Vassar Ct 6 NR20 . . . . . . .68 F6
Vaunce's La IP21 . . . . . . .131 B8
Vaunces La IP21 . . . . . . .131 B8
Vauxhall St NR2 . . . . . . .162 C5
Vauxhall Terr NR30 . . . .169 C6
Vawdrey Rd NR8 . . . . . . .155 F1
Veltshaw Cl PE31 . . . . . .133 B4
Venables Cl NR1 . . . . . . .163 B7
Venta Icenorum (Roman
Town)* NR14 . . . . .89 E6
Ventura Cl IP26 . . . . .98 F5
Vera Cl 10 NR13 . . . . .72 E7
Vera Rd
New Rackheath NR13 . . . . . .72 E7
Norwich NR6 . . . . .158 B4
Verdon's La NR18 . . . . . . .87 F2

Verdun Rd PE13 152 D5
Veronica Gn 9 NR31 170 B6
Vervain Cl 23 NR31 94 C6
Vetch Cl NR18 173 D4
Viburnum Way 6 NR31 170 B6
Vicar St NR18 173 B4
Vicarage Cl
Costessey NR8 156 F5
Foulden IP26 82 A1
1 Potter Heigham NR29 56 F6
Vicarage La
Bungay NR35 124 C8
Hoveton NR12 164 E5
Vicarage Mdws NR19 154 D4
Vicarage Rd
Cromer NR27 139 B6
Deopham NR18 86 D3
East Ruston NR12 24 A3
Foulden IP26 82 A2
Hockham IP24 102 D3
Norwich NR3 158 C1
Paston NR28 143 D2
Salhouse NR13 55 A2
Sheringham NR26 138 C6
Thetford IP24 176 D5
Wingfield IP21 131 E3
Worstead NR28 38 A5
Vicarage St NR28 151 C5
Vicarage Wlk 11 IP25 84 E3
Viceroy Cl PE31 140 C4
Victor Charles Cl IP27 175 B7
Victoria Arc NR30 169 C3
Victoria Ave
Brandon IP27 175 C3
Hunstanton PE36 132 D5
Victoria Cl Diss IP22 177 E3
Heacham PE31 133 E6
Taverham NR8 156 C8
Victoria Cotts PE31 133 D6
Victoria Ct
Sheringham NR26 138 E7
22 Watton IP25 84 D3
Victoria Gdns 7 NR30 169 D2
Victoria Hill IP23 130 C1
Victoria La
Deopham NR18 86 F3
Fakenham NR21 141 E4
Victoria Pl 17 PE13 152 C4
Victoria Rd Diss IP22 177 D4
5 Great Yarmouth NR30 169 D2
Great Yarmouth NR31 170 D3
Mundesley NR11 143 C6
3 Taverham NR8 155 C1
Taverham NR8 156 C8
Terrington St John PE34 42 C2
Wisbech PE13 152 C4
Victoria St
Caister-on-Sea NR30 168 F4
2 Downham Market PE38 172 A5
Great Yarmouth NR30 169 D6
Norwich NR1 178 A1
Sheringham NR26 138 D7
Victoria Terr PE34 146 C4
Victoria Way NR5 157 B2
Victory La PE34 60 C8
Victory Rd
Downham Market PE38 172 B4
Wisbech PE13 152 B3
Vienna Wlk NR19 154 C1
Viking Cl
Great Yarmouth NR31 170 D2
Swaffham PE37 153 D2
Viking Rd 1 NR31 94 C8
Village Cl 4 NR4 161 C5
Villarome NR30 168 C5
Villavon Way 4 NR13 73 D6
Villebois Rd PE33 63 B4
Vimy Dr NR18 173 D4
Vimy Ridge NR18 173 D4
Vince's Rd IP22 177 F4
Vincent Cl 6 IP26 98 E1
Vincent Pl 16 IP25 84 D3
Vincent Rd
Norwich NR1 163 A7
Sheringham NR26 138 E7
Vincents Rd NR9 69 A4
Vine Cl
Coney Weston IP31 127 B5
Hemsby NR29 167 B8
Vine Ct NR21 141 B4
Vine Hill PE34 61 C2
Vinery Cl 1 PE34 146 C5
Violet Cl
Attleborough NR17 174 C5
18 Great Yarmouth NR31 94 C6
Violet Dr NR26 138 B6
Violet Elvin Ct NR5 161 F5
Violet Rd NR3 158 F1
Violet Way NR19 154 C4
Virginia Cl NR7 159 C4
Vong La Grimston PE32 28 B1
Roydon PE32 45 A8
Vulcan Rd N NR6 158 C5
Vulcan Rd S NR6 158 C4

W

Waddington Ct 6 NR2 162 B7
Waddington St NR2 162 B7
Waddling La NR32 111 F7
Wade Cl NR11 150 C5
Wadehall La NR34 111 B1
Wades Way NR28 22 E5
Wadham Cl NR31 170 B3
Wadham Rd NR31 170 B3
Waggon & Horses La
NR3 178 B3
Wagtail Cl 2 NR31 170 A6
Wagtail Way IP24 176 D1
Wainford Mills Rd
Bungay NR35 124 C8
Wainford NR35 109 C1
Wainford Rd NR35 124 C8
Wakefield Rd NR5 161 C5
Wakehurst Cl 6 NR4 161 F1
Wakes La NR19 154 D5
Walcot Cl NR5 161 A7
Walcot Rd IP22 177 E6
Walcot Rise IP22 177 F5
Walcott Road N12 23 E4
Walcup's La PE32 29 D2
Waldeck Rd NR4 162 A3
Waldegrave 6 NR5 161 A8
Waldemar Ave NR6 158 B5
Waldemar Pk NR6 158 B5
Wales Bank PE14 59 A1
Wales Ct PE38 172 C5
Walk The
Great Yarmouth NR31 170 B6
Hickling NR12 39 F3
Oulton NR11 35 A8
Walker St 1 PE30 146 E6
Walkers Cl PE31 135 D2
Walks The NR34 111 A4
Walkway The NR12 24 A7
Wall La PE31 29 C4
Wall Rd Erpingham NR11 20 F3
Norwich NR3 158 E2
Wallace Cl
Dereham NR19 154 B6
King's Lynn PE30 147 D4
Wallace Twite Way
PE31 140 C3
Wall's La NR25 7 F3
Waller Cl NR13 72 D5
Wallers La NR20 33 C3
Wallgate La NR21 17 D5
Walnut Ave 5 PE33 43 E2
Walnut Ave N 2 PE33 43 E2
Walnut Cl
Brandon IP27 175 E2
Foulden IP26 82 A2
Hopton IP22 127 F5
Taverham NR8 155 D2
Walnut Gr
1 Fakenham NR21 141 E4
Watton IP25 84 D4
Walnut Hill NR14 73 A1
Walnut Pl PE33 82 A5
Walnut Rd PE14 41 E3
Walnut Tree Ave 24
NR29 57 D4
Walnut Wlk PE33 63 B4
Walnuts The
Grimston PE32 28 B1
Norwich NR4 162 A2
Walpole Bank PE14 41 C3
Walpole Cross Keys Prim Sch
PE34 42 A6
Walpole Gdns 4 NR2 178 A2
Walpole Highway Prim Sch
PE14 59 F8
Walpole La PE14 41 F4
Walpole Rd
Great Yarmouth NR30 169 D7
King's Lynn PE30 146 E7
Walpole St NR2 178 A2
Walpole Way 8 PE33 43 E2
Walpole Wr Gdns*
PE14 41 E3
Walsham Cl 3 PE30 147 D5
Walsingham Abbey Grounds
& Shirehall Mus*
NR22 16 F7
Walsingham Ct 2 PE13 152 A7
Walsingham Dr NR8 155 E3
Walsingham Prim Sch
NR22 16 F8
Walsingham Rd
Binham NR21 6 C1
Burnham Thorpe PE31 135 F2
Grear Balsingham NR22 17 B8
Walsoken Rd PE14 59 D3
Walter Howes Cres
PE32 44 C3
Walters Cl NR31 171 D5
Walters Rd NR8 156 C8
Walton Cl PE30 148 C4
Walton Rd
Norwich NR1 162 E3
St John's Fen End PE14 60 A5
West Walton PE14 59 F5
Wisbech PE13 152 E7
Waltons Way IP27 175 D2
Wangford Rd IP27 113 F3
Wansbrough Rd 10
NR15 106 E3
Wanton La PE34 144 A5
Waples Way NR19 154 D3
Wapping NR29 167 A2
Warbler Cl 6 NR31 94 C7
Ward Rd NR13 55 B1
Ward's Chase PE34 79 B8
Wardley Hill Rd NR35 109 D4
Warham Rd Binham NR21 6 E2
Wells-next-the-Sea
NR23 136 E4
Warham St Mary's Halt Sta
NR23 5 F4
Waring Rd NR5 161 B6
Warner Ave NR19 154 E7
Warnes Cl 4 NR27 139 C6
Warnett Rd NR7 159 D1
Warren Ave
Fakenham NR21 141 F4
Norwich NR6 158 A5
Warren Cl
Brandon IP27 175 D3
High Kelling NR25 8 E3
15 Horsford NR10 53 A3
Thetford IP24 176 A3
Watlington PE33 61 D5
Warren Ct 7 NR27 139 C6
Warren Dr NR11 143 B5
Warren Gn NR13 72 F8
Warren Loke NR31 93 E3
Warren Pl 4 NR19 154 D1
Warren Rd
Great Yarmouth NR31 171 D8
High Kelling NR25 8 E3
Hopton on Sea NR31 171 D5
Shouldham PE33 62 D4
Southrepps NR11 22 C6
Warren The
Cromer NR27 139 C6
Horsham St Faith &
Newton St Faith NR10 53 D2
Little Snoring NR21 17 C3
Norwich NR6 158 E4
Warren View NR14 109 D8
Warren's La NR17 174 C6
Warren's Rd PE34 145 D6
Warren's Way 5 NR16 105 F5
Warrens Yd NR23 136 C6
Warstade Way PE37 153 B4
Warwick Dr NR18 173 C5
Warwick St NR2 162 B5
Wash La Alburgh IP20 122 E7
Aslacton NR15 106 A1
Banham NR16 119 D6
Burgh St Peter NR34 111 C4
Clenchwarton PE34 145 E6
Gissing IP22 120 E5
Hales NR14 109 E6
Hinderclay IP22 128 C4
Howe NR15 90 C2
Redgrave IP22 129 A5
St Peter, South Elmham
NR35 123 F3
Saxlingham Nethergate
NR15 107 D8
Shelfanger IP22 120 B2
Shotesham NR15 89 F1
Topcroft NR35 108 A4
Wacton NR15 106 B2
Whissonsett NR20 31 E2
Wash National Nature
Reserve The* PE30 26 B5
Wash Rd PE14 95 E4
Washbridge 10 NR19 154 D5
Washpit Dro
South Acre PE32 64 D8
Swaffham PE37 153 C8
West Rudham PE31 29 F6
Watch House Hill
NR35 124 C8
Watch House La NR12 23 E4
Water End La PE32 48 D2
Water Gdns The PE13 152 A5
Water La Barnham IP24 125 E6
Barsham NR21 16 F4
Botesdale IP22 128 D1
Cringleford NR4 161 D1
Garboldisham IP22 128 A8
Great & Little Plumstead
NR13 73 A5
Ingham NR12 24 D2
4 King's Lynn PE30 146 D5
Letheringsett with Glandford
NR25 8 A2
Middleton PE32 44 C1
Mundesley NR11 143 C4
Neatishead NR12 55 E7
Runton NR27 10 A5
Thelnetham IP22 128 B5
Thetford IP24 176 C4
Water Mdw Cl NR29 167 A3
Water Mdw Way 2
PE38 172 A6
Water Mill La IP21 131 A4
Water Moor La NR21 141 C6
Water Sports Ctr PE34 43 C3
Water Twr Rd NR14 88 E4
Waterbank Rd 10 NR26 138 D7
Watercress La NR20 68 E6
Waterden Cl 5 PE30 147 A8
Waterfield Ave NR21 141 D5
Waterfield Cl 2 NR21 141 C5
Waterfield Mdws
NR28 151 E5
Waterheath Rd NR34 110 E5
Watering La PE33 43 E2
Watering Piece La
NR29 56 C7
Watering Rd IP21 131 B1
Watering The 3 NR3 162 D8
Wateringpit La NR12 55 A8
Waterland Cl NR30 168 C7
Waterlees Rd
Walsoken PE13 59 A6
2 Wisbech PE13 152 E7
Waterloo Ave 4 IP22 129 D7
Waterloo Cl 3 NR10 53 D2
Waterloo Pk Ave NR3 158 C1
Waterloo Pk Cl 6 NR3 158 C1
Waterloo Rd
Great Yarmouth NR30 169 E2
Hainford NR10 53 D6
Horsham St Faith NR10 53 E2
Waterloo Rd *continued*
Norwich NR3 162 D8
Waterloo St 13 PE30 146 E5
Waterlow Rd PE34 42 C4
Waterman Rd NR2 161 F7
Waterman's La PE38 79 D1
Waterman's Way PE38 79 A4
Watermeadow Cl 3
NR14 91 F1
Watermill Cl NR11 9 F1
Watermill Gn IP24 176 C3
Watermill La PE37 82 A6
Waters La NR29 167 A7
Watersfield Way
NR19 154 D2
Waterside PE30 146 F7
Waterside The NR6 157 D3
Waterworks Rd
Norwich NR2 162 A7
Old Hunstanton PE36 132 F7
Watery La
Beeston with Bittering
PE32 48 B3
Grimston PE32 45 B8
Guist NR20 33 A4
Matlask NR11 20 D5
Necton PE37 66 B4
Scarning NR19 154 A1
Shipdham IP25 67 C2
Wathen Way NR10 150 C1
Watkin Rd NR4 89 E8
Watling Cl NR30 168 E6
Watling Rd
Attleborough NR17 174 F6
Norwich NR7 159 D1
Watlings The NR19 67 B6
Watlington Prim Sch
PE33 61 D5
Watlington Rd PE33 61 F6
Watlington Sta PE33 61 D5
Watson Gr 9 NR2 162 B8
Watsons Cl NR31 171 E4
Watson-Watt Gdns
NR11 143 A7
Wattlefield Rd
Tacolneston NR16 105 C6
Wymondham NR18 88 A1
Watton Jun Sch IP25 84 D3
Watton Rd Ashill IP25 84 A6
Barford NR9 69 E2
Colney NR4 160 F4
Great Cressingham IP25 83 D4
Great Ellingham NR17 103 D8
Great Melton NR9 70 B2
Griston IP25 85 A2
Hingham NR9 86 B5
Hockham IP24 102 E4
Larling NR16 118 A8
Little Cressingham IP25 83 F2
Little Melton NR9 160 B4
North Pickenham PE37 83 C8
Shipdham IP25 67 B1
Shropham NR17 103 A4
Stow Bedon NR17 102 D7
Swaffham PE37 153 D2
Thompson IP25 102 A8
Waunci Cres NR31 170 D2
Wavell Rd NR19 154 C7
Waveney Cl
Hoveton NR12 164 E6
Hunstanton PE36 132 D3
Wells-next-the-Sea
NR23 136 D4
Waveney Dr
10 Belton NR31 94 A6
Wroxham/Hoveton
NR12 164 D5
Waveney Fst Sch NR31 94 A5
Waveney Hill NR32 111 F3
Waveney Hts IP21 131 C6
Waveney Rd
Bungay NR35 124 B8
Diss IP22 177 E3
Ditchingham NR35 109 B2
Great Yarmouth NR31 169 C1
Hunstanton PE36 132 C3
King's Lynn PE30 147 D5
Waveney Valley Swimming
Pool NR35 124 B7
Waverley Rd NR4 162 A2
Waxham Ct NR12 40 A5
Waxham Rd NR12 40 B5
Waxworks 28 NR30 169 D4
Wayford Rd NR12 38 F4
Wayland Ave 4 IP25 84 C3
Wayland Cl NR17 174 D5
Wayland Com High Sch
IP25 84 D3
Wayland Ct NR17 174 C5
Wayland Hospl NR17 174 A7
Wayland Rd NR17 103 C8
Wayland Way NR16 119 D7
Wayland Wlk PE38 172 B7
Weasenham La 1 PE13 152 D2
Weasenham Prim Sch
PE32 47 D8
Weasenham Rd
Great Massingham PE32 29 E1
Litcham PE32 47 E7
Weatherby Rd NR5 160 D8
Weavers Cl 4 NR10 53 D2
Weavers Croft 8 IP20 122 D2
Weavers Ct IP22 177 D5
Weavers View NR12 37 F1
Webb Dr 4 NR13 72 E7
Webbs Cl 2 NR28 151 E5
Webdell Ct 3 NR1 162 E1
Webster Cl
5 Norwich NR5 161 B8
8 Stoke Holy Cross NR14 89 F4
Webster Way NR30 168 D6
Wedgewood Ct NR31 170 C3
Wedgwood Dr PE13 152 D5
Weedon Way PE30 147 D4
Weeting Castle*
IP27 114 E8
Weeting Heath National
Nature Reserve*
IP27 114 C7
Weeting VC Prim Sch
IP27 175 B8
Welbeck Ave 8 NR29 57 D4
Welbeck Rd PE13 152 E4
Welborne Rd NR20 68 F5
Welden Rd NR19 154 B4
Welgate Cl 11 NR20 68 E6
Welgate Rd NR20 68 E5
Welholme's Cl 13 NR15 106 E3
Well Cl NR9 51 A6
Well Creek Rd PE14 77 F6
Well End PE14 77 A7
Well Hall La PE32 45 A6
Well Hill NR19 68 C5
Well La NR9 51 A6
Well Loke NR3 158 B3
Well Medieval Village of*
PE32 45 B7
Well Opening 24 NR30 169 D2
Well Rd Cantley NR13 92 D6
Great Yarmouth NR30 169 D2
Well St Docking PE31 134 C5
Great Yarmouth NR30 169 D4
Thetford IP24 176 D3
Witton NR28 23 D3
Wellbeck NR15 90 F2
Wellbeck Rd NR15 91 A2
Wellesley Ave NR1 163 B7
Wellesley Ave N 4 NR1 163 B7
Wellesley Ave S NR1 163 B6
Wellesley Fst Sch
NR1 163 B7
Wellesley Rd
Great Yarmouth NR30 169 D5
8 Long Stratton NR15 106 D3
Wellesley St 11 PE30 146 E5
Wellingham Rd
Litcham PE32 47 F6
Tittleshall PE32 48 A8
Wellington Cl
Brandon IP27 175 D3
Gimingham NR11 22 F8
Wellington Cres NR21 15 C3
Wellington La NR2 162 C6
Wellington Pl 12 NR30 169 D4
Wellington Rd
Briston NR24 142 B4
East Dereham NR19 154 D5
3 Feltwell IP26 98 E1
Great Yarmouth NR30 169 E2
6 Long Stratton NR15 106 D3
Norwich NR2 162 B6
Wellington Terr 1
PE13 152 C4
Wells Ave NR28 151 A3
Wells Cl 2 NR10 53 E5
Wells' La IP20 122 D1
Wells Maritime Mus*
NR23 136 D6
Wells next the Sea Prim Sch
NR23 136 E5
Wells next the Sea Sta
NR23 136 F4
Wells Rd
Burnham Overy Staithe
PE31 135 E7
Fakenham NR21 141 B4
Hindringham NR21 17 D6
Needham IP20 122 C1
North Creake NR21 4 D1
Stiffkey NR23 6 C6
Walsingham NR22 16 F8
Wighton NR23 5 F3
Wellspring Rd NR11 22 C8
Welney Wildfowl Refuge*
PE14 95 F6
Welsford Rd
5 Norwich NR4 89 D8
Norwich NR4 162 B1
Weltons Loke NR9 52 A6
Wendene NR5 160 F7
Wendling Rd NR19 48 F2
Wendover Rd NR13 72 D8
Wenman Ct 5 NR5 160 F8
Wensom Cl 3 PE33 61 D6
Wensum Cres NR6 157 D3
Wensum Ct NR21 32 C6
Wensum Dr NR20 49 F7
Wensum Gdns 1 NR20 50 B3
Wensum Mdws Mental
Health Hospl NR6 157 D4
Wensum Mid Sch
NR2 162 A7
Wensum Rd NR9 51 A4
Wensum St NR3 178 B3
Wensum Valley Cl
NR6 157 D4
Wensum Way
11 Belton NR31 94 A6
2 Fakenham NR21 141 E4
Wensum Wlk NR8 155 F3
Wentworth Cl 6 IP27 114 E1
Wentworth Gn NR4 161 F2
Wereham Row PE33 80 D3
Wesley Ave PE34 144 B5

Wesley Cl
Downham Market PE38 ...172 B5
4 Mattishall NR20 ...68 E6
Mundesley NR11 ...143 D5
Terrington St Clement PE34 ...144 B5
Wesley Rd
King's Lynn PE30 ...148 C5
Terrington St Clement PE34 ...144 B5
Wessex St NR2 ...178 A1
West Acre Gdns* PE32 ...46 D4
West Acre Rd PE37 ...153 A6
West Ave
Great Yarmouth NR31 ...170 C3
Ormesby St Margaret NR29 ...167 A3
West Carr Rd NR17 ...174 A4
West Church St NR16 ...119 A5
West Cl NR5 ...157 A2
West Cliff
Cromer NR27 ...139 B7
Sheringham NR26 ...138 D7
West Cres NR20 ...50 A5
West Croft NR9 ...88 C7
West Dereham Rd PE33 ...80 D3
West Dr Brandon IP27 ...175 A2
1 Friday Bridge PE14 ...77 A8
West Dro N PE14 ...59 D8
West Dro S PE14 ...59 E8
West Earlham Fst Sch NR5 ...161 D6
West Earlham Mid Sch NR5 ...161 D6
West End Briston NR24 ...142 F5
Costessey NR8 ...156 C4
Hilgay PE38 ...79 D1
Northwold IP26 ...99 B8
West End Ave
Brundall NR13 ...165 A4
Costessey NR8 ...156 C5
West End Ct 6 IP25 ...84 C3
West End St NR2 ...162 B7
West Flegg Mid Sch NR29 ...57 D5
West Gate NR18 ...173 B4
West Hall Rd
Dersingham PE31 ...140 D3
Mundford IP26 ...100 B4
West Harling Rd NR16 ...118 B4
West Head Rd PE34 ...78 F8
West Herne La IP22 ...128 D5
West La NR10 ...53 D1
West Lexham Hall PE32 ...47 C4
West Lynn Cty Prim Sch PE34 ...146 C5
West Parade
Norwich NR2 ...162 B6
Wisbech PE13 ...152 B7
West Pottergate NR2 ...162 B6
West Raynham Prim Sch NR21 ...30 F4
West Raynham Rd NR21 ...30 F4
West Rd
Caister-on-Sea NR30 ...168 D4
Dersingham PE31 ...140 D3
Great Yarmouth NR30 ...168 F1
Norwich NR5 ...157 A2
Ormesby St Margaret NR29 ...167 A2
Shouldham Thorpe PE33 ...62 C2
Tacolneston NR16 ...105 F4
Watton IP25 ...84 D3
West Caister NR30 ...168 B4
West Runton Sta NR27 ...10 A5
West St
North Creake NR21 ...4 D1
Wisbech PE13 ...152 C4
West Stree 18 NR30 ...169 D2
West Tofts Rd IP26 ...100 D3
West View
Dereham NR19 ...154 E1
South Pickenham PE37 ...83 D7
West View Dr NR13 ...74 A2
West View Rd NR13 ...165 E6
West Way
Downham Market PE38 ...172 B4
Stow Bardolph PE34 ...61 D1
Tacolneston NR16 ...105 E5
Wimbotsham PE34 ...79 D8
West Winch Prim Sch PE33 ...43 E2
West Winch Rd PE33 ...43 F4
West Wood Cotts NR21 ...32 B5
Westacre Dr NR6 ...158 E7
Westbourne Rd NR12 ...54 D7
Westbriggs Dro PE33 ...62 B5
Westbrook Ave 1 NR31 ...170 B6
Westcliff Ave NR27 ...139 A7
Westerley Cl NR30 ...168 D4
Westerley Way NR30 ...168 D4
Western Ave NR7 ...163 E6
Western Bypass NR11 ...150 B5
Western Cl 4 IP26 ...98 D1
Western Rd NR31 ...170 C4
Westfield Ave NR23 ...136 C6
Westfield Cl 2 NR29 ...57 C1
Westfield Inf Sch IP25 ...84 D3
Westfield La NR19 ...154 F1
Westfield Rd
Brundall NR13 ...165 D4
East Dereham NR19 ...154 E2
Swaffham PE37 ...153 B4
Wisbech PE13 ...152 E7

Westfields
Attleborough NR17 ...174 B4
King's Lynn PE30 ...147 C4
Narborough PE32 ...63 E7
Westfields Cl
Terrington St John PE14 ...60 C8
Tilney St Lawrence PE34 ...42 C1
Westgate
Hevingham NR10 ...53 B8
Hunstanton PE36 ...132 C4
Norwich NR6 ...157 F5
Shropham NR17 ...103 B4
Walsingham NR22 ...16 F8
Westgate Cl NR2 ...162 A4
Westgate Ct NR18 ...173 B4
Westgate Gn NR10 ...53 B8
Westgate Rd PE36 ...1 F6
Westgate St
Hevingham NR10 ...52 B8
Hilborough IP26 ...83 A3
Holme next the Sea PE36 ...2 A6
Shouldham PE33 ...62 D4
Southery PE38 ...97 A5
Westhall IP21 ...131 F1
Westhorpe Cl 3 PE30 ...147 A8
Westland Chase PE33 ...43 F1
Westlegate NR1 ...178 B2
Westmark PE30 ...147 C4
Westmead Ave PE13 ...152 E2
Westmead Rd NR21 ...141 C4
Weston Cl 1 NR13 ...73 C6
Weston Ct NR6 ...158 F6
Weston Miller Dr PE13 ...152 C7
Weston Rd Easton NR9 ...70 A7
Norwich NR3 ...158 C3
17 Wisbech PE13 ...152 C4
Weston Rise NR30 ...168 D5
Weston Sq 3 NR25 ...137 B6
Weston Terr NR26 ...138 E7
Weston Wood Cl NR7 ...163 E7
Weston Wood Rd NR7 ...163 D7
Westry Cl PE13 ...59 C5
Westwick Dr NR28 ...151 A4
Westwick Rd NR28 ...37 F5
Westwick St NR2 ...178 A3
Westwood Dr NR6 ...157 D6
Westwood Gdns NR18 ...173 A6
Westwood La NR21 ...32 B5
Weybourne Rd
Bodham NR25 ...9 A3
Sheringham NR26 ...138 B7
Weybourne Sta NR25 ...8 F5
Weynor Gdns NR25 ...8 E5
Wharf St PE12 ...41 B8
Wharton Dr NR28 ...151 E7
Whartons La 5 NR18 ...173 B3
Wheat Fields NR8 ...155 F2
Wheatacre Cl 9 NR10 ...53 A3
Wheatacres IP24 ...176 D5
Wheatcroft Way NR20 ...68 A8
Wheatfield Way NR15 ...106 F4
Wheatfields
Hillington PE31 ...28 B4
Rickinghall Superior IP22 ...128 E2
Wheatley Bank PE14 ...59 C5
Wheatley Dr PE30 ...148 B4
Wheatley Rd NR2 ...161 F7
Wheel Rd NR14 ...90 E4
Wheelbarrow La IP20 ...123 F1
Wheeler Rd NR3 ...158 A1
Wheelers La NR15 ...108 E8
Wheelwright Rd PE30 ...147 C5
Wheelwrights Cl NR13 ...92 E8
Wherry Cl NR28 ...151 E7
Wherry Rd
Bungay NR35 ...124 C8
Norwich NR1 ...178 C1
Wherry Reach 2 NR13 ...166 D4
Wherry Way NR30 ...169 C7
Whiffler Rd NR3 ...157 F2
Whimbrel Dr
8 Great Yarmouth NR31 ...94 C8
1 Great Yarmouth NR31 ...170 A7
Whimpwell St NR12 ...24 C4
Whin Comm Rd
Denver PE38 ...172 D1
Tottenhill PE33 ...61 F6
Whinburgh Rd NR19 ...67 F3
Whinchat Way 3 NR31 ...94 C7
Whinmere Rd NR12 ...39 E3
Whipp's La NR16 ...105 F7
Whisson Cl 1 PE30 ...147 A8
Whissonsett Rd NR20 ...48 E8
Whistle Dro IP28 ...112 D1
Whitby St 3 PE13 ...152 C5
White City Rd PE14 ...78 D6
White Clover Rd 26 NR31 ...94 C6
White Cross
Burgh & Tuttington NR11 ...36 E4
Hardingham NR9 ...86 E8
White Cross Rd PE37 ...153 C4
White Farm La NR7 ...163 C6
White Gate La NR11 ...11 D2
White Gates NR5 ...156 E1
White Hall Dr PE34 ...146 C4
White Hart St
2 Aylsham NR11 ...150 C7
East Harling NR16 ...118 C5
Foulden IP26 ...82 A2
White Heath Rd NR15 ...91 B3
White Horse Dr PE31 ...140 C4
White Horse La
Bixley NR14 ...89 F8
Trowse with Newton NR14 ...163 A1
Worstead NR28 ...38 B6

White Horse St IP27 ...175 A2
White House Ct NR3 ...158 B3
White House Dr 23 NR15 ...106 E3
White House Est NR27 ...139 D4
White House Farm La IP21 ...122 B2
White House Gdns 12 NR14 ...90 D5
White House La NR17 ...174 F5
White House Rd CB7 ...112 A7
White La PE33 ...63 A3
White Lion Rd
Coltishall NR12 ...54 D6
Wheatacre NR34 ...111 B4
White Lion St
Holt NR25 ...137 B6
Norwich NR2 ...178 A2
White Lodge Bsns Est NR4 ...89 E8
White Oaks PE37 ...65 E2
White Post Rd NR11 ...21 D5
White Rd
Barton Bendish PE33 ...63 D1
Methwold IP26 ...99 A5
White Rose Cl NR5 ...161 D8
White Sedge PE30 ...147 A8
White St NR29 ...57 D5
White Woman La NR6 ...159 A6
White Woman La Mid Sch NR6 ...158 F6
Whitecross La PE34 ...144 E4
Whitedike Dro IP26 ...113 B8
Whitefriars NR3 ...178 B4
Whitefriars CE Prim Sch PE30 ...146 D3
Whitefriars Rd PE30 ...146 D3
Whitefriars Terr PE30 ...146 D3
Whitegates Cl 6 NR9 ...88 D7
Whitegates Rd NR11 ...22 B7
Whitehall Rd NR2 ...162 B5
Whitehall Yd 8 NR26 ...138 D7
Whitehart La IP27 ...175 C4
Whitehart St 6 IP24 ...176 C4
Whitehorse La NR17 ...174 C5
Whitehorse Plain 7 NR30 ...169 C5
Whitehorse St
1 Fakenham NR21 ...141 C3
Wymondham NR18 ...173 B3
Whitehouse La
Earsham NR35 ...108 C1
Wicklewood NR18 ...87 C4
Whitelands NR21 ...141 D5
Whiteplot Rd IP26 ...98 D5
Whitethorn Cl 6 NR6 ...158 D5
Whiteway Rd PE31 ...135 B3
Whiting Rd NR4 ...162 D1
Whiting's La NR17 ...103 A6
Whitley Cl NR6 ...158 C6
Whitlingham Ctry Pk* NR7 ...163 E4
Whitlingham La NR14 ...163 C4
Whitsands Rd PE37 ...153 A5
Whittington Hill PE33 ...81 B2
Whittome Mill PE38 ...79 D1
Whitwell Rd
Norwich NR1 ...163 A7
Reepham NR10 ...149 A2
Sparham NR9 ...51 B6
Whitwell St NR10 ...149 C3
Whitworth Ave 1 NR17 ...174 C5
Whytehead Gdns IP22 ...177 D4
Wick Farm Cl 3 IP25 ...84 D3
Wick La NR29 ...57 D2
Wickhampton Rd NR13 ...93 A8
Wicklewood Prim Sch NR18 ...87 B5
Wicklewood Rd NR18 ...87 B6
Wickmere Rd NR11 ...20 C5
Wicks Yd 5 NR19 ...154 D5
Wiclewood Way PE31 ...140 C3
Widgeon Cl NR31 ...170 A6
Wier Ave NR20 ...68 F6
Wigg Rd NR21 ...141 B6
Wiggenhall Rd PE34 ...42 E3
Wiggenhall St Mary Magdalen Prim Sch PE34 ...61 B5
Wiggets La NR11 ...34 D7
Wiggs Rd NR14 ...110 F7
Wight Dr NR30 ...168 C6
Wightmans La NR31 ...170 D5
Wighton Halt Sta NR23 ...5 F3
Wigwam Hill IP22 ...129 C5
Wilberforce Rd
Norwich NR5 ...161 B6
Wisbech PE13 ...152 D5
Wilby Rd Norwich NR1 ...162 E1
Quidenham NR16 ...118 F8
Wild Flower Ctr* NR25 ...7 E3
Wild Radish Cl 18 NR14 ...89 B3
Wild Rd NR3 ...158 D1
Wildbriar Cl PE33 ...43 E1
Wilde Rd 1 NR13 ...72 E7
Wilderness Cl 3 IP20 ...122 D1
Wilderness La IP20 ...122 D2
Wildfields Cl PE34 ...145 D5
Wildfields Rd PE34 ...145 C6
Wildflower Way NR35 ...109 A2
Wilkins Ct NR5 ...161 C7
Wilkins Rd PE14 ...59 D3
Wilkinson Rd NR13 ...72 E7
Wilkinson Way NR28 ...151 D4
Wilks Farm Dr NR7 ...159 A5
Willbye Ave IP22 ...177 E5

William Booth Rd PE30 ...147 D5
William Booth St NR2 ...178 A2
William Brown Way 1 IP22 ...177 A5
William Bush Cl NR10 ...35 B2
William Childerhouse Way 6 NR5 ...160 E7
William Cl 5 Watton IP25 ...84 D3
6 Wymondham NR18 ...173 C6
William Cowper Cl NR19 ...154 E1
William Kett Cl NR1 ...163 A6
William Marriot Mus* NR25 ...137 E8
William Marshall CE Prim Sch PE14 ...95 D4
William Mear Gdns NR1 ...163 B6
William O'Callaghan Pl 11 NR19 ...154 D5
William Paston Rd NR28 ...151 D6
William Peck Rd 7 NR10 ...54 A2
William Rd
Fakenham NR21 ...141 F5
Wisbech PE13 ...152 C5
William St 9 PE30 ...146 E3
William Way NR19 ...154 C1
Williams Loke NR7 ...163 D8
Williams Way
3 Holt NR25 ...137 C5
5 North Walsham NR28 ...151 C6
Williamson Cl
Diss IP22 ...177 D6
Norwich NR7 ...159 C2
Williamson Cres 4 IP24 ...176 C2
Williman Cl PE31 ...133 D6
Willis St NR3 ...178 B4
Willoughby Way 5 NR13 ...72 E7
Willow Ave NR31 ...94 C7
Willow Cl
Brandon IP27 ...175 D2
Lingwood NR13 ...74 A2
Long Stratton NR15 ...106 E2
10 Mattishall NR20 ...68 E6
Middleton PE32 ...44 B4
North Walsham NR28 ...151 D7
Wortwell IP20 ...123 A4
Wymondham NR18 ...173 D5
Willow Cres 3 PE33 ...63 B4
Willow Ct
3 Attleborough NR17 ...174 B5
Beetley NR20 ...49 D4
Willow Dr
Clenchwarton PE34 ...145 E5
Dersingham PE31 ...140 D3
King's Lynn PE33 ...43 F4
Tilney All Saints PE34 ...42 E4
West Winch PE33 ...43 F1
Willow Gr
East Dereham NR19 ...154 D2
Sheringham NR26 ...138 E5
Willow Heath Rd PE33 ...80 B7
Willow Herb Wlk 4 NR18 ...173 E4
Willow La
Bedingham NR35 ...108 B3
Broome NR35 ...109 C3
Carbrooke IP25 ...85 B5
Norwich NR2 ...178 A3
Willow Pk PE30 ...147 C8
Willow Pl PE33 ...62 A5
Willow Rd
Downham Market PE38 ...172 B6
East Dereham NR19 ...154 B4
Hunstanton PE36 ...132 C3
King's Lynn PE30 ...148 D2
Willow Way
2 Ludham NR29 ...56 C5
18 Martham NR29 ...57 D4
Wisbech PE13 ...152 D3
Willow Wlk 5 IP20 ...122 D1
Willowbrook Cl 4 NR33 ...111 F1
Willows Ct 16 NR29 ...57 D4
Wilshere Ct 11 NR30 ...169 D3
Wilson Dr PE32 ...44 F3
Wilson Rd 5 NR1 ...163 B5
Wilson's Dro PE32 ...45 E3
Wilson's Way NR25 ...7 D6
Wilton Cres 2 PE30 ...148 C5
Wilton Rd Feltwell IP26 ...98 E1
Heacham PE31 ...133 C6
Wilton View NR28 ...151 D5
Wimbledon Ave IP27 ...175 A1
Wimbledon Way 2 PE38 ...172 B4
Wimbotsham Rd PE38 ...172 C6
Wimpole Dr PE30 ...148 E1
Winceby Cl 15 NR7 ...72 D4
Winch Rd PE32 ...45 C5
Winchcomb Rd NR2 ...161 F7
Winchester Twr NR2 ...162 C5
Winchester Way IP24 ...176 B5
Windermere Cl NR15 ...90 E2
Windermere Rd PE30 ...148 F2
Windle The NR13 ...74 C5
Windmill Ave NR20 ...68 A8
Windmill Cl
7 Poringland NR14 ...90 C4
Thetford IP24 ...176 D5
Windmill Ct 7 PE30 ...147 C5
Windmill Hill PE31 ...14 A3
Windmill La
Costessey NR8 ...157 A4
Syleham IP21 ...131 D4
Wretham IP24 ...102 B1

Windmill Rd
Gimingham NR11 ...22 F8
1 Marham PE33 ...63 B4
Norwich NR3 ...158 F2
Worstead NR28 ...38 A6
Wortwell IP20 ...123 A3
Windsor Ave NR30 ...169 D7
Windsor Chase NR8 ...155 D1
Windsor Cl 7 IP24 ...125 F6
Windsor Cres PE31 ...133 C5
Windsor Ct 4 IP25 ...84 D3
Windsor Dr
Dersingham PE31 ...140 D3
Wisbech PE13 ...152 D8
Windsor Pk
East Dereham NR19 ...154 D8
2 King's Lynn PE30 ...146 E3
Windsor Pk Gdns NR6 ...159 A6
Windsor Rd
Caister-on-Sea NR30 ...168 E6
Cantley NR13 ...92 C6
King's Lynn PE30 ...146 E3
Norwich NR6 ...158 A5
Windsor Rise PE36 ...132 C2
Windsor St 1 PE38 ...172 A5
Windsor Terr PE30 ...146 E3
Windsor Way NR31 ...170 B4
Windy Cres PE33 ...63 B3
Windy La NR15 ...107 B8
Windy Ridge PE33 ...63 B3
Winfarthing Ave PE30 ...146 D3
Winfarthing Rd
Banham NR16 ...119 D6
Shelfanger IP22 ...120 B2
Wing's La NR20 ...33 B7
Wingate Way NR2 ...162 C7
Wingfield PE30 ...147 D5
Wingfield Rd
Lakenheath IP27 ...113 E2
Norwich NR3 ...162 D8
Syleham IP21 ...131 D5
Weybread IP21 ...131 F6
Wings Rd IP27 ...113 E1
Winifred Ct NR26 ...138 E7
Winifred Rd NR31 ...169 B3
Winifred Way NR30 ...168 D8
Winmer Ave 6 NR29 ...58 B6
Winn's Cl NR25 ...137 A7
Winners Wlk NR8 ...155 E3
Winsford Way NR5 ...157 C1
Winstanley Rd 21 NR7 ...72 D4
Winston Churchill Dr PE30 ...147 C4
Winston Dr NR21 ...15 E6
Winter Gdns* NR30 ...169 E2
Winter Rd NR2 ...162 A6
Winterton Dures National Nature Reserve* NR29 ...58 B7
Winterton Fst Sch NR29 ...58 B6
Winterton Rd
Hemsby NR29 ...167 B8
Somerton NR29 ...57 F6
Wisbech & Fenland Mus* PE13 ...152 C4
Wisbech Castle* PE13 ...152 C4
Wisbech Gram Sch PE13 ...152 B5
Wisbech Rd
King's Lynn PE30 ...146 D2
Manea PE15 ...95 A2
Nordelph PE38 ...78 D4
Outwell PE14 ...77 F7
Walpole PE14 ...41 D4
Walsoken PE13 ...152 E8
Welney PE14 ...95 D5
Wissey View IP26 ...100 B4
Wistaria Rd PE13 ...152 F7
Wisteria Cl NR20 ...154 F4
Witard Cl NR7 ...159 D1
Witard Rd NR7 ...163 D8
Withersdale Rd IP20 ...123 A1
Withington St 1 PE12 ...41 B8
Withy Way NR8 ...155 E1
Witton Cl
Heacham PE31 ...133 C5
Reedham NR13 ...92 F5
Witton Gn NR13 ...92 F5
Witton La NR13 ...165 A8
Wittons La IP21 ...131 A3
Wiveton Rd NR25 ...7 D6
Woburn St NR2 ...162 C5
Wodehouse Cl 1 NR12 ...39 B4
Wodehouse Ct 11 IP25 ...84 D3
Wodehouse Rd
Bacton NR12 ...23 D4
Old Hunstanton PE36 ...132 E7
Wodehouse St NR3 ...162 E8
Wolfe Rd NR1 ...163 B7
Wolferton Dr PE37 ...153 B2
Wollaston Ave NR19 ...154 D7
Wolseley Rd NR31 ...169 B2
Wolterton Pk* NR11 ...20 E2
Wolterton Rd NR11 ...20 C2
Womersley Cl 5 NR1 ...163 B7
Womersley Rd NR1 ...163 B7
Wood Avens Way NR18 ...173 E4
Wood Cl Brandon IP27 ...175 D2
Kenninghall NR16 ...119 A4
Wood Dalling Rd
Guestwick NR20 ...34 A6
Reepham NR10 ...149 C6

Wood Dene Sch NR11 ......9 F3
Wood Dr **11** Beetley NR20 ..49 D4
11 Beetley NR20 ....49 D4
Wood Gn NR13 ....72 F8
Wood Hill NR8 ....156 D8
Wood La Aldeby NR34 ...110 E5
Bedingham NR35 ....108 C2
Bradenham IP25 ....66 D4
Bressingham IP22 ....119 E2
Bunwell NR16 ....105 D3
Burgh & Tuttington NR11 ..36 D5
Dickleburgh & Rushall
IP21 ....130 F6
Great Ellingham NR17 ...103 D8
Hepworth IP22 ....127 E2
Holme Hale IP25 ....66 B1
Honingham NR9 ....69 E8
Kelling NR25 ....8 C5
Little Eilingham NR17 ....86 B1
Long Stratton NR15 ....107 A2
Morley NR18 ....87 A1
Pulham Market IP21 ....121 E8
Scole IP21 ....130 F8
Starston IP20 ....122 C5
Strumpshaw NR13 ....73 F2
Swardeston NR14 ....89 C5
Thelnetham IP22 ....128 A2
Wicklewood NR18 ....87 B4
Wood Norton Rd
Foulsham NR20 ....33 C5
Stibbard NR21 ....32 E7
Wood Rising Rd NR9 ....86 A5
Wood St Norwich NR1 ...178 A1
Wisbech PE13 ....152 B6
Wood St Rd NR29 ....56 B8
Wood View NR28 ....151 A4
Wood View Ct NR5 .....157 A2
Wood View Rd NR6 .....157 E5
Wood's La NR20 ....49 B8
Woodbastwick Rd
Blofield NR13 ....165 E7
Blofield Heath NR13 .....73 C6
Woodbastwick NR13 .....55 E1
Woodbine Cl
North Walsham NR28 ...151 F5
Potter Heigham NR29 ...56 F7
Woodbridge Way
PE30 ....147 D4
Woodcock Cl NR3 .....158 D3
Woodcock La PE34 .....61 B7
Woodcock Mews **4**
NR31 ....170 A6
Woodcock Rd NR3 ....158 C3
Woodcock Rise IP27 ...175 F4
Woodcock's La NR9 ....88 A8
Woodcote Pk PE13 ....152 A4
Woodcroft Cl NR7 ....159 E2
Woodend Rd NR21 ....133 E5
Woodfarm La NR31 ....170 A2
Woodfield
Briston NR24 ....142 C4
1 East Dereham NR19 ...154 D1
Woodfield Rd NR25 ...137 C7
Woodforde Rd NR7 ...159 D2
Woodfordes Brewery &
Visitors Ctr* NR13 ....55 C2
Woodgate **12** NR4 ....89 B8
Woodgate La NR20 .....50 B3
Woodgate Rd NR20 ....50 A2

Woodgate Way PE31 ....134 F4
Woodhall Rd PE38 ......97 B8
Woodham Leas NR6 ...158 E6
Woodhill Rise NR5 ....161 C8
Woodhouse Cl **1** NR26 ..138 B6
Woodland Dr
Bungay NR35 ....124 A7
Ellingham NR35 ....109 E3
Norwich NR6 ....158 E6
Thorpe End NR13 ......72 D5
Woodland Farm Ind Units
NR10 ....53 A6
Woodland Gdns PE30 ..148 D5
Woodland La NR24 ....142 F2
Woodland Rd NR6 ....157 E6
Woodland Rise
Sheringham NR26 .....138 E5
12 Tasburgh NR15 ......106 F6
Woodland Rise W
NR26 ....138 D4
Woodland View Mid Sch
NR10 ....54 A2
Woodland View Mobile Home
Pk NR10 ....53 D6
Woodlands
53 Harleston IP20 .....122 D2
7 Thorpe Marriott NR8 ..155 B2
Woodlands Cl
Holt NR25 ....137 D7
4 Thetford IP24 ....176 E6
Woodlands Cres **1** NR7 ..72 D5
Woodlands Ct PE13 ...152 F7
Woodlands Dr IP24 .....20 ..176 D6
Woodlands Mid Sch
NR31 ....94 C6
Woodlands Rd NR5 ...157 A2
Woodlands Rise IP27 ..175 A2
Woodlands The IP25 ...84 A7
Woodlands Way Rd
NR12 ....55 D4
Woodlark Cl **2** IP24 ...176 D2
Woodpecker Dr **8** IP25 ..84 C3
Woodpecker Mews **5**
NR31 ....170 A6
Woodrising Rd NR9 ....85 D4
Woodrow Ave NR25 ...137 B5
Woodrow La NR15 ....121 A8
Woodrow Pl NR1 .....163 B6
Woodruff Cl **8** NR6 ...158 D5
Woods Cl **8** NR9 ......88 C7
Woods End NR17 .....174 C4
Woodside
Burnham Market PE31 ...135 A2
5 King's Lynn PE30 ...147 C4
North Walsham NR28 ...151 E4
Woodside Ave
Dersingham PE31 ......140 C5
Heacham PE31 ....133 D4
Woodside Cl
Attleborough NR17 ...174 C3
Dersingham PE31 .....140 C5
1 Taverham NR8 ......155 C1
Woodside Fst Com Sch
NR7 ....159 E1
Woodside Fst Sch NR9 ..88 D7
Woodside Pk NR17 ...174 C3
Woodside Rd NR7 ....159 E1
Woodstock La NR15 ..120 F8
Woodstock Way **8** NR29 ..57 D4
Woodton Prim Sch
NR35 ....108 C5

Woodton Rd NR35 ......108 A7
Woodview NR28 ....38 A4
Woodview Cl IP25 ......84 C4
Woodview Rd NR9 ......70 B5
Woodward Cl PE33 .....62 D4
Woodward Rd NR3 ....158 B2
Woodwark Ave **3** PE30 ..146 E6
Woodyard Cl **9** NR14 ...89 B3
Woodyard Sq The
NR35 ....108 C5
Wooll Dr NR28 ....151 D7
Woolner's La NR14 .....90 E7
Woolstencroft Ave
PE30 ....146 F7
Wootton Rd PE30 .....147 B7
Worcester Cl **3** NR29 ..167 A2
Worcester Rd PE13 ...152 C7
Worcester Way
Attleborough NR17 ...174 E4
Great Yarmouth NR31 ..170 B4
Wordsworth Cl PE38 ...172 D5
Wordsworth Gn IP24 ..176 E7
Wordsworth Rd
2 Diss IP22 ....177 E4
Norwich NR5 ....161 C6
Workhouse La
Foulsham NR20 ....33 D4
Tilney St Lawrence PE34 ...42 C1
Upwell PE14 ....77 D4
Workhouse Rd NR12 ....38 C3
Worlds End NR13 ......54 D4
Wormegay Prim Sch
PE33 ....62 A6
Wormegay Rd
Blackborough End PE32 ...44 C1
Wormegay PE32 ....62 D8
Worstead Prim Sch
NR28 ....38 A5
Worstead Rd NR28 .....38 B4
Worstead Sta NR28 ....37 F4
Wortham Cl **3** NR5 ...161 A8
Wortham Prim Sch
IP22 ....129 C4
Worthing Rd
North Elmham NR20 ....49 F7
Swanton Morley NR20 ...50 B6
Wramplingham Rd
NR18 ....173 D8
Wren Cl Brandon IP27 ...175 E3
Necton PE37 ....66 A3
Norwich NR7 ....161 E2
Wren Dr
2 Great Yarmouth NR31 ...94 C7
Great Yarmouth NR31 ..170 A6
Wrench Cl **4** NR11 ...150 D6
Wrench Rd NR5 ......161 D6
Wreningham Prim Sch
NR16 ....88 D1
Wrens The **1** IP24 ...176 D2
Wretton Fen Dro PE33 ..80 D1
Wretton Rd PE33 ......80 F2
Wretton Row PE33 .....80 E3
Wright Ave NR19 ....154 D1
Wright Cl NR30 ......168 E7
Wright Dr NR19 .....154 C4
Wright's Cl Holt NR25 ..137 E7
North Walsham NR28 ...151 B4
Wright's La PE12 ......41 B8
Wright's Loke NR28 ....22 E5
Wright's Wlk **12** NR19 ..154 D5
Wrights Cl NR11 .....150 C7
Wroe The PE14 ....59 C1

Wroo Rd NR17 ....103 F5
Wroughton Fst Sch
NR31 ....170 B6
Wroughton Mid Sch
NR31 ....170 B7
Wroxham Ave PE37 ...153 C2
Wroxham Rd
Coltishall NR12 ....54 E6
Rackheath NR13 ....72 D8
Salhouse NR13 ....54 E2
Sprowston NR7 ....159 C5
Wroxham Sta NR12 ...164 C6
Wyatt St PE30 ....146 E5
Wyatt Way IP24 ......176 B7
Wycliffe Rd NR14 ....161 D3
Wylde Croft NR8 .....155 D2
Wymans Way NR21 ...141 E5
Wymer Dr NR11 .....150 C4
Wymer St NR2 ......162 B6
Wymers La NR13 .....74 B8
Wymondham Abbey (rems)*
NR18 ....173 B3
Wymondham Abbey Sta
NR18 ....173 A3
Wymondham Coll NR18 ..87 B1
Wymondham Heritage Mus*
NR18 ....173 C4
Wymondham High Sch
NR18 ....173 C5
Wymondham Leisure Ctr
NR18 ....173 C4
Wymondham Rd
Bracon Ash NR14 ......88 E2
Bunwell NR16 ....105 B5
East Carleton NR14 ....88 F4
Flordon NR15 ....106 C8
Kimberley NR18 ....87 B6
Morley NR18 ....87 A3
Wreningham NR16 ......88 B2
Wymondham NR18 ....105 A8
Wymondham Sta
NR18 ....173 C2
Wyndfields **10** PE37 ..65 F4
Wyndham Pk NR27 ....10 C5
Wyndham St NR26 ...138 D7
Wyngates NR13 .....165 F6
Wynne's La PE34 ....145 C4

Y

Yallop Ave NR31 .....171 D8
Yare Cl
Caister-on-Sea NR30 ...168 D6
Great Yarmouth NR30 ..169 C6
Yare Rd NR31 ....94 A6
Yare Valley Dr NR4 ...161 C2
Yare Valley Rise NR13 ..165 C3
Yare View Cl NR13 ....92 F4
Yarmouth Bsns Pk
NR31 ....169 B2
Yarmouth Rd
Blofield NR13 ....165 F6
Broome NR35 ....110 C2
Brundall NR13 ....165 C5
Caister-on-Sea NR30 ..168 E2
Corton NR32 ....171 D1
Dilham NR28 ....38 C4
Geldeston NR34 ......110 A3
Hales NR14 ....109 F8
Hemsby NR29 ....167 A6
Kirby Cane NR35 .....109 E3

Yarmouth Rd continued
Lound NR32 ....94 B3
Ludham NR29 ....56 C5
North Walsham NR28 ..151 C4
Norwich NR7 ....163 E5
Ormesby St Margaret
NR29 ....167 C1
Postwick with Witton
NR13 ....165 A5
Raveningham NR14 ...110 B8
Stalham NR12 ....39 B3
Thurlton NR14 ....93 A1
Toft Monks NR34 .....110 E5
Worstead NR28 ....38 A6
Yarmouth Stadium
NR30 ....168 E2
Yarmouth Way NR30 ..169 C3
Yarn Mews **2** NR3 ...178 B4
Yarrington Way NR5 ...160 E8
Yarrow Cl IP24 ......176 F5
Yarrow Rd Bintree NR20 ...33 B2
2 Dereham NR20 ......68 A8
Yaxham CE Prim Sch
NR19 ....68 C6
Yaxham Rd
East Dereham NR19 ...154 E4
Mattishall NR20 ....68 C6
Yaxham Sta NR19 .....68 A4
Yaxley Way NR5 ......161 A8
Yaxley's La NR11 ....150 C6
Yaxley's Rd NR30 ....169 B6
Yeats Way NR19 .....154 B6
Yelverton Cl NR6 ....157 D5
Yelverton Rd NR14 ....90 E5
Yesmere **16** NR14 ....89 B3
Yew Ct NR7 ....159 D4
Yew Tree Cl **24** NR31 ..94 C7
Yew Tree Ct NR20 ....69 B7
Yew Tree Rd NR17 ..174 C5
Yew Ave PE36 ....132 D5
York Gdns PE13 .....152 D6
York La **15** NR12 .....39 B4
York Rd **4** Cromer NR27 ..139 D5
Great Yarmouth NR30 ..169 D3
King's Lynn PE30 ....146 E3
Wisbech PE13 ....152 D6
York Row PE13 .....152 C5
York St NR2 ....162 B4
York Terr Cromer NR27 ..139 D5
Wisbech PE13 ....152 C6
York Villa Cl NR29 .....75 E8
York Way IP24 ......176 B5
Youell Ave NR31 ....170 D1
Young's Cres NR13 ...92 E7
Young's Row PE12 ....41 A8
Youngman's La NR10 ..37 C5
Youngmans Cl NR28 ..151 D3
Youngmans La NR12 ..38 E6
Youngmans Rd NR18 ..173 C8

Z

Zara Way NR19 .....154 C1
Zephyr Cl NR30 ....168 D7
Zig-Zag La NR15 ....108 C8
Zobel Cl NR3 ....157 F2
Zurich Cl NR31 .....171 E4